D0918350

The Illustrated Network

The Morgan Kaufmann Series in Networking

Series Editor, David Clark, M.I.T.

The Illustrated Network
Walter Goralski

P2P Networking and Applications
John Buford, Heather Yu, and Eng Lua

Broadband Cable Access Networks: The HFC Plant
David Large and James Farmer

Technical, Commercial, and Regulatory Challenges of QoS: An Internet Service Model Perspective
XiPeng Xiao

MPLS: Next Steps
Bruce S. Davie and Adrian Farrel

Wireless Networking
Anurag Kumar, D. Manjunath, and Joy Kuri

Bluetooth Application Programming with the Java APIs, Essentials Edition
Timothy J. Thompson, Paul J. Kline, and C Bala Kumar

Internet Multimedia Communications Using SIP
Rogelio Martinez Perea

Information Assurance: Dependability and Security in Networked Systems
Yi Qian, James Joshi, David Tipper, and Prashant Krishnamurthy

Network Simulation Experiments Manual, Second Edition
Emad Aboelela

Network Analysis, Architecture, and Design, Third Edition
James D. McCabe

Wireless Communications & Networking: An Introduction
Vijay K. Garg

Ethernet Networking for the Small Office and Professional Home Office
Jan L. Harrington

IPv6 Advanced Protocols Implementation
Qing Li, Tatuya Jinmei, and Keiichi Shima

Computer Networks: A Systems Approach, Fourth Edition
Larry L. Peterson and Bruce S. Davie

Network Routing: Algorithms, Protocols, and Architectures
Deepankar Medhi and Karthikeyan Ramaswami

Deploying IP and MPLS QoS for Multiservice Networks: Theory and Practice
John Evans and Clarence Filsfils

Traffic Engineering and QoS Optimization of Integrated Voice & Data Networks
Gerald R. Ash

IPv6 Core Protocols Implementation
Qing Li, Tatuya Jinmei, and Keiichi Shima

Smart Phone and Next-Generation Mobile Computing
Pei Zheng and Lionel Ni

GMPLS: Architecture and Applications
Adrian Farrel and Igor Bryskin

Network Security: A Practical Approach
Jan L. Harrington

Content Networking: Architecture, Protocols, and Practice
Markus Hofmann and Leland R. Beaumont

Network Algorithmics: An Interdisciplinary Approach to Designing Fast Networked Devices
George Varghese

Network Recovery: Protection and Restoration of Optical, SONET-SDH, IP, and MPLS
Jean Philippe Vasseur, Mario Pickavet, and Piet Demeester

Routing, Flow, and Capacity Design in Communication and Computer Networks
Michał Pióro and Deepankar Medhi

Wireless Sensor Networks: An Information Processing Approach
Feng Zhao and Leonidas Guibas

Communication Networking: An Analytical Approach
Anurag Kumar, D. Manjunath, and Joy Kuri

The Internet and Its Protocols: A Comparative Approach
Adrian Farrel

Modern Cable Television Technology: Video, Voice, and Data Communications, 2e
Walter Ciciora, James Farmer, David Large, and Michael Adams

Bluetooth Application Programming with the Java APIs
C Bala Kumar, Paul J. Kline, and Timothy J. Thompson

Policy-Based Network Management: Solutions for the Next Generation
John Strassner

MPLS Network Management: MIBs, Tools, and Techniques
Thomas D. Nadeau

Developing IP-Based Services: Solutions for Service Providers and Vendors
Monique Morrow and Kateel Vijayananda

Telecommunications Law in the Internet Age
Sharon K. Black

Optical Networks: A Practical Perspective, Second Edition
Rajiv Ramaswami and Kumar N. Sivarajan

Internet QoS: Architectures and Mechanisms
Zheng Wang

TCP/IP Sockets in Java: Practical Guide for Programmers
Michael J. Donahoo and Kenneth L. Calvert

TCP/IP Sockets in C: Practical Guide for Programmers
Kenneth L. Calvert and Michael J. Donahoo

Multicast Communication: Protocols, Programming, and Applications
Ralph Wittmann and Martina Zitterbart

MPLS: Technology and Applications
Bruce Davie and Yakov Rekhter

High-Performance Communication Networks, Second Edition
Jean Walrand and Pravin Varaiya

Internetworking Multimedia
Jon Crowcroft, Mark Handley, and Ian Wakeman

Understanding Networked Applications: A First Course
David G. Messerschmitt

Integrated Management of Networked Systems: Concepts, Architectures, and Their Operational Application
Heinz-Gerd Hegering, Sebastian Abeck, and Bernhard Neumair

Virtual Private Networks: Making the Right Connection
Dennis Fowler

Networked Applications: A Guide to the New Computing Infrastructure
David G. Messerschmitt

Wide Area Network Design: Concepts and Tools for Optimization
Robert S. Cahn

For further information on these books and for a list of forthcoming titles, please visit our Web site at *http://www.mkp.com.*

The Illustrated Network

How TCP/IP Works in a Modern Network

Walter Goralski

AMSTERDAM • BOSTON • HEIDELBERG • LONDON
NEW YORK • OXFORD • PARIS • SAN DIEGO
SAN FRANCISCO • SINGAPORE • SYDNEY • TOKYO
Morgan Kaufmann is an imprint of Elsevier

Morgan Kaufmann Publishers is an imprint of Elsevier.
30 Corporate Drive, Suite 400
Burlington, MA 01803

This book is printed on acid-free paper. ♾

Library of Congress Cataloging-in-Publication Data

Goralski, Walter.
The illustrated network: how TCP/IP works in a modern network/Walter Goralski.
p. cm.—(The Morgan Kaufmann series in networking)
Includes bibliographical references and index.
ISBN 978-0-12-374541-5 (alk. paper)
1. TCP/IP (Computer network protocol) 2. Computer networks. I. Title.
TK5105.585.G664 2008
004.6'2–dc22

2008046728

For information on all Morgan Kaufmann publications, visit our Website at *www.mkp.com* or *www.books.elsevier.com*

Printed in the United States
08 09 10 11 12 10 9 8 7 6 5 4 3 2 1

Contents

Part V Network Management

Part VI Security

Part VII Media

Foreword

Network consolidation has been an industry trend since the turn of the century. Reducing capital investment by converging data, voice, video, virtual private networks (VPNs), and other services onto a single shared infrastructure is financially attractive; but the larger benefit is in not having to maintain and operate multiple, service-specific infrastructures. Fundamental to network consolidation—supporting a diverse set of services with a single infrastructure—is a common encapsulating protocol that accommodates different service transport requirements. The Internet protocol (IP) is that protocol.

Everything over IP

Things move fast in the networking industry; technologies can go from cutting edge to obsolete in a decade or less (think ATM, frame relay, token ring, and FDDI among others). It is therefore amazing that TCP/IP is 35 years old and evolved from ideas originating in the early 1960s.

Yet while the protocol invented by Vint Cerf and Bob Kahn in 1973 has undergone—and continues to undergo—hundreds of enhancements and one version upgrade, its core functions are essentially the same as they were in the mid 1980s. TCP/IP's antiquity, in an industry that unceremoniously discards technologies when something better comes along, is a testament to the protocol's elegance and flexibility.

And there is no sign that IP is coming to the end of its useful life. To the contrary, so many new IP-capable applications, devices, and services are being added to networks every day that a newer version, IPv6, has become necessary to provide sufficient IP addresses into the foreseeable future. As this foreword is written, IPv6 is in the very early stages of deployment; readers will still be learning from this book when IPv6 is the only version most people know.

The story of how TCP/IP came to dominate the networking industry is well known. Cerf, Kahn, Jon Postel, and many others who contributed to the early development of TCP/IP did so as a part of their involvement in creating ARPANET, the predecessor of the modern Internet. The protocol stack became further embedded in the infant industry when it was integrated into Unix, making it popular with developers.

But its acceptance was far from assured in those early years. Organizations such as national governments and telcos were uncomfortable with the informal "give it a try and see what works" process of the Working Groups—primarily made up of enthusiastic graduate students—that eventually became the Internet Engineering Task Force (IETF). Those cautious organizations wanted a networking protocol developed under a rigorous standardization process. The International Organization for Standardization (ISO) was tapped to develop a "mature" networking protocol suite, which was eventually to become the Open Systems Interconnection (OSI).

The ISO's *modus operandi* of establishing dense, thorough standards and releasing them only in complete, production-ready form took time. Even strong OSI advocates began using TCP/IP as a temporary but working solution while waiting for the ISO standards committees to finish their work. By the time OSI was ready, TCP/IP was so widely deployed, proven, and understood that few network operators could justify undertaking a migration to something different.

OSI survives today mainly in a few artifacts such as IS–IS and the ubiquitous OSI reference model. TCP/IP, in the meantime, is becoming an almost universal communications transport protocol.

The Illustrated Network

I am a visual person. I admire the capability of my more verbally oriented colleagues to easily discuss, in detail, a networking scenario, but I need to draw pictures to keep up.

When the first volume of the late W. Richard Stevens's *TCP/IP Illustrated* was released in 1994, it immediately became one of my favorite books, and continues to be at the top of my list of recommended books both for the student and for the reference shelf. Stevens's use of diagrams, configurations, and data captures to teach the TCP/IP protocol suite makes the book not just a textbook but a comprehensive set of case studies. It's about as visual as you can get without sitting in front of a protocol analyzer and watching packets fly back and forth.

But while the Stevens book has always been excellent for illustrating the behavior of individual TCP/IP components, it does not step back from that narrow focus to show you how these components interact at a large scale in a real network.

This is where Walt Goralski steps up. The book you are holding takes the same bottom-up approach (Stevens' words) to teaching the protocol suite: Each chapter builds on the previous, and each chapter gives you an intimate look at the protocol in action. But through an unprecedented collaboration with Juniper Networks, Goralski shows you not just interactions between a few devices in a lab but a production-scale view of a modern working network. The result is a practical, real-life, highly visual exploration of TCP/IP in its natural state.

The Illustrated Network: How TCP/IP Works in a Modern Network is destined to become one of the classics on practical IP networking and a cornerstone of the required reading lists of students and professionals alike.

Jeff Doyle
Westminster, Colorado

Preface

This is not a book on how to use the Internet. It is a book about how the Internet is made *useful for you*. The Internet is a public global network that runs on TCP/IP, which is frequently called the Internet Protocol Suite. A networking protocol is a set of rules that must be followed to accomplish something, and TCP/IP is actually a synthesis of the first two protocols that launched the Internet in its infancy, the Transmission Control Protocol (TCP) and the Internet Protocol (IP), which of course, allowed the transmission of information across the then youthful Internet. TCP/IP is the heart and soul of modern networks, and this book illustrates how that is accomplished. By using TCP/IP, we can observe how modern networks operate by following the transmission of modern data across all sorts of Internet connections.

Audience

This book is intended as a technical introduction into networking in general and the Internet in particular. I will not pretend that someone who has had no previous experience with either can easily plow through the entire book. But anyone who is experienced enough to check their email online, browse a Web site, download a movie or song, or chat with people around the world should have no trouble tackling the content of this book.

There are questions at the end of each chapter, but this is not a textbook per se. It can be used as a textbook as a first course in computer networking at the high school or undergraduate level. It will fit in with the computer science and electrical engineering departments. It is also explicitly intended for those entering the telecommunications industry or working for a company where the Internet is an essential part of the business plan (of which there are more and more each day).

Only one chapter uses C language code, and that only to provide information for the reader. Mathematical concepts that are not taught in high school are not used. There is no calculus, probability theory, and stochastic process concepts used in any chapter. The "pocket calculator" examples of public key encryption and Diffie-Hellman key distribution were carefully designed to illustrate the concepts, and yet make the mathematics as simple as possible.

What Is Unique about This Book?

What's in this book that you won't find in a half-dozen other books about TCP/IP? The list is not short.

1. This book uses the same network topology and addresses for every example and chapter.

2. This book treats IPv4 and IPv6 as equals.
3. This book covers the routing protocols as well as TCP/IP applications.
4. This book discusses ISPs as well as corporate LANs.
5. This book covers services provided as well as the protocols that provide them.
6. This book covers topics (MPLS, IPSec, etc.) not normally covered in other books on TCP/IP.

Why was the book written this way? Even in the Internet-conscious world we live in today, few study the entire network, the routers, TCP/IP, the Internet, and a host of related topics as part of their general education. What they do learn might seem like a lot, but when considered in relation to the enormous complexity of each of these topics, what is covered in general computer "literacy" or basic programming courses is really only a drop in the bucket.

As I was writing this book, and printing it out at my workplace, a silicon chip engineer-designer found a few chapters on top of the printer bin, and he began reading it. When I came to retrieve the printout, he was fascinated by the sample chapters. He wanted the book then and there. And as we talked, he made me realize that thousands of people are entering the networking industry every day, many from other occupations and disciplines. As the Internet grows, and society's dependence on the digital communication structure continues, more and more people need this overview of how modern networks operate.

The intellectually curious will not be satisfied with this smattering of and condensation of networking knowledge in a single volume. I'm hoping they will seek ways to increase their knowledge in specific areas of interest. This book covers hundreds of networking topics, and volumes have been written devoted to the intricacies of each one. For example, there are 20 to 30 solid books written on MPLS complexities and evolution, while the chapter here runs at about the same number of pages. My hope is that this book and this method of "illustrating" how a modern network works will contribute to more people seeking out those 20 to 30 books now that they know how the overall thing looks and works.

Like everyone else, I learned about networks, including routers and TCP/IP, mostly from books and from listening to others tell me what they knew. The missing piece, however, was being able to play with the network. The books were great, the discussions led to illumination of how this or that operated, but often I never "saw" it working. This book is a bit of a synthesis of the written and the seen. It attempts to give the reader the opportunity to see common tasks in a real, working, hands-on environment of the proper size and scale, and follow what happens behind the scenes. It's one thing to read about what happens when a Web site is accessed, but another to see it in action.

The purpose of this book is to allow you to see what is happening on a modern network when you access a Web site, write an email, download a song, or talk on the phone over the Internet. From that observation you will learn how a modern network works.

What You Won't Find in This Book

It might seem odd to list things that the book does not cover. But rather than have readers slog through and then find they didn't find what they were after, here's what you will not find in this edition of the book.

You will find no mention of the exciting new peer-to-peer protocols that distribute the server function around the network. There is no mention of the protocols used by chat rooms or services. The book does not explore music or movie download services. In other words, you won't find YouTube, IRC, iTunes, or even eBay mentioned in this book.

These topics are, of course, interesting and/or important. But the limitations of time and page count forced me to focus on essential topics. The other topics could easily form the foundation for *The Illustrated Network, Volume II: Beyond the Basics*.

The Illustrated Network

Many people frustrated with simple lab setups and restricted "live" networks have wished for a more complex and realistic yet secure environment where they can feel free to explore the TCP/IP protocols, layers, and applications without worrying that what they are seeing is limited to a quiet lab, or what they do might bring the whole network to its knees.

The days are long gone when an interested party could take over the whole network, from clients to servers to routers, and play with them at night or over the weekend. Networks are run on a normal business-hour schedule, especially now that the Web makes "prime time" on one side of the world when the other half is trying to get some sleep.

Many times I have encountered a new feature or procedure and said to myself, "I wish I could play with this and see what happens." But only after nearly 40 years of networking experience (I hooked up my first modem, about the size of a microwave oven, in 1966), have I finally arrived at the point where I could say, "I want to do this . . . ," and someone didn't tell me it could not be done.

Juniper Networks Inc., my employer, was in a unique position to help me with my plans to not merely talk about TCP/IP, or show contrived examples of the protocols in action, but to "illustrate" each piece with a series of clients, servers, routers, and connections (including the public Internet). They had the routers and links, and employed all the Unix and Windows-based hosts that I could possibly need. (In retrospect, there was probably some overkill in the network, as most chapters used only a couple of routers.) We decided not to upgrade the XP hosts to Vista, which was relatively new at the time, and I kept Internet Explorer 6 active, more or less out of convenience.

In any case, with the blessings of Juniper Networks, I set about creating the kind of network I needed for this book. It took a while, but in the end it was well worth it. We assembled a collection of five routers connected with SONET links,

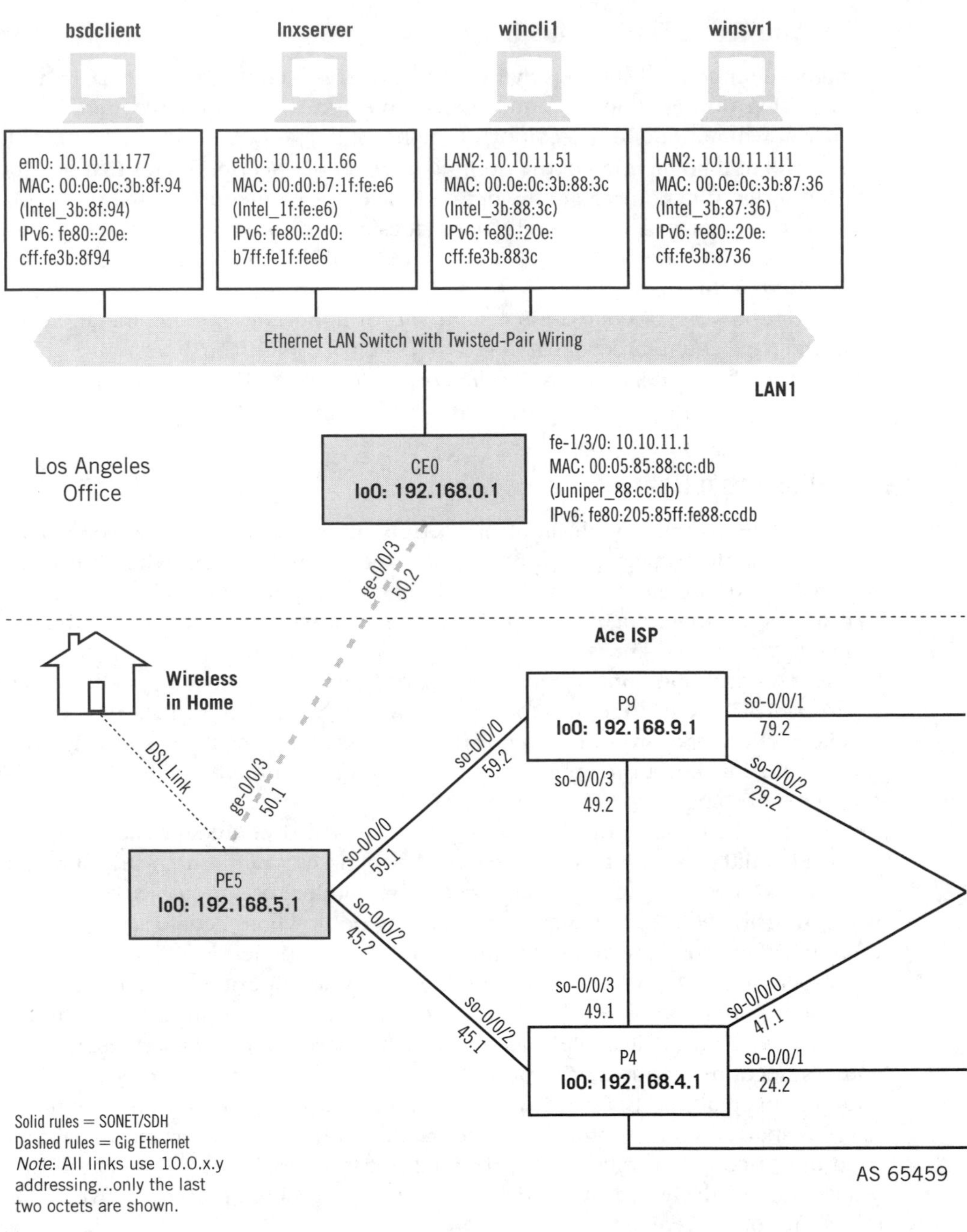
bsdclient
lnxserver
wincli1
winsvr1
em0: 10.10.11.177
MAC: 00:0e:0c:3b:8f:94
(Intel_3b:8f:94)
IPv6: fe80::20e:
cff:fe3b:8f94
eth0: 10.10.11.66
MAC: 00:d0:b7:1f:fe:e6
(Intel_1f:fe:e6)
IPv6: fe80::2d0:
b7ff:fe1f:fee6
LAN2: 10.10.11.51
MAC: 00:0e:0c:3b:88:3c
(Intel_3b:88:3c)
IPv6: fe80::20e:
cff:fe3b:883c
LAN2: 10.10.11.111
MAC: 00:0e:0c:3b:87:36
(Intel_3b:87:36)
IPv6: fe80::20e:
cff:fe3b:8736
Ethernet LAN Switch with Twisted-Pair Wiring
LAN1
Los Angeles
Office
CE0
lo0: 192.168.0.1
fe-1/3/0: 10.10.11.1
MAC: 00:05:85:88:cc:db
(Juniper_88:cc:db)
IPv6: fe80:205:85ff:fe88:ccdb
ge-0/0/3
50.2
Ace ISP
Wireless
in Home
DSL Link
ge-0/0/3
50.1
P9
lo0: 192.168.9.1
so-0/0/1
79.2
so-0/0/0
59.2
so-0/0/3
49.2
so-0/0/2
29.2
so-0/0/0
59.1
PE5
lo0: 192.168.5.1
so-0/0/2
45.2
so-0/0/3
49.1
so-0/0/0
47.1
so-0/0/2
45.1
P4
lo0: 192.168.4.1
so-0/0/1
24.2
Solid rules = SONET/SDH
Dashed rules = Gig Ethernet
Note: All links use 10.0.x.y
addressing...only the last
two octets are shown.
AS 65459

FIGURE P.1

The illustrated Network.

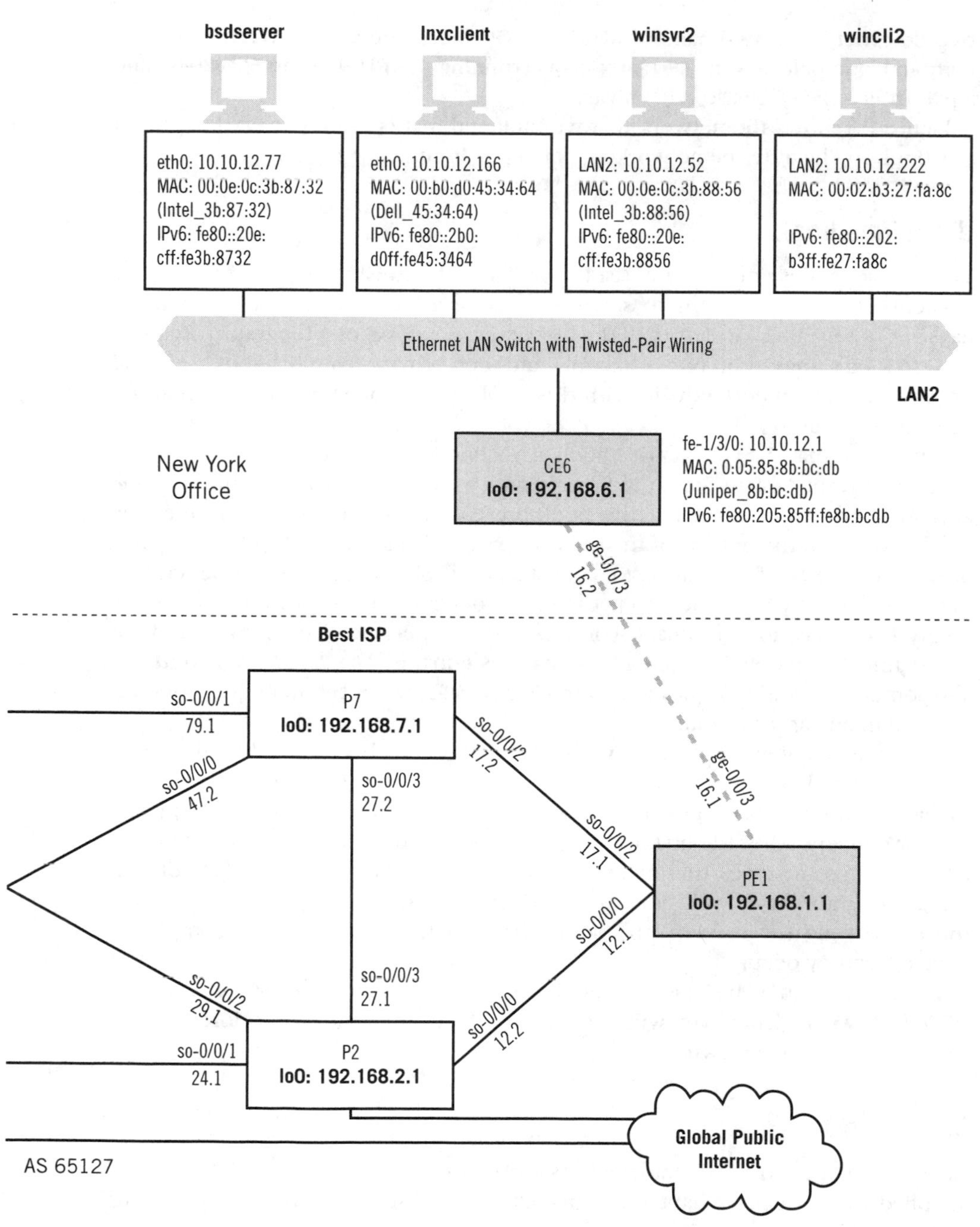

bsdserver
eth0: 10.10.12.77
MAC: 00:0e:0c:3b:87:32
(Intel_3b:87:32)
IPv6: fe80::20e:
cff:fe3b:8732
lnxclient
eth0: 10.10.12.166
MAC: 00:b0:d0:45:34:64
(Dell_45:34:64)
IPv6: fe80::2b0:
d0ff:fe45:3464
winsvr2
LAN2: 10.10.12.52
MAC: 00:0e:0c:3b:88:56
(Intel_3b:88:56)
IPv6: fe80::20e:
cff:fe3b:8856
wincli2
LAN2: 10.10.12.222
MAC: 00:02:b3:27:fa:8c
IPv6: fe80::202:
b3ff:fe27:fa8c
Ethernet LAN Switch with Twisted-Pair Wiring
LAN2
New York
Office
CE6
lo0: 192.168.6.1
fe-1/3/0: 10.10.12.1
MAC: 0:05:85:8b:bc:db
(Juniper_8b:bc:db)
IPv6: fe80:205:85ff:fe8b:bcdb
ge-0/0/3
16.2
Best ISP
so-0/0/1
79.1
P7
lo0: 192.168.7.1
so-0/0/2
17.2
ge-0/0/3
16.1
so-0/0/0
47.2
so-0/0/3
27.2
so-0/0/2
17.1
PE1
lo0: 192.168.1.1
so-0/0/0
12.1
so-0/0/2
29.1
so-0/0/3
27.1
so-0/0/0
12.2
so-0/0/1
24.1
P2
lo0: 192.168.2.1
Global Public
Internet
AS 65127

two Ethernet LANs, two pairs of Windows XP clients and servers (Home and Pro editions), one pair of Red Hat Linux hosts (running the RH 9 kernel 2.4.20-8), and a pair of FreeBSD (release 4.10) hosts.

Figure P.1 shows the network that we built and that is used in every chapter of this book to illustrate the networking concepts discussed.

Using This Book

This book is designed to be read from start to finish, chapter by chapter, sequentially. It seems funny to say this, because a lot of technical books these days are not meant to be "read" in the same way as a novel or a biography. Readers tend to look things up in books like this, and then browse from the spot they land on, which you can certainly do with this book, but probably more on a chapter-by-chapter level.

But I hope that the story in this book is as coherent as a mystery, if not as exciting as an adventure tale. From the first chapter, which offers readers a unique look at layered protocols, to the last, this book presents a story that proceeds in a logical fashion from the bottom of the Internet protocol suite to the top (and beyond, in some cases). So if you can, read from start to finish, as the chapters depend on previous ones. If you are new to networking concepts, or just beginning, I recommend this consecutive approach. For those more experienced, bobbing in and out is just fine, but remember that all emphasis is equal in *The Illustrated Network*, and sometimes you may question a topic's coverage, when the item questioned is covered in an earlier chapter.

As you're reading, you'll discover that generally, each chapter has the same structure. The beginning chapters, however, diverge from this format more than the later chapters do, as they require general exploration of the protocol, application, or concept. After the first few chapters, I begin the tasks of illustrating how it all works. In some cases, this involves not only the network built for this book, but the global Internet as well. Note that network configuration specifics, especially those involving the routers, vary somewhat, but these changes are completely detailed as they occur.

The companion Web site for this book is *www.elsevierdirect.com/companions/9780123745415*. There you will find many of the capture files to explore some of the protocols on your own.

Source Code

Chapter 3 on network technologies uses examples from wireless network captures supplied by Aeropeek. Chapter 12 on sockets uses listings from utility programs written by Michael J. Donahoo and Kenneth L. Calvert for their excellent book, *TCP/IP Sockets in C* (Morgan Kaufmann, 2001). Thanks to both groups for letting me use their material in this book.

ACKNOWLEDGMENTS

I would like to thank various leaders in their respective fields who have given me their time and read and reviewed selected chapters of this work. Their comments have made this a much better book than it would have been without their involvement. Any errors that remain are mine.

I would like to thank colleagues at Juniper Networks, Inc., who gave their time and effort to create this network. In many cases, they also helped with the book. It starts at the top with Scott Kriens, who has created an environment where creativity and exploration are encouraged. Thanks, Scott!

The list goes on to include June Loy, Aviva Garrett, Michael Tallon, Patrick Ames, Jason Lloyd, Mark Whittiker, Kent Ketell, and Jeremy Pruitt.

Finally I would like to thank my lead technical reviewers, Joel Jaeggli and Robin Pimentel, for the careful scrutiny they gave the book and the many fine corrections and comments they provided.

Lead Technical Reviewers

Joel Jaeggli works in the security and mobile connectivity group within Nokia. His time is divided between the operation of the nokia.net (AS 14277) research network and supporting the strategic planning needs of Nokia's security business. Projects with former employer, the University of Oregon, included the Network Startup Resource Center, Oregon Route views project, the Beyond BGP Project, and the Oregon Videolab. He is an active participant in several industry-related groups including the IETF (working group chair) and NANOG (two terms on the program committee). Joel frequently participates as an instructor or presenter at regional and international network meetings on Internet services and security-related topics.

Robin Pimentel is currently a network engineer at Facebook, where he helps the production network sustain growth alongside Facebook's user and application growth. Previously, Robin worked on the production network teams at Google and Yahoo. Robin also spent 6 years at Teradyne where he performed many networking, security, and Unix infrastructure engineering roles. Prior to his career in computer networks, Robin worked at Cadence Design Systems and Intel Corporation. While working in the chip sector, Robin specialized in silicon place and route, VHDL-based behavioral logic validation, and gate-level logic validation for on-chip memories.

About the Author

Walter Goralski has worked in the telecommunications and networking industry since 1970. He spent 14 years in the Bell System. After that he worked with minicomputers and LANs at Wang Laboratories and with the Internet at Pace University, where he was a graduate professor for 15 years. He joined Juniper Networks as a senior staff engineer in 2000 after 8 years as a technical trainer. Goralski is the author of 10 books about networking, including the bestselling *SONET/SDH* (now in its third edition). He has a master's degree in computer science from Pace University.

PART I

Networking Basics

All networks, from the smallest LAN to the global Internet, consist of similar components. Layered protocols are the rule, and this part of the book examines protocol suites, network devices, and the frames used on links that connect the devices.

CHAPTER

Protocols and Layers

1

What You Will Learn

In this chapter, you will learn about the protocol stack used on the global public Internet and how these protocols have been evolving in today's world. We'll review some key basic definitions and see the network used to illustrate all of the examples in this book, as well as the packet content, the role that hosts and routers play on the network, and how graphic user and command line interfaces (GUI and CLI, respectively) both are used to interact with devices.

You will learn about standards organizations and the development of TCP/IP RFCs. We'll cover encapsulation and how TCP/IP layers interact on a network.

This book is about what actually happens on a real network running the protocols and applications used on the Internet today. We'll be looking at the entire network—everything from the application level down to where the bits emerge from the local device and race across the Internet. A great deal of the discussion will revolve around the TCP/IP protocol suite, the protocols on which the Internet is built. The network that will run these protocols is shown in Figure 1.1.

Like most authors, I'll use TCP/IP as shorthand for the entire Internet protocol stack, but you should always be aware that the suite consists of many protocols, not just TCP and IP. The protocols in use are constantly growing and evolving as the Internet adapts to new challenges and applications. In the past few years, four trends have become clear in the protocol evolution:

Increased use of multimedia—The original Internet was not designed with proper quality of service assurances to support digital voice and video. However, the Internet now carries this as well as bulk and interactive data. (In this book, "data" means non-voice and non-video applications.) In the future, all forms of information should be able to use the Internet as an interactive distribution medium without major quality concerns.

Increasing bandwidth and mobility—The trend is toward higher bandwidth (capacity), even for mobile users. New wireless technologies seem to promise

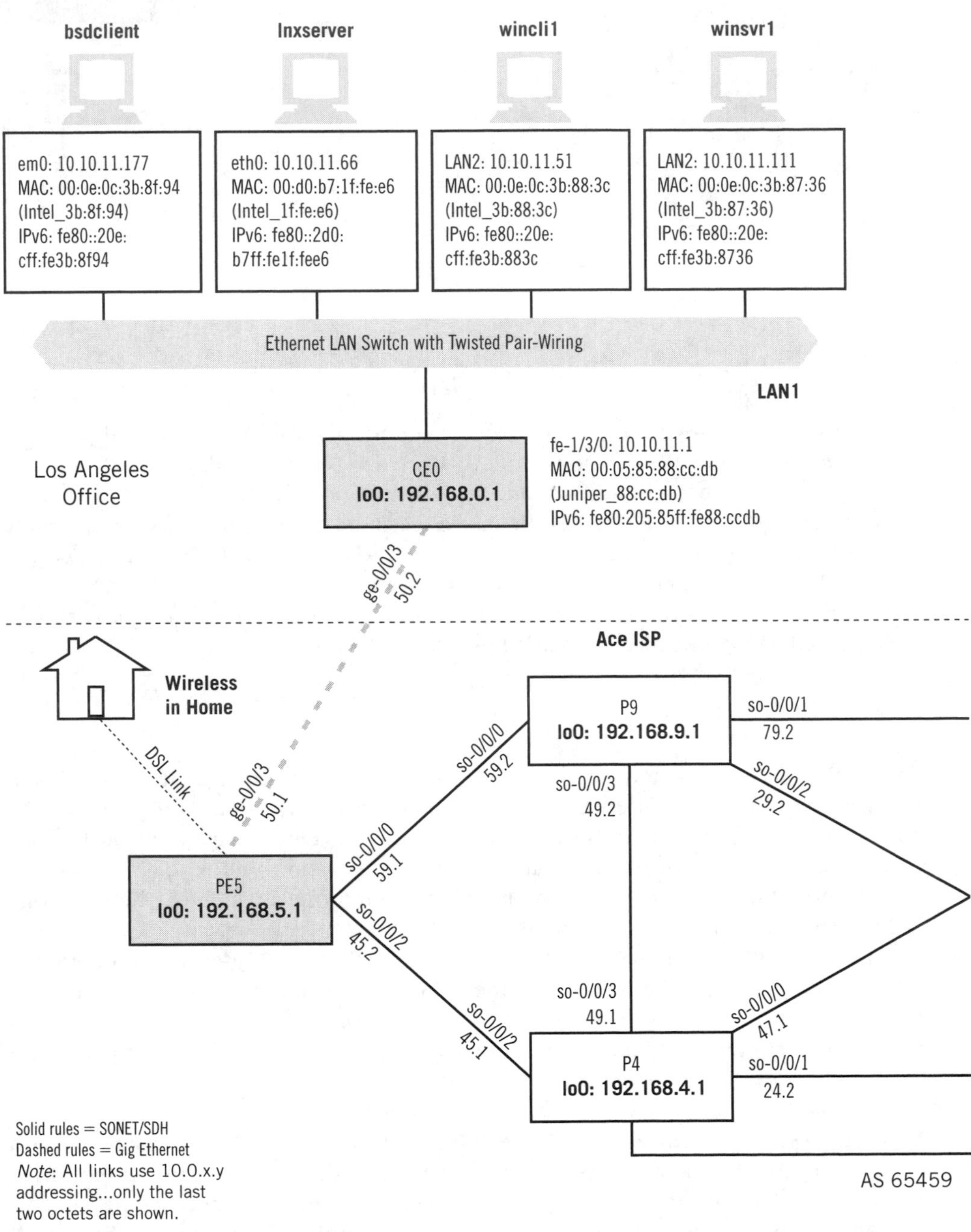

FIGURE 1.1

The Illustrated Network, showing the routers, links, and hosts on the network. Many of the layer addresses used in this book appear in the figure as well.

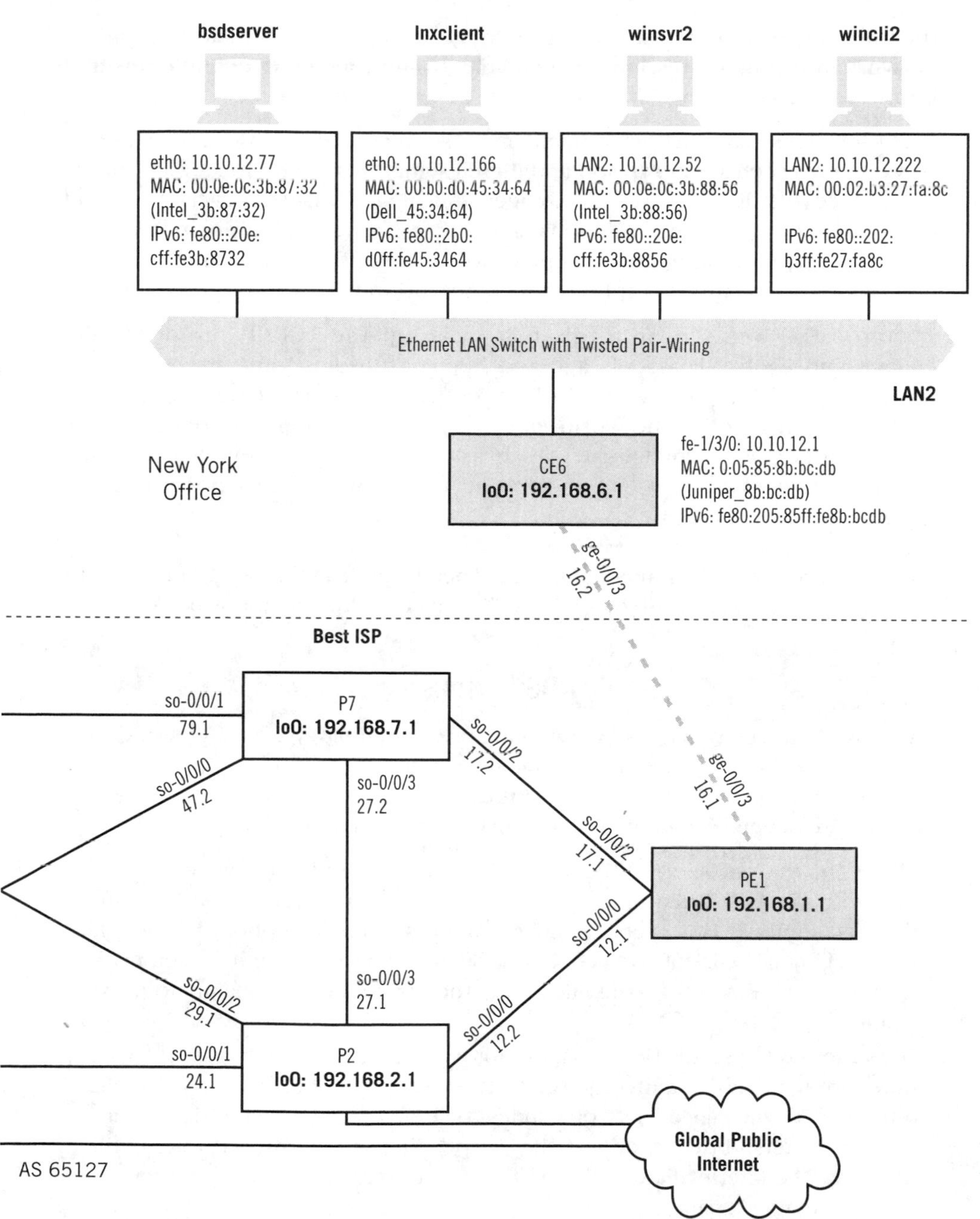
bsdserver
lnxclient
winsvr2
wincli2
eth0: 10.10.12.77
MAC: 00:0e:0c:3b:87:32
(Intel_3b:87:32)
IPv6: fe80::20e:
cff:fe3b:8732
eth0: 10.10.12.166
MAC: 00:b0:d0:45:34:64
(Dell_45:34:64)
IPv6: fe80::2b0:
d0ff:fe45:3464
LAN2: 10.10.12.52
MAC: 00:0e:0c:3b:88:56
(Intel_3b:88:56)
IPv6: fe80::20e:
cff:fe3b:8856
LAN2: 10.10.12.222
MAC: 00:02:b3:27:fa:8c
IPv6: fe80::202:
b3ff:fe27:fa8c
Ethernet LAN Switch with Twisted Pair-Wiring
LAN2
New York
Office
CE6
lo0: 192.168.6.1
fe-1/3/0: 10.10.12.1
MAC: 0:05:85:8b:bc:db
(Juniper_8b:bc:db)
IPv6: fe80:205:85ff:fe8b:bcdb
ge-0/0/3
16.2
Best ISP
so-0/0/1
79.1
P7
lo0: 192.168.7.1
so-0/0/2
17.2
ge-0/0/3
16.1
so-0/0/0
47.2
so-0/0/3
27.2
so-0/0/2
17.1
PE1
lo0: 192.168.1.1
so-0/0/0
12.1
so-0/0/2
29.1
so-0/0/3
27.1
so-0/0/0
12.2
so-0/0/1
24.1
P2
lo0: 192.168.2.1
Global Public
Internet
AS 65127

the "Internet everywhere." Users are no longer as restricted to analog telephone network modem bit rates, and new end-electronics, last-mile technologies, and improved wiring and backbones are the reason.

Security—Attacks have become much more sophisticated as well. The use of privacy tools such as encryption and digital signatures are no longer an option, but a necessity. E-commerce is a bigger and bigger business every year, and on-line banking, stock transactions, and other financial manipulations make strong security technologies essential. Identity verification is another place where new applications employ strong encryption for security purposes.

New protocols—Even the protocols that make up the TCP/IP protocol suite change and evolve. Protocols age and become obsolete, and make way for newer ways of doing things. IPv6, the eventual successor for IPv4, is showing up on networks around the world, especially in applications where the supply of IPv4 addresses is inadequate (such as cell phones). In every case, each chapter attempts to be as up-to-date and forward-looking as possible in its particular area.

We will talk about these trends and more in later chapters in this book. For now, let's take a good look at the network that will be illustrated in the rest of this book.

Key Definitions

Any book about computers and networking uses terminology with few firm definitions and rules of usage. So here are some key terms that are used over and over throughout this book. Keep in mind that these terms may have varying interpretations, but are defined according to the conventions used in this book.

- **Host:** For the purposes of this book, a host is any endpoint or end system device that runs TCP/IP. In most cases, these devices are ordinary desktop and laptop computers. However, in some cases hosts can be cell phones, handheld personal digital assistants (PDAs), and so on. In the past, TCP/IP has been made to run on toasters, coffee machines, and other exotic devices, mainly to prove a point.
- **Intermediate system:** Hosts that do not communicate directly pass information through one or more intermediate systems. Intermediate systems are often generically called "network nodes" or just "nodes." Specific devices are labeled "routers," "bridges," or "switches," depending on their precise roles in the network. The intermediate nodes on the Illustrated Network are routers with some switching capabilities.
- **System:** This is just shorthand for saying the device can be a host, router, switch, node, or almost anything else on a network. Where clarity is important, we'll always specify "end system" or "intermediate system."

THE ILLUSTRATED NETWORK

Each chapter in this book will begin with a look at how the protocol or chapter contents function on a real network. The Illustrated Network, built in the Tech Pubs department of Juniper Networks, Inc., in Sunnyvale, California, is shown in Figure 1.1.

The network consists of systems running three different operating systems (Windows XP, Linux, and FreeBSD Unix) connected to Ethernet local area networks (LANs). These systems are deployed in pairs, as either *clients* (for now, defined as "systems with users doing work in front of them") and *servers* (for now, defined as "systems with administrators, and usually intended only for remote use"). When we define the *client* and *server* terms more precisely, we'll see that the host's role at the protocol level depends on which host initiates the connection or interaction. The hosts can be considered to be part of a corporate network with offices in New York and Los Angeles.

Addressing information is shown for each host, router, and link between devices. We'll talk about all of these addresses in detail later, and why the hosts in particular have several addresses in varying formats. (For example, the hosts only have *link-local* IPv6 address, and not global ones.)

The LANs are attached to Juniper Networks' *routers* (also called intermediate nodes, although some are technically *gateways*), which in turn are connected in our network to other routers by point-to-point synchronous optical network (SONET) links, a type of wide area network (WAN) link. Other types of links, such as asynchronous transfer mode (ATM) or Ethernet, can be used to connect widely separated routers, but SONET links are very common in a telecommunications context. There is a link to the global Internet and to a home-based wireless LAN as well. The home office link uses digital

Major Parts of the Illustrated Network

The Illustrated Network is composed of four major components. At the top are two Ethernet LANs with the hosts of our fictional organization, one in New York and one in Los Angeles. The offices have different ISPs (a common enough situation), and the site routers link to Ace ISP on the West Coast and Best ISP on the East Coast with Gigabit Ethernet links (more on links in the next chapter). The two ISPs link to each other directly and also link to the "global public Internet." Just what this is will be discussed once we start looking at the routers themselves.

One employee of this organization (the author) is shown linking a home wireless network to the West Coast ISP with a high-speed ("broadband") digital subscriber line (DSL) link. The rest of the links are high-speed WAN links and two Gigabit Ethernet (GE) links. (It's becoming more common to use GE links across longer distances, but this network employs other WAN technologies.)

The Illustrated Network is representative of many LANs, ISPs, and users around the world.

subscriber line (DSL), a form of dedicated broadband Internet access, and not dial-up modem connectivity.

This network will be used throughout this book to illustrate how the different TCP/IP protocols running on hosts and routed networks combine to form the Internet. Some protocols will be examined from the perspective of the hosts and LAN (on the local "user edge") and others will be explored from the perspective of the service provider (on the global "network edge"). Taken together, these viewpoints will allow us to see exactly how the network works, inside and out.

Let's explore the Illustrated Network a little, from the user edge, just to demonstrate the conventions that will be used at the beginning of each chapter in this book.

Remote Access to Network Devices

We can use a host (client or server system running TCP/IP) to remotely access another device on the local network. In the context of this book, a *host* is a client or server system. We can loosely (some would say *very* loosely) define *clients* as typically the PCs on which users are doing work, and that's how we'll use the term for now. On the other hand, *servers* (again loosely) are devices that usually have administrators tending them. Servers are often gathered in special equipment racks in rooms with restricted access (the "server room"), although print servers are usually not. We'll be more precise about the differences between clients and servers as the "initiating protocol" later in this book.

Let's use host `lnxclient` to remotely access the host `bsdserver` on one of the LANs. We'll use the secure shell application, `ssh`, for remote access and log in (the `-l` option) as `remote-user`. There are other remote access applications, but in this book we'll use `ssh`. We'll use the command-line interface (CLI) on the Linux host to do so.

```
[root@lnxclient admin]# ssh -l remote-user@bsdserver
Password:
Last login: Sun Mar 17 16:12:54 2008 from securepptp086.s
Copyright (c) 1980, 1983, 1986, 1988, 1990, 1991, 1993, 1994
The Regents of the University of California. All rights reserved.
FreeBSD 4.10-RELEASE (GENERIC) #0: Tue May 25 22:47:12 GMT 2004
Welcome to FreeBSD!...
```

We can also use a host to access a *router* on the network. As mentioned earlier, a *router* is a type of intermediate system (or network node) that forwards IP data units along until they reach their destination. A router that connects a LAN to an Internet link is technically a *gateway*. We'll be more precise about these terms and functions in later chapters dealing with routers and routing specifically.

Let's use host `bsdclient` to remotely access the router on the network that is directly attached to the LAN, router `CE0` ("Customer Edge router #10"). Usually, we'd do this to configure the router using the CLI. As before, we'll use the secure shell application, `ssh`, for remote access and log in as `remote-user`. We'll again use the CLI on the Unix host to do so.

```
bsdclient> ssh -l remote-user@CEO
remote-user@ce0's password:
--- JUNOS 8.4R1.3 built 2007-08-06 06:58:15 UTC
remote-user@CEO>
```

These examples show the conventions that will appear in this book when command-line procedures are shown. All prompts, output, and code listings appear `like this`. Whenever a user types a command to produce some output, the command typed will appear `like this`. We'll see CLI examples from Windows hosts as well.

Illustrated Network Router Roles

The intermediate systems or network nodes used on the Illustrated Network are routers. Not all of the routers play the same role in the network, and some have switching capabilities. The router's role depends on its position in the network. Generally, smaller routers populate the edge of the network near the LANs and hosts, while larger routers populate the ISP's network core. The routers on our network have one of three network-centric designations; we have LAN switches also, but these are not routers.

- **Customer edge (CE):** These two routers belong to us, in our role as the customer who owns and operates the hosts and LANs. These CE routers are smaller than the other routers in terms of size, number of ports, and capabilities. Technically, on this network, they perform a gateway role.
- **Provider edge (PE):** These two routers gather the traffic from customers (typically there are many CE routers, of course). They are not usually accessible by customers.
- **Provider (P):** These six routers are arranged in what is often called a "quad." The two service providers on the Illustrated Network each manage two providers' routers in their network core. Quads make sure traffic flows smoothly even if any one router or one link fails on the provider's core networks.
- **Ethernet LAN switches:** The network also contains two Ethernet LAN switches. We'll spend a lot of time exploring switches later. For now, consider that switches operate on Layer 2 frames and routers operate on Layer 3 packets.

Now, what is this second example telling us? First of all, it tells us that routers, just like ordinary hosts, will allow a remote user to log in if they have the correct user ID and password. It would appear that routers aren't all that much different from hosts. However, this can be a little misleading. Hosts generally have different roles in a network than routers. For now, we'll just note that for security reasons, you don't want it to be easy for people to remotely access routers, because intruders can cause a lot of damage after compromising just a single router. In practice, a lot more security than just passwords is employed to restrict router access.

Secure remote access to a router is usually necessary, so not running the *process* or *entity* that allows remote access isn't an option. An organization with a large network could have routers in hundreds of locations scattered all over the country (or even the world). These devices need *management*, which includes tasks such as changing the configuration of the routers. Router configuration often includes details about the protocols' operation and other capabilities of the router, which can change as the network evolves. Software upgrades need to be distributed as well. Troubleshooting procedures often require direct entry of commands to be executed on the router. In short, remote access and file transfer can be very helpful for router and network management purposes.

File Transfer to a Router

Let's look at the transfer of a new router configuration file, for convenience called `routerconfig.txt`, from a client host (`wincli2`) to router `CE0`. This time we'll use a GUI for the file transfer protocol (FTP) application, which will be shown as a figure, as in Figure 1.2. First, we have to remotely access the router.

The main window section in the figure shows remote access and the file listing of the default directory on the router, which is `/var/home/remote` (the router uses the Unix file system). The listing in the lower right section is the contents of the default

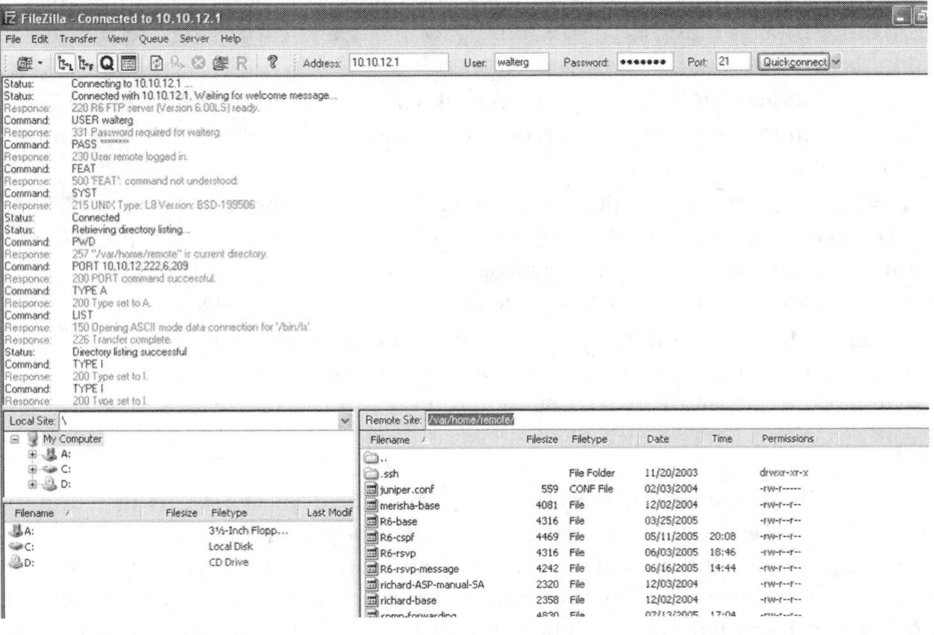

FIGURE 1.2

Remote access for FTP using a GUI. Note how the different panes give different types of information, yet bring it all together.

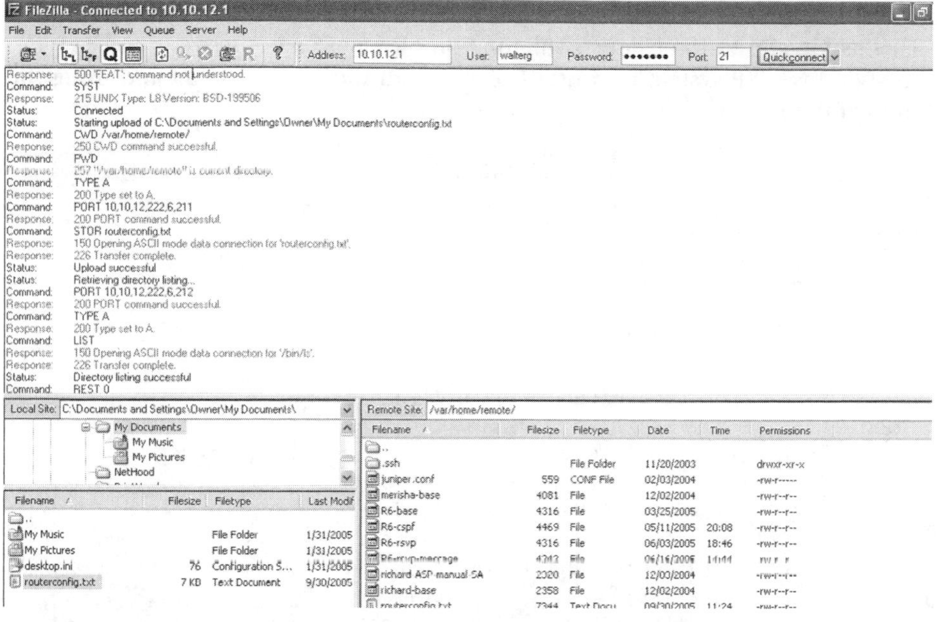

FIGURE 1.3

File transfer with a GUI. There are commands (user mouse clicks that trigger messages), responses (the server's replies), and status lines (reports on the state of the interaction).

directory, not part of the command/response dialog between host and router. The lower left section shows the file system on the host, which is a Windows system. Note that the file transfer is not encrypted or secured in any way.

Most "traditional" Unix-derived TCP/IP applications have both CLI and GUI interfaces available, and which one is used is usually a matter of choice. Older Unix systems, the kind most often used on the early Internet, didn't typically have GUI interfaces, and a lot of users prefer the CLI versions, especially for book illustrations. GUI applications work just as well, and don't require users to know the individual commands well. When using the GUI version of FTP, all the user has to do is "drag and drop" the local `routerconfig.txt` file from the lower left pane to the lower right pane of the window to trigger the commands (which the application produces "automatically") for the transfer to occur. This is shown in Figure 1.3.

With the GUI, the user does not have to issue any FTP commands directly.

CLI and GUI

We'll use both the CLI and GUI forms of TCP/IP applications in this book. In a nod to tradition, we'll use the CLI on the Unix systems and the GUI versions when Windows systems are used in the examples. (CLI commands often capture details that are not easily seen in GUI-based applications.) Keep in mind that you can use GUI applications on Unix and the CLI on Windows (you have to run `cmd` first to access the Windows CLI). This listing shows the router configuration file transfer of `newrouterconfig.txt` from the Windows XP system to router `CE6`, but with the Windows CLI and using the IP address of the router.

```
C:\Documents and Settings\Owner> ftp 10.10.12.1
Connected to 10.10.12.1.
220 R6 FTP server (version 6.00LS) ready.
User (10.10.12.1:none)):walterg
331 Password required for walterg.
Password: ********
ftp> dir
200 PORT command successful.
150 Opening ASCII mode data connection for '/bin/ls'.
total 128
drwxr-xr-x 2 remote staff 512 Nov 20 2004 .ssh
-rw-r--r-- 1 remote staff 4316 Mar 25 2006 R6-base
-rw-r--r-- 1 remote staff 4469 May 11 20:08 R6-cspf
-rw-r--r-- 1 remote staff 4316 Jun 3 18:46 R6-rsvp
-rw-r--r-- 1 remote staff 4242 Jun 16 14:44 R6-rsvp-message
-rw-r----- 1 remote staff 559 Feb 3 2005 juniper.conf
-rw-r--r-- 1 remote staff 4081 Dec 2 2005 merisha-base
-rw-r--r-- 1 remote staff 2320 Dec 3 2005 richard-ASP-manual-SA
-rw-r--r-- 1 remote staff 2358 Dec 2 2005 richard-base
-rw-r--r-- 1 remote staff 7344 Sep 30 11:28 routerconfig.txt
-rw-r--r-- 1 remote staff 4830 Jul 13 17:04 snmp-forwarding
-rw-r--r-- 1 remote staff 3190 Jan 7 2006 tp6
-rw-r--r-- 1 remote staff 4315 May 5 12:49 wjg-ORA-base-TP6
-rw-r--r-- 1 remote staff 4500 May 6 09:47 wjg-tp6-with-ipv6
-rw-r--r-- 1 remote staff 4956 May 8 13:42 wjg-with-ipv6
226 transfer complete
ftp: 923 bytes received in 0.00Seconds 923000.00Kbytes/sec.
ftp> bin
200 Type set to I
ftp> put newrouterconfig.text
200 PORT command successful.
150 Opening ASCII mode data connection for "newrouterconfig.txt".
226 Transfer complete.
ftp: 7723 bytes received in 0.00Seconds 7344000.00Kbytes/sec.
ftp>_
```

In some cases, we'll list CLI examples line by line, as here, and in other cases we will show them in a figure.

Ethereal and Packet Capture

Of course, showing a GUI or command line FTP session doesn't reveal much about how the network functions. We need to look at the bits that are flowing through the network. Also, we need to look at applications, such as the file transfer protocol, from the network perspective.

To do so, we'll use a packet capture utility. This book will use the Ethereal packet capture program in fact and by name throughout, although shortly after the project began, Ethereal became Wireshark. The software is the same, but all development will now be done through the Wireshark organization. Wireshark (Ethereal) is available free of charge at *www.wireshark.org*. It is notable that Wireshark, unlike a lot of similar applications, is available for Windows as well as most Unix/Linux variations.

Ethereal is a network protocol analyzer program that keeps a copy of every packet of information that emerges from or enters the system on a particular interface. Ethereal also parses the packet and shows not only the bit patterns, but what those bit groupings mean. Ethereal has a summary screen, a pane for more detailed information, and a pane that shows the raw bits that Ethereal captured. The nicest feature of Ethereal is that the packet capture stream can be saved in a standard *libpcap* format file (usually with a `.cap` or `.pcap` extension), which is common among most protocol analyzers. These files can be read and parsed and replayed by `tcpdump` and other applications or Ethereal on other systems.

Figure 1.4 shows the same router configuration file transfer as in Figure 1.2 and 1.3, and at the same time. However, this time the capture is not at the user level, but at the network level.

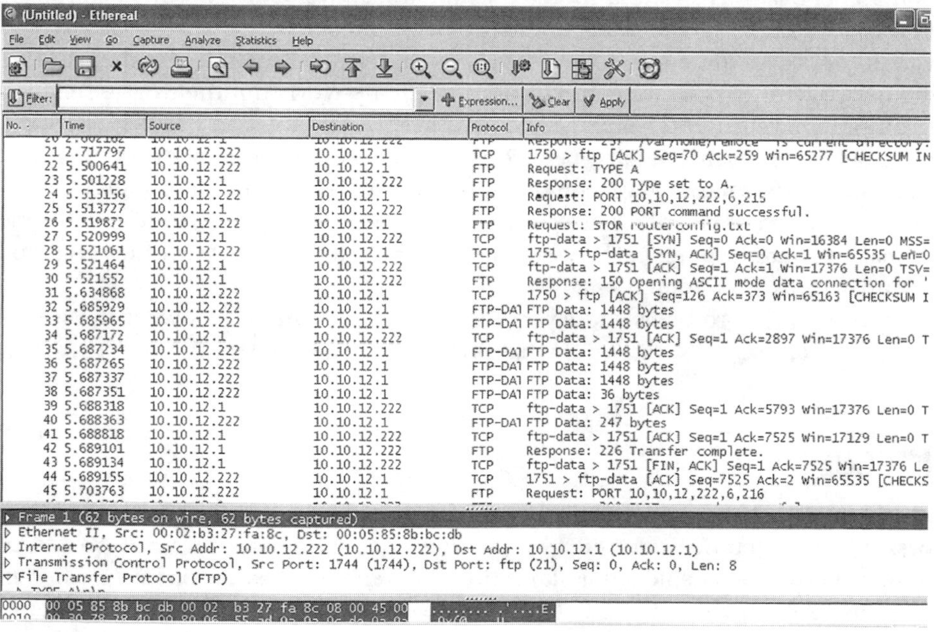

FIGURE 1.4

Ethereal FTP capture of the file transfer shown earlier from the user perspective.

Each packet captured is numbered sequentially and given a time stamp, and its source and destination address is listed. The protocol is in the next column, followed by the interpretation of the packet's meaning and function. The packet to request the router to `STOR routerconfig.txt` is packet number 26 in the sequence.

Already we've learned something important: that with TCP/IP, the number of packets exchanged to accomplish even something basic and simple can be surprisingly large. For this reason, in some cases, we'll only show a section of the panes of the full Ethereal screen, only to cut down on screen clutter. The captured files are always there to consult later.

With these tools—CLI listings, GUI figures, and Ethereal captures—we are prepared to explore all aspects of modern network operation using TCP/IP.

First Explorations in Networking

We've already seen that an authorized user can access a router from a host. We've seen that routers can run the `ssh` and `ftp` server applications `sshd` and `ftpd`, and the suspicion is that they might be able to run even more (they can just as easily be `ssh` and `ftp` clients). However, the router application suite is fairly restrictive. You usually don't, for example, send email to a router, or log in to a router and then browse Web sites. There is a fundamental difference in the roles that hosts and routers play in a network. A router doesn't have all of the application software you would expect to find on a client or server, and a router uses them mainly for management purposes. However, it does have all the layers of the protocol suite.

TCP/IP networks are a mix of hosts and routers. Hosts often talk to other devices on the network, or expose their applications to the network, but their basic function is to run programs. However, network systems like routers exist to keep the network running, which is their primary task. Router-based applications support this task, although in theory, routers only require a subset of the TCP/IP protocol suite layers to perform their operational role. You also have to manage routers, and that requires some additional software in practice. However, don't expect to find chat or other common client applications on a router.

What is it about protocols and layers that is so important? That's what the rest of this chapter is about. Let's start with what protocols are and where they come from.

PROTOCOLS

Computers are systems or devices capable of running a number of processes. These processes are sometimes referred to as *entities*, but we'll use the term processes. Computer networks enable communication between processes on two different devices that are capable of sending and receiving information in the form of bits (0s and 1s). What pattern should the exchange of bits follow? Processes that exchange bit streams must agree on a *protocol*. A protocol is a set of rules that determines all aspects of data communication.

A protocol is a standard or convention that enables and controls the connection, communication, and transfer of information between two communications endpoints, or hosts. A protocol defines the rules governing the syntax (what can be communicated), semantics (how it can be communicated), and synchronization (when and at what speed it can be communicated) of the communications procedure. Protocols can be implemented on hardware, software, or a combination of both.

Protocols are not the same as standards: some standards have never been implemented as workable protocols, while some of the most useful protocols are only loosely defined (this sometimes makes interconnection an adventure). The protocols discussed in this book vary greatly in degree of sophistication and purpose. However, most of the protocols specify one or more of the following:

Physical connection—The host typically uses different hardware depending on whether the connection is wired or wireless, and some other parameters might require manual configuration. However, protocols are used to supply details about the network connection (speed is part of this determination). The host can usually detect the presence (or absence) of the other endpoint devices as well.

Handshaking—A protocol can define the rules for the initial exchange of information across the network.

Negotiation of parameters—A protocol can define a series of actions to establish the rules and limits used for communicating across the network.

Message delimiters—A protocol can define what will constitute the start and end of a message on the network.

Message format—A protocol can define how the content of a message is structured, usually at the "field" level.

Error detection—A protocol can define how the receiver can detect corrupt messages, unexpected loss of connectivity, and what to do next. A protocol can simply fail or try to correct the error.

Error correction—A protocol can define what to do about these error situations. Note that error recovery usually consists of both error-detection and error-correction protocols.

Termination of communications—A protocol can define the rules for gracefully stopping communicating endpoints.

Protocols at various layers provided the abstraction necessary for Internet success. Application developers did not have to concern themselves overly with the physical properties of the network. The expanded use of communications protocols has been a major contributor to the Internet's success, acceptance, flexibility, and power.

Standards and Organizations

Anyone can define a protocol. Simply devise a set of rules for any or all of the phases of communication and convince others to make hardware or software that implements the new method. Of course, an implementer could try to be the only source of a given protocol, a purely *proprietary* situation, and this was once a popular way to develop protocols. After all, who knew better how to network IBM computers than IBM? Today, most closed protocols have given way to *open* protocols based on published *standards*, especially since the Internet strives for connectivity between all types of computers and related devices and is not limited to equipment from a certain vendor. Anyone who implements an open protocol correctly from public documents should in most cases be able to interoperate with other versions of the same protocol.

Standards promote and maintain an open and competitive market for network hardware and software. The overwhelming need for *interoperability* today, both nationally and internationally, has increased the set of choices in terms of vendor and capability for each aspect of data communications. However, proprietary protocols intended for a limited architecture or physical network are still around, of course. Proprietary protocols might have some very good application-specific protocols, but could probably not support things like the Web as we know it. Making something a standard does not guarantee market acceptance, but it is very difficult for a protocol to succeed without a standard for everyone to follow. Standards provide essential guidelines to manufacturers, vendors, service providers, consultants, government agencies, and users to make sure the interconnectivity needed today is there.

Data communication standards fall into two major categories: *de jure* ("by rule or regulation") and *de facto* ("by fact or convention").

De jure—These standards have been approved by an officially recognized body whose job is to standardize protocols and other aspects of networking. *De jure* standards often have the force of law, even if they are called *recommendations* (for these basic standards, it is recommended that nations use their own enforcement methods, such as fines, to make sure they are followed).

De facto—Standards that have *not* been formally approved but are widely followed fall into this category. If someone wants to do something different, such as a manufacturer of network equipment, this method can be used to quickly establish a new product or technology. These types of standards can always be proposed for *de jure* approval.

When it comes to the Internet protocols, things are a bit more complicated. There are very few official standards, and there are no real penalties involved for not following them (other than the application not working as promised). On the Internet, a "*de facto* standard" forms a *reference implementation* in this case. *De facto* standards are also often subportions or implementation details for formal standards, usually when the formal standard falls short of providing all the information needed to create a working program. Internet standard proposals in many cases require running code at some stages of the process: at least the *de facto* code will cover the areas that the standard missed.

The standards for the TCP/IP protocol suite now come from the Internet Engineering Task Force (IETF), working in conjunction with other Internet organizations. The IETF is neither strictly a de facto nor de jure standards organization: There is no force of law behind Internet standards; they just don't work the way they should if not done correctly. We'll look at the IETF in detail shortly. The Internet uses more than protocol standards developed by the IETF. The following organizations are the main ones that are the sources of these other standards.

Institute of Electrical and Electronics Engineers

This international organization is the largest society of professional engineers in the world. One of its jobs is to oversee the development and adaptation of international standards, often in the local area network (LAN) arena. Examples of IEEE standards are all aspects of wireless LANs (IEEE 802.11).

American National Standards Institute

Although ANSI is actually a private nonprofit organization, and has no affiliation with the federal government, its goals include serving as the national institution for coordinating voluntary standardization in the United States as a way of advancing the U.S. economy and protecting the public interest. ANSI's members are consumer groups, government and regulatory bodies, industry associations, and professional societies. Other countries have similar organizations that closely track ANSI's actions. The indispensable American Standard Code for Information Interchange (ACSII) that determines what bits mean is an example of an ANSI standard.

Electronic Industries Association

This is a nonprofit organization aligned with ANSI to promote electronic manufacturing concerns. The EIA has contributed to networking by defining physical connection interfaces and specifying electrical signaling methods. The popular Recommended Jack #45 (RJ-45) connector for twisted pair LANs is an example of an EIA standard.

ISO, or International Standards Organization

Technically, this is the International Organization for Standardization in English, one of its official languages, but is always called the *ISO*. "ISO" is not an acronym or initialism for the organization's full name in either English or French (its two official languages). Rather, the organization adopted ISO based on the Greek word *isos*, meaning *equal*. Recognizing that the organization's initials would vary according to language, its founders chose ISO as the universal short form of its name. This, in itself, reflects the aim of the organization: to equalize and standardize across cultures. This multinational body's members are drawn from the standards committees of various governments. They are a voluntary organization dedicated to agreement on worldwide standards. The ISO's major contribution in the field of networking is with the creation of a *model* of data networking, the *Open Systems Interconnection Reference Model (ISO-RM)*, which also forms the basis for a working set of protocols. The United States is represented by ANSI in the ISO.

International Telecommunications Union–Telecommunication Standards Sector

A global economy needs international standards not only for data networks, but for the global *public switched telephone network* (PSTN). The United Nations formed a committee under the International Telecommunications Union (ITU), known as the Consultative Committee for International Telegraphy and Telephony (CCITT), that was eventually reabsorbed into the parent body as the ITU-T in 1993. All communications that cross national boundaries must follow ITU-T "recommendations," which have the force of law. However, inside a nation, local standards can apply (and usually do). A network architecture called asynchronous transfer mode (ATM) is an example of an ITU-T standard.

In addition to these standards organizations, networking relies on various *forums* to promote new technologies while the standardization process proceeds at the national and international levels. Forum members essentially pledge to follow the specifications of the forum when it comes to products, services, and so forth, although there is seldom any penalty for failing to do so. The Metro Ethernet Forum (MEF) is a good example of the modern forum in action.

The role of regulatory agencies cannot be ignored in standard discussions. It makes no sense to develop a new service for wireless networking in the United States, for example, if the Federal Communications Commission (FCC) has forbidden the use of the frequencies used by the new service for that purpose. Regulated industries include radio, television, and wireless and cable systems.

Request for Comment and the Internet Engineering Task Force

What about the Internet itself? The Internet Engineering Task Force (IETF) is the organization directly responsible for the development of Internet standards. The IETF has its own system for standardizing network components. In particular, Internet standards cover many of the protocols used by devices attached to the Internet, especially those closer to the user (applications) than to the physical network.

Internet standards are formalized regulations followed and used by those who work on the Internet. They are specifications that have been tested and must be followed. There is a strict procedure that all Internet components follow to become standards. A specification starts out as an *Internet draft*, a working document that often is revised, has no official status, and has a 6-month life span. Developers often work from these drafts, and much can be learned from the practical experience of implementation of a draft. If recommended, the Internet authorities can publish the draft as a *request for comment (RFC)*. The term is historical, and does not imply that feedback is required (most of the feedback is provided in the drafting process). Each RFC is edited, assigned a number, and available to all. Not all RFCs are standards, even those that define protocols.

This book will make heavy use of RFCs to explain all aspects of TCP/IP and the Internet, so a few details are in order. RFCs have various *maturity levels* that they go through in their lifetimes, according to their *requirement levels*. The RFC life-cycle maturity levels are shown in Figure 1.5. Note that the timeline does not always apply, or is not applied in a uniform fashion.

A specification can fall into one of six maturity levels, after which it passes to historical status and is useful only for tracking a protocol's development. Following introduction as an Internet draft, the specification can be a:

Proposed standard—The specification is now well understood, stable, and sufficiently interesting to the Internet community. The specification is now usually tested and implemented by several groups, if this has not already happened at the draft level.

Draft standard—After at least two successful and independent implementations, the proposed standard is elevated to a draft standard. Without complications, and with modifications if specific problems are uncovered, draft standards normally become Internet standards.

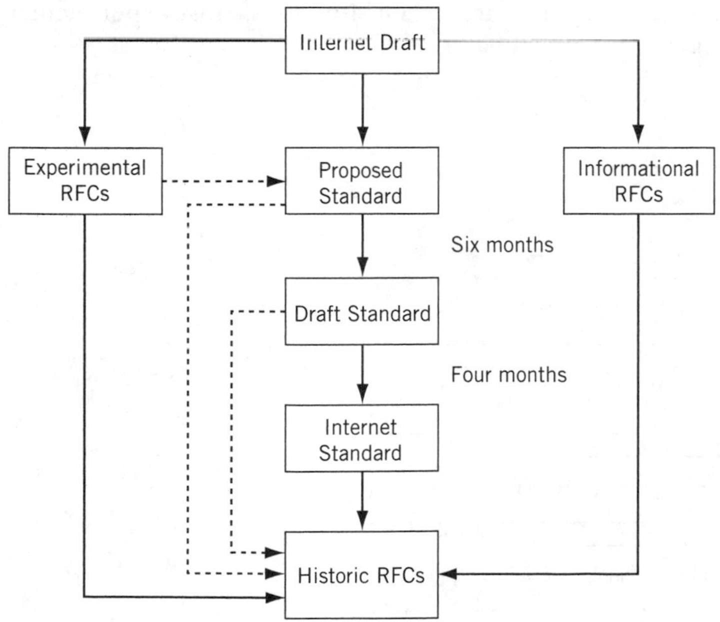

FIGURE 1.5

The RFC life cycle. Many experimental RFCs never make it to the standards track.

Internet standard—After demonstrations of successful implementation, a draft standard becomes an Internet standard.

Experimental RFCs—Not all drafts are intended for the "standards track" (and a huge number are not). Work related to an experimental situation that does affect Internet operation comprise experimental RFCs. These RFCs should *not* be implemented as part of any functional Internet service.

Informational RFCs—Some RFCs contain general, historical, or tutorial information rather than instructions.

RFCs are further classified into one of five requirement levels, as shown in Figure 1.6.

Required—These RFCs must be implemented by all Internet systems to ensure minimum conformance. For example, IPv4 and ICMP, both discussed in detail in this book, are required protocols. However, there are *very* few required RFCs.

Recommended—These RFCs are not required for minimum conformance, but are very useful. For example, FTP is a recommended protocol.

Elective—RFCs in this category are not required and not recommended. However, systems can use them for their benefit if they like, so they form a kind of "option set" for Internet protocols.

Limited Use—These RFCs are only used in certain situations. Most experimental RFCs are in this category.

RFC Requirement Levels
Required: All systems must implement
Recommended: All systems should implement
Elective: Not required nor recommended
Limited Use: Used in certain situations, such as experimental
Not Recommended: Systems should not implement

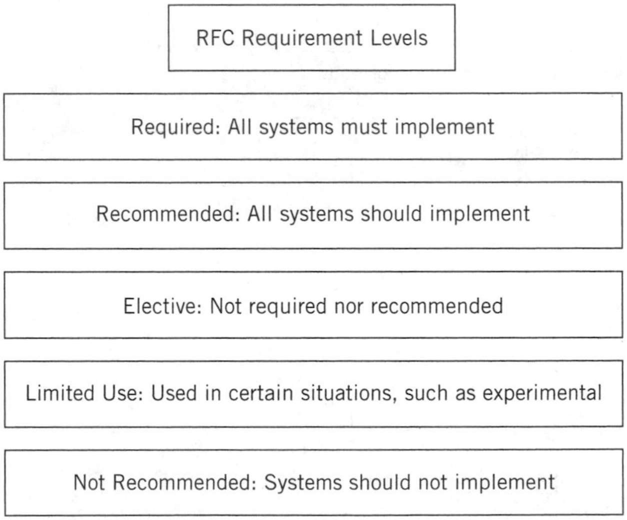

FIGURE 1.6

RFC requirement levels. There are very few RFCs that are required to implement an Internet protocol suite.

Not Recommended—These RFCs are inappropriate for general use. Most historic (obsolete) RFCs are in this category.

RFCs can be found at *www.rfc-editor.org/rfc.html*. Current Internet drafts can be found at *www.ietf.org/ID.html*. *Expired* Internet drafts can be found at *www.watersprings.org/pub/id/index-all.html*.

INTERNET ADMINISTRATION

As the Internet has evolved from an environment with a large student user population to a more commercialized network with a broad user base, the groups that have guided and coordinated Internet issues have evolved. Figure 1.7 shows the general structure of the Internet administration entities.

Internet Society (ISOC)—This is an international nonprofit organization formed in 1992 to support the Internet standards process. ISOC maintains and supports the other administrative bodies described in this section. ISOC also supports research and scholarly activities relating to the Internet.

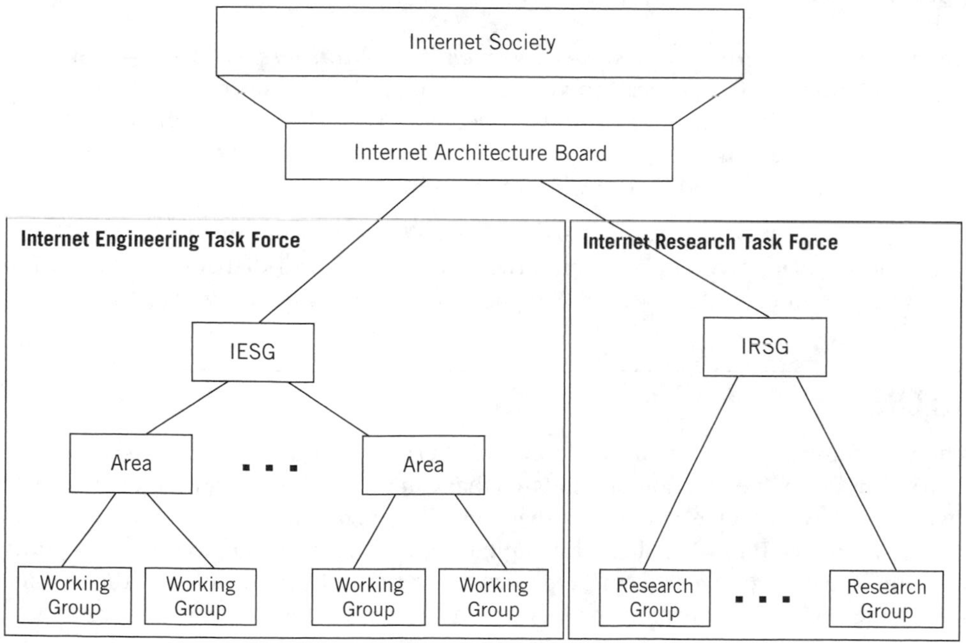

FIGURE 1.7

Internet administration groups, showing the interactions between the major components.

Internet Architecture Board (IAB)—This group is the technical advisor to ISOC. The IAB oversees the continued development of the Internet protocol suite and plays a technical advisory role to members of the Internet community involved in research. The IAB does this primarily through the two organizations under it. In addition, the RFC editor derives authority from the IAB, and the IAB represents the Internet to other standards organizations and forums.

Internet Engineering Task Force (IETF)—This a forum of *working groups* managed by the Internet Engineering Steering Group (IESG). The IETF identifies operational problem areas and proposes solutions. They also develop and review the specifications intended to become Internet standards. The working groups are organized into areas devoted to a particular topic. Nine areas have been defined, although this can change: applications, Internet protocols, routing, operations, user services, network management, transport, IPv6, and security. The IETF has taken on some of the roles that were invested in ISOC.

Internet Research Task Force (IRTF)—This is another forum of working groups, organized directly under the Internet Research Steering Group (IESG) for management purposes. The IRTF is concerned with long-term research topics related to Internet protocols, applications, architecture, and technology.

Two other groups are important for Internet administration, although they do not appear in Figure 1.7.

Internet Corporation for Assigned Names and Numbers (ICANN)—This is a private nonprofit corporation that is responsible for the management of all Internet *domain names* (more on these later) and Internet addresses. Before 1998, this role was played by the Internet Assigned Numbers Authority (IANA), which was supported by the U.S. government.

Internet Network Information Center (InterNIC)—The job of the InterNIC, run by the U.S. Department of Commerce, is to collect and distribute information about IP names and addresses. They are at *http://www.internic.net*.

LAYERS

When it comes to communications, all of these standard organizations have one primary function: the creation of standards that can be combined with others to create a working network. One concern is that these organizations be able to recommend solutions that are both flexible and complete, even though no single standards entity has complete control over the entire process from top to bottom. The way this is done is to divide the communications process up into a number of functional layers.

Data communication networks rely on *layered* protocols. In brief, processes running on a system and the communication ports that send and receive network bits are logically connected by a series of layers, each performing one major function of the networking task.

The key concept is that each layer in the protocol stack has a distinct purpose and function. There is a big difference between the application layer protocols we've seen, such as FTP and SSH, and a lower-level protocol such as Ethernet on a LAN. Each protocol layer handles part of the overall task.

For example, Ethernet cards format the bits sent out on a LAN at one layer, and FTP client software communicates with the FTP server at a higher layer. However, the Ethernet card does not tell the FTP application which bits to send out the interface. FTP addresses the higher-end part of the puzzle: sending commands and data to the FTP server. Other layers take care of things like formatting, and can vary in capability or form to address differences at every level. You don't use different Web browsers depending on the type of links used on a network. The whole point is that not all networks are Ethernet (for example), so a layered protocol allows a "mix and match" of whatever protocols are needed for the network at each layer.

Simple Networking

Most programming languages include statements that allow the programmer to send bits out of a physical connector. For example, suppose a programming language allowed you to program a statement like `write(port 20$, "test 1")`. Sure enough, when compiled, linked, and run, the program would spit the bits representing the string "test 1" out the communications port of the computer. A similar statement like `read(port 20$, STUFF)` would, when compiled, linked, and run, wait until something appeared in the buffer of the serial port and store the bits in the variable called STUFF.

A simple network using this technique is shown in Figure 1.8. (There is still some software in use that does networking this way.)

However, there are some things to consider. Is there anything attached to the port at all? Or are the bits just falling into the "bit bucket"? If there was a link attached, what if someone disconnected it while the bits are in flight? What about other types of errors? How would we know that the bits arrived safely?

Even assuming that the bits got there, and some listening process received them, does the content make sense? Some computers store bits differently than others, and "test 1" could be garbled on the other system. How many bits are sent to represent the

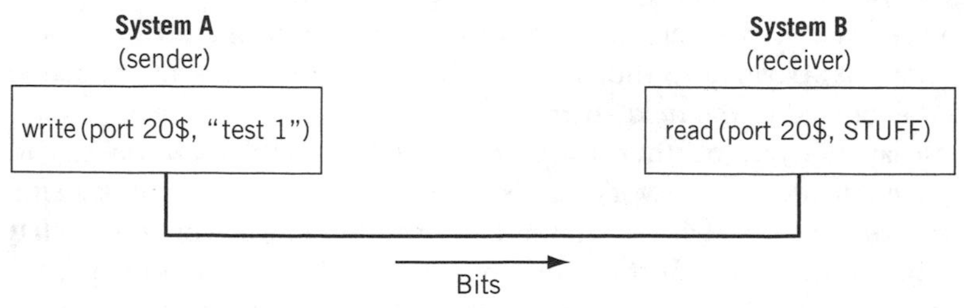

FIGURE 1.8

An extremely simple network with a distinctly non-layered approach to networking.

number 1? How do we know that a "short integer" used by the sender is the same as the "short integer" used by another? (In fairness, TCP/IP does little to address this issue directly.)

We see that the networking task is not as simple as it seems. Now, each and every networked application program could conceivably include every line of code that is needed to solve all of these issues (and there are even others), but that introduces another factor into the networking equation. Most hosts attached to a network have only one communications port active at any one time (the "network interface"). If an "all-in-one" network application is using it, perhaps to download a music file, how can another application use the same port for email? It can't.

Besides the need to multiplex in various ways, another factor influencing layers is that modern operating systems do not allow direct access to hardware. The need to go through the operating system and multiplex the network interface leads to a centralization of the networking tasks in the end system.

Protocol layers make all of these issues easier to deal with, but they cannot be added haphazardly. (You can still create a huge and ugly "layer" that implements everything from hardware to transport to data representation, but it would work.) As important as the layers are, the tasks and responsibilities assigned to those layers are even *more* important.

Protocol Layers

Each layer has a separate function in the overall task of moving bits between processes. These processes could be applications on separate systems, but on modern systems a lot of process-to-process communication is not host-to-host. For example, a lot of printer management software runs as a Web browser using a special loopback TCP/IP address to interface with the process that gathered status information from the printer.

As long as the boundary functions between adjacent layers are respected, layers can be changed or even completely rewritten without having to change the whole application. Layers can be combined for efficiency, "mixed-and-matched" from different vendors, or customized for different circumstances, all without having to rework the entire stack from top to bottom.

Nearly every layer has some type of multiplexing field to allow the receiver to determine the type of *payload*, or content of the data unit at a particular layer. A key point in networking is that the payload and control information at one layer is just a "transparent" (meaningless) payload to the layer below. Transparent bits, as the name implies, are passed unchanged to the next layer.

How can protocol layers work together? Introducing a bunch of new interfaces and protocols seems to have made the networking task harder, not easier. There is a simple method called *encapsulation* that makes the entire architecture workable. What is encapsulation? Think of the layers of the protocol suite in terms of writing a letter and the systems that are involved in letter delivery. The letter goes inside an envelope which is gathered with others inside a mailbag which is transported with others inside a truck or plane. It sounds like a very complicated way to deliver one message, but this system makes the overall task of delivering many messages easier, not harder. For example, there now can be facilities that only deal with mailbags and do not worry about an individual letter's language or the transportation details.

THE TCP/IP PROTOCOL SUITE

The protocol stack used on the Internet is the Internet Protocol Suite. It is usually called TCP/IP after two of its most prominent protocols, but there are other protocols as well. The *TCP/IP model* is based on a five-layer model for networking. From bottom (the link) to top (the user application), these are the physical, data link, network, transport, and application layers. Not all layers are completely defined by the model, so these layers are "filled in" by external standards and protocols. The layers have names but no numbers, and although sometimes people speak of "Layer 2" or "Layer 3," these are not TCP/IP terms. Terms like these are actually from the OSI Reference Model.

The TCP/IP stack is *open*, which means that there are no "secrets" as to how it works. (There are "open systems" too, but with TCP/IP, the systems do not have to be "open" and often are not.) Two compatible end-system applications can communicate regardless of their underlying architectures, although the connections between layers are not defined.

The OSI Reference Model

The TCP/IP or Internet model is not the only standard way to build a protocol suite or stack. The Open Standard Interconnection (OSI) reference model is a seven-layer model that loosely maps into the five layers of TCP/IP. Until the Web became widely popular in the 1990s, the OSI reference model, with distinctive names and numbers for its layers, was proposed as the standard model for all communication networks. Today, the OSI reference model (OSI-RM) is often used as a learning tool to introduce the functions of TCP/IP.

The TCP/IP stack is comprised of modules. Each module provides a specific function, but the modules are fairly independent. The TCP/IP layers contain relatively independent protocols that can be used depending on the needs of the system to provide whatever function is desired. In TCP/IP, each higher layer protocol is supported by lower layer protocols. The whole collection of protocols forms a type of hourglass shape, with IP in the middle, and more and more protocols up or down from there.

Suite, Stack, and Model

The term "protocol stack" is often used synonymously with "protocol suite" as an implementation of a reference model. However, the term "protocol suite" properly refers to a collection of all the protocols that can make up a layer in the reference model. The Internet protocol suite is an example of the Internet or TCP/IP reference model protocols, and a TCP/IP protocol stack implements one or more of these protocols at each layer.

The TCP/IP Layers

The TCP/IP protocol stack models a series of protocol layers for networks and systems that allows communications between any types of devices. The model consists of five separate but related layers, as shown in Figure 1.9. The Internet protocol suite is based on these five layers. TCP/IP says most about the network and transport layers, and a lot about the application layer. TCP/IP also defines how to interface the network layer with the data link and physical layers, but is not directly concerned with these two layers themselves.

The Internet protocol suite assumes that a layer is there and available, so TCP/IP does not define the layers themselves. The stack consist of protocols, not implementations, so describing a layer or protocols says almost nothing about how these things should actually be built.

Not all systems on a network need to implement all five layers of TCP/IP. Devices using the TCP/IP protocol stack fall into two general categories: a *host* or *end system* (ES) and an *intermediate node* (often a router) or an *intermediate system* (IS). The

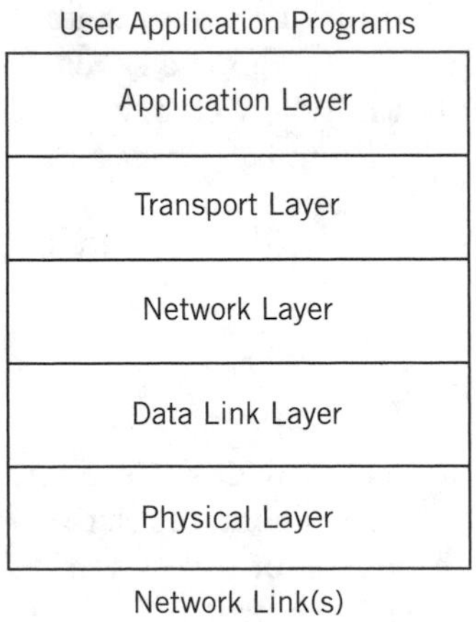

User Application Programs

Application Layer
Transport Layer
Network Layer
Data Link Layer
Physical Layer

Network Link(s)

FIGURE 1.9

The five layers of TCP/IP. Older models often show only four layers, combining the physical and data link layers.

intermediate nodes usually only involve the first three layers of TCP/IP (although many of them still have all five layers for other reasons, as we have seen).

In TCP/IP, as with most layered protocols, the most fundamental elements of the process of sending and receiving data are collected into the groups that become the layers. Each layer's major functions are distinct from all the others, but layers can be combined for performance reasons. Each implemented layer has an *interface* with the layers above and below it (except for the application and physical layers, of course) and provides its defined service to the layer above and obtains services from the layer below. In other words, there is a *service interface* between each layer, but these are not standardized and vary widely by operating system.

TCP/IP is designed to be comprehensive and flexible. It can be extended to meet new requirements, and has been. Individual layers can be combined for implementation purposes, as long as the service interfaces to the layers remain intact. Layers can even be split when necessary, and new service interfaces defined. Services are provided to the layer above after the higher layer provides the lower layer with the command, data, and necessary parameters for the lower layer to carry out the task.

Layers on the same system provide and obtain services to and from adjacent layers. However, a *peer-to-peer protocol process* allows the same layers on different systems to communicate. The term *peer* means every implementation of some layer is essentially equal to all others. There is no "master" system at the protocol level. Communications between peer layers on different systems use the defined protocols appropriate to the given layer.

In other words, *services* refer to communications between layers within the same process, and *protocols* refer to communications between processes. This can be confusing, so more information about these points is a good idea.

Protocols and Interfaces

It is important to note that when the layers of TCP/IP are on different systems, they are *only* connected at the physical layer. Direct peer-to-peer communication between all other layers is impossible. This means that all data from an application have to flow "down" through all five layers at the sender, and "up" all five layers at the receiver to reach the correct process on the other system. These data are sometimes called a *service data unit* (SDU).

Each layer on the sending system adds information to the data it receives from the layer above and passes it all to the layer below (except for the physical layer, which has no lower layers to rely on in the model and actually has to send the bits in a form appropriate for the communications link used).

Likewise, each layer on the receiving system unwraps the received message, often called a *protocol data unit* (PDU), with each layer examining, using, and stripping off the information it needs to complete its task, and passing the remainder up to the next layer (except for the application layer, which passes what's left off to the application program itself). For example, the data link layer removes the wrapper meant for it, uses it to decide what it should do with this data unit, and then passes the remainder up to the network layer.

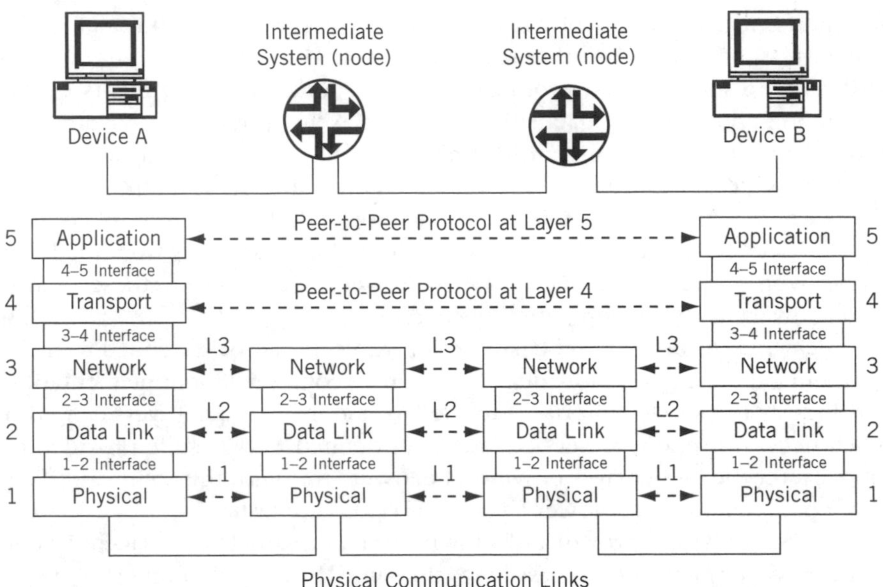

FIGURE 1.10

Protocols and interfaces, showing how devices are only physically connected at the lowest layer (Layer 1). Note that functionally, intermediate nodes only require the bottom three layers of the model.

The whole interface and protocol process is shown in Figure 1.10. Although TCP/IP layers only have names, layer numbers are also used in the figure, but only for illustration. (The numbers come from the ISO-RM.)

As shown in the figure, there is a natural grouping of the five-layer protocol stack at the network layer and the transport layer. The lower three layers of TCP/IP, sometimes called the network support layers, must be present and functional on all systems, regardless of the end system or intermediate node role. The transport layer links the upper and lower layers together. This layer can be used to make sure that what was sent was received, and what was sent is useful to the receiver (and not, for example, a stray PDU misdirected to the host or unreasonably delayed).

The process of encapsulation makes the whole architecture workable. Encapsulation of one layer's information inside another layer is a key part of how TCP/IP works.

Encapsulation

Each layer uses encapsulation to add the information its peer needs on the receiving system. The network layer adds a header to the information it receives from the transport at the sender and passes the whole unit down to the data link layer. At the receiver, the network layer looks at the control information, usually in a *header*, in the data it receives from the data link layer and passes the remainder up to the transport layer for further processing. This is called encapsulation because one layer has no idea what the structure or meaning of the PDU is at other layers. The PDU has several more or less official names for the structure at each layer.

The exception to this general rule is the data link layer, which adds both a *header* and a *trailer* to the data it receives from the network layer. The general flow of encapsulation in TCP/IP is shown in Figure 1.11. Note that on the transmission media itself (or communications link), there are only bits, and that some "extra" bits are added by the communication link for its own purposes. Each PDU at the other layers is labeled as data for its layer, and the headers are abbreviated by layer name. The exception is the second layer, the data link layer, which shows a header and trailer added at that level of encapsulation.

Although the intermediate nodes are not shown, these network devices will only process the data (at most) through the first three layers. In other words, there is no transport layer to which to pass network-layer PDUs on these systems for data communications (management is another issue).

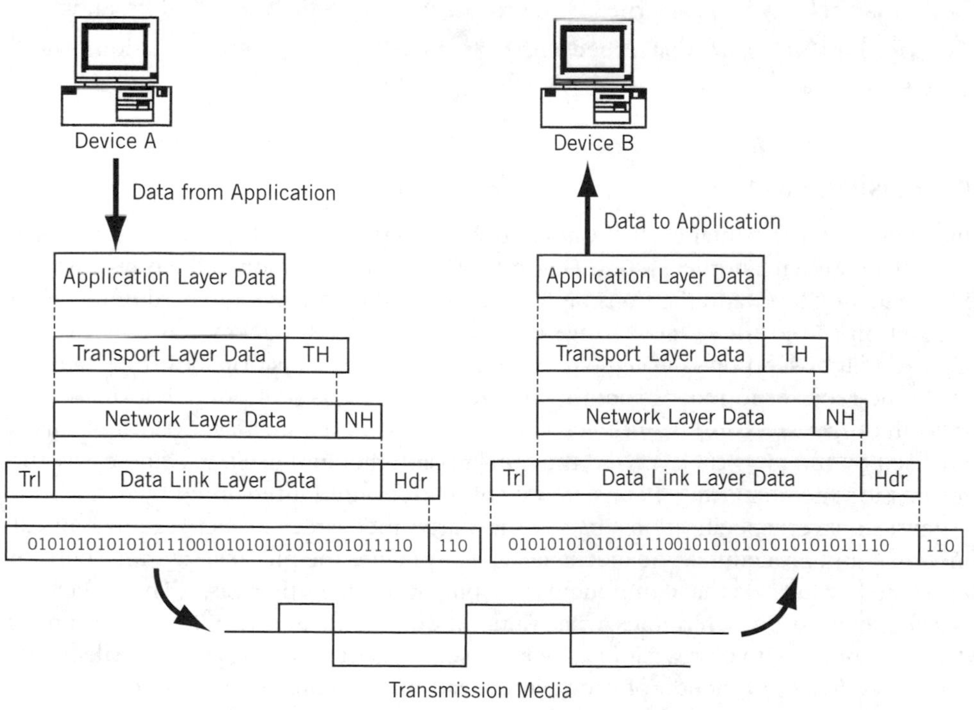

FIGURE 1.11

TCP/IP encapsulation and headers. The unstructured stream of bits represents frames with distinct content.

THE LAYERS OF TCP/IP

TCP/IP is mature and stable, and is the only protocol stack used on the Internet. This book is all about networking with TCP/IP, but it is easy to get lost in the particulars of TCP/IP if some discussion of the general tasks that TCP/IP is intended to accomplish is not included. This section takes a closer look at the TCP/IP layers, but only as a general guide to how the layers work.

TCP/IP Layers in Brief

- **Physical Layer:** Contains all the functions needed to carry the bit stream over a physical medium to another system.
- **Data Link Layer:** Organizes the bit stream into a data unit called a "frame" and delivers the frame to an adjacent system.
- **Network Layer:** Delivers data in the form of a packet from source to destination, across as many links as necessary, to non-adjacent systems.
- **Transport Layer:** Concerned with process-to-process delivery of information.
- **Application Layer:** Concerned with differences in internal representation, user interfaces, and anything else that the user requires.

The Physical Layer

The physical layer contains all the functions needed to carry the bit stream over a physical medium to another system. Figure 1.12 shows the position of the physical layer to the data link layer and the transmission medium. The transmission medium forms a pure "bit pipe" and should not change the bits sent in any way. Now, transmission "on the wire" might send bits through an extremely complex transform, but the goal is to enable the receiver to reconstruct the bit stream exactly as sent. Some information in the form of *transmission framing* can be added to the data link layer data, but this is only used by the physical layer and the transmission medium itself. In some cases, the transmission medium sends a constant idle bit pattern until interrupted by data.

Physical layer specifications have four parts: mechanical, electrical or optical, functional, and procedural. The mechanical part specifies the physical size and shape of the connector itself so that components will plug into each other easily. The electrical/optical specification determines what value of voltage or line condition determines whether a pin is active or what exactly represents a 0 or 1 bit. The functional specification specifies the function of each pin or lead on the connector (first lead is send, second is receive, and so on). The procedural specification details the sequence of actions that must take place to send or receive bits on the interface. (For Ethernet, the send pair is activated, then a "preamble" is sent, and so forth.) The Ethernet twisted-pair interfaces from the IEEE are common implementations of the physical layer that includes all these elements.

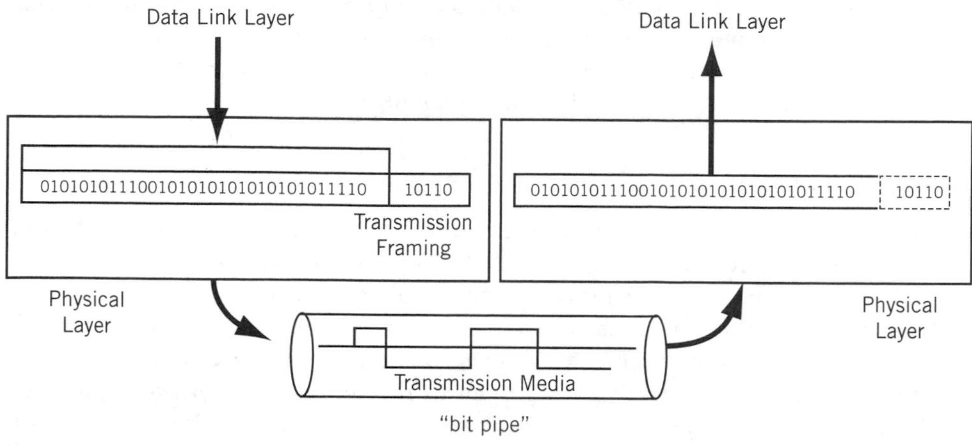

FIGURE 1.12

The physical layer. The transmission framing bits are used for transmission media purposes only, such as low-level control.

There are other things that the physical layer must determine, or be configured to expect.

Data rate—This transmission rate is the number of bits per second that can be sent. It also defines the duration of a symbol on the wire. Symbols usually represent one or more bits, although there are schemes in which one bit is represented by multiple symbols.

Bit synchronization—The sender and receiver must be *synchronized* at the symbol level so that the number of bits expected per unit time is the same. In other words, the sender and receiver *clocks* must be synchronized (timing is in the millisecond or microsecond range). On modern links, the timing information is often "recovered" from the received data stream.

Configuration—So far we've assumed simple *point-to-point links*, but this is not the only way that systems are connected. In a *multipoint configuration*, a link connects more than two devices, and in a multisystem *bus/broadcast* topology such as a LAN, the number of systems can be very high.

Topology—The devices can be arranged in a number of ways. In a full *mesh* topology, all devices are directly connected and *one hop* away, but this requires a staggering amount of links for even a modest network. Systems can also be arranged as a *star* topology, with all systems reachable through a central system. There is also the *bus* (all devices are on a common link) and the *ring* (devices are chained together, and the last is linked to the first, forming a ring).

Mode—So far, we've only talked about one of the systems as the sender and the other as the receiver. This is operation in *simplex mode*, where a device can only send or receive, such as with weather sensors reporting to a remote weather station. More realistic devices use *duplex mode*, where all systems can send or receive with equal facility. This is often further distinguished as *half-duplex* (the system can send and receive, but not at the same time) and *full-duplex* (simultaneous sending and receiving).

The Data Link Layer

Bits are just bits. With only a physical layer, System A has no way to tell System B, "Get ready some bits," "Here are the bits," and "Did you get those bits okay?" The data link layer solves this problem by organizing the bit stream into a data unit called a frame.

It is important to note that frames are the data link layer PDUs, and these are not the same as the physical layer transmission frames mentioned in the previous section. For example, network engineers often speak about *T1 frames* or *SONET frames*, but these are distinct from the data link layer frames that are carried inside the T1 or SONET frames. Transmission frames have control information used to manage the physical link itself and has little to do directly with process-to-process communications. This "double-frame" arrangement might sound redundant, but many transmission frames originated with voice because digitized voice has no framing at the "data link" layer.

The data link layer moves bits across the link and can add reliability to the raw communications link. The data link layer can be very simple, or make the link appear error-free to the layer above, the network layer. The data link layer usually adds both a header and trailer to the data presented by the network layer. This is shown in Figure 1.13.

The frame header typically contains a source and destination address (known as the "physical address" since it refers to the physical communication port) and some control information. The control information is data passed from one data link layer to the

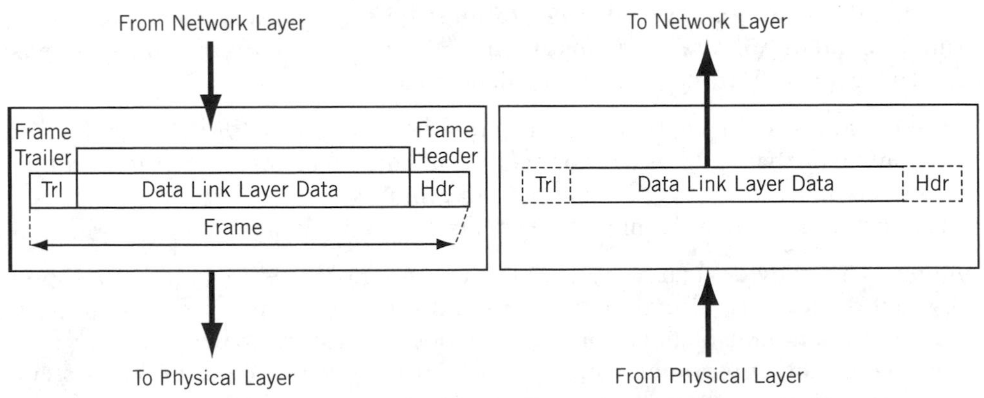

FIGURE 1.13

The data link layer, showing that data link layer frames have both header and trailer.

other data link layer, and not user data. The body of the frame contains the sequence of bits being transferred across the network. The trailer usually contains information used in detecting bit errors (such as cyclical redundancy check [CRC]). A maximum size is associated with the frame that cannot be exceeded because all systems must allocate memory space (buffers) for the data. In a networking context, a buffer is just special memory allocated for communications.

The data link layer performs framing, physical addressing, and error detection (error *correction* is another matter entirely, and can be handled in many ways, such as by resending a copy of the frame that had the errors). However, when it comes to frame error detection and correction in the real world, error detection bits are sometimes ignored and frames that defy processing due to errors are simply discarded. This does not mean that error detection and correction are not part of the data link layer standards: It means that in these cases, ignoring and discarding are the chosen methods of implementation. In discard cases, the chore of handling the error condition is "pushed up the stack" to a higher layer protocol.

This layer also performs *access control* (this determines whose turn it is to send over or control the link, an issue that becomes more and more interesting as the number of devices sharing the link grows). In LANs, this *media access control* (MAC) forms a sublayer of the data link layer and has its own addressing scheme known (not surprisingly) as the MAC layer address or *MAC address*. We'll look at MAC addresses in the next chapter. For now, it is enough to note that LANs such as Ethernet do not have "real" physical layer addresses and that the MAC address performs this addressing function.

In addition, the data link layer can perform some type of *flow control*. Flow control makes sure senders do not overwhelm receivers: a receiver must have adequate time to process the data arriving in its buffers. At this layer, the flow control, if provided, is link-by-link. (We'll see shortly that end-to-end—host-to-host—flow control is provided by the transport layer.) LANs do not usually provide flow control at the data link layer, although they can.

Not all destination systems are directly reachable by the sender. This means that when bits at the data link layer are sent from an originating system, the bits do not arrive at the destination system as the "next hop" along the way. Directly reachable systems are called *adjacent systems*, and adjacent systems are always "one hop away" from the sender. When the destination system is not directly reachable by the sender, one or more intermediate nodes are needed. Consider the network shown in Figure 1.14.

Now the sender (System A) is not directly connected to the receiver (System B). Another system, System 3, receives the frame and must forward it toward the destination. This system is usually called a *switch* or *router* (there are even other names), depending on internal architecture and network role. On a WAN (but not on a LAN), this second frame is a different frame because there is no guarantee that the second link is identical to the first. Different links need different frames. Identical frames are only delivered to systems that are directly reachable, or adjacent, to the sender, such as by an Ethernet switch on a LAN.

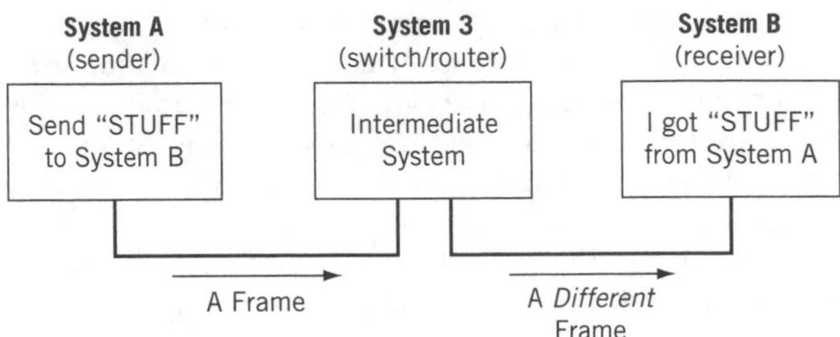

FIGURE 1.14

A more complex network. Note that the frames are technically different even if the same medium is used on both links.

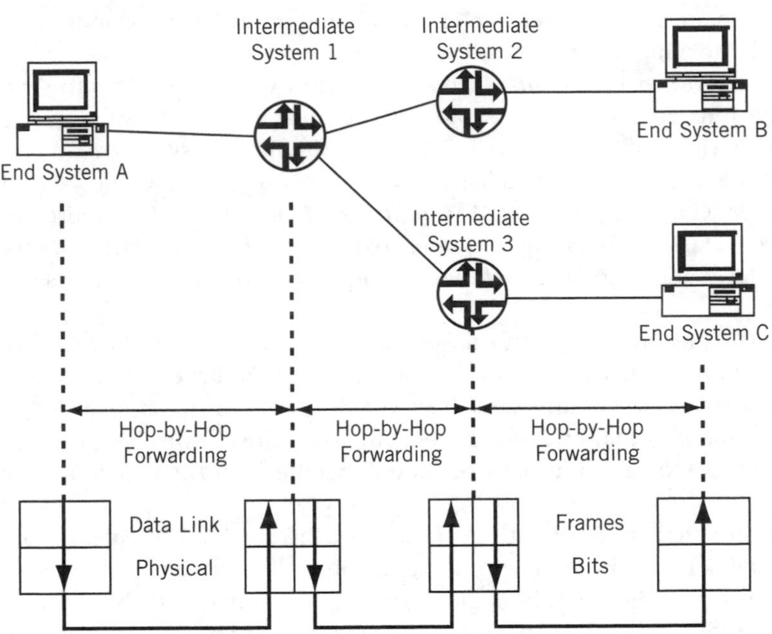

FIGURE 1.15

Hop-by-hop forwarding of frames. The intermediate systems also have a Layer 3, but this is not shown in the figure for clarity.

Networking with intermediate systems is called *hop-by-hop* delivery. A "hop" is the usual term used on the Internet or a router network to indicate the forwarding of a packet between one router or another (or between a host and router). Frames can "hop" between Layer 2 switches, but the term is most commonly used for Layer 3 router hops (which can consist of multiple switch-to-switch frame "hops"). There can be more than one intermediate system between the source and destination end systems, of course, as shown in Figure 1.15. Consider the case where End System A is sending a bit stream to End System C.

Note that the intermediate systems (routers) have *two* distinct physical and data link layers, reflecting the fact that the systems have two (and often more) communication links, which can differ in many ways. (The figure shows a typical WAN configuration with point-to-point links, but routers on LANs, and on some types of public data service WANs, can be deployed in more complicated ways.)

However, there is something obviously missing from this figure. There is no connection between the data link layers on the intermediate systems! How does the router know to which output port and link to forward the data in order to ultimately reach the destination? (In the figure, note that Intermediate System 1 can send data to either Intermediate System 2 or Intermediate System 3, but only through Intermediate System 3, which forwards the data, is the destination reachable.)

These forwarding decisions are made at the TCP/IP network layer.

The Network Layer

The network layer delivers data in the form of a *packet* from source to destination, across as many links as necessary. The biggest difference between the network layer and the data link layer is that the data link layer is in charge of data delivery between *adjacent* systems (directly connected systems one hop away), while the network layer delivers data to systems that are not directly connected to the source. There can be many different types of data link and physical layers on the network, depending on the variety of the link types, but the network layer is essentially the same on all systems, end systems, and intermediate systems alike.

Figure 1.16 shows the relationship between the network layer and the transport layer above and the data link layer below. A packet header is put in place at the sender and interpreted by the receiver. A router simply looks at the packet header and makes a forwarding decision based on this information. The transport layer does not play a role in the forwarding decision.

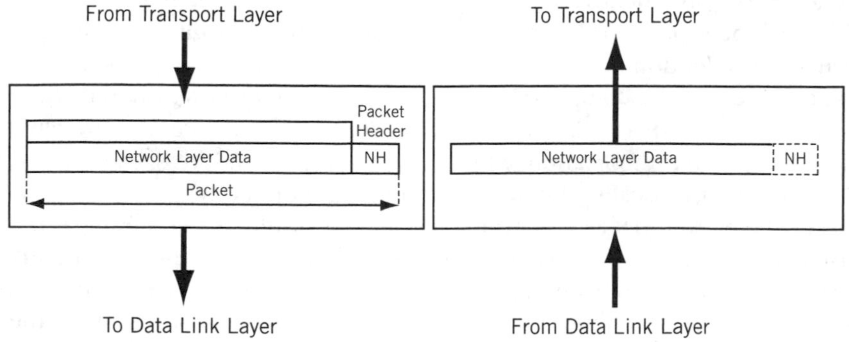

FIGURE 1.16

The network layer. These data units are packets with their own destination and source address formats.

How does the network layer know where the packet came from (so the sender can reply)? The key concept at the network layer is the *network address*, which provides this information. In TCP/IP, the network address is the *IP address*.

Every system in the network receives a network address, whether an end system or intermediate system. Systems require at least one network address (and sometimes many more). It is important to realize that this network address is different from, and independent of, the physical address used by the frames that carry the packets between adjacent systems.

Why should the systems need two addresses for the two layers? Why can't they just both use either the data link ("physical") address or the network address at *both* layers? There are actually several reasons. First, LAN addresses like those used in Ethernet come from one group (the IEEE), while those used in TCP/IP come from another group (ICANN). Also, the IP address is universally used on the Internet, while there are many types of physical addresses. Finally, there is no systematic assignment of physical addresses (and many addresses on WANs can be duplicates and so have "local significance only"). On the other hand, IP network addresses are globally administered, unique, and have a portion under which many devices are grouped. Therefore, many devices can be addressed concisely by this *network portion* of the IP address.

A key issue is how the network addresses "map" to physical addresses, a process known generally as *address resolution*. In TCP/IP, a special family of address resolution protocols takes care of this process.

The network address is a logical address. Network addresses should be organized so that devices can be grouped under a part of that address. In other words, the network address should be organized in a fashion similar to a telephone number, for example, 212-555-1212 in the North American public switched telephone network (PSTN). The sender need only look at the area code or "network" portion of this address (212) to determine if the destination is local (area codes are the same) or needs to be sent to an intermediate system to reach the 212 area code (source and destination area codes differ).

For this scheme to work effectively, however, all telephones that share the 212 area code should be grouped together. The whole telephone number beginning with 212 therefore means "*this* telephone in the 212 area code." In TCP/IP, the network address is the beginning of the device's complete IP address. A group of hosts is gathered under the network portion of the IP address. IP network addresses, like area codes, are globally administered to prevent duplication, while the rest of the IP address, like the rest of the telephone number, is locally administered, often independently.

In some cases, the packet that arrives at an intermediate system inside a frame is too large to fit inside the frame that must be sent out. This is not uncommon: different link and LAN types have different maximum frame sizes. The network layer must be able to *fragment* a data unit across multiple frames and reassemble the fragments at the destination. We'll say more about *fragmentation* in a later chapter.

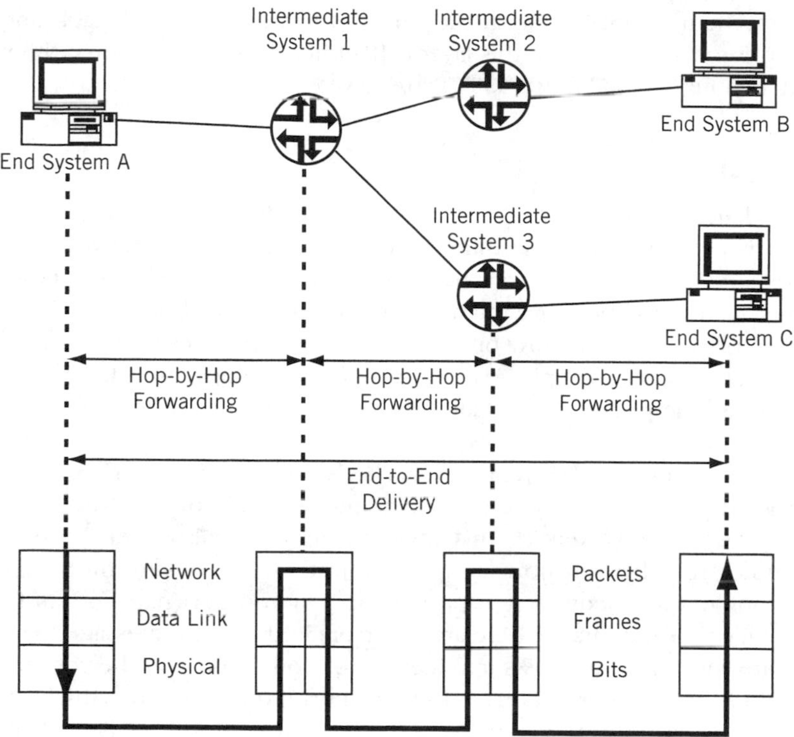

FIGURE 1.17

Source-to-destination delivery at the network layer. The intermediate systems now have all three required layers.

The network layer uses one or more *routing tables* to store information about reachable systems. The routing tables must be created, maintained, and purged of old information as the network changes due to failures, the addition or deletion of systems and links, or other configuration changes. This whole process of building tables to pass data from source to destination is called *routing*, and the use of these tables for packet delivery is called *forwarding*. The forwarding of packets inside frames always takes place hop by hop. This is shown in Figure 1.17, which adds the network layer to the data link layers already present and distinguishes between hop-by-hop forwarding and end-to-end delivery.

On the Internet, the intermediate systems that act at the packet level (Layer 3) are called *routers*. Devices that act on frames (Layer 2) are called *switches*, and some older telephony-based WAN architectures use switches as intermediate network nodes. Whether a node is called a switch or router depends on how they function internally.

In a very real sense, the network layer is at the very heart of any protocol stack, and TCP/IP is no exception. The protocol at this layer is IP, either IPv4 or IPv6 (some think that IPv6 is distinct enough to be known as TCPv6/IPv6).

The Transport Layer

Process-to-process delivery is the task of the transport layer. Getting a packet to the destination system is not quite the same thing as determining which process should receive the packet's *content*. A system can be running file transfer, email, and other network processes all at the same time, and all over a single physical interface. Naturally, the destination process has to know on which process the sender originated the bits inside the packet in order to reply. Also, systems cannot simply transfer a huge multimegabit file all in one packet. Many data units exceed the maximum allowable size of a packet.

This process of dividing message content into packets is known as *segmentation*. The network layer forwards each and every packet independently, and does not recognize any relationship between the packets. (Is this a file transfer or email packet? The network layer does not care.) The transport layer, in contrast, can make sure the whole *message*, often strung out in a sequence of packets, arrives in order (packets can be delivered out of sequence) and intact (there are no errors in the entire message). This function of the transport layer involves some method of flow control and error control (error detection *and* error correction) at the transport layer, functions which are absent at the network layer. The transport-layer protocol that performs all of these functions is TCP.

The transport-layer protocol does not have to do any of this, of course. In many cases, the content of the packet forms a complete unit all by itself, called a *datagram*. (The term "datagram" is often used to refer to the whole IP packet, but not in this book.) Self-contained datagrams are not concerned with sequencing or flow control, and these functions are absent in the User Datagram Protocol (UDP) at the transport layer.

So there are two very popular protocol packages at the transport layer:

- *TCP*—This is a connection-oriented, "reliable" service that provides ordered delivery of packet contents.
- *UDP*—This is a connectionless, "unreliable" service that does *not* provide ordered delivery of packet contents.

In addition to UDP and TCP, there are other transport-layer protocols that can be used in TCP/IP, all of which differ in terms of how they handle transport-layer tasks. Developers are not limited to the standard choices for applications. If neither TCP nor UDP nor any other defined transport-layer service is appropriate for your application, you can write your own transport-layer protocols and get others to adapt it (or use your application package exclusively).

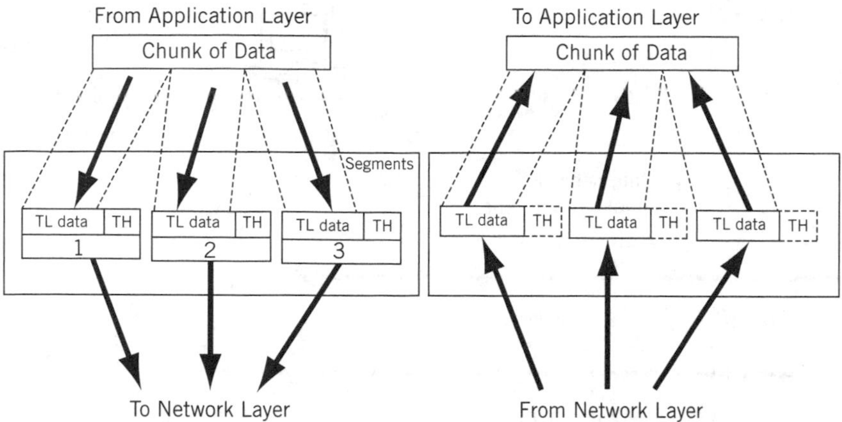

FIGURE 1.18

The transport layer, showing how data are broken up if necessary and reassembled at the destination.

In TCP/IP, it is often said that the network layer (IP itself) offers an "unreliable" or "best effort" service, while the transport layer adds "reliability" in the form of flow and error control. Later in this book, we'll see why these terms are unfortunate and what they really mean.

The network layer gets a single packet to the right system, and the transport layer gets the entire message to the right process. Figure 1.18 shows the transport layer breaking up a message at the sender into three pieces (each labeled "TL data" for transport-layer data and "TH" for transport-layer header). The figure then shows the transport layer reassembling the message at the receiver from the various *segments* that make up a message. In TCP/IP, there are also data units known as *datagrams*, which are always handled as self-contained units. There are profound differences between how the transport layer treats segments and datagrams, but this figure is just a general illustration of segment handling.

The functions that the transport layer, which in some protocols is called the end-to-end layer, might have to include follow:

Process addressing and multiplexing—Also known as "service-point addressing," the transport layer has to decide which process originated the message and to which process the message must be delivered. These are also known as *port addresses* in TCP/IP. Port addresses are an important portion of the application *socket* in TCP/IP.

Segment handling—In cases where each message is divided into segments, each segment has a sequence number used to put the message back together at the destination. When datagrams are used, each data unit is handled independently and sequencing is not necessary.

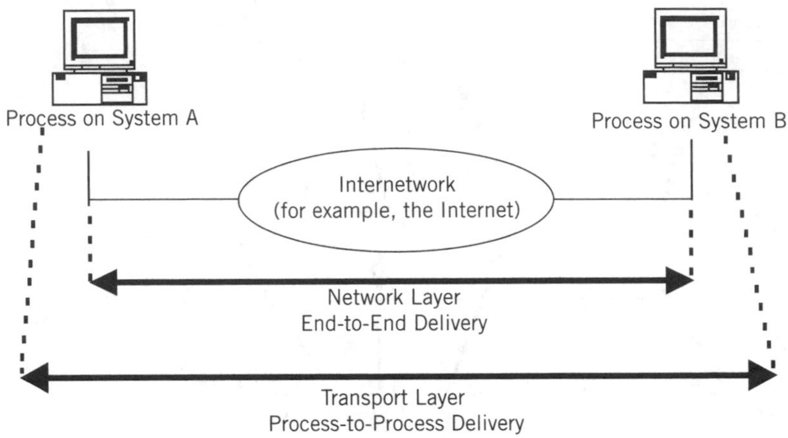

FIGURE 1.19

Reliable process-to-process delivery with the transport layer.

Connection control—The transport layer can be *connectionless* or *connection-oriented* (in fact, several layers can operate in either one of these ways). Connectionless (CL) layers treat every data unit as a self-contained, independent unit. Connection-oriented (CO) layers go through a three-phase process every time there is data to send to a destination after an idle period (connection durations can vary). First, some control messages establish the connection, then the data are sent (and exchanged if replies are necessary), and finally the connection is closed. Many times, a comparison is made between a telephone conversation ("dial, talk, hang up") with connections and an intercom ("push and talk any time") for connectionless communications, but this is not precise. Generally, segments are connection-oriented data units, and datagrams are connectionless data units.

Flow control—Just as with the data link layer, the transport layer can include flow control mechanisms to prevent senders from overwhelming receivers. In this case, however, the flow control is end-to-end rather than link-by-link. Datagrams do not require this service.

Error control—This is another function that can be performed at the data link layer, but again end-to-end at the transport layer rather than link-by-link. Communications links are not the only source of errors, which can occur inside a system as well. Again, datagrams do not require this service.

Figure 1.19 shows the relationship between the network layer and transport layer more clearly. The network layer operates from network interface to network interface, while the transport layer is more specific and operates from process to process.

The Application Layer

It might seem that once data are transferred from end-system process to end-system process, the networking task is pretty much complete. There is a lot that still needs to be done at the application level itself. In models of protocol stacks, it is common to place another layer between the transport layer and the user, the application layer. However, the TCP/IP protocol stack really stops at the transport layer (where TCP and UDP are). It is up to the application programmer to decide what should happen at the client and server level at that point, although there are individual RFCs for guidance, such as for FTP.

Although it is common to gather these TCP/IP applications into their own layer, there really is no such thing in TCP/IP as an application layer to act as some kind of "glue" between the application's user and the network.

In nearly all TCP/IP stacks, the application layer is part of the application process. In spite of the lack of a defined layer, a TCP/IP application might still have a lot to do, and in some ways the application layer is the most complex "layer" of all.

There are two major tasks that the application often needs to accomplish: session support and conversion of internal representation. Not all applications need both, of course, and some applications might not need either, but this overview includes both major functions.

Session Support

A session is a type of *dialog controller* between two processes that establishes, maintains, and synchronizes (controls) the interaction (dialog). A session decides if the communication can be half-duplex (both ends take turns sending) or full-duplex (both ends can send whenever they want). It also keeps a kind of "history" of the interaction between endpoints, so that when things go wrong or when the two communicate again, some information does not have to be resent.

In practical terms, the session consists of all "state variables" necessary to construct the history of the connection between the two devices. It is more difficult, but not impossible, to implement sessions in a connectionless environment because there is no easy way to associate the variables with a convenient label.

Internal Representation Conversion

The role of internal representation conversion is to make sure that the data exchange over the network is useful to the receivers. If the internal representation of data differs on the two systems (integer size, bit order in memory, etc.), the application layer translates between the formats so the application program does not have to. This layer can also provide encryption and compression functions, although it is more common to implement these last two functions separately from the network.

Standard protocol specifications can use the Abstract Syntax Notation 1 (ASN.1) definitions for translation purposes. ASN.1 can be used in programming, network

Architecture A		Architecture B
a	text "a"	a
00000001	integer 259	
00000011		00000011
		00000001

FIGURE 1.20

Internal representation differences. Integers can have different bit lengths and can be stored differently in memory.

management, and other places. ASN.1 defines various things such as which bit is "first on the wire" regardless of how it is stored internally, how many bits are to be sent for the numbers 0 through 255 (8), and so on. Everything can be translated into ASN.1, sent across the network, and translated back to whatever internal format is required at the destination.

The role of internal representation conversion is shown in Figure 1.20. The figure shows four sequential memory locations, each storing the letter "a" followed by the integer 259. Note that not only are there differences between the amount of memory addressed at once, but also in the *order* of the bits for numerics.

In some protocol stacks, the application program can rely on the services of a fully functional conversion for internal representation to perform these services. However, in TCP/IP, every network application program must do these things for itself.

Applications in TCP/IP

TCP/IP does not provide session or presentation services directly to an application. Programmers are on their own, but this does not mean they have to create everything from scratch. For example, applications can use a character-based presentation service called the Network Virtual Terminal (NVT), part of the Internet's telnet remote access specification. Other applications can use Sun's External Data Representation (XDR) or IBM's (and Microsoft's) NetBIOS programming libraries for presentation services. In this respect, there are many presentation layer services that TCP/IP can use, but there is no formal presentation service standard in TCP/IP that all applications must use.

Host TCP/IP implementations typically provide a range of applications that provide users with access to the data handled by the transport-layer protocols. These applications use a number of protocols that are not part of TCP/IP proper, but are used with TCP/IP. These protocols include the Hyper-Text Transfer Protocol (HTTP) used by Web browsers, the Simple Message Transfer Protocol (SMTP) used for email, and many others.

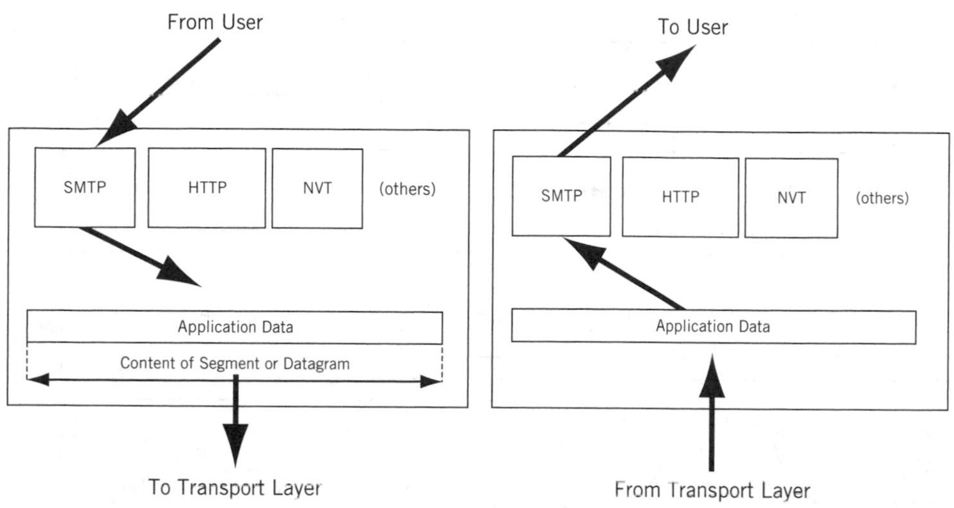

FIGURE 1.21

TCP/IP applications, showing how multiple applications can all share the same network connection.

In TCP/IP, the application protocol, the application service, and the user application itself often share the same name. The file transfer protocol in TCP/IP, called FTP, is at once an application protocol, an application service, and an application run by a user. It can sometimes be confusing as to just which aspect of FTP is under discussion.

The role of TCP/IP applications is shown in Figure 1.21. Note that this "layer" sits on top of the TCP/IP protocol stack and interfaces with programs or users directly.

Some protocols provide separate layers for sessions, internal representation conversion, and application services. In practice, these are seldom implemented independently. It just makes more sense to bundle them together by major application, as in TCP/IP.

THE TCP/IP PROTOCOL SUITE

To sum up, the five layers of TCP/IP are physical, data link, network, transport, and application. The TCP/IP stack is a hierarchical model made up of interactive modules. Each module provides a specific function. In TCP/IP, the layers contain relatively independent protocols that can be "mixed and matched" depending on the needs of the system to provide whatever function is desired. TCP/IP is hierarchical in the sense that each higher layer protocol is supported by one or more lower layer protocols.

Figure 1.22 maps some of the protocols used in TCP/IP to the various layers of TCP/IP. Every protocol in the figure will be discussed in this book, most in chapters all their own.

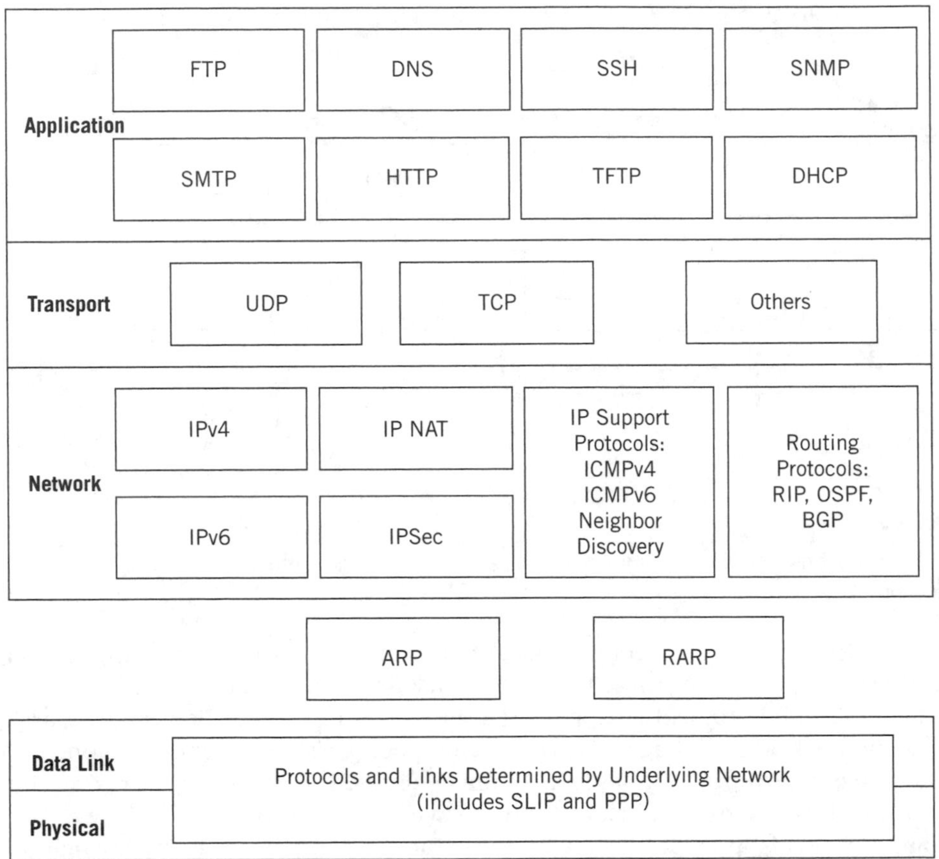

FIGURE 1.22

TCP/IP protocols and layers. Note the position of some protocols between layers.

With few exceptions, the TCP/IP protocol suite does not really define any low-level protocols below the network layer. TCP/IP usually specifies how to put IP packets into frames and how to get them out again. Many RFCs define IP *mapping* into these lower-layer protocols. We'll talk more about this mapping process in Chapter 2.

QUESTIONS FOR READERS

Refer to Figure 1.23 to help you answer the following questions.

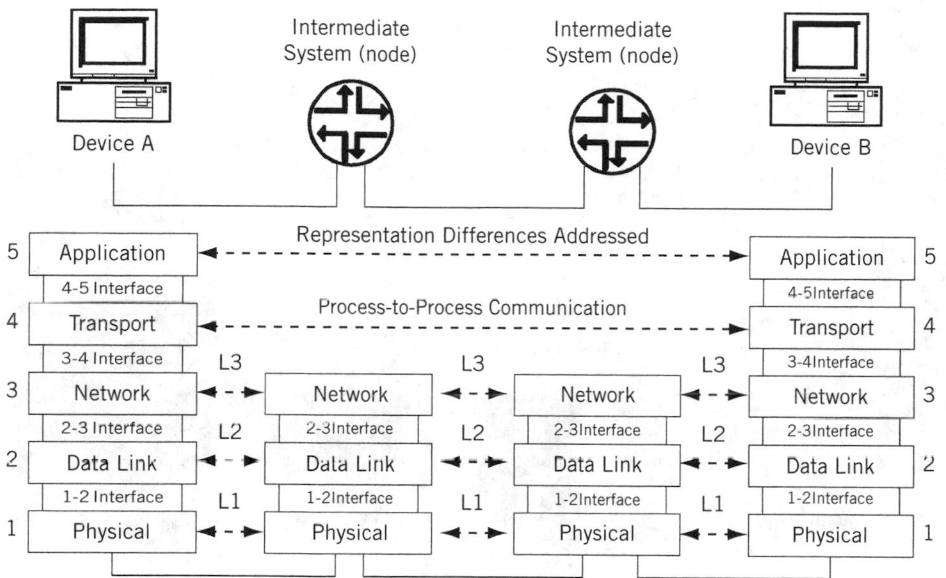

FIGURE 1.23

Summary of layered communications.

1. What are the differences between network-layer delivery and transport-layer delivery?
2. What are the main characteristics of a peer-to-peer process?
3. What are port addresses, logical addresses, and physical addresses?
4. What are the functions of the data link layer in the Internet model?
5. Which two major types of services can be provided at the application "layer"?

CHAPTER

TCP/IP Protocols and Devices

2

What You Will Learn

In this chapter, you will learn more about the TCP/IP protocol stack and the tools used in this book to investigate the Illustrated Network. We'll look at more details of TCP/IP and explore how TCP/IP devices provide internetworking from LAN to LAN.

You will learn about the types of devices used to connect LANs (such as bridges and routers) and conclude with the concept of VLANs and Metro Ethernet services.

The LANs on the Illustrated Network, including the LAN in the home office, are connected using routers as the network nodes. Each LAN forms a discrete network by itself, with its own clients and servers. When previously separate LANs are connected, or a previously complete LAN is segmented, the result is often called an *internetwork*.

Routers can be used to build an internetwork of LANs, but this is not the only way. Routers operate at the packet layer (Layer 3 of the TCP/IP model), and LANs can be linked or segmented at other layers of a protocol stack as well. Some routers can also function at these other layers, as the routers on the Illustrated Network can (i.e., routers often include functions other than pure routing). However, in many cases, different devices are used to link and segment LANs, devices that are not really routers at all.

This chapter will take a closer look at the Illustrated Network in several areas. First, we'll take a closer look at the individual layers and protocols that make up the TCP/IP protocol stack. Then, we'll investigate how devices handle internetworking from LAN to LAN at each protocol layer. Finally, we'll describe some other devices or methods that can be used between LANs, ending with a concept known as a virtual LAN or VLAN. VLANs are used by service providers to support a service known as Metropolitan Ethernet or Metro Ethernet.

Figure 2.1 shows the areas of the Illustrated Network we will be investigating in this chapter. The protocol stacks and layers run mainly on the host clients and servers, so the devices on the two LANs are shaded, along with the customer edge routers. We'll also mention the Gigabit Ethernet links and a Metro Ethernet, so those are highlighted as well.

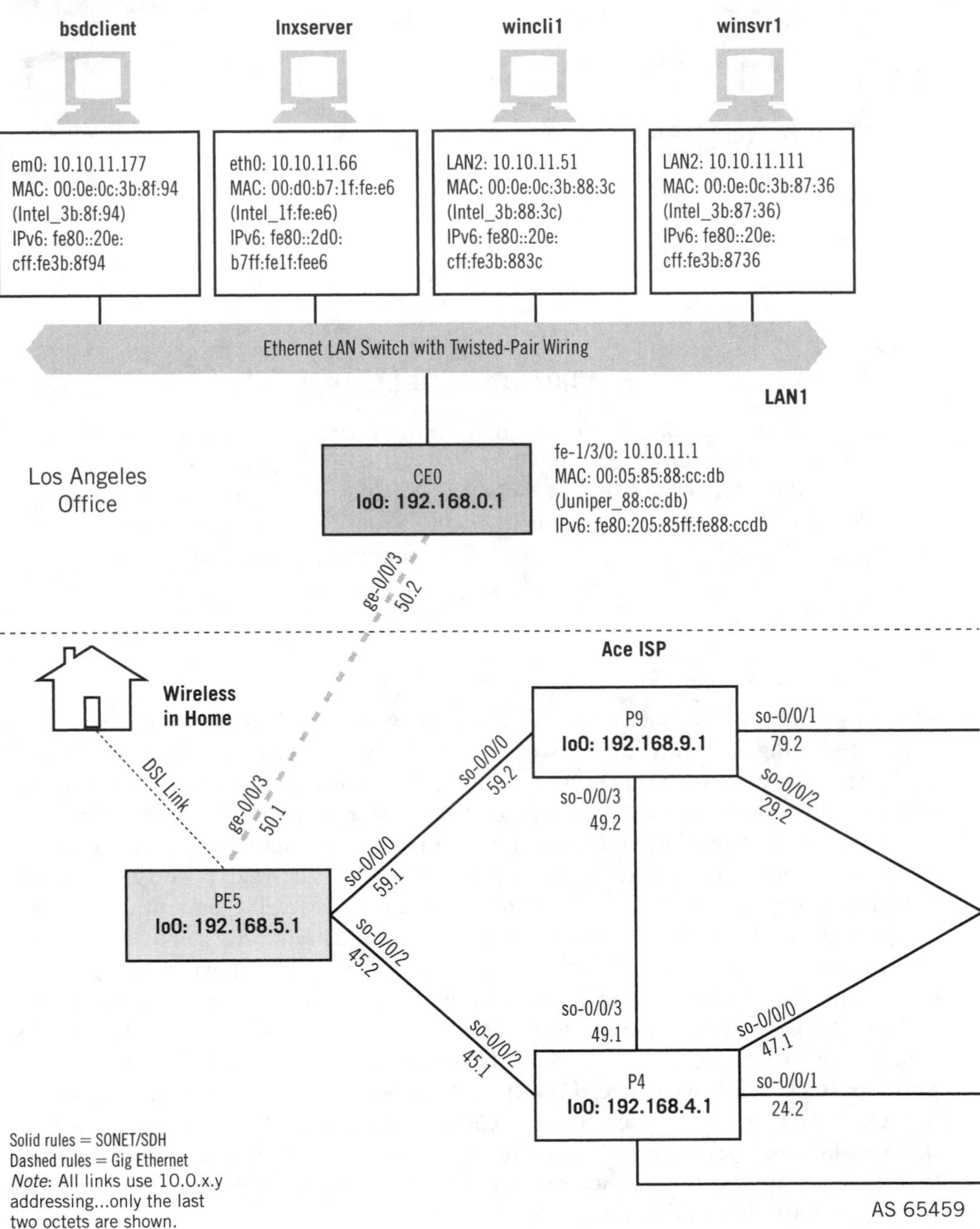

FIGURE 2.1

Internetworking on the Illustrated Network LAN. Note that there are two geographically separate LANs in New York and Los Angeles that must communicate.

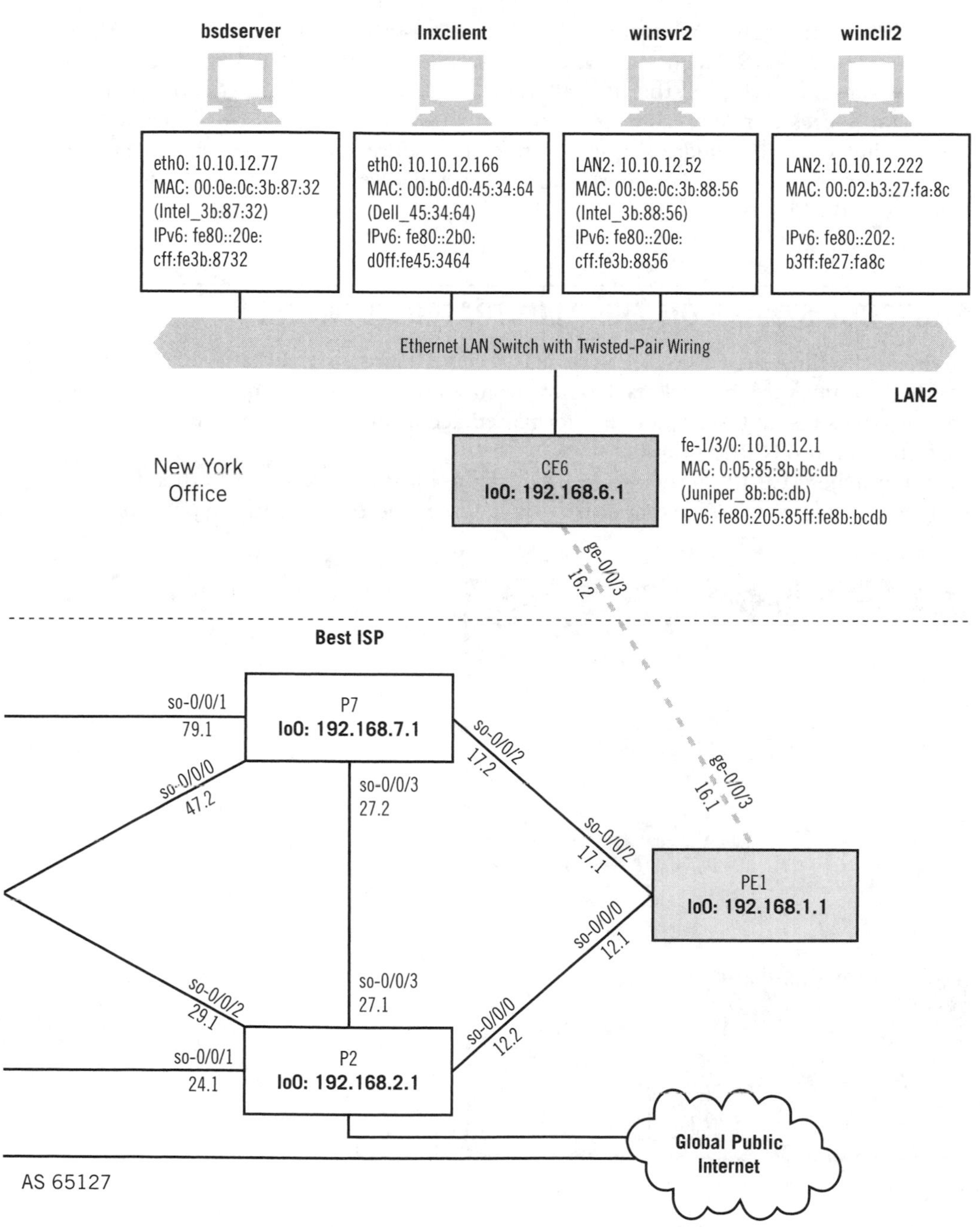

bsdserver
lnxclient
winsvr2
wincli2
eth0: 10.10.12.77
MAC: 00:0e:0c:3b:87:32
(Intel_3b:87:32)
IPv6: fe80::20e:
cff:fe3b:8732
eth0: 10.10.12.166
MAC: 00:b0:d0:45:34:64
(Dell_45:34:64)
IPv6: fe80::2b0:
d0ff:fe45:3464
LAN2: 10.10.12.52
MAC: 00:0e:0c:3b:88:56
(Intel_3b:88:56)
IPv6: fe80::20e:
cff:fe3b:8856
LAN2: 10.10.12.222
MAC: 00:02:b3:27:fa:8c
IPv6: fe80::202:
b3ff:fe27:fa8c
Ethernet LAN Switch with Twisted-Pair Wiring
LAN2
New York
Office
CE6
lo0: 192.168.6.1
fe-1/3/0: 10.10.12.1
MAC: 0:05:85:8b:bc:db
(Juniper_8b:bc:db)
IPv6: fe80:205:85ff:fe8b:bcdb
ge-0/0/3
16.2
Best ISP
so-0/0/1
79.1
P7
lo0: 192.168.7.1
so-0/0/2
17.2
ge-0/0/3
16.1
so-0/0/0
47.2
so-0/0/3
27.2
so-0/0/2
17.1
PE1
lo0: 192.168.1.1
so-0/0/0
12.1
so-0/0/2
29.1
so-0/0/3
27.1
so-0/0/0
12.2
so-0/0/1
24.1
P2
lo0: 192.168.2.1
Global Public
Internet
AS 65127

Each host in Figure 2.1 has three types of addresses associated with the interface connected to the LAN. The first is the IPv4 address. For example, the LAN interface on host `lnxserver` is `eth0` and the IPv4 address is `10.10.11.66`. The next address is the hardware address, or MAC address on a LAN: `00:d0:b7:1f:fe:e6`. Finally, each host lists the link-local IPv6 address based on this MAC address, or `fe80::2d0:b7ff:fe1f:fee6` for `lnxserver`. We'll talk more about IPv4 and IPv6 addressing and packets in Chapters 4 through 6.

PROTOCOL STACKS ON THE ILLUSTRATED NETWORK

LANs on the Illustrated Network send and receive frames, mainly Ethernet II frames. Inside the frames are the packets that flow from source to destination. The packets, and the messages inside the packets, are formatted according to the individual protocols that make up the TCP/IP protocol stack.

What major TCP/IP protocols are used on the Illustrated Network? Ethereal has a convenient summary screen that displays whenever Ethereal is capturing packets. Let's

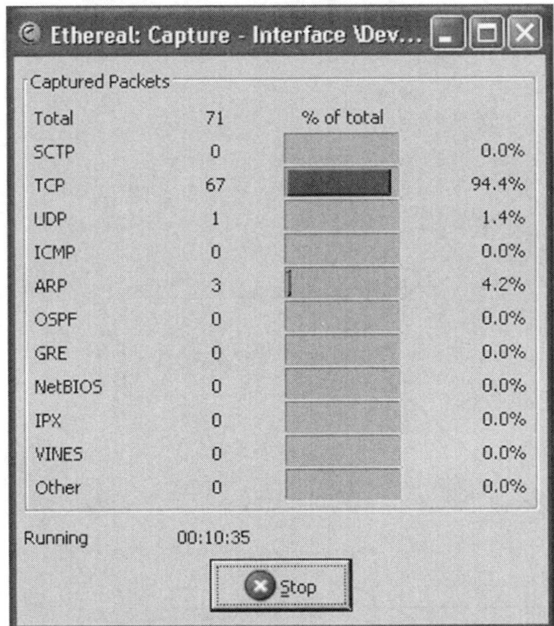

FIGURE 2.2

Ethereal capture summary, showing the number of packets used by different protocols. Often a very few types predominate.

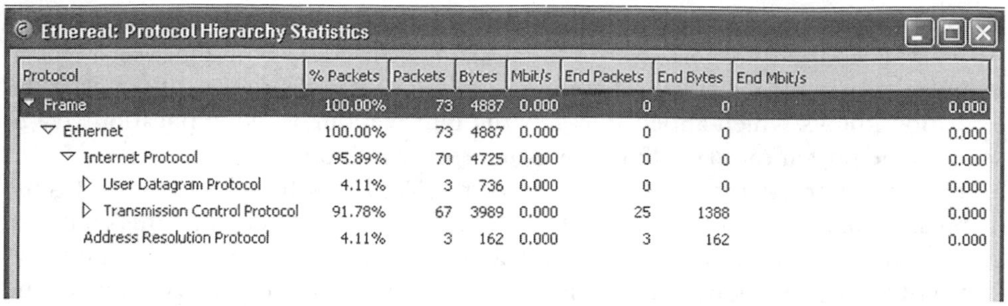

Ethereal: Protocol Hierarchy Statistics

Protocol	% Packets	Packets	Bytes	Mbit/s	End Packets	End Bytes	End Mbit/s
Frame	100.00%	73	4887	0.000	0	0	0.000
Ethernet	100.00%	73	4887	0.000	0	0	0.000
Internet Protocol	95.89%	70	4725	0.000	0	0	0.000
User Datagram Protocol	4.11%	3	736	0.000	0	0	0.000
Transmission Control Protocol	91.78%	67	3989	0.000	25	1388	0.000
Address Resolution Protocol	4.11%	3	162	0.000	3	162	0.000

FIGURE 2.3

Ethereal protocol hierarchy statistics. We'll be working almost exclusively with Ethernet frames on the Illustrated Network, but not always.

run Ethereal on `wincli2` and see what kind of protocols we capture when we remotely access router `CE6` and find the IP address associated with `winsrv1`. The summary screen is shown in Figure 2.2.

Most of the packets we have captured contain TCP. There are a couple from the User Datagram Protocol (UDP) and Address Resolution Protocol (ARP). The relationship between Ethernet II frames, IP packets, and these protocols is clearer when we look at the Ethereal protocol hierarchy statistics screen, as shown in Figure 2.3.

It is easy to see in the figure that all of the frames are Ethernet (II) frames, and that all but 3 of the 73 packets captured are IP packets. The 70 IP packets include 67 TCP packets and 3 UDP packets. We'll explore more about how all of these protocols fit together in this chapter.

LAYERS, PROTOCOLS, PORTS, AND SOCKETS

We'll take a closer look at frames in Chapter 3. For now, all we need to know is that layered protocols like TCP/IP function in a specific way. Frames are sent on LANs and inside the frame are packets. The packets carry the information from device to device. This information can be application data, but there are also packets that perform control and administrative tasks as well as data transfer.

Layering is not a magical solution to network protocol implementation. There is usually only one network interface on a host, so all applications must share this common interface, which has the network (IP) address. But how are arriving packets distributed to the proper application? The packets are all for this IP address, but which application layer process gets the information inside the packet?

The transport-layer protocol that should process the information inside the packet is indicated by the value in the *protocol* field of the IPv4 header. (We'll talk about IPv4 now, and detail the fields in the IPv4 and IPv6 headers in a later chapter.)

Inside the transport layer data unit, the receiving application is indicated by the *port* number in the transport layer header (again, we'll discuss these header fields in full in later chapters). By looking at the protocol and port fields, the TCP/IP stack at the destination knows which application gets the information. If two applications try to use the same port at the same time, this is an error condition.

Another important application layer concept in TCP/IP is the *socket*. A socket is the combination of the IP address and port number. We've already seen that this combination will uniquely identify an application. The socket is also the way that programmers often write networking application, using the socket as a kind of entry point to the other layers of the protocol stack. Often, sockets are built into the application programming interface (API).

An API is an important part of the application layer interface, but not all APIs are socket-based. Sockets are not even tied to the protocols themselves. Sockets and ports are important enough in TCP/IP to merit a detailed examination in a later chapter of this book. For now, we'll just look where the port number is carried and how the socket identifier is determined.

How can we find the port and socket in an IP packet inside an Ethernet frame? Let's use Ethereal to find them.

First, we'll use a little "echo" client and server utility on the Linux hosts to generate the frames for this exercise. (Note: This "echo" utility is not the same as the `/bin/echo` program on Linux systems.) We can invoke the server on the `lnxserver` host and use the client to send a simple string to be echoed back by the server process. We'll use Tethereal (the text version of Ethereal) this time, just to show that the same information is available in either the graphical or text-based version.

First, we'll run the Echo server process, which normally runs on port 7, on port 55555. This will help us easily locate the data we are looking for in the Ethereal capture.

```
[root@lnxserver admin]# ./echo 55555
```

We have to run Tethereal on each end as well, if we want to compare frames. The command is the same on the client and server. We'll use the verbose (`-V`) switch to see the MAC layer information as packets arrive.

```
[root@lnxclient admin]# /usr/sbin/tethereal –V
Capturing on eth0
```

Now we can invoke the Echo client to bounce the string `TESTING123` off the server process.

```
[root@lnxclient admin]# ./echo 10.10.11.66 TESTING123 55555
Received: TESTING123
[root@lnxclient admin]#
```

What did we get? Let's look at the frames leaving the client. We only need to examine the information pertaining to the port and socket. Only one of the frames captured is shown.

```
[root@lnxclient admin]# /usr/sbin/tethereal -V
Capturing on eth0

. . .

Frame 4 (52 bytes on wire, 52 bytes captured)
   Arrival Time: May 16, 2008 13:32:59.702046000
   Time delta from previous packet: 57.243134000 seconds
   Time relative to first packet: 62.239970000 seconds
   Frame Number: 4
   Packet Length: 52 bytes
   Capture Length: 52 bytes
Ethernet II, Src: 00:b0:d0:45:34:64, Dst: 00:05:85:8b:bc:db
   Destination: 00:05:85:8b:bc:db (Juniper__8b:bc:db)
   Source: 00:b0:d0:45:34:64 (Dell_45:34:64)
   Type: IP (0x0800)
Internet Protocol, Src Addr: 10.10.12.166 (10.10.12.166), Dst Addr: 10.10.11.66
(10.10.11.66)
   Version: 4
   Header length: 20 bytes
   Differentiated Services Field: 0x00 (DSCP 0x00: Default; ECN: 0x00)
      0000 00.. = Differentiated Services Codepoint: Default (0x00)
      .... ..0. = ECN-Capable Transport (ECT): 0
      .... ...0 = ECN-CE: 0
   Total Length: 38
   Identification: 0x0000
   Flags: 0x04
      .1.. = Don't fragment: Set
      ..0. = More fragments: Not set
   Fragment offset: 0
   Time to live: 64
   Protocol: UDP (0x11)
   Header checksum: 0x0ecc (correct)
   Source: 10.10.12.166 (10.10.12.166)
   Destination: 10.10.11.66 (10.10.11.66)
User Datagram Protocol, Src Port: 32825 (32825), Dst Port: 55555 (55555)
   Source port: 32825 (32825)
   Destination port: 55555 (55555)
   Length: 18
   Checksum: 0x1045 (correct)
Data (10 bytes)
0000 54 45 53 54 49 4e 47 31 32 33 TESTING123
```

Table 2.1 Port and Sockets		
Value	**lnxclient**	**lnxserver**
IP address	10.10.12.166	10.10.11.66
Port	32825	55555
Socket	10.10.12.166:32825	10.10.11.66:55555

Let's look at the fields that are emphasized. First, we have captured an Ethernet II frame with an IPv4 packet inside. The frame's type field value of `0x800` determines this. In the IP packet, the message from the client to the server, which starts on the next line, the source address is `10.10.12.166` (`lnxclient`) and the destination address is `10.10.11.66` (`lnxserver`), as they should be.

We can ignore the rest of the IP header fields for now, and skip down to where the source and destination port are highlighted. The source port chosen by the client is `32825` and the port on the server that will receive the data is `55555`. We decided that `55555` would be the server port, and the client chose a port number to use based on certain rules, which we will talk about in a later chapter.

Now that we know the IP addresses and ports used, we can determine the socket at each host. This is shown in Table 2.1.

THE TCP/IP PROTOCOL STACK

The layering of TCP/IP is important if IP packets are to run on almost any type of network. The IP packet layer is only one layer, and from the TCP/IP perspective, the layer or layers below the IP layer are not as important as the overall flow of packets from one host (end system) to another across the network.

Layering means that you only have to adapt one type of packet to an underlying network type to get the entire TCP/IP suite. Once the packet has been "framed," you need not worry about TCP/UDP, or any other protocol: they come along for the ride with the layering. Only the IP layer has to deal with the underlying hardware.

All that really matters is that the device at the receiving end understands the type of IP packet encapsulation used at the sending end. If only one form of packet encapsulation was used, the IP packets could remain inside the frame with a globally unique MAC address from source to destination. Network nodes could forward the frame without having to deal with the packet inside. We'll talk more about the differences between forwarding frames and forwarding packets later on in this book.

TCP/IP is considered to be a *peer protocol* stack, which means that every implementation of TCP/IP is considered to have the same capabilities as every other. There are no "restricted" or "master" versions of TCP/IP that anyone need be concerned about. So, for example, there is no special server stack needed.

However, this does not mean that all protocol stacks function in precisely the same way. TCP/IP, like many other protocol stacks, is implemented according to a model known as the *client-server model*.

THE CLIENT–SERVER MODEL

The hosts that run TCP/IP usually fall into one of two major categories: The host could be *client* or the host could be a *server*. However, this is mostly an application-layer model issue because most computers are fully multitasking-capable today. It is possible that the same host could be running the client version of a program for one application (e.g., the Web browser) and the server version of another program (e.g., a file transfer server) at the same time. Dedicated servers are most common on the Internet, but almost all client computers can act as servers for a variety of applications.The details are not as important as the interplay among layers and applications.

Peer-to-Peer Models

The client-server model is not the only way to implement a protocol stack. Many applications implement a peer-to-peer model. Peer applications have exactly the same capabilities whether used as a client or as a server. Distributed file-sharing systems on the Internet typically function as both client (fetching files for the user) and as a server (allowing user files to be shared by others).

The differences between client-server and peer-to-peer models are mainly application layer differences. A desktop computer that runs a Web browser and has file sharing turned on is both client and server, but is not now peer-to-peer. As an aside, in X-windows, which is not discussed in this book, the terms "client" and "server" are actually reversed and users sit in front of "X-servers" and access "X-clients."

TCP/IP LAYERS AND CLIENT–SERVER

TCP/IP has five layers. The bottom layers are the physical layer and underlying network layer. The underlying network technologies at the network layer are the topic of the next chapter. Above the data link layer is the IP layer itself. The IP layer forms and routes the IP packet (also called a datagram in a lot of documentation) and IP is the major protocol at this layer.

The transport layer of TCP/IP consists of two major protocols: the Transmission Control Protocol (TCP) and the User Datagram Protocol (UDP). TCP is a *reliable* layer added on top of the *best-effort* IP layer to make sure that even if packets are lost in transit, the hosts will be able to detect and resend missing information. TCP data units are called *segments*. UDP is as best-effort as IP itself, and UDP data units are called *datagrams*. The messages that applications exchange are made up of strings of segments or datagrams. Segments and datagrams are used to chop up application content, such as huge, multimegabyte files, into more easily handled pieces.

TCP is reliable in the sense that TCP always resends corrupt or lost segments. This strategy has many implications for delay-sensitive applications such as voice or video.

TCP is a *connection-oriented layer* on top of the *connectionless* IP layer. This means that before any TCP segment can be sent to another host, a TCP connection must be established to that host. Connectionless IP has no concept of a connection, and simply forwards packets without any understanding if the packets ever really got where they were going.

In contrast to TCP, UDP is a connectionless transport layer on top of connectionless IP. UDP segments are simply forwarded to a destination under the assumption that sooner or later a response will come back from the remote host. The response forms an implied or formal acknowledgment that the UDP segment arrived.

At the top of the TCP/IP stack is the application, or application services, layer. This is where the client–server concept comes into play. The applications themselves typically come in client or server versions, which is not true at other layers of TCP/IP. While a host computer might be able to run client processes and server processes at the same time, in the simplest case, these processes are two different applications.

Client–server application implementation can be extremely simple. A server process can start and basically sit and "listen" for clients to "talk" to the server. For example, a Web server is brought up on a host successfully whether there is a browser client pointed at it or not. The Web server process issues a *passive open* to TCP/IP and essentially remains idle on the network side until some client requests content. However, the Web browser (the client) process issues an *active open* to TCP/IP and attempts to

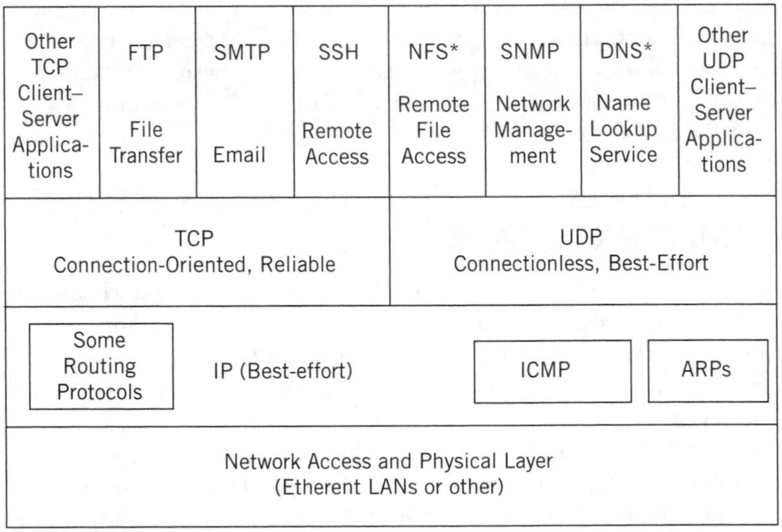

Other TCP Client–Server Applica-tions
FTP File Transfer
SMTP Email
SSH Remote Access
NFS* Remote File Access
SNMP Network Manage-ment
DNS* Name Lookup Service
Other UDP Client–Server Applica-tions
TCP Connection-Oriented, Reliable
UDP Connectionless, Best-Effort
Some Routing Protocols
IP (Best-effort)
ICMP
ARPs
Network Access and Physical Layer (Etherent LANs or other)

*In some instances, NFS and DNS use TCP.

FIGURE 2.4

The TCP/IP protocol stack in detail. The many possible applications on top and many possible network links on the bottom all funnel through the IP "hourglass."

send packets to a Web site immediately. If the Web site is not reachable, that causes an error condition.

To sum up the simplest application cases: Clients talk and servers listen (and usually reply). It is very easy to program an application that either talks or listens, although TCP/IP specifications allow for the transition of passive and active open from one state to another. We'll talk more about client and server application and passive and active opens in the chapter on sockets.

A more detailed look at the TCP/IP protocol stack is shown in Figure 2.4. The TCP/IP stack bridges the gap between interface connector on the network side (hardware) and the memory address space of the application on the host (software).

The names of the protocol data units used at each layer are worth reviewing. The unit of the network layer is the frame. Inside the frame is the data unit of the IP layer, the packet. The unit of the transport layer is the segment in TCP and datagram in UDP. The segment or datagram by definition is the content of the information-bearing packet. Finally, applications exchange messages. Segments and datagrams taken together form the messages that the applications are sending to each other.

This is a good place to explore some of the operational aspects of the TCP/IP protocol stack above the network access (or data link) layer.

THE IP LAYER

The connectionless IP layer routes the IP packets independently through the collection of network nodes such as routers that make up the "internetwork" that connects the LANs. Packets at the IP layer do not follow "paths" or "virtual circuits" or anything else set up by signaled or manually defined connections for packet flow in other types of network layers. However, this also means that the packets' content might arrive out of sequence, or even with gaps in the sequence due to lost packets, at the destination.

IP does not care to which application a packet belongs. IP delivers all packets without a sense of priority or sensitivity to loss. The whole point of IP is to get packets from one network interface to another. IP itself is not concerned with the lack of guaranteed *quality of service* (QoS) parameters such as bandwidth availability or minimal delay, and this is characteristic of all connectionless, best-effort networks. Even the basics, such as sequenced delivery of packet content, priorities, and guaranteed delivery in the form of acknowledgments (if these are needed by the application), must be provided by the higher layers of the TCP/IP protocol stack. These reliable transport functions are not functions of the IP layer, and some are not even functions of TCP.

Two other major protocols run at the IP layer besides IPv4 or IPv6 (or both). The routers that form the network nodes in a TCP/IP network must be able to send error messages to the hosts if a router must discard a packet (e.g., due to lack of buffer space because of congestion). This protocol is known as the Internet Control Message Protocol (ICMP). ICMP messages are sent inside IP packets, but ICMP is still considered a different protocol and not a separate layer.

The other major protocol placed at the IP layer has many different functions depending on the type of network that IP is running on. This is the Address Resolution Protocol (ARP). The main function of ARP is to provide a method for IPv4, which technically knows only about packets, to find out the proper network layer address to place in the frame header destination field. On LANs, this is the MAC address. Without this address, the network beneath the IP layer could not deliver the frame containing the IP packet to the proper destination. (IPv6 does not use ARP: IPv6 uses multicast for this purpose.)

On a LAN, ARP is a way for IPv4 to send a broadcast message onto the LAN asking, in effect, "Who has IP address 192.168.13.84?" Each system, whether host or router, on the LAN will examine the ARP message (all systems must pay attention to a broadcast) and the system having the IP address in question will reply to the sender's MAC address found in the source field of the frame. This target system will also cache the IP address information so that it knows the MAC address of the sender (this cuts down on ARP traffic on the network). The MAC layer address needed by the sending system is found in the source address field of the frame carrying the ARP reply packet.

ARP messages are broadcast to every host in what is called the network layer *broadcast domain*. The broadcast domain can be a single physical group (e.g., all hosts attached to a single group of hubs) or a logical grouping of hosts forming a *virtual LAN* (VLAN). More will be said about broadcast domains and VLANs later in this chapter.

THE TRANSPORT LAYER

The two main protocols that run above the IP layer at the transport layer are TCP and UDP. Lately, UDP has been assuming more and more prominence on the Internet, especially with applications such as voice and multicast traffic such as video. One reason is that TCP, with its reliable resending, is not particularly well suited for *real-time* applications (real time just means that the network delays must be low and stable or else the application will not function properly). For these applications, late-arriving data are worse than data that do not arrive at all, especially if the late data cause all the data "behind" it to also arrive late. (Of course, in spite of these limitations, TCP is still widely used for audio streaming and similar applications.)

Transmission Control Protocol

TCP's built-in reliability features include sequence numbering with resending, which is used to detect and resend missing or out-of-sequence segments. TCP also includes a complete flow control mechanism (called *windowing*) to prevent any sender from overwhelming a receiver. Neither of these built-in TCP features is good for real-time audio and video on the Internet. These applications cannot "pause" and wait for missing segments, nor should they slow down or speed up as traffic loads vary on the Internet. (The fact that they do just points out the incomplete nature of TCP/IP when it comes to quality of service for these applications and services.)

TCP contains all the functions and mechanisms needed to make up for the best-effort connectionless delivery provided by the IP layer. Packets could arrive at a host with errors, out of their correct sequence, duplicated, or with gaps in sequence due to lost (or discarded) packets. TCP must guarantee that the data stream is delivered to the destination application error-free, with all data in sequence and complete. Following the practice used in connection-oriented networks, TCP uses acknowledgments that periodically flow from the destination to the source to assure the sender that all is well with the data received to that point in time.

On the sending side, TCP passes segments to the IP layer for encapsulation in packets, which the IP layer in hosts and routers route connectionlessly to the destination host. On the receiving side, TCP accepts the incoming segments from the IP layer and delivers the data they represent to the proper application running above TCP in the exact order in which the data were sent.

User Datagram Protocol

The TCP/IP transport layer has another major protocol. UDP is as connectionless as IP. When applications use UDP instead of TCP, there is no need to establish, maintain, or tear down a connection between a source and destination before sending data. Connection management adds overhead and some initial delay to the network. UDP is a way to send data quickly and simply. However, UDP offers none of the reliability services that TCP does. UDP applications cannot rely on TCP to ensure error-free, guaranteed (via acknowledgments), in-sequence delivery of data to the destination.

For some simple applications, purely connectionless data delivery is good enough. Single request–response message pairs between applications are sent more efficiently with UDP because there is no need to exchange a flurry of initial TCP segments to establish a connection. Many applications will not be satisfied with this mode of operation, however, because it puts the burden of reliability on the application itself.

UDP is often used for short transactions that fit into one datagram and packet. Real-time applications often use UDP with another header inside called the real-time transport protocol (RTP). RTP borrows what it needs from the TCP header, such as a sequence number to detect (but not to resend) missing packets of audio and video, and uses these desirable features in UDP.

THE APPLICATION LAYER

At the top of the TCP/IP protocol stack, at the application layer, are the basic applications and services of the TCP/IP architecture. Several basic applications are typically bundled with the TCP/IP software distributed from various sources and, fortunately, are generally interoperable.

The standard application services suite usually includes a file transfer method (File Transfer Protocol: FTP), a remote terminal access method (Telnet, which is not commonly used today, and others, which are), an electronic mail system (Simple Mail

Transfer Protocol: SMTP), and a Domain Name System (DNS) resolver for domain name to IP address translation (and vice versa), and more. Many TCP/IP implementations also include a way of accessing files remotely (rather than transferring the whole file to the other host) known as the Network File System (NFS). There is also the Simple Network Management Protocol (SNMP) for network operations. For the Web, the server and browser applications are based on the Hypertext Transfer Protocol (HTTP). Some of these applications are defined to run on TCP and others are defined to run on UDP, and in many cases can run on either.

BRIDGES, ROUTERS, AND SWITCHES

The TCP/IP protocol stack establishes an architecture for internetworking. These protocols can be used to connect LANs in the same building, on a campus, or around the world. Not all internetworking devices are the same. Generally, network architects seeking to extend the reach of a LAN can choose from one of four major interconnection devices: repeaters, bridges, routers, and switches.

Not long ago, the network configuration and the available devices determined which type of internetworking device should be used. Today, network configurations are growing more and more complex, and the devices available often combine the features of several of these devices. For example, the routers on the Illustrated Network have all the features of traditional routers, plus some switching capabilities.

In their simplest forms, repeaters, bridges, and routers operate at different layers of the TCP/IP protocol stack, as shown in Figure 2.5. Roughly, repeaters forward bits from one LAN segment to another, bridges forward frames, and routers forward packets.

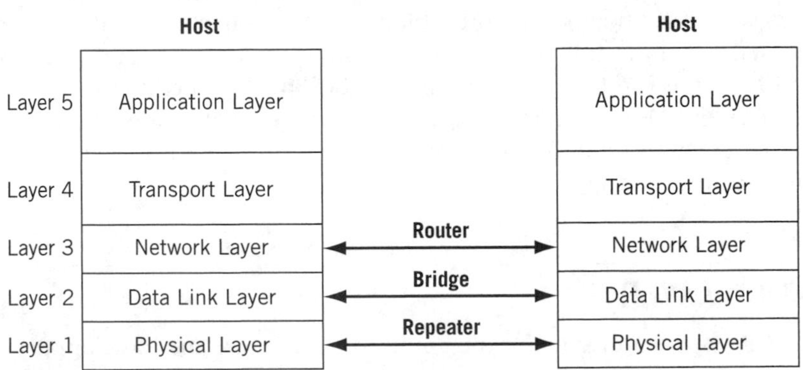

FIGURE 2.5

Repeater, bridge, and router. A repeater "spits bits," while a bridge deals with complete frames. A router operates at the packet level and is the main mode of the Internet.

Switches are important enough to deserve a separate discussion at the end of this section.

This section will explore the major characteristics of internetworking with bridges, routers, and switches. It will show how the LAN collision and broadcast domains are defined. This section will also show how the IP layer in particular and other protocols in TCP/IP interact in a routing environment.

Segmenting LANs

Network administrators and designers are often faced with a need to increase the amount of bandwidth available to users, increase the number of users supported, or extend the coverage of a LAN. The good news is that this means that the network is popular and useful, but the bad news is that there are lots of ways that these goals can be accomplished, some better than others.

Sometimes the answer is relatively straightforward. If a 100-Mbps Fast Ethernet is congested, moving everyone to Gigabit Ethernet will provide an instant increase in bandwidth (close to the theoretical tenfold increase with lots of tuning). However, this also usually means replacing adapter cards and replacing the "hubs" to support the new bandwidth and frames. This type of wholesale upgrade can be very expensive.

Hub

We avoid the use of the term "hub" in this book. Repeaters were called hubs when there were no others types of hubs. When bridges and switches and other LAN devices came along, it was better to call a repeater a repeater. Today the term "hub" can mean a repeater, bridge, switch, or a hybrid device like a multispeed repeater (which is really many single-speed repeaters connected by a bridge). The term "hub" never had a specific meaning.

Another way to give each user more bandwidth (and at the same time increase users and coverage) is to *segment* the LAN. Segmenting does not require replacing all of the user equipment. As the name implies, segmenting breaks the LAN into smaller portions and then reconnects them with an internetworking device.

Another consequence of the different protocol layers at which the various internetworking devices function is the number of LAN collision and broadcast domains created. Ethernet's CSMA/CD access method can result in collisions when stations on the LAN try to send at almost the same time. Collisions "waste" bandwidth because they destroy the frames, and the colliding stations must wait and try to send again. (Actually, unless they are oversubscribed, CSMA/CD systems offer better performance than token-passing or other methods.) Even when Ethernets do not generate collisions, broadcast

Table 2.2 Collision and Broadcast Domains		
Internetwork Device	**Collision Domains**	**Broadcast Domains**
Repeater	One	One
Bridge	Many	One
Router	Many	Many
Switch	Many	Depends on VLAN configuration

frames must be examined by each receiver because the destination address cannot be used to determine interest in content. Bandwidth is wasted if broadcast frames are sent to systems that have no interest in the content of the broadcast message. (In TCP/IP, ARPs are the major type of broadcast frames that systems send and receive.)

It should be noted that although CSMA/CD is part of Gigabit Ethernet, it is essentially nonexistent and not present at all in 10-Gigabit Ethernet.

Extending a LAN by forward bits still creates a single collision and broadcast domain. The number of collision and broadcast domains created by all the internetworking devices discussed is shown in Table 2.2. We'll look at why this is true of each device in detail shortly.

The use of these devices is not mutually exclusive. In other words, a router can be used to segment a LAN into two (or more) segments, and each resulting segment can be divided further with bridges. In an extreme case, each individual user or system has the full media bandwidth available. This is what switches can do.

Repeaters are a type of special case in that they do not segment a LAN at all. Repeaters do not furnish more bandwidth for users; they just extend the reach of the LAN. Repeaters are included in the table as a "baseline" for comparison. Repeaters forward bits from one segment to another and have no intelligence with regard to data format. If the frame contains errors, violates rules about minimum or maximum frame sizes, or anything else is wrong, the repeaters forward the frame anyway.

Note that wireless LAN devices connected to an attachment point share the same properties as a repeater network. And repeaters, technically obsolete on wired networks, have renewed life on wireless networks, especially what are called "ad hoc" wireless networks.

A 100BaseT Ethernet LAN consists of at least one multiport repeater (often called a "hub") with twisted-pair wires connected directly to each system. All systems see all frames, for better or worse. There are strict limits to the size to which a network made up of repeater-connected LAN segments can grow. The more systems there are that can send, the less of the total shared bandwidth each system has. Ethernet limits the number of systems that each LAN segment can have (the number varies by specific Ethernet type). Finally, there are distance limits to the electrical signals that repeaters propagate.

Bridges

Ethernet specifications limit the number of systems on a LAN segment and the overall distance spanned. To add devices to a LAN that has reached the maximum in one or both of these categories, a bridge can be used to connect LAN segments. Bridged networks normally filter frames and do not forward all frames onto all segments connected to the bridge. This is why bridges create more than one collision domain. However, the LAN segments linked by the bridge still normally form one broadcast domain. Although the word "bridge" is often applied to products, pure bridges are at least as obsolete as hubs.

The filtering process employed by a bridge differs according to specific LAN technology. Ethernet uses *transparent bridging* to connect LAN segments. A transparent bridge looks at the destination MAC address to decide if the frames should be:

- *Forwarded*—The frame is sent only onto the LAN segment where the destination is located. The bridge examines the source MAC address fields to find specific device locations.
- *Filtered*—The frame is dropped by the bridge. No message is sent back to the source.
- *Flooded*—The frame is sent to every LAN segment attached to the bridge. This is done for broadcast and multicast traffic.

When bridges are used to connect LAN segments, the media bandwidth is shared only by the devices on each segment. Because the broadcast domain is preserved, the bridged LANs still function as one big LAN. Bridges also discard frames with errors, as well as frames that violate LAN protocol length rules, and thus protect the other LAN segments when things go wrong.

Bridges are certainly an improvement over repeaters, but still have a number of issues. The common ARPs used to associate IP addresses at Layer 3 with LAN MAC addresses at Layer 2 pass through all bridges, but broadcasts due to protocols are not usually the issue. However, multicast traffic is also flooded, and multimedia applications such as videoconferences can easily overwhelm a bridged network. Some issues are more mundane: printers, which generate very little traffic, sometimes remain invisible in a bridged network.

Ethernet bridges must also be *spanning tree bridges*. These bridges can detect loops in the interconnected topology of LAN segments and bridges. Loops are a problem in bridged networks because some frames are always flooded onto all segments. Flooding multiplies the total number of frames on the network. Loops multiply frames over and over until a saturation point is reached.

Routers

Bridges add functions to an interconnected LAN because they operate at a higher layer of the protocol stack than repeaters. Bridges run at Layer 2, the frame layer, and can do everything a repeater can do, and more, because bridges create more collision domains. In the same way, routers add functionality to bridges and operate at Layer 3, the packet layer. Routers not only create more collision domains, they create more LAN broadcast domains as well.

In a LAN with repeaters or bridges, all of the systems belong to the same *subnet* or subnetwork. Layer 3 addresses in their simplest form—and IP addresses are a good example of this—consist of a *network* and system (*host*) portion of the address. LANs connected by routers have multiple broadcast domains, and each LAN segment belongs to a different subnetwork.

Because of the presence of multiple subnets, TCP/IP devices must behave differently in the presence of a router. Bridges connecting TCP/IP hosts are transparent to the systems, but routers connecting hosts are not. At the very least, the host must know the address of at least one router, the default router, to send packets beyond the local subnet. As we'll soon see, use of the default router requires the use of a default route, a route that matches all IPv4/IPv6 packets.

Bridges are sometimes called "protocol independent" devices, which really means that bridges can be used to connect LAN segments regardless of whether TCP/IP is used or not. However, routers must have Layer 3 software to handle whichever Layer 3 protocols are in use on the LAN. Many routers, especially routers that connect to the Internet, can and do understand only the IP protocol. However, many routers can handle multiple Layer 3 protocols, including protocols that are not usually employed with routed networks.

LAN Switches

The term "switch" in networking has threatened to become as overused as "hub." When applied to LANs, a switch is still a device with a number of common characteristics that can be compared to bridges and routers.

The LAN switch is really a complex bridge with many interfaces. LAN switching is the ultimate extension of multiport bridging. A LAN switch has every device on its own segment, giving each system the entire media bandwidth all for itself. Multiple systems can transmit simultaneously as long as there are no "port collisions" on the LAN switch. Port collisions occur when multiple source ports try to send a frame to the same output port at the same time.

All of the ports on the switch establish their own broadcast domain. However, when broadcast frames containing ARPs or multicast traffic arrive, the switch floods the frames to all other ports. Unfortunately, this makes LAN switching not much better than a repeater or a bridge when it comes to dealing with broadcast and multicast traffic (but there is an improvement because broadcast traffic cannot cause collisions that would force retransmissions).

To overcome this problem, a LAN switch can allow multiple ports to be assigned to a broadcast domain. The broadcast domains on a LAN switch are configurable and each floods broadcast and multicast traffic only within its own domain. As a matter of fact, it is not possible for *any* frames to cross the boundary of a broadcast domain: Another external device, such as a router, is always required to internetwork the domains.

When LAN switches define multiple broadcast domains they are creating virtual LANs (VLANs). Not all LAN switches can define VLANs, especially smaller ones, but many can. A VLAN defines membership to a LAN logically, through configuration, not physically by sharing media or devices.

On a WAN, the term "switch" means a class of network nodes that behave very differently than routers. We'll look more closely at how "fast packet network" devices, such as Frame Relay and ATM switches as network nodes, differ from routers in a later chapter.

Virtual LANs

A VLAN, according to the official IEEE definition, defines broadcast domains at Layer 2. VLANs, as a Layer 2 entity, really have little to do with the TCP/IP protocol stack, but VLANs make a huge difference in how switches and routers operate on a TCP/IP network.

Routers do not propagate broadcasts as bridges do, so a router automatically defines broadcast domains on each interface. Layer 2 LAN switches logically create broadcast domains based on configuration of the switch. The configuration tells the LAN switch what to do with a broadcast received on a port in terms of what other ports should receive it (or if it should even be flooded to all other ports).

When LAN switches are used to connect LAN segments, the broadcast domains cannot be determined just by looking at the network diagram. Systems can belong to different, the same, or even multiple, broadcast domains. The configuration files in the

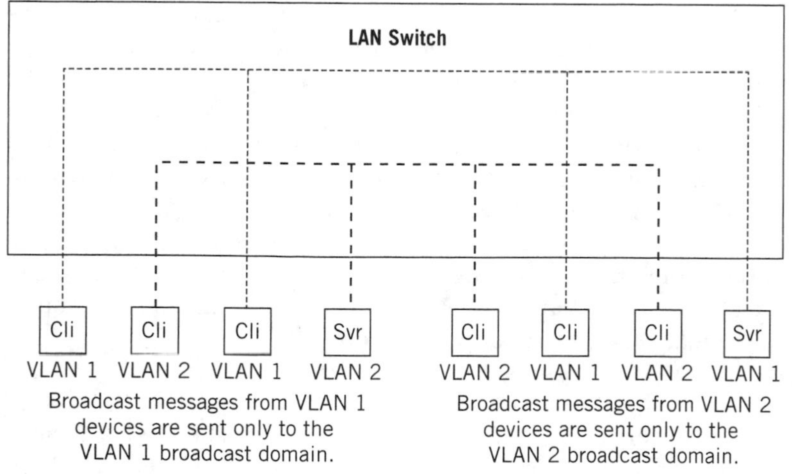

FIGURE 2.6

VLANs in a LAN switch. Broadcast domains are now logical entities connected by "virtual bridges" in the device.

LAN switches determine the boundaries of these domains as well as their members. Each broadcast domain is a type of "virtual bridge" within the switch. This is shown in Figure 2.6.

Each virtual bridge configured in the LAN switch establishes a distinct broadcast domain, or VLAN. Frames from one VLAN cannot pass directly to another VLAN on the LAN switch (or else you create one big VLAN or broadcast domain). Layer 3 internetworking devices such as routers must be used to connect the VLANs, allowing internetworking and at the same time keeping the VLAN broadcast domains distinct. All devices that can communicate directly without a router (or other Layer 3 or higher device) share the same broadcast domain.

VLAN Frame Tagging

VLAN devices can come in all shapes and sizes, and configuration of the broadcast domains can be just as variable. Interoperability of LAN switches is compromised when there are multiple ways for a device to recognize the boundaries of broadcast domains. To promote interoperability, the IEEE established IEEE 802.1Q to standardize the creation of VLANs through the use of frame *tagging*.

Some care is needed with this aspect of VLANs. VLANs are not really a formal networking concept, but they are a nice feature that devices can support. One key VLAN feature is the ability to place switch ports in virtual broadcast domains. The other key feature is the ability to *tag* Ethernet frames with a VLAN identifier so that devices can easily distinguish the boundaries of the broadcast domains. These devices and tags are not codependent, but you have to use both features to establish a useful VLAN.

Multiple tags can be placed inside Ethernet frames. There is also a way to assign priorities to the tagged frames, often called IEEE 802.1p, but officially known as IEEE 802.1D-1998. Internetworking devices, not just LAN switches, can read the tags and establish VLAN boundaries based on the tag information.

VLAN tags add 4 bytes of information between the Source Address and Type/Length fields of Ethernet frames. The maximum size of the modified Ethernet frame is increased from 1518 to 1522 bytes, so the frame check sequence must be recalculated when the VLAN tag is added. VLAN identifiers can range from 0 to 4095.

The use of VLAN "q in q" tags increases the available VLAN space (ISPs often assign each customer a VLAN identifier, and customers often have their own VLANs as well). In this case, multiple tags are placed in an Ethernet frame. The format and position of VLAN tags according to IEEE 802.3ac are shown in Figure 2.7.

VLANs are built for a variety of reasons. Among them are:

Security—Frames on an Ethernet segment are delivered everywhere, and devices only process (look inside) MAC frames that are addressed to them. Nothing stops a device from monitoring everything that arrives on the interface (that's essentially how Ethereal works). Sensitive information, or departmental traffic, can be isolated with virtual LANs.

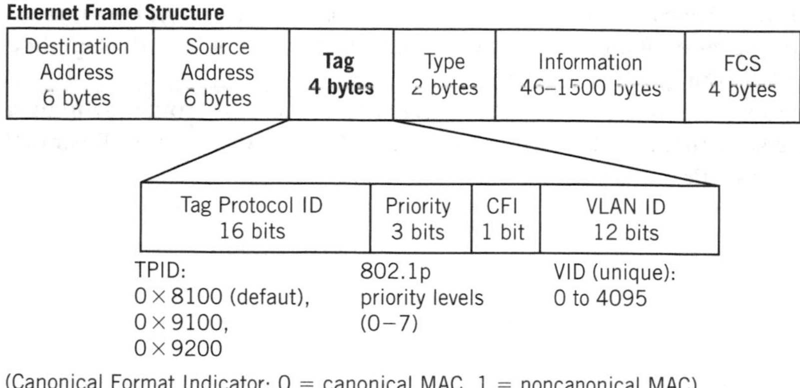

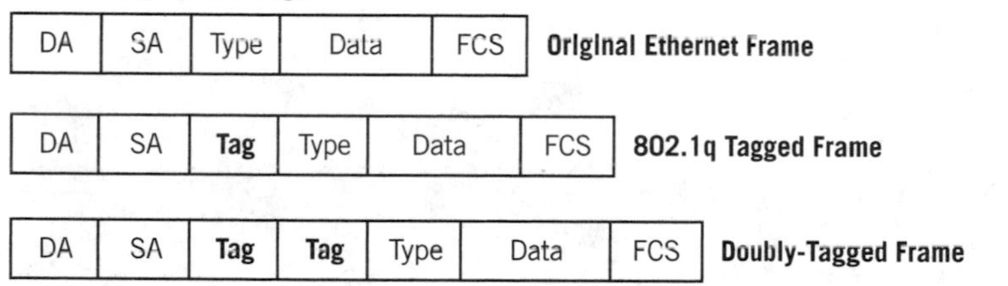

FIGURE 2.7

VLAN tags and frames. Note that frames can contain more than one tag, and often do.

Cutting down on broadcasts—Some network protocols are much worse than others when it comes to broadcasts. These broadcast frames can be an issue because they rarely carry user data and each and every system on the segment must process the content of a broadcast frame. VLANs can isolate protocol broadcasts so that they arrive only at the systems that need to hear them. Also, a number of hosts that might otherwise make up a very large logical network (e.g., Page 19 what we will call later a "/19-sized wireless subnet") could use VLANs because they can be just plain noisy.

Router delay—Older routers can be much slower than LAN switches. VLANs can be used to establish logical boundaries that do not need to employ a router to get traffic from one LAN segment to another. (In fairness, many routers today route at "wire speed" and do not introduce much latency into a network.)

The Illustrated Network uses Gigabit Ethernet links to connect the customer-edge routers to the ISP networks. Many ISPs would assign the frame arriving from LAN1 and LAN2 a VLAN ID and tag the frames at the provider-edge routers. If the sites are close enough, some form of Metro Ethernet could be configured using the tag information. However, the sites are far enough apart that we would have to use some other method to create a single LAN out of LAN1 and LAN2.

In a later chapter, we'll use VLAN tagging, along with some other router switching features, to create a "virtual private LAN" between LAN1 and LAN2 on the Illustrated Network, mainly for security purposes.

QUESTIONS FOR READERS

Figure 2.8 shows some of the concepts discussed in this chapter and can be used to help you answer the following questions.

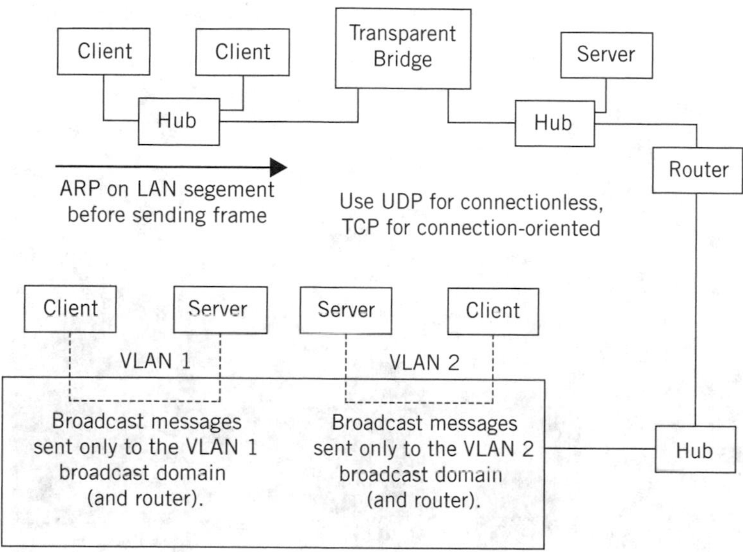

FIGURE 2.8

Hubs, bridges, and routers can connect LAN segments to form an internetwork.

1. What is the main function of the ARP message on a LAN?
2. What is the difference between TCP and UDP terms of connection overhead and reliability?
3. What is a transparent bridge?
4. What is the difference between a bridge and a router in terms of broadcast domains?
5. What is the relationship between a broadcast domain and a VLAN?

CHAPTER

Network Link Technologies

3

What You Will Learn

In this chapter, you will learn more about the links used to connect the nodes of the Illustrated Network. We'll investigate the frame types used in various technologies and how they carry packets. We'll take a long look at Ethernet, and mention many other link types used primarily in private networks.

You will learn about SONET/SDH, DSL, and wireless technologies as well as Ethernet. All four link types are used on thc Illustrated Network.

This chapter explores the physical and data link layer technologies used in the Illustrated Network. We investigate the methods used to link hosts and intermediate nodes together over shorter LAN distances and longer WAN distances to make a complete network.

For most of the rest of the book, we'll deal with packets and their contents. This is our only chance to take a detailed look at the frames employed on our network, and even peer inside them. Because the Illustrated Network is a real network, we'll emphasize the link types used on the network and take a more cursory look at link types that might be very important in the TCP/IP protocol suite, but are not used on our network. We'll look at Ethernet and the Synchronous Optical Network/Synchronous Digital Hierarchy (SONET/SDH) link technologies, and explore the variations on the access theme that digital subscriber line (DSL) and wireless technologies represent.

We'll look at public network services like frame relay and Asynchronous Transfer Mode (ATM) in a later chapter. In this book, the term *private network* is used to characterize network links that are owned or directly leased by the user organization, while a *public network* is characterized by shared user access to facilities controlled by a service provider. The question of *Who owns the intermediate nodes?* is often used as a rough distinguisher between private and public network elements.

Because of the way the TCP/IP protocol stack is specified, as seen in Chapter 1, we won't talk much about physical layer elements such as modems, network interface cards (NICs), and connectors. As important as these aspects of networking are, they

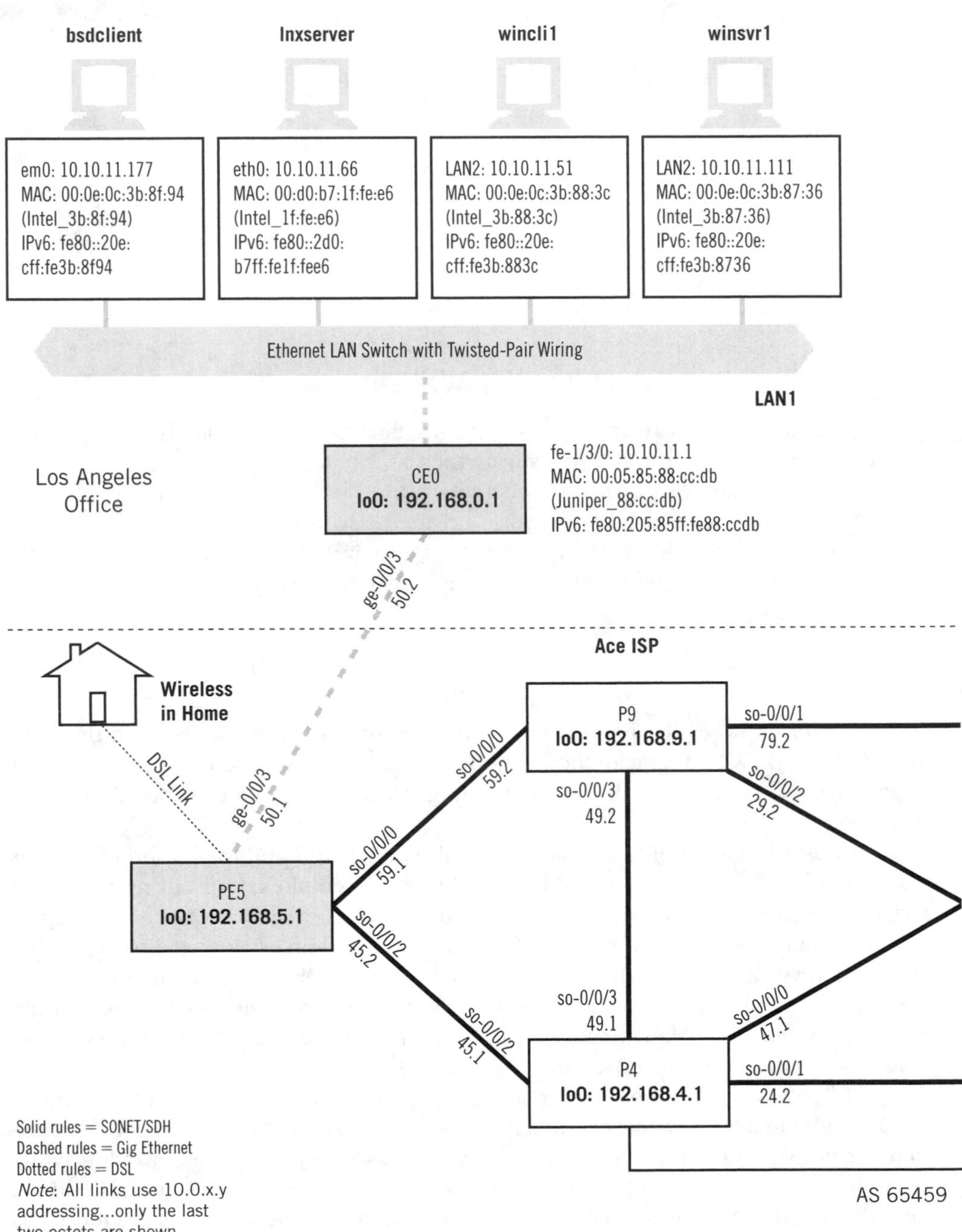

FIGURE 3.1

Connections used on the Illustrated Network. SONET/SDH links are indicated by heavy lines, Ethernet types by dashed lines, and DSL is shown as a dotted line. The home wireless network is not given a distinctive representation.

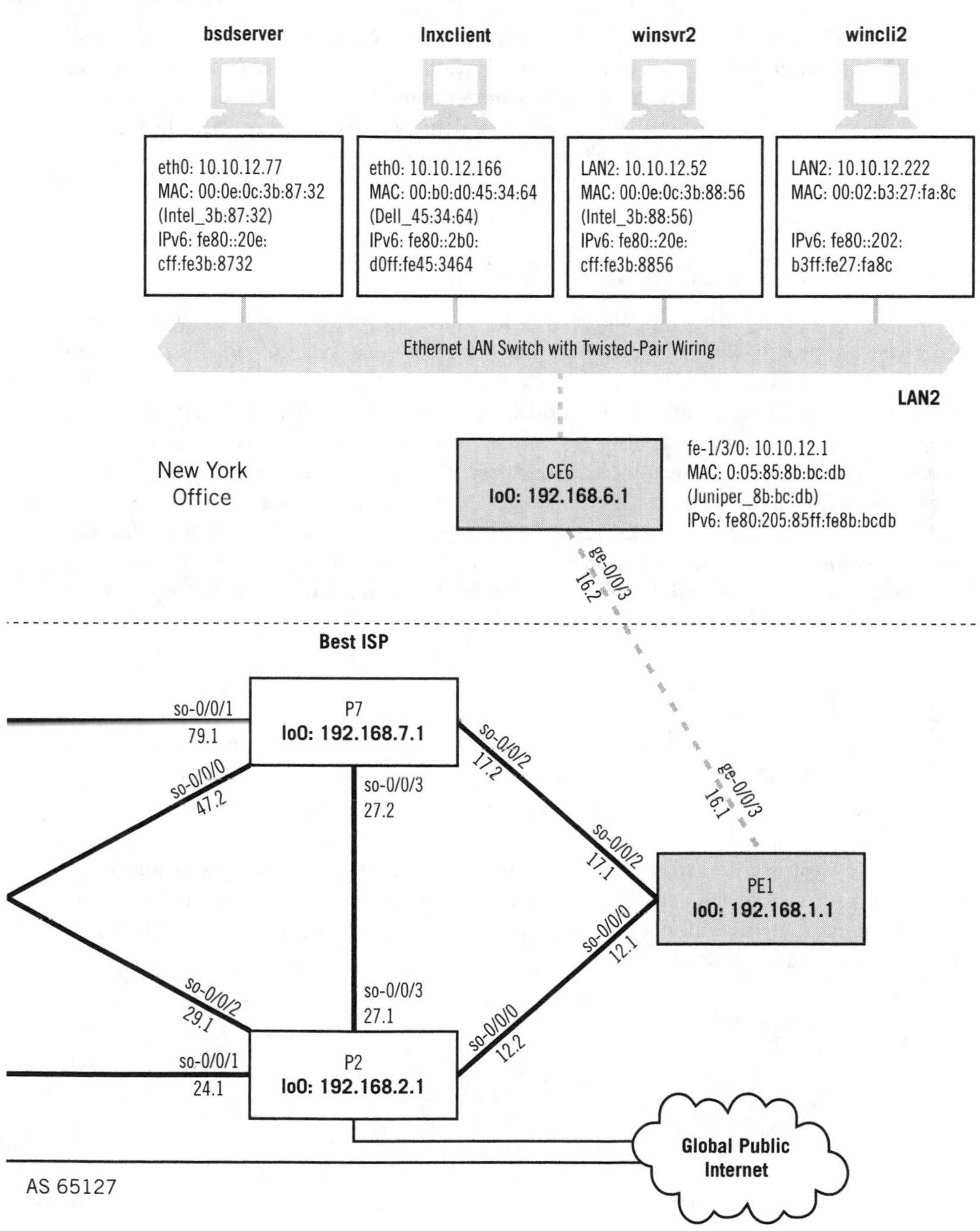

bsdserver
lnxclient
winsvr2
wincli2
eth0: 10.10.12.77
MAC: 00:0e:0c:3b:87:32
(Intel_3b:87:32)
IPv6: fe80::20e:
cff:fe3b:8732
eth0: 10.10.12.166
MAC: 00:b0:d0:45:34:64
(Dell_45:34:64)
IPv6: fe80::2b0:
d0ff:fe45:3464
LAN2: 10.10.12.52
MAC: 00:0e:0c:3b:88:56
(Intel_3b:88:56)
IPv6: fe80::20e:
cff:fe3b:8856
LAN2: 10.10.12.222
MAC: 00:02:b3:27:fa:8c
IPv6: fe80::202:
b3ff:fe27:fa8c
Ethernet LAN Switch with Twisted-Pair Wiring
LAN2
New York
Office
CE6
lo0: 192.168.6.1
fe-1/3/0: 10.10.12.1
MAC: 0:05:85:8b:bc:db
(Juniper_8b:bc:db)
IPv6: fe80:205:85ff:fe8b:bcdb
ge-0/0/3
16.2
Best ISP
so-0/0/1
79.1
P7
lo0: 192.168.7.1
so-0/0/0
47.2
so-0/0/3
27.2
so-0/0/2
17.2
ge-0/0/3
16.1
so-0/0/2
17.1
PE1
lo0: 192.168.1.1
so-0/0/0
12.1
so-0/0/2
29.1
so-0/0/3
27.1
so-0/0/0
12.2
so-0/0/1
24.1
P2
lo0: 192.168.2.1
Global Public
Internet
AS 65127

have little to do directly with how TCP/IP protocols or the Internet operates. For example, a full exploration of all the connector types used with fiber-optic cable would take many pages, and yet add little to anyone's understanding of TCP/IP or the Internet. Instead, we will concentrate on the structure of the frames sent on these link types, which *are* often important to TCP/IP, and present some operational details as well.

ILLUSTRATED NETWORK CONNECTIONS

We will start by using Ethereal (Wireshark), the network protocol analyzer introduced in the last chapter, to investigate the connections between systems on the Illustrated Network. It runs on a variety of platforms, including all three used in the Illustrated Network: FreeBSD Unix, Linux, and Windows XP. Ethereal can display real-time packet interpretations and, if desired, also save traffic to files (with a variety of formats) for later analysis or transfer to another system. Ethereal is most helpful when examining all types of Ethernet links. The Ethernet links are shown as dashed lines in Figure 3.1.

The service provider networks' SONET links are shown as heavy solid lines, and the DSL link to the home office is shown as a dotted line. The wireless network inside the home is not given a distinctive representation in the figure. Note that ISPs today typically employ more variety in WAN link types.

Displaying Ethernet Traffic

On the Illustrated Network, all of the clients and servers with detailed information listed are attached to LANs. Let's start our exploration of the links used on the Illustrated Network by using Ethereal both ways to see what kind of *frames* are used on these LANs.

Here is a capture of a small frame to show what the output looks like using tethereal, the text-based version of Ethereal. The example uses the verbose mode (-V) to force tethereal to display all packet and frame details. The example shows, highlighted in bold, that Ethernet II frames are used on LAN1.

```
[root@lnxserver admin]# /usr/sbin/tethereal -V
    Frame 2 (60 bytes on wire, 60 bytes captured)
    Arrival Time: Mar 25, 2008 12:14:36.383610000
    Time delta from previous packet: 0.000443000 seconds
    Time relative to first packet: 0.000591000 seconds
    Frame Number: 2
    Packet Length: 60 bytes
    Capture Length: 60 bytes
Ethernet II, Src: 00:05:85:88:cc:db, Dst: 00:d0:b7:1f:fe:e6
    Destination: 00:d0:b7:1f:fe:e6 (Intel_1f:fe:e6)
    Source: 00:05:85:88:cc:db (Juniper__88:cc:db)
    Type: ARP (0x0806)
    Trailer: 00000000000000000000000000000000...
```

```
Address Resolution Protocol (reply)
    Hardware type: Ethernet (0x0001)
    Protocol type: IP (0x0800)
    Hardware size: 6
    Protocol size: 4
    Opcode: reply (0x0002)
    Sender MAC address: 00:05:85:88:cc:db (Juniper__88:cc:db)
    Sender IP address: 10.10.11.1 (10.10.11.1)
    Target MAC address: 00:d0:b7:1f:fe:e6 (Intel_1f:fe:e6)
    Target IP address: 10.10.11.66 (10.10.11.66)
```

Many details of the packet and frame structure and content will be discussed in later chapters. However, we can see that the source and destination MAC addresses are present in the frame. The source address is `00:05:85:88:cc:db` (the router), and the destination (the Linux server) is `00:d0:b7:1f:fe:e6`. Ethereal even knows which organizations have been assigned the first 24 bits of the 48-bit MAC address (Intel and Juniper Networks). We'll say more about MAC addresses later in this chapter.

Figure 3.2 shows the same packet, and the same information, but in graphical format. Only a small section of the entire window is included. Note how the presence of Ethernet II frames is indicated, parsed on the second line in the middle pane of the window.

Why use text-based output when a graphical version is available? The graphical output shows the raw frame in hex, something the text-based version does not do, and the interpretation of the frame's fields is more concise.

However, the graphical output is not always clearer. In most cases, the graphical representation can be more cluttered, especially when groups of packets are involved. The graphical output only parses one packet at a time on the screen, while a whole string of packets can be parsed with tethereal (but printouts of graphical information can be formatted like tethereal).

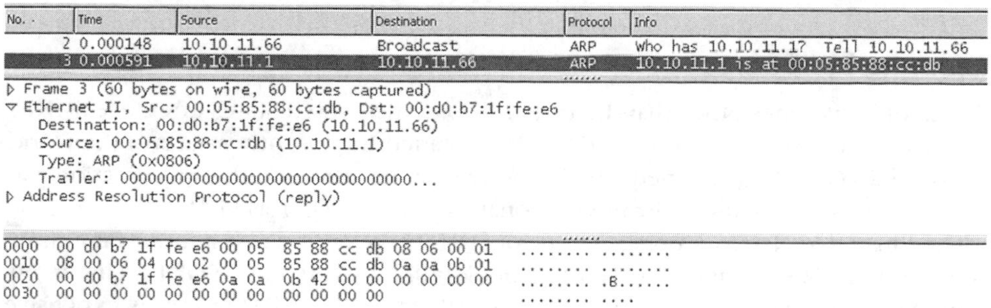

No.	Time	Source	Destination	Protocol	Info
2	0.000148	10.10.11.66	Broadcast	ARP	Who has 10.10.11.1? Tell 10.10.11.66
3	0.000591	10.10.11.1	10.10.11.66	ARP	10.10.11.1 is at 00:05:85:88:cc:db

```
▷ Frame 3 (60 bytes on wire, 60 bytes captured)
▽ Ethernet II, Src: 00:05:85:88:cc:db, Dst: 00:d0:b7:1f:fe:e6
    Destination: 00:d0:b7:1f:fe:e6 (10.10.11.66)
    Source: 00:05:85:88:cc:db (10.10.11.1)
    Type: ARP (0x0806)
    Trailer: 000000000000000000000000000000000...
▷ Address Resolution Protocol (reply)
```

```
0000  00 d0 b7 1f fe e6 00 05  85 88 cc db 08 06 00 01   ........ ........
0010  08 00 06 04 00 02 00 05  85 88 cc db 0a 0a 0b 01   ........ ........
0020  00 d0 b7 1f fe e6 0a 0a  0b 42 00 00 00 00 00 00   ........ .B......
0030  00 00 00 00 00 00 00 00  00 00 00 00               ........ ....
```

FIGURE 3.2

Graphical interface for Ethereal. There are three main panes. Top to bottom: (1) a digest of the packets header and information, (2) parsed details about frame and packet contents, and (3) the raw frame captured in hexadecimal notation and interpreted in ASCII.

In addition, many network administrators of Internet servers do not install or use a graphical interface, and perform their tasks from a command prompt. If you're not sitting in front of the device, it's more expedient to run the non-GUI version. Tethereal is the only realistic option in these cases. We will use both types of Ethereal in the examples in this book.

In our example network, what about LAN2? Is it also using Ethernet II frames? Let's capture some packets on `bsdserver` to find out.

```
bsdserver# tethereal -V
Capturing on em0
Frame 1 (98 bytes on wire, 98 bytes captured)
    Arrival Time: Mar 25, 2008 13:05:00.263240000
    Time delta from previous packet: 0.000000000 seconds
    Time since reference or first frame: 0.000000000 seconds
    Frame Number: 1
    Packet Length: 98 bytes
    Capture Length: 98 bytes
Ethernet II, Src: 00:0e:0c:3b:87:32, Dst: 00:05:85:8b:bc:db
    Destination: 00:05:85:8b:bc:db (Juniper__8b:bc:db)
    Source: 00:0e:0c:3b:87:32 (Intel_3b:87:32)
    Type: IP (0x0800)
Internet Protocol, Src Addr: 10.10.12.77 (10.10.12.77), Dst Addr: 10.10.12.1
(10.10.12.1)
    Version: 4
    Header length: 20 bytes
    ....
```

Yes, an Ethernet II frame is in use here as well. Even though we're running Ethereal (tethereal) on a different operating system (FreeBSD) instead of on Linux, the output is nearly identical (the differences are due to a slightly different version of Ethereal on the servers). However, LANs are not the only type of connections used on the Illustrated Network.

Displaying SONET Links

What about link types other than Ethernet? ISPs in the United States often use SONET fiber links between routers separated by long distance. In most other parts of the world, SDH is used. SONET was defined initially in the United States, and the specification was adapted, with some changes, for international use by the ITU-T as SDH.

The Illustrated Network uses SONET, not SDH. There are small but important differences between SONET and SDH, but this book will only reference SONET. Line monitoring equipment that allows you to look directly at SONET/SDH frames is expensive and exotic, and not available to most network administrators. So we'll take a different approach: We'll show you the information that's available on a router with a SONET interface. This will show the considerable bandwidth available even in the slowest of SONET links, which runs at 155 Mbps and is the same as the basic SDH speed.

SONET and SDH

The SONET fiber-optic link standard was developed in the United States and is mainly used in places that follow the digital telephony system used in the United States, such as Canada and the Philippines. SDH, on the other hand, is used in places that follow the international standards developed for the digital telephony system in the rest of the world. SDH *must* be used for all international links, even those that link to SONET networks in the United States.

The differences between SONET and SDH transmission frame structures, nomenclature, alarms, and other details are relatively minor. In most cases, equipment can handle SONET/SDH with equal facility.

We can log in to router CE0 and monitor a SONET interface for a minute or so and see what's going on.

Routers and Users

Usually, network administrators don't let ordinary users casually log in to routers, even edge routers, and poke around. Even if they were allowed to, the ISP's core routers would still remain off limits. But this is *our* network, and we can do as we please, wherever we please.

```
Admin>ssh ce0
adminCE6's password: *********
--- JUNOS 8.4R1.3 built 2007-08-06 06:58:15 UTC
admin@ce0> monitor interface so-0/0/1
R2                                 Seconds: 59               Time: 13:36:05
                                                            Delay: 2/0/3
Interface: so-0/0/1, Enabled, Link is Up
Encapsulation: PPP, Keepalives, Speed: OC3
Traffic statistics:                                         Current delta
  Input bytes:               166207481 (576 bps)                [2498]
  Output bytes:              171979817 (48 bps)                 [2713]
  Input packets:             2868777 (0 pps)                      [39]
  Output packets:            2869671 (0 pps)                      [39]
Encapsulation statistics:
  Input keepalives:          477607                                [6]
  Output keepalives:         477717                                [7]
  LCP state: Opened
Error statistics:
  Input errors:              0                                     [0]
  Input drops:               0                                     [0]
  Input framing errors:      0                                     [0]
```

```
  Input runts:             0                                          [0]
  Input giants:            0                                          [0]
  Policed discards:        0                                          [0]
  L3 incompletes:          0                                          [0]
  L2 channel errors:       0                                          [0]
  L2 mismatch timeouts:    0                                          [0]
  Carrier transitions:     1                                          [0]
  Output errors:           0                                          [0]
  Output drops:            0                                          [0]
  Aged packets:            0                                          [0]
Active alarms : None
Active defects: None
SONET error counts/seconds:
  LOS count                1                                          [0]
  LOF count                1                                          [0]
  SEF count                3                                          [0]
  ES-S                     1                                          [0]
  SES-S                    1                                          [0]
SONET statistics:
  BIP-B1                   0                                          [0]
  BIP-B2                   0                                          [0]
  REI-L                    0  BIP-B3              Z                   [0]
```

Not much is happening yet on our network in terms of traffic, but the output is still informative. The first column shows cumulative values and the second column shows the change since the last monitor "snapshot" on the link. "Live" traffic during these 59 seconds, in this case mostly a series of *keepalive* packets, is shown in parentheses, both in bytes per second and in packets per second (the example rounds the 39 packets in 59 seconds, or 0.66 packets per second, down to 0 packets per second). The frames carried on the link, listed as encapsulation, belong to a protocol called Point-to-Point Protocol (PPP). Six PPP keepalives have been sent in the 59-second window, and seven have been received (they are exchanged every 10 seconds), adding to the total of more than 477,000 since the link was initialized. The cumulative errors also occurred as the link was initializing itself, and it is reassuring that there are no new errors.

Displaying DSL Links

The Illustrated Network also has a broadband DSL link from an ISP that is used to allow a home office to attach to the router network. This link is shown in red in Figure 3.1. If the permissions are set up correctly, the home user will be able to access network resources on LAN1 and LAN2. DSL links are much faster than ordinary dial-up lines and are always available, just like a leased access line. The DSL link terminates at home in a DSL router (more properly, a *residential gateway*), and the distribution of information to devices in the home can be by wired or wireless LAN.

On the network end of the DSL link, the link terminates at a DSL access multiplexer (DSLAM), typically using IP or ATM technology.

At the user end of the DSL link on the Illustrated Network, the office in the home uses both a wired and a wireless network. This is a common arrangement today: People with laptops can wander, but desktop PCs usually stay put. The wireless network encapsulates packets and sends them to a special device in the home (a wireless access point, often built into a DSL router).

What kind of frames does the DSL link use? That's hard to determine, because the DSL modem is upstream of the DSL router in most cases (sometimes on the side of the house, sometimes closer to the service provider). The wired LAN between DSL router and computer uses the same type of Ethernet frames we saw on LAN1 and LAN2. On a wired LAN, Ethereal will always capture Ethernet II frames, as shown in Figure 3.3.

What can we learn about DSL itself? Well, we can access the DSL router using a Web browser and see what kinds of information are available. Figure 3.4 shows the basic setup screen of the Linksys DSL router (although it's really not doing any real routing, just functioning as a simple gateway between ISP and home LAN).

Because this is a working LAN, I've restored the default names and addresses for this example. The router itself is `WRT54G` (a product designation), and the ISP does not expect only one host to use the DSL link, so no host or domain name is required. We'll talk about the maximum transmission unit (MTU) size later in this chapter. This is set automatically on the link.

The DSL router itself uses IPv4 address 192.168.1.1. We'll talk about what the subnet mask does in Chapter 4. The router hands out IP addresses as needed to devices on the home network, starting with 192.168.1.100, and it uses the Dynamic Host Configuration Protocol (DHCP) to do this. We'll talk about DHCP in Chapter 18.

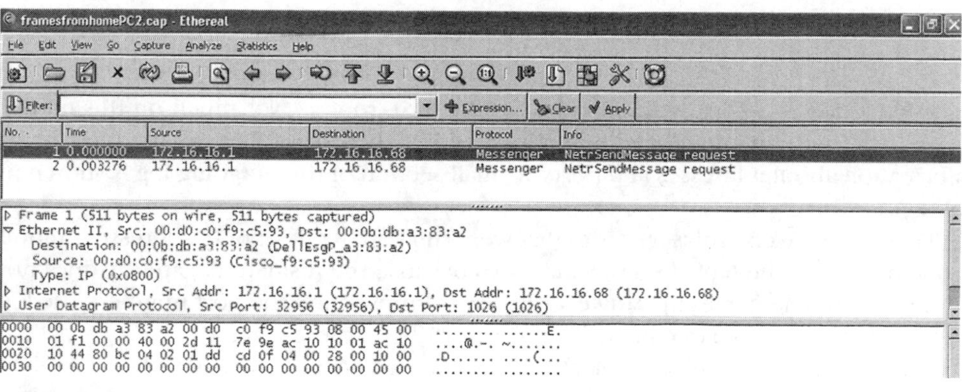

FIGURE 3.3

Ethernet frames on a wired LAN at the end of a DSL link. Capturing raw DSL frame "on the wire" is not frequently done, and is difficult without very expensive and specialized equipment.

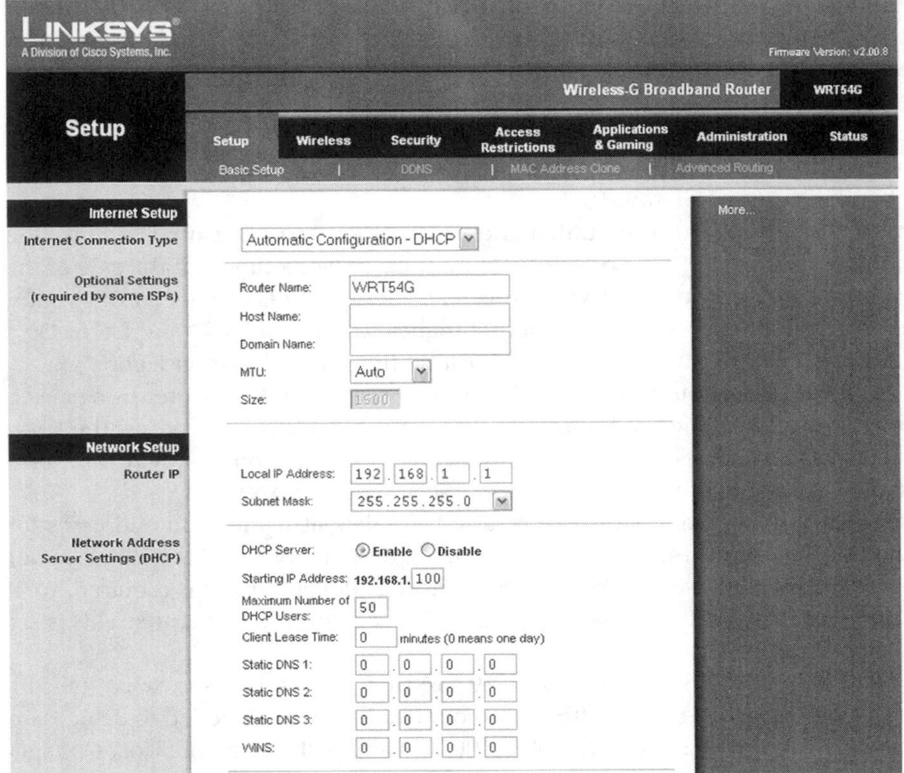

FIGURE 3.4

Basic setup screen for a DSL link. We'll talk about all of these configuration parameters and protocols, such as subnet masks and DHCP, in later chapters.

What kinds of statistics are available on the DSL router? Not much on this model. There are simple incoming and outgoing logs, but these capture only the most basic information about addresses and ports. A small section of the outgoing log is shown in Table 3.1.

These are all Web browser entries that were run with names, not IP addresses (Yahoo is one of them). The table lists the addresses because the residential gateway does not bother to look the names up. However, instead of presenting the port numbers, the log interprets them as a service name (www is port 80 on most servers).

We'll take a more detailed look at DSL later in this chapter. Now, let's take a look at the fourth and last link type used on the Illustrated Network: the four available wireless links used to hook a laptop and printer up to the home office DSL router.

The wireless implementation is a fairly straightforward bridging exercise. A single wireless interface is bridged in software with the Ethernets in the box. The wireless network is a single broadcast/collision domain.

Table 3.1 Outgoing Log Table from DSL Router

LAN IP	Destination URL/IP	Service/Port Number
192.168.1.101	202.43.195.13	www
192.168.1.101	64.86.142.99	www
192.168.1.101	202.43.195.52	www
192.168.1.101	64.86.142.120	www

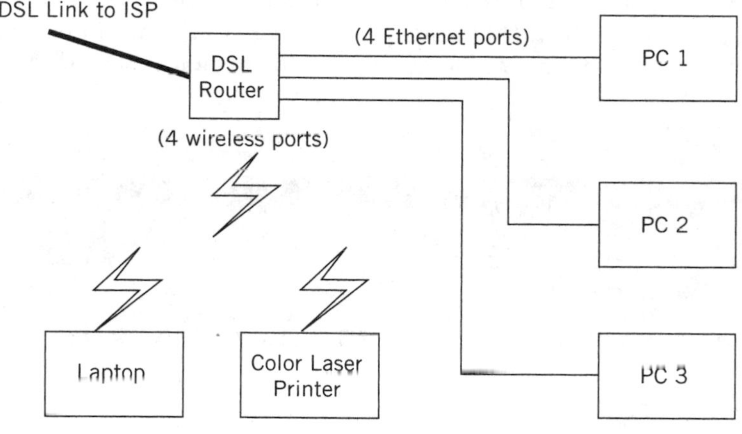

FIGURE 3.5

The home office network for the Illustrated Network. Devices must have either Ethernet ports or wireless interfaces (some have both). Not all printers are network-capable or wireless.

Displaying Wireless Links

The physical arrangement of the home office equipment used on the Illustrated Network is shown in Figure 3.5. In addition to the three wired PCs (used for various equipment configurations), there are two wireless links. One is used by the laptop for mobility, and the other is used to share a color laser printer. The DSL router does not have "ports" in the same sense as wired network devices, but it only supports up to four wireless devices.

The wireless link from the laptop to the DSL router, which uses something called IEEE 802.11g (sometimes called Wireless-G), is a distinct Layer 2 network technology and should not use Ethernet II frames. Let's make sure.

Capturing traffic at the wireless frame level requires special software and special drivers for the wireless network adapter card. The examples in this chapter use information from a wireless packet sniffer called Airopeek NX from Wildpackets.

A sample capture of a data packet and frame from a wireless link is shown in Figure 3.6.

Wireless LANs based on IEEE 802.11 use a distinct frame structure and a complex data link layer protocol. We'll talk about 802.11 shortly, but for now we should just note that the Illustrated Network uses USB-attached wireless NICs, and few wireless sniffers support these types of adapters.

The frame addressing and encapsulation on wireless LANs is much more complicated than Ethernet. Note that the 802.11 MAC frame has *three* distinct MAC addresses, labeled Destination, BSSID, and Source. The wireless LAN has to keep track of source, destination, and wireless access point (Base Station System ID, or BSSID) addresses. Also note that these are not really Ethernet II frames. The frames on the wireless link are structured according to the IEEE 802.2 LLC header. These have "SNAP SAP," indicated by *0xAA*, in the frame, in contrast to Ethernet II frames, which are indicated by *0x01*.

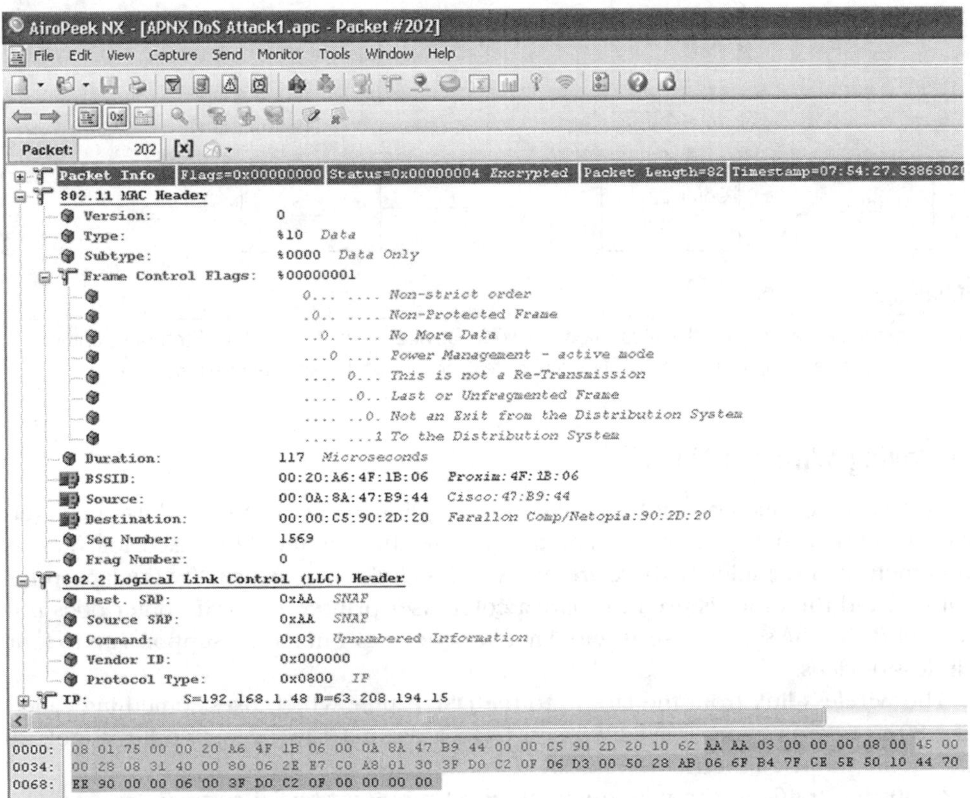

FIGURE 3.6

Data frame and packet on a wireless link. Note that the IEEE 802.11 MAC header is different from the Ethernet in many ways and uses the IEEE 802.2 LLC inside.

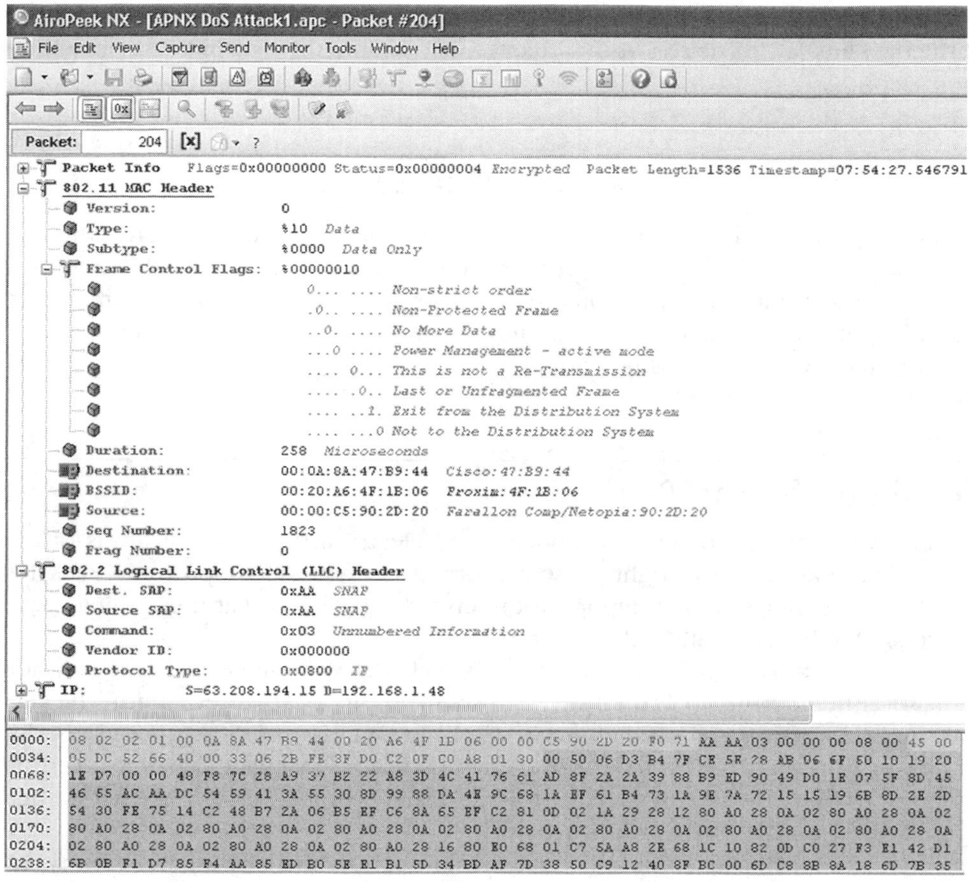

FIGURE 3.7

The next data frame in the sequence, showing how the contents of the address fields shift based on direction and type of wireless frame.

The address fields in 802.11 also "shift" their meaning, as shown in Figure 3.7. The fields are now BSSID, Source, and Destination. This is another capture from Airopeek NX, showing the next data frame sent in the captured exchange. The address fields have different meanings based on whether they are sent *to* the wireless router or are received *from* the wireless router.

Frames and the Link Layer

In summary, we have seen that the connections on the Illustrated Network consist of several types of links. There are wired Ethernet LANs and Gigabit Ethernet links, SONET links and DSL links, and even a wired LAN in the home network. We've looked at some of the frame types that carry information back and forth on the network connections.

There are many more types of frames that can carry IP packets between systems at the data link layer. The rest of this chapter will explore the data link layer in a little more depth.

RFCs and Physical Layers

Internet RFCs usually describe not how the physical (or data link) layers in a TCP/IP network should function, but how to place packets inside data link frames and get them out again at the other end of the link to the adjacent system. It is always good to remember that frames flow between *adjacent* (directly connected or reachable) systems on a network.

THE DATA LINK LAYER

Putting the world of connectors, modems, and electrical digital signal levels of the physical layer aside, let's go right to the data link layer of the TCP/IP protocol stack. It's not that these things are not important to networking; it's just that these things have nothing directly to do with TCP/IP.

The data link layer of TCP/IP takes an IP packet at the source and puts it inside whichever frame structure is used between systems (e.g., an Ethernet frame). The data link layer then passes the frame to the physical layer, which sends the frame as a series of bits over the link itself. At the receiver, the physical and data link layers recover the frame from the arriving sequence of bits and extract the packet. The packet is then passed to the receiving network (IP) layer.

Interfaces for IP packets have been defined for all of the following network types, for both LAN and WAN:

Ethernet—Originally from Digital Equipment Corporation, Intel, and Xerox (sometimes called DIX Ethernet).

IEEE (Institute of Electrical and Electronics Engineers) 802.3—Ethernet-based LANs, including all its variations, such as Gigabit Ethernet.

Synchronous Optical Network, Synchronous Digital Hierarchy (SONET/SDH)—A high-speed, optical WAN transport.

IEEE 802.11 Wireless LANs—Includes any technology, such as WiFi, based on variations of this.

Token Ring—LANs from IBM, the same as IEEE 802.5.

Point-to-Point Protocol (PPP)—This protocol is from the IP developers themselves, and is not limited to carrying IP packets.

X.25—An international standard, public, switched, connection-oriented network protocol.

Frame Relay—An international standard, public, switched, connection-oriented network protocol based on X.25.

Asynchronous Transfer Mode (ATM)—An international standard, public, switched, connection-oriented network protocol based on cells instead of frames.

Fiber Distributed Data Interface (FDDI)—A LAN-like network ring running at 100 Mbps.

Switched Multimegabit Data Services (SMDS)—A high-speed, connectionless, LAN-like, public network service.

Integrated Services Digital Network (ISDN)—A public switched network similar to X.25.

Digital Subscriber Line (DSL)—Based on some older Integrated Services Digital Network (ISDN)-related technologies and used for high-speed Internet access.

Serial Line Interface Protocol (SLIP) and Compressed SLIP (CSLI)—An older way of sending IP packets over a dial-up, asynchronous modem arrangement (also from the IP developers).

Cable Modems (CMODEMs)—A method of sending IP packets over a cable TV infrastructure.

IPoFW IP over Firewire (IEEE 1394)—A popular PC interface for peripheral devices. There are other interfaces as well, such as ARCnet and IEEE 802.4 LANs, but the point is that TCP/IP is not tied to any specific type of network at the lower layers. The TCP/IP protocol stack is very flexible and encompassing, much more so than almost anything else that could be used on a global network.

In the future, this list will get even longer as newer transports for IP packets are standardized and older ones remain (in spite of diminishing interest, standards like these tend to stay in place because no one cares enough to move them to "historic" RFCs). Some of the newer network types that might find their way onto many networks in the future follow:

VDSL—VDSL is a "very-high-speed" form of DSL that uses fiber feeders to reach less than a mile from the home (often called fiber to the neighborhood, or FTTN). Most VDSL service offerings deliver television, telephone, and high-speed Internet access over a unified residential cabling system through a special residential gateway box. On the Illustrated Network, the home office DSL link is actually VDSL, but this service is not as widely available as other forms of DSL.

GE-PONS—These Gigabit Ethernet Passive Optical Network (GE-PONS) nodes are part of a global push toward Fiber to the Home (FTTH), an approach that has been—somewhat ironically—slowed by the popularity of DSL over copper wires. Based on IEEE 802.3ah standards, this technology can support gigabit speeds in both directions and might take advantage of the popularity of voice over IP (VoIP).

BPL—In some places, high-speed Internet access is provided by the electric utility as part of broadband power line (BPL) technology. Delivered over the same socket as power, BPL services might form a nice adjunct to wireless services, which are hard to cost-justify in sparsely populated areas and over rough terrain.

The advantage of not tying the network layer to any specific type of links at the lower layers is flexibility (IP can run on anything). A new type of network interface can be added without great effort. Also, it makes linking these various network types into an internetwork that much easier.

All TCP/IP implementations must be able to support at least one of the defined interface types. Most implementations of TCP/IP will do fine today with only a handful of interface types, and, as we have seen, Ethernet frames are perhaps the most common of all data-link frame formats for IP packets, especially at the endpoints of the network.

The rest of this chapter provides a closer look at the four link types used on the Illustrated Network, as well as PPP, the major IEFT data-link protocol that we saw used on SONET. The coverage is not intended to be exhaustive, but will be enough to introduce the technologies.

Although all four link types are covered, the coverage is not equal. There is much more information about Ethernet and wireless than SONET or DSL. The main reason is that expensive and exotic line monitoring equipment is needed in order to burrow deep enough in the lower layers of the protocol stacks used in SONET and DSL to show the transmission frames. End users, and even many smaller ISPs, do just fine diagnosing problems on SONET and DSL links with basic Ethernet and IP monitoring tools. Then again, point-to-point links are a bit easier to diagnose than shared media networks. (Is the line protocol up in both directions? Is the distance okay? Is the bit error rate acceptable? Okay, it's not the link layer . . .)

SONET and DSL are distinguished from Ethernet and wireless LANs with regard to addressing. SONET and DSL are point-to-point technologies and use much simpler link-level addressing schemes than LAN technologies. There are only two ends in a point-to-point connection, and you always know which end you are. Anything you send is intended for the other end of the link, and anything you receive comes from the other end as well.

THE EVOLUTION OF ETHERNET

The original Ethernet was developed at the Xerox Palo Alto Research Center (PARC) in the mid-1970s to link the various mainframes and minicomputers that Xerox used in their office park campus environment of close-proximity buildings. The use of WAN protocols to link all of these buildings did not appeal to Xerox for two reasons. First, an efficient WAN infrastructure would have demanded a mesh of leased telephone lines, which would have been enormously expensive given the number of computers. Second, leased telephone lines did not have the bandwidth (usually these carried only up to 9600 bps, and at most 56 Kbps, in the late 1970s) needed to link the computers.

Their solution was to invent the *local* area network, the LAN. However, Xerox was not interested in actually building hardware and chipsets for their new invention, which was named *Ethernet.* Instead, Bob Metcalf, the Ethernet inventor, left Xerox and recruited two other companies, one to make chipsets for Ethernet and the other to make the hardware components to employ these chipsets. The two companies were chip-maker Intel and computer-maker Digital Equipment Corporation (DEC). Ethernet v1.0 was rolled out in 1980, followed by Ethernet v2.0 in 1982, which fixed some annoying problems in v1.0. This is why, in our examples, Ethereal keeps showing that IP packets are inside Ethernet II frames when they leave and arrive at hosts.

DIX Ethernet, the proprietary version, ran over a single, thick coaxial cable "bus" that snaked through a building or campus. Transmitting and receiving devices (transceivers) were physically clamped to the coaxial cable (with "vampire taps") at predetermined intervals. Transceivers usually had multiple ports for attaching the transceiver cables that led to the actual PC or minicomputer linked by the Ethernet LAN. The whole LAN ran at an aggregate speed of 10 Mbps, an unbelievable rate for the time. But Ethernet had to be fast, because up to 1024 computers could share this single coaxial cable bus to communicate using a media access method known as carrier-sense multiple access with collision detection (CSMA/CD). DIX Ethernet had to be distinguished from all other forms of Ethernet, which were standardized by the IEEE starting in 1984.

The IEEE first standardized a slightly different arrangement for 10-Mbps CSMA/CD LANs (IEEE 802.3) in 1984. Why the IEEE felt compelled to change the proprietary Ethernet technology during the standardization process is somewhat of a puzzle. Some said the IEEE always did this, but around the same time the IEEE essentially rubberstamped IBM's proprietary Token Ring LAN specification as IEEE 802.5. The changes to the hardware of DIX Ethernet were minor. There was no v1.0 support at all (i.e., all IEEE 802.3 LANs were DIX Ethernet v2.0) and the terminology was changed slightly. The DIX transceiver became the IEEE 802.3 "media attachment unit" (MAU), and so on.

However, throughout the 1980s and into the 1990s, as research into network capabilities matured, the IEEE added a number of variations to the original IEEE 802.3 CSMA/CD hardware specification. The original specification became 10Base5 (which meant 10-Mbps transport, using baseband signaling, with a 500-meter LAN segment). This was joined by a number of other variants designed to make LAN implementation more flexible and—especially—less expensive. New IEEE 802.3 variations included 10Base2 (with 200-meter segments over thin coaxial cable), the wildly popular 10BaseT (with hubs instead of segments linked to PCs by up to 100 meters of unshielded twisted-pair copper wire), and versions that ran on fiber-optic cable. Eventually, all of these technologies except those on coaxial cable went first to 100 Mbps (100BaseT), then 1000 Mbps (Gigabit Ethernet), which run over twisted pair for short spans and can use fiber for increasingly long hauls, now in the SONET/SDH ranges.

Today, IEEE 802.3ae 10G-base-er (extended range) LAN physical layer links can span 40 km. Another, "zr," is not standardized, but can stretch the span to 80 km. And interestingly, 10-Gbps Ethernet is back on coaxial cable as "10Gbps cx4."

Ethernet II and IEEE 802.3 Frames

Today, of course, the term "Ethernet" essentially means the same as "IEEE 802.3 LAN." In addition to changing the hardware component names and creating IEEE 802.3 10BaseT, the IEEE also changed the Ethernet *frame* structure for reasons that remain obscure. It was this development that had the most important implication for those implementing the TCP/IP protocol stack on top of Ethernet LANs.

The DIX Ethernet II frame structure was extremely simple. There were fields in the frame header for the source and destination MAC (the upper part of the data link layer, used on LANs) address, a type field to define content (packet) structure, a variable-length data field, and an error-detecting trailer. The source and destination addresses were required for the mutually adjacent systems on a LAN (a point-to-point-oriented data link layer with just a "destination" address would not work on LANs: Who sent this frame?). The type field was required so the recipient software would know the structure of the data inside the frame. That is, the destination NIC could examine the type field and determine if the frame contents were an IP packet, some other type of packet, a control frame, or almost anything else. The destination NIC card could then pass the frame contents to the proper software module (the network layer) for further processing on the frame data contents. The type field value for IP packets was set as `0x0800`, the bit string `00001000 00000000`.

However, the IEEE 802 committee changed the simple DIX Ethernet II frame structure to produce the IEEE 802.3 CSMA/CD frame structure. Gone was the DIX Ethernet II type (often called "Ethertype") field, and in its place was a same-sized `length` field. This action somewhat puzzled observers of LAN technology. DIX Ethernet II frames worked just fine without an explicit length field. The total frame length was determined by the positions of the starting and ending frame delimiters. The data were always after the header and before the trailer. Simple enough for software to figure out.

Now, with IEEE 802.3 it was even easier to figure out the length of a received frame (the software just had to look at the `length` field value). However, it was now impossible for the receiving software to figure out just what the structure of the frame data was by looking only at the frame header. Clearly, a place in the IEEE 802.3 CSMA/CD frame had to be found to put the DIX Ethernet II `type` field, since receivers had to have a way to figure out which software process understood the frame content's data structure. Other protocols did not understand IP packet structures, and vice versa.

The IEEE 802.3 committee "robbed" some bytes from the payload area, bytes which in DIX Ethernet were data bytes. Since the overall length of the frame was already fixed, and this set the length of the frame data to 1500 bytes (the same as in DIX Ethernet), the outcome was to *reduce* the allowed length of the data contents of an IEEE 802.3 frame. A simplified picture of the two frame types indicating the location of the `0x0800` `type` field and the length of the `data` field is shown in Figure 3.8.

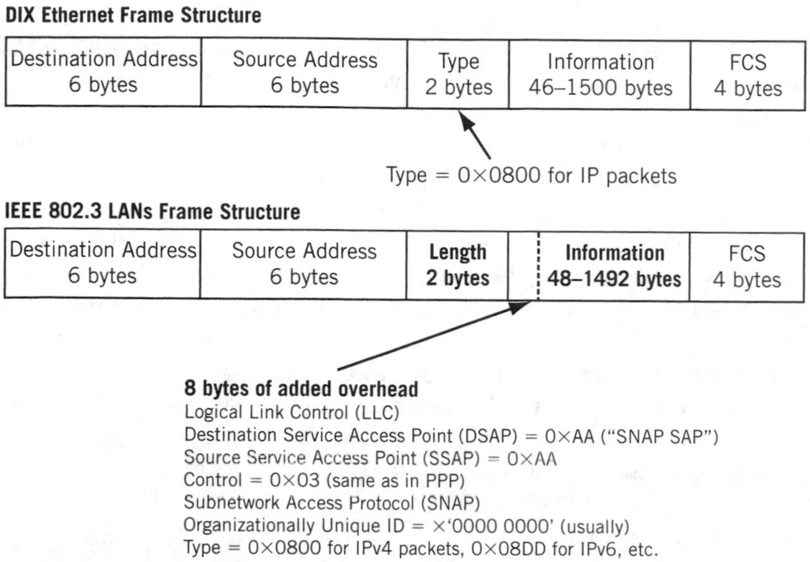

DIX Ethernet Frame Structure

Destination Address 6 bytes	Source Address 6 bytes	Type 2 bytes	Information 46–1500 bytes	FCS 4 bytes

Type = 0×0800 for IP packets

IEEE 802.3 LANs Frame Structure

Destination Address 6 bytes	Source Address 6 bytes	**Length 2 bytes**		**Information 48–1492 bytes**	FCS 4 bytes

8 bytes of added overhead
Logical Link Control (LLC)
Destination Service Access Point (DSAP) = 0×AA ("SNAP SAP")
Source Service Access Point (SSAP) = 0×AA
Control = 0×03 (same as in PPP)
Subnetwork Access Protocol (SNAP)
Organizationally Unique ID = ×'0000 0000' (usually)
Type = 0×0800 for IPv4 packets, 0×08DD for IPv6, etc.

FIGURE 3.8

Types of Ethernet frames. The frames for Gigabit and 10 Gigabit Ethernet differ in detail, but follow the same general structure.

MAC Addresses

The MAC addresses used in 802 LAN frames are all 48 bits (6 bytes) long. The first 24 bits (3 bytes) are assigned by the IEEE to the manufacturer of the NIC (manufacturers pay for them). This is the Organizationally Unique Identifier (OUI). The last 24 bits (3 bytes) are the NIC manufacturer's serial number for that NIC. Some protocol analyzers know the manufacturer's ID (which is not public but seldom suppressed) and display this along with the address. This is how Ethereal displays MAC addresses not only in hex but starting with "Intel_" or "Juniper_."

Note that both frame types use the same, familiar source and destination MAC address, and use a 32-bit (4-byte) frame check sequence (FCS) for frame-level error detection. The FCS used in both cases is a standard, 32-bit cyclical redundancy check (CRC-32). The important difference is that the DIX Ethernet frame indicates information type (frame content) with a 2-byte `type` field (`0x0800` means there is an IPv4 packet inside and `0x86DD` means there is an IPv6 packet inside) and the IEEE 802.3. CSMA/CD frame places this Ethertype field at the end of an additional 8 bytes of overhead called the Subnetwork Access Protocol (SNAP) header. Another 3 bytes are the OUI given to the NIC vendor when they registered with the IEEE, but this field is not always used for that purpose.

The 802.3 frame must subtract these 8 bytes from the IP packet length so that the overall frame length is still the same as for DIX Ethernet II. This is because the maximum length of the frame is universal in almost all forms of Ethernet. The maximum

IEEE 802.3 frame data is 1492 due to the 8 extra bytes needed to represent the `type` field. Any IP packet larger than this will not fit in a single frame, and must *fragment* its payload into more than one frame and have the payload reassembled at the receiver.

That's not all there is to it. LAN implementers and vendors quickly saw that the IEEE 802.3 hardware arrangement was more flexible (and less expensive) than DIX Ethernet. They also saw that the DIX Ethernet II frame structure was simpler and could carry slightly more user data than the complex IEEE 802.3 frame structure. Being practical people, the vendors simply used the flexible IEEE 802.3 hardware with the simple DIX Ethernet II frame structure, creating the mixture that is commonly seen today on most LANs.

Today, just because the *hardware* is IEEE 802.3 compliant (e.g., 100BaseT), does not mean that the frame structure used to carry IP packets is *also* IEEE 802.3 compliant. The frame structure is most likely Ethernet II, as we have seen. (It's worth pointing out that Ethernet frame content *other* than IP usually uses the 802.3 frame format. However, the Illustrated Network is basically an IP-only network.)

THE EVOLUTION OF DSL

IP packet interfaces have been defined for many LAN and WAN network technologies. As soon as a new transport technology reaches the commercial-deployment stage, IP is part of the scheme, if for no other reason than regardless of what is in the middle, TCP/IP in Ethernet frames is at both ends. DSL technologies are a case in point. Originally designed for the "national networks" that would offer everything that the Internet does today, but from the telephone company as part of the Integrated Services Digital Network (ISDN) initiatives of the 1980s, DSL was adapted for "broadband" Internet access when the grand visions of the telephone companies as content providers were reduced to the reality of a restricted role as ISPs and little more. (Even the term "broadband" is a topic of much debate: A working definition is "speeds fast enough to allow users to watch video without getting a headache or becoming disgusted," speeds that keep dropping as video coding and compression techniques become better.)

DSL once included a complete ATM architecture, with little or no TCP/IP. Practical considerations forced service providers to adapt DSLs once again, this time for the real consumer world of Ethernet LANs running TCP/IP. And a tortured adaptation it proved to be. The problem was deeper than just taking an Ethernet frame and mapping it to a DSL frame (even DSL bits are organized into a distinctive transport frame). Users had to be assigned unique IP addresses (not necessary on an isolated LAN), and the issues of bridging versus routing versus switching had to be addressed all over again. This was because linking two LANs (the home user client LAN, even if it had but one PC, and the server LAN) over a WAN link (DSL) was not a trivial task. The server LAN could be the service provider's "home server" or anyplace else the user chose to go on the Internet.

Also, ATM logical links (called permanent virtual circuits, or PVCs) are normally provisioned between the usual local exchange carrier's DSLAM and the Internet access

Networking Visions Today and Yesterday

Today, when anyone can start a Web site with a simple server and provide a service to one and all over the Internet, it is good to remember that things were not always supposed to be this way. Not so long ago, the control of services on a public global network was supposed to be firmly under the control of the service provider. Many of these "fast-packet" networking schemes were promoted by the national telephone companies, from broadband ISDN to ATM to DSL. They all envisioned a network much like the Internet is today, but one with all the servers "in the cloud" owned and operated by the service providers. Anyone wanting to provide a service (such as a video Web site) would have to go to the service provider to make arrangements, and average citizens would probably be unable to break into that tightly controlled and expensive market.

This scheme avoided the risk of controversial Web site content (such as copyrighted material available for download), but with the addition of restrictions and surveillance. Also, the economics for service providers are much different when they control content from when they do not.

Today, ISPs most often provide transport and connectivity between Web sites and servers owned and operated by almost anyone. ISP servers are usually restricted to a small set of services directly related to the ISP, such as email or account management.

provider's aggregation router. This can be very costly because IP generally has much better statistical multiplexing properties and there can be long hauls through the ATM networks before the ATM link is terminated.

The solution was to scrap any useful role for ATM (and any non-TCP/IP infrastructure) except as a passive transport for IP packets. This left ATM without any rationale for existence, because most of the work was done by running PPP over the DSL link between a user LAN and a service provider LAN.

PPP and DSL

Why is PPP used with DSL (and SONET)? The core of the issue is that ISPs needed some kind of *tunneling* protocol. Tunneling occurs when the normal message-packet-frame encapsulation sequence of the layers of a networking protocol suite are violated. When a message is placed inside a packet, then inside a frame, and this frame is placed inside *another* type of frame, this is a tunneling situation. Although many tunneling methods have been standardized at several different TCP/IP layers, tunneling works as long as the tunnel endpoints understand the correct sequence of headers and content (which can also be encrypted for *secure* tunnels).

In DSL, the tunneling protocol had to carry the point-to-point "circuits" from the central networking location to the customer's premises and across the shared media

LAN to the end user device (host). There are many ways to do this, such as using IP-in-IP tunneling, a virtual private network (VPN), or lower level tunneling. ISPs chose PPP as the solution for this role in DSL.

Using PPP made perfect sense. For years, ISPs had used PPP to manage their WAN dial-in users. PPP could easily assign and manage the ISP's IP address space, compartmentalize users for billing purposes, and so on. As a LAN technology, Ethernet had none of those features. PPP also allowed user authentication methods such as RADIUS to be used, methods completely absent on most LAN technologies (if you're on the LAN, it's assumed you belong there).

Of course, keeping PPP meant putting the PPP frame inside the Ethernet frame, a scheme called Point-to-Point Protocol over Ethernet (PPPoE), described in RFC 2516. Since tunneling is just another form of encapsulation, all was well.

PPP is not the only data link layer framing and negotiation procedure (PPP is not a full data link layer specification) from the IETF. Before PPP became popular, the Serial Line Internet Protocol (SLIP) and a closely related protocol using compression (CSLIP, or Compressed SLIP) were used to link individual PCs and workstations not connected by a LAN, but still running TCP/IP, to the Internet over a dial-up, asynchronous analog telephone line with modems. SLIP/CSLIP was also once used to link routers on widely separated TCP/IP networks over asynchronous analog leased telephone lines, again using modems. SLIP/CSLIP is specified in RFC 1055/STD 47.

PPP Framing for Packets

PPP addresses many of the limitations of SLIP, and can run over both asynchronous links (as does SLIP) and synchronous links. PPP provides for more than just a simple frame structure for IP packets. The PPP standard defines management and testing functions for line quality, option negotiation, and so on. PPP is described in RFC 1661, is protocol independent, and is not limited to IP packet transport.

The PPP control signals, known as the PPP Link Control Protocol (LCP), need not be supported, but are strongly recommended to improve performance. Other control information is included by means of a Network Control Protocol (NCP), which defines management procedures for frame content protocols. The NCP even allows protocols other than IP to use the serial link at the same time. The LCP and NCP subprotocols are a distinguishing feature of PPP.

The use of LCP and NCP on a PPP link on a TCP/IP network follows:

- The source PPP system (user) sends a series of LCP messages to configure and test the serial link.
- Both ends exchange LCP messages to establish the link options to be used.
- The source PPP system sends a series of NCP messages to establish the Network Layer protocol (e.g., IP, IPX, etc.).
- IP packets and frames for any other configured protocols are sent across the link.
- NCP and LCP messages are used to close the link down in a graceful and structured manner.

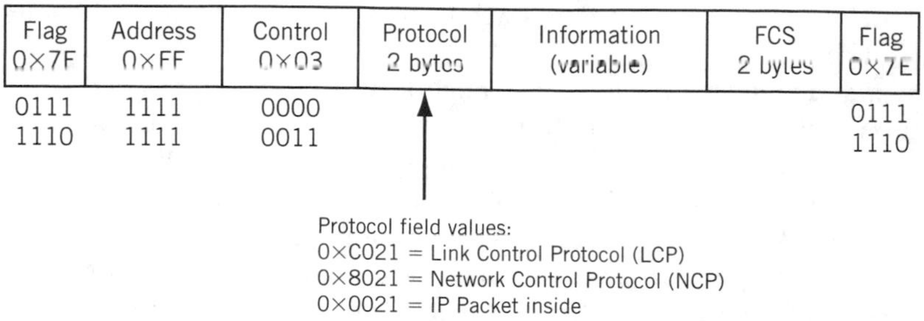

Flag 0×7F	Address 0×FF	Control 0×03	Protocol 2 bytes	Information (variable)	FCS 2 bytes	Flag 0×7E
0111 1110	1111 1111	0000 0011				0111 1110

Protocol field values:
0×C021 = Link Control Protocol (LCP)
0×8021 = Network Control Protocol (NCP)
0×0021 = IP Packet inside

FIGURE 3.9

The PPP frame. The flag bytes (0×7E) essentially form an "idle pattern" on the link that is "interrupted" by frames carrying information.

The benefits are to create a more efficient WAN transport for IP packets. The structure of a PPP frame is shown in Figure 3.9.

The Flag field is `0x7E` (`0111 1110`), as in many other data link layer protocols. The Address field is set to `0xFF` (`1111 1111`), which, by convention, is the "all-stations" or broadcast address. Note that none of the other fields in the Point-to-Point Protocol header have a source address for the frame. Point-to-point links only care about the destination, which is always `0xFF` in PPP and essentially means "any device at the other end of this link that sees this frame." This is one reason why serial interfaces on routers sometimes do not have IP addresses (but many serial interfaces, especially to other routers, have them anyway—this is the only way to make the serial links "visible" to the IP layer and network operations).

The Control field is set to `0x03` (`0000 0011`), which is the Unnumbered Information (UI) format, meaning that there is no sequence numbering in these frames. The UI format is used to indicate that the connectionless IP protocol is in use. The Protocol field identifies the format and use of the content of the PPP frame itself. For LCP messages, the Protocol field has the value `0xC021` (`1100 0000 0010 0001`), for NCP the field has the value `0x8021` (`1000 0000 0010 0001`), and for IP packets the field has the value `0x0021` (`0000 0000 0010 0001`).

Following the header is a variable-length Information field (the IP packet), followed by a PPP frame trailer with a 16-bit, frame check sequence (FCS) for error control, and finally an end-of-frame Flag field.

PPP frames may be compressed, field sizes reduced, and used for many specific tasks, as long as the endpoints agree.

DSL Encapsulation

How are IP packets encapsulated on DSL links? DSL specifications establish a basic DSL frame as the physical level, but IP packets are not placed directly into these frames. IP packets are placed inside PPP frames, and then the PPP frames are encapsulated inside Ethernet frames (this is PPP over Ethernet, or PPPoE). Finally, the Ethernet frames are placed inside the DSL frames and sent to the DSL Access Module (DSLAM) at the telephone switching office.

Once at the switching office, it might seem straightforward to extract the Ethernet frame and send it on into the "router cloud." But it turns out that almost all DSLAMs are networked together by ATM, a technology once championed by the telephone companies. (Some very old DSLAMs use another telephone company technology known as frame relay.) ATM uses *cells* instead of frames to carry information.

So the network/data-link/physical layer protocol stack used between DSLAMs and service provider routers linked to the Internet usually looks like five layers instead of the expected three:

- IP packet containing user data, which is inside a PPP frame, which is inside an
- Ethernet frame running to the DSL router (PPPoE), which is inside a series of
- ATM cells, which are sent over the physical medium as a series of bits.

We'll take a closer look at frame relay and ATM in a later chapter on public network technologies that can be used to link routers together.

Forms of DSL

Entire books are devoted to the variations of DSL and the DSL protocol stacks used by service providers today. Instead of focusing on all the details of these variations, this section will take a brief look at the variation of DSL that can be used when IP packets make their way from a home PC onto the Internet.

DSL often appears as "xDSL" where the "x" can stand for many different letters. DSL is a modern technology for providing broadband data services over the same twisted-pair (TP), copper telephone lines that provide voice service. DSL services are often called "last-mile" (and sometimes "first-mile") technologies because they are used only for short connections between a telephone switching station and a home or office. DSL is not used between switching stations (SONET is often used there).

DSL is an extension of the Integrated Services Digital Network (ISDN) technology developed by the telephone companies for their own set of combined voice and data services. They operate over short ranges (less than 18 kilofeet) of 24 American Wire Gauge (AWG) voice wire to a telephone central office. DSLs offer much higher speeds than traditional dial-up modems, up to 52 mbps for traffic sent "downstream" to the user and usually from 32 kbps to 1 Mbps from traffic sent "upstream" to the central office. The actual speed is distance limited, dropping off at longer distances.

At the line level, DSLs use one of several sophisticated modulation techniques running in premises DSL router chipsets and DSLAMs at the telephone switching office. These include the following:

- Carrierless Amplitude Modulation (CAP)
- Discrete Multitone Technology (DMT)
- Discrete Wavelet Multitone (DWM)
- Simple Line Code (SLC)
- Multiple Virtual Line (MVL)

DSL can operate in a duplex (symmetrical) fashion, offering the same speeds upstream and downstream. Others, mainly targeted for residential Internet browsing customers, offer higher downstream speeds to handle relatively large server replies to upstream mouse clicks or keystrokes. However, standard VDSL and VDSL2 have much less asymmetry than other methods. For example, 100-Mbps symmetric operation is possible at 0.3 km, and 50 Mbps symmetric at 1 km.

The DSLAMs connect to a high-speed service provider backbone, and then the Internet. DSLAMs aggregate traffic, typically for an ATM network, and then connect to a router network. On the interface to the premises, the DSLAM demultiplexes traffic for individual users and forwards it to the appropriate users.

In order to support traditional voice services, most DSL technologies require a signal filter or "splitter" to be installed on the customer premises to share the twisted-pair wiring. The DSLAM splits the signal off at the central office. Splitterless DSL is very popular, however, in the form of "DSL Lite" or several other names.

In Table 3.2, various types of DSL are compared. The speeds listed are typical, as are the distance (there are many other factors that can limit DSL reach) and services offered.

VDSL requires a fiber-optic feeder system to the immediate neighborhood, but VDSL can provide a full suite of voice, video, and data services. These services include the highest Internet access rates available for residential services, and integration between voice and data services (voice mail alerts, caller ID history, and so on, all on the TV

Table 3.2 Types of DSL

Type	Meaning	Typical Data Rate	Mode	Distance	Applications
IDSL	ISDN DSL	128 Kbps	Duplex	18k ft on 24 AWG TP	ISDN services: voice and data; Internet access
HDSL	High-speed DSL	1.544 to 42.048 Mbps	Duplex	12k ft on 24 AWG TP	T1/E1 service, feeder, WAN access, LAN connections, Internet access
SDSL	Symmetric DSL	1.544 to 2.048 Mbps	Duplex	12k ft on 24 AWG TP	Same as HDSL
ADSL	Asymmetric DSL	1.5 to 6 Mbps 16 to 640 kbps	Down Up	18k ft on 24 AWG TP	Internet access, remote LAN access, some video applications.
DSL Lite (G.Lite)	"Splitterless" ADSL	1.5 to 6 Mbps 16 to 640 kbps	Down Up	18k ft on 24 AWG TP	Same as ADSL, but does not require a premises "splitter" for voice services
VDSL	Very-high-speed DSL	13 to 52 Mbps 1.5 to 2.3 Mbps	Down Up	1k to 4.5k ft depending on speed	Same as ADSL plus full voice and video services, including HDTV

screen). VDSL is used on the Illustrated Network to get packets from the home office's PCs to the ISP's router network (the overall architecture is not very different from DSL in general). From router to router over WAN distances, the Illustrated Network uses a common form of transport for the Internet in the United States: SONET.

THE EVOLUTION OF SONET

SONET is the North American version of the international SDH standard and defines a hierarchy of fast transports delivered on fiber-optic cable. One of the most exciting aspects of SONET when it first appeared around 1990 was the ability to deploy SONET links in self-healing rings, which nearly made outages a thing of the past. (The vast majority of link failures today involve signal "backhoe fade," a euphemism for accidental cable dig-ups.)

Before networks composed almost entirely of fiber-optic cables came along, network errors were a high-priority problem. Protocols such as IP and TCP had extensive error-detection and error-correction (the two are distinct) methods built into their operation, methods that are now quietly considered almost a hindrance in modern networks.

Now, SONET rings do not inherently protect against the common problem of a lack of equipment or route diversity, but at least it's possible. Not all SONET links are on rings, of course. The links on the Illustrated Network are strictly point-to-point.

A Note about Network Errors

Before SONET, almost all WAN links used to link routers were supplied by a telephone company that subscribed to the Bell System standards and practices, even if the phone company was not part of the sprawling AT&T Bell System. In 1984, the Bell System engineering manual named a bit error rate (BER) of 10^{-5} (one error in 100,000 bits sent) as the target for dial-up connections, and put leased lines (because they could be "tuned" through predictable equipment) at 10 times better, or 10^{-6} (one error in every 1,000,000 bits).

SONET/SDH fiber links typically have BERs of 1000 (10^3) to 1 million (10^6) times better than those common in 1984. Since 1000 days is about 3 years, converting a copper link to fiber meant that all the errors seen yesterday are now spread out over the next 3 years (a BER of 10^{-9}) to 3000 years (10^{-12}). LAN error rates, always much lower than those of WANs due to shorter spans and less environmental damage, are in about the same range. Most errors today occur on the modest-length (a kilometer or mile) access links between LAN and WAN to ISP points of presence, and most of those errors are due to intermittently failing or faulty connectors.

The only real alternatives for SONET/SDH high-speed WAN links are newer versions of Ethernet, especially in a metropolitan Ethernet context. The megabit-speed T1 (1.544 Mbps) or E1 (2.048 Mbps) links are used for the local loop. However, even those copper-based circuits are usually serviced by newer technologies and carried over SONET/SDH fiber on the backbone.

How are IP packets carried inside SONET frames? The standard method is called Packet over SONET/SDH (POS). The procedures used in POS are defined in three RFCs:

- RFC1619, PPP over SONET/SDH
- RFC1661, the PPP
- RFC1662, PPP in HDLC-like framing

Packet over SONET/SDH

SONET/SDH frames are not just a substitute for Ethernet or PPP frames. SONET/SDH frames, like T1 and E1 frames, carry unstructured bit information, such as digitized voice telephone calls, and are not usually suitable for direct packet encapsulation. In the case of IP, the packets are placed inside a PPP frame (technically, a type of High-Level Data Link Control ["HDLC-like"] PPP frame with some header fields allowed to vary in HDLC fixed for IP packet payloads). The PPP frame, delimited by a stream of special 0x7E interframe fill (or "idle" pattern) bits, is then placed into the payload area of the SONET/SDH frame.

Figure 3.10 shows a series of PPP frames inside a SONET frame running at 51.84 Mbps. Although SONET (and SDH) frames are always shown as two-dimensional arrays

		SONET Frame Payload Area
SONET Frame 1	SONET Frame Overhead	7E 7E 7E 7E 7E 7E 7E 7E 7E 7E 7E 7E 7E 7E 7E 7E 7E 7E | **PPP Hdr** | **IP packet....** | **IP trailer** | 7E 7E 7E 7E 7E 7E 7E 7E 7E 7E 7E 7E 7E 7E 7E 7E 7E 7E 7E 7E 7E 7E 7E 7E 7E 7E 7E 7E 7E 7E 7E 7E 7E 7E | **PPP Hdr** | **IP packet** ....
SONET Frame 2	SONET Frame Overhead	.... | **IP trailer** | 7E 7E 7E 7E 7E 7E 7E 7E 7E 7E 7E 7E 7E 7E 7E 7E 7E 7E 7E 7E 7E 7E 7E 7E 7E 7E 7E 7E 7E 7E 7E 7E 7E 7E | **PPP Hdr** | **IP packet** .... | **IP trailer** | 7E 7E
SONET Frame 3	SONET Frame Overhead	7E 7E 7E 7E 7E 7E 7E 7E 7E 7E 7E 7E 7E 7E 7E 7E 7E 7E | **PPP Hdr** | **IP packet** | **IP trailer** | 7E 7E 7E 7E 7E 7E 7E 7E 7E 7E 7E 7E 7E 7E 7E 7E 7E 7E 7E | **PPP Hdr** | **IP packet** ....
SONET Frame 4	SONET Frame Overhead	.... | **IP trailer** | 7E 7E 7E 7E 7E 7E 7E 7E 7E 7E 7E 7E 7E 7E 7E 7E 7E 7E 7E 7E 7E 7E 7E 7E 7E 7E 7E 7E 7E 7E 7E 7E 7E 7E | **PPP Hdr** | **IP packet** .... | **IP trailer** | 7E 7E

FIGURE 3.10

Packet over SONET, showing how the idle pattern of 0x7E surrounds the PPP frames with IP packets inside.

of bits, the figure is not very accurate. It doesn't show any of the SONET framing bytes, and IP packets are routinely set to around 1500 bytes long, so they would easily fill an entire 774-byte, basic SONET transmission-frame payload area. Even the typical network default maximum IP packet size of 576 bytes is quite large compared to the SONET payload area. However, many packets are not that large, especially acknowledgments.

One other form of transport used on the Illustrated Network is common on IP networks today. Wireless links might some day be more common than anything else.

WIRELESS LANs AND IEEE 802.11

Wireless technologies are the fastest-growing form of link layer for IP packets, whether for cell phones or home office LANs. Cell phone packets are a bit of a challenge, and wireless LANs are evolving rapidly, but this section will focus on wireless LANs, if only because wireless LANs are such a good fit with Ethernet. This section will be a little longer than the others, only because the latest wireless LANs are newer than the previous methods discussed.

The basic components of the IEEE 802.11 wireless LAN architecture are the wireless stations, such as a laptop, and the access point (AP). The AP is not strictly necessary, and a cluster of wireless stations can communicate directly with each other without an AP. This is called an IEEE 802.11 independent, basic service set (IBSS) or ad hoc network. One or more wireless stations form a basic service set (BSS), but if there is only one wireless station in the BSS, an AP is necessary to allow the wireless station to communicate. An AP has both wired and wireless connections, allowing it to be the access "point" between the wireless station and the world. In a typical home wireless network (an arbitrarily low limit), one BSS supports up to four wireless devices, and the AP is bundled with the DSL router or cable modem with the high-speed link for Internet access. (The DSL router or cable modem can have multiple wired connections as well.) In practice, the number of systems you can connect to a given type of AP depends on your performance needs and the traffic mix.

A wireless LAN can have multiple APs, and this arrangement is sometimes called an infrastructure wireless LAN. This type of LAN has more than one BSS, because each AP establishes its own BSS. This is called an extended service set (ESS), and the APs are often wired together with an Ethernet LAN or an Ethernet hub or switch. The three major types of IEEE 802.11 wireless LANs—ad hoc (IBSS), BSS, and ESS—are shown in Figure 3.11.

Wi-Fi

An intended interoperable version of the IEEE 802.11 architecture is known as *Wi-Fi*, a trademark and brand of the Wi-Fi Alliance. It allows users with properly equipped wireless laptops to attach to APs maintained by a service provider in restaurants, bookstores, libraries, and other locations, usually to access the Internet. In some places, especially downtown urban areas, a wireless station can receive a strong signal from two or

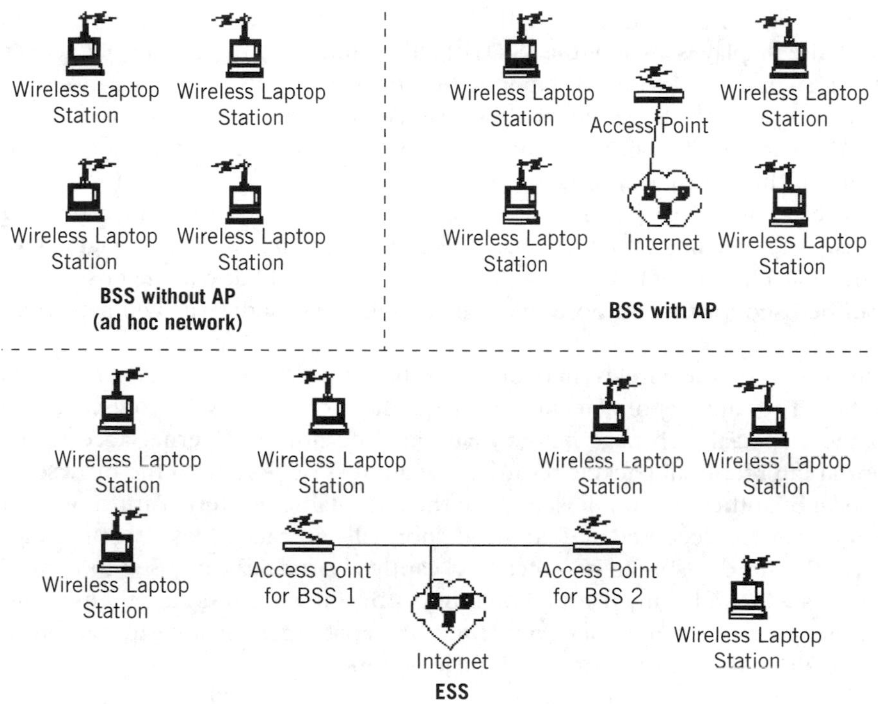

FIGURE 3.11

Wireless LAN architectures. Most home networks are built around an access point built into a DSL router/gateway.

more APs. While a wireless station can belong to more than one BSS through its AP at the same time, this is not helpful when the APs are offering different network addresses (and perhaps prices for attachment). This collection of Wi-Fi networks is sometimes called the "Wi-Fi jungle," and will only become worse as wireless services turn up more and more often in parks, apartment buildings, offices, and so on. How do APs and wireless stations sort themselves out in the Wi-Fi jungle?

If there are APs present, each wireless station in IEEE 802.11 needs to *associate* with an AP before it can send or receive frames. For Internet access, the 802.11 frames contain IP packets, of course. The network administrator for every AP assigns a *Service Set Identifier* (SSID) to the AP, as well as the channels (frequency ranges) that are associated with the AP. The AP has a MAC layer address as well, often called the BSSID.

The AP is required to periodically send out *beacon frames*, each including the AP's SSID and MAC layer address (BSSID), on its wireless channels. These channels are scanned by the wireless station. Some channels might overlap between multiple APs, because the "jungle" has no central control, but (hopefully) there are other channels that do not. In practice, interference between overlapping APs is not a huge problem in the absence of a high volume of traffic. When you "view available networks" in Windows XP, the display is a list of the SSIDs of all APs in range. To get Internet access, you need to associate your wireless station with *one* of these APs.

After selecting an AP by SSID, the wireless host uses the 802.11 association protocol to join the AP's subnet. The wireless station then uses DHCP to get an IP address, and becomes part of the Internet through the AP.

If the wireless Internet access is not free, or the wireless LAN is intended for restricted use (e.g., tenants in a particular building), the wireless station might have to authenticate itself to the AP. If the pool of users is small and known, the host's MAC address can be used for this purpose, and only certain MAC addresses will receive IP addresses.

Once the user is on the wireless network, many hotels use the *captive portal* form of authentication. The captive portal technique makes the user with a Web browser (HTTP client) to see a special Web page before being granted normal Internet access. The captive portal intercepts all packets regardless of address or port, until the browser is used as a form of authentication device. Once the acceptable use terms are viewed or the payment rates are accepted and arranged, "normal" Internet access is granted for a fixed period of time. It should be noted that captive portals can be used to control wired access as well, and many places (hotel rooms, business centers) use them in this fashion. In many cases, the normal device "firewall" capabilities must be turned off or configured to allow the captive portal Web page to appear.

Another post-access approach employs usernames and passwords—these are popular at coffee shops and other retail establishments. In both cases, there is usually a central *authentication server* used by many APs, and the wireless host communicates with this server using either RADIUS (RFC 2138) or DIAMETER (RFC 3588). Once authenticated, the users' traffic is commonly encrypted to preserve privacy over the airwaves, where signals can usually be picked up easily and without the knowledge of end users.

When accessing the office remotely, even if captive portal or some other method is used, most organizations add something to secure tunneling based on PPTP (Microsoft's Point-to-Point Tunneling Protocol) or PPPoE to run proprietary VPN client software. We've already mentioned PPPoE, and PPTP with VPNs will be explored later in this book.

IEEE 802.11 MAC Layer Protocol

IEEE 802.11 defines two MAC sublayers: the distributed coordination function (DCF) and the point coordination function (PCF). The PCF MAC is optional and runs on top of the DCF MAC, which is mandatory. PCF is used with APs and is very complex, while DCF is simpler and uses a venerable access method known as *carrier sense multiple access with collision avoidance* (CSMA/CA). Note that while Ethernet LANs *detect* collisions between stations sending at the same time with CSMA/CD, wireless LANs *avoid* collisions. Collision *detection* is not appropriate for wireless LANs for a number of reasons, the most important being the *hidden terminal problem*.

To understand the hidden terminal problem, consider the two wireless laptops and AP shown in Figure 3.12. (The problem does not only occur with an AP, but the figure

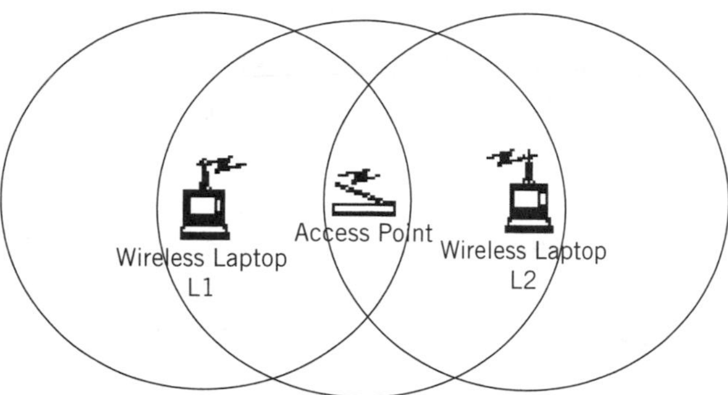

FIGURE 3.12

Hidden terminals on wireless LANs. This can be a problem in larger home networks, and special "LAN extender" devices can be used to prevent the problem.

shows this situation.) Both laptops are within range of the AP, but not of each other (there are many reasons for this, from distance to signal fading). Obviously, if L1 is sending a frame to the AP, L2 could also start sending a frame, because the carrier sensing shows the network as "clear." However, a collision occurs at the AP and both frames have errors, although both L1 and L2 think their frames were sent just fine.

Now, the AP clearly knows what's going on. It just needs a way to tell the wireless stations when it's okay to send (or not). CSMA/CD can use an optional method known as *request to send* (RTS) and *clear to send* (CTS) to avoid these types of undetected collisions. When a sender wants to send a data frame, it must first reserve the channel by sending a short RTS frame to the AP, telling the AP how long it will take to send the data, and receive an acknowledgement frame (ACK) that all went well. If the sender receives a short CTS control frame back, then it can send. Other stations hear the CTS as well, and refrain from sending during this time period.

The way that RTS/CTS works for sending data to an access point is shown in Figure 3.13.

There are two time notations in the figure: DIFS and SIFS. The *distributed inter-frame space* (DIFS) is the amount of time a wireless station waits to send after sensing that the channel is clear. The station waits a bit "just in case" because wireless LANs, unlike Ethernet, do not detect collisions and cease sending, so collisions are very debilitating and must be avoided at all costs. The *short inter-frame spacing* (SIFS) is also used between frames for collision avoidance. There is also a duration timer in all 802.11 frames, measured in microseconds, that tells the other stations how long it will take to send the frame and receive a reply. Stations avoid link access during this time period.

While RTS/CTS does reduce collisions, it also adds delay and reduces the available bandwidth on a channel. In practice, each wireless station sets an RTS threshold so that CTS/RTS is used only when the frame is longer than this value. Many wireless stations set the threshold so high that the value is larger than the maximum frame length, and the RTS/CTS is skipped for all data.

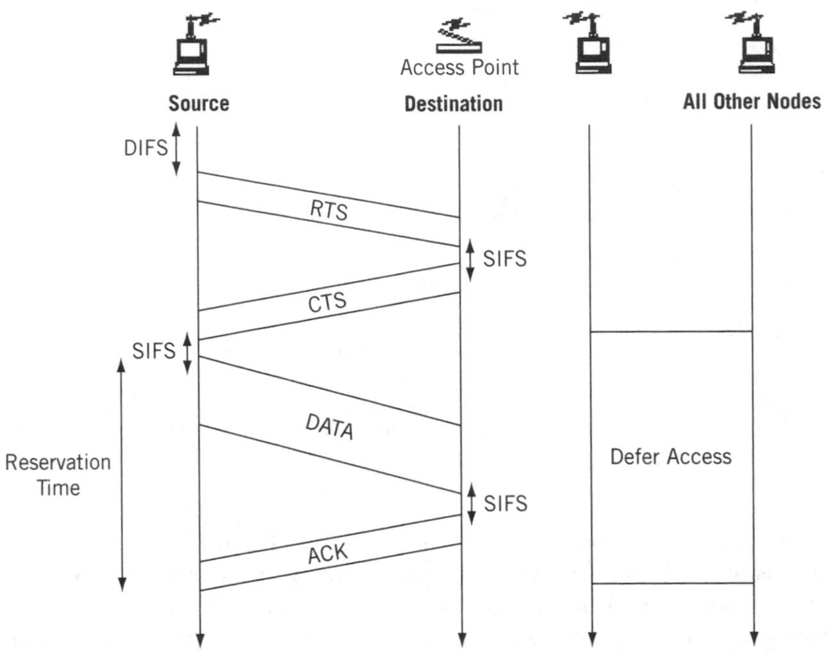

FIGURE 3.13

RTS and CTS in wireless LANs showing how all other nodes must defer access to the medium. The CTS is heard by all other nodes, although this is not detailed in the figure.

Frame Control	Duration	Address 1	Address 2	Address 3	Seq. Control	Address 4	Payload	FCS
2 bytes	2 bytes	6 bytes	6 bytes	6 bytes	2 bytes	6 bytes	0–2312 bytes	4 bytes

FIGURE 3.14

IEEE 802.11 frame structure. Note the potential number of address fields (four) in contrast to the two used in Ethernet II frames.

The IEEE 802.11 Frame

Although the IEEE 802.11 frame shares a lot with the Ethernet frame (which is one reason some packet sniffers can parse wireless frames as if they were Ethernet), there are a number of unique fields in 802.11. There are nine main fields, and the *frame control* (FC) field has 10 fields. The nine major fields of the IEEE 802.11 MAC frame are shown in Figure 3.14. The only fields in the two FC bytes that we will talk about are the *From DS* and *To DS* fields. (In some cases, the first three fields of the 802.11 MAC frame, the version, type, and subtype, are presented separately from the frame control flags, which are all bits.)

Frame control (FC)—This field is 2 bytes long and contains, among other things, two important flag bits: To DS (distribution system) and From DS.

Duration—This byte gives the duration of the transmission in all frame types except one. In one control frame, this "D" byte gives the ID of the frame.

Addresses—There are four possible address fields, each 6 bytes long and structured the same as Ethernet MAC addresses. The fourth field is only present when multiple APs are in use in an ESS. The meaning of each address field depends on the value of the DS flags in the FC field, discussed later.

Sequence control—This 2-byte field gives the sequence number of the frame and is used in flow control.

Payload—This field can be from 0 to 2312 bytes long. Usually it is fewer than 1500 bytes and holds an IP packet, but there are other types of payloads. The precise type and subtype of the content is determined by the content of the FC field.

CRC—The frame cyclical redundancy check is a 4-byte CRC-32, used to determine the nature of the acknowledgement sent.

Why does the wireless frame need to define four address fields? Mainly because the arrangements of wireless stations can be complicated. Is there an AP in the BSS? Is there more than one AP? What type of frame is being sent? Data? Control? Management? The number of address fields present, and what they represent, depend on the answers to these questions.

How do receivers know exactly how many addresses are used and what they represent? That's where the two DS flags in the FC field come in. The meaning of the address fields (and possible presence of the Address 4 field) depends on the values of these two bits. Actually, there are *five* types of MAC addresses used in wireless LANs:

BSSID—This is usually the MAC address of the AP, but it is generated randomly in an IBSS or ad hoc network.

Transmitter Address (TA)—The TA is the MAC address of the individual station that has just sent the frame.

Receiver Address (RA)—The RA is the MAC address of the immediate receiver of the frame. This can be a group or broadcast address.

Source Address (SA)—The SA is the MAC address of the individual station that originated the frame. Due to the possible role played by the AP, the SA is not necessarily the same as the TA.

Destination Address (DA)—The DA is the MAC address of the final destination of the frame, and can also be a group or broadcast as well as an individual station. Again, due to the AP(s), this address might not match the RA.

Table 3.3 DS Bits and Wireless LAN Data Frame Address Fields

Type of Network	From DS	To DS	Address 1	Address 2	Address 3	Address 4
Ad hoc (IBSS)	0	0	DA (= RA)	SA	BSSID	N/A
To AP	0	1	RA (= BSSID)	SA	DA	N/A
From AP	1	0	DA (= RA)	BSSID	SA	N/A
ESS (multiple APs)	1	1	RA	TA	DA	SA

The interplay among these address types and the meaning of the two DS flags for data frames is shown in Table 3.3.

A look back at Figures 3.6 and 3.7 will show that these address patterns are reflected in the screen captures. The last two bits of the frame control flags are the DS bits, which are 01 (To AP) and 10 (From AP), respectively. The Proxima AP is passing the frame between the Cisco and Farallon wireless stations.

The Address 4 field appears only when there are multiple APs. Usually, data frames in a simple BSS with AP use DS bit combinations `01` and `10` to make their way through the AP from one wireless station to another.

QUESTIONS FOR READERS

Figure 3.15 shows some of the concepts discussed in this chapter and can be used to help you answer the following questions.

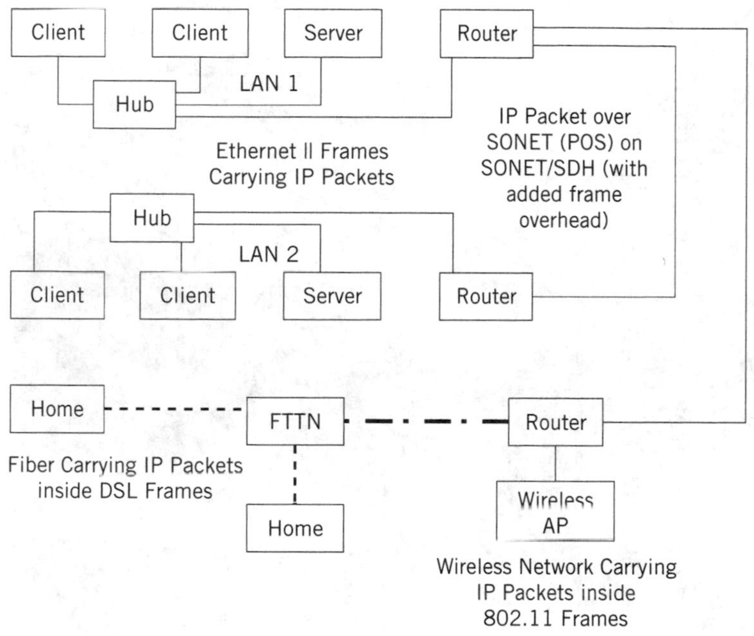

FIGURE 3.15

IP packets are carried in many different types of frames, and some of those frames are tucked inside lower level transmission frames.

1. Both LAN1 and LAN2 use Ethernet II frames. What would happen if frame types on the two LANs were different?
2. SONET/SDH still has its own overhead bytes when IP packets are carried inside the SONET/SDH framcs. Why is the SONET/SDH overhead still necessary?
3. What is the captive portal method of wireless access permission and how does it work?
4. Ethernet LANs can extend to metropolitan area distances and perhaps beyond. If Metro Ethernet evolved to remove all distance limits, what are the advantages and disadvantages of *always* using Ethernet frames for IP packets?
5. Why are more than two addresses used in wireless frames in some cases? Which cases require more than two addresses?

PART

II

Core Protocols

All hosts attached to the Internet run certain core protocols to enable their applications to function properly. This part of the book examines these protocols and shows how the router forms the glue that holds the Internet together.

HAPTER

IPv4 and IPv6 Addressing

4

What You Will Learn

In this chapter, you will learn about the addressing used in IPv4 and IPv6. We'll assign addresses of both types to various interfaces on the hosts and routers of the Illustrated Network. We'll mention older classful IPv4 addressing and the current classless system. We will start to explore the differences between IPv4 and IPv6 addressing and why both exist.

You will learn about the important concept of subnetting and supernetting and other aspects of IP addressing. We'll detail the IP subnet mask as well.

In many ways, IPv4 and IPv6 are distinct protocols with important differences. Nevertheless, both IPv4 and IPv6 are valid IP layer addresses, some networks use both IPv4 and IPv6, and the packet data content is the same in both. Network engineers often deal with both every day, and we will too. In the future, the importance of IPv6 will only grow.

IPv4 addressing was fairly straightforward to understand before the Internet exploded all over the world. Then the original ("classful") rules for assigning networks IPv4 addresses didn't work as well, and routers were getting overwhelmed by the size and resources needed to maintain routing and forwarding tables.

This chapter investigates both IPv4 and IPv6 addressing, and the host and router interfaces on the Illustrated Network have both IPv4 and IPv6 addresses (see Figure 4.1). We'll assign these addresses manually in this chapter.

We'll start the discussion by describing the classless Internet routing (CIDR) rules created so that we did not run out of IPv4 addresses in 1994, shortly after the Web exploded onto the scene. Then we'll describe the older classful system, and, finally, we'll talk about IPv6 addressing. This chapter also explores important aspects of IP addressing subnetting and supernetting.

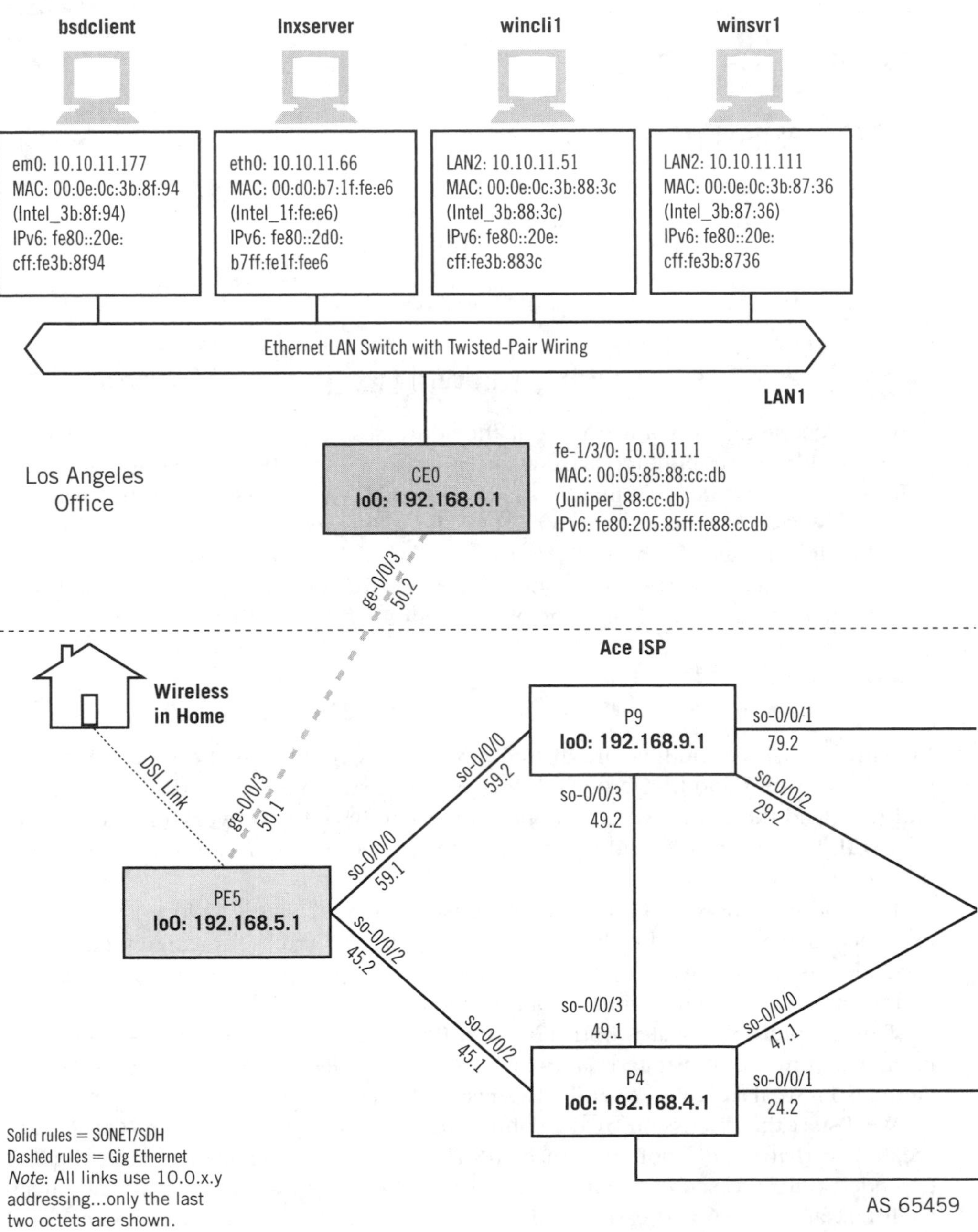

FIGURE 4.1

The Illustrated Network IP addressing, showing the interfaces on the LANs and customer-edge routers that we will be working with. Note that in most cases, all of the network interfaces will have both IPv4 and IPv6 addresses.

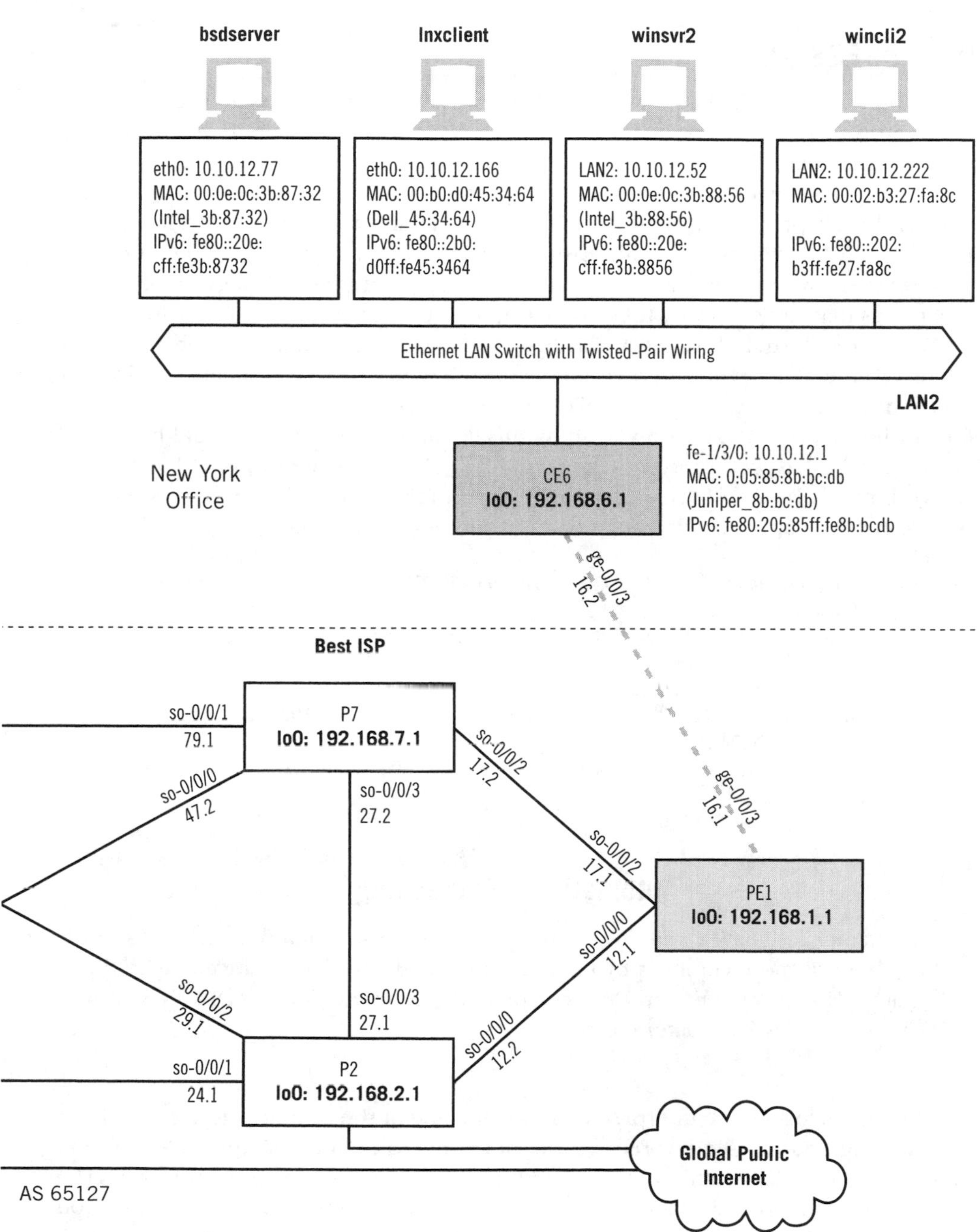

bsdserver
lnxclient
winsvr2
wincli2
eth0: 10.10.12.77
MAC: 00:0e:0c:3b:87:32
(Intel_3b:87:32)
IPv6: fe80::20e:
cff:fe3b:8732
eth0: 10.10.12.166
MAC: 00:b0:d0:45:34:64
(Dell_45:34:64)
IPv6: fe80::2b0:
d0ff:fe45:3464
LAN2: 10.10.12.52
MAC: 00:0e:0c:3b:88:56
(Intel_3b:88:56)
IPv6: fe80::20e:
cff:fe3b:8856
LAN2: 10.10.12.222
MAC: 00:02:b3:27:fa:8c
IPv6: fe80::202:
b3ff:fe27:fa8c
Ethernet LAN Switch with Twisted-Pair Wiring
LAN2
New York
Office
CE6
lo0: 192.168.6.1
fe-1/3/0: 10.10.12.1
MAC: 0:05:85:8b:bc:db
(Juniper_8b:bc:db)
IPv6: fe80:205:85ff:fe8b:bcdb
ge-0/0/3
16.2
Best ISP
so-0/0/1
79.1
P7
lo0: 192.168.7.1
so-0/0/2
17.2
ge-0/0/3
16.1
so-0/0/0
47.2
so-0/0/3
27.2
so-0/0/2
17.1
PE1
lo0: 192.168.1.1
so-0/0/0
12.1
so-0/0/2
29.1
so-0/0/3
27.1
so-0/0/0
12.2
so-0/0/1
24.1
P2
lo0: 192.168.2.1
Global Public
Internet
AS 65127

IP ADDRESSING

In Chapter 2 we worked a lot with the Linux and Windows clients and servers. Let's start with our FreeBSD hosts and routers to look at IPv4 and IPv6 addresses on the device's interfaces.

Figure 4.1 shows through shading the portion of the network we'll be working with in this chapter. All of the ISP routers have IP addresses, of course, both IPv4 and IPv6, but we'll only look at the addressing of the customer routers. Although it can be important, we won't worry about the addressing used internally by service providers. The things that can go wrong there are far beyond this introductory discussion.

When the Illustrated Network was first configured, we manually assigned an IPv4 address to the `bsdserver` Ethernet interface (`em0`) with `ifconfig`. The only tricky part was translating the prefix length used on our network (`/24`) to a decimal network mask for this host (this was done only to show this common method). We could have used `10.10.12.77/24` as well, or even hex (`0xffffff00`). We'll talk about prefix lengths and network masks later on in this chapter. The `ifconfig` command generates no output, but we can look at the result using `ifconfig` without any parameters.

```
bsdserver# ifconfig em0 inet 10.10.12.77 netmask 255.255.255.0
bsdserver# ifconfig
em0: flags=8843<UP,BROADCAST,RUNNING,SIMPLEX,MULTICAST> mtu 1500
        options=3<RXCSUM,TXCSUM>
        inet6 fe80::20e:cff:fe3b:8732%em0 prefixlen 64 scopeid 0x1
        inet 10.10.12.77 netmask 0xffffff00 broadcast 10.10.12.255
        ether 00:0e:0c:3b:87:32
        media: Ethernet autoselect (100baseTX <full-duplex>)
        status: active
```

Automatic IP Addressing

This chapter assigns IPv4 and IPv6 addresses manually on each device. This is still done, but it is more common by far to assign IP addresses automatically with the Dynamic Host Configuration Protocol, or DHCP. Routers can use DHCP as well. We'll look at DHCP in a later chapter.

The interface flags are interpreted on the first line of the output. Interface `em0` is up and running, and can send or receive, but not at the same time (simplex). It can send and receive broadcasts and multicast, and has a Maximum Transmission Unit (MTU) of 1500 bytes (a normal Ethernet frame). If a packet is queued for output and is too large for this 1500-byte frame, then the packet content must be fragmented into multiple frames, each in its own packet. We'll talk about fragmentation in detail in a later chapter. The option line says that the frame check sequence is generated when transmitting and checked when receiving.

Note that we got an IPv6 address (the `inet6` line) as well. This is called the ***link-local*** (`0xfe80`) IPv6 address. It is based on the MAC address and generated automatically, with a prefix length (`prefixlen`) of `/64`. Newer versions of FreeBSD function this way, as long as the local router is properly configured to run IPv6. You can use the `ifconfig` command with the `inet6` option to assign a specific IPv6 address to the interface. (There's a lot more to IPv6 addressing, such as *router-assigned prefixes*, but we're keeping it very basic here.)

The next line lists the IPv4 address, netmask, and the address used as an IP broadcast address to send packets to every device on the network. The MAC address has a line all its own, followed by the type of media: 100-Mbps, twisted-pair Ethernet, capable of sending and receiving (`full-duplex`) at the same time (but `em0` will not do that). The interface is `active` as well as `up`, which means that it is sending and receiving bits.

Linux uses slightly different syntax to assign IPv4 addresses to interfaces. Let's assign an IPv4 address to the `lnxclient` Ethernet interface (`eth0`) using `ifconfig`. In this case, the network mask format is easier to read. We'll look at the interface before the address is assigned, and then after, and find something very different from FreeBSD with regard to the network broadcast address.

```
[root@lnxclient admin]# ifconfig
eth0        Link encap:Ethernet  HWaddr 00:B0:D0:45:34:64
            UP BROADCAST RUNNING MULTICAST  MTU:1500  Metric:1
            RX packets:43993 errors:0 dropped:0 overruns:1 frame:0
            TX packets:0 errors:0 dropped:0 overruns:0 carrier:0
            collisions:0 txqueuelen:100
            RX bytes:7491082 (7.1 Mb)  TX bytes:0 (0.0 b)
            Interrupt:5 Base address:0xec00
[root@lnxclient admin]# ifconfig eth0 10.10.12.166 netmask 255.255.255.0
[root@lnxclient admin]# ifconfig
eth0        Link encap:Ethernet  HWaddr 00:B0:D0:45:34:64
            inet addr:10.10.12.166  Bcast:10.255.255.255  Mask:255.255.255.0
            UP BROADCAST RUNNING MULTICAST  MTU:1500  Metric:1
            RX packets:44000 errors:0 dropped:0 overruns:1 frame:0
            TX packets:0 errors:0 dropped:0 overruns:0 carrier:0
            collisions:0 txqueuelen:100
            RX bytes:7492614 (7.1 Mb)  TX bytes:0 (0.0 b)
            Interrupt:5 Base address:0xec00
```

This output gives much the same information as FreeBSD, but provides more details for traffic statistics and error conditions. The last line of output gives details about how the interface card communicates with the operating system and has nothing directly to do with the network. Note that no automatic IPv6 addresses are generated. All versions of the Linux kernel newer than 2.2, regardless of distribution, now support ways to give an interface an IPv6 address, but we will not do that.

However, Linux has also done something very odd with the broadcast address. We'll talk more about broadcast address formats later in this chapter, but it is supposed to be formed by setting all of the host bits that follow the network bits in the IP address to 1.

Now, we set a network mask for 24 bits (255.255.255.0), but Linux has set all the bits in the field to a string of 1 bits in the broadcast mask to the last 24 bits of the IPv4 address, or 10.255.255.255. As we saw with FreeBSD, the correct broadcast address for this network mask should be 10.10.12.255.

This means, as we'll soon discover, that this older version of Linux expects *classful* IPv4 addresses, and today we mostly use *classless* IPv4 addresses. (There was some debate as to whether this was a "broken" version or install, but the behavior is consistent and all else seems well.)

To fix the broadcast address so that the network functions properly (yes, it matters), we'll have to specify a broadcast address for lnxclient (and do the same for lnxserver).

```
[root@lnxclient admin]# ifconfig eth0 broadcast 10.10.12.255
[root@lnxclient admin]# ifconfig
eth0       Link encap:Ethernet  HWaddr 00:B0:D0:45:34:64
           inet addr:10.10.12.166  Bcast:10.10.12.255  Mask:255.255.255.0
           UP BROADCAST RUNNING MULTICAST  MTU:1500  Metric:1
           RX packets:44000 errors:0 dropped:0 overruns:1 frame:0
           TX packets:0 errors:0 dropped:0 overruns:0 carrier:0
           collisions:0 txqueuelen:100
           RX bytes:7492614 (7.1 Mb)  TX bytes:0 (0.0 b)
           Interrupt:5 Base address:0xec00
```

Let's move on to the Windows devices. In Windows, IPv4 and IPv6 address assignment can be awkward. In Windows XP, you typically use the graphical interface to assign IPv4 addresses, subnet masks, and default gateways. The method is well-documented in many places and need not be detailed here. You can easily view the current IP addresses by running the Windows ipconfig command. Here's the result on wincli2.

```
Microsoft Windows XP [Version 5.1.2600]
(C) Copyright 1985-2001 Microsoft Corp.
C:\Documents and Settings\Owner>ipconfig
Windows IP Configuration
Ethernet adapter Local Area Connection:
          Connection-specific DNS Suffix  . :
          IP Address  . . . . . . . . . . : 10.10.12.222
          Subnet Mask . . . . . . . . . . : 255.255.255.0
          Default Gateway . . . . . . . . : 10.10.12.1
```

Unlike the Unix-based output, Windows XP associates a default gateway with the interface. This information is properly part of the host routing and forwarding routing table, and we'll talk more about default gateways in a later chapter on routing.

How can we give the LAN interface an IPv6 address? In XP, the graphical version depends on the service packs installed. The easiest way is to use the command prompt to first install the IPv6 protocol stack as a dual stack on the host. XP can generate a series of IPv6 addresses automatically as well (you can also set them manually). It should be noted that in Vista, IPv6 is typically turned on by default.

```
C:\Documents and Settings\Owner>ipv6 install
Installing. . .
Succeeded.
C:\Documents and Settings\Owner>
```

Once IPv6 support is available, the output of the `ipconfig` command shows some very interesting things.

```
C:\Documents and Settings\Owner>ipconfig
Windows IP Configuration
Ethernet adapter Local Area Connection:
         Connection-specific DNS Suffix  . :
         IP Address  .   .   . . . . . . . : 10.10.12.222
         Subnet Mask .   .   . . . . . . . : 255.255.255.0
         IP Address  .   .   . . . . . . . : fe80::202:b3ff:fe27:fa8c%4
         Default Gateway .   . . . . . . . : 10.10.12.1
```

Tunnel adapter Automatic Tunneling Pseudo-Interface:

```
         Connection-specific DNS Suffix  . :
         IP Address  .   .   . . . . . . . : fe80::5efe:10.10.12.222%2
         Default Gateway .   . . . . . . . :
```

Not only has the IPv6 installation created an IPv6 address for the LAN interface, it is a site-local address based on the MAC address of the interface (see Chapter 3). The "%" number is just an index for the order in which certain types of IPv6 addresses were generated by the IPv6 installation.

On working networks, more than just the automatic tunnel IPv6 address is usually created. It is not unusual to see a `Tunnel adapter Teredo Tunneling Pseudo-Interface`. Teredo is a Microsoft initiative, defined in RFC 3904, that allows devices to reach the IPv6 Internet from behind a network address translation (NAT) device. There is often a `Tunnel adapter 6to4 Tunneling Pseudo-Interface` as well, depending on how the routers are configured. A full discussion of these Windows IPv6 interfaces is beyond the scope of this book, but we'll discuss IPv6 tunneling in more detail in Chapter 9.

The customer edge routers are Juniper Networks routers. The configuration files on these routers look very different from those on a Cisco router. Juniper Networks router configurations are more like C language programs and are organized with braces in indented stanzas. However, Juniper Networks router configurations can be rendered in "`set`" language that looks more like Cisco's style. For example, on router CE0, the addressing on interface `fe-1/3/0` is more complex than on a host:

```
admin@CE0> show interface fe-1/3/0
unit 0 {
   family inet {
         address 10.10.11.1/24;
    }
```

```
    family inet6 {
        address FC00:ffb3:d5:b:205:85ff:fe88:ccdb/64;
    }
}
user@CE0>
```

In this format, all statements configured under another statement (indented) apply to that higher level statement. Thus, both `family inet` and `family inet6` apply to `unit 0`, but only the address `10.10.11.1/24` applies to `family inet`. The form is used often in this book, and becomes more familiar with repetition.

This form can also be shown in the following more compact format, which is the style we will use in this book:

```
admin@CE0> set interface fe-1/3/0 unit 0 family inet address 10.10.11.1/24;
admin@CE0> set interface fe-1/3/0 unit 0 family inet6 address
    FC00:ffb3:d5:b:205:85ff:fe88:ccdb/64;
```

This output is for logical `unit 0`, the simplest case. Juniper Networks router interfaces can have logical units numbered from 0 to 65535, and each can have more than one IPv4 or IPv6 address. The LAN interface on CE6 looks very much the same, except for the address specifics.

We'll talk about the specifics of the IPv4 and IPv6 address formats, network marks, and prefix lengths, and other topics, in the rest of this chapter. At the end, we'll see just what the complex IPv6 address format is telling us about the Illustrated Network.

One type of address we *won't* be exploring in this chapter is the *anycast* address. To understand anycast addresses, consider that there are three major types of IP addresses.

Unicast—This type of IP address is used to identify a single network interface. It establishes a one-to-one relationship between the network address and network endpoint (interface). So each unicast address uniquely identifies a network source or destination.

Broadcast/Multicast—This type of IP address is used to identify a changeable *group* of interfaces. Broadcast addresses are used to send a message to every reachable interface, and *broadcast domains* are typically defined physically. Multicast addresses are not limited to a single domain and multicast groups are established logically. IPv6 relies on multicast addresses for many of the discovery features of IPv6 and things that are done with broadcasts in IPv4. In both multicast and broadcast, there is a many-to-one association between network address and network endpoints. Consequently, one address identifies a group of network endpoints, and information is replicated by routers to reach them all.

Anycast—This type of IP address, formally defined in IPv6, is used to identify a defined *set* of interfaces, usually on different devices. Anycast addresses are used to deliver packets to the "nearest" interface, where nearness is defined as a routing parameter. The same can be done in IPv4, but not as elegantly. However, multicasts deliver to many interface destinations, while anycasts deliver to only one, although many might be reachable. Anycasts are useful for redundancy purposes, so servers can exist around the world, all with the same address, but traffic is only sent to the one that is the "closest" to the source.

This book uses mainly unicast IP addresses. Multicast and anycast addresses will be introduced and used as necessary.

THE NETWORK/HOST BOUNDARY

We just saw that the mask determines where the boundary between the network and host portions of the IP address lies. This boundary is important: If it is set too far to the right, there are lots of networks, but none of them can have many hosts. If it is set too far to the left, then there are plenty of hosts allowed, but fewer networks overall.

In IP, the address boundary is moveable, and always has been. But in the past, right through the big Internet explosion in the mid-1990s, the network/host boundary in IPv4 could only be in one of three places. This produced lots of networks that were too small in terms of hosts, and many that were far too large, capable of holding millions of hosts. Not only that, but there were so many small networks, each of which needing a separate routing table entry in each and every core Internet router, that the Internet threatened to drown under its own weight.

In a nutshell, the inability to aggregate Class C blocks drove routing table pressure and the unsustainable rate of allocation of Class A and Class B addresses. This would have caused IPv4 exhaustion by 1994 to 1995, as projected in 1990.

So the rules were changed to allow the network/host boundary in IPv4 and IPv6 addresses to be set almost anywhere (there are still some basic rules). When applied to the former, fixed, IPv4 octet boundaries, if you moved the "natural" boundary of the mask to the *right* of its normal position, this was called *subnetting* and the address space gets smaller. (Actually, even the older "natural" IPv4 addresses could always be subnetted.) And if you moved the "natural" boundary of the mask to the *left* of its normal position, this was called *supernetting* and the address space became larger.

In this chapter, we will talk about subnetting and supernetting in detail. Supernetting is more commonly called "aggregation" today, but we'll call it supernetting in this chapter just to make the contrast with subnetting explicit. We will also talk about the current system of rules for hosts and routers concerning the positioning of the boundary between the network and host portion of the IP address, variable-length subnet masking (VLSM), and classless interdomain routing (CIDR). But first, let's look at the IPv4 address in detail.

THE IPv4 ADDRESS

The IPv4 address is a network layer concept and has nothing to do with the addresses that the data link layer uses, often called the *hardware address* on LANs. IPv4 addresses must be mapped to LAN hardware addresses and WAN serial link addresses. However, there is no real relationship between LAN media access control (MAC) or WAN serial link addresses in the frame header and the IPv4 addresses used in the packet header, with the special exception of multicast addresses.

The original IPv4 addressing scheme established in RFC 791 is known as *classful* addressing. The 32 bits of the IPv4 address fall into one of several classes based on the value of the initial bits in the IPv4 address. The major classes used for addresses were A, B, and C. Class D was (and is) used for IPv4 multicast traffic, and Class E was "reserved" for experimental purposes. Each class differs in the number of IPv4 address bits assigned to the *network* and the *host* portion of the IP address. This scheme is shown in Figure 4.2.

Note that with Class A, B, and C, we are referring to the size of the blocks being allocated as well as the region from which they were allocated by IANA. However, Classes D and E refer to the whole respective region. Multicast addresses, when they were assigned for applications, for example, were assigned one at a time like (for instance) port numbers. (We'll talk about port numbers in a later chapter.) In the rest of this chapter, references to Classes A, B, and C are concerned with address space sizes and not locations.

The 4 billion (actually 4,294,967,296) possible IPv4 addresses are split up into five classes. The five classes are not equal in size, and Class A covers a full half of the whole

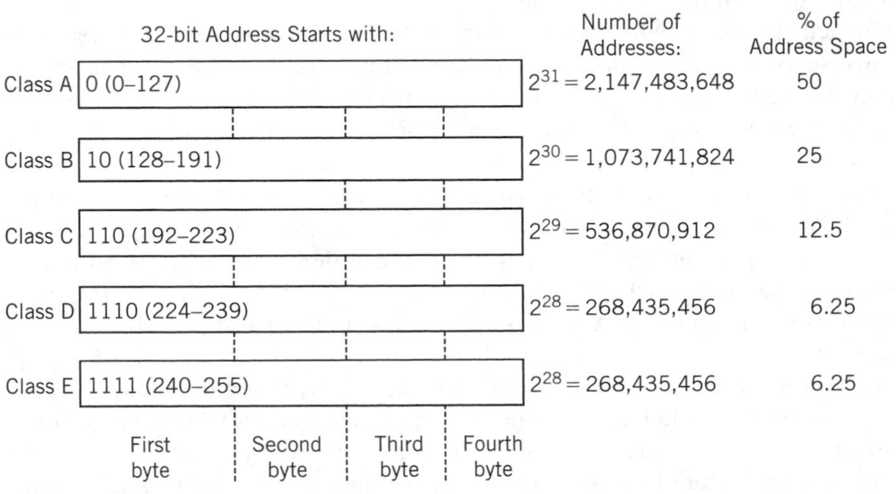

FIGURE 4.2

Classful IPv4 addressing, showing the number of addresses possible and percentage of the total address space for each class. Class D is still the valid IPv4 address range used for multicasting.

IPv4 address space. Class E addresses are "experimental" and some of them have been used for that purpose, but they are seldom seen today.

In practice, only the Class D addresses are still used on the Internet in a classful manner. Class D addresses are the IPv4 multicast addresses (`224.0.0.0` to `239.255.255.255`), and we'll talk about those as needed. We will nonetheless talk about classful IPv4 addressing in this book, especially later on in this chapter when subnetting is considered and when mentioning the routing protocol RIPv1. However, the significance of classful IPv4 addressing is strictly historical. Classful addressing comes up occasionally, and at least some introduction is necessary.

This chapter, and this book, emphasizes *classless* IP addresses, the current way of interpreting the 32-bit IPv4 address space. This scheme assumes that no classes exist and is how routers on the Internet interpret IPv4 addresses. In classless addressing, the IPv4 network *mask* or *prefix* determines the boundary between the network and host portion of the IP address instead of the initial IP address bits. On a host, it is still often called a network mask, because hosts don't care about classful or classless, but it is called a prefix on a router.

Hosts really don't deal with the differences between classful and classless IP addresses. Routers, on the other hand, must. Because this book deals with networks as a whole, including routers, some understanding of both classful and classless IPv4 addressing is beneficial.

Dotted Decimal

IPv4 addresses are most often written in dotted decimal notation. In this format, each 8-bit byte in the 32-bit IPv4 address is converted from binary or hexadecimal to a decimal number between 0 (0000 0000 or 0x00) and 255 (1111 1111 or 0xFF). The numbers are then written as four decimal numbers with dots between them: W.X.Y.Z.

For example, 1010 1100 0001 0000 1100 1000 0000 0010 (0xAC 10 C8 02) becomes 172.16.200.2. And 1011 1111 1111 1111 0000 1110 0010 1100 (0xBF FF 0E 2C) becomes 191.255.14.44, and so on.

Hosts on the same network (essentially a LAN) must have the prefix (network portion) of their IP addresses (IPv4 or IPv6) be the same. This is how routers route packets between networks that form the Internet: by the network portion of the IP address. The whole IP address specifies the host on the network, and the network portion identifies the LAN. The boundary between network and host IP address bits is moveable for either classful or classless IP addresses. An IP address can be expressed in dotted decimal, binary, octal, or hexadecimal. While all are correct and mean the same thing, it's most common to use *dotted decimal* notation for IPv4 and hexadecimal (hex) for IPv6. (In fact, some RFCs, such as those for HTTP [covered in Chapter 22], require dotted decimal for IPv4 addresses.)

The basic concepts of classful IPv4 addressing are shown in Figure 4.3 for the three most common classes—A, B, and C. The figure shows the Internet name assigned to the IPv4 address, the *default* network mask and prefix length for each of the three common classes, and the IPv4 address in dotted decimal.

Note that when no network mask is given, the class of the address is determined by the value of the initial bits of the address, as already described. The network mask can move this boundary, but in practice only to the *right* in classful addressing.

Classless IPv4 addressing, on the other hand, as used on routers, does not derive a default subnet mask or prefix length. The prefix length for classless IPv4 addressing must be given (by the netmask) to properly place the boundary between NetID and HostID portions of the IPv4 address.

IP addresses, both IPv4 and IPv6, can be public or private. Public network address spaces are assigned by a central authority and should be unique. Private network addresses are very useful, but are not guaranteed to be unique. Therefore, the use of private network address spaces has to be carefully managed, because routers on the Internet would not work properly if a LAN showed up in two places at the same time. Nevertheless, the use of private address spaces in IP is popular for perceived security reasons. The security aspects are often overemphasized: The expansion of the locally available address space is the key reason for private address use. (If you have one IP address and three hosts, you have a problem without private addressing.) But private address spaces must be translated to public addresses whenever a packet makes it way onto the global public Internet.

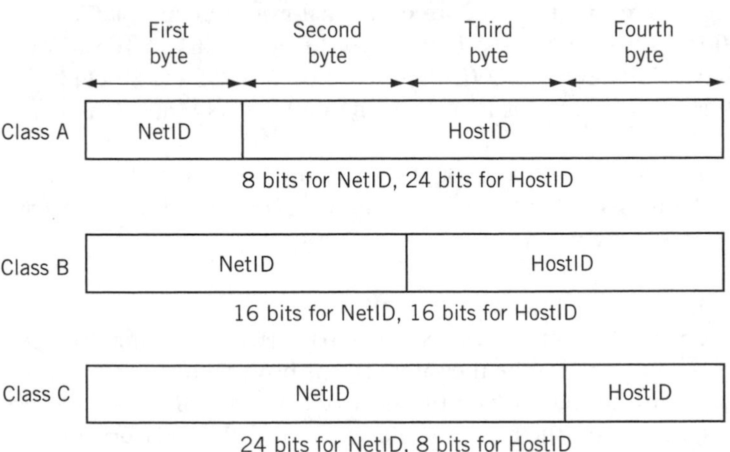

FIGURE 4.3

The classful IPv4 address for classes A, B, and C. Note how the boundary between network identifier and host identifier moves to the right, allowing more networks and fewer hosts in each class.

Moreover, private IP addresses are not routable outside a local network, so a router is not allowed to advertise a route to a private address space onto the public Internet. Note that private addresses are just as routable as public ones within your own network (as on the Illustrated Network), or by mutual consent with another party. They are not generally routable on the global public Internet due to their lack of uniqueness and usual practices.

Almost all networks today rely on private network addresses to prevent public IPv4 address exhaustion, so these addresses are not just to test networks and labs any longer. Customer-edge routers often translate between a large pool of private (internal) and a smaller pool of public (external) addresses and insulate the local LAN from the outside world. We'll talk more about private IPv4 address in the next section of this chapter.

When obtaining a public IP address, a user or organization receives an address space that should be globally unique on the Internet. (Sadly, you often find yourself "blackholed" to nowhere for some ISP to route your packets because someone else used your address space internally for some private network without permission!) This first piece is the network portion (prefix) of an IP address space, such as 191.255.0.0. This example uses a so-called "Martian" IPv4 address, which is a valid IP address, but not used on the Internet. Technically, the address space beginning with 191.255 is reserved, but could be assigned in the future. The 0.0 ending means an IP network is referenced, and not a host (in this case, but hosts sometimes have IPv4 addresses that end with 0). Some TCP/IP protocol stacks struggle with IPv4 addresses ending in 0 or 255, so it is best to avoid them. The host portion of the IPv4 address is assigned locally, usually by the LAN network administrator. For example, a host could be assigned IPv4 address 191.255.14.44.

The examples in this chapter use the manual, *static* IP address assignment method. When this method is used with public IP addresses, the organization still either obtains the IP network address range on its own, or uses the range of IP addresses assigned to the organization by its ISP. The Dynamic Host Configuration Protocol (DHCP) makes it possible to assign IP addresses to devices in a *dynamic* fashion. DHCP is the method many organizations use either for security reasons (to make it harder to find device IP addresses) or to assign a unique IP address to a device only when it actually needs to access the Internet. There are many more uses for dynamic IP address allocations on the Internet, and much more to discuss, and DHCP will be explored in a later chapter.

When the topic is routers, IP addresses are often written in the <*netid, hostid/prefix*> form to determine the netid/hostid boundary. To completely identify a particular host on a particular network, the whole address is needed. When all 32 bits of the IPv4 address are given, and the prefix is not, this is called a *host address* on a router. In classless routing, there is no fixed separation point between the network and host portion of the IP address: It is completely determined by the prefix, which must be known. In dotted decimal notation, the full range of possible IP addresses can run from 0.0.0.0 to 255.255.255.255. Prefixes can run from /0 (a special, but useful, case) to /31. Until recently, the /31 prefix was often useless to routers, as we will see in a later chapter, and the /32 prefix is the same as the host address.

Private IPv4 Addresses

RFC 1918 established private address spaces for Classes A, B, and C to be used on private IP networks, and these are still respected in classless IP addressing. Books such as this one, where it is not desirable to use public IP addresses for examples, use RFC 1918 addresses throughout, much like using "555" telephone numbers in movies and on TV. The private IP address ranges follow:

- *Class A:* `10.0.0.0` through `10.255.255.255` (`10.0.0.0/8`, or just `10/8`)
- *Class B:* `172.16.0.0` through `172.31.255.255` (`172.16.0.0/12`, or just `172.16/12`)
- *Class C:* `192.168.0.0` through `192.168.255.255` (`192.168.0.0/16`, or just `192.168/16`)

There are three very important points that should always be kept in mind regarding private addresses. First, these addresses should never be announced by a routing protocol on a local router to the public Internet. However, these addresses are frequently assigned and used when they are isolated or translated. We'll look at network address translation (NAT) in a later chapter. In summary,

- Private IP addresses are not routable outside the local network (they cannot be advertised to the public Internet).
- They are widely used on almost all networks today (even our small home network with DSL uses private IP addresses).
- Private addresses are usually translated with NAT at an edge router to map the private addresses used on a LAN to the public address space used by the ISP.

Understanding IPv4 Addresses

IP addresses and their prefixes are read in a certain way and have special meanings depending on how they are written and used. For example, the classful IPv4 address `192.168.19.48` is read as "host 48 on IP network 192.168.19.0." In a classless environment, as on a router, the prefix length, in this case `/24`, must be known. Routers often drop trailing zeros, `192.168.19.0/24` is the same as `192.168.19/24`. All IP network addresses must have the bits in the host address field set to `0` and this address cannot be assigned to any host. (Typically, nothing on a host prevents this address assignment. It just won't work properly.) Note that while the table is describing a particular `/24` address in the examples, it's not the address itself but its location in the field specified by the mask that is critical.

Table 4.1 lists some specific forms of IPv4 addresses, what they look like, and whether they can be used as a source or destination address or have some other special use.

IPv4 addresses in example formats such as `0.0.0.46` and `192.168.14.0` are never actually seen as packet header addresses. Loopback addresses are used on hosts and routers for testing and aren't even numbered on the interface. All systems "know" that packets sent to the loopback addresses (any IPv4 address starting with `127`) are not sent out the network interface.

Table 4.1 Special Forms of IPv4 Addresses, Showing How Some Are Limited in Application to Source or Destination

Special Address	NetID	HostID	Example	Use
Network itself	Non-0	All zeros (0s)	192.168.14.0	Used by routers: on a host, means "some host," but it is not used.
Directed broadcast	Non-0	All ones (1s)	192.168.14.255	Destination only: used by routers to send to all host on this network.
Limited broadcast	All 1s	All 1s	225.255.255.255	Destination only: direct broadcast when NetID is not known.
This host on this network	All 0s	All 0s	0.0.0.0	Source only: used when host does not know its IPv4 address.
Specific host on this network	All 0s	Non-0	0.0.0.46	Destination only: defined, but not used
Loopback	127	Any	127.0.0.0	Destination only: packet is not sent out onto network.

When these forms are not used in their defined roles (e.g., when something like `172.16.255.255` is used as a packet source address instead of a destination), the result is usually an error.

THE IPv6 ADDRESS

In addition to IPv4 (often written as just IP), there is IP version 6 (IPv6). IPv6 was developed as IPng ("IP:The Next Generation" because the developers were supposedly fans of the TV show "Star Trek:The Next Generation"). (IPv5 existed and is defined in RFC 1819 as the Streams 2 [ST2] protocol.)

This section is not intended to be an exhaustive investigation of IPv6. The emphasis here is on the IPv6 header and address, and how IPv6 will affect router operation. IPv6 has been around since about 1995, but pressure to transition from IPv4 to IPv6 is mostly recent. (The exhaustion of the IPv4 address space has been delayed mainly through the use of NAT and DHCP.) Today, the pressure for transition from IPv4 to IPv6 comes mainly from network service providers and operators and other groups with large internal networks, such as cellular telephone network operators.

In some applications, major IPv6 addresses are confined to the core of large IP networks, and customers and users still see only IPv4 addresses. Nevertheless, there is nothing to fear about learning IPv6, and some familiarity with IPv6 will probably be expected in the future.

Features of IPv6 Addressing

The major features of IPv6, such as IPSec, have nearly all been back-ported into IPv4. However, the major design features of IPv6 follow:

- An increase in the size of the IP address from 4 bytes (32 bits) to 16 bytes (128 bits).
- An increase in the size of the IP header from 24 bytes (192 bits) to 40 bytes (320 bits). (Although aside from the address fields, the header is actually smaller than in IPv4.)
- Enhanced security capabilities using IPSec (if needed).
- Provision of special "mobile" and autoconfiguration features.
- Provision for support of *flows* between routers and hosts for interactive multimedia.
- Inclusion of header compression and extension techniques.

The IPv6 address increases the size of the IP address from 4 bytes (32 bits) to 16 bytes (128 bits). For backward compatibility, all currently assigned public IP addresses are supported as a subset of the IPv6 address space. The IPv6 address size increases the overall IP packet header size (and total TCP/IP overhead) from the current 24 bytes (192 bits) to 40 bytes (320 bits). However, the IPv6 header is much simpler than the IPv4 header.

IPv6 includes autoconfigured address and special support for mobile (not always wireless) users. A new mobile feature called *chained headers* might allow the faster forwarding of IPv6 packets through routers, and forbids intermediate fragmentation of IPv6 packets in routers. The path MTU size must always be respected in IPv6 routers.

IPv6 features support for what are called "flows." Flows were included in IPv6 because forwarding packets at wirespeed was originally considered impossible. *Flow caching* (the association of IPv6 packets into flows with similar TCP/IP header fields) was thought to be the workaround. However, flow caching is now widely discredited in the IPv4 world and flows are now established and applied to stateful firewall filters (Chapter 28). The flow field in IPv6 is normally set to all 0s.

IPv6 is a good fit for a dynamic environment. There are many *address discovery* options bundled with IPv6, including support for autoconfiguration, finding the maximum path MTU size (to avoid the need for fragmentation, which IPv6 routers will not do), finding other hosts' MAC addresses without ARP broadcasts, and finding routers other than the default.

The last major feature in IPv6 is a standard for header compression and extension. At first, these two features may seem contradictory, but they are actually complementary. Header compression addresses situations where the 40 bytes of the IPv6 header consists mostly of "empty" or repeated fields (like all-0 bit fields). In IPv6, there is a standard way of compressing the 40 bytes of the header down to 20 or so. There is also a way to extend these IPv6 header fields for future new features (IPv4 also has header extension options).

Most networks with a choice will be content to sit and wait before making a transition to IPv6. Naturally, networks concerned with IPv4 address exhaustion (such as huge, IP-based cell telephone networks) will convert to IPv6 right away, as large networks in China have. For the vast majority of TCP/IP users, IPv6 is a long way off, and IPv4 will be around for many years.

IPv6 Address Types and Notation

There are no broadcast addresses at all in IPv6, even directed broadcasts (these were favorites of IPv4 hackers). In IPv6, multicast addresses serve the same purpose as broadcasts do in IPv4. The difference between IPv6 anycast and multicast is that packets sent to an anycast IPv6 address are delivered to *one* of several interfaces, while packets sent to a multicast IPv6 address are delivered to *all* of many interfaces.

There is no such thing as dotted decimal notation for IPv6. All IPv6 addresses are expressed in hexadecimal. They could be expressed in binary as well, but 128 0s and 1s are tedious to write down. IPv6 addresses are written in 8 groups of 16 bits each, or 8 groups of 4 hexadecimal numbers, separated by colons. Some examples of IPv6 addresses (which appear over and over) follow:

```
FEDC:BA98:7654:3210:FEDC:BA98:7654:3210
1080:0000:0000:0000:0008:0800:200C:417A
```

Because this is still a lot to write or type, there are several ways to abbreviate IPv6 addresses. For example, any group can leave out leading 0s, and all-0 groups can be expressed as just a single 0. A long string of leading 0s can simply be replaced by a double colon (::). In fact, as long as there is no ambiguity, groups of 0s anywhere in the IPv6 address can be expressed as ::. The double colon can only be used once in an IPv6 address.

Even with these conventions, the first IPv6 address given earlier cannot be compressed at all. The second address can be expressed as

```
1080::8:800:200C:417A
```

This is better than writing out all 128 bits, even as hexadecimal. Because only one set of double colons can ever be used inside an IPv6 address,

```
1080:0000:0000:9865:0000:0000:0000:4321
```

could be written as

```
1080:0:0:9865::4321
```

or

```
1080::9865:0:0:0:4321
```

but *never* as

```
1080::9865::4321
```

(How big are the missing groups of 0s to the left or right of `9865`?)

A special case in IPv6 is made for using IPv4 addresses as IPv6 addresses. For example, the IPv4 address 10.0.0.1 could be written in IPv6 as

```
0:0:0:0:0:0:A00:1
```

or even

```
::A00:1
```

IPv4 addresses in IPv6 can still be written in dotted decimal as

```
::10.0.0.1
```

The double colon at the start is the sign that this is an IPv6 address even though it looks just like an IPv4 address. Many routers and other devices allow this convention.

IPv6 Address Prefixes

The first few bits of an IPv6 address do reveal something about the IPv6 address, although IPv6 addressing is in no way classful. IPv6 addresses have an *address type*, and the type is determined by the *format prefix* of the IPv6 address. There are reserved addresses in IPv6 as well, for things like loopback (`::1`), multicast (starting with FF), and so on. There is also an *unspecified address* consisting of all 0s (`0:0:0:0:0:0:0:0`, compressed as just `::`) that can be used as a source address by an IPv6 device that has not yet been assigned an IPv6 address. IPv6 address space is also reserved for OSI-RM Network Service Attachment Point (NSAP) addresses, and IPX addresses used with Novell NetWare.

All of these format prefixes are supposed to be given in hexadecimal, not binary. An IPv6 address that begins with `1101` means `0001 0001 0000 0001`, and is the same as `11::1`.... An IPv6 multicast address begins with `FF` and means `1111 1111:1111 1111`.

There are several basic forms of IPv6 address. Like many IPv4 addresses, IPv6 address spaces are often handed out by ISPs to their customers, usually starting with `200x`. There are also ways to assign variable-length fields for the registry identifier (the authority that assigned this IPv6 address space to the ISP), provider identifier (the ISP), subscriber identifier (the customer), subnet identifier (a group of physical links), and the interface identifier (such as the MAC address). However, most ISPs will assign IPv6 addresses just as they do IPv4 addresses (i.e., as a network address space and prefix length). *Provider independent* IPv6 addresses are not handed out by ISPs.

There used to be two types of local IPv6 addresses: *site-local* and *link-local*. Local IPv6 addresses are addresses without global significance, and they can be used over and over again as long as they do not cause confusion to hosts or routers. Local addresses start with the same 7 bits: `1111 111` or `FE` in hexadecimal (overall, the first 10 bits are important). Site-local addresses are now *deprecated* (the Internet word for "more than obsolete"). Link-local addresses can be used between two devices that are part of the same broadcast domain or on a point-to-point link.

Private IPv6 addresses usually begin with `FC00` (the full form is `FC00::/7`) and are called ***unique local-unicast addresses*** (ULA or ULA local or even ULA-L). Usually, link-local IPv6 addresses end with a 64-bit representation (called EUI-64 by the IEEE) of the 48-bit MAC address. The EUI-64 is a concatenation of the 24-bit OUI used in the MAC address with the 40-bit extension formed by prepending the 16 bits `0xFFFE` to the lower 24 bits of the MAC address.

SUBNETTING AND SUPERNETTING

Let's take a look at all aspects of finding and moving the boundary between network and host bits in the IP address. The moveable boundary is an important one, because routers performing indirect delivery generally only need to look at the NetID or *prefix* of the entire IP address to determine the next hop and then find the output interface to send the packet on its way. Of course, direct delivery requires both prefix and host addressing examination, which is why the location of the NetID/HostID boundary is so important.

How do routers and hosts know *precisely* where the boundary between prefix and host address is in the IP address? Only when this prefix/host boundary is known will the device know if the next hop is a router. And that, as we'll see in a later chapter, makes all the difference.

In the following discussions, the examples used are chosen for their simplicity, not for completeness.

Subnetting in IPv4

The IP address space was originally classful. (Of course, they didn't know it was classful back then—it was just the IP address space). As such, it contained a number of special purpose and private addresses. These characteristics of the first three classes, which have already been discussed, are summarized in Table 4.2.

Even before the Web exploded and everyone needed an IP network address for their PCs and Web sites, it was obvious that Class A and B addresses would quickly become exhausted, leaving only Class C addresses for most networks. However, these addresses only allow 254 hosts per IP network (0 and 255 were for the network and broadcast addresses). Many networks quickly exceeded this limit.

Also, Internet core routers must have a separate routing table entry for every reachable IP network. If most IP networks are Class C networks, then all Internet core routers would potentially have to hold in memory (and maintain!) a list of more than 2 million entries. Even with inexpensive memory, routing and forwarding tables of this size

Table 4.2 Classful IPv4 Addresses and Default Masks

Class	Initial Bits	Range	Default Mask
A	0	0 to 127	255.0.0.0
B	10	128 to 191	225.255.0.0
C	110	192 to 223	255.255.255.0

Note: The value of the initial bits automatically limits the range of addresses possible in each class.

pose challenges. For example, in 1993 there were fewer than 10,000 routes on most backbone routers, and this did not grow to 100,000 until about 2001. Now, it is not uncommon to add 2000 routes *per week*.

Subnetting Basics

IP address subnetting applies to any IP address. The original application of subnetting was so that point-to-point links between routers did not require a full `/24` address for each link. Subnetting also allowed a single Class C IP address to be used on small LANs having fewer than 254 hosts connected by routers instead of bridges. Bridges would simply shuttle frames among all of the ports on the bridge, but routers, as packet layer devices, determine the output interface for a packet based on the network portion of the IP address. If only one address is assigned to the entire site, but two LANs on the site are connected through a router, then the address must be subnetted so that the router functions properly. Basically, you need to create two distinct address spaces, and the IP host addresses assigned on each LAN segment must be correct as well. The LAN segments now become *subnets* of the main IP address space.

Subnetting is done using an IP address *mask*. The mask is a string of bits as long as the IP address (32 bits in the case of IPv4). If the mask bit is a 1 bit, the corresponding bit in the IP address is part of the network portion of the IP address. If the address bit is part of the host portion, the corresponding mask bit is set to a 0 bit. A mask of `255.255.0.0` means that the first 16 bits of the IP address are part of the network address and the last 16 bits are part of the host portion of the address.

All subnet masks must end in 0, 128, 192, 224, 240, 248, 252, 254, or 255—the values of each bit position as they are "turned on" left to right in any octet. Strangely, subnet masks were once allowed to turn on bits that were "noncontiguous" (not starting at the left of the address without gaps). This is no longer true, and the effect is to restrict masks to the ending values listed. Note that `255.224.0.0` is a valid subnet mask, as is `255.255.248.0` and `255.255.255.252`. Once the 1 bits stop, the rest of the subnet mask must be set to all 0 bits.

Subnet masks can be written in as many forms as there are for IP addresses: dotted decimal notation, bit string, octal, or hexadecimal. Seeing subnet masks in either dotted decimal or hexadecimal notation, or the newer *prefix* "slash" notation, also known as

Table 4.3 Use of Default or "Natural" Subnet Masks*			
Original Class	**Default Mask**	**Network/Host Bits**	**Example Interpretation**
A	255.0.0.0	8/24 (/8 prefix)	10.24.215.86 is host 0.24.215.86 on network 10.0.0.0
B	255.255.0.0	16/16 (/16 prefix)	172.17.44.200 is host 0.0.44.200 on network 172.17.0.0
C	255.255.255.0	24/8 (/24 prefix)	192.168.27.3 is host 0.0.0.3 on network 192.168.27.0

** The more bits, the more network identifiers; the fewer bits, the fewer host identifiers possible.*

CIDR notation, are the most common. Sometimes the default mask for an IP address class is called the "natural mask" for that type of address. In all cases it is possible to change the default mask to move the boundary between the network and host portions of the IP address to wherever the device needs to see it. All devices, whether hosts or routers, which need to route the packets within the subnetted network, must have identical masks. All routing protocols in wide use today exchange subnet mask information together with routing information.

The use of the default masks for the original classful IP address space is shown in Table 4.3. The more bits, the more network identifiers, and the fewer bits, the fewer host identifiers possible.

Subnetting moves the boundary between the network and host for a particular classful IP address to the *right* of the position where the boundary is normally found. We will see later that supernetting moves the boundary between network and host for a particular classful IP address to the *left* of this position. CIDR (which uses VLSM) can move the boundary anywhere.

It is important to realize that subnetting does not change anything with respect to the outside world. Internet routers still deliver the packets as before. It is the customer or site router that applies the subnet mask and delivers packets to the subnets. Instead of the usual two parts of the IP address, network, and host, we now have network, subnet, and host. However, even at the beginning of the classful era, Class A blocks were subnetted into `/16`s and `/24`s internally as appropriate.

Look at a simple LAN (`192.168.15.0`) before and after subnetting, as shown in Figure 4.4. The subnet creates two equal-sized subnets, but the Internet routers deliver packets as before. The subnet adds one "extra" bit to the default Class C mask. If this bit is 0, the first subnet is intended, and if the bit is 1, then the second subnet is intended. The hosts must be numbered according to the subnet, naturally, and all have the same subnet mask so they can determine which addresses are still on their subnet (same NetID) and which are not (different NetID).

Many implementations will not allow the assignment of the first subnet address (the network) or the last (broadcast). A LAN with 254 hosts subnetted into two subnets only yields 126 host addresses per subnet, not 127.

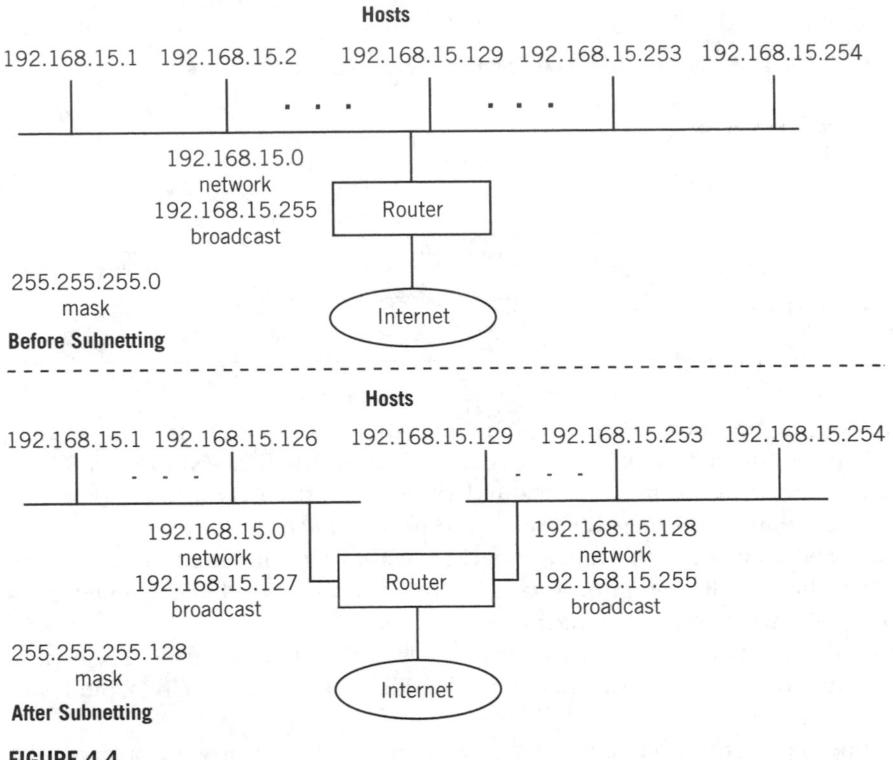

FIGURE 4.4

Subnetting a LAN, showing how the value of the initial bits determines the subnet. Host addresses, if assigned manually, must follow the subnet mask convention.

A sometimes tricky subnet issue is determining exactly what the subnet address (all 0 bits after the mask) and broadcast address (all 1 bits after the mask) are for a given IP address and subnet mask. This can be difficult because subnet masks do not always fall on byte boundaries as do classful addresses. An IP address like `172.31.0.128` might not look like the address of the network itself, but it might be. A network address, in some implementations of TCP/IP, cannot be assigned to a host. (`172.31.0.128` with a subnet mask of `255.255.255.128` is a network address.)

Consider the address `172.18.0.126` with a subnet mask of `255.255.255.192`. What is the subnet and broadcast address for this subnet? What range of host addresses can be assigned to this subnet? These questions come up all the time, and there are utilities available on the Internet that do this quickly. But here's one way to do it by hand.

The first thing to do is to mask out the network portion of the IP address with the subnet mask by writing down the mask bits. Then the subnet portion of the address can be easily marked off by "turning on" the masked bits. Next, it is easy to form the subnet and broadcast address for the subnet by setting the rest of the bits in the address (the host bits) first to all 0 bits (network) and then to all 1 bits (broadcast). The resulting address range forms the limits of the subnet.

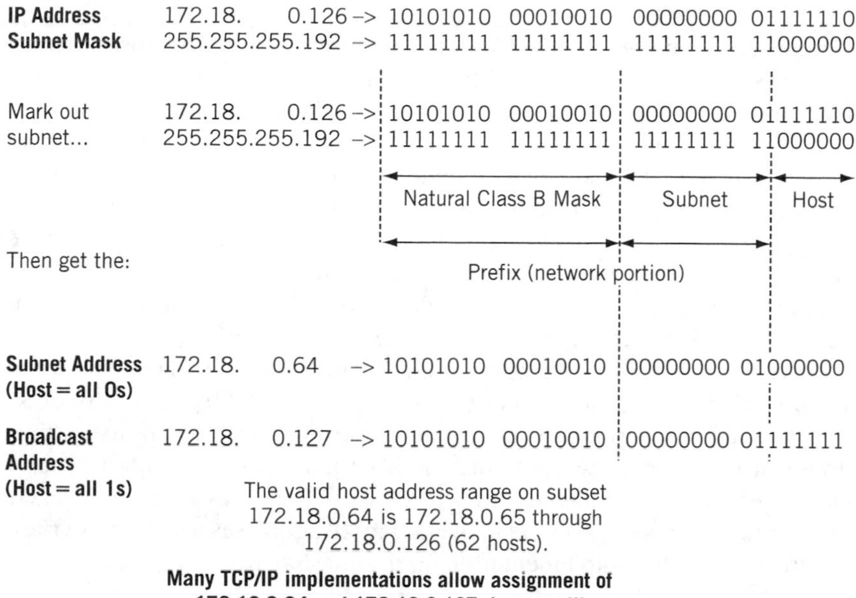

FIGURE 4.5

Finding subnet host address range, showing those available for host assignment. Many routers allow the use of subnet and broadcast addresses as if they were host addresses.

Let's look at an example. Figure 4.5 shows how to derive the network and broadcast address answers for IP address `172.18.0.126` with the subnet mask `255.255.255.192`.

These answers are important when subnetting the IP address space because care is needed to assign host addresses to the proper subnets (and router interfaces). Having a "discontiguous" classful major network that has been subnetted so that part of the space is reached through one interface of the router ("`10.24.0.0` over here..."), and the other part of the subnetted major network is reached through another interface ("`10.25.0.0` over there ...") can be a problem unless care is taken with the subnets and the masks that establish them.

CIDR and VLSM

Today, the standard methods for moving the network/host address boundary are variable-length subnet masking (VLSM) for host addressing and routing inside a routing domain, and classless interdomain routing (CIDR) for routing between routing domains. (We'll talk more about routing domains later in this book. For now, think of a routing domain as an ISP's collection of routers.) And although treated separately here for introductory reasons, it is important to realize that VLSM is the fundamental mechanism of CIDR.

CIDR (defined in RFC 1519) and VLSM (defined in RFC 1860) address more general issues than simple subnetting. We've been looking at addresses from the host perspective in this chapter so far. Let's discuss CIDR from the router perspective.

CIDR was an immediate answer to two problems: first, the impending exhaustion of the Class A and Class B address space, and second, the rapid increase in Internet core routing table sizes to handle the many Class C addresses required to handle new users.

In CIDR, a block of *contiguous* IP addresses from the former classful address space are assigned in a group, such as groups of Class C addresses. This allows a service provider or large customer to configure IP networks from a few hosts up to 16,384 hosts. The number of contiguous addresses needed is determined by a simple count of the number of host addresses required. The original CIDR plan, applied to Class C addresses, is shown in Table 4.4. Contiguous address numbers flow seamlessly between former class boundaries, allowing assignment of address "chunks" for larger networks.

The CIDR RFC does *not* "subtract" two host addresses for the network itself (final bits all 0s) and a broadcast address (final bits all 1s). CIDR applies mainly to router operation, and routers do not assume any structure of the IP addresses in the packets they route. The limitation on assigning the high and low IP addresses to a host interface is a function of the host TCP/IP implementation (and some, like routers, do not enforce any limitations at all).

CIDR changed the terminology that applied to IP addresses. Routes to IP networks are now represented by *prefixes*. A prefix consists of an IP network address, followed by a slash (/), and followed with an indication of how many of the leftmost contiguous bits in the address are part of the network mask applied for routing purposes. For example, before CIDR, the Class C address `192.168.64.0` would ordinarily have a mask of `255.255.255.0`. Subnetting could add bits to this major network mask, but only in the fixed patterns and values outlined in the previous section. CIDR enabled a "CIDR-ized" network address to be represented as `192.168.64.0/18`, and that was all the information needed. Sometimes this is abbreviated even further to just `192.168.64/18`, but the

Table 4.4 Address Grouping under CIDR*

Number of Hosts Needing Addresses	Class C Addresses Given by Registry
Fewer than 256	1 Class C network
Fewer than 512 but more than 256	2 contiguous Class C networks
Fewer than 1024 but more than 512	4 contiguous Class C networks
Fewer than 2048 but more than 1024	8 contiguous Class C networks
Fewer than 4096 but more than 2048	16 contiguous Class C networks
Fewer than 8192 but more than 4096	32 contiguous Class C networks
Fewer than 16,384 but more than 8192	64 contiguous Class C networks

**Contiguous address numbers flow seamlessly between former class boundaries, allowing assignment of address "chunks" for larger networks.*

two forms are equivalent. The notation just means that a "subnet mask 18 bits long should be applied to 192.168.64.0." This is the same as writing "192.168.64.0 with mask 255.255.192.0" but in more compact form.

Table 4.5 shows all possible prefix lengths, their netmasks in dotted decimal, and the number of classful networks the prefix represents. It also shows the number of usable IPv4 addresses that can be assigned to hosts once the network address itself and the directed broadcast address are subtracted. We'll talk about the special 0/0 address and prefix length in Chapter 8. All possible mask lengths are shown for /1 to /32. The /0 mask matches the whole Internet and is discussed in the routing chapters.

Even when CIDR was used, all bits after the IP network address had to be zero, an aspect of IP addressing that did not change. For example, 192.168.64.0/18 was a valid IP network address, but 192.168.64.0/17 was not (due to the presence of the "1" bit for the "64" in the 17th bit position). This aspect of CIDR is shown in Figure 4.6. The IP network 192.168.64.0/18 is a CIDR "supernet" because the mask contained fewer bits than the natural mask in classful IP addressing.

Table 4.5 CIDR Prefixes and Addressing*

Prefix Length	Dotted Decimal Netmask	Number of Classful Networks	Number of Usable IPv4 Addresses
/1	128.0.0.0	128 Class A's	2,147,483,646
/2	192.0.0.0	64 Class A's	1,073,741,822
/3	224.0.0.0	32 Class A's	536,870,910
/4	240.0.0.0	16 Class A's	268,435,454
/5	248.0.0.0	8 Class A's	134,217,726
/6	252.0.0.0	4 Class A's	67,108,862
/7	254.0.0.0	2 Class A's	33,554,430
/8	255.0.0.0	1 Class A or 256 Class B's	16,777,214
/9	255.128.0.0	128 Class B's	8,388,606
/10	255.192.0.0	64 Class B's	4,194,302
/11	255.224.0.0	32 Class B's	2,097,150
/12	255.240.0.0	16 Class B's	1,048,574
/13	255.248.0.0	8 Class B's	524,286
/14	255.252.0.0	4 Class B's	262,142
/15	255.254.0.0	2 Class B's	131,070
/16	255.255.0.0	1 Class B or 256 Class C's	65,534
/17	255.255.128.0	128 Class C's	32,766

(*Continued*)

Table 4.5 CIDR Prefixes and Addressing* (*Continued*)

Prefix Length	Dotted Decimal Netmask	Number of Classful Networks	Number of Usable IPv4 Addresses
/18	255.255.192.0	64 Class C's	16,382
/19	255.255.224.0	32 Class C's	8,190
/20	255.255.240	16 Class C's	4,094
/21	255.255.248.0	8 Class C's	2,046
/22	255.255.252.0	4 Class C's	1,022
/23	255.255.254.0	2 Class C's	510
/24	255.255.255.0	1 Class C	254
/25	255.255.255.128	1/2 Class C	126
/26	255.255.255.192	1/4 Class C	62
/27	255.255.255.224	1/8 Class C	30
/28	255.255.255.240	1/16 Class C	14
/29	255.255.255.248	1/32 Class C	6
/30	255.255.255.252	1/64 Class C	2
/31	255.255.255.254	1/128 Class C	0
/32	255.255.255.255	1/256 Class C (1 host)	– (1 host route)

**All possible mask lengths are shown, for /1 to /32. The /0 mask matches the whole Internet and will be discussed in the routing chapters.*

The /31 Prefix

In many cases, a /31 prefix that allows only two IPv4 addresses on a subnet is useless. Hosts are not normally assigned addresses that indicate the network itself (the lowest address on the subnet) or the directed broadcast (the highest address on the subnet). Because a /31 prefix only allows the final bit to be 0 or 1, this prefix is not useful for a subnet with hosts. Most subnets normally use a /30 prefix at most, which yields two useful host addresses in addition to the low and high addresses.

However, many router networks employ the /31 prefix to address the endpoints of a point-to-point link such as SONET/SDH. There are no hosts to worry about, and only the router network need worry about the use of internal address spaces. With /31 prefixes, a single Class C address space can be used to provide addresses for 128 (256 divided by 2) point-to-point inter-router links, not just 64 (256 divided by 4).

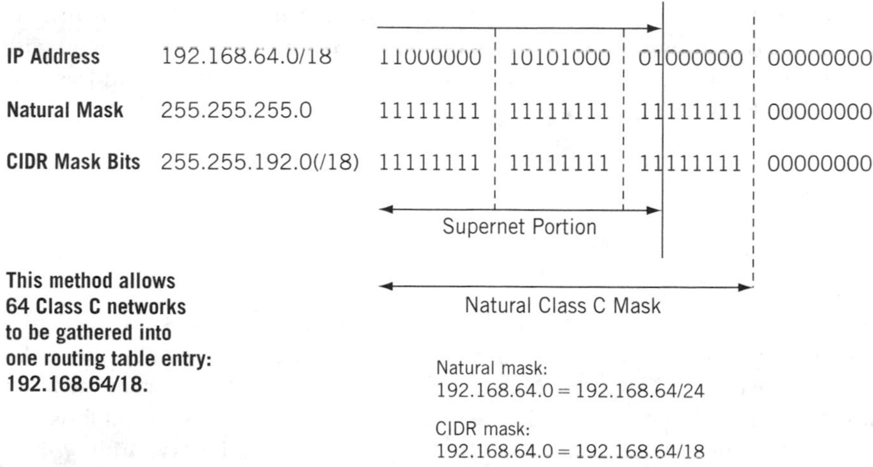

FIGURE 4.6

CIDR in operation. Basically, supernetting moves the natural mask to the left while subnetting moves it to the right.

CIDR allowed the creation of a network such as `192.168.64.0/18` with 16,384 hosts (14 bits remain for the host portion of the `192.168.64.0` network) instead of requiring 64 separate IP network addresses to be assigned and configured. CIDR did more than allow the grouping of contiguous Class C addresses into bigger networks than possible before. Once the principle was established, CIDR allowed the *aggregation* of all possible IP addresses under the specified prefix into this one compact notation. This kept routing table sizes under control in the late 1990s.

Where does VLSM fit in? As mentioned, VLSM applied more to hosts and a single routing domain. Basically, in the days of classful IP addressing, all subnets of the same address had to have the same mask length. So you could, for example, subnet `10.0.0.0/8` into `10.0.0.0/16` subnets, but *every* device on *every* subnet had to have the same `/16` mask. This could be okay if all the subnetted LANs had roughly the same number of hosts, but what about point-to-point links between routers on the subnet? They could get by with a `/31` or `/30` mask because there were only two endpoints, but they had to have room for the same thousands of hosts as the rest of the `/16`.

Note that the Illustrated Network is an offender: The links between our routers use `/24` masks for point-to-point links. We would not do this in the real world, but it will help our understanding of simple examples when we turn to routing later in this book.

IPv6 ADDRESSING DETAILS

Let's take a quick look at some of the differences between IPv4 and IPv6 addressing. The use of the IPv6 address space is determined by the value of the first few bits of an IPv6 address. Routing in IPv6 is similar to IPv4 with CIDR and VLSM, but there are a few points to be made to clarify this.

IPv6 addresses can be *provider based*, *provider independent*, or for *local use*. All provider-based IPv6 addresses for "aggregatable" global unicast packets begin with either 0010 (2) or 0011 (3) in the first four bit positions of the 128-bit IPv6 address.

Typical IPv6 address prefixes would look like:

```
2001:0400::/23
2001:05FF::/29
2001:0408::/35
```

and so on.

The 64 bits that make up the low-order bits of the IPv6 address must be in a format known as the EUI-64 (64-bit Extended Unique Identifier). Normally, the 48-bit MAC address consists of 3 bytes (24 bits) assigned to the manufacturer and 3 bytes (24 bits) for the serial number of the NIC itself. A typical MAC address would look like 0000:900F:C27E. The next to the last bit in the first byte of this address is the *global/local* bit, and is usually set to a 0 bit (global). This means that the MAC address is globally assigned and is using the native address assigned by the manufacturer. In EUI-64 format, this bit is flipped and usually ends up being set to a 1 bit (the *meaning* is flipped too, so in IPv6, 1 here means *global*). This would make the first byte 02 instead of 00. For example, 0000:900F:C27E becomes 0200:900F:C27E (not always, but this is just a simple example).

To convert a MAC address to a 64-bit address that can be used on an interface for the host portion of an IPv6 address, we insert the string FFFE between the manufacturer and the serial number fields of the MAC address (between the first and the last 3 bytes). The MAC address becomes 0200:90FF:FE0F:C27E. This is more easily shown as follows:

- MAC address: 0200:900F:C27E
- Split in half: 0200:90 0F:C27E
- Insert FFFE: FF FE
- Form EUI-64: 0200:90FF:FE0F:C27E

Link-local IPv6 addresses begin with 1111 1110 1000 (FE80 in hexadecimal, making the first two bytes FE80 if all of the trailing 6 bits in the second byte are 0 bits). ULA local addresses are in the form FC00::/7. In IPv6, interfaces are expected to have multiple addresses, a shift from IPv4. It's common to find three IPv6 addresses on an interface: global, link local, and site local. It is also common to use multiple link-local addresses, one based on the MAC and the other based on random numbers.

Both forms usually end with the 48-bit IEEE MAC address, but again with the added FFFE bits to form the EUI-64 identifier. The FC00 ULA address forms are used as the *private addresses* in IPv6 (just as 10.0.0.0 and the others in IPv4), and that's how they are used in this book.

IPv6 addresses appear in sources and outputs about equally with capitals (FE80) or lower case (fe80), and we'll see both. (In the RFCs, however, these are universally capitalized.) The major formats of the IPv6 address are shown in Figure 4.7.

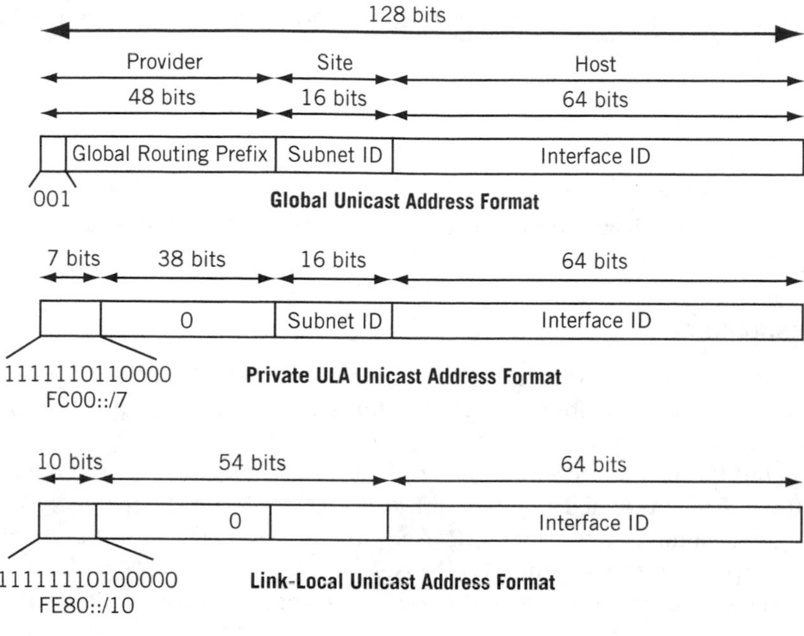

FIGURE 4.7

Major IPv6 address formats, showing how the value of the initial bits determine format. The FC00 address format is often used as private IPv6 address.

Two routers connected by a small LAN can use the link-local IPv6 address of `FE80::<EUI-64 formatted MAC address>` on their interfaces. This type of address is never advertised by an IPv6 router attached to the Internet, and it cannot be used across subnets. On point-to-point links, a distinguishing identifier of the interface card other than the MAC address can be used at the end of the link-local address.

ULA-L addresses can include a 16-bit subnet field, so these forms of private IPv6 addresses *can* be used across subnets (through routers), but these addresses are not usually advertised onto the Internet. Using link-local and ULA-local IPv6 addresses, an organization can build an entire global network, but usually only if none of the traffic tries to travel across the Internet. If it does, IPv6 provider-based addresses are needed. This is similar to building a complete corporate network in IPv4 using the `10.0.0.0` private address space, but using Network Address Translation (NAT) for traffic that must travel across the Internet. However, in IPv6, hosts are assigned multiple addresses, some global and some local. In this case, the lower order bits (80 bits) of the site-local address (subnet and interface) are just pasted onto the higher fields (48 bits) of the provider-based forms of the IPv6 address.

What about private masks and routing in IPv6? As shown above, prefix masks in IPv6 have the same general form as prefix masks in IPv4. Here is a sample IPv6 link-local host address (this time in lower case hex notation) and one possible network prefix for it:

```
fe80::90:69ff:fea0:8000/128
fe80:: /64
```

As in keeping with all of the addresses used in this book, this IPv6 address is a private address. The `/64` mask tells the router that the first 64 bits of the address are to be used for routing purposes.

IP Address Assignment

Most people get IP addresses from their ISP. But where do ISPs get their IP addresses? Large organizations can still apply for their own IP addresses independent from any ISP. To whom do they apply?

IP addresses (and the Internet domain names associated with them) were initially handed out by the Internet Assigned Number Authority (IANA). Today the Internet Corporation for Assigned Names and Numbers (ICANN), an international nonprofit organization, oversees the process of assigning IP addresses.

Actual IP addresses are handed out by the following Regional Internet Registries (RIRs):

- ARIN (American Registry for Internet Numbers) at *www.arin.net*—ARIN has handed out IP addresses for North and South America, the Caribbean, and Africa below the Sahara since 1997.
- RIPE NCC (Reseaux IP European Network Coordination Center) at *www.ripe.net*—RIPE assigns IP addresses in Europe and surrounding areas.
- APNIC (Asian Pacific Network Information Center) at *www.apnic.net*—APNIC assigns IP addresses in 62 countries and regions in Central Asia, Southeast Asia, Indochina, and Oceania.
- LACNIC (Latin American and Caribbean Network Information Center) at *www.lacnic.net*—LACNIC assigns IP addresses from ARIN in 38 countries, including Mexico.
- AfriNIC (African Network Information Center) at *www.afrinic.net*—AfriNIC took over assignment of African IP addresses from ARIN.

All of these Internet Registries databases (who has what IP address space?) combined are known as the Internet Routing Registry (IRR). Internet domain names comprise a related activity, but (like IP addresses) names must be globally unique and (unlike IP addresses) can be almost anything.

For the latest information on IP address assignment, which is always subject to change, see *www.icann.org*.

When it comes to IPv6, in particular, IANA still hands out addresses to the registries, which pass them along to IPv6 ISPs, who allocate IPv6 addresses to their customers.

The current policy is given at *www.arin.net/policy.* An older policy is used in this chapter (see *www.arin.net/policy/ipv6_policy.html*) and uses these prefixes at each step of the process:

- `2001::/16` is reserved for IANA.
- IANA hands out a `/23` prefix to each registry.
- Registry hands out a `/32` or shorter prefix to an IPv6 ISP.
- ISP allocates a `/48` prefix for each customer site.
- Local administrators add 16 bits for each LAN on their network, for a `/64` prefix.

This scheme is shown in Figure 4.8. When the LAN is included, most IPv6 addresses have `/64` network masks. This is the prefix length used on the Illustrated Network. IPv6 routers can perform the following tasks:

- Route traffic to a particular ISP based on the first 32 bits of the IPv6 destination address.
- Route traffic to a particular site based on the first 48 bits of the IPv6 destination address.
- Route traffic to a particular LAN based on the first 64 bits of the IPv6 destination address.

In practice, IPv6 core routers can look at (and build forwarding tables based on) `/32` or shorter prefixes, routers inside a particular AS (routing domain) can look at `/48` prefixes, and site routers on the customer edge can look at `/64` prefixes to get traffic right to the destination LAN.

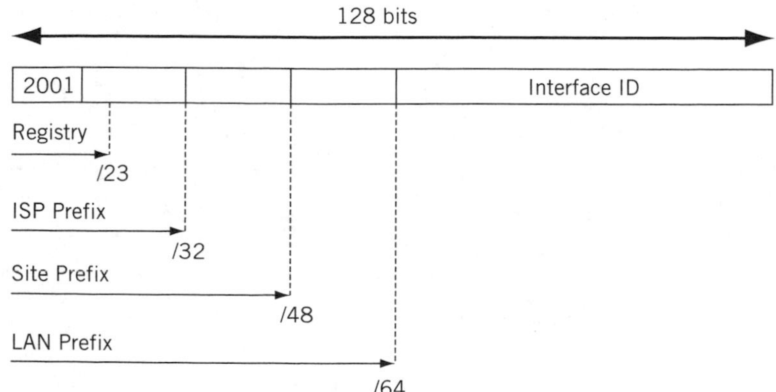

FIGURE 4.8

IPv6 address allocation, showing how various bits should be assigned by different entities. In some places, mobile phone providers are heavy users of IPv6 addresses.

Now we can better understand the IPv6 address assigned to `CE0` that we saw at the beginning of the chapter:

```
FC00:ffb3:d5:b:205:85ff:fe88:ccdb
```

or

```
FC00:FFB3:00D5:000B:0205:75FF:FE88:CCDB
```

Let's break it down one element at a time and see where it all comes from:

- *Registry*—We use `FC00` instead of `2001` to indicate a private ULA-local IPv6 address.
- *ISP*—We add Best ISP's AS number of `65459` (`0xFFB3`) for LAN 1 or Ace ISP's AS number `65127` (`0xFE67`) for LAN2.
- *Site*—We add telephony area code `213` (`0x00D5`) for the Los Angeles or `212` (`0x00D4`) for New York sites. (We could always use more of the phone number, but this is enough.)
- *LAN*—We add 11 (`0x000B`) for LAN1 or 12 (`0x000C`) for LAN 2. These are borrowed from the IPv4 addresses.
- *EUI-64*—We add `0x0205 85FF FE88 CCDB` for the hardware MAC address.

The mask is `/64`, naturally. Keep in mind that in the real world, none of this complex coding would be done.

QUESTIONS FOR READERS

Figure 4.9 shows some of the concepts discussed in this chapter and can be used to help you answer the following questions.

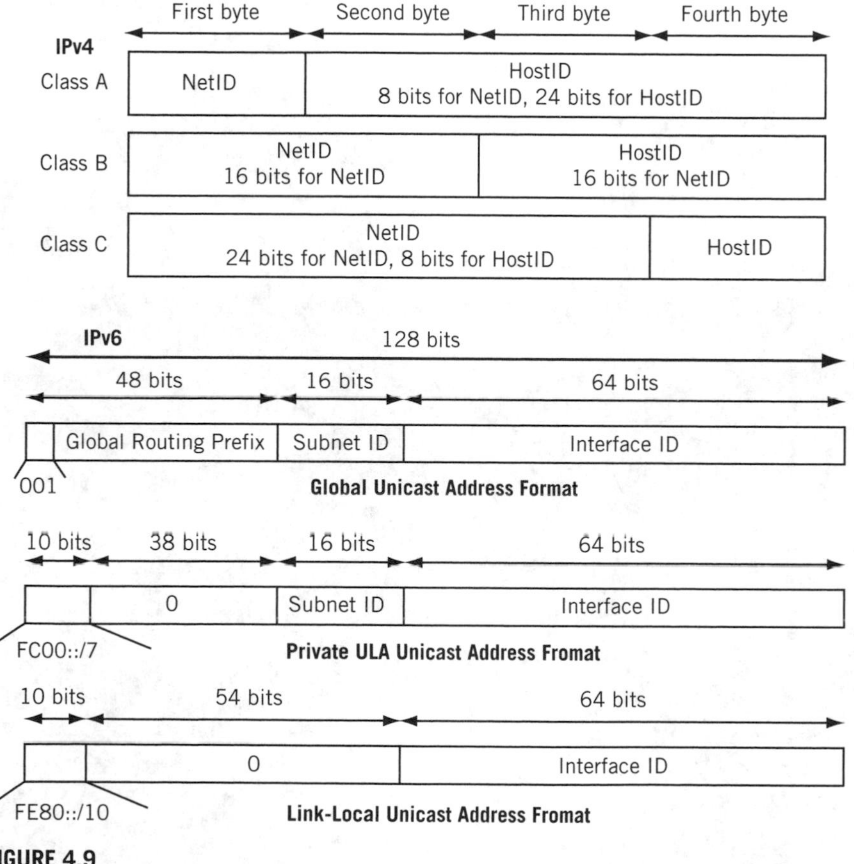

FIGURE 4.9

Some major IPv4 and IPv6 address formats, showing classes in IPv4 and FE80 FC00 IPv6 addresses.

1. How many bits make up IPv4 and IPv6 addresses?
2. Which special address formats make up the IPv4 network itself and directed broadcast (all hosts on the subnet) addresses?
3. How many hosts can be configured with an IPv4 network mask of `255.255.255.240`?
4. What are the differences in format and use between IPv6 link-local and private ULA-local addresses?
5. How many "double colons" (: :) can appear in an IPv6 address?

CHAPTER

Address Resolution Protocol

5

What You Will Learn

In this chapter, you will learn about the hardware addressing used in the data link layer frame and how it is found by the sender. We'll talk a lot about the hardware addresses used on LANs, the MAC addresses.

You will learn about the ARP protocol, which is how IP stacks on LANs identify the hardware address that the destination field of the frame should use.

The Internet, or any internetwork, is made up of a combination of physical networks such as LANs and internetworking devices such as routers. A packet sent by a host might pass through several different physical networks before finally reaching its destination.

The hosts and routers at the network layer are identified by their network addresses (also called logical addresses). In TCP/IP, the network or logical address is the IP address, as we saw in the last chapter. These addresses are usually implemented in software, and must be globally unique on the Internet. At the data link layer, the interface that sends and receives frames is identified by the physical or hardware address. An example of a hardware address is the 48-bit MAC address we have been seeing at the frame level. (See Figure 5.1.)

The hardware address and the network address are two different identifiers with different sizes, but we need both of them. Layered protocol stacks can use different types of packets (such as IPv4 and IPv6) on the same Ethernet. Also, IPv4 packets can be sent over an Ethernet link and then over a point-to-point link with a very different frame structure.

However, we need some way to map back and forth between addresses at the network and hardware levels. In TCP/IP, this mapping is provided by the address resolution protocols (the technical term is *bindings*). ARP results are stored in an *ARP cache* on a host so that the entire process does not have to be constantly repeated.

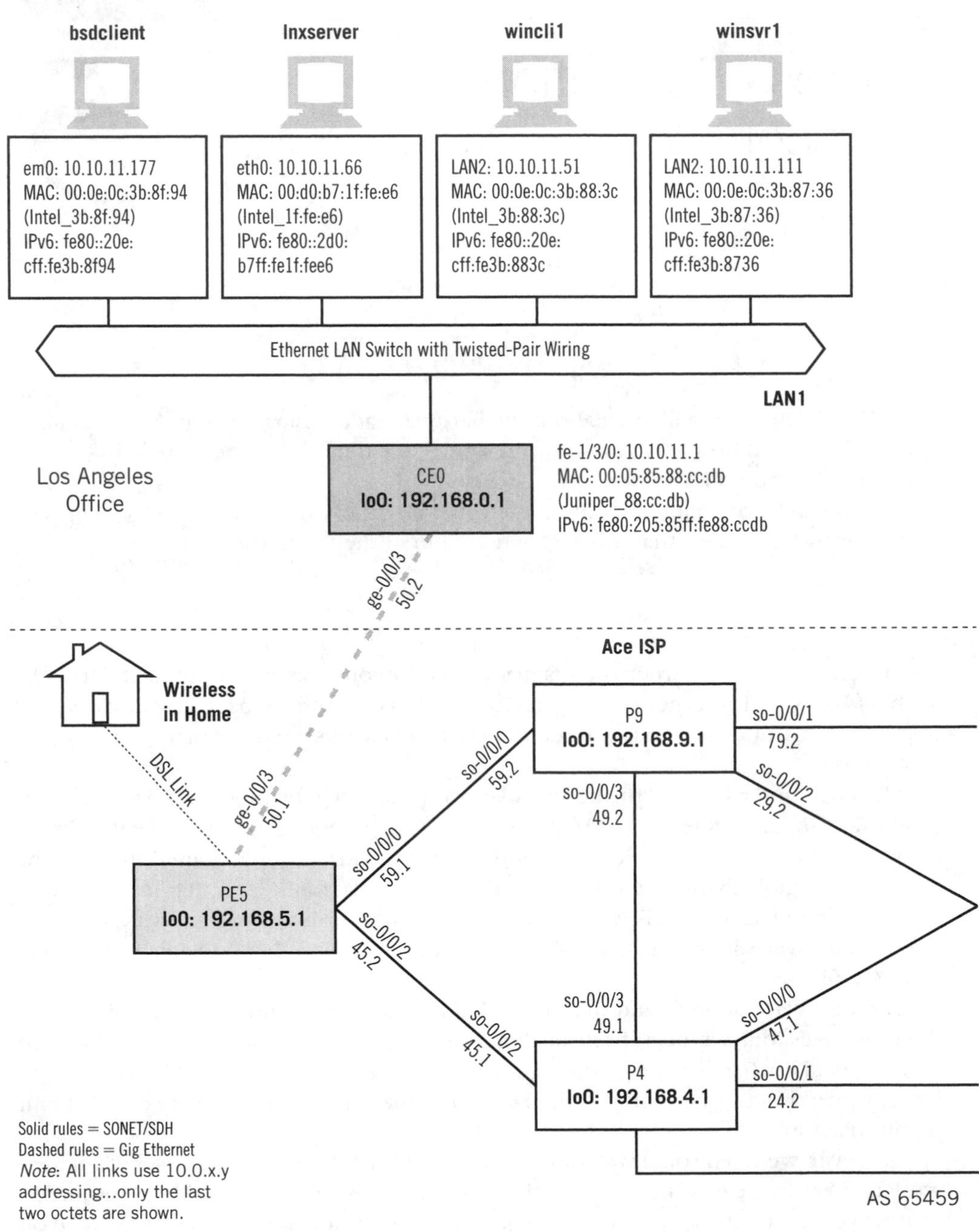

FIGURE 5.1

ARP on the Illustrated Network, showing that devices on the LANs employ ARP to determine hardware (MAC) addresses.

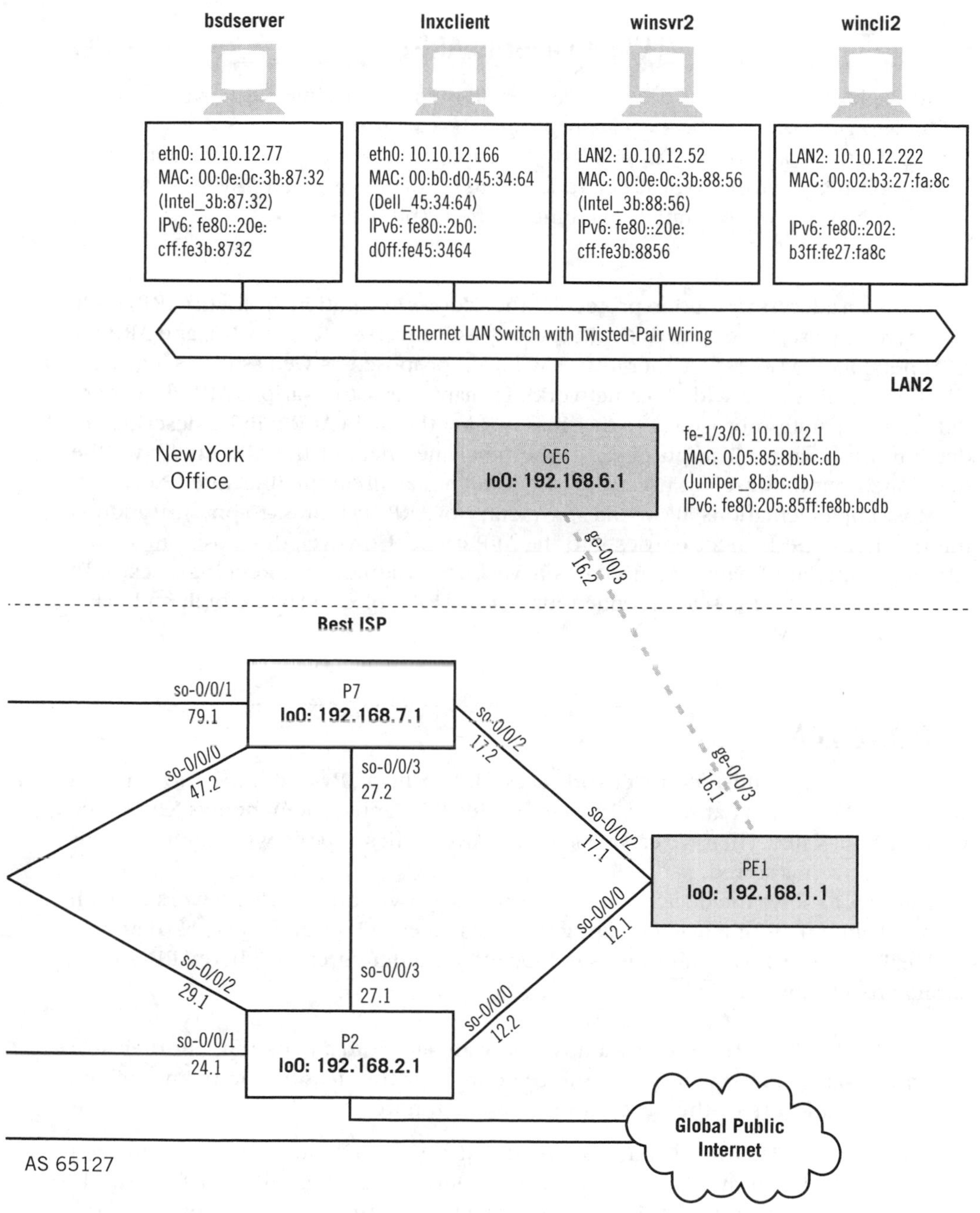
bsdserver
lnxclient
winsvr2
wincli2
eth0: 10.10.12.77
MAC: 00:0e:0c:3b:87:32
(Intel_3b:87:32)
IPv6: fe80::20e:
cff:fe3b:8732
eth0: 10.10.12.166
MAC: 00:b0:d0:45:34:64
(Dell_45:34:64)
IPv6: fe80::2b0:
d0ff:fe45:3464
LAN2: 10.10.12.52
MAC: 00:0e:0c:3b:88:56
(Intel_3b:88:56)
IPv6: fe80::20e:
cff:fe3b:8856
LAN2: 10.10.12.222
MAC: 00:02:b3:27:fa:8c
IPv6: fe80::202:
b3ff:fe27:fa8c
Ethernet LAN Switch with Twisted-Pair Wiring
LAN2
New York
Office
CE6
lo0: 192.168.6.1
fe-1/3/0: 10.10.12.1
MAC: 0:05:85:8b:bc:db
(Juniper_8b:bc:db)
IPv6: fe80:205:85ff:fe8b:bcdb
ge-0/0/3
16.2
Best ISP
so-0/0/1
79.1
P7
lo0: 192.168.7.1
so-0/0/0
47.2
so-0/0/3
27.2
so-0/0/2
17.2
ge-0/0/3
16.1
so-0/0/2
17.1
PE1
lo0: 192.168.1.1
so-0/0/0
12.1
so-0/0/2
29.1
so-0/0/3
27.1
so-0/0/0
12.2
so-0/0/1
24.1
P2
lo0: 192.168.2.1
Global Public
Internet
AS 65127

What Layer Is ARP?

Although often shown at the same layer as IP because the messages ride inside frames, as in this book, the ARPs are really in a class all by themselves. Some authors describe them as a "high" data link layer function, but they are more of a boundary function between the logical network and its physical hardware. Also, ARPs are not really protocols, but rather mapping methods (bindings).

The main address resolution protocol is the Address Resolution Protocol (ARP) itself, but there are also Reverse ARP (RARP), proxy ARP, Inverse ARP (InARP), and ARP for ATM networks (ATMARP). Other ARPs have been proposed as well (such as a generic "WARP" for ARPs on a wide area network). In many ways, the various ARP flavors are not really separate protocols. For that reason, only the main ARP will be described in detail in this chapter. The purposes of the other members of the ARP family will be mentioned, but they are not used very often, and not at all on the Illustrated Network.

Most implementations allow the *static* entry of ARP IP-address-to-physical-address information as permanent entries into the ARP cache. However, this poses an administrative nightmare (many organizations have a hard enough time keeping track of IP addresses alone) and is seldom done today. Most ARP tables today are built and maintained dynamically.

ARP AND LANs

Let's see how the Illustrated Network uses ARP to map IPv4 addresses to physical addresses. We can look at some ARPs sent by FreeBSD, Linux, and Windows XP, and see what they look like. Then we can examine the ARP caches and see what information is kept and how it is stored.

Figure 5.1 shows the devices on the Illustrated Network that we'll be working with in this chapter. This time we'll be using the hosts on each LAN and a pair of routers.

We'll use these hosts and routers to look at four different cases where ARP is used, as shown in Figure 5.2.

Host to host—The ARP sender is a host and wants to send a packet to another host on the same LAN. In this case, the IP address of the destination is known and the MAC address of the destination must be found.

Host to router—The ARP sender is a host and wants to send a packet to another host on a different LAN. A forwarding (routing) table is used to find the IP address of the router. In this case, the IP address of the router is known and the MAC address of the router must be found.

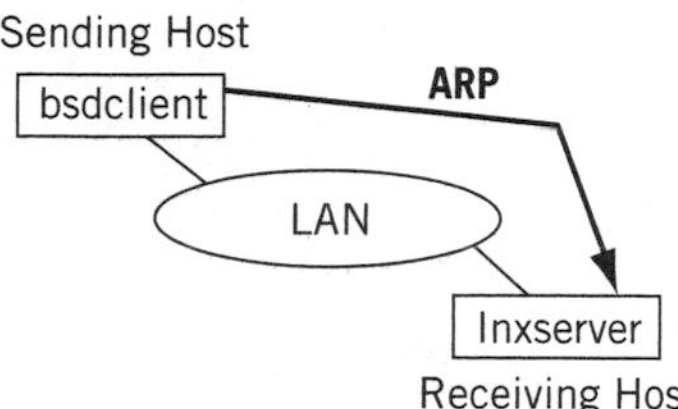
Case 1: Find the address
of a host on the same
subnet as the source.
Sending Host
bsdclient
ARP
LAN
lnxserver
Receiving Host

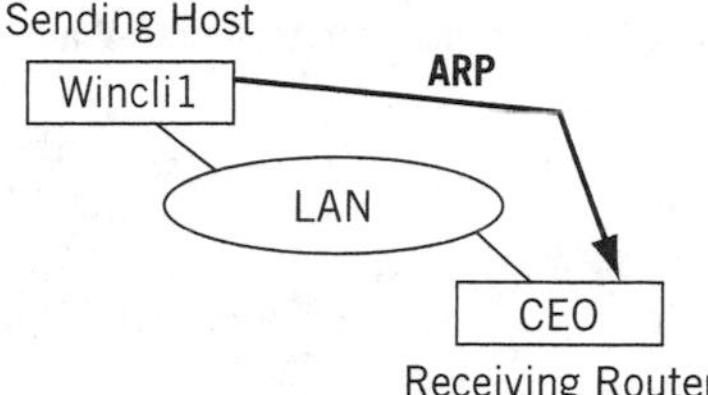
Case 2: Find the address
of a router on the same
subnet as the source.
Sending Host
Wincli1
ARP
LAN
CE0
Receiving Router

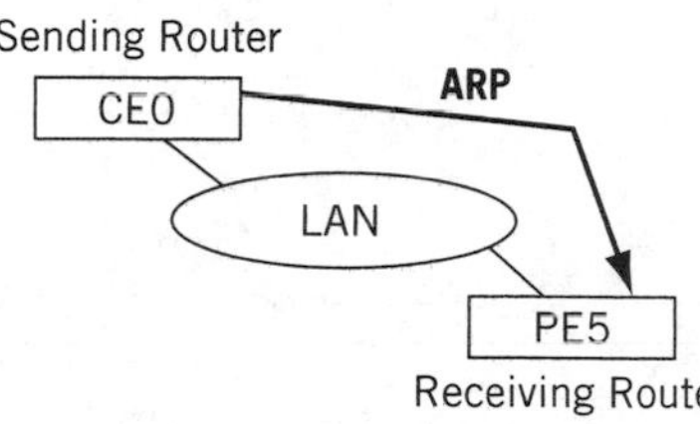
Case 3: Find the address
of a router on the same
subnet as the source router.
Sending Router
CE0
ARP
LAN
PE5
Receiving Router

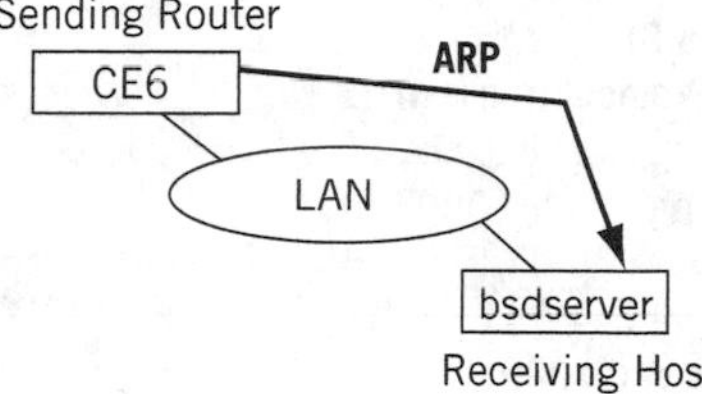
Case 4: Find the address
of a host on the same
subnet as the source router.
Sending Router
CE6
ARP
LAN
bsdserver
Receiving Host

FIGURE 5.2

Four ARP scenarios. Note that routers employ ARP just as hosts do, and that an ARP stays on the same subnet as the sender.

Router to router—The ARP sender is a router and wants to forward a packet to another router on the same LAN. A forwarding (routing) table is used to find the IP address of the router. In this case, the IP address of the router is known and the MAC address of the destination router must be found.

Router to host—The ARP sender is a router and wants to forward a packet to a host on the same LAN. In this case, the IP address of the host is known (from the IP destination address on the packet) and the MAC address of the host must be found.

Let's look at Case 1 in detail because the others are more or less variations on this basic theme. In Case 1, ARP is used when a host wants to send to another host on the same IP subnet and the MAC address of the destination is not already known. We'll start the LAN2 host `lnxclient` sending a short message to `winsrv2` (it doesn't really matter what the message is). Because this is the first time that these devices have communicated in a long time, an ARP request is broadcast on LAN2 and the sender waits for a reply.

Now let's capture the ARP request and response pair on the `lnxclient` host at IPv4 address 10.10.12.166. We'll set a filter to only capture and display ARP packets.

```
root@lnxclient admin]# /usr/sbin/tethereal -V arp
Capturing on eth0
Frame 1 (42 bytes on wire, 42 bytes captured)
   Arrival Time: May  5, 2008 22:13:40.148457000
   Time delta from previous packet: 0.000000000 seconds
   Time relative to first packet: 0.000000000 seconds
   Frame Number: 1
   Packet Length: 42 bytes
   Capture Length: 42 bytes
Ethernet II, Src: 00:b0:d0:45:34:64, Dst: ff:ff:ff:ff:ff:ff
   Destination: ff:ff:ff:ff:ff:ff (Broadcast)
   Source: 00:b0:d0:45:34:64 (Dell_45:34:64)
   Type: ARP (0x0806)
Address Resolution Protocol (request)
   Hardware type: Ethernet (0x0001)
   Protocol type: IP (0x0800)
   Hardware size: 6
   Protocol size: 4
   Opcode: request (0x0001)
   Sender MAC address: 00:b0:d0:45:34:64 (Dell_45:34:64)
   Sender IP address: 10.10.12.166 (10.10.12.166)
   Target MAC address: 00:00:00:00:00:00 (00:00:00_00:00:00)
   Target IP address: 10.10.12.52 (10.10.12.52)
Frame 2 (106 bytes on wire, 106 bytes captured)
   Arrival Time: May  5, 2008 22:13:40.148642000
   Time delta from previous packet: 0.000185000 seconds
   Time relative to first packet: 0.000185000 seconds
   Frame Number: 2
   Packet Length: 106 bytes
   Capture Length: 106 bytes
Ethernet II, Src: 00:0e:0c:3b:88:56, Dst: 00:b0:d0:45:34:64
   Destination: 00:b0:d0:45:34:64 (Dell_45:34:64)
   Source: 00:0e:0c:3b:88:56 (00:0e:0c:3b:88:56)
   Type: ARP (0x0806)
   Trailer: 00000000000000000000000000000000...
Address Resolution Protocol (reply)
   Hardware type: Ethernet (0x0001)
   Protocol type: IP (0x0800)
   Hardware size: 6
   Protocol size: 4
   Opcode: reply (0x0002)
   Sender MAC address: 00:0e:0c:3b:88:56 (00:0e:0c:3b:88:56)
   Sender IP address: 10.10.12.52 (10.10.12.52)
   Target MAC address: 00:b0:d0:45:34:64 (Dell_45:34:64)
   Target IP address: 10.10.12.166 (10.10.12.166)
```

We'll look at the fields of an ARP in detail later. For now, note that the ARP request, indicated by a `0x0806` in the Ethertype field goes out as a broadcast frame with an all-zero MAC address field. It's looking for the MAC address that goes with IP address `10.10.12.52` (`winsrv2`), the target IP address. The ARP reply frame returns the reply with the correct MAC address plugged into the all-zero field (and with the MAC address as the source address in the frame).

The results of an ARP pair between the `bsdclient` host (`10.10.11.177`) and the `lnxserver` host (`10.10.11.66`) is almost the same, but not quite. The frame sent in reply to the ARP is smaller than before.

```
bsdclient# tethereal -V arp
Capturing on em0
Frame 1 (42 bytes on wire, 42 bytes captured)
   Arrival Time: May 5, 2008 22:24:04.518213000
   Time delta from previous packet: 0.000000000 seconds
   Time since reference or first frame: 0.000000000 seconds
   Frame Number: 1
   Packet Length: 42 bytes
   Capture Length: 42 bytes
Ethernet II, Src: 00:0e:0c:3b:8f:94, Dst: ff:ff:ff:ff:ff:ff
   Destination: ff:ff:ff:ff:ff:ff (Broadcast)
   Source: 00:0e:0c:3b:8f:94 (10.10.11.177)
   Type: ARP (0x0806)
Address Resolution Protocol (request)
   Hardware type: Ethernet (0x0001)
   Protocol type: IP (0x0800)
   Hardware size: 6
   Protocol size: 4
   Opcode: request (0x0001)
   Sender MAC address: 00:0e:0c:3b:8f:94 (10.10.11.177)
   Sender IP address: 10.10.11.177 (10.10.11.177)
   Target MAC address: 00:00:00:00:00:00 (00:00:00_00:00:00)
   Target IP address: 10.10.11.66 (10.10.11.66)
Frame 2 (60 bytes on wire, 60 bytes captured)
   Arrival Time: May 5, 2008 22:24:04.518421000
   Time delta from previous packet: 0.000208000 seconds
   Time since reference or first frame: 0.000208000 seconds
   Frame Number: 2
   Packet Length: 60 bytes
   Capture Length: 60 bytes
Ethernet II, Src: 00:d0:b7:1f:fe:e6, Dst: 00:0e:0c:3b:8f:94
   Destination: 00:0e:0c:3b:8f:94 (10.10.11.177)
   Source: 00:d0:b7:1f:fe:e6 (10.10.11.66)
   Type: ARP (0x0806)
   Trailer: 000000000000000000000000000000000000
Address Resolution Protocol (reply)
   Hardware type: Ethernet (0x0001)
```

```
Protocol type: IP (0x0800)
Hardware size: 6
Protocol size: 4
Opcode: reply (0x0002)
Sender MAC address: 00:d0:b7:1f:fe:e6 (10.10.11.66)
Sender IP address: 10.10.11.66 (10.10.11.66)
Target MAC address: 00:0e:0c:3b:8f:94 (10.10.11.177)
Target IP address: 10.10.11.177 (10.10.11.177)
```

The reply from the Linux system is only 60 bytes, 46 bytes less than the response from the Windows XP server in the first example. That's interesting; let's take a closer look at what Windows XP is doing. Figure 5.3 shows a graphical capture of the reply from `winsrv2` (`10.10.12.52`) to an ARP request from `wincli2` (`10.10.12.222`).

The reply is indeed 106 bytes long, but the extra bits are all zeros. The only difference in the replies is the number of trailing zeroes in the frame. And we can also see that the ARP software can deal with these easily.

We've already mentioned that ARP results are cached. The devices that send the ARP requests cache the results, and the device that receives the ARP usually also caches the MAC address in the arriving ARP request. The idea is that if one device in a pair

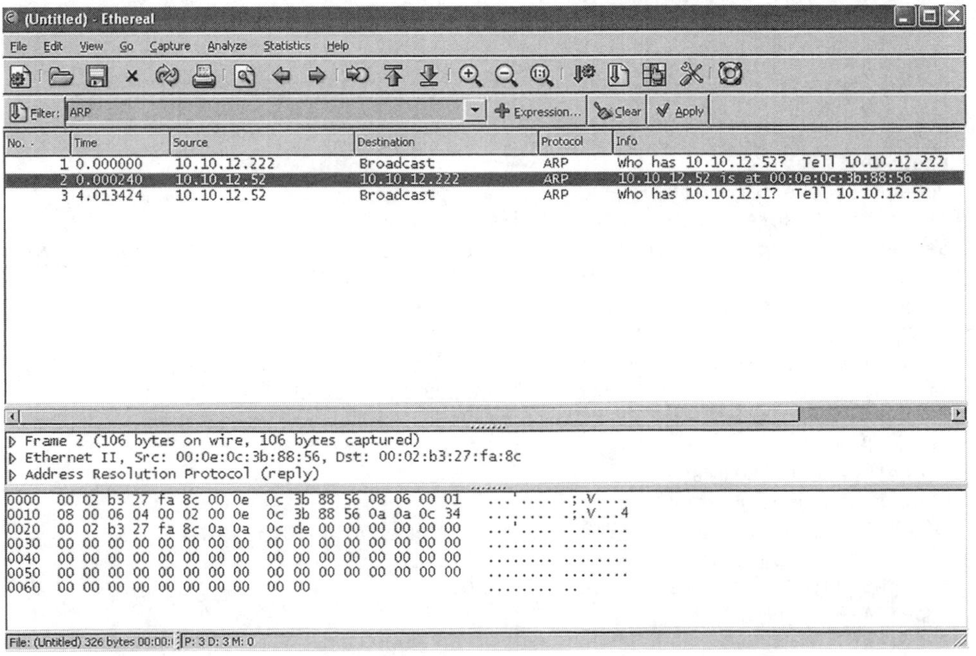

FIGURE 5.3

Windows XP ARP reply capture. The ARP message, in this case an ARP reply, is encapsulated directly inside the Ethernet frame.

sends in one direction, the other device in the pair will probably send in the opposite direction as well.

Let's look at the ARP cache on the `bsdserver` host (`10.10.12.77`) using the `-a` (all) option.

```
bsdserver# arp -a
? (10.10.12.1) at 00:05:85:8b:bc:db on em0 [ethernet]
? (10.10.12.52) at 00:0e:0c:3b:88:56 on em0 [ethernet]
? (10.10.12.166) at 00:b0:d0:45:34:64 on em0 [ethernet]
? (10.10.12.222) at 00:02:b3:27:fa:8c on em0 [ethernet]
```

All four other devices on LAN2 are represented. The question marks are there because we have no DNS running at the moment. Let's see if we can add to the cache by sending a ping to the Windows XP server (`winsrv1`) on LAN1.

```
bsdserver# ping 10.10.11.111
PING 10.10.11.111 (10.10.11.111): 56 data bytes
64 bytes from 10.10.11.111: icmp_seq=0 ttl=126 time=0.403 ms
64 bytes from 10.10.11.111: icmp_seq=1 ttl=126 time=0.413 ms
64 bytes from 10.10.11.111: icmp_seq=2 ttl=126 time=0.376 ms
^C
--- 10.10.11.111 ping statistics ---
3 packets transmitted, 3 packets received, 0% packet loss
round trip min/avg/max/stddev = 0.376/0.397/0.413/0.016 ms
bsdserver# arp -a
? (10.10.12.1) at 00:05:85:8b:bc:db on em0 [ethernet]
? (10.10.12.52) at 00:0e:0c:3b:88:56 on em0 [ethernet]
? (10.10.12.166) at 00:b0:d0:45:34:64 on em0 [ethernet]
? (10.10.12.222) at 00:02:b3:27:fa:8c on em0 [ethernet]
```

Nothing was added to the ARP cache on the FreeBSD server. Why should it be? The other host is only reachable through a router, and the router's ARP entry is already there (`10.10.12.1`). These types of ARPs, the most common, are only used when the destination is on the same LAN subnet as the source.

Usually, entries in the ARP cache are deleted when no communication occurs with another device, usually after 300 seconds (5 minutes) of silence between the devices. We can force the ARP cache to empty by using the `-d` (delete) option.

```
bsdserver# arp -d -a
10.10.12.1 (10.10.12.1) deleted
10.10.12.52 (10.10.12.52) deleted
10.10.12.166 (10.10.12.166) deleted
10.10.12.222 (10.10.12.222) deleted
```

In Linux, the command to display the ARP cache is the same (`arp`), but the `-e` option displays the result in the "default" Linux format (using no option gives the same result). The "C" means that the entry is "complete."

```
[root@lnxserver admin]# /sbin/arp
Address          HWtype        HWaddress          Flags Mask       Iface
10.10.11.1       ether       00:05:85:88:CC:DB     C               eth0
10.10.11.111     ether       00:0E:0C:3B:88:3C     C               eth0
10.10.11.177     ether       00:0E:0C:3B:8F:94     C               eth0
10.10.11.51      ether       00:0E:0C:3B:87:36     C               eth0
[root@lnxserver admin]# /sbin/arp -e
Address          HWtype        HWaddress          Flags Mask       Iface
10.10.11.1       ether       00:05:85:88:CC:DB     C               eth0
10.10.11.111     ether       00:0E:0C:3B:88:3C     C               eth0
10.10.11.177     ether       00:0E:0C:3B:8F:94     C               eth0
10.10.11.51      ether       00:0E:0C:3B:87:36     C               eth0
```

In Linux, use of the `-a` option displays the results in "BSD" style. The output is still slightly different, however.

```
[root@lnxserver admin]# /sbin/arp -a
? (10.10.11.1) at 00:05:85:88:CC:DB [ether] on eth0
? (10.10.11.111) at 00:0E:0C:3B:88:3C [ether] on eth0
? (10.10.11.177) at 00:0E:0C:3B:8F:94 [ether] on eth0
? (10.10.11.51) at 00:0E:0C:3B:87:36 [ether] on eth0
```

Windows XP displays the ARP cache with `arp -a` as well. This output is from `winsrv2` on LAN2.

```
C:\Documents and Settings\Owner>arp -a
Interface: 10.10.12.52 --- 0x1003
  Internet Address      Physical Address        Type
10.10.12.1            00-05-85-8b-bc-db        dynamic
10.10.12.77           00-0e-0c-3b-87-32        dynamic
10.10.12.166          00-b0-d0-45-34-64        dynamic
10.10.12.222          00-02-b3-27-fa-8c        dynamic
```

The term *dynamic* distinguishes these entries from statically defined entries.

There is no separate ARP for IPv6. MAC addresses can be embedded in the IPv6 addresses, but this does not solve the problem of a source host knowing the physical address of a destination host or router. When a host uses IPv4-derived IPv6 addresses, such as `::10.10.11.111`, IPv4 ARP information can be used to supply the MAC addresses for IPv6.

The address resolution process in IPv6 uses ICMPv6 messages and is part of the Neighbor Discovery (ND) process. Generally, a multicast Neighbor Solicitation message is sent and a unicast Neighbor Advertisement message is received in reply. We'll talk more about this process in the chapter on ICMPv6. For now, let's just verify that IPv6 address resolution uses ICMPv6 messages.

Ethereal can capture and display IPv6 traffic as well as IPv6. Let's send a test message using the link-local IPv6 addresses from `winsrv1` to `wincli1`, and capture the address resolution in action. We'll capture everything but only display ICMPv6 messages. The result is shown in Figure 5.4.

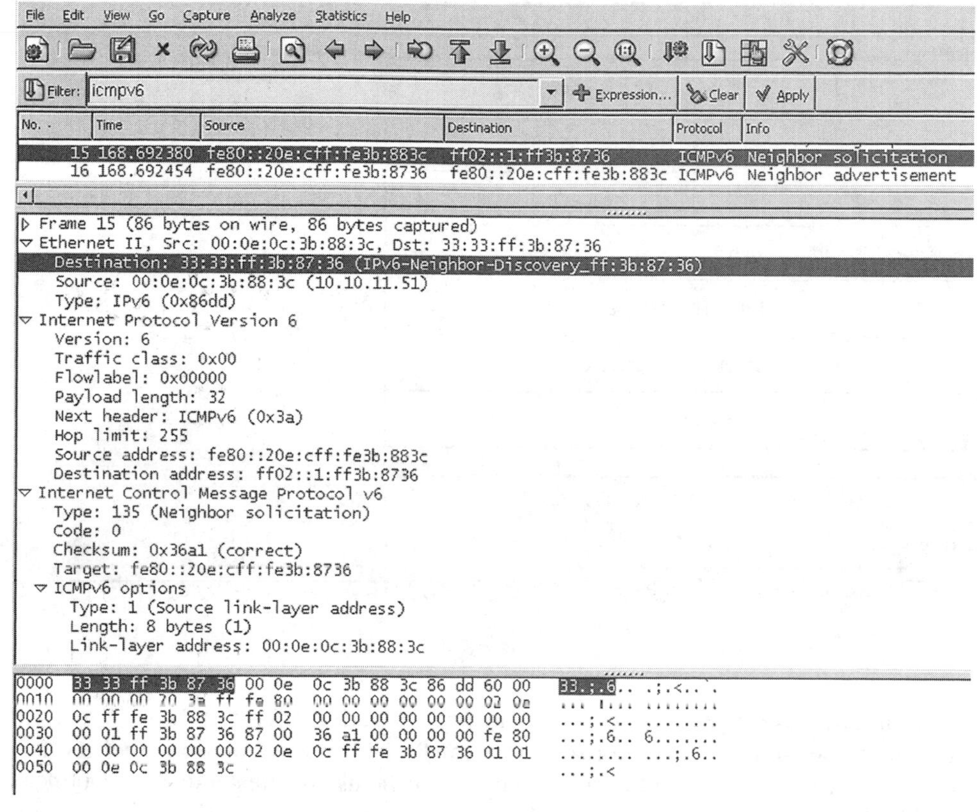

FIGURE 5.4

IPv6 address resolution with ICMPv6, showing that the Neighbor Solicitation frame is sent to the special IPv6 Neighbor Discovery address.

Figure 5.4 shows the details of the Neighbor Solicitation message. The frame destination address is highlighted in the figure, showing that a special multicast frame address is used instead of the ARP broadcast frame address. The major differences between this procedure and the ARP process in IPv4 are that ICMPv6 is used in IPv6, and the solicitation message is sent to the IPv6 multicast group address associated with the target address.

ARP PACKETS

ARP uses packets, but these are not IP packets. ARP messages ride inside Ethernet frames, or any LAN frame, in exactly the same way as IP packets. There is no need to use an IP address here anyway: ARP frames are valid only for a particular LAN segment and never leave the local LAN (i.e., ARP messages cannot be routed). The structure of an ARP message is shown in Figure 5.5.

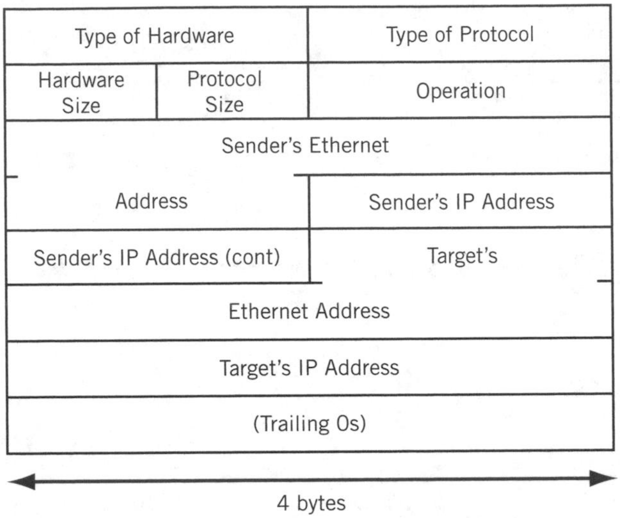

Type of Hardware		Type of Protocol	
Hardware Size	Protocol Size	Operation	
Sender's Ethernet			
Address		Sender's IP Address	
Sender's IP Address (cont)		Target's	
Ethernet Address			
Target's IP Address			
(Trailing 0s)			

4 bytes

FIGURE 5.5

The ARP message's fields. The message is placed directly inside a frame, such as an Ethernet frame.

This figure is because the 28-byte ARP message includes fields 1, 2, 4, and 6 bytes in length, and does not readily lend itself to "normal" 32-bit representation. The first five fields form a type of message header. The next four fields are the sender's and target's IP and MAC addresses. Usually, it's the target's MAC address that needs to be found with the ARP process. And as we have already seen, the ARP message can end with a variable number of trailing zeros.

On an Ethernet LAN, ARP messages have their own Ethertype value (`0x0806`). However, some ARP implementations used the "regular" Ethertype for IP packets (`0x0800`) because the IP implementation itself can easily decide if the information inside the frame is IPv4 (packet starts with `0x04`) or an ARP message (packet starts with `0x0001` for Ethernet).

The main fields are present in both ARP request and ARP reply messages:

Type of Hardware—This 2-byte field is used to identify the style of hardware address. (The Ethernet-style MAC address, with value = 1, is the most common, of course.)

Type of Protocol—This 2-byte field identifies the type of Layer 3, or network layer, protocol that is being queried. (ARP messages, because they are not IP packets, can be used for more than IP addresses.) This uses the same set of values as the Ethertype field, so IP is `0x0800`.

Hardware Size—This byte identifies the size, in bytes, of the hardware address. The Ethernet MAC address is 6 bytes long.

Protocol Size—This byte identifies the size, in bytes, of the Layer 3 protocols. IPv4 addresses are 4 bytes long.

Operation—This 2-byte field identifies the ARP message's intent. For example, an ARP request ("Who has this IPv4 address?") has the operation value of 1 and a reply value of 2.

The rest of the fields do not have a fixed size. Their size is determined by the value in the Hardware Size and Protocol Size fields. On our Ethernet LANs, the hardware address size is 6 bytes (MAC) and the protocol address size is 4 bytes (IPv4). In that case, the sizes and functions of these fields are as follows.

Sender's Ethernet Address—This 6-byte field holds the sender's Ethernet address. It should be the same as the source address in the Ethernet frame.

Sender's IP Address—This 4-byte field holds the sender's Ethernet address. (This is how targets fill in their own ARP caches without requiring more ARPs.)

Target's Ethernet Address—This 6-byte field holds the target's Ethernet address. This field in set to all 0 bits in a request. The reply will have this field filled in and the operation changed to "reply."

Target's IP Address—This 4-byte field holds the target's IPv4 address.

EXAMPLE ARP OPERATION

What the ARP process adds to TCP/IP is a mechanism for a source device to ask, "Who has IP address `10.10.12.52` (this was our first example from the Illustrated Network) and what is the physical (hardware) address associated with it?"

ARP messages are broadcast frames sent to all stations. The proper destination IP layer realizes that the destination IP address in the packet matches its own and replies directly to the sender. The target device replies by simply reversing the source and destination IP address in the ARP packet. The target also uses its own hardware address as the source address in the frame and message.

The ARP process is shown in Figure 5.6. The steps are numbered and taken from the example earlier in this chapter, where `lnxclient` ARPs to find the MAC address of `winsvr2`.

1. The system `lnxclient` (`10.10.12.166`) assembles an ARP request and sends it as a broadcast frame on the LAN. Because it is unknown, the requested MAC address field in the ARP message uses all zeros (0s), which are placeholders.

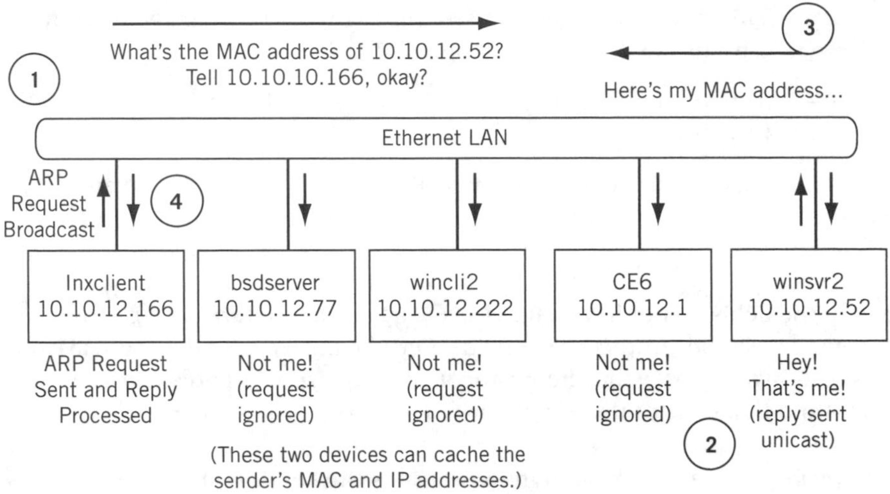

FIGURE 5.6

The ARP request and reply process. The message asks for the MAC address associated with the destination, and the sender's address that should receive the reply. Other devices that hear the reply can cache the information.

2. All devices attached to the LAN receive and process the broadcast, even the router `CE6`. But only the device with the target's IP address in the ARP message (`winsvr2` at `10.10.12.52`) replies to the ARP. The target also caches the MAC address associated with `10.10.12.166` (the source address in the broadcast frame).

3. The target system `winsvr2` sends a unicast ARP reply message back to `lnxclient`. The reply has the MAC address requested both in the frame (as a source address) and in the ARP message field sent as 0s.

The originating source system and the target system will cache the hardware address of the destination and proceed to send "live" IP packets with the information, at the same time supplying the proper frame address as a parameter to the network access layer software.

Figure 5.7 shows how the ARP request and reply message shown at the beginning of this chapter look like "on the wire." The field values can be compared to the ARP message format shown in Figure 5.5. Again, the `lnxclient` to `winsrv2` ARP pair are used as the example. Trailing zeros are not shown.

ARP operation is completely transparent to the user. ARP operation is usually triggered when a user runs some TCP/IP application, such as FTP, and the frame's destination MAC address is not in the ARP cache.

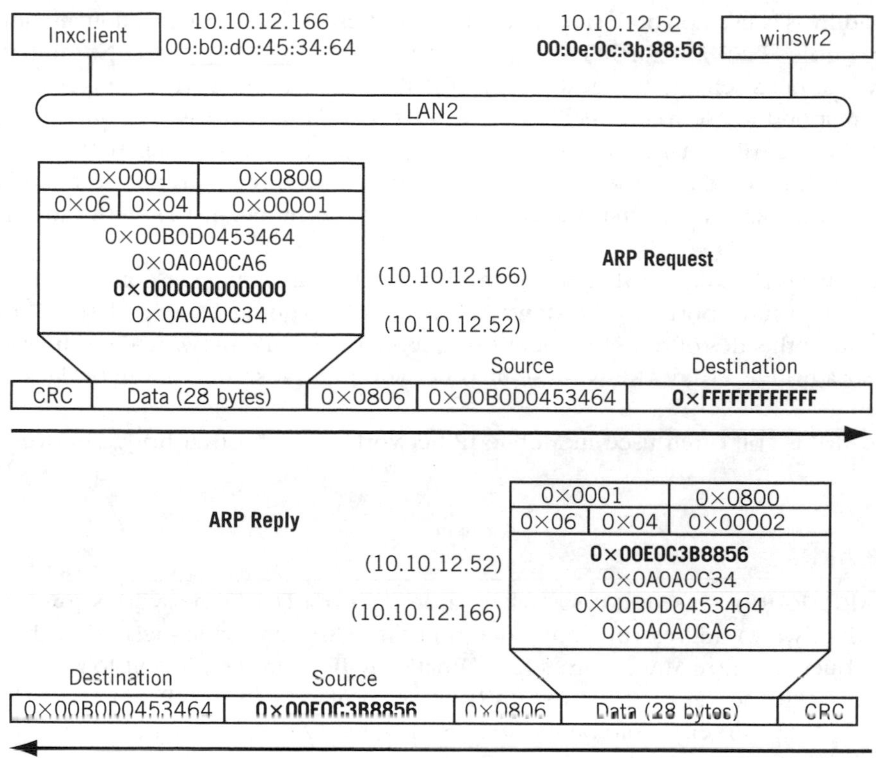

FIGURE 5.7

ARP exchange example, showing how the requested information is provided by the destination's reply.

ARP VARIATIONS

ARP is a fairly straightforward procedure to determine the LAN hardware address that goes with a given IP address. However, there are more network types than LANs and there are more "addresses" that need to be associated with IP addresses than "hardware" addresses. Consequently, there are a few other types of ARPs that have evolved to deal with other IP network situations.

Proxy ARP

Proxy ARP is an older technique (it was called the "ARP Hack") that was used in early routers, and is still supported in some routers today. LANs connected by bridges had hosts that did not (and could not) use different IP network addresses. The same IP network address is used on both sides of a bridge, so there is one broadcast domain, and ARPs are shuttled back and forth. This practice wasted bandwidth on the LANs (and on any WAN link between the bridges). Proxy ARP allowed the router that replaced the bridge to respond to ARP requests directly with its own MAC address, without having to propagate the ARP packets onto the other LAN segment. Hosts then sent frames to the router, but acted as if they were sending the frames directly to the destination host. Proxy ARP makes sure that the router received the frame, just as with indirect delivery.

Routers normally require that the same IP subnet address not be configured on more than one router port. Proxy ARP was a method of assigning a single Class A, B, or C address to both sides of router without using subnet masking, allowing the router to function as a bridge. Proxy ARP was useful as networking transitioned from bridges to routers.

Proxy ARP is still often used in Mobile IP networks, which often bridge between devices.

Reverse ARP

Reverse ARP (RARP) is used in cases where a device on a TCP/IP network knows its physical (hardware) address but must determine the IP address associated with it. A RARP request ("I have MAC address X . . . What's my IP address?") is sent to a device running the RARP server process. The RARP server replies with the IP address of the device. The RARP server should be located on the local LAN segment, but it does not have to be.

RARP messages use the same packet format as ARP, but the Ethertype is `0x0835`, and the operation field is 3 for a RARP request and 5 for a RARP reply. Of course, the information to be supplied is the IP address. As with ARP, the request is broadcast and the reply is unicast. RARP is defined in RFC 903.

RARP was frequently used for diskless network devices on TCP/IP networks such as workstations, X-terminals, routers, and hubs. These devices needed to obtain variable configuration information such as the IP address for an external source whenever they were rebooted or powered on. In addition, the amount of configuration information you could obtain through RARP was very limited. Today, with almost every device having flash memory to store configuration information during reboot when power is off, the need for RARP is greatly diminished.

Even in cases where configuration information or IP addresses need to be assigned dynamically, there are better ways to achieve the same result than with RARP, such as BOOTP and DHCP. Both will be discussed in Chapter 18 of this book.

ARPs on WANs

On most WANs, ARP is still used, but as a limited multicast rather than a broadcast. ARP has a couple of variations used to address WAN environments such as frame relay and ATM networks. These public network technologies use *virtual circuits* (a type

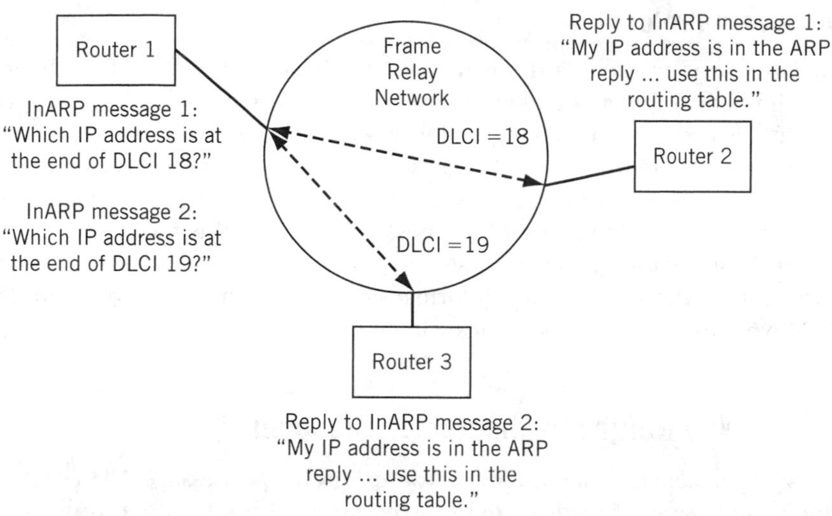

FIGURE 5.8

Inverse ARP (InARP) exchange over a frame relay network. In this case, the hardware address (DLCI) is known and the sender needs to determine the IP address.

of logical connection) at the frame (frame relay) or cell (ATM) level instead of MAC addresses. The issue in frame relay and ATM (both called *non-broadcast multiaccess* [NBMA] link networks) is to find the virtual circuit number, such as the Data Link Connection Identifier (DLCI) in frame relay, associated with a particular IP address.

InARP (Inverse ARP) was developed for use on frame relay networks. Instead of using ARP to determine MAC-layer LAN addresses, TCP/IP networks linked by frame relay networks use InARP to determine the IP address at the other end of a frame relay DLCI number to use when sending IP packets. InARP is used as soon as frame relay DLCI are created. The replies are used to build the routing table in the frame relay access device (router). The InARP process is shown in Figure 5.8. InARP is essentially an adaptation of the reverse ARP (RARP) process used on LANs.

ATMARP is a similar method used to find the ATM virtual path identifier (VPI) and/or virtual channel identifier (VCI) over an ATM network.

ARP AND IPv6

IPv6 really has no need for a separate ARP function. Instead, the Neighbor Discovery protocol (ND, sometimes NDP) described in RFC 2461 performs the functions of the IPv4 ARP in IPv6.

ND is really a superset of most of the functions of IPv4's ARP, ICMP Redirect, and ICMP Router Discovery features. This section will discuss some of the features of NDP, but most of this will be covered in the chapter on ICMP.

Neighbor Discovery Protocol

The Neighbor Discovery protocol is the way that IPv6 hosts and routers find things out about their immediate neighborhood, typically the LAN segment. A lot of effort was expended in IPv4 to find out configuration necessities such as default routers, any alternate routers, MAC addresses of adjacent hosts, and so on. In some cases, these addresses could not be found automatically with IPv4 and had to be entered manually (the default router). IPv6 was designed to be almost automatic in this regard.

When an IPv6 host comes up for the first time, the host advertises its MAC layer address and asks for neighbor and router information. Because these messages are in the form of ICMPv6 messages, only the basics will be presented here.

Why Neighbor *and* Router Discovery?

Why does IPv6 have separate neighbor and router discovery messages? After all, IPv4 did fine using a single broadcast frame structure for host-host and router-host address discovery.

IPv6 is more sophisticated than IPv4 when it comes to devices and networks. In IPv6, devices can be located on a local *multiple access link* (LAN), which are considered *on link*, or *off link*. Generally, there are a lot more hosts on a network than routers. IPv6 directs messages that discover host addresses only to the local hosts, while messages to discover one or more default routers are processed only by the routers.

Instead of a single mass broadcast, neighbor discover in IPv6 is done with *multicast groups*. We'll talk about multicast in more detail in a later chapter.

Many routers today forward packets in hardware, but broadcasts have to be processed by software. IPv6 routers can ignore the numerous messages sent from host to host on a LAN. This makes the use of the network resources with IPv6 more efficient.

The ARP function in IPv6 is performed by four messages in ND. The Router Solicitation/Router Advertisement mechanism is noteworthy in that it provides the key for host IPv6 address configuration, default route selection, and potentially even bootstrap configuration information.

Neighbor Solicitation—This message is sent by a host to find out the MAC layer address of another host. It is also used for Duplicate Address detection (Does another host have the same IPv6 address?) and for Neighbor Unreachability Detection (Is the other host still there?). The receiving host must reply with a Neighbor Advertisement.

Neighbor Advertisement—This message contains the MAC layer address of the host and is sent in reply to a Neighbor Solicitation message. Hosts also send unsolicited Neighbor Advertisement when they first start up or if any of the advertised information changes.

Router Solicitation—This message is sent by a host to find routers. The receiving router must reply with a Router Advertisement.

Router Advertisement—This message contains the MAC layer address of the router and is sent in reply to a Router Solicitation message. Routers also send an unsolicited Router Advertisement when they first start up if any of the advertised information changes.

ND Address Resolution

ND functions are performed only for local IPv6 addresses (the hop limit is set to 1 for these messages). ND messages, unlike ARP, are not broadcast ("Everyone pay attention to this") but rather multicast ("Only those interested pay attention to this").

When an IPv6 host or router starts up, it joins several multicast groups. The IPv6 mode must join the *all-nodes* group. It must also join a *solicited-node* group for each interface running IPv6 or IPv6 address that the node has. Joining these groups allows the device to receive packets without having all the details of its address established. This is a much more sophisticated arrangement than the ARP method used in IPv4. The IPv6 device must keep these multicast groups active until all of its addressing details have been resolved.

When an IPv6 device needs to resolve the MAC layer address of another host on the LAN, a Neighbor Solicitation message is sent to the solicited-node multicast address. The IPv6 solicited-node multicast address is formed by taking the low-order 24 bits of the IPv6 address and adding the 104-bit prefix `FF02::1` to it. Thus, for the link-local IPv6 address `fe80::20e:cff:fe3b:883c`, the IPv6 multicast group address used is `fe02::1:fe3b:883c`.

But what multicast address should the message use in the Ethernet frame? That multicast address is formed by prepending `33:33` to the lower 24 bits of the IPv6 address. Each device with an IP address registers this form with the local NIC and expects to receive ND messages this way initially. For the IPv6 multicast group address `fe02::1:fe3b:883c`, the multicast address used in the Ethernet destination field is `33:33:fe:3b:88:3c`.

An example of the address resolution pair capture earlier in this chapter is shown in Figure 5.9. Note the use of multicast IPv6 and frame addresses in the Neighbor Solicitation request and the way the information is supplied in the unicast Neighbor Announcement reply.

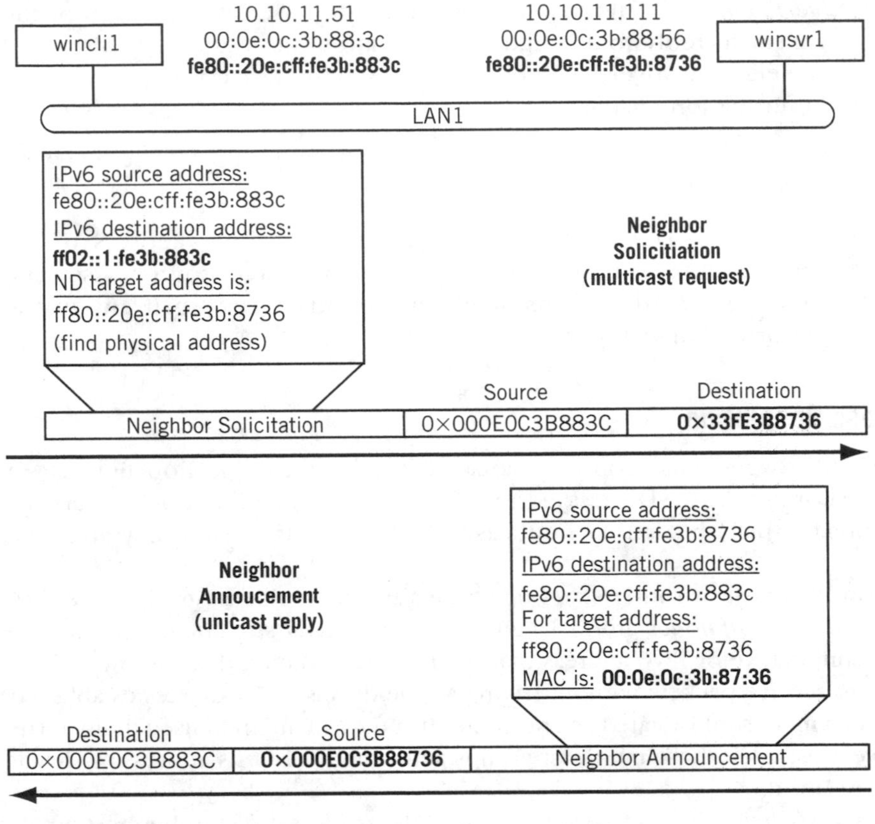

FIGURE 5.9

IPv6 neighbor discovery and address resolution, showing how the request uses multicast frame and packet addresses.

If no response is received, the sender can generate the Neighbor Solicitation message several times. When a Neighbor Advertisement message is received by the sender, the content is used to update the IPv6 Neighbor cache (the equivalent of the IPv4 ARP cache).

More details on ND message formats and operation are discussed in the ICMP chapter.

QUESTIONS FOR READERS

Figure 5.10 shows some of the concepts discussed in this chapter and can be used to help you answer the following questions.

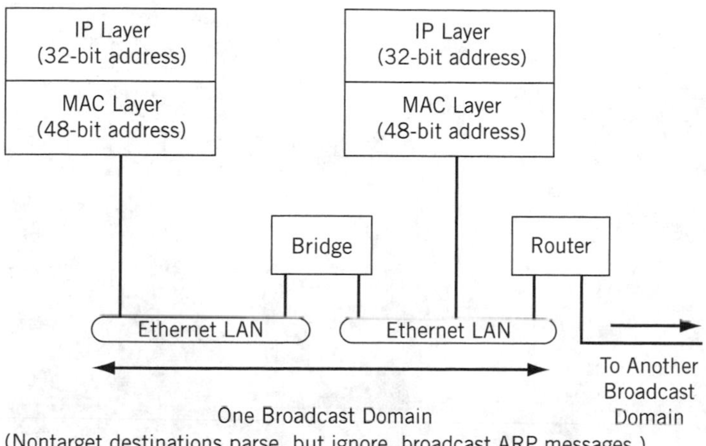

FIGURE 5.10

ARP messages are used to coordinate IP addresses with lower layer addressing.

1. Why can't the same address structure and value be used for network layer and hardware addresses?
2. Why do ARPs have to pass through bridges, but should not pass through routers?
3. Why does a receiver place the sender's MAC address in its own ARP cache?
4. What is Proxy ARP used for?
5. What is the advantage of using multicast groups instead of broadcasts for address resolution?

CHAPTER

6

IPv4 and IPv6 Headers

What You Will Learn

In this chapter, you will learn about the IP layer. We'll start with the fields in the IPv4 and IPv6 packet headers. We'll discuss most of the fields in detail and show how many of them relate to each other.

You will learn about fragmentation, and how large content is broken up, spread across a sequence of many packets, and reassembled at the destination. We'll also talk about some of the perceived hazards of this fragmentation process.

Thus far, we've created a network of hosts and routers, linked them with a variety of architectures and link types (LANs and WANs), and discussed the frame formats and methods used to distribute packets among the nodes. We've considered the IPv4 and IPv6 address formats, and the ways that they map to lower, link layer addresses. Now it's time to concentrate on the IP layer itself.

Even casual users of the TCP/IP protocol suite are familiar with the basic IP packet, or, as it was initially called (and still often is) the *datagram.* An IP datagram or packet is the connectionless IP network-layer protocol data unit (PDU). When TCP/IP came along, packets were often associated with connection-oriented data networks such as X.25, the international packet data network standard. To emphasize the connectionless nature of IP, then a radical approach to network layer operation, the TCP/IP developers decided to invent a new term for the IP packet. Through analogy with the telegram (a terse message sent hop by hop through a network of point-to-point links), they came up with the term "datagram."

The IP layer of the whole TCP/IP protocol stack is the very heart of TCP/IP. The frames that are sent and delivered across the network from host to router and router to host contain IP packets. However, like almost all statements about nearly any network protocol, there are exceptions to the general "frames contain IP packets" rule. As shown in the last chapter, an important class of IP layer protocols known as the Address Resolution Protocols (ARPs) does not technically use IP packets, but ARP messages are very close in structure to IP packets. Also, the Internet Control Message Protocol (ICMP) uses IP packets and is included in the IP layer. We'll look at ICMP in the next chapter.

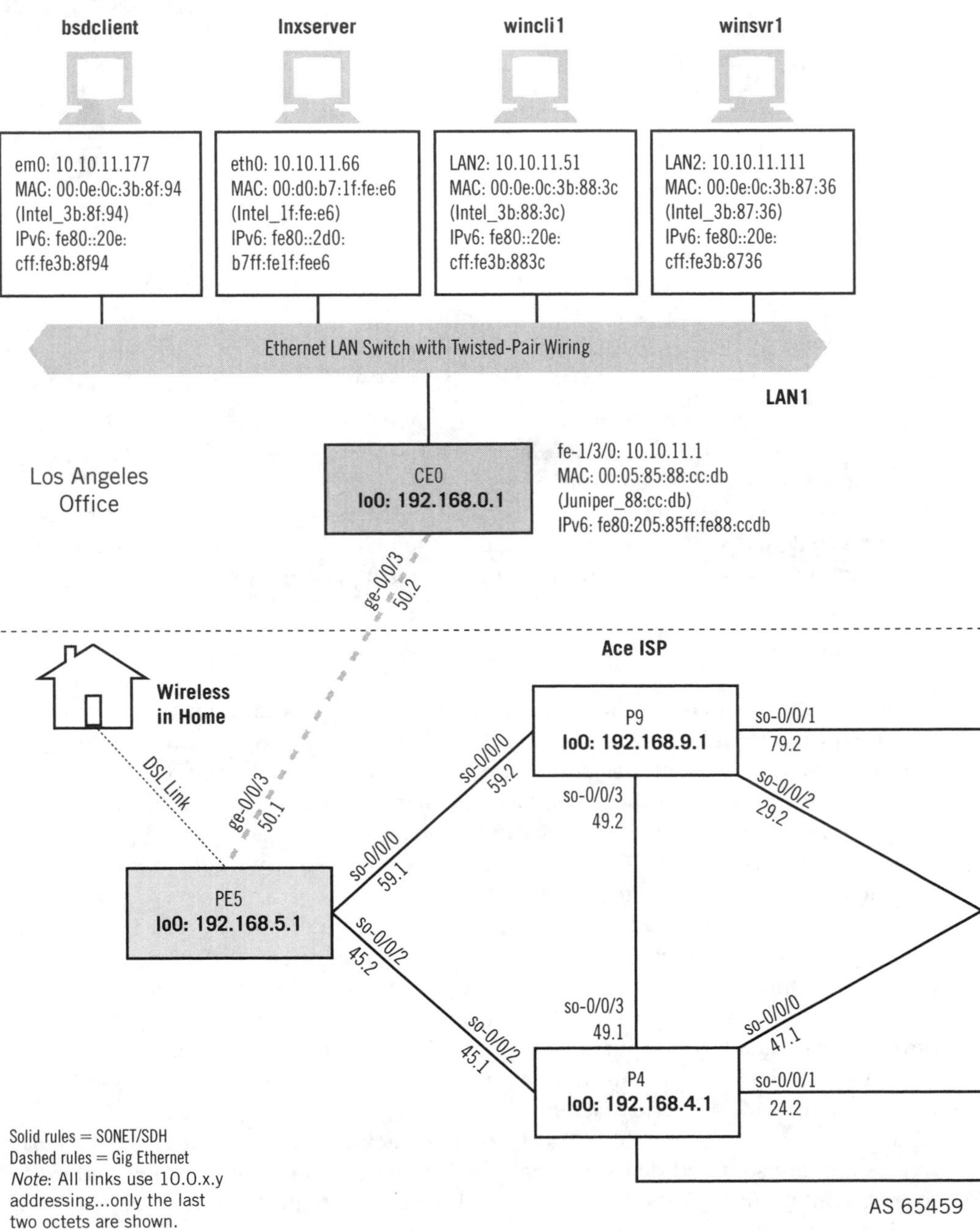

FIGURE 6.1

The LANs on the Illustrated Network use both IPv4 and IPv6 packets. We'll be looking at the headers generated by the hosts on the LANs.

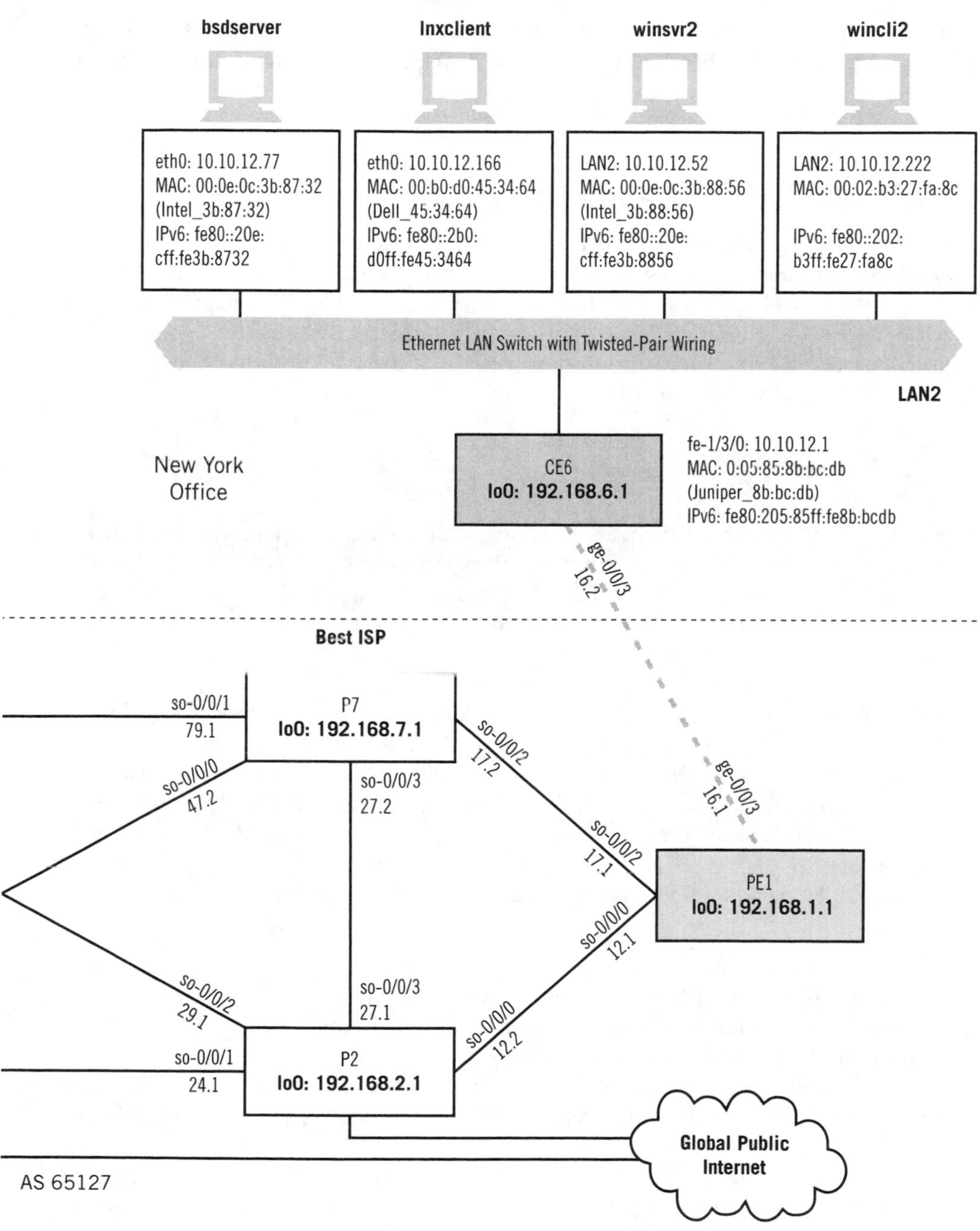

bsdserver
lnxclient
winsvr2
wincli2
eth0: 10.10.12.77
MAC: 00:0e:0c:3b:87:32
(Intel_3b:87:32)
IPv6: fe80::20e:
cff:fe3b:8732
eth0: 10.10.12.166
MAC: 00:b0:d0:45:34:64
(Dell_45:34:64)
IPv6: fe80::2b0:
d0ff:fe45:3464
LAN2: 10.10.12.52
MAC: 00:0e:0c:3b:88:56
(Intel_3b:88:56)
IPv6: fe80::20e:
cff:fe3b:8856
LAN2: 10.10.12.222
MAC: 00:02:b3:27:fa:8c
IPv6: fe80::202:
b3ff:fe27:fa8c
Ethernet LAN Switch with Twisted-Pair Wiring
LAN2
New York
Office
CE6
lo0: 192.168.6.1
fe-1/3/0: 10.10.12.1
MAC: 0:05:85:8b:bc:db
(Juniper_8b:bc:db)
IPv6: fe80:205:85ff:fe8b:bcdb
ge-0/0/3
16.2
Best ISP
so-0/0/1
79.1
P7
lo0: 192.168.7.1
so-0/0/2
17.2
ge-0/0/3
16.1
so-0/0/0
47.2
so-0/0/3
27.2
so-0/0/2
17.1
PE1
lo0: 192.168.1.1
so-0/0/0
12.1
so-0/0/2
29.1
so-0/0/3
27.1
so-0/0/0
12.2
so-0/0/1
24.1
P2
lo0: 192.168.2.1
Global Public
Internet
AS 65127

Both IPv4 and IPv6 packet structures will be detailed in this chapter. However, for the sake of simplicity, whenever the term "IP" is used without qualification, "IPv4" is implied.

PACKET HEADERS AND ADDRESSES

Let's take a close look at the packets used on the Illustrated Network. We'll look at the IPv4 header and addresses first. We worked with the Windows clients and servers a lot in the last few chapters, and we'll work with them again in this chapter. But we'll also work with the Unix devices and tethereal captures in this chapter, especially for fragmentation and IPv6. And, as we'll soon see, one of the biggest differences between IPv4 and IPv6 is how fragmentation is handled.

Fragmentation

People talk loosely about the pros and cons of "IP packet fragmentation," but this terminology is not correct. It is not the IP packet itself that is fragmented, but the packet *content*. If the payload is too large to fit inside a single IP packet (as determined by the IP layer implementation), the content is spread across several packets, each with its own IP header.

In some cases, as we will see in this chapter, the content of an IP packet must be further broken up to traverse the next link on the network. However, it's not really the IP packet that is fragmented. The original packet is discarded, and a string of IP packets is created that preserves the packet content and overall header fields, but changes specifics. When we say that "the packet is the data unit that flows end-to-end through the network," it is not the packet that is unchanged, but the content.

Naturally, if packet content is kept small enough, no fragmentation is necessary.

Figure 6.1 shows the parts of the Illustrated Network that we'll be using for our investigation of IP headers and fragmentation. The LAN clients and servers are highlighted, as are the local customer-edge routers.

Let's start with IPv4. We can just start a flow of IPv4 packets between a client and server and capture them. Then we can parse the packets until we find something of interest.

Let's take a good look at all the fields in an IPv4 packet header. We've already captured plenty of them. This example is from the FTP transfer from host (`wincli2`, with address `10.10.12.222`) to router (`CE6`, with address `10.10.12.1`) that we first saw in Chapter 2. Figure 6.2 shows a frame from the actual data transfer itself, frame 35, in fact.

The Ethernet frame is of type `0x0800` to show it carries an IPv4 packet. All of the lines from "Internet Protocol" to the line before "Transmission Control Protocol" interpret

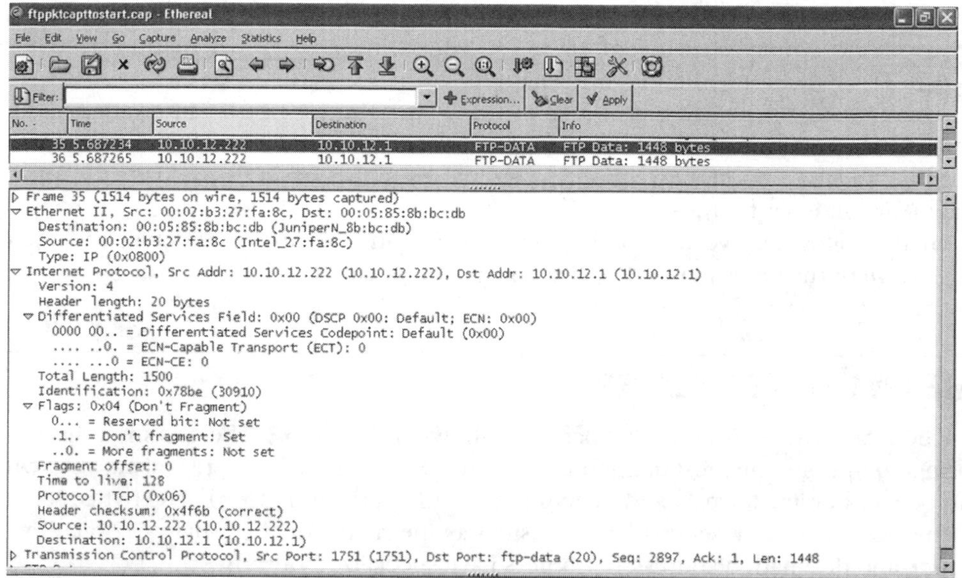

FIGURE 6.2

Capture of IPv4 header fields. The frame is broken out to show the content and meaning of every field in the IPv4 header. Note that the DF (Don't Fragment) bit is set on the packet.

fields in the IPv4 header. The source and destination addresses are listed first. Although we'll see that they are not the first fields in the header, they are definitely the fields that most frequently are of interest.

Ethereal interprets a field in the IPv4 header called the Type of Service (TOS) field according to something called Differentiated Services (DiffServ). DiffServ is only one way to interpret these fields. The figure shows that there are three things indicated by the 8 bits in the TOS field:

Differentiate Services Code Point (DSCP)—The default is zero, which means this packet does not require special handling by any router or host other than IP's normal best-effort service.

Explicit-Congestion-Notification Capable Transport (ECT)—This bit is set by devices when the transport is able to provide an indication of network congestion to network-attached devices. The value of zero shows that Ethernet is not an ECT, so packets cannot tell devices when the LAN is congested.

ECN Congestion Explicit (ECT-CE)—On transport that can report congestion, this bit is set when some predefined criteria for network congestion is met. This is often a percentage of output buffer fullness. On Ethernet this bit is always zero.

We'll say a little more about DSCP and quality of service (QOS) in a later chapter. However, the incomplete support for and variations in QOS implementations rule out QOS or DSCP as a topic for an entire chapter.

There are also four flag bits shown in the figure. The two most important are the bits that indicate this packet content is not to be fragmented (the DF bit is set to 1) and that there are no more frames carrying pieces of this packet's payload (the More Fragments bit is set to 0).

In the following, we talk about fragmentation in IPv4 in more detail, and then explore all of the fields in the IPv4 header in more detail.

THE IPv4 PACKET HEADER

The general structure of the IPv4 packet is shown in Figure 6.3. The minimum header (using no options, the most common situation) has a length of 20 bytes (always shown in a 4-bytes-per-line format), and a maximum length (very rarely seen) of 60 bytes. Some of the fields are fairly self-explanatory, such as the fields for the 4-byte (32-bit) IPv4 source and destination address, but others have specialized purposes.

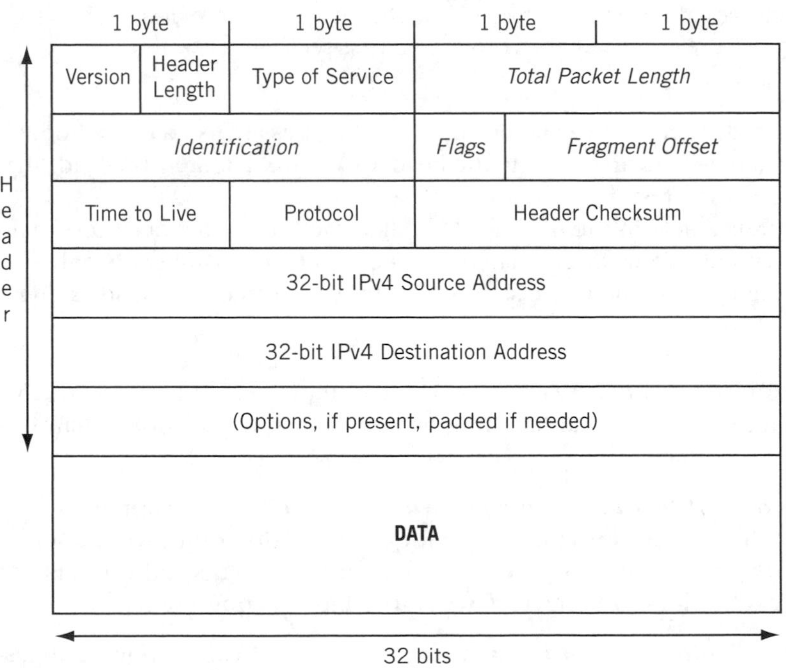

FIGURE 6.3

IPv4 Packet and Header

Version—Currently set to `0x04` for IPv4.

Header Length—Technically, this is the *Internet* header length (IHL). It is the length of the IP header in 4-byte (32-bit) units known as "words," and includes any option fields present and padding needed to align the header on a 32-bit boundary. In Figure 6.2, this is 20 bytes, which is most common.

Type of Service (TOS)—Contains parameters that affect how the packet is handled by routers and other equipment. Never widely used, it was redefined as Differentiated Services (DiffServ or DS) code points and is still hampered because of a lack of widespread implementation, especially from one routing domain to another. The meaning of these bits, which are all set to 0 in Figure 6.2, was detailed earlier in this chapter.

The next four fields, shown in italics in Figure 6.3, figure directly in the fragmentation process. Fragmentation, introduced in Chapter 4, occurs when a packet is forwarded onto a data link and the packet content will not fit inside a single frame. In these cases, the packet content must be fragmented and spread across several frames, then reassembled at the destination host. Fragmentation will be discussed in detail in the next section of this chapter.

Total Packet Length—This is the length of the whole packet in bytes. The maximum value for this two-byte field is 65,535 bytes. This length is approached by no common TCP/IP implementation or network MTU size. The packet in Figure 6.2 is 1500 bytes long, the most common length due to the prevalence of Ethernet LANs.

Identification—A 16-bit number set for each packet to help the destination host reassemble like-numbered fragments. Even intact, single packets could be fragmented by routers (sometimes repeatedly) on their way to a destination, so this field must be filled in. This field is set to `0x78be` (`30910`) in Figure 6.2.

Flags—Only the first 3 bits of this field are defined. Bit 1 is reserved and must be set to 0. Bit 2 (DF) is set to 0 if fragmentation is allowed or 1 if fragmentation is *not* allowed. Bit 3 (MF) is set to 0 if the packet is the last fragment, or 1 if there are more fragments to come. Note that the MF field does not imply any sequencing of the arriving fragments, nor does it guarantee that the set is complete. Other fields are examined to determine sequencing and completeness. The packet in Figure 6.2 will generate an error when it encounters a device that wants to fragment the packet content.

Fragment Offset—When a packet is fragmented, the fragments must fall on an 8-byte boundary. That is, an 800-byte packet can be fragmented into two packets of 400 bytes each, but not as eight packets of 100 bytes each, since 100 is not evenly divisible by 8. This field contains the number of 8-byte units, or *blocks*, in the packet fragment. The offset is 0 in Figure 6.2.

The rest of the IP header fields do not deal with fragmentation.

Time to Live (TTL)—This 8-bit field value is supposed to be the number of *seconds*, up to 255 maximum, that a packet can take to reach the destination. Each router is supposed to decrement this field by a preconfigured amount which must be greater than 0. If a packet arriving at a router has this field set to 0, it is discarded and never routed. Unfortunately, there is no standard way to track time across a group of routers, so most TCP/IP networks interpret this field as a simple *hop count* between routers and simply decrement this field by 1. The TTL in Figure 6.2 is 128, a fairly typical value.

Protocol—This 8-bit field contains the number of the transport-layer protocol that is to receive and process the data content of the packet. The protocol number for TCP is 6 and UDP is 17, but almost 200 have been defined. The packet in Figure 6.2 carries TCP.

Header Checksum—An error-detection field for the IP header only, not the packet data fields. If the computed checksum does not match at the receiver, the header is damaged and not routed. Figure 6.2 not only shows the header checksum of `0x4f6b`, but Ethereal tells us that it is correct.

Source and Destination Addresses—The 32-bit IPv4 addresses of the source and destination hosts. The packet in Figure 6.2 is sent from 10.10.12.222 to 10.10.12.1.

Options—The IPv4 options are seldom used today for data transfer and will not be described further, nor do they appear in Figure 6.2.

Padding—When options *are* used, the padding field makes sure the header ends on a 32-bit boundary. That is, the header must be an integer number of 4-byte "words." The header in Figure 6.2 is not padded, and few are since options use is unusual.

FRAGMENTATION AND IPv4

Let's look at IPv4 fragmentation on the Illustrated Network. We can determine how the MTU size and fragmentation affect IPv4 data transfer rates.

It's not all that important (and not all that interesting) to show the fragmentation process with a capture. Moreover, it is difficult to convey a sense of what's going on with a series of snapshots, even when Ethereal parses the fragmentation fields. Appreciating the effects of a small MTU size on data transfers is more important.

Let's use the `bsdclient` on LAN1 and `bsdserver` on LAN2 to show what fragmentation does to data throughput. We'll use FTP to transfer a small file (about 30,000 bytes) called `test.stuff` from the server to the client. Why so small a file? Just to show that if fragmentation plays a role in small transfers, the effects will be magnified with larger files. First, we'll use the default MTU sizes.

```
bsdclient# ftp 10.10.12.77
Connected to 10.10.12.77.
220 bsdserver FTP server (Version 6.00LS) ready.
Name (10.10.12.77:admin): admin
331 Password required for admin.
Password:
230 User admin logged in.
Remote system type is UNIX.
Using binary mode to transfer files.
ftp> get test.stuff
local: test.stuff remote: test.stuff
150 Opening BINARY mode data connection for 'test.stuff' (29752 bytes).
100%
|***************************************************************************
**********************| 29752 00:00 ETA
226 Transfer complete.
29752 bytes received in 0.01 seconds (4.55 MB/s)
```

This is about 4.5 MBps (or about 36 Mbps) and transfer time of about 1/100th of a second. Not too bad. (Keep in mind that 1/100th of a second is about the smallest interval that can be reported without special hardware.) This is good throughput, but remember there are only two routers involved, connected by a SONET link at 155 Mbps and the LAN runs at 100 Mbps. There is also no other traffic on the network, so the transfer rate is totally dependent on the ability of the host to fill the pipe from server to client.

Now let's change to Maximum Transmission Unit size at the server connected to LAN2 (the server LAN) from the default of 1500 to 256 bytes. How much of a difference will this make?

```
ftp> get test.stuff
local: test.stuff remote: test.stuff
150 Opening BINARY mode data connection for 'test.stuff' (29752 bytes).
100%
|***************************************************************************
**********************| 29752 00:00 ETA
226 Transfer complete.
29752 bytes received in 1.30 seconds (22.29 KB/s)
ftp>
```

The transfer time is up to 1.3 seconds, about 130 times longer than before! And the transfer rate fell from about 36 Mbps to about 184 *KILOBITS* per second, three orders of magnitude less than before. This is the "performance penalty" of fragmentation. (It should be pointed out that these numbers are not precise, and there are many other reasons that file transfers speed up or slow down. However, the point is entirely valid.)

We can view a lot of packet statistics, including fragment statistics, using the `netstat` utility. With `netstat`, we can monitor an interface in real time, display the host routing table, observe running network processes, and so on. We'll do more with `netstat` later. For now, we'll just see how many fragments our 30,000-byte file transfer has generated.

To do this, we'll look at the IP statistics on the client before and after the file transfer has been run with the small MTU size. We'll set the counters to zero first.

```
bsdclient# netstat -sp ip
ip:
        0 total packets received
        0 bad header checksums
        0 with size smaller than minimum
        0 with data size < data length
        0 with ip length > max ip packet size
        0 with header length < data size
        0 with data length < header length
        0 with bad options
        0 with incorrect version number
        0 fragments received
        0 fragments dropped (dup or out of space)
        0 fragments dropped after timeout
        0 packets reassembled ok
        [many more lines deleted for clarity...]
```

Now we'll reset the counters, run the transfer again, and check the IP statistics.

```
bsdclient# netstat -sp ip
ip:
        57 total packets received
        0 bad header checksums
        0 with size smaller than minimum
        0 with data size < data length
        0 with ip length > max ip packet size
        0 with header length < data size
        0 with data length < header length
        0 with bad options
        0 with incorrect version number
        171 fragments received
        0 fragments dropped (dup or out of space)
        0 fragments dropped after timeout
        57 packets reassembled ok
        [many more lines deleted for clarity...]
```

The file was transferred as 171 fragments that were reassembled into 57 packets. Let's take a closer look at fragmentation of the MTU size in IPv4.

Fragmentation and MTU

If an IP packet is too large to fit into the frame for the outgoing link, the packet content must be fragmented to fit into multiple "transmission units." The Maximum Transmission Unit (MTU) size is a key concept in all TCP/IP networks, often complicated by the fact that different types of links (LAN or WAN) have very different MTU sizes. Many of these are shown in Table 6.1. The link protocols shown in italics have "tunable" (configurable) MTU sizes instead of defined defaults, but almost all interfaces allow you to lower the MTU size. The figures shown are the usual maximums. The 9000-byte packet size is not standard in Gigabit Ethernet, but common.

Hosts reassemble any arriving fragmented packets to avoid routers pasting together and then tearing apart packets repeatedly as they are forwarded from link to link. Fragments themselves can even be fragmented further as a packet makes its way from, for example, Gigabit Ethernet to frame relay to Ethernet.

Fragmentation is something that all network administrators used to try to avoid. As a famous paper circulated in 1987 asserted bluntly, "Fragmentation [is] considered harmful." As recently as 2004, an Internet draft (*http://ietfreport.isoc.org/all-ids/draft-mathis-frag-harmful-00.txt*) took this one step further with the title, "Fragmentation Considered Very Harmful." The paper asserts that most of the harm occurs when a fragment of packet content, especially the first, is lost on the network. And a number of older network attacks involved sending long sequences of fragments to targets, never finishing the sequence, until the host or router ran out of buffer space and crashed. Also,

Table 6.1 Typical MTU Sizes*

Link Protocol	Typical MTU Limit	Maximum IP Packet
Ethernet	1518	1500
IEEE 802.3	1518	1492
Gigabit Ethernet	9018	9000
IEEE 802.4	8191	8166
IEEE 802.5 (Token Ring)	4508	4464
FDDI	4500	4352
SMDS/*ATM*	9196	9180
Frame relay	4096	4091
SDLC	2048	2046

**Frame overhead accounts for the differences between the theoretic limit and maximum IP packet size.*

because of the widespread use of *tunnels* (see Chapter 26), there are link layers that really need an MTU larger than 1500 to support encapsulation, and you can't fragment MTUs inside a tunnel.

There are several reasons for the quest to determine the smallest of the MTU sizes on the links between source and destination. This "minimum" MTU size can be used between a source and destination in order to avoid fragmentation. The main reasons today follow:

- Fragmentation is processor intensive. Early routers were hard pressed to both route and fragment. Even today, high link speeds force routers to concentrate on routing and minimize "housekeeping" tasks.
- Many hosts struggle to reassemble fragments. Fragmentation puts the reassembly burden on the receiving host, which can be a cell phone, watch, or something else. This requires processing power and delays the processing of the packet.
- Fragmentation fields are favorite targets for hacking. TCP/IP implementation behaviors are not spelled out in detail for many situations where the fragmentation fields are set to inconsistent or contradictory values. Many a host and router have been hung by exploiting this variable behavior.
- Fragments can be lost, out-of-sequence, or errored. The more pieces there are, the more things that can go wrong. The worse occurs when the first fragment is lost on the network.
- Early IP implementations avoided fragmentation by setting the default IP packet size very low, to only 576 bytes. All link protocols then in common use could handle this small packet size, and many IP implementations to this day still use this default packet size. Naturally, the smaller the MTU size, the greater the number of packets sent for a given message, and the greater the chances something can go wrong.

Fragmentation behavior changes in IPv6. In IPv6, routers do not perform fragmentation.

Fragmentation and Reassembly

The point has already been made that fragmentation is a processor-intensive operation. Naturally, if all hosts sending packets were aware of the *minimum* MTU size on a path from source to destination before sending an IP packet, the problem would be solved. There are ways to determine the path MTU size.

Path MTU Determination

The commonly used method to determine this path MTU is slow, but it works. The method involves "testing" the path to the destination before sending "live" packets to a destination system where the path MTU is not known. The source system sends out an echo packet. (The echo service just bounces back the content of the packet to the sender.) The echo packet is usually the MTU size of the source system's own TCP/IP network, which could be 1500 bytes for Ethernet, 4500 for Token Ring, and so on. This packet has the DF bit set in the Flags field in the IPv4 header. If the echo packet comes back successfully, then the MTU size is fine and can be used for "live" data.

However, if the current path through the routers includes a smaller MTU size on a link or network that the packet must traverse as the packet makes its way to the destination, the router attached to this smaller MTU size network *must* discard the packet, since the DF bit is set. The router sends an ICMP error message back to the source indicating the error condition, which is that the packet was discarded because the DF bit was set. The source can then adjust the packet size downward and try again. This process can be repeated several times, trying to find the optimal path MTU.

This path MTU determination method works, but it is awkward and slow. The live data basically wait until the path MTU size is determined for a destination. And because each packet is independently routed, if there are multiple paths through the router network (and there usually are, this being the whole point of using routers), the MTU size may change with every possible path that an IP packet can take from the source to the destination. However, this method is better than nothing.

A FRAGMENTATION EXAMPLE

Figure 6.4 shows a router on a TCP/IP network. The arriving IP packet is coming from a WAN link with a configured MTU size of 4500 bytes. The destination system is attached to the router by means of an Ethernet LAN, which has an MTU size of 1500 bytes,

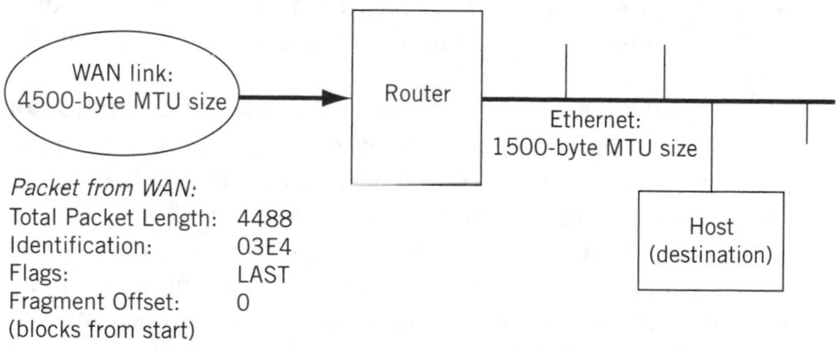

Packet from LAN:	*Frag #1:*	*Frag #2:*	*Frag #3:*
Total Packet Length:	4488	4488	4488
Identification:	03E4	03E4	03E4
Flags:	MORE	MORE	LAST
Fragment Offset: (blocks from start)	0	187	374

(187 8-byte blocks = 1496 bytes)

FIGURE 6.4

An IPv4 fragmentation example, showing the various header field values for each of the three fragments loaded into the frames.

Obviously, the 4500-byte packet must be fragmented across three Ethernet frames to reach the destination host.

Figure 6.4 shows the portions of the IP packet data and the values of the fragmentation fields for each fragment. The figure also shows how the destination system interprets the fragmentation fields to reassemble the entire packet at the destination.

We've already looked at the problems with fragmentations from the router and network perspective. From the perspective of the receiving host, there are two main reasons that fragmentation should be avoided. One is the need to wait for undelivered fragments, and the other is the lack of knowledge on the part of a destination of the reassembled datagram size. Let's look at the destination host reassembly process to explore the "performance penalty" that fragmentation involves.

A fragmented packet is always reassembled at the destination host and never by routers. (Why put together packets that might require fragmentation all over again?) However, because all packets are independently routed, the pieces of a packet can arrive out of sequence. When the first fragment arrives, local buffer memory is allocated for the reassembly process. The Fragment Offset of the arriving packet indicates exactly where in the sequence the newly arrived fragment should be placed.

At a busy destination, such as a Web server, many different packets from several sources can arrive in fragments. All of these pieces can be subjected to the reassembly process at the same time. The destination host IP layer software will associate packets having matching Identification, Source, Destination, and Protocol fields as belonging to the same packet.

However, the Total Length field in a packet fragment's header only indicates the length of that particular fragment, not the entire packet before fragmentation. It is only when the destination system receives the *last* fragment that the total length of the original packet can be determined.

If a packet is partially reassembled and the final piece to complete the set has not arrived, IP includes a tunable reassembly time-out parameter. If the reassembly timer expires, the remaining packet fragments are discarded. If the final piece of the packet arrives after the time-out, this packet fragment must be discarded as well.

This description of the reassembly process shows the twin problems of memory allocation woes from packet size uncertainties and delays due to the reassembly time-out.

Arriving IP packets have no way to inform the destination system that "I am the first of 10 fragments." If so, it would be easy for the destination system to allocate memory for reassembly that was the best-fit for remaining contiguous buffer space. But all packet fragments can indicate is "I am the first of many," "I am the second of many," and so on, until one finally says, "I am the last of many." This uncertainty of reassembled size makes many TCP/IP implementations allocate as large a block of memory as available for reassembly. Obviously, a fragmented packet may have been quite large to begin with, because it was fragmented in the first place. But the net result is that local buffers become quite fragmented. And if smaller blocks of memory are allocated, the resulting non-contiguous pieces must be moved to an adequate sized memory buffer before the transport layer can process the reassembled datagram.

The reassembly time-out value must have a value low enough to make the recovery process delay of the transport layer reasonable. The transport layer contains session (connection) information that will detect a missing packet in a sequence of segments (the contents of the packets), and TCP always requests missing information to be resent. Too long a value for the reassembly timer makes this retransmission process very inefficient. Too short a value leads to needlessly discarded packets. In most TCP/IP implementations, the reassembly timer is set by the software vendor and cannot be changed. This is yet another reason to avoid fragmentation.

Reassembly "deadlock" used to be a problem as well. When memory was a scarce commodity in hosts, all available local buffer memory could end up holding partially assembled fragments. An arriving fragment could not be accepted even if it completed a set and the system eventually hung. However, in these days of cheap and plentiful memory, this rarely happens.

Limitations of IPv4

The limitations of IPv4 are often cast solely in terms of address space. As important as that is, it is only part of the story. Address space is not the only IPv4 limitation. Some others follow:

- The fragmentation fields are present in every IPv4 packet.
- Fragmentation is always done with a performance penalty and is best avoided. Yet the fields involved—all 6 bytes worth and more than 25% of the basic 20-byte IPv4 header—must be present in each and every packet.
- IPv4 Options were seldom used and limited in scope.
- The IPv4 Type of Service field was never used as intended.
- The IPv4 Time To Live field was also never used as intended.
- The 8-bit IPv4 Type field limited IPv4 packet content to 256 possibilities.

All of these factors contributed to the structure of the IPv6 packet header.

The IPv6 Header Structure

Let's go back to our Windows devices and capture some IPv6 packets. Then we can examine those headers and compare them to IPv4 headers.

```
bsdserver# ping6 fc00:fe67:d4:b:205:85ff:fe8b:bcdb
PING6(56=40+8+8 bytes) fc00:fe67:d4:b:20e:cff:fe3b:8732 -->
fc00:fe67:d4:b:205:85ff:fe8b:bcdb
16 bytes from fc00:fe67:d4:b:205:85ff:fe8b:bcdb, icmp_seq=0 hlim=64
 time=16.027 ms
16 bytes from fc00:fe67:d4:b:205:85ff:fe8b:bcdb, icmp_seq=1 hlim=64
 time=0.538 ms
16 bytes from fc00:fe67:d4:b:205:85ff:fe8b:bcdb, icmp_seq=2 hlim=64
 time=0.655 ms
```

```
16 bytes from fc00:fe67:d4:b:205:85ff:fe8b:bcdb, icmp_seq=3 hlim=64
 time=0.622 ms
^C
--- fc00:fe67:d4:b:205:85ff:fe8b:bcdb ping6 statistics ---
4 packets transmitted, 4 packets received, 0% packet loss
round-trip min/avg/max/std-dev = 0.538/4.461/16.027/6.678 ms
```

Here is the first packet we captured:

```
bsdserver# tethereal -V
Capturing on em0
Frame 1 (70 bytes on wire, 70 bytes captured)
   Arrival Time: May 23, 2008 18:39:58.914560000
   Time delta from previous packet: 0.000000000 seconds
   Time since reference or first frame: 0.000000000 seconds
   Frame Number: 1
   Packet Length: 70 bytes
   Capture Length: 70 bytes
Ethernet II, Src: 00:0e:0c:3b:87:32, Dst: 00:05:85:8b:bc:db
   Destination: 00:05:85:8b:bc:db (JuniperN_8b:bc:db)
   Source: 00:0e:0c:3b:87:32 (Intel_3b:87:32)
   Type: IPv6 (0x86dd)
Internet Protocol Version 6
   Version: 6
   Traffic class: 0x00
   Flowlabel: 0x00000
   Payload length: 16
   Next header: ICMPv6 (0x3a)
   Hop limit: 64
   Source address: fc00:fe67:d4:b:20e:cff:fe3b:8732 (fc00:fe67:d4:b:20e:
cff:fe3b:8732)
   Destination address: fc00:fe67:d4:b:205:85ff:fe8b:bcdb (fc00:fe67:d4:
b:205:85ff:fe8b:bcdb)
Internet Control Message Protocol v6
   Type: 128 (Echo request)
   Code: 0
   Checksum: 0x7366 (correct)
   ID: 0x0565
   Sequence: 0x0000
   Data (8 bytes)

0000 6e b9 73 44 43 f4 0d 00              n.sDC...
```

In contrast to the IPv4 header, there are only eight lines (and eight fields) in the IPv6 header. Since the packet is simple enough, let's look at the header fields in detail as we examine the meaning and values in this IPv6 packet.

The IPv6 header is shown in Figure 6.5. Besides the new expanded, 16-byte IP source and destination addresses, there are only six other fields in the entire IPv6 header. This simpler header structure makes for faster packet processing in most cases.

1 byte	1 byte	1 byte	1 byte
Version / Traffic Class		Flow Label	
Payload Length		Next Header	Hop Limit
128-bit IPv6 Source Address			
128-bit IPv6 Destination Address			

FIGURE 6.5

The IPv6 header fields. Note the reduction in field number of how the address fields occupy most of the header.

IPv6 packets have their own frame Ethertype value, `0x86dd`, making it easy for receivers that must handle both IPv4 and IPv6 on the same interface to distinguish the frame content.

Version—A 4-bit field for the IP version number (`0x06`).

Traffic Class—A 12-bit field that identifies the major class of the packet content (e.g., voice or video packets). Our capture shows this field as the default at 0, meaning that it is ordinary bulk data (as FTP should carry) and requires no special handling at devices.

Flow Label—A 16-bit field used to label packets belonging to the same flow (those with the same values in several TCP/IP header parameters). The flow label here is 0, but this is common.

Payload Length—A 16-bit field giving the length of the packet in bytes, excluding the IPv6 header. The payload of this packet, an ICMP message, is 16 bytes long.

Next Header—An 8-bit field giving the type of header immediately following the IPv6 header (this served the same function as the Protocol field in IPv4). This packet carries an ICMPv3 message, so the value is `0x3a`.

Hop Limit—An 8-bit field set by the source host and decremented by 1 at each router. Packets are discarded if the hop limit is decremented to zero (this replaces the IPv4 Time To Live field). The hop limit here is `64`, half of the FTP value in our IPv4 example. Generally, implementers choose the default to use, but values such as 64 or 128 are common.

IPv4 AND IPv6 HEADERS COMPARED

Figure 6.6 shows the fields in the IPv4 packet header compared to the fields in the IPv6 header.

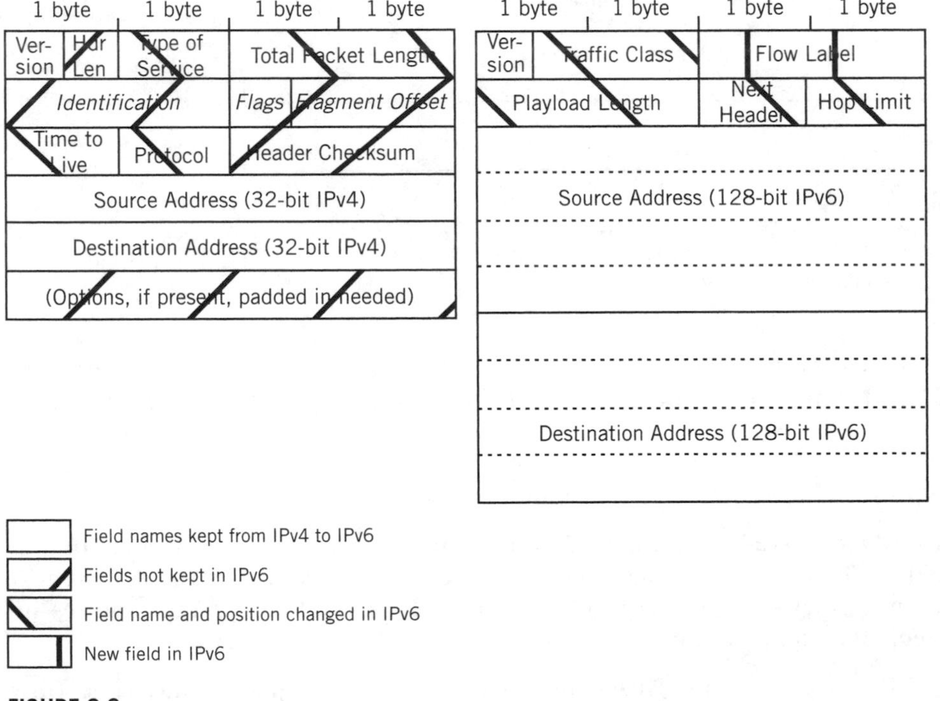

FIGURE 6.6

IPv4 and IPv6 headers compared, showing how the old fields and new fields relate to each other.

IPv6 Header Changes

In summary, the following are some of the most important changes to the IP header in IPv6.

- Longer addresses (32 bits to 128 bits). No fragmentation fields.
- No header checksum field. No header length field (there is a fixed length header).
- Payload length given in bytes, not "blocks" (32-bit units). Time to Live (TTL) field becomes Hop Limit.
- Protocol field becomes Next Header (determines content format). 64-bit alignment of the packet, not 32-bit alignment. A Flow Label field has been added.
- No Type of Service bits (which were seldom respected anyway). Many of the IPv4 fields vanish completely, especially the fields used for packet fragmentation. IPv6 addresses fragmentation performance penalties and problems by forbidding it altogether in routers. Source hosts can still fragment, however, if the source host wants to send packets larger than the Path MTU size to a destination. In IPv6, as in IPv4, fragmentation issues can be avoided altogether by making all packets 1280 bytes long—the minimum established by RFC 2460—but this results in many "extra" packets.
- The IPv4 header Checksum field is absent because destination host error checking is the preferred method of error detection in today's more reliable networks, and almost all transmission frames provide better error detection than the IP layer. There is no header length field because all IPv6 headers are the same length. The Payload Length field excludes the IPv6 header fields and is measured in bytes, rather than the awkward 4-byte units of IPv4.
- The TTL field, never interpreted as time anyway, is gone as well. In its place is the Hop Limit field, a simple indication of the number of routers that a packet can pass through before it should reach the destination host. The Protocol field of IPv4 has become the Next Header field in IPv6. The term "next header" is more accurate because the information inside the IPv6 packet is not necessarily a higher layer protocol (e.g., TCP segment) in IPv6. There are many other possibilities.
- The entire packet must be an integer number of 64-bit (8-byte) units. The 32-bit unit for IPv4 was established when many high-performance computers were 32-bit machines, meaning memory access and internal bus operations moved 32-bit units (called a "word") around. Today high-performance computers often support 64-bit words. It only made sense to align the new IPv6 header for ease and speed of processing on the newer architecture computers.
- Finally, in place of the ToS field in IPv4, the IPv6 header defines a Flow Label field. Flows are used by routers to pick out IPv6 packets containing delay-sensitive data such as voice, video, and multimedia. The Type of Service field was usually ignored by routers in IPv4, and other uses were not standardized.

- The IPv6 specification includes a concept known as Extension Headers. Extension Headers essentially take the place of the Options in the IPv4 packet header. IPv6 Extension Headers are only present when necessary and are designed to be extensible (new functions may be defined in the future), but the term "extensible Extension Headers" is awkward.
- The current Extension Headers include a Hop-by-Hop Option Header, examined by every router handling the IPv6 packet and an Authentication Header for enhanced security on TCP/IP networks (these are used in IPv4 as part of IPSec). There is also a Fragmentation header for the use of the source host when there is no way to prevent the source from sending packets larger than the path MTU size (IPv6 routers cannot fragment, but hosts can). Also, there used to be a Routing Header specifying the IP addresses of the routers on the path from source to destination (similar to "source routing" in token ring LANs), but this is deprecated by RFC 5095. There are several others, but these show the kinds of capabilities included in the IPv6 Extension Headers.

IPv6 AND FRAGMENTATION

What would happen if we put IPv6 into a situation where it has to fragment packet content to make it fit into a frame? Let's use the Illustrated Network to find out. Two useful ping parameters are the size of the packet to bounce off a remote device and the count of packets sent. We'll capture the packets sent when `bsdserver` sends a 2000-byte packet (too large for an Ethernet frame) to the router.

```
bsdserver# ping6 -s 2000 -c 1 fc00:fe67:d4:b:205:85ff:fe8b:bcdb
PING6(2048=40+8+2000 bytes) fc00:fe67:d4:b:20e:cff:fe3b:8732 -->
fc00:fe67:d4:b:205:85ff:fe8b:bcdb
2008 bytes from fc00:fe67:d4:b:205:85ff:fe8b:bcdb, icmp_seq=0 hlim=64
 time=2.035 ms

--- fc00:fe67:d4:b:205:85ff:fe8b:bcdb ping6 statistics ---
1 packets transmitted, 1 packets received, 0% packet loss
round-trip min/avg/max/std-dev = 2.035/2.035/2.035/0.000 ms
bsdserver#
```

This makes 2008 bytes with the IPv6 header. Here's what we have (the data fields, which contain test strings, have been omitted):

```
bsdserver# tethereal -V
Capturing on em0
Frame 1 (1510 bytes on wire, 1510 bytes captured)
   Arrival Time: May 25, 2008 08:39:21.231993000
   Time delta from previous packet: 0.000000000 seconds
   Time since reference or first frame: 0.000000000 seconds
   Frame Number: 1
```

```
   Packet Length: 1510 bytes
   Capture Length: 1510 bytes
Ethernet II, Src: 00:0e:0c:3b:87:32, Dst: 00:05:85:8b:bc:db
   Destination: 00:05:85:8b:bc:db (JuniperN_8b:bc:db)
   Source: 00:0e:0c:3b:87:32 (Intel_3b:87:32)
   Type: IPv6 (0x86dd)
Internet Protocol Version 6
   Version: 6
   Traffic class: 0x00
   Flowlabel: 0x00000
   Payload length: 1456
   Next header: IPv6 fragment (0x2c)
   Hop limit: 64
   Source address: fc00:fe67:d4:b:20e:cff:fe3b:8732 (fc00:fe67:d4:b:20e:
     cff:fe3b:8732)
   Destination address: fc00:fe67:d4:b:205:85ff:fe8b:bcdb (fc00:fe67:d4:
     b:205:85ff:fe8b:bcdb)
Fragmentation Header
   Next header: ICMPv6 (0x3a)
   Offset: 0
   More fragments: Yes
   Identification: 0x000000e5
Internet Control Message Protocol v6
   Type: 128 (Echo request)
   Code: 0
   Checksum: 0x74df
   ID: 0x0e60
   Sequence: 0x0000
   Data (1440 bytes) (OMITTED)

Frame 2 (622 bytes on wire, 622 bytes captured)
   Arrival Time: May 25, 2008 08:39:21.232007000
   Time delta from previous packet: 0.000014000 seconds
   Time since reference or first frame: 0.000014000 seconds
   Frame Number: 2
   Packet Length: 622 bytes
   Capture Length: 622 bytes
Ethernet II, Src: 00:0e:0c:3b:87:32, Dst: 00:05:85:8b:bc:db
   Destination: 00:05:85:8b:bc:db (JuniperN_8b:bc:db)
   Source: 00:0e:0c:3b:87:32 (Intel_3b:87:32)
   Type: IPv6 (0x86dd)
Internet Protocol Version 6
   Version: 6
   Traffic class: 0x00
   Flowlabel: 0x00000
   Payload length: 568
   Next header: IPv6 fragment (0x2c)
   Hop limit: 64
   Source address: fc00:fe67:d4:b:20e:cff:fe3b:8732 (fc00:fe67:d4:
     b:20e:cff:fe3b:8732)
```

```
    Destination address: fc00:fe67:d4:b:205:85ff:fe8b:bcdb (fc00:fe67:
      d4:b:205:85ff:fe8b:bcdb)
Fragmentation Header
    Next header: ICMPv6 (0x3a)
    Offset: 1448
    More fragments: No
    Identification: 0x000000e5
Data (560 bytes) (OMITTED)

(Frames 3 and 4, the echoed frames sent back in response, are mirror
images of Frames 1 and 2 and have been omitted for brevity.)

bsdserver#
```

Because the host cannot pack 2000 bytes into an Ethernet frame, the IPv6 host does the fragmenting *before* it sends the bits onto the LAN. There are no fragmentation fields in the IPv6 header, however, so IPv6 includes a second header (next header) that carries the information needed for the destination to reassemble the fragments (in this case, two of them). The important fields are highlighted in bold in the preceding code.

The first frame (the capture says "packet") is 1510 bytes long, including 1456 bytes of payload (given in the Payload Length field). The Next Header value of `0x2c` indicates that the next header is an IPv6 fragment header. The Fragmentation Header fields are listed in full:

- *Next Header* (`0x3a`)—The header following the Fragmentation Header is an ICMPv6 message header.
- *Offset* (`0`)—This is the first fragment of a series.
- *More Fragments* (Yes)—There are more fragments to come.
- *Identification* (`0x000000e5`)—Only reassemble fragments that share this identifier value.

The data field in the ICMPv6 message is 1440 bytes long. The rest of the 1510 bytes are from the various headers pasted onto these bytes.

Frame 2 holds the rest of the 2000 bytes in the ping. This frame is 622 bytes long and carries 568 bytes of payload. The Next Header is still an IPv6 fragment (`0x2c`). The Fragmentation Header fields follow:

- *Next header* (`0x3a`)—The header following the Fragmentation Header is an ICMPv6 message header.
- *Offset* (`1448`)—These bytes start 1448 bytes after the content of the first frame. (The "extra" 8 bytes are for the ICMPv6 header.)
- *More Fragments* (No)—The contents of this packet complete the series.
- *Identification* (`0x000000e5`)—This fragment goes with the previous one with this identifier value.

The data field in the ICMPv6 message is 560 bytes long. Along with the 1440 bytes in the first fragment, these add up to the 2000 bytes sent.

QUESTIONS FOR READERS

Figure 6.7 shows some of the concepts discussed in this chapter and can be used to help you answer the following questions.

1 byte		1 byte	1 byte		1 byte
Ver-sion	Hdr Len	Type of Service	Total Packet Length		
Identification			*Flags*	*Fragment Offset*	
Time to Live		Protocol	Header Checksum		
Source Address (32-bit IPv4)					
Destination Address (32-bit IPv4)					
(Options, if present, padded if needed)					

1 byte		1 byte	1 byte	1 byte
Ver-sion	Traffic Class		Flow Label	
Playload Length			Next Header	Hop Limit
Source Address (128-bit IPv6)				
Destination Address (128-bit IPv6)				

FIGURE 6.7

The IPv4 and IPv6 packet header fields. IPv6 can employ most IPv4 options as "next header" fields following the basic header.

1. Why are diagnostics like ping messages routinely given high hop-count values such as 64 or 128?
2. Without any IPv4 options in use, what value should be seen in the Header Length field most of the time?
3. How does an IP receiver detect missing fragments?
4. Is there any way for an IP receiver to determine how many fragments are supposed to arrive?
5. Since almost all the IPv4 header fields are options in IPv6, is it correct to say that the IPv6 header is "simplified"?

CHAPTER

7

Internet Control Message Protocol

What You Will Learn

In this chapter, you will learn about ICMP messages, their types, and (in many cases) the codes used in each type. We'll look at which ICMP messages are routinely blocked at firewalls and which are essential for proper device operation.

You will learn about the common ping utility for determining device accessibility ("reachability") on an IP network. We'll discuss the mechanics of both ping and traceroute, and use several ping examples to illustrate ICMP on the network.

The only function of the IP layer is to provide addressing for and route the IP packet. That's all. Once an IP packet has been dealt with, the IP layer just looks for the next packet. But IP is a connectionless, "best effort," or "unreliable" method of packet delivery. The terms "best effort" and "unreliable" often make it sound like IP is casual about the delivery of packets, which is why they are in quotes so that no one takes them too literally. IP's best effort is usually just fine, given the low error rates on modern transports, and it is mostly unreliable with regard to a lack of guarantees, as has been pointed out. Besides, there is nothing wrong with letting other layers, such as the TCP segments or the Ethernet frames, have the major responsibility for error detection and correction.

This is not to say that IP should be oblivious to errors. The network layer, in its ubiquitous and key position at the heart of the protocol stack, should know about packet errors and is in a good position to let layers above know what's going on (although IP lets the upper layers decide what to do about the condition).

And there's plenty that can still go wrong, and not just with regard to bit errors. A packet might wander the router cloud until the TTL field hits zero. A destination server might be down. A destination server might no longer *exist*. The "do not fragment" bit might forbid fragmentation when it is needed to send a packet, stopping the routing process cold. In all of these situations, the sender should be informed of the condition.

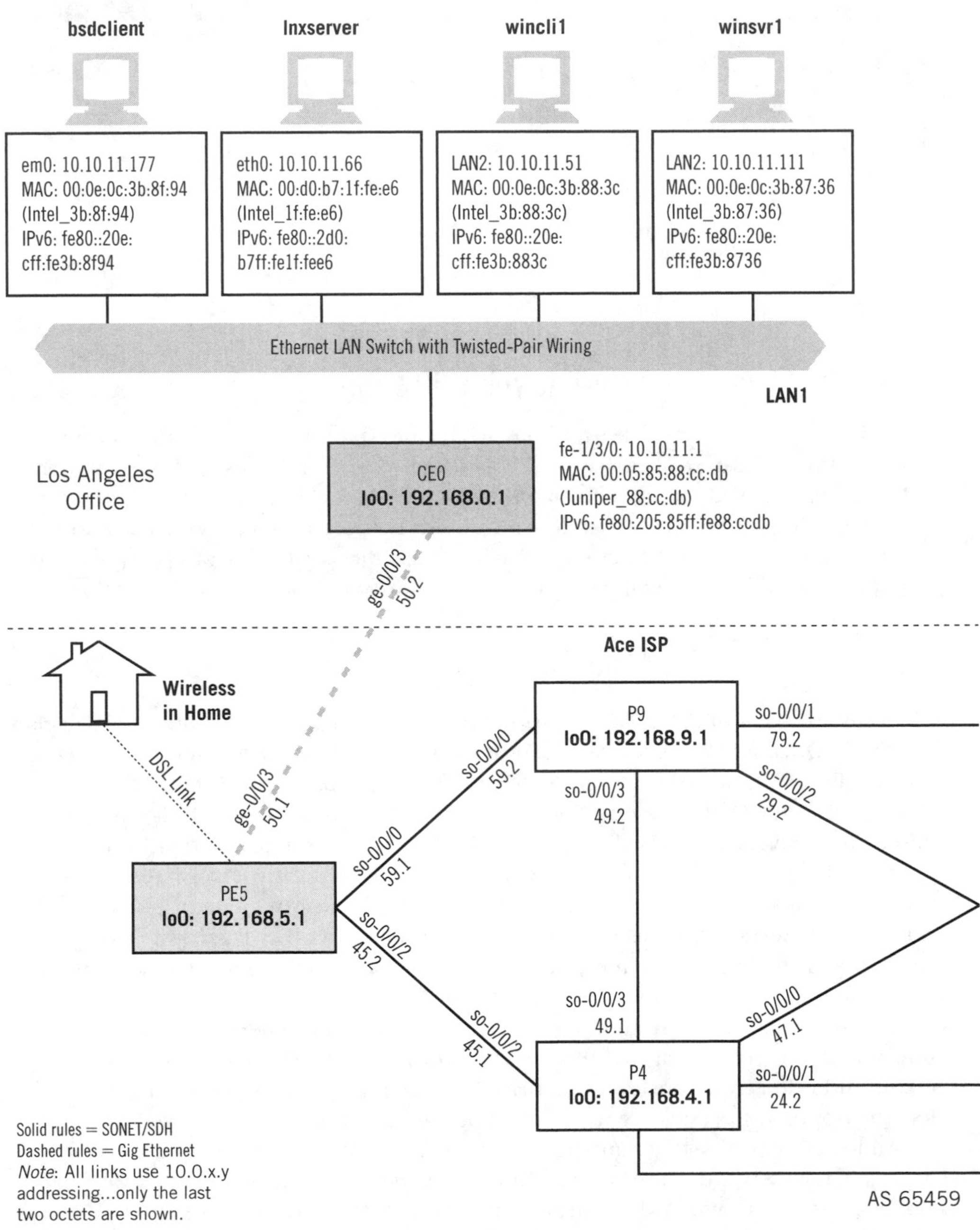

FIGURE 7.1

ICMP is used on all devices on the Illustrated Network, routers, and hosts. In this chapter, we'll work with the hosts on the LANs.

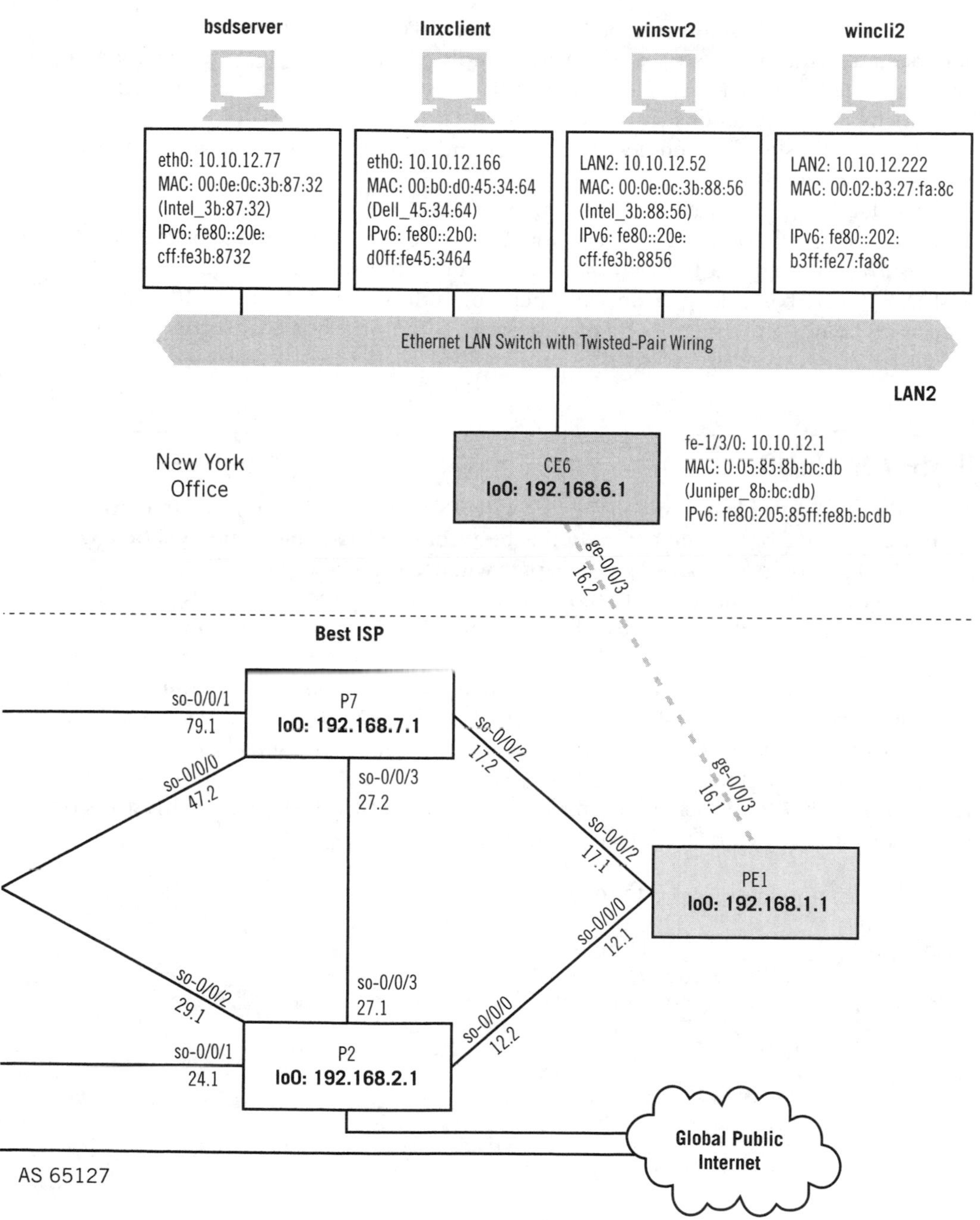

bsdserver
lnxclient
winsvr2
wincli2
eth0: 10.10.12.77
MAC: 00:0e:0c:3b:87:32
(Intel_3b:87:32)
IPv6: fe80::20e:
cff:fe3b:8732
eth0: 10.10.12.166
MAC: 00:b0:d0:45:34:64
(Dell_45:34:64)
IPv6: fe80::2b0:
d0ff:fe45:3464
LAN2: 10.10.12.52
MAC: 00:0e:0c:3b:88:56
(Intel_3b:88:56)
IPv6: fe80::20e:
cff:fe3b:8856
LAN2: 10.10.12.222
MAC: 00:02:b3:27:fa:8c
IPv6: fe80::202:
b3ff:fe27:fa8c
Ethernet LAN Switch with Twisted-Pair Wiring
LAN2
New York
Office
CE6
lo0: 192.168.6.1
fe-1/3/0: 10.10.12.1
MAC: 0:05:85:8b:bc:db
(Juniper_8b:bc:db)
IPv6: fe80:205:85ff:fe8b:bcdb
ge-0/0/3
16.2
Best ISP
so-0/0/1
79.1
P7
lo0: 192.168.7.1
so-0/0/2
17.2
ge-0/0/3
16.1
so-0/0/0
47.2
so-0/0/3
27.2
so-0/0/2
17.1
PE1
lo0: 192.168.1.1
so-0/0/0
12.1
so-0/0/2
29.1
so-0/0/3
27.1
so-0/0/0
12.2
so-0/0/1
24.1
P2
lo0: 192.168.2.1
Global Public
Internet
AS 65127

Without error condition feedback from the network, the natural response to an unexpected result (in this case, a reply) is to simply repeat the original message. Sometimes this might work, especially if the condition is transient, but semipermanent or permanent error conditions must be reported to the source. Otherwise, repetitive sending might result in an endless error loop, and certainly adds unnecessary traffic loads to the network.

This chapter explores aspects of IP's built-in error reporting protocol, the Internet Control Message Protocol (ICMP). Note that ICMP does not deal with "error messages," but "*control* messages," a better term to cover all of the roles that have evolved for ICMP. We'll start by looking at one indispensable utility used on all TCP/IP network: ping. We'll be using the same LAN-based hosts as in the previous chapter, as shown in Figure 7.1.

ICMP AND PING

The easiest way to look at ICMP on the Illustrated Network is with ping and traceroute. Both utilities have been used before in this book, but because traceroute will be used again in the chapters on routing, this chapter will use ICMP and ping.

The ping utility is just a way to "bounce" packets off a target device and see if it is there—that is, it has the IP address that was provided, is powered on, and alive. The device might still not function in the correct way (i.e., the router might not be routing properly), but at least the device is present and accounted for. It is routine to ping a newly installed device, host, router, or anything else, just to see if it responds. If it doesn't, network administrators have a place to start troubleshooting.

Let's use ping from the `lnxclient` to the `bsdserver`, both on LAN2 to start exploring ICMP. Windows XP only sends four pings by default, but Unix systems will just keep going until stopped with `^C` (which is what was done here).

```
[root@lnxclient admin]# ping 10.10.12.77
PING 10.10.12.77 (10.10.12.77) 56(84) bytes of data.
64 bytes from 10.10.12.77: icmp_seq=1 ttl=64 time=0.549 ms
64 bytes from 10.10.12.77: icmp_seq=2 ttl=64 time=0.169 ms
64 bytes from 10.10.12.77: icmp_seq=3 ttl=64 time=0.171 ms
64 bytes from 10.10.12.77: icmp_seq=4 ttl=64 time=0.187 ms
64 bytes from 10.10.12.77: icmp_seq=5 ttl=64 time=0.216 ms
^C

--- 10.10.12.77 ping statistics ---
5 packets transmitted, 5 received, 0% packet loss, time 3996ms
rtt min/avg/max/mdev = 0.169/0.258/0.549/0.146 ms
[root@lnxclient admin]#
```

The output shows the ICMP sequence numbers and round-trip time (`rtt`) for the group in terms of minimum, average, maximum, and even the maximum deviation from the mean. We do not have DNS on the network, so we have to use IP addresses. Most ping implementations will accept host names, and some (such as Cisco routers) will even do a reverse DNS lookup when given an IP address and report the host name in the result. This can be very helpful when an IP address is entered incorrectly or assigned to a different device than anticipated.

We can look at the ICMP packets used with ping in more detail. Let's use both LANs this time, and ping from wincl1 (10.10.11.51) on LAN1 to wincli2 (10.10.12.222) on LAN2. With XP, we won't have to worry about stopping the sequence.

```
C:\Documents and Settings\Owner> ping 10.10.12.222

Pinging 10.10.12.222 with 32 bytes of data:

Reply from 10.10.12.222: bytes=32 time<1ms TTL=126
Reply from 10.10.12.222: bytes=32 time<1ms TTL=126
Reply from 10.10.12.222: bytes=32 time<1ms TTL=126
Reply from 10.10.12.222: bytes=32 time<1ms TTL=126

Ping statistics for 10.10.12.222:
   Packets: Sent = 4, Received = 4, Lost = 0 (0% less),
Approximate round-trip times in milliseconds:
   Minimum = 0ms, Maximum = 0ms, Average - 0ms
```

Due to the way the Windows operating systems handle timing, it's not unusual to have RTTs of 0.

What does this group of packets look like at the target? Figure 7.2 shows us.

We can see that the four pings are accomplished with eight packets sent over the network. Look at the last column in the upper part of the figure. Ping employs messages in request-reply pairs using the ICMP protocol. An Echo request is sent out which basically tells the receiver to "send an ICMP Echo message back to me, okay?" Once the reply is received, the next request is sent, statistics compiled as the procedure goes along, and so on.

The details of Frame 1 show that the ICMP message is carried directly inside an IP packet (and then Ethernet II frame). But ICMP is not often shown as a transport layer protocol. That would make ICMP function at the same level as things like TCP and UDP, and this is simply not true. ICMP, as we will find, is concerned with network layer problems, so portraying ICMP as a type of special protocol associated with IP is not really a mistake.

So technically, because IPv4 packets carry ICMP messages as protocol number 1, ICMP is as valid a layer above IP as TCP or UDP or any other of the 200 or so defined IP protocols that can be carried inside IP packets. But because every IP implementation must include ICMP (and IPv6 has ICMPv6), it makes sense to bundle ICMP and IP together. This also implies that ICMP messages do not report their own errors.

What if no reply is received by the source of a ping? The source then times out and another ICMP Echo request message is sent. Naturally, no statistics can be generated, and we get a "host unreachable" message in most cases. We can force a timeout simply by trying to ping a nonexistent address (this could also be the result of a simple typo).

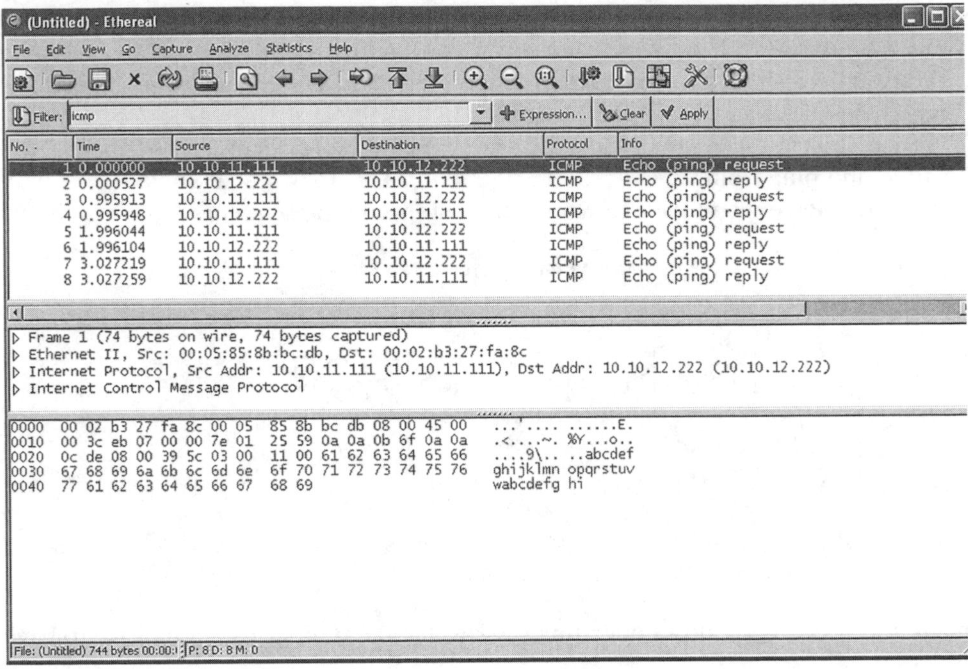

FIGURE 7.2

Ping ICMP requests and replies showing details of the ping echo request in the middle pane. Note that the content of the packet is the ICMP message, not TCP or UDP.

```
[root@lnxclient admin]# ping 10.10.12.55
PING 10.10.12.55 (10.10.12.55) 56(84) bytes of data.
From 10.10.12.166 icmp_seq=1 Destination Host Unreachable
From 10.10.12.166 icmp_seq=2 Destination Host Unreachable
From 10.10.12.166 icmp_seq=3 Destination Host Unreachable

--- 10.10.12.55 ping statistics ---
3 packets transmitted, 0 received, +3 errors, 100% packet loss, time 5022ms,
pipe 3
[root@lnxclient admin]#
```

Many ping implementations report either "unreachable" or "unknown" errors. The *unreachable* report implies that the target was once known to the source and reachable, but isn't "reachable" at the moment. The *unknown* report implies that the source has never heard of the target address or port. However, unreachable reports are often returned by a host source pinging a new device, which obviously should be unknown.

Most network people treat both error condition reports the same way: Something is just plain wrong.

Ping remains the first choice for checking connectivity on the Internet, between hosts, and between host and router. On LANs, the first troubleshooting step is "can you ping it?" If you cannot, there's no sense of going further. If you can, and things like applications still do not function as expected, at least the troubleshooting process can continue productively.

Firewalls sometimes screen out ICMP messages in the name of security. In these cases, even a failed ping does not prove that a device is not working properly. However, diagnostics become more complex, although not impossible. Of course, screening out *all* ICMP messages from a site usually also eliminates correct error reporting and proper operation of the device. After we list the ICMP message types, we'll discuss which ICMP messages are essential.

Ping works with IPv6, too. On most Unix hosts, it's called `ping6`. When used with the special IPv6 multicast address `ff02::1`, the `%em0` addition probes for the IPv6 address of every interface on the LAN, a form of forced ***neighbor discovery*** in IPv6. Here's what it looks like on LAN2 when run from the `bsdserver`.

```
bsdserver# ping6 ff02::1%em0
PING6(56=40+8+8 bytes) fe80::20e:cff:fe3b:8732%em0 --> ff02::1%em0
16 bytes from fe80::20e:cff:fe3b:8732%em0, icmp_seq=0 hlim=64 time=0.154 ms
16 bytes from fe80::202:b3ff:fe27:fa8c%em0, icmp_seq=0 hlim=128 time=0.575
ms(DUP!)
16 bytes from fe80::5:85ff:fe8b:bcdb%em0, icmp_seq=0 hlim=64 time=1.192
ms(DUP!)
16 bytes from fe80::20e:cff:fe3b:8856%em0, icmp_seq=0 hlim=64 time=0.097
ms(DUP!)
^C

-- ff02::1%em0 ping6 statistics --
1 packets transmitted, 1 packets received, +3 duplicates, 0% packet loss
round-trip min/avg/max/std-dev = 0.071/2.520/39.406/8.950 ms
bsdserver#
```

All four systems on LAN2 are listed, except for `lnxclient`, which does not have an IPv6 address. But hosts `winsrv2` (`fe80::20e:cff:fe3b:8856`), `wincli2` (`fe80::202:b3ff:fe27:fa8c`), router `TP6` (`fe80::5:85ff:fe8b:bcdb`), and even `bsdserver` (`fe80::20e:cff:fe3b:8732`) itself have all replied. Oddly, the Windows XP client replies with a hop limit of 128.

IPv6 traffic (and ICMPv6) is also visible to Ethereal, so we can explore the format of these packets a little further. Figure 7.3 shows how the exchange of the `ping6 ff02::1%em0` packets looks like from `wincli2` when run from `bsdserver`. Note that this only captures the exchange of packets that `wincli2` processes.

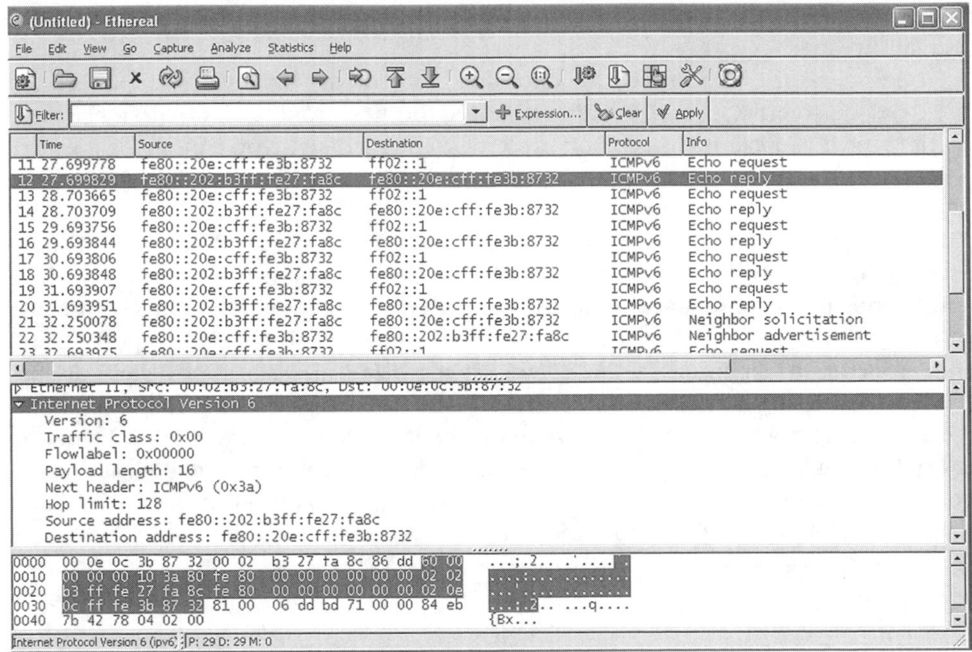

FIGURE 7.3

ICMPv6 capture showing the ICMPv6 echo reply message from `wincli2`. The header details are shown in the middle pane.

IPv6 uses its own version of ICMP, called (not surprisingly) ICMPv6. The ICMPv6 Echo reply message, sent in response to the ping to multicast group `ff02::1`, is highlighted in the figure. From the source address, we can tell this is from `wincli2`. We looked at the details of the IPv6 header in the last chapter. Note that the hop limit is 128 in the reply, and that the protocol number for ICMP is `0x3a` (58 decimal).

THE ICMP MESSAGE FORMAT

ICMP is usually considered to be part of the IP layer itself, and that is how ICMP is presented here. Hosts are supposed to set the IPv4 packet header TOS field to 0 if the packet carries an ICMP message, and routers are supposed to set the precedence field to 6 or 7.

Figure 7.4 shows the format of two ICMP messages. All ICMP messages start with the same three fields: an 8-bit Type and Code, followed by a 16-bit Checksum. Then, depending on the value of the Type, the details of what follows varies. So to be more informative, a second ICMP message is shown. The second message displays the format used for a very common network condition, Destination Unreachable, which we saw earlier.

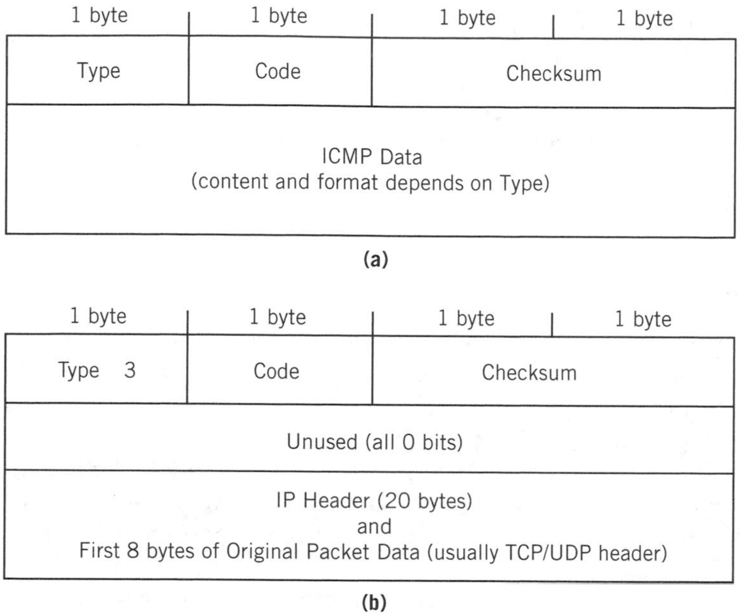

1 byte	1 byte	1 byte	1 byte
Type	Code	Checksum	
ICMP Data (content and format depends on Type)			

(a)

1 byte	1 byte	1 byte	1 byte
Type 3	Code	Checksum	
Unused (all 0 bits)			
IP Header (20 bytes) and First 8 bytes of Original Packet Data (usually TCP/UDP header)			

(b)

FIGURE 7.4

ICMP message format, showing how a specific message such as Destination Unreachable uses the fields following the initial three. (a) General format of ICMP message. (b) Format of Destination Unreachable ICMP message.

Destinations on a TCP/IP network can be unreachable for a number of reasons. The host could be down, or have a new IP address that is not yet known to all systems. The destination's Internet name could have been typed incorrectly (but still maps to an existing IP address), the only link to the site could have failed, and so on.

ICMP Message Fields

The fields that appear in all ICMP messages follow:

Type—This 8-bit field defines the major purpose of the ICMP message. Most indicate error conditions, but two of the most common type values, 8 and 0, mean Echo Request and Echo Reply, respectively. A Type value of 3 means Destination Unreachable. All Types determine the format of the rest of the ICMP message beyond the first three fields.

Code—This 8-bit field gives additional information about the condition in the Type field. This is often not necessary, and many Types have only a Code = 0 defined. Other Types have many Code values defined to allow the source to focus on the real problem. For example, Destination Unreachable (Type = 3) has 16 codes (0–15) defined.

Checksum—This is the same type of checksum as used for the IP packet header. This points out that ICMP, although considered part of IP itself, is really just as much a separate layer as anything else in TCP/IP and so must provide for its own error checking.

ICMP Types and Codes

There are about 40 defined ICMP message types, and message types 41 through 255 are reserved for future use. Only a handful of the types have more than a Code value of 0 defined, but these are the more important ICMP message types.

There are two major categories of ICMP messages: error messages (reports that do not expect a response) and queries (messages sent with the expectation of a matching response). Some others do not fall neatly into either category. The structure of the fields following the checksum depends on the type of ICMP message. These two formats are shown in Figure 7.5.

Note that the Destination Unreachable format shown in Figure 7.4 is an ICMP error message and does not generate a reply. The fields that appear following the initial three in the ICMP Destination Unreachable message are very common.

Unused—This 32-bit field must be set to all 0 bits for Destination Unreachable, but in other ICMP messages it is often used as a sequence number to allow requests and responses to be coordinated by senders and receivers.

IP Header and More—The last 28 bytes of the ICMP Destination Unreachable message consist of the original IP header (usually 20 bytes, but can be up to 60 bytes) and the first 8 bytes of the segment inside the packet. Usually, this includes the ports used by the TCP or UDP segment. This practice allows senders to realize exactly what field value is objectionable. It's one thing to say "Port unreachable," but better to say "Hey! The port in the UDP segment you sent, which is port 6735, can't be reached here right now..."

Usually, the error messages have the all-zero unused byte followed by the 28-byte header and packet data, but not always. Identifiers track Query message request/response pairs, and the sequence numbers help sort out queries sent by the same process (the process identifier, the PID, is often the ICMP Query identifier in Unix systems).

The suite of the 40 ICMP message types can be implemented by hosts or routers. Some of the types are mandatory, some are optional, some are for experimental use, and some are obsolete. In some cases, specifications explicitly state that hosts or routers be able to transmit and receive (process) ICMP messages, but not in all cases.

1 byte	1 byte	1 byte	1 byte
Type	Code	Checksum	
Content Depends on Type/Code*			
IP Header (20 bytes) and First 8 bytes of Original Packet Data (usually TCP/UDP header)			

(a)

**Usually all 0 (unused) except for:*
Type 3/Code 4: Destination unreachable, fragmentation needed
(fields are 2 bytes unused and 2-byte link MTU size)
Type 3/Code 5: Destination unreachable, redirect (field is router IP address)
Type 12/Code 0: Parameter problem (field is 4-bit pointer to parameter, rest all 0)

1 byte	1 byte	1 byte	1 byte
Type 3	Code	Checksum	
Identifier for Request/Response pairs (usually PID in Unix)		Sequence Number (set to 0 initially and incremented)	
Content depends on Query Type			

(b)

FIGURE 7.5

ICMP error and query messages. Note that error messages include the IP header that generated the error. (a) ICMP error message. (b) ICMP query message.

Let's take a look at what the specifications say about ICMP messages. First, we'll look at error messages, and then query messages, and then all the rest.

ICMP Error Messages

ICMP Error messages report semipermanent network conditions. The five ICMP error messages are displayed in Table 7.1, which shows how routers and hosts should handle each type.

Time-exceeded errors result from TTL expiration (Code = 0) or when fragments cannot be completed quickly enough at a receiver (Code = 1). Parameter problems are usually sent in regard to IP options. The codes are for a bad IP header (0), missing a required option field (1), or a bad length (2).

Which of these message types are essential to device operation and should not be blocked? Generally, the Destination Unreachable is essential (it is used by traceroute), and used in MTU path calculations. Of the others, the Redirect message is most often

Table 7.1 ICMP Error Messages

Type	Meaning	Codes	Data	Router Sends	Router Receives	Host Sends	Host Receives
3	Destination Unreachable	0–15	IP hdr + 8 bytes	M	M	M	M
4	Source Quench	0	IP hdr + 8 bytes	Obs	Obs	Obs	Obs
5	Redirect	0–3	IP hdr + 8 bytes	M	M	Opt	Opt
11	Time Exceeded	0–1	IP hdr + 8 bytes	M	M	Opt	Opt
12	Parameter Problem	0–2	IP hdr + 8 bytes	M	M	M	M

Obs, obsolete; Opt, optional; M, mandatory.

Table 7.2 ICMP Destination Unreachable Codes

Code	Meaning
0	Network is unreachable (the router's links to it might have failed).
1	Host is unreachable (the router can't reach the host; it might be turned off).
2	Requested protocol is unreachable (the process might not be running on the host).
3	Port is unreachable (the remote application might not be running on the host).
4	Fragmentation needed at router but DF flag is set (used for path MTU determination).
5	Source route has failed (source route path might go through down link or router).
6	Destination network is unknown (different than Code = 0; router can't find it).
7	Destination host is unknown (different than Code = 1; router can't find host).
8	Source host is isolated (source host is not allowed to send onto the network).
9	Communication with this network is administratively forbidden (due to firewall).
10	Communication with this host is administratively forbidden (due to firewall).
11	Network is unreachable with specified Type of Service (router can't forward).
12	Host is unreachable with specified Type of Service (router can't forward).
13	Communication administratively prohibited (by route filtering).
14	Host precedence violation (the first-hop router does not support this precedence).
15	Precedence cut-off in effect (requested precedence too low for router network).

blocked, because it does just as it says, that is, it tells another device to send packets somewhere else.

Many ICMP errors are Destination Unreachable errors. The 16 codes for this error type and their meanings are shown in Table 7.2, which includes a likely cause for the condition.

The precedence bits are in the TOS field of the IPv4 packet header, and are distinct from the TOS bits themselves (and are almost universally ignored anyway).

ICMP Query Messages

ICMP Query messages are used to question conditions on the network. These messages are used in pairs, and each request anticipates a response. The 10 ICMP Query messages are listed in Table 7.3, which shows how routers and hosts should handle each type.

These ICMP messages in Table 7.3 allow routers and hosts to query for timestamp, address mask, and domain name information. Echo requests and replies have special uses described in the section of this chapter on ping.

Table 7.3 ICMP Query Messages

Type	Meaning	Codes	Data	Router Sends	Router Receives	Host Sends	Host Receives
0	Echo reply	0	Varies	M	M	M	M
8	Echo request	0	Varies	M	M	M	M
13	Timestamp request	0	12 bytes	Opt	Opt	Opt	Opt
14	Timestamp reply	0	12 bytes	Opt	Opt	Opt	Opt
15	Information request	0	0 bytes	Obs	Obs	Obs	Obs
16	Information reply	0	0 bytes	Obs	Obs	Obs	Obs
17	Mask request	0	4 bytes	M	M	Opt	Opt
18	Mask reply	0	4 bytes	M	M	Opt	Opt
37	Domain name request	0	0 bytes	M	M	M	M
38	Domain name reply	0	0 bytes	M	M	M	M

Obs, obsolete; Opt, optional; M, mandatory.

Which of these should be allowed to pass through firewalls? Sites most often allow Echo messages (used by ping), although some allow only incoming Echo replies but not Echo requests (which allows my devices to ping yours, but not the other way around). The timestamp reply is also used by `traceroute`, and if these messages are blocked, asterisks (*) appear instead of times in the `traceroute` report (we'll look at `traceroute` operation in detail in Chapter 9).

Table 7.4 Other ICMP Query Messages

Type	Meaning	Codes	Data	Router Sends	Router Receives	Host Sends	Host Receives
1	Unassigned	NA	NA	NA	NA	NA	NA
2	Unassigned	NA	NA	NA	NA	NA	NA
6	Alternate host address	0	(4 bytes)	(Prohibited)	(Prohibited)	Opt	Opt
9	Router advertisement	0	Varies	M	Opt	Prohibited	Opt
10	Router solicitation	0	0 bytes	M	M	Opt	Opt
19	Reserved–security	NA	NA	NA	NA	NA	NA
20–29	Reserved–robustness	NA	NA	NA	NA	NA	NA
30	Traceroute	0–1	Varies	Opt	Opt	M	M
31	Datagram conversion error	0–11	Varies	?	?	?	?
32	Mobile host redirect	0	Varies	Opt	Opt	Opt	Opt
33	IPv6 where-are-you	0	?	Opt	Opt	Opt	Opt
34	IPv6 I-am-here	0	?	Opt	Opt	Opt	Opt
35	Mobile registration request	0, 16	Varies	Opt	Opt	Opt	Opt
36	Mobile registration reply	0, 16	Varies	Opt	Opt	Opt	Opt
39	SKIP	0	Varies	Opt	Opt	Opt	Opt
40	Photurius	0–3	Varies	Exp	Exp	Exp	Exp

Exp, expired; Obs, obsolete; Opt, optional; M, mandatory; NA, not applicable.

Other ICMP Messages

Some ICMP messages do not fall neatly into either the error or query category. These messages are typically used in specialized circumstances. The other 25 ICMP messages are listed in Table 7.4, again showing how routers and hosts should handle each type.

The messages displayed in Table 7.4 are less intuitive than others. Many of the other messages are relatively new, apply to special circumstances, and not much has been published about their use.

Very little has been written on the use of the alternate host address message and the table is filled in with more suggestions than anything else. Router advertisement and solicitation messages are defined in RFC 1256 as part of "neighbor discovery" for IPv4 and a way around network administrators needing to know local router addresses.

The traceroute message was introduced in RFC 1393 and was supposed to be a more formal way to perform a traceroute, but never really caught on. RFC 1393 describes an alternate traceroute method that uses a single packet with an IP header Traceroute option field and uses the answering ICMP Type = 30 messages from routers to gather the same information while using far fewer messages. However, support for this method is not mandatory on routers, making this form of traceroute problematic.

Datagram conversion errors are part of the "Next Generation Internet" protocol using 64-bit addresses described in RFC 1475 and occurring when packets cannot be converted to the new format. The mobile-related messages (32, 36, and 37) are part of Mobile IP (or "IP Mobility"). SKIP is the Simply Key Management for Internet Protocols and is used for Internet security. So is Photurius, an experimental aspect of IPSec that has four codes: one reserved (0), one for an unknown IPSec Security Parameter Index (SPI, 1), one for failed authentication (2), and one for failed decryption (3).

SENDING ICMP MESSAGES

Few TCP/IP protocols have been the subject of as much tinkering and add-on functionality as ICMP. The original specification of ICMP was in RFC 792 and refined in RFC 1122 (Host Network Requirements) and RFC 1812 (Router Requirements). RFC 1191 added path MTU discovery functions to ICMP, RFC 1256 added router discovery, and RFC 1393 extended traceroute functions with a special message type not often used.

But at heart, ICMP is a collection of predefined messages to indicate very specific conditions. If the sender of a packet receives an ICMP message that involves ICMP itself (the query messages), then ICMP deals with it directly. Otherwise, other protocols are notified. (Unreachable ports are reported to UDP, which lacks the segment tracking that TCP has, and so forth.) The precise response of an application to an ICMP message can vary, but usually the error is reported to the user so that corrective action (even if it's just "Stop doing that!") can be taken.

When ICMP Must Be Sent

Systems that detect a packet error and discard the packet may or may not send an ICMP message back to the originating host. Usually it depends on whether the error is transient or semipermanent.

Things like invalid checksums are ignored in TCP/IP, because these are considered to be transient failures that should not persist. The philosophy is that if the data are important, the sender will simply resend. Transient errors are unlikely to repeatedly manifest themselves in a chain of packets, and thus do not indicate a network-wide problem.

However, semipermanent errors such as invalid IP addresses need to be reported to the originator. These are fundamental problems with the network or in the way that the application is trying to use the network. The sender must either stop or change the content of the packets.

It is important to realize that the presence of many ICMP messages on a network does not mean that things are not working well, nor does the lack of ICMP messages mean that the network is working fine.

Most users see only a handful of ICMP message types, especially those used for ping and `traceroute`, such as the Time Exceeded, Timestamp Reply, Destination Unreachable, and Echo messages.

When ICMP Must *Not* Be Sent

ICMP also establishes situations when ICMP messages must *not* be sent. Transients like checksum errors or intermittent link-level failures are clear examples, but ICMP goes further than this. Generally, error messages should not be sent if they will generate more network traffic and add little new information to what is obvious to the sender.

For example, RFC 1122 says that ICMP error message should never be sent if a receiver gets the following:

- ICMP error message (e.g., errors in ICMP checksums should not be reported as errors)
- Internet Group Management Protocol (IGMP) message (IGMP is for multicast, and multicast traffic tends to multiply exponentially on the network, and one error could trigger many error messages)
- Packet with a broadcast or multicast destination address (another traffic-oriented rule)
- Link-layer frame with broadcast or multicast address
- Packet with a special source address (all zeros, loopback, and so on)
- Any fragment other than the first fragment of a fragmented packet

PING

Most people who know little about how TCP/IP works usually know of the ICMP-based application known as ping. The original metaphor was the "ping" of a naval sonar unit. Ping is a simple Echo query-and-response ICMP message that is used to see if another device is up and reachable over the network. A successful ping means that network administrators looking at problems can relax a great deal: The network routers on the path and at least two hosts are running just fine.

Ping implementations and the parameters supported vary greatly among operating systems and routers (most routers support ping). Some only send four packets and quit, unless told to send more. Others send constantly until told to stop. The parameters can usually set many of the IPv4 packet header fields such as TTL, TOS, and so on to specific values.

Usually, Unix versions use the PID as the Identifier field in the ping message, but Linux increments this based on application calls. Unix ping messages are usually 56 bytes long, but Windows implementations use only 32 bytes. The payload of the ping message echoed back to the sender typically consists of an 8-byte timestamp and a fill pattern. The timestamp can be used to roughly calculate round-trip delays through the network (in milliseconds).

Ping has some quirks that users should be aware of. First, small pings (maybe 56 or 64 bytes in the packet) often work fine, while larger pings with more realistic payload sizes do not go through reliably. That's what users care about—the network is struggling with real data packets. Seeing a small ping getting through reliably is not always helpful.

Also, the round-trip times are not often vital information. You expect round-trip times to go up as packet sizes increase, and that's typically what is observed. The same is true if the network is heavily loaded. But this is a relative, not absolute, observation. Only when round-trip times are longer than expected, or if they vary by huge amounts, is there an indication that something is wrong.

Part of the reason that round-trip times are not reliable is that routers (in particular) and even hosts might process ICMP Echo requests at a lower priority than other traffic. In fact, in many router architectures, ICMP message processing requires a trip to the control-plane processor, while transit traffic is forwarded in the forwarding-plane hardware.

We'll be using ping extensively in many chapters in this book.

TRACEROUTE

Traceroute is not an ICMP-based network utility in the same sense that ping is. However, because traceroute uses ICMP messages to perform its functions, and for many people the next step after ping is traceroute, this is the place to discuss this utility. We'll use traceroute heavily in Chapter 9 and throughout the rest of the book.

After ping has been used to verify that an IP address is reachable over the network, the next logical step is to determine *how* the packets make their way to the destination and back. In other words, we would like to trace the route from source to destination (the reverse path is normally the same). Yes, IP networks route around failures and routing tables can change, but paths are usually stable on the order of hours if not days when things are not going completely haywire. Of course, paths might also simply be asymmetric, yet stable, so it is not only path changes that are challenging for traceroute interpretation.

Traceroute implementations vary even more than those for ping. Some have graphical displays and use other Internet utilities to display location and administrative information about the routers and networks uncovered. This in turn has made many network administrators so nervous that they routinely block traceroute ICMP messages with firewalls or route filters to hide topology details. In fairness, the Internet is no longer a teaching tool or good place to explore the limits of knowledge, and there are so many disruptive or even malicious people on the Internet, that a certain amount of anxiety is completely understandable (which is why a network such as the one used for this book makes so much sense).

On Unix-based systems, traceroute often sends a sequence of three UDP packets (a typical default is three) to an invalid port on another host (this number starts at 33434). The utility can also use ICMP Echo requests, which is what the Windows version does. Some versions even use TCP (a utility called `tcptraceroute`).

Whatever the type of packet, the TTL field is initially set to 1 in the three packet set, so the first router along the path should generate an ICMP Time Exceeded message to the sender. The round-trip delay in the timestamp field and IP address of the router is recorded by the sender and another set of packets is sent, this time with the TTL set to 2. These packets are discarded by the second router, and another ICMP message is sent back. The process is repeated until the destination host is reached and the host returns a Destination Port Unreachable message, or until a firewall is encountered that blocks the ICMP messages or unsolicited UDP traffic. (These messages mimic port scans and are sometimes blocked, as mentioned earlier in this chapter.)

The end result should be a list of the routers on the path from source to destination (or the firewall) that also records round-trip delays. In some cases (sometimes many cases), some routers will not respond to the TTL "timeout" with an ICMP message, but simply silently discard the offending packet. If the packet does not return within the timeout window (Cisco routers use a default timeout of 2 seconds), most traceroute implementations indicate this with an asterisk (*) or some other placeholder and just keep going, trying to reach the next router. (The appearance of the asterisk does *not* necessarily mean that the packet was lost.)

One nagging traceroute issue is the number of messages exchanged over the network needed to reveal fairly basic information. RFC 1393 describes an alternate traceroute method that uses a single packet with an IP header Traceroute option field and uses the answering ICMP Type = 30 messages from routers to gather the same information while using far fewer messages. However, support for this method is not mandatory on routers.

We'll use traceroute a lot in many of the chapters of this book too.

PATH MTU

ICMP messages also play a role in path MTU discovery. We've already mentioned the MTU as a critical link parameter determined by the maximum frame size. Packets, including all headers, that fit inside the smallest frame size on the path from source to destination do not have to be fragmented and do not incur any of the penalties that fragmentation involves.

But tuning the path MTU size to packet size has another network benefit: This practice maximizes throughput and minimizes the overhead required to move large messages from system to system. Overhead bytes are those that do no useful work in terms of data transfer, but are necessary for the data transfer to take place at all.

Consider a data transfer using 68-byte MTUs, once the smallest size possible. If usual IP and TCP headers are used, which are 20 bytes each, they will take up 40 bytes of the packet, leaving only 28 bytes for data. So a whopping 59% (40/68) of the packet is made of overhead. And a minimum of 35,715 packets need to be sent, routed, and processed to transfer every megabyte of data. Bumping this MTU size up to 576 bytes (a typical default value and the functional minimum for IPv4) cuts the overhead down to about 7% (40/576) and requires only 1866 packets per megabyte of data, about 5% of the previous number of packets.

Using the typical Internet frame size of 1500, the overhead shrinks to about 2.5% and the number of packets required for a megabyte of data becomes a respectable 685. Larger MTUs have proportional benefits. (It is sometimes pointed out that bigger packets are not always more efficient; they can add delay for smaller units of traffic, a phenomenon often called "serial delay," and on high bit error links, larger packets almost guarantee that a bit error requiring a resend will occur during frame transmission. On older, more error-prone networks, throughput shrank to zero as packet size grew.)

The 576-btye MTU size was selected as a compromise between latency ("delay") and throughput for modems and low-speed serial SLIP implementation. This is directly related to the serialization delay discussed below. And use of an MTU size smaller than 512 precludes the use of the Dynamic Host Configuration Protocol (DHCP).

Now, TCP can adjust this message size, no matter what the default, but UDP traffic, which is growing, cannot. Of course, every link from host to router to router to host can have a different MTU size. That is what path MTU discovery is all about. It works via the following:

- Setting the DF flag in the IP header to 1 (don't fragment)
- Sending a large packet to the destination to which the path MTU is being determined
- Seeing if any router responds with an ICMP Destination Unreachable message with Code = 4 (fragmentation required but don't fragment bit is set)
- Repeating the first three steps with a smaller packet size

The process stops when a message is received from the destination host, showing that a path MTU of this size works. Again, paths are fluid on TCP/IP router networks, but they are remarkably stable considering all that can go wrong. By the way, it is assumed that the path MTU for outbound packets is the same as the path MTU size for inbound packets, but this is *not* true just often enough to make the process unnecessarily haphazard.

Table 7.5 Path MTU Plateaus for Various Network Link Types

Plateau Size in Bytes	Description
65535	Maximum MTU and packet size
32000	A value established "just in case"
17914	16-Mbps IBM token ring LANs
8166	IEEE 802.4 token bus LANs
4352	FDDI (100 Mbps fiber rings)
2314	Wireless IEEE 802.11b native frame (often "adjusted" to 1492)
2002	4-Mbps IEEE 802.5 token ring (recommended value)
1492	IEEE 802.3 LANs (also used in 802.2)
1006	SLIP
508	Arcnet (proprietary LAN from Datapoint)
296	Some point-to-point links use this value
68	Minimum MTU size

The path MTU "seed" or probe size and adjustment steps are not randomly chosen. A series of "plateaus" representing common link MTU limits has been established. Some of these are shown in Table 7.5.

In practice, as important as the path MTU size is, little is often done about the MTU size except to change the default to 1500 bytes if the default value is less (it usually is). This is because most networks that hold the source and destination networks are Ethernet LANs that do not support 9000-byte jumbo frames. Between routers, WAN links typically support larger MTU sizes (around 4500 bytes or larger), but that does no good if the end system can only handle 1500-byte frames. However, WAN links with MTUs greater than 1500 bytes allow the use of tunnel encapsulation of 1500-byte MTU packets without the need for fragmentation, so the larger MTU is not actually wasted.

ICMPv6

A funny thing happened to ICMP on its way to IPv6. It didn't work. ICMP, now officially called ICMPv4, is built around the IPv4 packet header and things that could go wrong with it. And not only is the IPv6 packet header different, as well as many fields and address sizes, but many functions added to IPv4 that affected ICMPv4 were scattered in separate RFCs and implementation varied. These functions are systematized in ICMPv6.

ICMPv6 makes some major changes to ICMPv4:

- New ICMPv6 messages and procedures replace ARPs.
- There are ICMPv6 messages to help with automatic address configuration.

- Path MTU discovery is automatic, and a new Packet Too Big message is sent to the source for over-large packets because IPv6 routers do not fragment.
- There is no Source Quench in ICMPv6 (it is obsolete in ICMPv4, but still exists).
- IGMP for multicast is included in ICMPv6.
- ICMPv6 helps detect nonfunctioning routers and inactive partner hosts.
- ICMPv6 is so different that it now has its own IP protocol number. IPv6 uses the next header value of 58 for ICMPv6 messages.

Basic ICMPv6 Messages

The general ICMPv6 message format is similar to ICMPv4, but somewhat simpler. The structure of a generic ICMPv6 message and the common Destination Unreachable message are shown in Figure 7.6. ICMPv6 error messages are in the range 0 to 127. Some of the most common are shown in the figure as well.

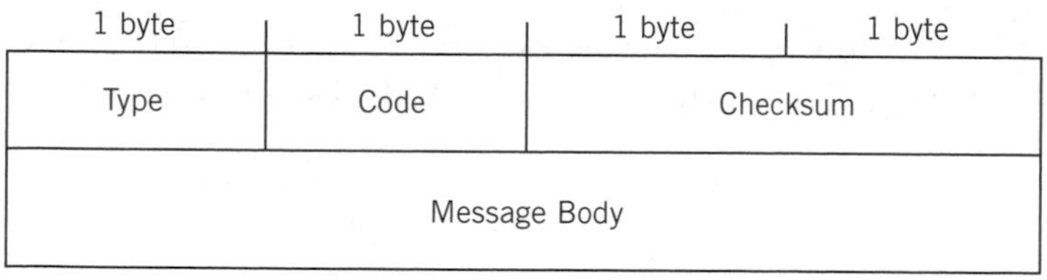

1 byte	1 byte	1 byte	1 byte
Type	Code	Checksum	
Message Body			

(a)

Basic ICMPv6 Type field values:
1 Destination Unreachable
2 Packet Too Big
3 Time Exceeded
4 Parameter Problem
5 Redirect
128 Echo Request
129 Echo Reply

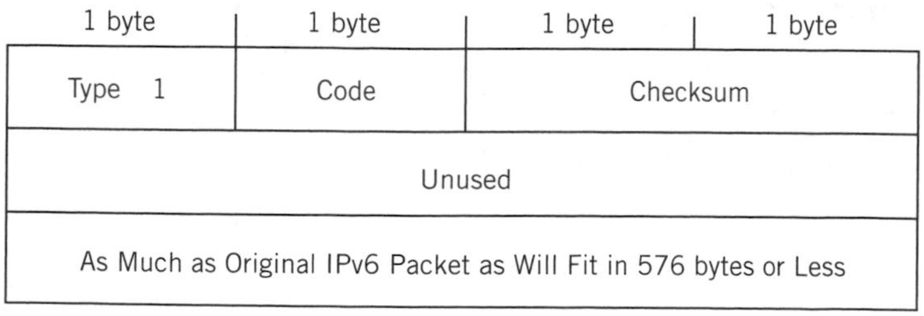

1 byte	1 byte	1 byte	1 byte
Type 1	Code	Checksum	
Unused			
As Much as Original IPv6 Packet as Will Fit in 576 bytes or Less			

(b)

FIGURE 7.6

ICMPv6 message formats, which can be compared to the IPv4 versions in Figure 7.4. (a) Generic ICMPv6 message format. (b) ICMPv6 Destination Unreachable message.

Table 7.6 Destination Unreachable Codes for ICMPv6

Code	Meaning
0	No route to destination
1	Communication with destination administratively prohibited
2	Next destination in the IPv6 Routing header is not a neighbor, and this is a strict route (routing headers are not currently supported)
3	Address unreachable
4	Port unreachable

Destination Unreachable

In ICMPv6, the Destination Unreachable message type is Type = 1. The codes that can be compared to Table 7.2 IPv4 codes number only five and are listed in Table 7.6.

Packet Too Big

A router sends an ICMPv6 Packet Too Big message to the source when the packet is bigger than the MTU for the next-hop link. The next-hop link's MTU size is reported in the message. In ICMPv4, this type of information was supplied in the Destination Unreachable message. The format of the Packet Too Big message is shown in Figure 7.7.

Time Exceeded

An ICMPv6 Time Exceeded message is sent by a router when the Hop Limit field of the IPv6 header reaches 0 (ICMPv6 Code = 0) or when the receiver's fragment reassembly timeout (senders can still fragment under IPv6) has expired (ICMPv6 Code = 1). The

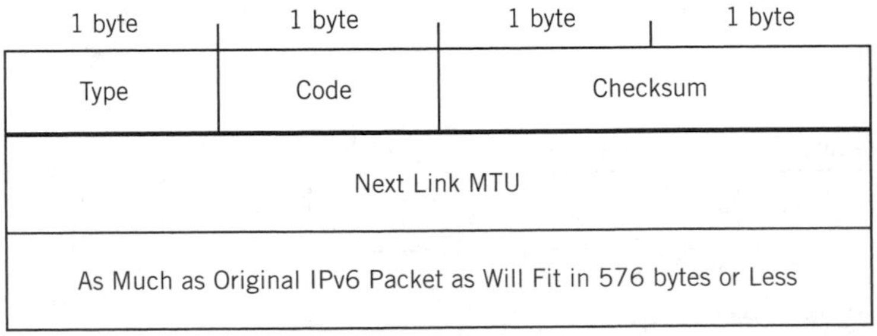

1 byte	1 byte	1 byte	1 byte
Type	Code	Checksum	
Next Link MTU			
As Much as Original IPv6 Packet as Will Fit in 576 bytes or Less			

FIGURE 7.7

ICMPv6 Packet Too Big format, showing details of the fields used.

Table 7.7 Parameter Problem Codes and Meanings

Code	Meaning
0	Erroneous header field encountered
1	Unrecognized next header type encountered
2	Unrecognized IPv6 option encountered

format is the same as for the ICMPv6 Destination Unreachable message, except that the Type is 3.

Parameter Problem

As in ICMPv4, an ICMPv6 Parameter Problem message is sent by a host or router that cannot process a packet due to a header field problem. The codes are listed in Table 7.7.

Echo Request and Reply

Under IPv6, ping becomes "pingv6" (the name is not important) and uses ICMPv6 Echo Request and Reply messages, but with Type = 128 used for requests and Type = 129 used for replies.

Neighbor Discovery and Autoconfiguration

ICMPv6 provides a number of neighbor discovery functions that help with:

- Location of routers
- IPv6 parameter configuration
- Location of local hosts
- Neighbor unreachability detection
- Automatic address configuration and duplicate detection

These ICMPv6 functions use the following message types:

Router Solicitation Type = 133 messages are sent by a host to ask neighbor routers to make their presence known and provide link and Internet parameters, similar to the ICMPv4 Router Solicitations. The message is sent to the all-router link-local IPv6 multicast address.

Router Advertisement Type = 134 messages are sent periodically by every router and in response to a host's Router Solicitation, similar to the ICMPv4 Router Advertisements. The message is sent either to the all-nodes IPv6 multicast address (unsolicited) or to the querying host (solicited).

Neighbor Solicitation Type = 135 messages are used, as ARP in IPv4, to find the link-layer address of a neighbor, verify the neighbor is still reachable with the cached entry, or check that no other node has this IPv6 address. These messages also detect unresponsive neighbors.

Neighbor Advertisement Type = 136 messages are sent in response to Neighbor Solicitation messages and resemble the ARP response. Nodes can also announce changes in link-layer addresses by sending unsolicited.

Neighbor Advertisements. Redirect Type = 137 messages perform the same role as the ICMPv4 redirect.

Routers and Neighbor Discovery

IPv6 routers provide their hosts with basic configuration and parameter information using Router Advertisement messages sent to the all-hosts link-local IPv6 multicast address. Hosts do not have to wait for these periodic router messages and can send a Router Solicitation message at startup. This reply is sent to the host's link-local address.

Each router will supply data that includes the following:

- Link-layer router address
- MTU for any links that have variable MTUs
- List of all prefixes and lengths used on the LAN (the specification says "link")
- Prefixes that a host can use to create its addresses
- Default Hop Limit value to use on packets
- Values for miscellaneous timers
- Location of a DHCP server where the host should fetch more information

Note that the Router Advertisement (RA) will indicate the availability of a DHCP server for stateless configuration (RA option O), or the requirement to perform stateful configuration (RA option M). The location of the DHCPv6 server is not specified, merely that it's available and what the requirements are for use.

Interface Addresses

Each IPv6 interfaces has a *list* of addresses and prefixes associated with it, including a unique link-local address. In theory, this should allow LANs to easily migrate from one ISP to another simply by changing prefixes and allowing the older prefix to age-out of the host. In practice, migration between IPv6 service providers is not as simple. DNS entries do not just "flop over," and host and router configuration (and firewalls!) have static configuration parameters. The point is that router advertisements assign a lifetime, which must be refreshed, to advertised prefixes. This also makes it easier to move hosts from LAN to LAN.

Each host can use some of the prefixes and lengths advertised by the routers (if they are flagged for this use) to construct host addresses. A private (ULA local) or global address can be constructed by appending a unique interface identifier to the advertised prefix and added to the list of the host's IPv6 addresses.

Router advertisements can also direct a host to a DHCP server that can assign addresses chosen by a network administrator.

Neighbor Solicitation and Advertisement

One of the problems with ARP in IPv4 was that it was essentially a frame-level protocol that did not fit in well with the IP layer at all. In IPv6,"ARPs" are ICMPv6 messages. ICMPv6 packets can be handled easily at the IPv6 layer, and can be authenticated and even encrypted with IPSec techniques.

In addition to finding neighbor link-layer addresses, the Neighbor Solicitation and Advertisement messages are used to find "dead" routers and partner hosts, and detect duplicate IPv6 addresses.

Neighbor Solicitation messages are sent to the solicited-node IPv6 multicast address, which is formed by appending the last 3 bytes of an IPv6 link-local address to a multicast prefix. The use of the multicast address cuts down on the number of hosts that has to pay attention to the "ARP" message (in fact, only the target system should process the request). The sender also includes its own link-layer address with the message.

Duplicate IP addresses are always a problem. Before a system can claim an IPv6 address or any other address *not* constructed by adding a link-local address to a prefix, the system sends a Neighbor Solicitation message asking whether any neighbor already has that IPv6 address. This message uses the special IPv6 Unspecified Source address as the source address, because you can't ask about a source address by using the source address! If the address is in use, the response is multicast to inform all devices. Addresses that are manually assigned are tested in the same fashion.

Dead routers and hosts are detected by a sending unicast Router and Neighbor Solicitation message to the device in question.

QUESTIONS FOR READERS

Figure 7.8 shows some of the concepts discussed in this chapter and can be used to help you answer the following questions.

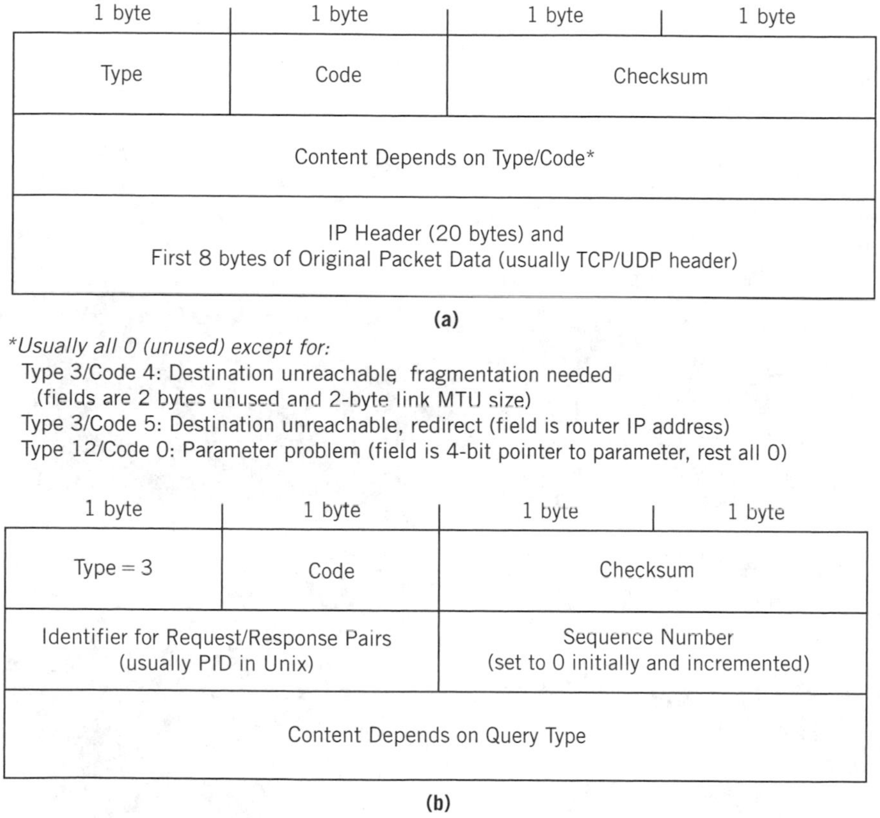

1 byte	1 byte	1 byte	1 byte
Type	Code	Checksum	
Content Depends on Type/Code*			
IP Header (20 bytes) and First 8 bytes of Original Packet Data (usually TCP/UDP header)			

(a)

*Usually all 0 (unused) except for:
Type 3/Code 4: Destination unreachable, fragmentation needed
(fields are 2 bytes unused and 2-byte link MTU size)
Type 3/Code 5: Destination unreachable, redirect (field is router IP address)
Type 12/Code 0: Parameter problem (field is 4-bit pointer to parameter, rest all 0)

1 byte	1 byte	1 byte	1 byte
Type = 3	Code	Checksum	
Identifier for Request/Response Pairs (usually PID in Unix)		Sequence Number (set to 0 initially and incremented)	
Content Depends on Query Type			

(b)

FIGURE 7.8

ICMP error and query messages in general. (a) Error message. (b) Query message.

1. How many types of error-reporting messages are there in ICMP? How many pairs of query messages are there in ICMP?
2. Which pair of ICMP messages can be used to obtain the subnet mask?
3. Which kind of ICMP message notifies a host that there is a problem in the packet header?
4. Which fields are used for the ICMP checksum calculation?
5. A ping sent to IP address `10.10.12.77` (the address assigned to `bsdserver`) on LAN2 is successful. Later, it turns out that the `bsdserver` was powered off for maintenance at the time. What could have happened?

CHAPTER

Routing

8

What You Will Learn

In this chapter, you will learn how routing works. We'll look at both direct delivery of packets to a destination without a router and indirect delivery through a router, both of which happen all the time. Routers provide indirect delivery between LANs while bridges essentially provide direct delivery only. Packet switching, on the other hand, is a related form of indirect delivery that will be explored in a later chapter.

You will learn about the role of *routing tables* and *forwarding tables* in the routing process. Technically, routers use the information in the routing table to create a forwarding table to forward packets to the *next hop* based on a metric, but many people use the terms *routing* and *forwarding* loosely, often using one term for both. We'll try to use the terms as defined here consistently in this chapter, but there is no real formal definition of either term.

The Internet is the largest router-based network in the world. Router-based networks, as we'll see in this chapter, are characterized by certain features and methods of operation. The most obvious feature of a router-based network is that the most essential network nodes are routers and not bridges or switches or more exotic devices. This does not mean that there are no bridges, switches, and other types of network devices. It just means that routing is the most important function in moving packets from source to destination. This chapter is an introduction to routing as a process.

Figure 8.1 shows the areas of the Illustrated Network we will be investigating in this chapter. The LANs and customer-edge routers are highlighted, but the other routers play a large but unseen part in this chapter. We'll look at the role of the service-provider routers in the chapters on routing protocols. For now, we'll focus on how sending devices decide whether the destination is on their own network or whether the packets must be sent to a router for forwarding through a routing network.

We'll talk about forwarding tables in later chapters that investigate routing and routers more deeply. For now, let's take a look at the simple routing tables that are used on the Illustrated Network's hosts and routers.

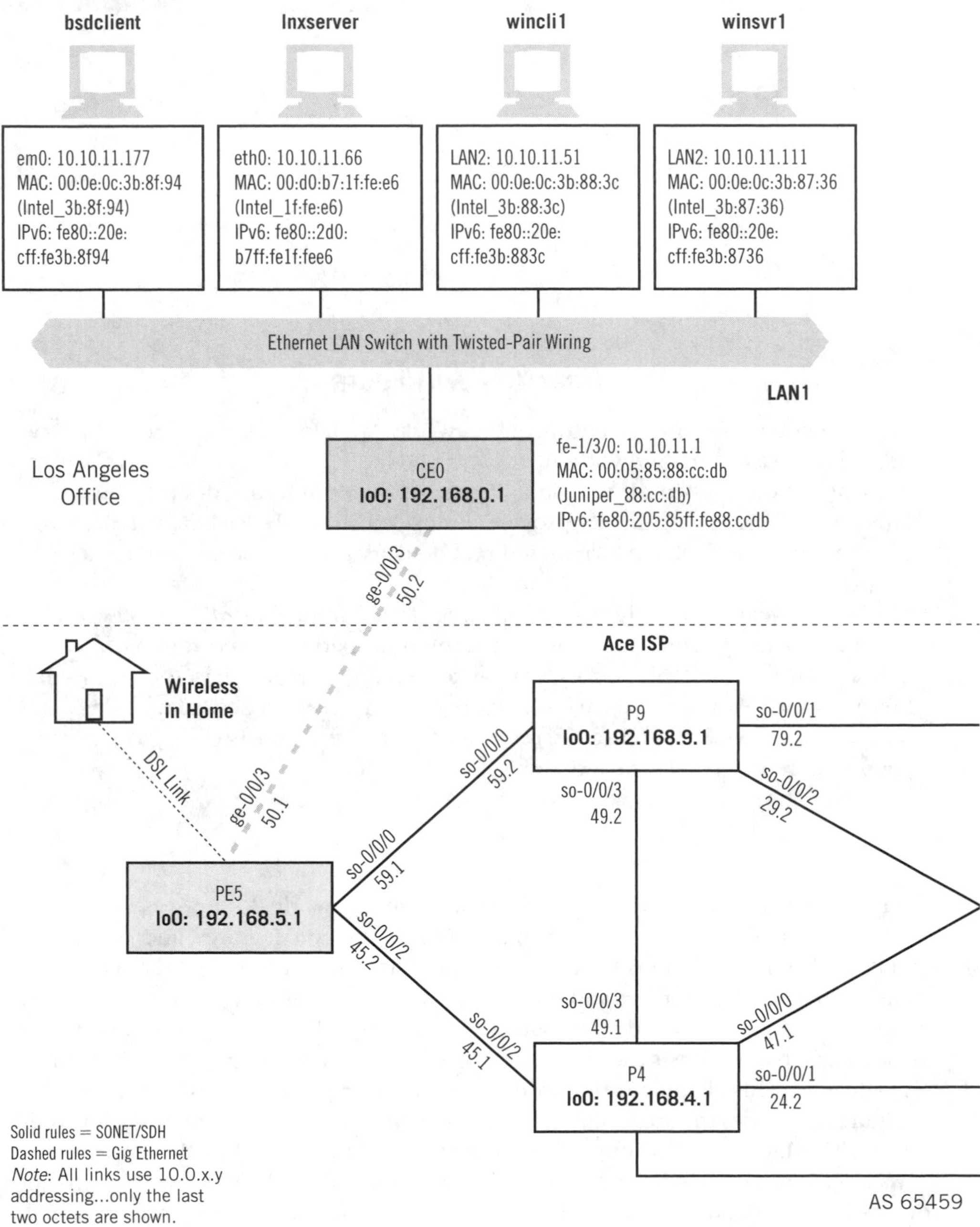

FIGURE 8.1

The Illustrated Network LAN internetworking, showing how the routers are connected and the links available to forward (route) packets through the network.

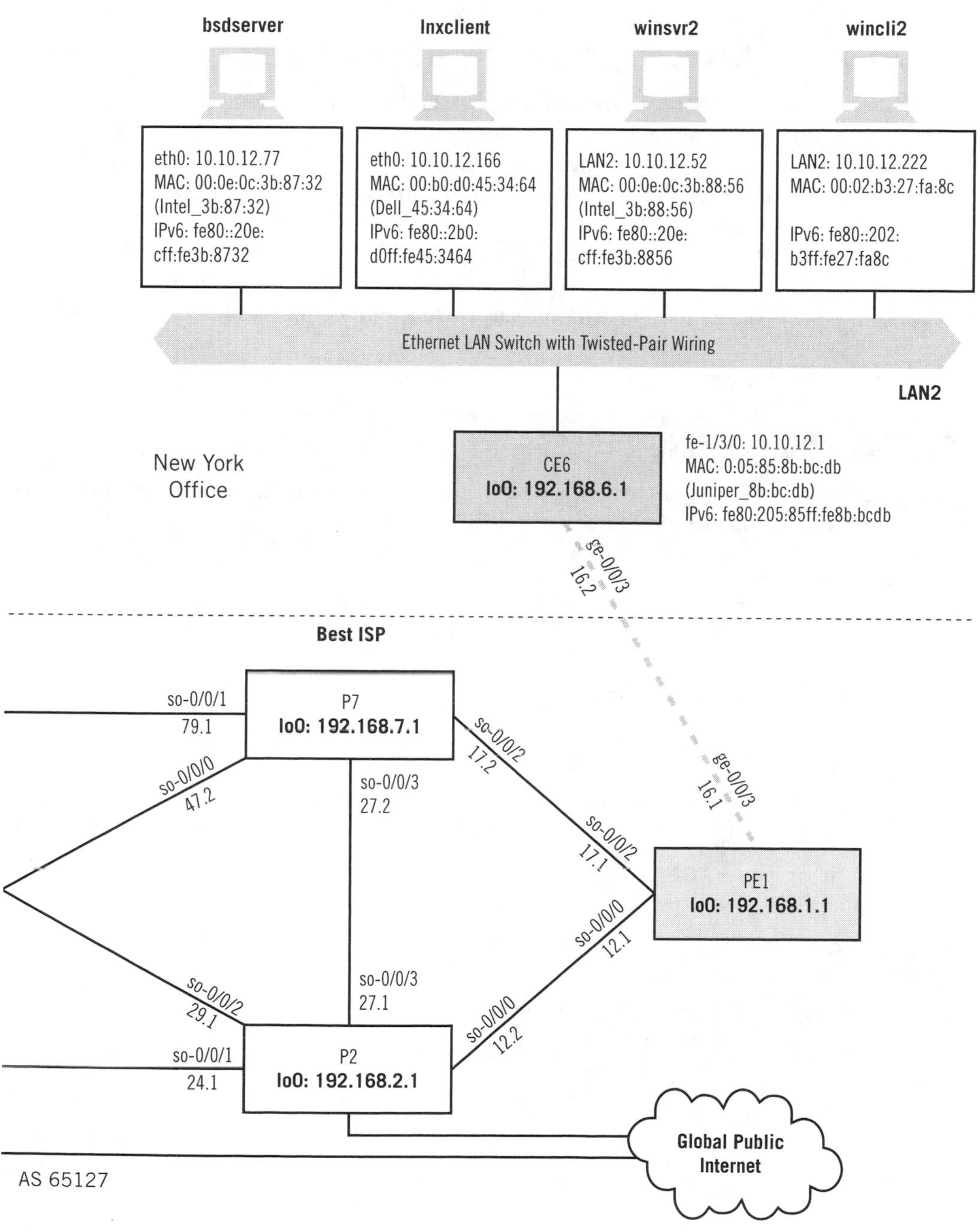

bsdserver
lnxclient
winsvr2
wincli2
eth0: 10.10.12.77
MAC: 00:0e:0c:3b:87:32
(Intel_3b:87:32)
IPv6: fe80::20e:
cff:fe3b:8732
eth0: 10.10.12.166
MAC: 00:b0:d0:45:34:64
(Dell_45:34:64)
IPv6: fe80::2b0:
d0ff:fe45:3464
LAN2: 10.10.12.52
MAC: 00:0e:0c:3b:88:56
(Intel_3b:88:56)
IPv6: fe80::20e:
cff:fe3b:8856
LAN2: 10.10.12.222
MAC: 00:02:b3:27:fa:8c
IPv6: fe80::202:
b3ff:fe27:fa8c
Ethernet LAN Switch with Twisted-Pair Wiring
LAN2
New York
Office
CE6
lo0: 192.168.6.1
fe-1/3/0: 10.10.12.1
MAC: 0:05:85:8b:bc:db
(Juniper_8b:bc:db)
IPv6: fe80:205:85ff:fe8b:bcdb
ge-0/0/3
16.2
Best ISP
so-0/0/1
79.1
P7
lo0: 192.168.7.1
so-0/0/0
47.2
so-0/0/3
27.2
so-0/0/2
17.2
ge-0/0/3
16.1
so-0/0/2
17.1
PE1
lo0: 192.168.1.1
so-0/0/0
12.1
so-0/0/2
29.1
so-0/0/3
27.1
so-0/0/0
12.2
so-0/0/1
24.1
P2
lo0: 192.168.2.1
Global Public
Internet
AS 65127

Routing Table and Forwarding Table

There are really two different types of network tables used in routers and hosts, and we'll distinguish them in this chapter. The routing table holds all of the information that a device knows about network addresses and interfaces, and is usually held in a fairly user-friendly format such as a standard set of tables or even a database, often with metrics (costs) associated with each route.

A forwarding table, on the other hand, is usually a machine-coded internal one that contains the routes actually used by the device to reach destinations. In most cases, the routing one holds more information than is distilled in the forwarding table.

ROUTERS AND ROUTING TABLES

The router that attaches LAN1 to the world is CE0, a Juniper Networks router. Let's look at the information in the routing table on CE0.

```
admin@CE0> show route
inet.0: 5 destinations, 5 routes (5 active, 0 holddown, 0 hidden)
+ = Active Route, - = Last Active, * = Both

0.0.0.0/0          *[Static/5] 3d 02:59:20
                 > via ge-0/0/3.0
10.0.50.0/24       *[Direct/0] 2d 14:25:52
                 > via ge-0/0/3.0
10.0.50.1/32       *[Local/0] 2d 14:25:52
                  Local via ge-0/0/3.0
10.10.11.0/24      *[Direct/0] 2d 14:25:52
                 > via fe-1/3/0.0
10.10.11.1/32      *[Local/0] 2d 14:25:52
                  Local via fe-1/3/0.0

inet6.0: 5 destinations, 6 routes (6 active, 0 holddown, 0 hidden)
+ = Active Route, - = Last Active, * = Both

::/0               *[Static/5] 2d 13:50:23
                    > via ge-0/0/3.0
fe80::/64          *[Direct/0] 2d 14:25:53
                    > via fe-1/3/0.0
fe80::205:85ff:fe88:ccdb/128
                   *[Local/0] 2d 14:25:53
                     Local via fe-1/3/0.0
fc00:fe67::/32     *[Static/5] 2d 13:50:23
                    > via ge-0/0/3.0
fc00:ffb3:d4:b::/64*[Direct/0] 2d 10:45:08
                    > via fe-1/3/0.0
fc00:ffb3:d4:b:205:85ff:fe88:ccdb/128
                   *[Local/0] 2d 10:45:08
                     Local via fe-1/3/0.0
```

Because both IPv4 and IPv6 addresses are configured, we have both IPv4 and IPv6 routing tables. There's a lot of information here that we'll detail in later chapters on routing protocols, so let's just look at the basics of CE0's routing tables. Only physical addresses are used for now, on the LAN1 interface fe-1/3/0 and the Gigabit Ethernet link to the provider routers, ge-0/0/3. Later, we'll also assign an address to the router's *loopback* interface, but not in this example.

In both tables, there are local, direct, and static entries. Local entries are the full 32- or 128-bit addresses configured on the interfaces. Direct entries are for the network portions of the interface address, so they have prefixes shorter than 32 or 128 bits. For example, the entry for the fe-1/3/0 interface has a local entry of 10.10.11.1/32 and a direct entry of 10.10.11.0/24. Both were derived from the configuration of the address string 10.10.11.1/24 to the interface (technically, a string like 10.10.11.1/24 is neither 32-bit host address nor 24-bit network address, but a concatenation of address and network mask).

Static entries are entries that are placed in the routing table by the network administrator, and they stay there no matter what else the router learns about the network. In this case, the static entry is also the *default route*, a type of "router of last resort" that is used if no other entry in the routing table seems to represent the correct place to forward the packet. The default route matches the entire IPv4 address space, so nothing escapes the default. Note that the highlighted default route for IPv4 is 0.0.0.0/0 (or 0/0) and sends packets out via interface ge-0/0/3 onto the service provider router network.

The local and direct entries for the ge-0/0/3 interface make up the last two entries in this simple five-entry routing table. The default entry basically says to the router, "If you don't know where else to forward the packet, send it out here." This seems trivial, but only because router CE0 has only two interfaces. Backbone routers can have very complicated routing tables.

Each route in the table has a *preference* associated with the route. A lower value means the route is somehow "better" than another route to the same place having a higher value. The value of 0 associated with local/direct entries means that no other route can be a better way of reaching the locally attached interface, which only makes sense.

Routing table entries often have a *metric* associated with them. Why do routes need both preferences and metrics? Preference indicates *how* the router knows about a route; the metric assigns a *cost* of using the route, no matter how it was learned. Both preference and metric are considered in determining the active route to a destination. Generally, only active routes are loaded into the forwarding table. We'll look at this process more closely in the later chapters of routing. An asterisk (*) marks routes that are both currently active and have been active the last time the router recomputed its routes to use in the forwarding table.

There are no metrics in the CE0 routing tables. Why? Because metrics are usually assigned by routing protocols and we don't have any routing protocols running yet on CE0. Static routes can be configured with metrics, but they still work fine without them.

The six entries in the IPv6 routing table mimic the five entries in the IPv4 table, and the default ::0 static route is highlighted. The only unassigned or "extra" entry is the fe80::/64 direct route (which is generated automatically) for the link-local prefix for LAN1.

HOSTS AND ROUTING TABLES

Routers are not the only network devices that have routing tables. Hosts have them as well. It's how they know whether to send a packet inside a frame directly to the destination or to send the packet and frame to a router so it can be forwarded to its destination.

The following code block shows what the routing table on bsdserver looks like. We can display it with the netstat -r command (the r option displays network statistics about the routing table). We'll use netstat -nr in this chapter because the n option forces the output to use IP addresses instead of DNS names. This is a good practice because when trouble strikes the network, chances are that DNS will be down (or provides the wrong information), so it's best to get used to seeing IP addresses in these reports.

```
bsdserver# netstat -nr
Routing tables

Internet:
Destination        Gateway           Flags        Refs       Use        Netif Expire
default            10.10.12.1        UGSc         0          0          em0
10.10.12/24        link#1            UC           0          0          em0
localhost          localhost         UH           0          144        lo0

Internet6:
Destination                 Gateway                  Flags       Netif Expire
localhost.booklab.          localhost.booklab.       UH          lo0
fe80::%em0                  link#1                   UC          em0
fe80::20e:cff:fe3b          00:0e:0c:3b:87:32        UHL         lo0
fe80::%lo0                  fe80::1%lo0              Uc          lo0
fe80::1%lo0                 link#4                   UHL         lo0
fc00::                      link#1                   UC          em0
fc00::20e:cff:fe3b          00:0e:0c:3b:87:32        UHL         lo0
fc00:fe67:d4:b::            link#1                   UC          em0
fc00:fe67:d4:b:205          00:05:85:8b:bc:db        UHLW        em0
fc00:fe67:d4:b:20e          00:0e:0c:3b:87:32        UHL         lo0
ff01::                      localhost.booklab.       U           lo0
ff02::%em0                  link#1                   UC          em0
ff02::%lo0                  localhost.booklab.       UC          lo0
```

The IPv4 routing table is even simpler than the CE0 router's, which we might have expected, because the host only has one interface (em0). The third entry (localhost) is for the loopback interface (lo0), so there are really only two. The 10.10.12/24 entry points to link#1, which is the em0 interface that attaches bsdserver to LAN1. It says Gateway above the column, but it really means "what is the next hop for this packet?"

Why does it say "gateway" and not "router"? Because technically it *is* a gateway, not a router. A gateway, as mentioned before, connects one or more LANs to the Internet (and can route from LAN to LAN, not just onto or off of the Internet). A router, on the other hand, can have nothing but other routers connected to it. People speak very loosely, of course, and usually the terms "gateway" or "router" can be used without confusion.

So the default entry does point to a router, in this case CE6, which is the gateway to the world on LAN2. The Refs and Use columns are usage indicators, and there is no Expire value because this information, as on router CE0, was not learned via a routing protocol and therefore will not get "stale" and need to be refreshed.

The flags commonly seen in FreeBSD follow:

- U (Up)—The route is the active route.
- H (Host)—The route destination is a single host.
- G (Gateway)—Send packets for this destination here, and it will figure out where to forward it.
- S (Static)—A manually configured route that was not generated by protocol or other means.
- C (Clone)—Generates a new route based on this one for devices that we connect to. Normally used for the local network(s).
- W (Was cloned)—A route that was autoconfigured based on a LAN clone route.
- L (Link)—The route references hardware.

Although listed as default, the actual entry value for the default route is 0.0.0.0/0 or 0/0. We can force numeric displays in netstat by using the n option, but we won't use that here (generally, the fewer options you have to remember to use, the better).

Where's the Metric?

Note the netstat -nr on the host did not display any metric values, and show route on the router didn't either. In the case of CE0, that was explained by the fact that we have no routing protocol running to provide metrics for routes (destination networks). But even if a routing protocol were running, netstat never shows any metrics associated with routes. Does that mean hosts have no metrics or do not bother to compute them? Not necessarily, as we'll soon see in the case of Windows XP.

Why is the Internet6 routing table so much larger than either the Internet (IPv4) table on bsdserver or the tables on router CE0? It is larger because of the IPv6 neighbor discovery feature that populates the table with all of the local IPv6 hosts on LAN2. An easy way to spot them is by their MAC addresses in the Gateway column. There are also number link-local (fe80) and private (fc00) entries absent in IPv4, as well as multicast addresses beginning with ff.

Let's look at the routing table on lnxclient for comparison. We don't have IPv6 running, so the table includes the IPv4 address only. Most of the information is the same as in FreeBSD, just arranged differently.

```
[root@lnxclient admin]# netstat -nr
Kernel IP routing table
Destination     Gateway         Genmask         Flags   MSS Window    irtt Iface
10.10.12.0      *               255.255.255.0   U       0 0           0 eth0
127.0.0.0       *               255.0.0.0       U       0 0           0 lo
default         10.10.12.1      0.0.0.0         UG      0 0           0 eth0
[root@lnxclient admin]#
```

The `Gateway` column has asterisks because we don't have DNS running and the address is the same as the `Destination`. Only the default gateway entry (`10.10.12.1`) is different than the entry (`0.0.0.0/0`). Instead of prefixes, `lnxclient` uses netmask (`Genmask`) notation for the table entries, but either way, the network is `10.10.12.0/24`.

The flags used in Linux follow (note the slightly different meanings compared to FreeBSD):

- G (Gateway)—The route uses a gateway.
- U (Up)—The interface to be used is up.
- H (Host)—Only a single host can be reached by the route.
- D (Dynamic)—The route is not a static route, but a dynamic route learned by a routing protocol.
- M (Modified)—This flag is set if the entry was changed by an ICMP redirect message.
- ! (Exclamation)—The route will reject (drop) all packets sent to it.

Linux hosts have the maximum segment size (`MSS`), `Window` size, and initial round-trip time (`irtt`) lists associated with the route, but these are not IP parameters. They're most useful for TCP, and we'll talk about them in the TCP chapter. And confusingly, a value of 0 in these columns does not mean that their *values* are zero (which would make for an interesting network), but that the *defaults* are used. The `Iface` column shows the interface used to reach the destination address space, with `lo` being loopback.

Finally, Windows hosts have routing tables as well. You can display the routing table contents with the `route print` command or with the same `netstat -nr` command using in Unix-based systems. This output is from `wincli1` and lists only the IPv4 routes.

```
C:\Documents and Settings\Owner>route print
Route Table
===========================================================================
Interface List
0x1 . . . . . . . . . . . . . . . MS TCP Loopback interface
0x2 . . .00 0e 0c 3b 88 3c. . . Intel(R) PRO/1000 MT Desktop Adapter -
Packet Scheduler Miniport
===========================================================================
```

```
===========================================================================
Active Routes:
Network  Destination       Netmask          Gateway       Interface     Metric
         0.0.0.0           0.0.0.0          10.10.11.1    10.10.11.51   10
         10.10.11.51       255.255.255.255  127.0.0.1     127.0.0.1     10
         10.255.255.255    255.255.255.255  10.10.11.51   10.10.11.51   1
         127.0.0.0         255.0.0.0        127.0.0.1     127.0.0.1     1
         224.0.0.0         240.0.0.0        10.10.11.51   10.10.11.51   10
         255.255.255.255   255.255.255.255  127.0.0.1     127.0.0.1     1
Default Gateway:        10.10.11.1
===========================================================================
Persistent Routes:
Network Address     Netmask          Gateway Address     Metric
     10.10.12.0     255.255.255.0    10.10.11.1          1
```

The table looks different, yet is still very familiar. There is an entry for the default gateway (10.10.11.1), which is also listed separately for emphasis. One oddity is the classful broadcast address entry (10.255.255.255), but this can be changed. There are explicit loopback (127.0.0.0/8) and multicast (224.0.0.0/4) entries, and a 255.255.255.255/32 entry, as well as for the host itself (10.10.11.51/32), which point to the loopback interface.

Instead of relying on a flag, Windows just shows you Active Routes. But there is also a Persistent Route that is always in the table, no matter what. This was entered in the table manually, like a static route, and makes sure that any packets sent to LAN2 go to the router at 10.10.11.1. It would still work with only a default route, but this shows how a static route shows up in Windows.

Note that even though no routing protocol is running in the host, wincli1 assigns metrics to all the routes. These can be changed, but they are always there. But what about when netstat -nr is used on the Windows host? We didn't see any metrics on the Unix-based systems. Take a look at what we get with netstat -nr.

This output is from wincli1 and lists only the IPv4 routes.

```
C:\Documents and Settings\Owner>netstat -nr
Route Table
===========================================================================
Interface List
0x1 . . . . . . . . . . . . . . . MS TCP Loopback interface
0x2 . . .00 0e 0c 3b 88 3c. . . Intel(R) PRO/1000 MT Desktop Adapter -
Packet Scheduler Miniport
===========================================================================
===========================================================================
Active Routes:
Network  Destination       Netmask          Gateway       Interface     Metric
         0.0.0.0           0.0.0.0          10.10.11.1    10.10.11.51   10
         10.10.11.51       255.255.255.255  127.0.0.1     127.0.0.1     10
         10.255.255.255    255.255.255.255  10.10.11.51   10.10.11.51   1
         127.0.0.0         255.0.0.0        127.0.0.1     127.0.0.1     1
```

```
          224.0.0.0        240.0.0.0         10.10.11.51  10.10.11.51  10
          255.255.255.255  255.255.255.255   127.0.0.1    127.0.0.1    1
Default Gateway:        10.10.11.1
===========================================================================
Persistent Routes:
Network Address     Netmask          Gateway Address    Metric
     10.10.12.0     255.255.255.0    10.10.11.1         1
```

That's right—the output is identical, and *does* show the metrics. However, Windows appears to be the only implementation that shows the metrics associated with routes when `netstat` is used.

Let's take a more detailed look at how routing tables are used to determine whether packets should be sent to the destination directly or to a router for forwarding. We'll see how IP and MAC addresses are used in the packets and frames as well.

DIRECT AND INDIRECT DELIVERY

When routers are used to connect or segment Ethernet LANs, the Ethernet frame that leaves a source may or may not be the same frame that arrives at the destination. If the source and destination host are on the same LAN, then a method sometimes known as *direct delivery* is used and the frame is delivered locally. This means that the source and destination MAC addresses are the same in the frame that is sent from the source and in the frame that arrives at the destination.

Let's see if we can verify that frames are delivered locally, without a router, when the IP address prefix is the same on the destination and on the source. In this case, the MAC addresses on the frame that leave the source and the ones in the frame that arrive at the destination should be the same.

We can also check and make sure that the frames use different MAC addresses when the source and destination hosts are on different IP networks and the frames pass through a router. We can even check and make sure that the frames came from the router.

First, let's use the Windows client and server (which are located in pairs on the two LANs) to generate some packets to capture with Ethereal. We'll use a little utility called "ping" (discussed more fully in Chapter 7) to bounce some packets off the Windows IPv4 addresses.

Ethereal is running on `wincli2`. When we send some pings to the client (`10.10.12.222`) from the Windows server (`10.10.12.52`), what we see is shown in Figure 8.2.

The MAC address `00:02:b3:27:fa:8c` is associated with IPv4 address `10.10.12.222`, and the MAC layer address `00:0e:0c:3b:88:56` is associated with IPv4 address `10.10.12.52`. If we looked at the same stream of pings on the server, the MAC address and IP address associations would be the same. The frame sent is the same as the one that arrives.

What about a packet sent to other IP networks? We'll use a little "echo" client and server utility on the Linux hosts to generate the frames for this exercise. We'll say more

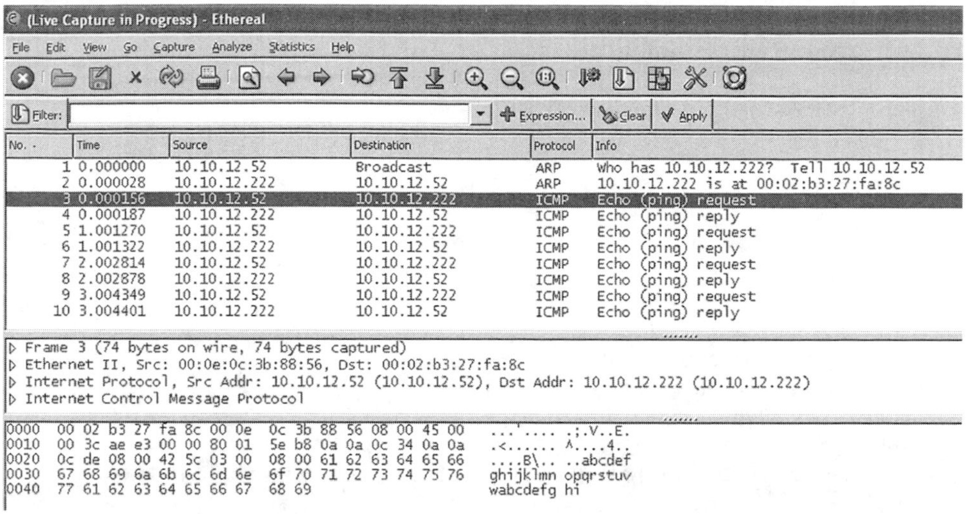

```
(Live Capture in Progress) - Ethereal
File Edit View Go Capture Analyze Statistics Help
Filter:                                   Expression... Clear Apply
No. Time      Source        Destination   Protocol Info
 1 0.000000  10.10.12.52   Broadcast     ARP   Who has 10.10.12.222?  Tell 10.10.12.52
 2 0.000028  10.10.12.222  10.10.12.52   ARP   10.10.12.222 is at 00:02:b3:27:fa:8c
 3 0.000156  10.10.12.52   10.10.12.222  ICMP  Echo (ping) request
 4 0.000187  10.10.12.222  10.10.12.52   ICMP  Echo (ping) reply
 5 1.001270  10.10.12.52   10.10.12.222  ICMP  Echo (ping) request
 6 1.001322  10.10.12.222  10.10.12.52   ICMP  Echo (ping) reply
 7 2.002814  10.10.12.52   10.10.12.222  ICMP  Echo (ping) request
 8 2.002878  10.10.12.222  10.10.12.52   ICMP  Echo (ping) reply
 9 3.004349  10.10.12.52   10.10.12.222  ICMP  Echo (ping) request
10 3.004401  10.10.12.222  10.10.12.52   ICMP  Echo (ping) reply

▷ Frame 3 (74 bytes on wire, 74 bytes captured)
▷ Ethernet II, Src: 00:0e:0c:3b:88:56, Dst: 00:02:b3:27:fa:8c
▷ Internet Protocol, Src Addr: 10.10.12.52 (10.10.12.52), Dst Addr: 10.10.12.222 (10.10.12.222)
▷ Internet Control Message Protocol

0000  00 02 b3 27 fa 8c 00 0e  0c 3b 88 56 08 00 45 00   ...'.... .;.V..E.
0010  00 3c ae e3 00 00 80 01  5e b8 0a 0a 0c 34 0a 0a   .<...... ^....4..
0020  0c de 08 00 42 5c 03 00  08 00 61 62 63 64 65 66   ....B\.. ..abcdef
0030  67 68 69 6a 6b 6c 6d 6e  6f 70 71 72 73 74 75 76   ghijklmn opqrstuv
0040  77 61 62 63 64 65 66 67  68 69                     wabcdefg hi
```

FIGURE 8.2

MAC addresses and direct delivery. Note that the MAC layer addresses in the frame that is sent are the same as in the frame that will arrive at the destination.

about where this little utility came from in the chapter on sockets (Chapter 12). For now, just note that this is *not* the usual Linux echo utility bundled with most distributions. With this utility, we can invoke the server on the `lnxserver` host and use the client to send a simple string to be echoed back by the server process. We'll use tethereal (the text version of Ethereal) this time, just to show that the same information is available in either the graphical or text-based version.

First, we'll run the Echo server process, which normally runs on port 7, on port 55555:

```
[root@lnxserver admin]# ./Echo 55555
```

We have to run tethereal on each end too, if we want to compare frames. The command is the same on the client and server. We'll use the verbose (`–V`) switch to see the MAC layer information as packets arrive.

```
[root@lnxclient admin]# /usr/sbin/tethereal-V
Capturing on eth0
```

Now we can invoke the Echo client to bounce the string `TESTING123` off the server process.

```
[root@lnxclient admin]# ./Echo 10.10.11.66 TESTING123 55555
Received: TESTING123
[root@lnxclient admin]#
```

What did we get? Let's look at the frames leaving the client. We only need to examine the Layer 2 and IP address information.

```
[root@lnxclient admin]# /usr/sbin/tethereal-V
Capturing on eth0
Frame 1 (74 bytes on wire, 74 bytes captured)
    Arrival Time: May 5, 2008 13:39:34.102363000
    Time delta from previous packet: 0.000000000 seconds
    Time relative to first packet: 0.000000000 seconds
    Frame Number: 1
    Packet Length: 74 bytes
    Capture Length: 74 bytes
Ethernet II, Src: 00:b0:d0:45:34:64, Dst: 00:05:85:8b:bc:db
    Destination: 00:05:85:8b:bc:db (Juniper__8b:bc:db)
    Source: 00:b0:d0:45:34:64 (Dell_45:34:64)
    Type: IP (0x0800)
Internet Protocol, Src Addr: 10.10.12.166 (10.10.12.166), Dst Addr: 10.10.11.66
(10.10.11.66)
    Version: 4
    Header length: 20 bytes... [much more information not shown]
```

We can see that the Ethernet frame leaving the Linux client has source MAC address 00:b0:d0:45:34:64 and destination MAC address 00:05:85:8b:bc:db. The packet inside the frame has the source IPv4 address 10.10.12.166 and destination address 10.10.11.66, as expected.

How do we know that the destination MAC address 00:05:85:8b:bc:db is not associated with the destination address 10.10.11.66? We can simply look at the frame that arrives at the Linux server.

```
[root@lnxserver admin]# /usr/sbin/tethereal -V
Capturing on eth0
Frame 1 (74 bytes on wire, 74 bytes captured)
    Arrival Time: May 5, 2008 13:39:34.104401000
    Time delta from previous packet: 0.000000000 seconds
    Time relative to first packet: 0.000000000 seconds
    Frame Number: 1
    Packet Length: 74 bytes
    Capture Length: 74 bytes
Ethernet II, Src: 00:05:85:88:cc:db, Dst: 00:d0:b7:1f:fe:e6
    Destination: 00:d0:b7:1f:fe:e6 (Intel_1f:fe:e6)
    Source: 00:05:85:88:cc:db (Juniper__88:cc:db)
    Type: IP (0x0800)
Internet Protocol, Src Addr: 10.10.12.166 (10.10.12.166), Dst Addr: 10.10.11.66
(10.10.11.66)
    Version: 4
    Header length: 20 bytes...(much more information not shown)
```

Note that the frame arriving at 10.10.11.66 has the MAC address 00:d0:b7:1f:fe:e6, which is not the one used as the destination MAC address in the frame leaving the 10.10.12.166 client (that address is 00:b0:d0:45:34:64).

Table 8.1 Frame IP and MAC Addresses

	MAC Source Address	IP Source Address	MAC Destination Address	IP Destination Address
Frame leaving client	00:b0:d0:45:34:64 (Linux client)	10.10.12.166 (Linux client)	00:05:85:8b:bc:db (Juniper router)	10.10.11.66 (Linux server)
Frame arriving at server	00:05:85:88:cc:db (Juniper router)	10.10.12.166 (Linux client)	00:d0:b7:1f:fe:e6 (Linux server)	10.10.11.66 (Linux server)

Now, if the MAC address associated with the frame leaving the 10.10.12.166 client is 00:bo:do:45:34:64, then the MAC address associated with the same IP address on the server LAN cannot magically change to 00:05:85:88:cc:db. As expected, the IP packet is identical (except for the decremented TTL field), but the *frame* is different. This is sometimes called *indirect delivery* of packets because the packet is sent through one or more network nodes and not directly to the destination.

These relationships are displayed in Table 8.1, which shows how the MAC addresses relate to the IP subnet addresses.

Tethereal not only gives the MAC addresses, but also parses the 24-bit OUI and helpfully lists Intel as the owner of 00:d0:b7 and Juniper as the owner of 00:05:85. We can verify this on the Linux client or server. Let's look at the client's ARP cache.

```
[root@lnxclient admin]# /sbin/arp -a
? (10.10.12.1) at 00:05:85:8b:bc:db [ether] on eth0
[root@lnxclient admin]#
```

The question mark (?) just means that our routers do not have names in DNS.

The Illustrated Network uses two small LAN switches for LAN1 and LAN2, but the nodes used for internetworking are routers. Let's take a closer look at just what a router does and how it delivers packets from LAN to LAN over an internetwork.

Routing

Routing is done entirely with IP addresses, of course. Many books make extensive use of the concepts of *direct routing* and *indirect routing* of packets. This can be confusing, since direct "routing" of packets does not require a router. In this chapter, the terms *direct delivery* and *indirect delivery* are used instead. A host can use direct delivery to send packets directly to another host, perhaps using a VLAN, or use indirect delivery if the destination host is reachable only through a router.

How does the source host know whether the destination host is reachable through direct (local) delivery or indirect (remote) delivery through a router? The answer has a lot to do with the way bridges and routers differ in their fundamental operation, and how routers use the IP address to determine how to handle packets. Here's an example using the Illustrated Network's actual MAC and IP addresses.

Direct Delivery without Routing

Let's look at a packet sent from `wincli` on LAN1 to `winsvr1`. Both of these hosts are on LAN1, so no routing is needed. The IPv4 addresses are `10.10.11.51` for `wincli1` and `10.10.11.111` for `winsvr1`, and both use the same `255.255.255.0` mask. Therefore, both addresses have the same network portion of the IPv4 address, `10.10.11.0/24`.

The host software knows that no router is needed to handle a packet sent from the source host to the destination host because the IP addresses of the source and destination hosts have the *same IP network portion* (prefix) in both source and destination IP addresses. This is a simple and effective way to let hosts know whether they are on the same LAN. The packet can be placed in a frame and sent directly to the destination using the local link. This is shown in Figure 8.3.

In Figure 8.3, a packet is followed from client to server when both are on the same LAN segment and there is no router between client and server. All direct delivery means is that the packet and frame do not have to pass through a router on the way from source to destination.

The TCP/IP protocol stack on the client builds the TCP header and IP header. In Figure 8.3, the IP packet is placed inside an Ethernet MAC frame. The MAC source and destination addresses are shown as well. The client knows its own MAC address, and if

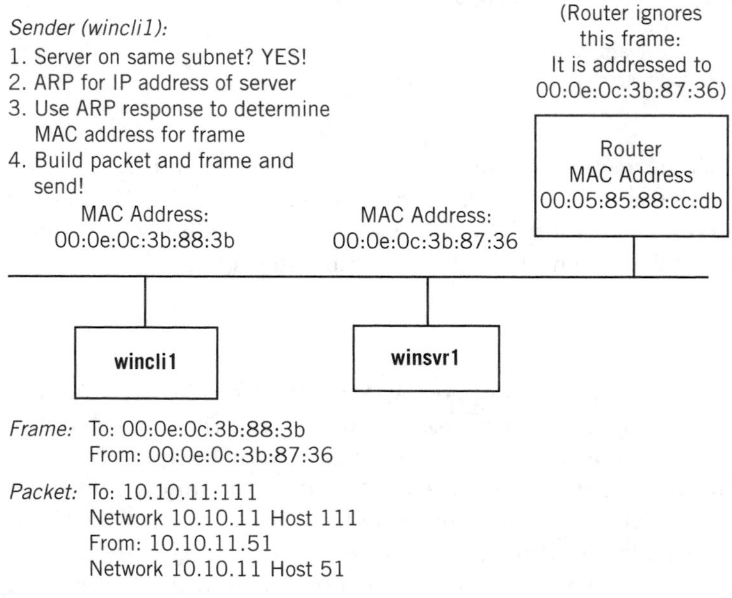

FIGURE 8.3

Direct delivery of packets on a LAN. Note that the MAC address does not change from source to destination, and that the router ignores the frame.

the server's MAC address is not cached, an ARP broadcast message that asks, "Who has IP address `10.10.11.111`?," is used to determine the MAC address of the server.

The source host knew to ask for the MAC address of the destination host because the destination host is on the same LAN as the source. Hosts with the same IP network addresses must be on the same LAN segment. Destination hosts on the same LAN are simply "asked" to provide their MAC addresses. The destination MAC address in the frame is the MAC address that corresponds to the destination IP address in the IP packet inside the MAC frame.

What would be different when the client and server are on different LANs and must communicate through a router?

Indirect Delivery and the Router

It is one thing to say that the router is the network node of the Internet, but exactly what does this mean? What is the role of the router on the Internet? Routers route IP packets to perform *indirect delivery* (through the *forwarding*) of packets from source to destination.

Unlike direct delivery, where the packets are sent between devices on the same LAN, indirect delivery employs one or more routers to connect source and destination. The source and destination could be near in terms of distance, perhaps on separate floors of the same building. All that really matters is whether there is a router between source and destination or not.

Figure 8.4 shows a simple network consisting of two LANs connected by routers. The routers are connected by a serial link using PPP, but SONET would do just as well. Of course, the Internet consists of thousands of LANs and routers, but all of the essentials of routing can be illustrated with this simple network.

The routing network has been simplified to emphasize the architectural features without worrying about the details. The routers are just Router 1 and Router 2, not `CE0` and `CE6`. But the LANs are still LAN1 and LAN2, and we'll trace a packet from `wincli1` on LAN1 to `winsvr2` on LAN2.

Both LAN segments in Figure 8.4 are implemented with Ethernet hubs and unshielded twisted pair (UTP) wiring, but are shown as shared media cables, just to make the adjacencies clearer. Each host in the figure has a network interface card (NIC) installed. It is important to realize that it is the *interface* that has the IP address, not the entire host, but in this example each host has only one interface. However, the routers in the figure have more than one network interface and therefore more than one IP network address. A router is a network device that belongs to two or more networks at the same time, which is how they connect LANs. A typical router can have 2, 8, 16, or more interfaces. Each interface usually gets an IP address and typically represents a separate "network" as the term applies to IP, but there are exceptions.

Each NIC in a host or router has a MAC address, and these are given in Figure 8.4. The routers are only shown with network layers and IP layers, because that's all they need for packet forwarding (most routers do have application layers, as we have seen). Because the routers in this example are in different locations, they are connected by a

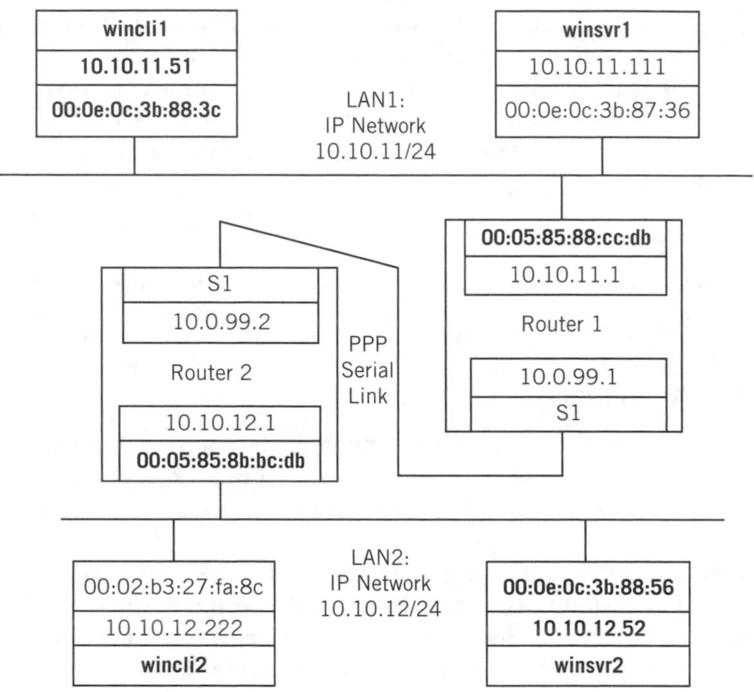

FIGURE 8.4

Indirect delivery using a router. Note the different MAC and link-level addresses in place between source and destination.

serial link. The serial link is running PPP and packets are placed inside PPP frames on this link between the routers. There is no need for global uniqueness on serial ports, since they are point-to-point links in the example, so each is called "S1" (Serial1) at the network layer. They don't even require IP addresses, but these are usually provided to make the link visible to network management and make routing and forwarding tables a lot simpler.

All of the pieces are now in place to follow a packet between client and server on the "internetwork" in Figure 8.4 using indirect delivery of packets with routers. Let's see what happens when a client process running on `wincli1` wants to send a packet to a server process running on `winsvr2`. The application is unimportant. What is important is that the source host knows that the destination host (server) is not on the same LAN. Once the IP address of the server is obtained, it is obvious to the source that the destination IP network address (`10.10.12.52`) is different than the source IP network address (`10.10.11.51`).

The source client software now knows that the packet going to `10.10.12.52` must be sent through at least one router, and probably several routers, using indirect delivery. It is called indirect delivery (or indirect routing) *because the packet destination*

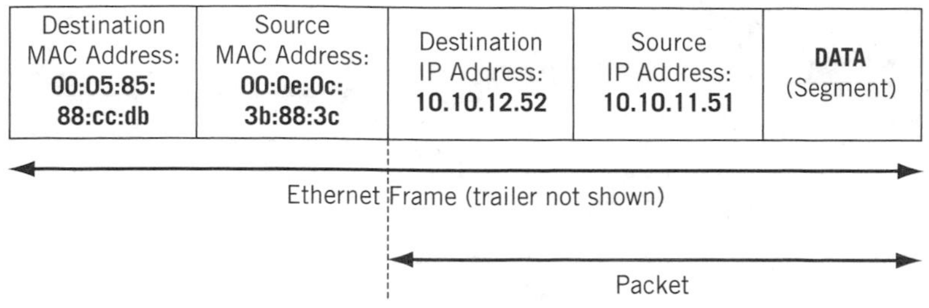

FIGURE 8.5

Frame and packet sent to Router1, showing source and destination IP and MAC addresses.

address is the destination IP address of `winsvr2`, *but the initial frame destination address is the MAC address of the Router1.* The packet is sent *indirectly* to the destination host inside a frame sent to the router. The address fields of the frame and packet constructed and sent on the LAN by `wincli1` are shown in Figure 8.5.

Note that the *frame* is sent to Router1's MAC address (`00:05:85:88:cc:db`), but the *packet* is sent to `10.10.12.52` (`winsvr2`). This is how routing works. (Bridges, or direct delivery even in routing, always has frames in which the destination MAC address is the same as the IP address it represents.)

How did the source host, `wincli1`, know the MAC address of the correct router? There could be several routers on a LAN, if for no other reason than redundancy. All that `wincli1` did was use the routing table to look up the IP address of the destination. But there's no specific entry for a network associated with `10.10.12.52`. However, TCP/IP configuration on a host often includes configuration of at least one *default gateway* to be used when packets must leave the local LAN. The default gateway (a router in this case) can be set statically, or dynamically using the Dynamic Host Configuration Protocol (DHCP), or even other ways. In this example network, the default gateway IP address has been entered statically when the host was configured for TCP/IP.

Since the default gateway is by definition on the same LAN as the source host (they share the same IP address prefix), the source host can just send an ARP to get the MAC address of the interface on the router attached to that LAN. Note that the IP address of the router is used only to get the MAC address of the router, not so that the source host `wincli1` can send packets to the router (the packets are being forwarded to `winsvr2`).

When this packet is sent, the router pays attention to the frame when it arrives, but `winsrv1` ignores it (the frame is not for `00:0e:0c:3b:87:36`). Router1 looks at the packet inside the frame and knows that the destination host is not directly connected to Router1. The *next hop* to the destination is another router. How does Router1 know? In much the same way as `wincli1`: Router1 compares the destination IP address to the IP addresses assigned to its local interfaces. These are `10.10.11.0/24` and `10.0.99.0/24`. The packet's destination IP address of `10.10.12.0/24` does not belong to either of the two networks local to Router1.

However, a router can have many interfaces, not just the two in this example. Which output port should the router use to forward the packet? The network portion of the IP

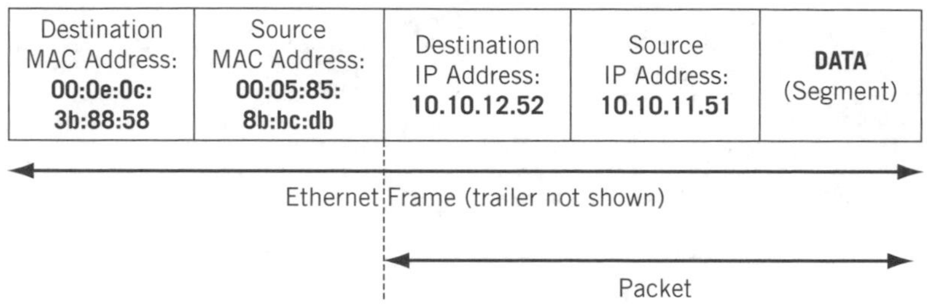

FIGURE 8.6

Frame sent by Router2 to `winsvr2`, showing source and destination IP and MAC addresses.

address is looked up in the forwarding table according to certain rules to find out the IP address of the next-hop router and the output interface leading to this router. (In practice, Router1 might simply have a default route pointed at the serial WAN interface.) The rules used for these lookups will be discussed in more detail in a later chapter. For now, assume that Router1 finds out that the next hop for the packet to `winsvr2` is Router2, and that Router2 is reached on serial port S1.

Router1 now encapsulates the packet from `wincli1` to `winsvr2` inside a PPP frame for transport on the serial link. Another key feature distinguishing routers from bridges, as we have seen, is an IPv4 router's ability to *fragment* a packet for transport on an output link. Fragmentation depends on every router knowing the maximum transmission unit (MTU) frame size for the link types on all of the router's interfaces. Ethernet LANs, for example, all have an MTU size of 1500 bytes (1518 bytes, including the LAN frame header). Serial links usually have MTU sizes larger than that, so this example assumes that Router1 does not have to fragment the content of the packet it received from the LAN.

When the packet sent by `wincli1` to `winsvr2` arrives at Router2 on the serial link from Router1, Router2 knows that the next hop for this packet is *not* another router. Router2 can deliver the packet directly to `winsvr2` using direct delivery. How does it know? Because the network portion of the IP address in the packet destination, `10.10.12.52/24`, is on the same network as the router on one of its interfaces, `10.10.12.1/24`. In brief, it has a route that covers the destination network on one of its interfaces.

The frame containing the packet is sent onto the LAN with the structure shown in Figure 8.6. Note that in this case the MAC address of the *source* is Router2, and the MAC address of the destination is the MAC address of `winsrv2`. Again, Router2 can always use ARP to get the MAC address associated with IP address `10.10.12.52` if the MAC address of the destination host is not in the local ARP cache on the router. The source and destination IP addresses on the packet do not change in this example, of course. `Winsvr2` must be able to reply to the sender, `wincli1` in this case. (We'll talk about cases using NAT, when the source and destination packet addresses do and must change, in the chapter on NAT.)

It is assumed that there is no problem with MTU sizes in this example. However, MTU sizes are often important, especially when the operational differences between IPv4 and IPv6 routers, when it comes to fragmentation, are considered.

QUESTIONS FOR READERS

Figure 8.7 shows some of the concepts discussed in this chapter and can be used to help you answer the following questions.

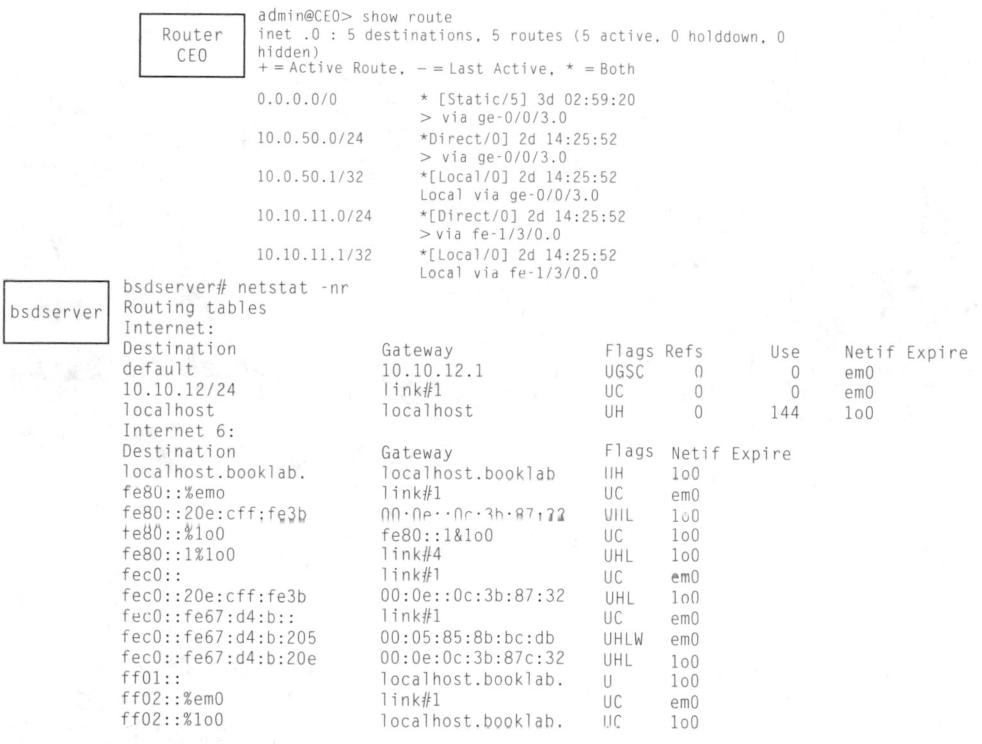

```
Router CEO

admin@CEO> show route
inet .0 : 5 destinations, 5 routes (5 active, 0 holddown, 0
hidden)
+ = Active Route, - = Last Active, * = Both

0.0.0.0/0          * [Static/5] 3d 02:59:20
                   > via ge-0/0/3.0
10.0.50.0/24       *Direct/0] 2d 14:25:52
                   > via ge-0/0/3.0
10.0.50.1/32       *[Local/0] 2d 14:25:52
                   Local via ge-0/0/3.0
10.10.11.0/24      *[Direct/0] 2d 14:25:52
                   >via fe-1/3/0.0
10.10.11.1/32      *[Local/0] 2d 14:25:52
                   Local via fe-1/3/0.0

bsdserver

bsdserver# netstat -nr
Routing tables
Internet:
Destination          Gateway               Flags Refs    Use   Netif Expire
default              10.10.12.1            UGSC     0      0   em0
10.10.12/24          link#1                UC       0      0   em0
localhost            localhost             UH       0    144   lo0
Internet 6:
Destination          Gateway               Flags  Netif Expire
localhost.booklab.   localhost.booklab     UH     lo0
fe80::%emo           link#1                UC     em0
fe80::20e:cff:fe3b   00:0e::0c:3b:87:32    UHL    lo0
fe80::%lo0           fe80::1&lo0           UC     lo0
fe80::1%lo0          link#4                UHL    lo0
fec0::               link#1                UC     em0
fec0::20e:cff:fe3b   00:0e::0c:3b:87:32    UHL    lo0
fec0::fe67:d4:b::    link#1                UC     em0
fec0::fe67:d4:b:205  00:05:85:8b:bc:db     UHLW   em0
fec0::fe67:d4:b:20e  00:0e:0c:3b:87c:32    UHL    lo0
ff01::               localhost.booklab.    U      lo0
ff02::%em0           link#1                UC     em0
ff02::%lo0           localhost.booklab.    UC     lo0
```

FIGURE 8.7

The routing table output from router CEO (IPv4 only) and host bsdserver.

1. What is the difference between a routing table and a forwarding table?
2. In the IPv6 routing table for router CEO, what is the IPv6 address associated with interface ge-0/0/3?
3. In the IPv6 routing table for router CEO, what is the precise IP address value of the default route for IPv4 and IPv6?
4. Why are there so many entries in the IPv6 host routing table on bsdserver?
5. What is a "persistent" route? What is a "static" route?

CHAPTER

Forwarding IP Packets

9

What You Will Learn

In this chapter, you will learn how routers forward IP packets. We'll start with the logical steps a router follows to forward ("route") a packet out the next-hop interface. Then we'll look at router architectures to see how specialized devices (there are "software-only" routers) accomplish routing and forwarding.

Finally, you will learn about how IPv4 routers transition to handling IPv6 routing and various methods to *tunnel* IPv6 packets through links connected by IPv4-only routers. Tunnels were introduced in Chapters 3 and 4 and occur when the normal encapsulation sequence of packet-inside frame is violated in some fashion.

This chapter is really a continued investigation into many of the concepts introduced in the previous chapter. Figure 9.1 highlights the network components we'll be working with in this chapter.

The routers on our network are Juniper Networks routers. These routers have a different "look and feel" compared to other routers, most of which use a more "Cisco-like" interface and display. For example, the routing tables seem very long and detailed compared to Cisco routers' default displays.

```
admin@CE6> show route 10.10/16

inet.0: 34 destinations, 35 routes (34 active, 0 holddown, 0 hidden)
+ = Active Route, - = Last Active, * = Both

10.10.11.0/24      *[OSPF/10] 1w5d 18:25:05, metric 6
                    > via ge-0/0/3.0
10.10.12.0/24      *[Direct/0] 2w2d 00:15:44
                    > via fe-1/3/0.0
10.10.12.1/32      *[Local/0] 2w2d 00:15:44
                      Local via fe-1/3/0.0
```

We'll talk about the routing table entry marked Open Shortest Path First (OSPF) in Chapter 14. This route was learned by a routing protocol running between the routers on our network, and we'll see how OSPF is configured in a later chapter. Note that

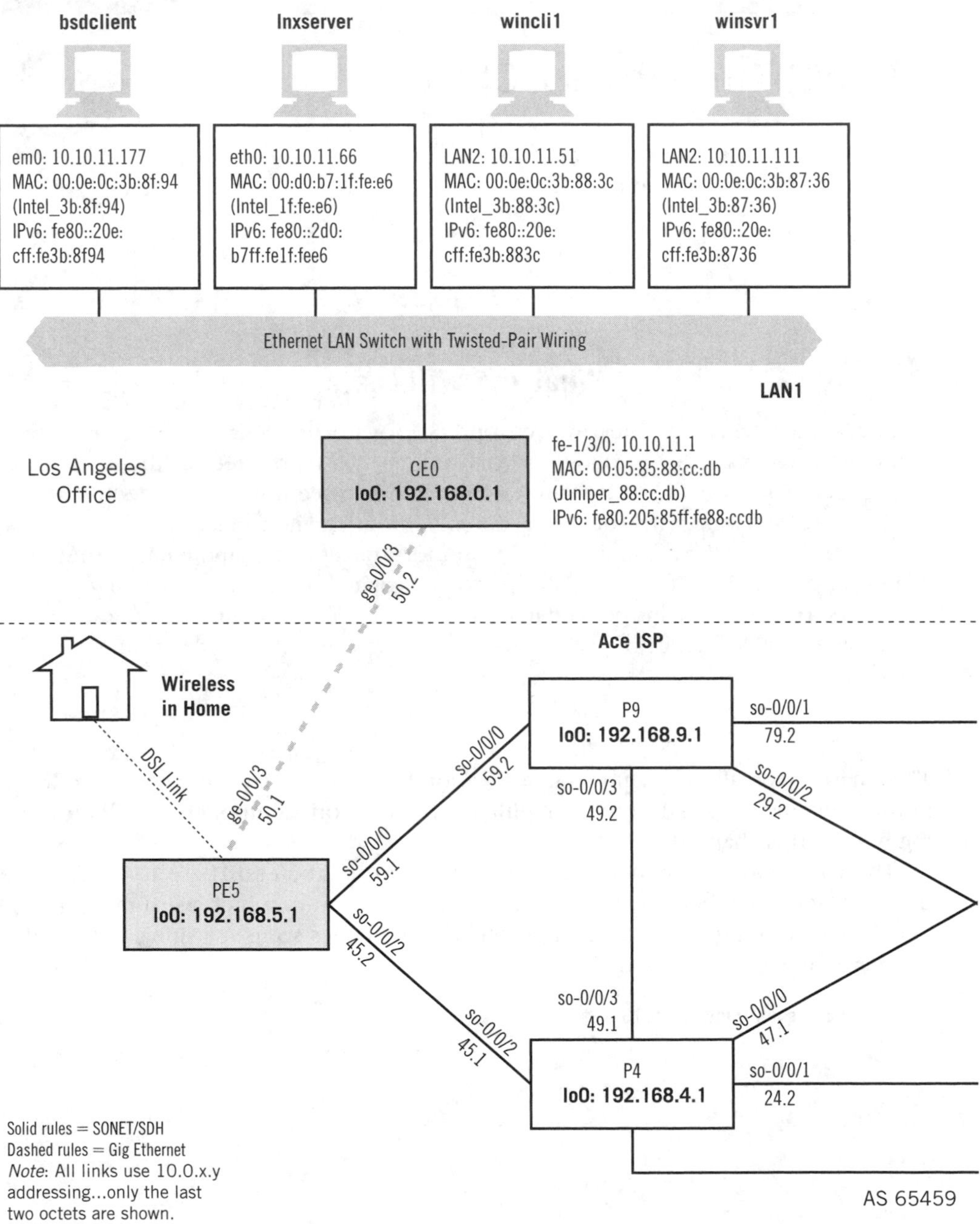

FIGURE 9.1

Forwarding packets across the network. Note that we'll be using the customer-edge routers CE0 and CE6 in this chapter.

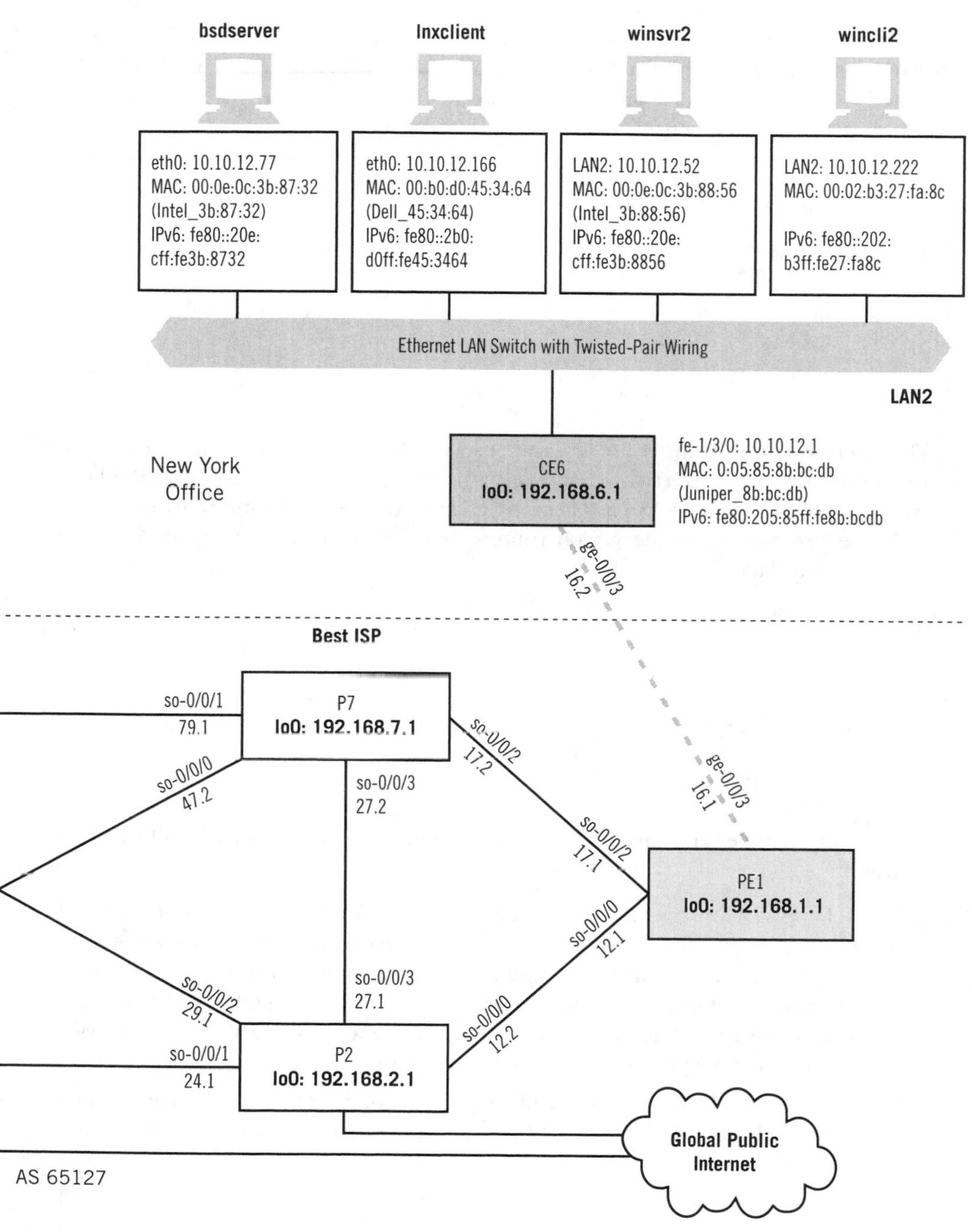
bsdserver
eth0: 10.10.12.77
MAC: 00:0e:0c:3b:87:32
(Intel_3b:87:32)
IPv6: fe80::20e:
cff:fe3b:8732
lnxclient
eth0: 10.10.12.166
MAC: 00:b0:d0:45:34:64
(Dell_45:34:64)
IPv6: fe80::2b0:
d0ff:fe45:3464
winsvr2
LAN2: 10.10.12.52
MAC: 00:0e:0c:3b:88:56
(Intel_3b:88:56)
IPv6: fe80::20e:
cff:fe3b:8856
wincli2
LAN2: 10.10.12.222
MAC: 00:02:b3:27:fa:8c
IPv6: fe80::202:
b3ff:fe27:fa8c
Ethernet LAN Switch with Twisted-Pair Wiring
LAN2
New York
Office
CE6
lo0: 192.168.6.1
fe-1/3/0: 10.10.12.1
MAC: 0:05:85:8b:bc:db
(Juniper_8b:bc:db)
IPv6: fe80:205:85ff:fe8b:bcdb
ge-0/0/3
16.2
Best ISP
P7
lo0: 192.168.7.1
so-0/0/1
79.1
so-0/0/0
47.2
so-0/0/3
27.2
so-0/0/2
17.2
ge-0/0/3
16.1
so-0/0/2
17.1
PE1
lo0: 192.168.1.1
so-0/0/0
12.1
so-0/0/2
29.1
so-0/0/3
27.1
so-0/0/0
12.2
P2
lo0: 192.168.2.1
so-0/0/1
24.1
Global Public
Internet
AS 65127

the entry has a *preference* of 10 (which makes it more "costly" to use than direct/local interface routes [0] or static routes [5]). Traffic to destinations on LAN1 is sent to PE1 over the ge-0/0/3 interface. A preference is distinct from the metric or cost of a route itself; preference applies to routes learned in different ways.

We can make the routing table display more Cisco-like by using the terse option:

```
admin@CE6> show route 10.10/16 terse

inet.0: 34 destinations, 35 routes (34 active, 0 holddown, 0 hidden)
+ = Active Route, - = Last Active, * = Both

A Destination       P Prf    Metric 1     Metric 2     Next hop        AS path
* 10.10.11.0/24     O  10    6                         >ge-0/0/3.0
* 10.10.12.0/24     D   0                              >fe-1/3/0.0
* 10.10.12.1/32     L   0                              Local
```

The asterisk (*) means the route is active (used for forwarding), and the P field is for protocol. One metric is used (two are allowed), the next-hops are the same (thankfully!), and we'll talk about what an AS path is in the chapter on the BGP routing protocol.

Let's use traceroute to see which routers CE6 uses to reach LAN1, attached to router CE0 at interface 10.10.11.1.

```
admin@CE6> traceroute 10.10.11.1

traceroute to  10.10.11.1  (10.10.11.1), 30 hops max, 40 byte packets
 1  10.0.16.1  (10.0.16.1)   0.743 ms  0.681 ms  0.573 ms
 2  10.0.12.2  (10.0.12.2)   0.646 ms  0.647 ms  0.620 ms
 3  10.0.24.2  (10.0.24.2)   0.656 ms  0.664 ms  0.632 ms
 4  10.0.45.2  (10.0.45.2)   0.690 ms  0.677 ms  0.695 ms
 5  10.10.11.1  (10.10.11.1)   0.846 ms  0.819 ms  0.775 ms
```

Each router handles the three-packet set generated by the source (CE6) in one of three ways:

1. If the packet is not for this router (the device does not have 10.10.11.1 configured locally), and the TTL is 1 or 0, then the router creates an ICMP Time-Exceeded message, sets the source address to the router's receiving interface address, sets the destination address to the source's, and sends the ICMP packet out the interface listed as the route back to the source in the forwarding table. This does not have to be the same as the receiving interface, but it usually is.
2. If the packet is not for this router and the TTL is not 1 or 0, then the router decrements the TTL field and forwards the packet out the interface leading to the next hop on the way to the destination address.
3. If the packet is for this router or device, then it sends back an ICMP Port Unreachable message.

Why a TTL of 1 or 0? Some routers decrement the TTL immediately and others only as part of the forwarding process, right before output queuing. This way both types of router handle the packet consistently.

When the source receives a Time-Exceeded message, it records the results of the round-trip time for the three packets, checks to see if it has a DNS entry for the IP address, and prints a line of output with a "hop" number and the rest of the statistics. When it receives a Port Unreachable message, the traceroute utility prints the final results and exits.

Because we don't yet have DNS running, all the IPv4 addresses are repeated twice. From the network diagram, we can see that the packets flowed from CE6 to PE1 (not surprisingly) at 10.0.16.1 and then through P2 (10.0.12.2), P4 (10.0.24.2), PE5 (10.0.45.2) and on to CE0 (10.10.11.1, the local interface target, is used instead of 10.0.50.2). (We'll see what happens when one of the P routers or links between them fails in a later chapter.)

We have IPv6 running on the LANs and routers CE0 and CE6. Let's see what happens on CE6 when we ping the LAN1 interface address four times using the LAN2 interface IPv6 source address. Recall that the private ULA IPv6 addresses on LAN1 start with fc00:ffb3:d5:a.

```
admin@CE6> ping count 4 inet6 source fc00:fe67:d4:b:205:85ff:fe8b:bcdb
fc00:ffb3:d5:a:205:85ff:fe88:ccdb
PING6(56=40+8+8 bytes) fc00:fe67:d4:b:205:85ff:fe8b:bcdb -> fc00:ffb3:d5:
a:205:85ff:fe88:ccdb
-- fc00:ffb3:d5:a:205:85ff:fe88:ccdb ping6 statistics --
4 packets transmitted, 0 packets received, 100% packet loss
```

What happened? Well, for one thing, we have no routes to any IPv6 addresses on LAN1 in the IPv6 routing table. And if they're not in the routing table, they won't be in the forwarding table.

```
admin@CE6> show route table inet6 fc00:ffb3:d5:a::/64
admin@CE6>
```

What can we do about this? Well, we could add some static routes to the IPv6 tables on each router, or we could run an IPv6 routing protocol between the routers to share the routing information (we'll do this in a later chapter). Or, we can configure an IPv6 over IPv4 tunnel between routers CE6 and CE0 (and back). We know we have connectivity with IPv4 between the edge routers, as shown with traceroute.

Here's how to configure an IPv6-over-IPv4 tunnel on routers CE0 and CE6. It basically tells the router to take any traffic for LAN1 or LAN2 IPv6 addresses, put them inside IPv4 packets with the LAN IPv4 interface addresses, and send them out as if they were IPv4 packets. We'll apply the tunnels on a logical interface known as the Generic Routing Encapsulation (GRE) interfaces, abbreviated gr- on Juniper Networks routers. Only the final configuration statements are shown.

```
[edit interfaces gr-1/0/0]
admin@CE6# set interfaces gr-1/0/0
admin@CE6# set unit 0 tunnel source 10.10.12.1;
    /*source address on LAN2 interface*/
```

```
admin@CE6# set unit 0 tunnel destination 10.10.11.1;
    /*destination address on LAN1 interface*/
admin@CE6# set unit 0 family inet6 address fc00:ffb3::/32
    /*LAN1 addresses*/
[edit interfaces gr-1/0/0]
admin@CE0# set interfaces gr-1/0/0
admin@CE0# set unit 0 tunnel source 10.10.11.1;
    /*source address on LAN1 interface*/
admin@CE0# set unit 0 tunnel destination 10.10.12.1;
    /*destination address on LAN2 interface*/
admin@CE0# set unit 0 family inet6 address fc00:ffb3::/32
    /*LAN2 addresses*/
```

Now we should be able to ping and traceroute an IPv6 address on LAN1 (in this case, `fc00:ffb3:d5:a:20e:cff:fe3b:8f95` for `bsdclient`) from the customer-edge router on LAN2. And we can. Note that, because of the tunnel, the destination seems to be only two hops away.

```
admin@CE6> ping inet6 count 4 source fc00:fe67:d4:b:205:85ff:fe8b:bcdb
fc00:ffb3:d5:a:20e:cff:fe3b:8f95
PING6(56=40+8+8 bytes) fc00:fe67:d4:b:205:85ff:fe8b:bcdb -->
fc00:ffb3:d5:a:20e:cff:fe3b:8f95
16 bytes from fc00:fe67:d4:b:205:85ff:fe8b:bcdb, icmp_seq=0 hlim=64
time=0.900 ms
16 bytes from fc00:fe67:d4:b:205:85ff:fe8b:bcdb, icmp_seq=1 hlim=64
time=0.728 ms
16 bytes from fc00:fe67:d4:b:205:85ff:fe8b:bcdb, icmp_seq=2 hlim=64
time=0.856 ms
16 bytes from fc00:fe67:d4:b:205:85ff:fe8b:bcdb, icmp_seq=3 hlim=64
time=0.838 ms

admin@CE6> traceroute inet6 source fc00:fe67:d4:b:205:85ff:fe8b:bcdb
fc00:ffb3:d5:a:20e:cff:fe3b:8f95
traceroute6 to fc00:ffb3:d5:a:20e:cff:fe3b:8f95 (fc00:ffb3:d5:a:205:85ff:
fe88:ccdb) from fc00:fe67:d4:b:205:85ff:fe8b:bcdb, 30 hops max, 12 byte
packets
 1  fc00:ffb3:d4:b:205:85ff:fe88:ccdb (fc00:ffb3:d4:b:205:85ff:fe88:ccdb)
1.059 ms  0.979 ms  0.819 ms
 2  fc00:ffb3:d5:a:20e:cff:fe3b:8f95 (fc00:ffb3:d5:a:20e:cff:fe3b:8f95)
0.832 ms 0.887 ms  0.823 ms
```

Let's take a look at the some basic types of router architectures that can be used to implement these packet-forwarding strategies.

ROUTER ARCHITECTURES

There are three main steps that a router must follow to process and forward a packet to the next hop. Processing a packet means to check an incoming packet for errors and other parameters, looking up the destination address in a forwarding table to determine the proper output port for the packet, and then sending the packet out on that port.

But how are the input ports connected to the output ports? In smaller routers, which can even be implemented on PC or laptop computers with two or more interfaces, software simply examines the packet headers and forwards the packets where they need to go. Windows PCs can do this, and often do on home networks. In Linux, there is a command to allow the "host" to forward packets without processing the content of the packet more fully.

```
[root@lnxserver admin]# echo "1" > /proc/sys/net/ipv4/ip_forward
```

Linux IP Forwarding

If you enter the `ip_forward` command from the shell command prompt, the setting is not "remembered" after a reboot. If the host is to function as a gateway as well as host, place the command in an initialization script.

Small routers, such as those for DSL or small-edge LANs, can allow the incoming packet to sit in a memory buffer somewhere and adjust header fields, perform tunnel encapsulation, and so on, and then queue the packet for output. Larger routers, such as those used by ISPs or on the Internet backbones, must route as fast as they can, usually at *wire speeds* (this means that the device processes data without reducing overall transmission speed, so even if the packets arrive as fast as the input line allows, under maximum load, there is minimal delay through the router).

Instead of *software-based* forwarding architectures, these larger routers use *hardware-based* forwarding fabric architectures. The differences are important, so we'll take a look at them in more detail.

Basic Router Architectures

When it comes to architecture, routers look very much like a PC. This was one of the reasons for the initial success of routers: Routers could be fabricated out of simple, off-the-shelf parts and did not require extensive or customized chipsets or hardware. So these routers have a CPU, memory, interfaces, peripheral ports—in short, usually everything but a hard drive. Small routers do not even have floppy drives or other forms of external storage. This makes sense: Routers don't need to store much of anything. A forwarding table needs to be in memory at all times, because it's much too slow to try and fetch a piece of the table off a hard drive when needed. A lot of routers boot themselves from special servers, and have nonvolatile random access memory (NVRAM) that keeps whatever information they need to remember whenever their power is cut or turned off. Volatile memory like normal RAM is always erased when power is lost, but NVRAM is like a disk.

The chief distinction is that at the heart of such routers is a general-purpose computer. The architecture for large modern routers does not have a "center."

Routers do not have to worry about adding cards for video, graphics, or other tasks either. The slots in the chassis just handle various types of networking interfaces such as Ethernet, ATM, SONET/SDH (Synchronous Optical Network/Synchronous Digital Hierarchy), or other types of point-to-point WAN links. Most interface modules have multiple ports, depending on the type of interface that they support. In a lot of high-end router models, the interface cards are complex devices all by themselves and often called *blades*. Interfaces usually can be added as needed for the networking environment—one or more LAN cards for the routers that handle customers and one or more WAN cards for connection to other routers. Backbone routers often have only WAN cards and no customers at all.

Another difference between a software-based router and a common PC is that PCs almost always have only a single CPU. Because of the central role of these chips in running all of the hardware and software on the computer, single-CPU architectures require very powerful CPU chips.

Some routers use a variety of CPU chips, and because the tasks are shared among the processors, these CPU chips do not have to be tremendously powerful either. Each CPU set is chosen to fit the mission of the router. They have enough horsepower for the home and small office, and these chips are stable, plentiful, and inexpensive.

Some routers use different types of memory. Figure 9.2 shows the general layout of the motherboard of a generic software-based router. Many router motherboards have four types of memory intended for specific purposes. Each type of memory and its location on the motherboard is shown in the figure. This architecture is also very similar to the network processor engine (NPE) for larger Cisco router architectures. A lot of architectures forgo packet memory because of the bandwidth available in their shared

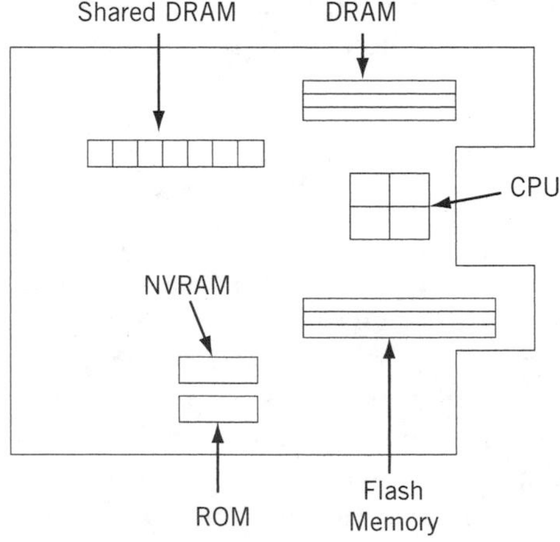

FIGURE 9.2

Software-based architecture for small routers, showing the various types of memory used.

memory architecture or because the CPU itself contains a dedicated packet handling architecture.

Every router ships with at least the factory default minimum of DRAM (dynamic random access memory) and flash memory, but more can be added in the factory or in the field. Generally, the DRAM can be doubled or increased fourfold, depending on model, and flash memory can be doubled.

RAM/DRAM is sometimes called *working storage* because in the days before hard drives and other types of external storage, memory was all that computers had for storing information outside of the immediate CPU. In a router, the RAM/DRAM performs the same functions for the router's CPU as the memory in a PC does for its CPU. So when the router is up and running, the RAM/DRAM contains an image of the operating system software, the running configuration (called *running-config* in routers using the Cisco configuration conventions) file, the routing table and associated tables built after startup, and the packet buffer. If this seems like a lot of work for one type of memory, this just shows the flexibility of function in a general-purpose architecture router.

The RAM acronym often used by router vendors is somewhat misleading. Almost all RAM in a router today is DRAM, since static memory—regular RAM—became obsolete some time ago. But people are used to the old RAM acronym, and it's included in a lot of literature just for familiarity.

In addition to the DRAM near the CPU, these types of routers include shared DRAM or shared memory. Also known as *packet memory*, the shared DRAM handles the packet buffers in the router. Splitting the packet buffers from the other DRAM improves I/O performance, because the shared DRAM is physically closer to the interfaces that handle the packets.

Nonvolatile RAM (NVRAM) is memory that retains information even when power is cut off to the router. Routers use NVRAM to store a copy of the router configuration file. Without NVRAM, the router would never be able to remember its proper configuration when it was restarted. NVRAM is where the startup configuration (called *startup-config* on routers using the Cisco configuration conventions) is stored.

Flash memory is another form of nonvolatile memory. But although flash memory is different from NVRAM, flash memory can also be erased and reprogrammed as needed. In many routers, flash memory is used to hold one or more copies of the router's operating system: In the case of Cisco, this is called the Internetwork Operating System, or IOS.

ROM is read-only memory and is therefore nonvolatile, but, as might be expected, ROM cannot be changed. Routers use ROM to hold what is called the *bootstrap* program. Normally, flash memory and NVRAM hold all of the information that the router needs to come up again properly with the current configuration after a shutdown or other power loss. But if there is a catastrophe, the bootstrap program in ROM can be used to boot the router into a minimum configuration. ROM used for this purpose is also called ROMMON (ROM monitor) and usually has a distinctive `rommon>>` prompt taken from early Unix systems. ROMMON at least gets the router to the point where simple commands can be typed in through a system console terminal (monitor). In smaller routers, ROM holds only a minimal subset of the router's operating system software. In larger routers, the ROM often holds a full copy of the router's operating system software.

Another Router Architecture

In contrast to the basic router architecture just explored, no one would accuse a large Internet backbone router of looking or acting like a PC. Routers based on a central CPU just about run out of gas once link speeds move into the multigigabit ranges with OC-48 (2.4 Gbps) and OC-192 (10 Gbps). And with 10 Gigabit Ethernet and OC-768 (40 Gbps), a change to the basic architecture of the router for the Internet backbone is necessary. Many Internet backbone routers share the same basic architecture, whether they come from Cisco or Juniper Networks or someone else. However, the terminology used for the components varies considerably from vendor to vendor. Because the Illustrated Network uses Juniper Networks routers as its network nodes, we'll use the Juniper Networks architecture and terminology in this section, but only as an example, not necessarily as an endorsement.

Larger network routers, oddly enough, do have hard drives. In fact, many Internet backbone routers have a complete PC built right in (some even have two PCs). But wait a minute. Isn't the PC architecture much too slow for heavy duty, "wire-speed" routing? And isn't a hard drive useless when it comes to routing because the forwarding table has to be in memory? Right on both counts. The PC in the backbone router, called the routing engine (RE) in Juniper Networks routers, does not forward packets at all. Packets are routed and forwarded by the packet-forwarding engine (PFE), which is where all the specialized ASICs are located. The RE controls the router, handles the routing protocols, and performs all of the other tasks that can be handled more leisurely than wire-speed packet transit traffic. Packets are forwarded from input to output port using the forwarding table (FT) in the hardware fabric.

The fundamental principle in large router design is the idea that the functions of a router can be split into two distinct parts: one portion for handling routing and control operations and another for forwarding packets. By separating these two operations, the router hardware can be designed and optimized to perform each function well.

This division of labor makes perfect sense. It has already been pointed out several times that no one really sends traffic to a router. The vast majority of packets just pass through the router. So transit packets never leave the hardware-based *fabric* linking input and output ports and control packets, such as those for the routing protocols, which only come along every few seconds or so, and can be handled as required by the RE.

Just like other routers, large backbone routers can handle various types of networking interfaces. But these routers are normally intended for mainly customer traffic aggregation or for an ISP backbone, although many corporations are attracted to edge-oriented routers with this architecture as well. And anywhere in an enterprise where there is a requirement for sustained 2-Gbps operation, routing is probably not being done in software.

The overall concept of the division between routing engine (routing protocol control and management) and packet-forwarding engine (line-rate routing transit traffic) with a hardware-based "switching" fabric is shown in Figure 9.3.

The section of the router that is designed to handle the general routing operations (and control-plane management tasks) is the RE. The RE is designed to handle all the routing protocols, user interaction, system management, and OAM&P (operations,

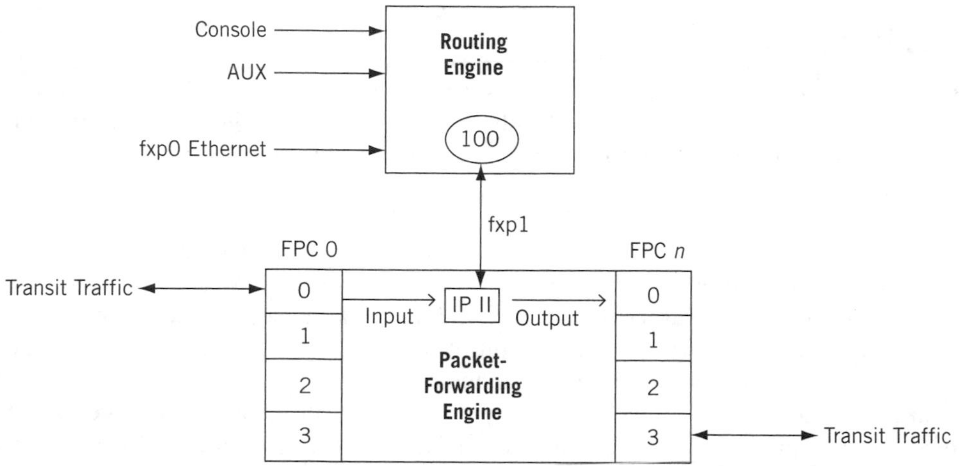

FIGURE 9.3

A hardware-based router with a switching fabric architecture. Note that the figure uses the architecture and terminology of Juniper Networks routers, which are used on the Illustrated Network.

administration, maintenance, and provisioning), and so on. The second section in Juniper Networks routers is the PFE, and is specifically designed to handle the forwarding of packets across the router from input to output interface. Transit packets never enter the routing engine at all.

The communications channel between the routing engine and the PFE is a standard 100-Mbps Fast Ethernet. This might seem somewhat surprising at first, because the interfaces on a Juniper Networks router can be many gigabits per second. But only control information needs to enter the routing engine. The vast majority of packets only transits the PFE at wire speeds. There are many advantages to using a standard interface, even internally. A standard interface is easier to implement than creating a new proprietary interface, and standard chipsets are readily available, inexpensive, and so on.

The routing engine of a Juniper Networks router contains the router's operating system, the JUNOS Internet software, the command line interface (CLI) for configuration and control, and the routing table (RT) itself. The routing table in a Juniper Networks router contains all of the routing information gathered from all routing protocols running on the router, as well as miscellaneous information such as interface addresses, static routes, and so forth.

It might not seem that the RE would have to be very powerful, or have a large hard drive, but it usually does. This is because of the increasing expense of converging a growing routing table.

The PFE is where the forwarding table resides. The forwarding table contains all the active route information that is actually used to determine the packet's next hop without needing to send the packet to the routing engine.

ROUTER ACCESS

Users don't generally communicate directly *with* routers, but rather *through* routers. The situation is different for network administrators and managers, however, who must communicate directly with the individual routers in order to install, configure, and manage the routers.

Routers are key devices on the Internet and almost any type of network. Many backbone routers handle packets for hundreds or thousands of users, and some handle packets for even more. So when a router goes down, or even slows down due to congestion or a problem, the users go wild and the network managers react immediately. For this reason, network managers need multiple and foolproof ways to access the routers they are responsible for in order to manage them.

Larger routers, and many smaller ones, do not normally come with a keyboard, mouse, and monitor. Nevertheless, there are usually three ways that a network administrator can communicate with a router.

The Console Port

This port is for a serial terminal that is at the same location as the router and attached by a short cable from the serial port on the terminal to the console port on the router. The terminal is usually a PC or Unix workstation running a terminal emulation program. There are several physical connector types used for this port on Cisco routers. Network administrators sometimes have to carry around several different connector types so they can be sure to have the proper connector for the router they need to manage. (Usually, after initial installation, the console ports are connected to a terminal server on a management network so that access does not have to be right where the router is.)

The Auxiliary Port

This port is for a serial terminal that is at a remote location. Connection is made through a pair of modems, one connected to the router and the other connected to the terminal. There is little difference, if any, between the auxiliary (AUX) and console ports in terms of characteristics. They are separate because routers might require simultaneous local and remote access that would be impossible if there were only one serial port on the router.

The Network

The router can always be managed over the same network on which it is routing packets. This is often called "in-band management" in contrast to the console and AUX ports, which are "out-of-band." This just means that the network access method shares the link to the router "in the same bandwidth" as user packets transiting the router. There are often three ways to access a router over the network: through Telnet

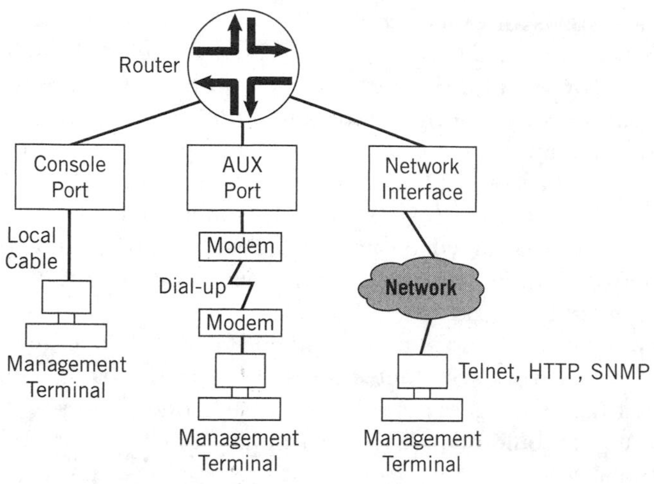

FIGURE 9.4

The three router access methods. Note that the console port requires access to the router, while the others allow remote access.

(called VTY lines on a Cisco router), with a more secure remote access program called secure shell (SSH), using a Web browser (HTTP is the protocol), or with SNMP (Simple Network Management Protocol), a protocol invented expressly for remote router management.

These arrangements are shown in Figure 9.4. Small routers usually only have a console port. With the proper cables, these console ports can be hooked up to a modem for remote access, but obviously cannot be used simultaneously for local access. On some routers, the console ports are labeled "Admin" or "Management." It is tempting to try and access a console or AUX ports using the normal graphical interface provided by Windows, a Mac, or Unix X-Windows. But the console and AUX ports only understand a simple, character-based serial protocol. On Windows PCs, for example, only HyperTerminal (or another serial terminal emulation program) can communicate with a router through the console or AUX ports.

FORWARDING TABLE LOOKUPS

In the connectionless, best-effort world of IP, every packet is forwarded independently, hop by hop, toward the destination. Each router determines the next hop for the destination address in the packet header based on information gathered into the routing table and distilled into the forwarding table. The essential operation of a router is the looking up of the packet's destination IP address in this table to determine the next hop.

It's unusual that a packet address is an exact match for a table entry. Otherwise, routing and forwarding tables would need an entry for every host in the world—all 32 bits for IPv4 and 128 bits for IPv6! So in the current classless (prefix) world of IP addressing, the host-hop destination is chosen by the *longest match* rule. Figure 9.5 shows how the next-hop address and interface information are used with the ARP process (cache or query) to forward the packet in a frame toward the destination.

Consider a packet sent to 10.10.11.77 (bsdclient) from LAN2. Remember, the network is 10.10.11.0/24. Suppose the Best ISP edge router, PE1, has the entries shown in Table 9.1 about 10.10/16 networks in its tables; the longest match determines the correct interface that should forward the packet.

Which interface is the "best" next hop toward the destination? It would be easy if we had an entry like 10.10.11/24 to work with, but routers closer to the backbone use *aggregate* addresses in their tables. In most cases, Internet backbone routers will accept prefixes of /24 or shorter. (It would be nice to accept only /19 or shorter, but not many could get away with that.)

So where should the router send a packet for network 10.10.11.0/24? Which next hop should it use? All three table entries are "close" to the destination address, but which one is "best"?

According to the longest-match rule, the router will send the packet for 10.10.11.77 to 10.10.17.2 on interface so-0/0/2. But how exactly does it work?

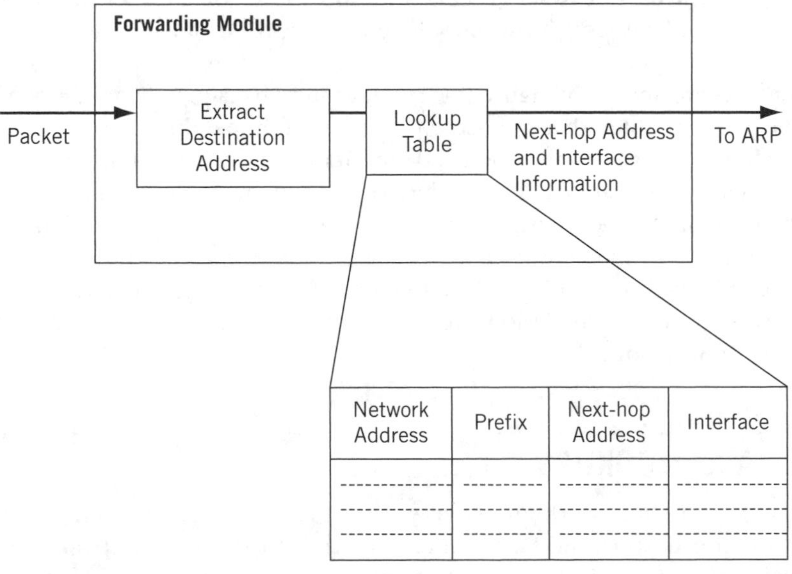

FIGURE 9.5

How the longest match rule applies to a forwarding table lookup. More specific (longer) routes are preferred to less specific (shorter) routes.

Table 9.1 Tables for Router PE1

Network (Network Bits in Bold)	Prefix	Next-Hop Address	Interface
10.10.0 (00001010 00001010 0000xxxx xxxx)	/20	10.0.12.2	so-0/0/0
10.10.8 (00001010 00001010 00001xxx xxxx)	/21	10.0.19.2	so-0/0/1
10.10.8 (00001010 00001010 000010xx xxxx)	/22	10.0.17.2	so-0/0/2

Routers today can "mix and match" prefixes of differing lengths in a routing or forwarding table and still send packets to the correct next hop. In the table, 10.10.8/21 and 10.10.8/22 are different routes, as would be 10.10.8/23 and 10.10.8/24.

Now, the 32-bit destination address, 10.10.11.77, in bits is 00001010 00001010 00001011 01001101. There is, of course, no subnet mask associated with a host address. Looking at the table, the first 20 bits are exactly the same in all three entries, as well as the destination address. But which is the *longest* match? The router will keep comparing the addresses in the table to the destination address bit by bit until the table runs out of entries. The last match is the longest match, no matter if it's all 32 bits, or none (the default 0/0 entry matches everything).

The 21st bit is a 1 bit in the table entry for 10.10.8/21, and so is the 21st bit in the destination address. The 22nd bit is a 0 bit in the table entry for 10.10.8/22, and so is the 22nd bit in the destination address. There is no longer entry. This makes the /22 entry the longest match for the destination address, and the packet is forwarded to 10.10.17.2. The rest of the bits are used for local delivery of the packet on LAN2.

The longest match is also often called the *best match* or the *more specific route* for a given destination IP address. But whatever it is called, the point is the same: The longest-match next hop is always used in favor of a potential, but shorter match, next hop.

What if there were other entries such as 10.10.8/23 or 10.10.8/24? It doesn't matter. The 1 bit in the 23rd position will not match these entries, which all have 0s at the end of the entry. The same longest match rules apply at each router.

DUAL STACKS, TUNNELING, AND IPv6

So far, we've seen how routers forward packets, what the routers look like internally, and how the longest match determines the output port. But most of this chapter dealt with IPv4. But what about IPv6 packets? It's one thing to say that some routers can handle both IPv4 and IPv6, but what about older or smaller routers and hosts that don't integrate IPv6 support and handle IPv4 only? This chapter ends with a consideration of the role of the router in a world that is slowly making its way toward IPv6.

The transition to IPv6 will be a long one for most networks. There might be networks where it will be necessary to mix hosts and routers that run IPv4 only, IPv6 only, and a combination of the two. Why would a host need to run both IPv4 and IPv6? Well, a Web site that only ran IPv6 would be forever unreachable by IPv4 browsers. Routers, of course, can be used to build separate IPv4 and IPv6 router networks. For example,

LAN1 and LAN2 could have two routers each—one for IPv4 and one for IPv6 traffic. But a lot of newer routers should be able to handle both IPv4 and IPv6 packets, and many do.

There are two main strategies that have emerged for dealing with mixed IPv4 and IPv6 environments. These are *dual protocol stacks* and *tunneling*.

Dual Protocol Stacks

All of the hosts on the Illustrated Network, as we have seen, are capable of assigning both an IPv6 and IPv4 address to their network interfaces. This is possible because they all implement a sort of "split" IP network layer. For example, if the Ethernet Type field is set to `0x0800` the packet is handed off to the IPv4 process, and if the Type field is set to `0x86DD`, then the packet is handed off to the IPv6 process. This is shown conceptually in Figure 9.6.

The dual protocol stack must provide error messages that are IPv6 "aware," and routing protocols have to adapt to IPv6 addresses as well (as we'll see). And in spite of the figure, which is a very common representation, the TCP/UDP layer is also dual.

Dual protocols stacks are not new with IPv6. This method was frequently used whenever two or more protocol stacks had to share a single host interface. In fact, very complex arrangements were not unknown, with IBM's (and Microsoft's) NetBios sharing the network with Novell's NetWare and IP itself (for Internet access).

Tunneling

Tunneling is a much misunderstood topic in general. This section talks about IPv6 tunnels, but networks also feature IPSec tunnels, VPN tunnels, and possibly even more. But they all employ tunnels. ***Tunneling occurs whenever the normal sequence of encapsulation headers is violated.*** That's all.

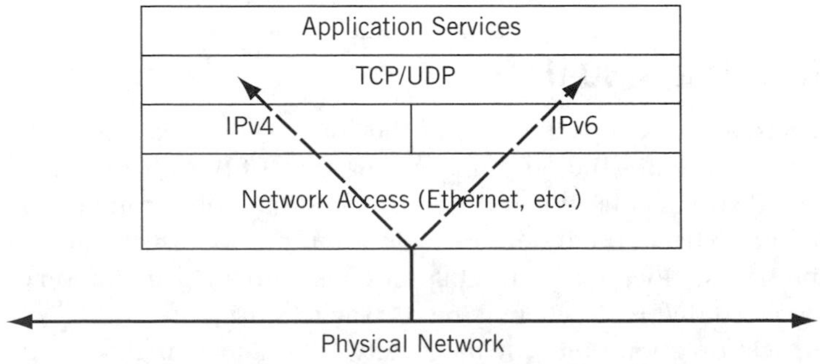

FIGURE 9.6

Dual protocol stacks for IPv4 and IPv6 sharing a single network connection. Technically, TCP and UDP have to be adjusted for an IPv6 environment.

Normally, a message is broken up into segments, which are put inside packets placed inside frames that are sent as a sequence of bits to an adjacent system. The receiver usually expects that the frame contains a packet, and so on, but what if it doesn't? Then the device is using tunneling.

We've already seen a form of tunneling in action. When we put PPP frames inside Ethernet frames, we put a frame inside a frame and violated the normal OSI-RM sequence of headers. That's okay, *as long as the receiver knows the sequence of headers the sender is generating*.

Not all devices need to know the exact sequence of encapsulations used by the sender and receiver. Only the *endpoints* (usually hosts, but not always) need to know how to encapsulate the data at one end and process the headers correctly at the destination. In between, inside the tunnel, all other devices can treat the data units as usual.

Tunneling in a mixed IPv4 and IPv6 network is used to transport IPv6 packets over a series of IPv4 routers or to an IPv4 host. There is a lot of variation in tunnels to support IPv4/IPv6 operation. For example, a native IPv6 backbone might tunnel IPv4 to reduce address consumption in the network core. For the sake of simplicity, let's consider four types of tunnels and two major scenarios for their use:

1. *Host to router*—Hosts with dual-stack capabilities can tunnel IPv6 packets to a dual-stack router that is only reachable over a series IPv4-only device.
2. *Router to router*—Routers with dual-stack capabilities can tunnel IPv6 packets over an IPv4 infrastructure to other routers.
3. *Router to host*—Routers with dual-stack capabilities can tunnel IPv6 packets over an IPv4 infrastructure to a dual-stack destination host.
4. *Host to host*—Hosts with dual-stack capabilities can tunnel IPv6 packets over an IPv4 infrastructure to other dual-stack IP hosts without an intervening router.

The four types of tunnels are shown in Figure 9.7. When the IPv6 packet is sent to a router (the first two tunneling methods), the endpoint of the tunnel is not the same as the destination, so the destination address of the IPv6 packet does not indicate the same device as the IPv4 tunnel endpoint address that carries the IPv6 packet. The source host or router must have the tunnel endpoint's IPv4 address configured. This is called *configured tunneling*.

In contrast, the last two methods send the encapsulated IPv6 packet directly to the destination host, so the IPv4 and IPv6 addresses used correspond to the same host. This lets the IPv6 destinations use IPv4-compatible addresses that are derived automatically by the devices. This is called *automatic tunneling* because it does not require explicit configuration.

Automatic tunneling uses a special form of the IPv6 address. The 32-bit IPv4 address is simply prepended with 96 zero bits in the form `0:0:0:0:0:0:`*`<IPv4 address>`*. This format is abbreviated as `::`*`<IPv4 address>`*.

All dual-stack IP hosts recognize this format and encapsulate the IPv6 packet inside an IPv4 packet using the embedded IPv4 address, creating an end-to-end tunnel. The

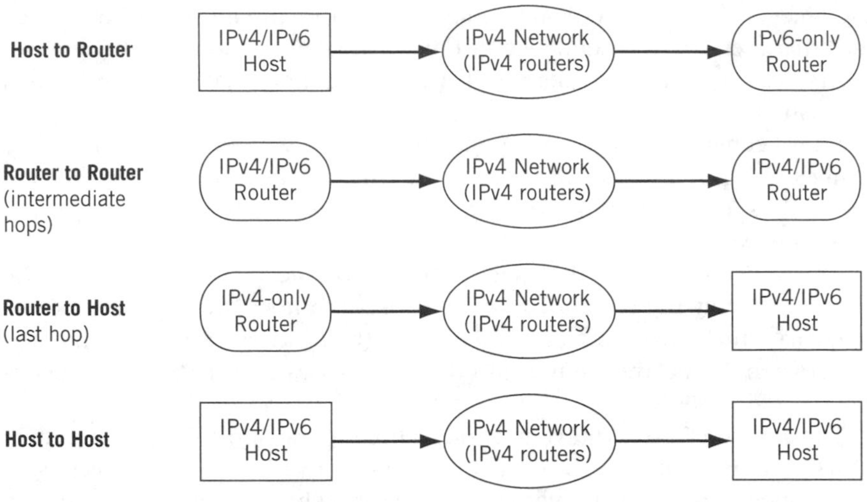

FIGURE 9.7

The various types of IPv6 tunnels, showing host and router situations that can be used to connect.

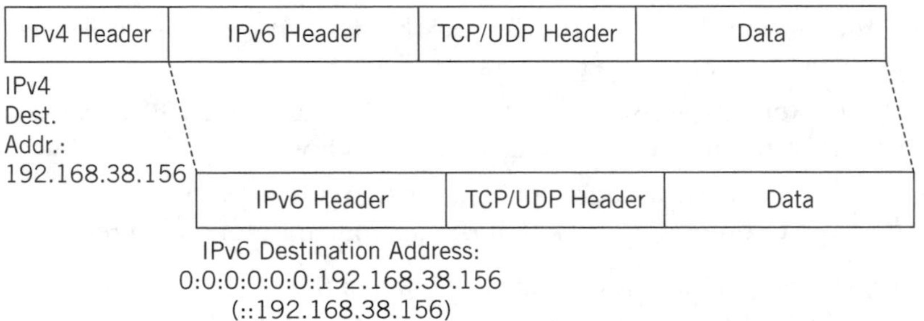

FIGURE 9.8

The special IPv6 tunnel-addressing format for dual-stack routers.

receiver simply strips off the IPv4 header and processes the IPv6 header and packet inside.

Hosts that only run IPv6 can use dual-stack routers to communicate using this special form of IPv6 address also. Dual-stack routers recognize the IPv6 traffic and use the last 32 bits to create the IPv4 address for the IPv4 "wrapper." Figure 9.8 shows how this special addressing format works. Naturally, this requires IPv6-only hosts to have valid and routable IPv4 addresses, which clearly marks the format as a transitional method. If the IPv6 address is not in this special address form, then a configured tunnel must be used, or, if every device on the path from source to destination uses dual protocol stacks, or IPv6 only, well-formed IPv6 addresses can be used.

TUNNELING MECHANISMS

The theory of tunneling IPv6 packets through a collection of IPv4 routers is one thing. Exactly how to do it is another. There are several tunnel *mechanisms* that embody the concepts discussed previously.

Manually configured tunnels—These are defined in RFC 2893, and both endpoints of the tunnel must have both IPv4 and IPv6 addresses. These tunnels are usually used between dual-stack edge routers.

Generic Routing Encapsulation (GRE) tunnels—GRE tunnels were designed to transport non-IP protocols over an IP network. But GRE is also a good way to carry IPv6 across the IPv4 routers. We used a GRE tunnel earlier in this chapter.

IPv4-compatible (6over4) tunnels—Also defined in RFC 2893, these are the automatic tunnels based on IPv4-compatible IPv6 addresses using the `::<IPv4 address>` form of IPv6 address.

6to4 tunnels—Another form of automatic tunnel defined in RFC 3065. They use an IPv4 address embedded in the IPv6 address to identify the tunnel endpoint.

Intra-site Automatic Tunnel Addressing Protocol (ISATAP) tunnels—ISATAP tunnels are a mechanism much like 6to4 tunneling, but for local site (campus) networks. An ISATAP address uses a special prefix and the IPv4 address to identify the endpoint.

The differences between the 6to4 tunnel and the ISATAP tunnel address are shown in Figure 9.9.

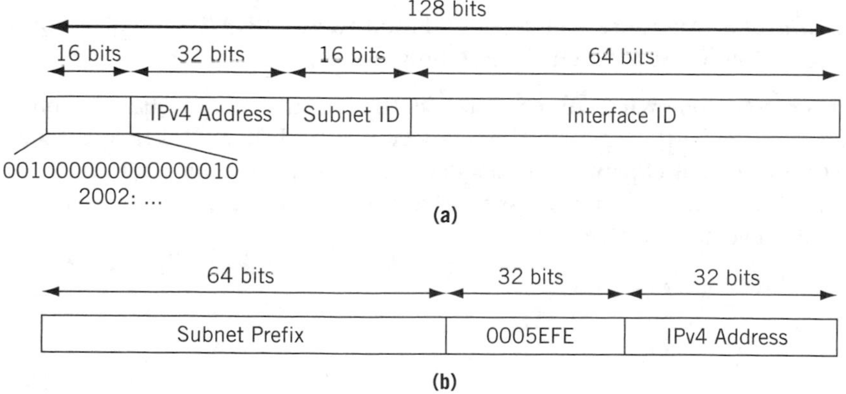

FIGURE 9.9

The differences between 6to4 and ISATAP tunnel addressing, showing how the 128 bits of the IPv6 address are structured in each case. (a) 6to4 tunneling address format (b) ISATAP tunneling address format

TRANSITION CONSIDERATIONS

Routers occupy a key position during the transition period between IPv4 and IPv6. There are still a lot of routers, mostly older ones, that do not handle IPv6 or understand only the `::<IPv4 address>` form of IPv6 address. How will IPv4 and IPv6 routers and hosts interoperate?

A transition plan has been put in place and contains some distinct terminology that is new. The IPv4 to IPv6 transition plan defines the following terms for nodes:

- *IPv4-only Node*—A host or router that implements only IPv4.
- *IPv6/IPv4 (dual) Node*—A host or router that implements both IPv4 and IPv6.
- *IPv6-only Node*—A host or router that implements only IPv6.
- *IPv6 Node*—A host or router that implements IPv6. Both IPv4/IPv6 dual nodes and IPv6-only nodes are included in this category.
- *IPv4 Node*—A host or router that implements IPv4. Both IPv4/IPv6 dual nodes and IPv4-only nodes are included in this category.

In addition, the plan defines three types of addresses:

1. *IPv4-compatible IPv6 address*—An address assigned to an IPv6 node that can be used in both IPv6 and IPv4 packets. The `::<IPv4 address>` format is used for this type of IP address. For example, an address such as `::10.10.11.66` is used when there is no IPv6 router available.
2. *IPv4-mapped IPv6 address*—An address assigned to an IPv4-only node represented as an IPv6 address. These addresses always identify IPv4-only nodes, never IPv4/IPv6 or IPv6-only nodes. These are provided when an IPv6 application requests the host name for a node with an IPv4 address only. For example, `::FFFF:10.10.12.166` is an IPv4-mapped IPv6 address.
3. *IPv6-only address*—An address globally assigned to any IPv4/IPv6 or IPv6-only node. These addresses never identify IPv4-only nodes.

These terms can be somewhat confusing, but all they mean is that hosts and routers can be classified either as IPv4 devices, IPv6 devices, or both IPv4 and IPv6 devices. The IPv4/IPv6 devices are capable of understanding and using both IPv4 and IPv6. However, the IPv6-only address (an address that has no relationship to an IPv4 address) can be used in an IPv6/IPv4 device.

QUESTIONS FOR READERS

Figure 9.10 shows some of the concepts discussed in this chapter and can be used to help you answer the following questions.

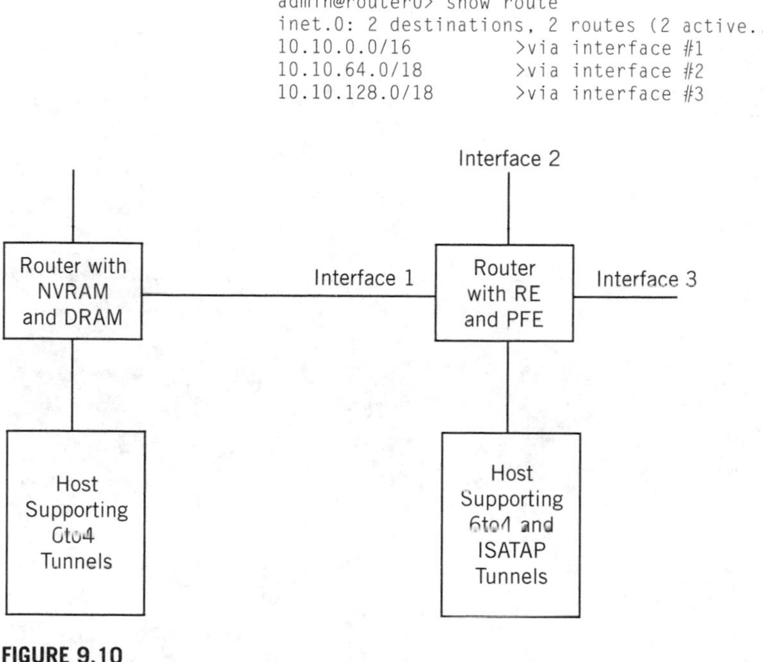

FIGURE 9.10

A simple network of routers and hosts, showing architecture, a routing table, and tunnel support.

1. Which router, based on the architecture in the figure, is probably a small site router? Which is probably a large Internet backbone router?
2. Which output interface, based on the routing table shown in the figure, will packets arriving from the directly attached host for IPv4 address `10.10.11.1` use for forwarding? Assume longest match is used.
3. Which output interface will packets for `10.10.192.10` use? Assume the longest match is used.
4. Which IPv6 tunneling protocol can be used between the two hosts? How many bits will be used for the subnet identifier?
5. Do the routers require IPv6 support to deliver packets between the two hosts?

CHAPTER

User Datagram Protocol

10

What You Will Learn

In this chapter, you will learn about UDP, one of the major transport layer protocols in the TCP/IP stack. We'll talk about datagrams and the structure of the UDP header.

You will learn about ports and sockets and how they are used at the transport layer.

The User Datagram Protocol (UDP) is one the major transport layer protocols that rides on top of IPv4 or IPv6. Most explorations of the TCP/IP transport layer treat the other major protocol, the connection-oriented Transmission Control Protocol (TCP) first and present connectionless UDP later. But the complexities of TCP, and the reasons for these often sophisticated procedures, are better understood after appreciating the basic connectionless service provided by UDP. In addition, certain concepts that are shared by both UDP and TCP, such as ports, can be introduced in UDP and so reduce the number of new ideas that must be covered during TCP discussions to a more manageable level.

The UDP acronym shows the effects of early Internet efforts to distinguish connectionless packet delivery ("It's a datagram, not a packet!") from more conventional connection-oriented schemes in use at the time. The data unit of UDP is not a packet anyway, but a *datagram*, the content of a connectionless packet (many authors call IP packets datagrams as well, but we do not in this book). UDP datagrams have their own headers, naturally, and the UDP header is about as simple as a header can get. That's only to be expected, because UDP operation is also very simple, making UDP ideal for a first look at end-to-end functions on a network.

In recent years, UDP's popularity as a transport layer protocol for applications has been growing. The simple and fast operation of UDP makes it ideal for delay-sensitive traffic like voice samples (the digital representation of analog speech), multicast digital video, and other types of "real-time" traffic that cannot be resent if lost on the network. This use of UDP is not as originally intended, and there are other things that need to be done before UDP is ready for voice and video, but in the true spirit of Internet innovation, UDP was adapted for these new circumstances.

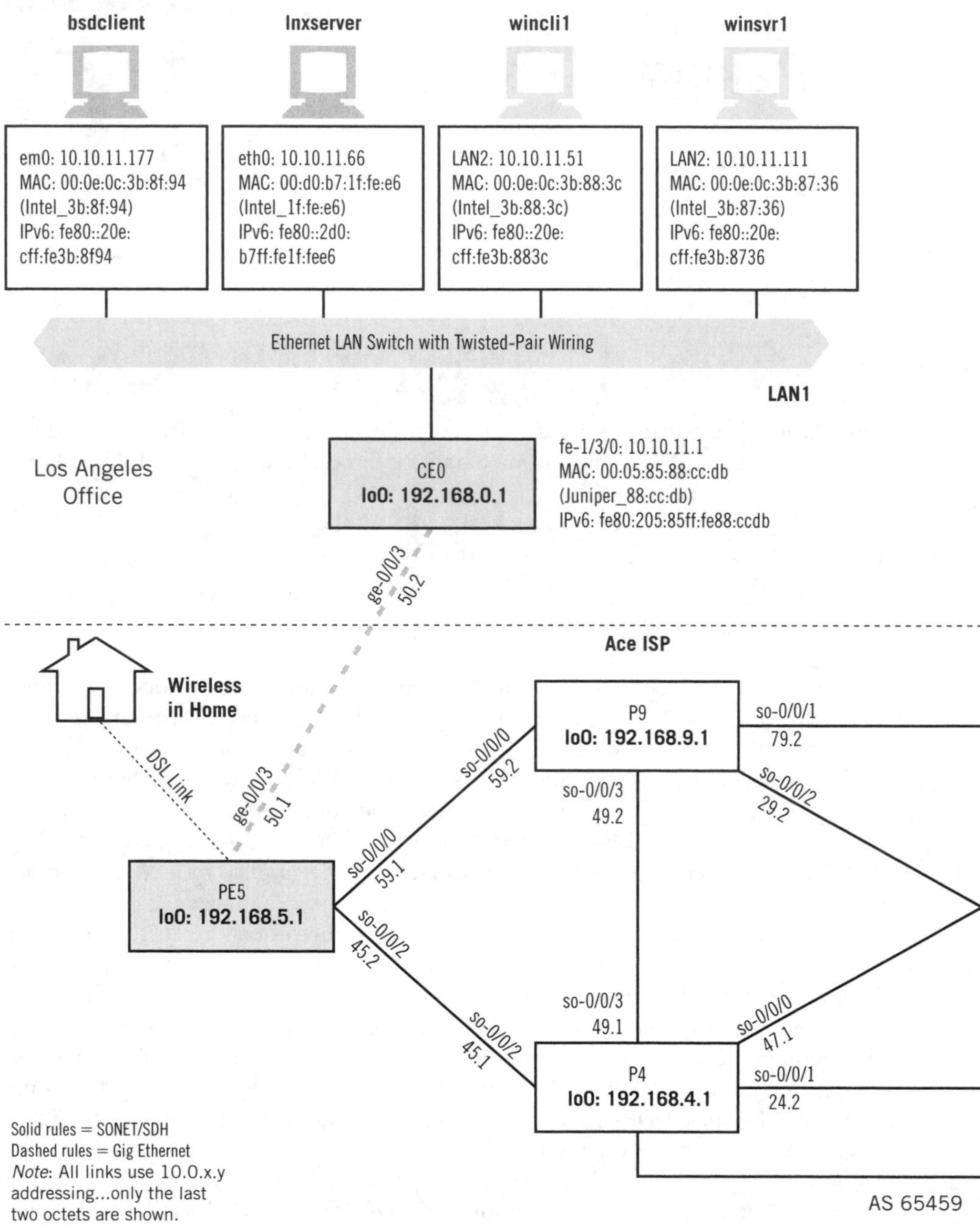

FIGURE 10.1

UDP ports and sockets on the Illustrated Network. Note that this chapter mainly uses the Unix-based hosts on the network to explore UDP.

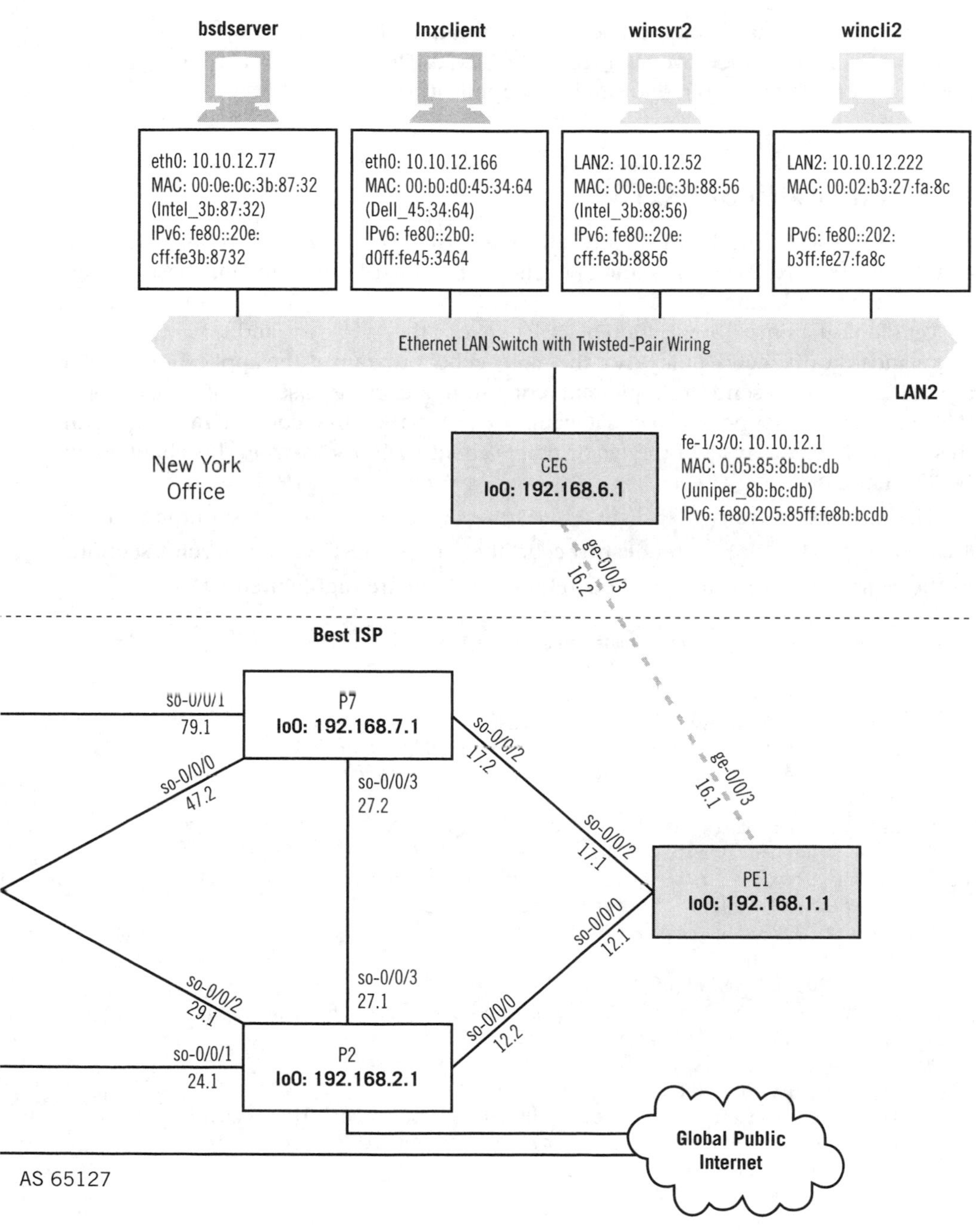
bsdserver
lnxclient
winsvr2
wincli2
eth0: 10.10.12.77
MAC: 00:0e:0c:3b:87:32
(Intel_3b:87:32)
IPv6: fe80::20e:
cff:fe3b:8732
eth0: 10.10.12.166
MAC: 00:b0:d0:45:34:64
(Dell_45:34:64)
IPv6: fe80::2b0:
d0ff:fe45:3464
LAN2: 10.10.12.52
MAC: 00:0e:0c:3b:88:56
(Intel_3b:88:56)
IPv6: fe80::20e:
cff:fe3b:8856
LAN2: 10.10.12.222
MAC: 00:02:b3:27:fa:8c
IPv6: fe80::202:
b3ff:fe27:fa8c
Ethernet LAN Switch with Twisted-Pair Wiring
LAN2
New York
Office
CE6
lo0: 192.168.6.1
fe-1/3/0: 10.10.12.1
MAC: 0:05:85:8b:bc:db
(Juniper_8b:bc:db)
IPv6: fe80:205:85ff:fe8b:bcdb
ge-0/0/3
16.2
Best ISP
so-0/0/1
79.1
P7
lo0: 192.168.7.1
so-0/0/2
17.2
so-0/0/0
47.2
so-0/0/3
27.2
ge-0/0/3
16.1
so-0/0/2
17.1
PE1
lo0: 192.168.1.1
so-0/0/0
12.1
so-0/0/2
29.1
so-0/0/3
27.1
so-0/0/0
12.2
so-0/0/1
24.1
P2
lo0: 192.168.2.1
Global Public
Internet
AS 65127

UDP is used by many common network applications, including DNS, IPTV streaming media applications, voice over IP (VoIP), the Trivial File Transfer Protocol (TFTP), and online games. UDP is required for multicast applications.

UDP PORTS AND SOCKETS

Figure 10.1 shows the hosts on the Illustrated Network that we'll be using in this chapter to explore UDP ports and sockets. We'll primarily use the Unix-based hosts, both FreeBSD and Linux.

Let's look at a simple application of UDP between the `lnxclient` and `lnxserver` hosts. The standard Unix "echo" utility (not the same "echo" program as the application used in a previous chapter) sends a simple text string from a client to a server using UDP port 7. The server just bounces a UDP datagram back with the same content. But even with this simple interaction, all of the major points about UDP discussed in this chapter can be illustrated.

The capture is from `lnxserver` (`10.10.11.66`). The server is responding to the `lnxclient` (`10.10.12.166`) request to echo the string "TEST." The important sections of the request and response packets relevant to UDP are highlighted.

```
[root@lnxserver admin]# /usr/sbin/tethereal -V port 7
Capturing on eth0
Frame 1 (60 bytes on wire, 60 bytes captured)
   Arrival Time: May 6, 2008 16:31:30.947137000
   Time delta from previous packet: 0.000000000 seconds
   Time relative to first packet: 0.000000000 seconds
   Frame Number: 1
   Packet Length: 60 bytes
   Capture Length: 60 bytes
Ethernet II, Src: 00:05:85:88:cc:db, Dst: 00:d0:b7:1f:fe:e6
   Destination: 00:d0:b7:1f:fe:e6 (Intel_1f:fe:e6)
   Source: 00:05:85:88:cc:db (Juniper__88:cc:db)
   Type: IP (0x0800)
   Trailer: 0000000000000000000000000000
Internet Protocol, Src Addr: 10.10.12.166 (10.10.12.166), Dst Addr:
10.10.11.66 (10.10.11.66)
   Version: 4
   Header length: 20 bytes
   Differentiated Services Field: 0x00 (DSCP 0x00: Default; ECN: 0x00)
      0000 00.. = Differentiated Services Codepoint: Default (0x00)
      .... ..0. = ECN-Capable Transport (ECT): 0
      .... ...0 = ECN-CE: 0
   Total Length: 32
   Identification: 0x0000
   Flags: 0x04
      .1.. = Don't fragment: Set
      ..0. = More fragments: Not set
   Fragment offset: 0
```

```
   Time to live: 62
   Protocol: UDP (0x11)
   Header checksum: 0x10d2 (correct)
   Source: 10.10.12.166 (10.10.12.166)
   Destination: 10.10.11.66 (10.10.11.66)
User Datagram Protocol, Src Port: 32787 (32787), Dst Port: echo (7)
   Source port: 32787 (32787)
   Destination port: echo (7)
   Length: 12
   Checksum: 0xac26 (correct)
Data (4 bytes)

0000  54 45 53 54                    TEST

Frame 2 (46 bytes on wire, 46 bytes captured)
   Arrival Time: May 6, 2008 16:31:30.948312000
   Time delta from previous packet: 0.001175000 seconds
   Time relative to first packet: 0.001175000 seconds
   Frame Number: 2
   Packet Length: 46 bytes
   Capture Length: 46 bytes
Ethernet II, Src: 00:d0:b7:1f:fe:e6, Dst: 00:05:85:88:cc:db
   Destination: 00:05:85:88:cc:db (Juniper__88:cc:db)
   Source: 00:d0:b7:1f:fe:e6 (Intel_1f:fe:e6)
   Type: IP (0x0800)
Internet Protocol, Src Addr: 10.10.11.66 (10.10.11.66), Dst Addr:
10.10.12.166 (10.10.12.166)
   Version: 4
   Header length: 20 bytes
   Differentiated Services Field: 0x00 (DSCP 0x00: Default; ECN: 0x00)
   0000 00.. = Differentiated Services Codepoint: Default (0x00)
     .... ..0. = ECN-Capable Transport (ECT): 0
     .... ...0 = ECN-CE: 0
   Total Length: 32
   Identification: 0x0000
   Flags: 0x04
     .1.. = Don't fragment: Set
     ..0. = More fragments: Not set
   Fragment offset: 0
   Time to live: 64
   Protocol: UDP (0x11)
   Header checksum: 0x0ed2 (correct)
   Source: 10.10.11.66 (10.10.11.66)
   Destination: 10.10.12.166 (10.10.12.166)
User Datagram Protocol, Src Port: echo (7), Dst Port: 32787 (32787)
   Source port: echo (7)
   Destination port: 32787 (32787)
   Length: 12
   Checksum: 0xac26 (correct)
Data (4 bytes)

0000  54 45 53 54                 TEST
```

The DF bit in the packet is set, and the UDP checksum field is used. Technically, the UDP checksum is optional, and the client decides whether to use it. The server responds with a checksum because the client used a checksum in the request. In fact, Windows XP and FreeBSD do the same.

The UDP checksum was made optional to cut processing on reliable networks like small LAN segments to a bare minimum. Today, client and server on the same LAN segment are not very common, and processing the checksum is not a burden for modern computing devices. Also, UDP checksum calculation can be offloaded to modern Ethernet chipsets, so it's less "expensive" than it used to be. Currently, use of the UDP checksum is common, and most traditional texts say it "should" be used with IPv4. Use of the UDP checksum is mandatory with IPv6.

Note that the program uses client UDP port `32787`. This is in the range of ports known as ***registered ports***. We'll talk about those, and the ***dynamic port*** range of 49152 to 65535, later in this chapter. The dynamic port range that a Unix system uses is a kernel-tunable parameter and can be changed using tweaks to the `/etc/sysctl.conf` file, but information on exactly how to do it is scarce and beyond the scope of this book.

We can see the sockets in use on a Linux host by using the `netstat -lp` command to display listening sockets. (Although the options imply these are listening ports, it is the socket information that is displayed.)

```
root@lnxserver admin]# netstat -lp
Active Internet connections (only servers)
Proto Recv-Q Send-Q Local Address              Foreign Address     State
       PID/Program name
tcp        0      0 *:32768                    *:*                 LISTEN
       1664/
tcp        0      0 localhost.localdo:32769 *:*                    LISTEN
       1783/xinetd
tcp        0      0 localhost.localdoma:783 *:*                    LISTEN
       1853/spamd -d -c -a
tcp        0      0 *:sunrpc                   *:*                 LISTEN
       1645/
tcp        0      0 *:x11                      *:*                 LISTEN
       2103/X
tcp        0      0 *:ssh                      *:*                 LISTEN
       1769/sshd
tcp        0      0 localhost.localdoma:ipp *:*                    LISTEN
       6813/cupsd
tcp        0      0 localhost.localdom:smtp *:*                    LISTEN
       1826/
udp        0      0 *:32768                    *:*
       1664/
udp        0      0 *:echo                     *:*
       1923/Echo
udp        0      0 *:sunrpc                   *:*
       1645/
```

```
udp        0      0 *:631                   *:*
       6813/cupsd
udp        0      0 localhost.localdoma:ntp *:*
       1800/
udp        0      0 *:ntp                   *:*
       1800/
Active UNIX domain sockets (only servers)
Proto RefCnt Flags      Type      State         I-Node PID/Program name
Path
unix  2      [ ACC ]    STREAM    LISTENING     2663   1939/
/tmp/jd_sockV4
unix  2      [ ACC ]    STREAM    LISTENING     2839   2053/
/tmp/.gdm_socket
unix  2      [ ACC ]    STREAM    LISTENING     2714   2016/
/tmp/.font-unix/fs7100
unix  2      [ ACC ]    STREAM    LISTENING     2542   1872/
/tmp/.iroha_unix/IROHA
unix  2      [ ACC ]    STREAM    LISTENING     2849   2103/X
/tmp/.X11-unix/X0
unix  2      [ ACC ]    STREAM    LISTENING     2535   1862/gpm
/dev/gpmctl
```

The output is difficult to parse, but we can see our little echo utility (highlighted, and the second line of the UDP section) patiently waiting for clients on port 7 (the output identifies it as the standard "echo" port). UDP, being a stateless protocol, is not technically in a "listening" state, but that's what the server socket essentially does. The asterisks (*:*) mean that communications will be accepted from another IP address and port.

The command to reveal the same type of information on bsdserver is sockstat.

```
bsdserver# sockstat
USER     COMMAND    PID    FD PROTO  LOCAL ADDRESS        FOREIGN ADDRESS
root     sendmail    88    4  tcp4   *:25                 *:*
root     sendmail    88    6  tcp4   *:587                *:*
root     sshd        83    4  tcp4   *:22                 *:*
root     inetd       79    4  tcp4   *:21                 *:*
root     inetd       79    5  tcp4   *:23                 *:*
root     syslogd     72    5  udp4   *:514                *:*

USER     COMMAND    PID    FD PROTO  LOCAL ADDRESS        FOREIGN ADDRESS
root     sendmail    88    5  tcp46  *:25                 *:*
root     sshd        83    3  tcp46  *:22                 *:*
root     syslogd     72    4  udp6   *:514                *:*
USER     COMMAND    PID    FD PROTO  ADDRESS
admin    sshd     48218    3  stream sshd[48216]:4
root     sshd     48216    4  stream sshd[48218]:3
smmsp    sendmail    91    3  dgram  syslogd[72]:3
root     sendmail    88    3  dgram  syslogd[72]:3
root     syslogd     72    3  dgram  /var/run/log
```

The little "echo" port is not listed because it is not running on this host. Note that the `syslogd` process in FreeBSD listens on *both* the UDP and TCP ports (in this case, port 514) for clients.

What about Windows XP? The command here is `netstat -a` (all), but be prepared to be surprised. Windows hosts listen to a larger number of sockets than Unix systems. It depends on exactly what the system is doing, but even on our "quiet" test network, `winsrv2` has 25 TCP and 19 UDP processes waiting to spring into action. They range from `Netbios` (an old IBM and Microsoft LAN protocol) to Microsoft-specific functions. Heavily loaded systems have even higher numbers.

What about looking at UDP with IPv6? It's not really necessary. We are now high enough in the TCP/IP protocol stack not to worry about differences between IPv4 and IPv6. (In practical terms, we still have to worry about DNS a bit, but we'll talk about that in Chapter 19.) With the exception of the checksum use and something called the *pseudo-header*, UDP is the same in both.

WHAT UDP IS FOR

UDP was defined in RFC 768 and refined in RFC 1122. All implementations must follow both RFCs to make interoperability reliable, and all do. UDP uses IP protocol ID 17. Any IPv4 or IPv6 packet received with 17 in the protocol ID field is given to the local UDP service.

UDP is defined as stateless (no session information is kept by hosts) and unreliable (no guarantees of any QoS parameters, not even delivery). This does *not* mean that UDP traffic is somehow lower priority on the network or through routers. It's not as if UDP traffic is routinely tossed by stressed-out routers. It just means that if the application using UDP needs to keep track of a session history ("How many datagrams did you get before that link failed?") or guaranteed delivery ("I'm not sending any more until I know if you got the datagrams I sent."), then the *application* itself must do it, because UDP can't and won't.

Nevertheless, there is a whole class of applications that use UDP, some almost exclusively. These are applications that are invoked to exchange quick, request-response pairs of messages, such as DNS ("Quick! What IP address goes with `www.example.com`?"). These applications could suffer while waiting for all the overhead that TCP requires to set up a connection between hosts before sending a message.

Multicast allows one source to send a *single* packet stream to multiple destinations (TCP is strictly a one-source-to-one-destination protocol), so UDP must be used for multicast data transfer as well. Multicast is not only used with video or audio, but also in applications such as the Dynamic Host Configuration Protocol (DHCP).

In other words, UDP is a low-overhead transport for applications that do not need, or cannot have, the "point-to-point" connections or guaranteed delivery that TCP provides.

Packets carrying UDP traffic in IPv4 sometimes have the DF (Don't Fragment) bit set in the IPv4 header. However, no one should be surprised or upset to find a UDP datagram riding inside an IPv4 packet without the DF bit set.

THE UDP HEADER

Figure 10.2 shows the UDP header. There are only four fields, and the data inside the datagram (the message) are optional.

The header is only 8 bytes (64 bits) long. First are the 2-byte Source Port field and the 2-byte Destination Port field. These fields are the datagram counterparts of the source and destination IP addresses at the packet level. But unlike IP addresses, there is no structure to the port fields: All values between 0 and 65,353 are represented as pure numerics. This does not mean that all port numbers, source and destination, are the same, however. Port values can be divided into well-known, registered, and dynamic port numbers.

The Length field gives the length in bytes of the UDP datagram, and includes the header fields along with any data. The minimum length is 8 (the header alone), and the maximum value is 65,353. However, the achievable maximum UDP datagram lengths are determined by the size of the send and receive buffers on the host end systems, which are usually set to around 8000 bytes (although they can be changed).

As already mentioned, hosts are required to handle 576-byte IP packets at a minimum, but many protocols (the most common being DNS and DHCP) limit the maximum size of the UDP datagram that they use to 512 bytes or less.

The Checksum field is the most interesting field in the UDP header. This is because the checksum is *not* a simple value calculated on the UDP header fields and data, if present. The UDP checksum is computed on what is called the *pseudo-header*. The pseudo header fields for IPv4 are shown in Figure 10.3.

The all-zero byte is used to provide alignment of the pseudo-header, and the data field must be padded to align it with a 16-bit boundary. The 12 bytes of the UDP pseudo-header are prepended to the UDP datagram, and the checksum is computed on the whole object. For this computation, the Checksum field itself is set to zero, and the 16-bit result placed in the field before transmission. If the checksum computes to zero, an all-1s value is sent, and all-1s is not a computable checksum. The pseudo-header fields are not sent with the datagram.

1 byte	1 byte	1 byte	1 byte
Source Port		Destination Port	
Length (including header)		Checksum	
Datagram Data (optional)			

FIGURE 10.2

The four UDP header fields. Technically, use of the checksum is optional, but it is often used today.

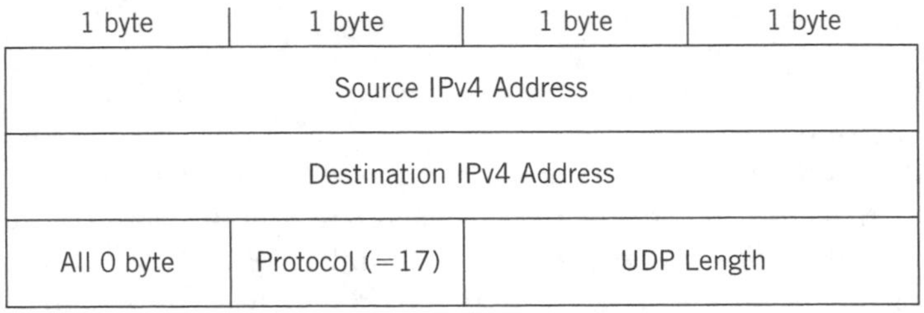

1 byte	1 byte	1 byte	1 byte
Source IPv4 Address			
Destination IPv4 Address			
All 0 byte	Protocol (=17)	UDP Length	

FIGURE 10.3

The UDP IPv4 pseudo-header. These fields are used for checksum computation and include fields in the IP header.

At the receiver, the value of the Checksum is copied and the field again set to zero. The checksum is again computed on the pseudo-header and compared to the received value. If they match, the datagram is processed by the receiving application indicated by the destination port number. If they do not match, the datagram is silently discarded (i.e., no error message is sent to the source).

Naturally, using 32-bit IPv4 addresses to compute transport layer checksums will not work in IPv6, although the procedure is the same. RFC 2460 establishes a different set of pseudo-header fields for IPv6. The IPv6 pseudo-header is shown in Figure 10.4.

The Next Header value is not always 17 for UDP, because other extension headers could be in use. Length is the length of the upper layer header and the data it carries.

IPv4 AND IPv6 NOTES

The presence of the IP source and destination address in an upper layer checksum computation strikes many as a violation of the concept of protocol layer independence. (The same concern applies to NAT, discussed in Chapter 27.) In fact, a lot of TCP/IP books mention that including packet level fields in the end-to-end checksum helps assure (when the checksum is correct at the receiver) that the message has not only made its way to right port, but to the correct system.

The presence of a pseudo-header also shows how late in the development process that TCP and UDP were separated from IP. Not only that, but the transport layer and network layer (or, to give them more intuitive names, the end-to-end layer and routing layer) have *always* been tightly coupled in any working network.

The use of the UDP checksum is not required for IPv4, but highly recommended. It is required in IPv6, of course. In IPv4, servers that receive client datagrams with the checksum field set are supposed to reply using the checksum, but this is not always enforced. If the IPv4 checksum field is not used, it is set to all 0 bits (recall that all 0 checksums are sent as all-1s).

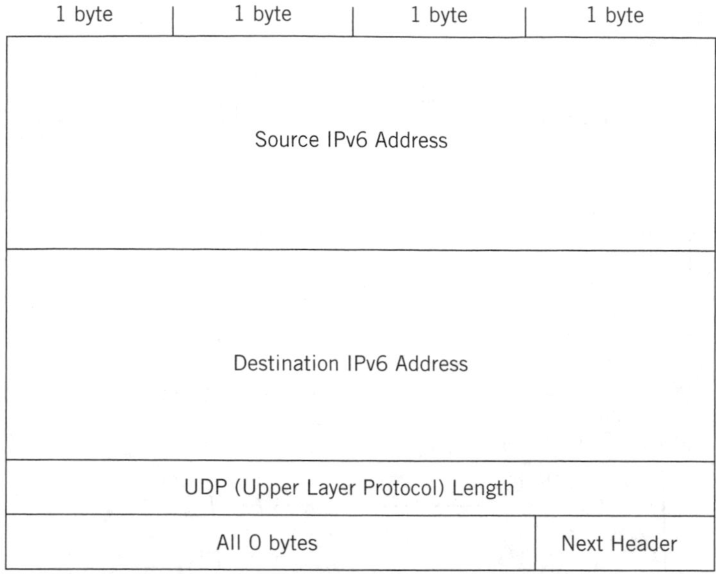

FIGURE 10.4

The UDP IPv6 pseudo-header. Use of the UDP checksum is not optional in IPv6.

PORT NUMBERS

Each application running above UDP (and TCP) and IP is indexed by its port number, allowing for the multiplexing of the IP layer. Just as frames with different types of packets inside (on Ethernet, IPv4 is `0x0800` and IPv6 is `0x86DD`) are multiplexed onto a single LAN interface, the individual IPv4 or IPv6 packets are multiplexed and distributed by the protocol number (UDP is IP protocol number 17, and TCP is 6).

The port numbers in turn multiplex and distribute datagrams from applications, allowing them to share a single UDP or TCP process, which is usually integrated closely with the operating system. This function of frame Ethertype, packet protocol, and datagram port is shown in Figure 10.5. The figure shows how IPv4 data for DNS makes its way from frame through IPv4 through UDP to the DNS application listening on UDP port 53.

Well-Known Ports

Port numbers can run from 0 to 65353. Port numbers from 0 to 1023 are reserved for common TCP/IP applications and are called *well-known ports*. The use of well-known ports allows client applications to easily locate the corresponding server application processes on other hosts. For example, a client process wanting to contact a DNS

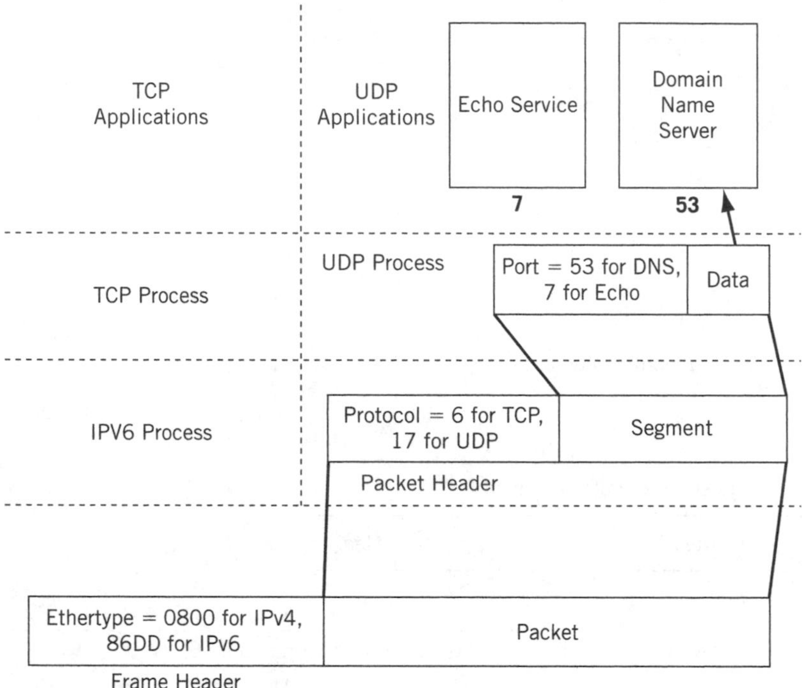

FIGURE 10.5

UDP port multiplexing and distribution, showing how a single IP layer (IPv6 in this case) can be used by multiple transport protocols and applications.

process running on a server must send the datagram to some destination port. The well-known port number for DNS is 53, and that's where the server process should be listening for client requests. These ports are sometimes called "privileged" ports, although a number of applications that formerly ran in "privileged" mode, such as HTTP servers, do not run this way anymore except when binding to the port. It should be noted that it is getting harder and harder to register new applications in the space below 1023 (these often use registered ports in the range 1024 to 49151).

Ports used on servers are ***persistent*** in the sense that they last for a long time, or at least as long as the application is running. Ports used on clients are *ephemeral* ("lasting a short time," although the term technically means "lasting a day") in the sense that they "come and go" as the user runs client applications.

Technically, UDP port numbers are independent from TCP port numbers. In practice, most of the applications indexed by port numbers are the same in UDP or TCP (although a few applications can use either protocol), excepting a handful that are maintained for historical reasons. This does not imply that applications can use TCP or UDP as they choose. It just means that it's easier to maintain one list rather than two. But no matter what port numbers are used, UDP port 1000 is a different application than TCP port 1000, even though both applications might perform the same function.

Some of the more common well-known port numbers are shown in Table 10.1. In the table, the UDP and TCP port numbers are identical.

Port numbers above 1023 can be either *registered* or *dynamic* (also called *private* or *non-reserved*). Registered ports are in the range 1024 to 49151. Dynamic ports are in the range 49152 to 65535. As mentioned, most new port assignments are in the range from 1024 to 49151.

Registered port numbers are non-well-known ports that are used by vendors for their own server applications. After all, not every possible application capability will be reflected in a well-known port, and software vendors should be free to innovate. Of course, if another vendor chooses the same port number for a server process, and they are run on the same system, there would be no way to distinguish between these two seemingly identical applications.

- *Well-known ports*—Ports in the range 0 to 1023 are assigned and controlled.
- *Registered ports*—Ports in the range 1024 to 49151 are not assigned or controlled, but can be registered to prevent duplication.
- *Dynamic ports*—Ports in the range 49152 to 65535 are not assigned, controlled, or registered. They are used for temporary or private ports. They are also known as private or non-reserved ports. Clients should choose ephemeral port numbers from this range, but many systems do not.

Table 10.1 Some Well-Known Ports Used by UDP and TCP Services and Functions

Port Number	Service	Meaning
7	Echo	Used to echo data back to the sender
9	Discard	Used to discard data at receiver
13	Daytime	Reports time information in user-friendly format
17	Quote	Returns a "quote of the day" (rarely used today)
19	Chargen	Character generator
53	DNS	Domain Name Service
67	DHCP server	Server port used to send configuration information
68	DHCP client	Client port used to receive configuration information
69	TFTP	Trivial file transfer
161	SNMP	Used to receive network management queries
162	SNMP traps	Used to receive network problem reports
1011–1023	Reserved	Reserved for future use

Vendors can register their application's ports with ICANN. Other software vendors are supposed to respect these registered values and register their own server application port numbers from the pool of unused values. Some registered UDP and TCP protocol numbers are shown in Table 10.2.

The private, or dynamic, port numbers are used by clients and *not* servers. Datagrams sent from a client to a server are typically only sent to well-known or registered ports (although there are exceptions). Server applications are usually long lived, while client processes come and go as users run them. Client applications therefore are free to choose almost any port number not used for some other purpose (hence the term "dynamic"), and many use different source port numbers every time they are run. The server has no trouble replying to the proper client because the server can just reverse the source and destination port numbers to send a reply to the correct client (assuming the IP address of the client is correct).

All TCP/IP implementations must know the range of well-known, registered, and private ports when choosing a port number to use. Unix systems hold this information is the `/etc/services` file. Windows users can find this `C:\%SystemRoot%\system32\drivers\etc\SERVICES` file, where *%SystemRoot%* will be automatically referred to a folder such as `WinNT` or `WINDOWS`. Most ports are the same for UDP or TCP, but some are unique to one or the other. For example, FTP control uses TCP port 21.

Table 10.2 Selected Registered UDP and TCP Ports with Service and Brief Description of Meaning

Port Number	Service	Brief Description of Use
1024	Reserved	Reserved for future use
1025	Blackjack	Network version of blackjack
1026	CAP	Calendar access protocol
1027	Exosee	ExoSee
1029	Solidmux	Solid Mux Server
1102	Adobe 1	Adobe Server 1
1103	Adobe 2	Adobe Server 2
44553	Rbr-debug	REALBasic Remote Debug
46999	Mediabox	MediaBox Server
47557	Dbbrowse	Databeam Corporation
48620–49150	Unassigned	These ports have not been registered
49151	Reserved	Reserved for future use

Here is the beginning of the file from winsvr2:

```
# Copyright (c) 1993-1999 Microsoft Corp.
#
# This file contains port numbers for well-known services defined by IANA
#
# Format:
#
# <service name>  <port number>/<protocol>  [aliases...]   [#<comment>]
#

echo           7/tcp
echo           7/udp
discard        9/tcp        sink null
discard        9/udp        sink null
systat        11/tcp        users            #Active users
systat        11/tcp        users            #Active users
daytime       13/tcp
daytime       13/udp
qotd          17/tcp        quote            #Quote of the day
qotd          17/udp        quote            #Quote of the day
chargen       19/tcp        ttytst source    #Character generator
chargen       19/udp        ttytst source    #Character generator
ftp-data      20/tcp                         #FTP, data
ftp           21/tcp                         #FTP. control
telnet        23/tcp
[many more lines not shown...]
```

For the latest global list of well-known, registered, and private port numbers, see *www.iana.org/assignments/port-numbers*. The port numbers are the same for IPv4 and IPv6.

The Socket

The combination of IPv4 or IPv6 address and port numbers forms an abstract concept called a *socket*. We've mentioned the socket concept briefly before, and will do so again and again in later chapters. The socket concept is important for many reasons, and a later chapter will explore some of them more completely. For now, all that is important to mention is that, for each client-server interaction, there is a socket on each host at the endpoints of the network. The sockets at each end uniquely identify that particular client-server interaction, although the same sockets can be used for subsequent interactions.

Sockets are usually written in IPv4 and IPv6 by adding a colon (:) to the IP address, although sometimes a dot (.) is used instead. In IPv6, it is also necessary to add brackets to avoid confusion with the :: notation, such as in [FC00:490:f100:1000::1]:80. A UDP socket on lnxclient, for example, would be 10.10.12.166:17, while one on bsdserver would be 10.10.12.77:17.

Action	Condition	Outcome
UDP request sent to server	Server available	Sender gets UDP reply from server
UDP request sent to server	Port is closed on server	Sender gets ICMP "Port unreachable" message
UDP request sent to server	Server host does not exist	Sender gets ICMP "Host unreachable" message
UDP request sent to server	Port is blocked by firewall/router	Sender gets ICMP "Port unreachable— Administrative prohibited"message
UDP request sent to server	Port is blocked by silent firewall/router	(timeout)
UDP request sent to server	Reply is lost on way back	(timeout)

FIGURE 10.6

UDP protocol actions, showing the request–reply outcomes.

UDP OPERATION

The delivery of UDP datagrams is by no means certain. The lack of an expected response on the part of a server to a UDP client request is handled by a simple timeout. Responses are not always expected, as might be the case with streaming audio and video. The client might resend the datagram, but in many cases this might not be the best strategy.

In some cases, lack of response is not a reliable indication that anything is wrong with the network or remote host. Routers routinely filter out unwanted packets, and many do so silently, while others send the appropriate ICMP "administratively prohibited" message.

In general, there are five major possible results when an application sends a UDP request, shown in Figure 10.6. Note that *any* of the replies can be lost on the way back to the sender, generating a timeout.

UDP OVERFLOWS

We've looked at UDP as a sort of quick-and-dirty request–response interaction between hosts over a network. Delivery is not guaranteed, but neither is an important network property called *flow control*. A lot of nonsense has been written about flow control, which is a very simple idea. It just means that no sender should ever be able to overwhelm a receiver with traffic. In other words, receivers must have a way to tell senders to slow down. UDP, of course, has no such mechanism.

The confusion over flow control often comes from treating flow control as a synonym for a related concept called *congestion control*. While flow control is strictly a local property of individual senders and receivers, congestion control is a global property of the network. No sender overwhelms a receiver: There's just too much traffic in the router network for things to work properly.

Congestion control often uses flow control to accomplish its goals (source quench was a not-too-sophisticated mechanism). There's not much else a router can use other than flow control to tell senders to shut up for a while. But that's no excuse for treating the two as one and the same.

What has this to do with UDP? Well, it is possible for UDP receivers' buffers, which are usually fixed, to overflow with unexpected UDP datagrams and be forced to discard traffic. Most UDP implementations include a way to display "UDP socket overflows" or discarded UDP datagrams.

But what if an application needs guaranteed delivery, sequencing, and flow control to work properly, and we don't want to add these to the application? Files cannot use quick request-response messages to transfer themselves over a network. That's the job of TCP, which is the topic of the next chapter.

QUESTIONS FOR READERS

Figure 10.7 shows some of the concepts discussed in this chapter and can be used to help you answer the following questions.

1 byte	1 byte	1 byte	1 byte
Source Port		Destination Port	
Length (including header)		Checksum	
Datagram Data (optional)			

(a)

1 byte	1 byte	1 byte	1 byte
Source IPv4 Address			
Destination IPv4 Address			
All 0 byte	Protocol (=17)	UDP Length	

(b)

FIGURE 10.7

The UDP header (a) and pseudo-header (b) fields for IPv4.

1. Which UDP header field does UDP use for demultiplexing?
2. What is UDP's only attempt at error control?
3. A socket is comprised of which two TCP/IP components?
4. What is the registered port range? Is this assigned or controlled?
5. What is the dynamic or private port range? Are these assigned or controlled?

CHAPTER

Transmission Control Protocol

11

What You Will Learn

In this chapter, you will learn about the TCP transport layer protocol, which is the connection-oriented, more reliable companion of UDP. We'll talk about all the fields in the TCP header (which are many) and how TCP's distinctive three-way handshake works.

You will learn how TCP operates during the data transfer and disconnect phase, as well as some of the options that have been established to extend TCP's use for today's networking conditions.

The Transmission Control Protocol (TCP) is as complex as UDP is simple. Some of the same concepts apply to both because both TCP and UDP are end-to-end protocols. Sockets and ports, well-known, dynamic, and private, apply to both. TCP is IP protocol 6, but the ports are usually the same as UDP and run from 0 to 65,535. The major difference between UDP and TCP is that TCP is connection oriented. And that makes all the difference.

Internet specifications variously refer to connections as "virtual circuits," "flows," or "packet-switched services," depending on the context. These subtle variations are unnecessary for this book, and we simply use the term "connection." A connection is a logical relationship between two endpoints (hosts) on a network. Connections can be *permanent* (although the proper term is "semipermanent") or on demand (often called "switched"). Permanent connections are usually set up by manual configuration of the network nodes. (On the Internet, this equates to a series of very specific static routes.) On-demand connections require some type of *signaling protocol* to establish connections on the fly, node by node through the network from the source (the "caller") host to the destination (the "callee") host.

Permanent connections are like intercoms: You can talk right away or at any time and know the other end is there. However, you can only talk to that specific endpoint on that connection. On-demand connections are like telephone calls: You have to wait until the other end "answers" before you talk or send any information, but you connect to (call) anyone in the world.

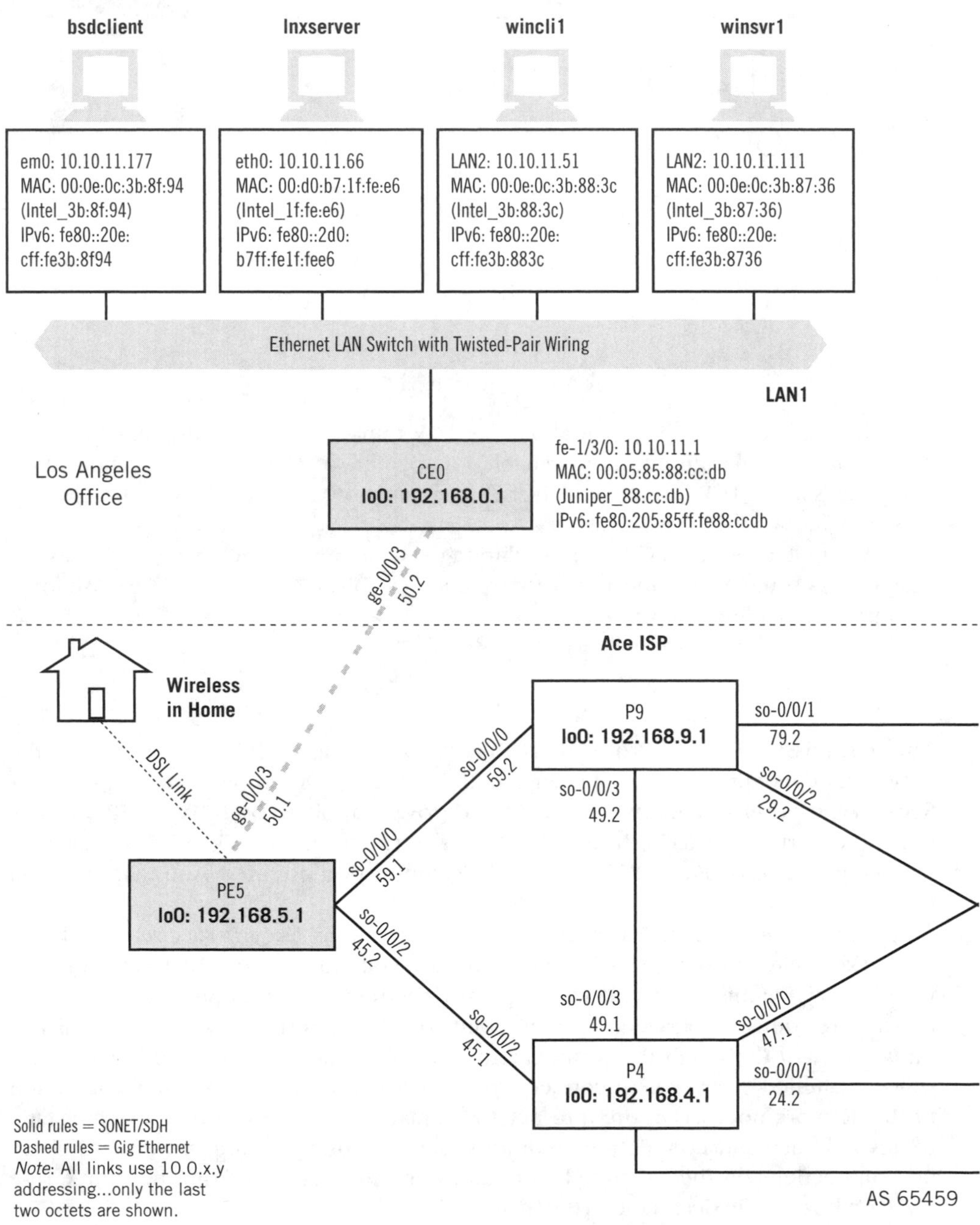

FIGURE 11.1

TCP client–server connections, showing that this chapter uses a client and server pair on the same LAN.

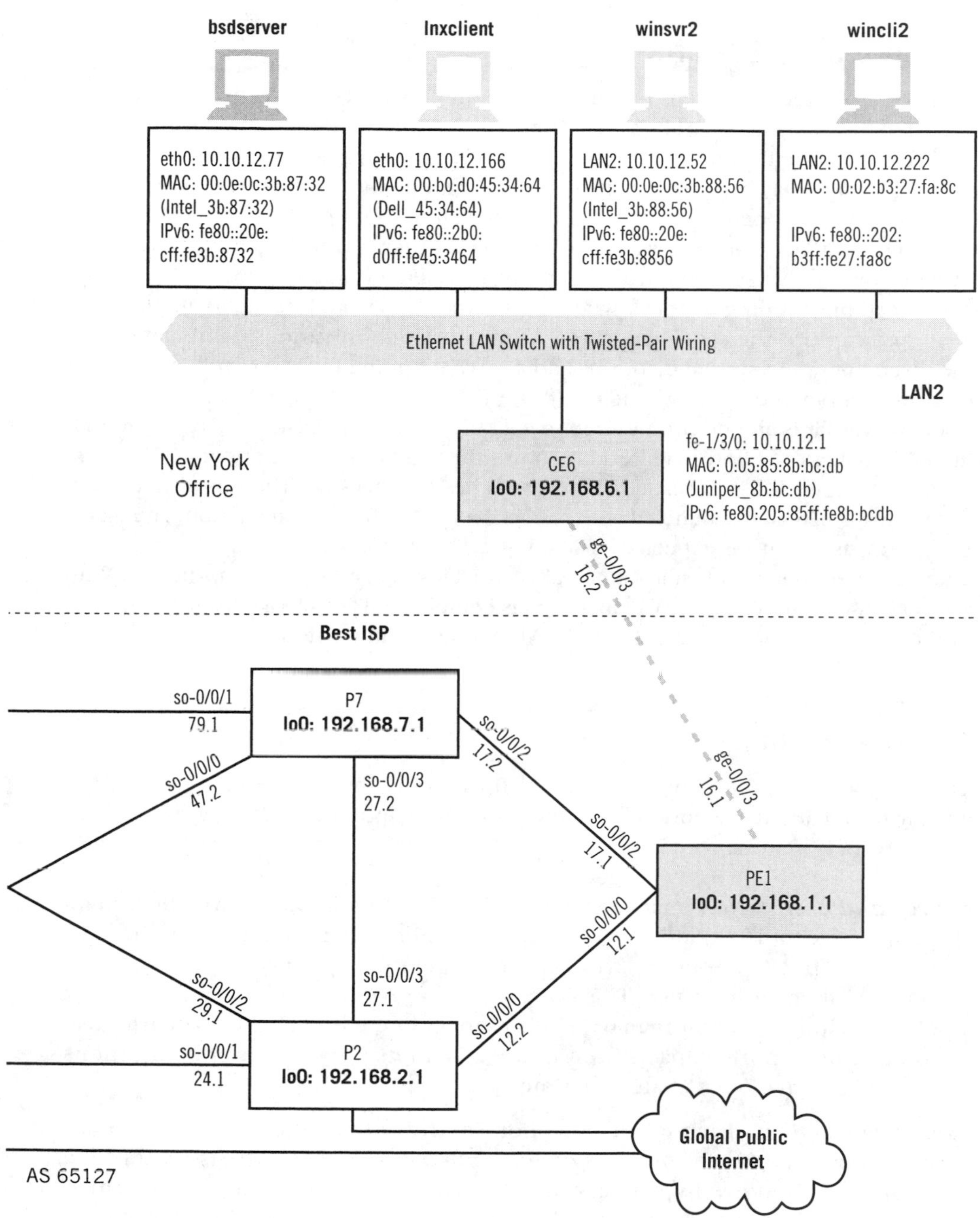
bsdserver
eth0: 10.10.12.77
MAC: 00:0e:0c:3b:87:32
(Intel_3b:87:32)
IPv6: fe80::20e:
cff:fe3b:8732
lnxclient
eth0: 10.10.12.166
MAC: 00:b0:d0:45:34:64
(Dell_45:34:64)
IPv6: fe80::2b0:
d0ff:fe45:3464
winsvr2
LAN2: 10.10.12.52
MAC: 00:0e:0c:3b:88:56
(Intel_3b:88:56)
IPv6: fe80::20e:
cff:fe3b:8856
wincli2
LAN2: 10.10.12.222
MAC: 00:02:b3:27:fa:8c
IPv6: fe80::202:
b3ff:fe27:fa8c
Ethernet LAN Switch with Twisted-Pair Wiring
LAN2
New York
Office
CE6
lo0: 192.168.6.1
fe-1/3/0: 10.10.12.1
MAC: 0:05:85:8b:bc:db
(Juniper_8b:bc:db)
IPv6: fe80:205:85ff:fe8b:bcdb
ge-0/0/3
16.2
Best ISP
so-0/0/1
79.1
P7
lo0: 192.168.7.1
so-0/0/2
17.2
ge-0/0/3
16.1
so-0/0/0
47.2
so-0/0/3
27.2
so-0/0/2
17.1
PE1
lo0: 192.168.1.1
so-0/0/0
12.1
so-0/0/2
29.1
so-0/0/3
27.1
so-0/0/0
12.2
so-0/0/1
24.1
P2
lo0: 192.168.2.1
Global Public
Internet
AS 65127

TCP AND CONNECTIONS

As much as router discussions become talks about IP packets and headers, host discussions tend to become talks about TCP. However, a lot of the demonstrations involving TCP revolve around things that can go wrong. What happens if an acknowledgment (ACK) is lost? What happens when two hosts send almost simultaneous connection requests (SYN) to open a connection? With the emphasis on corner cases, many pages written on TCP become exercises in exceptions. Yet there is much to be learned about TCP just by watching it work in a normal, error-free environment.

Instead of watching to check whether TCP recovers from lost segments (it does), we'll just capture the sequence of TCP segments used on various combinations of the three operating system platforms and see what's going on. Later, we'll use an FTP data transfer between `wincli2` and `bsdserver` (both on LAN2) to look at TCP in action. In many ways it is an odd protocol, but we'll only look at the basics and examine FTP in detail in a later chapter. Figure 11.1 shows these hosts on the network.

As before, we'll use Ethereal to look at frames and packets. There is also a utility called `tcpdump`, which is bundled with almost every TCP/IP implementation. The major exception, as might be expected, is Windows. The Windows version, `windump`, is not much different than our familiar Ethereal, so we'll just use Ethereal to capture our Windows TCP sessions. Because TCP operation is complicated, let's look at some details of TCP operation before looking at how TCP looks on the Illustrated Network.

THE TCP HEADER

The TCP header is the same for IPv4 and IPv6 and is shown in Figure 11.2. We've already talked about the port fields in the previous chapter on UDP. Only the features unique to TCP are described in detail.

Source and destination port—In some Unix implementations, source port numbers between 1024 and 4999 are called ephemeral ports. If an application does not specify a source port to use, the operating systems will use a source port number in this range. This range can be expanded and changed (but not always), and 49,152 through 65,535 is more in line with current standards. Use of ephemeral ports impacts firewall use and limits the number of connections a host can have open at any one time.

Sequence number—Each new connection (re-tries of failed connections do not count) uses a different *initial sequence number* (ISN) as the basis for tracking segments. Windows uses a very simple time-based formula to compute that ISN, while Unix ISNs are more elaborate (ISNs can be spoofed by hackers).

Acknowledgment number—This number must be greater than or equal to zero (even a TCP SYN consumes one sequence number) except for the all 1's ISN. All segments on an established connection must have this bit set. If there is no

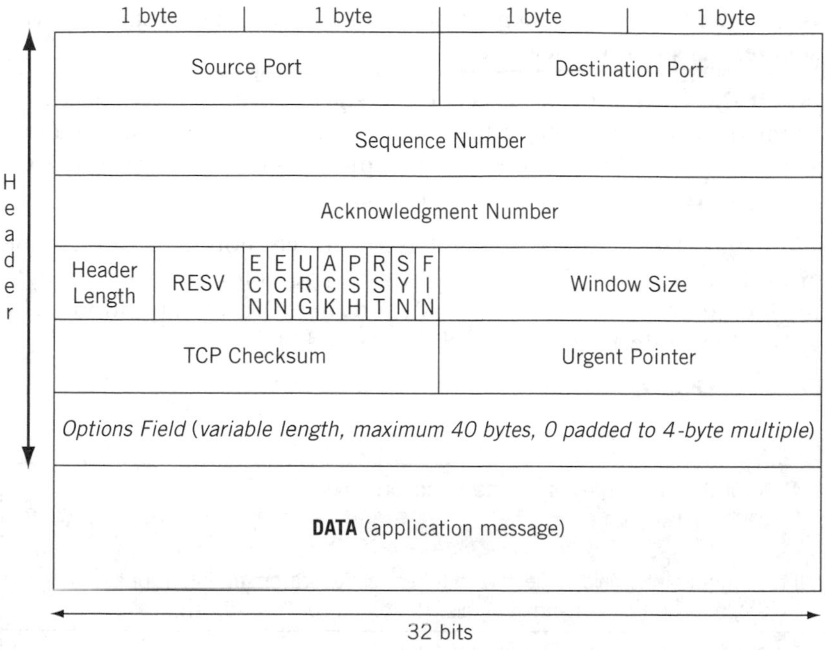

FIGURE 11.2

The TCP header fields. Note that some fields are a single bit wide, and others, like the options field, can be up to 40 bytes (320 bits) long.

actual data in the received segment, the acknowledgment number increments by 1. (Every byte in TCP is still counted, but that's not all that contributes to the sequence number field.)

Header length—The TCP header length in 4-byte units.

Reserved—Four bits are reserved for future use.

ECN flags—The two explicit congestion notification (ECN) bits are used to tell the host when the network is experiencing congestion and send windows should be adjusted.

URG, ACK, PSH, RST, SYN, FIN—These six single-bit fields (Urgent, Acknowledgment, Push, Reset, Sync, and Final) give the receiver more information on how to process the TCP segment. Table 11.1 shows their functions.

Window size—The size of receive window that the destination host has set. This field is used in TCP flow control and congestion control. It should not be set to zero in an initial SYN segment.

Checksum—An error-checking field on the entire TCP segment and header as well as some fields from the IP datagram (the pseudo-header). The fields are the same as in UDP. If the checksum computed does not match the received value, the segment is silently discarded.

Urgent pointer—If the URG control bit is set, the start of the TCP segment contains important data that the source has placed before the "normal" contents of the segment data field. Usually, this is a short piece of data (such as CTRL-C). This field points to the first nonurgent data byte.

Options and padding—TCP options are padded to a 4-byte boundary and can be a maximum of 40 bytes long. Generally, a 1-byte Type is followed by a 1-byte Length field (including these initial 2 bytes), and then the actual options. The options are listed in Table 11.2.

Table 11.1 TCP Control Bits by Abbreviation and Function

Bit	Function
URG	If set, the Urgent Pointer field value is valid (often resulting from an interrupt-like CTRL-C). Seldom used, but intended to raise the priority of the segment.
ACK	If set, the Acknowledgment Number field is valid.
PSH	If set, the receiver should not buffer the segment data, but pass them directly to the application. Interactive applications use this, but few others.
RST	If set, the connection should be aborted. A favorite target of hackers "hijacking" TCP connections, a series of rules now govern proper reactions to this bit.
SYN	If set, the hosts should synchronize sequence numbers and establish a connection.
FIN	If set, the sender had finished sending data and initiated a close of the connection.

Table 11.2 TCP Option Types, Showing Abbreviation (Meaning), Length, and RFC in Which Established

Type	Meaning	Total Length and Description	RFC
0	EOL	1 byte, indicates end of option list (only used if end of options is not end of header)	793
1	NOP	1 byte, no option (used as padding to align header with Header-Length Field)	793
2	MSS	4 bytes, the last 2 of which indicate the maximum payload that one host will try to send another. Can only appear in SYN and does not change.	793 879

Table 11.2 *(continued)*

Type	Meaning	Total Length and Description	RFC
3	WSCALE	3 bytes, the last establishing a multiplicative (scaling) factor. Supports bit-shifted window values above 65,535.	1072
4	SACKOK	2 bytes, indicating that selective ACKs are permitted.	2018
5	SACK	Of variable length, these are the selective ACKs.	1072
6	Echo	6 bytes, the last 4 of which are to be echoed.	1072
7	Echo reply	6 bytes, the last 4 of which echo the above.	1072
8	Timestamp	10 bytes, the last 8 of which are used to compute the retransmission timer through the RTT calculation. Makes sure that an old sequence number is not accepted by the current connection.	1323
9	POC perm	2 bytes, indicating that the partial order service is permitted.	1693
10	POC profile	3 bytes, the last carrying 2-bit flags.	1693
11	CC	6 bytes, the last 4 providing a segment connection count.	1644
12	CCNEW	6 bytes, the last 4 providing new connection count.	1644
13	CCECHO	6 bytes, the last 4 echoing previous connection count.	1644

TCP MECHANISMS

It might not be obvious why TCP connections should be such a complication. One of the reasons is that TCP adds more to connectionless IP than connection capability. The TCP service also provides aspects of what the ISO-RM defines as Session Layer services, services that include the history (a popular term is "state variables") of the connection progress. Connections also provide a convenient structure with which to associate QoS parameters, although every layer of any protocol stack always has some QoS duties to perform, even if it is only error checking.

Officially, TCP is a virtual circuit service that adds reliability to the IP layer, reliability that is lacking in UDP. TCP also provides sequencing and flow control to the host-to-host interaction, which in turn provides a congestion control mechanism to the routing network as a whole (as long as TCP, normally an end-to-end concern, is aware of the congested condition). The flow control mechanism in TCP is a *sliding window* procedure that prevents senders from overwhelming receivers and applies in both directions of a TCP connection.

TCP was initially defined in RFC 793, refined in RFCs 879, 1106, 1110, and 1323 (which obsoleted RFC 1072 and RFC 1185). RFCs 1644 and 1693 extended TCP to support *transactions*, which can be loosely understood as "connection-oriented request-response pairs that cannot use UDP." RFC 3168 added *explicit congestion notification* (ECN) bits to the TCP header. These bits were "added" by redefining bits 6 and 7 in the TOS field of the packet header.

TCP and Transactions

It is important to note that TCP does not use the term "transaction" to describe those peculiar interactions that require coordinated actions among multiple hosts on the network. A familiar "transaction" is an accounting process that is not complete until *both* one account has been debited and another has been credited. Database transactions are a completely different notion than what a transaction means in TCP.

But this is not the purpose of transactions for TCP (T/TCP)! TCP "transactions" are a way to sneak a quick burst of request-response data into an exchange of connection setup segments, similar to the way that UDP works.

TCP headers can be between 20 bytes (typical) and 60 bytes long when options are used (not often). A *segment*, which is the content of a TCP data unit, is essentially a portion of the application's send buffer. As bytes accumulate in the send buffer, they will exceed the *maximum segment size* (MSS) established for the connection. These bytes receive a TCP header and are sent inside an IP packet. There are also ways to "push" a partially full send buffer onto the network.

At the receiver, the segment is added to a receive buffer until complete or until the application has enough data to process. Naturally, the amount of data exchanged varies greatly.

Let's look at how TCP works and then examine the header fields that make it all happen. It might seem strange to talk about major TCP features before the TCP header has been presented, but the operation of many of the fields in the TCP header depend on terminology and concepts used during TCP connection and other procedures.

CONNECTIONS AND THE THREE-WAY HANDSHAKE

TCP establishes end-to-end connections over the unreliable, best-effort IP packet service using a special sequence of three TCP segments sent from client to server and back called a *three-way handshake*. Why three ways? Because packets containing the TCP segment that ask a server to accept another connection and the server's response might be lost on the IP router network, leaving the hosts unsure of exactly what is going on.

Once the three segments are exchanged, data transfer can take place from host to host in either direction. Connections can be dropped by either host with a simple exchange of segments (four in total), although the other host can delay the dropping until final data are sent, a feature rarely used.

TCP uses unique terminology for the connection process. A single bit called the SYN (synchronization) bit is used to indicate a connection request. This single bit is still embedded in a complete 20-byte (usually) TCP header, and other information, such as the *initial sequence number* (ISN) used to track segments, is sent to the other host. Connections and data segments are acknowledged with the ACK bit, and a request to terminate a connection is made with the FIN (final) bit.

The entire TCP connection procedure, from three-way handshake to data transfer to disconnect, is shown in Figure 11.3. TCP also allows for the case where two hosts performs an active open at the same time, but this is unlikely.

This example shows a small file transfer to a server (with the server sending 1000 bytes back to the client) using 1000-byte segments, but only to make the sequence numbers and acknowledgments easier to follow. The whole file is smaller than the

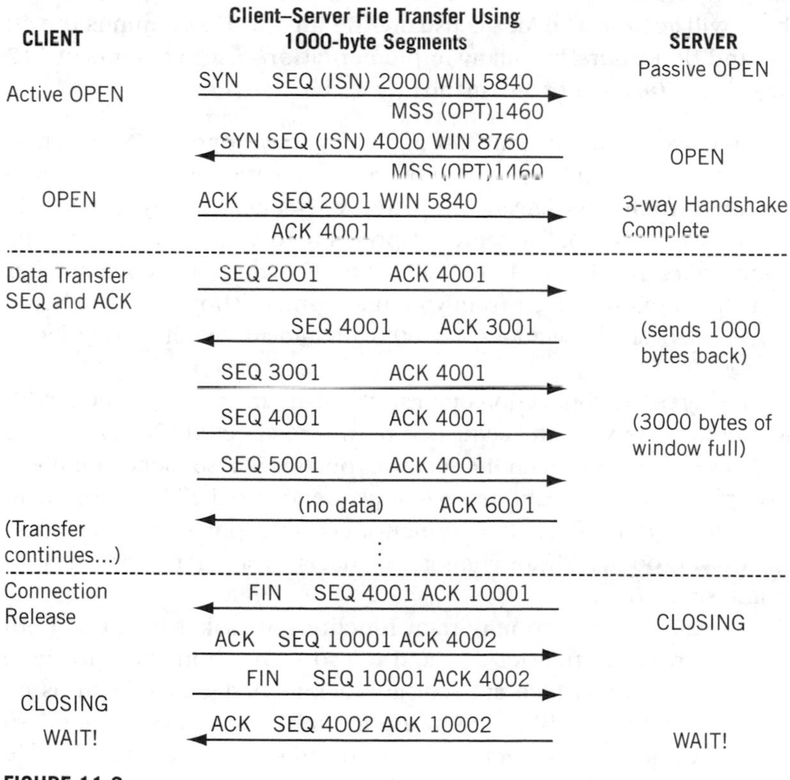

FIGURE 11.3

Client–server interaction with TCP, showing the three connection phases of setup, data transfer, and release (disconnect).

server host's receive window and nothing goes wrong (but things often go wrong in the real world).

Note that to send even one exchange of a request-response pair inside segments, TCP has to generate *seven* additional packets. This is a lot of packet overhead, and the whole process is just slow over high latency (delay) links. This is one reason that UDP is becoming more popular as networks themselves become more reliable.

Connection Establishment

Let's look at the normal TCP connection establishment's three-way handshake in some detail. The three messages establish three important pieces of information that both sides of the connection need to know.

1. The ISNs to use for outgoing data (in order to deter hackers, these should not be predictable).
2. The buffer space (window) available locally for data, in bytes.
3. The Maximum Segment Size (MSS) is a TCP Option and sets the largest segment that the local host will accept. The MSS is usually the link MTU size minus the 40 bytes of the TCP and IP headers, but many implementations use segments of 512 or 536 bytes (it's a *maximum*, not a demand).

A server issues a passive open and waits for a client's active open SYN, which in this case has an ISN of 2000, a window of 5840 bytes and an MSS of 1460 (common because most hosts are on Ethernet LANs). The window is almost always a multiple of the MSS (1460 × 4 = 5840 bytes). The server responds with a SYN and declares the connection open, setting its own ISN to 4000, and "acknowledging" sequence number 2001 (it really means "the next byte I get from you in a segment should be numbered 2001"). The server also established a window of 8760 bytes and an MSS of 1460 (1460 × 6 = 8760 bytes).

Finally, the client declares the connection open and returns an ACK (a segment with the ACK bit set in the header) with the sequence number expected (2001) and the acknowledgment field set to 4001 (which the server expects). TCP sequence numbers count every byte on the data stream, and the 32-bit sequence field allows more than 4 billion bytes to be outstanding (nevertheless, high-speed transports such as Gigabit Ethernet roll this field over too quickly for comfort, so special "scaling" mechanisms are available for these link speeds).

TCP's three-way handshake has two important functions. It makes sure that both sides know that they are ready to transfer data and it also allows both sides to agree on the initial sequence numbers, which are sent and acknowledged (so there is no mistake about them) during the handshake. Why are the initial sequence numbers so important? If the sequence numbers are not randomized and set properly, it is possible for malicious users to hijack the TCP session (which can be reliable connections to a bank, a store, or some other commercial entity).

Each device chooses a random initial sequence number to begin counting every byte in the stream sent. How can the two devices agree on both sequence number values in about only three messages? Each segment contains a separate sequence number field and acknowledgment field. In Figure 11.3, the client chooses an initial sequence number (ISN) in the first SYN sent to the server. The server ACKs the ISN by adding one to the proposed ISN (ACKs always inform the sender of the *next* byte expected) and sending it in the SYN sent to the client to propose its own ISN. The client's ISN could be rejected, if, for example, the number is the same as used for the previous connection, but that is not considered here. Usually, the ACK from the client both acknowledges the ISN from the server (with server's ISN + 1 in the acknowledgment field) and the connection is established with both sides agreeing on ISN. Note that no information is sent in the three-way handshake; it should be held until the connection is established.

This three-way handshake is the universal mechanism for opening a TCP connection. Oddly, the RFC does not insist that connections begin this way, especially with regard to setting other control bits in the TCP header (there are three others in addition to SYN and ACK and FIN). Because TCP really expects some control bits to be used during connection establishment and release, and others only during data transfer, hackers can cause a lot of damage simply by messing around with wild combinations of the six control bits, especially SYN/ACK/FIN, which asks for, uses, and releases a connection all at the same time. For example, forging a SYN within the window of an existing SYN would cause a reset. For this reason, developers have become more rigorous in their interpretation of RFC 793.

Data Transfer

Sending data in the SYN segment is allowed in transaction TCP, but this is not typical. Any data included are accepted, but are not processed until after the three-way handshake completes. SYN data are used for round-trip time measurement (an important part of TCP flow control) and *network intrusion detection* (NID) evasion and insertion attacks (an important part of the hacker arsenal).

The simplest transfer scenario is one in which nothing goes wrong (which, fortunately, happens a lot of the time). Figure 11.4 shows how the interplay between TCP sequence numbers (which allow TCP to properly sequence segments that pop out of the network in the wrong order) and acknowledgments allow both sides to detect missing segments.

The client does not need to receive an ACK for each segment. As long as the established receive window is not full, the sender can keep sending. A single ACK covers a whole sequence of segments, as long as the ACK number is correct.

Ideally, an ACK for a full receive window's worth of data will arrive at the sender just as the window is filled, allowing the sender to continue to send at a steady rate. This timing requires some knowledge of the round-trip time (RTT) to the partner host and some adjustment of the segment-sending rate based on the RTT. Fortunately, both of these mechanisms are available in TCP implementations.

What happens when a segment is "lost" on the underlying "best-effort" IP router network? There are two possible scenarios, both of which are shown in Figure 11.4.

In the first case, a 1000-byte data segment from the client to the server fails to arrive at the server. Why? It could be that the network is congested, and packets are being dropped by overstressed routers. Public data networks such as frame relay and ATM (Asynchronous Transfer Mode) routinely discard their frames and cells under certain conditions, leading to lost packets that form the payload of these data units.

If a segment is lost, the sender will not receive an ACK from the receiving host. After a timeout period, which is adjusted periodically, the sender resends the last unacknowledged segment. The receiver then can send a single ACK for the entire sequence, covering received segments beyond the missing one.

But what if the network is *not* congested and the lost packet resulted from a simple intermittent failure of a link between two routers? Today, most network errors are caused by faulty connectors that exhibit specific intermittent failure patterns that steadily worsen until they become permanent. Until then, the symptom is sporadic lost packets on the link at random intervals. (Predictable intervals are the signature of some outside agent at work.)

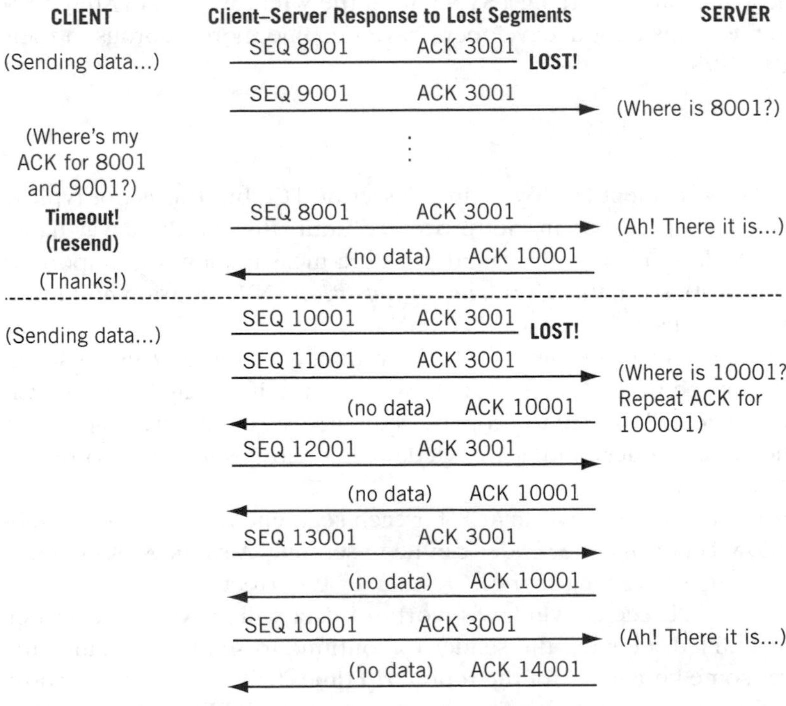

FIGURE 11.4

How TCP handles lost segments. The key here is that although the client might continue to send data, the server will not acknowledge all of it until the missing segment shows up.

Waiting is just a waste of time if the network is not congested and the lost packet was the result of a brief network "hiccup." So TCP hosts are allowed to perform a "fast recovery" with duplicate ACKs, which is also shown in Figure 11.4.

The server cannot ACK the received segments 11,001 and subsequent ones because the missing segment 10,001 prevents it. (An ACK says that all data bytes up to the ACK have been received.) So every time a segment arrives beyond the lost segment, the host only ACKs the missing segment. This basically tells the other host "I'm still waiting for the missing 8001 segment." After several of these are received (the usual number is three), the other host figures out that the missing segment is lost and not merely delayed and resends the missing segment. The host (the server in this case) will then ACK all of the received data.

The sender will still slow down the segment sending rate temporarily, but only in case the missing segment was the result of network congestion.

Closing the Connection

Either side can close the TCP connection, but it's common for the server to decide just when to stop. The server usually knows when the file transfer is complete, or when the user has typed `logout` and takes it from there. Unless the client still has more data to send (not a rare occurrence with applications using persistent connections), the hosts exchange four more segments to release the connection.

In the example, the server sends a segment with the FIN (final) bit set, a sequence number (whatever the incremented value should be), and acknowledges the last data received at the server. The client responds with an ACK of the FIN and appropriate sequence and acknowledgment numbers (no data were sent, so the sequence number does not increment).

The TCP releases the connection and sends its own FIN to the server with the same sequence and acknowledgment numbers. The server sends an ACK to the FIN and increments the acknowledgment field but not the sequence number. The connection is down.

But not really. The "best-effort" nature of the IP network means that *delayed duplicated* could pop out of a router at any time and show up at either host. Routers don't do this just to be nasty, of course. Typically, a router that hangs or has a failed link rights itself and finds packets in a buffer (which is just memory) and, trying to be helpful, sends them out. Sometimes routing loops cause the same problem.

In any case, late duplicates must be detected and disposed of (which is one reason the ISN space is 32 bits—about 4 billion—wide). The time to wait is supposed to be twice as long as it could take a packet to have its TTL go to zero, but in practice this is set to 4 minutes (making the packet transit time of the Internet 2 minutes, an incredibly high value today, even for Cisco routers, which are fond of sending packets with the TTL set to 255).

The wait time can be as high as 30 minutes, depending on TCP/IP implementation, and resets itself if a delayed FIN pops out of the network. Because a server cannot accept other connections from this client until the wait timer has expired, this often led to "server paralysis" at early Web sites.

Today, many TCP implementations use an *abrupt close* to escape the wait-time requirement. The server usually sends a FIN to the client, which first ACKs and then sends a RST (reset) segment to the server to release the connection immediately and bypass the wait-time state.

FLOW CONTROL

Flow control prevents a sender from overwhelming a receiver with more data than it can handle. With TCP, which resends all lost data, a receiver that is discarding data that overflows the receive buffers is just digging itself a deeper and deeper hole.

Flow control can be performed by either the sender or the receiver. It sounds strange to have senders performing flow control (how could they know when receivers are overwhelmed?), but that was the first form of flow control used in older networks.

Many early network devices were printers (actually, teletype machines, but the point is the same). They had a hard enough job running network protocols and printing the received data, and could not be expected to handle flow control as well. So the senders (usually mainframes or minicomputers with a lot of horsepower for the day) knew exactly what kind of printer they were sending to and their buffer sizes. If a printer had a two-page buffer (it really depended on byte counts), the sender would know enough to fire off two pages and then wait for an acknowledgment from the printer before sending more. If the printer ran out of paper, the acknowledgment was delayed for a long time, and the sender had to decide whether it was okay to continue or not.

Once processors grew in power, flow control could be handled by the receiver, and this became the accepted method. Senders could send as fast as they could, up to a maximum window size. Then senders had to wait until they received an acknowledgment from the receiver. How is that flow control? Well, the receiver could delay the acknowledgments, forcing the sender to slow down, and usually could also force the sender to shrink its window. (Receivers might be receiving from many senders and might be overwhelmed by the aggregate.)

Flow control can be implemented at any protocol level or even every protocol layer. In practice, flow control is most often a function of the transport layer (end to end). Of course, the application feeding TCP with data should be aware of the situation and also slow down, but basic TCP could not do this.

TCP is a "byte-sequencing protocol" in which every byte is numbered. Although each segment must be acknowledged, one acknowledgment can apply to multiple segments, as we have seen. Senders can keep sending until the data in all unacknowledged segments equals the window size of the receiver. Then the sender must stop until an acknowledgment is received from the receiving host.

This does not sound like much of a flow control mechanism, but it is. A receiver is allowed to *change* the size of the receive window during a connection. If the receiver finds that it cannot process the received window's data fast enough, it can establish a new (smaller) window size that must be respected by the sender. The receiver can even "close" the window by shrinking it to zero. Nothing more can be sent until the receiver has sent a special "window update ACK" (it's not ACKing new data, so it's not a real ACK) with the new available window size.

The window size should be set to the network bandwidth multiplied by the round-trip time to the remote host, which can be established in several ways. For example, a 100-Mbps Ethernet with a 5-millisecond (ms) round-trip time (RTT) would establish a 64,000-byte window on each host (100 Mbps × 5 ms = 0.5 Mbits = 512 kbits = 64 kbytes). When the window size is "tuned" to the RTT this way, the sender should receive an ACK for a window full of segments just in time to optimize the sending process.

"Network" bandwidths vary, as do round-trip times. The windows can always shrink or grow (up to the socket buffer maximum), but what should their initial value be? The initial values used by various operating systems vary greatly, from a low of 4096 (which is not a good fit for Ethernet's usual frame size) to a high of 65,535 bytes. FreeBSD defaults to 17,520 bytes, Linux to 32,120, and Windows XP to anywhere between 17,000 and 18,000 depending on details.

In Windows XP, the `TCPWindowSize` can be changed to any value less that 64,240. Most Unix-based systems allow changes to be made to the `/etc/sysctl.conf` file. When adjusting TCP transmit and receive windows, make sure that the buffer space is sufficient to prevent hanging of the network portion on the OS. In FreeBSD, this means that the value of `nmbclusters` and socket buffers must be greater than the maximum window size. Most Linux-based systems autotune this based on memory settings.

TCP Windows

How do the windows work during a TCP connection? TCP forms its segments in memory sequentially, based on segment size, each needing only a set of headers to be added for transmission inside a frame. A conceptual "window" (it's all really done with pointers) overlays this set of data, and two moveable boundaries are established in this series of segments to form three types of data. There are segments waiting to be transmitted, segments sent and waiting for an acknowledgment, and segments that have been sent and acknowledged (but have not been purged from the buffer).

As acknowledgments are received, the window "slides" along, which is why the process is commonly called a "sliding window."

Figure 11.5 shows how the sender's sliding window is used for flow control. (There is another at the receiver, of course.) Here the segments just have numbers, but each integer represents a whole 512, 1460, or whatever size segment. In this example, segments 20 through 25 have been sent and acknowledged, 26 through 29 have been sent but not acknowledged, and segments 30 through 35 are waiting to be sent. The send buffer is therefore 15 segments wide, and new segments replace the oldest as the buffer wraps.

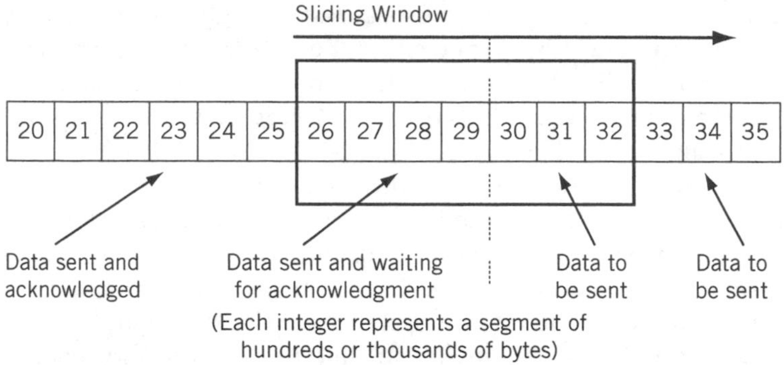

FIGURE 11.5

TCP sliding window.

Flow Control and Congestion Control

When flow control is used as a form of congestion control for the whole network, the network nodes themselves are the "receivers" and try to limit the amount of data that senders dump into the network.

But now there is a problem. How can routers tell the hosts using TCP (which is an end-to-end protocol) that there is congestion on the network? Routers are not supposed to play around with the TCP headers in transit packets (routers have enough to do), but they *are* allowed to play around with IP headers (and often have to).

Routers know when a network is congested (they are the *first* to know), so they can easily flip some bits in the IPv4 and IPv6 headers of the packets they route. These bits are in the TOS (IPv4) and Flow (IPv6) fields, and the hosts can read these bits and react to them by adjusting windows when necessary.

RFC 3168 establishes support for these bits in the IP and TCP headers. However, support for explicit congestion notification in TCP and IP routers is not mandatory, and rare to nonexistent in routers today. Congestion in routers is usually indicated by dropped packets.

PERFORMANCE ALGORITHMS

By now, it should be apparent that TCP is not an easy protocol to explore and understand. This complexity of TCP is easy enough to understand: Underlying network should be fast and simple, IP transport should be fast and simple as well, but unless every application builds in complex mechanisms to ensure smooth data flow across the network, the complexity of networking must be added to TCP. This is just as well, as the data transfer concern is end to end, and TCP is the host-to-host layer, the last bastion of the network shielding the application from network operations.

To look at it another way, if physical networks and IP routers had to do all that the TCP layer of the protocol stack does, the network would be overwhelmed. Routers would be overwhelmed by the amount of state information that they would need to carry, so we delegate carrying that state information to the hosts. Of course, applications are many, and each one shouldn't have to do it all. So TCP does it. By the way, this consistent evolution away from "dumb terminal on a smart network" like X.25 to "smart host on a dumb network" like TCP/IP is characteristic of the biggest changes in networking over the years.

This chapter has covered only the basics, and TCP has been enhanced over the years with many algorithms to enhance the performance of TCP in particular and the network in general. ECN is only one of them. Several others exist and will only be mentioned here and not investigated in depth.

Delayed ACK—TCP is allowed to wait before sending an ACK. This cuts down on the number of "stand-alone" ACKs, and lets a host wait for outgoing data to "piggyback" an acknowledgment onto. Most implementations use a 200-ms wait time.

Slow Start—Regardless of the receive window, a host computes a second *congestion window* that starts off at one segment. After each ACK, this window doubles in size until it matches the number of segments in the "regular" window. This prevents senders from swamping receivers with data at the start of a connection (although it's not really very slow at all).

Defeating Silly Window Syndrome Early—TCP implementations processed receive buffer data slowly, but received segments with large chunks of data. Receivers then shrunk the window as if this "chunk" were normal. So windows often shrunk to next to nothing and remained here. Receivers can "lie" to prevent this, and senders can implement the Nagle algorithm to prevent the sending of small segments, even if PUSHed. (Applications that naturally generate small segments, such as a remote login, can turn this off.)

Scaling for Large Delay-Bandwidth Network Links—The TCP window-scale option can be used to count more than 4 billion or so bytes before the sequence number field wraps. A timestamp option sent in the SYN message helps also. Scaling is sometimes needed because the Window field in the TCP header is 16 bits long, so the maximum window size is normally 64 kbytes. Larger windows are needed for large-delay times, high-bandwidth product links (such as the "long fat pipes" of satellite links). The scaling uses 3 bytes: 1 for type (scaling), 1 for length (number of bytes), and 2 for a shift value called S. The shift value provides a binary scaling factor to be applied to the usual value in the Window field. Scaling shifts the window field value S bits to the left to determine the actual window size to use.

Adjusting Resend Timeouts Based on Measured RTT—How long should a sender wait for an ACK before resending a segment? If the resend timeout is too short, resends might clutter up a network slow in relaying ACKs because it is teetering on the edge of congestion. If it is too long, it limits throughput and slows recovery. And a value just right for TCP connection over the local LAN might be much too short for connections around the globe over the Internet. TCP adjusts its value for changing network conditions and link speeds in a rational fashion based on measured RTT, how fast the RTT has change in the past.

TCP AND FTP

First we'll use a Windows FTP utility on `wincli2` (`10.10.12.222`) to grab the 30,000-byte file `test.stuff` from the server `bsdserver` (`10.10.12.77`) and capture the TCP (and FTP) packets with Ethereal. Both hosts are on the same LAN segment, so the process should be quick and error-free.

The session took a total of 91 packets, but most of those were for the FTP data transfer itself. The Ethereal statistics of the sessions note that it took about 55 seconds from first packet to last (much of which was "operator think time"), making the average about 1.6 packets per second. A total of 36,000 bytes were sent back and forth, which sounds like a lot of overhead, but it was a small file. The throughput on the 100 Mbps LAN2 was about 5,200 bits per second, showing why networks with humans at the controls have to be working very hard to fill up even a modestly fast LAN.

We've seen the Ethereal screen enough to just look at the data in the screen shots. And Ethereal lets us expand all packets and create a PDF out of the capture file. This in turn makes it easy to cut-and-paste exactly what needs to be shown in a single figure instead of many.

For example, let's look at the TCP three-way handshake that begins the session in Figure 11.6.

```
No. - Time       Source         Destination    Protocol  Info
  1 0.000000   10.10.12.222   10.10.12.77    TCP       2790 > ftp [SYN] Seq=0 Ack=0 Win=65535 Len=0 MSS=1460
  2 0.000185   10.10.12.77    10.10.12.222   TCP       ftp > 2790 [SYN, ACK] Seq=0 Ack=1 Win=57344 Len=0 MSS=1460
  3 0.000216   10.10.12.222   10.10.12.77    TCP       2790 > ftp [ACK] Seq=1 Ack=1 Win=65535 [CHECKSUM INCORRECT] Len=0

▷ Frame 1 (62 bytes on wire, 62 bytes captured)
▷ Ethernet II, Src: 00:02:b3:27:fa:8c, Dst: 00:0e:0c:3b:87:32
▷ Internet Protocol, Src Addr: 10.10.12.222 (10.10.12.222), Dst Addr: 10.10.12.77 (10.10.12.77)
▽ Transmission Control Protocol, Src Port: 2790 (2790), Dst Port: ftp (21), Seq: 0, Ack: 0, Len: 0
    Source port: 2790 (2790)
    Destination port: ftp (21)
    Sequence number: 0    (relative sequence number)
    Header length: 28 bytes
  ▷ Flags: 0x0002 (SYN)
    Window size: 65535
    Checksum: 0xe658 (correct)
  ▽ Options: (8 bytes)
      Maximum segment size: 1460 bytes
      NOP
      NOP
      SACK permitted
```

FIGURE 11.6

Capture of three-way handshake. Note that Ethereal sets the "relative" sequence number to zero instead of presenting the actual ISN value.

The first frame, from 10.10.12.222 to 10.10.12.77, is detailed in the figure. The window size is 65,535, the MSS is 1460 bytes (as expected for Ethernet), and selective acknowledgments (SACK) are permitted. The server's receive window size is 57,344 bytes. Figure 11.7 shows the relevant TCP header values from the capture for the initial connection setup (which is the FTP control connection).

Ethereal shows "relative" sequence and acknowledgment numbers, and these always start at 0. But the figure shows the last bits of the actual hexadecimal values, showing how the acknowledgment increments the value in sequence and acknowledgment number (the number increments from 0x...E33A to 0x...E33B), even though no data have been sent.

Note that Windows XP uses 2790 as a dynamic port number, which is really in the registered port range and technically should not be used for this purpose.

This example is actually a good study in what can happen when "cross-platform" TCP sessions occur, which is often. Several segments have bad TCP checksums. Since we are on the same LAN segment, and the frame and packet passed error checks correctly, this is probably a quirk of TCP pseudo-header computation and no bits were changed on the network. There is no ICMP message because TCP is above the IP layer. Note that the application just sort of shrugs and keeps right on going (which happens not once, but several times during the transfer). Things like this "non-error error" happen all the time in the real world of networking.

At the end of the session, there are really two "connections" between wincli2 and bsdserver. The FTP session rides on top of the TCP connection. Usually, the FTP session is ended by typing BYE or QUIT on the client. But the graphical package lets the user just click a disconnect button, and takes the TCP connection down without ending the FTP session first. The FTP server objects to this breach of protocol and the FTP server process sends a message with the text, You could at least say goodbye, to the client. (No one will see it, but presumably the server feels better.)

TCP sessions do not have to be complex. Some are extremely simple. For example, the common TCP/IP "echo" utility can use UDP or TCP. With UDP, an echo is a simple

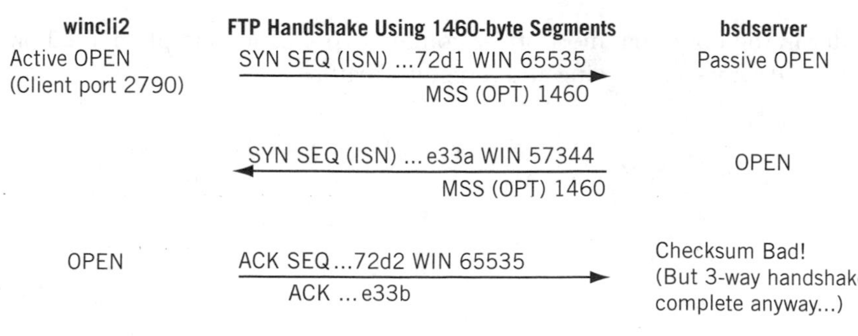

FIGURE 11.7

FTP three-way handshake, showing how the ISNs are incremented and acknowledged.

No.	Time	Source	Destination	Protocol	Info
1	0.000000	10.10.12.166	Broadcast	ARP	Who has 10.10.12.1? Tell 10.10.12.166
2	0.000380	10.10.12.1	10.10.12.166	ARP	10.10.12.1 is at 00:05:85:8b:bc:db
3	0.000405	10.10.12.166	10.10.11.66	TCP	33146 > echo [SYN] Seq=0 Ack=0 Win=5840 Len=0 MSS=1460 TSV=
4	0.001094	10.10.11.66	10.10.12.166	TCP	echo > 33146 [SYN, ACK] Seq=0 Ack=1 Win=5792 Len=0 MSS=1460
5	0.001148	10.10.12.166	10.10.11.66	TCP	33146 > echo [ACK] Seq=1 Ack=1 Win=5840 Len=0 TSV=956616151
6	0.001315	10.10.12.166	10.10.11.66	ECHO	Request
7	0.001635	10.10.11.66	10.10.12.166	TCP	echo > 33146 [ACK] Seq=1 Ack=11 Win=5792 Len=0 TSV=8272323
8	0.001934	10.10.11.66	10.10.12.166	ECHO	Response
9	0.002073	10.10.12.166	10.10.11.66	TCP	33146 > echo [ACK] Seq=11 Ack=11 Win=5840 Len=0 TSV=9566161
10	0.002127	10.10.12.166	10.10.11.66	TCP	33146 > echo [FIN, ACK] Seq=11 Ack=11 Win=5840 Len=0 TSV=95
11	0.002431	10.10.11.66	10.10.12.166	TCP	echo > 33146 [FIN, ACK] Seq=11 Ack=12 Win=5792 Len=0 TSV=82
12	0.002462	10.10.12.166	10.10.11.66	TCP	33146 > echo [ACK] Seq=12 Ack=12 Win=5840 Len=0 TSV=9566161

FIGURE 11.8

Echo using TCP, showing all packets of the ARP, three-way handshake, data transfer, and connection release phases.

exchange of two segments, the request and reply. In TCP, the exchange is a 10-packet sequence.

This is shown in Figure 11.8, which captures the echo "TESTstring" from `lnxclient` to `lnxserver`. It includes the initial ARP request and response to find the server.

Why so many packets? Here's what happens during the sequence.

Handshake (packets 3 to 5)—The utility uses dynamic port 33,146, meaning Linux is probably up-to-date on port assignments. The connection has a window of 5840 bytes, much smaller than the FreeBSD and Windows XP window sizes. The MMS is 1460, and the exchange has a rich set of TCP options, including timestamps (TSV) and windows scaling (not used, and not shown in the figure).

Transfer (packets 6 to 9)—Note that each ECHO message, request and response, is acknowledged. Ethereal shows relative acknowledgment numbers, so ACK=11 means that 10 bytes are being ACKed (the actual number is `0x0A8DA551`, or 177,055,057 in decimal.

Disconnect (packets 10 to 12)—A typical three-way "sign-off" is used.

We'll see later in the book that most of the common applications implemented on the Internet use TCP for its sequencing and resending features.

QUESTIONS FOR READERS

Figure 11.9 shows some of the concepts discussed in this chapter and can be used to help you answer the following questions.

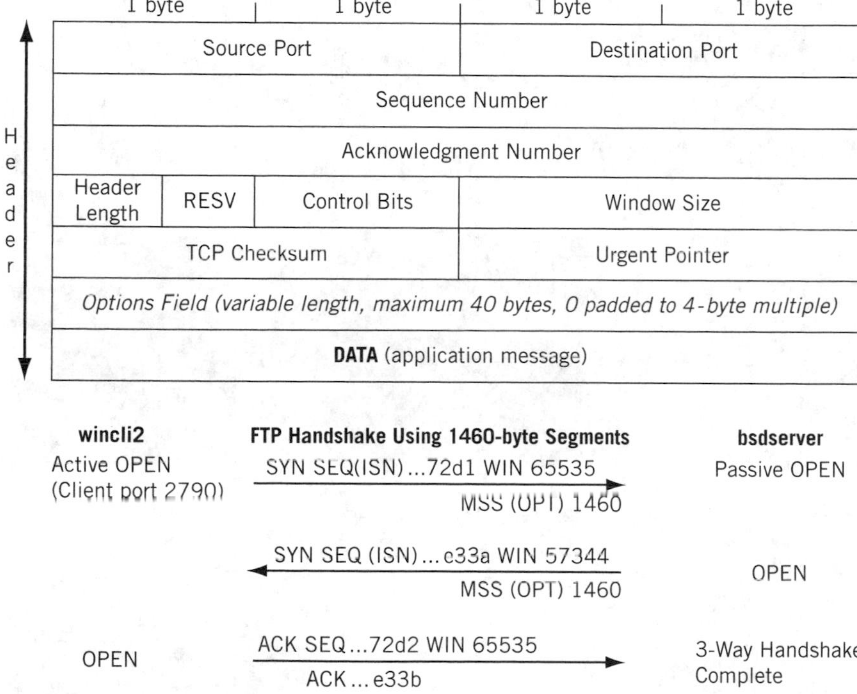

FIGURE 11.9

The TCP header fields and three-way handshake example.

1. What are the three phases of connection-oriented communications?
2. Which fields are present in the TCP header but absent in UDP? Why are they not needed in UDP?
3. What is the TCP flow control mechanism called?
4. What does it mean when the initial sequence and acknowledgment numbers are "relative"?
5. What is the silly window syndrome? What is the Nagle algorithm?

CHAPTER

Multiplexing and Sockets

12

What You Will Learn

In this chapter, you will learn about how multiplexing (and demultiplexing) and sockets are used in TCP/IP. We'll see how multiplexing allows many applications can share a single TCP/IP stock process.

You will learn how layer and applications interact to make multiplexing and the socket concept very helpful in networking. We'll use a small utility program to investigate sockets and illustrate the concepts in this chapter.

Now that we've looked at UDP and TCP in detail, this chapter explores two key concepts that make understanding how UDP and TCP work much easier: *multiplexing* and *sockets*. Technically, the term should be "multiplexing and demultiplexing," but because mixing things together makes little sense unless you can get them back again, most people just say "multiplexing" and let it go at that.

Why is multiplexing necessary? Most TCP/IP hosts have only one TCP/IP stack process running, meaning that every packet passing into or out of the host uses the same software process. This is due to the fact that the hosts usually have only one network connection, although there are exceptions. However, a host system typically runs many (technically, if other systems can access them, the host system is a server). All these applications share the single network interface through multiplexing.

LAYERS AND APPLICATIONS

Both the source and destination port numbers, each 16 bits long, are included as the first fields of the TCP or UDP segment header. Well-known ports use numbers between 0 and 1023, which are reserved expressly for this purpose. In many TCP/IP implementations, there is a process (usually `inetd` or `xinetd`, the "Internet daemon") that listens for *all* TCP/IP activity on an interface. This process then launches to FTP or other application processes on request, using the well-known ports as appropriate.

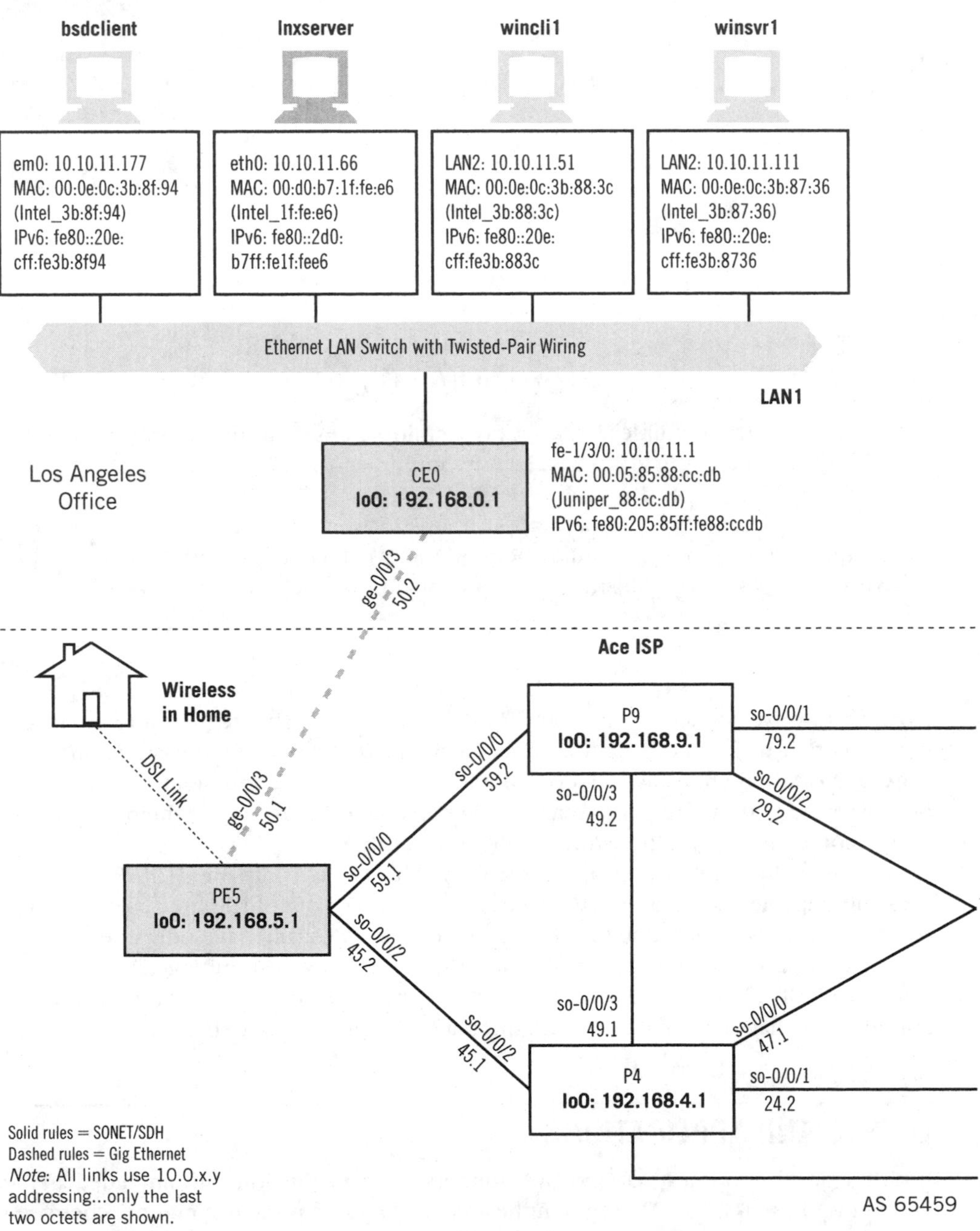

FIGURE 12.1

Sockets between Linux client and server, showing the devices used in this chapter to illustrate socket operation.

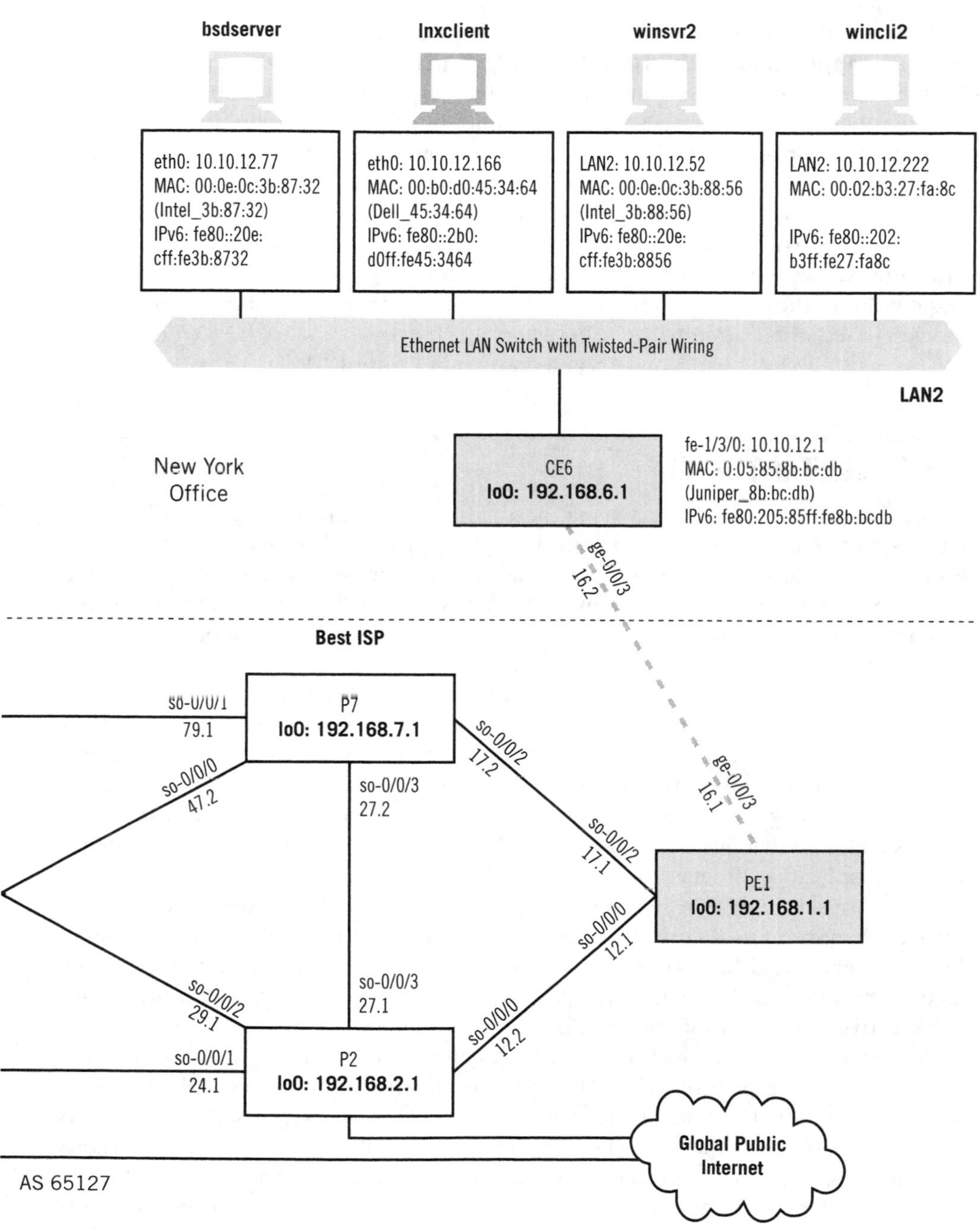
bsdserver
lnxclient
winsvr2
wincli2
eth0: 10.10.12.77
MAC: 00:0e:0c:3b:87:32
(Intel_3b:87:32)
IPv6: fe80::20e:
cff:fe3b:8732
eth0: 10.10.12.166
MAC: 00:b0:d0:45:34:64
(Dell_45:34:64)
IPv6: fe80::2b0:
d0ff:fe45:3464
LAN2: 10.10.12.52
MAC: 00:0e:0c:3b:88:56
(Intel_3b:88:56)
IPv6: fe80::20e:
cff:fe3b:8856
LAN2: 10.10.12.222
MAC: 00:02:b3:27:fa:8c
IPv6: fe80::202:
b3ff:fe27:fa8c
Ethernet LAN Switch with Twisted-Pair Wiring
LAN2
New York
Office
CE6
lo0: 192.168.6.1
fe-1/3/0: 10.10.12.1
MAC: 0:05:85:8b:bc:db
(Juniper_8b:bc:db)
IPv6: fe80:205:85ff:fe8b:bcdb
ge-0/0/3
16.2
Best ISP
so-0/0/1
79.1
P7
lo0: 192.168.7.1
so-0/0/0
47.2
so-0/0/3
27.2
so-0/0/2
17.2
ge-0/0/3
16.1
so-0/0/2
17.1
PE1
lo0: 192.168.1.1
so-0/0/0
12.1
so-0/0/2
29.1
so-0/0/3
27.1
so-0/0/0
12.2
so-0/0/1
24.1
P2
lo0: 192.168.2.1
Global Public
Internet
AS 65127

However, the well-known server port numbers can be *statically mapped* to their respective application on the TCP/IP server, and that's how we will explore them in this introduction to sockets. With static mapping, the DNS (port number 53) or FTP (port number 21) server processes (for example) must be running on the server at all times in order for the server TCP protocol to accept connections to these application form clients. Things are more complex when both IPv4 and IPv6 are running, but this chapter considers the situation for IPv4 for simplicity.

This chapter will be a little different than the others. Instead of jumping right in and capturing packets and then analyzing them, the socket packet capture is actually the whole point of the chapter. So we'll save that until last. In the meantime, we'll develop a socket-based application to work between the `lnxclient` (`10.10.12.166` on LAN2) and `lnxserver` (`10.10.11.66` on LAN1), as shown in Figure 12.1.

THE SOCKET INTERFACE

Saying that applications share a single network connection through multiplexing is not much of an explanation. *How* does the TCP/IP process determine the source and destination application for the contents of an arriving segment? The answer is through sockets. Sockets are the combination of IP address and TCP/UDP port number. Hosts use sockets to identify TCP connections and sort out UDP request–response pairs, and to make the coding of TCP/IP applications easier.

The server TCP/IP application processes that "listen" through passive opens for connection requests use well-known port numbers, as already mentioned. The client TCP/IP application processes that "talk" through active opens and make connection requests must choose port numbers that are not reserved for these well-known numbers. Servers listen on a socket for clients talking to that socket. There is nothing new here, but sockets are more than just a useful concept. The *socket interface* is the most common way that application programs interact with the network.

There are several reasons for the socket interface concept and construct. One reason has already been discussed. Suppose there are two FTP sessions in progress to the same server, and both client processes are running over the same network connection on a host with IP address `192.168.10.70`. It is up to the client to make sure that the two processes use different client port numbers to control the sessions to the server. This is easy enough to do. If the clients have chosen client port numbers `14972` and `14973`, respectively, the FTP server process replies to the two client sockets as `192.168.10.79:14972` and `192.168.10.70:14973`. So the sockets allow simultaneous file transfer sessions to the same client from the same FTP server. If the client sessions were distinguished only by IP address or port number, the server would have no way of uniquely identifying the client FTP process. And the FTP server's socket address is accessed by all of the FTP clients at the same time without confusion.

Now consider the server shown in Figure 12.2. Here there is a server that has more than one TCP/IP interface for network access, and thus more than one IP address. Yet these servers may still have only one FTP (or any other TCP/IP application) server process

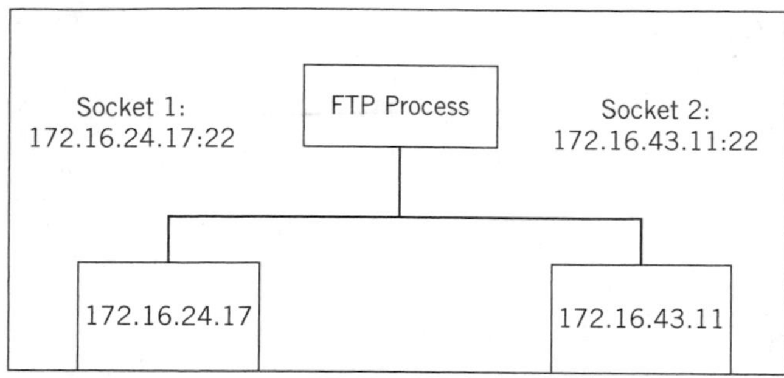

FIGURE 12.2

The concept of sockets applied to FTP. Note how sockets allow a server with two different IP addresses to access the FTP server process using the same port.

running. With the socket concept, the FTP server process has no problem separating client FTP sessions from different network interfaces because their socket identifiers will differ on the server end. Since a TCP connection is always identified by both the client and server IP address and the client and server port numbers, there is no confusion.

This illustrates the sockets concept in more depth, but not the use of the socket interface in a TCP/IP network. The socket interface forms the boundary between the application program written by the programmer and the network processes that are usually bundled with the operating system and quite uniform compared to the myriad of applications that have been implemented with programs.

Socket Libraries

Developers of applications for TCP/IP networks will frequently make use of a *sockets library* to implement applications. These applications are not the standard "bundled" TCP/IP applications like FTP, but other applications for remote database queries and the like that must run over a TCP/IP network. The sockets library is a set of programming tools used to simplify the writing of application programs for TCP or UDP. Since these "custom" applications are not included in the regular application services layer of TCP/IP, these applications must interface directly with the TCP/IP stack. Of course, these applications must also exist in the same client–server, active–passive open environment as all other TCP/IP applications.

The socket is the programmer's identifier for this TCP/IP layer interface. In Unix environments, the socket is treated just like a file. That is, the socket is created, opened, read from, written to, closed, and deleted, which are exactly the same operations that a programmer would use to manipulate a file on a local disk drive. Through the use of the socket interface, a developer can write TCP/IP networked client–server applications without thinking about managing TCP/IP connections on the network.

The programmer can use sockets to refer to any remote TCP/IP application layer entity. Many developers use socket interfaces to provide "front-end" graphical interfaces

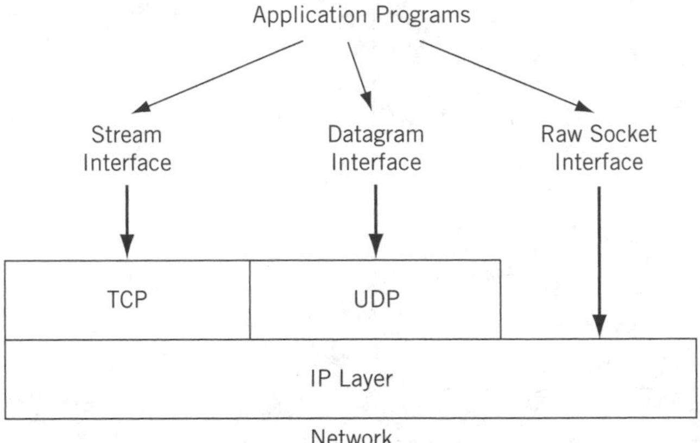

FIGURE 12.3

The three socket types. Note that the raw socket interface bypasses TCP and UDP. (The socket program often builds its own TCP or UDP header.)

to common remote TCP/IP server processes such as FTP. Of course, the developers may choose to write applications that implement both sides of the client-server model.

The socket can interface with either TCP (called a "stream" socket), UDP (called a "datagram" socket), or even IP directly (called the "raw" socket). Figure 12.3 shows the three major types of socket programming interfaces. There are even socket libraries that allow interfaces with the frames of the network access layer below IP itself. More details must come from the writers of the sockets libraries themselves, since socket libraries vary widely in operational specifics.

TCP Stream Service Calls

When used in the stream mode, the socket interface supplies the TCP protocol with the proper service *calls* from the application. These service calls are few in number, but enough to completely activate, maintain, and terminate TCP connections on the TCP/IP network. Their functions are summarized in the following:

OPEN—Either a passive or active open is defined to establish TCP connections.

SEND—Allows a client or server application process to pass a buffer of information to the TCP layer for transmission as a segment.

RECEIVE—Prepares a receive buffer for the use of the client or server application to receive a segment from the TCP layer.

STATUS—Allows the application to locate information about the status of a TCP connection.

CLOSE—Requests that the TCP connection be closed.

ABORT—Asks that the TCP connection discard all data in buffers and terminate the TCP connection immediately.

These commands are invoked on the application's behalf by the socket interface, and therefore are not seen by the application programmer. But it is always good to keep in mind that no matter how complicated a sockets library of routines might seem to a programmer, at heart the socket interface is a relatively simple procedure.

THE SOCKET INTERFACE: GOOD OR BAD?

However, the very simplicity of socket interfaces can be deceptive. The price of this simplicity is isolating the network program developers from any of the details of how the TCP/IP network actually operates. In many cases, the application programmers interpret this "transparency" of the TCP/IP network ("treat it just like a file") to mean that the TCP/IP network really does not matter to the application program at all.

As many TCP/IP network administrators have learned the hard way, nothing could be further from the truth. Every segment, datagram, frame, and byte that an application puts on a TCP/IP network affects the performance of the network for everyone. Programmers and developers that treat sockets "just like a file" soon find out that the TCP/IP network is not as fast as the hard drive on their local systems. And many applications have to be rewritten to be more efficient just because of the seductive transparency of the TCP/IP network using the socket interface.

For those who have been in the computer and network business almost from the start, the socket interface controversy in this regard closely mirrors the controversy that erupted when COBOL, the first "high-level" programming language, made it possible for people who knew absolutely nothing about the inner workings of computers to be trained to write application programs. Before COBOL, programmers wrote in a low-level assembly language that was translated (assembled) into machine instructions. (Some geniuses wrote directly in machine code without assemblers, a process known as "bare metal programming.")

Proponents then, as with sockets, pointed out the efficiencies to be enjoyed by freeing programmers from reinventing the wheel with each program and writing the same low-level routines over and over. There were gains in production as well—programmers who wrote a single instruction in COBOL could rely on the compiler to generate about 10 lines of underlying assembly language and machine code. Since programmers all wrote about the same number of lines of code a day, a 10-fold gain in productivity could be claimed.

The same claims regarding isolation are often made for the socket interface. Freed from concerns about packet headers and segments, network programmers can concentrate instead on the real task of the program and benefit from similar productivity gains. Today, no one seriously considers the socket interface to be an isolation liability, although similar claims of "isolation" are still heard when programmers today can generate code by pointing and clicking at a graphical display in Visual Basic or another even higher level "language."

The "Threat" of Raw Sockets

A more serious criticism of the socket interface is that it forms an almost perfect tool for hackers, especially the raw socket interface. Many network security experts do not look kindly on the kind of abuses that raw sockets made possible in the hands of hackers.

Why all the uproar over raw sockets? With the stream (TCP) and datagram (UDP) socket interfaces, the programmer is limited with regard to what fields in the TCP/UDP or IP header that they can manipulate. After all, the whole goal is to relieve the programmer of addressing and header field concerns. Raw sockets were originally intended as a protocol research tool only, but they proved so popular among the same circle of trusted Internet programmers at the time that use became common.

But raw sockets let the programmer pretty much control the entire content of the packet, from header to flags to options. Want to generate a SYN attack to send a couple of million TCP segments with the SYN bit sent one after the other to the same Web site, and from a phony IP address? This is difficult to do through the stream socket, but much easier with a raw socket. Consequently, this is one reason why you can find and download over the Internet hundreds of examples using TCP and UDP sockets, but raw socket examples are few and far between. Not only could users generate TCP and UPD packets, but even "fake" ICMP and traceroute packets were now within reach.

Microsoft unleashed a storm of controversy in 2001 when it announced support for the "full Unix-style" raw socket interface in Windows XP. Limited support for raw sockets in Windows had been available for years, and third-party device drivers could always be added to Windows to support the full raw socket interface, but malicious users seldom bestirred themselves to modify systems that were already in use. However, if a "tool" was available to these users, it would be exploited sooner or later.

Many saw the previous limited support for raw sockets in Windows as a blessing in disguise. The TCP/UDP layers formed a kind of "insulation" to protect the Internet from malicious application programs, a protective layer that was stripped away with full raw socket support. They also pointed out that the success of Windows NT servers, and then Windows 95/98/Me, all of which lacked full raw socket support, meant that no one *needed* full raw sockets to do what needed doing on the Internet. But once full raw sockets came to almost everyone's desktop, these critics claimed, hackers would have a high-volume, but poorly secured, operating system in the hands of consumers.

Without full raw sockets, Windows PCs could not spoof IP addresses, generate TCP segment SYN attacks, or create fraudulent TCP connections. When taken over by email-delivered scripts in innocent-looking attachments, these machines could become "zombies" and be used by malicious hackers to launch attacks all over the Internet.

Microsoft pointed out that full raw sockets support was *possible* in previous editions of Windows, and that "everybody else had them." Eventually, with the release of Service Pack 2 for Windows XP, Microsoft restricted the traffic that could be *sent* over the raw socket interface (receiving was unaffected) in two major ways: TCP data could not be sent and the IP source address for UDP data must be a valid IP address. These changes should do a lot to reduce the vulnerability on Windows XP in this regard.

Also, in traditional Unix-based operating systems, access to raw sockets is a privileged activity. So, in a sense the issue is not to hamper raw sockets, but to prevent unauthorized access to privileged modes of operation. According to this position, all raw socket restrictions do is hamper legitimate applications and form an impediment to effectiveness and portability. Restrictions have never prevented a subverted machine from spoofing traffic before Windows XP or since.

Socket Libraries

Although there is no standard socket programming interface, there are some socket interfaces that have become very popular for a number of system types. The original socket interface was developed for the 1982 version of the Berkeley Systems Distribution of Unix (BSD 4.1c). It was designed at the time to be used with a number of network protocol architectures, not just TCP/IP alone. But since TCP/IP was bundled with BSD Unix versions, sockets and TCP/IP have been closely related. A number of improvements have been made to the original BSD socket interface since 1982. Some people still call the socket interfaces "Berkeley sockets" to honor the source of the concept.

In 1986, AT&T, the original developers of Unix, introduced the Transport Layer Interface (TLI). The TLI interface was bundled with AT&T UNIX System V and also supported other network architectures besides TCP/IP. However, TLI is also almost always used with TCP/IP network interface. Today, TLI remains somewhat of a curiosity.

WinSock, as the socket programming interface for Windows is called, is a special case and deserves a section of its own.

THE WINDOWS SOCKET INTERFACE

One of the most important socket interface implementations today, which is not for the Unix environment at all, is the Windows Socket interface programming library, or WinSock. WinSock is a dynamic link library (DLL) function that is linked to a Windows TCP/IP application program when run. WinSock began with a 16-bit version for Windows 3.1, and then a 32-bit version was introduced for Windows NT and Windows 95. All Microsoft DLLs have well-defined application program interface (API) calls, and in WinSock these correspond to the sockets library functions in a Unix environment.

It is somewhat surprising, given the popularity of the TCP/IP protocol architecture for networks and the popularity of the Microsoft Windows operating system for PCs, that it took so long for TCP/IP and Windows to be used together. For a while, Microsoft (and the hardcover version of Bill Gates's book) championed the virtues of multimedia CD-ROMs over the joys of surfing the Internet, but that quickly changed when the softcover edition of the book appeared and Microsoft got on the Internet bandwagon (much to the chagrin of Internet companies like Netscape). In fairness to Microsoft, there were lots of established companies, such as Novell, that failed to foresee the rise of the Internet and TCP/IP and their importance in networking. There were several reasons for the late merging of Windows and TCP/IP.

TCP/IP and Windows

First, TCP/IP was always closely associated with the Unix world of academics and research institutions. As such, Unix (and the TCP/IP that came with it) was valued as an open standard that was easily and readily available, and in some cases even free. Windows, on the other hand, was a commercial product by Microsoft intended for corporate or private use of PCs. Windows came to be accepted as a proprietary, de facto standard, easily and readily available, but never for free. Microsoft encouraged developers to write applications for Windows, but until the release of Windows for Workgroups (WFW) these applications were almost exclusively "stand-alone" products intended to run complete on a Windows PC. Even with the release of Windows for Workgroups, the network interface bundled with WFW was not TCP/IP, but NetBIOS, a network interface for LANs jointly owned by IBM and Microsoft.

Second, in spite of Windows multitasking capabilities (the ability to run more than one process at a time), Windows used a method of multitasking known as "non-preemptive multitasking." In non-preemptive multitasking, a running process had to "pause" during execution on its own, rather than the operating system taking control and forcing the application to pause and give other processes a chance to execute. Unix, in contrast, was a preemptive multitasking environment. With preemptive multitasking, the Unix operating system keeps track of all running processes, allocating computer and memory resources so that they all run in an efficient manner. This system is characterized by more work for the operating system, but it is better for all the applications in the long run. Windows was basically a multitasking GUI built on top of a single-user operating system (DOS).

Sockets for Windows

The pressure that led to the development of the WinSock interface is simple to relate. Users wanted to hook their Windows-based PCs into the Internet. The Internet only understands one network protocol, TCP/IP. So WinSock was developed to satisfy this user need. At first the WinSock interface was used almost exclusively to Internet-enable Windows PCs. That is, the applications developed in those pre-Web days to use the WinSock interface were simple client process interfaces to enable Windows users to Telnet to Internet sites, run FTP client process programs to attach to Internet FTP servers, and so on. This might sound limited, but before WinSock, Windows users were limited to dialing into ports that offered asynchronous terminal text interfaces and performed TCP/IP conversion for Windows users.

There were performance concerns with those early Windows TCP/IP implementations. The basic problem was the performance of multitasked processes in the Microsoft Windows non-preemptive environment. Most TCP/IP processes, client or server, do not worry about when to run or when to pause, as the Unix operating system handles that. With Windows applications written for the WinSock DLL, all of the TCP/IP processes worried about the decision of whether to run or pause, since the Windows operating system could not "suspend" or pause them on its own. This voluntary giving up of execution time was a characteristic of Windows, but not of most TCP/IP implementations.

Also, Unix workstations had more horsepower than PC architectures in those early days, and the Unix operating system has had multitasking capabilities from the start. Originally, Unix required a whole minicomputer's resources to run effectively. When PCs came along in the early 1980s, they were just not capable of having enough memory or being powerful enough to run Unix effectively (a real embarrassment for the makers of AT&T PCs for a while). By the early 1990s, when the Web came along, early Web sites often relied on RISC processors and more memory than Windows PCs could even address in those days.

It is worth pointing out that most of these limitations were first addressed with Windows 95, the process continued with Windows NT, and finally Windows XP and Vista. Today, no one would hesitate to run an Internet server on a Windows platform, and many do.

SOCKETS ON LINUX

Any network, large or small, can use sockets. In this section, let's look at some socket basics on Linux systems.

We could write socket client and server applications from scratch, but the truth is that programmers hate to write anything from scratch. Usually, they hunt around for code that does something pretty close to what they want and modify it for the occasion (at least for noncommercial purposes). There are plenty of socket examples available on the Internet, so we downloaded some code written by Michael J. Donahoo and Kenneth L. Calvert. The code, which comes with no copyright and a "use-at-your-own-risk" warning, is taken from their excellent book, *TCP/IP Sockets in C* (Morgan Kaufmann, 2001).

We'll use TCP because there should be more efficiency derived from a connection-oriented, three-way handshake protocol like TCP than in a simple request–response protocol like UDP. This application sends a string to the server, where the server socket program bounces it back. (If no port is provided by the user, the client looks for well-known port 7, the TCP Echo function port.) First, we'll list out and compile my version of the client socket code (`TCPsocketClient` and `DieWithError.c`) on `lnxclient`. (Ordinarily, we would put all this is its own directory.)

```
[root@lnxclient admin]# cat TCPsocketClient.c
#include <stdio.h>      /* for printf() and fprintf() */
#include <sys/socket.h> /* for socket(), connect(), send(), and recv() */
#include <arpa/inet.h>  /* for sockaddr_in and inet_addr() */
#include <stdlib.h>     /* for atoi() and exit() */
#include <string.h>     /* for memset() */
#include <unistd.h>     /* for close() */

#define RCVBUFSIZE 32   /* Size of receive buffer */
```

```
void ErrorFunc(char *errorMessage);  /* Error handling function */

int main(int argc, char *argv[])
{
    int sock;                          /* Socket descriptor */
    struct sockaddr_in echoServAddr;   /* Echo server address */
    unsigned short echoServPort;       /* Echo server port */
    char *servIP;                      /* Server IP address (dotted quad) */
    char *echoString;                  /* String to send to echo server */
    char echoBuffer[RCVBUFSIZE];       /* Buffer for echo string */
    unsigned int echoStringLen;        /* Length of string to echo */
    int bytesRcvd, totalBytesRcvd;     /* Bytes read in single recv()
                                          and total bytes read */

    if ((argc < 3) || (argc > 4))      /* Test for correct number of
                                          arguments  */
    {
       fprintf(stderr, "Usage: %s <Server IP> <Echo Word> [<Echo Port>]\n",
               argv[0]);
       exit(1);
    }

    servIP = argv[1];         /* First arg: server IP address (dotted quad) */
    echoString = argv[2];     /* Second arg: string to echo */

    if (argc == 4)
        echoServPort = atoi(argv[3]); /* Use given port, if any */
    else
        echoServPort = 7;  /* 7 is the well-known port for the echo
                              service */

    /* Create a reliable, stream socket using TCP */
    if ((sock = socket(PF_INET, SOCK_STREAM, IPPROTO_TCP)) < 0)
        DieWithError("socket() failed");

    /* Construct the server address structure */
    memset(&echoServAddr, 0, sizeof(echoServAddr));     /* Zero out
                                                           structure */
    echoServAddr.sin_family    = AF_INET;               /* Internet address
                                                           family */
    echoServAddr.sin_addr.s_addr = inet_addr(servIP);   /* Server
                                                           IP address */
    echoServAddr.sin_port   = htons(echoServPort);      /* Server port */

    /* Establish the connection to the echo server */
    if (connect(sock, (struct sockaddr *) &echoServAddr,
      sizeof(echoServAddr)) < 0)
       DieWithError("connect() failed");

    echoStringLen = strlen(echoString);        /* Determine input length */
```

```
    /* Send the string to the server */
    if (send(sock, echoString, echoStringLen, 0) != echoStringLen)
        DieWithError("send() sent a different number of bytes than expected");

    /* Receive the same string back from the server */
    totalBytesRcvd = 0;
    printf("Received: ");              /* Setup to print the echoed string */
    while (totalBytesRcvd < echoStringLen)
    {
        /* Receive up to the buffer size (minus 1 to leave space for
           a null terminator) bytes from the sender */
        if ((bytesRcvd = recv(sock, echoBuffer, RCVBUFSIZE - 1, 0)) <= 0)
            DieWithError("recv() failed or connection closed prematurely");
        totalBytesRcvd += bytesRcvd;   /* Keep tally of total bytes */
        echoBuffer[bytesRcvd] = '\0';  /* Terminate the string! */
        printf(echoBuffer);            /* Print the echo buffer */
    }

    printf("\n");    /* Print a final linefeed */

    close(sock);
    exit(0);
}

[root@lnxclient admin]# cat DieWithError.c
#include <stdio.h>  /* for perror() */
#include <stdlib.h> /* for exit() */

void DieWithError(char *errorMessage)
{
    perror(errorMessage);
    exit(1);
}

[root@lnxclie3nt admin]#
```

The steps in the program are fairly straightforward. First, we create a stream socket, and then establish the connection to the server. We send the string to echo, wait for the response, print it out, clean things up, and terminate. Now we can just compile the code and get ready to run it.

```
[root@lnxclient admin]# gcc –o TCPsocketClient TCPsocketClient.c DieWithError.c
[root@lnxclient admin]#
```

Before we run the program with **TCPsocketoClient** *<ServerIPAddress>* *<StringtoEcho>* *<ServerPort>*, we need to compile the server portion of the code on `lnxserver`. The code in these two files is more complex.

```
[root@lnxserver admin]# cat TCPsocketServer.c
#include <stdio.h>      /* for printf() and fprintf() */
#include <sys/socket.h> /* for socket(), bind(), and connect() */
#include <arpa/inet.h>  /* for sockaddr_in and inet_ntoa() */
#include <stdlib.h>     /* for atoi() and exit() */
#include <string.h>     /* for memset() */
#include <unistd.h>     /* for close() */

#define MAXPENDING 5    /* Maximum outstanding connection requests */

void ErrorFunc(char *errorMessage);      /* Error handling function */
void HandleTCPClient(int clntSocket);    /* TCP client handling function */

int main(int argc, char *argv[])
{
    int servSock;                    /* Socket descriptor for server */
    int clntSock;                    /* Socket descriptor for client */
    struct sockaddr_in echoServAddr; /* Local address */
    struct sockaddr_in echoClntAddr; /* Client address */
    unsigned short echoServPort;     /* Server port */
    unsigned int clntLen;            /* Length of client address data
                                        structure */

    if (argc != 2)     /* Test for correct number of arguments */
    {
        fprintf(stderr, "Usage:  %s <Server Port>\n", argv[0]);
        exit(1);
    }

    echoServPort = atoi(argv[1]);  /* First arg:  local port */

    /* Create socket for incoming connections */
    if ((servSock = socket(PF_INET, SOCK_STREAM, IPPROTO_TCP)) < 0)
        DieWithError("socket() failed");

    /* Construct local address structure */
    memset(&echoServAddr, 0, sizeof(echoServAddr));   /* Zero out
                                                          structure */
    echoServAddr.sin_family = AF_INET;                /* Internet address
                                                          family */
    echoServAddr.sin_addr.s_addr = htonl(INADDR_ANY); /* Any incoming
                                                          interface */
    echoServAddr.sin_port = htons(echoServPort);      /* Local port */

    /* Bind to the local address */

    if (bind(servSock, (struct sockaddr *) &echoServAddr,
        sizeof(echoServAddr)) < 0)
        DieWithError("bind() failed");

    /* Mark the socket so it will listen for incoming connections */
    if (listen(servSock, MAXPENDING) < 0)
        DieWithError("listen() failed");
```

```
    for (;;) /* Run forever */
    {
        /* Set the size of the in-out parameter */
        clntLen = sizeof(echoClntAddr);

        /* Wait for a client to connect */
        if ((clntSock = accept(servSock, (struct sockaddr *) &echoClntAddr,
                               &clntLen)) < 0)
            DieWithError("accept() failed");

        /* clntSock is connected to a client! */

        printf("Handling client %s\n", inet_ntoa(echoClntAddr.sin_addr));

        HandleTCPClient(clntSock);
    }
    /* NOT REACHED */
}

[root@lnxserver admin]# cat HandleTCPClient.c
#include <stdio.h>      /* for printf() and fprintf() */
#include <sys/socket.h> /* for recv() and send() */
#include <unistd.h>     /* for close() */

#define RCVBUFSIZE 32   /* Size of receive buffer */

void DieWithError(char *errorMessage);  /* Error handling function */

void HandleTCPClient(int clntSocket)
{
    char echoBuffer[RCVBUFSIZE];        /* Buffer for echo string */
    int recvMsgSize;                    /* Size of received message */

    /* Receive message from client */
    if ((recvMsgSize = recv(clntSocket, echoBuffer, RCVBUFSIZE, 0)) < 0)
        DieWithError("recv() failed");

    /* Send received string and receive again until end of transmission */
    while (recvMsgSize > 0)      /* zero indicates end of transmission */
    {
        /* Echo message back to client */
        if (send(clntSocket, echoBuffer, recvMsgSize, 0) != recvMsgSize)
            DieWithError("send() failed");

        /* See if there is more data to receive */
        if ((recvMsgSize = recv(clntSocket, echoBuffer, RCVBUFSIZE, 0)) < 0)
            DieWithError("recv() failed");
    }
    close(clntSocket);    /* Close client socket */
}

[root@lnxserver admin]#
```

The server socket performs a passive open and waits (forever, if need be) for the client to send a string for it to echo. It's the `HandleTCPClient.c` code that does the bulk of this work. We also need the `ErrorFunc.c` code, as before, so we have three files to compile instead of only two, as on the client side.

```
[root@lnxserver admin]# gcc -o TCPsocketServer TCPsocketServer.c
HandleTCPClient.c DieWithError.c
[root@lnxserver admin]#
```

Now we can start up the server on `lnxserver` using the syntax **TCPsocketServer** `<ServerPort>`. (Always check to make sure the port you choose is not in use already!)

```
[root@lnxserver admin]# ./TCPsocketServer 2005
```

The server just waits until the client on `lnxclient` makes a connection and presents a string for the server to echo. We'll use the string *TEST.*

```
[root@lnxclient admin]# ./TCPsocketClient 10.10.11.66 TEST 2005
Received: TEST
[root@lnxclient admin]#
```

Not much to that. It's very fast, and the server tells us that the connection with `lnxclient` was made. We can cancel out of the server program.

```
Handling client 10.10.12.166
^C
[root@lnxserver admin]#
```

We've also used Ethereal to capture any TCP packets at the server while the socket client and server were running. Figure 12.4 shows what we caught.

So that's the attraction of sockets, especially for TCP. Ten packets (two ARPs are not shown) made their way back and forth across the network just to echo "TEST" from one system to another. Only two of the packets actually do this, as the rest are TCP connection overhead.

But the real power of sockets is in the details, or lack of details. Not a single line of C code mentioned creating a TCP or IP packet header, field values, or anything else. The stream socket interface did it all, so the application programmer can concentrate on the task at hand and not be forced to worry about network details.

	Time	Source	Destination	Protocol	Info
1	0.000000	10.10.12.166	10.10.11.66	TCP	32919 > 2005 [SYN] Seq=0 Ack=0 Win=5840 Len=0 MSS=1460 TS
4	0.000608	10.10.11.66	10.10.12.166	TCP	2005 > 32919 [SYN, ACK] Seq=0 Ack=1 Win=5792 Len=0 MSS=14
5	0.000897	10.10.12.166	10.10.11.66	TCP	32919 > 2005 [ACK] Seq=1 Ack=1 Win=5840 Len=0 TSV=3286109
6	0.001074	10.10.12.166	10.10.11.66	TCP	32919 > 2005 [PSH, ACK] Seq=1 Ack=1 Win=5840 Len=4 TSV=32
7	0.001103	10.10.11.66	10.10.12.166	TCP	2005 > 32919 [ACK] Seq=1 Ack=5 Win=5792 Len=0 TSV=1992372
8	0.001233	10.10.11.66	10.10.12.166	TCP	2005 > 32919 [PSH, ACK] Seq=1 Ack=5 Win=5792 Len=4 TSV=19
9	0.001454	10.10.12.166	10.10.11.66	TCP	32919 > 2005 [ACK] Seq=5 Ack=5 Win=5840 Len=0 TSV=3286109
10	0.001597	10.10.12.166	10.10.11.66	TCP	32919 > 2005 [FIN, ACK] Seq=5 Ack=5 Win=5840 Len=0 TSV=32
11	0.001651	10.10.11.66	10.10.12.166	TCP	2005 > 32919 [FIN, ACK] Seq=5 Ack=6 Win=5792 Len=0 TSV=19
12	0.001853	10.10.12.166	10.10.11.66	TCP	32919 > 2005 [ACK] Seq=6 Ack=6 Win=5840 Len=0 TSV=3286109

FIGURE 12.4

The socket client–server TCP stream captured. This is a completely normal TCP connection accomplished with a minimum of coded effort.

QUESTIONS FOR READERS

Figure 12.5 shows some of the concepts discussed in this chapter and can be used to help you answer the following questions.

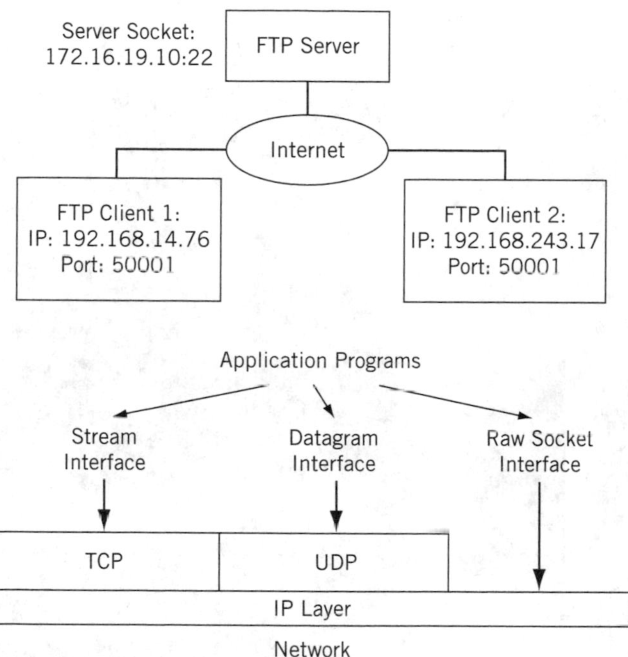

FIGURE 12.5

A socket in an FTP server and the various types of socket programming interfaces.

1. In the figure, two clients have picked the same ephemeral port for their FTP connection to the server. What is it about the TCP connection that allows this to happen all the time without harm?
2. What if the user at the *same* client PC ran two FTP sessions to the same server process? What would have to be different to make sure that both TCP control (and data) connections would not have problems?
3. What is the attraction of sockets as a programming tool?
4. Why can't the same type of socket interface be used for both TCP and UDP?
5. Are fully supported raw sockets an overstated threat to the Internet and attached hosts?

Routing and Routing Protocols

Internet service providers (ISPs) use routers and routing protocols to connect pieces of the Internet together. This part explores IGPs such as RIP, OSPF, and IS-IS, and also BGP. It includes a look at multicast routing protocols and MPLS, a method of IP switching.

CHAPTER

Routing and Peering

13

What You Will Learn

In this chapter, you will learn about how routing differs from switching, the other network layer technology. We'll compare connectionless and connection-oriented networking characteristics and see how *quality of service* (QoS) can be supported on both.

You will learn what a *routing protocol* is and what they do. We'll investigate the differences between interior and exterior routing protocols as the terms apply to an ISP. We'll also talk about *routing policies* and the role they play on the modern Internet.

In Chapter 9, we introduced the concept of forwarding packets hop by hop across a network of interconnected routers and LANs. This process is loosely called "routing," and that chapter comprised a first look at routing tables (and the associated forwarding tables). In this chapter, we'll discuss how ISPs manipulate their routing tables with routing policies to influence the flow of traffic on the Internet. This chapter will focus more closely on the routing tables on hosts. In Chapters 14 and 15, we discuss in more detail the routing tables and routing policies on the network routers.

This chapter will look at the routing tables on the hosts on the LANs, as shown in Figure 13.1. But we'll also discuss, for the first time, how the two ISPs on the network (called Ace ISP and Best ISP) relate to each other and how their routing tables ensure that traffic flows most efficiently between LAN1 and LAN2. For example, it's obviously more effective to send LAN1–LAN2 traffic over the link between P4 and P2 instead of shuttling onto the Internet from P4 and relying on routers beyond the control of either Best or Ace ISP to route the packets back to P2. (Of course, traffic could flow from P4 to P7, or even end up at P9 to be forwarded to P7, but this is just an example.) But how do the routers know how P2 and P4 are connected? More importantly, how do the routers PE5 and PE1 know how the other routers are connected? What keeps router PE5 from forwarding Internet-bound traffic to P9 instead of P4? And, because P9 is also connected to P4, why should it be a big deal anyway?

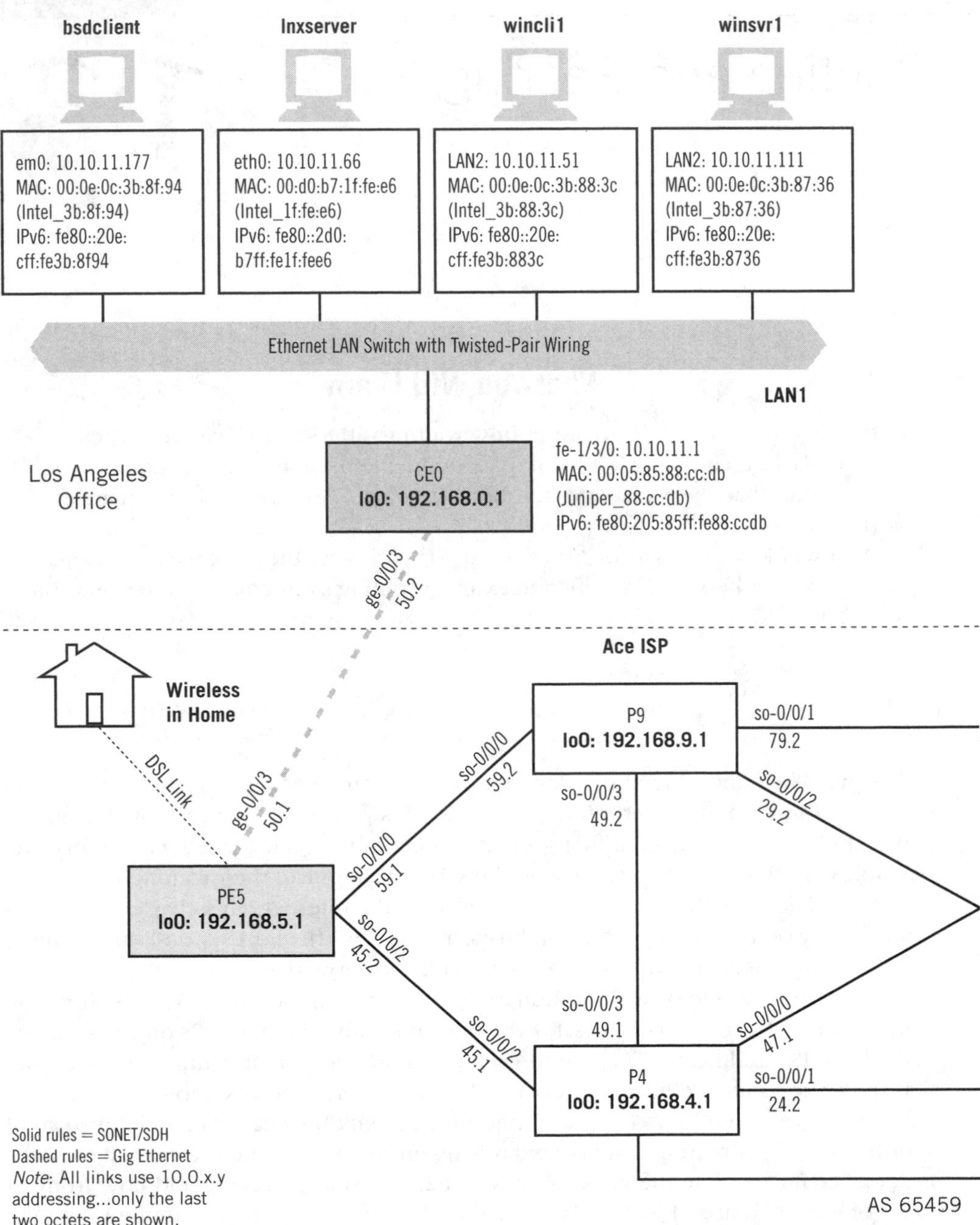

FIGURE 13.1

The hosts on the LANs have routing tables as well as the routers. The ISPs on the Illustrated Network have chosen to implement an ISP peering arrangement.

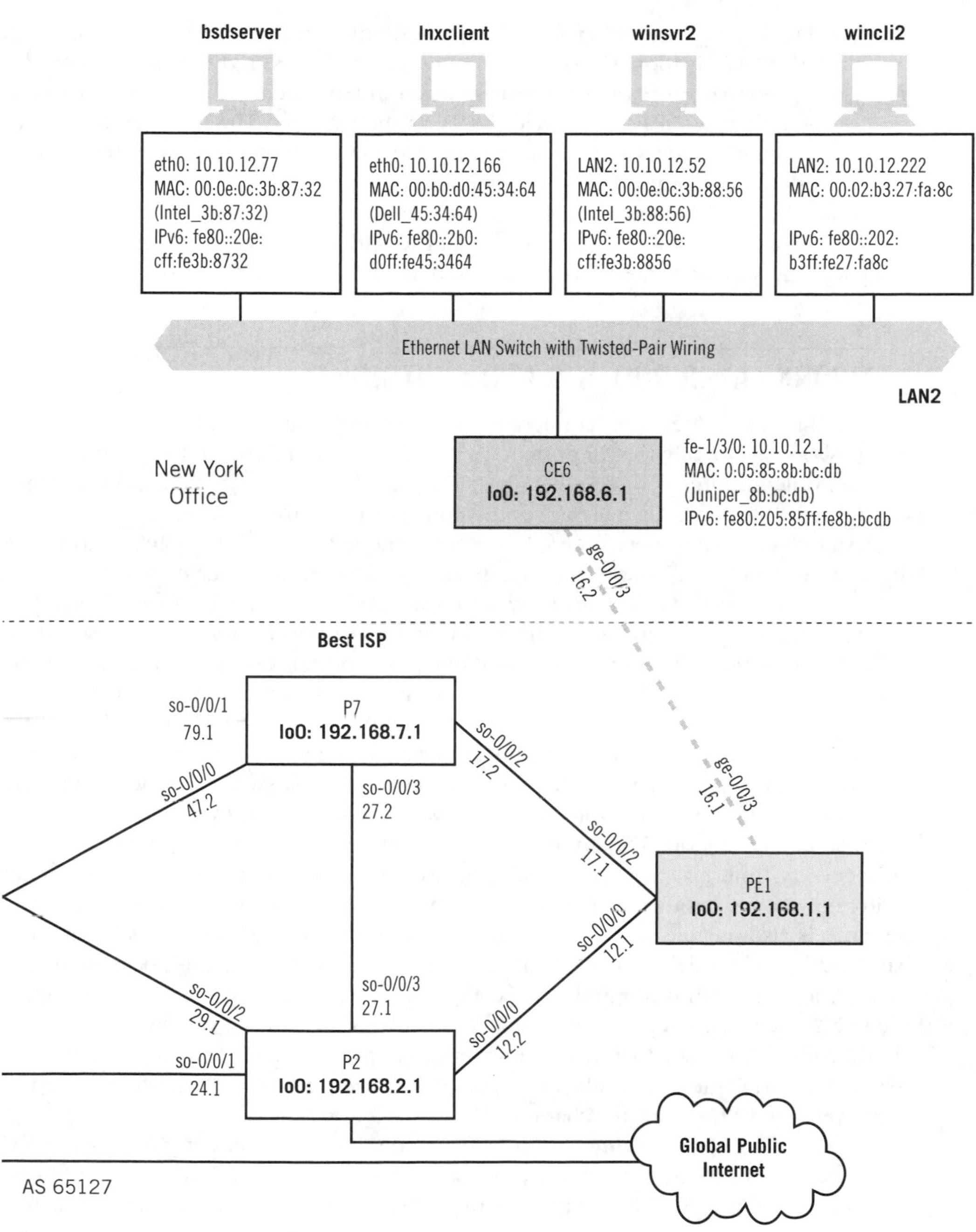
bsdserver
lnxclient
winsvr2
wincli2
eth0: 10.10.12.77
MAC: 00:0e:0c:3b:87:32
(Intel_3b:87:32)
IPv6: fe80::20e:
cff:fe3b:8732
eth0: 10.10.12.166
MAC: 00:b0:d0:45:34:64
(Dell_45:34:64)
IPv6: fe80::2b0:
d0ff:fe45:3464
LAN2: 10.10.12.52
MAC: 00:0e:0c:3b:88:56
(Intel_3b:88:56)
IPv6: fe80::20e:
cff:fe3b:8856
LAN2: 10.10.12.222
MAC: 00:02:b3:27:fa:8c
IPv6: fe80::202:
b3ff:fe27:fa8c
Ethernet LAN Switch with Twisted-Pair Wiring
LAN2
New York
Office
CE6
lo0: 192.168.6.1
fe-1/3/0: 10.10.12.1
MAC: 0:05:85:8b:bc:db
(Juniper_8b:bc:db)
IPv6: fe80:205:85ff:fe8b:bcdb
ge-0/0/3
16.2
Best ISP
so-0/0/1
79.1
P7
lo0: 192.168.7.1
so-0/0/0
47.2
so-0/0/3
27.2
so-0/0/2
17.2
ge-0/0/3
16.1
so-0/0/2
17.1
PE1
lo0: 192.168.1.1
so-0/0/0
12.1
so-0/0/2
29.1
so-0/0/3
27.1
so-0/0/0
12.2
so-0/0/1
24.1
P2
lo0: 192.168.2.1
Global Public
Internet
AS 65127

This chapter will begin to answer these questions, and the next two chapters will complete the investigation. However, it should be mentioned right away that connectionless routers that route (forward) each packet independently through the network are not the only way ISPs can connect LANs on the Internet. The network nodes can be connection-oriented switches that forward packets along fixed paths set up through the network nodes from source to destination.

We've already discussed connectionless and connection-oriented services at the transport layer (UDP and TCP). Let's see what the differences are between connectionless and connection-oriented services at the network layer.

NETWORK LAYER ROUTING AND SWITCHING

Are the differences between connection-oriented and connectionless networking at the network layer really that important? Actually, yes. The difference between the way connectionless router networks handle traffic (and link and node failures) is a major reason that IP has basically taken over the entire world of networking.

A *switch* in modern networking is a network node that forwards packets toward a destination depending on a locally significant connection identifier over a fixed path. This fixed path is called a *virtual circuit* and is set up by a signaling protocol (a *switched virtual circuit*, or SVC) or by manual configuration (a *permanent virtual circuit*, or PVC). A *connection* is a logical association of two endpoints. Connections only need be referenced, not identified by "to" and "from" information. A data unit sent on "connection 22" can only flow between the two endpoints where it is established—there is no need to specify more. (We've seen this already at Layer 2 when we looked at the connection-oriented PPP frame.) As long as there is no confusion in the switch, connection identifiers can be reused, and therefore have what is called *local significance only*.

Packets on SVCs or PVCs are often checked for errors hop by hop and are resent as necessary from node to node (the originator plays no role in the process). Packet switching networks offer guaranteed delivery (as least as error-free as possible). The network is also reliable in the sense that certain performance guarantees in terms of bandwidth, delay, and so on can be enforced on the connection because packets always follow the same path through the network. A good example of a switched network is the public switched telephone network (PSTN). SVCs are normal voice calls and PVCs are the leased lines used to link data devices, but frame relay and ATM are also switched network technologies. We'll talk about *public switched network* technologies such as frame relay and ATM in a later chapter.

On the other hand, a *router* is a network node that independently forwards packets toward a destination based on a globally unique address (in IP, the IP address) over a dynamic path that can change from packet to packet, but usually is fairly stable over time. Packets on router networks are seldom checked for errors hop by hop and are only resent (if necessary) from host to host (the originator plays a key role in the process). Packet routing networks offer only "best-effort" delivery (but as error-free as possible). The network is also considered "unreliable" in the sense that certain performance guarantees in terms of bandwidth, delay, and so on cannot be enforced from end to end because packets often follow different paths through the network. A good example of a router-based network is the global, public Internet.

CONNECTION-ORIENTED AND CONNECTIONLESS NETWORKS

Many layers of a protocol stack, especially the lower layers, offer a choice of connection-oriented or connectionless protocols. These choices are often independent. We've seen that connectionless IP can use connection-oriented PPP at Layer 2. But what is it that makes a *network* connectionless? Not surprisingly, it's the implantation of the network layer. IP, the Internet protocol suite's network layer protocol, is connectionless, so TCP/IP networks are connectionless.

Connection-oriented networks are sometimes called *switched networks*, and connectionless networks are often called *router-based networks*. The signaling protocol messages used on switched networks to set up SVCs are themselves routed between switches in a connectionless manner using globally unique addresses (such as telephone numbers). These call setup messages must be routed, because obviously there are no connection paths to follow yet. Every switched network that offers SVCs must also be a connectionless, router-based network as well.

One of the major reasons to build a connectionless network like the Internet was that it was inherently simpler than connection-oriented networks that must route signaling setups messages and forward traffic on connections. The Internet essentially handles everything as if it were a signaling protocol message. The differences between connection-oriented switched networks and connectionless router networks are shown in Table 13.1.

Table 13.1 Switched and Connectionless Networks Compared by Major Characteristics

Characteristic	Switched Network	Connectionless Network
Design philosophy	Connection oriented	Connectionless
Addressing unit	Circuit identifiers	Network and host address
Scope of address	Local significance	Globally unique
Network nodes	Switches	Routers
Bandwidth use	As allowed by "circuit"	Varies with number and size of frames
Traffic processing	Signaling for path setup	Every packet routed independently
Examples	Frame relay, ATM, ISDN, PSTN, most other WANs	IP, Ethernet, most other LANs

Note that every characteristic listed for a connectionless network applies to the signaling network for a switched network. It would not be wrong to think of the Internet as a signaling network with packets that can carry data instead of connection (call) setup information. The whole architecture is vastly simplified by using the connectionless network for everything.

The simplified router network, in contrast to the switched network, would automatically route around failed links and nodes. In contrast, connection-oriented networks lost every connection that was mapped to a particular link or switch. These had to be re-established through signaling (SVCs) or manual configuration (PVCs), both of which involved considerable additional traffic loads (SVCs) or delays (PVCs) for all affected users. One of the original aims of the early "Internet" was explicitly to demonstrate that packet networks were more robust when faced with failures. Therefore, connectionless networks could be built more cheaply with relatively "unreliable" components and still be resistant to failure. Today, "best-effort" and "unreliable" packet delivery over the Internet is much better than any other connection-oriented public data network not so long ago.

Of course, an Internet router has to maintain a list of every possible reachable destination in the world (and so did signaling nodes in connection-oriented networks), but processors have kept up with the burden imposed by the growth in the scale of the routing tables. A switch only has to keep track of local associations of two endpoints (connections) currently established. We'll talk about multiprotocol label switching (MPLS) in Chapter 17 as an attempt to introduce the efficiencies of switching into router-based networking. (MPLS does not really relieve the main burdens of interdomain routing, but we will see that MPLS has *traffic engineering* capabilities that allow ISPs to shift the paths that carry this burden.)

In only one respect is there even any discussion about the merits of connection-oriented networks versus the connectionless Internet. This is in the area of the ability of connectionless router networks to deliver *quality of service* (QoS).

Quality of Service

It might seem odd to talk about QoS in a chapter on connectionless Internet routing and forwarding. But the point is that in spite of the movement to converge all types of information (voice and video as well as data) onto the Internet, no functional interdomain QoS mechanism exists. QoS is at heart a queue management mechanism, and only by applying these strategies across an entire routing domain will QoS result in any route optimization at all. Even then, no ISP can impose its own QoS methodology on any other.

One of the biggest challenges in quality of service (QoS) discussions is that there is no universal, accepted agreement of just what network QoS actually means. Some sources define QoS quite narrowly, and others define it more broadly. For the purposes of this discussion, a broader definition is more desirable. We'll use six parameters in this book.

CoS or QoS?

Should the term for network support of performance parameters be "class of service" (CoS) or "quality of service" (QoS)? Many people use the terms interchangeably, but in this book QoS is used to mean that parameters can take on almost any value between maximum and minimum. CoS, on the other hand, establishes groups of parameters based on real world values (e.g., bandwidth at 10, 100, or 1000 Mbps with associated delays), and is offered as a "class" to customers (e.g., bronze, silver, or gold service).

Our working definition of QoS in this book is the "ability of an application to specify required values of certain parameters to the network, values without which the application will not be able to function properly." The network either agrees to provide these parameters for the applications data flow, or not. These parameters include things like minimum bandwidth, maximum delay, and security. It makes no sense to put delay-sensitive voice traffic onto a network that cannot deliver delays less than 2 or 3 seconds one way (voice suffers at delays far less than full seconds), or to put digital, wide-screen video onto a network of low-bandwidth, dial-up analog connections.

Table 13.2 shows some typical example values that are used often. In some cases, an array of values is offered to customers as a CoS.

Bandwidth is usually the first and foremost QoS parameters, for the simple reason that bandwidth was for a long time the *only* QoS parameter that could be delivered by networks with any degree of consistency. It has also been argued that, given enough bandwidth (just how much is part of the argument), every other QoS parameter becomes irrelevant.

Jitter is just delay variation, or how much the end-to-end network latency varies from time to time due to effects such as network queuing and link failures, which cause alternate routes to be used. Information loss is just the effect of network errors. Some

Table 13.2 The Six QoS Parameters

QoS Parameter	Example Values (Typical)
Bandwidth (minimum)	1.5 Mbps, 155 Mbps, 1 Gbps
Delay (maximum)	50-millisecond (ms) round-trip delay, 150-ms delay
Jitter (delay variation)	10% of maximum delay, 5-ms variation
Information loss (error effects)	1 in 10,000 packets undelivered
Security	All data streams encrypted and authenticated

applications can recover from network errors by retransmission and related strategies. Other applications, most notably voice and video, cannot realistically resend information and must deal with errors in other ways, such as the use of forward error correction codes. Either way, the application must be able to rely on the network to lose only a limited amount of information, either to minimize resends (data) or to maximize the quality of the service (voice/video).

Availability and reliability are related. Some interpret reliability as a local network quality and availability as global quality. In other words, if my local link fails often, I cannot rely on the network, but global availability to the whole pool of users might be very good. There is another way that reliability is important in TCP/IP. IP is often called an *unreliable* network layer service. This does not imply that the network fails often, but that, at the IP layer, the network cannot be relied on to deliver any QoS parameter values at all, not even minimum bandwidth. But keep in mind that a system built of unreliable components can still be reliable, and QoS is often delivered in just this fashion.

Security is the last QoS parameter to be added, and some would say that it is the most important of all.

Many discussions of QoS focus on the first four items on the parameter list. But reliability and security also belong with the others, for a number of reasons. Security concerns play a large part in much of IPv6. And reliability can be maximized in IP routing tables. There are several other areas where security and reliability impact QoS parameters; the items discussed here are just a few examples.

Service providers seldom allow user application to pick and choose values from every QoS category. Instead, many service providers will gather the typical values of the characteristics for voice, video, and several types of data applications (bulk transfer, Web access, and so on), and bundle these as a *class of service* (CoS) appropriate for that traffic flow. (On the other hand, some sources treat QoS and CoS as synonyms.) Usually, the elements in a CoS suite that a service provider offers have distinctive names, either by type (voice, video) or characteristic ("gold" level availability), or even in combination ("silver-level video service").

The promise of widespread and consistent QoS has been constantly derailed by the continuing drop in the cost (and availability) of network links of higher and higher bandwidth. Bandwidth is a well-understood network resource (some would say the *only* well-understood network resource), and those who control network budgets would rather spend a dollar on bandwidth (known effects, low risk, etc.) than on other QoS schemes such as DiffServ (spotty support, difficult to implement, etc.).

HOST ROUTING TABLES

Now that we've shown that the Illustrated Network is firmly based on connectionless networking concepts, let's look at the routing tables (*not* switching tables) on some of the hosts. Host routing tables can be very short. When initially configured, many of them have only four types of entries.

Loopback—Usually called `lo0` on Unix-based systems (and routers), this is the prefix `127/8` in IPv4 and `::1` in IPv6. Not only used for testing, the loopback is a stable interface on a router (or host) that should not change even if the interface addresses do.

The host itself—There will be one entry for every interface on the host with an IP address. This is a `/32` address in IPv4 and a `/128` address in IPv6.

The network—Each host address has a network portion that gets its own routing table entry.

The default gateway—This tells the host which router to use when the network portion of the destination IP address does not match the network portion of the source address.

Gateway or Edge Router?

A lot of texts simply say that the term "router" is the new term for "gateway" on the Internet, but that this old term still shows up in a number of acronyms (such as IGP). Other sources use the term "gateway" as a kind of synonym for what we've been calling the customer-edge router, meaning a router with only two types of routing decisions, that is, local or Internet. A DSL "router" is really just a "gateway" in this terminology, translating between local LAN protocols and service provider protocols. On the other hand, a backbone router without customer LANs is definitely a router in any sense of the term.

In this book, we'll use the terms "gateway" and "router" interchangeably, keeping in mind that the gateway terminology is still used for the entry or egress point of a particular subnet.

Routing Tables and FreeBSD

FreeBSD systems keep this fundamental information in the `/etc/default/rc.conf` file. But this information can be manipulated with the `ifconfig` command, which we've used already. However, interface information does not automatically jump into the routing table unless the changes are made to the `rc.conf` file. (If the `network_interfaces` variable is kept to the default of `auto`, the system finds its network interfaces at boot time.)

Let's use the `netstat -nr` command to take a closer look at the routing table on `bsdserver`.

```
bsdserver# netstat -nr
Routing tables

Internet:
Destination         Gateway             Flags     Refs      Use  Netif Expire
default             10.10.12.1          UGSc        1       97   em0
10.10.12/24         link#1              UC          2       0    em0
```

```
10.10.12.1          00:05:85:8b:bc:db  UHLW       2       0     em0    335
10.10.12.52         00:0e:0c:3b:88:56  UHLW       0       4     em0   1016
127.0.0.1           127.0.0.1          UH         0    6306     lo0

Internet6:
Destination                        Gateway                Flags   Netif Expire
::1                                ::1                    UH      lo0
fe80::%em0/64                      link#1                 UC      em0
fe80::20e:cff:fe3b:8732%em0        00:0e:0c:3b:87:32      UHL     lo0
fe80::%xl0/64                      link#2                 UC      xl0
fe80::2b0:d0ff:fec5:9073%xl0       00:b0:d0:c5:90:73      UHL     lo0
fe80::%lo0/64                      fe80::1%lo0            Uc      lo0
fe80::1%lo0                        link#4                 UHL     lo0
ff01::/32                          ::1                    U       lo0
ff02::%em0/32                      link#1                 UC      em0
ff02::%xl0/32                      link#2                 UC      xl0
ff02::%lo0/32                      ::1                    UC      lo0
```

FreeBSD merges the routing and ARP tables, which is why hardware addresses (and their timeouts) appear in the output. The `C` and `c` flags are host routes, and the `S` is a static entry.

To manually configure an Ethernet interface and add the route to the routing table, we use the `ifconfig` and `route` commands.

```
bsdserver# ifconfig em0 inet 10.10.12.77/24
bsdserver# route add -net 10.10.12.77 10.10.12.1
```

Routing and Forwarding Tables

Remember, the routing tables we're looking at here are tables of routing information and mainly for human inspection. Generally, everything the system learns about the network from a routing protocol is put into the routing table. But not all of the information is used for packet forwarding.

At the software level, the system creates a forwarding table in a much more compact and machine-useable format. The forwarding table is used to determine the output, the next-hop interface (if the system is not the destination). However, we'll use the friendly routing tables to illustrate the routing process, as is normally done.

Routing Tables and RedHat Linux

RedHat Linux systems keep most network configuration information in the `/etc/sysconfig` and `/etc/sysconfig/network-scripts` directories. The hostname, default gateway, and other information are kept in the `/etc/sysconfig/network` file. The Ethernet interface-specific information, such as IP address and network mask for eth0, is in the /etc/sysconfig/network-scripts/ifcfg-eth0 file (loopback is in ifcfg-lo0).

Let's look at the lnxclient routing table with the netstat -nr command.

```
[root@lnxclient admin]# netstat -nr
Kernel IP routing table
Destination  Gateway     Genmask        Flags  MSS  Window  irtt  Iface
10.10.12.0   0.0.0.0     255.255.255.0  U        0  0          0  eth0
127.0.0.0    0.0.0.0     255.0.0.0      U        0  0          0  lo
0.0.0.0      10.10.12.1  0.0.0.0        UG       0  0          0  eth0
```

Oddly, the host address isn't here. This system does not require a route for the interface address bound to the interface. The loopback entries are slightly different as well. Only network entries are in the Linux routing table. If we added a second Ethernet interface (eth1) with IPv4 address 172.16.44.98 and a different default router (172.16.44.1), we'd add that information with the ipconfig and route commands.

```
[root@lnxclient admin]# ifconfig eth1 172.16.44.98 netmask 255.255.255.0
[root@lnxclient admin]# route add default gw 172.16.44.0 eth1
```

We're not running IPv6 on the Linux systems, so no IPv6 information is displayed.

Routing and Windows XP

Windows XP, of course, handles things a little differently. We've already used ipconfig to assign addresses, and Windows XP uses the route print command to display routing table information, such as on wincli2.

```
C:\Documents and Settings\Owner>route print
===========================================================================
Interface List
0x1 ........................... MS TCP Loopback interface
0x2 ...00 02 b3 27 fa 8c ...... Intel(R) PRO/100 S Desktop Adapter - Packet
Scheduler Miniport
===========================================================================
===========================================================================
Active Routes:
Network Destination        Netmask          Gateway       Interface  Metric
          0.0.0.0          0.0.0.0       10.10.12.1    10.10.12.222      20
       10.10.12.0    255.255.255.0     10.10.12.222    10.10.12.222      20
     10.10.12.222  255.255.255.255        127.0.0.1       127.0.0.1      20
   10.255.255.255  255.255.255.255     10.10.12.222    10.10.12.222      20
        127.0.0.0        255.0.0.0        127.0.0.1       127.0.0.1      1
        224.0.0.0        240.0.0.0     10.10.12.222    10.10.12.222      20
  255.255.255.255  255.255.255.255     10.10.12.222    10.10.12.222      20
Default Gateway:        10.10.12.1
===========================================================================
Persistent Routes:
  None
```

The table is an odd mix of loopbacks, multicast, and host and router information. Persistent routes are static routes that are not purged from the table. We can delete information, add to it, or change it. If no gateway is provided for a new route, the system attempts to figure it out on its own.

The IPv6 routing table is not displayed with `route print`. To see that, we need to use the `IPv6 rt` command. The table on `wincli2` reveals only a single entry for the link-local-derived IPv6 address of the default router.

```
C:\Documents and Settings\Owner>ipv6 rt
::/0 -> 5/fe80:5:85ff:fe8b:bcdb pref 256 life 25m52s <autoconf>
```

This won't even let us ping the `wincli1` system on LAN1, even though we know to what router to send the IPv6 packets.

```
C:\Documents and Settings\Owner>ping6 fe80::20c:cff:fe3b:883c

Pinging fe80::20c:cff:fe3b:883c with 32 bytes of data:

No route to destination.
   Specify correct scope-id or use -s to specify source address.
No route to destination.
   Specify correct scope-id or use -s to specify source address.
No route to destination.
   Specify correct scope-id or use -s to specify source address.
No route to destination.
   Specify correct scope-id or use -s to specify source address.

Ping statistics for fe80::20c:cff:fe3b:883c:
   Packets: Sent = 4, Received = 0, Lost = 4 (100% loss)
```

What's wrong? Well, we're using link-local addresses, for one thing. Also, we have no way to get the routing information known about LAN2 and router CE6 to LAN1 and router CE0. That's the job of the Interior Gateway Protocols (IGPs), the types of routing protocols that run between ISP's routers. Why do we need them? Let's look at the Internet first, and then we'll use an IPG in the next chapter so that the IPv6 ping works.

THE INTERNET AND THE AUTONOMOUS SYSTEM

Before taking a more detailed look at the routing protocols that TCP/IP uses to ensure that every router knows how to forward packets closer to their ultimate destination, it's a good idea to have a firm grasp of just what routing protocols are trying to accomplish on the modern Internet. The Internet today is composed of interlocking network pieces, much like a jigsaw puzzle of global proportions. Each piece is called an *autonomous system* (AS), and it's convenient to think of each ISP as an AS, although this is not strictly true.

Routing Protocols and Routing Policies

A routing *protocol* is run on a router (and can be run on a host) to allow the router to dynamically learn about its network neighborhood and pass this knowledge on until every router has built a consistent view of the network "map" and the least cost ("best") place to forward traffic toward any reachable destination. Until the protocol *converges* there is always the possibility that some routers do not have the latest view of the network and might forward packets incorrectly. Actually, it's possible that some of the "maps" never converge and that some less-than-optimal path might be taken. But that need not be a disaster, although the reasons are far beyond this simple introduction.

A routing *policy* can be defined as "a rule implemented on the router to determine the handling of routing protocol information." An example of an ISP's routing policy rule is to "accept no routing protocol updates from hosts or routers not part of this ISP's network." This rule, intended to minimize the effects of malicious users, can be combined with others to create an overall routing policy for the whole ISP.

The term should not be confused with *policy routing*. Policy routing is usually defined as the forwarding of packets based not only on destination address, but also on some other fields in the TCP/IP header, especially the IPv4 ToS bits. Confusingly, policy routing can be made more effective with routing policies, but this book will not deal with policy routing or QoS issues.

Routing protocols do not and cannot blend all these ASs together into a seamless whole all on their own. Routing *protocols* allow routers or networks to share adjacency information with their neighbors. They establish the global connectivity between routers, within an AS and without, and ASs in turn establish the global connectivity that characterizes the Internet. Routing *policies* change the behavior of the routing protocols so AS connectivity is made into what the ISPs want (usually, ISPs add some term like "AS connectivity is made more effective and efficient" but many times routing policy doesn't do this, as we'll see).

Routers are the network nodes of the global public Internet, and they pass IP address information back and forth as needed. The result is that every router knows how to reach every IP network (really, the IP prefix) anywhere in the world, or at least those that advertise that they are willing to accept traffic for that prefix. They also know when a link or router has failed, and thus other networks might then be (temporarily) unreachable. Routers can dynamically route around failed links and routers, unless the destination network is connected to the Internet by only one link or happens to be right there on the local router.

There are no users on the router itself that originate or read email (as an example), although routers routinely take on a client or a server role (or both) for configuration and administrative purposes. Routers almost always just pass IP packet traffic through from one interface to another, input port to output port, while trying to ensure that the packets are making progress through the network and moving one step closer to its destination. It is said that routers route packets "hop by hop" through the Internet. In a very real sense, routers don't care if the packet ever reaches the destination or not: All the router knows is that if the IP address prefix is X, that packet goes out port Y.

THE INTERNET TODAY

There is really no such thing as *the* Internet today. The *concept* of "the Internet" is a valid one, and people still use the term all the time. But the Internet is no longer a thing to be charted and understood and controlled and administered. What we have is an interlocking grid of ISPs, an *ISP "grid-net,"* so to speak. Actually, the graph of the Internet is a bit less organized than this, although ISPs closer to the core have a higher level of interconnection than those at the edge. This is an interconnected mesh of ISPs and related Internet-connected entities such as government bureaus and learning institutions. Also, keep in mind that in addition to the "big-I internet," there are other internetworks that are not part of this global, public whole.

If we think of the Internet as a unity, and have no appreciation of actual ISP connectivity, then the role of routing protocols and routing policies on the Internet today cannot be understood. Today, Internet talk is peppered with terms like *peers*, *aggregates*, *summaries*, *Internet exchange points (IXPs)*, *backbones*, *border routers*, *edge routers*, and *points of presence (POPs)*. These terms don't make much sense in the context of the Internet as a unified network.

The Internet as the spaghetti bowl of connected ISPs is shown in Figure 13.2. There are large national ISPs, smaller regional ISPs, and even tiny local ISPs. There are also pieces of the Internet that act as exchange points for traffic, such as the Network Access Points NAPs and IXPs. IXPs can by housed in POPs, formal places dedicated for this purpose, and in various *collocation facilities*, where the organizations rent floor space for a rack of equipment ("broom closet") or larger floor space for more elaborate arrangements, such as redundant links and power supplies. The IXPs are often run by former telephone companies.

Each cloud, except the one at the top of the figure, basically represents an ISP's AS. Within these clouds, the routing protocol can be an IGP such as OSPF, because it is presumed that each and every network device (such as the backbone routers) in the cloud is controlled by the ISP. However, between the clouds, an EGP such as BGP must be used, because no ISP can or should be able to directly control a router in another ISP's network.

The ISPs are all chained together by a complex series of links with only a few hard and fast rules (although there are exceptions). As long as local rules are followed, as determined by contract, the smallest ISP can link to another ISP and thus give their users the ability to participate in the global public Internet. Increasingly, the nature of the linking between these ISPs is governed by a series of agreements known as *peering arrangements*. Peers are equals, and national ISPs may be peers to each other, but

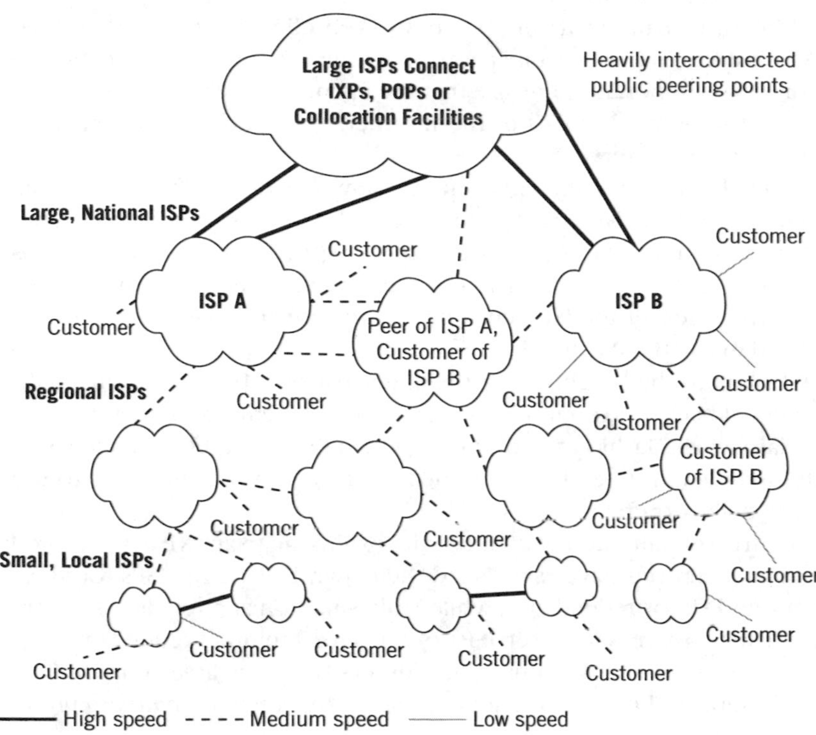

FIGURE 13.2

The haphazard way that ISPs are connected on today's Internet, showing IXPs at the top. Customers can be individuals, organizations, or other ISPs.

treat smaller ISPs as just another customer, although it's not all that unusual for small regional ISPs to peer with each other.

Peering arrangements detail the reciprocal way that traffic is handed off from one ISP (and that means AS) to another. Peers might agree to deliver each other's packets for no charge, but bill non-peer ISPs for this privilege, because it is assumed that the national ISP's backbone will be shuttling a large number of the smaller ISPs' packets. But the national ISP won't be using the small ISP much. A few examples of national ISPs, peer ISPs, and customer ISPs are shown in the figure. This is just an example, and very large ISPs often have plenty of very small customers and some of those will be attached to more than one other ISP and employ high capacity links. There will also be "stub AS" networks with no downstream customers.

Millions of PCs and Unix systems act as clients, servers, or both on the Internet. These hosts are attached to LANs (typically) and linked by routers to the Internet. The LANs and "site routers" are just "customers" to the ISPs. Now, a customer of even moderate size could have a topology similar to that of an ISP with a distinct border, core, and aggregation or services routers. Although all attached hosts conform to the client-server architecture, many of them are strictly Web clients (browsers) or Web servers (Web sites), but the Web is only one part of the Internet (although probably the most important one). It is important to realize that the clients and servers are on LANs, and that routers are the network nodes of the Internet. The number of client hosts greatly exceeds the number of servers.

The link from the client user to the ISP is often a simple cable or DSL link. In contrast, the link from a server LAN's router to the ISP could be a leased, private line, but there are important exceptions to this (Metro Ethernet at speeds greater than 10 Mbps is very popular). There are also a variety of Web servers within the ISP's own network. For example, the Web server for the ISP's customers to create and maintain their own Web pages is located inside the ISP cloud.

The smaller ISPs link to the backbones of the larger, national ISPs. Some small ISPs link directly to national backbones, but others are forced for technical or financial reasons to link in a "daisy-chain" fashion to other ISPs, which link to other ISPs, and so on until an ISP with direct access to an IXP is reached. Peering bypasses the need to use the IXP structure to deliver traffic.

Many other countries obtain Internet connectivity by linking to an IXP in the United States, although many countries have established their own IXPs. Large ISPs routinely link to more than one IXP for redundancy, while truly small ones rarely link to more than one other ISP for cost reasons. Peer ISPs often have multiple, redundant links between their border routers. (Border routers are routers that have links to more than one AS.) For a good listing of the world's major IXPs, see *http://en.wikipedia.org* under Internet Exchange Point.

Speeds vary greatly in different parts of the Internet. Client access by way of low-speed dial-up telephone lines is typically 33.6 to 56 kbps. Servers are connected by Metro Ethernet or by medium-speed private leased lines, typically 1.5 Mbps. The high-speed backbone links between national ISPs run at yet higher speeds, and between the IXPs themselves, speeds of 155 Mbps (known as OC-3c), 622 Mbps (OC-12c), 2.4 Gbps (OC-48c), and 10 Gbps (OC-192c) can be used, although "$n \times 10$" Gbps Ethernet trunks are less expensive. Higher speeds are always needed, both to minimize large Web site content-transfer latency times (like video and audio files) and because the backbones concentrate and aggregate traffic from millions of clients and servers onto a single network.

THE ROLE OF ROUTING POLICIES

Today, it is impossible for all routers to know all details of the Internet. The Internet now consists of an increasing number of *routing domains*. Each routing domain has its own internal and external routing policies. The sizes of routing domains vary greatly, from only one IP address space to thousands, and each domain is an AS. Many ISPs have only one AS, but national or global ISPs might have several AS numbers. A global ISP might have one AS for North America, another for Europe, and one for the rest of the world. Each AS has a uniquely assigned AS number, although there can be various, logical "sub-ASs" called *confederations* or *subconfederations* (both terms are used) inside a single AS.

We will not have a lot to say about routing policies, as this is a vast and complex topic. But some basics are necessary when the operation of routers on the network is considered in more detail.

An AS forms a group of IP networks sharing a unified *routing policy framework*. A routing policy framework is a series of guidelines (or hard rules) used by the ISP to formulate the actual routing policies that are configured on the routers. Among different ASs, which are often administered by different ISPs, things are more complex. Careful coordination of routing policies is needed to communicate complicated policies among ASs.

Why? Because some router somewhere must know all the details of all the IPv4 or IPv6 addresses used in the routing domain. These routes can be aggregated (or summarized) as shorter and shorter prefixes for advertisement to other routers, but some routers must retain all the details.

Routes, or prefixes, not only need to be advertised to another AS, but need to be accepted. The decision on which routes to advertise and which routes to accept is determined by routing policy. The situation is summarized in the extremely simple exchange of routing information between two peer ASs shown in Figure 13.3. (Note that the labels "AS #1" and "AS #2" are not saying "this is AS1" or "this is AS2"—AS numbers are reserved and assigned centrally.) The routing information is transferred by the routing protocol running between the routers, usually the Border Gateway Protocol (BGP).

The exchange of routing information is typically bidirectional, but not always. In some cases, the routing policy might completely suppress or ignore the flow of routing information in one direction because of the routing policy of the sender (suppress the advertising of a route or routes) or the receiver (ignore the routing information from the sender). If routing information is not sent or accepted between ASs, then clients or servers in one AS cannot reach other hosts on the networks represented by that routing information in the other AS.

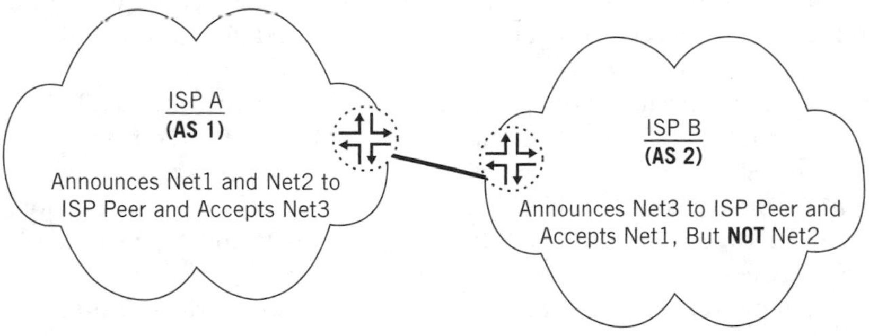

FIGURE 13.3

A simple example of a routing policy, showing how routes are announced (sent) and accepted (received). ISP A and ISP B are peers.

Economic considerations often play a role in routing policies as well. In the old days, there were always subsidies and grants available for continued support for the research and educational network. Now the ISP grid-net has ISPs with their own customers, and they can also be customers of other ISPs as well. Who pays whom, and how much?

PEERING

Telephony faced the same problem and solved it with a concept called *settlements*. This is where one telephone company bills the call originator and shares a portion of the billed amount with other telephone companies as an *access charge*. Access charges compensate the other telephone companies, long distance and local, that carry the call for the loss of the use of their own facilities (which could otherwise make money for the company directly) for the duration of the call. Now, in the IP world the source and destination share the cost of delivering packets, but the point is that telephony solved a similar issue and the terminology has been borrowed by the ISPs, which are often telephone companies as well.

The issue on the Internet becomes one of how one ISP should compensate another ISP for delivering packets that originate on the other ISP (if at all). The issue is complicated because the "call" is now a stream of packets, and an ISP might just be a transit ISP for packets that originate in one ISP's AS and are destined for a third ISP's AS.

ISP peers have tried three ways to translate this telephony "settlements" model to the Internet. First, there are very popular bilateral (between two sides) settlements based on the "call," usually defined as some aspect of IP packet flows. In this settlement arrangement, the first ISP, where the packet originates at a client, gets all of the revenue from the customer. However, the first ISP shares some of this money with the other ISP (where the server is located). Second, there is the idea of *sender keeps all* (SKA), where the flow of packets from client to server one way is supposedly balanced by the flow of packets from client to server the other way. So each ISP might as well just keep all of the revenue from their customers. Finally, there are *transit fees*, which are just settlements between one ISP and another, usually paid by a smaller ISP to a larger (because this traffic flow is seldom symmetrical).

Unfortunately, none of these methods have worked out well on the Internet. TCP/IP is not telephony and routers are not telephone switches. There are often many more than just two or three ISPs involved between client and server. There is no easy way to track and account for the packets that should constitute a "call," and even TCP sessions leave a lot to be desired because a simple Web page load might involve many rapid TCP connections between client and server. It is often hard to determine the "origin" because a packet and packets do not always follow stable network paths. Packets are often dropped, and it seems unfair to bill the originating ISP for resent packets replacing those that were not delivered by the billing ISP in the first place. Finally, dynamic routing might not be symmetric: So-called "hot potato" routing seeks to pass packets off to another ISP as soon as possible. So the path from client to server often passes through different ISPs rather than keeping requests and replies all on one ISP's network. This common practice has real consequences for QoS enforcement.

These drawbacks of the telephony settlements model resulted in a movement to more simplistic arrangements among ISP *peers*, which usually means ISPs of roughly equal size. These are often called *peering arrangements* or just *peering*. There is no strict definition of what a peer is or is not, but it often describes two ISPs that are directly connected and have instituted some routing policies between them. In addition, there is nearly endless variation in settlement arrangements. These are just some of the broad categories. The key is that any traffic that a small network can offload onto a peer costs less than traffic that stays on internal transit links.

Economically, there is often also a sender-keeps-all arrangement in place, and no money changes hands. An ISP that is not a peer is just another *customer* of the ISP, and customers pay for services rendered. An interesting and common situation arises when three peers share a "transit peer" member. This situation is shown in Figure 13.4. There are typically no financial arrangements for peer ISPs providing transit services to the third peer, so peer ISPs will not provide transit to a third peer ISP (unless, of course, the third peer ISP is willing to pay and become a customer of one of the other ISPs).

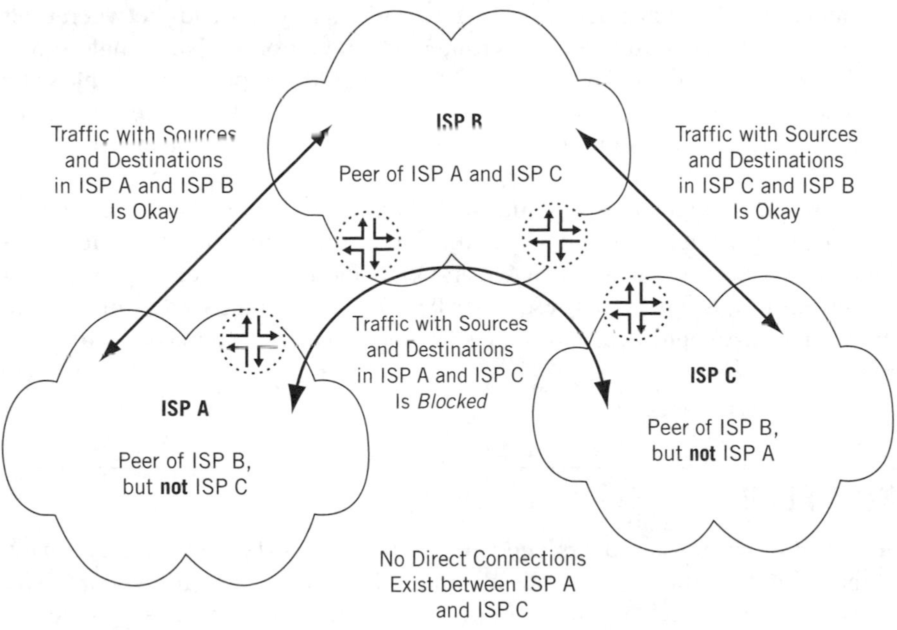

FIGURE 13.4

ISPs do not provide free transit services, and generally are either peers or customers of other ISPs. Unless "arrangements" are made, ISP B will routinely block transit traffic between ISP A and ISP C.

All three of these ISPs are "peers" in the sense that they are roughly equal in terms of network resources. They could all be small or regional or national ISPs. ISP A peers with ISP B and ISP B peers with ISP C, but ISP A has no peering arrangement (or direct link) with ISP C. So packet deliveries from hosts in ISP A to ISP B (and back) are allowed, as are packet deliveries from hosts in ISP C to and from ISP B. But ISP B has routing policies in place to prevent transit traffic from ISP A to and from ISP C through ISP B. How would that be of any benefit to ISP B? Unless ISP A and ISP C are willing to peer with each other, or ISP A or ISP C is willing to become a customer of ISP B, there will be no routing information sent to ISP A or ISP C to allow these ISPs to reach each other through ISP B. The routing policies enforced on the routers in ISP B will make sure of this, telling ISP A (for example) "you can't get to ISP C's hosts through me!"

The real world of the Internet, without a clearly defined hierarchy, complicates peering drastically. Peering is often a political issue. The politics of peering began in 1997, when a large ISP informed about 15 other ISPs that its current, easy-going peering arrangements would be terminated. New agreements for transit traffic were now required, the ISP said, and the former peers were effectively transformed into customers. As the trend spread among the larger ISPs, direct connections were favored over public peering points such as the IXPs.

This is one reason that Ace ISP and Best ISP in Figure 13.1 at the beginning of the chapter maintain multiple links between the four routers in the "quad" between their border routers. Suppose for a moment that routers P2 and P4 only have a single, direct link between them to connect the two ISPs. What would happen if that link were down? Well, at first glance, the situation doesn't seem very drastic. Both have links to "the Internet," which we know now is just a collection of other ISPs just like Ace and Best.

Can LAN1 reach LAN2 through "the Internet"? Maybe. It all depends on the arrangements between our two ISPs and the ISPs at the end of the "Internet" links. These ISPs might not deliver transit traffic between Ace and Best, and may even demand payment for these packets as "customers" of these other ISPs. The best thing for Ace and Best to do—if they don't have multiple backup links in their "quad"—is to make more peers of other ISPs.

PICKING A PEER

All larger ISPs often want to be peers, and peers of the biggest ISPs around. (For many, buying transit and becoming a customer of some other ISP is a much less expensive and effective way to get access to the global public Internet if being a transit provider is not your core business.) When it comes to peering, bigger is better, so a series of mergers and acquisitions (it is often claimed that there are no mergers, only acquisitions) among the ISPs took place as each ISP sought to become a "bigger peer" than another. This consolidation decreased the number of huge ISPs and also reduced the number of potential peers considerably.

Potential partners for peering arrangements are usually closely examined in several areas. ISPs being considered for potential peering must have high capacity backbones, be of roughly the same size, cover key areas, have a good network operations center (NOC), have about the same quality of service (QoS) in terms of delay and dropped packets, and (most importantly), exchange traffic roughly symmetrically. Nobody wants their routers, the workhorse of the ISP, to peer with an ISP that supplies 10,000 packets for every 1000 packets it accepts. Servers, especially Web sites, tend to generate much more traffic than they consume, so ISPs with "tight" networks with many server farms or Web hosting sites often have a hard time peering with anyone. On the other hand, ISPs with many casual, intermittent client users are courted by many peering suitors. Even if match is not quite the same in size, if the traffic flows are symmetrical, peering is always possible. The peering situation is often as shown in Figure 13.5. Keep in mind that other types of networks (such as cable TV operators and DSL providers) have different peering goals than presented here.

Without peering arrangements in place, ISPs rely on public exchange and peering points like the IXPs for connectivity. The trend is toward more private peering between pairs of peer ISPs.

Private peering can be accomplished by installing a WAN link between the AS border routers of the two ISPs. Alternatively, peering can be done at a collocation site where the two peers' routers basically sit side by side. Both types of private peering are common.

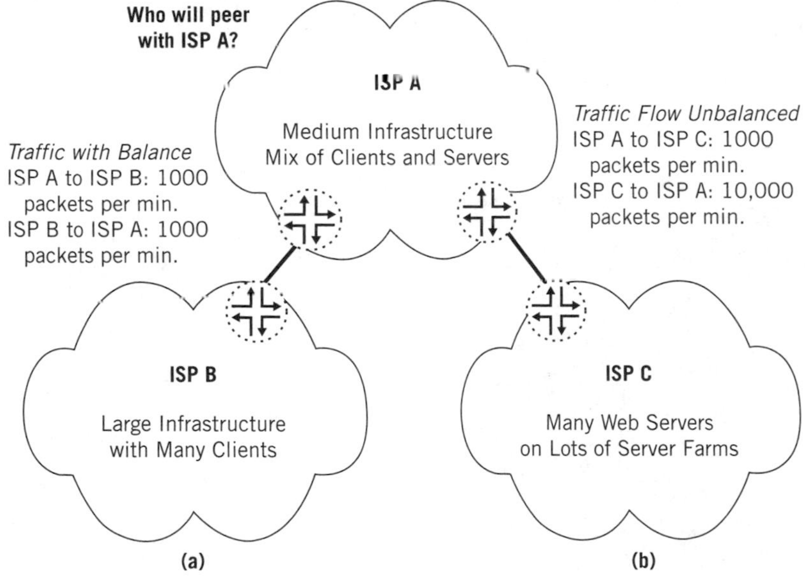

FIGURE 13.5

Good and bad peering candidates. Note that the goal is to balance the traffic flow as much as possible. Generally, the more servers the ISP maintains, the harder it is to peer. (a) ISP A will propose peering to ISP B; (b) ISP A will not want to peer with ISP C but will take them on as a customer.

The Internet today has more routes than there were *computers* attached to the Internet in early 1989. Routing policies are necessary whether the peering relationship is public or private (through an IXP or through a WAN link between border routers). Routing information simply cannot be easily distributed everywhere all at once. Even the routing protocols play a role. Some routing protocols send much more information than others, although protocols can be "tuned" by adjusting parameters and with routing policies.

Routing policies help interior gateway protocols (IGPs) such as OSPF and IS–IS distribute routing information within an AS more efficiently. The flow of routing information between routing domains must be controlled by routing policies to enforce the public or private peering arrangements in place between ISPs.

In the next chapter, we'll see how an IGP works within an AS or routing domain.

QUESTIONS FOR READERS

Figure 13.6 shows some of the concepts discussed in this chapter and can be used to help you answer the following questions.

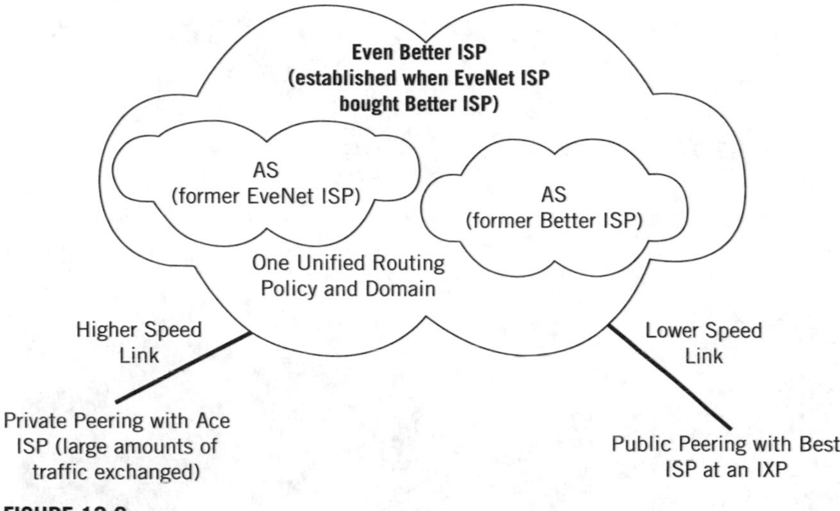

FIGURE 13.6

Even Better ISP, showing peering arrangements and routing domains.

1. What is an Internet autonomous system (AS)?
2. Why might a single ISP like Even Better ISP have more than one routing domain?
3. What is the purpose of a routing policy?
4. What does "ISP peering" mean?
5. What is the difference between public and private peering? Are both necessary?

CHAPTER

IGPs: RIP, OSPF, and IS–IS

14

What You Will Learn

In this chapter, you will learn about the role of IGPs and how these routing protocols are used in a routing domain or autonomous system (AS). We'll use OSPF and RIP, but mention IS–IS as well.

You will learn how a routing policy can distribute the information gathered from one routing protocol into another, where it can be used to build routing and forwarding tables, or *announced* (sent) to other routers. We'll create a routing policy to announce our IPv6 routes to the other routers.

As is true of many chapters in this book, this chapter's content is more than enough for a whole book by itself. Only the basics of IGPs are covered here, but they are enough to illustrate the function of an internal routing protocol on our network.

In this chapter, we'll configure an IGP to run on the Juniper Networks routers that make up the Illustrated Network. In Chapter 9 we saw output that showed OSPF running on router CE6 as part of Best ISP's AS. So first we'll show how OSPF was configured on the routers in AS 65127 and AS 65459. We could configure IS–IS on the other AS, but that would make an already long chapter even longer. Because we closed the last chapter with IPv6 ping messages not working, let's configure RIPng, the version of RIP that is for IPv6. This is not an endorsement of RIPng, especially given other available choices. It's just an example.

Why not add OSPFv3 (the version of OSPF used with IPv6) for IPv6 support? We certainly could, but suppose the smaller site routers only supported RIP or RIPng? (RIP is usually bundled with basic software, but other IGPs often have to be purchased.) Then we would have no choice but to run RIPng to distribute the IPv6 addresses. If we configure RIPng to run on the ASs between on-site routers CE0 and CE6, we can always extend RIPng support right to the Unix hosts (the IPv6 hosts just need to point to CE0 or CE6 as their default routers).

In this chapter, we'll use the routers heavily, as shown in Figure 14.1.

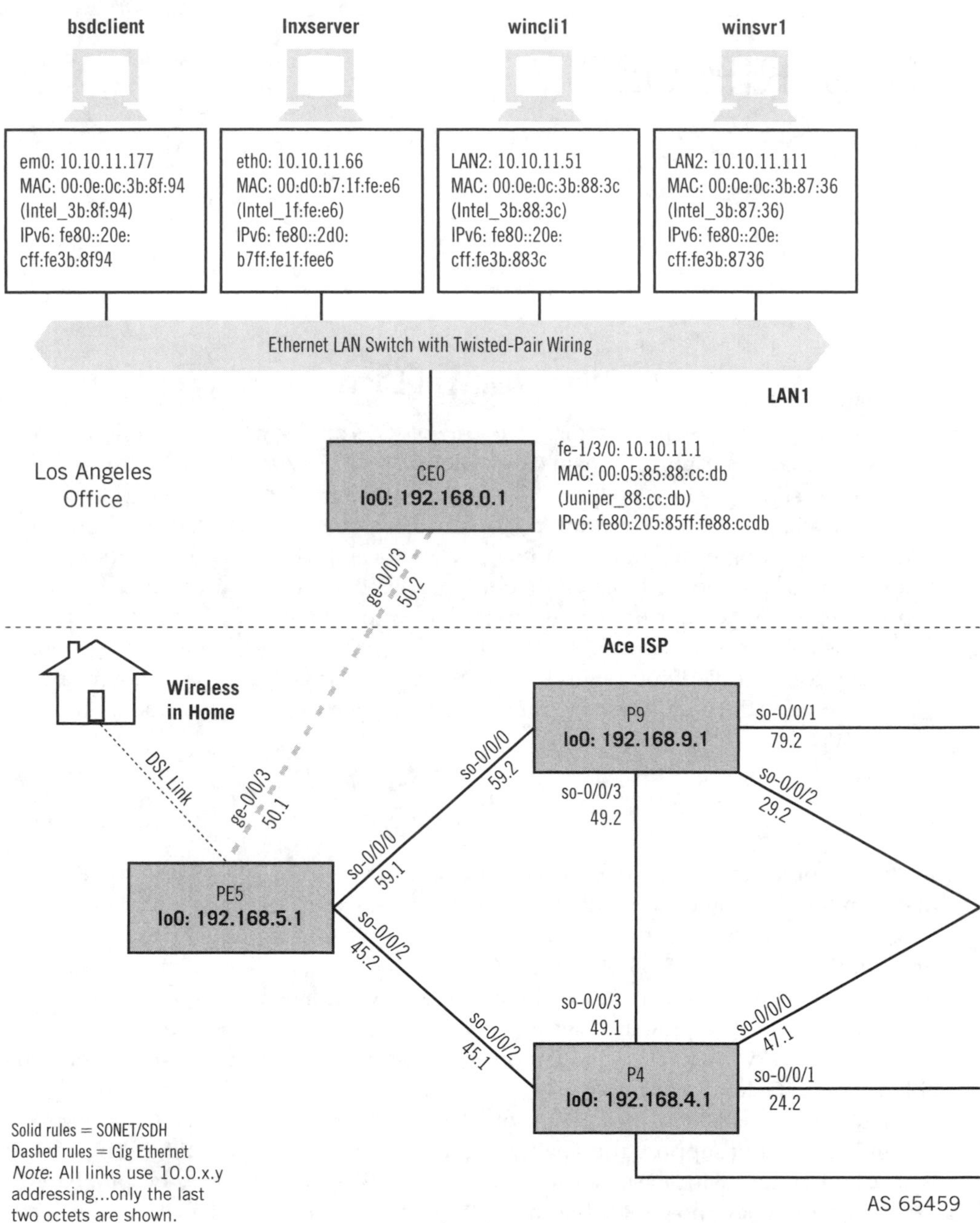

FIGURE 14.1

The routers on the Illustrated Network, showing routers on which OSPF and RIPng will be running. The IGPs will not be running between the two AS routing domains; instead, an EGP will run.

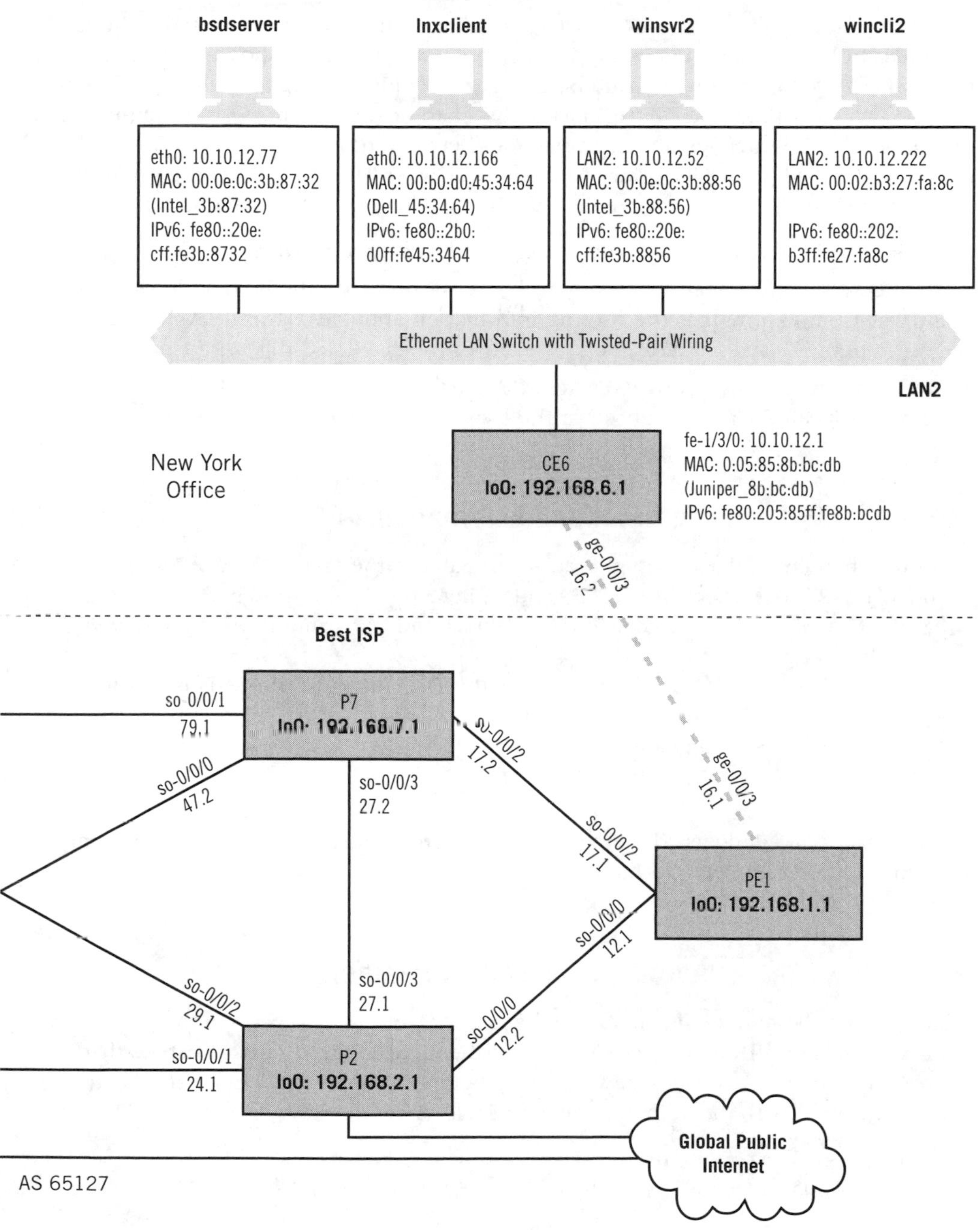
bsdserver
lnxclient
winsvr2
wincli2
eth0: 10.10.12.77
MAC: 00:0e:0c:3b:87:32
(Intel_3b:87:32)
IPv6: fe80::20e:
cff:fe3b:8732
eth0: 10.10.12.166
MAC: 00:b0:d0:45:34:64
(Dell_45:34:64)
IPv6: fe80::2b0:
d0ff:fe45:3464
LAN2: 10.10.12.52
MAC: 00:0e:0c:3b:88:56
(Intel_3b:88:56)
IPv6: fe80::20e:
cff:fe3b:8856
LAN2: 10.10.12.222
MAC: 00:02:b3:27:fa:8c
IPv6: fe80::202:
b3ff:fe27:fa8c
Ethernet LAN Switch with Twisted-Pair Wiring
LAN2
New York
Office
CE6
lo0: 192.168.6.1
fe-1/3/0: 10.10.12.1
MAC: 0:05:85:8b:bc:db
(Juniper_8b:bc:db)
IPv6: fe80:205:85ff:fe8b:bcdb
ge-0/0/3
16.2
Best ISP
so 0/0/1
79.1
P7
lo0: 192.168.7.1
so-0/0/2
17.2
so-0/0/0
47.2
so-0/0/3
27.2
ge-0/0/3
16.1
so-0/0/2
17.1
PE1
lo0: 192.168.1.1
so-0/0/0
12.1
so-0/0/3
27.1
so-0/0/2
29.1
so-0/0/1
24.1
P2
lo0: 192.168.2.1
so-0/0/0
12.2
Global Public
Internet
AS 65127

Unfortunately, when it comes to networks, a lot of things are interrelated, although we'd like to learn them sequentially. For example, we've already shown in Chapter 9 that OSPF is configured on the routers, although we didn't configure it. Also, although both ASs will run the same IGP (RIPng) in this chapter, the ASs are *not* running RIPng or any other IGP in between (e.g., on the links between routers P9 and P7). That's the job of the EGP, which we'll explore in the next chapter. There is a lot going on in this chapter, so let's list the topics covered here (and in Chapter 15), so we don't get lost.

1. We'll talk about ASs and the role of IGP and EGPs on a network.
2. We'll configure RIPng as the IGP in both ASs, starting with the IPv6 address on the interfaces and show that the routing information about LAN1 and LAN2 ends up everywhere. We will not talk about the role of the EGP in all this until Chapter 15.
3. We'll compare three major IGPs: RIP, OSPF, and IS–IS. In the OSPF section, we'll show how OSPF was configured in the two ASs for Chapter 9.

Internal and External Links

In this chapter, we'll add RIPng as an IGP on all but the links between AS 65459 and AS 65127. This affects routers P9 and P4 in AS 65459 and routers P7 and P2 in AS 65127. IGPs run on internal (*intra*-AS) links, and EGPs run on external (*inter*-AS) links.

In Chapter 15, we'll configure BGP as the EGP on those links. This chapter assumes that BGP is up and running properly on the external links between P9 and P4 in AS 65459 and P7 and P2 in AS 65127.

We'll use our Windows XP clients for this exercise, just to show that the "home version" of XP is completely comfortable with IPv6.

Autonomous System Numbers

Ace and Best ISP on the Illustrated Network use AS numbers (ASNs) in the private range, just as our IP addresses. IANA parcels them out to the various registries that assign them as needed to those who apply. Before 2007, AS numbers were 2-byte (16-bit) values with the following ranges of relevance:

- **0:** Reserved (can be used to identify nonrouted networks)
- **1–43007:** Allocated by ARIN, APNIC, AfriNIC, and RIPE NCC
- **43008–48127:** Held by IANA
- **48128–64511:** Reserved by IANA
- **64512–65534:** Designated by IANA for private use
- **65535:** Reserved

Since 2007, ASNs are allocated as 4-byte values. Because each field can run from 0 to 65535, the current way of designating ASNs is as two numbers in the form *nnnnn.nnnnnn*. The full range of ASNs now is from 0.0 to 65535.65535 (0 to 4,294,967,295 in decimal).

For example, 0.65525 is how the former 2-byte ASN 65535 would be written today. In this book, we'll drop the leading "0," and just use the "legacy" 2-byte AS format for Ace and Best ISP: 65459 and 65127.

Now, let's see what it takes to get RIPng up and running on these routers. So far, the link-local fe80 addresses have been fine for running ping and for neighbor discovery from router to host, but these won't be useful for LAN1 to LAN2 communications with IPv6. For this, we'll use routable `fc00` private ULA IPv6 addresses. Once we get RIPng up and running with routable addresses on our hosts and routers, we should be able to successfully ping from LAN1 to LAN2 using only IPv6 addresses. While we'll be configuring IGPs on both Ace and Best ISP's AS routing domains, we *won't* be running IGPs between them. That's the job of the EGP (Border Gateway Protocol, or BGP), and we'll add that in Chapter 15.

We need to create four routable IPv6 addresses and prefixes—two for the hosts and two for the router's LAN interfaces (both are `fe-1/3/0`). We've already done this in Chapter 4. The site IPv6 addresses, and the IPv4 and MAC addresses used on the same interfaces, are shown in Table 14.1. We don't need to change the link-local addresses on the link between the routers because, well, they are link-local.

We know from Chapter 13 that we have these IPv6 addresses configured on `wincli1` and `wincli2`. We have to do three things to enable RIPng on the routers:

- Configure routable addresses on interface `fe-1/3/0`
- Configure the RIPng protocol to run on the site (customer-edge) routers (CE0 and CE6), the provider-edge routers (PE5 and PE1), and the internal links on the provider-backbone routers (P9, P7, P4, and P2).
- Create and apply a routing policy on CE0 and CE6 to advertise the `fe-1/3/0` IPv6 addresses with RIPng.

Table 14.1 Routable IPv6 Addresses Used on the Network

System	IPv4 Network Address	MAC Address	IPv6 Address
wincli1	10.10.11/24	02:0e:0c:3b:88:3c	fc00:ffb3:d5:b:20e:cff:fe3b:883c
CE0 (fe-1/3/0)	10.10.11/24	00:05:85:88:cc:db	fc00:ffb3:d5:b:205:85ff:fe88:ccdb
CE6 (fe-1/3/0)	10.10.12/24	00:05:85:8b:bc:db	fc00:fe67:d4:c:205:85ff:fe8b:bcdb
Wincli2	10.10.12/24	00:02:b3:27:fa:8c	fc00:fe67:d4:c:202:b3ff:fe27:fa8c

The configurations are completely symmetrical, so one of each type will do for illustration purposes. Let's use router CE0 as the customer-edge router. First, the addresses for IPv4 (`family inet`) and IPv6 (`family net6`) must be configured on LAN interface `fe-1/3/0`.

```
set interfaces fe-1/3/0 unit 0 family inet address 10.10.11.1/24
set interfaces fe-1/3/0 unit 0 family inet6 address fe80::205:85ff:fe88:ccdb/64
set interfaces fe-1/3/0 unit 0 family inet6 address fc00:fe67:d4:c:205:85ff:fe88:
    ccdb/64
```

Note that the link-local address is fine as is. We usually have many addresses on an interface in most IPv6 implementations, including multicast. We just added the second address to it. Now we can configure RIPng itself on the link between CE0 and PE5. We have to explicitly tell RIPng to announce (export) the routing information specified in the `send-ipv6` routing policy (which we'll write shortly) and tell it the RIPng "neighbor" (routing protocol partner) is found on interface `ge-0/0/3` logical unit 0.

```
set protocols ripng group ripv6group export send-ipv6
set protocols ripng group ripv6group neighbor ge-0/0/3.0
```

Because RIPv2 and RIPng use multicast addresses, we specify the router's neighbor location with the *physical* address information (`ge-0/0/3`) instead of unicast address. And because Juniper Network's implementation of RIP always listens for routing information but never advertises or announces routes unless told, we'll have to write a routing policy to "export" the IPv6 addresses we want into RIPng. There's only one interface needed in this case, `fe-1/3/0.0` to LAN1. It seems odd to say `from` when sending, but in a Juniper Networks routing policy, `from` really means "out of"—"Out of all the interfaces, this applies to interface `fe-1/3/0`."

```
set policy-options policy-statement send-ipv6 from interface fe-1/3/0.0
set policy-options policy-statement send-ipv6 from family inet6
set policy-options policy-statement send-ipv6 then accept
```

All this routing policy says is that "if the routing protocol (which is RIPng) running on the LAN1 interface (`fe-1/3/0`) wants to advertise an IPv6 route (from family inet6), let it (accept)."

We also have to configure RIPng on the other routers. We know that we can't run RIPng on the external links on the border routers (P7, P9, P2, and P4), but we can show the full configurations on PE5 and PE1. These routers have to run RIPng on *three* interfaces, not just one, so that RIPng routing information flows from site router to backbone (and from backbone to site router). Let's look at PE5 (PE1 is about the same).

```
set interfaces fe-1/3/0 unit 0 family inet address 10.10.50.1/24
set interfaces fe-1/3/0 unit 0 family inet6 address fe80::205:85ff:fe85:aafe/64
set interfaces fe-1/3/0 unit 0 family inet6 address fc00:fe67:d4:c:205:85ff:fe85:
    aafe/64
```

We have IPv6 addresses on the SONET links to P9 and P4, so-0/0/0 and so-0/0/2, but the details are not important. What is important is that we run RIPng on all three interfaces.

```
set protocols ripng group ripv6group export send-ipv6
set protocols ripng group ripv6group neighbor ge-0/0/3.0
set protocols ripng group ripv6group neighbor so-0/0/0.0
set protocols ripng group ripv6group neighbor so-0/0/2.0
```

The routing policy now will export the interface IPv6 addresses we want into RIPng. This policy has one *term* for each interface and is more complex than the one for the site routers.

```
set policy-options policy-statement send-ipv6 term A from interface ge-0/0/3.0
set policy-options policy-statement send-ipv6 term A from family inet6
set policy-options policy-statement send-ipv6 term A then accept
set policy-options policy-statement send-ipv6 term B from interface so-0/0/0.0
set policy-options policy-statement send-ipv6 term B from family inet6
set policy-options policy-statement send-ipv6 term B then accept
set policy-options policy-statement send-ipv6 term C from interface so-0/0/2.0
set policy-options policy-statement send-ipv6 term C from family inet6
set policy-options policy-statement send-ipv6 term C then accept
```

The policy simply means this: "Out of all interfaces, look at ge-0/0/3, so-0/0/0, and so-0/0/2. If the routing protocol running on those links (which is RIPng) wants to advertise an IPv6 route (from family inet6), let it (accept)."

The backbone routers run RIPng on their internal interfaces, but the configurations and policies are very similar to those on the provider-edge routers. We don't need to list those.

When all the configurations are committed and made active on the routers, we form an *adjacency* and exchange IPv6 routing information with each neighbor according to the policy. The IPv6 routing table on CE0 now shows the prefix of LAN2 (fc00:fe67:d4:c::/64) learned from CE6 with RIPng.

```
admin@CE0# show route table inet6 fc00:fe67:d4:c::/64

inet6.0: 38 destinations, 38 routes (38 active, 0 holddown, 0 hidden)
+ = Active Route, - = Last Active, * = Both

fc00:ffbe:d5:b::/64 *[RIPng/100] 01:15:19, metric 6, tag 0
                to fc00:ffbe:d5:b::a00:3b01 via so-0/0/0.0
                > to fc00:ffbe:d5:b::a00:2d01 via so-0/0/2.0
```

What does all this mean? We've learned this route with RIPng, and its *preference* is 100 (high compared to local interfaces, which are 0). When routes are learned in different ways from different protocols, the route with the *lowest* preference will be the active route. The metric of 6 (hops) essentially shows that LAN2 is 6 routers away from LAN1. If there are different paths with different metrics through a collection of routers, the hop to the path with the lowest metric becomes the active route. More advanced routing protocols can compute metrics on the basis of much more than simply number of routers (hops).

Note the right angle bracket (>) to the left of the `so-0/0/2.0` link to router P9. Remember, there are *two* ways for PE5 to forward packets to LAN2: through router P4 at the end of link `so-0/0/0.0` and through router P9 at the end of link `so-0/0/0.0`. The > indicates that packets are being forwarded to router P9. (Usually, all other things being equal, a router chooses the link with the lower IP address.) However, the other link is available if the active link or router fails. (If we want to forward packets out *both* links, we can turn on *load balancing* and the links will be used in a round-robin fashion.)

But even with RIPng up and running among the routers, we still have to give non-link-local addresses to the hosts. Right now, if we try to use `ping6` on LAN2 to ping a different IPv6 private address on LAN1, we'll still get an error condition. Let's try it from `wincli2` on LAN2 to `wincl1` on LAN1.

```
C:\Documents and Settings\Owner>ping6 fe80::20c:cff:fe3b:883c

Pinging fe80::20c:cff:fe3b:883c with 32 bytes of data:

No route to destination.
  Specify correct scope-id or use -s to specify source address.
No route to destination.
  Specify correct scope-id or use -s to specify source address.
No route to destination.
  Specify correct scope-id or use -s to specify source address.
No route to destination.
  Specify correct scope-id or use -s to specify source address.

Ping statistics for fe80::20c:cff:fe3b:883c:
    Packets: Sent = 4, Received = 0, Lost = 4 (100% loss)
```

Like the routers, the Windows XP hosts need routable addresses. We assign an interface (by index shown by `ipconfig`) that is a routable IPv6 address with the `ipv6 adu` command. But the address is still shown with `ipconfig`.

```
C:\Documents and Settings\Owner>ipconfig

Ethernet adapter Local Area Connection:

        Connection-specific DNS Suffix  . :
        IP Address. . . . . . . . . . . . : 10.10.12.222
        Subnet Mask . . . . . . . . . . . : 255.255.255.0
```

```
IP Address . . . . . . . . . . . . : fc00:fe67:d5:c:202:b3ff:fe27:fa8c
IP Address . . . . . . . . . . . . : fe80::202:b3ff:fe27:fa8c%5
Default Gateway  . . . . . . . . . : 10.10.12.1
                                    fe80::5:85ff:fe8b:bcdb%5
                                    fc00:fe67:d5:c:205:85ff:fe8b:bcdb
```

How did the host know the default gateway to use for IPv6? We probed for neighbors earlier, but even if we had not, IPv6 router advertisement (which was configured with RIPng on the routers, and the main reason we did it) takes care of that.

Now we should be able to ping end to end from `wincli2` to `wincli1` by IPv6 address.

```
C:\Documents and Settings\Owner>ping6 fc00:ffb3:d4:b:20e:cff:fe3b:883c

Pinging fc00:ffb3:d.4:b:20e:cff:fe3b:883c
from fc00:fe67:d5:c:202:b3ff:fe27:fa8c with 32 bytes of data:

Reply from fc00:ffb3:d4:b:20e:cff:fe3b:883c: bytes=32 time<1ms
Reply from fc00:ffb3:d4:b:20e:cff:fe3b:883c: bytes=32 time<1ms
Reply from fc00:ffb3:d4:b:20e:cff:fe3b:883c: bytes=32 time<1ms
Reply from fc00:ffb3:d4:b:20e:cff:fe3b:883c: bytes=32 time<1ms

Ping statistics for fc00:ffb3:d4:b:20e:cff:fe3b:883c:
    Packets: Sent = 4, Received = 4, Lost = 0 (0% loss),
Approximate round trip times in milli-seconds:
    Minimum = 4ms, Maximum = 5ms, Average = 4ms
```

The reverse also works as well. In the rest of this chapter, let's take a closer look at how the IGPs perform their task of distributing routing information within an AS. Remember, how the IGP routing information gets from AS to AS with an EGP is the topic of Chapter 15.

INTERIOR ROUTING PROTOCOLS

Routers initially know only about their immediate environments. They know the IP addresses and prefixes configured on their local interfaces, and at most a little more statically defined information. Yet all routers must know all the details about everything in their routing domain to forward packets rationally, hop by hop, toward a given destination. So routers offer to and ask their *neighbor routers* (adjacent routers one hop away) about the routing information they know. Little by little, each router then builds up a detailed routing information database about the TCP/IP network.

How do routers exchange this routing information within a domain and between routing domains? With *routing protocols*. Within a routing domain, several different routing protocols can be used. Between routing domains on the Internet, another routing protocol is used. This chapter focuses on the routing protocols used *within* a routing domain and the next chapter covers the routing protocol used *between* routing domains.

Interior routing protocols, or IGPs, run between the routers inside a single routing domain, or autonomous system (AS). A large organization or ISP can have a single AS, but many global networks divide their networks into one or more ASs. IGPs run within these routing domains and do not share information learned across AS boundaries except physical interface addresses if necessary.

Modern routing protocols require minimal configuration of *static routes* (routes configured and maintained by hand). Today, *dynamic* routing protocols allow adjacent (directly connected) routers to exchange routing table information periodically to build up the topology of the router network as a whole by passing information received by adjacent neighbors on to other routers.

IGPs essentially "bootstrap" themselves into existence, and then send information about their IP addresses and interfaces to other routers directly attached to the source router. These neighbor, or adjacent, routers distribute this information to their neighbors until the network has *converged* and all routers have the identical information available.

When changes in the network as a result of failed links or routers cause the routing tables to become outdated, the routing tables differ from router to router and are inconsistent. This is when routing loops and black holes happen. The faster a routing protocol converges, the better the routing protocol is for large-scale deployment.

THE THREE MAJOR IGPs

There are three main IGPs for IPv4 routing: RIP, OSPF, and IS–IS. The Routing Information Protocol (RIP), often declared obsolete, is still used and remains a popular routing protocol for small networks. The newer version of RIP, known as RIPv2, should always be used for IPv4 routing today. Open Shortest Path First (OSPF) and Intermediate System–Intermediate System (IS–IS) are similar and much more robust than RIP. There are versions of all three for IPv6: OSPFv3, RIPng (sometimes seen as RIPv6), and IS–IS works with either IPv4 or IPv6 today.

RIP is a *distance-vector* routing protocol, and OSPF and IS–IS are *link-state* routing protocols. Distance-vector routing protocols are simple and make routing decisions based on one thing: How many routers (hops) are there between here and the destination? To RIP, link speeds do not matter, nor does congestion near another router. To RIP, the "best" route always has the fewest number of hops (routers).

Link-state protocols care more about the network than simply the number of routers along the path to the destination. They are much more complex than distance-vector routing protocols, and link-state protocols are much more suited for networks with many different link speeds, which is almost always the case today. However, link-state protocols require an elaborate database of information about the network on each router. This database includes not only the local router addressing and interfaces, but each and every router in the immediate area and often the entire AS.

ROUTING INFORMATION PROTOCOL

The RIP is still used on all types of TCP/IP networks. The basics of RIP were spelled out in RFC 1058 from 1988, but this is misleading. RIP was in use long before 1988, but no one bothered to document RIP in detail. RIP is bundled with almost all implementations of TCP/IP, so networks often run only RIP. Why pay for something when RIP was available for free?

RIP version 1 (RIPv1) in RFC 1058 has a number of annoying limitations, but RIP is so popular that doing away with RIP is not a realistic consideration. RFC 1388 introduced RIP version 2 (RIPv2 or sometimes RIP-2) in 1993. RIPv2 addressed RIPv1 limitations, but could not turn a distance-vector protocol into a link-state routing protocol such as OSPF and IS–IS.

RIPv2 is backward compatible with RIPv1, and most RIP implementations run RIPv2 by default and allow RIPv1 to be configured. In this chapter, the term "RIP" by itself means "a version of RIP runs RIPv2 by default but can also be configured as RIPv1 as required."

Router vendor Cisco was deeply dissatisfied with RIPv1 limitations and so created its own vendor-specific (proprietary) version of an IGP routing protocol, which Cisco called the Interior Gateway Routing Protocol (IGRP). IGRP improved upon RIPv1 in several ways, but "pure" IGRP could only run between Cisco routers. As good as IGRP was, IGRP was still basically implemented as a distance-vector protocol. As networks grew more and more complex in terms of link speeds and router capacities, it was possible to switch to a link-state protocol such as OSPF or IS–IS, but many network administrators at the time felt these new protocols were not stable or mature enough for production networks. Cisco then invented Enhanced IGRP (EIGRP) as a sort of "hybrid" routing protocol that combined features of both distance-vector and link-state routing protocols all in one (proprietary) package.

Due to the proprietary nature of IGRP and EIGRP, only the basics of these routing protocols are covered in this chapter.

Distance-Vector Routing

RIP and related distance-vector routing protocols are classified as "Bellman–Ford" routing protocols because they all choose the "best" path to a destination based on the *shortest path* computation algorithm. It was first described by R. E. Bellman in 1957 and applied to a distributed network of independent routers by L. R. Ford, Jr. and D. R. Fulkerson in 1962. Every version of Unix today bundles RIP with TCP/IP, usually as the *routed* ("route management daemon") process, but sometimes as the *gated* process.

All routing protocols use a *metric* (measure) representing the relative "cost" of sending a packet from the current router to the destination. The lowest relative cost is the "best" way to send a packet. Distance-vector routing protocols have only one metric: distance. The distance is usually expressed in terms of the number of routers between the router with the packet and the router attached to the destination network. The

Table 14.2 Example RIP Routing Table

Network	Next Hop Interface	Cost
10.0.14.0	Ethernet 1 (E1)	2
172.16.15.0	Serial 1 (S1)	1
192.168.44.0	Ethernet 2 (E2)	3
192.168.66.0	Serial 2 (S2)	INF (15)
192.168.78.0	Locally attached	0

distance metric is carried between routers running the same distance-vector routing protocol as a *vector*, a field in a routing protocol update packet.

A simple example of how distance-vector, or hop-count, routing works will illustrate many of the principles that all routing protocols simple and complex must deal with. All routing protocols must pass along network information received from adjacent routers to all other routers in a routing domain, a concept known as *flooding*. Flooding is the easiest way to ensure consistency of routing tables, but convergence time might be high as routers at one end of a chain of routers wait for information from routers at the far end of the chain to make its way through the routers in between. Flooding also tends to maximize the bandwidth consumed by the routing protocol itself, but there are ways to reduce this.

RIP floods updates every 30 seconds. Note that routing information takes at least 30 seconds to reach the *closest* neighbor if that is the routing update interval used. Long chains of routers can take quite a long time to converge (several minutes) when a network address is added or when a link fails.

When this network converges, each routing table will be consistent and each router will be reachable from every other router over one of the interfaces. The network topology has been "discovered" by the routing protocol. An example of the information in one of these tables is shown in Table 14.2.

Routers can have alternatives other than those shown in the table. For example, the cost to reach network `192.168.44.0` from this router could be the same (3) over E1 as it is over E2. The E1 interface is most likely in the table because the update from the neighbor router saying "send `192.168.44.0` packets here" arrived before the update from another router saying the same thing, or the entry was already in the table. When costs are equal, routing tables tend to keep what they know.

Broken Links

The distance-vector information has now been exchanged and the routers all have a way to reach each other. Usually, the routing protocol will update an internal database in the router just for that routing protocol and one or more entries based on the database are made in the routing table, which might contain information from other routing protocols as well. The routing table information is then used to compute the "best" routes to be used in the forwarding table (sometimes called the switching table) of the router. This chapter blurs the distinctions between routing protocol database, routing table, and forwarding table for the sake of simplicity and clarity.

What will happen to the network if a link "breaks" and can no longer be used to forward traffic? In a static routing world, this would be disastrous. But when using a dynamic routing protocol, even one as simple as a distance-vector routing protocol, the network should be able to converge around the new topology.

The routers at each end of the link, since they are locally connected to the interface (direct), will notice the outage first because routers constantly monitor the state of their interfaces at the physical level. Distance-vector protocols note this absent link by noting that the link now has an "infinite" cost. All routers formerly reachable through the link are now an infinite distance away.

Distance-Vector Consequences

In some cases, distance-vector updates are generated so closely in time by different routers that a link failure can cause a routing loop to occur, and packets can easily "bounce" back and forth between two adjacent routers until the packet TTL expires, even though the destination is reachable over another link. The "bouncing effect" will last until the network converges on the new topology.

However, this convergence can take some time, since routers not located at the end of a failed link have to gradually increase their costs to infinity one "hop" at a time. This is called "counting to infinity," and can drag out convergence time considerably if the value of "infinity" is set high enough. On the other hand, a low value of "infinity" will limit the maximum number of routers that can form the longest path through the network from source to destination.

In order to minimize the effects of bouncing and counting to infinity, most implementations of distance-vector routing protocols such as RIP also implement *split horizon* and *triggered updates*.

Split Horizon

If Router A is sending packets to Router B to reach Router E, then it makes no sense at all for Router B to try to reach Router E through Router A. All Router A will do is turn around and send the packet right back to Router B. So Router A should never advertise a way to reach Router E to Router B.

A more sophisticated form of split horizon is known as *split horizon with poison reverse*. Split horizon with poison reverse eliminates a lot of counting to infinity problems due to single link failures. However, many multiple link failures will still cause routing loops and counting to infinity problems even when split horizon with poison reverse is in use.

Triggered Updates

With triggered updates, a router running a distance-vector protocol such as RIP can remain silent if there are no changes to the information in the routing table. If a link failure is detected, triggered updates will send the new information. Triggered updates, like split horizon, will not eliminate all cases of routing loops and counting to infinity. However, triggered updates always help the counting process to reach infinity much faster.

RIPv1

A RIP packet must be 512 bytes or smaller, including the header. RIP packets have no implied sequence, and each update packet is processed independently by the router receiving the update. A router is only required to keep *one* entry associated with each route. But in practice, routers might keep up to four or more routes (next hops) to the same destination so that convergence time is lowered.

RIPv1 required routers running RIP to *broadcast* the entire contents of their routing tables at fixed intervals. On LANs, this meant that the RIPv1 packets were sent inside broadcast MAC frames. But broadcast MAC frames tell not only every router on the LAN, but every *host* on the LAN, "pay attention to this frame." Inside the frame, the host would find a RIPv1 update packet, and probably ignore the contents. But every 30 seconds, every host on the LAN had to interrupt its own application processing and start throwing away RIPv1 packets.

Each host *could* keep the information inside the RIPv1 update packet. Some hosts on LANs with RIPv1 routers have as elaborate a routing table as the routers themselves. Hackers loved RIPv1: With a few simple coding changes, any host could impersonate a RIPv1 router and start pumping out fake routing information, as many college and university network administrators discovered in the late 1980s. (This is one reason you don't run RIP on host interfaces.)

Many people see RIP updates vary from 30 seconds and assume that timers are off. In fact, table updates in RIP are initiated on each router at *approximate* 30-second intervals. Strict synchronization is avoided because RIP traffic spikes can easily lead to discarded RIP packets. The *update timer* usually adds or subtracts a small amount of time to the 30-second interval to avoid RIP router synchronization.

Network devices running RIP can be either *active* or *passive (silent)* mode. Active RIP devices will listen for RIP update packets and also generate their own RIP update packets. Passive RIP devices will only listen for RIP updates and never generate their own update packets. Many hosts, for example, which must process the broadcast RIP updates sent on a LAN, are purely passive RIP devices.

RIPv1 Limitations

RIPv1 had a number of limitations that made RIPv1 difficult to use in large networks. The larger the routing domain, the more severe and annoying the limitations of RIPv1 become.

Wasted Space—All of the RIPv1 packet fields are larger than they need to be, sometimes many times larger. There are almost three times as many 0 bits as information bits in a RIP packet.

Limited Metrics—As a network grows, the distance-vector might require a metric greater than 15, which is unreachable (infinite).

No Link Speed Allowances—The simple hop count metric will always result in packets being sent (as an example) over two hops using low-speed, 64-kbps links rather than three hops using SONET/SDH links.

No Authentication—RIPv1 devices will accept RIPv1 updates from any other device. Hackers love RIPv1 for this very reason, but even an innocently misconfigured router can disrupt an entire network using RIPv1.

Subnet Masks—RIPv1 requires the use of the same subnet mask because RIPv1 updates do not carry any subnet mask information.

Slow Convergence—Convergence can be very slow with RIPv1, often 5 minutes or more when links result in long chains of routers instead of neat meshes. And "circles" of RIPv1 routers maximize the risk of counting to infinity.

RIPv2

RIPv2 first emerged as an update to RIPv1 in RFC 1388 issued in January 1993. This initial RFC was superseded by RFC 1723 in November 1994. The only real difference between RFC 1388 and RFC 1723 is that RFC 1723 deleted a 2-byte Domain field from the RIPv2 packet format, designating this space as unused. No one was really sure how to use the Domain field anyway. The current RIPv2 RFC is RFC 2453 from November 1998.

RIPv2 was not intended as a replacement for RIPv1, but to extend the functions of RIPv1 and make RIP more suitable for VLSM. The RIP message format was changed as well to allow for authentication and multicasting.

In spite of the changes, RIPv2 is still RIP and suffers from many of the same limitations as RIPv1. Most router vendors support RIPv2 by default, but allow interfaces or whole routers to be configured for backward compatibility with RIPv1. RIPv2 made major improvements to RIPv1:

- Authentication between RIP routers
- Subnet masks to be sent along with routes
- Next hop IP addresses to be sent along with routes
- Multicasting of RIPv2 messages

The RIPv2 packet format is shown in Figure 14.2.

Command Field (1 byte)—This is the same as in RIPv1: A value of 1 is for a Request and a value of 2 is for a Response.

Version Number (1 byte)—RIPv1 uses a value of 1 in this field, and RIPv2 uses a value of 2.

1 byte	1 byte	1 byte	1 byte
Command	Version	Unused (set to all zeros)	
Address Family Identifier		Authentication or Route Tag	
IP Address			
Subnet Mask			
Next Hop			
Metric			
(Repeats multiple times,up to a maximum of 25)			
Address Family Identifier		Authentication or Route Tag	
IP Address			
Subnet Mask			
Next Hop			
Metric			

Route Entry

Route Entry

32 bits

FIGURE 14.2

RIPv2 packet format, showing how the subnet mask is included with the routing information advertised.

Unused (2 bytes)—Set to all zero bits. This was the Domain field in RFC 1388. Now officially unused in RFC 1723, this field is ignored by routers running RIPv2 (but this field must be set to all 0 bits for RIPv1 routers).

Address Family Identifier (AFI) (2 bytes)—This field is set to a value of 2 when IP packet and routing information is exchanged. RIPv2 also defined a value of 1 to ask the receiver to send a copy of its entire routing table. When set to all 1s (0xFFFF), the AFI field is used to indicate that the 16 bits following the AFI field, ordinarily set to 0 bits, now carry information about the type of authentication being used by RIPv2 routers.

Authentication or Route Tag (2 bytes)—When the AFI field is not 0xFFFF, this is the Route Tag field. The Route Tag field identifies *internal* and *external* routes in RIPv2. Internal routes are those learned by RIP itself, either locally or through other RIP routers. External routes are routes learned from another routing protocol such as OSPF or BGP.

IPv4 Address (4 bytes)—This field and the three that follow can be repeated up to 25 times in the RIPv2 Response packet. This field is almost the same as in

RIPv1. This address can be a host route, a network address, or a default route. A RIPv2 Request packet has the IP address of the originator in this field.

Subnet Mask (4 bytes)—This field, the biggest change in RIPv2, contains the subnet mask that goes with the IP address in the previous field. If the network address does not use a subnet mask different from the natural classful major network mask, then this field can be set to all zeroes, just as in RIPv1.

Next Hop (4 bytes)—This field contains the next hop IP address that traffic to this IP address space should use. This was a vast improvement over the "implied" next hop used in RIPv1.

Metric (4 bytes)—Unfortunately, the metric field is unchanged. The range is still 1 to 15, and a metric value of 16 is considered unreachable.

RIPv2 is still RIP. But RIPv2's additions for authentication, subnet masks, next hops, and the ability to multicast routing information increase the sophistication of RIP and have extended RIP's usefulness.

Authentication

Authentication was added in RIPv2. The Response messages contain the routing update information, and authenticating the responder to a Request message is a good way to minimize the risk of a routing table becoming corrupted either by accident or through hacker activities. However, there were really only 16 bits available for authentication, hardly adequate for modern authentication techniques. So the authentication actually takes the place of one routing table entry and authenticates the entire update message. This gives 16 bytes (128 bits) for authentication, which is not state of the art, but is better than nothing.

The really nice feature of RIPv2 authentication is that router vendors can add their own Authentication Type values and schemes to the basics of RIPv2, and many do. For example, Cisco and Juniper Networks routers can be configured to use MD5 (Message Digest 5) authentication encryption to RIPv2 messages. Thus, most routers can have three forms of authentication on RIP interfaces: none, simple password, or MD5. Naturally, the MD5 authentication keys used must match up on the routers.

Subnet Masks

The biggest improvement from RIPv1 to RIPv2 was the ability to carry the subnet mask along with the route itself. This allowed RIP to be used in classless IP environments with VLSM.

Next Hop Identification

Consider a network where there are several site routers with only one or a few small LANs. The small routers run RIPv2 between themselves and their ISP's router, but might run a higher speed link to one router and a lower speed link to another. The higher speed link might be more hops away than the lower speed link.

The next hop field in RIPv2 is used to "override" the ordinary metric method of deciding active routes in RIP. RIPv2 routers check the next hop field in the routing update message. If the next hop field is set for a particular route, the RIP router will use this as the next hop for the route, regardless of distance-vector considerations.

This RIPv2 next hop mechanism is sometimes called *source routing* in some documents. But true source routing information is always set by a host, not a router. This is just RIPv2 *next hop identification*.

Multicasting

Multicasting is a kind of "halfway" distribution method between unicast (one source to one destination) and broadcast (one source to all possible destinations). Unlike broadcasts that are received by all nodes on the subnet, only devices that *join* the RIPv2 multicast group will receive packets for RIPv2. (We'll talk more about multicast in Chapter 16.) RIPv2 multicasting also offers a way to filter out RIPv2 messages from a RIPv1 only router. This can be important, since RIPv2 messages look very much like RIPv1 messages. But RIPv2 messages are all *invalid* by RIPv1 standards. RIPv1 devices would either discard RIPv2 messages because the mandatory all-zero fields are not all zeroes, or accept the routes and ignore the additional RIPv2 information such as the subnet mask. RIPv2 multicasting makes sure that only RIPv2 devices see the RIPv2 information. So RIPv1 and RIPv2 routers can easily coexist on the same LAN, for instance. The multicast group used for RIPv2 routers is `224.0.0.9`.

RIPv2 is still limited in several ways. The 15 maximum-hop count is still there, as well as counting to infinity to resolve routing loops. And RIPv2 does nothing to improve on the fixed distance-vector values that are a feature of all versions of RIP.

RIPng for IPv6

The version of RIP used with IPv6 is called *RIPng*, where "ng" stands for "next generation." (IPv6 itself was often called IPng in the mid-1990s.) RIPng uses exactly the same hop count metric as RIP as well as the same logic and timers. So RIPng is still a distance-vector RIP, with two important differences.

1. The packet formats have been extended to carry the longer IPv6 addresses.
2. IPv6 security mechanisms are used instead of RIPv2 authentication.

The overall format of the RIP packet is the same as the format of the RIPv2 packet (but RIPng cannot be used by IPv4). There is a 32-bit header followed by a set of 20-byte route entries. The header fields must be the same as those used in RIPv2: There is a 1-byte Command code field, followed by a 1-byte Version field (now 6), and then 2 unused bytes of bits that must still be set to all 0 bits. However, the 20-byte router entry fields in RIPng are totally different that those in RIPv2.

IPv6 addresses are 16 bytes long, leaving only 4 bytes for any other information that must be associated with the IPv6 route. First, there is a 2-byte Route Tag field with the same use as in RIPv2: The Route Tag field identifies *internal* and *external* routes. Internal routes are those learned by RIP itself, either locally or through other RIP routers.

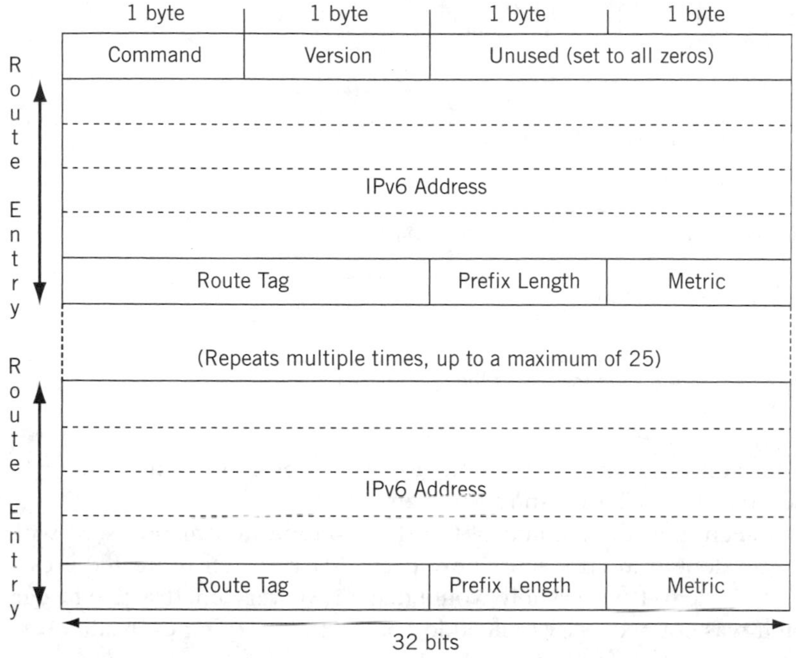

FIGURE 14.3

RIPng for IPv6 packet fields. Note the large address fields and different format than RIPv2 fields

External routes are routes learned from another routing protocol such as OSPF or BGP. Then there is a 1-byte Prefix Length field that tells the receiver where the boundary between network and host is in the IPv6 address. Finally, there is a 1-byte Metric field (this field was a full 32 bits in RIPv1 and RIPv2). Since infinity is still 16 in RIPng, this is not a problem.

The fields of the RIPng packet are shown in Figure 14.3. The combination of IPv6 address and Prefix Length do away with the need for the Subnet Mask field in RIPv2 packets. The Address Format Identifier (AFI) field from RIPv2 is not needed in RIPng, since only IPv6 routing information can be carried in RIPng.

But IPv6 still needs a Next Hop field. This RIPv2 field contained the next-hop IP address that traffic to this IP address space should use, and was a vast improvement over the "implied" next hop used in RIPv1. Now, IPv6 does not always need this Next Hop information, but in many cases the next hop should be included in an IPv6 routing information update. An IPv6 Next Hop needs another 128 bits (16 bytes). The creators of RIPng decided to essentially reproduce the same route entry structure for the IPv6 Next Hop, but use a special value of the last field (the Metric) to indicate that the first 16 bytes in the route entry was an IPv6 Next Hop, not the route itself. The value chosen for the metric was 256 (0xFF) because this was far beyond the legal hop count limit (15) for RIP.

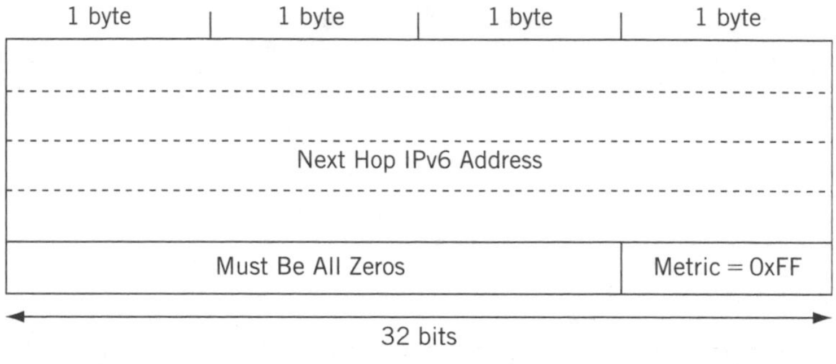

FIGURE 14.4

The Next Hop in IPv6 with RIPng. Note the use of the special metric value.

When the route entry used is an IPv6 Next Hop, the 3 bytes preceding the `0xFF` Metric must be set to all 0 bits. This is shown in Figure 14.4.

At first it might seem that the amount of the IPv6 routing information sent with RIPng must instantly double in size, since now each 20-byte IPv6 route requires a 20-byte IPv6 Next Hop field. This certainly would make IPv6 very unattractive to current RIP users. But it was not necessary to include a Next Hop entry for each and every IPv6 route because the creators of RIPng used a clever mechanism to optimize the use of the Next Hop entry.

A Next Hop always qualifies any IPv6 routes that follow it in the string of route entries until another Next Hop entry is reached or the packet stream ends. This keeps the number of "extra" Next Hop entries needed in RIPng to an absolute minimum. And due to the fact that the Next Hop field in RIPv2 has only specialized use, a lot of IPv6 routes need no Next Hop entry at all.

The decision to replace RIPv2 authentication with IPv6 security mechanisms was based on the superior security used in IPv6. When used with RIPng updates, the IPv6 Authentication Header protects both the data inside the packet and the IP addresses of the packet, but this is not the case with RIPv2 authentication no matter which method is used. And IPv6 encryption can be used to add further protection.

A NOTE ON IGRP AND EIGRP

Cisco routers often use a proprietary IGP known as the Interior Gateway Routing Protocol (IGRP) instead of RIP. Later, features were added to IGRP in the form of Enhanced IGRP (EIGRP). In spite of the name, EIGRP was a complete redesign of IGRP. This section will only give a brief outline of IGRP and EIGRP, since IGRP/EIGRP interoperability with Juniper Networks routers is currently impossible.

IGRP and EIGRP might appear to be open standards, but this is only due to the wide-ranging deployment of Cisco routers. Cisco has never published the details of IGRP internals (EIGRP is based on these), and is not likely to.

IGRP improves on RIP in several areas, but IGRP is still essentially a distance-vector routing protocol. EIGRP, on the other hand, is advertised by Cisco as a "hybrid" routing protocol that includes aspects of link-state routing protocols such as OSPF and IS–IS among the features of EIGRP. Today not many, even those with all-Cisco networks, would consider running EIGRP over OSPF or IS–IS.

Open Shortest Path First

OSPF is not a distance-vector protocol like RIP, but a *link-state* protocol with a set of metrics that can be used to reflect much more about a network than just the number of routers encountered between source and destination. In OSPF, a router attempts to route based on the "state of the links."

OSPF can be equipped with metrics that can be used to compute the "shortest" path through a group of routers based on link and router characteristics such as highest throughput, lowest delay, lowest cost (money), link reliability, or even more. OSPF is still used very cautiously, with default metrics based entirely on link bandwidth. Even with this conservative use, OSPF link states are an improvement over simple hop counts.

Distance-vector routing protocols like RIP were fine for networks comprised of equal speed links, but struggled when networks started to be built out of WAN links with a wide variety of available speeds. When RIP first appeared, almost all WANs were composed of low-speed analog links running at 9600 bps. Even digital links running at 56 or 64 kbps were mainly valued for their ability to carry five 9600-bps channels on the same physical link. Commercial T1s at 1.544 Mbps were not widely available until 1984, and then only in major metropolitan areas. Today, the quickest way to send packets from one router to another is not always through the fewest number of routers.

The "open" in OSPF is based on the fact that the Shortest Path First (SPF) algorithm was not owned by anyone and could be used by all. The SPF algorithm is often called the *Dijkstra algorithm* after the computer and network pioneer that first worked it out from graph theory. Dijkstra himself called the new method SPF, first described in 1959, because compared to a distance-vector protocol's counting to infinity to produce convergence, his algorithm always found the "shortest path first."

OSPF version 1 (OSPFv1), described in RFC 1131, never matured beyond the experimental stage. The current version of OSPF, OSPFv2, which first appeared as RFC 1247 in 1991, and is now defined by RFC 2328 issued in 1998, became the recommended replacement for RIP (although a strong argument could be made in favor of IS–IS, discussed later in this chapter).

Link States and Shortest Paths

Link-state protocols are all based on the idea of a *distributed map* of the network. All of the routers that run a link-state protocol have the same copy of this network map, which is built up by the routing protocol itself and not imposed on the network from an outside source. The network map and all of the information about the routers and links (and the routes) are kept in a *link-state database* on each router. The database is not a "map" in the usual sense of the word: Records represent the topology of the network as a series of links from one router to another. The database must be identical on all of the routers in an *area* for OSPF to work.

Initially, each router only knows about a piece of the entire network. The local router knows only about itself and the local interfaces. So *link-state advertisements* (LSAs), the OSPF information sent to all other routers from the local router, always identify the local router as the source of the information.

The OSPF routing protocol "floods" this information to all of the other routers so that a complete picture of the network is generated and stored in the link-state database. OSPF uses *reliable flooding* so that OSPF routers have ways to find out if the information passed to another router was received or not.

The more routers and links that OSPF has to deal with, the larger the link-state database that has to be maintained. In large router networks, the routing information could slow traffic. OSPFv2 introduced the idea of *stub areas* into an OSPF routing domain. A stub area could function with a greatly reduced link-state database, and relied on a special *backbone area* to reach the entire network.

What OSPF Can Do

By 1992, OSPF had matured enough to be the recommended IGP for the Internet and had delivered on its major design goals.

Better Routing Metrics for Links

OSPF employs a configurable link metric with a range of valid values between 1 and 65,535. There is no limit on the total cost of a path between routers from source to destination, as long as all the routers are in the same AS. Network administrators, for example, could assign a metric of 10,000 to a low-bandwidth link and 10 to a very high-bandwidth Metro Ethernet or SONET/SDH link. In theory, these values could be manually assigned through a central authority. In practice, most implementations of OSPF divide a *reference bandwidth* by the actual bandwidth on the link, which is known through the router's interface configuration. The default reference bandwidth is usually 100 Mbps (Fast Ethernet). Since the metric cannot be less than 0, all links at 100 Mbps or faster use a 1 as a link metric and thus revert to a simple hop count when computing longest cost paths. The reference bandwidth is routinely raised to accommodate higher and higher bandwidths, but this requires a central authority to carry out consistently.

Equal-Cost Multipaths

There are usually multiple ways to reach the same destination network that the routing protocol will compute as having the same cost. When equal-cost paths exist, OSPF routers can find and use equal-cost paths. This means that there can be multiple next hops installed in a forwarding table with OSPF. OSPF does not specify how to use these multipaths: Routers can use simple round-robin per packet, round-robin per flow, hashing, or other mechanisms.

Router Hierarchies

OSPF made very large routing domains possible by introducing a two-level hierarchy of areas. With OSPF, the concepts of an "edge" and "backbone" router became common and well understood.

Internal and External Routes

It is necessary to distinguish between routing information that originated within the AS (internal routing information) and routing information that came from another AS (external routing information). Internal routing information is generally more trusted than external routing information that might have passed from ISP to ISP across the Internet.

Classless Addressing

OSPF was first designed in a classful Internet environment with Class A, B, and C addresses. However, OSPF is comfortable with the arbitrary network/host boundaries used by CIDR and VLSM.

Security

RIPv1 routers accepted updates from anyone, and even RIPv2 routers only officially used simple plain-text passwords that could be discovered by anyone with access to the link. OSPF allows not only for simple password authentication, but strong MD5 key mechanisms on routing updates.

ToS Routing

The original OSPF was intended to support the bit patterns established for the Type of Service (ToS) field in the IP packet header. Routers at the time had no way to enforce ToS routing, but OSPF anticipated the use of the Internet for all types of traffic such as voice and video and went ahead and built into OSPF ways to distribute multiple metrics for links. So OSPF routing updates can include ToS routing information for five IP ToS service classes, defined in RFC 1349. The service categories and OSPF ToS values are normal service (ToS = 0), minimize monetary cost (2), maximize reliability (4), maximize throughput (8), and minimize delay (16). Since all current implementations of OSPF support only a ToS value of 0, no more need be said about the other ToS metrics.

By the way, here's all we did on the customer- and provider-edge routers in each AS to configure OSPF to run on every router interface. Now, in a real network, we wouldn't necessarily configure OSPF to run on all of the router's internal or management interfaces, but it does no harm here.

```
set protocols ospf area 0.0.0.0 interface all
```

All OSPF routers do not have to be in the same area, and in most real router networks, they aren't. But this is a simple network and only configures an OSPF *backbone area*, 0.0.0.0. The provider routers in our ISP cores (P9, P7, P4 and P2), which are called

AS border routers, or ASBRs, run OSPF on the *internal* links within the AS, but not on the *external* links to the other AS (this is where we'll run the EGP).

The relationship between the OSPF use of a reference bandwidth and ToS routing should be clarified. Use of the OSPF link reference bandwidth is different from and independent of ToS support, which relies on the specific settings in the packet headers. OSPF routers were supposed to keep separate link-state databases for each type of service, since the least-cost path in terms of bandwidth could be totally different from the least-cost path computed based on delay or reliability. This was not feasible in early OSPF implementations, which struggled to maintain the single, normal ToS = 0 database. And it turned out that the Internet users did not want lots of bandwidth or low delay or high reliability when they sent packets. Internet users wanted lots of bandwidth *and* low delay *and* high reliability when they sent packets. So the reference bandwidth method is about all the link-state that OSPF can handle, but that is still better than nothing.

OSPF Router Types and Areas

OSPFv2 introduced areas as a way to cut down on the size of the link-state database, the amount of information flooded, and the time it takes to run the SPF algorithm, at least on areas other than the special backbone area.

An OSPF area is a logical grouping of routers sharing the same 32-bit Area ID. The Area ID can be expressed in dotted decimal notation similar to an IP address, such as 192.168.17.33. The Area ID can also be expressed as a decimal equivalent, so Area 261 is the same as Area 0.0.1.5. When the Area ID is less than 256, usually only a single number is used, but Area 249 is still really Area 0.0.0.249.

There are five OSPF area types. The position of a router with respect to OSPF areas is important as well. The area types are shown in Figure 14.5.

The OSPF Area `0` (`0.0.0.0`) is very special. This is the backbone area of an OSPF routing domain. An OSPF routing domain (AS) can consist of a single area, but in that case the single area must be Area `0`. Only the backbone area can generate the summary routing topology information that is used by the other areas. This is why all interarea traffic must pass through the backbone area. (There are *backdoor links* that can be configured on some routers to bypass the backbone area, but these violate the OSPF specification.) In a sense, the backbone area knows everything. Not so long ago, only powerful high-end routers could be used on an OSPF backbone. On the Illustrated Network, each AS consists of only an Area 0.

If an area is not the backbone area, it can be one of four other types of areas. All of these areas connect to the backbone area through an Area Border Router (ABR). An ABR by definition has links in two or more areas. In OSPF, routers always form the boundaries between areas. A router with links outside the OSPF routing domain is called an autonomous system boundary router (ASBR). Routing information about destination IP addresses not learned from OSPF are always advertised by an ASBR. Even when static routes, or RIP routes, are redistributed by OSPF, that router technically becomes an ASBR. ASBRs are the source of *external routes* that are outside of the

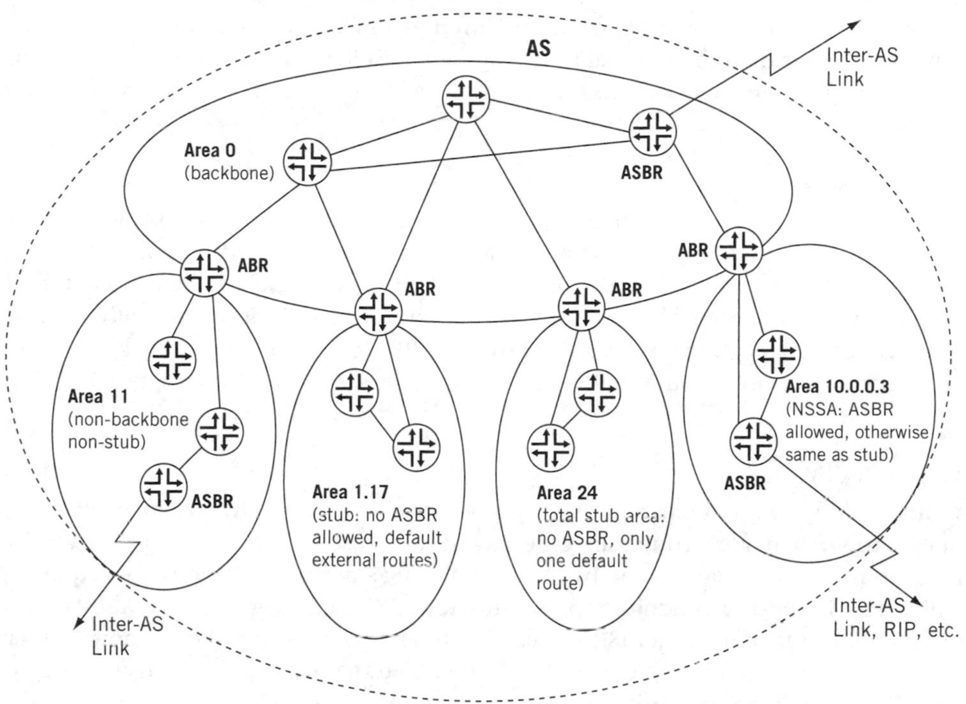

FIGURE 14.5

OSPF area types, showing the various ways that areas can be given numbers (decimal, IP address, or other). Note that ABRs connect areas and ASBRs have links outside the AS or to other routing protocols.

OSPF routing domain, and external routes are often very numerous in an OSPF routing domain attached to the global Internet. If a router is not an ABR or ASBR, it is either an *internal router* and has all of its interfaces within the same area, or a *backbone router* with at least one link to the backbone. However, these terms are not as critical to OSPF configurations as to ABRs or ASBRs. That is, not all backbone routers are ABRs or ASBRs; backbone routers can also be internal routers, and so on.

Non-backbone, Non-stub Areas

These areas are really smaller versions of the backbone area. There can be links to other routing domains (ASBRs) and the only real restriction on a non-backbone, non-stub area is that it cannot be Area 0. Area 11 in Figure 14.5 is a non-backbone, non-stub area.

Stub Area

Stub areas cannot have links outside the AS. So there can be no ASBRs in a stub area. This minimizes the amount of external routing information that needs to be distributed into the link-state databases of the stub area routers. Because an AS might be an ISP on the

Internet, the number of external routes required in an OSPF routing domain is usually many times larger than the internal routes of the AS itself. Stub area routers only obtain information on routes external to the AS from the ABR. Area 1.17 in Figure 14.5 is a stub area.

Total Stub Area

This is also called a "totally stubby area." Recall that stub areas cannot have ASBRs within them, by definition. But stub areas can only reach other ASBRs, which have the links leading to and from other ASs, through an ABR. So why include detailed external route information in the stub area router's link-state database? All that is really needed is the proper default route as advertised by the ABR. Total stub areas only know how to reach their ABR for a route that is not within their area. Area 24 in Figure 14.5 is a total stub area.

Not-So-Stubby Area

Banning ASBRs from stub areas was very restrictive. Even the advertisement of static routes into OSPF made a router an ASBR, as did the presence of a single LAN running RIP, if the routes were advertised by OSPF. And as ISPs merged and grew by acquiring smaller ISPs, it became difficult to "paste" the new OSPF area with its own ASBRs onto the backbone area of the other ISP. The easiest thing to do was to make the new former AS a stub area, but the presence of an ASBR prevented that solution. The answer was to introduce the concept of a not-so-stubby area (NSSA) in RFC 1587. An NSSA can have ASBRs, but the external routing information introduced by this ASBR into the NSSA is either kept within the NSSA or translated by the ABR into a form useful on the backbone Area 0 and to other areas. Area 10.0.0.3 in Figure 14.5 is an NSSA.

OSPF Designated Router and Backup Designated Router

An OSPF router can also be a Designated Router (DR) and Backup Designated Router (BDR). These have nothing to do with ABRs and ASBRs, and concern only the relationship between OSPF routers on links that deliver packets to more than one destination at the same time (mainly LANs).

There are two major problems with LANs and public data networks like ATM and frame relay (called non-broadcast multiple-access, or NBMA, networks). First is the fact that the link-state database represents links and routers as a directed graph. A simple LAN with five OSPF routers would need $N(N - 1)/2$, or $5(4)/2 = 20$ link-state advertisements just to represent the links between the routers, even though all five routers are mutually adjacent on the LAN and any frame sent by one is received by the other four. Second, and just as bad, is the need for flooding. Flooding over a LAN with many OSPF routers is chaotic, as link-state advertisements are flooded and "reflooded" on the LAN.

To address these issues, multiaccess networks such as LANs always elect a designated router for OSPF. The DR solves the two problems by representing the multiaccess network as a single "virtual router" or "pseudo-node" to the rest of the network and managing the process of flooding link-state advertisements on the multiaccess network. So each router on a LAN forms an OSPF adjacency only with the DR (and also the Backup DR [BDR] as mentioned later). All link-state advertisements go only to the DR (and BDR), and the DR forwards them on to the rest of the network and internetwork routers.

Each network that elects a DR also elects a BDR that will take over the functions of the DR if and when the DR fails. The DR and BDR form OSPF adjacencies with all of the other routers on the multiaccess network and the DR and BDR also form an adjacency with each other.

OSPF Packets

OSPF routers communicate using IP packets. OSPF messages ride directly inside of IP packets as IP protocol number 89. Because OSPF does not use UDP or TCP, the OSPF protocol is fairly elaborate and must reproduce many of the features of a transport protocol to move OSPF messages between routers.

There can be one of five OSPF packet types inside the IP packet, all of which share a common OSPF header. The structure of the common OSPF header is shown in Figure 14.6.

The version field is 2, for OSPFv2, and the type has one of the five values. The packet length is the length of the OSPF packet in bytes. The Router ID is the IP address selected as OSPF Router ID (usually the loopback interface address), and the Area ID is the OSPF area of the router that originates the message. The checksum is the same as the one used on IP packets and is computed on the whole OSPF packet.

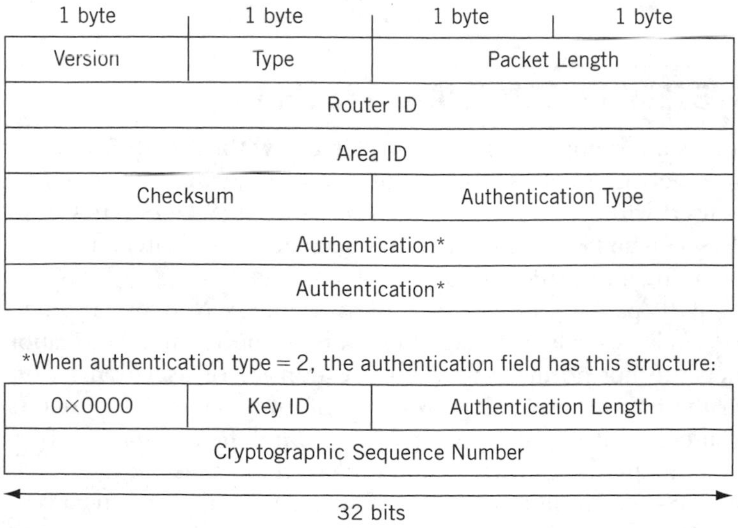

1 byte	1 byte	1 byte	1 byte
Version	Type	Packet Length	
Router ID			
Area ID			
Checksum		Authentication Type	
Authentication*			
Authentication*			

*When authentication type = 2, the authentication field has this structure:

0×0000	Key ID	Authentication Length	
Cryptographic Sequence Number			

32 bits

FIGURE 14.6

OSPF packet header fields, showing how the structure can vary with type.

The Authentication Type (or AuType) is either none (0), simple password authentication (1), or cryptographic authentication (2). The simple password is an eight-character plain-text password, but the use of AuType = 2 authentication gives the authentication field the structure shown in the figure. In this case, the Key ID identifies the secret key and authentication algorithm (MD5) used to create the message digest, the Authentication Data Length specifies the length of the message digest appended to the packet (which does not count as part of the packet length), and the Cryptographic Sequence Number always increases and prevents hacker "replay" attacks.

OSPFv3 for IPv6

The changes made to OSPF for IPv6 are minimal. It is easy to transition from OSPF for IPv4 to OSPF for IPv6. There is new version number, OSPF version 3 (OSPFv3), and some necessary format changes, but less than might be expected. The basics are described in RFC 2740.

OSPF for IPv6 (often called OSPFv6) will use link local IPv6 addresses and IPv6 multicast addresses. The IPv6 link-state database will be totally independent of the IPv4 link-state database, and both can operate on the same router.

Naturally, OSPFv6 must make some concessions to the larger IPv6 addresses and next hops. But the common LSA header has few changes as well. The Link State Identifier field is still there, but is now a pure identifier and not an IPv4 address. There is no longer an Options field, since this field also appears in the packets that need it, and the LSA Header Type field is enlarged to 16 bits. Naturally, when LSAs carry the details of IPv6 addresses, those fields are now large enough to handle the 128 bit IPv6 addresses.

INTERMEDIATE SYSTEM–INTERMEDIATE SYSTEM

OSPF is not the only link-state routing protocol that ISPs use within an AS. The other common link-state routing protocol is IS–IS (Intermediate System–Intermediate System). When IS–IS is used with IP, the term to use is *Integrated IS*. IS–IS is not really an IP routing protocol. IS–IS is an ISO protocol that has been adapted ("integrated") for IP in order to carry IP routing information inside non-IP packets.

IS–IS packets are not IP packets, but rather ConnectionLess Network Protocol (CLNP) packets. CLNP packets have ISO addresses, not IP source and destination addresses. CLNP packets are not normally used for the transfer of user traffic from client to server, but for the transfer of link-state routing information between routers. IS–IS does not have "routers" at all: Routers are called *intermediate systems* to distinguish them from the *end systems* (ES) that send and receive traffic.

The independence of IS–IS from IP has advantages and disadvantages. One advantage is that network problems can often be isolated to IP itself if IS–IS is up and running between two routers. One disadvantage is that there are now sources and destinations on the network (the ISO addresses) that are not even "ping-able." So if a link between two routers is configured with incorrect IP addresses (such as `10.0.37.1/24` on one router and `10.0.38.2/24` on the other), IS–IS will still come up and exchange routing information over the link, but IP will not work correctly, leaving the network administrators wondering why the routing protocol is working but the routes are broken.

Our network does not use IS–IS, so much of this section will be devoted to introducing IS–IS terminology, such as link-state protocol (LSP) data unit instead of OSPF's link-state advertisement (LSA), and contrasting IS–IS behavior with OSPF.

The IS–IS Attraction

If IS–IS is used instead of OSPF as an IGP within an AS, there must be strong reasons for doing so. Why introduce a new type of packet and addressing to the network? And even the simple task of assigning ISO addresses to routers can be a complex task. Yet many ISPs see IS–IS as being much more flexible than OSPF when it comes to the structure of the AS.

IS–IS routers can form both Level 1 (L1) and Level 2 (L2) adjacencies. L1 links connect routers in the same IS–IS area, and L2 links connect routers in different areas. In contrast to OSPF, IS–IS does not demand that traffic sent between areas use a special backbone area (Area 0.0.0.0). IS–IS does not care if interarea traffic uses a special area or not, as long as it gets there. The same is true when a larger ISP acquires a smaller one and it is necessary to "paste" new areas onto existing areas. With IS–IS, an ISP can just paste the new area wherever it makes sense and configure IS–IS L1/L2 routers in the right places. IS–IS takes care of everything.

A backbone area in IS–IS is simply a contiguous collection of routers in different areas capable of running L2 IS–IS. The fact that the routers must be directly connected (contiguous) to form the backbone is not too much as a limitation (most core routers on the backbone usually have multiple connections). Each and every IS–IS backbone router can be in a different area. If an AS structure similar to centralized OSPF is desired, this is accomplished in IS–IS by running certain (properly connected) routers as L2-only routers in one selected area (the backbone), connecting areas adjacent to the central area with L1/L2 routers, and making the other the routers in the other areas L1-only routers. The IS–IS attraction is in this type of flexibility compared to OSPF.

IS–IS and OSPF

ISO's idea of a network layer protocol was CLNP. To distribute the routing information, ISO invented ES–IS to get routing information from routers to and from clients and servers, and IS–IS to move this information between routers.

IS–IS came from DEC as part of the company's effort to complete DECnet Phase V. Standardized as ISO 10589 in 1992, it was once thought that IS–IS would be the natural progression from RIP and OSPF to a better routing protocol. (OSPF was struggling at the time.) To ease the transition from IP to OSI-RM protocols, Integrated IS–IS (or Dual IS–IS) was developed to carry routing information for both IP and ISO-RM protocols.

OSPF rebounded, ironically by often borrowing what had been shown to work in IS–IS. Today OSPF is the recommended IGP to run on the Internet, but IS–IS still has adherents for reasons of flexibility. Of course, OSPF has much to recommend it as well.

Similarities of OSPF and IS–IS

- Both IS–IS and OSPF are link-state protocols that maintain a link-state database and run an SPF algorithm based on Dijkstra to compute a shortest path tree of routes.
- Both use Hello packets to create and maintain adjacencies between neighboring routers.
- Both use areas that can be arranged into a two-level hierarchy or into interarea and intraarea routes.
- Both can summarize addresses advertised between their areas.
- Both are classless protocols and handle VLSM.
- Both will elect a designated router on broadcast networks, although IS–IS calls it a designated intermediate system (DIS).
- Both can be configured with authentication mechanisms.

Differences between OSPF and IS–IS

Many of the differences between IS–IS and OSPF are terminology. The use of the terms IS and ES have been mentioned. IS–IS has a subnetwork point of attachment (SNPA) instead of an interface, protocol data units (PDUs) instead of packets, and other minor differences. OSPF LSAs are IS–IS link-state PDUs (LSPs), and LSPs are packets all on their own and do not use OSPF's LSA-OSPF header-IP packet encapsulation.

But all IS–IS and OSPF differences are not trivial. Here are the major ones.

Areas—In OSPF, ABRs sit on the borders of areas, with one or more interfaces in one area and other interfaces in other areas. In IS–IS, a router (IS) is either totally in one area or another, and it is the links between the routers that connect the areas.

Route Leaking—When L2 information is redistributed into L1 areas, it is called *route leaking*. Route leaking is defined in RFC 2966. A bit called the Up/Down bit is used to distinguish routes that are local to the L1 area (Up/Down = 0) from those that have been leaked in the area from an L1/L2 router (Up/Down = 1). This is necessary to prevent potential routing loops. Route leaking is a way to make IS–IS areas with LI only routers as "smart" as OSPF routers in not-so-stubby-areas (NSSAs).

Network Addresses—CLNP does not use IP addresses in its packets. IS–IS packets use a single *ISO area address* (Area ID) for the entire router because the router must be within one area or another. Every IS–IS router can have up to three different area ISO addresses, but this chapter uses one ISO address per router. The ISO Area ID is combined with an *ISO system address* (System ID) to give the ISO *Network Entity Title*, or NET. Every router must be given an ISO NET as described in ISO 8348.

Network Types—OSPF has five different link or network types that OSPF can be configured to run on: point-to-point, broadcast, non-broadcast multi-access (NBMA), point-to-multipoint, and virtual links. In contrast, IS–IS defines only two types of links or *subnetworks*: broadcast (LANs) and point-to-point (called "general topology"). This only distinguishes links that can support multicasting (broadcast) and use a designating router (DIS) and links that do not support multicasting.

Designated Intermediate System (DIS)—Although IS–IS technically uses a DIS, many still refer to these devices as a designated router (DR). The DIS or DR represents the entire multiaccess network link (such as a LAN) as a single *pseudo-node*. The pseudo-node (a "virtual node" in some documentation) does not really exist, but there are LSPs that are issued for the entire multiaccess network as if the pseudo-node were a real device. Unlike OSPF, all IS–IS routers on a pseudo-node (such as a LAN) are always fully adjacent to the pseudo-node. This is due to the lack of a backup DIS, and new DIS elections must take place quickly.

LSP Handling—IS–IS routers handle LSPs differently than OSPF routers handle LSAs. While OSPF LSAs age from zero to a maximum (MaxAge) value of 3600 seconds (1 hour), IS–IS LSPs age downward from a MaxAge of 1200 seconds (20 minutes) to 0. The normal refresh interval is 15 minutes. Since IS–IS does not use IP addresses, multicast addresses cannot be used in IS–IS for LSP distribution. Instead, a MAC destination address of `0180.c200.0014` (AllL1ISs) is used to carry L1 LSPs to L1 ISs (routers), and a MAC destination address of `0180.c200.0015` (AllL2ISs) is used to carry L2 LSPs to L2 ISs (routers).

Metrics—Like OSPF, IS–IS can use one of four different metrics to calculate least-cost paths (routes) from the link-state database. For IS–IS, these are default (all routers must understand the default metric system), delay, expense, and error (reliability in OSPF). Only the default metric system is discussed here, as with OSPF, and that is the only system that most router vendors support. The original IS–IS specification used a system of metric values that could only range from 0 to 63 on a link, and paths (the sum of all link costs along the route) could have a maximum cost of 1023. Today, IS–IS implementations allow for "wide metrics" to be used with IS–IS. This makes the IS–IS metrics 32 bits wide.

IS–IS for IPv6

One advantage that IS–IS has over OSPF is that IS–IS is not an IP protocol and is not as intimately tied up with IPv4 as OSPF. So IS–IS has fewer changes for IPv6: IPv4 is already strange enough.

With IPv6, the basic mechanisms of RFC 1195 are still used, but two new Type-Length-Vector (TLVs, which define representation) types are defined for IPv6.

IPv6 Interface Address (type 232)—This TLV just modifies the interface address field for the 16-byte IPv6 address space.

IPv6 Reachability (type 236)—This TLV starts with a 32-bit wide metric. Then there is an Up/Down bit for route leaking, an I/E bit for external (other routing protocol or AS) information, and a "sub-TLVs present?" bit. The last 5 bits of this byte are reserved and must be set to 0. There is then 1 byte of Prefix Length (VLSM) and from 0 to 16 bytes of the prefix itself, depending on the value of the Prefix Length field. Zero to 248 bytes of sub-TLVs end the TLV.

Both types have defined sub-TLVs fields, but none of these has yet been standardized.

QUESTIONS FOR READERS

Figure 14.7 shows some of the concepts discussed in this chapter and can be used to help you answer the following questions.

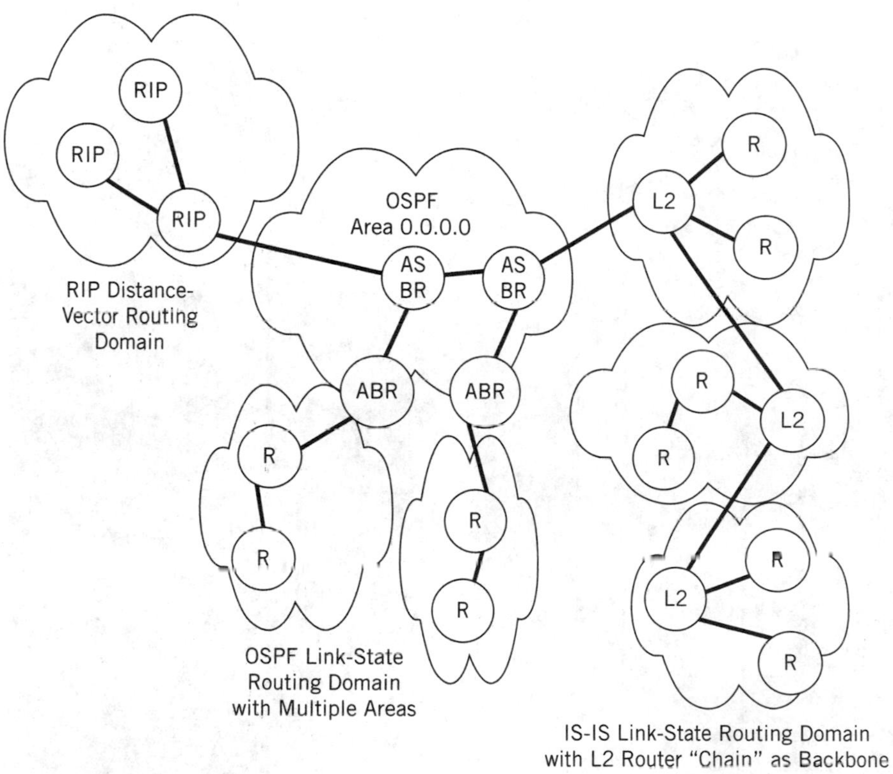

FIGURE 14.7

Three IGPs and some of their major characteristics.

1. Why does RIP continue to be used in spite of its limitations?
2. What is the difference between distance-vector and link-state routing protocols?
3. It is often said that it is easier to configure a backbone area in IS–IS than in OSPF. What is the basis for this statement?
4. What are the similarities between OSPF and IS–IS?
5. What are the major differences between OSPF and IS–IS?

CHAPTER

Border Gateway Protocol 15

What You Will Learn

In this chapter, you will learn about the BGP and the essential role it plays on the Internet. With BGP, routing information is circulated outside the AS and to all routing domains. We'll see how a simple routing policy change can make a destination unreachable.

You will learn about the differences between the Internet BGP (IBGP) and the Exterior Gateway Protocol (EBGP), and why both are needed. We'll also look at BGP attributes and message formats.

The EGP used on the Internet is the Border Gateway Protocol (BGP). IGPs run between the routers inside a routing domain (single AS). BGP runs between different autonomous services (ASs). BGP runs on links between the border routers of these routing domains and shares information about the routes within the AS or learned by the AS with the AS on the other side of the "border."

BGP makes sure that every network and interface in any AS located anywhere on the Internet is reachable from every other place. BGP does not generate any routing information on its own, unlike the IGPs, which essentially "bootstrap" themselves into existence. BGP relies on an underlying IGP (or static routes) as the source of the BGP-distributed information.

BGP runs on the border routers of Ace ISP's AS 65459 (routers P9 and P4) and Best ISP's AS 65127 (routers P7 and P2). These are highlighted in Figure 15.1. An IGP such as OSPF or IS–IS runs on the direct links between routers P9 and P4 and routers P7 and P2, but these are interior links. BGP runs on the other links between the backbone routers.

BGP AS A ROUTING PROTOCOL

There *are* EGPs defined other than BGP. The Inter-Domain Routing Protocol (IDRP) from ISO is the EGP that was to be used with IS–IS as an IGP. IDRP is also sometimes promoted as the successor to BGP, or the best way to carry IPv6 routing information

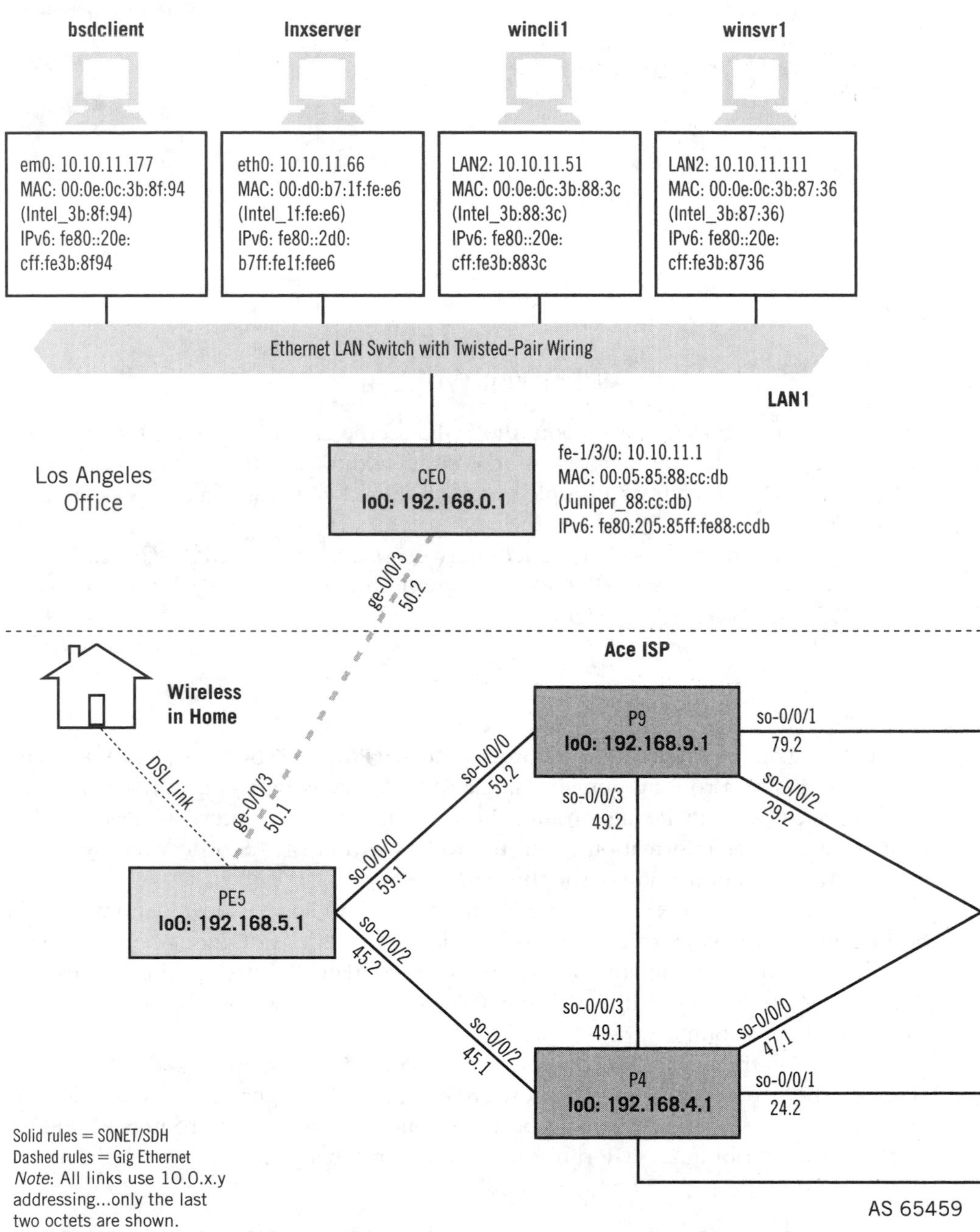

FIGURE 15.1

BGP on the Illustrated Network.

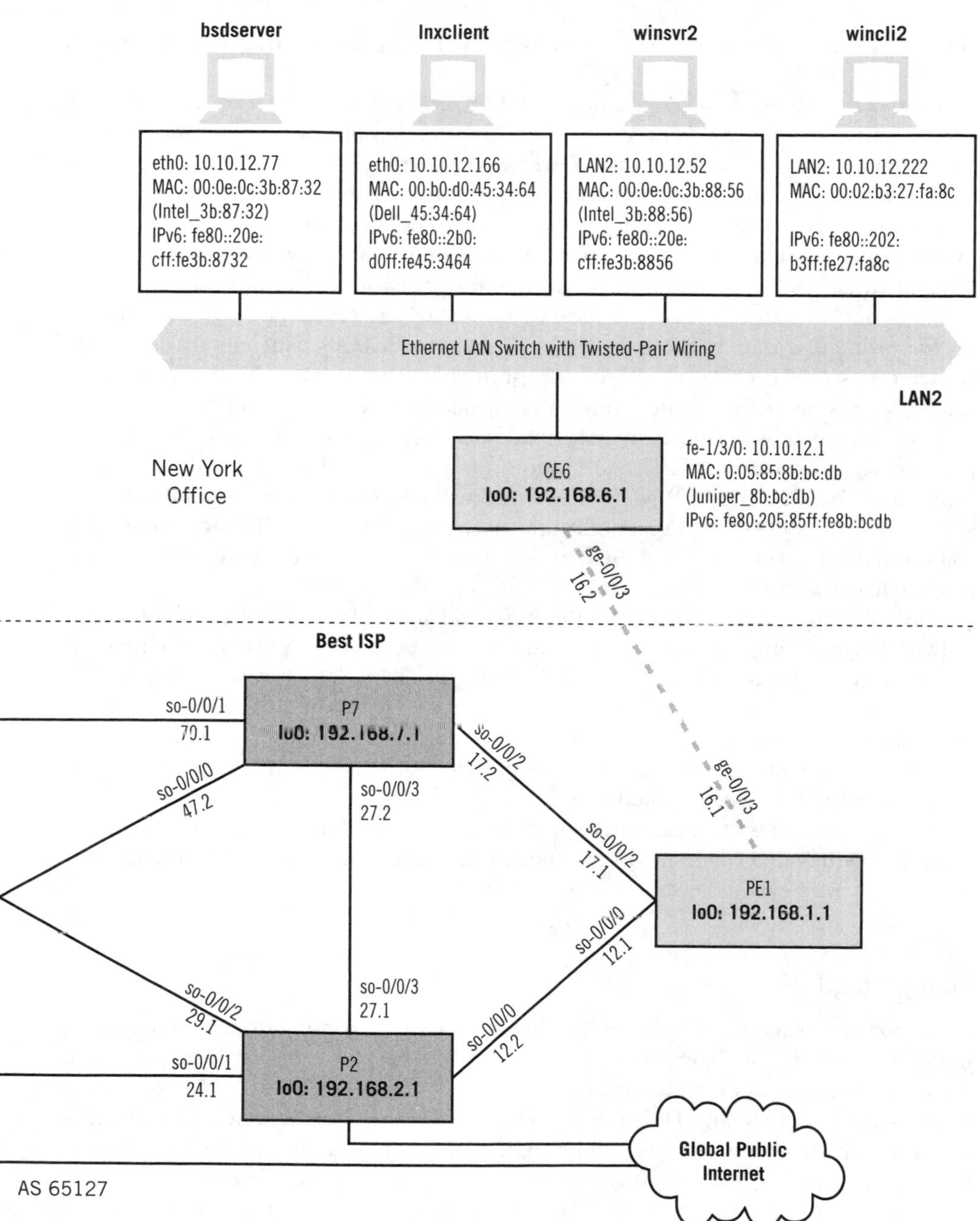
bsdserver
lnxclient
winsvr2
wincli2
eth0: 10.10.12.77
MAC: 00:0e:0c:3b:87:32
(Intel_3b:87:32)
IPv6: fe80::20e:
cff:fe3b:8732
eth0: 10.10.12.166
MAC: 00:b0:d0:45:34:64
(Dell_45:34:64)
IPv6: fe80::2b0:
d0ff:fe45:3464
LAN2: 10.10.12.52
MAC: 00:0e:0c:3b:88:56
(Intel_3b:88:56)
IPv6: fe80::20e:
cff:fe3b:8856
LAN2: 10.10.12.222
MAC: 00:02:b3:27:fa:8c
IPv6: fe80::202:
b3ff:fe27:fa8c
Ethernet LAN Switch with Twisted-Pair Wiring
LAN2
New York
Office
CE6
lo0: 192.168.6.1
fe-1/3/0: 10.10.12.1
MAC: 0:05:85:8b:bc:db
(Juniper_8b:bc:db)
IPv6: fe80:205:85ff:fe8b:bcdb
ge-0/0/3
16.2
Best ISP
so-0/0/1
79.1
P7
lo0: 192.168.7.1
so-0/0/2
17.2
ge-0/0/3
16.1
so-0/0/0
47.2
so-0/0/3
27.2
so-0/0/2
17.1
PE1
lo0: 192.168.1.1
so-0/0/0
12.1
so-0/0/2
29.1
so-0/0/3
27.1
so-0/0/0
12.2
so-0/0/1
24.1
P2
lo0: 192.168.2.1
Global Public
Internet
AS 65127

between ISP ASs. However, when it comes to the Internet today, the only EGP worth considering is BGP.

In a very real sense, BGP is not a routing protocol at all. BGP does not really carry routing information from AS to AS, but information *about* routes from AS to AS. Generally, a route that passes through fewer ASs (ISPs) than another is considered more attractive, although there are many other factors (BGP attributes) to consider. BGP is a routing protocol without real routes or metrics, and both of those derive from the IGP. BGP is not a link-state protocol, because the state of links in many AS clouds would be difficult to convey and maintain across the entire network (and links would tend to "average out" to a sort of least common denominator anyway). But it's not a distance-vector protocol either, because more attributes than just AS path length determine active routes. BGP is called a "path-vector" protocol (a vector has a direction as well as value), but mainly because a new term was needed to describe its operation.

BGP information is not even described as a "route." BGP carries network layer reachability information (NLRI). BGP "routes" do not have metrics, like IGP routes, but *attributes*. Together, the BGP NLRI and their attributes allow other ASs to make decisions about the best way to reach a route (network) in another AS. Once a packet is routed to the correct AS through BGP information, the packet is delivered locally using the IGP information.

The differences between BGP and IGPs should always be remembered. Some new to BGP struggle with BGP terminology and concepts because they attempt to interpret BGP features in terms of more familiar IGP features. BGP does not work like an IGP because BGP is *not* an IGP and should not work like an IGP. When BGP passes information from one AS border router to another AS border router inside an AS, a form known as interior BGP (IBGP) is used. When BGP passes information from one AS to another AS, the form of BGP used is called exterior BGP (EBGP).

This chapter does not deal much with routing policies for BGP based on multiple attributes, which determine how the routers use BGP to route packets. Complex routing policies are beyond the scope of this book.

Configuring BGP

It's important to keep in mind exactly what is meant by a routing domain and routing policy. For example, is CE0 part of AS 65459 or not? This is not as simple a question as it sounds, because there might be a dozen routers behind CE0 that the Ace ISP knows nothing about. But the interface to PE5 is firmly under the control of Ace, and generally all customer site routers are considered part of the ISP's routing domain in the sense that a routing policy on PE5 can always control the routing behavior of CE0.

This does not mean something like preventing the users on LAN1 from running Internet Chat or something. This type of application-level detailing is not what a routing policy is for. Corporate policies of this type (application policing) are best handled by an appliance on site. ISP routing policies determine things like where the

10.10.11.0/24 route to LAN1 is advertised or held back, and which routes are accepted from other sources.

Let's see how easy it is to configure BGP on the border routers. Each of them is essentially identical in basic configuration, so let's use P9 as an example.

```
set protocols bgp group ebgp-to-as65127 type external;
set protocols bgp group ebgp-to-as65127 peer-as 65127;
set protocols bgp group ebgp-to-as65127 neighbor 10.0.79.1;
set protocols bgp group ebgp-to-as65127 neighbor 10.0.29.1;

set protocols bgp group ibgp-mesh type internal;
set protocols bgp group ibgp-mesh local-address 192.168.9.1;
set protocols bgp group ibgp-mesh neighbor 192.168.4.1;
set protocols bgp group ibgp-mesh neighbor 192.168.5.1;
```

BGP configurations are organized into groups that have user-defined names (ebgp-to-as65127 and ibgp-mesh) Note that there are two types of BGP running on the border routers: EBGP and IBGP. EBGP must know the other AS number and IBGP must know the local address to use as a source address (routers typically have many IP addresses). Note that EBGP uses link addresses and IBGP uses the router's "loopback" address, in this case the address assigned to the routing engine. We'll see why this is usually done when we discuss EBGP and IBGP later in this chapter.

We showed at the end of the previous chapter that we could ping IPv6 addresses from the Windows XP client on LAN1 to the Windows XP client on LAN2. Let's see if the same works for the IPv4 addresses on the Unix hosts. All is well between bsdclient and bsdserver.

```
bsdclient# ping 10.10.12.77
PING 10.10.12.1 (10.10.12.77): 56 data bytes
64 bytes from 10.10.12.77: icmp_seq=0 ttl=255 time=0.600 ms
64 bytes from 10.10.12.77: icmp_seq=1 ttl=255 time=0.477 ms
64 bytes from 10.10.12.77: icmp_seq=2 ttl=255 time=0.441 ms
64 bytes from 10.10.12.77: icmp_seq=3 ttl=255 time=0.409 ms
^C
--- 10.10.12.77 ping statistics ---
4 packets transmitted, 4 packets received, 0% packet loss
round-trip min/avg/max/stddev = 0.409/0.482/0.600/0.072 ms
```

The default behavior for BGP is to advertise all active routes that it learns by its own operation, so no special advertising policies are needed on the backbone routers. Because there are direct links in place between the two ISPs to connect the Los Angeles office (LAN1) with the New York office (LAN2), each ISP relies on the routing protocol metrics to make sure traffic flowing between LAN1 (10.10.11/24) and LAN2 (10.10.12/24) is not forwarded onto the Internet. That is, the cost of forwarding a LAN1-LAN2 packet between the provider backbone routers will always be less than using the Internet at large.

However, one day the users on LAN1 and LAN2 discover a curious thing: no one can reach servers on the other LAN. Pings to the local router work fine, but pings to remote hosts on the other LAN produce no results at all.

```
bsdserver# ping 10.10.12.1
PING 10.10.12.1 (10.10.12.1): 56 data bytes
64 bytes from 10.10.12.1: icmp_seq=0 ttl=255 time=0.599 ms
64 bytes from 10.10.12.1: icmp_seq=1 ttl=255 time=0.476 ms
64 bytes from 10.10.12.1: icmp_seq=2 ttl=255 time=0.401 ms
64 bytes from 10.10.12.1: icmp_seq=3 ttl=255 time=0.443 ms
^C
--- 10.10.12.1 ping statistics ---
4 packets transmitted, 4 packets received, 0% packet loss
round-trip min/avg/max/stddev = 0.401/0.480/0.599/0.071 ms
bsdserver# ping 10.10.11.177
PING 10.10.11.177 (10.10.11.177): 56 data bytes
^C
--- 10.10.11.177 ping statistics ---
5 packets transmitted, 0 packets received, 100% packet loss
```

The remote router cannot be pinged either (presumably, no security prevents them from pinging to another site router's port).

```
bsdserver# ping 10.10.11.1
PING 10.10.11.1 (10.10.11.1): 56 data bytes
^C
--- 10.10.11.1 ping statistics ---
7 packets transmitted, 0 packets received, 100% packet loss
```

The Power of Routing Policy

There are many things that could be wrong in this situation. In this case, the cause of the problem is ultimately determined to be a feud between the Ace ISP and Best ISPs running the service provider routers. The issue (greatly exaggerated here) is a server located on LAN2 in New York. This essential server provides full-motion video, huge database files, and all types of other information to the clients in Los Angeles on LAN1. Naturally, a lot more packets flow from Best ISP's AS to Ace ISP's AS than the other way around. So, the Ace ISP (AS 65459) controlling border routers P9 and P4 decided that Best ISP (AS 65127) should pay for all these "extra" packets they were delivering from the New York server. Shortly before the LANs stopped communicating, they sent a bill to Best ISP—turning AS 65127 from a peer into a customer.

Naturally, Best ISP was not happy about this new arrangement and refused to pay. So, Ace ISP decided to do a simple thing: they applied a routing policy and did not send any information about the LAN1 network (`10.10.11/24`) to AS 65127's border routers (P7 and P2). If the border routers don't know how to send packets back to LAN1 from the servers on LAN2, Ace ISP will be getting what they paid Best ISP for—which is nothing. (In the real world, the customer paying for LAN1 and LAN2 connectivity would be asked to pay for the asymmetrical traffic load.)

Without the correct routing information available on the routers on both ASs, no one on LAN2 can find a route to LAN1. Even if there were still some connectivity between the sites through Ace and Best ISPs' links to the Internet, this means that the symptom would show up as a sharply increased network delay (and related application timeouts), as packets now wander through many more hops than before. Something would still clearly be wrong.

This large effect comes from a very simple cause. Let's look at the routing tables and policies on P2 and P7 (and P9 and P4) and see what has happened. Best ISP has applied a very specific routing policy to their external BGP session with Ace ISP's border routers. Here's what it looks like on P7.

```
set policy-statement no-10-10-11 term1 from route-filter 10.10.11.0/24 exact;
set policy-statement no-10-10-11 term1 then reject;
```

This basically says, "Out of all the routing protocol information, find (filter) the information matching the network 10.10.11.0/24 exactly and nothing else; then discard (reject) this information and do not use it in the routing or forwarding tables."

This *import policy* on P7 and P2 (Best ISP's routers) is applied on links from neighbor border routers P4 and P9 (Ace ISP's routers). The effect is to block BGP in AS 65127 from learning anything at all about network 10.10.11/24 from P4 and P9. Normally, Best ISP's backbone routers would pass the information about the route to LAN1 through P7 and P2 to all other routers in the AS, including CE6 (LAN2's site router). Without this information, no forwarding table can be built on CE6 to allow packets to reach LAN1. Problem solved: no packets for LAN1 can flow through Best ISP's router network.

Note that Best ISP (AS 65127) still advertises its own LAN2 network (10.10.12/24) to Ace ISP, and Ace ISP's routers accept and distribute the information. So, on LAN1 the site router CE0 still knows about both LANs.

```
admin@CE0# show route 10.10/16
inet.0: 38 destinations, 38 routes (38 active, 0 holddown, 0 hidden)
+ = Active Route, - = Last Active, * = Both
10.10.11.0/24 *[Direct/0] 00:03:31
> via fe-1/3/0.0
10.10.11.1/32 *[Local/0] 00:03:31
Local via fe-1/3/0.0
10.10.12.0/24 *[BGP/170] 00:00:09
> via ge-0/0/3.0
```

But this makes no difference: Packets can get to LAN2 through CE6 (and from anywhere else in Best ISP's AS), but they have no way to get back if they have a source address of 10.10.12.x. Let's verify this on CE6.

```
admin@CE6# show route 10.10/16
inet.0: 38 destinations, 38 routes (37 active, 0 holddown, 1 hidden)
+ = Active Route, - = Last Active, * = Both
```

```
10.10.12.0/24 *[Direct/0] 00:25:42
> via fe-1/3/0.0
10.10.12.1/32 *[Local/0] 00:25:42
Local via fe-1/3/0.0
```

How are packets to get back to `10.10.11/24`? They can't. (The former route to LAN1 is now *hidden* because the network is no longer reachable.) This simple example shows the incredible power of BGP and routing policies on the Internet.

BGP AND THE INTERNET

BGP is the glue of the Internet. Generally, an ISP cannot link to another ISP unless both run BGP. Contrary to some claims, customer networks (even large customer networks with many routers and multiple ASs) do not have to run BGP between their own networks and to their ISP (or ISPs). Smaller customers especially can define a limited number of static routes provided by the ISP, and larger customers might be able run IGP passively (no adjacency formed) on the border router's ISP interface. It depends on the complexity of the customer and ISP network. A customer with only one link to a single ISP generally does not need BGP at all. But if a routing protocol is needed, it will be BGP.

When a customer network links to two ISPs and runs BGP, routing policies are immediately needed to prevent the large ISPs from seeing the smaller network as a transit AS to each other. This actually happened a number of times in the early days of BGP, when small corporate networks new to BGP suddenly found themselves passing traffic between two huge national ISPs whose links to each other had failed. Why pass traffic through two or three other ISPs when "Small Company, Inc." has a BGP path a single AS long? BGP routing policies are immediately put in place to not advertise routes learned for one national ISP to the other. As long as "you can't get there from here," all will be fine at the little network in the middle.

BGP *summarizes* all that is known about the IP address space inside the local AS and *advertises* this information to other ASs. The other ASs pass this information along, until all ASs running BGP know exactly what is where on the Internet. Without BGP, a single default route must handle all destinations outside the AS. This is okay when a single router leads to the Internet, but inadequate for networks with numerous connections to other ASs and ISPs.

BGP was not the original EGP used on the Internet. The first exterior gateway protocol was Exterior Gateway Protocol (EGP). EGP is still around, but only on isolated portions of the original Internet—such as for the U.S. military. An appreciation of EGP's limitations helps to understand why BGP works the way it does.

EGP and the Early Internet

In the early 1980s, the Internet had grown to include almost 1000 computers. Several noted that distance-vector routing protocols such as the original Gateway-to-Gateway Protocol (GGP), an IGP, would not scale to a large network environment. If every router needed to know everything about every route, convergence times when links failed would be very high. GGP routing changes had to happen globally and in a coordinated fashion. But the Internet, even in the 1980s, was a huge network with many different types of computers and routers run by many different organizations.

The answer divided the emerging Internet into independent but interconnected ASs. As seen in Chapter 14, the AS is identified by a 4-byte (32-bit) number assigned by the same authorities that assign IP addresses. We'll use a shorthand such as `65127` instead of the full (and proper) `0.65127` to indicate legacy 2-byte AS numbers. The AS range `64512` through `65535` is reserved for private AS numbers. Inside the AS, the network was assumed to be under the control of a single network administrator. Within the AS, local network matters (addressing, links, new routers, and so on) could be addressed locally with GGP. But GGP ran only within the AS. Between ASs, some way had to be found to communicate what networks were reachable within and through one AS to the other AS.

EGP was the solution. EGP ran on the border routers (gateways), with links to other ASs. EGP routers just sent a list of other routers and the classful major networks that the router could reach. This cut down on the amount of information that needed to be sent between ASs. Today, aggregation should be used as often as possible with BGP instead of classful major network routes, but the intent and result are the same. So, if a BGP router knows about networks `10.10.1.0/24` through `10.10.127.0/24` it can aggregate the route as `10.10.0.0/17` and advertise that one route (NRLI) instead of 128 separate routing updates. Even if a network such as `10.10.11.0/24` is not included in the range, the more specific advertisement of `10.10.11.0/24` and the longest match rule will make sure traffic finds its way to the right place—as long as the route is advertised properly. Nevertheless, there are many reasons people do not aggregate as much as they should, and many of their reasons are flawed. For example, trying to protect a network against "prefix hijacking" is a bad reason not to aggregate.

There is no need for an EGP to reproduce the features of an IGP. An IGP needs to tell every router in the AS which router has which interfaces and what IP addresses are attached to these interfaces or reachable through that router (such as static routes). All that other ASs need to know is which IP addresses are reachable in a particular AS and how to get to a border router on, or nearer to, the target AS.

The Birth of BGP

EGP suffered from a number of limitations, too technical to recount. After some initial attempts to upgrade EGP, it was decided to create a better EGP (as a class of routing protocol, contrasted with IGPs) than EGP: BGP. BGP was defined in 1989 with RFC 1105 (BGP1 or BGP-1 or BGPv1), revised in 1990 as RFC 1163 (BGP2), and revised again in 1991 as RFC 1267 (BGP3). The version of BGP used today on the Internet, BGP4, emerged in 1994 as RFC 1654 and was extended for classless operation in 1995 as RFC 1771. The baseline BGP specification today is RFC 4271. This chapter describes BGP4.

BGP has been extended for new roles on the Internet. BGP *extended communities* are used with virtual private networks (VPNs). Communities are simply labeled that so they can be used to associate NLRIs that do not share other traits. For example, a community value can be assigned to small customers and another community value used to identify a small customer with multiple sites. There are few limits to the community "tags'" usage. And BGP routes are often the only ones that can use multiprotocol label switching (MPLS) label-switched paths (LSPs). BGP is as easily extensible as IS–IS and OSPF to support new functions and add routing information that needs to be circulated between ASs.

Many organizations find themselves suddenly forced to adapt BGP in a hurry, for instance, when they have to multihome their networks. Also, when they deploy VPNs or MPLS or any one of the many newer technologies used to potentially span ISPs and ASs, BGP is needed. The problem with IGPs is that they cannot easily share information across routing domain boundaries.

BGP AS A PATH-VECTOR PROTOCOL

One of the problems with EGP was that the metrics looked very much like RIP hop counts. Simple distance vectors were not helpful at the AS level, because hop counts did not distinguish the fast links that began appearing in major ISP network backbones. Destinations that were "close" over two or three 56- or 64-kbps links actually took much longer to reach than through four or five hops over 45-Mbps links, and distance vectors had no protection against routing loops.

Link-state protocols could have dealt with the problem by implementing some of the alternate ToS metrics described for OPSF and IS–IS. However, these would rely not only on consistent implementation among all ISPs but the proper setting of bits in IP packets. In the world of independent highly competitive ISPs, this consistency was next to impossible. So, BGP was developed as a *path-vector* protocol. This means that one of the most important attributes BGP uses to choose the active route is the length of the AS path reported in the NLRI.

To create this AS list, BGP routing updates carry a complete list of transit networks (ASs) that must be traversed between the AS receiving the update and the AS that can deliver the packet using its IGP. A loop occurs when an AS path list contains the same AS that is receiving the update, so this update is rejected and loops are prevented. If the update is accepted, that AS will add its own AS to the list when advertising the routing update to other ASs. This lets an AS apply routing policies to the updates and avoid using routes that lead through an AS that is not the preferred way to reach a destination.

Path vectors do not mean that all ASs are created equal. Numerous small ASs might get traffic through faster than one huge AS. But more aspects of a route are described in BGP than just the length of the AS path to the destination. The system allows each AS to represent the route with a different metric that means something to the AS originating the route.

But more ASs generate more and longer path information. RFC 1774 in 1995 estimated that 100,000 routes generated by 3000 ASs would have paths about 20 ASs long. There was a concern about router memory and processor requirements to store and maintain all of this information, especially in smaller routers.

Several mechanisms are built into BGP to address this. ISPs would not usually accept a BGP route advertisement with a mask more than 19 bits long (`/19`). This was called the *universally reachable* address level. The price for compact routing tables and maintenance was a loss of routing accuracy, and many ISPs relaxed this policy. Most today accept `/24` prefixes (although they can accept more specific addresses from their own customers, of course). The other BGP mechanisms to cut down on routing table size and maintenance complexity are route reflectors, confederations (also called sub-confederations), and route damping (or dampening). All of these are beyond the scope of this chapter, but should be mentioned.

IBPG AND EBGP

BGP is an EGP that runs between individual routing domains, or ASs. When BGP *speakers* (the term for routers configured to peer with BGP neighbors) are in different ASs, the routers use an *exterior* BGP (EBPG) session to exchange information. When BGP peers are within the same AS, the routers use *interior* BGP (IBGP). These terms often appear as E-BPG/I-BGP or eBGP/iBGP.

IBGP is not some IGP version of BGP. It is used to allow BGP routers to exchange BGP routing information inside the same AS. IBGP sessions are usually only required when an AS is *multihomed* or has multiple links to other ASs. (However, we used them on the Illustrated Network anyway, and that's fine too.) An AS with only a single link to one other AS need only run EBGP on the border router and relies on the IGP to distribute routes learned by EBPG to the other routers. In the case where there is only one exit point for the entire AS, a single static default route to the border router can be used effectively instead. The reason that IBGP is needed is shown in Figure 15.2.

Without IBGP, all routes learned by EBGP must be dumped into the IGP to make sure all routes are known in the entire AS. This can easily overwhelm the IGP. For this reason, it is usual to create an IBGP mesh between routers on the backbone (other routers can make do with a handful of default routes).

EBGP sessions typically peer to the physical interface address of the neighbor router. These are often point-to-point WAN links, and are the only way to reach another AS. If the link is down, the other AS is unreachable over that link. So, there is little point in trying to keep a BGP session going to the peer.

On the other hand, IBGP sessions usually peer to the stable "loopback" interface address of the peer router. An IBGP peer can typically be reached over more than one physical interface within the AS, so even if an IBGP peer's "closest" interface is down the BGP sessions can stay up because BGP packets use the IGP routing table to find an alternate route to the peer.

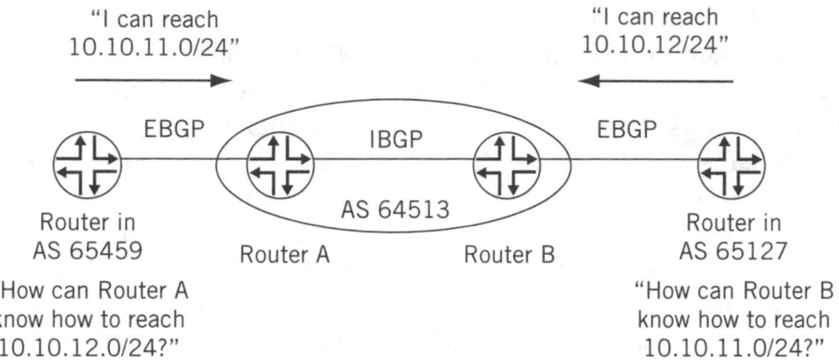

FIGURE 15.2

The need for IBGP. Note that if only EBGP is running, the AS in the middle must dump all BGP routes into the IGP to advertise them throughout the network.

Two BGP neighbors, EBGP or IBGP, first exchange their entire BGP routing tables—subject to the policies on each router. After that, only incremental or partial table information is exchanged when routing changes occur. BGP keepalives are exchanged because in stable networks long periods of time might elapse before something interesting happens.

IGP Next Hops and BGP Next Hops

BGP uses NLRIs as the way one AS tells another, "I know how to reach IP address space `192.168.27.0/24` and `172.16.44.0/24` and…" The AS does not say that it is the AS that has assigned that IP address space locally. Many of the addresses might be from other ASs beyond the AS advertising the routes. The AS path allows an AS to figure out how far away a destination is through the AS that has advertised the route, or NLRI.

With an IGP, the next hop associated with a route is usually the IP address of the physical interface on the next hop router. But the BGP next hop (also sometimes called the "protocol next hop") is often the IP address of the *router* that is advertising the BGP NLRI information. The BGP next hop is the address of the BGP peer, most often the loopback interface address (the *BGP Identifier*) for IBGP and the physical interface address in the other AS for EBGP. The BGP next hop is the way one BGP router tells another, "If you have a packet for this IP address space, send it here."

The IGP has to know how to reach the next hop, whether it's a BGP next hop or not. But the next hop for EBGP is often at the end of a link to the other AS and is not running an IGP (it's not an internal link). So, how is the IGP to know about it? Well, BGP routes could be "dumped" into the IGP—but there are a lot more external routes than internal, and the whole point is to keep the IGP and EGP separate to some extent. This brings up an interesting point about the relationship of BGP and the IGP and a practice known as next hop self.

BGP and the IGP

There is a well-known unreachable condition in BGP that must be solved with a simple routing policy know as *next hop self*, or just NHS. An EBGP route (NLRI) normally arrives from another AS with the physical address of the remote interface as the BGP next hop. If the EBGP route is readvertised through IBPG, it is likely that the BGP next hop will be completely unknown to the IGP routing tables inside the receiving AS. A router within an AS does not care how to reach a physical interface IP address in another AS. Next hop self is just a way to have the router advertising the route through IBGP use *itself* as the next hop for the EBGP route. The idea is not BGP "next-hop-is-the-physical-interface-in-another-AS" but BGP "next-hop-is-me-in-this-AS" or BGP "next-hop-self."

BGP is not a routing protocol built directly on top of IP. BGP relies on TCP connections to reach its peers, and so resembles an IP application more than an IGP routing protocol. Without the IGP to provide connectivity, TCP sessions for the BGP messages cannot be established except on links to adjacent routers. BGP does not flood information with IBPG. So, what an IBGP router learns from its IBGP peers is never passed along to another IBGP neighbor.

To fully distribute BGP information among the routers within an AS, a full mesh of IBGP connections (adjacencies) is necessary. Every IBGP router must send complete routing information to every other IBGP router in the AS. In a large AS with many external links to other ASs, this meshing requirement can add a lot of overhead traffic and configuration maintenance to the network. This is where route reflectors and confederations come in (these concepts are far beyond the scope of this chapter and will not be discussed further).

The main reasons BGP was built this way were to keep BGP as simple as possible and to prevent routing loops inside the AS. The dependency on TCP and the lack of flooding means that IBGP must communicate directly with every other router that needs to know BGP routing information. This does not mean that every router must be adjacent (connected by a direct link), because TCP can be routed through many routers to reach its destination. What it does mean is that routers connected by IBGP inside an AS must create a *full mesh* of IGBP peering sessions. This need to create a full mesh and *synchronize* BGP with the IGP is shown in Figure 15.3.

In the figure, Ace ISP and Best ISP are no longer peers. Now they are both customers of National ISP. Naturally, everyone on LAN2 still has to know how to reach LAN2 at `10.10.11.0/24` (and vice versa, of course). EBGP advertises LAN1 to National ISP, and IBGP from border router to border router makes sure that LAN2 on Best ISP can reach `10.10.11.0/24`. But what about an internal router inside National ISP's AS? There are only two ways to allow everyone in National ISP's service area to access LAN1 (presumably to buy something, although there *are* cases concerning LAN1 security where the route might not be advertised everywhere). With a full mesh of IBGP sessions in National ISP, there is no need to dump all external routes into the IGP (the IGP should only handle routes within the AS).

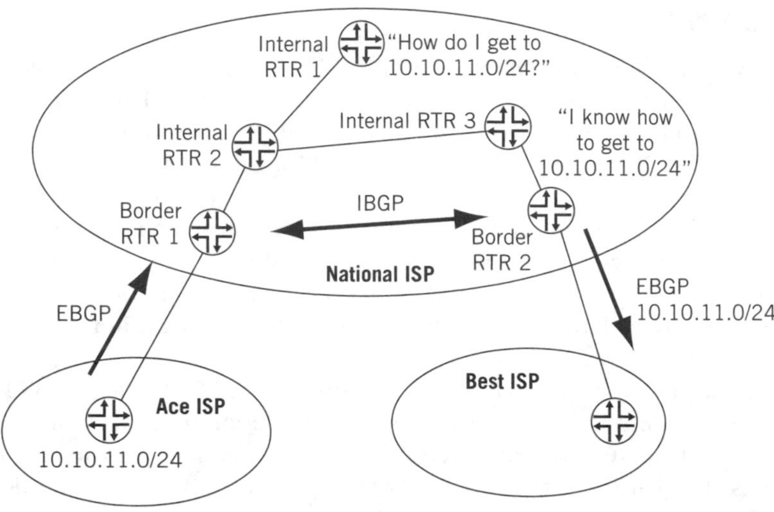

FIGURE 15.3

The need for a full IBGP mesh. Note that the routers inside National ISP do not necessarily know how to reach 10.10.11.0/24 (LAN1).

OTHER TYPES OF BGP

The major types of BGP are EBGP for external peers outside the AS and IBGP for internal peers within the same AS. These are usually the only types of BGP mentioned in most sources. But there are other variations of BGP used in other situations.

One BGP variation that is becoming very important, especially where VPNs are concerned, is Multiprotocol BGP (often seen as MBGP or MP-BGP). Multiprotocol BGP originally extended BGP to support IP multicast routes and routing information. But MBGP is also used to support IP-based VPN information and to carry IPv6 routing information, such as from RIPng and OSPF for IPv6. MBGP work on IPv6 is just starting, so no special consideration of using BGP for IPv6 appears in this chapter other than to note than MBGP is used for this purpose. MBGP is currently defined in RFC 4760.

There is also Multihop BGP, sometimes seen as *EBGP multihop*. Multihop BGP is only used with EBGP and allows an EBGP peer in another AS to be more than one hop away. Usually, EBGP peers are directly connected by a point-to-point WAN link. But sometimes it is necessary to peer with a router beyond the border router that actually terminates the link. Normally, BGP packets have a TTL of 1 and thus never travel beyond the adjacent router. Multihop BGP packets have a TTL greater than 1 and the peer is beyond the adjacent router. Multihop BGP is also used in load balancing situations when there is more than one link between two border routers, and for "route-view"-style route collectors.

Finally, there is a slight change in behavior of the BGP that runs between confederations. In most cases, the version of BGP that runs between confederations is just called EBGP. However, there are slight differences in the EBGP that runs between ASs and the EBGP that runs between confederations—which are always inside the same AS. Sometimes the variant of BGP that runs between confederations is known as Confederation BGP, or CBGP, although use of this term is not common.

BGP ATTRIBUTES

The information that all forms of BGP carry is associated with a route (NLRI) as a series of *attributes*. This is the major difference between BGP and IGPs. IGP routes carry the route, next hop, metric, and maybe an optional tag (or two). BGP routes can carry a considerable amount of information, all intended to allow an AS to choose the "best" way to reach a destination.

Most implementations of BGP will understand 10 attributes, and some use and understand even more. Every BGP attribute is characterized by two major parameters. An attribute is either well known or optional. Well-known attributes must be understood and processed by every implementation of BGP regardless of vendor. Optional attributes are exactly that: there is no guarantee that a given BGP implementation will understand or process that particular attribute. BGP implementations that do not support an optional attribute simply pass that information on if that is what is called for, or ignore it.

In addition, a well-known BGP attribute is either mandatory or discretionary. Mandatory BGP attributes must be present in every BGP update message for EBGP, IBGP, or something else. Discretionary BGP attributes appear only in some types of BGP update messages, such as those used by EBGP only.

Finally, optional BGP attributes are transitive or nontransitive. Transitive BGP optional attributes are passed from peer to peer even if the router does not support that option. Nontransitive BGP optional attributes can be ignored by the receiver BGP process if not supported and not sent along to peers. The ten BGP attributes discussed in this chapter are listed in Table 15.1 and their characteristics are described in the list that follows.

Table 15.1 BGP Attributes

Attribute and Type Code	Well-Known Mandatory	Well-Known Discretionary	Optional Transitive	Optional Nontransitive
ORIGIN (1)	X			
AS_PATH (2)	X			
NEXT_HOP (3)	X			
LOCAL_PREF (4)		X		
ATOMIC_AGGR (5)		X		
AGGREGATOR (6)			X	
COMMUNITY (7)			X	
MED (8)				X
ORIGINATOR_ID (9)				X
CLUSTER_LIST (10)				X

ORIGIN—This attribute reflects where BGP obtained knowledge of the route in the first place. This can be the IGP, EGP, or "incomplete."

AS_PATH—This forms a sequence of AS numbers that leads to the originating AS for the NLRI. The main use of the AS Path is for loop avoidance among ASs, but it is common to artificially extend the AS Path attribute through a routing policy so that a particular path through a certain router looks very unattractive. The AS Path attribute can consist of an ordered list of AS numbers (AS_SEQUENCE) or just a collection of AS numbers in no particular order (AS_SET).

NEXT_HOP—The BGP Next Hop (or "protocol next hop") is quite distinct from an IGP's next hop. Outside an AS, the BGP Next Hop is most likely the border router—not the actual router inside the other AS that has this network on a local interface. Next Hop Self is the typical way to make sure that the BGP Next Hop is reachable.

LOCAL_PREF—The Local Preference of the NLRI is relative to other routes learned by IBGP within an AS and therefore is not used by EBGP. When routes are advertised with IBGP, traffic will flow toward the AS exit point (border router) that advertised the highest Local Preference for the route. It is used to establish a preferred exit link to another AS.

MULTI_EXIT_DISC (MED)—The Multi-Exit Discriminator (MED) attribute is the way one AS tries to influence another when it goes to choosing among multiple exit points (border routers) that link to the AS. A MED is the closest thing to a purely IGP metric that BGP has. Changing MEDs is one of the most common ways one ISP tries to make another ISP use the links it wants between the ISPs, such as higher speed links ("use this address on this link to reach me, unless it's down, then use this one..."). MED values are totally arbitrary.

ATOMIC_AGGREGATE and AGGREGATOR—These two attributes work together. Both are used when routing information is aggregated for BGP. A common goal on the Internet today is to represent as many networks (routes) with as few routing table entries as possible. So, as routing information makes its way through the Internet each AS will often try to condense (aggregate) the routing information as much as possible with as short a VLSM as can be properly contrived.

COMMUNITY—The BGP Community attribute is sort of a "club for routes." Communities make it easier to apply policies to routes as a group. There might be a community that applies to an ISP's customers. In that case, it is not necessary to list every customer's IP address in a policy to set Local Pref or MED (for example) as long as they all are assigned to a unique "customer" community value. Community values are often used today as a way for one ISP to inform a peer ISP of the value of the Local Pref for the route inside the originating ISP's

AS (Local Pref is not present in EBGP). The Community attribute was originally Cisco specific, but was standardized in RFC 1997. Communities just make it easier for a router to find all NLRIs associated with (for example) a particular VPN.

ORIGINATOR_ID and CLUSTER_LIST—These attributes are used by BGP route reflectors. Both of these attributes are used to prevent routing loops when route reflectors are in use. The Originator ID is a 32-bit value created by the route reflector and is the originator of the route within the local AS. If the originator router sees that its own ID is a received route, a loop has occurred and the route is ignored. The Cluster List is a list of the route reflection cluster IDs of the clusters through which the route has passed. If a route reflector sees it own cluster ID in the Cluster List, a loop has occurred and the route is ignored.

BGP AND ROUTING POLICY

BGP is a policy-driven protocol. What BGP does and how BGP does it can be almost totally determined by routing policy. It is difficult to make BGP do exactly what an ISP wants without the use of routing policies.

Want BGP to advertise customers on static routes or running OSPF, IS-IS, or RIP? Redistribute statics, OSPF, IS-IS, and RIP into BGP? Want to artificially extend an AS path to make an AS look very unattractive for transit traffic? Write a routing policy to prepend the AS multiple times. Want to change the community attribute to add or subtract information? Use a routing policy. Concerned about the shear amount of routes advertised? Write a routing policy to aggregate the routes any way that makes sense. Want to advertise a more specific route along with a more general aggregate (called "punching a hole" in the advertised address space)? Write a routing policy. BGP depends on routing policy to behave the way it should.

BGP Scaling

A global corporation today might have 3000 routers large and small spread around the world. Even with multiple ASs, there could be 1000 routers within an AS that might all need IBGP information—no matter how the routes have been aggregated. To fully mesh 1000 IBGP routers within an AS requires 499,500 IBGP sessions. A network 100 times larger than a 10-router network requires more than 10,000 times more IBGP sessions. Adding one router adds 1000 additional IBGP sessions to the network.

This problem with the exponential growth of IBGP sessions is the main BGP scaling issue. There are two ways to deal with this issue: the use of router reflectors (RR) and confederations.

What is the difference between RRs and confederations? At the risk of offending BGP purists, it can be loosely stated that RRs are a way of grouping BGP routers inside an AS and running IBGP between the RR clusters. Confederations are a way of grouping BGP routers inside an AS and running EBGP between the confederation "sub-ASs." Because of the differences between RRs and confederations, it is even possible to have both configured at the same time in the same AS. There is also BGP route damping, which is not a way of dealing with BGP scaling directly but rather a way to deal with the effects of BGP scaling in terms of the amount of routing information that needs to be distributed to IBGP and EBGP peers when a router or link fails.

BGP MESSAGE TYPES

BGP messages types are simpler than those used by OSPF and IS–IS because of the presence of TCP. TCP handles all of the details of connection setup and maintenance, and before a BGP peering session is established the router performs the usual TCP three-way handshake using TCP port 179 on one router. The other router uses a port that is not well known, and it is just a matter of whose TCP SYN message arrives first that determines which BGP peer is technically the "server." All BGP messages are then unicast over the TCP connection. There are only four BGP message types.

Open—Used to exchange version numbers (usually four, but two routers can agree on an earlier version), AS numbers (same for IBGP, different for EBGP), hold time until a Keepalive or Update is received (the smaller value is used if they differ), the BGP identifier (Router ID, usually the loopback interface address), and options such as authentication method (if used).

Keepalive—Keepalive messages are used to maintain the TCP session when there are no Updates to send. The default time is one-third of the hold time established in the Open message exchange.

Update—This advertises or withdraws routes. The Update has fields for the NLRI (both prefix and VLSM length), path attributes, and withdrawn routes by prefix and length.

Notification—These are for errors and always close a BGP connection. For example, a BGP version mismatch in the Open message closes the connection, which must then be reopened when one router or the other adjusts its version support.

The maximum TCP segment size for a BGP message is 4096 bytes and the minimum is 19 bytes. All BGP messages have a common header, as shown in Figure 15.4.

The Marker is a 16-byte field used for synchronizing BGP connections and in authentication. If no authentication is used and the message is an Open, this field is set to all 1s. The Length is a 16-bit field that contains the length of the message, including the header, in bytes. Finally, the Type is an 8-bit field set to 1 (Open), 2 (Update), 3 (Notification), or 4 (Keepalive).

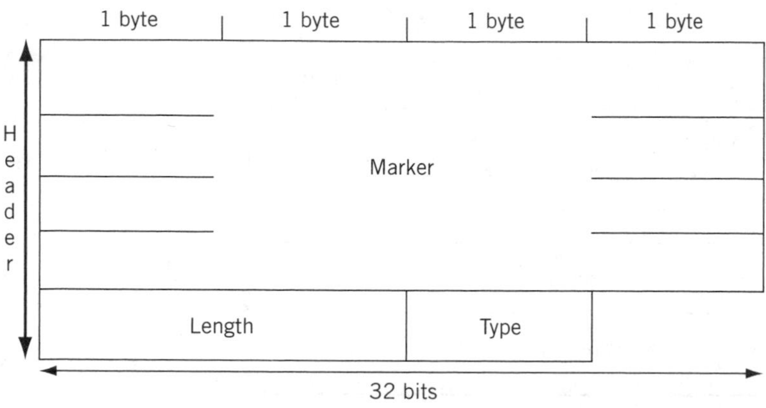

FIGURE 15.4

The BGP message header carried inside a TCP segment.

BGP MESSAGE FORMATS

A data portion follows the header in all but the Keepalive messages. Keepalives consist of only the BGP message headers and so need not be discussed further in this section.

The Open Message

Once a TCP connection has been established between two BGP speakers, Open messages are exchanged between the BGP peers. If the Open is acceptable to a router, a Keepalive is sent to confirm the Open. Once Keepalives are exchanged, peers can exchange Updates, Keepalives, and Notification messages. The format of the Open message is shown in Figure 15.5.

The Open message has an 8-bit Version field, a 2-byte My Autonomous System field, a 2-byte Hold Time value (0 or at least 3 seconds), a 32-bit BGP Identifier (router ID), an 8-bit Optional Parameters Length field (set to 0 if no options are present), and the optional parameters themselves in the same TLV format used by IS–IS in the previous chapter. BGP options are not discussed in this chapter.

The Update Message

The Update message is used to advertise NLRIs (routes) to a BGP peer, to withdraw multiple routes that are now unreachable (or *unfeasible*), or both. The format of the Update message is shown in Figure 15.6. Because of the peculiar "skew" the 19-byte BGP header puts on subsequent fields, this message is shown in a different format than the others. There are two distinct sections to the Update message. They are used to Withdraw and Advertise routes.

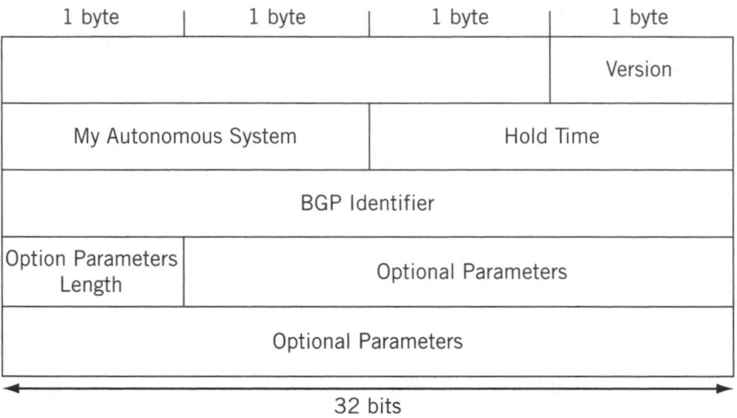

FIGURE 15.5

The BGP Open message showing optional fields at the end.

Unfeasible Routes Length (2 bytes)
Withdrawn Routes (variable length)
Total Path Attribute Length (2 bytes)
Path Attribute (variable length)
Network Layer Reachability Information (variable length)

FIGURE 15.6

The BGP Update message. This is the main way routes are advertised with BGP.

The Update message starts with a 20-byte field indicating the total length of the Withdrawn Routes field in bytes. If there are no Withdrawn Routes, this field is set to zero. If there are Withdrawn Routes, the routes follow in a variable-length field with the list of Withdrawn Routes. Each route is a Length/Prefix pair. The length indicates the number of bits that are significant in the following prefix and form a mask/prefix pair.

The next field is a 2-byte Total Path Attribute Length field. This is the length in bytes of the Path Attributes field that follows. A value of zero means that nothing follows.

The variable-length Path Attributes field lists the attributes associated with the NRLIs that follow. Each Path attribute is a TLV of varying length, the first part of which

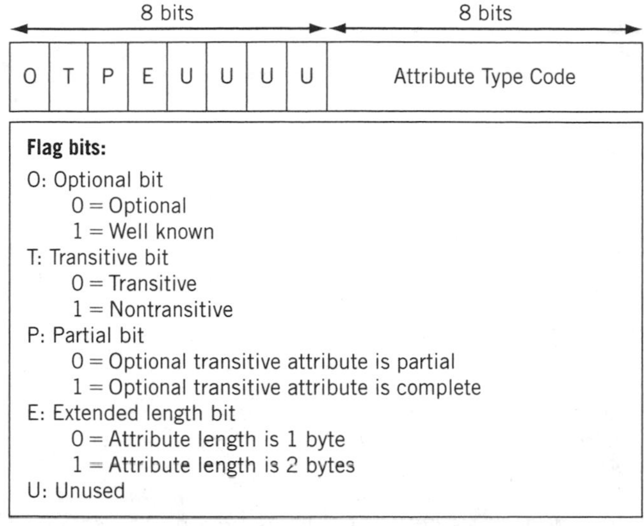

FIGURE 15.7

The BGP Attribute Type format. This is how NRLIs are grouped.

is the 2-byte Attribute Type. There is a structure to the Attribute Type field, as shown in Figure 15.7. There are four flag bits, four unused bits, and then an 8 bit Attribute Type code.

There are other attribute codes in use with BGP, but these are not discussed in this chapter. One of the most important of these other attributes is the Extended Community attribute used in VPNs.

The Update message ends with a variable-length NLRI field. Each NLRI (route) is a Length/Prefix pair. The length indicates the number of bits that is significant in the following prefix. There is no length field for this list that ends the Update message. The number of NLRIs present is derived from the known length of all of the other fields.

So, instead of saying "here's a route and these are its attributes..." for every NLRI advertised the Update message basically says "here's a group of path attributes and here are the routes that these apply to..." This cuts down on the number of messages that needs to be sent across the network. In this way, each Update message forms a unit of its own and has no further fragmentation concerns.

The Notification Message

Error messages in BGP have an 8-bit Error Code, an 8-bit Subcode, and a variable-length Data field determined by the Error Code and Subcode. The format of the BGP Notification message is shown in Figure 15.8.

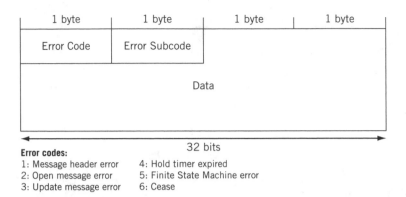

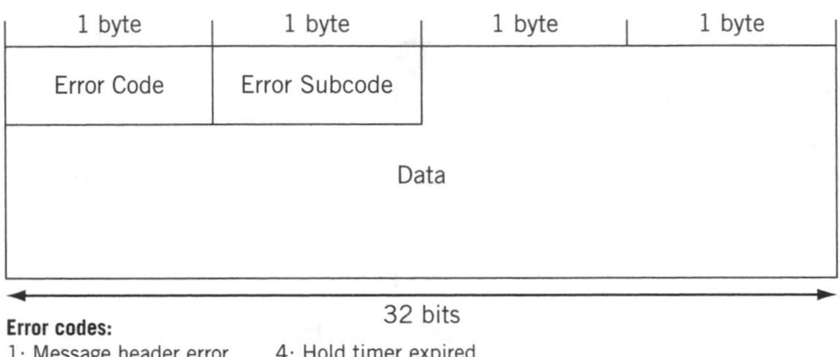

Error codes:
1: Message header error
2: Open message error
3: Update message error
4: Hold timer expired
5: Finite State Machine error
6: Cease

FIGURE 15.8

The BGP Notification message format. BGP benefits from using TCP as a transport protocol.

A full discussion of BGP Notification codes and subcodes is beyond the scope of this chapter. The major Error Codes are Message Header Error (1), Open Message Error (2), Update Message Error (3), Hold Timer Expired (4), Finite State Machine Error (5), used when the BGP implementation gets hopelessly confused about what it should be doing next, and Cease (6), used to end the session.

QUESTIONS FOR READERS

Figure 15.9 shows some of the concepts discussed in this chapter and can be used to help you answer the following questions.

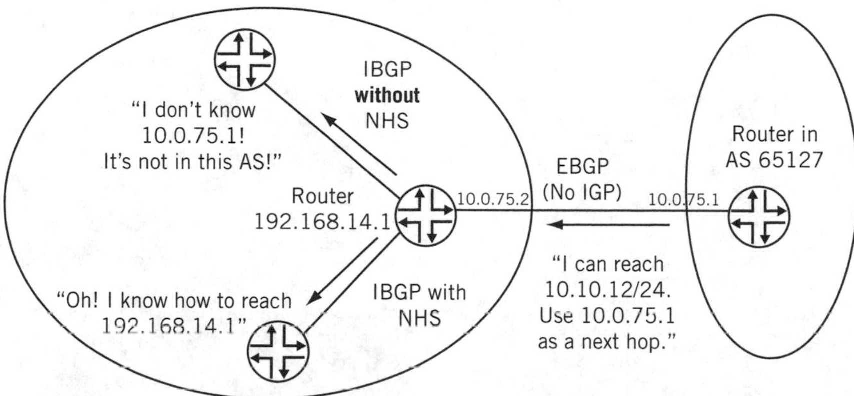

FIGURE 15.9

How Next Hop Self allows internal routers to forward packets for BGP routes. Border router 192.168.14.1 substitutes its own address for the "real" next hop.

1. BGP distributes "reachability" information and not routes. Why doesn't BGP distribute route information?
2. What does it mean to say that the BGP is a "path-vector" protocol?
3. What is "next hop self" and why is it important in BGP?
4. Which two major BGP router configurations are employed to deal with BGP scaling?
5. What are the ten major BGP attributes?

CHAPTER

Multicast

16

What You Will Learn

In this chapter, you will learn how multicast routing protocols allow multicast traffic to make its way from a source to interested receivers through a router-based network. We'll look at both dense and parse multicast routing protocols, as well as some of the other protocols used with them (such as IGMP).

You will learn how the PIM rendezvous point (RP) has become the key component in a multicast network. We'll see how to configure an RP on the network and use it to deliver a simple multicast traffic stream to hosts.

If the Internet and TCP/IP are going to be used for everything from the usual data activities to voice and video, something must be done about the normal *unicast* packet addressing reflecting one specific source and one specific destination. Almost everything described in this book so far has featured unicast, although multicast addresses have been mentioned from time to time—especially when used by routing protocols.

The one-to-many operation of multicast is a technique between the one-to-one packet delivery operation of unicast and the one-to-all operation of broadcast. Broadcasts tend to disrupt hosts' normal processing because most broadcasts are not really intended for every host yet each receiving host must pay attention to the broadcast packet's content. Many protocols that routinely used broadcasts, such as RIPv1, were replaced by versions that used multicast groups instead (RIPv2, OSPF). Even the protocols in IPv4 that still routinely use broadcast, such as ARPing to find the MAC address that goes with an IP address, have been replaced in IPv6 with multicast-friendly versions of the same procedure.

Multicast protocols are still not universally supported on much of the Internet. Then how do large numbers of people all watch the same video feed from a Web server (for example) at the same time? Today, this is normally accomplished with numerous unicast links, each running from the server to every individual host. This works, but it does not scale. Can a server handle 100, 1000, or 1,000,000 simultaneous users? Many-to-many multicast applications, such as on-line gaming and gambling sites, use

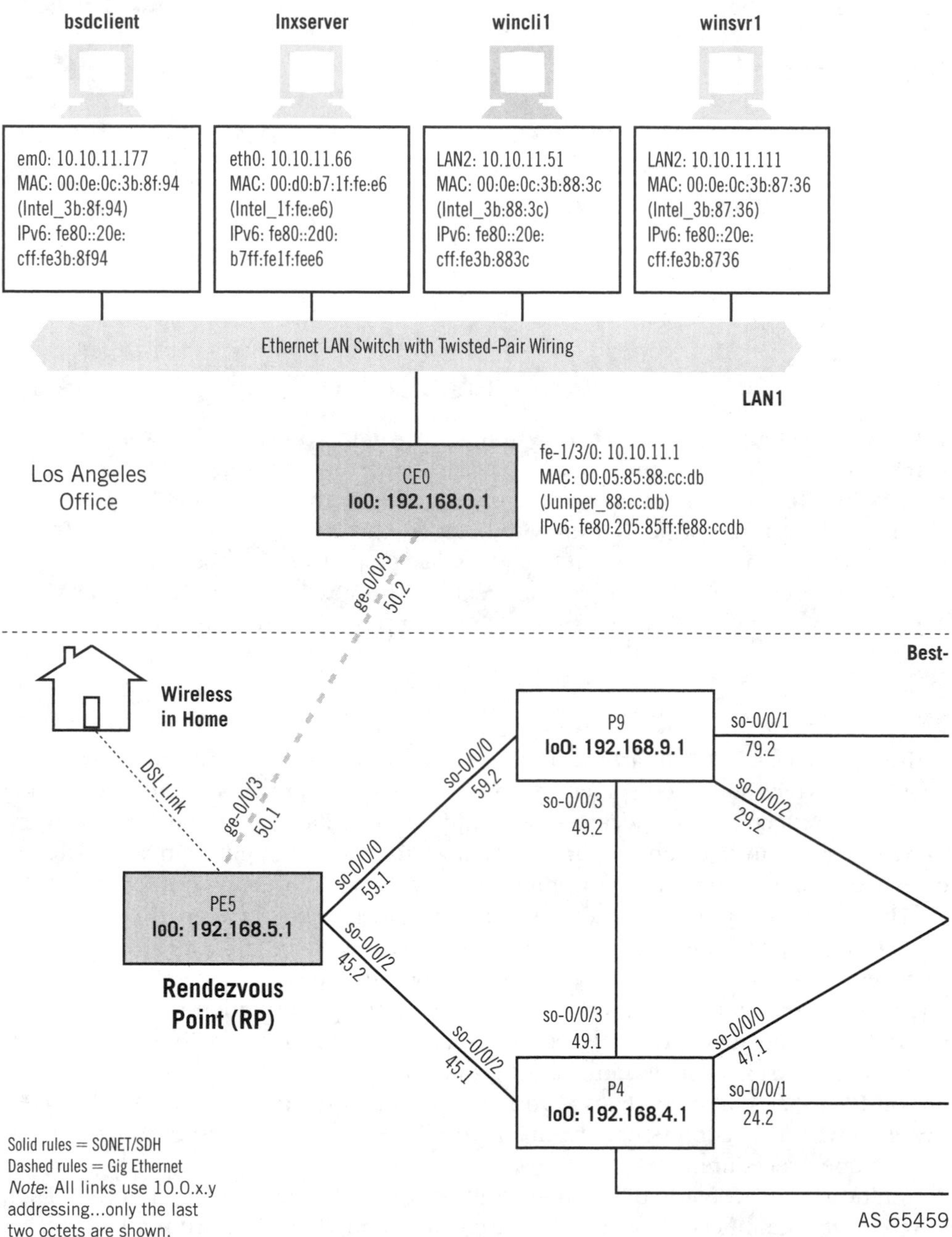

FIGURE 16.1

Portion of the Illustrated Network used for the multicast examples. The RP will be router PE5, and the ISPs have merged into a single AS for this chapter.

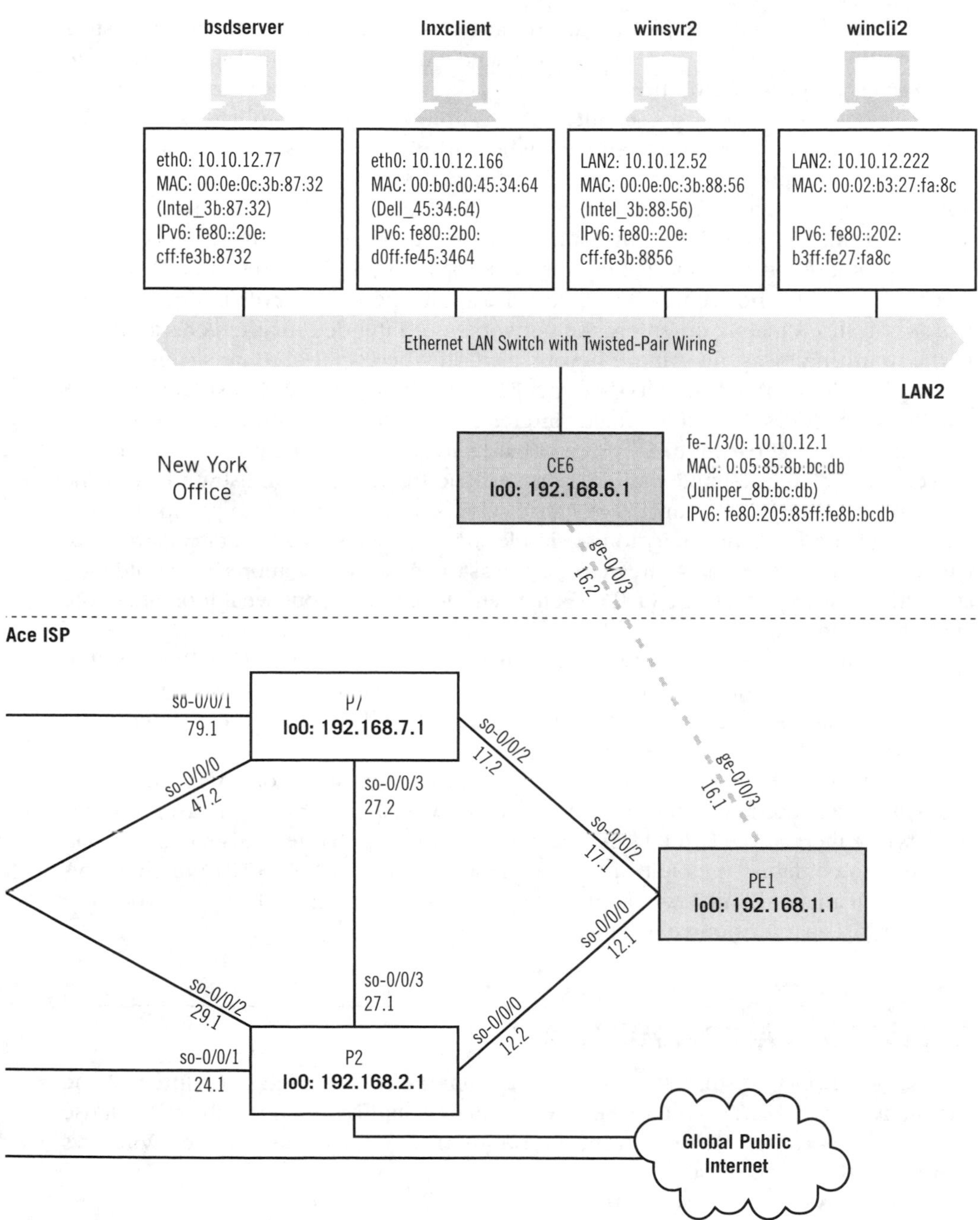
bsdserver
lnxclient
winsvr2
wincli2
eth0: 10.10.12.77
MAC: 00:0e:0c:3b:87:32
(Intel_3b:87:32)
IPv6: fe80::20e:
cff:fe3b:8732
eth0: 10.10.12.166
MAC: 00:b0:d0:45:34:64
(Dell_45:34:64)
IPv6: fe80::2b0:
d0ff:fe45:3464
LAN2: 10.10.12.52
MAC: 00:0e:0c:3b:88:56
(Intel_3b:88:56)
IPv6: fe80::20e:
cff:fe3b:8856
LAN2: 10.10.12.222
MAC: 00:02:b3:27:fa:8c
IPv6: fe80::202:
b3ff:fe27:fa8c
Ethernet LAN Switch with Twisted-Pair Wiring
LAN2
New York
Office
CE6
lo0: 192.168.6.1
fe-1/3/0: 10.10.12.1
MAC: 0.05.85.8b.bc.db
(Juniper_8b:bc:db)
IPv6: fe80:205:85ff:fe8b:bcdb
ge-0/0/3
16.2
Ace ISP
so-0/0/1
79.1
P7
lo0: 192.168.7.1
so-0/0/2
17.2
ge-0/0/3
16.1
so-0/0/0
47.2
so-0/0/3
27.2
so-0/0/2
17.1
PE1
lo0: 192.168.1.1
so-0/0/0
12.1
so-0/0/2
29.1
so-0/0/3
27.1
so-0/0/0
12.2
so-0/0/1
24.1
P2
lo0: 192.168.2.1
Global Public
Internet

multiple point-to-point meshes of links in most cases. Even if modern server clusters could do this, could all the routers and links handle this traffic? Multicast uses the *routers* to replicate packets, not the servers.

However, interdomain (or even intersubnet) multicasting is a problem. IP multicast is widely leveraged on localized subnets where it's solely a question of host support. Many-to-many applications have some fundamental scaling challenges and multicast does not address these very well. For example, how does each host in a shared tree of multicast traffic manage the receipt of perhaps 50 video streams from participants?

Today, multicast is a key component of local IPv6 and IPv4 resource discovery mechanisms and is not confined to enterprise applications. However, multicast *applications* are used mainly on enterprise networks not intended for the general public. In the future, multicast must move beyond a world where special routers (not all routers can handle multicast packets) use special parts of the Internet (most famously, the MBONE, or multicast backbone) to link interested hosts to their sources. Multicast must become an integral part of every piece of hardware and software on the Internet.

Let's look at a few simple multicast packets and frames on the Illustrated Network. We don't have any video cameras or music servers on the network to pump out content, but we do have the ability to use simple socket programs to generate a stream of packets to multicast group addresses as easily as to unicast destinations. We could look at multicast as used by OSPF or IPv6 router announcements, but we'll look at simple applications instead.

We'll look at IPv4 first, and then take a quick look at IPv6 multicasting. We'll use the devices shown in Figure 16.1 to illustrate multicast protocols, introducing the terms used in multicast protocols as we go. We'll explore all of the terms in detail later in the chapter.

This chapter uses `wincli2` and `lxnclient` on LAN2 and `wincli1` on LAN1. The router `PE5` will serve as our PIM sparse-mode RP. To simplify the number of multicast protocols used, we've merged the two ISPs into Best-Ace ISP for this chapter. This means we will not need to configure the Multicast Source Discovery Protocol (MSDP), which allows receivers in an AS to find RPs in another AS. A full investigation of MSDP is beyond the scope of this chapter, but we will go over the basics.

A FIRST LOOK AT IPv4 MULTICAST

This section uses two small socket programs from the source cited in Chapter 12: the excellent *TCP/IP Sockets in C* by Michael J. Donahoo and Kenneth L. Calvert. We'll use two programs run as MulticastReceiver and MulticastSender, and two free Windows multicast utilities, wsend and wlisten.

Let's start with two hosts on the same LAN. We'll use `lnxclient (10.10.12.166)` and `wincli2 (10.10.12.222)` for this exercise (both clients, but there's no heavy multicasting going on). We'll set the Linux client to multicast the text string `HEY` once every 3 seconds onto the LAN using multicast group address `239.2.2.2` (multicasts use special IP addresses for destinations) and UDP port `22222` (multicast applications often use UDP, and cannot use TCP). Naturally, we'll set the multicast receiver socket program on the Windows XP client to receive traffic sent to that group.

It should be noted that the multicast group addresses used here are *administratively scoped* addresses that should only reach a limited number of hosts and not be used on the global public Internet, much like private IP addresses. However, we won't discuss how the traffic to these groups is limited. This is mainly because there are some operational disagreements about how to apply administratively scoped boundaries. We are using scoped addresses primarily as an analogy for private IP addresses. We could also have used GLOP addresses (discussed in this chapter) or addresses from the dynamic multicast address block.

The receiver socket program does *not* generate any special messages to say, "Send me content addressed to group `239.2.2.2`." We know it's going to be there. Later, we'll see that a protocol called Internet Group Management Protocol (IGMP) sends join or leave messages and knows what content is carried at this time by group `239.2.2.2` because of the Session Announcement Protocol and Source Description Protocol (SAP/SDP) messages it receives. In reality, multicast is a *suite* of protocols—and much more is required to create a complete multicast *application*. However, this little send-and-receive exercise will still reveal a lot about multicast. Figure 16.2 shows a portion of the Ethereal capture of the packet stream, detailing the UDP content inside the IP packet.

No.	Time	Source	Destination	Protocol	Info
1	0.000000	10.10.12.166	239.2.2.2	UDP	Source port: 32789 Destination port: 22222
2	3.010159	10.10.12.166	239.2.2.2	UDP	Source port: 32789 Destination port: 22222
3	5.966049	10.10.12.222	224.0.0.22	IGMP	V3 Membership Report
4	6.020324	10.10.12.166	239.2.2.2	UDP	Source port: 32789 Destination port: 22222
5	6.671757	10.10.12.222	224.0.0.22	IGMP	V3 Membership Report
6	9.030488	10.10.12.166	239.2.2.2	UDP	Source port: 32789 Destination port: 22222
7	12.040651	10.10.12.166	239.2.2.2	UDP	Source port: 32789 Destination port: 22222
8	14.534613	10.10.12.222	10.10.12.77	FTP	Request: TYPE I
9	14.535018	10.10.12.77	10.10.12.222	FTP	Response: 200 Type set to I.
10	14.750163	10.10.12.222	10.10.12.77	TCP	3373 > ftp [ACK] Seq=8 Ack=20 Win=64889 [CHECI
11	15.050822	10.10.12.166	239.2.2.2	UDP	Source port: 32789 Destination port: 22222
12	18.060977	10.10.12.166	239.2.2.2	UDP	Source port: 32789 Destination port: 22222
13	19.075860	10.10.12.222	224.0.0.22	IGMP	V3 Membership Report
14	19.672152	10.10.12.222	224.0.0.22	IGMP	V3 Membership Report
15	21.071140	10.10.12.166	239.2.2.2	UDP	Source port: 32789 Destination port: 22222
16	24.081295	10.10.12.166	239.2.2.2	UDP	Source port: 32789 Destination port: 22222
17	27.091454	10.10.12.166	239.2.2.2	UDP	Source port: 32789 Destination port: 22222

```
▷ Frame 15 (60 bytes on wire, 60 bytes captured)
▷ Ethernet II, Src: 00:b0:d0:45:34:64, Dst: 01:00:5e:02:02:02
▷ Internet Protocol, Src Addr: 10.10.12.166 (10.10.12.166), Dst Addr: 239.2.2.2 (239.2.2.2)
▽ User Datagram Protocol, Src Port: 32789 (32789), Dst Port: 22222 (22222)
    Source port: 32789 (32789)
    Destination port: 22222 (22222)
    Length: 11
    Checksum: 0x7ffa (correct)
  Data (3 bytes)

0000  01 00 5e 02 02 02 00 b0  d0 45 34 64 08 00 45 00   ..^..... .E4d..E.
0010  00 1f 00 00 40 00 01 11  72 1a 0a 0a 0c a6 ef 02   ....@... r.......
0020  02 02 80 15 56 ce 00 0b  7f fa 48 45 59 00 00 00   ....V... ..HEY...
0030  00 00 00 00 00 00 00 00  00 00 00 00               ........ ....
```

FIGURE 16.2

Multicast packet capture, showing the MAC address format used and the port in the UDP datagram. Some IGMPv3 messages appear also.

The Ethernet frame destination address is in a special form, starting with `01` and ending in `02:02:02`—which corresponds to the `239.2.2.2` multicast group address. We'll explore the rules for determining this frame address in material following. Note that the packet is addressed to the entire group, not an individual host (as in unicast). How does the network know where to send replicated packets? Two strategies (discussed later in the chapter) are to send content everywhere and then stop if no one says they are listening (flood-and-prune, or dense mode), or to send content only to hosts that have indicated a desire to receive the content (sparse mode).

The figure also shows that the Windows XP receiver (`10.10.12.222`) is generating IGMPv3 membership reports sent to multicast group address `224.0.0.22` (the IGMP multicast group). XP does this to keep the multicast content coming, even though the socket sender program has no idea what it means. These messages from XP to the IGMP group sometimes cause consternation with Windows network administrators, who are not always familiar with multicast and wonder where the `224.0.0.22` "server" could be.

Now let's set our multicast group send program to span the router network from LAN1 to LAN2. We'll start the socket utility sending on `wincli1 (10.10.11.51)`, using multicast group `239.1.1.1` and UDP port `11111`. The listener will still be `wincli2 (10.10.12.222)`.

This is easy enough, and Ethereal on `wincli1` shows a steady stream of multicast traffic being dumped onto LAN1. However, the Ethereal capture on `wincli2` (which had no problem receiving a multicast stream only moments ago) now receives absolutely nothing. What's wrong?

The problem is that the routers between LAN1 and LAN2 are not running a multicast routing protocol. The router on LAN1 at `10.10.11.1` adjacent to the source receives every multicast packet sent by `wincli1`. But the destination address of `239.1.1.1` is meaningless when considered as a unicast address. No entry exists in the unicast routing table, and there is yet no multicast "routing table" (more properly, table for multicast interface state) on the router network.

Before we configure multicast for use on our router network and allow multicast traffic to travel from LAN1 to LAN2, there are many new terms and protocols to explain—a few of which we've already mentioned (IGMP, SAP/SDP, how a multicast group maps to a frame destination address, and so on.) Let's start with the basics.

MULTICAST TERMINOLOGY

Multicast in TCP/IP has developed a reputation of being more difficult to understand than unicast. Part of the problem is the special terminology used with multicast, and the implication that if something is not universally supported, it must be complicated and difficult to understand. But there is nothing in multicast that is more complex than subnet masking, multicast sockets are nearly the same as unicast sockets (except that they don't use TCP sockets), and many things that routing protocols do with multicast packets are now employed in unicast as well (the reverse-path forwarding, or RFP

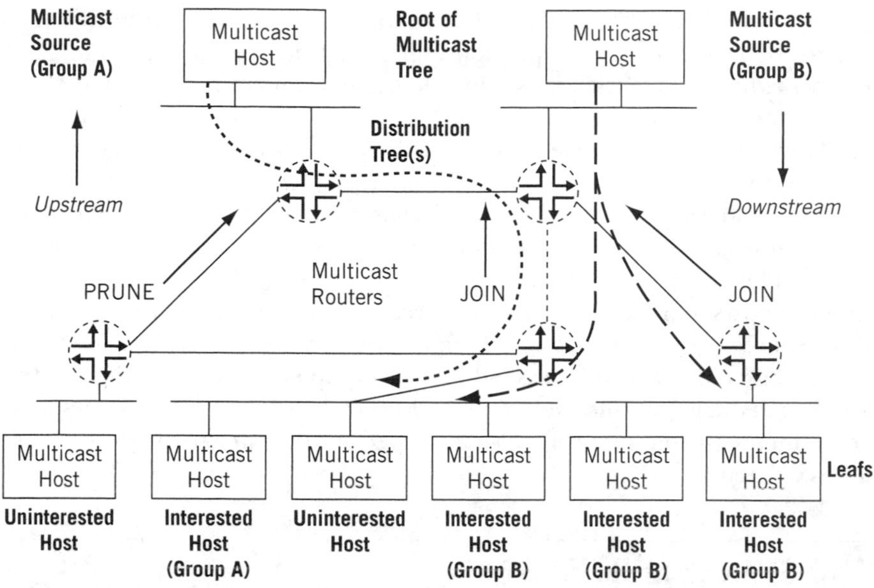

FIGURE 16.3

Examples of multicast terminology showing how multicast trees are "rooted" at the source. JOINs are also sent using IGMP from receivers to local routers.

check). Figure 16.3 shows a general view of some of the terms commonly used in an IP multicast network.

The key component of the multicast network is the multicast-capable router, which replicates the packets. The routers in the IP multicast network, which has exactly the same topology as the unicast network it is based on, use a *multicast routing protocol* to build a *distribution tree* to connect receivers (this term is preferred to the multimedia implications of *listeners*, but the listener term is also used) to *sources*. The distribution tree is rooted at the source. The interface on the router leading toward the source is the *upstream* interface, although the less precise terms *incoming* or *inbound* interface are also used. There should be only one upstream interface on the router receiving multicast packets. The interface on the router leading toward the receivers is the *downstream* interface, although the less precise terms *outgoing* or *outbound* interface are used as well. There can be 0 to $N - 1$ downstream interfaces on a router, where N is the number of logical interfaces on the router. To prevent looping, the upstream interface should never receive copies of downstream multicast packets.

Routing loops are disastrous in multicast networks because of the repeated replication of packets. Modern multicast routing protocols need to avoid routing loops, packet by packet, much more rigorously than in unicast routing protocols.

Each subnetwork with hosts on the router that has at least one interested receiver is a *leaf* on the distribution *tree*. Routers can have multiple *leafs* or *leaves* (both terms are used) on different interfaces and must send a copy of the IP multicast packet out on each interface with a leaf. When a new leaf subnetwork is added to the tree (i.e., the interface to the host subnetwork previously received no copies of the multicast packets), a new *branch* is built, the leaf is joined to the tree, and replicated packets are now sent out on the interface.

When a branch contains no leaves because there are no interested hosts on the router interface leading to that IP subnetwork, the branch is *pruned* from the distribution tree, and no multicast packets are sent out from that interface. Packets are replicated and sent out from multiple interfaces only where the distribution tree branches at a router, and no link ever carries a duplicate flow of packets.

Collections of hosts all receiving the same stream of IP packets, usually from the same multicast source, are called *groups*. In IP multicast networks, traffic is delivered to multicast groups based on an IP multicast address or group address. The groups determine the location of the leaves, and the leaves determine the branches on the multicast network. Some multicast routing protocols use a special RP router to allow receivers to find sources efficiently.

DENSE AND SPARSE MULTICAST

Multicast addresses represent groups of receivers, and two strategies can be employed to ensure that all receivers interested in a multicast group receive the traffic.

Dense-Mode Multicast

The assumption here is that almost all possible subnets have at least one receiver wanting to receive the multicast traffic from a source, so the network is *flooded* with traffic on all possible branches and then pruned back as branches do not express an interest in receiving the packets—explicitly (by message) or implicitly (timeout silence). This is the *dense mode* of multicast operation. LANs are appropriate environments for dense-mode operation. In practice, although PIM-DM is worth covering (and we'll even configure it!) there aren't a lot of scenarios in which people would seriously consider it. Periodic blasting of source content is neither a very scalable nor efficient use of resources.

Sparse-Mode Multicast

The assumption here is that very few of the possible receivers want packets from this source, so the network establishes and sends packets only on branches that have at least one leaf indicating (by message) a desire for the traffic. This is the *sparse mode* of multicast operation. WANs (like the Internet) are appropriate networks for sparse-mode operation. Sparse-mode multicast protocols use the special RP router to allow receivers to find sources efficiently.

Specific networks can run whichever mode makes sense. A low-volume multicast application can make effective use of dense mode, even on a WAN. A high-volume application on a LAN might still use sparse mode for efficiency.

Some multicast routing protocols, especially older ones, support only dense-mode operation—which makes them difficult to use efficiently on the public Internet. Others allow sparse mode as well. If sparse-dense mode is supported, the multicast routing protocol allows some special dense multicast groups to be used to the RPs—at which point the router operates in sparse mode.

MULTICAST NOTATION

To avoid multicast routing loops, every multicast router must always be aware of the interface that leads to the source of that multicast group content by the shortest path. This is the upstream (incoming) interface, and packets should never be forwarded back toward a multicast source. All other interfaces are potential downstream (outgoing) interfaces, depending on the number of branches on the distribution tree.

Routers closely monitor the status of the incoming and outgoing interfaces, a process that determines the multicast forwarding state. A router with a multicast forwarding state for a particular multicast group is essentially "turned on" for that group's content. Interfaces on the router's outgoing interface list (OIL) send copies of the group's packets received on the incoming interface list for that group. The incoming and outgoing interface lists might be different for different multicast groups.

The multicast forwarding state in a router is usually written in (S,G) or (*,G) notation. These are pronounced "S comma G" and "star comma G," respectively. In (S,G), the S refers to the unicast IP address of the source for the multicast traffic, and the G refers to the particular multicast group IP address for which S is the source. All multicast packets sent from this source have S as the source address and G as the destination address.

The asterisk (*) in the (*,G) notation is a wild card indicating that the source sending to group G is unknown. Routers try to track down these sources when they have to in order to operate more efficiently.

MULTICAST CONCEPTS

The basic terminology of multicast is complicated by the use of several related concepts. Many of these apply to how the routers on a multicast-capable network handle multicast packets and have little to do with hosts on LANs, but they are important concepts nonetheless.

Reverse-Path Forwarding

Unicast forwarding decisions are typically based on the destination address of the packet arriving at a router. The unicast routing table is organized by destination subnet and mainly set up to forward the packet toward the destination.

In multicast, the router forwards the packet away from the source to make progress along the distribution tree and prevent routing loops. The router's multicast forwarding state runs more logically by organizing tables based on the reverse path, from the receiver back to the root of the distribution tree. This process is known as reverse-path forwarding (RPF).

The router adds a branch to a distribution tree depending on whether the request for traffic from a multicast group passes the RPF check. Every multicast packet received must pass an RPF check before it is eligible to be replicated or forwarded on any interface.

The RPF check is essential for every router's multicast implementation. When a multicast packet is received on an interface, the router interprets the source address in the multicast IP packet as the destination address for a unicast IP packet. The source multicast address is found in the unicast routing table, and the outgoing interface is determined. If the outgoing interface found in the unicast routing table is the same as the interface that the multicast packet was received on, the packet passes the RPF check. Multicast packets that fail the RPF check are dropped because the incoming interface is not on the shortest path back to the source.

Routers can build and maintain separate tables for RPF purposes. The router must have some way to determine its RPF interface for the group, which is the interface topologically closest to the root. The distribution tree should follow the shortest-path tree topology for efficiency. The RPF check helps to construct this tree.

The RPF Table

The RPF table plays the key role in the multicast router. The RPF table is consulted for every RPF check, which is performed at intervals on multicast packets entering the multicast router. Distribution trees of all types rely on the RPF table to form properly, and the multicast forwarding state also depends on the RPF table.

The routing table used for RPF checks can be the same routing table used to forward unicast IP packets, or it can be a separate routing table used only for multicast RPF checks. In either case, the RPF table contains only unicast routes because the RPF check is performed on the source address of the multicast packet (not the multicast group destination address), and a multicast address is forbidden from appearing in the source address field of an IP packet header. The unicast address can be used for RPF checks because there is only one source host for a particular stream of IP multicast content for a multicast group address, although the same content could be available from multiple sources.

Populating the RPF Table

If the same routing table used to forward unicast packets is also used for the RPF checks, the routing table is populated and maintained by the traditional unicast routing protocols such as Border Gateway Protocol (BGP), Intermediate System-to-Intermediate System (IS–IS), OSPF, and Routing Information Protocol (RIP). If a dedicated multicast

RPF table is used, this table must be populated by some other method. Some multicast routing protocols, such as the Distance Vector Multicast Routing Protocol (DVMRP), essentially duplicate the operation of a unicast routing protocol and populate a dedicated RPF table. Others, such as Protocol Independent Multicast (PIM), do not duplicate routing protocol functions and must rely on some other routing protocol to set up this table—which is why PIM is protocol independent.

Some traditional routing protocols (such as BGP and IS-IS) now have extensions to differentiate between different sets of routing information sent between routers for unicast and multicast. For example, there is multiprotocol BGP (MBGP) and multitopology routing in IS-IS (M-ISIS). Multicast Open Shortest Path First (MOSPF) also extends OSPF for multicast use, but goes further than MBGP or M-ISIS and makes MOSPF into a complete multicast routing protocol on its own. When these routing protocols are used, routes can be tagged as multicast RPF routers and used by the receiving router differently than the unicast routing information.

Using the main unicast routing table for RPF checks provides simplicity. A dedicated routing table for RPF checks allows a network administrator to set up separate paths and routing policies for unicast and multicast traffic, allowing the multicast network to function more independently of the unicast network. The following section discusses in further detail how PIM operates, although the concepts could be applied to other multicast routing protocols.

Shortest-Path Tree

The distribution tree used for multicast is rooted at the source and is the shortest-path tree (SPT) as well. Consider a set of multicast routers without any active multicast traffic for a certain group (i.e., they have no multicast forwarding state for that group). When a router learns that an interested receiver for that group is on one of its directly connected subnets, the router attempts to join the tree for that group.

To join the distribution tree, the router determines the unicast IP address of the source for that group. This address can be a simple static configuration in the router, or use more complex methods.

To build the SPT for that group, the router executes an RPF check on the source address in its routing table. The RPF check produces the interface closest to the source, which is where multicast packets from this source for this group should flow into the router.

The router next sends a join message out on this interface using the proper multicast protocol to inform the upstream router that it wishes to join the distribution tree for that group. This message is an (S,G) join message because both S and G are known. The router receiving the (S,G) join message adds the interface on which the message was received to its OIL for the group and performs an RPF check on the source address. The upstream router then sends an (S,G) join message out the RPF interface toward the source, informing the upstream router that it also wants to join the group.

Each upstream router repeats this process, propagating joins out the RPF interface—building the SPT as it goes. The process stops when the join message does the following:

- Reaches the router directly connected to the host that is the source, or
- Reaches a router that already has multicast forwarding state for this source-group pair.

In either case, the branch is created, each of the routers has multicast forwarding state for the source-group pair, and packets can flow down the distribution tree from source to receiver. The RPF check at each router ensures that the tree is an SPT.

SPTs are always the shortest path, but they are not necessarily short. That is, sources and receivers tend to be on the periphery of a router network (not on the backbone) and multicast distribution trees have a tendency to sprawl across almost every router in the network. Because multicast traffic can overwhelm a slow interface, and one packet can easily become a hundred or a thousand on the opposite side of the backbone, it makes sense to provide a shared tree as a distribution tree so that the multicast source could be located more centrally in the network (on the backbone). This sharing of distribution trees with roots in the core network is accomplished by a multicast rendezvous point.

Rendezvous Point and Rendezvous-Point Shared Trees

In a shared tree, the root of the distribution tree is a router (not a host), and is located somewhere in the core of the network. In the primary sparse-mode multicast routing protocol, Protocol Independent Multicast sparse mode (PIM-SM), the core router at the root of the shared tree is the RP. Packets from the upstream source and join messages from the downstream routers "rendezvous" at this core router.

In the RP model, other routers do not need to know the addresses of the sources for every multicast group. All they need to know is the IP address of the RP router. The RP router knows the sources for all multicast groups.

The RP model shifts the burden of finding sources of multicast content from each router—the (S,G) notation—to the network—the (*,G) notation knows only the RP. Exactly how the RP finds the unicast IP address of the source varies, but there must be some method to determine the proper source for multicast content for a particular group.

Consider a set of multicast routers without any active multicast traffic for a certain group. When a router learns that an interested receiver for that group is on one of its directly connected subnets, the router attempts to join the distribution tree for that group back to RP (not to the actual source of the content). In some sparse-mode protocols, the shared tree is called the rendezvous-point tree (RPT).

When the branch is created, packets can flow from the source to the RP and from the RP to the receiver. Note that there is no guarantee that the shared tree (RPT) is the shortest path tree to the source. Most likely it is not. However, there are ways to "migrate" a shared tree to an SPT once the flow of packets begins. In other words, the forwarding state can transition from (*,G) to (S,G). The formation of both types of trees depends heavily on the operation of the RPF check and the RPF table.

PROTOCOLS FOR MULTICAST

Multicast is not a single protocol used for a specific function, like FTP. Nor is multicast a series of separate protocols that can be used as desired between adjacent hosts and routers to perform a function, like IS-IS and OSPF. Multicast is a series of related protocols that must be carefully coordinated across and between an AS and often among hosts.

The family of multicast protocols is due to the complexity of source discovery and the mechanisms used to perform this task. Most hosts can send and receive multicast frames and packets on a LAN as easily as they handle broadcast or unicast. Routers must be capable of sending copies of a single received packet out on more than one interface (replication), and many low-end routers cannot do this. In addition, routers must be able to use unicast routing tables for multicast purposes, or construct special tables for multicast information (again, many low-end routers cannot do this).

Multicast routers must be able to maintain state on each interface with regard to multicast traffic. That is, the router must know which multicast groups have active receivers on an outgoing interface (called downstream interfaces) and which interface is the "closest" to the source (called *upstream interface*). These interfaces vary from group to group, one group can have more than one potential source (for redundancy purposes), and special routers might be employed for many groups (the RPs).

Multicast Hosts and Routers

Multicast tasks are very different for hosts versus routers. At this juncture, we will extend the multicast discussion beyond IPv4 to IPv6 and hosts. General points follow.

- Hosts must be able to join and leave multicast groups. The major protocols here are various versions of the Internet Group Management Protocol (IGMP) in IPv4 and Multicast Listener Discovery (MLD) in IPv6.
- Hosts (users) must know the content of multicast groups. The related Session Announcement Protocol and Session Description Protocol (SAP/SDP, defined in RFC 2974 and RFC 2327) are the standard protocols used to describe the content and some other aspects of multicast groups. These should *not* be used as a method of multicast source discovery.
- Routers must be able to find the sources of multicast content, both in their own multicast (routing) domain and in others. For sparse modes, this means finding the RPs. These can be configured statically, or use protocols such as Auto-RP, anycast RP (RFC 3446), bootstrap router (BSR), or MSDP (RFC 3618). For IPv6, *embedded RP* is used instead of MSDP—which is not defined for IPv6 use. (This point actually applies to ASM, not SSM, discussed in material following.)
- Routers must be able to prevent loops that replicate the same packet over and over. The techniques here are not really protocols, and include the use of scoping (limiting multicast packet hops) and RPF checks.

- Routers must provide missing multicast information when feasible. Multicast networks can use Pragmatic General Multicast (PGM) to add some TCP features lacking in UDP to multicast networks. However, the only assurance is that you know you missed something. Application-specific mechanisms can do the same thing with simple sequence numbers.

Fortunately, only a few of these protocols are really used for multicast at present on the Internet. The only complication is that some of the special protocols used for IPv4 multicasting do not work with IPv6, and thus different protocols perform the same functions.

Multicast Group Membership Protocols

Multicast group membership protocols allow a router to know when a host on a directly attached subnet, typically a LAN, wants to receive traffic from a certain multicast group. Even if more than one host on the LAN wants to receive traffic for that multicast group, the router has to send only one copy of each packet for that multicast group out on that interface because of the inherent broadcast nature of LANs. Only when the router is informed by the multicast group membership protocol that there are no interested hosts on the subnet can the packets be withheld and that leaf pruned from the distribution tree.

Internet Group Management Protocol for IPv4

There is only one standard IPv4 multicast group membership protocol: the Internet Group Management Protocol (IGMP). However, IGMP has several versions that are supported by hosts and routers. There are currently three versions of IGMP.

IGMPv1—The original protocol defined in RFC 1112. An explicit join message is sent to the router, but a timeout is used to determine when hosts leave a group. This process wastes processing cycles on the router, especially on older or smaller routers.

IGMPv2—Among other features, IGMPv2 (RFC 2236) adds an explicit leave message to the join message so that routers can more easily determine when a group has no interested listeners on a LAN.

IGMPv3—Among other features, IGMPv3 (RFC 3376) optimizes support for a single source of content for a multicast group or source-specific multicast (SSM). (RFC 1112 supported both many-to-many and one-to-many multicast, but one-to-many is considered the more viable model for the Internet at large.)

Although the various versions of IGMP are backward compatible, it is common for a router to run multiple versions of IGMP on LAN interfaces because backward compatibility is achieved by dropping back to the most basic of all versions run on a LAN. For example, if one host is running IGMPv1, any router attached to the LAN running IGMPv2 drops back to IGMPv1 operation—effectively eliminating the IGMPv2 advantages. Running multiple IGMP versions ensures that both IGMPv1 and IGMPv2 hosts find peers for their versions on the router.

Multicast Listener Discovery for IPv6

IPv6 does not use IGMP to manage multicast groups. Multicast groups are an integral part of IPv6, and the Multicast Listener Discovery (MLD) protocol is an integral part of IPv6. Some IGMP functions are assumed by ICMPv6, but IPv6 hosts perform most multicast functions with MLD. MLD comes in two versions: MLD version 1 (RFC 2710) has basic functions, and MLDv2 (RFC 3590) supports SSM groups.

Multicast Routing Protocols

There are five multicast routing protocols.

Distance-Vector Multicast Routing Protocol

This is the first of the multicast routing protocols and hampered by a number of limitations that make this method unattractive for large-scale Internet use. DVMRP is a dense-mode-only protocol that uses the flood-and-prune, or implicit join method, to deliver traffic everywhere and then determines where uninterested receivers are. DVMRP uses source-based distribution trees in the form (S,G).

Multicast Open Shortest Path First

This protocol extends OSPF for multicast use, but only for dense mode. However, MOSPF has an explicit join message, and thus routers do not have to flood their entire domain with multicast traffic from every source. MOSPF uses source-based distribution trees in the form (S,G).

PIM Dense Mode

This is Protocol Independent Multicast operating in dense mode (PIM DM), but the differences from PIM sparse mode are profound enough to consider the two modes separately. PIM also supports sparse-dense mode, but there is no special notation for that operational mode. In contrast to DVMRP and MOSPF, PIM dense mode allows a router to use any unicast routing protocol and performs RPF checks using the unicast routing table. PIM dense mode has an implicit join message, so routers use the flood-and-prune method to deliver traffic everywhere and then determine where the uninterested receivers are. PIM dense mode uses source-based distribution trees in the form (S,G), as do all dense-mode protocols.

PIM Sparse Mode

PIM sparse mode allows a router to use any unicast routing protocol and performs RPF checks using the unicast routing table. However, PIM sparse mode has an explicit join message, so routers determine where the interested receivers are and send join messages upstream to their neighbors—building trees from receivers to RP. The Protocol

Table 16.1 Major Characteristics of Multicast Routing Protocols

Multicast Routing Protocol	Dense Mode	Sparse Mode	Implicit Join	Explicit Join	(S,G) SBT	(*,G) Shared Tree
DVMRP	Yes	No	Yes	No	Yes	No
MOSPF	Yes	No	No	Yes	Yes	No
PIM-DM	Yes	No	Yes	No	Yes	No
PIM-SM	No	Yes	No	Yes	Yes, maybe	Yes, initially
CBT	No	Yes	No	Yes	No	Yes

Independent Multicast sparse mode uses an RP router as the initial source of multicast group traffic and therefore builds distribution trees in the form (*,G), as do all sparse-mode protocols. However, PIM sparse mode migrates to an (S,G) source-based tree if that path is shorter than through the RP for a particular multicast group's traffic.

Core-Based Trees

Core-based trees (CBT) share all of the characteristics of PIM sparse mode (sparse mode, explicit join, and shared [*,G] trees), but are said to be more efficient at finding sources than PIM sparse mode. CBT is rarely encountered outside academic discussions and the experimental RFC 2201 from September 1997. There are no large-scale deployments of CBT, commercial or otherwise. The differences among the five multicast routing protocols are summarized in Table 16.1.

It is important to realize that retransmissions due to a high bit-error rate on a link or overloaded router can make multicast as inefficient as repeated unicast.

Any-Source Multicast and SSM

RFC 1112 originally described both one-to-many (for radio and television) and many-to-many (for videoconferences and application on-line gaming) multicasts. This model is now known as *Any-Source Multicast* (ASM). To support many-to-many multicasts, the *network* is responsible for source discovery. So, whenever a host expresses a desire to join a group the network must find all the sources for that group and deliver them to the receiver.

Source discovery is especially complex with interdomain scenarios (source in one AS, receiver/s in another). And most plans to commercialize Internet multicasts, such as bringing radio station and television channel multicasts directly onto the Internet, revolve around the one-to-many model exclusively. So, the one-to-many scenario has been essentially split off from the all-embracing RFC 1112 vision and become Source-Specific Multicast (SSM, defined in FC 3569).

As the name implies, SSM supports multicast content delivery from only one specific source. In SSM, source discovery is not the responsibility of the network but of the

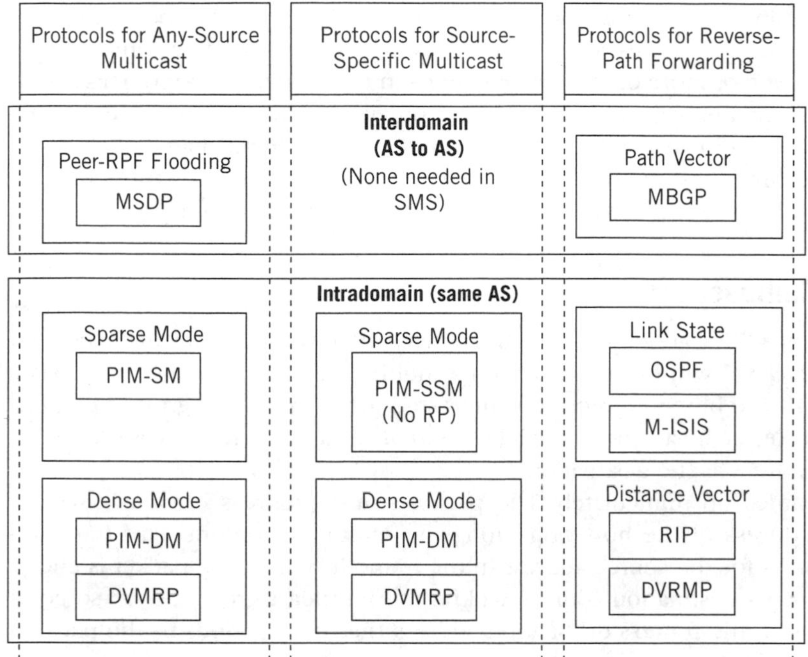

FIGURE 16.4

Suite of multicast protocols showing how those for ASM, SSM, and RFP checks fit together and are used.

receivers (hosts). This eliminates much of the complexity of multicast mechanisms required in ASM and the use of MSDP. It also eliminates some of the scaling considerations associated with traffic on (*,G) groups.

ASM and SSM are not protocols but service models. Most of what is described in this chapter applies to ASM (the more general model). But keep in mind that SSM does away with many of the procedures covered in detail here that apply to ASM, including RPs, RPTs, and MSDP. Figure 16.4 shows the current suite of multicast protocols and how they all fit together.

Multicast Source Discovery Protocol

MSDP, described in RFC 3618, is a mechanism to connect multiple PIM-SM domains (usually, each in an AS). Each PIM-SM domain can have its own independent RPs, and these do not interact in any way (so MSDP is not needed in SSM scenarios). The advantages of MSDP are that the RPs do not need any other resource to find each other and that domains can have receivers only and get content without globally advertising group membership. In addition, MSDP can be used with protocols other than PIM-SM.

MSDP routers in a PIM-SM domain peer with their MSDP router peers in other domains. The peering session uses a TCP connection to exchange control information. Each domain has one or more of these connections in its "virtual topology." This allows domains to discover multicast sources in other domains. If these sources are deemed of interest to receivers in another domain, the usual source-tree mechanism in PIM-SM is used to deliver multicast content—but now over an interdomain distribution tree. More details about MSDP are beyond the scope of this introductory chapter.

Frames and Multicast

Multicasting on a LAN is a good place to start an investigation of multicasting in general. Consider a single LAN, without routers, with a multicast source sending to a certain group. The rest of the hosts are receivers interested in the multicast group's content. So, the multicast source host generates packets with its unicast IP address as the source and the group address as the destination.

One issue comes up immediately. The packet source address obviously will be the unicast IP address of the host originating the multicast content. This translates to the MAC address for the source address in the frame in which the packet is encapsulated. The packet's destination address will be the multicast group. So far, so good. But what should be the frame's destination address that corresponds to the packet's multicast group address?

Using the LAN broadcast MAC address defeats the purpose of multicast, and hosts could have access to many multicast groups. Broadcasting at the LAN level makes no sense. Fortunately, there is an easy way out of this. The MAC address has a bit that is set to 0 for unicast (the LAN term is *individual address*) and to a 1 to indicate that this is a multicast address. Some of these addresses are reserved for multicast groups for specific vendors or MAC-level protocols. Internet multicast applications use the range 0x01-00-5E-00-00-00 to 0x01-00-5E-FF-FF-FF. TCP/IP multicast receivers listen for frames with one of these addresses when the application joins a multicast group and stops listening when the application terminates or the host leaves the group.

So, 24 bits are available to map IPv4 multicast addresses to MAC multicast addresses. But all IPv4 addresses, including multicast addresses, are 32 bits long. There are 8 bits left over. How should IPv4 multicast addresses be mapped to MAC multicast addresses to minimize the chance of "collisions" (two different multicast groups mapped to the same MAC multicast address)?

All IPv4 multicast addresses begin with the same four bits (1110), so we only have to really worry about 4 bits (not 8). We shouldn't drop the last bits of the IPv4 address, because these are almost guaranteed to be host bits—depending on subnet mask. But the high-order bits, the rightmost bits, are almost always network bits and we're only worried about one LAN for now.

One other bit of the remaining 24 MAC address bits is reserved (an initial 0 indicates an Internet multicast address), so let's just drop the 5 bits following the initial 1110 in the IPv4 address and map the 23 remaining bits (one for one) into the last 23 bits of the MAC address. This procedure is shown in Figure 16.5.

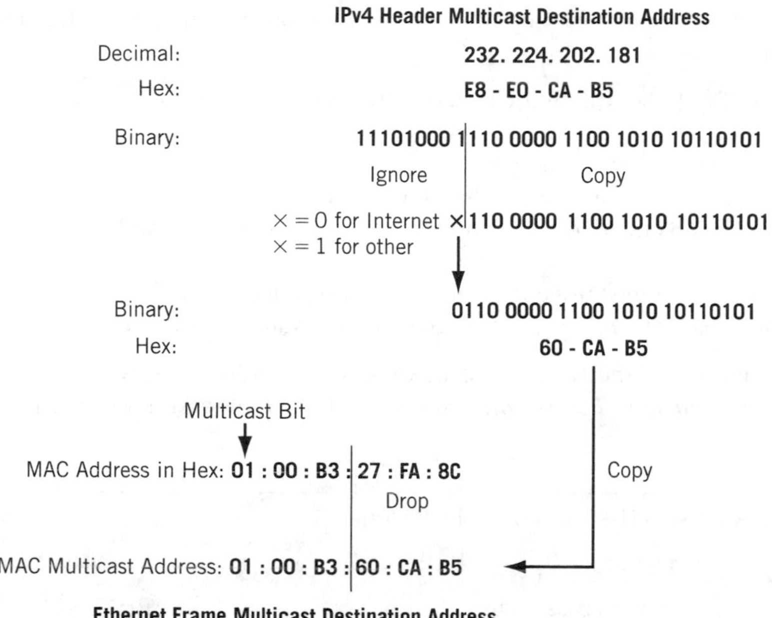

FIGURE 16.5

How to convert from IPv4 header multicast to Ethernet MAC multicast address formats.

Note that this process means that there are 32 (2^5) IPv4 multicast addresses that could map to the same MAC multicast addresses. For example, multicast IPv4 addresses `224.8.7.6` and `229.136.7.6` translate to the same MAC address (0x01-00-5E-08-07-06). This is a real concern, and because the host will accept frames sent to both multicast groups, the IP software must reject one or the other. This problem does not exist in IPv6, but is always a concern in IPv4.

Once the MAC address for the multicast group is determined, the operating system essentially orders the NIC card to join or leave the multicast group and accept frames sent to the address as well as the host's unicast address or ignore that multicast group's frames. It is possible for a host to receive multicast content from more than one group at the same time, of course. The procedure for IPv6 multicast packets inside frames is nearly identical, except for the MAC destination address 0x3333 prefix and other points outlined in the previous section.

IPv4 Multicast Addressing

The IPv4 addresses (Class D in the classful addressing scheme) used for multicast usage range from `224.0.0.0` to `239.255.255.255`. Assignment of addresses in this range is controlled by the Internet Assigned Numbers Authority (IANA). Multicast addresses can never be used as a source address in a packet (the source address is always the unicast

IP address of the content originator). Certain subranges within the range of addresses are reserved for specific uses.

- `224.0.0.0/24`—The link-local multicast range (these packets never pass through routers)
- `224.2.0.0/16`—The SAP/SDP range
- `232.0.0.0/8`—The Source-Specific Multicast (SSM) range
- `233.0.0.0/8`—The AS-encoded statically assigned GLOP range defined in RFC 3180
- `239.0.0.0/8`—The administratively scoped multicast range defined in RFC 2365 (these packets *may* pass through a certain number of routers)

For a complete list of currently assigned IANA multicast addresses, refer to the *www.iana.org/assignments/multicast-addresses* Web site. If multicast addresses had

Table 16.2 Multicast Addresses Used for Various Protocols

Address	Purpose	Comment
224.0.0.0	Reserved base address	RFC 1112
224.0.0.1	All systems of this subnet	RFC 1112
224.0.0.2	All routers on this subnet	
224.0.0.3	Unassigned	
224.0.0.4	DVMRP routers on this subnet	RFC 1075
224.0.0.5	All OSPF routers on this subnet	RFC 1583
224.0.0.6	All OSPF DRs on this subnet	RFC 1583
224.0.0.7	All ST (Streams protocol) routers on this subnet	RFC 1190
224.0.0.8	All ST hosts on this subnet	RFC 1190
224.0.0.9	All RIPv2 routers on this subnet	RFC 1723
224.0.0.10	All Cisco IGRP routers on this subnet	(Cisco)
224.0.0.11	All Mobile IP agents	
224.0.0.12	DHCP server/relay agents	RFC 1884
224.0.0.13	All PIM routers	(IANA)
224.0.014-224.0.0.21	Assigned to various routing protocols and router features	(IANA)
224.0.0.22	IGMP	(IANA)
224.0.0.23-244.0.0.255	See *www.iana.org/assignments/multicast-addresses*	(IANA)

been assigned in the same manner that unicast addresses were allocated, the Class D address space would have been exhausted long ago. However, IANA allocates static multicast addresses only for protocols. Routers cannot forward packets in these ranges. Some of these addresses are outlined in Table 16.2.

A simple dynamic address allocation mechanism is used in the SAP/SDP block to prevent multicast address exhaustion. Applications, such as the Session Directory Tool (SDR), use this mechanism to randomly select an unused address in this range. This dynamic allocation mechanism for global multicast addresses is similar to the DHCP function, which dynamically assigns unicast addresses on a LAN.

However, some applications require static multicast addresses. So, GLOP (described in RFC 3180) provides static multicast ranges for organizations that already have an AS number. (GLOP is not an acronym or abbreviation—it's just the name of the mechanism.) GLOP uses the 2-byte AS number to derive a `/24` address block within the 233/8 range. It's worth noting that there are no GLOP addresses set aside for 4-byte AS numbers. The static multicast range is derived from the following form:

```
233.[first byte of AS].[second byte of AS].0/24
```

For example, AS 65001 is allocated `233.253.233.0/24`—and only this AS can use it. The following is an easy way to compute this address.

1. Convert the AS number to hexadecimal (65001 = 0xFDE9).
2. Convert the first byte back to decimal (0xFD = 253).
3. Convert the second byte back to decimal (0xE9 = 233).

Addresses in the 239/8 range are defined as administratively scoped. Packets sent to these addresses should not be forwarded by a router outside an administratively defined boundary (usually a domain).

Addresses in the 232/8 range are reserved for SSM. A nice feature of SSM is that the multicast group address no longer needs to be globally unique. The source-group "channel," or tuple, provides uniqueness because the receiver is expressing interest in only one source for the group.

SSM has solved the multicast addressing allocation headache. With SSM, as well as GLOP, administrative scoping, and SAP/SDP, IPv4 multicast address allocation is sufficient until IPv6 becomes more common.

IPv6 Multicast Addressing

In IPv6, the number of multicast (and unicast) addresses available is not an issue. All IPv6 multicast addresses start with `1111 1111` (`0xFF`). As in IPv4, no IPv6 packet can have an IPv6 multicast address as a source address. There is really no such thing as a "broadcast" in IPv6. Instead, devices must belong to certain multicast groups and pay attention to packets sent to these groups. The structure of the IPv6 multicast address is shown in Figure 16.6.

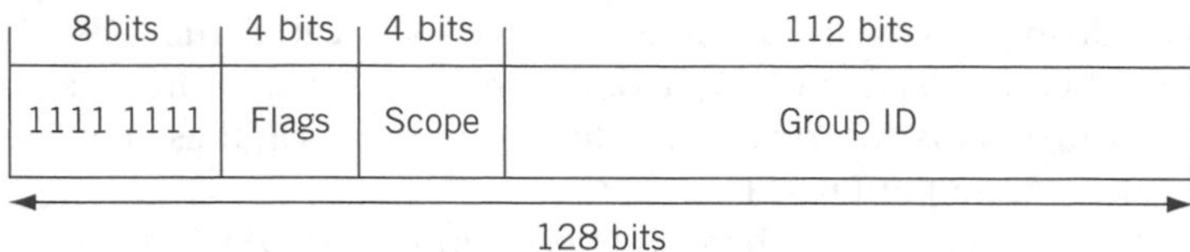

FIGURE 16.6

The IPv6 multicast address format. Note the presence of the scope field.

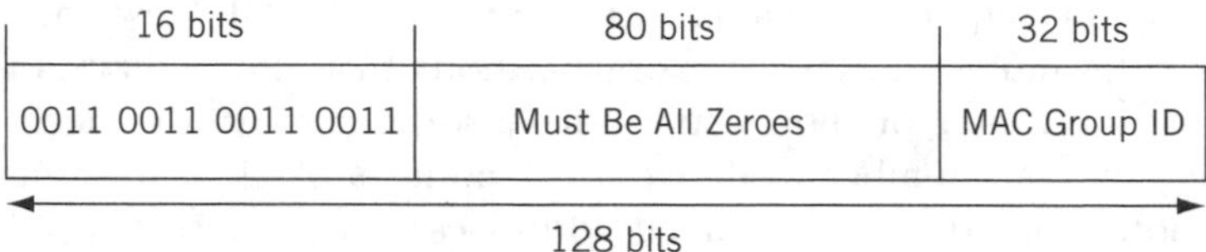

FIGURE 16.7

The IPv6 multicast group addresses showing how the MAC group ID is embedded.

Format Prefix

This 8-bit field is simply `1111 1111` (`0xFF`).

Flags

As of RFC 2373, the only flag defined for this 4-bit field is Transient (T). If 0, the multicast address is a permanently assigned well-known address allocated by IANA. If 1, the multicast address is not permanently assigned (transient).

Scope

This 4-bit field establishes the multicast packets' boundaries. RFC 2372 defines several well-known scopes, including node-local (1), link-local (2), site-local (3), organization-local (8), and global (E). Packets sent to `0xFF02:`*`X`* are confined to a single link and cannot pass through a router (this issue came up in the IGP chapter with RIPng).

Group ID

The IPv6 multicast group ID is 112 bits long. Permanently assigned group IDs are valid regardless of the scope value, whereas transient group IDs are valid *only* within a particular scope. The 122 bits of the Group ID field pose a challenge to the 48-bit MAC address (and only 23 of those bits were used in IPv4). But the solution is much simpler than in IPv4. RFC 2373 recommends using the low-order 32 bits of the Group ID and setting the high-order 16 bits to `0x3333`. This is shown in Figure 16.7.

Naturally, there are 80 more bits that could be used in the Group ID field. For now, RFC 2373 recommends setting the 80+ bits available for multicast group IDs to 0s. If there is a problem with 32 bits for multicast groups, which can be as many as 4 billion, probably in the future the RFC group will think about extending the bits.

PIM-SM

The most important multicast routing protocol for the Internet today is PIM sparse mode, defined in RFC 2362. PIM-SM is ideal for a number of reasons, such as its protocol-independent nature (PIM can use regular unicast routing tables for RPF checks and other things), and it's a nice fit with SSM (in fact, not much else fits at all with SSM). So, we'll look at PIM-SM in a little more detail (also in addition, because that's what we'll be using on the Illustrated Network's routers).

If a potential receiver is interested in the content of a particular multicast group, it sends an IGMP Join message to the local router—which must know the location of the network RPs servicing that group. If the local router is not currently on the distribution tree for that group, the router sends a PIM Join message (not an IGMP message) through the network until the router becomes a leaf on the shared tree (RPT) to the RP. Once multicast packets are flowing to the receiver, the routers all check to see if there is a shorter path from the source to the destination than through the RP. If there is, the routers will transition the tree from an RPT to an SPT using PIM Join and Prune messages (technically, they are PIM Join/Prune messages, but it is common to distinguish them). The SPT is rooted at the designated router of the source. All of this is done transparently to the receivers and usually works very smoothly.

There are other reasons to transition from an RPT to an SPT, even if the SPT is actually longer than the RPT. An RP might become quite busy, and the shortest path might not be optimal as determined by unicast routing protocols. A lot of multicast discussion at ISPs involves issues such as how many RPs there should be (how many groups should each service?) and where they should be located (near their sources? centrally?). A related issue is how routers know about RPs (statically? Auto-RP? BSR?), but these discussions have no clear or accepted answers.

There is only one PIM-SM feature that needs to be explained. How does traffic get from the sender's local router to the RP? The rendezvous point could create a tree directly to every source, but if there is a lot of sources, there is a lot of state information to maintain. It would be better if the senders' local routers could send the content directly to the RP.

But how? The destination address of all multicast packets is a group address and not a unicast address. So, the source's router (actually, the DR) encapsulates the multicast packets inside a unicast packet sent to the RP and tunnels the packet to the RP in this form. The RP decapsulates the multicast content and makes it available for distribution over the RPT tree.

There is much more to PIM-SM that has not been detailed here, such as PIM-SM for SSM (sometimes seen as PIM-SSM). But it is enough to explain the interplay among host receivers, IGMP (in IPv4), MLD (in IPv6), PIM itself, the RP, and the source.

The Resource Reservation Protocol and PGM

A lot of books and material on multicast include long discussions of the Resource Reservation Protocol (RSVP), and some multicast routers and hosts still use RSVP to signal the network that the multicast packet stream they will be receiving will consume a certain amount of resources on the network. However, the most common use of RSVP today is not with multicast but with Multiprotocol Label Switching (MPLS)—and that's where we'll put RSVP.

RVSP makes sense for multicast in a restricted bandwidth environment. But the need for RSVP was undermined (as was ATM) by the embarrassment of bandwidth available on LANs and router backbones (the video network YouTube today uses more bandwidth than the entire Internet had in 2000). On slow networks, the biggest shortcoming is that you can't reserve bandwidth you don't have. If you do anyway, you're really just performing admission control (limited to those who are allowed to connect over the network) and hosing the other applications. Everything works better with enough bandwidth.

However, this is not to say that multicast is fine using UDP in all cases—especially when multicast content must cross ISP boundaries, where bandwidth on these heavily used links is often consumed by traffic. Nothing is more annoying when receiving multicast content, voice, or video than dropped packets causing screen freezes and unpredictable silences. So, routers and hosts can use Pragmatic General Multicast (PGM), described in RFC 3208. PGM occupies the same place in the TCP/IP stack as TCP itself. PGM runs on sender and receiver hosts, and on routers (which perform the PGM router assist function).

As mentioned, the goal of PGM is not to make multicast UDP streams as reliable as TCP. The PGM goal is to allow senders or routers (performing router assist functions) to supply missing multicast packets if possible (such as for stock-ticker applications) or to assure receivers that the data is indeed missing and not just delayed (it does this by simply sequencing multicast packets). The issue is that you have to carry all of this state information in routers, which is not good for scaling.

Multicast Routing Protocols

Now we can go back to the network. We'll have to run a multicast routing protocol on our routers. We'll run PIM, which is the most popular multicast protocol. But PIM can be configured in dense "send-everywhere" mode or sparse "only if you ask" mode. Which should we use?

Let's consider our router configuration. Nothing is easier to configure than dense mode. We can just configure PIM dense mode (PIM-DM) to run on every router interface (even the LAN interfaces if we like—the PIM messages won't hurt anything), except for the network management interface on Juniper Networks routers (fxp0.0). Multicast traffic is periodically flooded everywhere and pruned back as IGMP membership reports come in on local area network interfaces. This is just an exercise for our lab network. You definitely should not try this at home. The following is the configuration on router `CE6`:

```
set protocols pim interface all mode dense;
set protocols pim interface fxp0.0 disable;
```

It is not necessary to configure IGMP on the LAN interface. As long as PIM is configured, IGMPv2 is run on all interfaces that support broadcasts (including frame relay and ATM). Of course, if a different version of IGMP—such as IGMPv1 or IGMPv3 (`wincli` was running IGMPv3, as shown in Figure 16.2)—is desired, this must be explicitly configured.

It is more interesting and meaningful to configure the PIM sparse mode, because that is what is used, with few exceptions, on the Internet. There are two distinct configurations: one for the RP router and the other on all the non-RP routers. We'll use simple static configuration to locate the RP router, but that's not what is typically done in the real world. The configuration on the RP router, which is router PE5 in this example, follows:

```
set protocols pim rp local address 192.168.5.1;
set protocols pim rp interface all mode sparse;
set protocols pim rp interface fxp0.0 disable;
```

The `local` keyword means that the local router is the RP. The address is the RP address that will be used in PIM messages between the routers. The configuration on the non-RP router, such as `P9`, follows:

```
set protocols pim rp static address 192.168.5.1;
set protocols pim rp interface all mode sparse;
set protocols pim rp interface fxp0.0 disable;
```

The static keyword means that another router is the RP, located at the IP address given. The RP address is used in PIM messages between the routers.

Once PIM is up and running on the rest of the router network (we don't need MSDP because the RP is known everywhere within the merged Best-Ace ISP routing domain and this precludes interdomain ASM use anyway), `wincli2` receives multicast traffic from `wincli1`, as shown in Figures 16.8 and 16.9.

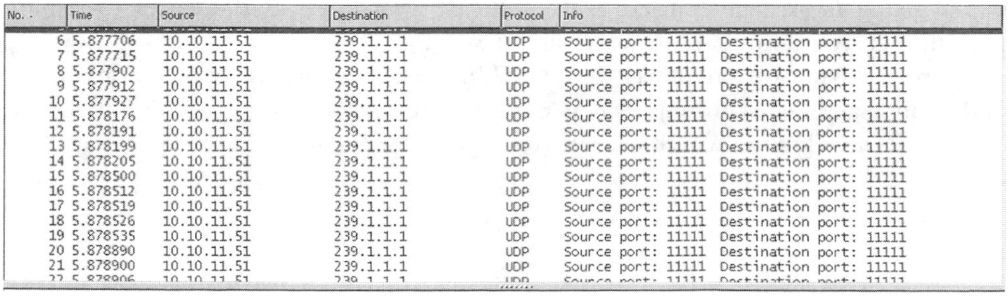

No.	Time	Source	Destination	Protocol	Info
6	5.877706	10.10.11.51	239.1.1.1	UDP	Source port: 11111 Destination port: 11111
7	5.877715	10.10.11.51	239.1.1.1	UDP	Source port: 11111 Destination port: 11111
8	5.877902	10.10.11.51	239.1.1.1	UDP	Source port: 11111 Destination port: 11111
9	5.877912	10.10.11.51	239.1.1.1	UDP	Source port: 11111 Destination port: 11111
10	5.877927	10.10.11.51	239.1.1.1	UDP	Source port: 11111 Destination port: 11111
11	5.878176	10.10.11.51	239.1.1.1	UDP	Source port: 11111 Destination port: 11111
12	5.878191	10.10.11.51	239.1.1.1	UDP	Source port: 11111 Destination port: 11111
13	5.878199	10.10.11.51	239.1.1.1	UDP	Source port: 11111 Destination port: 11111
14	5.878205	10.10.11.51	239.1.1.1	UDP	Source port: 11111 Destination port: 11111
15	5.878500	10.10.11.51	239.1.1.1	UDP	Source port: 11111 Destination port: 11111
16	5.878512	10.10.11.51	239.1.1.1	UDP	Source port: 11111 Destination port: 11111
17	5.878519	10.10.11.51	239.1.1.1	UDP	Source port: 11111 Destination port: 11111
18	5.878526	10.10.11.51	239.1.1.1	UDP	Source port: 11111 Destination port: 11111
19	5.878535	10.10.11.51	239.1.1.1	UDP	Source port: 11111 Destination port: 11111
20	5.878890	10.10.11.51	239.1.1.1	UDP	Source port: 11111 Destination port: 11111
21	5.878900	10.10.11.51	239.1.1.1	UDP	Source port: 11111 Destination port: 11111

FIGURE 16.8

Receiving a stream of multicast traffic from wincli1 across the router network on wincli2.

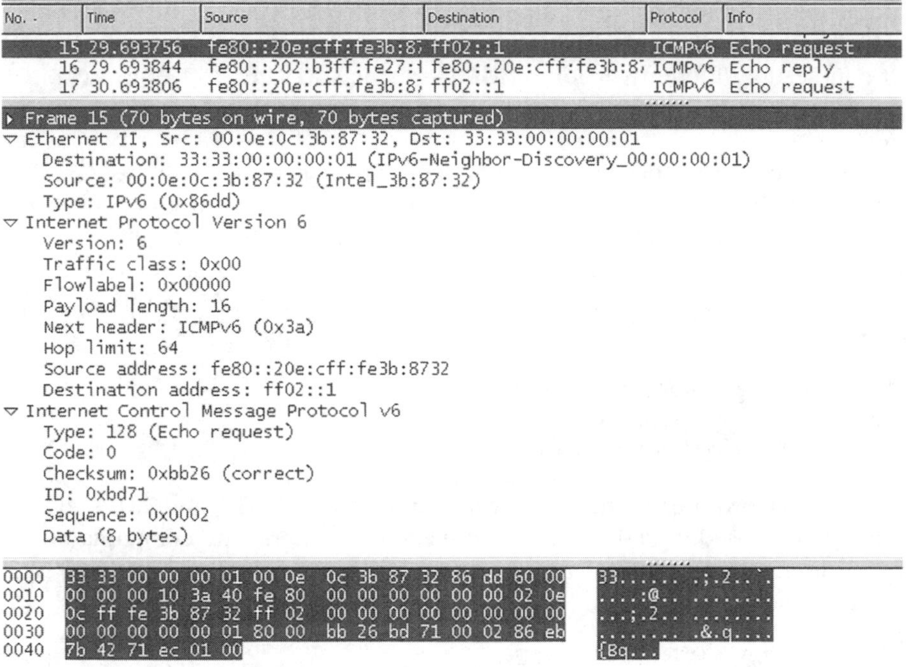

FIGURE 16.9

ICMPv6 multicast packets for neighbor discovery, showing how the MAC address is embedded in the IPv6 source address field.

IPv6 Multicast

In contrast to IPv4, where multicast sometimes seems like an afterthought compared to the usual unicast business of the network, IPv6 is fairly teeming with multicast. You have to do a lot to add multicast to IPv4, but IPv6 simply will not work without multicasting. Of course, a lot of this multicast use is confined to single subnets. So, despite being more heavily used, IPv6 multicast is not necessarily easier to deploy (even though you don't have to worry about MSDP).

Figure 16.10 shows a multicast IPv6 neighbor discovery packet, which contains an ICMPv6 message (an echo request). As expected, the packet is sent to IPv6 multicast address `0xFF02::1`, and the frame is sent to the address beginning `0x33:33`.

QUESTIONS FOR READERS

Figure 16.10 shows some of the concepts discussed in this chapter and can be used to help you answer the following questions.

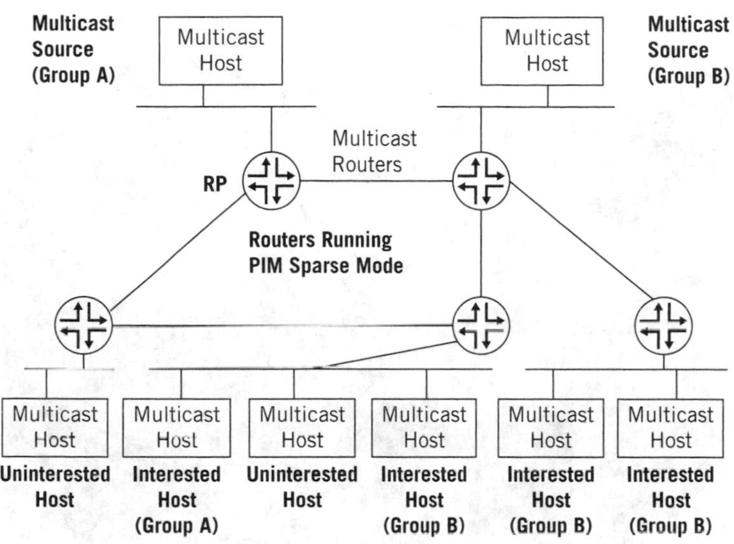

FIGURE 16.10

A group of routers running PIM sparse mode with sources and receivers.

1. Generally, it is a good idea for RPs to be centrally located on the router network. Why does this make sense?
2. In Figure 16.10, does the rightmost host, which is interested in Group B content, have to get it initially from the RP when the source is closer?
3. Would the RP be required if the routers were running PIM dense mode?
4. Will the leftmost router with the uninterested host constantly stream multicast traffic onto the LAN anyway?
5. Is the uninterested host on the LAN in the middle able to listen in on Group A and Group B traffic without using IGMP to join the groups?

CHAPTER

MPLS and IP Switching

17

What You Will Learn

In this chapter, you will learn how the desire for convergence has led to the development of various IP switching techniques. We'll also compare and contrast frame relay and ATM switched networks to illustrate the concepts behind IP switching.

You will learn how MPLS is used to create LSPs to switch (instead of route) IP packet through a routing domain. We'll see how MPLS can form the basis for a type of VPN service offering.

One of the reasons TCP/IP and the Internet have grown so popular is that this architecture is the promising way to create a type of "universal network" well suited for and equally at home with voice, video, and data. The Internet started as a network exclusively for data delivery, but has proved to be remarkably adaptable for different classes of traffic. Some say that more than half of all telephone calls are currently carried for part of their journey over the Internet, and this percentage will only go higher in the future. Why not watch an entire movie or TV show over the Internet? Many now watch episodes they missed on the Internet. Why not everything? As pointed out in the previous chapter, multicast might not be used to maximum effect for this but video delivery still works.

When a service provider adds television (or video in general) to Internet access and telephony, this is called a "triple play" opportunity for the service provider. (Adding wireless services over the Internet is sometimes called a "quadruple play" or "home run.")

This desire for networking convergence is not new. When the telephone was invented, there were more than 30 years' worth of telegraph line infrastructure in place from coast to coast and in most major cities throughout the United States. The initial telephone services used existing telegraph links to distribute telegrams, but this was not a satisfactory solution. The telegraph network was optimized for the dots and dashes of Morse code, not the smooth analog waveforms of voice. Early attempts to run voice over telegraph lines stumbled not over bandwidth, but with the crosstalk induced

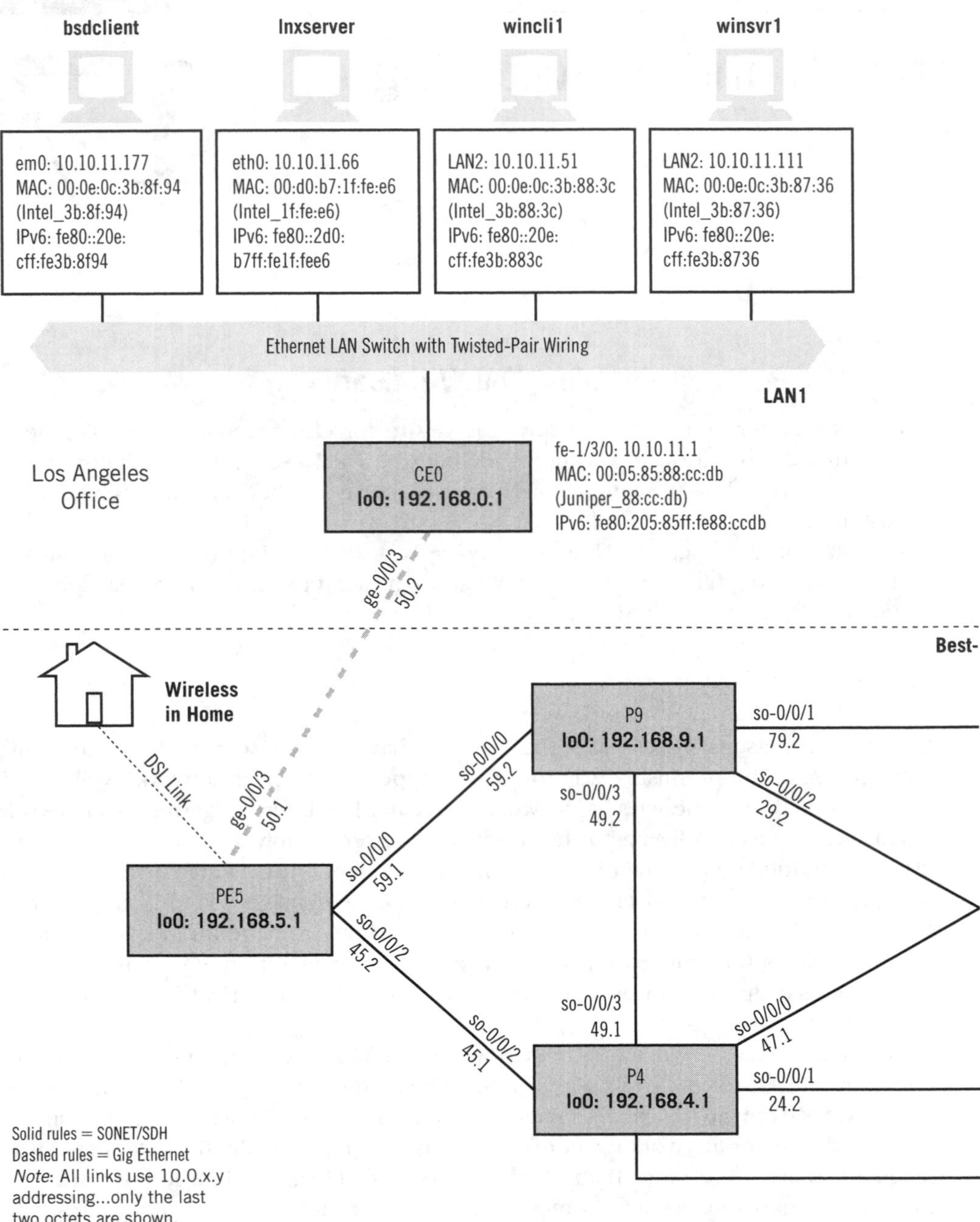

FIGURE 17.1

The routers on the Illustrated Network will be used to illustrate MPLS. Note that we are still dealing with the merged Best-Ace ISP and a single AS.

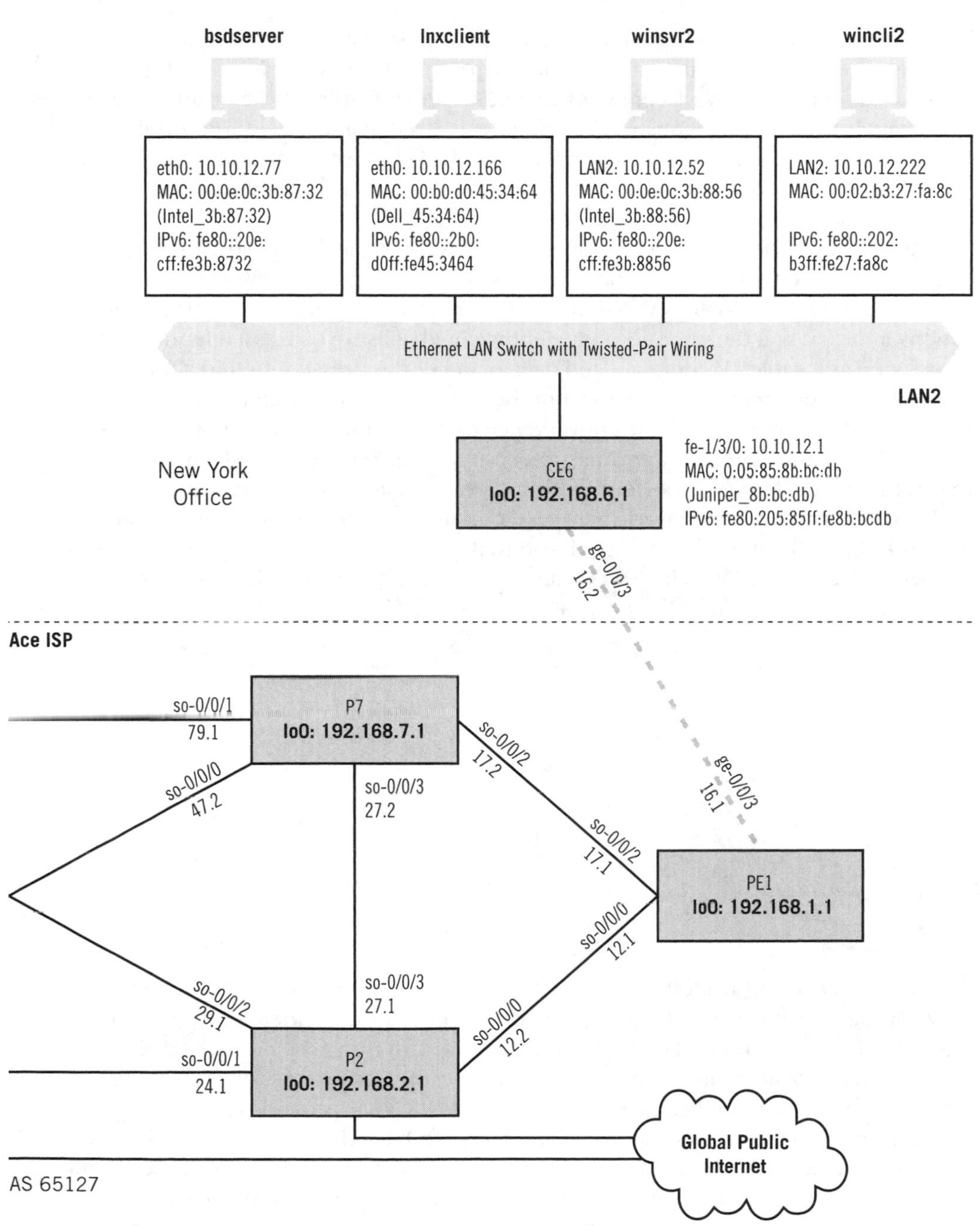
bsdserver
lnxclient
winsvr2
wincli2
eth0: 10.10.12.77
MAC: 00:0e:0c:3b:87:32
(Intel_3b:87:32)
IPv6: fe80::20e:
cff:fe3b:8732
eth0: 10.10.12.166
MAC: 00:b0:d0:45:34:64
(Dell_45:34:64)
IPv6: fe80::2b0:
d0ff:fe45:3464
LAN2: 10.10.12.52
MAC: 00:0e:0c:3b:88:56
(Intel_3b:88:56)
IPv6: fe80::20e:
cff:fe3b:8856
LAN2: 10.10.12.222
MAC: 00:02:b3:27:fa:8c
IPv6: fe80::202:
b3ff:fe27:fa8c
Ethernet LAN Switch with Twisted-Pair Wiring
LAN2
New York
Office
CE6
lo0: 192.168.6.1
fe-1/3/0: 10.10.12.1
MAC: 0:05:85:8b:bc:db
(Juniper_8b:bc:db)
IPv6: fe80:205:85ff:fe8b:bcdb
ge-0/0/3
16.2
Ace ISP
so-0/0/1
79.1
P7
lo0: 192.168.7.1
so-0/0/2
17.2
ge-0/0/3
16.1
so-0/0/0
47.2
so-0/0/3
27.2
so-0/0/2
17.1
PE1
lo0: 192.168.1.1
so-0/0/0
12.1
so-0/0/2
29.1
so-0/0/3
27.1
so-0/0/0
12.2
so-0/0/1
24.1
P2
lo0: 192.168.2.1
Global Public
Internet
AS 65127

by the pulses of Morse code running in adjacent wires. The solution was to twist and pair telephone wires and maintain adequate separation from telegraph wire bundles.

So, two separate networks grew up: telephone and telegraph. When cable TV came along much later, the inadequate bandwidth of twisted-pair wire led to a third major distinct network architecture—this one made of coaxial cable capable of delivering 50 or more (compared to the handful of broadcast channels available, that was a lot) television channels at the same time.

Naturally, communications companies did not want to pay for, deploy, and maintain three separate networks for separate services. It was much more efficient to use one converged infrastructure for everything. Once deregulation came to the telecommunications industry, and the same corporate entity could deliver voice as a telephony company, video as a cable TV company, and data as an ISP, the pressure to find a "universal" network architecture became intense. But the Internet was not the only universal network intended to be used for the convergence of voice, video, and data over the same links. Telecommunications companies also used frame relay (FR) and asynchronous transfer mode (ATM) networks to try to carry voice, video, and data on the same links.

Let's see if we can "converge" these different applications onto the Illustrated Network. This chapter will use the Illustrated Network routers exclusively. This is shown in Figure 17.1, which also reveals something interesting when we run traceroute from `bsdclient` on LAN1 to `bsdserver` on LAN2.

```
bsdclient# traceroute bsdserver

traceroute to bsdserver (10.10.12.77), 64 hops max, 44 byte packets
 1  10.10.11.1 (10.10.11.1)  0.363 ms  0.306 ms  0.345 ms
 2  10.0.50.1 (10.1.36.2)  0.329 ms  0.342 ms  0.346 ms
 3  10.0.45.1 (10.0.45.1) 0.330 ms  0.341 ms  0.346 ms
 4  10.0.24.1 (10.0.24.1) 0.332 ms  0.343 ms  0.345 ms
 5  10.0.12.1 (10.0.12.1) 0.329 ms  0.342 ms  0.347 ms
 6  10.0.16.2 (10.0.16.2) 0.330 ms  0.341 ms  0.346 ms
 7  10.10.12.77 (10.10.12.77)  0.331 ms  0.343 ms  0.347 ms
bsdclient#
```

The packets travel from PE5 to P4 and then on to P2 and PE1. Why shouldn't they flow through P9 and P7? Well, they could, but without load balancing turned on (and it is not) PE5 has to choose P9 or P4 as the next hop. All things being equal, if all other metrics are the same, routers typically pick to lowest IP address. A look at the network diagram shows this to be the case here.

There are obviously other users on the Best-Ace ISP's network, not just those on LAN1 and LAN2. However, it would be nice if the customer-edge (site) routers CE0 and CE6 were always seven hops away and never any more (in other words, no matter how traffic is routed there are always six routers between LAN1 and LAN2). This is because most of the traffic flows between the two sites, as we have seen (on many LANs, vast quantities of traffic usually flow among a handful of destinations).

Before the rise of the Internet, the company owning LAN1 and LAN2 would pay a service provider (telephone company or other "common carrier") to run a point-to-point link between New York and Los Angeles and use it for data traffic. They might also do the same for voice, and perhaps even for video conferences between the two sites. The nice thing about these leased line links (links used exclusively for voice are called tie lines) is that they make the two sites appear to be directly connected, reducing the number of hops (and network processing delay) drastically.

But leased lines are an expensive solution (they are paid for by the mile) and are limited in application (they only connect the two sites). What else could a public network service provider offer as a convergence solution to make the network more efficient?

We'll take a very brief look at the ideas behind some public network attempts at convergence (frame relay and ATM) and then see how TCP/IP itself handles the issue. We'll introduce Multiprotocol Label Switching (MPLS) and position this technology as a way to make IP router networks run faster and more efficiently with IP switching.

CONVERGING WHAT?

Convergence is not physical convergence through channels, which had been done for a very long time. Consider a transport network composed of a series of fiber optic links between SONET/SDH multiplexers. The enormous bandwidth on these links can be (and frequently is) channelized into multiple separate paths for voice bits, data bits, and video bits on the same physical fiber. But this is not convergence.

In this chapter convergence means the combination of voice, video, and data on the same physical channel. Convergence means more than just carrying channels on the same physical transport. It means combining the bits representing voice, video, and data into one stream and carrying them all over the total bandwidth on the same "unchannelized" fiber optic link. If there are voice, video, and data channels on the link, these are now virtual channels (or logical channels) and originate and terminate in the same equipment—not only at the physical layer, but at some layer above the lowest.

On modern Metro Ethernet links, the convergence is done by combining the traffic from separate VLANs on the same physical transport. The VLANs can be established based on traffic type (voice, video, and data), customer or customer site, or both (with an inner and outer VLAN label.) In this chapter, we'll talk about MPLS—which can work with VLANs or virtual channels.

Fast Packet Switching

Before there was MPLS, there was the concept of *fast packet switching* to speed up packet forwarding on converged links and through Internet network nodes. Two major technologies were developed to address this new technology, and they are worth at least a mention because they still exist in some places.

Frame Relay

Frame relay was an attempt to slim down the bulky X.25 public packet switching standard protocol stack for public packet networks for the new environment of home PCs and computers at every work location in an organization. Although it predated modern layered concepts, X.25 essentially defined the data units at the bottom three layers—physical interface, frame structure, and packet—as an international standard. It was mildly successful compared to the Internet, but wildly successful for a world without the Web and satellite or cell phones. In the mid-1980s, about the only way to communicate text to an off-shore oil platform or ships at sea was with the familiar but terse "GA" (go ahead) greeting on a teletype over an X.25 connection.

The problem with X.25 packets (called PLP, Packet Layer Protocol, packets) was that they weren't IP packets, and so could not easily share or even interface with the Internet, which had started to take off when the PC hit town. But IP didn't have a popular WAN frame defined (SLIP did not really use frames), so the X.25 Layer 2 frame structure, High-level Data Link Control (HDLC)—also used in ISDN—was modified to make it more useful in an IP environment populated by routers. In fact, routers, which struggled with full X.25 interfaces, could easily add frame relay interfaces.

One of the biggest parts of X.25 dropped on the way to frame relay was error resistance. Today, network experts have a more nuanced and sophisticated understanding of how this should be done instead of the heavyweight X.25 approach to error detection and recovery.

Frame relay was once popularly known as "X.25 on steroids," a choice of analogies that proved unfortunate for both X.25 and frame relay. But at least frame relay switch network nodes could relay frames faster than X.25 switches could route packets. Attempts were made to speed X.25 up prior to the frame relay makeover, such as allowing a connection-request message to carry data, which was then processed and a reply returned by the destination in a connection-rejected message, thus making X.25 networks as efficient for some things as a TCP/IP network with UDP. However, an X.25 network was still much more costly to build and operate than anything based on the simple Internet architecture. The optimization to X.25 that frame relay represented is shown in Figure 17.2.

Even with frame relay defined, there was still one nagging problem: Like X.25 before it, frame relay was connection oriented. Only signaling protocol messages were connectionless, and many frame relay networks used "permanent virtual circuits" set up

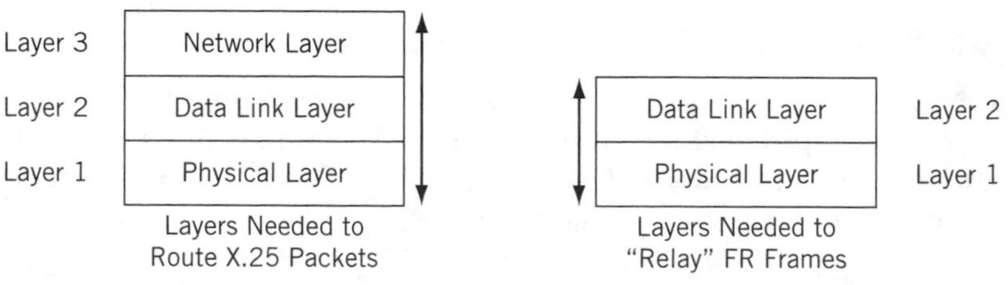

FIGURE 17.2

How X.25 packet routing relates to frame relaying. Note that frame relay has no network layer, leaving IP free to function independently.

with a labor-intensive process comparable to configuring router tables with hundreds of static entries in the absence of mature routing protocols.

Connections were a large part of the reason that X.25 network nodes were switches and not routers. A network node that handled only frame relay frames was still a switch, and connections were now defined by a simple identifier in the frame relay header and called "virtual circuits." But a connection was still a connection. In the time it took a frame relay signaling message exchange to set up a connection, IP with UDP could send a request and receive a reply. Even for bulk data transfer, connections over frame relay had few attractions compared to TCP for IP.

The frame relay frame itself was tailor-made for transporting IP packets over public data networks run by large telecommunications carriers rather than privately owned routers linked by dedicated bandwidth leased by the mile from these same carriers. The frame relay frame structure is shown in Figure 17.3.

- *DLCI*—The Data Link Connection Identifier is a 10-bit field that gives the connection number.
- *C/R*—The Command/Response bit is inherited from X.25 and not used.
- *EA*—The Extended Address bit tells whether the byte is the last in the header (headers in frame relay can be longer than 2 bytes).
- *FECN and BECN*—The Forward/Backward Explicit Congestion Notification bits are used for flow control.
- *DE*—The Discard Eligible bit is used to identify frames to discard under congested conditions.

Unlike a connectionless packet, the frame relay frame needs only a connection identifier to allow network switch nodes to route the frame. In frame relay, this is the DLCI. A connection by definition links two hosts, source and destination. There is no

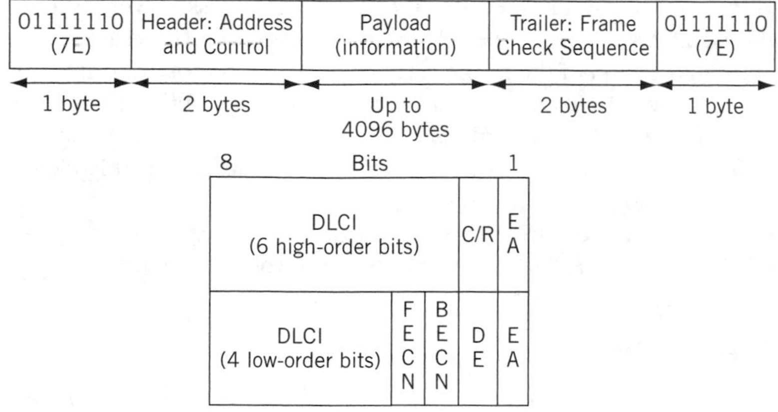

FIGURE 17.3

The basic 2-byte frame relay frame and header. The DLCI field can come in larger sizes.

sense of "send this *to* DLCI 18" or "this is *from* DLCI 18." Frames travel *on* DLCI 18, and this implies that connections are inherently unidirectional (which they are, but are usually set up and released in pairs) and that the connection identifiers in each direction did not have to match (although they typically did, just to keep network operators sane).

One of the things that complicate DLCI discussions is that unlike globally unique IP addresses, DLCIs have local significance only. This just means that the DLCI on a frame relay frame sent from site A on DLCI 25 could easily arrive at site B on DLCI 38. And in between, the frame could have been passed around the switches as DLCI 18, 44, or whatever. Site A only needs to know that the local DLCI 25 leads to site B, and site B needs to know that DLCI 38 leads to site A, and the entire scheme still works. But it is somewhat jarring to TCP/IP veterans.

This limits the connectivity from each site to the number of unique DLCIs that can operate at any one time, but the DLCI header field can grow if this becomes a problem. And frame relay connections were never supposed to be used all of the time.

What about adding voice and video to frame relay? That was actually done, especially with voice. Frame relay was positioned as a less expensive way of linking an organization's private voice switches (called private branch exchanges, or PBXs) than with private voice circuits. Voice was not always packetized, but at least it was "framerized" over these links. If the links had enough bandwidth, which was not always a given, primitive videoconferencing (but not commercial-quality video signals that anyone would pay to view) could be used as well.

Frame relay suffered from three problems, which proved insurmountable. It was not particularly IP friendly, so frame relay switches (which did not run normal IP routing protocols) could not react to TCP/IP network conditions the way routers could. The router and switches remained "invisible" to each other. And in spite of efforts to integrate voice and video onto the data network, frame relay was first and foremost a data service and addressed voice and video delay concerns by grossly overconfiguring bandwidth in almost all cases. Finally, the telecommunications carriers (unlike the ISPs) resisted easy interconnection of the frame relay network with those of other carriers, which forced even otherwise eager customers to try to do everything with one carrier (an often impossible task). It was a little like cell phones without any possibility of roaming, and in ironic contrast to the carrier's own behavior as an ISP, this closed environment was not what customers wanted or needed.

Frame relay still exists as a service offering. However, outside of just another type of router WAN interface, frame relay has little impact on the Internet or IP world.

Asynchronous Transfer Mode

The Asynchronous Transfer Mode (ATM) was the most ambitious of all convergence methods. It had to be, because what ATM essentially proposed was to throw everything out that had come before and to "Greenfield" the entire telecommunications structure the world over. ATM was part of an all-encompassing vision of networking known as broadband ISDN (B-ISDN), which would support all types of voice, video, and data applications though virtual channels (and virtual connections). In this model, the Internet would yield to a global B-ISDN network—and TCP/IP to ATM.

Does this support plan for converged information sound familiar? Of course it does. It's pretty much what the Internet and TCP/IP do today, without B-ISDN or ATM. But when ATM was first proposed, the Internet and TCP/IP could do none of the things that ATM was supposed to do with ease. How did ATM handle the problems of mixing support for bulk data transfer with the needs of delay-sensitive voice and bandwidth-hungry (and delay-sensitive) video?

ATM was the international standard for what was known as cell relay (there were cell relay technologies other than ATM, now mostly forgotten). The cell relay name seems to have developed out of an analogy with frame relay. Frame relay "relayed" (switched) Layer 2 frames through network nodes instead of independently routing Layer 3 packets. The efficiency of doing it all at a lower layer made the frame relay node faster than a router could have been at the time.

Cell relay took it a step further, doing everything at Layer 1 (the actual bit level). But there was no natural data unit at the physical layer, just a stream of bits. So, they invented one 53 bytes long and called it the "cell"—apparently in comparison to the cell in the human body—which is very small, can be generic, and everything else is built up from them. Technically, in data protocol stacks, cells are a "shim" layer slipped between the bits and the frames, because both bits and frames are still needed in hardware and software at source and destination.

Cell relay (ATM) "relayed" (switched) cells through network nodes. This could be done entirely in hardware because cells were all exactly the same size. Imagine how fast ATM switches would be compared to slow Layer 3 routers with two more layers to deal with! And ATM switches had no need to allocate buffers in variable units, or to clean up fragmented memory. The structure of the 5-byte ATM cell header is shown in Figure 17.4 (descriptions follow on next page). The call payload is always 48 bytes long.

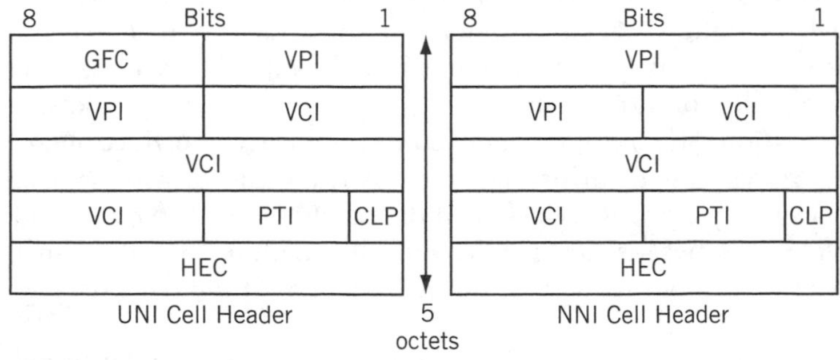

FIGURE 17.4

The ATM cell header. Note the larger VPI fields on the network (NNI) version of the header.

- *GFC*—The Generic Flow Control is a 4-bit field used between a customer site and ATM switch, on the User-Network Interface (UNI). It is not present on the Network-Network Interface (NNI) between ATM switches.
- *VPI*—The Virtual Path Identifier is an 8- or 12-bit field used to identify paths between sites on the ATM network. It is larger on the NNI to accommodate aggregation on customer paths.
- *VCI*—The Virtual Connection Identifier is a 16-bit field used to identify paths between individual devices on the ATM network.
- *PTI*—The Payload Type Indicator is a 3-bit field used to identify one of eight traffic types carried in the cell.
- *CLP*—The Cell Loss Priority bit serves the same function as the DE bit in frame relay, but identifies cells to discard when congestion occurs.
- *HEC*—The Header Error Control byte not only detects bit errors in the entire 40-bit header, but can also *correct* single bit errors.

In contrast to frame relay, the ATM connection identifier was a two-part virtual path identifier (VPI) and virtual channel identifier (VCI). Loosely, VPIs were for connections between sites and VCIs were for connections between devices. ATM switches could "route" cells based on the VPI, and the local ATM switch could take care of finding the exact device for which the cell was destined.

Like frame relay DLCIs, ATM VPI/VCIs have local significance only. That is, the VPI/VPI values change as the cells make their way from switch to switch and depending on direction. Both frame relay and ATM switch essentially take a data unit in on an input port, look up the header (DLCI or VPI/VCI label) in a table, and output the data unit on the port indicated in the table—but also with a new label value, also provided by the table.

This distinctive label-swapping is characteristic of switching technologies and protocols. And, as we will see later, switching has come to the IP world with MPLS, which takes the best of frame relay and ATM and applies it directly to IP without the burden of "legacy" stacks (frame relay) or phantom applications (ATM and B-ISDN).

The tiny 48-byte payload of the ATM cell was intentional. It made sure that no delay-sensitive bits got stuck in a queue behind some monstrous chunk of data a thousand times larger than the 48 voice or video bytes. Such "serialization delay" introduced added delay and delay variation (jitter) that rendered converged voice and video almost useless without more bandwidth than anyone could realistically afford. With ATM, all data encountered was a slightly elevated delay when data cells shared the total bandwidth with voice and video. But because few applications did anything with data (such as a file) before the entire group of bits was transferred intact ATM pioneers deemed this a minor inconvenience at worst.

All of this sounded too good to be true to a lot of networking people, and it turned out that it was. The problem was not with raw voice and video, which could be molded into any form necessary for transport across a network. The issue was with data, which came inside IP packets and had to be broken down into 48-byte units—each of which had a 5-byte ATM cell header, and often a footer that limited it to only 30 bytes.

This was an enormous amount of overhead for data applications, which normally added 3 or 4 bytes to an Ethernet frame for transport across a WAN. Naturally, no hardware existed to convert data frames to cells and back—and software was much too slow—so this equipment had to be invented. Early results seemed promising, although the frame-to-cell-and-back process was much more complex and expensive than anticipated. But after ATM caught on, prices would drop and efficiencies would be naturally discovered. Once ATM networks were deployed, the B-ISDN applications that made the most of them would appear. Or so it seemed.

However, by the early 1990s it turned out that making cells out of data frames was effective as long as the bandwidth on the link used to carry both voice and video along with the data was limited to less than that needed to carry all three at once. In other words, if the link was limited to 50 Mbps and the voice and video data added up to 75 Mbps, cells made sense. Otherwise, variable-length data units worked just fine. Full-motion video was the killer at the time, with most television signals needing about 45 Mbps (and this was not even high-definition TV). Not only that, but it turned out that the point of diminishing ATM returns (the link bandwidth at which it became slower and more costly to make cells than simply send variable-length data units) was about 622 Mbps—lower than most had anticipated.

Of course, one major legacy of the Internet bubble was the underutilization of fiber optic links with more than 45 Mbps, and in many cases greatly in excess of 622 Mbps. And digital video could produce stunning images with less and less bandwidth as time went on. And in that world, in many cases, ATM was left as a solution without a problem. ATM did not suffer from lack of supporters, but it proved to be the wrong technology to carry forward as a switching technology for IP networks.

Why Converge on TCP/IP?

Some of the general reasons TCP/IP has dominated the networking scene have been mentioned in earlier chapters. Specifically, none of the "new" public network technologies were particularly TCP/IP friendly—and some seemed almost antagonistic. ATM cells, for instance, would be a lot more TCP/IP friendly if the payload were 64 bytes instead of 48 bytes. At least a lot of TCP/IP traffic would fit inside a single ATM cell intact, making processing straightforward and efficient.

At 48 bytes, everything in TCP/IP had to be broken up into at least two cells. But the voice people wanted the cell to be 32 bytes or smaller, in order to keep voice delays as short as possible. It may be only a coincidence that 48 bytes is halfway between 32 and 64 bytes, but a lot of times reaching a compromise instead of making a decision annoys both parties and leaves neither satisfied with the result. So, ATM began as a standard by alienating the two groups (voice and data) that were absolutely necessary to make ATM a success.

But the real blow to ATM came because a lot of TCP/IP traffic would not fit into 64-byte frames. ACKs would fit well, but TCP/IP packet sizes tend to follow a bimodal distribution with two distinct peaks at about 64 and between 1210 and 1550 bytes. The upper cluster is smaller and more spread out, but this represents the vast bulk of all traffic on the Internet.

Then new architectures allowed otherwise normal IP routers to act like frame relay and ATM switches with the addition of IP-centric MPLS. Suddenly, all of the benefits of frame relay and ATM could be had without using unfamiliar and special equipment (although a router upgrade might be called for).

MPLS

Rather than adding IP to fast packet switching networks, such as frame relay and ATM, MPLS adds fast packet switching to IP router networks. We've already talked about some of the differences between routing (connectionless networks) and switching networks in Chapter 13. Table 17.1 makes the same type of comparisons from a different perspective.

The difference in the way CoS is handled is the major issue when convergence is concerned. Naturally, the problem is to find the voice and video packets in the midst of the data packets and make sure that delay-sensitive packets are not fighting for bandwidth along with bulk file transfers or email. This is challenging in IP routers because there is no fixed path set up through the network to make it easy to enforce QoS at every hop along the way. But switching uses stable paths, which makes it easy to determine exactly which routers and resources are consumed by the packet stream. QoS is also challenging because you don't have administrative control over the routers outside your own domain.

MPLS and Tunnels

Some observers do not apply the term "tunnel" to MPLS at all. They reserve the term for wholesale violations on normal encapsulations (packet in frame in a packet, for example). MPLS uses a special header (sometimes called a "shim" header) between packet and frame header, a header that is not part of the usual TCP/IP suite layers.

However, RFCs (such as RFC 2547 and 4364) apply the tunnel terminology to MPLS. MPLS headers certainly conform to general tunnel "rules" about stack encapsulation violations. This chapter will not dwell on "MPLS tunnel" terminology but will not avoid the term either. (This note also applies to MPLS-based VPNs, discussed in Chapter 26.)

But QoS enforcement is not the only attraction of MPLS. There are at least two others, and probably more. One is the ability to do *traffic engineering* with MPLS, and the other is that MPLS *tunnels* form the basis for a certain *virtual private network* (VPN) scheme called *Layer 3 VPNs*. There are also *Layer 2 VPNs*, and we'll look at them in more detail in Chapter 26.

MPLS uses tunnels in the generic sense: The normal flow of the layers is altered at one point or another, typically by the insertion of an "extra" header. This header is added at one end router and removed (and processed) at the other end. In MPLS, routers form the

Table 17.1 Comparing Routing and Switching on a WAN		
Characteristic	**Routing**	**Switching**
Network node	Router	Switch
Traffic flow	Each packet routed independently hop by hop	Each data unit follows same path through network
Node coordination	Routing protocols share information	Signaling protocols set up paths through network
Addressing	Global, unique	Label, local significance
Consistency of address	Unchanged source to destination	Label is swapped at each node
QoS	Challenging	Associated with path

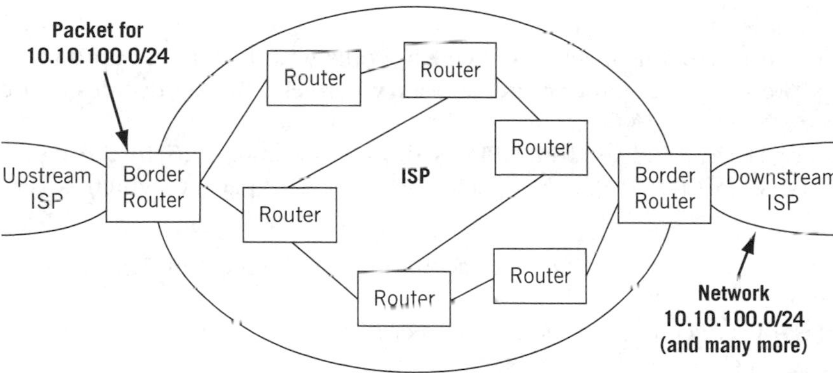

FIGURE 17.5

The rationale for MPLS. The LSP forms a "shortcut" across the routing network for transit traffic. The Border Router knows right away, thanks to BGP, that the packet for 10.10.100.0/24 must exit at the other border router. Why route it independently at every router in between?

endpoints of the tunnels. In MPLS, the header is called a *label* and is placed between the IP header and the frame headers—making MPLS a kind of "Layer 2 and a half" protocol.

MPLS did not start out to be the answer to everyone's dream for convergence or traffic engineering or anything else. MPLS addressed a simple problem faced by every large ISP in the world, a problem shown in Figure 17.5.

MPLS was conceived as a sort of BGP "shortcut" connecting border routers across the ISP. As shown in the figure, a packet bound for `10.10.100.0/24` entering the border router from the upstream ISP is known, thanks to the IBGP information, to have to exit the ISP at the other border router. In practice, of course, this will apply to many border routers and thousands of routes (usually most of them), but the principle is the same.

Only the local packets with destinations within the ISP technically need to be routed by the interior routers. Transit packets can be sent directly to the border router,

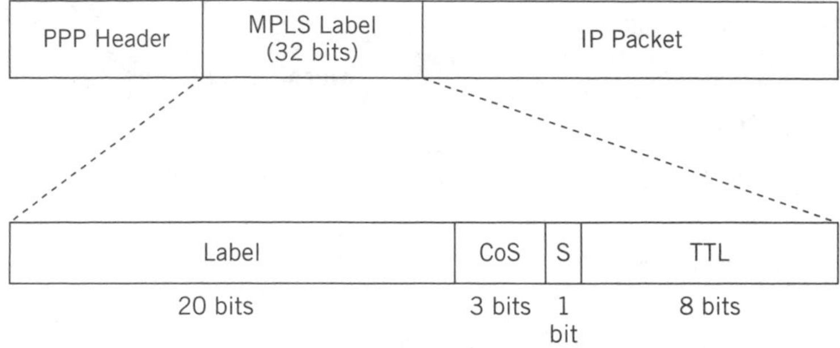

FIGURE 17.6

The 32-bit MPLS label fields. Note the 3-bit CoS field, which is often related to the IP ToS header. The label field is used to identify flows that should be kept together as they cross the network.

if possible. MPLS provides this mechanism, which works with BGP to set up tunnels through the ISP between the border routers (or anywhere else the ISP decides to use them).

The structure of the label used in MPLS is shown in Figure 17.6. In the figure, it is shown between a Layer 2 PPP frame and the Layer 3 IP packet (which is very common).

- *Label*—This 20-bit field identifies the packets included in the "flow" through the MPLS tunnel.
- *CoS*—Class-of-Service is a 3-bit field used to classify the data stream into one of eight categories.
- *S*—The Stack bit lets the router know if another label is *stacked* after the current 32-bit label.
- *TTL*—The Time-to-Live is an 8-bit field used in exactly the same way as the IP packet header TTL. This value can be copied from or into the IP packet or used in other ways.

Certain label values and ranges have been reserved for MPLS. These are outlined in Table 17.2.

The MPLS architecture is defined in RFC 3031, and MPLS label stacking is defined in RFC 3032 (more than one MPLS label can precede an IP packet). General traffic engineering in MPLS is described in RFC 2702, and several drafts add details and features to these basics.

What does it mean to use traffic engineering on a router network? Consider the Illustrated Network. We saw that traffic from LAN1 to LAN2 flows through backbone routers P4 and P2 (reverse traffic also flows this way). But notice that P2 and P4 also have links to and from the Internet. A lot of general Internet traffic flows through routers P2 and P4 and their links, as well as LAN1 and LAN2 traffic.

Table 17.2 MPLS Label Values and Their Uses

Value or Range	Use
0	IPv4 Explicit Null. Must be the last label (no stacking). Receiver removes the label and routes the IPv4 packet inside.
1	Router Alert. The IP packet inside has information for the router itself, and the packet should not be forwarded.
2	IPv6 Explicit Null. Same as label 0, but with IPv6 inside.
3	Implicit Null. A "virtual" label that never appears in the label itself. It is a table entry to request label removal by the downstream router.
4–15	Reserved.
16–1023 and 10000–99999	Ranges used in Juniper Networks routers to manually configure MPLS tunnels (not used by the signaling protocols).
1024–9999	Reserved.
100000–1048575	Used by signaling protocols.

So, it would make sense to "split off" the LAN1 and LAN2 traffic onto a less utilized path through the network (for example, from PE5 to P9 to P7 to PE1). This will ease congestion and might even be faster, even though in some configurations there might be more hops (for example, there might be other routers between P9 and P7).

Why Not Include CE0 and CE6?

Why did we start the MPLS tunnels at the provider-edge routers instead of directly at the customer edge, on the premises? Actually, as long as the (generally) smaller site routers support the full suite of MPLS features and protocols there's no reason the tunnel could not span LAN to LAN.

However, MPLS traditionally begins and ends in the "provider cloud"—usually on the PE routers, as in this chapter. This allows the customer routers to be more independent and less costly, and allows reconfiguration of MPLS without access to the customer's routers. Of course, in some cases the customer might want ISP to handle MPLS management—and then the CE routers certainly could be included on the MPLS path.

There are ways to do this with IGPs, such as OSPF and IS-IS, by adjusting the link metrics, but these solutions are not absolute and have global effects on the network. In contrast, an MPLS tunnel can be configured from PE5 to PE1 through P9 and P7 and only affect the routing on PE5 and PE1 that involves LAN1 and LAN2 traffic, exactly the effect that is desired.

MPLS Terminology

Before looking at how MPLS would handle a packet sent from LAN1 to LAN2 over an MPLS tunnel, we should look at the special terminology involved with MPLS. In no particular order, the important terms are:

LSP—We've been calling them tunnels, and they are, but in MPLS the tunnel is called a *label-switched path*. The LSP is a unidirectional connection following the same path through the network.

Ingress router—The *ingress router* is the start of the LSP and where the label is *pushed* onto the packet.

Egress router—The *egress router* is the end of the LSP and where the label is *popped* off the packet.

Transit or intermediate router—There must be at least one *transit* (sometimes called *intermediate*) *router* between ingress and egress routers. The transit router(s) *swaps* labels and replaces the incoming values with the outgoing values.

Static LSPs—These are LSPs set up by hand, much like *permanent virtual circuits* (PVCs) in FR and ATM. They are difficult to change rapidly.

Signaled LSPs—These are LSPs set up by a signaling protocol used with MPLS (there are two) and are similar to *switched-virtual circuits* (SVCs) in FR and ATM.

MPLS domain—The collection of routers within a routing domain that starts and ends all LSPs form the MPLS domain. MPLS domains can be nested, and can be a subset of the routing domain itself (that is, all routers do not have to understand MPLS; only those on the LSP).

Push, pop, and swap—A *push* adds a label to an IP packet or another MPLS label. A *pop* removes and processes a label from an IP packet or another MPLS label. A *swap* is a pop followed by a push and replaces one label by another (with different field values). Multiple labels can be added (push push . . .) or removed (pop pop . . .) at the same time.

Penultimate hop popping (PHP)—Many of LSPs can terminate at the same border router. This router must not only pop and process all the labels but route all packets inside, *plus* all other packets that arrive from within the ISP. To ease the load of this border router, the router one hop upstream from the egress router (known as the *penultimate* router) can pop the label and simply route the packet to the egress router (it *must* be one hop, so the effect is the same). PHP is an optional feature of LSPs, and keep in mind that the LSP is still considered to terminate at the egress router (not at the penultimate).

Constrained path LSPs—These are *traffic engineering* (TE) LSPs set up by a signaling protocol that must respect certain TE constraints imposed on the network with regard to delay, security, and so on. TE is the most intriguing aspect of MPLS.

IGP shortcuts—Usually, LSPs are used in special router tables and only available to routes learned by BGP (transit traffic). Interior Gateway Protocol (IGP) shortcuts allow LSPs to be installed in the main routing table and used by traffic within the ISP itself, routes learned by OSPF or another IGP.

Signaling and MPLS

There are two signaling protocols that can be used in MPLS to automatically set up LSPs without human intervention (other than configuring the signaling protocols themselves!). The Resource Reservation Protocol (RSVP) was originally invented to set up QoS "paths" from host to host through a router network, but it never scaled well or worked as advertised. Today, RSVP has been defined in RFC 3209 as RSVP for TE and is used as a signaling protocol for MPLS. RSVP is used almost exclusively as RSVP-TE (most people just say RSVP) by routers to set up LSPs (explicit-path LSPs), but can still be used for QoS purposes (constrained-path LSPs).

The Label Distribution Protocol (LDP), defined in RFC 3212, is used exclusively with MPLS but cannot be used for adding QoS to LSPs other than using simple constraints when setting up paths. On the other hand, LDP is trivial to configure compared to RSVP. This is because LDP works directly from the tables created by the IGP (OSPF or IS–IS). The lack of QoS support in LDP is due to the lack of any intention in the process. The reason for the LDP paths created from the IGP table to exist is only simple adjacency. In addition, LDP does not offer much if your routing platform can forward packets almost as fast as it can switch labels. Today, use of LDP is deprecated (see the admonitions in RFC 3468) in favor of RSVP-TE.

A lot of TCP/IP texts spend a lot of time explaining how RSVP-TE works (they deal with LDP less often). This is more of an artifact of the original use of RSVP as a host-based protocol. It is enough to note that RSVP messages are exchanged between all routers along the LSP from ingress to egress. The LSP label values are determined, and TE constraints respected, hop by hop through the network until the LSP is ready for traffic. The process is quick and efficient, but there are few parameters that can be configured even on routers that change RSVP operation significantly (such as interval timers)—and none at all on hosts.

Although not discussed in detail in this introduction to MPLS, another protocol is commonly used for MPLS signaling, as described in RFC 2547bis. BGP is a routing protocol, not a signaling protocol, but the extensions used in multiprotocol BPG (MPBGP) make it well suited for the types of path setup tasks described in this chapter. With MPBGP, it is possible to deploy BGP- and MPLS-based VPNs without the use of any other signaling protocol. LSPs are established based on the routing information distributed by MPBGP from PE to PE. MPBGP is backward compatible with "normal" BGP, and thus use of these extensions does not require a wholesale upgrade of all routers at once.

Label Stacking

Of all the MPLS terms outlined in the previous section, the one that is essential to understand is the concept of "nested" LSPs; that is, LSPs which include one or more other LSPs along their path from ingress to egress. When this happens, there will be more than one label in front of the IP packet for at least part of its journey.

It is common for many large ISPs to stack three labels in front of an IP packet. Often, the end of two LSPs is at the same router and two labels are pushed or popped at once. The current limit is eight labels.

There are several instances where this stacking ability comes in handy. A larger ISP can buy a smaller ISP and simply "add" their own LSPs onto (outside) the existing ones. In addition, when different signaling protocols are used in core routers and border routers, these domains can be nested instead of discarding one or the other.

The general idea of nested MPLS domains with label stacking is shown in Figure 17.7. There are five MPLS domains, each with its own way of setting up LSPs: static, RSVP, and LDP. The figure shows the number of labels stacked at each point and the order

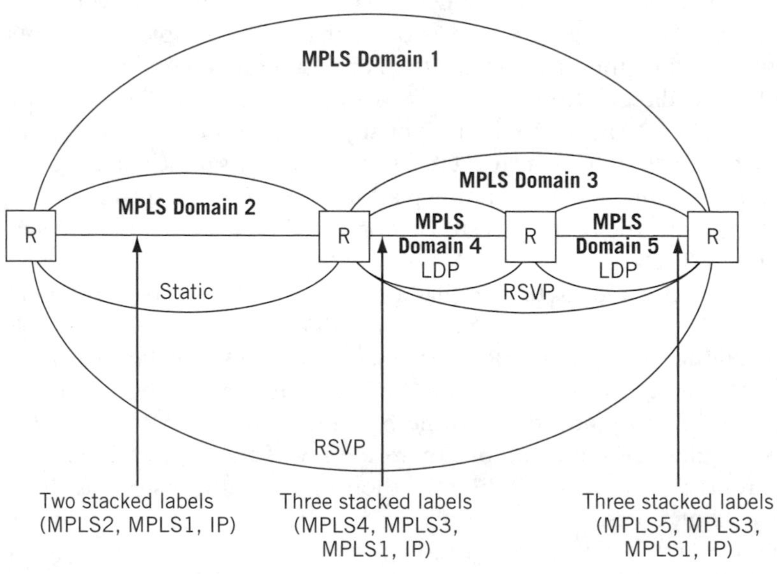

FIGURE 17.7

MPLS domains, showing how the domains can be nested or chained, and how multiple labels are used.

they are stacked in front of the packet. All of the routers shown (in practice, there will be many more) pop and process multiple labels. MPLS domains can be nested for geographical, vendor, or organizational reasons as well.

MPLS and VPNs

MPLS forms the basis for many types of VPNs used on IP networks today, especially Layer 3 VPNs. LSPs are like the PVCs and SVCs that formed "virtually private" links across a shared public network such as FR or ATM. LSPs are not really the same as private leased-line links, but they appear to be to their users.

Of course, while the path is constrained, the MPLS-based Layer 3 VPN is not actually doing anything special to secure the content of the tunnel or to protect its integrity. So, this "security" value is limited to constraining the path. This reduces the places where snooping or injection can occur, but it does not replace other Layer 3 VPN technology for security (such as IPSec, discussed in Chapter 29).

Nevertheless, VPNs are often positioned as a security feature on router networks. This is because, like "private" circuits, hackers cannot hack into the middle of an LSP (VPN) just by spoofing packets. There are labels to be dealt with, often nested labels. The ingress and egress routers are more vulnerable, but it's not as easy to harm VPNs or the sites they connect as it is to disrupt "straight" router networks.

So, VPNs have a lot in common with MPLS and LSPs—except that the terms are different! For example, the transit routers in MPLS are now provider (P) routers in VPNs. VPNs are discussed further in the security chapters.

MPLS Tables

The tables used to push, pop, and swap labels in multiprotocol label switching are different from the tables used to route packets. This makes sense: MPLS uses switching, and packets are routed.

Most MPLS tables are little more than long lists of labels with two key pieces of information attached: the output interface to the next-hop router on the LSP and the new value of the label. Other pieces of information can be added, but this is the absolute minimum.

What does an MPLS switching table look like? Suppose we did set up an LSP between LAN1 and LAN2 to carry packets from PE5 to PE1 through backbone routers P9 and P7 instead of through P4 and P2?

Figure 17.8 shows how the MPLS switching tables might be set up to switch a packet from LAN1 to LAN2. Note that this has nothing to do with routed traffic going back from LAN2 to LAN1! (In the real world, we would set up an LSP going from LAN2 to LAN1 as well.)

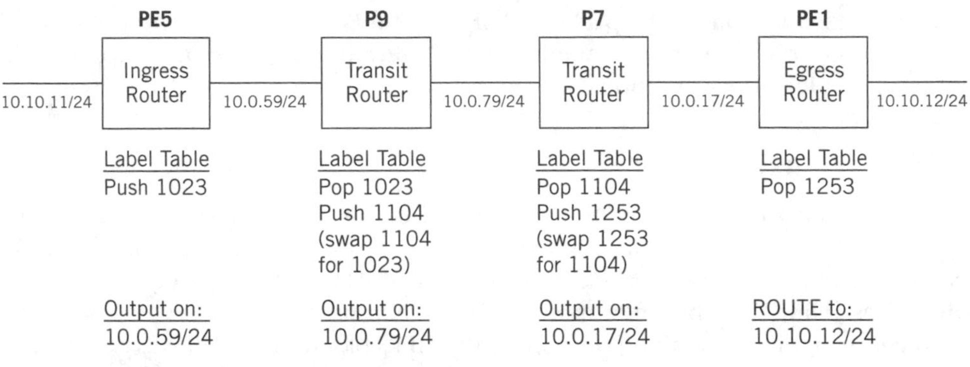

FIGURE 17.8

Label tables for a static LSP from PE5 (ingress) to PE1 (egress).

CONFIGURING MPLS USING STATIC LSPS

Let's build the static LSP from LAN1 to LAN2 from PE5 to P9 to P7 to PE1 that was shown in Figure 17.8. Then we'll show how that affects the routing table entries and run a traceroute for packets sent from `10.10.11.0/24` (LAN1) to `10.10.12.0/24` (LAN2).

The Ingress Router

Let's start by configuring the LSP on PE5, the ingress router, so that packets from LAN1's address space get an MPLS label value of `1023` and are sent to `10.0.59.2` as a next hop on the link to P9 (`so-0/0/0`).

```
set protocols mpls static-path LAN1-to-LAN2 10.10.11.0/24 next-hop 10.0.59.2;
set protocols mpls static-path LAN1-to-LAN2 10.10.11.0/24 push 1023;
set protocols mpls static-path LAN1-to-LAN2 interface so-0/0/0;
```

Once the configuration is committed, the static LSP shows up as a static route naturally (signaled LSPs are referenced by signaling a protocol, RSVP or LDP).

```
admin@PE5# show route table inet.0 protocol static
10.10.11.0/24      *[Static/5]  00:01:42
                    > to 10.0.59.2 via so-0/0/0. push 1023
```

The Transit Routers

This is how the LSP is configured on P9, the first transit (or intermediate) router.

```
set protocols mpls interface so-0/0/0 label-map 1023 next-hop 10.0.79.1;
set protocols mpls interface so-0/0/0 label-map 1023 swap 1104;
```

Note that this table is not organized by destination, as on the PE router, but by the interface that the MPLS data unit arrives on. There can be many labels, but this "label map" looks for 1023, swaps it for label 1104, and forwards it to 10.0.79.1. Note that there was no need to look anything up in the main routing table (in Juniper Networks routers, the interface addresses are held in hardware). Transit LSPs are identified by the use of swap in the static router entry, but this time in MPLS "label table" mpls.0.

```
admin@P9# show route table mpls.0 protocol static
1023            *[Static/5]  00:01:57
                > to 10.0.79.1 via so-0/0/1. swap 1104
```

The link to P7 is so-0/0/1, as expected. The configuration on the P7, the second transit router, is very similar.

```
set protocols mpls interface so-0/0/1 label-map 1104 next-hop 10.0.17.1;
set protocols mpls interface so-0/0/1 label-map 1104 swap 1253;
```

If we wanted to configure PHP, this is the router where we would enable it. The statement swap 3 is the "magic word" that enables PHP. MPLS label value 3 says to the local router, "Don't really push a 3 on the packet, but instead pop the label and route the packet inside." The use of the label at least makes it easier to remember that the end of the LSP is really on PE1.

The Egress Router

The configuration on the egress router, PE1, is essentially the opposite of that on the ingress router but more similar to that on a transit router.

```
set protocols mpls interface so-0/0/2 label-map 1253 next-hop 10.0.12.0/24;
set protocols mpls interface so-0/0/2 label-map 1253 pop;
admin@PE1# set protocols mpls interface so-0/0/2 label-map 1253 next-hop 10.10.12.0/24;
admin@PE1# set protocols mpls interface so-0/0/2 label-map 1253 pop;
```

There is no need to tell the router what label value to pop: if it got this far, the label value is 1253. Note that the next hop is the IP address of LAN2, which is the entire point of the exercise. When PHP is used, there is no need for a label map for that LSP on the egress router. When PHP is not used, the egress LSPs are identified by the use of pop in the static router entry in mpls.0.

```
admin@PE1# show route table mpls.0 protocol static
1253            *[Static/5]  00:02:17
                > to 10.10.12.0/24 via ge-0/0/3. pop
```

Static LSPs are fine, but offer no protection at all against link failure. And consider how many interfaces, labels, and other information have to be maintained and entered by hand. In MPLS classes, most instructors make students suffer through a complex static LSP configuration (some of which *never* work correctly) before allowing the use of RSVP-TE and LDP to "automatically" set up LSPs anywhere or everywhere. It is a lesson that is not soon forgotten. (In fact, dynamic LSP configuration using RVSP-TE is so simple that it is not even used as an example in this chapter.)

Traceroute and LSPs

How do we know that our static LSP is up and running properly? A `ping` that works proves nothing about the LSP because it could have been routed, not switched. Even one that fails proves nothing except the fact that something is broken.

But `traceroute` is the perfect tool to see if the LSP is up and running correctly. The following is what it looked like before we configured the LSP.

```
bsdclient# traceroute bsdserver
traceroute to bsdserver (10.10.12.77), 64 hops max, 44 byte packets
 1  10.10.11.1 (10.10.11.1)  0.363 ms  0.306 ms  0.345 ms
 2  10.0.50.1 (10.1.36.2) 0.329 ms  0.342 ms  0.346 ms
 3  10.0.45.1 (10.0.45.1) 0.330 ms  0.341 ms  0.346 ms
 4  10.0.24.1 (10.0.24.1) 0.332 ms  0.343 ms  0.345 ms
 5  10.0.12.1 (10.0.12.1) 0.329 ms  0.342 ms  0.347 ms
 6  10.0.16.2 (10.0.16.2) 0.330 ms  0.341 ms  0.346 ms
 7  10.10.12.77 (10.10.12.77)  0.331 ms  0.343 ms  0.347 ms
bsdclient#
```

Let's look at it now, after the LSP.

```
bsdclient# traceroute bsdserver
traceroute to bsdserver (10.10.12.77), 64 hops max, 44 byte packets
 1  10.10.11.1 (10.10.11.1)  0.363 ms  0.306 ms  0.345 ms
 2  10.0.59.1 (10.0.59.1)  0.329 ms  0.342 ms  0.346 ms
 3  10.0.16.2 (10.0.16.2) 0.330 ms  0.343 ms  0.0347 ms
 4  10.10.12.77 (10.10.12.77)  0.331 ms  0.343 ms  0.347 ms
bsdclient#
```

Only four routers have "routed" the packet. On the backbone, the packet is switched based on the MPLS tables, and so forms one router hop. But at least we can see that the packets are sent toward P9 (`10.0.59.1`) and not P4 (`10.0.50.1`).

The details of the path of MPLS LSPs are not visible from the hosts. Why should they be? LSPs are tools for the service providers on our network. Only on the routers, running a special version of traceroute, can we reveal the hop-by-hop functioning of the LSP. When run on PE5 to trace the path to the link to CE6, traceroute "expands" the path and provides details—showing that the CE6 is still five routers away from CE0 (and that there are still six routers and seven hops between LAN1 and LAN2).

```
admin@PE5> traceroute 10.10.16.1
traceroute to 10.10.12.0 (10.10.12.0), 30 hops max, 40 byte packets
 1  10.10.12.1 (10.10.12.1)  0.851 ms  0.743 ms  0.716 ms
    MPLS Label=1023 CoS=0 TTL=1 S=1
 2  10.0.59.1 (10.0.59.1)  0.799 ms  0.753 ms  0.721 ms
    MPLS Label=1104 CoS=0 TTL=1 S=1
 3  10.0.79.1 (10.0.79.1)  0.832 ms  0.769 ms  0.735 ms
    MPLS Label=1253 CoS=0 TTL=1 S=1
 4  10.0.17.1 (10.0.17.1)  0.854 ms  0.767 ms  0.734 ms
 5  10.0.16.1 (10.0.16.1)  0.629 ms !N  0.613 ms !N  0.582 ms !N
admin@PE5>
```

Just to show that the LSP we set up is unidirectional, watch what happens when we run `traceroute` in ***reverse*** from `bsdserver` on LAN2 to `bsdclient` on LAN1.

```
bsdserver# traceroute bsdclient
traceroute to bsdclient (10.10.11.177), 64 hops max, 44 byte packets
 1  10.10.12.1 (10.10.12.1)  0.361 ms  0.304 ms  0.343 ms
 2  10.0.16.1 (10.1.16.1) 0.331 ms  0.344 ms  0.347 ms
 3  10.0.12.2 (10.0.12.2) 0.329 ms  0.340 ms  0.345 ms
 4  10.0.24.2 (10.0.24.2) 0.333 ms  0.344 ms  0.346 ms
 5  10.0.45.2 (10.0.45.2) 0.329 ms  0.342 ms  0.347 ms
 6  10.0.50.2 (10.0.50.2) 0.330 ms  0.341 ms  0.346 ms
 7  10.10.11.177 (10.10.11.177)  0.331 ms  0.343 ms  0.347 ms
bsdclient#
```

Packets flow through backbone routers P2 and P4, as they did before the MPLS LSP was set up! The "old" route is used, showing that MPLS is the basis for traffic engineering on a router network.

QUESTIONS FOR READERS

Figure 17.9 shows some of the concepts discussed in this chapter and can be used to help you answer the following questions.

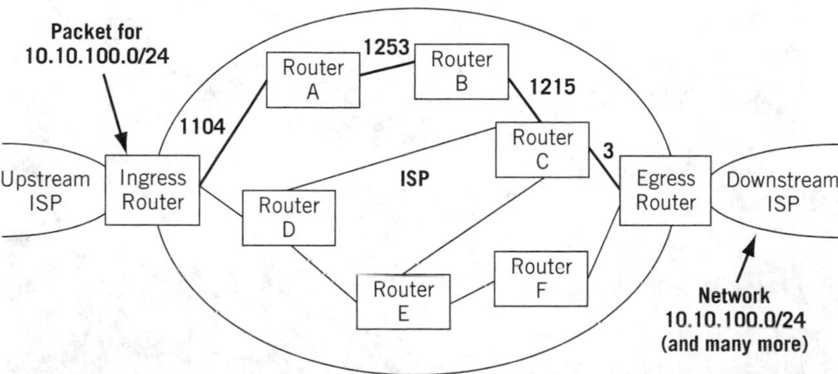

FIGURE 17.9

An MPLS LSP from ingress to ingress router, showing label value to path. The LSP runs along the heavy lines through the routers designated. The label values used on each link are also shown.

1. Does the LSP in Figure 17.9 use the shortest path in terms of number of routers from ingress to egress?
2. What does *traffic engineering* mean as the term applies to MPLS?
3. Is there an LSP set up on the reverse path from egress to ingress router?
4. Which label is used on the LSP between routers A and B? Is this label added to another, or swapped?
5. Is PHP used on the LSP? How can you tell?

PART

IV

Application Level

Every host on the Internet typically runs a set of basic client-server applications. This part of the book examines each one in detail.

CHAPTER

Dynamic Host Configuration Protocol

18

What You Will Learn

In this chapter, you will learn how IP addresses are assigned in modern IP networks. You will learn how the Dynamic Host Configuration Protocol (DHCP) and related protocols, such as BOOTP, combine to allow IP addresses to be assigned to devices dynamically instead of by hand.

You will learn how users often struggle to find printers and servers whose IP addresses "jump around," and you will learn means of dealing with this issue.

When TCP/IP first became popular, configuration was never trivial and often complex. Whereas many clients needed only a handful of parameters, servers often required long lists of values. Operating systems had quickly outgrown single floppies, and most hosts now needed hard drives just to boot themselves into existence. Routers were in a class by themselves, especially when they connected more than two subnets—and in the days of expensive memory and secondary storage (hard drives), routers usually needed to load not only their configuration from a special server, but often their entire operating systems.

A once-popular movement to "diskless workstations" hyped devices that put all of their value into hefty processors while dispensing with expensive (and failure-prone) hard drives altogether. Semiconductor memory was not only prohibitively expensive in adequate quantities but universally volatile, meaning that the content did not carry over a power failure if shut down. How could routers and diskless workstations find the software and configuration information they needed when they were initially powered on?

RFC 951 addressed this situation by defining BOOTP, the bootstrap protocol, to find servers offering the software and configuration files routers and other devices needed on the subnet. The basic functions were extended in RFC 1542, which described relay agents that could be used to find BOOTP servers almost anywhere on a network. BOOTP did a good job at router software loading, but the configuration part (notably the IP addresses) assigned by the device's physical address had to be laboriously maintained by the BOOTP server administrator.

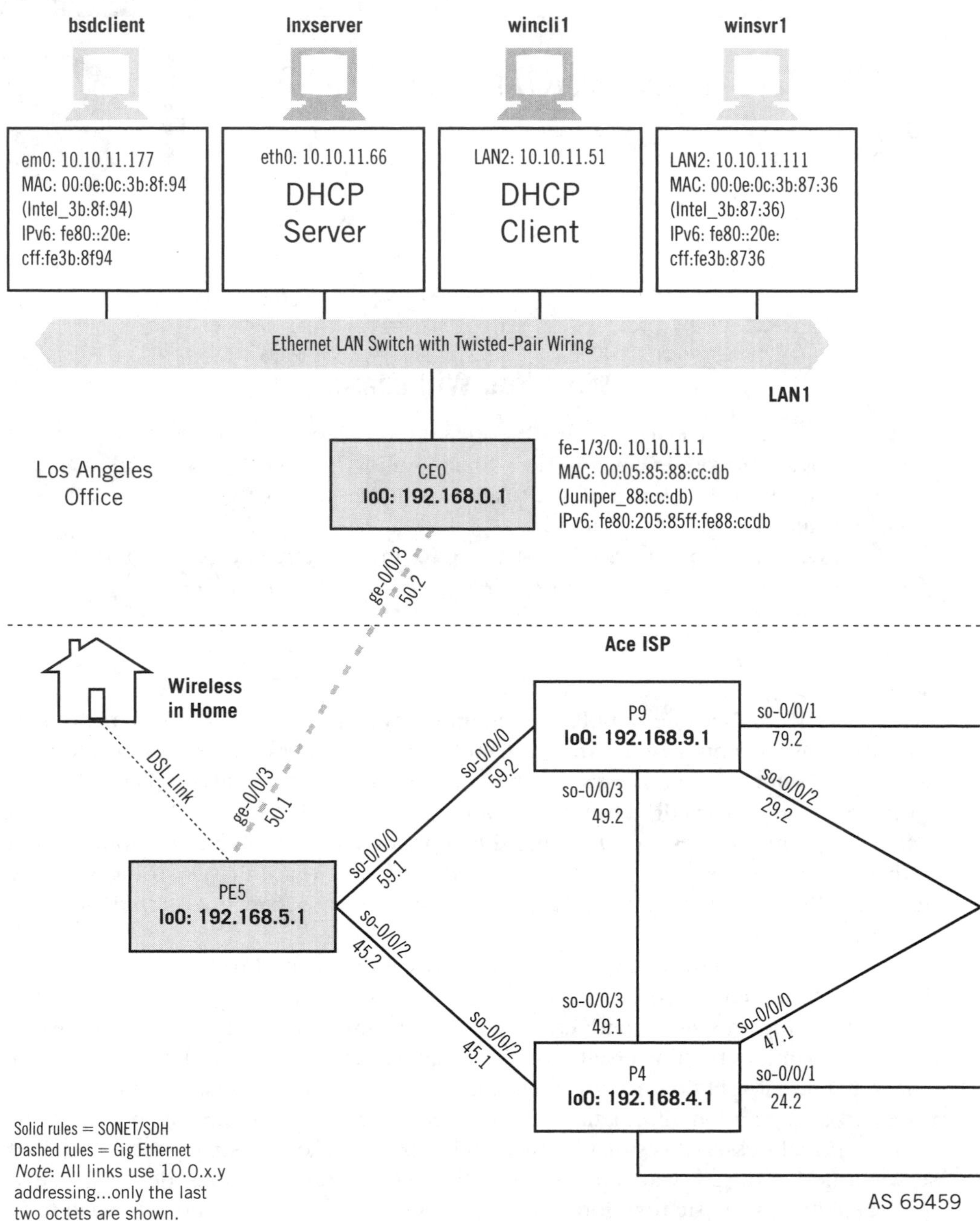

FIGURE 18.1

DHCP devices and configuration on the Illustrated Network showing the host used as DHCP relay agent.

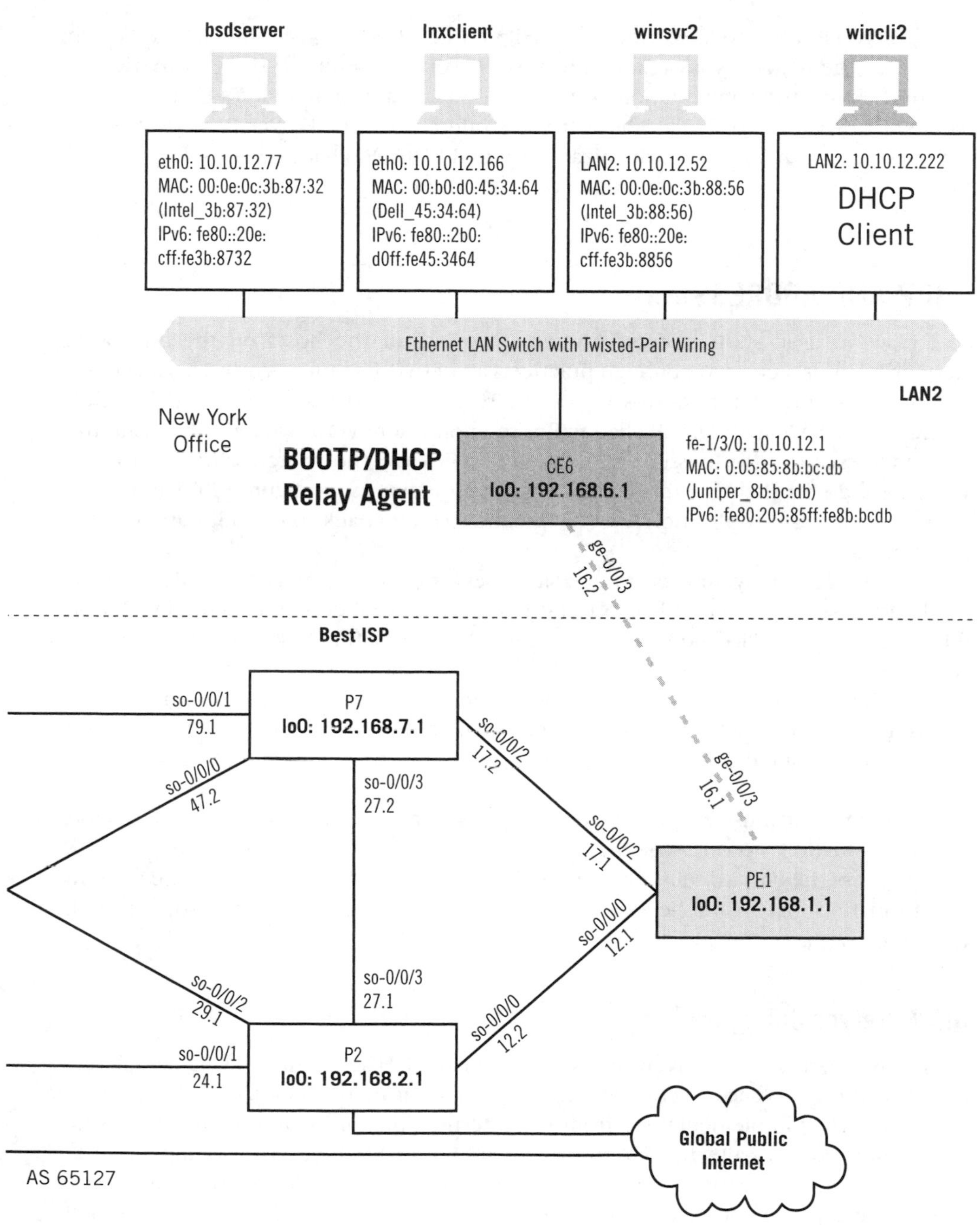
bsdserver
lnxclient
winsvr2
wincli2
eth0: 10.10.12.77
MAC: 00:0e:0c:3b:87:32
(Intel_3b:87:32)
IPv6: fe80::20e:
cff:fe3b:8732
eth0: 10.10.12.166
MAC: 00:b0:d0:45:34:64
(Dell_45:34:64)
IPv6: fe80::2b0:
d0ff:fe45:3464
LAN2: 10.10.12.52
MAC: 00:0e:0c:3b:88:56
(Intel_3b:88:56)
IPv6: fe80::20e:
cff:fe3b:8856
LAN2: 10.10.12.222
DHCP
Client
Ethernet LAN Switch with Twisted-Pair Wiring
LAN2
New York
Office
BOOTP/DHCP
Relay Agent
CE6
lo0: 192.168.6.1
fe-1/3/0: 10.10.12.1
MAC: 0:05:85:8b:bc:db
(Juniper_8b:bc:db)
IPv6: fe80:205:85ff:fe8b:bcdb
ge-0/0/3
16.2
Best ISP
so-0/0/1
79.1
P7
lo0: 192.168.7.1
so-0/0/2
17.2
ge-0/0/3
16.1
so-0/0/0
47.2
so-0/0/3
27.2
so-0/0/2
17.1
PE1
lo0: 192.168.1.1
so-0/0/0
12.1
so-0/0/2
29.1
so-0/0/3
27.1
so-0/0/0
12.2
so-0/0/1
24.1
P2
lo0: 192.168.2.1
Global Public
Internet
AS 65127

So, BOOTP was updated and clarified in RFC 2131 to become DHCP, which automated the IP address assignment process, making the entire system more friendly and useful for host configuration. RFC 2132 described all parameters that could be used with BOOTP and DHCP. The real value offered by DHCP over BOOTP was the ability to release an address. Dynamically assigned BOOTP devices received an address that had no upper bound on how long they could use it.

DHCP AND ADDRESSING

So far, we've used static address assignment on all of the hosts on the Illustrated Network. This is a common enough practice: Lab network testing is often hard enough without worrying about address leases expiring, host addresses changing, and cluttering up the LAN with DHCP chatter. But the point here is to dynamically assign the host addresses on the Illustrated Network (we'll leave the routers alone), so that's what we'll do for this chapter. We'll use the equipment as configured in Figure 18.1. Note that for these application-level chapters we can go back to two ISPs and routing domains.

We'll use IPv4 only and set up our Linux server (`lnxserver`) as a DHCP server for the IP address ranges on both LAN1 and LAN2. First, we'll configure Windows XP on the same LAN to find its address using the DHCP server. Naturally, as with multicast this won't help the hosts on LAN2 find the DHCP server. So, we'll configure LAN2 router CE6 as a BOOTP and DHCP relay agent by sending DHCP messages to the Linux DHCP server and sending back the replies. Finally, we'll configure the Windows XP client on LAN2 to use dynamic IP address assignment and to make sure the entire configuration works.

Once again, it must be pointed out that this network exists solely for this book. In a real situation, no one would really make clients in Los Angeles rely on a DHCP server across the country (although it would certainly work). Considering the amount of information that would be exposed, it would at least be carried over some sort of encrypted path.

DHCP Server Configuration

Linux-based DHCP servers run `/usr/sbin/dhcpd`, the DHCP daemon, using parameters found in the `/etc/dhcpd.conf` file. The configuration guide bundled with the most common DHCP implementation, from the Internet Software Consortium (ISC), is 36 pages long and gives all sorts of options that are not needed for basic configurations.

There are even freeware implementations of DHCP servers for Windows XP. These feature the expected point-and-click GUI setup interface, and are just as useful as their Unix-based cousins.

The following is a fairly minimal configuration file for a DHCP server. Note that we can assign the default router address as an option for the subnet. If this option is not present, users will have to enter their default "gateway" information manually.

```
[root@lnxserver admin]# /cat  /etc/dhcpd.conf
# dhcpd.conf
#
# global options
ddns-update-style interim;
default-lease-time 600;
max-lease-time 7200;

subnet 10.10.11.0 netmask 255.255.255.0 {
   range 10.10.11.200 10.10.11.210;
   option routers 10.10.11.1;
}
subnet 10.10.12.0 netmask 255.255.255.0 {
   range 10.10.12.210 10.10.12.220;
   option routers 10.10.12.1;
}
```

Although we are not using DHCP to dynamically update DNS entries, and we don't even have a DNS server on the LAN yet, the ISC implementation insists on having a line in the configuration referencing dynamic DNS update "style." And although a lot of TCP/IP references mention DHCP's "unhelpful" error messages, we found the error messages when we tried to start dhcpd with a missing semicolon (;) or a missing ddns-update-style line to be `explicit` and `welcome`.

By the way, this lack of DNS is one reason many hands-on Internet services workshops start with DNS first. But there is no requirement for this, as the order of the chapters in this book illustrates.

But what DNS name should be associated with a DHCP address? Typically, a generic name such as *dhcp1.example.com* is associated with the DHCP address. However, this is not appropriate for servers, and only barely tolerable for clients, which usually have more informative names in DNS. And generally, you don't want to hand out changing IP addresses to routers, servers, or the DHCP server itself.

Ordinarily, we would include an option line for the DNS server's names, but we haven't configured those yet on the network. Options can be global or applied to only a subset of the network, a nice feature. We'd also usually have a host entry for our servers so that they would get the same IPv4 addresses every time. For testing, it's common to override the default lease time and maximum lease time (which are fairly high) for which a host can ask to use the address. We've made them 10 minutes and an hour, respectively, here.

The most important lines are those that establish the address pool for hosts on LAN1 (`10.10.11.0`) that ask for an IPv4 address. This information is set in the subnet and range lines. We've made the range different from any of the IPv4 addresses used before, just so it's easy to see if Windows XP is really picking up the DHCP address.

We've also set up an address pool for LAN2 (`10.10.12.0`), just to save time. We haven't configured the LAN2 router as a DHCP relay agent yet, but we will.

Setting up a DHCP client is much easier than setting up the server. Windows XP, for example, makes it very easy to reconfigure a PC to obtain an IPv4 address (including the default router) from the network's DHCP server (as shown in Figure 18.2).

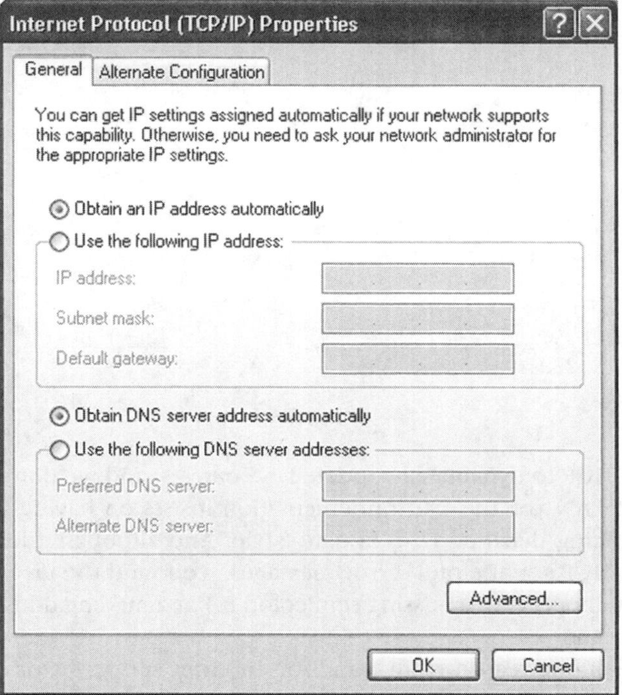

FIGURE 18.2

Configuring Windows to use DHCP, as is commonly done. Note that the IP address and DNS server to be used are assigned.

Now let's run the DHCP server on `lnxserver` and see what address the Windows XP host `wincli1` is assigned.

```
C:\Documents and Settings\Owner>ipconfig
Windows IP Configuration
Ethernet adapter Local Area Connection:

    Connection-specific DNS Suffix . :
    IP Address . . . . . . . . : 10.10.11.200
    Subnet Mask . . . . . . . . : 255.255.255.0
    Default Gateway . . . . . . . : 10.10.11.1
```

As expected, the address assigned is within the range specified, and is the first address in that range.

Router Relay Agent Configuration

The configuration stanza to make a Juniper Network router a DHCP relay agent is under the BOOTP hierarchy level. This makes sense because DHCP relay agents are all BOOTP relay agents as well. We'll talk more about BOOTP later in this chapter.

The router can act as a relay agent globally or for a group of interfaces. This just makes the CE6 router into a DHCP relay agent for the LAN2 interface. There is no need to do anything for LAN1 on the network because the DHCP server handles all of those hosts locally.

```
set forwarding-options helpers bootp description "DHCP relay agent for
   lnxserver on LAN1";
set forwarding-options helpers bootp server 10.10.11.66;
set forwarding-options helpers bootp interface fe-1/3/0;
```

That's all there is to it. As long as there's a way to reach network 10.10.11/24 from LAN2 and a way to get back to 10.10.12/24 from CE0, DHCP messages should have no problem crossing the network like any other packets.

Getting Addresses on LAN2

Without a relay agent running on the LAN2 router, we can fire up wincli2 all we want and it will never receive an IP address from a DHCP server. One is not present on LAN2, and the router will not route DHCP messages unless told to.

Now that we have the relay agent running, we can check the IPv4 address on wincli2. Note that the lowest IP address in the range is not always the first one handed out by the DHCP server. In this case, the host asks for its "old" address of 10.10.12.222, and the server attempts to assign the closest address it has to that one.

```
C:\Documents and Settings\Owner>ipconfig
Windows IP Configuration
Ethernet adapter Local Area Connection:

      Connection-specific DNS Suffix . :
      IP Address . . . . . . . . : 10.10.12.220
      Subnet Mask . . . . . . . . : 255.255.255.0
      Default Gateway . . . . . . . : 10.10.12.1
```

DHCP is such an important part of LANs and the Internet today that a closer look at the functioning of DHCP through a router relay agent is a good idea. The complete sequence of events, captured on wincli2 as it received its DHCP address, is shown in Figure 18.3.

We'll talk about DHCP messages and sequences in detail later in this chapter. Note that the sequence starts with wincli2 sending a broadcast DHCP discover message onto LAN2 with the "unknown" source address of 0.0.0.0. The host asks for its "old" address, 10.10.12.222. The router, acting as relay agent, forwards the request to the DHCP server (10.10.11.66, lnxserver) on LAN1, which replies to the relay agent and wants to assign address 10.10.12.220 to wincli2. The relay agent sends an ARP (No. 2) to see if anyone on LAN2 already has 10.10.12.220 (it could have been assigned statically). The relay agent then offers the host this IP address (No. 3), and the DHCP server itself (No. 4) sends a ping to check on 10.10.12.220 itself (note that there is no reply to the ping from wincli2).

No.	Time	Source	Destination	Protocol	Info
1	0.000000	0.0.0.0	255.255.255.255	DHCP	DHCP Discover - Transaction ID 0xae286763
2	0.002869	10.10.12.1	Broadcast	ARP	Who has 10.10.12.220? Tell 10.10.12.1
3	0.605057	10.10.12.1	10.10.12.220	DHCP	DHCP Offer - Transaction ID 0xae286763
4	0.617837	10.10.11.66	10.10.12.220	ICMP	Echo (ping) request
5	2.601820	0.0.0.0	255.255.255.255	DHCP	DHCP Discover - Transaction ID 0xae286763
6	2.605344	10.10.12.1	10.10.12.220	DHCP	DHCP Offer - Transaction ID 0xae286763
7	10.602050	0.0.0.0	255.255.255.255	DHCP	DHCP Discover - Transaction ID 0xae286763
8	10.606884	10.10.12.1	10.10.12.220	DHCP	DHCP Offer - Transaction ID 0xae286763
9	10.607177	0.0.0.0	255.255.255.255	DHCP	DHCP Request - Transaction ID 0xae286763
10	10.612208	10.10.12.1	10.10.12.220	DHCP	DHCP ACK - Transaction ID 0xae286763
11	10.614933	10.10.12.220	Broadcast	ARP	Who has 10.10.12.220? Gratuitous ARP
12	10.930007	10.10.12.220	Broadcast	ARP	Who has 10.10.12.220? Gratuitous ARP
13	11.930094	10.10.12.220	Broadcast	ARP	Who has 10.10.12.220? Gratuitous ARP

FIGURE 18.3

DHCP messages sent through a router relay agent. Note the use of broadcast and the "unknown" source IP address.

It takes a while for the host to gather the information about possible multiple DHCP servers, and there are two pairs of repeated DHCP discover messages from "`0.0.0.0`" and DHCP offers from the relay agent (Nos. 5–8). In each exchange, the host asks for its old IP address (`10.10.12.222`) in the DHCP discover message, and the relay agent assigns `10.10.12.220` in the DHCP offer message.

Finally, wincli2 accepts the DHCP information and assigned address, and sends a DHCP request message (No. 9) for configuration information for `10.10.12.220`, but it is still using the `0.0.0.0` address. The relay agent replies with a DHCP acknowledgement (No. 10), which basically contains the same information as before.

The sequence ends with a series of gratuitous ARPs to the relay agent (Nos. 11–13) for address `10.10.12.220`, the host's new address (see the source IP address field). This tells the DHCP relay agent that everything has worked out. The details of one of the DHCP discover messages sent by the host (all of them are essentially the same) are shown in Figure 18.4.

The details of one of the DHCP offer messages sent by the relay agent on behalf of the DHCP server (all of these are essentially the same too) are shown in Figure 18.5.

Using DHCP on a Network

As we have seen, what DHCP brings to TCP/IP for the first time is a measure of mobility. With the proper DHCP servers available, a user could unplug a host from one Ethernet LAN subnet, move it across the country, plug it into another subnet, expect the configuration data to be loaded properly, and become productive on the new subnet immediately.

Once ISPs began offering dial-up Internet access to the general public with home PCs, the benefits of DHCP became instantly obvious. Suppose an ISP had a pool of 254 IPv4 addresses, that is, what used to be a Class C address. But the ISP also has 300 customers. Obviously, 254 IP addresses cannot be statically assigned to 300 hosts. However, all of them cannot be on-line at the same time because the ISP has only 200 dial-in modem ports (a situation that was not uncommon before the Web took over the planet). So, DHCP quickly became the means of choice in assigning IP addresses dynamically to a pool of users.

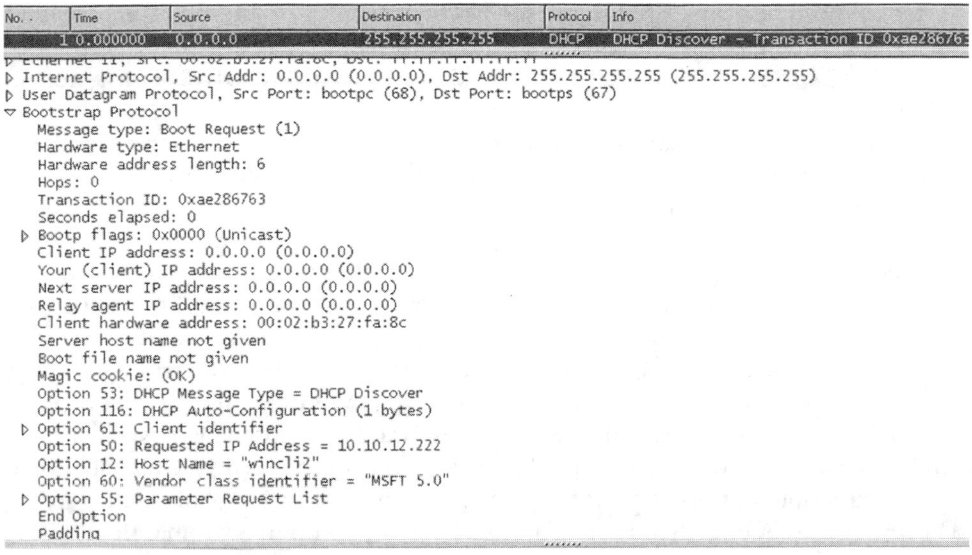

No. Time Source Destination Protocol Info
1 0.000000 0.0.0.0 255.255.255.255 DHCP DHCP Discover - Transaction ID 0xae28676
Internet Protocol, Src Addr: 0.0.0.0 (0.0.0.0), Dst Addr: 255.255.255.255 (255.255.255.255)
User Datagram Protocol, Src Port: bootpc (68), Dst Port: bootps (67)
Bootstrap Protocol
Message type: Boot Request (1)
Hardware type: Ethernet
Hardware address length: 6
Hops: 0
Transaction ID: 0xae286763
Seconds elapsed: 0
Bootp flags: 0x0000 (Unicast)
Client IP address: 0.0.0.0 (0.0.0.0)
Your (client) IP address: 0.0.0.0 (0.0.0.0)
Next server IP address: 0.0.0.0 (0.0.0.0)
Relay agent IP address: 0.0.0.0 (0.0.0.0)
Client hardware address: 00:02:b3:27:fa:8c
Server host name not given
Boot file name not given
Magic cookie: (OK)
Option 53: DHCP Message Type = DHCP Discover
Option 116: DHCP Auto-Configuration (1 bytes)
Option 61: Client identifier
Option 50: Requested IP Address = 10.10.12.222
Option 12: Host Name = "wincli2"
Option 60: Vendor class identifier = "MSFT 5.0"
Option 55: Parameter Request List
End Option
Padding

FIGURE 18.4

The DHCP discover message details. Note the use of the bootstrap protocol (BOOTP) and the numerous options.

```
No.   Time        Source        Destination       Protocol  Info
    1 0.000000    0.0.0.0       255.255.255.255   DHCP      DHCP Discover - Transaction ID 0xae286763
    2 0.002869    10.10.12.1    Broadcast         ARP       Who has 10.10.12.220?  Tell 10.10.12.1
    3 0.605057    10.10.12.1    10.10.12.220      DHCP      DHCP Offer    - Transaction ID 0xae286763
    4 0.617837    10.10.11.66   10.10.12.220      ICMP      Echo (ping) request
    5 2.601820    0.0.0.0       255.255.255.255   DHCP      DHCP Discover - Transaction ID 0xae286763

▷ User Datagram Protocol, Src Port: bootps (67), Dst Port: bootpc (68)
▽ Bootstrap Protocol
    Message type: Boot Reply (2)
    Hardware type: Ethernet
    Hardware address length: 6
    Hops: 1
    Transaction ID: 0xae286763
    Seconds elapsed: 0
  ▷ Bootp flags: 0x0000 (Unicast)
    Client IP address: 0.0.0.0 (0.0.0.0)
    Your (client) IP address: 10.10.12.220 (10.10.12.220)
    Next server IP address: 10.10.11.66 (10.10.11.66)
    Relay agent IP address: 10.10.12.1 (10.10.12.1)
    Client hardware address: 00:02:b3:27:fa:8c
    Server host name not given
    Boot file name not given
    Magic cookie: (OK)
    Option 53: DHCP Message Type = DHCP Offer
    Option 54: Server Identifier = 10.10.11.66
    Option 51: IP Address Lease Time = 10 minutes
    Option 1: Subnet Mask = 255.255.255.0
    Option 3: Router = 10.10.12.1
    End Option
    Padding

0110  00 00 00 00 00 00 63 82  53 63 35 01 02 36 04 0a   ......c. Sc5..6..
0120  0a 0b 42 33 04 00 00 02  58 01 04 ff ff ff 00 03   ..B3.... X.......
0130  04 0a 0a 0c 01 ff 00 00  00 00 00 00 00 00 00 00   ........ ........
0140  00 00 00 00 00 00 00 00  00 00 00 00 00 00 00 00   ........ ........
0150  00 00 00 00 00 00                                  ......
```

FIGURE 18.5

The DHCP offer message details, showing the use of the "magic cookie."

Organizations that employed proxy servers to protect their Internet users (or limit Internet users) could do the same thing, and often did. In fact, any time the pool of potential users exceeds the number of IP addresses available, DHCP is a potential solution.

The heavy use of changing IP addresses among ISPs was one major reason ISPs refused to support servers on the customer's premises (asymmetric traffic loads, especially over always-on but asymmetrical DSL links, was the other one). Servers were typically included in DNS, to make them easy to remember, and this required a high degree of stability of IP addresses because changes had to propagate literally around the world. Naturally, dynamic server addresses, changing rapidly, challenged DNS procedures and capabilities. Servers could get static IP addresses, if they could be found, and running one server process like a Web server on an otherwise all-client host made the box into a server. The simplest thing for an ISP to do was to ban servers on the customer's premises, unless extra fees for DNS "maintenance" were paid (in truth, there was little maintenance the ISP had to do except initially). Officially, home servers were "not supported"; since ISPs had little way of making sure that a server was present this essentially meant, "If you call and try to open a trouble ticket on it, we won't listen."

When DHCP is configured on a client in many operating systems, it usually isn't even required to name it. Just check off or click on "obtain an IP address automatically" and you're in business.

BOOTP still exists, and some devices still use BOOTP alone. BOOTP is often combined with the Trivial File Transfer Protocol (TFTP), defined in RFC 1350 (RFCs 2347, 2348, and 2349 all discuss TFTP options). And the best way to understand why DHCP works the way it does is to begin with BOOTP.

BOOTP

Diskless workstations were expected to have only basic IP, UDP, and TFTP capabilities at start-up, although of course they needed Ethernet and rudimentary operating system functions as well. The original vision for BOOTP was to have the process complete in three steps.

The BOOTP client broadcast a request for information from port UDP 68 to a boot server listening on port 67. (BOOTP uses well-known ports for both client and server because server replies can be broadcast, but typically are not.)

The boot server returned the client's IP address and, as an option, the location of a file to be downloaded (presumably, the rest of the client's software was in this file). The client used TFTP and the boot server listening on UDP port 69 to download the software.

RARP, discussed in Chapter 5, provides the IP address that goes with a physical address (such as the MAC address). RARP provides an IP address to a diskless client, but *only* an IP address. And RARP broadcasts never pass through a router, whereas BOOTP requests, in proper configurations, will (this requires a relay agent, as in DHCP).

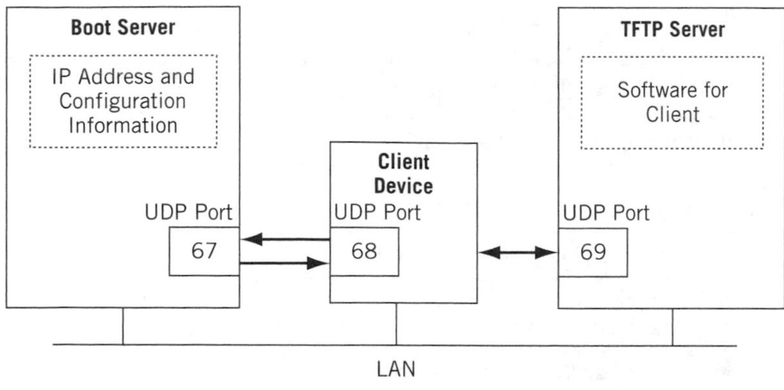

FIGURE 18.6

BOOTP and TFTP servers, showing the ports used by the servers and client.

BOOTP Implementation

Diskless workstations never became a popular line, and most users saw them as a return to the "bad old days" of "dumb terminals" and considered a full-blooded PC on the desktop as a sign of status. And soon enough the cost differential for diskless devices as opposed to full-fledged workstations or desktops shrunk to zero and then went negative. Applications for devices with no local storage still exist, but there is no cost benefit associated with them.

Once almost all PCs began to ship with minimal hard disks it became more common to split the boot server functions between two separate servers. The boot server still listened on UDP port 67 for client broadcast requests sent on port 68, and this was usually all PCs needed. But for truly diskless devices one or more TFTP servers provided the files needed for further operation, usually separated by type. This arrangement is shown in Figure 18.6.

BOOTP was very flexible. Clients could start with some or no information, accept any boot server or pick a particular one, and use no file (a default) or a specific download file.

BOOTP Messages

All BOOTP requests and replies are sent as 300-byte UDP messages. These are shown in Figure 18.7. Fields shown in bold must be filled in for a BOOTP request, and those in italic represent optional information supplied by the client.

Opcode—This byte is set to 1 for a request and 2 for a reply.

Hardware Type—This byte is set to 1 for Ethernet, and uses the same values as the hardware type field in an ARP message.

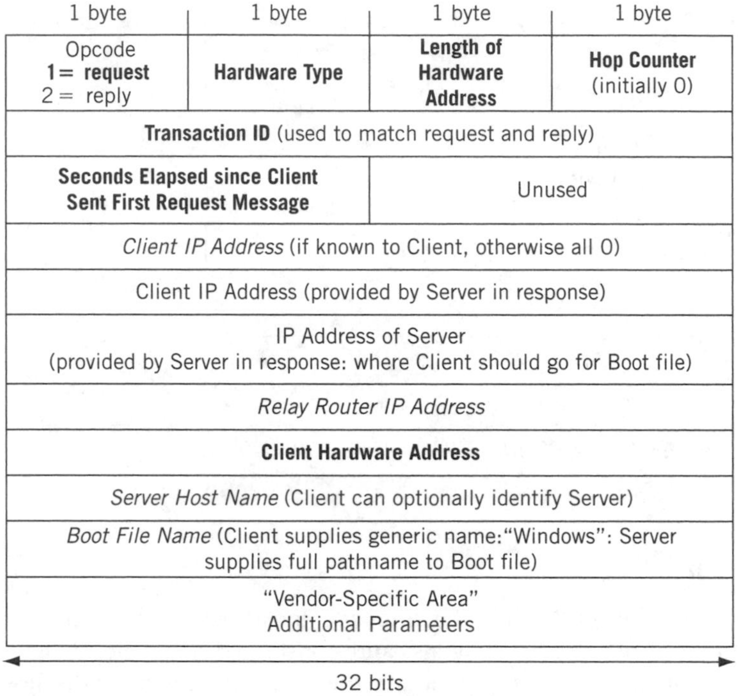

1 byte	1 byte	1 byte	1 byte
Opcode **1= request** 2= reply	**Hardware Type**	**Length of Hardware Address**	**Hop Counter** (initially 0)
Transaction ID (used to match request and reply)			
Seconds Elapsed since Client Sent First Request Message		Unused	
Client IP Address (if known to Client, otherwise all 0)			
Client IP Address (provided by Server in response)			
IP Address of Server (provided by Server in response: where Client should go for Boot file)			
Relay Router IP Address			
Client Hardware Address			
Server Host Name (Client can optionally identify Server)			
Boot File Name (Client supplies generic name:"Windows": Server supplies full pathname to Boot file)			
"Vendor-Specific Area" Additional Parameters			

32 bits

FIGURE 18.7

Request.

Hardware Address Length—This byte is set to 6 for Ethernet.

Hop Counter—The client sets this to 0, but a proxy BOOTP server (or *relay agent*, described later) can use this field when the BOOTP message is sent beyond the local Ethernet.

Transaction ID—A random 4-byte number chosen by the client and used to match replies to their requests. Multiple servers can reply, and only the first is accepted by the client.

Seconds Elapsed—A 2-byte field set by the client to the amount of time since the bootstrap process began. It starts at 0 and gradually increases if the request is not answered. A secondary server can monitor this value, and if it gets too high will assume the primary BOOTP server is down and reply to the client.

Client IP Address—Set to all 0 bits unless the client knows its IP address, in which case it is placed here.

"Your" Client IP Address—If the previous field is 0, the server supplies the client's IP address in this field.

Server IP Address—Filled in by the server.

Relay Router IP Address—If a BOOTP relay agent is used, the router fills in the address of the port the request was received on. This allows the server to reply to the proper relay agent.

Client Hardware Address—The same 16-byte address is in the frame source address, but the BOOTP process has no easy access to this information (which is three layers away) so it is placed here.

Server Hostname—The server optionally can use these 64 bytes (null terminated) to identify itself to the client.

Boot File Name—The server optionally can use these 128 bytes (null terminated) to identify the path to and the name of the boot file.

Vendor-Specific Area—These 64 bytes are used for BOOTP extensions, defined in RFC 1533.

BOOTP Relay Agents

BOOTP requests are broadcast, and broadcasts will not be forwarded through a router. Yet maintaining BOOTP servers on all subnets, which are often quite small, can be burdensome in many organizations. So, BOOTP allows the use of relay agents, which can be hosts but are usually routers having the added capability to forward BOOTP requests to a centrally located server.

The router BOOTP relay agent is allowed to broadcast the request onto other subnets, using the hop count to control endless looping, but it is more common for the relay agent to maintain a list of the IP addresses of one or more boot servers to which to forward the requests. The way it all fits together is shown in Figure 18.8.

The relay agent receiving a BOOTP broadcast checks the Relay Router field. If it is set to 0, the relay agent inserts the port's IP address (if the field is non-zero, another relay router has already processed this request). The BOOTP server will use the address to reply to the proper relay agent.

The relay agent can send the request to one or more preconfigured BOOTP servers. The relay agent usually replaces the broadcast IP address with the BOOTP server's destination address.

BOOTP "Vendor-Specific Area" Options

The fields in the BOOTP request and reply do not cover a lot of things client hosts often need to know to function properly. For example, how is the subnet mask and default router address conveyed to the client?

RFC 1533 kept the vendor-specific purpose of the field but added several optional functions that can be used to supply needed information to a client. The "magic cookie"

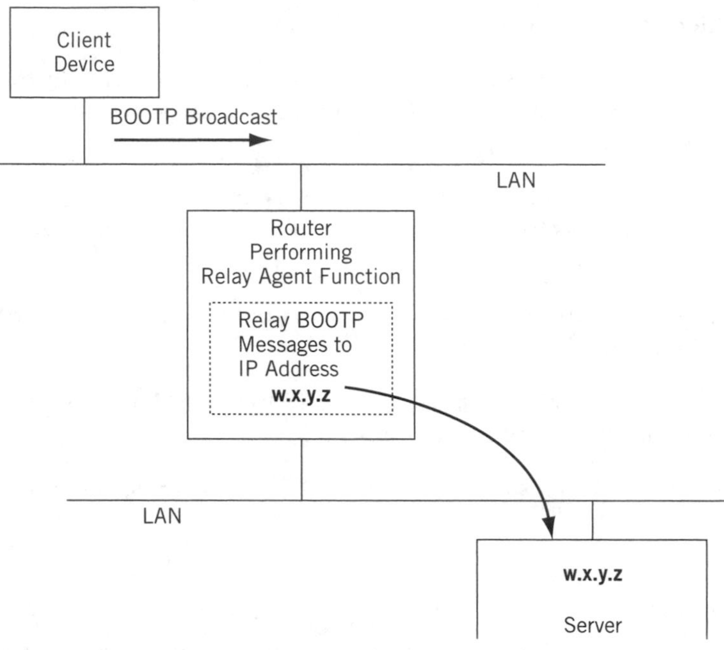

FIGURE 18.8

BOOTP relay agent (router), showing how the relay agent forwards broadcast BOOTP messages to a unicast IP address.

IPv4 address of 99.130.83.99 is used to signal clients that there is useful information in this area.

Each item begins with a 1-byte Tag (for example, Tag = 1 is for the subnet mask) and Length (subnet mask = 4 bytes) field. Tag = 0 is used to pad items to a 32-bit boundary, and Tag = 255 is used pad out the end of the list.

Once a client has used BOOTP to obtain an IP address, subnet mask, and default router address, it is ready to begin the software download phase if needed. The TFTP protocol is used for this process.

TRIVIAL FILE TRANSFER PROTOCOL

Many books discuss TFTP in the context of full FTP. But TFTP is best understood in the context of the BOOTP environment. In particular, TFTP differs greatly from usual FTP operation (FTP is discussed in Chapter 20). In contrast to full FTP, TFTP

- Uses UDP port 69
- Uses uniformly sized 512-byte blocks of data, except for the last (If the file is a multiple of 512 bytes, a final, empty block signals end-of-file.)

- Numbers blocks starting from 1
- Acknowledges every block
- Uses no authentication

Today, of course, the lack of authentication means that use of TFTP requires special considerations. And it still makes more sense to use Trivial File Transfer Protocol for BOOTP software downloads because in many cases the client and server are on the same low-error-rate LAN.

Once a client knows where to go and what to get, a TFTP transaction starts with a read request (RRQ) to download a file or write request (WRQ), used if the client is going to save information back onto the TFTP server. The requests are sent to UDP port 69 on the server, and a dynamic port is used on the client.

The server does not use port 69 throughout the process, but identifies a server port to use for the rest of the procedure. Data transfer proceeds through an exchange of sequenced data blocks and answering ACKs, one-for-one, echoing the data block number. Any non–full-data block ends the exchange.

The default block size can be changed using the options at the end of the read or write request. A size of 1468 (a 1500-byte Ethernet frame minus the 20 IP, 8 UDP, and 4 TFTP header bytes) is common. Other options include a resend timeout value (UDP has none of its own) and the total size of the file to be transferred. This value is offered in the client write request, but is set to 0 in a read request and sent by the server in response. A client is allowed to abort the transfer if the file size the server wants to transfer is too large.

TFTP Messages

TFTP really only has requests (RQ), data blocks (DATA), and ACKs, but these are employed to yield a total of six message types.

- Read request (RRQ)
- Write request (WRQ)
- Data block (DATA)
- Acknowledgment (ACK)
- Error (ACK)
- Option acknowledgment (OACK)

The six operation codes are used in the Trivial File Transfer Protocol header, shown in Figure 18.9.

The fields in RRQ and WRQ can vary in size and are thus delimited with all-0 bytes. Oddly, there are no codes for the modes or for the strings `netascii` and `octet` (there was also a `mail` mode initially).

TFTP Download

TFTP lives up to its name. A simple TFTP transfer is shown in Figure 18.10. In the figure, it is assumed that no options are used.

TFTP message inside UDP

2 bytes	N bytes	1 byte	N bytes	1 byte
Opcode 1 = RRQ 2 = WRQ	Filename	0	Mode	0

2 bytes	2 bytes	0–512 bytes
Opcode 3 = DATA	Block Number	Data

2 bytes	2 bytes
Opcode 4 = ACK	Block Number

2 bytes	2 bytes	N bytes	1 byte
Opcode 5 = Error	Error Number	Error Message	0

2 bytes	N bytes	1 byte	N bytes	1 byte	
Opcode 6 = OACK	Option A	0	Option B	0	. . .

FIGURE 18.9

The six TFTP messages. Note that the content is extremely variable depending on opcode.

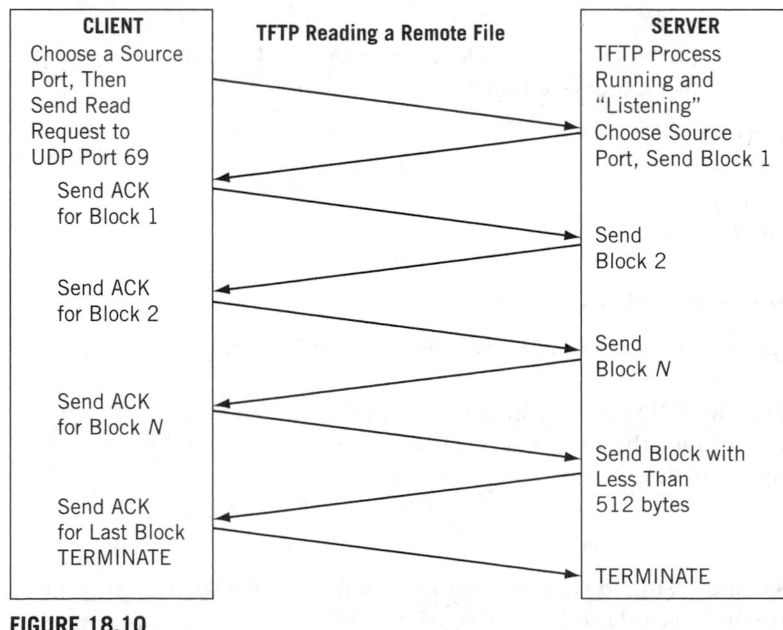

FIGURE 18.10

TFTP file transfer. Compared to full FTP, this exchange is very simple.

DHCP

It might seem odd to spend so much time in a chapter on DHCP discussing BOOTP and TFTP. But much of what DHCP does and the way it accomplishes its functions is similar to the operation of these two earlier protocols. DHCP involves a more complex exchange of messages between client and server, but the intention was always that servers could provide both BOOTP and DHCP functions with a minimum of recoding.

DHCP was referenced in BOOTP RFCs 1533 and 1534, but as an "extension" of BOOTP capabilities. Currently, RFC 2131 describes DHCP and distinguishes it from BOOTP. Not only does a DHCP server allocate addresses to clients, but it also maintains parameters for individual clients and entire client groups, greatly enhancing the efficiency of the entire system. In general, DHCP is designed to:

- Be a mechanism. No "policy" or ideas about IP address allocation schemes are assumed by DHCP. However, DHCP can be the mechanism on which such policies are built.
- Do away with manual configuration. A user should always be able to simply plug their devices into the network and work. (The requirement to configure DHCP, if not the default, is beyond DHCP's control.)
- Handle many subnets from one server. DHCP employs the BOOTP relay agent concept, mostly implemented in routers, for this purpose.
- Allow multiple servers. For redundancy and reliability, clients and servers must be able to deal with more than one DHCP server.
- Coexist with statically addressed hosts. As mentioned, dynamically addressed servers are a challenge for DNS and the user in general. DHCP must allow these hosts to function properly.
- Support BOOTP. DHCP can use BOOTP relay agents and must be able to service BOOTP clients.
- Guarantee unique addresses. No address can ever be assigned to two clients at the same time.
- Retain client information. The servers must retain all client parameters in case of failures or between shutdown and start-up.

If the addresses handed out by DHCP were permanent, there would be little difference between static assignment or the way that BOOTP operates. But the DHCP association between client and address is called a *binding*, or, more commonly, a *lease*. And like any lease, it must be renewed periodically or become available for assignment to a new client.

The pool of IP addresses handed out by the DHCP server is called a *scope*. A collection of scopes gathered for administrative purposes is known as a *superscope*.

DHCP Operation

The format of the DHCP message is shown in Figure 18.11, which should be compared to the BOOTP message in Figure 18.7. Many BOOTP clients have no problem interacting with DHCP servers, and that was the intent all along.

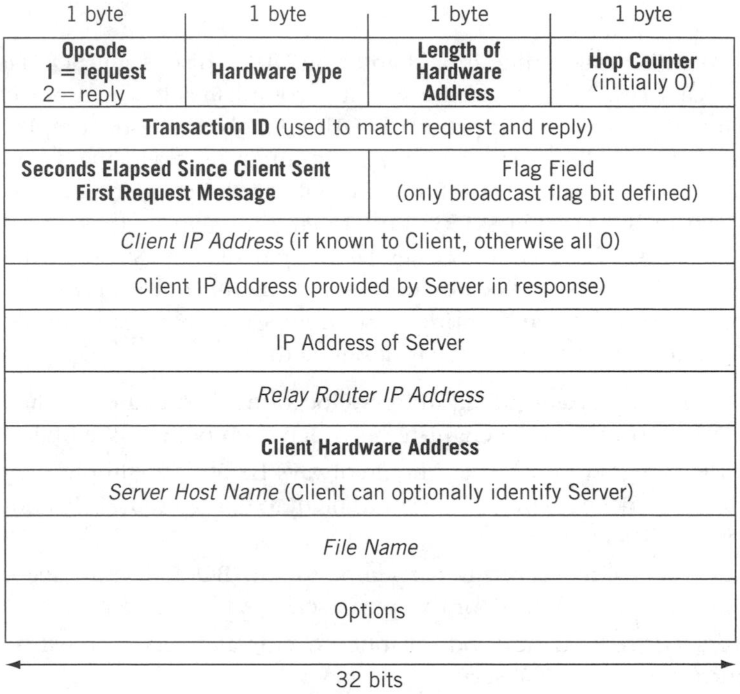

1 byte	1 byte	1 byte	1 byte
Opcode **1 = request** 2 = reply	**Hardware Type**	**Length of Hardware Address**	**Hop Counter** (initially 0)
Transaction ID (used to match request and reply)			
Seconds Elapsed Since Client Sent First Request Message		Flag Field (only broadcast flag bit defined)	
Client IP Address (if known to Client, otherwise all 0)			
Client IP Address (provided by Server in response)			
IP Address of Server			
Relay Router IP Address			
Client Hardware Address			
Server Host Name (Client can optionally identify Server)			
File Name			
Options			

32 bits

FIGURE 18.11

DHCP message format, showing similarities with the BOOTP message.

The fields are the same in form and content as those for BOOTP, with a few exceptions. Opcode DHCP uses the same operation codes as BOOTP (1 = request and 2 = reply). DHCP is indicated by the use of an Option Tag value of 53. This allowed DHCP to use BOOTP relay agents transparently.

Flags—These 16 bits were unused in BOOTP. Only one flag is defined for DHCP, the rightmost bit, or BROADCAST flag. All other bits must be set to 0. A tricky issue in dynamic configuration was the fact that some clients discarded unicast packets until configuration was complete, and so the DHCP messages were rejected with their addresses! The BROADCAST bit told servers to broadcast replies to these DHCP clients.

Options—The BOOTP "vendor-specific" fields in what is now the DHCP options field, were greatly extended to become DHCP parameters. Client ID Option DHCP clients can be identified other than by hardware MAC address, as in BOOTP. Some other identifier, such as a fully qualified domain name, could be used instead. This helped if NIC cards were replaced. In practice, those cards are very reliable and this option is not used much.

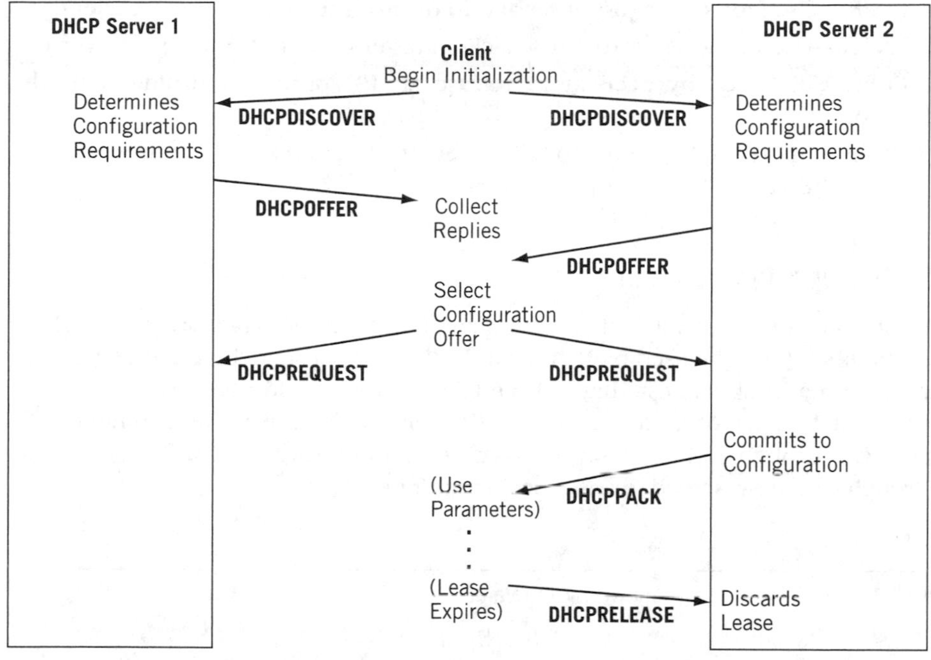

FIGURE 18.12

Typical DHCP message flow when there are two potential DHCP servers from which to choose.

The client ID option is used for several things: It provides better logging, supports dynamic DNS, and allows for hosts with more than one network interface (such as laptops with wired and wireless capability). Care must be taken that you don't produce collisions, because two hosts with the same client ID will get the same IP address.

Once a host is configured to seek out configuration information using DHCP, the message flow is straightforward—even with two "competing" DHCP servers on a LAN. The usual flow of messages is shown in Figure 18.12.

DHCP, in contrast to BOOTP, uses a complex sequence of messages between clients and servers, all tucked neatly inside the "BOOTP" options field at the end of the message. There are eight major DHCP messages types (all using either request or reply operation codes, of course).

- DHCPDISCOVER—Used by clients to discover DHCP servers, and usually includes a list of the parameters for which the client needs values, such as IP addresses, subnet mask, and default router.
- DHCPOFFER—Used by servers to offer the needed values to clients.
- DHCPREQUEST—Used by a client to request a reply from one server. The request is sent to all servers, even those not selected.
- DHCPDECLINE—Used by a client to refuse to accept one or more values from a server, usually because they are not valid for the client.

- DHCPACK—Used for server responses and to furnish the parameters to a client.
- DHCPNAK—Used by a server to refuse a client request. (Clients must start over.)
- DHCPRELEASE—Used by a client to release an IP address, returning it to the server pool.
- DHCPINFORM—Used by clients to tell servers the client has an IP address already, but needs the values for other parameters.

DHCP Message Type Options

DHCP clients can request values for more than 60 different parameters from a DHCP server. The first 49 can be used by BOOTP or DHCP, and these include the very fundamental IP subnet mask request (Tag = 1) and default router address (Tag = 3).

Options 50 through 61 are reserved for DHCP only. These are outlined in Table 18.1. Tag numbers through 127 are reserved for current and future standard options. Tags 128 through 254 are reserved for site-specific options.

Table 18.1 DHCP Parameters Shown by Tag Value

Tag	Parameter	Description
50	Requested IP address	Client asks for a specific IP address.
51	IP address lease time	Client's request or time granted by server.
52	Option overload	The Server Host Name or Boot File Name fields are carrying DHCP options to save space in the message.
53	DHCP message type	This is how the DISCOVER, OFFER, or REQUEST formats are determined.
54	DHCP server identifier	Client tells which server was accepted.
55	Parameter request list	Client's list of needed parameters.
56	Message	Used for errors. Server sends errors with DHCPNAK, and client uses DHCPDECLINE.
57	Max. DHCP message size	Largest DHCP message the client can accept.
58	Renewal time (T1)	Client will try to renew lease after this time.
59	Rebinding time (T2)	If lease renewal fails, client tries any server after this elapsed time (T2 must be greater than T1).
60	Class identifier	Vendor code describing client. Servers can reply based on this class.
61	Client identifier	Unique identifier for this client used by server to determine parameters.

DHCP AND ROUTERS

DHCP takes advantage of the BOOTP relay agent concept. In fact, router configuration of DHCP can be complicated because many routers mention only BOOTP relay agents and assume administrators know they are the same.

A DHCP relay agent is usually a router, but it could also be a dual-homed host that uses a router to reach the DHCP server. A typical configuration using a router as a relay agent was shown in Figure 18.1.

The DHCP relay agent listens for broadcast BOOTP request messages and sends them to the server. The relay agent then receives replies from the DHCP server and replies to the client.

DHCPv6

We haven't done anything with DHCP in IPv6. There's a reason for that, and it has to do with the way IPv6 configures itself on a host.

A lot of what DHCP does in IPv4 can also be done with RARP and ICMP. Yet DHCP is all over the place in IPv4. IPv6 includes elaborate neighbor and router discovery protocols that allow IPv6 hosts to invent link-local IPv6 addresses and multicast groups for configuration purposes. Yet, just like IPv4 DHCP for IPv6 exists as DHCPv6. There are at least three reasons DHCPv6 continues to make sense in IPv6.

- Not all networks support the multicasts needed for IPv6 autoconfiguration, like those consisting of point-to-point links or ATM and frame relay.
- Some small IPv6 networks might not have a router, which is required for IPv6 autoconfiguration.
- Network managers might desire more control over device configuration than afforded by IPv6 autoconfiguration.

DHCPv6 will not be used on the Illustrated Network. There is no BOOTP support because it is not really needed in IPv6. In truth, a lot of DHCP parameters are superfluous in IPv6. It is enough for this chapter to point out that DHCPv6 can be triggered by options in the IPV6 Router Advertisement messages, which we first introduced in Chapter 5.

DHCPv6 and Router Advertisements

DHCPv6 and its relationship to IPv6 addressing are described in a series of RFCs, most notably RFC 3315 and 3726. DHCPv6 can provide stateless or stateful address autoconfiguration information to IPv6 hosts. Stateless address autoconfiguration is used to configure both link-local and additional non–link-local addresses through the exchange of Router Solicitation and Router Advertisement messages with routers. Stateful address autoconfiguration is used to configure non–link-local addresses through the use of a configuration protocol such as DHCP.

How does a host know which one it can use? We did not emphasize it then, but our discussion of the IPv6 Router Advertisement protocol in Chapter 7 mentioned the M and O bit flags. The Router Advertisement message can set the following:

Managed Address Configuration Flag, known as the M flag—When set to 1, this bit instructs the host to use the configuration protocol to obtain a stateful (non-link-local) address.

Other Stateful Configuration Flag, known as the O flag—When set to 1, this bit instructs the host to use the configuration protocol to obtain more configuration settings.

There can be four different situations.

1. Both M and O flags are 0. This is used when the local network has no DHCPv6 infrastructure. IPv6 hosts use Router Advertisements and other methods, such as manual configuration, to get non-link-local addresses and other settings.
2. Both M and O flags are 1. In this case, DHCPv6 is used to obtain both addresses and other configuration settings. This is known as the "DHCPv6 stateful" situation, and DHCPv6 is used to assign stateful addresses to the IPv6 hosts.
3. M flag is 0, O flag is 1. DHCPv6 is not used to provide addresses, but only other configuration settings, such as the location of DNS servers. The routers are set to advertise non-link-local prefixes from which the IPv6 hosts can configure stateless addresses. This is known as "DHCPv6 stateless" because stateful addresses are not provided.
4. M flag is 1, O flag is 0. DHCPv6 is used to provide addresses, but no other settings. This combination is allowed but unlikely, because IPv6 hosts need to know other things, such as the addresses of the DNS servers.

Because we're not using DHCPv6 on the Illustrated Network, we won't detail the DHCPv4 message formats and exchange patterns—which are different for stateful and stateless operation.

DHCPv6 Operation

All DHCP servers and relay agents are required to join the local All-DHCP-Agents multicast group, and all servers must join the local All-DHCP-Servers group. All relay agents also join the local All-DHCP-Relays group.

DHCPv6 servers and agents send to UDP port 546, and clients send to UDP port 547. There are six message types defined for DHCPv6, and one nice feature is that the operation code (or message type byte) comes first in the message instead of being buried in the old BOOTP options field (as is DHCP for IPv4).

QUESTIONS FOR READERS

Figure 18.13 shows some of the concepts discussed in this chapter and can be used to help you answer the following questions.

BOOTP Message Format and Fields

Opcode	**Hardware Type**	**Length of Hw Address**	**Hop Counter**
Transaction ID (used to match request and reply)			
Seconds Elapsed Since Client Sent First Request Message		Unused	
Client IP Address (if known to Client, otherwise all 0)			
Client IP Address (provided by Server in response)			
IP Address of Server (Server response: where Client should go for Boot file)			
Relay Router IP Address			
Client Hardware Address			
Server Host Name (Client can optionally identify Server)			
Boot File Name (Client supplies generic name — "Windows")			
"Vendor-Specific Area" Additional Parameters			

DHCP Message Format and Fields

Opcode	**Hardware Type**	**Length of Hw Address**	**Hop Counter**
Transaction ID (used to match request and reply)			
Seconds Elapsed Since Client Sent First Request Message		Flag Field	
Client IP Address (if known to Client, otherwise all 0)			
Client IP Address (provided by Server in response)			
IP Address of Server			
Relay Router IP Address			
Client Hardware Address			
Server Host Name (Client can optionally identify Server)			
File Name			
Options			

FIGURE 18.13

The BOOTP and DHCP messages compared.

1. The client sets the BOOTP hop count to zero initially. If that is the case, what is the hop counter used for?
2. What is the hardware type and hardware address length for Ethernet?
3. How is the relay router IP address field used?
4. What is the client ID option in DHCP?
5. What is the "magic cookie" IP address in BOOTP?

CHAPTER

19

The Domain Name System

What You Will Learn

In this chapter, you will learn how DNS gives the Internet a more user-friendly way to access resources. We'll see how names are associated with IP addresses and how applications find this information.

You will learn how DNS servers provide information about local networks, and how this information is distributed and shared on the Internet. We'll also use show tools to help examine DNS.

The Domain Name System (DNS) is the distributed database used by the TCP/IP protocol suite to translate hostnames to IP addresses (both IPv4 and IPv6) and provide related information, such as email routing information. DNS has been around as part of the Internet for so long that it is easy to forget that in the early days users needed a file named `/etc/hosts` (no extension) unless they wanted to type in the 32-bit IP address that went along with the hostname.

Today, the database is distributed because no single site on the Internet knows everyone's hostname and IP address. Of course, placing every host's IP address in a single text file would be impractical now, but people can still type `www.juniper.net` anywhere on the Internet and access the main Web page for the site. The correct functioning of DNS is so ingrained in expectations that many users do not even realize that when DNS fails typing, `http://207.17.137.68` yields the same result as the `www` entry. For many, when DNS disappears the Internet might as well have vanished as well (except for some local and cached IP addresses, this is probably true enough).

Microsoft support services report that well over 70% of all calls, no matter what the reported symptom, end up being DNS calls. How can something as apparently simple as DNS cause such problems? Two big reasons are that the details of DNS functioning have changed a lot recently, and that many users and administrators know very little about the inner workings of DNS.

Because of the abundance of new terminology, special operations, and new types of servers, this chapter requires us to discuss some of the basics of DNS before looking

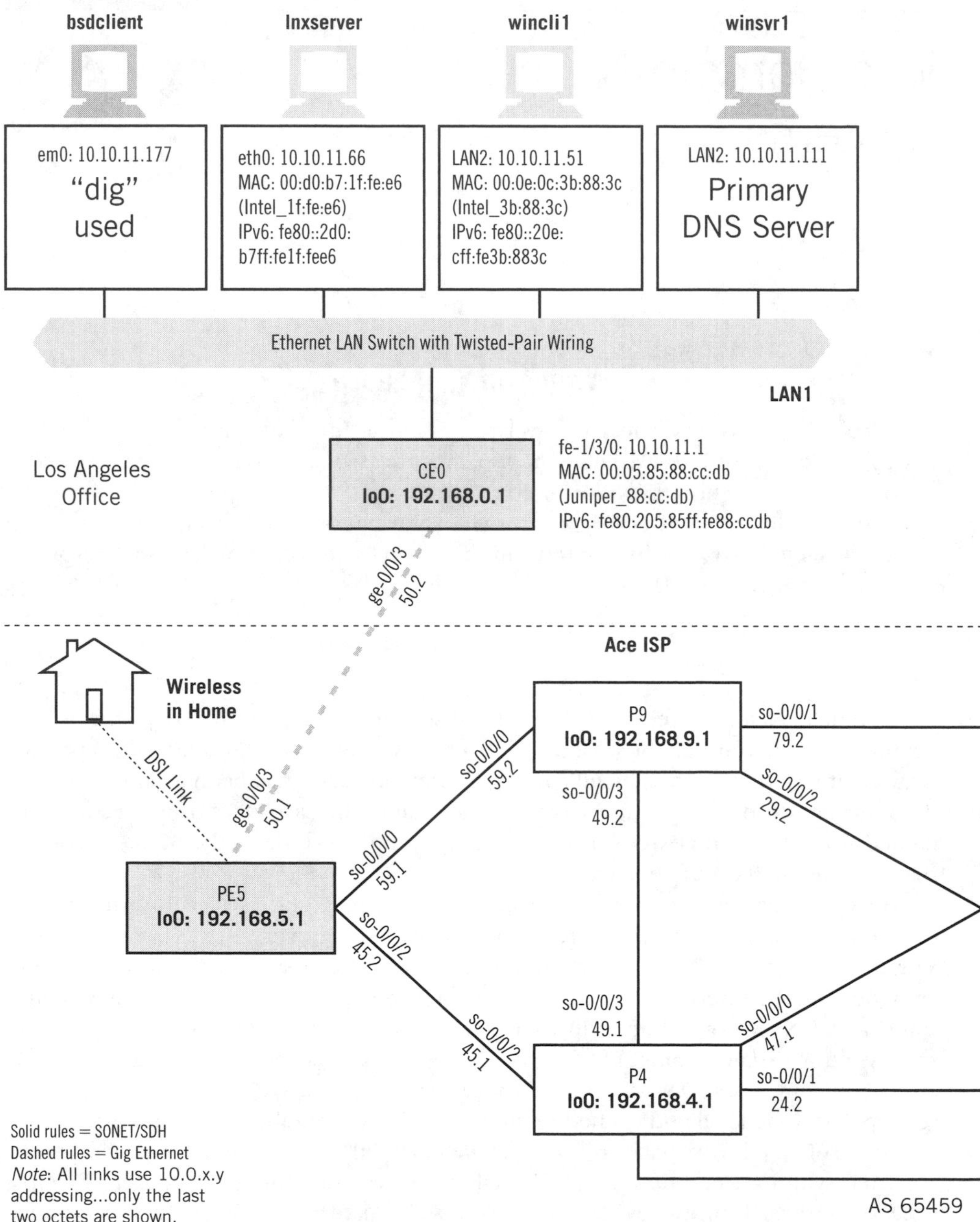

FIGURE 19.1

DNS on the Illustrated Network, showing the hosts used as primary and secondary DNS servers and utilities.

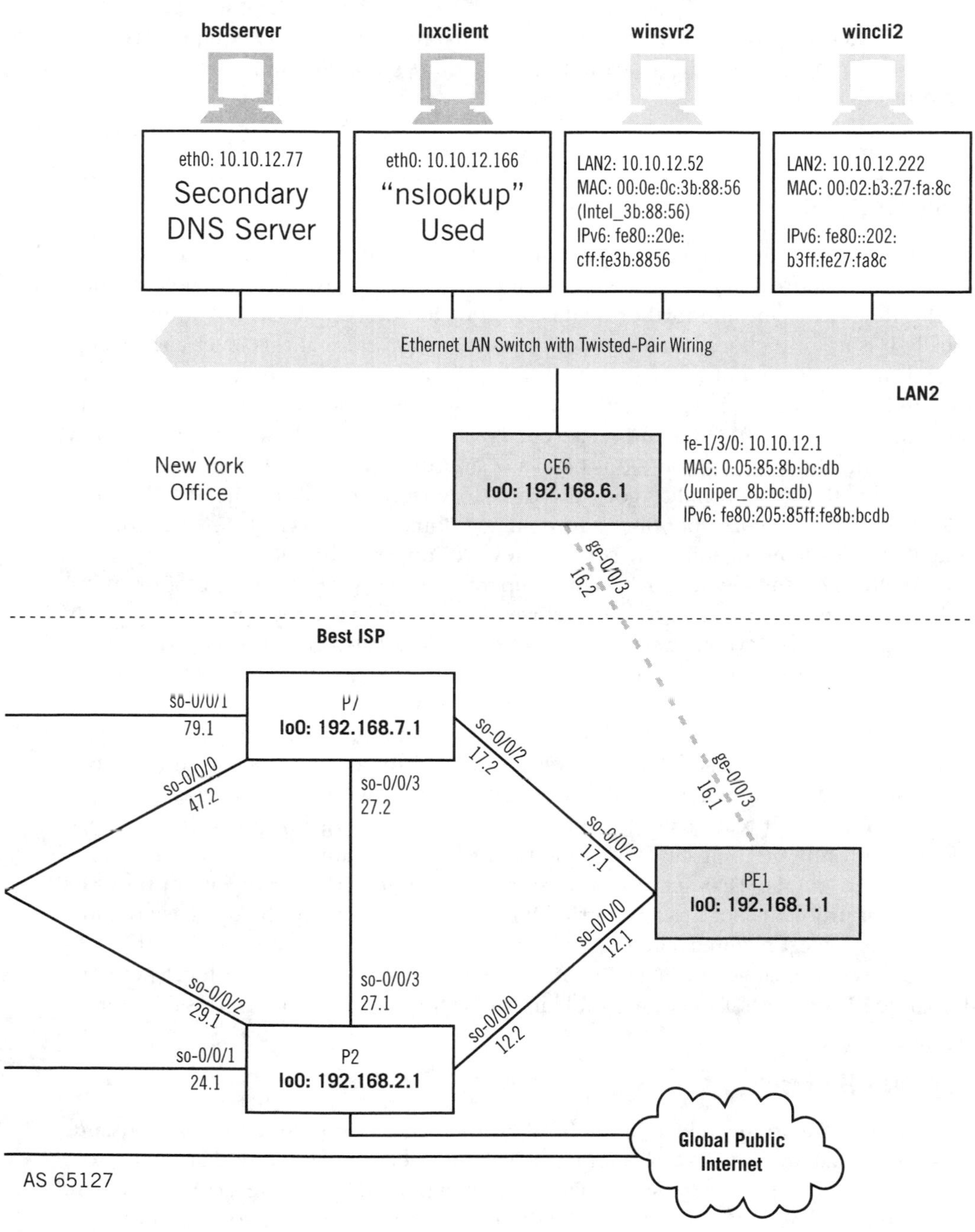
bsdserver
lnxclient
winsvr2
wincli2
eth0: 10.10.12.77
Secondary DNS Server
eth0: 10.10.12.166
"nslookup" Used
LAN2: 10.10.12.52
MAC: 00:0e:0c:3b:88:56
(Intel_3b:88:56)
IPv6: fe80::20e:
cff:fe3b:8856
LAN2: 10.10.12.222
MAC: 00:02:b3:27:fa:8c
IPv6: fe80::202:
b3ff:fe27:fa8c
Ethernet LAN Switch with Twisted-Pair Wiring
LAN2
New York Office
CE6
lo0: 192.168.6.1
fe-1/3/0: 10.10.12.1
MAC: 0:05:85:8b:bc:db
(Juniper_8b:bc:db)
IPv6: fe80:205:85ff:fe8b:bcdb
ge-0/0/3
16.2
Best ISP
so-0/0/1
79.1
P7
lo0: 192.168.7.1
so-0/0/2
17.2
so-0/0/0
47.2
so-0/0/3
27.2
ge-0/0/3
16.1
so-0/0/2
17.1
PE1
lo0: 192.168.1.1
so-0/0/0
12.1
so-0/0/2
29.1
so-0/0/3
27.1
so-0/0/0
12.2
so-0/0/1
24.1
P2
lo0: 192.168.2.1
Global Public Internet
AS 65127

at how DNS is employed on a network. In this chapter, we'll use the equipment in the roles shown in Figure 19.1. Discussion will be kept to a minimum and exploration is maximized in this chapter.

DNS BASICS

Recall that two things are globally administered in TCP/IP: the network portion of the IPv4 or IPv6 address and the domain name that goes along with it. The host portion of the IP address and the further qualification of the domain name are administered locally. It is up to the local administrator to prevent duplicates at this level, and in large organizations this is not as easy as it sounds. (In some cases there are valid reasons for duplicates to exist in an organization, such as due to "split horizon" issues.) Very large organizations often depend on several layers of administration (perhaps division, department, and so on) to dole out blocks of addresses and domain names correctly. Along with this responsibility goes the duty to ensure that all of the detailed host addressing and the corresponding fully qualified domain names (FQDNs) is correct so that all of the clients can find the servers they are supposed to find.

Usually each site—whether it be a company, university, or other type of organization—maintains its own database of information and runs a server process (typically on a dedicated system) other systems can query. You can also get a third party (not the ISP) to manage a zone for you, and that is a service most registrars will do for a nominal fee (if not free) with the registration of a domain name.

At one time, connection to the Internet required an organization to provide at least two DNS servers for the site. The goal was resilience, but because missing authoritative name serves can cause all sorts of performance issues two non-topologically diverse name serves do not really solve anything. Now, very small organizations (or individual users) often rely on their ISP to provide the DNS service and point all of their hosts at these two "public" DNS servers for hostname resolution. This arrangement poses its own set of problems, such as a recurring ISP charge to "maintain" the database records (surely the lowest maintenance task on the Internet) and the need to update the ISP's database when changes to FQDN or IP addressing take place on the local network. Dynamic IP addresses also cause problems for DNS, as detailed later in this chapter.

The DNS Hierarchy

DNS servers are arranged in a hierarchical fashion. That is, the hundreds of thousands of systems that are *authoritative* for the FQDNs in their *zone* are found at the bottom of the DNS "pyramid." For ease of maintenance, when two or more DNS servers are involved only one of them is flagged as the primary server for the zone, and the rest become secondary DNS servers. Both are authoritative for the zone. ISPs typically run their own DNS servers, often for their customers, with the actual number of systems for each ISP depending on the size of the ISP. At the top of the pyramid is the "backbone." There are root servers for the root zone and others for `.com`, `.edu`, and so on.

DNS servers above the local authoritative level refer other name servers to the systems beneath them, and when appropriate each name server will cache information. Information provided to hosts from any but the authoritative DNS system for the domain is considered *non-authoritative*, a designation not reflecting its reliability, but rather its derived nature.

Authoritative and non-authoritative servers can be further classified into categories. Authoritative servers can be:

- *Primary*—The primary name server for a zone. Find its information locally in a disk file.
- *Secondary*—One or more secondary name servers for the zone. They get their information from the primary.
- *Stub*—A special secondary that contains only name server data and not host data.
- *Distribution*—An internal (or "stealth server") name server known only by IP address.

Keep in mind that the primary and secondary distinction is relevant only to the operator of the systems and not to the querier, who treats them all the same. Non-authoritative servers (technically, only the *response* is non-authoritative) can be:

- *Caching*—Contain no local zone information. Just caches what it learns from other queries and responses it handles.
- *Forwarder*—Performs the queries for many clients. Contains a huge cache.

Root Name Servers

The root servers that stand at the tip of the DNS pyramid deserve more explanation in terms of operation and organization. Today, the root servers are the entry points to the DNS service and rely more on caching than the passive databases that once characterized the root server system. With the explosion of the Internet, it made little sense to maintain records with the same "priority" for sites that are constantly bombarded with traffic and those that are seldom visited. The current database in a root name server is small.

The current root servers only know which name server a local DNS needs to ask next to resolve a query. So, any query for a `.com` sent to a root name server produces a list of name servers that might know the answer. The continuous caching of these answers means that there is less need to query the root servers after the first query.

Root Server Operation

The root server operators are not involved in the policymaking regarding Internet names and addresses, nor in modification of the data. They just take what is originated by one of their number (Verisign Global Registry Services) and propagate it to the others. The operators are encouraged to explore diversity in organizational structure, locations, hardware, and software, while maintaining expected levels of physical system security and over-provisioning of capacity. They maintain their own infrastructure for emergencies, including telephone hotlines, encrypted email, and secure credentials. The root servers use distributed *anycast* where practical, making many separate systems all over the world appear and act as one system with one IP address. The use of anycast helps minimize the effects of denial-of-service attacks.

We haven't talked about anycast before. In *anycast*, as in multicast, there is a one-to-many association between addresses and *destinations* (multicast has *groups*) on the network. Each destination address identifies a set of receiver endpoints, but (in contrast to multicast) only *one* of them (determined to be the "nearest" or the "best") is chosen at any particular time to receive information from a particular sender. For example, in contrast to a broadcast (which goes to everyone) or a multicast (which goes to all interested listeners) sent onto a LAN, a message to an anycast address goes to only one of a set of hosts and is then considered delivered. Anycast ("send this to any one of these") is more suited to connectionless protocols (such as UDP) than stateful protocols (such as TCP) that have to maintain state information.

Root server operators often struggle to overcome a lot of misconceptions, even on the part of people who should know better. Contrary to what some believe, all Internet traffic does *not* flow through the root servers (nor do they determine routes), not every DNS query goes to a root server, the "A" system is not special, and there *are* many more than just 13 *machines*.

Table 19.1 DNS Root Servers Listed by Operator, Locations, and IP Address

Server	Operator	Locations
A	Verisign	Dulles, VA
B	Information Sciences Institute	Marina Del Rey, CA
C	Cogent Communications	Herndon, VA; Los Angeles; New York; Chicago
D	University of Maryland	College Park, MD
E	NASA Ames Research Center	Mountain View, CA
F	Internet Systems Consortium, Inc.	43 sites all over the world
G	U.S. DoD NIC	Vienna, VA
H	U.S. Army Research Lab	Aberdeen, MD
I	Autonomica/NORDUnet	31 sites all over the world
J	Versign	41 sites all over the world
K	Réseaux IP Européens–Network Coordination Center	17 sites all over the world
L	ICANN	Los Angeles; Miami
M	WIDE Project	6 sites around the world

Root Server Details

Table 19.1 shows the 13 root name servers (A through M), who operates them, their locations, and their IP addresses (IPv4 and IPv6, where applicable). For the latest information, which changes from time to time (for example, the IPv4 address of `B.root-servers.net` changed in 2004), see *www.root-servers.org.*

Note that many of the root servers, although all grouped under a single name, are actually many systems spread throughout the world. This is where anycast is useful.

In the past, the willingness of DNS servers to accept updates from any source when offered was a major security weakness. Modern DNS servers accept only authorized and digitally signed updates, and higher level DNS servers never accept dynamic updates from anyone. One interesting initiative is the continuing development of DNS Security (DNSSec). DNS is still a tempting target on the Internet, and although DNSSec raises the bar the target remains attractive.

DNS IN THEORY: NAME SERVER, DATABASE, AND RESOLVER

DNS consists of three essential components: the name server, the database of DNS resource records, and the resolver. An application interacts with name servers through a resolver. This is an application program that resides on user workstations and sends requests for DNS information when necessary. Resolvers must be able to find at least one name server, usually the local name server, and local DNS servers provide authoritative answers for local systems. The resolver must also be able to use the information returned by the local name server, if the resource records needed are not local or cached, to pursue the query using referral information leading to other DNS name servers on the Internet.

The resource records of the Domain Name Space are grouped and formatted with a strict tree-structured name space. Information is associated with each type of resource record. The sets of local information (the zones) in this structure are distributed among all DNS servers. The name servers essentially answer resolver queries using the information in its zones or from other zones. A resolver query gives the name of interest and stipulates the type of information needed.

The name servers themselves maintain the structure of the Domain Name Space and the sets of information about the hosts in the zones. Any name server can cache anything it sees about any part of any Internet domain, but generally a particular name server knows only about a tiny fraction of the Internet zones. But there are pointers to other name servers that can be used to answer a resolver query. Name servers can distribute zone information to other name servers to provide redundancy. Finally, DNS name servers periodically refresh their zone information, from local files (the primary) or from other name servers (the secondaries) through a zone transfer.

Other important DNS concepts are relative name and absolute name (FQDN). A resolver request for the IP address for the relative name Web server would produce many addresses on many networks around the world. The relative name is part of the complete absolute name, perhaps *webserver.example.com*. Most resolvers step through an ordered list of preconfigured suffixes, append them one at a time to the relative name, and attempt to find the IP address without the absolute name. Absolute names always end in a dot (.).

Like all good protocols using query/response pairs, DNS uses UDP (port 53). However, DNS also uses TCP (and port 53 there, too) for zone transfers between name servers. These transfers can be considerable in large organizations, and although LANs usually feature very low-error rates the risk of corrupt DNS information more than justifies the use of TCP for the zone transfers. TCP is also used if a response is larger than 512 bytes. And flow control is a really good reason to use TCP for zone transfers, because they can occur over essentially arbitrary distances.

Adding a New Host

Whenever a new host is added to a zone, the DNS administrator must add the resource records (minimally the name and IP address of the host) to a file on the primary name server. The primary name server is then told to read the configuration files, and when the secondaries query the primary (typically every 3 hours), the secondaries find newer information on the primary and perform a zone transfer. The DNS Notify feature enhances the basic zone status check and zone transfer mechanisms. This lets the primary server notify the secondaries when the database has changed. A related feature allows part of a zone to be transferred and not the entire zone information.

How can all of the local name servers find each other? They can't. But every name server must be able to find and contact the root name servers on the Internet. Their positions at the top of the DNS pyramid allow the root name servers to answer queries directly from the zone they have loaded, if with non-authoritative information. Of course, there's always a chance a user on one side of the world will attempt to contact a server or Web site that has just been linked to the Internet and has the zone information such as the IP address available only in the local name server on the network with the Web site.

Recursive and Iterative Queries

If DNS database information is spread throughout the Internet, and the local name servers cannot find each other and the root name servers don't have gigantic databases, how can all hosts in the world find out anything at all? It is because of the way the local DNS name server handles a query from a resolver.

DNS queries can be sent out asking for another name server to handle the query recursively or iteratively (some texts say "non-recursively"). Most local DNS servers function recursively by default. In fact, recursive operation maximizes the amount of information available for caching on name servers, although iterative operation will maximize the amount of information available to a particular name server. Many local name servers use recursive queries (they can be asked to handle a query iteratively), and higher level name servers use iterative queries (root servers always answer queries iteratively).

Recursive DNS queries are handled by the receiving name server waiting until it receives an answer to its own queries. Iterative queries are handled with an immediate "I don't know the answer, but here's where you can look next" response. In the recursive case, the name server "in the middle" can find and cache the information, whereas in the iterative case, it cannot. This might sound confusing, but we'll look at a detailed example of how DNS usually works in the following sections.

Delegation and Referral

Large organizations, or large ISPs operating the DNS servers for their customers, often delegate part of the domain name space to a separate system. For example, a huge *bigcompany.com* might have headquarters records on the main DNS but delegate DNS chores for maintaining and housing *east.bigcompany.com* (on the east coast) and *west.bigcompany.com* (on the west) to its two main divisions. So, there are three DNS servers in all, perhaps called *hqns.bigcompany.com*, *ns1.east.bigcompany.com* on the east coast and *ns2.west.bigcompany.com* on the west coast. There could be many LANs for which one of these name servers is authoritative, such as the LANs for accounting, marketing, sales, and so on.

Figure 19.2 shows the flow of DNS-related actions (solid arrows) and the responses they invoke (dashed arrows) among the DNS name servers mentioned in the *bigcompany.com* example the first time someone looks for the Web site. The initial user resolver query to the LAN's local name server and the eventual response are also shown. The following is the sequence in detail.

The local user on the `wincli1` Web browser (me) requests a Web page from *www.sales.west.bigcompany.com* (the example is valid, but the name has been changed). The browser invokes the local name resolver software in the PC and passes this name to it.

The local resolver checks its cache to see if there is already an IP address stored for this name. (If there is, the quest is over, but we've assumed that this is the first time the user has asked for the Web site so it's not cached.) The resolver also checks to see if there is a local host table file. (Again, let's assume there is no static mapping for the name.)

The resolver generates a recursive query (typically) and sends it to the local name server, which we've set up as `ns1.booklab.englab.jnpr.net` on `winsrv1` using the name server's IP address, which it knows because the server is local (it's `10.10.11.111`). The local DNS system receives the request and checks its cache. If present, the DNS returns a non-authoritative response to the resolver. It would also check to see if there are zone resource records for the request name, but because they are completely different domains there are no zone records.

The local DNS generates an iterative request containing the name sought and sends it to a root name server. The root name server doesn't resolve the name, but returns the name and IP address of the name server for the `.com` domain. The local DNS (which is performing the bulk of the work, we should note) now sends an iterative request to the name server for the `.com` domain.

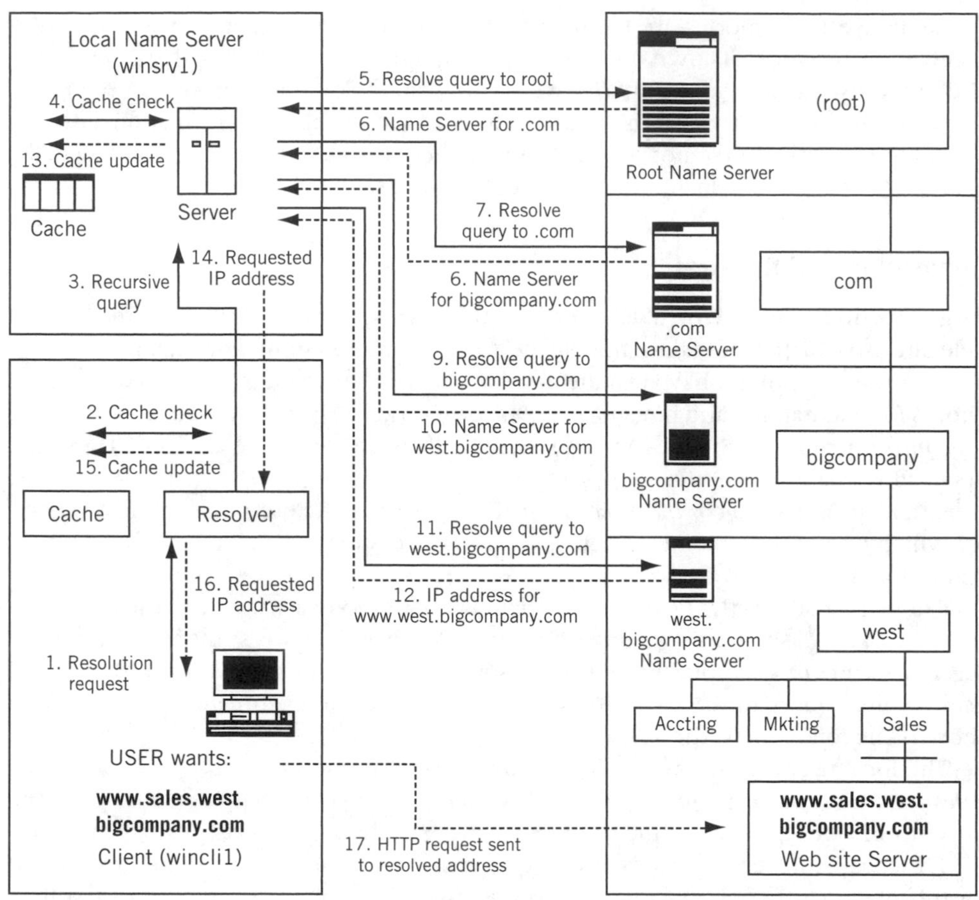

FIGURE 19.2

Example DNS query and response message flow. Messages sent to the servers are shown as solid arrows and replies as dashed arrows.

The `.com` name server returns the name and IP address for the name server for the `bigcompany.com` domain. The local DNS then generates an iterative request to the name server for the `bigcompany.com` domain. The `bigcompany.com` name server looks to see if it has that information. It notices that the requested name is in a separate zone, the `west.bigcompany.com` subdomain.

The local DNS next generates an iterative request to the name server for the `west.bigcompany.com` domain. This name server is authoritative for the *www.sales.west.bigcompany.com* information. It returns the address information for the host to the local DNS. The local DNS system (`winsrv1`) caches the information.

The local DNS returns the resolution to the client's resolver software (`wincli1`). The local resolver also caches the information. The local resolver supplies the address information to the browser. The browser can now send an HTTP request to the correct IP address.

It's actually a tribute to the entire DNS server collection that all of this usually happens very quickly. Note how using recursion on the PC maximized the amount of DNS information available for caching and how iteration elsewhere minimized the amount of information needing to be stored permanently.

Glue Records

There was one key step in the chain of delegation and referral in Figure 19.2 that did not use DNS to find an IP address. Notice that the `bigcompany.com` name server did not use DNS to find the IP address of the `west.bigcompany.com` name server. Delegation must use an address (A) resource record to indicate the IP addresses of name servers responsible for zones below the current level. These are called glue records in DNS and are the answer to an interesting question involving dynamic IP address allocation.

When DHCP first became available, many organizations configured a pool of IP addresses to be assigned only to active users on the Internet. Many organizations included their DNS servers in this pool, and quickly found out that DNS stopped working. Why? Simply, the glue records used by intermediate name servers to find the local authoritative servers didn't work anymore. In other words, the headquarters can't use DNS to find the zone resource records for delegated zones! Glue records serve that purpose.

This is one main reason users whose ISPs use DHCP with dynamic IP addresses for host configuration cannot establish their own DNS name server at home. These users would form delegated zones from the main ISP. And without a local DNS server users who want to place their own server on-site need to work with the ISP to make this happen. Some people see this as part of an ISP plot to prevent users from running their own servers, creating hosting revenue for ISPs and others. But it's really just the glue records.

You need a DNS service provider willing to upgrade the glue records when your address changes. In practice, dynamic DNS service providers can do this, but it also means that the TTL on the records must be low enough so that they flow over in short order. Ideally, they would also provide a secondary DNS.

DNS IN PRACTICE: RESOURCE RECORDS AND MESSAGE FORMATS

When implemented as a series of resolvers and name servers, DNS databases consist of resource records (RRs) entered into a zone file and loaded onto the authoritative name server. Any other DNS name server can cache this information as a non-authoritative source, and a special reverse zone file is used to enable resolvers to look up a host name by IP address. RRs all end in in-addr.arpa. A DNS RR contains the following fields.

Name—The FQDN or portion that is represented by the entry. For example, `bigcompany.com`.

TTL (Time to Live)—How long in seconds the record can be cached. Many ISPs use 2 or even 3 days for this field (172,800 or 259,000). If no value is entered, the default can be short (as little as 1 hour).

Class—Today, the only class that counts is `IN` for Internet address. This is usually entered only once, in the first record, and is inherited by all subsequent records for that name.

Record-Type—There are many record types, usually indicated by a short abbreviation, such as `A` for address and `NS` for name server. The types fall into four categories:

Table 19.2 Common DNS Resource Record Types and Their Uses and Meanings

Use	Record Type	Meaning
Zone	SOA	Start of Authority records identify the zone and set parameters.
	NS	Gives an authoritative name server for the zone, and delegates subdomains. Not the IP address of the name server, but a text field.
Basic	A	Maps the name to the IPv4 address. Each device address requires a separate A record.
	AAAA	Used to allow an IPv4 name server to return an IPv6 address. Intended as a transitional type.
	A6	Now obsolete, these were used to map a name to an IPv6 address.
	PTR	Used to map an IP address to a host name in reverse zone lookups.
	DNAME	Formerly used for redirection for reverse lookups in IPv6 DNS servers due to longer nature of IPv6 addresses. Now obsolete.
	MX	Mail Exchanger records point from a name to A records that are the mail exchanger for the name.
Security	KEY	The public key for the DNS name.
	NXT	Used for negative answers with DNSSec.
	SIG	The signature for an authenticated zone.
Optional	CNAME	Maps an alias name to a canonical ("real") name. For example, www.example.com and ftp.example.com might both be running on the host server.example.com.
	LOC	Geographical location.
	NAPTR	Name Authority Pointer is used to allow regular expression rewrites of the domain name.
	RP	Contact information for responsible person.
	SRV	Gives locations of well-known services.
	TXT	To add comments and information to the record.

zone, basic, security, and optional. A list of the more common record types appears in Table 19.2.

Record-Data—Depending on the type, this information varies. For a name server, this is the domain name of the name server. For a host, this is the IP address.

Comments—These are optional and begin with a semicolon (;) and are never returned with data.

This is not an exhaustive list. Some defined record types are seldom used (HINFO is supposed to mention host model and operating system) or are perceived as security risks (WKS records list the "well-known services" available at the host).

Some readers might have noticed the elaborate form of the IPv6 addresses used on the Illustrated Network. This is because IPv6 once used something called the binary label syntax. IPv6 addresses use the first bits (really, whole words) of the 128-bit IPv6 address to indicate the ISP. The A6 records included a referral field to allow a name server to refer to the ISP's name server for the "network" portion of the IPv6 address. The A6 record also gave the number and value of the bits present in the A6 record itself. This prevented the laborious entry of many redundant bits into the resource records. It also made shifting service providers easier. So, a query for an A6 record might only get the last 64 bits of an IPv6 address. A further referral query to the name server in the A6 record is necessary for the first 64 bits. The DNAME records do the same for the Pv6 host name. This now obsolete system was used for the IPv6 addresses.

The same DNS message format is used for queries and responses. The DNS query message goes out with a 12 octet header and a variable number of questions. The DNS response message essentially pastes on a variable number of three types of response fields: answer RRs, RRs identifying authoritative servers, and RRs with additional information. Figure 19.3 shows the general format of the DNS message.

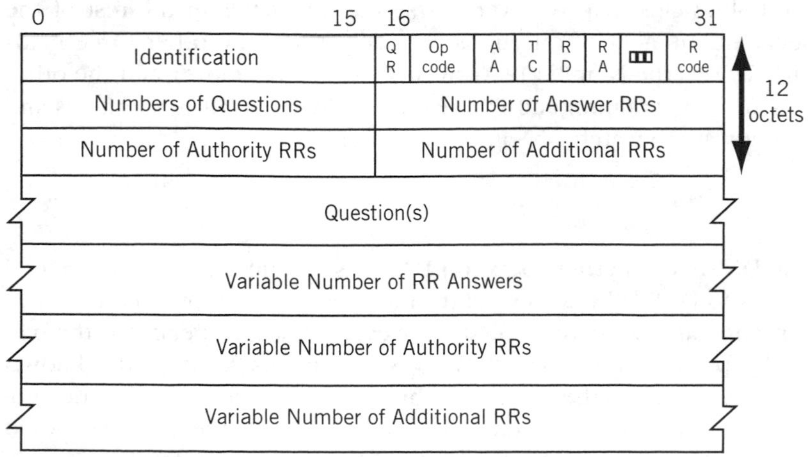

FIGURE 19.3

DNS message format. Note that the last four fields are variable in size.

DNS Message Header

The 16-bit identification field, set by the client and returned by the server, allows for coordination of outstanding requests and responses. The 16-bit Flags field is quite complex:

QR—A 1-bit field where 0 = query and 1 = response.

Opcode—A 4-bit field where 0 = standard query. Other values are for an inverse query (1) and a server status request (2).

AA—A 1-bit flag that indicates that the name server is authoritative for the zone (1 = true).

TC—A 1-bit flag meaning that the reply has been truncated. UDP limits DNS responses to 512 octets, except when Extension Mechanism for DNS (EDNS0, defined in RFC 2671) is used. EDNS0 identifies the requester's UDP packet size.

RD—A 1-bit flag for "recursion desired." If this bit is set in a query, the receiving name server is supposed to keep trying to find the answer. If this bit is not set, the name server returns a list of other name servers to contact unless it can provide an authoritative answer.

RA—A 1-bit flag for "recursion available." Some name servers will refuse to act recursively, and this bit is cleared in response to let other systems know about server refusal.

Pad—A 3-bit field that must be set to 000.

Rcode—A 4-bit field for the return code. The most common values are for no error (0) and a name error (3).

The next four 16-bit fields help receivers parse the four fields in the rest of the message. In a query, the number of questions is usually 1 and the other three fields are 0. A reply typically sets the Number of Answers field to 1 (or more), and the other two are 0. Utilities such as tcpdump and Ethereal normally parse all of the fields and flags. There are other ways to watch DNS in action, however.

DNSSec

As indispensable as DNS is for Internet operation, DNS was not (unfortunately) designed to be secure. Threats to DNS fall into several distinct classes, many of which are just well-known security threats redirected at DNS. However, a few are specific to the particular way the DNS protocol functions. RFC 3833 documents some of the known threats to DNS and tries to assess the extent to which DNSSec will succeed in defending against these threats. Although this section uses some concepts we haven't covered yet, DNSSec is important enough to introduce in this chapter on DNS itself.

In particular, DNSSec was designed to protect Internet DNS resolvers (the clients) from forged DNS data, which can point people looking for a particular Web site (such as their bank) to the wrong IP address. This forged information can be put in place by a process called DNS cache poisoning. In DNSSec, all answers to queries are digitally signed (we'll talk more about digital signatures and certificates in Chapters 22 and 23). The digital signature can be checked by the resolver to see if the information is identical to the information on the authoritative DNS server for the site. DNSSec, although designed primarily to protect IP addresses, can be used to protect other information (such as the cryptographic certificates stored in DNS). RFC 4367 describes how to use DNS to distribute certificates, including those used for email, so it is possible to use DNSSec as a global infrastructure for secure email.

However, DNSSec does not say anything about the confidentiality of data. That is, all DNSSec responses are authenticated but not encrypted (we'll talk more about the differences in Chapter 29). It also really doesn't protect against denial-of-service attacks directly, although DNSSec does provide some benefit through the authentication features of the digital signature. Other methods must be used to protect bulk data, such as a large zone transfer. Of course (per RFC 4367) DNSSec cannot prevent users from making false assumptions about domain names, such as the idea that the organization's name plus *.com* is always the company (or bank) Web site they are looking for. But at least DNSSec can authenticate that the data provided by DNS is actually from the domain owner.

The current DNSSec specifications describe DNSSec-bis. The most important are RFC 4033, RFC 4034, and RFC 4035.

DNS Tools: nslookup, dig, and host

The Berkeley Internet Name Domain (BIND), developed for the Unix environment, is both resolver and name server. When BIND is running as name server, the process is named. Entire books have been written about DNS and BIND, so this chapter can only look at a few of the things that can be explored with a few simple DNS tools and utilities.

BIND configuration statements for a zone are in named.conf, usually found in `/etc`—where the name servers to be contacted (in `resolv.conf`) are also located. A "hints" file (variously named *named.ca, named.root,* or *root.cache*) has information about the root servers and essentially "primes" the DNS cache at start-up.

The nslookup utility program allows a user to interact with a DNS name server directly. Options allow the user to display detailed query and response information as needed. Originally a testing tool, nslookup functions in both interactive and non-interactive mode. Today, the use of nslookup is deprecated, and it is not included in many operating system distributions. Its functionality has been taken over by dig and host.

The Domain Internet Groper (dig) DNS query tool is more general than nslookup, and is often used with other tools. It has a consistent output format that is easily parsed with other programs, and is available for Windows 2000/XP (but not 98/ME).

Over time, dig developed a distinct "feature sprawl" that offended some who favored clean and mean Internet tools. The host utility by Eric Wassenaar is intended to be an evolutionary step for both nslookup and dig. The examples in this chapter will use dig as well as nslookup, if only because of the familiarity of the nslookup format.

DNS IN ACTION

Putting a functioning DNS system on the Illustrated Network will allow us to do things such as ping *winsrv1.booklab.englab.jnpr.net* instead of having to know the IP address and use ping 10.10.11.111. We'll go against common wisdom and make a Windows XP system (winsrv1) our primary DNS server, and we will use the FreeBSD server (bsdserver) as the secondary DNS for LAN1 and LAN2. Windows XP Pro does not support DNS natively, so we'll use a GUI-based DNS server package called SimpleDNS instead of BIND.

Once DNS is up and running, we have to ensure that all hosts know where to find it. On lnxclient, and most Unix hosts, we just add them to the /etc/resolv.conf file.

```
search booklab.englab.jnpr.net englab.jnpr.net jnpr.net
nameserver 10.10.11.111
nameserver 10.10.12.77
```

Now, let's see how DNS works to find local hosts.

```
[root@lnxclient admin]# nslookup
Note:  nslookup is deprecated and may be removed from future releases.
Consider using the 'dig' or 'host' programs instead.  Run nslookup with
the '-sil[ent]' option to prevent this message from appearing.
> winsrv1
Server:         10.10.11.111
Address:        10.10.11.111#53

Name:   winsrv1.booklab.englab.jnpr.net
Address: 10.10.11.111
> winscli1
Server:         10.10.11.111
Address:        10.10.11.111#53

Name:   wincli1.booklab.englab.jnpr.net
Address: 10.10.11.51
> bsdserver
Server:         10.10.11.111
Address:        10.10.11.111#53

Name:   bsdserver.booklab.englab.jnpr.net
Address: 10.10.12.77
>
```

Note the "warning" about continued use of nslookup. But it still works. Of course, if we pause the DNS on winsrv1, we can still get a response from bsdserver (as long as a zone transfer has taken place).

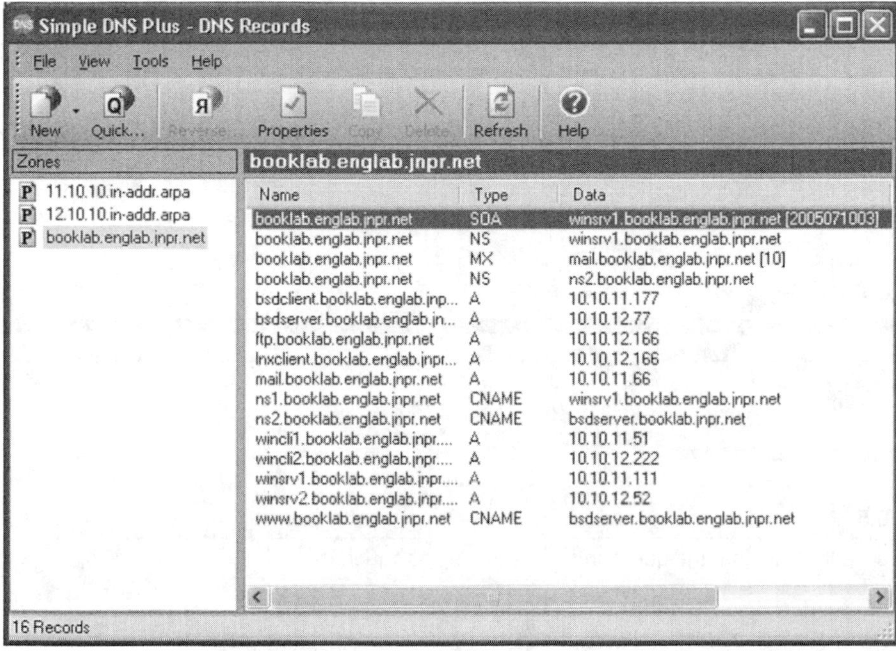

FIGURE 19.4

DNS records on `winsrv1` using a GUI. Note the various record types (the name servers in particular).

```
> lnxserver
Server: 10.10.12.77
Address: 10.10.12.77#53

Non-authoritative answer:
Name: lnxserver.booklab.englab.jnpr.net
Address: 10.10.11.66
```

Simple DNS has a nice GUI, in contrast to the text files used in most Unix DNS versions (as shown in Figure 19.4).

The Ethereal capture in Figure 19.5 shows the utter simplicity of the DNS message exchanges. There's even a nice log of these messages, as shown in Figure 19.6 (it also tracks DHCP leases when dynamic DNS is used).

Now we can finally `ping` on the Illustrated Network the "normal" way.

```
[root@lnxclient admin]# ping wincli1.booklab.englab.jnpr.net
PING wincli1.booklab.englab.jnpr.net (10.10.11.51) 56(84) bytes of data.
64 bytes from wincli1.booklab.englab.jnpr.net (10.10.11.51): icmp_seq=1
 ttl=126 time=0.768 ms
64 bytes from wincli1.booklab.englab.jnpr.net (10.10.11.51): icmp_seq=2
 ttl=126 time=0.283 ms
```

```
No.  Time      Source        Destination   Protocol Info
  1 0.000000  10.10.12.166  10.10.11.111  DNS      Standard query A wincli1.booklab.englab.jnpr.net
  2 0.002286  10.10.11.111  10.10.12.166  DNS      Standard query response A 10.10.11.51
  3 8.343237  10.10.12.166  10.10.11.111  DNS      Standard query A bsdclient.booklab.englab.jnpr.net
  4 8.345109  10.10.11.111  10.10.12.166  DNS      Standard query response A 10.10.11.177

▷ Frame 2 (107 bytes on wire, 107 bytes captured)
▷ Ethernet II, Src: 00:0e:0c:3b:87:36, Dst: 00:05:85:88:cc:db
▷ Internet Protocol, Src Addr: 10.10.11.111 (10.10.11.111), Dst Addr: 10.10.12.166 (10.10.12.166)
▷ User Datagram Protocol, Src Port: domain (53), Dst Port: 32808 (32808)
▽ Domain Name System (response)
    Transaction ID: 0x8948
  ▷ Flags: 0x8580 (Standard query response, No error)
    Questions: 1
    Answer RRs: 1
    Authority RRs: 0
    Additional RRs: 0
  ▽ Queries
    ▷ wincli1.booklab.englab.jnpr.net: type A, class inet
  ▽ Answers
    ▷ wincli1.booklab.englab.jnpr.net: type A, class inet, addr 10.10.11.51

0000  00 05 85 88 cc db 00 0e  0c 3b 87 36 08 00 45 00   ........ .;.6..E.
0010  00 5d 40 ba 00 00 80 11  cd ad 0a 0a 0b 6f 0a 0a   .]@..... .....o..
0020  0c a6 00 35 80 28 00 49  68 cb 89 48 85 80 00 01   ...5.(.I h..H....
0030  00 01 00 00 00 00 07 77  69 6e 63 6c 69 31 07 62   .......w incli1.b
0040  6f 6f 6b 6c 61 62 06 65  6e 67 6c 61 62 04 6a 6e   ooklab.e nglab.jn
0050  70 72 03 6e 65 74 00 00  01 00 01 c0 0c 00 01 00   pr.net.. ........
0060  01 00 01 51 80 00 04 0a  0a 0b 33                  ...Q.... ..3
```

FIGURE 19.5

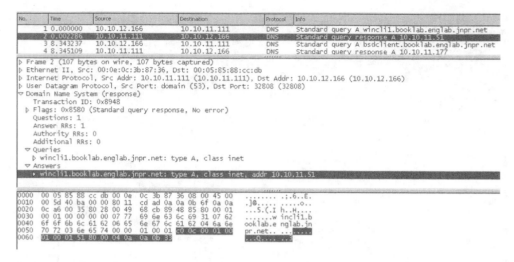

DNS server reply. Note that the question field shows up as "queries."

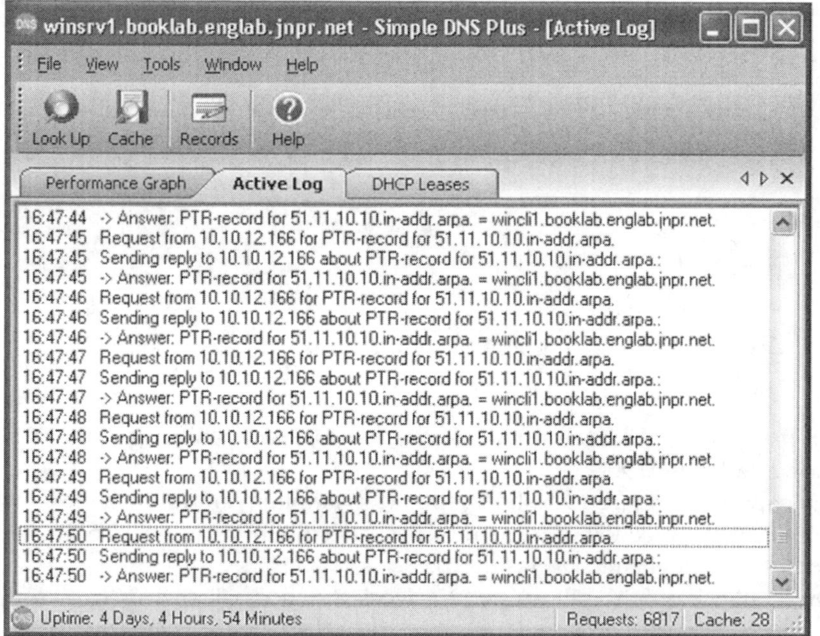

FIGURE 19.6

DNS server log showing the history of queries and responses.

```
64 bytes from wincli1.booklab.englab.jnpr.net (10.10.11.51): icmp_seq=3
 ttl=126 time=0.285 ms
64 bytes from wincli1.booklab.englab.jnpr.net (10.10.11.51): icmp_seq=4
 ttl=126 time=0.259 ms
64 bytes from wincli1.booklab.englab.jnpr.net (10.10.11.51): icmp_seq=5
 ttl=126 time=0.276 ms
64 bytes from wincli1.booklab.englab.jnpr.net (10.10.11.51): icmp_seq=6
 ttl=126 time=0.244 ms
64 bytes from wincli1.booklab.englab.jnpr.net (10.10.11.51): icmp_seq=7
 ttl=126 time=0.259 ms
^C

--- wincli1.booklab.englab.jnpr.net ping statistics ---
7 packets transmitted, 7 received, 0% packet loss, time 8080ms
rtt min/avg/max/mdev = 0.244/0.325/0.768/0.158 ms
[root@lnxclient admin]#
```

LAN1 is also running a DNS server on `lnxserver`, and to keep the configuration very simple only functions as a non-authoritative server. The configuration is short and sweet:

```
lnxserver$ cat /etc/named.conf
options {
  directory "/var/named";
};
// this is a caching only name server zone configuration
zone "." {
  type hint;
  file "named.ca";
};
zone "0.0.127.in-addr.local";
  type master;
  file "named.local";
};
```

The two zone statements only point to the root servers on the Internet (in the hints file *named.ca)* and make this server the master for its own loopback address. These two zones appear in all name server configurations.

We should also limit the hosts from which recursion can be performed on the caching name server. Otherwise, it might get used as a denial-of-service amplifier. That section would be:

```
allow-recursion { 127.0.0.1;
10.10.11.0/24;
};
```

We'll point to the lnxserver name server on wincli1 on LAN1 and use nslookup to verify that we can still find the Internet name servers. At the interactive DNS prompt (>), we'll set the type of query to send to ns for name servers and we will look for "com."

This is the root of the entire ".com" Domain Name Space (note that we ask for `com.` and not `.com` without the ending dot). Otherwise, the system would append a suffix and try to find *com.booklab.englab.jnpr.net* and return an error (unless we did have a system named "com" on the network).

```
> com.
Server: lnxserver.booklab.juniper.net
Address: 192.168.27.14

Non-authoritative answer:
com     nameserver = f.gtld-servers.net
com     nameserver = g.gtld-servers.net
com     nameserver = h.gtld-servers.net
com     nameserver = i.gtld-servers.net
com     nameserver = j.gtld-servers.net
com     nameserver = k.gtld-servers.net
com     nameserver = l.gtld-servers.net
com     nameserver = m.gtld-servers.net
com     nameserver = a.gtld-servers.net
com     nameserver = b.gtld-servers.net
com     nameserver = c.gtld-servers.net
com     nameserver = d.gtld-servers.net
com     nameserver = e.gtld-servers.net

a.gtld-servers.net    internet address = 192.5.6.30
a.gtld-servers.net    AAAA IPv6 address = 2001:503:a83e::2:30
b.gtld-servers.net    internet address = 192.33.14.30
b.gtld-servers.net    AAAA IPv6 address = 2001:503:231d::2:30
c.gtld-servers.net    internet address = 192.26.92.30
d.gtld-servers.net    internet address = 192.31.80.30
e.gtld-servers.net    internet address = 192.12.94.30
f.gtld-servers.net    internet address = 192.35.51.30
g.gtld-servers.net    internet address = 192.42.93.30
h.gtld-servers.net    internet address = 192.54.112.30
i.gtld-servers.net    internet address = 192.43.172.30
j.gtld-servers.net    internet address = 192.48.79.30
k.gtld-servers.net    internet address = 192.52.178.30
l.gtld-servers.net    internet address = 192.41.162.30
m.gtld-servers.net    internet address = 192.55.83.30
```

There are 13 servers, A through M, on the first part of the list. But instead of being called "root servers" these are "gltd servers." GLTD stands for generic top-level domains (sometimes seen as gTLD), and that's what the traditional Internet host name endings such as `.com`, `.mil`, `.org`, and so on are in DNS. There are also ccTLDs (country code TLDs), such as `.fr` for France and `.ca` for Canada.

Note that the A and B GTLD servers return AAAA record types, showing that the A6 and DNAME records (once so promising) are obsolete. We're not supposed to use nslookup (dig is not built into Windows XP, but can be installed as freeware). Let's see what dig can do, this time on the FreeBSD client.

```
bsdclient# dig

; <<>> DiG 8.3 <<>>
;; res options: init recurs defnam dnsrch
;; got answer:
;; ->>HEADER<<- opcode: QUERY, status: NOERROR, id: 10624
;; flags: qr rd ra; QUERY: 1, ANSWER: 13, AUTHORITY: 0, ADDITIONAL: 13
;; QUERY SECTION:
;;      ., type = NS, class = IN

;; ANSWER SECTION:
.                        12h46m16s IN NS  d.root-servers.net.
.                        12h46m16s IN NS  a.root-servers.net.
.                        12h46m16s IN NS  h.root-servers.net.
.                        12h46m16s IN NS  c.root-servers.net.
.                        12h46m16s IN NS  g.root-servers.net.
.                        12h46m16s IN NS  f.root-servers.net.
.                        12h46m16s IN NS  b.root-servers.net.
.                        12h46m16s IN NS  j.root-servers.net.
.                        12h46m16s IN NS  k.root-servers.net.
.                        12h46m16s IN NS  l.root-servers.net.
.                        12h46m16s IN NS  m.root-servers.net.
.                        12h46m16s IN NS  i.root-servers.net.
.                        12h46m16s IN NS  e.root-servers.net.

;; ADDITIONAL SECTION:
d.root-servers.net.      12h46m16s IN A  128.8.10.90
a.root-servers.net.      12h46m16s IN A  198.41.0.4
h.root-servers.net.      12h46m16s IN A  128.63.2.53
c.root-servers.net.      12h46m16s IN A  192.33.4.12
g.root-servers.net.      12h46m16s IN A  192.112.36.4
f.root-servers.net.      12h46m16s IN A  192.5.5.241
b.root-servers.net.      12h46m16s IN A  192.228.79.201
j.root-servers.net.      12h46m16s IN A  192.58.128.30
k.root-servers.net.      12h46m16s IN A  193.0.14.129
l.root-servers.net.      12h46m16s IN A  198.32.64.12
m.root-servers.net.      12h46m16s IN A  202.12.27.33
i.root-servers.net.      12h46m16s IN A  192.36.148.17
e.root-servers.net.      12h46m16s IN A  192.203.230.10

;; Total query time: 1 msec
;; FROM: bsdclient.booklab.englab.jnpr.net to SERVER: 10.10.11.66
;; WHEN: Fri Feb 22 10:10:00 2008
;; MSG SIZE  sent: 17  rcvd: 449

bsdclient#
```

That's a lot more detailed information, and it doesn't use an interactive prompt. By default, dig looks for root NS records and serves up flags, TTL information (in user-friendly units), and so on. Let's look at a more complete (or realistic) example and look for the IP address of the server for *www.amazon.com* (perhaps so you can prepare to order more copies of this book).

```
bsdclient# dig www.amazon.com

; <<>> DiG 8.3 <<>> www.amazon.com
;; res options: init recurs defnam dnsrch
;; got answer:
;; ->>HEADER<<- opcode: QUERY, status: NOERROR, id: 10904
;; flags: qr aa rd ra; QUERY: 1, ANSWER: 1, AUTHORITY: 0, ADDITIONAL: 0
;; QUERY SECTION:
;;      www.amazon.com, type = A, class = IN

;; ANSWER SECTION:
www.amazon.com.         1m7s IN A       207.171.175.35

;; Total query time: 95 msec
;; FROM: bsdclient.booklab.englab.jnpr.net to SERVER: 10.10.11.66
;; WHEN: Fri Feb 22 10:40:17 2008
;; MSG SIZE  sent: 32  rcvd: 48
```

dig got us an answer, but not an authoritative one (AUTHORITY: 0). To get the authoritative answer to the Amazon Web site, and not something from cache, we'll have to find the Amazon name servers and ask one of them.

```
bsdclient# dig www.amazon.com ns

; <<>> DiG 8.3 <<>> www.amazon.com ns
;; res options: init recurs defnam dnsrch
;; got answer:
;; ->>HEADER<<- opcode: QUERY, status: NOERROR, id: 44598
;; flags: qr rd ra; QUERY: 1, ANSWER: 4, AUTHORITY: 0, ADDITIONAL: 1
;; QUERY SECTION:
;;       www.amazon.com, type = NS, class = IN

;; ANSWER SECTION:
www.amazon.com.         21h7m55s IN NS  ns-40.amazon.com.
www.amazon.com.         21h7m55s IN NS  ns-30.amazon.com.
www.amazon.com.         21h7m55s IN NS  ns-20.amazon.com.
www.amazon.com.         21h7m55s IN NS  ns-10.amazon.com.

;; ADDITIONAL SECTION:
ns-40.amazon.com.       21h7m55s IN A   207.171.169.7
;; Total query time: 1 msec
;; FROM: bsdclient.booklab.englab.jnpr.net to SERVER: 10.10.11.66
;; WHEN: Fri Feb 22 10:38:37 2008
;; MSG SIZE  sent: 32  rcvd: 128
```

Amazon has four name servers (note we found these answers cached, because of the AUTHORITY: 0). We'll ask ns-40 about Amazon's Web site:

```
bsdclient# dig @ns-40.amazon.com www.amazon.com A

; <<>> DiG 8.3 <<>> @ns-40.amazon.com www.amazon.com A
; (1 server found)
;; res options: init recurs defnam dnsrch
;; got answer:
;; ->>HEADER<<- opcode: QUERY, status: NOERROR, id: 6717
;; flags: qr rd; QUERY: 1, ANSWER: 0, AUTHORITY: 1, ADDITIONAL: 0
;; QUERY SECTION:
;;     www.amazon.com, type = A, class = IN

;; AUTHORITY SECTION:
www.amazon.com.         1m7s IN A       207.171.166.48

;; Total query time: 3 msec
;; FROM: bsdclient.booklab.englab.jnpr.net to SERVER: 204.74.101.1
;; WHEN: Fri Feb 22 10:32:52 2008
;; MSG SIZE  sent: 32  rcvd: 112
```

Now `AUTHORITY: 1` appears. It's nice to know that Amazon's own name server is authoritative for itself. But let's not get too worried about authoritative answers. Cached information is usually just as good. In fact, look what happens when we repeat the query.

```
bsdclient# dig @ns-40.amazon.com www.amazon.com A

; <<>> DiG 8.3 <<>> @ns-40.amazon.com www.amazon.com A
; (1 server found)
;; res options: init recurs defnam dnsrch
;; got answer:
;; ->>HEADER<<- opcode: QUERY, status: NOERROR, id: 52895
;; flags: qr aa rd ra; QUERY: 1, ANSWER: 1, AUTHORITY: 0, ADDITIONAL: 0
;; QUERY SECTION:
;;      www.amazon.com, type = A, class = IN

;; ANSWER SECTION:
www.amazon.com.         1m7s IN A       207.171.175.35

;; Total query time: 91 msec
;; FROM: bsdclient.booklab.englab.jnpr.net to SERVER: 207.171.169.7
;; WHEN: Fri Feb 22 10:55:29 2008
;; MSG SIZE  sent: 32  rcvd: 48
```

Isn't the `ns-40` server still authoritative? Sure, but our earlier query just popped that information into the local cache. Why fetch up an authoritative reply when there's one just as good in cache? Caching can be a nuisance when trying to "force" authoritative answers, especially across the Internet.

Dig has been criticized for feature bloat. For comparison, the host DNS utility retains the clean and sparse Unix output philosophy.

```
bsdclient# host www.amazon.com
www.amazon.com has address 207.171.166.102
bsdclient#
```

Even at its most verbose, host is not as forthcoming as the other utilities.

```
bsdclient# host -v www.amazon.com ns-40.amazon.com
Using domain server:
Name: ns-40.amazon.com
Addresses: 207.171.169.7

Trying null domain
rcode = 0 (Success), ancount=1
The following answer is not verified as authentic by the server:
www.amazon.com  67 IN   A      207.171.175.29
```

This has been by no means an exhaustive look at how DNS acts. For more information, the excellent *DNS and BIND* by Cricket Liu (O'Reilly Media) should be considered definitive.

QUESTIONS FOR READERS

Figure 19.7 shows some of the concepts discussed in this chapter and can be used to help you answer the following questions.

No.	Time	Source	Destination	Protocol	Info
1	0.000000	10.10.12.166	10.10.11.111	DNS	Standard query A wincli1.booklab.englab.jnpr.net
2	0.002286	10.10.11.111	10.10.12.166	DNS	Standard query response A 10.10.11.51
3	8.343237	10.10.12.166	10.10.11.111	DNS	Standard query A bsdclient.booklab.englab.jnpr.net
4	8.345109	10.10.11.111	10.10.12.166	DNS	Standard query response A 10.10.11.177

```
▷ Frame 2 (107 bytes on wire, 107 bytes captured)
▷ Ethernet II, Src: 00:0e:0c:3b:87:36, Dst: 00:05:85:88:cc:db
▷ Internet Protocol, Src Addr: 10.10.11.111 (10.10.11.111), Dst Addr: 10.10.12.166 (10.10.12.166)
▷ User Datagram Protocol, Src Port: domain (53), Dst Port: 32808 (32808)
▽ Domain Name System (response)
    Transaction ID: 0x8948
  ▷ Flags: 0x8580 (Standard query response, No error)
    Questions: 1
    Answer RRs: 1
    Authority RRs: 0
    Additional RRs: 0
  ▽ Queries
    ▷ wincli1.booklab.englab.jnpr.net: type A, class inet
  ▽ Answers
    ▷ wincli1.booklab.englab.jnpr.net: type A, class inet, addr 10.10.11.51
```

```
0000  00 05 85 88 cc db 00 0e  0c 3b 87 36 08 00 45 00   ........ .;.6..E.
0010  00 5d 40 ba 00 00 80 11  cd ad 0a 0a 0b 6f 0a 0a   .]@..... .....o..
0020  0c a6 00 35 80 28 00 49  68 cb 89 48 85 80 00 01   ...5.(.I h..H....
0030  00 01 00 00 00 00 07 77  69 6e 63 6c 69 31 07 62   .......w incli1.b
0040  6f 6f 6b 6c 61 62 06 65  6e 67 6c 61 62 04 6a 6e   ooklab.e nglab.jn
0050  70 72 03 6e 65 74 00 00  01 00 01 c0 0c 00 01 00   pr.net.. ........
0060  01 00 01 51 80 00 04 0a  0a 0b 33                  ...Q.... ..3
```

FIGURE 19.7

A DNS server reply message parsed by Ethereal.

1. How many questions (queries) are usually present in a DNS request?
2. Is the message in the figure a query or a response?
3. What are the host names of the client and the DNS server on the Illustrated Network that correspond to the IP addresses in the figure?
4. The flag field value is `0x8580`. Is the DNS server authoritative for the zone?
5. Based on the flag field value, is recursion desired and available?

CHAPTER

File Transfer Protocol

20

What You Will Learn

In this chapter, you will learn how FTP provides a method to move files around the Internet. We'll examine various aspects of FTP as a protocol and as an application, showing how commands translate to protocol actions.

You will learn about the differences between FTP's active and passive modes of operation. We'll discuss how security concerns affect the operation of FTP.

The original Internet boasted three applications: electronic mail, remote computer access, and remote file access. Over time, not only have these three been joined by a host of others but the original applications have evolved to keep pace with expansion of the Internet and the environment of the modern world. As a simple example of this trend, these applications have all moved beyond their simple commands typed in at a prompt to graphical front ends. These GUIs make the applications more accessible to novices, but at the same time mask the details of protocol operation from users. Yet in most cases the original protocols are still there, running behind the scenes, as this look at the File Transfer Protocol (FTP) will show.

FTP transfers a copy of a file. The original file is usually still present on the source host, available for copying over and over as remote users request it. Copying files between two different computer systems has always been more difficult than it seems. Today, most users are familiar with the differences between Windows file formats and those used by Apple, which is why one can't usually take a floppy or CD from one and load it on the other. When other file systems are considered, such as the varieties of Unix and older formats used by minicomputer and mainframe vendors (many of which could not be copied between computer models from the same *vendor*), it is no wonder the FTP is one of the most elaborate and robust applications in TCP/IP (although format conversion is much less of a concern than it used to be).

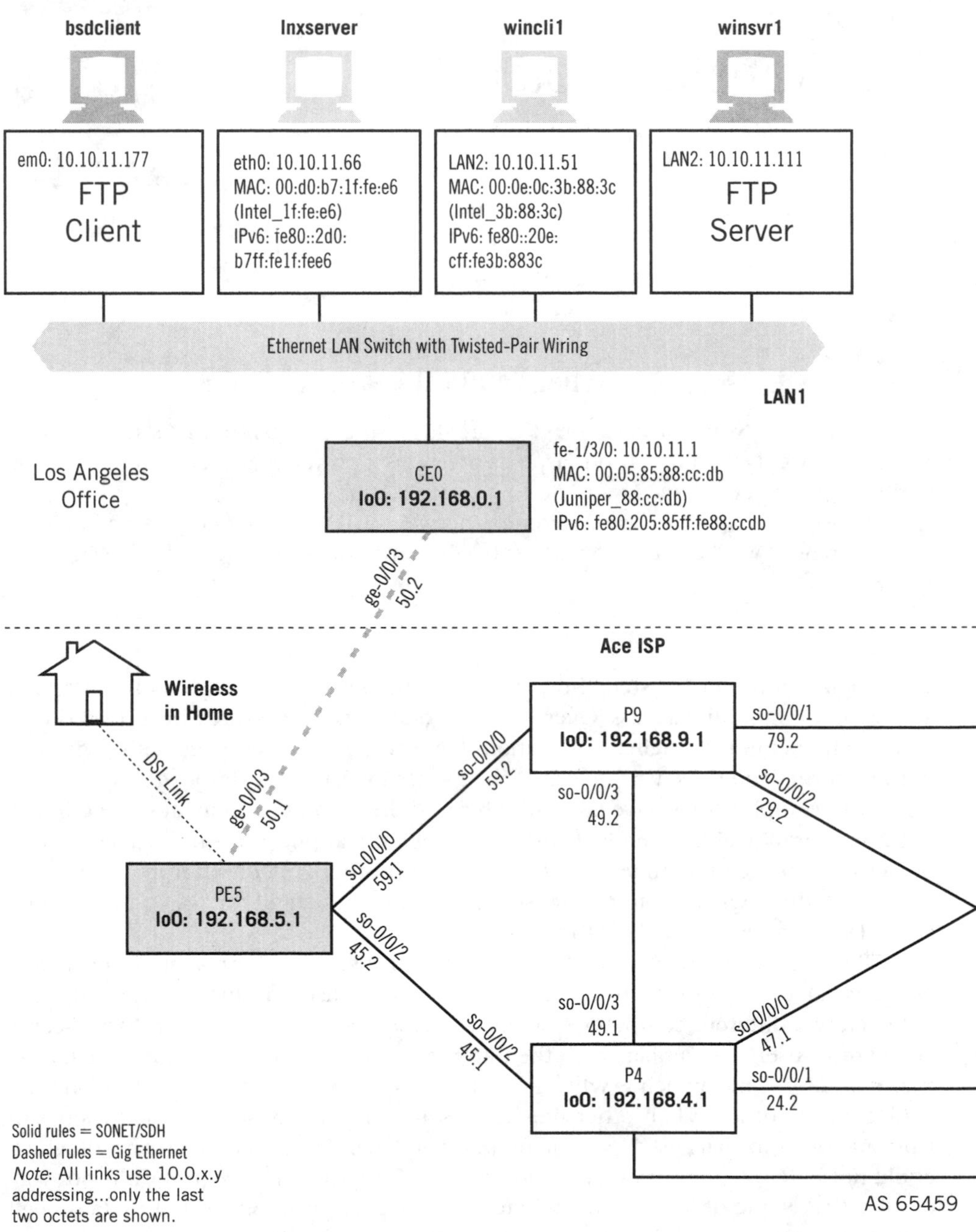

FIGURE 20.1

FTP client and servers on the Illustrated Network use Unix-based and Windows hosts.

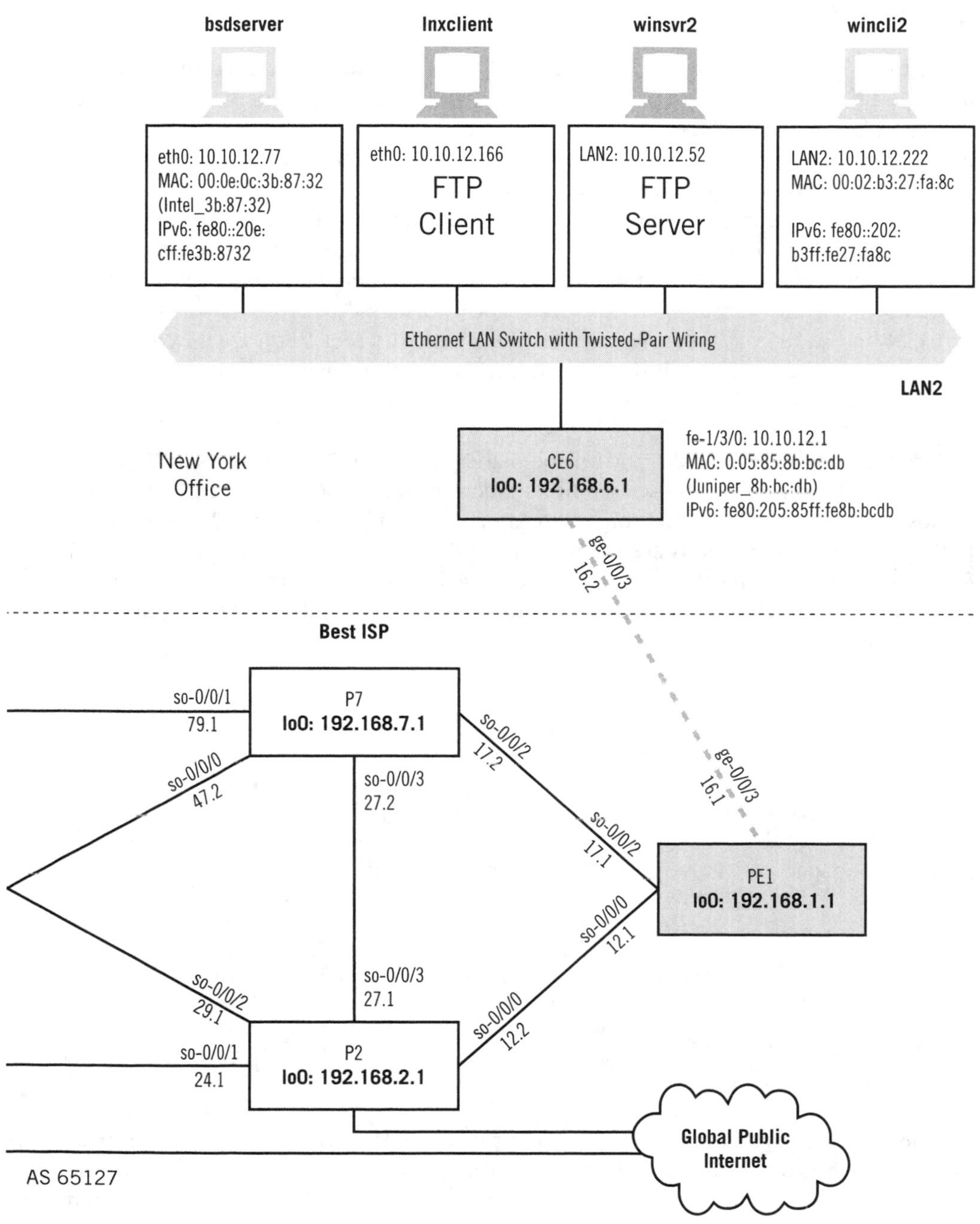
bsdserver
lnxclient
winsvr2
wincli2
eth0: 10.10.12.77
MAC: 00:0e:0c:3b:87:32
(Intel_3b:87:32)
IPv6: fe80::20e:
cff:fe3b:8732
eth0: 10.10.12.166
FTP
Client
LAN2: 10.10.12.52
FTP
Server
LAN2: 10.10.12.222
MAC: 00:02:b3:27:fa:8c
IPv6: fe80::202:
b3ff:fe27:fa8c
Ethernet LAN Switch with Twisted-Pair Wiring
LAN2
New York
Office
CE6
lo0: 192.168.6.1
fe-1/3/0: 10.10.12.1
MAC: 0:05:85:8b:bc:db
(Juniper_8b:bc:db)
IPv6: fe80:205:85ff:fe8b:bcdb
ge-0/0/3
16.2
Best ISP
so-0/0/1
79.1
P7
lo0: 192.168.7.1
so-0/0/0
47.2
so-0/0/3
27.2
so-0/0/2
17.2
ge-0/0/3
16.1
so-0/0/2
17.1
PE1
lo0: 192.168.1.1
so-0/0/0
12.1
so-0/0/2
29.1
so-0/0/3
27.1
so-0/0/0
12.2
so-0/0/1
24.1
P2
lo0: 192.168.2.1
Global Public
Internet
AS 65127

OVERVIEW

Of all the applications covered in this book, FTP is the one we've used most on the Illustrated Network. Whenever we had software to install, capture files to consolidate, or screen images to transfer, we used FTP to move them around. Every server device had a different FTP package installed, from the "native" FreeBSD and Linux CLI version to a couple of different GUI FTP servers for Windows XP.

That said, the "experimental" nature of the Illustrated Network should be noted. FTP is still useful for file transfers on the global public Internet (especially a form known as *anonymous FTP*), but in the real world it's better practice to use an authenticated form of file transfer such as SFTP or SCP (discussed at the end of this chapter). Let's take a look at how these applications look and feel. Then we'll explore the basics of FTP operation in a little more detail. This chapter makes FTP servers out of `winsrv1` and `winsrv2`. We'll access them from `bsdclient` and `lnxclient`, as shown in Figure 20.1.

The CLI versions of FTP depend on commands, of course. The GUI version depends on commands as well, but these are often hidden from the user (some show the commands executed after you click on a button or icon). This is not an FTP tutorial, and FTP application's commands are not part of the FTP protocol, but this will give a feel for the number of things FTP can do. You can look at the commands a client can use to tell the servers what to do in FreeBSD and Linux. These are the FTP `help` command listings. The following is FreeBSD:

```
bsdclient# ftp
ftp>> help
Commands may be abbreviated.  Commands are:

!          chmod       ftp     ls       msend     proxy     rhelp     system
$          close       get     macdef   newer     put       rmdir     tenex
account    cr          gate    mdelete  nlist     pwd       rstatus   trace
append     debug       glob    mdir     nmap      quit      runique   type
ascii      delete      hash    mget     ntrans    quote     send      umask
bell       dir         help    mkdir    open      recv      sendport  user
binary     disconnect  idle    mls      page      reget     site      verbose
bye        edit        image   mode     passive   rename    size      ?
case       epsv4       lcd     modtime  preserve  reset     status
cd         exit        less    more     progress  restart   struct
cdup       form        lpwd    mput     prompt    restrict  sunique
ftp>>
```

The list given by Linux is similar, but not the same. Most of the commands appear in both lists, but 6 are unique to Linux and 11 are unique to FreeBSD. Some are quite handy, such as the ability in FreeBSD's FTP to `preserve` the modification timestamp on downloaded files. Usually, the "extra" commands are used to determine how files are handled before or after they are transferred. The actual session commands are fairly consistent, and they both get the job done.

The biggest difference in FTP application-level operation is between the "regular" use of the `port` command and the use of the `passive` (PASV) command. Until recently, it was the server that supplied the port number assignment to use for the data connection and then opened the connection. But in *passive mode* the port number and open command used for the data connection is supplied by the client instead of the server, mainly to satisfy firewall rules and still allow FTP to function. We'll talk more about this later in this chapter, because it can cause problems when firewalls are in use, which should be just about always today.

First, let's see if the FreeBSD or Linux versions of Unix differ in how their FTP client implementations handle the PASV mode. In both cases, we'll fetch the same file from the FTP server running on `winsrv1`.

PORT and PASV

In both FreeBSD and Linux, passive mode is the default. The FTP passive command is a toggle that turns thc modc on and off as it is entered.

```
ftp> passive
Passive mode off.
ftp> passive
Passive mode on.
ftp>
```

The following shows a little 30,000-byte file called `testfile.zip` from the CLI on FreeBSD and Linux. This example uses a plain text password, but only for instructional purposes.

```
bsdclient# ftp
ftp> open 10.10.11.111
Connected to 10.10.11.111.
220 Fastream NETFile FTP Server Ready
Name (10.10.11.111:admin): walter
331 Password required for walter.
Password: (not shown)
230 User walter logged in.
Remote system type is UNIX.
Using binary mode to transfer files.
ftp> get testfile.zip
local: testfile.zip remote: testfile.zip
227 Entering Passive Mode (10,10,11,111,7,69).
150 Opening data connection for testfile.zip.
100%
|***************************************************************************
**************************| 30642       00:00 ETA
226 File sent ok
30642 bytes received in 0.10 seconds (306.08 KB/s)
ftp>
```

FTP Features

Most features that you get by default in some FTP applications (such as the transfer progress "tick marks") must be explicitly turned on in other FTP implementations.

We like the fact that the client shows we are in passive mode and tells me the port number I'm going to use to open the data connection to the server. We also like the tick mark progress bar and the statistics displayed. Let's look at what we get in Linux:

```
[root @lnxclient admin]# ftp
ftp> open 10.10.11.111
Connected to 10.10.11.111.
220 Fastream NETFile FTP Server Ready
500 'AUTH': command not understood.
500 'AUTH': command not understood.
KERBEROS_V4 rejected as an authentication type
Name (10.10.11.111:admin): walter
331 Password required for walter.
Password: (not shown)
230 User walter logged in.
Remote system type is UNIX.
Using binary mode to transfer files.
ftp> get testfile.zip
local: testfile.zip remote: testfile.zip
227 Entering Passive Mode (10,10,11,111,7,80).
150 Opening data connection for testfile.zip.
226 File sent ok
30642 bytes received in 0.0065 seconds (4.6e+03 Kbytes/s)
ftp>
```

Linux is more terse and tries to use Kerberos (a more secure authentication method), going back to simple userID and password only when it has to. We are comparing variants of the default FTP client on these systems rather than something built into the systems themselves or a high-quality FTP application. However, we'll look at the packet capture as well.

Let's see what these exchanges look like when captured by Ethereal. Figure 20.2 shows the packets from the time the user logs into the server until that data connection is used.

It is reassuring to note that the client does indeed use the port expected by the server (7 × 256 = 1792 + 98 = 1890), although the port is not in the currently accepted range for these ports. Figure 20.3 shows the same using the Linux client.

As expected with an application as widely used and as venerable as FTP, there are only a few differences here and there. Note that the Windows XP file server identifies

No.	Time	Source	Destination	Protocol	Info
12	5.684289	10.10.11.111	10.10.11.177	FTP	Response: 230 User walter logged in.
13	5.684326	10.10.11.177	10.10.11.111	FTP	Request: SYST
14	5.685414	10.10.11.111	10.10.11.177	FTP	Response: 215 UNIX Type: L8 Internet Component Suite
15	5.780771	10.10.11.177	10.10.11.111	TCP	3482 > ftp [ACK] Seq=35 Ack=147 Win=57920 [CHECKSUM INCORRECT] Len=0
16	14.698100	10.10.11.177	10.10.11.111	FTP	Request: TYPE I
17	14.699351	10.10.11.111	10.10.11.177	FTP	Response: 200 Type set to I.
18	14.699371	10.10.11.177	10.10.11.111	FTP	Request: SIZE testfile.zip
19	14.701099	10.10.11.111	10.10.11.177	FTP	Response: 213 30642
20	14.701151	10.10.11.177	10.10.11.111	FTP	Request: EPSV
21	14.702099	10.10.11.111	10.10.11.177	FTP	Response: 500 'EPSV': command not understood.
22	14.702115	10.10.11.177	10.10.11.111	FTP	Request: PASV
23	14.718089	10.10.11.111	10.10.11.177	FTP	Response: 227 Entering Passive Mode (10,10,11,111,7,98).
24	14.718147	10.10.11.177	10.10.11.111	TCP	1399 > 1890 [SYN] Seq=0 Ack=0 Win=57344 [CHECKSUM INCORRECT] Len=0 MS
25	14.718464	10.10.11.111	10.10.11.177	TCP	1890 > 1399 [SYN, ACK] Seq=0 Ack=1 Win=64512 Len=0 MSS=1460 WS=0 TSV=
26	14.718473	10.10.11.177	10.10.11.111	TCP	1399 > 1890 [ACK] Seq=1 Ack=1 Win=57920 [CHECKSUM INCORRECT] Len=0 TS
27	14.718491	10.10.11.177	10.10.11.111	FTP	Request: RETR testfile.zip
28	14.721213	10.10.11.111	10.10.11.177	FTP	Response: 150 Opening data connection for testfile.zip.
29	14.733956	10.10.11.111	10.10.11.177	FTP-DA1	FTP Data: 1448 bytes

```
▷ Frame 23 (114 bytes on wire, 114 bytes captured)
▷ Ethernet II, Src: 00:0e:0c:3b:87:36, Dst: 00:0e:0c:3b:8f:94
▷ Internet Protocol, Src Addr: 10.10.11.111 (10.10.11.111), Dst Addr: 10.10.11.177 (10.10.11.177)
▷ Transmission Control Protocol, Src Port: ftp (21), Dst Port: 3482 (3482), Seq: 215, Ack: 74, Len: 48
▽ File Transfer Protocol (FTP)
  ▷ 227 Entering Passive Mode (10,10,11,111,7,98).\r\n
```

FIGURE 20.2

FTP passive using FreeBSD, showing that the client initiates the data connection.

No.	Time	Source	Destination	Protocol	Info
15	6.651598	10.10.11.111	10.10.12.166	FTP	Response: 230 User walter logged in.
16	6.651766	10.10.12.166	10.10.11.111	TCP	33370 > ftp [ACK] Seq=60 Ack=177 Win=5840 Len=0 TSV=1529423567 TSER=2
17	6.651830	10.10.12.166	10.10.11.111	FTP	Request: SYST
18	6.661275	10.10.11.111	10.10.12.166	FTP	Response: 215 UNIX Type: L8 Internet Component Suite
19	6.699748	10.10.12.166	10.10.11.111	TCP	33370 > ftp [ACK] Seq=66 Ack=221 Win=5840 Len=0 TSV=1529423572 TSER=2
20	17.942524	10.10.12.166	10.10.11.111	FTP	Request: TYPE I
21	17.943808	10.10.11.111	10.10.12.166	FTP	Response: 200 Type set to I.
22	17.943983	10.10.12.166	10.10.11.111	TCP	33370 > ftp [ACK] Seq=74 Ack=241 Win=5840 Len=0 TSV=1529424696 TSER=2
23	17.944064	10.10.12.166	10.10.11.111	FTP	Request: PASV
24	17.957221	10.10.11.111	10.10.12.166	FTP	Response: 227 Entering Passive Mode (10,10,11,111,7,89).
25	17.957521	10.10.12.166	10.10.11.111	TCP	33371 > 1881 [SYN] Seq=0 Ack=0 Win=5840 Len=0 MSS=1460 TSV=1529424697
26	17.957834	10.10.11.111	10.10.12.166	TCP	1881 > 33371 [SYN, ACK] Seq=0 Ack=1 Win=64512 Len=0 MSS=1460 WS=0 TSV
27	17.957863	10.10.12.166	10.10.11.111	TCP	33371 > 1881 [ACK] Seq=1 Ack=1 Win=5840 Len=0 TSV=1529424697 TSER=0
28	17.958059	10.10.12.166	10.10.11.111	FTP	Request: RETR testfile.zip
29	17.963755	10.10.11.111	10.10.12.166	FTP	Response: 150 Opening data connection for testfile.zip.
30	17.966947	10.10.11.111	10.10.12.166	FTP-DA1	FTP Data: 1448 bytes
31	17.966951	10.10.11.111	10.10.12.166	FTP-DA1	FTP Data: 12 bytes
32	17.967154	10.10.11.111	10.10.12.166	FTP-DA1	FTP Data: 1448 bytes

```
▷ Frame 24 (114 bytes on wire, 114 bytes captured)
▷ Ethernet II, Src: 00:05:85:8b:bc:db, Dst: 00:b0:d0:45:34:64
▷ Internet Protocol, Src Addr: 10.10.11.111 (10.10.11.111), Dst Addr: 10.10.12.166 (10.10.12.166)
▷ Transmission Control Protocol, Src Port: ftp (21), Dst Port: 33370 (33370), Seq: 241, Ack: 80, Len: 48
▽ File Transfer Protocol (FTP)
  ▷ 227 Entering Passive Mode (10,10,11,111,7,89).\r\n
```

FIGURE 20.3

FTP passive using Linux. The port numbers are more in line with current practice.

itself as a "Unix Type" file server. FreeBSD tries an initial `EPSV`, the RFC 2428 extended passive command for IPv6, and network address translation (NAT) environments and FTP. (We'll talk all about `EPSV` later in the chapter.) It then uses, as Linux does from the start, the `PASV` command.

Linux is more in line with current client port usage conventions, using 33371 rather than FreeBSD, which still is using four-digit port numbers. In both cases, the data transfer does not use the well-known port 20 on the server side.

FTP AND GUIS

When it comes to Windows, `winsrv1` is running the FTP package Fastream and `winsrv2` is running FileZilla. We had no familiarity with these packages: they were just the first "shareware" ones we found when looking on the Web. Again, given the history of vulnerabilities in FTP servers and the possible consequences of having a server subverted you should not run random FTP software found on the Internet except in tightly controlled circumstances like these.

The Fastream NETFile FTP server is also an HTTP Web server and is free for personal use. It has a nice logging capability, which can display on-screen and save to a file at the same time. This is shown in Figure 20.4.

FileZilla has the most impressive array of log-in variations, as shown in Figure 20.5. We'll say more about SSL and SSH in later chapters. SFTP solves many of the problems running FTP with tunnels and NAT can cause.

In addition, almost all Web browsers can handle FTP as well as HTTP, the Web protocol. This is part of the "universal client" role of the browser.

For example, if we use the Web browser on `winsrv1` to "visit" the FTP server on `winsrv2` (`ftp://winsrv2`), we are still asked to log in (no anonymous user is defined on `winsrv2`, but if it had been, no log-in screen would appear. The log-in request is shown in Figure 20.6.

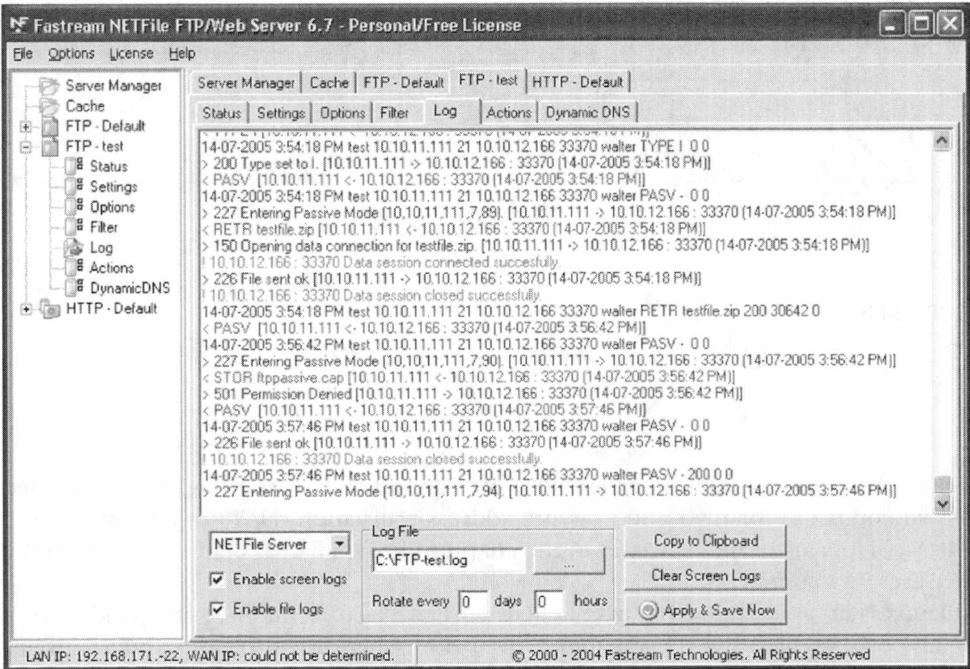

FIGURE 20.4

Fastream FTP logging. Note the amount of detail provided.

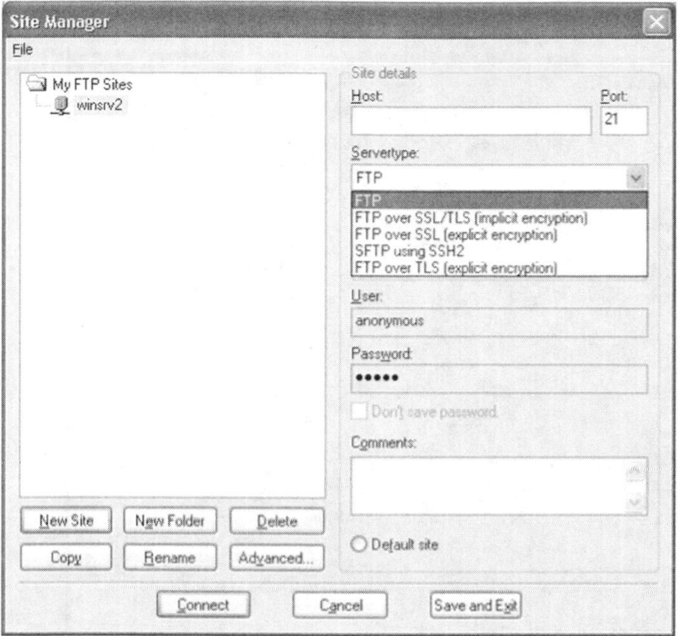

FIGURE 20.5

FileZilla FTP log-in variations. SFTP is part of SSH2, but is a separate protocol.

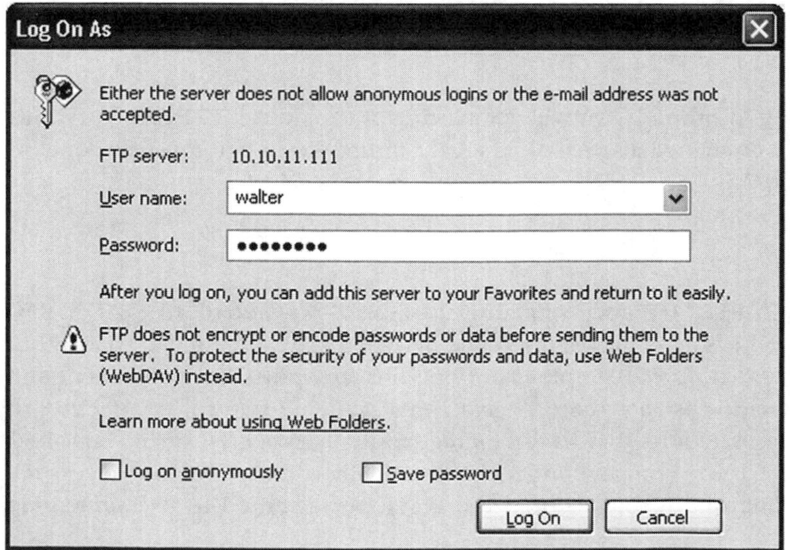

FIGURE 20.6

FTP browser log-in screen, showing how verbose a GUI can be compared to CLI implementations.

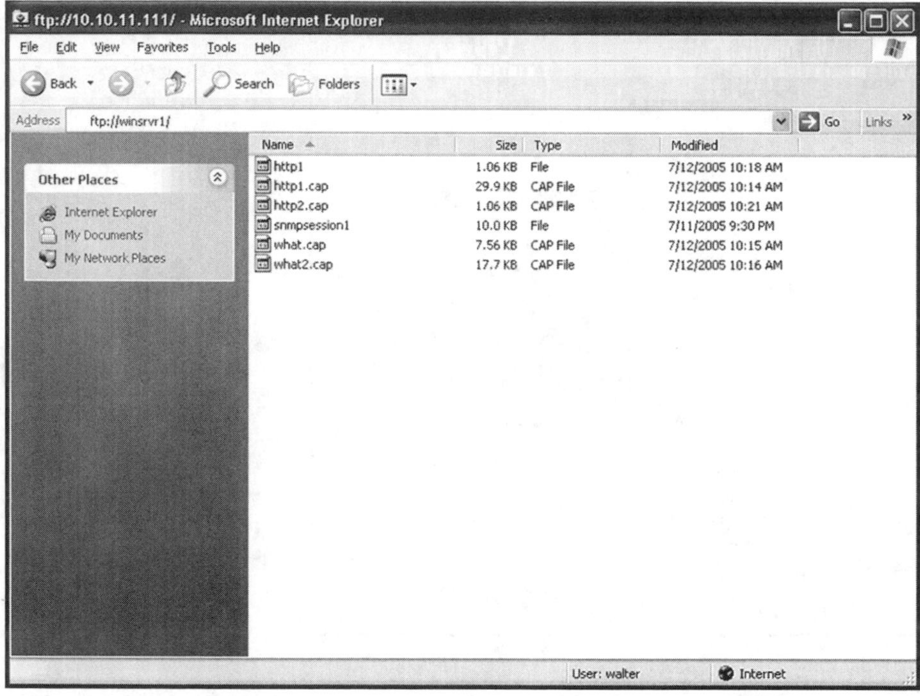

FIGURE 20.7

Browser FTP listing, showing how a browser can act as a "universal client."

But once we log in properly, we will get a listing of the default FTP directory. This directly, `C:\NFRoot`, contained a series of Ethereal capture files when this was done (as shown in Figure 20.7).

FTP Basics

FTP was defined in RFC 959 and updated in RFC 2228, RFC 2640, RFC 2773, RFC 3659 and several others. One major difference between FTP and almost every other application is the fact that FTP employs not one but *two* ports between client and server. One explanation is that there is always an available control connection to quickly countermand actions that have unintended or unexpected results. But RFC 959 simply notes that the control connection essentially uses the remote access telnet protocol, leading one to believe that the developers wanted to use something already existing.

The FTP control connection is set up in the usual client-server fashion. That is, an FTP server process (such as ftpd) is listening for clients' connection requests. The number of simultaneous clients an FTP server can accept varies and is usually a configurable parameter, but limits well above 100 are not unusual.

The FTP server requires a log-in from the user, and in many cases servers will allow a special log-in for *anonymous FTP.* The user is supposed to use their email address as a password, a primitive auditing measure. Anonymous FTP implementations used to allow users to simply press Enter and leave the anonymous password field blank, but many FTP implementations now demand at least something at the password prompt. Some do not allow more creative substitutes for an email address, and many FTP servers check for things such as the presence of dots and the at sign (@) to try to enforce some semblance of honesty. In many cases, the FTP server will accept a similar term such as `guest` or `visitor`. The point behind anonymous FTP is that users are not required to have a valid user ID or password on the remote system in order to be able to access files in some directories.

Of course, there are file areas on the FTP server that should only be accessed by authenticated users of the remote system. Private IDs can be combined with anonymous FTP to protect certain areas of the file system while allowing public access to others. Of course, this does not stop people from *trying* to access files they had no business seeing, but if the file system permissions are set up correctly (or at all), FTP is highly secure. However, the best way to prevent access to sensitive files is *not* to put them on an FTP server with public access in the first place.

The well-known port of the control connection is TCP port 21. The client runs the FTP client program and uses an ephemeral port to begin the interaction with the server. This connection asks for the user ID and password, anonymous or not, and is nothing more than a normal remote log-in session using the Telnet application.

Once logged in, the user is placed in a default file system directory. Navigation outside this directory might be permitted, but usually there's a good reason to direct a user to this particular directory, and thus outside access should be unnecessary.

FTP Commands and Reply Codes

Users are sometimes surprised to see that FTP employs a very rich protocol all by itself. When run in interactive mode from the command line, FTP supplies its own prompt (like DNS) and supplies users with return codes for everything they type in.

The client and server have a conversation over the control connection, with the user at the client typing simple commands and sending them to the server process over the control connection. Some of the more common and helpful FTP commands are outlined in Table 20.1. These are the commands users type. But FTP sends four-character representations of these commands. For example, a `get` is a `RETR` (retrieve) and a `put` is `STOR` (store).

The server receives the command, takes the appropriate action (if allowed), and returns a numeric reply code. The reply codes are translated by the FTP client into text that can be understood easily and displayed at the prompt. The displayed text can vary from system to system because each FTP client implementation is free to interpret the reply codes, within reason, and display that text to the user. The meanings of the first and second digits of the reply codes are outlined in Table 20.2.

The third digit adds details. For example, the reply code `500` means that there is a syntax error and an unrecognized command has been sent to the server. The reply

Table 20.1 Common FTP Commands[a]

Command	Meaning
Open	Create an FTP connection between the two hosts.
Close	Close an FTP connection between two hosts.
Bye	End the FTP session.
Get	Retrieve a remote file from the remote host.
Put	Store a file on the remote host.
Mget	Get multiple files using wildcards (for example, mget a* fetches all files that being with the letter "a" in the current directory).
Mput	Put multiple files on the remote host using wildcards.
Glob	Enable wildcard interpretation. This is usually on by default.
Ascii	The file transferred is in ASCII representation (a common default).
Binary	The file is in image (binary) format (sometimes the default), and is useful for programs and formatted word processing files.
Cd	Change the directory on the remote host.
Dir	Get a directory listing from the remote host.
Ldir	Get a directory listing from the local host.
Hash	Display hash marks (dots) to show file transfer progress.

[a] *These commands are not part of the FTP protocol.*

code `501` means the syntax error is in the command arguments. If the reply code generates more than one line at the client (for example, if the valid arguments are listed), the reply code appears on the first line with a hyphen and is repeated at the end of the text.

The user then can type in another command. Common FTP replies, including the text that could be displayed with them, are:

- 125 Data connection open and transfer starting
- 200 Command okay
- 214 Help message (text follows)
- 331 User name okay, password required
- 425 Unable to open data connection
- 452 Error writing file
- 500 Command syntax error
- 501 Argument syntax error

Sessions end with the user typing `bye` or `quit` at the FTP prompt. The server should respond with a `221` reply, usually displayed as `221 Goodbye`. In some cases, the server

Table 20.2 FTP Protocol Reply Codes

Reply	Meaning
1xx	Positive response, but preliminary. Action begun, but wait for another reply before sending further commands.
2xx	Positive completion. New commands can be sent.
3xx	Positive response, but intermediate. Command accepted, but another command is required to complete the action.
4xx	Negative reply, but transient. Action did not take place, but the condition is temporary and the same command can be used again.
5xx	Negative reply, permanent. Action did not take place, and cannot be done. The command should not be sent again in that form.
x0x	Syntax error.
x1x	Information.
x2x	Reply refers to control or data connections.
x3x	Reply refers to authenticating and accounting commands, such as login.
x4x	Unspecified.
x5x	File system status information.

simply disappears, and one client we've used groused in the session log `You could at least say Goodbye`. But it is a sign of the robustness and stability of FTP that such breaches of protocol seldom mean that things do not work properly overall.

One advantage of running FTP from the command line instead of from a GUI is that the user can type in the entire array of FTP commands, which typically number 50 or more. GUI point-and-click clients can be prettier and easier, but do not always implement the full suite of FTP commands. (Some of the commands are seldom used or necessary today, such as `glob`, but might come in handy in certain situations.)

FTP Data Transfers

At some point in the FTP conversation between client and server port 21, the user will use a command that will trigger a file transfer. The transfer might not be the actual file itself, such as with `get` or `put`. Often, the user requests a file directory listing from the present working directory on the server with the `dir` command, usually to ensure that the desired file is there or to check the spelling after the first transfer attempt has failed. These actions require the server to set up an FTP *data connection*. (The control connection is just a Telnet remote access session and is inappropriate for bulk data transfer anyway.) The FTP model of control and data connections is shown in Figure 20.8.

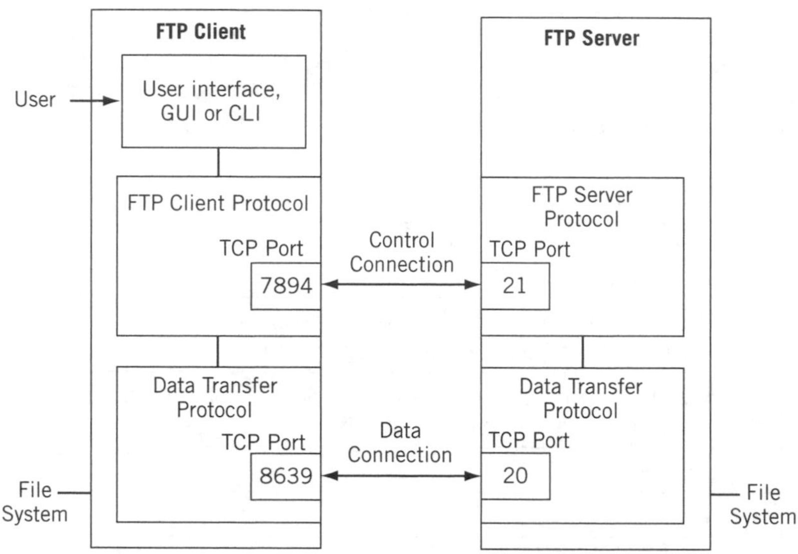

FIGURE 20.8

FTP control and data connections, showing how both are used in an FTP application.

Consider what happens when a user at an FTP client types in the dir command to receive a list of the contents of the remote host's directory. This requires the establishment of a data connection on the part of the server. The server normally uses well-known TCP port 20 as the server end of the data connection. But how does the client know which ephemeral port to listen on for the data?

The server sends an FTP `PORT` command over the control connection to the client with this information. This tells the client which port should be used at the client end for the data connection. So that there is no misunderstanding, the server includes the client's IP address as well. Thus, the command really supplies socket information. The PORT command is sent over the control connection and is formatted as if it were data to appear on a Telnet terminal, including control characters such as `\n` (new line).

The port number is expressed as two independent numbers. The first is multiplied by 256 and added to the second (which must be in the range 0–255) to give the client's port number. So, if the PORT command ends with the numbers `14, 234` (excluding the control characters) the port number the client should use for the data connection is 3818 ($14 \times 256 = 3584 + 234 = 3818$).

The client issues a passive open on port 3818, and the FTP server now sends a TCP SYN message to open the TCP session and send the `dir` listing as requested. The server usually closes the data connection as soon as the transfer is complete.

The control connection process of obtaining a simple `dir` listing from a remote FTP server is shown in Figure 20.9. Note that the client issues FTP commands and the server replies with codes.

The activity on the data connection is shown in Figure 20.10. Although in many cases the data connection uses well-known port 20 on the server, it does not have to.

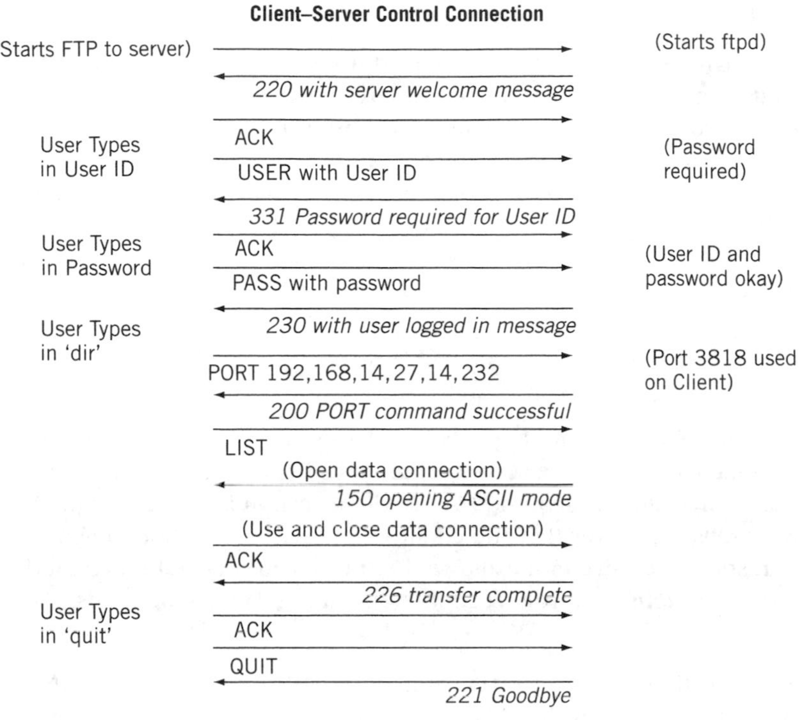

FIGURE 20.9

FTP control connection, showing how a directory listing proceeds.

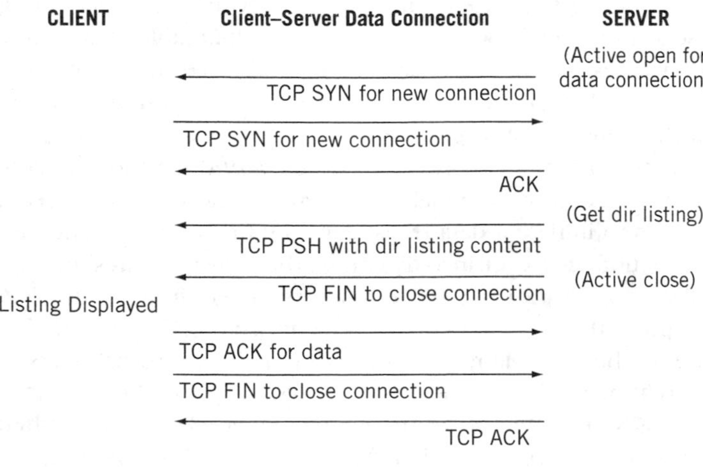

FIGURE 20.10

FTP data connection. The connection does not have to use port 20 on the server.

Passive and Port

Using the PORT command is not the only way the port used for the FTP data connection is determined. Today, the PORT command is considered in many cases to be an unacceptable security risk to an organization. This is because the PORT command requires an external FTP server to open a connection *to* an internal client. It is possible for a firewall to support incoming TCP connections for FTP, but with the common use of network address translation (see Chapter 27) it is simpler to use passive. (In larger installations using firewalls and NAT, collisions among the incoming port numbers are common anyway.)

FTP Passive

FTP supports two different methods of data connection establishment. In the normal *active* mode using PORT, the server (1) initiates the data connection, then (2) the client asks for a data transfer and (3) the client responds. In *passive* mode (PASV), the client tells the server that the client will initiate the data connection and the server responds. Passive mode allows the transfer to proceed when modern client devices are prohibited from accepting incoming data connections.

Consider the implication for a user sitting at a client host on a corporate LAN. We haven't talked about security in any detail, but in many cases the company will employ a *firewall* between internal LANs and the external world of the Internet. The firewall's job is to prevent malicious hackers or their code from attacking the hosts on the internal network.

One of the ways firewalls do this is to prevent any outside devices from establishing TCP connections to any internal client hosts on the LAN (publicly accessed servers are typically isolated, physically and logically, from purely internal hosts). Hosts accepting outside connections are seen, from the firewall's perspective, as vulnerable to any number of malicious worms or viruses. Many inexpensive firewalls also see an external FTP server's attempt to establish a TCP data connection to the client as a potential hostile attack. This attempt is blocked, and the transfer fails.

The PASV command reverses the procedure, and lets the *client* open the data connection to the server. Figure 20.11 shows the major difference between a client using the POST and PASV commands to initiate a data transfer. In both cases, the client uses port 4122 for the data connection. However, in active mode the *server* initiates the data connection and uses well-known port 20. In passive mode, the client initiates the data connection and listens on port 2020 instead of 20 for the connection.

However, all might still not be well. Many firewalls will not allow internal hosts to open connections to external ports that are not well known. After all, the malicious user could be on the local LAN and attacking someone else remotely. So, even when PASV is used the data connection set up might still fail.

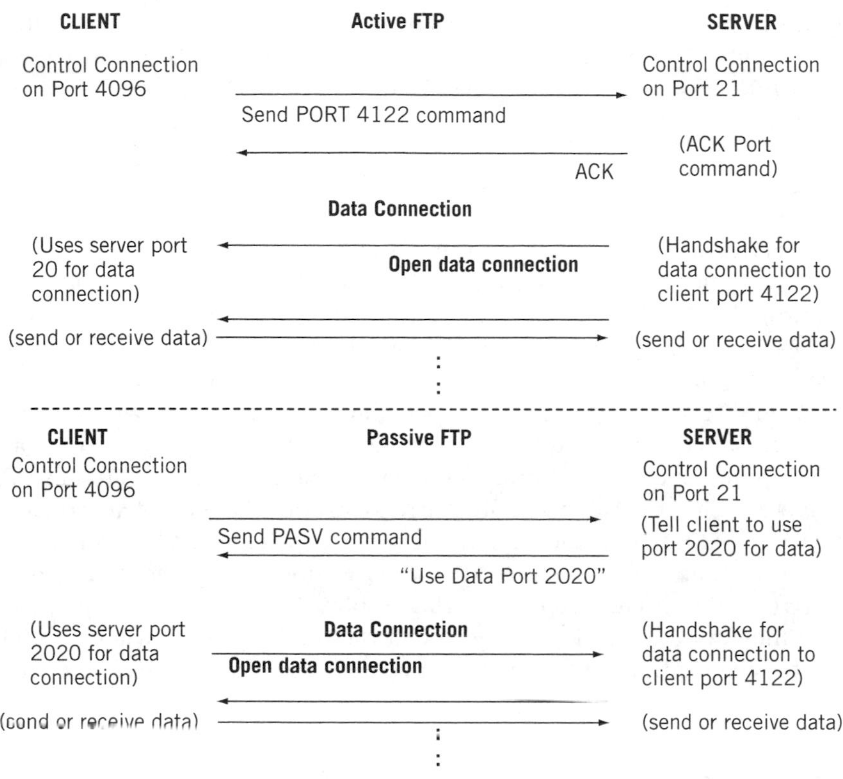

FIGURE 20.11

FTP active and passive. Note which side opens the data connection and which ports are used in each case.

More state-of-the-art firewalls will look at more than just TCP or UDP headers and can figure out that an FTP session is in progress. Many will only allow ports from a certain preconfigured pool to be used, but there is a lot of variation in implementation.

RFC 2428 defines the `EPRT` and `EPSV` commands to be used when IPv6 addresses and NAT is in use. Some FTP implementations use these forms of `PORT` and `PASS` by default. Network address translation can be particularly harsh on FTP because addresses can change. Some applications, such as FTP, send IP address and protocol ports inside messages as data. Unless NAT can change the addresses in the data stream to agree with its other changes, the application will fail. We'll talk more about NAT in a later chapter, but a full discussion of the interplay of NAT and FTP is beyond the scope of this book.

Sometimes the FTP application tries to get into the act and imposes certain conventions on the user. One FTP implementation insists on using `PASV` when it finds that private IPv4 addresses are being used, presumably because private addresses are only used behind a firewall or when NAT is used. This particular form of FTP also insists that the user enter the public "WAN" address space used, which can be problematic when a purely private TCP/IP network such as the Illustrated Network is being used! (Needless to say, this application was not very useful on the Illustrated Network.)

File Transfer Types

What about the actual files that can be transferred from server to client or from client to server? The original FTP specification listed multiple options as to file type, embedded control characters, structure, and transmission mode. In those days, there were many types of computer architectures. Today, those choices usually boil down to exactly two: `ascii` and `binary`. Either one can be the implementation default, but as time goes on, pure text files using ASCII are becoming rarer and rarer, whereas files with executable code and embedded HTML formatting are becoming more and more common. FTP helpfully puts in line formatting control characters if they are missing when performing an `ascii` transfer. Naturally, this renders code files completely useless (although many newer FTP-based applications make this much less of a concern).

Unless there is a compelling reason to do otherwise, most FTP transfers are better off using `binary` (the file is transferred as a string of bits, and FTP makes no effort to figure out what they mean). This doesn't mean that the transferred file will be useful, but it has a better chance than a file of program code transferred as a text note with `ascii`.

When Things Go Wrong

There is a huge benefit to keeping FTP data transfers off the control connection. The use of two connections allows users to abort a file transfer that is unintended or out of control (a misformed `mget` is usually the culprit). When the client is storing a file on a server, the use of the control connection is straightforward: The client stops sending data and sends an `ABOR` command to the sender on the control connection. The interrupt key is usually `cntl-C`, but others are possible depending on operating system. The `ABOR` command is sent as urgent TCP data to make sure it is handled promptly by the server.

When the server receives the `ABOR` command on the control connection, it should respond with 426 (transfer aborted) and 226 (abort successful) messages. The data transfer might continue sending data, and typically does, but the client will not acknowledge it and ignores everything received after the user abort.

There are only a few other things that can go wrong with FTP. A common mistake is to transfer binary files as text, and some FTP servers will warn the user if the file extension seems to indicate this might be going to happen. Other servers assume that users know what they are doing and simply perform the transfer.

There are two other parameters dealing with file transfer in FTP that can be changed and might cause problems when multiple files are transferred without restoring the settings. One is the *file-structure*. A transfer can use *file-structure* (the name is unfortunate) or *record-structure*. File-structure, the usual default, makes no assumptions about the file at all and simply views the content as a string of bytes. Record-structure, rarely used today, means that there is a record format to the file and is set by sending the `STRU R` command to the other host.

Even when the record-structure is set for the transfer, the actual formatting of the data depends on another setting—this one is called the *transmission mode*. Modes can be *stream* (the typical default), *block*, and *compressed*. The three modes combine with the file-structure to give four types of file transfer formatting.

Stream mode with file-structure—The file is set as a stream of bytes, and TCP provides data integrity. No headers or delimiters are inserted into the data stream, and the end of the transferred file is only indicated by closing the data connection normally. This is the most common way in which FTP works on the Internet today.

Stream mode with record-structure—The file is sent as a string of records, each one delimited by a 2-byte End of Record (EOR) control code (`0xFF01`). An End of File (EOF) code, `0xFF02` (or sometimes `0xFF03`), is used to indicate the end of the file to the receiver.

Block mode—The file is sent as a series of data blocks. Each block begins with a 3-byte header containing some descriptor flags and a 2-byte length field giving the block byte count. Flags are used to indicate EOR, EOF, and restart.

Compressed mode—Rarely supported today because modern compression methods have superseded this primitive function. The file is sent after removing repeated string of bytes. Today, files are compressed outside FTP and sent as `binary` data.

Finally, many FTP server implementations routinely check the domain name of the client to make sure it is valid before allowing the connection. Reverse DNS, as this is called, is not a robust security feature, and at times has caused problems as well on the network. Hackers can easily use phony IP addresses, the theory goes, but it's more difficult (and foolish) to map it to a public domain name and distribute the information by registering on the public DNS. This was a problem with some early Illustrated Network file transfers because no DNS was running on the network at all, and even when it was no Illustrated Network domain names were registered on the Internet. But "dumber" FTP versions worked just fine with only IP addresses.

FTP COMMANDS

One of the things that surprises people when they examine traces of FTP activity is that the FTP commands sent and received by client and server are not the same as the ones entered by the user at the client. We've already looked at some examples (cntl-C sends an `ABORT`), but maybe it's a good idea to look at them in more detail.

Table 20.3 FTP Commands for File Server Access with Meaning and Parameters

Command	Meaning	Parameter(s)
USER	User ID	User ID
PASS	User password	Password itself
ACCT	Provide an account for charging purposes	Account ID
REIN	Reinitialize to the start state	None
QUIT	End and log out	None
ABORT	Abort previous command and any file transfer	None

Table 20.4 FTP Commands for Remote Server File Management with Meaning and Parameters

Command	Meaning	Parameter(s)
CWD	Change to another directory	Directory path
CDUP	Change to the parent directory	None
DELE	Delete a file	File name
LIST	List file information	None, or directory name, or list of files
MKD	Make a directory	Directory name
NLST	List the files in a directory	None for current directory, or name
PWD	Show the name of the current working directory	None
RMD	Remove a directory	Directory name
RNFR	Rename a file (references current name)	Current file name
RNTO	Rename a file (references new name)	New file name
SMNT	Mount a different file system	File system identifier
ABORT	Abort previous command and any file transfer	None

Clients and servers do not have to implement all of the FTP commands, which are often added to. What happens if a server requires the user at the client to use an FTP command the client implementation does not support? A thorough client will implement the `quote` user command, which lets the user enter the exact formal command (and any parameters) necessary to continue. The input is then sent over the control connection exactly as entered.

The six FTP commands that control a user's access to a remote file server are outlined in Table 20.3. The 11 FTP commands that control a user's file access and management functions on the remote file server are outlined in Table 20.4. The working directory is the current directory.

Table 20.5 FTP Commands for Transfer Parameters, with Meaning and Parameters

Command	Meaning	Parameter(s)
TYPE	Identify the file type for transfer	A (ASCII), E (EBCDIC), I (binary image), N (nonprint), T (telnet), C (ASA)
STRU	File structure	F (file) or R (record)
MODE	Format used for transmission	S (stream), B (block), C (compressed)

Table 20.6 FTP Commands for File Transfer, with Meaning and Parameters

Command	Meaning	Parameter(s)
ALLO	Allocate enough space for the data to come	Integer number of bytes
APPE	Append a local file to the remote file	File names
EPSV	The extended version (RFC 2428) of the PASV command, used for IPv6 and NAT	IP address and port
EPRT	The extended version (RFC 2428) of the PORT command, used for IPv6 and NAT	IP address and port
PASV	Supply the network address and port number that will be used for the data connection initiated by the client	IP address and port
PORT	Supply the network address and port number that will be used for the data connection initiated by the server	IP address and port
REST	Identify a restart marker (followed by the transfer command to be restarted)	Marker value
RETR	Get (retrieve) a file	File name(s)
STOR	Put (store) a file	File name(s)
STOU	Create a version of the file with a unique name (store unique)	File name

The three FTP commands that set the type, structure, and mode of the file transfer are outlined in Table 20.5. The 10 FTP commands that actually control the file transfer are outlined in Table 20.6. Finally, the five FTP commands outlined in Table 20.7 supply useful information to the user.

Variations on a Theme

Few people use the command line interface for FTP unless they have to. However, it is common to use the CLI for instructional purposes (as done here). But today almost all FTP client software, and many servers, use GUI interfaces to let users simply point and

Table 20.7 FTP Commands for User Information, with Meaning and Parameters

Command	Meaning	Parameter(s)
HELP	Gives information about server implementation	None
NOOP	Request "OK" reply from server	None
SITE	Used in the popular WU-FTP implementation from Washington University (used in many Linux versions) to engage server-specific commands not in the FTP standard	None
SYST	Requests that the server identify its OS version	None
STAT	Request connection status and parameter information from server	None

click at directories and files and effect a transfer. Almost all still allow users to watch the interplay between mouse strokes and FTP commands and response codes, but few pay attention to them unless things go wrong.

GUI implementations of FTP tend to be much more sophisticated than their CLI cousins, especially when it comes to security variations. The heavy use of security on modern networks has spawned many variations of the simple FTP control and data connection process. Most of these variations have to do with how the user ID and password are packaged and sent from client to server, but some are more far-reaching than that. Many commercial FTP server implementations can be set up to function in any of the following environments:

- Simple FTP
- FTP over Secure Sockets Layer and Transport Layer Security (SSL/TLS), using implicit encryption
- FTP over SSL/TLS using explicit encryption
- FTP over TLS directly, using explicit encryption
- FTP bypassing the firewall

We'll have much more to say about these security variations later in this book. There is also Secure FTP (SFTP), a feature of Secure Shell 2 (SSH2). But this is a completely different protocol than FTP, as we'll see in Chapter 25 (on SSH).

A Note on NFS

If TCP/IP is indeed for everything, an employee at a branch bank should be able to use common TCP/IP applications to change a customer's information in the central bank's database. However, it makes no sense at all to access the master account file, transfer a copy of it to the branch host, update it, and then load it back up to the central location. Not only does this method transfer masses of information *not* needed, but it prevents (hopefully) anyone else from updating any other customer record at the same time.

Many applications don't want or need remote file *transfer*. They just need remote file *access*, usually to a particular record or even field. This is the idea behind the Network File System (NFS), pioneered by Sun Microsystems. NFS allows local file systems to be accessed by remote users as if they were local users and is a nice illustration of the power and utility of the socket interface.

NFS is actually part of an overall system that includes an extension of the socket concept known as remote procedure calls (RPCs). RPCs are a more sophisticated way of handling basic programming subroutine (or function) calls by allowing the subprogram (the procedure) to be called on a remote system across a network (hence the term *remote procedure call*).

RPCs do not use well-known ports. RPC server processes handle RPC client requests for server connections by *dynamically mapping* the server ports. In dynamic mapping, all connection requests handled by TCP go to *one* server process running at the application layer instead of several. This server process is capable of dynamically starting up the correct port server application process and allowing the TCP protocol to grant the connection. The single server application process running under dynamic mapping is known as the *port mapper*. These port mappers (usually run as the `rpcbind` process) are very common on most Unix implementations of TCP/IP.

Another part of the NFS is the External Data Representation (XDR) standard, a way of defining data types in terms of standard formats. The point is to allow remote file access between different platforms, from Unix to Windows to MACs and even more. NFS has been a part of the overall TCP/IP standardization process since 1998.

QUESTIONS FOR READERS

Figure 20.12 shows some of the concepts discussed in this chapter and can be used to answer the following questions.

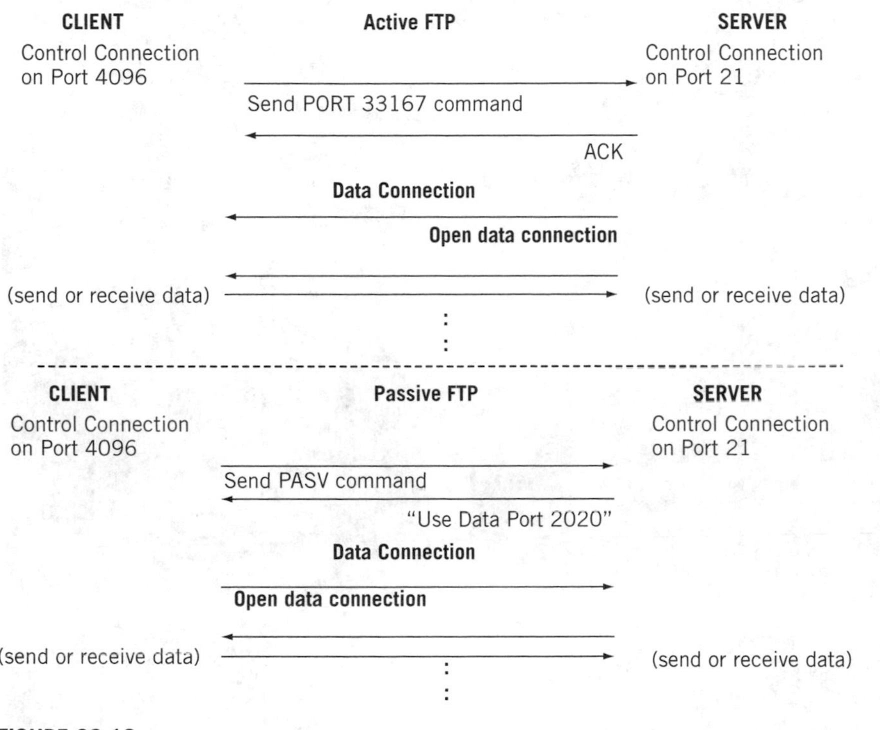

FIGURE 20.12

Simplified view of active and passive data transfer modes.

1. Who initiates the data connection in active and passive mode, respectively?
2. In the figure, for active mode what port will the client use on the server for data transfer?
3. In the figure, for passive mode what port will the client use on the server for data transfer?
4. In the figure, what port will the client use for the data connection in active mode?
5. In the figure, what port will the client use for the data connection in *passive* mode? How does the server know what it is?

CHAPTER

SMTP and Email

21

What You Will Learn

In this chapter, you will learn about the major architectures used to send and receive email on the Internet. We'll also see the five steps needed to send an email message.

You will learn about the protocols used with email applications, especially SMTP and POP3. We'll also describe MIME messages and discuss the important role of headers in email.

The Internet and TCP/IP are known to the greatest number of people through electronic mail (email) applications. Even those who cannot tell a router from a modem, or a packet from a frame, can check their email and send a message. A certain percentage of users still use the Internet mainly for email.

Email was one of the original applications the Internet was created to support (the others being file transfer and remote computer access). Things have come a long way since the original `mail` application, which is still supported on many Unix boxes:

```
>mail harry
We need to talk.
.
```

The modern email explosion has produced on-line ads, do-not-contact lists, spam, spam blockers, evil attachments, impounded attachments, and dozens of other moves and countermoves that make the email experience at once essential and yet daunting for many. Hardly anyone uses email except through a GUI today, and the mail user agents (MUAs)—the technical term for email client applications—are as varied as they are powerful, allowing users to schedule meetings, reserve conference rooms, or even request a projector for a certain time or place.

Email is a set of related and interconnected protocols that run on clients and servers to provide the global mesh of mailboxes and readers and writers upon which email depends. We'll look at several scenarios for sending and receiving email, using the devices on the network shown in Figure 21.1.

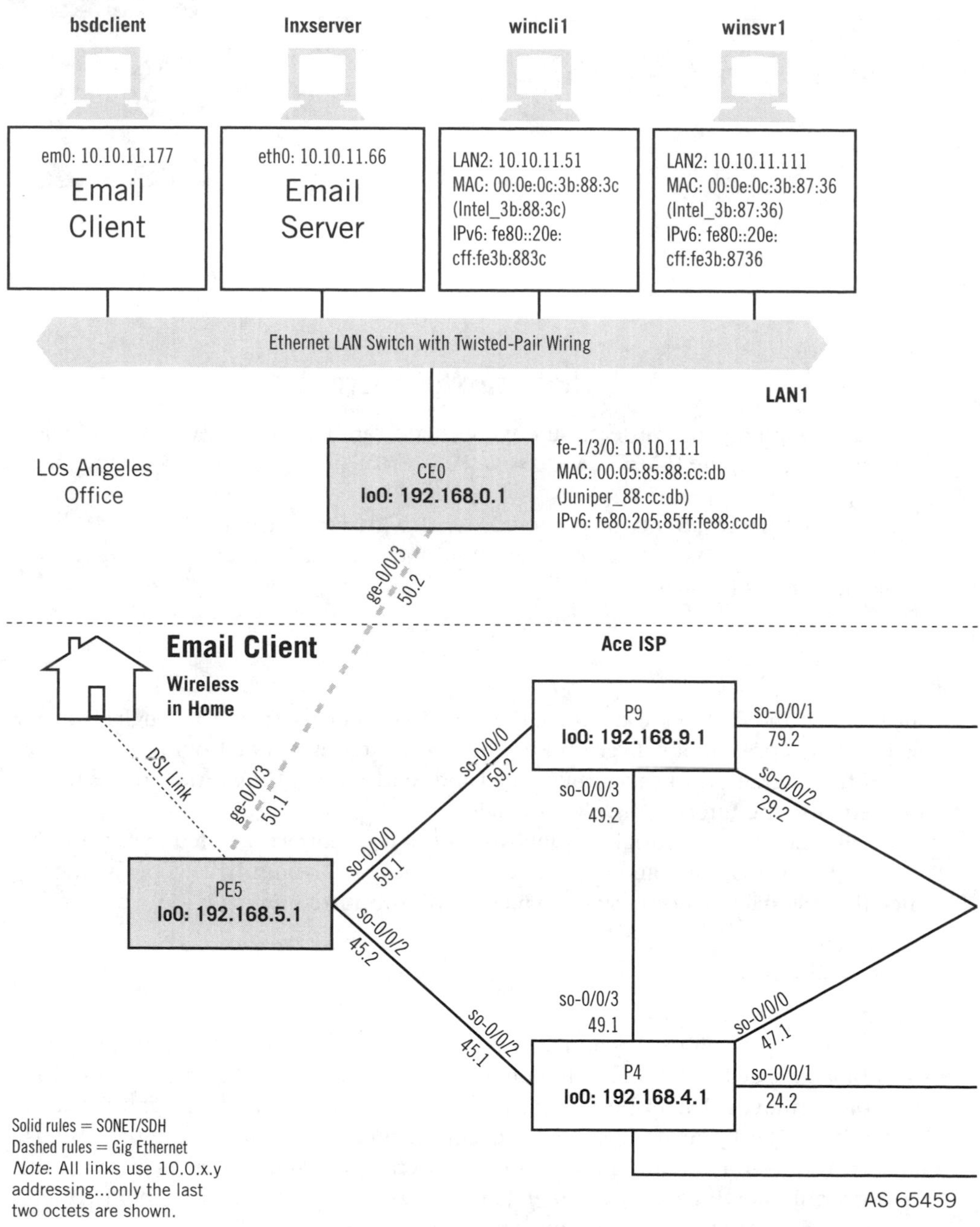

FIGURE 21.1

Email on the Illustrated Network, showing the Unix-based hosts used on email clients and servers.

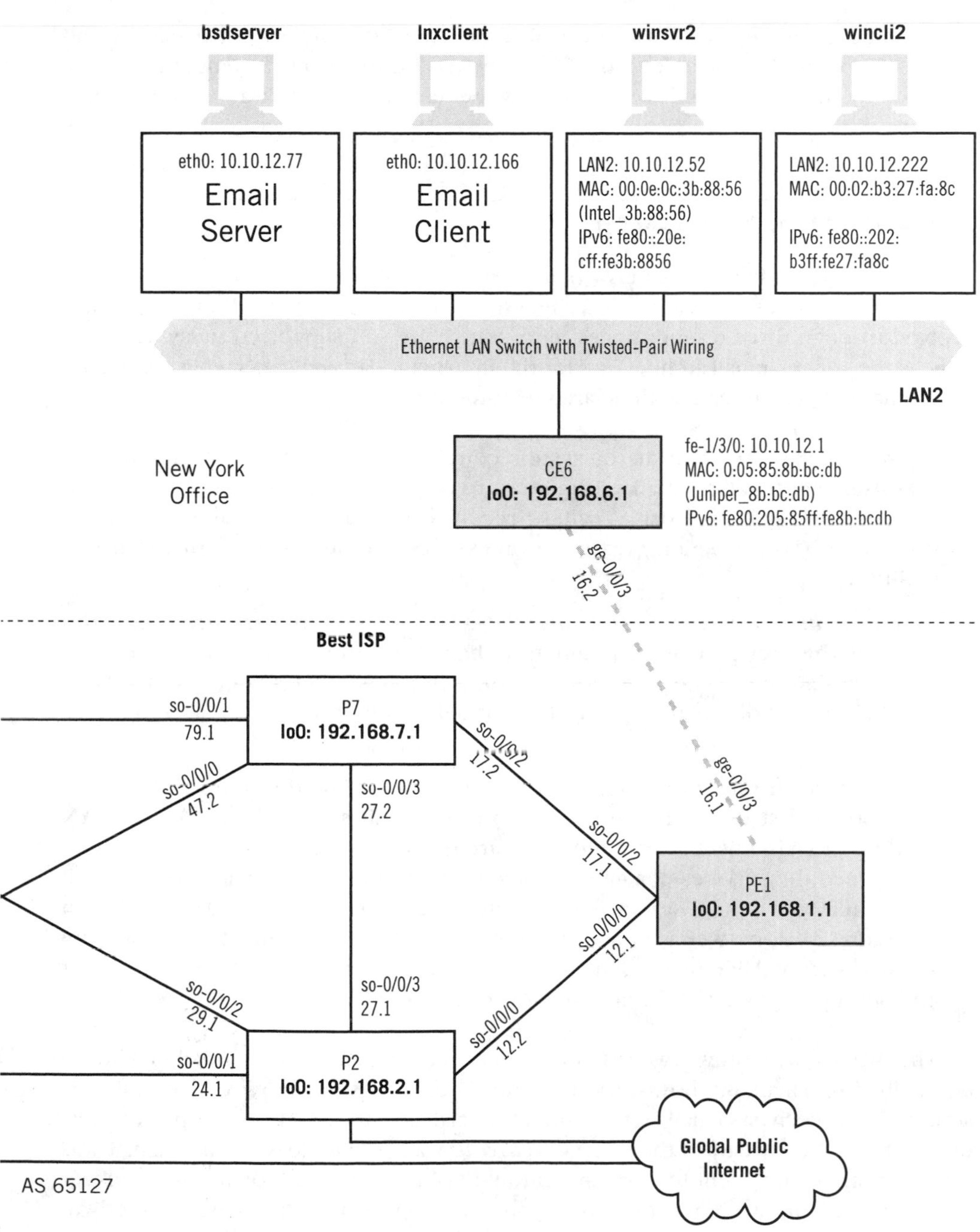

bsdserver
lnxclient
winsvr2
wincli2
eth0: 10.10.12.77
Email Server
eth0: 10.10.12.166
Email Client
LAN2: 10.10.12.52
MAC: 00:0e:0c:3b:88:56
(Intel_3b:88:56)
IPv6: fe80::20e:
cff:fe3b:8856
LAN2: 10.10.12.222
MAC: 00:02:b3:27:fa:8c
IPv6: fe80::202:
b3ff:fe27:fa8c
Ethernet LAN Switch with Twisted-Pair Wiring
LAN2
New York Office
CE6
lo0: 192.168.6.1
fe-1/3/0: 10.10.12.1
MAC: 0:05:85:8b:bc:db
(Juniper_8b:bc:db)
IPv6: fe80:205:85ff:fe8b:bcdb
ge-0/0/3
16.2
Best ISP
so-0/0/1
79.1
P7
lo0: 192.168.7.1
so-0/0/2
17.2
ge-0/0/3
16.1
so-0/0/0
47.2
so-0/0/3
27.2
so-0/0/2
17.1
PE1
lo0: 192.168.1.1
so-0/0/0
12.1
so-0/0/2
29.1
so-0/0/3
27.1
so-0/0/0
12.2
so-0/0/1
24.1
P2
lo0: 192.168.2.1
Global Public Internet
AS 65127

In some examples, we'll use the Unix-based host systems as email clients and servers. We won't leave Windows out, however. We'll use the email client at the home to office to show that Windows Outlook works essentially the same as older email systems.

ARCHITECTURES FOR EMAIL

What needs to be added to the network to create the TCP/IP email system shown in the figure? It all depends on the overall architecture used to support email, and these have evolved through three distinct stages, all of which are still supported today. The final stage is the general email architecture for the Internet today, and that's what we will be exploring in this chapter. The three architectures are:

Single shared system—The shared system could be a mainframe or minicomputer that users access. The email administrator creates *mailboxes* (restricted access files on the local hard drive) where received messages are stored. A special user agent (UA) program creates the messages and stores them in the user's mailbox.

Shared systems connected by the Internet—The second architecture takes into account the fact that users might not share the same local system. Another piece was added to the email architecture: the message transfer agent (MTA). The UA still handles mailboxes and messages locally, whereas the MTA handles communications between the two systems in the usual client/server fashion.

Email clients and servers connected by the Internet—The final step is to realize that today most users are connected to their email servers by a LAN or WAN (dial-up or DSL) link. Because receivers are not always present (even on a LAN), users need the services of a message access agent (MAA) to retrieve their email from their local email server. The architecture of this final scenario is shown in Figure 21.2, between typical users we can call "Alice" and "Bob." The flow shown is from Alice to Bob, but when Bob replies to Alice the roles of client and server (as well as MTA and MAA) are reversed.

This architecture shows two systems dedicated to managing users' email mailboxes and delivering email. But how does the sender's email system know which device is acting as the receiver's email system? Today, special DNS records provide this information, but in the early days of the Internet *relaying* was used to deliver email. Email was routed from email system to email system in a fashion similar to forwarding packets. Today, most email travels over the Internet from an originator's email system directly to the recipient's, minimizing complexity and delay.

But email servers are not necessary for the TCP/IP email protocol, the Simple Mail Transfer Protocol (SMTP), to operate. We can still use the original and simple Unix built-in applications (`sendmail` and `mail`) to send and retrieve email from (for example)

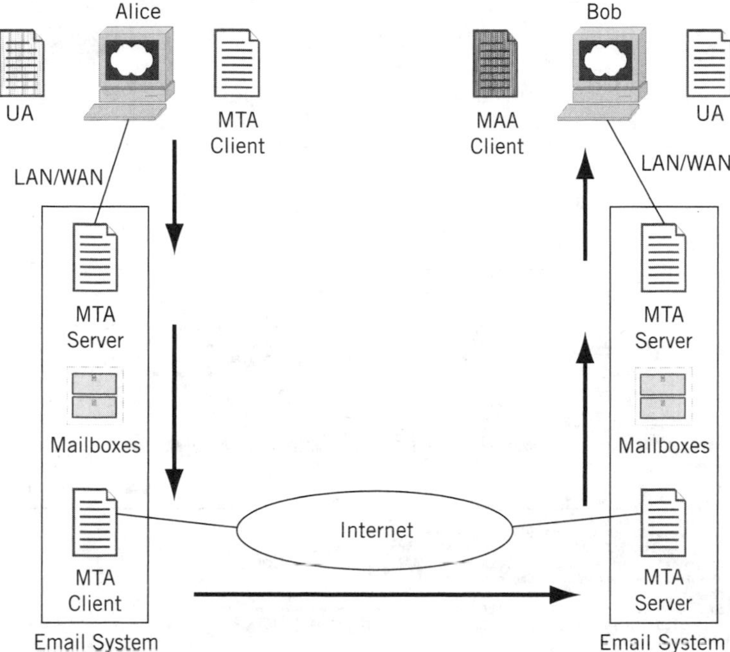

FIGURE 21.2

Email over the Internet, showing the role of client and server components.

bsdserver to bsdclient. It's nice to know that even today complex GUIs and massive directories are not needed to exchange email messages from the command prompt.

```
bsdserver# sendmail admin@bsdclient.booklab.englab.juniper.net
testing to 10.10.11.177
.
bsdserver#
```

This email is going to the admin user on bsdclient. The text of the message is "testing to 10.10.11.177" and the text entry ends with a single period on a line by itself. Shown in the following is what happens at the receiver, starting with the prompt indicating that mail has arrived (the period does not appear in the received text).

```
You have new mail.
bsdclient# mail
Mail version 8.1 6/6/93.  Type ? for help.
"/var/mail/admin": 2 messages 1 unread
    1 admin@bsdserver.engl  Fri Jan 18 22:38  22/1153
U   2 admin@bsdserver.engl  Fri Jan 18 22:56  22/1162
& 2
```

```
Message 2:
From admin@bsdserver.booklab.englab.juniper.net Fri Jan 18 22:56:47 2008
Date: Fri, 18 Jan 2008 22:50:47 -0700 (PDT)
From: Administrator<admin @bsdserver.booklab.englab.juniper.net>
To: undisclosed-recipients:;

testing to 10.10.11.177

&
```

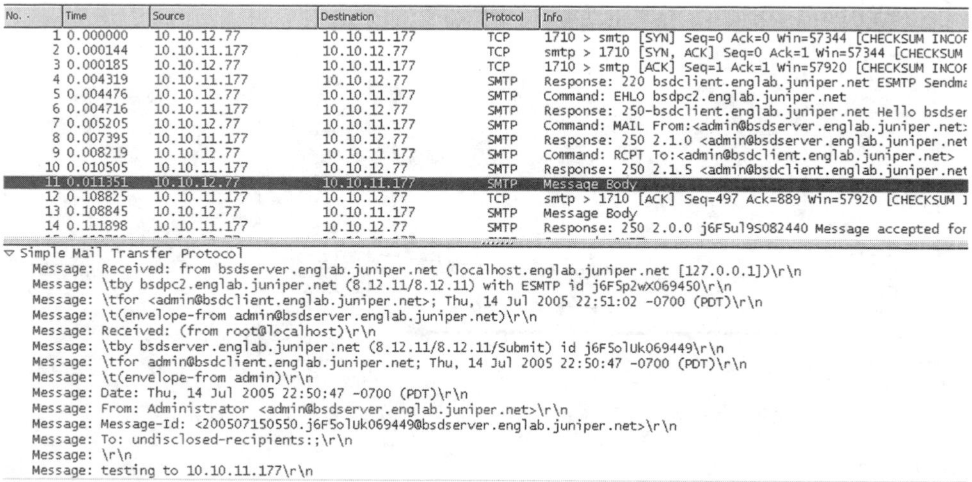

No.	Time	Source	Destination	Protocol	Info
1	0.000000	10.10.12.77	10.10.11.177	TCP	1710 > smtp [SYN] Seq=0 Ack=0 Win=57344 [CHECKSUM INCOF
2	0.000144	10.10.11.177	10.10.12.77	TCP	smtp > 1710 [SYN, ACK] Seq=0 Ack=1 Win=57344 [CHECKSUM
3	0.000185	10.10.12.77	10.10.11.177	TCP	1710 > smtp [ACK] Seq=1 Ack=1 Win=57920 [CHECKSUM INCOF
4	0.004319	10.10.11.177	10.10.12.77	SMTP	Response: 220 bsdclient.englab.juniper.net ESMTP Sendm
5	0.004476	10.10.12.77	10.10.11.177	SMTP	Command: EHLO bsdpc2.englab.juniper.net
6	0.004716	10.10.11.177	10.10.12.77	SMTP	Response: 250-bsdclient.englab.juniper.net Hello bsdser
7	0.005205	10.10.12.77	10.10.11.177	SMTP	Command: MAIL From:<admin@bsdserver.englab.juniper.net:
8	0.007395	10.10.11.177	10.10.12.77	SMTP	Response: 250 2.1.0 <admin@bsdserver.englab.juniper.net
9	0.008219	10.10.12.77	10.10.11.177	SMTP	Command: RCPT To:<admin@bsdclient.englab.juniper.net>
10	0.010505	10.10.11.177	10.10.12.77	SMTP	Response: 250 2.1.5 <admin@bsdclient.englab.juniper.net
11	0.011351	10.10.12.77	10.10.11.177	SMTP	Message Body
12	0.108825	10.10.11.177	10.10.12.77	TCP	smtp > 1710 [ACK] Seq=497 Ack=889 Win=57920 [CHECKSUM I
13	0.108845	10.10.12.77	10.10.11.177	SMTP	Message Body
14	0.111898	10.10.11.177	10.10.12.77	SMTP	Response: 250 2.0.0 j6F5ul9S082440 Message accepted for

```
▽ Simple Mail Transfer Protocol
    Message: Received: from bsdserver.englab.juniper.net (localhost.englab.juniper.net [127.0.0.1])\r\n
    Message: \tby bsdpc2.englab.juniper.net (8.12.11/8.12.11) with ESMTP id j6F5p2wX069450\r\n
    Message: \tfor <admin@bsdclient.englab.juniper.net>; Thu, 14 Jul 2005 22:51:02 -0700 (PDT)\r\n
    Message: \t(envelope-from admin@bsdserver.englab.juniper.net)\r\n
    Message: Received: (from root@localhost)\r\n
    Message: \tby bsdserver.englab.juniper.net (8.12.11/8.12.11/Submit) id j6F5olUk069449\r\n
    Message: \tfor admin@bsdclient.englab.juniper.net; Thu, 14 Jul 2005 22:50:47 -0700 (PDT)\r\n
    Message: \t(envelope-from admin)\r\n
    Message: Date: Thu, 14 Jul 2005 22:50:47 -0700 (PDT)\r\n
    Message: From: Administrator <admin@bsdserver.englab.juniper.net>\r\n
    Message: Message-Id: <200507150550.j6F5olUk069449@bsdserver.englab.juniper.net>\r\n
    Message: To: undisclosed-recipients:;\r\n
    Message: \r\n
    Message: testing to 10.10.11.177\r\n
```

FIGURE 21.3

Delivery of message using SMTP. Note the embedded control characters (starting with \) in the message body.

In this case, the mail was delivered directly from system to system. Only the SMTP MTA was used, with a minimal UA. Figure 21.3 shows the actual delivery of the message text itself. (Do not be concerned about the "undisclosed-recipients:" in the `To:` field. The `for` field in the message shows that the message is for the `admin` user on `bsdclient`.) Note that there is a lot more information carried in the message and displayed by the receiver than was entered by the sender. We'll talk more about these added email *headers* in detail later in this chapter.

Even when a complex GUI is used as an email front end, the same basic sequence of about 24 packets is used by SMTP to pass a small message off anywhere in the world. However, most people don't use the command prompt for this purpose. Modern email is more complex.

Sending Email Today

Today, there are five basic steps almost everyone uses to send and receive email. Although the procedures are absolutely symmetrical, and everyone is both sender and receiver when it comes to email, we'll follow a message one way from one person to another.

Email Message Composition

The user accesses a GUI email user agent (UA or sometimes MUA) to create the message. The email message contains two major parts: the *header* and the *body*. The header contains a series of fields that describes the message and controls how it is delivered and processed. The body of the message contains the actual information to be sent to the recipient. There can be multiple files accompanying the header and simple text of the message, and these are known as *attachments*. Most users do little more with the header than specify the email addresses of the intended recipients and subject line content. The UA takes care of making sure the entire message is in the correct standard format.

Submission of Email

When the user "sends" the newly created email, the sender's host (in a client role) does not need to set up a TCP connection directly to the receiver's host (in a server role). In fact, the user can compose a message and decide to submit it for delivery later, manually or automatically. Even when the message leaves the sender's host, the message is sent to the local email server using SMTP, and might sit there for a while rather than being forwarded across the Internet immediately. This allows for more efficient use of resources on the local email server. The server might require SMTP authentication of the user before accepting the message (we'll talk more about authentication later).

Delivery of Email

Once the local SMTP server has accepted the email message, the email server of the recipient(s) must be determined. DNS is used for this purpose, and the local email server performs a DNS query to access special Mail Exchanger (MX) records stored on a name server to provide this information. For example, an email sent to `walter@example.com` might be sent to a remote email server known as `pop3.example.com`. DNS provides both the name and IP address of this server.

SMTP also supports the ability to pass email messages through a specified sequence of SMTP servers to reach the destination. The intermediate servers are email *relay agents*. Relay agents are useful when a large organization has a single email server connected to the Internet (perhaps for ease of screening incoming messages) and yet has departments with their own email servers on each LAN. One way or another, the message makes its way to the destination email SMTP server that knows exactly who `walter@example.com` is. If the server cannot be contacted after a certain period of time, the mail is bounced back to the sender as undeliverable.

Email Processing

The receiving STMP server processes the incoming message, and if all seems well, places it into the recipient's mailbox. The message remains until the user retrieves it. If the recipient is unknown to the receiving server, the message is bounced back to the sender (also as undeliverable).

Email Access and Reading

The recipient's email application checks in periodically with the local SMTP server to see if any mail has arrived. This checking can be either automatic or when specifically run. If there is mail, the user can retrieve the mail, open it, and read it, and delete it. Usually, these are all separate steps. This step does not use SMTP, but a special mail access method and protocol such as POP3 or IMAP4 (both are used by TCP/IP MAAs).

All five of these steps are not always necessary. Some hosts act as mail servers all on their own, and the host-local-mail-server communication steps can be bypassed. Dial-in users often compose, send, and receive email all at once when they send mail. But usually all five steps are needed.

Four devices are involved in the five steps. They are the sender's client, the sender's local SMTP mail server, the recipient's local SMTP mail server, and the recipient's client. The relationship they have with one another and the protocols the email uses are shown in Figure 21.4. Note the symmetrical nature of the components so that two-way communication is possible.

Email Protocols

There are three common protocols used to deliver email over the Internet: the Simple Mail Transfer Protocol (SMTP), the Post Office Protocol (POP), and the Internet Message Access Protocol (IMAP). All three use TCP, and the last two are used for accessing electronic mailboxes. Special records stored in DNS servers play a role as well, using

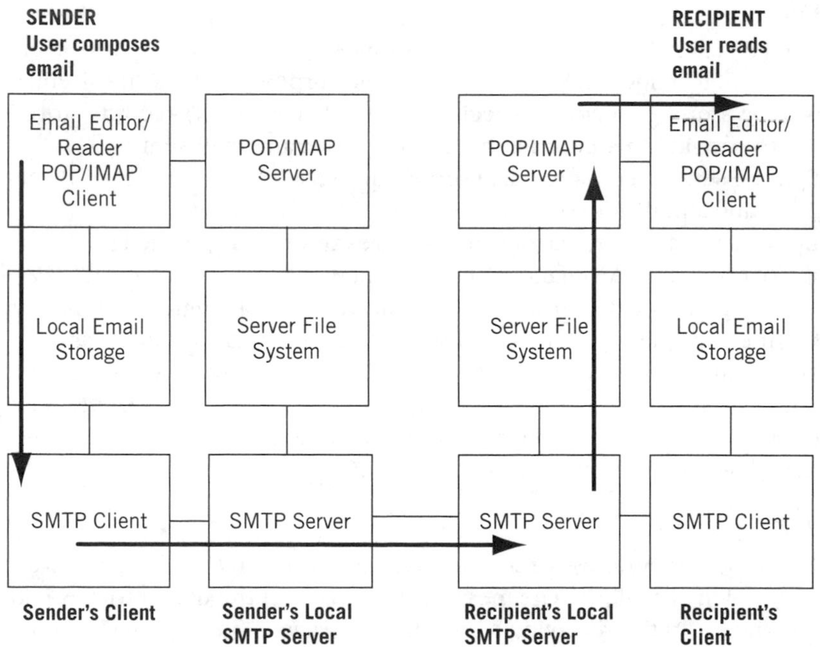

FIGURE 21.4

Email protocols and components, showing the components used to send an email message. Note the symmetrical nature of the sender and recipient so that the receiver can respond.

UDP. The current version of POP is version 3 (POP3) and the current version of IMAP is version 4 (IMAP4).

Although not a protocol, there is a series of Multipurpose Internet Mail Extensions (just MIME, never "MIMEs") for various types of email attachments (not just simple text). Finally, a number of related specifications add authentication to the basic email protocols. The way the protocols fit together is shown in Figure 21.5.

As we have seen, the original SMTP was designed as a simple host-to-host protocol. A user on one host created a message with a program called `sendmail` or `mail` and this text was sent directly to the destination host using SMTP as a Mail Transfer Agent (MTA). Of course, if the remote user was not running an email server process to accept the SMTP session, there was nothing for the sender to do but keep trying.

Modern email systems "decouple" the sender from the receiver so that email still goes through, even when the recipient is away for two weeks (but the messages keep piling up, just like regular mail). In addition, unlike almost every other TCP/IP application email operates *not* from host to host but from user to user. This means that users are not required to receive email on a particular host, nor is a particular host expected to have only one user with email capabilities. (We can even pick up email for a recipient from the *sending* host, and we'll do that later.) This user "mobility" poses special challenges for email addressing, which is why more than just a host name is required for correct email delivery.

The solution, of course, is to add another level to the hostname, this one identifying a particular user. So, for example, `walter@example.com` indicates a different mail destination than `goralski@example.com`. And, in fact, the actual host on which an email user is defined is not always added to the email address (which would yield something like `walter@bsdclient.example.com`). The email protocols all work together to make this work.

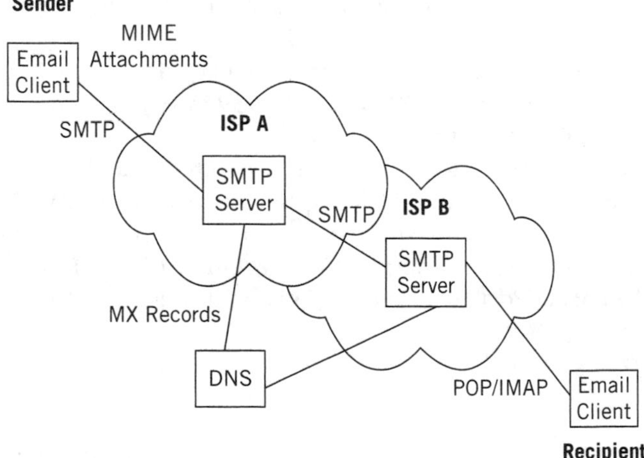

FIGURE 21.5

Email protocols, showing where they fit between sender and recipient.

There are older email address formats—FIDOnet, UUCP, email gateways (distinguished by the use of `user%` notations), and so on—but these are only of historical interest today. This is not to say that the evolution of email is not interesting, just that the history can be given very briefly and the discussion can turn to what is actually done with email on the Internet today.

The Evolution of Email in Brief

As expected with an application that has grown from a simple way to send text messages to an almost universal tool on the Internet, the email RFCs track a long evolutionary path as email changed with the times. In fact, email goes back to the days before TCP/IP and the Internet formally existed—all the way back to ARPAnet. Two very early documents, RFCs 95 and RFC 155, described physical mailing lists for distributing documents. Then the pioneers realized that the network itself could be used to distribute these documents, in the form of an electronic messaging application and associated protocols. In 1971, RFC 196 described the Mail Box Protocol for sending documents for remote printing.

By the mid-1970s, more sophisticated methods were developed, including some based on FTP. Today, the basic protocol for TCP/IP email is defined in RFC 821, and RFC 822 defines the format of the basic email message. RFC 974 added interactions with DNS to email transactions, and RFC 1869 added more capabilities as SMTP Service Extensions (ESMTP). Today, everyone still calls it SMTP, even when ESMTP is a more accurate term. Those same RFCs are still essentially in force today, although heavily added to in a number of ways and currently gathered as RFC 2821 and RFC 2822 (exactly 2000 away from the originals, an intentional numeration).

Email quickly grew to include various types of attachments, and modern users are used to these. RFCs 2045 through 2048 define basic MIME, which allows email to carry various types of email attachments. This series replaced RFCs 1521, 1522, and 1590, which had displaced RFC 1341.

Modern email protocols split the sending and retrieving task. The retrieval protocol POP3 has evolved through five RFCs, from RFC 1081 to RFC 1939. Another method, IMAP4 (often just IMAP), went from RFC 1730 to 2060.

Finally, RFC 2254 extended the SMTP authentication capabilities, and these were based on ESMTP in RFC 1869. Most modern SMTP applications support SMTP authentication, which defines an SMTP authentication server to advertise this function to SMTP clients. Today, the list of RFCs relating to MIME security (S/MIME) is a lengthy one and additional drafts are added all the time. And many RFCs address SMTP authentication.

SMTP Authentication

How do you know that the email you send goes only to the person intended? How do you know that the email you just got, supposedly from the president of your company, really came from that person? SMTP authentication was introduced to help prevent these email abuses, and others. It was based partly on ESTMP, and most implementations support SMTP authentication today. A lot of MUAs, which of course include the SMTP client, make it available. A server can support several forms of authentication, and the client application should pick one to use. The client can request a specific authentication method, but the server is free to reject its use.

SMTP authentication, which is advertised by an SMTP authentication server, requires clients to authenticate themselves, and both parties must mutually accept and support the chosen authentication procedure. Once successfully authenticated, the user can receive and send email.

Unfortunately, SMTP authentication does not fit very well into the SMTP protocol, mainly because it is based on the Simple Authentication and Security Layer (SASL) concept, which is more strictly aimed at direct client–server interactions. And several RFCs are needed to understand how it all works, some of which don't even mention any SMTP extensions, although they require use of the special ESMTP `EHLO` (Extended Hello) command.

The goal of SMTP authentication is to prevent username and password from crossing the network (the Internet) in plain text. A full discussion of STMP authentication depends on an understanding of how encryption provides authentication, topics which have not been covered yet. SMTP authentication is still evolving, and the mechanisms, methods, and procedures used will change as time goes on.

Simple Mail Transfer Protocol

A basic SMTP session between sender and local SMTP server is shown in Figure 21.6.

Like FTP, SMTP uses a system of client commands with parameters and numerical server responses, which is usually accompanied by some basic text as well. Oddly, if you know what you are doing, you can simply use a remote access method to connect to the SMTP server, and simply send the keywords and any parameters by typing them at the command prompt. The basic interaction between client and server when SMTP authentication is used is shown in Figure 21.7.

The client indicates to the server that it knows the server supports ESMTP (and wants to use it) with the SMTP `EHLO` command. The server offers a number of authentication schemes, including simple log in with password. The client selects this option with the `AUTH` command. The server then uses *base64 encoding* (a special type of character coding) to ask the user for username and password, one at a time. The client replies are also encoded with base64, not encrypted. If the user types in the password incorrectly, the authentication fails, but the user can usually try again before the server drops the connection altogether.

The 11 most common SMTP commands are outlined in Table 21.1. A few others are defined, but they are hardly used anymore.

SMTP reply codes resemble FTP reply codes. The first digit refers to the command status, the second classifies the reply, and the third adds details. The meanings of the first two digits are outlined in Table 21.2.

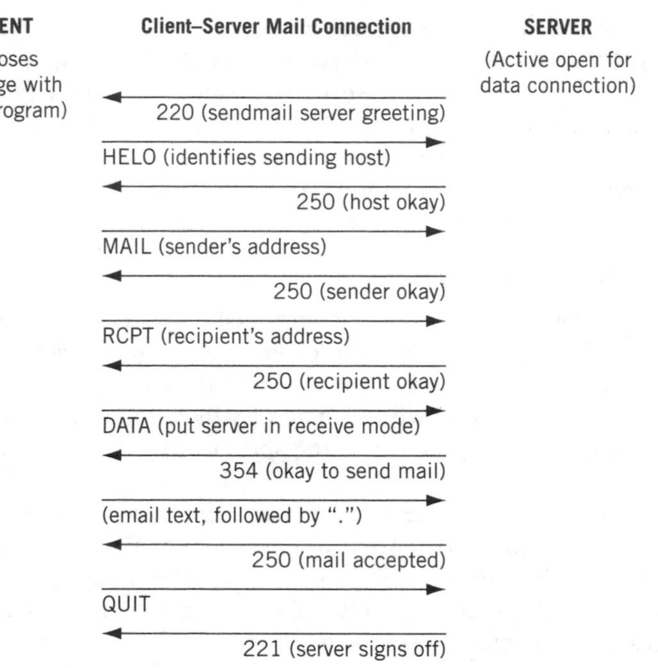

FIGURE 21.6

Basic STMP email exchange between a client and a server.

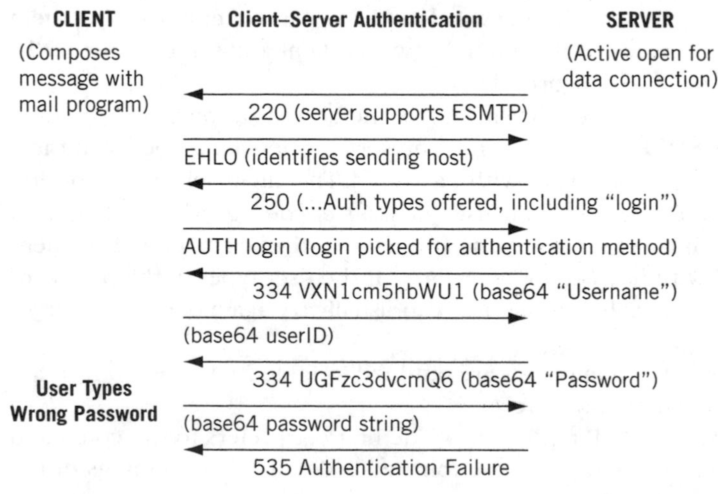

FIGURE 21.7

SMTP authentication. Note that SMTP uses a special coding known as base64.

Table 21.1 Common SMTP Commands and Meanings

Command	Meaning
HELO	Identifies the sender to the receiver.
EHLO	Identifies the sender with extended capabilities to the receiver.
MAIL FROM	Identifies the originator and starts a mail transaction.
RCPT TO	Identifies an individual recipient. Repeated for multiple recipients. Receiver, if possible, checks for the validity of the recipient.
DATA	Sender is ready to transmit lines of text. Maximum line length is 1000 characters, including final "new line" character or characters.
RSET	Aborts current mail transaction and clears all information.
NOOP	Asks for a positive reply.
QUIT	Asks for a positive reply to close the connection.
VRFY	Asks the receiver to validate recipient name.
EXPN	Asks the receiver to confirm name in a mailing list, and for list content. For information only (do not change recipient names).
HELP	Asks for implementation details, such as commands supported.

Table 21.2 SMTP Reply Codes and Meanings

Digit and Position	Meaning
1xx	Positive preliminary (not currently used)
2xx	Positive completion
3xx	Positive intermediate result
4xx	Transient negative (okay to try again)
5xx	Permanent negative ("stop doing that!")
x0x	For a problem, syntax error, or unknown command
x1x	Information request reply (such as to HELP)
x2x	Connection reply
x3x	Unspecified
x4x	Unspecified
x5x	Receiver status reply

MULTIPURPOSE INTERNET MAIL EXTENSIONS

MIME is a rather dry subject, but quite important, if for no other reason than that MIME formats are also used in transfer using the protocol of the World Wide Web, the Hypertext Transport Protocol (HTTP), which is examined in the next chapter. So, MIME deserves at least a quick look here.

A MIME message has a set of headers and one or more "body parts." Internet text mail messages also have headers, of course, with fields such as `To:`, `From:`, and `Date:`. MIME messages have additional introductory headers to describe the overall format and content of the message.

MIME Media Types

When there are multiple parts to a MIME message, one introductory header defines a string used to mark the boundaries between parts. After the boundary delimiter, which is chosen by the email application, there are additional headers to describe the part of the MIME message that follows. The overall structure of the information in each part is determined by the `Content-Type` MIME headers. The type can be an image, audio, text, or even a mixture of these.

There are seven standard media types, all of which have a variety of subtypes. Five of them are considered "discrete" (meaning that the format is consistent throughout the part), and two are "composite," meaning that the format changes independently in each component. The discrete types are:

- Text
- Image
- Video
- Audio
- Application

The composite types are:

- *Multipart*—Each component can have a different data type, usually discrete.
- *Message*—Used to "encapsulate" other information, such as a forwarded email message.

Some of the more common subtypes used in these seven major data types are outlined in Table 21.3.

MIME Encoding

The data type and subtype establish the format of the content of a MIME body part. But how should the data in each part be represented for transmission across the Internet? MIME defines a variety of coding methods, allowing hosts and MTAs to be as flexible as possible.

The default coding method is ASCII (as used in the United States). If another method is used, such as for formatted documents, this must be announced in a MIME `Content-Transfer-Encoding` header.

There are six major MIME encoding methods. These are listed in Table 21.4. The `quoted-printable` encoding extends the usual 7-bit ASCII code set to allow a few extra characters. Special hex characters are preceded by an = sign. So, `0x0C` (form feed) is sent in quoted `=printable` as `= 0C`.

`Base64` encoding is very common today. SMTP was originally a text-based transmission system. Yet a lot of email content is sent as simple bytes, such as audio and video,

Table 21.3 MIME Content Types and Subtypes

Type	Subtypes
text	plain, richtext, tab-separated-values, html, sgml
image	jpeg, gif, ief, tiff, g3fax, png
video	mpeg, quicktime, vnd.vivo
audio	basic, 32kadpcm, vnd.vivo
application	octet-stream, postscript, rtf, pdf, zip, macwriteii, msword, remote-printing, EDI-X12, EDIFACT, dec-dx, dca-rft, activemessage, applefile, mac-binhex40, news-message-id, mews-transmission, wordperfect5.1, mathematica, pgp-encrypted, pgp-signature, pgp-keys, andrew-inset, slate, set-payment, set-registration, sgml, wita, lotus-wordpro, lotus-1-2-3, lotus-organizer, ms-excel, powerbuilder-6
multipart	mixed, alternative, digest, parallel, appledouble, header-set, form-data, report, voice-message, signed, encrypted
message	rfc822, partial, external-body, news, http, delivery-status

Table 21.4 MIME Encoding Methods and Meanings

Method	Meaning
7bit	Ordinary ASCII as used in the United States.
quoted-printable	Adds a few special characters and coding to ASCII text.
base64	Content is mapped into a "text" package (very common).
8bit	Similar to 7bit, but can include 8-bit characters.
binary	True binary data.
x-(name)	Experimental encodings must have a name starting with "x".

and even as executable code (much to the chagrin of network administrators). `Base64` encoding converts a binary data stream to a sequence of "text" characters. This usually results in the size of the binary file growing by about 33% in terms of bytes. This is because 6 bits can indicate the numbers 0 through 63. But bytes are 8 bits, of course, at least where the Internet and TCP/IP are concerned.

An Example of a MIME Message

Consider a writer delivering a short story to an editor as an email attachment (been there, done that). What would the MIME headers that form the overall body of the email message look like? Well, they would resemble the following:

```
Content-Type: multipart/mixed;
    boundary = "--- = _NextPart_000_027HB582.0E7E0F6"
This is a message in MIME format.
--- = _NextPart 000_027HB582.0E7E0F6
Content-Type: text/plain
```

```
Please take a look at the attached short story. Thanks.

W
```

--- = _NextPart_000_027HB582.0E7E0F6
Content-Type: application/msword;
name = "new story.doc"
Content-Transfer-Encoding: base64
Content-Disposition: attachment;
filename = "new story.doc"

```
(Lots of nonsense characters form the base64 table.)
```

--- = _NextPart_000_027HB582.0E7E0F6

The lines in bold are the MIME headers.

USING POP3 TO ACCESS EMAIL

The original host-to-host SMTP did not allow for attachments, limited messages to 1000 bytes, was a purely connection-oriented application, and never imagined a world of personal computers and intermittent email checking. STMP was built for immediate email delivery to a specific host, sort of what we think of as instant messaging (IM) today. Email today is often delivered to mailboxes on mail servers, not directly to the end user, that is, users who might only have dial-up Internet access.

```
Filter:                                  Expression...  Clear  Apply
No. -  Time      Source        Destination   Protocol  Info
  1 0.000000  10.10.12.166  10.10.11.66   TCP   2447 > pop3 [SYN] Seq=0 Ack=0 Win=16384 [CHECKSUM
  2 0.001392  10.10.11.66   10.10.12.166  TCP   pop3 > 2447 [SYN, ACK] Seq=0 Ack=1 Win=5840 [CHECK
  3 0.001512  10.10.12.166  10.10.11.66   TCP   2447 > pop3 [ACK] Seq=1 Ack=1 Win=17520 [CHECKSUM
  4 0.036163  10.10.11.66   10.10.12.166  POP   Response: +OK POP3 lnxserver.englab.jnpr.net  serv
  5 0.037275  10.10.12.166  10.10.11.66   POP   Request: USER admin1
  6 0.037563  10.10.11.66   10.10.12.166  TCP   pop3 > 2447 [ACK] Seq=51 Ack=14 Win=5840 [CHECKSUM
  7 0.038817  10.10.11.66   10.10.12.166  POP   Response: +OK User name accepted, password please
  8 0.039279  10.10.12.166  10.10.11.66   POP   Request: PASS admin11
  9 0.063158  10.10.11.66   10.10.12.166  POP   Response: +OK Mailbox open, 1 messages
 10 0.064186  10.10.12.166  10.10.11.66   POP   Request: STAT
 11 0.065568  10.10.11.66   10.10.12.166  POP   Response: +OK 1 1108
 12 0.068662  10.10.12.166  10.10.11.66   POP   Request: LIST
 13 0.068888  10.10.11.66   10.10.12.166  POP   Response: +OK Mailbox scan listing follows
 14 0.073886  10.10.12.166  10.10.11.66   POP   Request: RETR 1
 15 0.075981  10.10.11.66   10.10.12.166  POP   Response: +OK 1108 octets
 16 0.089344  10.10.12.166  10.10.11.66   POP   Request: DELE 1
 17 0.089903  10.10.11.66   10.10.12.166  POP   Response: +OK Message deleted
 18 0.091310  10.10.12.166  10.10.11.66   POP   Request: QUIT
 19 0.094766  10.10.11.66   10.10.12.166  POP   Response: +OK Sayonara
 20 0.094839  10.10.11.66   10.10.12.166  TCP   pop3 > 2447 [FIN, ACK] Seq=1342 Ack=62 Win=5840 [C
 21 0.094923  10.10.12.166  10.10.11.66   TCP   2447 > pop3 [ACK] Seq=62 Ack=1343 Win=16179 [CHECK
 22 0.095627  10.10.12.166  10.10.11.66   TCP   2447 > pop3 [FIN, ACK] Seq=62 Ack=1343 Win=16179 [
 23 0.097023  10.10.11.66   10.10.12.166  TCP   pop3 > 2447 [ACK] Seq=1343 Ack=63 Win=5840 [CHECKS

▷ Transmission Control Protocol, Src Port: pop3 (110), Dst Port: 2447 (2447), Seq: 134, Ack: 40, Len: 45
▽ Post Office Protocol
  ▷ +OK Mailbox scan listing follows\r\n
    1 1108\r\n
    .\r\n

0000  00 00 39 c7 40 a0 00 50  bf 78 71 83 08 00 45 00   ..9.@..P .xq...E.
0010  00 55 fc b1 40 00 40 06  ba 99 0a 0a 0b 42 0a 0a   .U..@.@. .....B..
0020  0c a6 00 6e 09 8f 5d d3  2e fd 1c ca 63 6d 50 18   ...n..]. ....cmP.
0030  16 d0 5c c3 00 00 2b 4f  4b 20 4d 61 69 6c 62 6f   ..\...+O K Mailbo
0040  78 20 73 63 61 6e 20 6c  69 73 74 69 6e 67 20 66   x scan l isting f
File: pop3test3.pcap 4398 bytes 00:  P: 39 D: 39 M: 0
```

FIGURE 21.8

A POP3 capture, highlighting how the email listing is sent to the user.

These intermittent Internet users log in and access their mailbox with POP3 (commonly just called POP). POP3 does not send email: SMTP does that. But POP3 retrieves the email, and the IMAP4 protocol maintains and controls access to the mailbox accounts.

POP3 uses TCP port 110, and users are authenticated by userID and password. POP3 then places a lock on the mailbox to avoid access conflicts. The POP3 server then enters transaction mode for user access to messages. POP3 features include the ability to view a list of email messages and their sizes and to selectively retrieve or delete messages, but many implementations simply dump all waiting mail to the client. POP3 servers can be the same device as the SMTP mail server, but this is not a requirement.

Let's add POP3 to our network. We used the BSD hosts before, so let's make `lnxserver` (`10.10.11.66`) into our email server for the network. We can then compose a fairly long (1108 bytes) message and send it to user `admin1`. Figure 21.8 shows the sequence of packets used to retrieve the message from host `lnxclient` (`10.10.12.166`).

POP3 employs a characteristic `+OK` and not a code when responding normally to a client. The series of packets shown in Figure 21.8 is boiled down to its POP3 essentials in Figure 21.9.

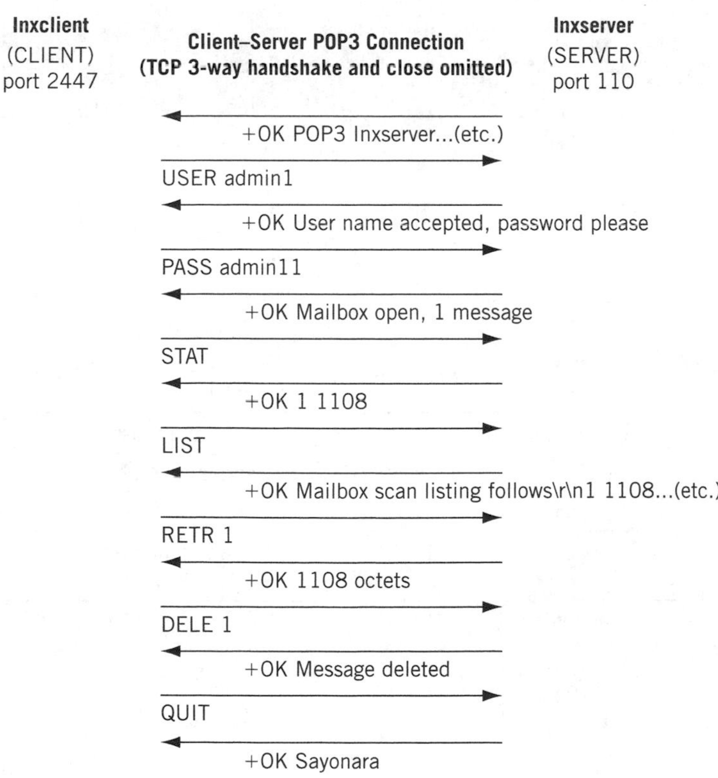

FIGURE 21.9

A POP3 connection used to fetch email, showing a more schematic view than the capture.

Note that the retrieval of the message (RETR) by the client and its deletion from the server (DELE) are separate steps. You don't have to delete email as you read it, of course. The `+OK Sayonara` is also part of the POP3 protocol implementation.

HEADERS AND EMAIL

We've mentioned email headers already and supplied some details about MIME headers (header extensions). Email has its own proper set of headers as well, and an Internet email message is little more than a sequence of headers and their values, one after the other, from the start of the email message to the end. Table 21.5 outlines the basic email header field names and groups established by RFC 822.

Now we have everything in place to examine the headers created when sending a short email message through our email server (`lnxserver`) from a client host to another user. We'll use the `admin` account on `lnxclient` to send a message to the `admin` user on

Table 21.5 RFC 822 Email Header Fields and Characteristics

Field Group	Field Name	Appearance	Occurrences per Message	Comment
Destination Address Field	To:	Usually present	1	Primary recipient list
	Cc:	Optional	1	Copy recipient
	Bcc:	Optional	1	"Blind" copy
Identification Fields	Message-ID:	Usually present	1	Unique code applied when sent
	In-Reply-To:	Optional, normal for replies	1	Provides method to coordinate responses
	References:	Optional	1	Other documents or message IDs
Informational Fields	Subject:	Usually present	1	Topic of the message
	Comments:	Optional	Unlimited	Describe message
	Keywords:	Optional	Unlimited	Useful search item
Origination Date	Date:	Mandatory	1	Date and time stamp for mail
Originator Fields	From:	Mandatory	1	Source address of "originator"
	Sender:	Optional	1	If different from "originator"
	Reply-To:	Optional	1	If absent, reply goes to "from"

Table 21.5 *(continued)*

Field Group	Field Name	Appearance	Occurrences per Message	Comment
Resent Fields	Resent-Date: Resent-From: Resent-Sender: Resent-To: Resent-Cc: Resent-Bcc: Resent-Message-ID:	Each time message is resent, this block is generated	Resent-Date: and Resent-Sender: are mandatory; all others optional	Special, used for forwarding an email message to others
Trace Fields	Received: Return-Path:	Inserted by email system	Unlimited	Used to trace the message through the email system

`lnxserver` (these are not necessarily the same users: they just share a mailbox name). Then we'll fetch the message from the email server mailbox using the `admin` account, showing that we can fetch our email almost anywhere, even from the sending host.

We can use the same basic `mail` program as we did on the BSD hosts. This time, we'll use the `-s` flag to create a subject for the message. The text is simple, and we end our message with a single dot as before.

```
[admin@lnxclient admin]$ mail –s "Here is another example"
        admin@lnxserver.booklab.englab.juniper.net

This is text...
.
Cc: (enter)
```

Now we'll use fetchmail to "fetch" the mail message with POP3 from the email server (`lnxserver`) and bring it back to `lnxclient`. Note that when we run the program and have email we get a version of the familiar "you've got mail" prompt.

```
[admin@lnxclient admin]$ fetchmail
Enter password for admin@lnxserver.booklab.englab.juniper.net: (not shown)
You have new mail in /var/spool/mail/admin
```

Usually, our complete email application would display the information and the message. But there's nothing magical about that. We can do the same with the command prompt, listing the mailbox content and displaying the email message with normal Unix commands.

```
[admin@lnxclient admin]$ ls –l /var/spool/mail/admin
-rw-------   1 admin    mail        3122 Jan 17 16:42 /var/spool/mail/admin
```

```
[admin@lnxclient admin]$ cat /var/spool/mail/admin
From admin@lnxserver.booklab.englab.juniper.net  Wed Jan 16 13:04:50 2008
Return-Path: <admin@lnxclient.booklab.englab.juniper.net>
Received: from localhost (localhost.localdomain [127.0.0.1])
        by lnxclient.booklab.englab.juniper.net (8.12.9/8.12.8) with ESMTP id
        jBGL4onD026830
        for <admin@localhost>; Wed, 16 Jan 2008 13:04:50 -0800
Received: from lnxserver.booklab.englab.juniper.net
        by localhost with POP3 (fetchmail-6.2.0)
        for admin@localhost (single-drop); Wed, 16 Jan 2008 13:04:50 -0800 (PST)
Received: from lnxclient.booklab.englab.juniper.net ([10.10.12.166])
        by lnxserver.booklab.englab.juniper.net (8.12.8/8.12.8) with ESMTP id
        jBGL4HFa027257
        for <admin@lnxserver.booklab.englab.juniper.net>; Wed, 16 Jan 2008
        13:04:17 -0800 (PST)
Received: from lnxclient.booklab.englab.juniper.net (localhost.localdomain
        [127.0.0.1])
        by lnxclient.booklab.englab.juniper.net (8.12.8/8.12.8) with ESMTP id
        jBGL4HnD026820
        for <admin@lnxserver.booklab.englab.juniper.net>; Wed, 16 Jan 2008
        13:04:17 -0800
Received: (from admin@localhost)
        by lnxclient.booklab.englab.juniper.net (8.12.8/8.12.8/Submit) id
        jBGL4HHf026818
        for admin@lnxserver.booklab.englab.juniper.net; Wed, 16 Jan 2008
        13:04:17 -0800
Date: Wed, 16 Jan 2008 13:04:17 -0800
From: admin@lnxclient.booklab.englab.juniper.net
Message-Id: <200801172104.jBGL4HHf-26818 @lnxclient.booklab.englab.juniper.net>
To: admin@lnxserver.booklab.englab.juniper.net
Subject: Here is another example
X-IMAPbase: 1134766876 8
Status: o
X-UID: 8
X-Keywords:

This is text...
```

The important fields are highlighted. Most of the other headers were added when the email was created, of course. Most useful is the series of `Received:` headers, which allows us to trace the message back to its origin. It might seem odd that there are *five* receiver headers along the trace for a message that has gone from client to email server and then back to client. But the application adds a `localhost` step at each end, at the sender (`admin@localhost`) and receiver (`from localhost`) to the message trace. The complete path of the message recorded in the headers (from "bottom to top") is:

1. The mail application receives the composed message from the local user.
2. The local mailbox receives the message using ESMTP.
3. The email server receives the message using ESMTP.

4. The other client retrieves the message from the email server using POP3 (`fetchmail`).
5. The local host transfers the message to the local mailbox using ESMTP.
6. The use of these protocols is highlighted in the headers.

HOME OFFICE EMAIL

Let's end our email discussion by showing that Windows uses the same protocols and headers to send and receive email over the Internet. This time, we'll send a message from `lnxclient` on the Illustrated Network to my home office host (which uses Outlook).

Almost all email applications have an option to view the complete headers. In Outlook, it's just "Message Header" in the singular, but the following is the result of viewing the message headers in Outlook. Only the headers are displayed, not the message text itself.

```
Microsoft Mail Internet Headers Version 2.0
Received: from beta.jnpr.net ([172.24.18.109]) by positron.jnpr.net with
    Microsoft SMTPSVC(5.0.2195.6713);
    Thu, 17 Jan 2008 07:37:14 -0700
Received: from merlot.juniper.net ([172.17.27.10]) by beta.jnpr.net over TLS
    secured channel with Microsoft SMTPSVC(6.0.3790.1830);
    Thu, 17 Jan 2008 07:37:13 -0700
Received: from lnxclient.englab.juniper.net (lnxclient.englab.junipor.net
   [10.10.12.166])
   by merlot.juniper.net (8.11.3/8.11.3) with ESMTP id k9JEbDH15244
   for <walterg@juniper.net>; Thu, 17 Jan 2008 07:37:13 -0700 (PDT)
   (envelope-from admin@lnxclient.englab.juniper.net)
Received: from lnxclient.englab.juniper.net (localhost.localdomain
   [127.0.0.1])
   by lnxclient.englab.juniper.net (8.12.8/8.12.8) with ESMTP id
   k9JEacUg026193
   for <walterg@juniper.net>; Thu, 17 Jan 2008 07:36:58 -0700
   Received: (from admin@localhost)
   by lnxclient.englab.juniper.net (8.12.8/8.12.8/Submit) id k9JEaSlp026191
   for walterg@juniper.net; Thu, 17 Jan 2008 07:36:28 -0700
Date: Thu, 17 Jan 2008 07:36:28 -0700
From: admin@lnxclient.englab.juniper.net
Message-Id: <200801171436.k9JEaSlp026191@lnxclient.englab.juniper.net>
To: walterg@juniper.net
Subject: here is an email example
Return-Path: admin@lnxclient.englab.juniper.net
X-OriginalArrivalTime: 17 Jan 2008 14:37:13.0230 (UTC) FILETIME=[10F80AE0:
  01C6F38C]
```

QUESTIONS FOR READERS

Figure 21.10 shows some of the concepts discussed in this chapter and can be used to answer the following questions.

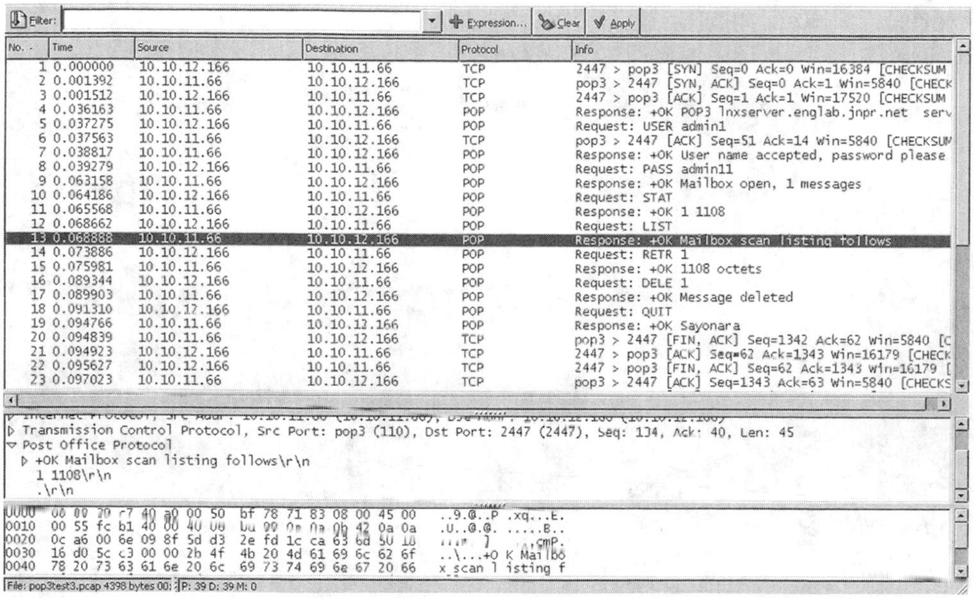

```
No. Time      Source        Destination   Protocol Info
 1 0.000000  10.10.12.166  10.10.11.66   TCP  2447 > pop3 [SYN] Seq=0 Ack=0 Win=16384 [CHECKSUM
 2 0.001392  10.10.11.66   10.10.12.166  TCP  pop3 > 2447 [SYN, ACK] Seq=0 Ack=1 Win=5840 [CHECK
 3 0.001512  10.10.12.166  10.10.11.66   TCP  2447 > pop3 [ACK] Seq=1 Ack=1 Win=17520 [CHECKSUM
 4 0.036163  10.10.11.66   10.10.12.166  POP  Response: +OK POP3 lnxserver.englab.jnpr.net  serv
 5 0.037275  10.10.12.166  10.10.11.66   POP  Request: USER admin1
 6 0.037563  10.10.11.66   10.10.12.166  TCP  pop3 > 2447 [ACK] Seq=51 Ack=14 Win=5840 [CHECKSUM
 7 0.038817  10.10.11.66   10.10.12.166  POP  Response: +OK User name accepted, password please
 8 0.039279  10.10.12.166  10.10.11.66   POP  Request: PASS admin11
 9 0.063158  10.10.11.66   10.10.12.166  POP  Response: +OK Mailbox open, 1 messages
10 0.064186  10.10.12.166  10.10.11.66   POP  Request: STAT
11 0.065568  10.10.11.66   10.10.12.166  POP  Response: +OK 1 1108
12 0.068662  10.10.12.166  10.10.11.66   POP  Request: LIST
13 0.068888  10.10.11.66   10.10.12.166  POP  Response: +OK Mailbox scan listing follows
14 0.073886  10.10.12.166  10.10.11.66   POP  Request: RETR 1
15 0.075981  10.10.11.66   10.10.12.166  POP  Response: +OK 1108 octets
16 0.089344  10.10.12.166  10.10.11.66   POP  Request: DELE 1
17 0.089903  10.10.11.66   10.10.12.166  POP  Response: +OK Message deleted
18 0.091310  10.10.12.166  10.10.11.66   POP  Request: QUIT
19 0.094766  10.10.11.66   10.10.12.166  POP  Response: +OK Sayonara
20 0.094839  10.10.11.66   10.10.12.166  TCP  pop3 > 2447 [FIN, ACK] Seq=1342 Ack=62 Win=5840 [C
21 0.094923  10.10.12.166  10.10.11.66   TCP  2447 > pop3 [ACK] Seq=62 Ack=1343 Win=16179 [CHECK
22 0.095627  10.10.12.166  10.10.11.66   TCP  2447 > pop3 [FIN, ACK] Seq=62 Ack=1343 Win=16179 [
23 0.097023  10.10.11.66   10.10.12.166  TCP  pop3 > 2447 [ACK] Seq=1343 Ack=63 Win=5840 [CHECKS

▷ Transmission Control Protocol, Src Port: pop3 (110), Dst Port: 2447 (2447), Seq: 134, Ack: 40, Len: 45
▽ Post Office Protocol
  ▷ +OK Mailbox scan listing follows\r\n
    1 1108\r\n
    .\r\n

0040  78 20 73 63 61 6e 20 6c  69 73 74 69 6e 67 20 66   x scan l isting f
File: pop3test3.pcap 4398 bytes 00: P: 39 D: 39 M: 0
```

FIGURE 21.10

POP3 session capture.

1. Which port does POP3 use?
2. Which password is provided by the user?
3. Was the email message deleted after it was retrieved?
4. How long was the message?
5. How many other messages are in the user's mailbox?

CHAPTER

Hypertext Transfer Protocol

22

What You Will Learn

In this chapter, you will learn about the HTTP protocol used on the Web, including the major message types and HTTP methods. We'll also discuss the status codes and headers used in HTTP.

You will learn how URLs are structured and how to decipher them. We'll also take a brief look at the use of cookies and how they apply to the Web.

After email, the World Wide Web is probably the most common TCP/IP application general users are familiar with. In fact, many users access their email through their Web browser, which is a tribute to the versatility of the protocols used to make the Web such a vital part of the Internet experience.

There is no need to repeat the history of the Web and browser, which are covered in other places. It is enough to note here that the Web browser is a type of "universal client" that can be used to access almost any type of server, from email to the file transfer protocal (FTP) and beyond. The unique addressing and location scheme employed with a browser along with several related protocols combine to make "surfing the Web" (it's really more like fishing or trawling) an essential part of many people's lives around the world.

The protocol used to convey formatted Web pages to the browser is the Hypertext Transfer Protocol (HTTP). Often confused with the Web page formatting standard, the Hypertext Markup Language (HTML), it is HTTP we will investigate in this chapter. The more one learns about how the Hypertext Transfer Protocol and the browser interact with the Web site and TCP/IP, the more impressed people tend to become with the system as a whole. The wonder is not that browsers sometimes freeze or open unwanted windows or let worms wiggle into the host but that it works effectively and efficiently at all.

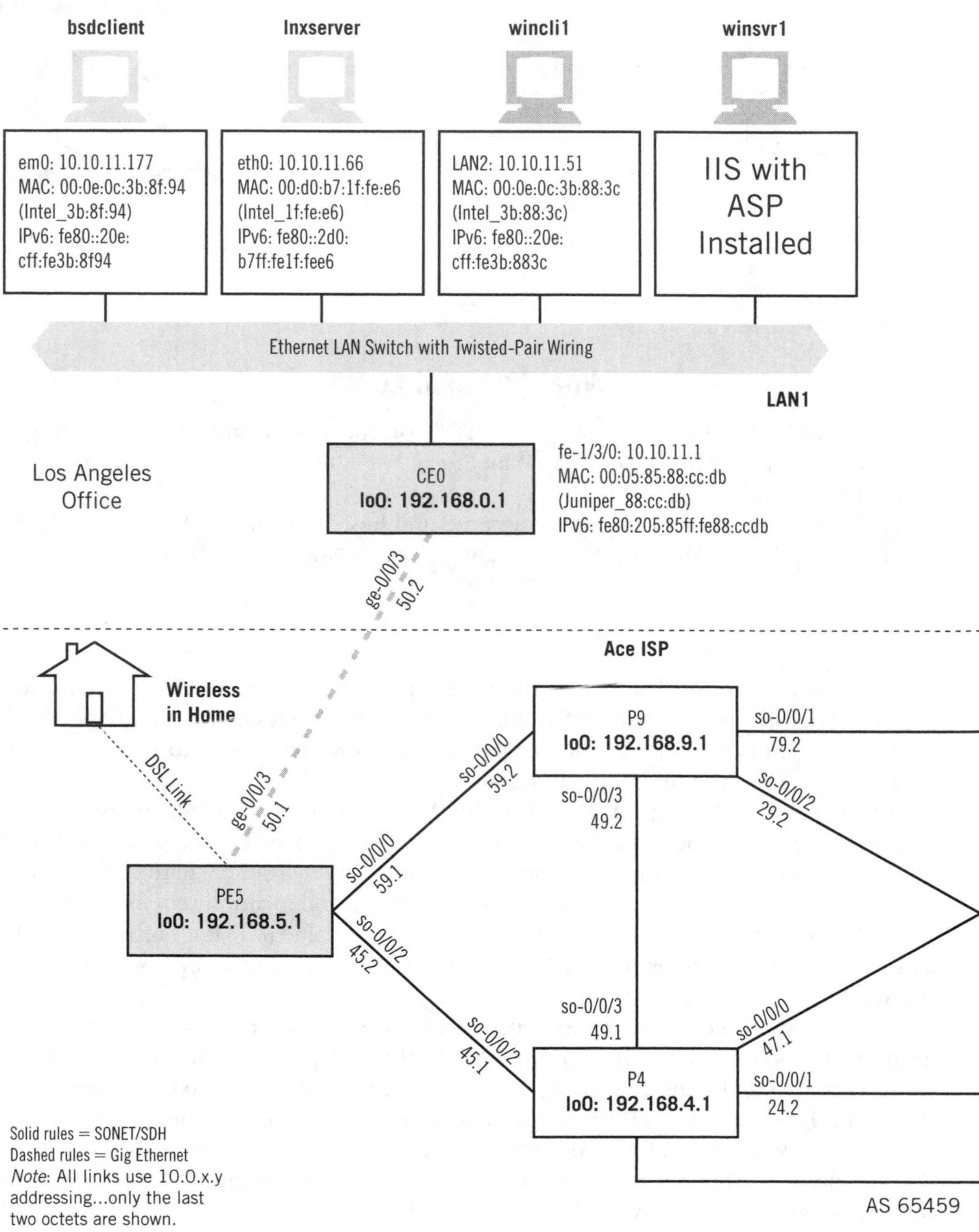

FIGURE 22.1

The Web servers on the Illustrated Network, also showing the major client browser hosts. Note that we'll be using IIS with ASP on the Windows platform and Apache with SSL on the Unix host.

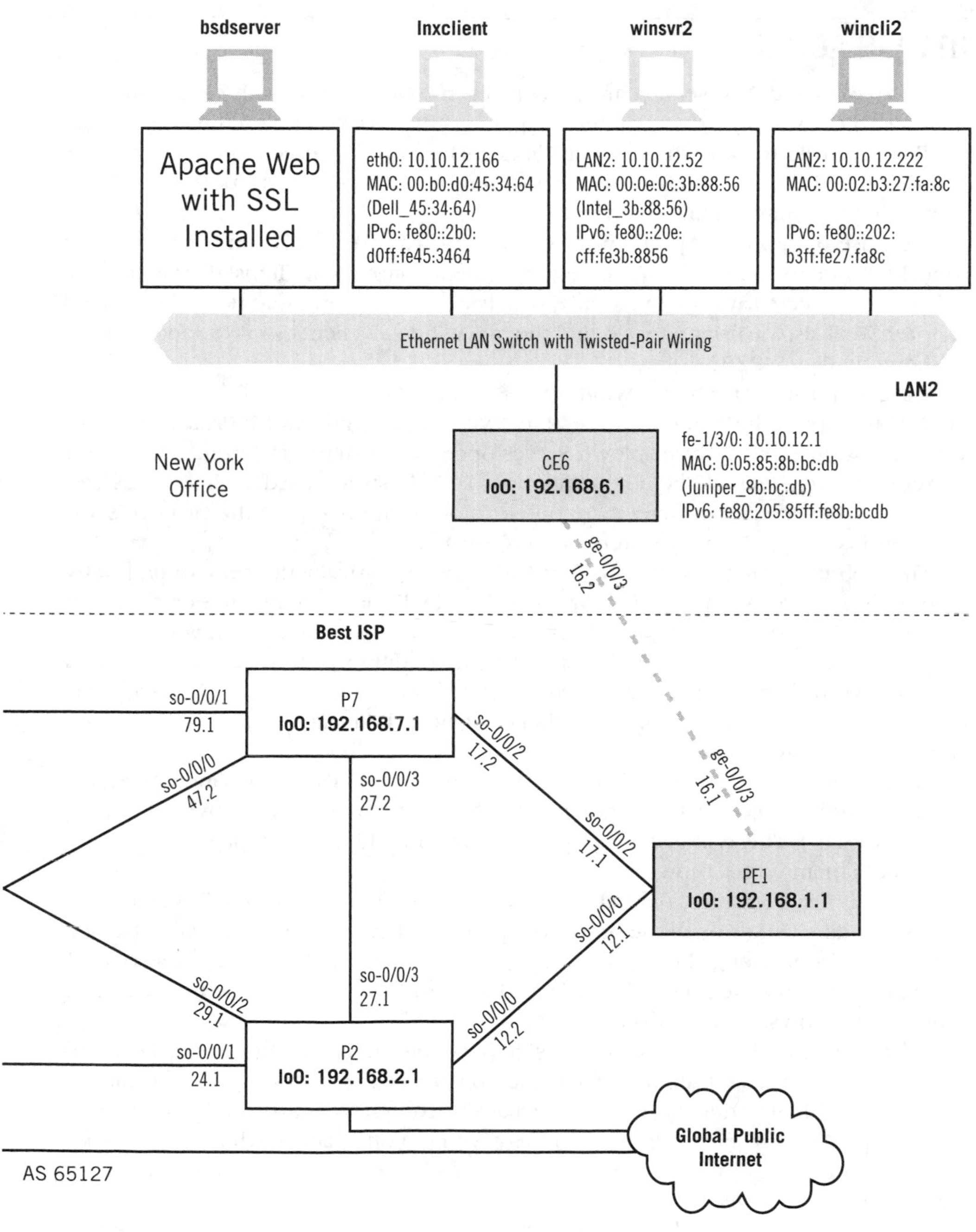
bsdserver
lnxclient
winsvr2
wincli2
Apache Web with SSL Installed
eth0: 10.10.12.166
MAC: 00:b0:d0:45:34:64
(Dell_45:34:64)
IPv6: fe80::2b0:d0ff:fe45:3464
LAN2: 10.10.12.52
MAC: 00:0e:0c:3b:88:56
(Intel_3b:88:56)
IPv6: fe80::20e:cff:fe3b:8856
LAN2: 10.10.12.222
MAC: 00:02:b3:27:fa:8c
IPv6: fe80::202:b3ff:fe27:fa8c
Ethernet LAN Switch with Twisted-Pair Wiring
LAN2
New York Office
CE6
lo0: 192.168.6.1
fe-1/3/0: 10.10.12.1
MAC: 0:05:85:8b:bc:db
(Juniper_8b:bc:db)
IPv6: fe80:205:85ff:fe8b:bcdb
ge-0/0/3
16.2
Best ISP
so-0/0/1
79.1
P7
lo0: 192.168.7.1
so-0/0/2
17.2
ge-0/0/3
16.1
so-0/0/0
47.2
so-0/0/3
27.2
so-0/0/2
17.1
PE1
lo0: 192.168.1.1
so-0/0/0
12.1
so-0/0/2
29.1
so-0/0/3
27.1
so-0/0/0
12.2
so-0/0/1
24.1
P2
lo0: 192.168.2.1
Global Public Internet
AS 65127

HTTP IN ACTION

Web browsers and Web servers are perhaps even more familiar than electronic mail, but nevertheless there are some interesting things that can be explored with HTTP on the Illustrated Network. In this chapter, Windows hosts will be used to maximum effect. Not that the Linux and FreeBSD hosts could not run GUI browsers, but the "purity" of Unix is in the command line (not the GUI).

We'll use the popular Apache Web server software and install it on `bsdserver`. Just to make it interesting (and to prepare for the next chapter), we'll install Apache with the Secure Sockets Layer (SSL) module, which we'll look at in more detail in the next chapter. We'll also be using `winsrv1` and the two Windows clients, `wincli1` and `wincli2`, as shown in Figure 22.1.

We could install Apache for Windows XP as well, because one of the goals of this book is to explore how much can be done with basic Windows XP Professional. But we don't want to go into full-blown server operating systems and build a complete Windows server. It should be noted that many Unix hosts are used exclusively as Web sites or email servers, but here we're only exploring the basics of the protocols and applications, not their ability or relative performance.

The Web has changed a lot since the early days of statically defined content delivered with HTTP. Now it's common for the Web page displayed to be built on fly on the server, based on the user's request. There are many ways to do this, from good old Perl to Java and beyond, all favored and pushed by one vendor or platform group or another. In Windows, the "in-house" dynamic Web page software is called Active Service Pages (ASP). ASP works differently than the others, but all of them vary in large or small ways, so that's not really a criticism.

So, we'll install Integrated Information Services (IIS), available for Windows XP Pro and a few other (free) packages, notably the .NET Framework and Software Development Kit (SDK). This will make it possible for us to build ASP Web pages on `winsrv1` and access them with a browser.

The ASP installation was rather torturous, but there are invaluable Web sites and books that take you through the process step by step. One book includes an extremely simple Web page along the lines of "Hello World!" (but the Web page is also small enough to demonstrate how HTTP fetches the page). Figure 22.2 shows how the page looks in the browser window on `wincli2`.

What does the HTTP exchange look like between the client and server? Let's capture it with Ethereal and see what we come up with. Figure 22.3 shows the result.

Not surprisingly, after the TCP handshake the content is transferred with a single HTTP request and response pair. The entire page fit in one packet, which is detailed in the figure. And just as it should, once TCP acknowledges the transfer the connection stays open (persistent).

Note that the dynamic date and time content is transferred as a static string of text. All of the magic of dynamic content takes place on the server's "back room" and does not involve HTTP in the least.

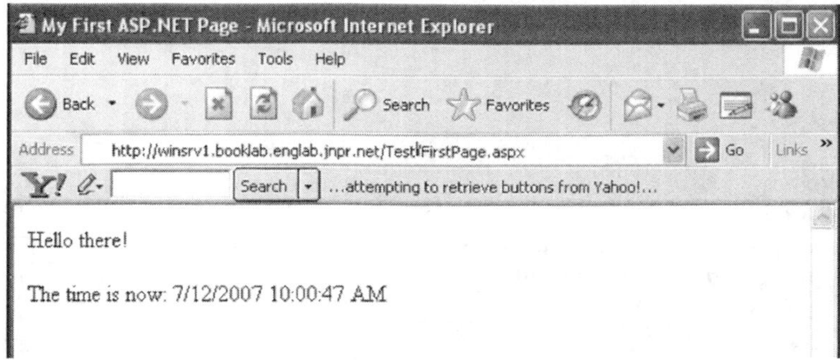

FIGURE 22.2

An ASP page from winsrv1. The "active" component means that the date and time on the page are kept current.

```
No.  Time      Source        Destination   Protocol Info
  1 0.000000  10.10.12.222  10.10.11.111  TCP      2858 > http [SYN] Seq=0 Ack=0 Win=65535 Len=0 MSS=1460
  2 0.000165  10.10.11.111  10.10.12.222  TCP      http > 2858 [SYN, ACK] Seq=0 Ack=1 Win=64512 Len=0 MSS=14
  3 0.000449  10.10.12.222  10.10.11.111  TCP      2858 > http [ACK] Seq=1 Ack=1 Win=65535 Len=0
  4 0.000717  10.10.12.222  10.10.11.111  HTTP     GET /Test/FirstPage.aspx HTTP/1.1
  5 0.003762  10.10.11.111  10.10.12.222  HTTP     HTTP/1.1 200 OK (text/html)
  6 0.172041  10.10.12.222  10.10.11.111  TCP      2858 > http [ACK] Seq=220 Ack=403 Win=65133 Len=0

▷ Transmission Control Protocol, Src Port: http (80), Dst Port: 2858 (2858), Seq: 1, Ack: 220, Len: 402
▼ Hypertext Transfer Protocol
  ▷ HTTP/1.1 200 OK\r\n
    Server: Microsoft-IIS/5.1\r\n
    Date: Tue, 12 Jul 2007 17:18:10 GMT\r\n
    X-Powered-By: ASP.NET\r\n
    X-AspNet-Version: 1.1.4322\r\n
    Cache-Control: private\r\n
    Content-Type: text/html; charset=utf-8\r\n
    Content-Length: 183\r\n
    \r\n
▽ Line-based text data: text/html
    <html>
    <head>
    <title>My First ASP.NET Page</title>

    </head>
    <body>
    <p>Hello there!</p>
    <p>The time is now: <span id="lblTime">7/12/2007 10:18:10 AM</span></p>
    </body>
    </html>

0030  fb 25 2e 0d 00 00 48 54  54 50 2f 31 2e 31 20 32   .%....HT TP/1.1 2
0040  30 30 20 4f 4b 0d 0a 53  65 72 76 65 72 3a 20 4d   00 OK..S erver: M
0050  69 63 72 6f 73 6f 66 74  2d 49 49 53 2f 35 2e 31   icrosoft -IIS/5.1
0060  0d 0a 44 61 74 65 3a 20  54 75 65 2c 20 31 32 20   ..Date:  Tue, 12
0070  4a 75 6c 20 32 30 30 35  20 31 37 3a 31 38 3a 31   Jul 2007  17:18:1
```

FIGURE 22.3

Capture of the HTTP for the ASP page, showing how the protocol identifies the "make and model" of the Web site (Microsoft IIS using ASP.NET).

What about more involved content? Let's see what the default Apache with SSL page looks like from `wincli2` when we install it on `bsdserver`. This is shown in Figure 22.4.

This is just the default index.html page showing that Apache installed successfully. There is no "real" SSL on this page, however. There is no security or encryption

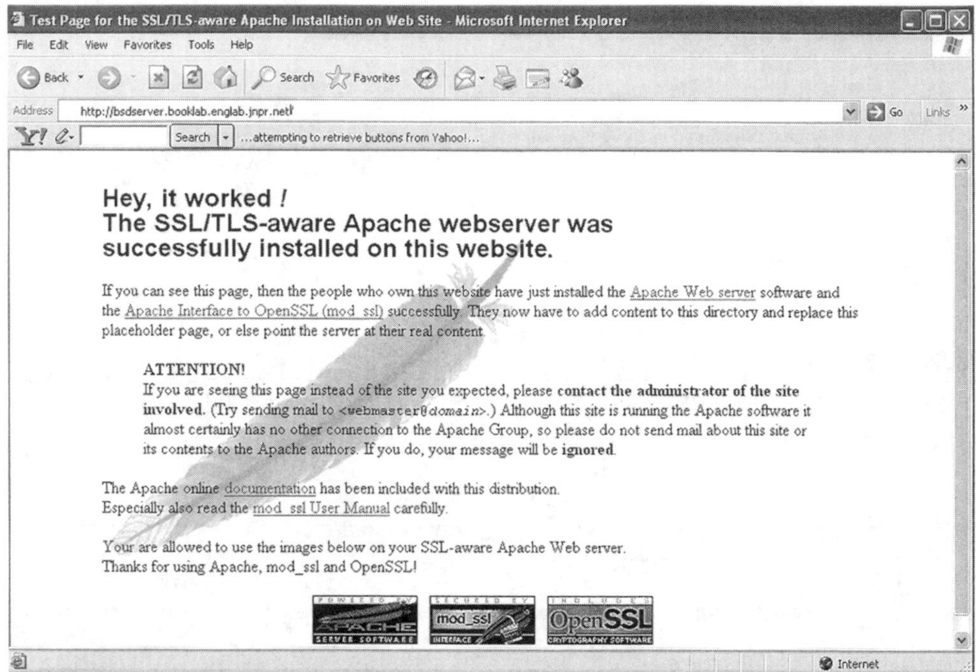

FIGURE 22.4

Apache HTTP "success" page displayed when the software is installed correctly.

No.	Time	Source	Destination	Protocol	Info
6	19.869191	10.10.12.222	10.10.12.77	TCP	2870 > http [SYN] Seq=0 Ack=0 Win=65535 Len=0 MSS=1460
7	19.869421	10.10.12.77	10.10.12.222	TCP	http > 2870 [SYN, ACK] Seq=0 Ack=1 Win=57344 Len=0 MSS=
8	19.869446	10.10.12.222	10.10.12.77	TCP	2870 > http [ACK] Seq=1 Ack=1 Win=65535 [CHECKSUM INCOR
9	19.869615	10.10.12.222	10.10.12.77	HTTP	GET / HTTP/1.1
10	19.874838	10.10.12.77	10.10.12.222	HTTP	HTTP/1.1 200 OK (text/html)
11	19.874961	10.10.12.77	10.10.12.222	HTTP	Continuation
12	19.874970	10.10.12.77	10.10.12.222	HTTP	Continuation
13	19.875008	10.10.12.222	10.10.12.77	TCP	2870 > http [ACK] Seq=284 Ack=3115 Win=65535 [CHECKSUM
14	19.878090	10.10.12.222	10.10.12.77	HTTP	GET /manual/images/apache_pb.gif HTTP/1.1
15	19.879332	10.10.12.222	10.10.12.77	TCP	2871 > http [SYN] Seq=0 Ack=0 Win=65535 Len=0 MSS=1460
16	19.879369	10.10.12.77	10.10.12.222	HTTP	HTTP/1.1 304 Not Modified
17	19.879614	10.10.12.77	10.10.12.222	TCP	http > 2871 [SYN, ACK] Seq=0 Ack=1 Win=57344 Len=0 MSS=
18	19.879634	10.10.12.222	10.10.12.77	TCP	2871 > http [ACK] Seq=1 Ack=1 Win=65535 [CHECKSUM INCOR
19	19.881509	10.10.12.222	10.10.12.77	HTTP	GET /manual/images/mod_ssl_sb.gif HTTP/1.1
20	19.882138	10.10.12.77	10.10.12.222	HTTP	HTTP/1.1 304 Not Modified
21	19.882186	10.10.12.222	10.10.12.77	HTTP	GET /manual/images/openssl_ics.gif HTTP/1.1
22	19.883464	10.10.12.77	10.10.12.222	HTTP	HTTP/1.1 304 Not Modified
23	19.886588	10.10.12.222	10.10.12.77	HTTP	GET /manual/images/feather.jpg HTTP/1.1
24	19.887160	10.10.12.77	10.10.12.222	HTTP	HTTP/1.1 304 Not Modified
25	20.102066	10.10.12.222	10.10.12.77	TCP	2871 > http [ACK] Seq=685 Ack=446 Win=65090 [CHECKSUM I
26	20.102104	10.10.12.222	10.10.12.77	TCP	2870 > http [ACK] Seq=970 Ack=3559 Win=65091 [CHECKSUM

```
▷ Frame 24 (277 bytes on wire, 277 bytes captured)
▷ Ethernet II, Src: 00:0e:0c:3b:87:32, Dst: 00:02:b3:27:fa:8c
▷ Internet Protocol, Src Addr: 10.10.12.77 (10.10.12.77), Dst Addr: 10.10.12.222 (10.10.12.222)
▷ Transmission Control Protocol, Src Port: http (80), Dst Port: 2871 (2871), Seq: 223, Ack: 685, Len: 223
▽ Hypertext Transfer Protocol
  ▷ HTTP/1.1 304 Not Modified\r\n
    Date: Tue, 12 Jul 2005 17:49:02 GMT\r\n
    Server: Apache/1.3.33 (Unix) mod_ssl/2.8.22 OpenSSL/0.9.7d\r\n
    Connection: Keep-Alive, Keep-Alive\r\n
    Keep-Alive: timeout=15, max=98\r\n
    ETag: "22c9a-1bc4-380f63c6"\r\n
```

FIGURE 22.5

HTTP Apache capture. Most of the text is transferred in only a few packets.

involved. What does the HTTP capture look like now? It's captured on `wincli2` (shown in Figure 22.5).

This exchange involved 21 packets, and would have been longer if the image had not been cached on the client (a simple "Not Modified" string is all that is needed to fetch it onto the page). Most of the text is transferred in packets 10 through 12, and then the images on the page are "filled in." We'll take a look at the SSL aspects of this Web site in the next chapter.

Before getting into the nuts and bolts of HTTP, there is a related topic that must be investigated first. This is an appreciation of the addressing system used by browsers and Web servers to locate the required information in whatever form it may be stored. There are three closely related systems defined for the Internet (not just the Web). These are uniform resource identifiers (URIs), locators (URLs), and names (URNs).

Uniform Resources

As if it weren't enough to have to deal with MAC addresses, IP addresses, ports, sockets, and email addresses, there is still another layer of addresses used in TCP/IP that has to be covered. These are "application layer" addresses, and unlike most of the other addresses (which are really defined by the needs of the particular protocol) application layer addresses are most useful to humans.

This is not to say that the addresses we are talking about here are the same as those used in DNS, where a simple correspondence between IP address `192.168.77.22` and the name `www.example.com` is established. As is fitting for the generalized Web browser, the addresses used are "universal"—and that was one name for them before someone figured out that they weren't really *universal* quite yet, but they were at least *uniform*.

So, labels were invented not only to tell the browser which host to go to and application use but what *resources* the browser was expecting to find and just where they were located. Let's start with the general form for these labels, the URI.

URIs

The generic term for resource location labels in TCP/IP is *URI*. One specific form of URI, used with the Web, is the URL. The use of URLs as an instance of URIs has become so commonplace that most people don't bother to distinguish the two, but they are technically distinct.

The latest work on URIs is RFC 2396, which updated several older RFCs (including RFC 1738, which defines URLs). In the RFC, a URI is simply defined as "a compact string of characters for identifying an abstract or physical resource." There is no mention of the Web specifically, although it was the popularity of the Web that led to the development of uniform resource notations in the first place.

When a user accesses `http://www.example.com` from a Web browser, that string is a URI as much as a URL. So, what's the difference between the URI and the URL?

URLs

RFC 1738 defined a URL format for use on the Web (although the RFC just says "Internet"). Newer URI rules all respect conventions that have grown up around URLs over the years. URLs are a subset of URIs, and like URIs, consist of two parts: a *method* used to access the resource, and the *location* of the resource itself. Together, the parts of the URL provide a way for users to access files, objects, programs, audio, video, and much more on the Web.

The method is labeled by a scheme, and usually refers to a TCP/IP application or protocol, such as `http` or `ftp`. Schemes can include plus signs (+), periods (.), or hyphens (-), but in practice they contain only letters. Methods are case insensitive, so `HTTP` is the same as `http` (but by convention they are expressed in lowercase letters).

The locator part of the URL follows the scheme and is separated from it by a colon and two forward slashes (`://`). The format or the locator depends on the type of scheme, and if one part of the locator is left out, default values come into play. The scheme-specific information is parsed by the received host based on the actual scheme (method) used in the URL.

Theoretically, each scheme uses an independently defined locator. In practice, because URLs use TCP/IP and Internet conventions many of the schemes share a common syntax. For example, both `http` and `ftp` schemes use the DNS name or IP address to identify the target host and expect to find the resource in a hierarchical directory file structure.

The most general form of URL for the Web is shown in Figure 22.6. There is very little difference between this format and the general format of a URI, and some of these differences are mentioned in the material that follows the figure.

The format changes a bit with method, so an FTP URL has only a `type=<typecode>` field as the single `<params>` field following the `<url-path>`. For example, a type code of `d` is used to request an FTP directory listing. The figure shows the general field for the `http` method.

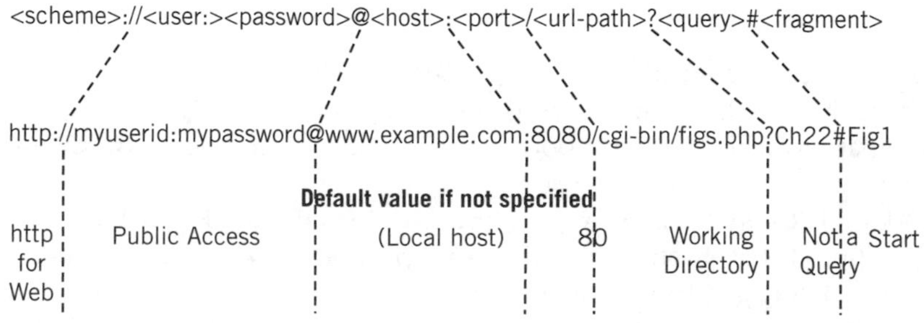

FIGURE 22.6

The fields of a complete URL, showing that the default values used in the fields are absent.

<scheme>—The method used to access the resource. The default method for a Web browser is `http`.

<user> and <password>—In a URI, this is the `authorization` field. A URL's authorization consists of a user ID and password separated by a colon (:). Many private Web sites require user authorization, and if not provided in the URL the user is prompted for this information. When absent, the user defaults to publicly available resource access.

<host>—Called the `networkpath` in a URI, the host is specified in a URL by DNS name or IP address (IPv6 works fine for servers using that address form).

<port>—This is the TCP or UDP port that together with the host information specifies the socket where the method appropriate to the scheme is found. For `http`, the default port is 80.

<url-path>—The URI specification calls this the `absolutepath`. In a URL, this is usually the directory path starting from the default directory to where the resource is to be found. If this field is absent, the Web site has a default directory into which the user is placed. The forward slash (/) before the path is not technically part of the path, but forms the delimiter and must follow the port. If the `url-path` ends in another slash, this means a directory and not a "file" (but most Web sites figure out whether the path ends at a file or directory on their own). A double dot (..) moves the user up one level from the default directory.

<params>—These parameters control how the method is used on the resource and are scheme specific. Each parameter has the form <parameter>=<value> and the parameters are separated by semicolons (;). If there are no parameters, the default action for the resource is taken.

<query>—This URL field contains information used by the server to form the response. Whereas parameters are scheme specific, query information is resource specific.

<fragment>—The field is used to indicate which particular part of the resource the user is interested in. By default, the user is presented with the start of the entire resource.

Most of the time, a simple URL, such as `ftp://ftp.example.com`, works just fine for users. But let's look at a couple of examples of fairly complex URLs to illustrate the use of these fields.

http://myself:mypassword@mail.example.com:32888/mymail/ShowLetter?MsgID-5551212#1

The user `myself`, authenticated with `mypassword`, is accessing the `mail.example.com` server at TCP port `32888`, going to the directory `/mymail`, and running the `ShowLetter` program. The letter is identified to the program as `MsgID-5551212`, and the first part of the message is requested (this form is typically used for a multipart MIME message).

www.examplephotos.org:8080/cgi-bin/pix.php?WeddingPM#Reception19

The user is going to a publicly accessible part of the site called `www.examplephotos.org`, which is running on TCP port `8080` (a popular alternative or addition to port 80). The resource is the PHP program `pix.php` in the `cgi-bin` directory below the default directory, and the URL asks for a particular page of photographs to be accessed (`WeddingPM`) and for a particular photograph (`Reception19`) to be presented.

www.sample.com/who%20are%20you%3F

File names that have embedded spaces and special characters that are the same as URL delimiters can be a problem. This URL accesses a file named `who are you?` in the default directory at the `www.sample.com` site. There are 21 "unsafe" URL characters that can be represented this way.

There are many other URL "rules" (as for Windows files), and quite a few tricks. For example, if we wanted to make a Web page at `www.loserexample.com` (IP address `192.168.1.1`) appear as if it is located at `www.nobelprizewinners.org`, we can translate the Web site's IP address to decimal (`192.168.1.1 = 0xC0A80101 =` 3232235777 decimal), add some "bogus" authentication information in front of it (which will be ignored by the Web site), and hope that no one remembers the URL formatting rules:

http://www.nobelprizewinners.org@3232235777

A lot of evil hackers use this trick to make people think they are pointing and clicking at a link to their bank's Web site when they are really about to enter their account information into the hacker's server! Well, if that's what a URL is for, why is a URN needed?

URNs

URNs extend the URI and URL concept beyond the Web, beyond the Internet even, right into the ordinary world. URIs and URLs proved so popular that the system was extended to become URNs. URNs, first proposed in RFC 2141, would solve a particularly vexing problem with URLs.

It may be a tautology, but a URL specifies resources by *location*. This can be a problem for a couple of reasons. First, the resource (such as a freeware utility program) could exist on many Web servers, but if it is not on the one the URL is pointing to the familiar `HTTP 404 - NOT FOUND` error results. And how many times has a Web site moved, changing name or IP address or both—leaving thousands of pages with embedded links to the stale information? (URLs do not automatically supply a helpful "You are being directed to our new site" message.)

As expected, URNs label resources by a *name* rather than a location. The familiar Web URL is a little like going by address to a particular house on a particular street and asking for Joe Smith. A URN is like asking for Joe Smith, getting an answer from a "resolver," and going to the current address where good old Joe is found. "Joe Smith" is an example of a URN in the human "namespace." Of course, if this is to work properly there can only be one Joe Smith in the world.

Any namespace that can be used to uniquely identify *any* type of resource can be used as a URN. But before you rush out to invent a URN system for automobiles, for example, keep in mind that designing URNs for new namespaces is not that easy.

Each URN must be recognized by some official body or another, and must be strictly defined by a formal language. It's not enough to say that the URN string will identify a car. It is necessary to define things such as the length of the string and just what is allowed in the string and what isn't (actually, there's a lot more to it than that).

For example, the International Standard Book Number (ISBN) system uniquely identifies books published all over the world. Part of the number identifies region of the world where the book is published, another part the publisher, yet another part the particular book, and finally there is a checksum digit that is computed in case someone makes a mistake writing down one of the other parts. The formal definition of the ISBN namespace would establish the length of these fields, and note that the ISBN must be 10 digits long and can only be made up of the digits 0 through 9, except for the last checksum digit, where the Roman numeral X is used for the checksum 10 (10 is a valid ISBN checksum "digit"). The general format of a URN is URN:<namespace-ID>:<resource-identifier>.

Note the lack of any sense of location. The namespace ID is needed to distinguish a 10-digit telephone number from a 10 digit ISBN numbers (for example), and the URN literally makes it obvious that the URN notation system is being employed.

Work on URNs has been slow. A resource identified by URN still has a location, and so must still provide one or more URLs (think of all the places where a certain book might be located) to the user. A series of RFCs, from RFC 3401 to RFC 3406, defines a system of URN "resolvers" called the *Dynamic Delegation Discovery System* (DDDS). For now, the Internet will have to make do with URLs.

HTTP

HTTP started out as a very simple protocol, based on the familiar scheme of a small set of commands issued by the client (browser) and reply codes and related information issued by the server (Web site). As indicated by the name, the original HTTP (and HTML) concerned itself with hyper*text*, the idea being to embed active links in textual information and allow users to spontaneously follow their instincts from page to page and site to site around the Internet and around the world. There were also graphics associated with the Web almost immediately, and this was a startling enough innovation to completely change the user perception of the Internet.

The original version of HTTP, now called HTTP 0.9, was just something people did if they wanted their Web sites to work, and nobody bothered to write down much about it. The people who wanted to know found out how it worked. This was fine for a few years, but once the Web got rolling RFC 1945 in 1996 defined HTTP 1.0 (a more full-blooded protocol)—which made "old" HTTP into HTPP 0.9. Then HTTP 1.1 came along in 1997 with RFC 2068, which was extended in 1999 with RFC 2616. And that was pretty much it. The basic HTTP 1.1 is what we live and work with on the Internet today.

However, it's always good to remember what HTTP is and isn't. HTTP is just a transport mechanism for Web stuff, and not only for varied *content*. HTTP is flexible enough to transport Web features such as cascading style sheets (CCSs), Java Applets, Active Server Pages (ASPs), Perl scripts, and any one of the half dozen of so languages and programming tools that have evolved to make Web servers more complex and paradoxically easier to configure and use.

The Evolution of HTTP

HTTP began as a simple TCP/IP request/response language using TCP to retrieve information from a server in a *stateless* manner (most TCP/IP applications are stateless). Because the server is stateless, the server has no idea of any history of the interaction between client and server. Therefore, any state information has to be stored in the client. We'll talk about *cookies* later, after looking at the basics of HTTP.

With HTTP 0.9, a basic browser accessed a Web page by issuing a `GET` command for the page desired (indicated in the URL), accompanied by a number of HTTP *headers*. This was sent over a TCP connection established between the browser port and port 80 (the default Web port) on the server. The server responded with the text-based Web page marked up in HTML and closed the TCP session. The initial browser command was usually `GET /index`.html.

But what about the graphics and audio in the reply, if included in the Web page? HTML is a *markup* language, meaning that special *tags* are inserted into an ordinary text file to control the appearance of the Web page on the browser screen. Once the initial request transfer was made in HTTP 0.9, the browser parsed the HTML tags and opened a separate TCP connection to the server for every *element* of the page. This is why the location of the graphics and associated media files are so important in HTML: they aren't really "there" on the page in any sense until HTTP is used to fetch them.

Naturally, the TCP overhead involved with all of this shuttling of information was staggering, especially on slow dial-up links and when Web pages grew to include 30 or more elements. Some Web sites shut down as the "listen" queues filled up, router links became saturated with TCP overhead, and browsers hung as frustrated users began pounding and clicking everything in sight (one old Internet Explorer message box begged "Stop doing that!").

Interim solutions were not particularly effective. Many solutions made use of massive caching of Web pages on "intermediate systems" that were closer to the perceived user pool, and many businesses used "proxy servers" (an old Internet security mechanism pressed into service as a caching storehouse). Caching Web pages became so common that Internet gurus felt compelled to remind everyone that the point of TCP was that it was an *end-to-end* protocol and that fetching Web pages from caches from proxy servers was not the same as the real thing.

So, HTTP evolved to make the entire process more efficient. HTTP 1.0 created a true messaging protocol and added support for MIME types, adapted for the Web, and addressed some of the issues with HTTP 0.9 (but not all). In addition, vendors had been incrementally adding features here and there haphazardly. HTTP 1.1 brought all of these changes under one specification. In particular, HTTP 1.1 added:

Persistent connections: A client can send multiple requests for related resources in a single TCP session.

Pipelining—Persistent connections permitted clients to pipeline requests to the server. If the browser requests images 1, 2, and 3 from the server, the client does not have to wait for a response to the image 1 request before requesting file 2. This allows the server to handle requests much more efficiently.

Multiple host name support—Web sites could now run more than one Web server per IP address and host name. Today, one Web server can handle requests for literally hundreds of individual Web sites, all running as "virtual hosts" on the server.

Partial resource selection—A client can ask for only part of a document of resource.

Content negotiation—The client and server can exchange information to allow the client to select the best format for a resource, such as MP3 or WAV format for audio files (the formats must be available on the server, of course). This negotiation is not the same as presenting format options to the user.

Better security—Authentication was added to HTTP interactions with RFC 2617.

Better support for caching and proxying—Rules were added to make caching of Web pages and the operation of proxy servers more uniform.

HTTP 1.1 is the current version of HTTP. With so many millions of Web sites in operation today, any fundamental changes to HTTP would be unthinkable. Instead, changes to HTTP are to be made through extensions to HTTP 1.1. Unfortunately, not everyone agrees about the best way to do this. An HTTP extension "framework" was written as RFC 2774 in 2000 but has never moved beyond the experimental stage.

HTTP Model

The simplest HTTP interaction is for a browser client to send a request directly to the Web site server (running `httpd`) and get a response over a TCP connection between client and server. With HTTP 1.1, the model was extended to allow for *intermediaries* in the path between client and server. These devices can be proxies, gateways, tunnel endpoints, and so on. Proxy servers are especially popular for the Web, and a company frequently uses them to improve response time for job-related queries and to provide security for the corporate LAN.

Like FTP, HTTP invites data from "untrustworthy" sources right in the front door, and the proxy tries to screen harmful pages out. The proxy also protects IP addresses and

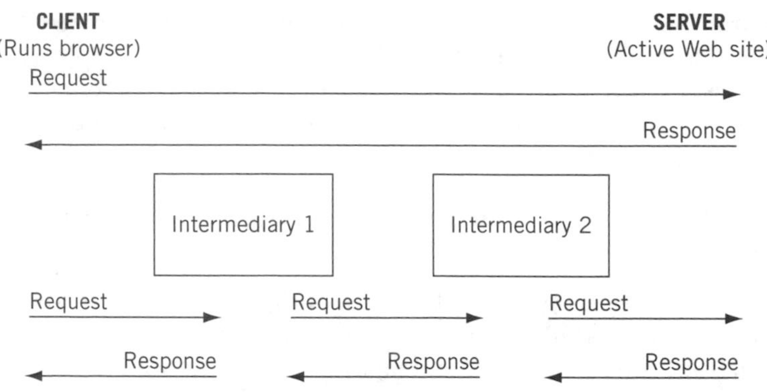

FIGURE 22.7

The HTTP models of interaction, showing how intermediaries can act on a request or response.

other types of information from leaving the site. (Some companies feared that workers would fritter away company time and so tried to limit Web access with proxies as well.) With an intermediary in place, the direct request/response becomes a four-step process.

1. *Browser request:* HTTP client sends the request to the intermediary.
2. *Intermediary request:* The intermediary makes changes to the request and forwards the request to the actual Web server.
3. *Web server response:* The Web site interprets the request and sends the reply back to the intermediary.
4. *Intermediary response:* The intermediary device processes the reply, makes changes, and forwards it to the client browser.

Generally, intermediaries become security devices that can perform a variety of functions, which we will explore later in this book. It is not unusual to find more than one intermediary on the path from HTTP client to server. In these scenarios, the request (and response) is *created* once but sent three times, usually with slightly different information. The difference between direct interactions and those with intermediaries is shown in Figure 22.7.

HTTP Messages

All HTTP messages are either requests or responses. Clients almost always issue requests, and servers almost always issue responses. Intermediaries can do both. The HTTP *generic message format* is similar to a text-based email message and is defined as a series of headers followed by an optional message body and trailer (which consists of more "headers"). The whole is introduced by a "start line."

```
<start-line>
<message-headers>
<empty-line>
[<message-body>]
[<message-trailers>]
```

The start line text identifies the nature of the message. HTTP headers can be presented in any order at all, and they follow a `<header-name>:<header-value>` convention. The message body frequently carries a file (called an *entity* in HTTP) found more often in responses than in requests. Special headers describe the encoding and other characteristics of the entity.

TRAILERS AND DYNAMIC WEB PAGES

Web pages were originally statically defined in HTML and passed out to whoever was allowed to see them. Web pages today are sometimes still created this way, but the most sophisticated Web pages create their content dynamically, on the fly, after a user has requested it. And for reasons of efficiency, the beginning can be streamed toward the browser before the end of the result has been determined. Pages that include current date and time stamps are good examples of dynamic Web page content, but of course many are much more complex.

Dynamic Web pages, however, pose a problem for persistent TCP connections. The browser has to know when the entire Web page response has been received. With a static Web page, the size is announced in a header at the start of the item. But dynamic page headers cannot list the size ahead of time, because the server does not know.

HTTP today uses *chunked encoding* to solve this problem. As soon as it is known, each piece of the response gets it own size (the chunk) and is sent to the browser. The last chunk has size 0, and can include optional "trailer" information consisting of a series of HTTP headers.

HTTP Requests and Responses

HTTP requests are a specific instance of the generic message format. They are introduced by a "request line."

```
<request-line>
<general-headers>
<request-headers>
<entity-headers>
<empty-line>
[<message-body>]
[<message-trailers>]
```

A typical initial request from a browser to the Web site is shown in Figure 22.8.

Request line	GET.index.html HTTP/1.1
General headers	Date: Mon, 04 July 2007 19:12:45 GMT Connection: close
Request headers	Host: www.example.com From: walterg@example.com Accept: text/html, text/plain User-Agent: MSIE6.0 (Windows XP)
Entity headers	
Message body	

FIGURE 22.8

The HTTP request message, showing some details of the general and request headers.

Status line	HTTP/1.1 200 OK
General headers	Date: Mon, 04 July 2007 19:12:48 GMT Connection: close
Response headers	Server: Apache/1/3/27 Accept-Range: bytes
Entity headers	Content-Type: text/html Content-Length: 170 Last-Modified: Fri, 01 July 2007 22:15:32 GMT
Message body	<html> <head> <title>Welcome to the Illustrated Network Site!</title> </head> <body> <p> This site under construction. Check back later... </p> </body> </html>

FIGURE 22.9

The HTTP response message, showing the headers usually included.

If the request is sent to an intermediary, such as a proxy server, the host name would appear in the request line as the resource's full URL: `GET http://www.example.com`. The use of the general, request, and entity headers are fairly self-explanatory. Request headers, however, can be conditional and are only filled if certain criteria are met. Each HTTP request to a server generates a response, and sometimes two (a preliminary response and then the full response). The format is only slightly different from the request.

```
<status-line>
<general-headers>
<response-headers>
<entity-headers>
<empty-line>
[<message-body>]
[<message-trailers>]
```

The status line has two purposes: It tells the client what version of HTTP is in use and summarizes the results of processing the client's request. The results are set as a status code and reason phrase associated with it. The structure of a typical HTTP response, sent in response to the request shown in Figure 22.8, is shown in Figure 22.9. The response headers provide details for the overall status summarized in the first line of the response.

HTTP Methods

HTTP commands, such as GET, are not called commands at all. HTTP is an *object-oriented* language, and instead of pointing out that *all* languages used for programming are to one extent or another object oriented we'll just mention that HTTP commands are called *methods*. (Yes, the URI method `http` has other HTTP methods beneath it.) Most HTTP messages use the first three methods almost exclusively. The HTTP methods are:

`GET`—Requests a resource from a Web site by URL. Sometimes also used to upload form data, but this is not a secure method. When the request headers contain conditionals, this situation is often called a *conditional GET*. When part of a resource is requested, this is sometimes called a *partial GET*.

`HEAD`—Formatted very much like a `GET`, the `HEAD` requests only the HTTP headers from the server (not the target itself). Clients use this to see if the resource is actually there before asking for a potentially monstrous file.

`POST`—Sends a block of data from the browser to the server, usually data from a form the user has filled out or some other application data. The URL sent must identify the function (program) that processes the data on the server.

`PUT`—Also sends data to the server, but asks the server to store the body of the data as a resource (file), which must be named in the URL. This can be used (with authentication) to store a file on the server, but FTP is most often used to accomplish this and thus PUT is not often used (or allowed).

`OPTIONS`—Requests information about communication options available on the Web server, with an asterisk (*) asking for details about the server itself. Not surprisingly, this method can be a security risk.

`DELETE`—Asks the server to delete the resource, which must be named in the URL. Not often used, for the same reasons as PUT.

`TRACE`—Used to debug Web applications, especially when proxy servers and gateways are in use. The client asks for a copy of the request it sent.

`CONNECT`—Reserved for future use with SSL tunneling.

The initial HTTP RFC 2068 also defined `PATCH`, `LINK`, and `UNLINK`, but these have been removed. However, some sources continue to list them. Most of the HTTP methods are

Table 22.1 HTTP Status Codes and Their Meanings

Code	Meaning
1xx	Informational, such as "request received" or "continuing process"
2xx	Successful reception, processing, acceptance, or completion
3xx	Redirection, indicating further action is needed to complete the request
4xx	Client error, such as the familiar 404, not found often, indicating syntax error
5xx	Server error when the Web site fails to fulfill a valid request

"safe" methods that can be repeated by impatient users without harm. The exception is the `POST` method, which should only be done once or side effects will result in inconsistent or just plain wrong information on the server.

HTTP Status Codes

The status codes used to provide status information to the browser are very similar to those used in FTP and email. Only the major (first) digit codes are listed in Table 22.1.

Each status code has an associated reason phrase. The reason phrases in the HTTP specification are "samples" that everyone copies and uses. They are intended as aids to memory and not as a full explanation of what is wrong when an error occurs. But a lot of browsers just display the 404 status code reason phrase, `Not Found`, and deem it adequate.

It's not necessary to list all of the HTTP status codes, but one does require additional comment. The 100 status code (reason phrase Continue) is often seen when a client is going to use the `POST` (or `PUT`) method to store a large amount of data on the server. The client might want to check to see whether the server can accept the data, rather than immediately sending it all. So, the request will have a special `Expect: 100-continue` header in it asking the server to reply with a `100 Continue` preliminary reply if all is well. After this response is received, the client can send the data.

That's the theory, anyway. In practice, it's a little different. Clients usually go ahead and send the data even if they *don't* get the `100 Continue` response from the server (hey, the browser has to do *something* with all of that data). And servers, perhaps thinking about all those users out there holding their breaths just waiting for `100 Continue` responses before they turn blue, often send out `100 Continue` preliminary responses for almost every request they get from a browser. But it was a fine idea.

HTTP Headers

It is not possible or necessary to list every HTTP header. Instead, we can just a take a look at the types of things HTTP headers do. First, some of the headers are *end-to-end* and others are *hop-by-hop*. As might be expected, the end-to-end headers are not changed as they make their way between client and server no matter how many

Table 22.2 HTTP General Headers and Their Uses

Header	Use
Cache-control	These contain a directive that establishes limits on how the request or response in cached. Only one directive can accompany a cache-control header, but multiple cache-control headers can be used.
Connection	These contain instructions that apply only to a particular connection. The headers are hop-by-hop and cannot be retained by proxies and used for other connections. The most common use is with the "close" parameters (Connection: close) to override a persistent connection and terminate the TCP session after the server response.
Date	Date and time the message originated, in RFC 822 email format.
Pragma	Implementation-specific directives similar to Unix programming. Often used for cache control in older versions of HTTP.
Trailer	When the response is chunked, this header is used before the data to indicate the presence of the trailer fields.
Transfer-encoding	Message body encoding, most often used with chunked transfers. This applies to the entire message, not a particular entity.
Upgrade	Clients can list connection protocols they support. If the server supports another in common, it can "upgrade" the connection and inform the client in the response.
Via	Used by intermediaries to allow client and server to trace the exact path.
Warning	Carries additional information about the message, usually from an intermediary device regarding cached information.

intermediary devices are between client and server. Hop-by-hop headers, on the other hand, have information relevant to each intermediary system.

General Headers

General headers are not supposed to be specific to any particular message or component. These convey information about the message itself, not about content. They also control how the message is handled and processed. However, in practice general headers are found in one type of message and not another. Some can have slightly different meanings in a request or response. The general headers are outlined in Table 22.2.

Request Headers

The request headers in an HTTP request message allow clients to supply information about themselves to the server, provide details about the request, and give the client more control over how the server handles the request and how (or if) the response is

Table 22.3 HTTP Request Headers and Their Uses

Header	Use
Accept	What media types the client will accept, including preference (q).
Accept-Charset	Similar to accept, but for character sets.
Accept-Encoding	Similar to accept, but for content encoding (especially compression).
Accept-Language	Similar to accept, but for language tags.
Authorization	Used to present authentication information ("credentials") to the server.
Expect	Tells the server what action the client expects next, usually "Continue."
From	Human user's email address. Optional, and for information only.
Host	Only mandatory header, used to specify DNS name/port of Web site.
If-Match	Usually in GET, server responds with entity only if it matches the value of the entity tags.
If-Modified-Since	Similar to If-Match, but only if the resource has changed in the time interval specified.
If-None-Match	Similar to If-Match, but the exact opposite.
If-Range	Used with Range header to check whether entity has changed and request that part of the entity.
If-Unmodified-Since	Opposite of If-Modified-Since.
Max-Forwards	Limits the number of intermediaries. Used with TRACE and OPTIONS. Value is decremented and when 0 must get a response.
Proxy-Authorization	Similar to Authorization, but used to present authentication information ("credentials") to a proxy server.
Range	Asks for part of an entity.
Referer	Never corrected to "referrer," this is used to supply the URL for the "back" button function to the server (also has privacy implications).
TE	Means "transfer encodings," and is often used with chunking.
User-Agent	Provides server with information about the client (name/version).

returned. This is the largest category of headers, and only the briefest description can be given of each. They are listed in Table 22.3.

Response Headers

HTTP response headers are the opposite of request headers and appear only in messages sent from server to browser. They expand on the information provided in the summary status line, as outlined in Table 22.4. Many response headers are sent only in answer to a specific type of request, or to certain headers within particular requests.

Table 22.4 HTTP Response Headers and Their Uses

Header	Use
Accept-Ranges	Tells client if server accepts partial content requests using Range request header. Typical values are in bytes, or "none" for no support.
Age	Tells the client the approximate age of the resource.
ETag	Gives the entity tag for the entity in the response.
Location	Gives client a new URL to use instead of one requested.
Proxy-Authenticate	Tells client how the proxy requires authentication, both method and parameters needed.
Retry-After	Tells client to try the request again later, seconds or by date/time.
Server	Server version of User-Agent request header, used for server details.
Vary	Used by caching devices to make decisions.
WWW-Authenticate	Tells client how the Web site requires authentication, both method and parameters needed.

Table 22.5 HTTP Entity Headers and Their Uses

Header	Use
Allow	Lists methods that apply to this resource.
Content-Encoding	Describes optional encoding method, usually the compression algorithm used so that the client can decompress the entity.
Content-Language	Specifies the human language used by the entity. It is optional and can specify multiple languages.
Content-Length	Size of the entity in bytes (octets). Not used in chunked transfers.
Content-Location	Resource location as URL. Optional, but used if entity is in multiple places.
Content-MD5	Used for message integrity checking with Message Digest 5.
Content-Range	Used for entities that are part of the complete resource.
Content-Type	Similar to MIME type and subtype, but not exactly the same.
Expires	Data and time after which entity is considered stale.
Last-Modified	Date and time server "believes" entity last changed.

Entity Headers

Finally, entity headers describe the resource carried in the body of the HTTP message. They usually appear in responses, but can appear in `PUT` and `POST` requests. Many of the entity headers have the same names as the MIME types they are based on, but with important differences. The entity headers are outlined in Table 22.5.

Use of the Last-Modified header is complicated by the fact that the server might not know when an entity was last modified, especially if the resource is "virtual." For dynamic content, this header should be the same as the time the message was generated.

Cookies

A Web server gets a request, processes a request, and returns a response in a completely stateless manner. Every request, even from the same client a moment later, looks brand new to the server.

Stateless servers are the easiest to operate. If they fail, just start them up again. No one cares where they left off. You can even transfer processing to another host and everything runs just fine, as long as the resources are there. Stateless servers are best for simple resource-retrieval systems.

That's how the Web started out, but unfortunately this is not how the Web is used today. Web sites have shopping carts that remember content and billing systems that remember credit card information. They also remember log-in information that would otherwise have to be entered every time an HTTP request was made.

How should the state information necessary for the Web today be stored? For better or worse, the answer today is in *cookies*. The term seems to have originated in older programs that required users to supply a "magic cookie" to make the program do something out of the ordinary ("Easter eggs" seem to be the GUI equivalent). According to others, an old computer virus put the image onscreen of Cookie Monster (of *Sesame Street* fame) announcing, "Want cookie!" The user had to type the word *cookie* to continue. The *cookie* term is also used in BOOTP/DHCP.

Cookies were initially developed by Netscape and were formalized as a Web *state management* system in RFC 2965, which replaced RFC 2109. Cookies are not actually part of HTTP, and remain an option, but few Web browsers can afford to reject all cookies out of hand (so to speak).

The idea behind cookies as a method of server state management is simple. If the server can't hold state information about the user and the session, let the client do it. When the server has a function that needs a state to be maintained over time, the server sends a small amount of data to the client (a cookie).

Cookies are presented when the server asks for them, and are updated as the session progresses. Cookies are just text strings and have no standard formats, in that only a particular server has to understand and parse them. In Windows XP, cookies are stored in the `cookies.txt` file under the user's *Documents and Settings* directory. Cookies just accumulate there until users clear them out (few do). If deleted, the file is built again from scratch. Looking at someone's cookies is a quick and dirty way to see where the browser (not necessarily the user) has gone recently.

Cookies, as indispensable as they are on the Web today, tend to have a somewhat unsavory reputation. They aren't perfect: If a cookie is established to allow access to a book-shop Web site at home, the cookie is not present on the user's office computer and the Web site has no idea who the user is because there is no cookie to give to the server. A lot of users assume they've done something wrong, but that's just the way cookies work.

Most browsers can be set to screen or reject cookies, mainly because cookies are a barely tolerated security risk to many people (many think the browser default should be to *reject* all cookies instead of accepting them). In particular, there are three big issues with cookies.

Sending of sensitive information— Banks routinely store user ID and password in a cookie. Even if it is encrypted when sent, the information is typically sitting on your computer in plain text (waiting for anyone to look at it).

User tracking abuse—Servers can set cookies for any reason, including tracking the sites a user visits rather than storing useful parameters. This is often seen as a violation of the right to privacy, and some Web browsers are silent when a cookie is set.

Third-party cookies—If a Web page contains a link (perhaps to a small image) to another Web site, the *second site* can set a cookie (called a *third-party cookie*) on your machine even though you've never visited (or intend to visit) the site. So, that must be how all those porn-site cookies got there.

Some people regard cookies as much ado about nothing, whereas others busily turn off all cookie support whenever they go on-line. But most people should at least consider disabling third-party cookies, which really have no legitimate use when it comes to HTTP state management

QUESTIONS FOR READERS

Figure 22.10 shows some of the concepts discussed in this chapter and can be used to answer the following questions.

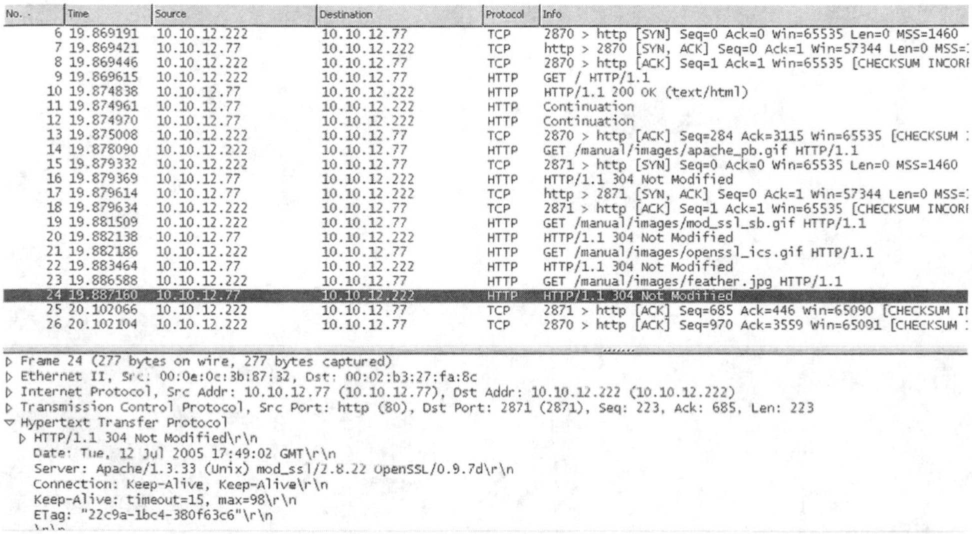

No.	Time	Source	Destination	Protocol	Info
6	19.869191	10.10.12.222	10.10.12.77	TCP	2870 > http [SYN] Seq=0 Ack=0 Win=65535 Len=0 MSS=1460
7	19.869421	10.10.12.77	10.10.12.222	TCP	http > 2870 [SYN, ACK] Seq=0 Ack=1 Win=57344 Len=0 MSS=:
8	19.869446	10.10.12.222	10.10.12.77	TCP	2870 > http [ACK] Seq=1 Ack=1 Win=65535 [CHECKSUM INCORI
9	19.869615	10.10.12.222	10.10.12.77	HTTP	GET / HTTP/1.1
10	19.874838	10.10.12.77	10.10.12.222	HTTP	HTTP/1.1 200 OK (text/html)
11	19.874961	10.10.12.77	10.10.12.222	HTTP	Continuation
12	19.874970	10.10.12.77	10.10.12.222	HTTP	Continuation
13	19.875008	10.10.12.222	10.10.12.77	TCP	2870 > http [ACK] Seq=284 Ack=3115 Win=65535 [CHECKSUM :
14	19.878090	10.10.12.222	10.10.12.77	HTTP	GET /manual/images/apache_pb.gif HTTP/1.1
15	19.879332	10.10.12.222	10.10.12.77	TCP	2871 > http [SYN] Seq=0 Ack=0 Win=65535 Len=0 MSS=1460
16	19.879369	10.10.12.77	10.10.12.222	HTTP	HTTP/1.1 304 Not Modified
17	19.879614	10.10.12.77	10.10.12.222	TCP	http > 2871 [SYN, ACK] Seq=0 Ack=1 Win=57344 Len=0 MSS=:
18	19.879634	10.10.12.222	10.10.12.77	TCP	2871 > http [ACK] Seq=1 Ack=1 Win=65535 [CHECKSUM INCORI
19	19.881509	10.10.12.222	10.10.12.77	HTTP	GET /manual/images/mod_ssl_sb.gif HTTP/1.1
20	19.882138	10.10.12.77	10.10.12.222	HTTP	HTTP/1.1 304 Not Modified
21	19.882186	10.10.12.222	10.10.12.77	HTTP	GET /manual/images/openssl_ics.gif HTTP/1.1
22	19.883464	10.10.12.77	10.10.12.222	HTTP	HTTP/1.1 304 Not Modified
23	19.886588	10.10.12.222	10.10.12.77	HTTP	GET /manual/images/feather.jpg HTTP/1.1
24	19.887160	10.10.12.77	10.10.12.222	HTTP	HTTP/1.1 304 Not Modified
25	20.102066	10.10.12.222	10.10.12.77	TCP	2871 > http [ACK] Seq=685 Ack=446 Win=65090 [CHECKSUM II
26	20.102104	10.10.12.222	10.10.12.77	TCP	2870 > http [ACK] Seq=970 Ack=3559 Win=65091 [CHECKSUM :

```
▷ Frame 24 (277 bytes on wire, 277 bytes captured)
▷ Ethernet II, Src: 00:0e:0c:3b:87:32, Dst: 00:02:b3:27:fa:8c
▷ Internet Protocol, Src Addr: 10.10.12.77 (10.10.12.77), Dst Addr: 10.10.12.222 (10.10.12.222)
▷ Transmission Control Protocol, Src Port: http (80), Dst Port: 2871 (2871), Seq: 223, Ack: 685, Len: 223
▽ Hypertext Transfer Protocol
  ▷ HTTP/1.1 304 Not Modified\r\n
    Date: Tue, 12 Jul 2005 17:49:02 GMT\r\n
    Server: Apache/1.3.33 (Unix) mod_ssl/2.8.22 OpenSSL/0.9.7d\r\n
    Connection: Keep-Alive, Keep-Alive\r\n
    Keep-Alive: timeout=15, max=98\r\n
    ETag: "22c9a-1bc4-380f63c6"\r\n
    \r\n
```

FIGURE 22.10

The Apache server capture.

1. Which version of Apache is the server using?
2. Which ports are the client and server using?
3. Completely parse the following URL: *http://www.examplebooks.com:8888/cgi-bin/ebook.php?HTTPforChimps#page345*.
4. Completely parse the following URL:

   ftp://ftp.freestuff.com/Is%20This%20Really%20Free%3F.
5. What is a cookie used for? Examine your `cookies.txt` file.

CHAPTER

Securing Sockets with SSL

23

What You Will Learn

In this chapter, you will learn about the secure sockets layer (SSL) and how it is used on Web sites. We investigate the layers and operation of the SSL protocol and discuss the SSL's use of certificates.

You will learn about the public key infrastructure (PKI) and how public keys are used for encryption. We present a simple example of public key encryption and decryption using only a pocket calculator and no advanced mathematics.

Web site security and user authentication were not much of a concern in the HTTP chapter. But the popularity of the Web for e commerce is based on trusting that the transactions sent over the Internet are secure. To most users, this means two things:

Server authentication—The identity of the server is vouched for in some way (such as a *certificate*), so that users have confidence that the Web site is not run by a bunch of hackers collecting credit card or password information.

Safe passage—Data that passes back and forth between client and server cannot be read (decrypted) by hackers sniffing odd interfaces here and there.

In this chapter, we explore the SSL, the most widely deployed security protocol on the Web (and in the world) today. Many users notice the little yellow lock that appears in the lower right-hand corner of most Web browsers, and a large percentage of those realize that this means the browser has deemed this site "secure," but few bother to investigate just what that means.

SSL AND WEB SITES

In the last chapter, we configured the hosts `bsdserver` and `winsvr1` to act as a Web site using Apache. In this chapter, we'll explore the security aspects of the Web software. We'll be using the same equipment as in the previous chapter, as shown in Figure 23.1.

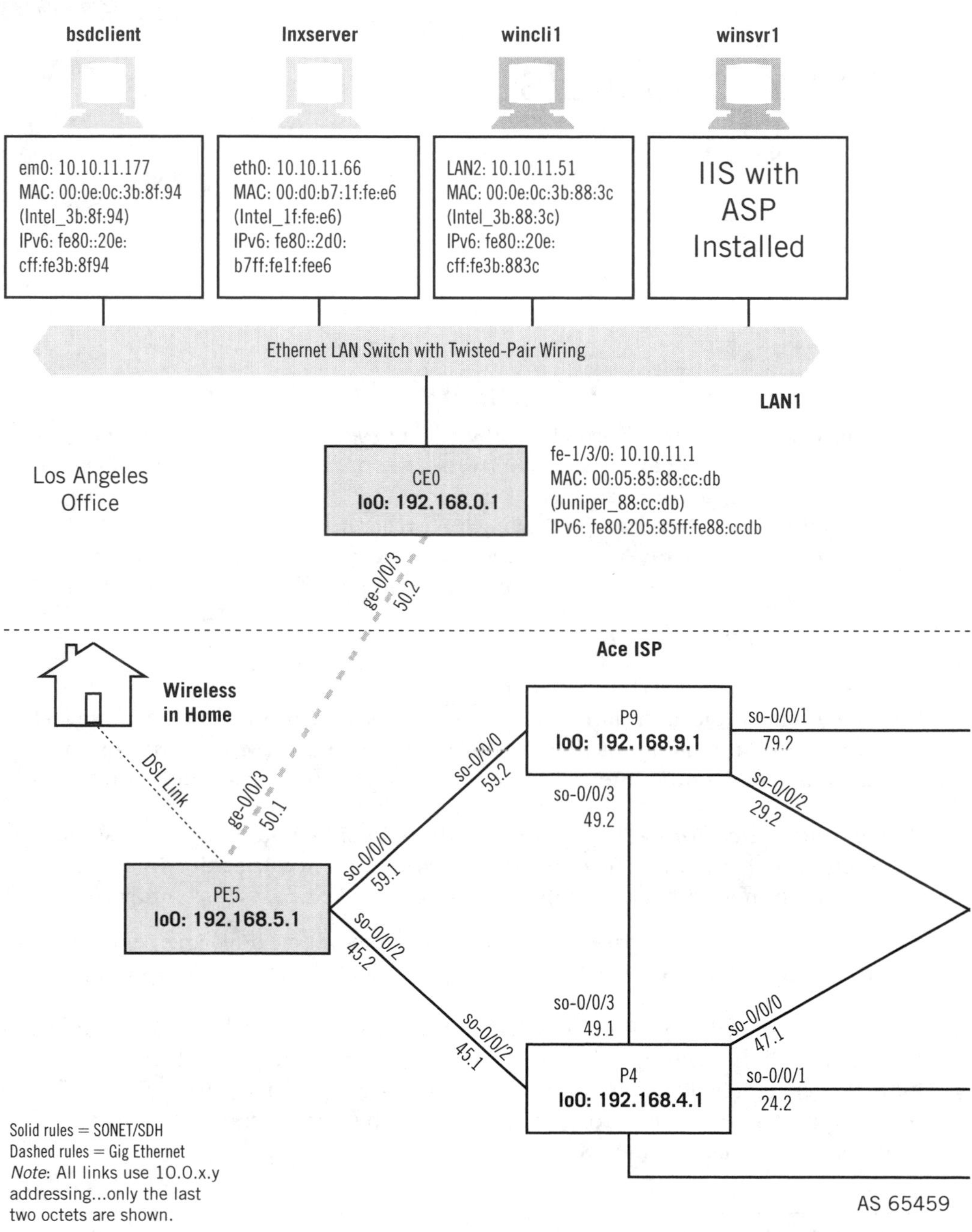

FIGURE 23.1

Web sites on the Illustrated Network showing that the Apache Web server supports SSL.

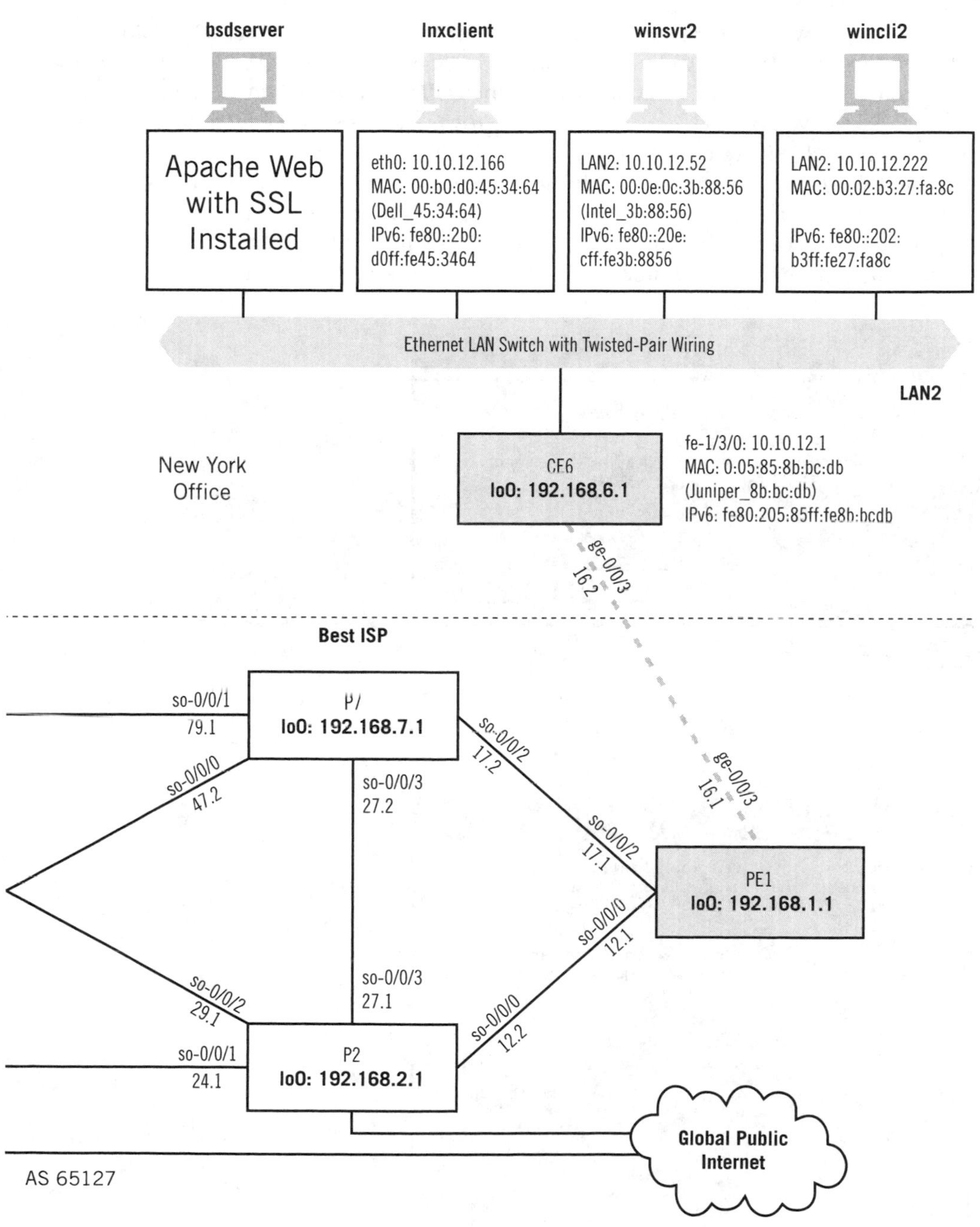

bsdserver
lnxclient
winsvr2
wincli2
Apache Web with SSL Installed
eth0: 10.10.12.166
MAC: 00:b0:d0:45:34:64
(Dell_45:34:64)
IPv6: fe80::2b0:
d0ff:fe45:3464
LAN2: 10.10.12.52
MAC: 00:0e:0c:3b:88:56
(Intel_3b:88:56)
IPv6: fe80::20e:
cff:fe3b:8856
LAN2: 10.10.12.222
MAC: 00:02:b3:27:fa:8c
IPv6: fe80::202:
b3ff:fe27:fa8c
Ethernet LAN Switch with Twisted-Pair Wiring
LAN2
New York Office
CE6
lo0: 192.168.6.1
fe-1/3/0: 10.10.12.1
MAC: 0:05:85:8b:bc:db
(Juniper_8b:bc:db)
IPv6: fe80:205:85ff:fe8b:bcdb
ge-0/0/3
16.2
Best ISP
so-0/0/1
79.1
P7
lo0: 192.168.7.1
so-0/0/2
17.2
ge-0/0/3
16.1
so-0/0/0
47.2
so-0/0/3
27.2
so-0/0/2
17.1
PE1
lo0: 192.168.1.1
so-0/0/0
12.1
so-0/0/2
29.1
so-0/0/3
27.1
so-0/0/0
12.2
so-0/0/1
24.1
P2
lo0: 192.168.2.1
Global Public Internet
AS 65127

The Apache Web server software uses a type of SSL called OpenSSL. What happens when we use the Apache Web server with the OpenSSL module on `bsdserver`? Let's try it from `wincli2` and see what happens. In the HTTP chapter, when we accessed the default Apache Web page (`index.html`) at *http://bsdserver.booklab.englab.jnpr.net*, the page mentioned SSL but did not display a security lock.

When we type in a request for the *secure* part of the `bsdserver` by using `https`, as in `https://bsdserver.booklab.englab.jnpr.net`, we get a default security alert right away from IE (as shown in Figure 23.2). It seems odd to warn about a secure connection, but that's what it does.

FIGURE 23.2

A security alert in IE, oddly "alerting" the user that the information *cannot* be viewed by others. Note that these warnings can be disabled.

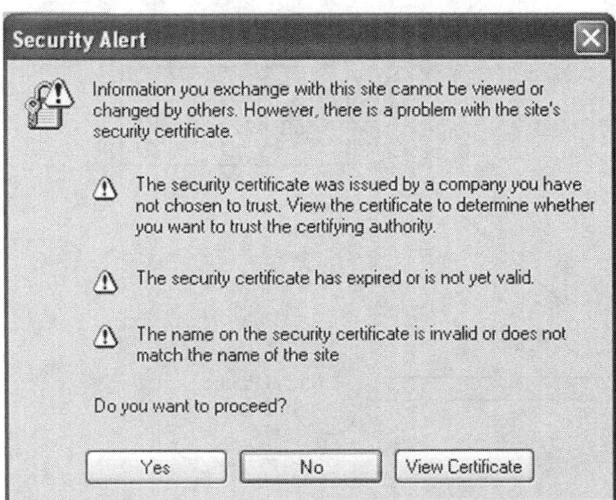

FIGURE 23.3

A certificate security warning. Often the certificate has expired and has not yet been renewed.

Most people choose not to see this warning over and over and click the box, but it's good to see that the browser knows that it's going to establish a secure connection. If we okay the operation, the first thing that is noticeable is how much slower the server is to respond compared to the "regular" default Web page display—which is just about instantaneous because the two hosts are on the same LAN. Of course, the `bsdserver` is not the fastest platform, or the platform of choice, for commercial Web site hosting.

A lot is going on between server and client, but eventually the browser receives the *site certificate* and in this case immediately objects to the certificate provided by `bsdserver`. This is shown in Figure 23.3.

The certificate must pass three major tests, and the certificate used for testing OpenSSL with Apache is wanting in all three categories. First, the issuing "company" does not exist. Second, the certificate has expired. Third, the name on the certificate has nothing to do with `bsdserver`. The user can view the certificate, and ultimately decide to proceed or essentially abort the request for the page. If we view the certificate used for testing in Apache SSL, the reasons for the warnings become obvious (as shown in Figure 23.4).

The testing certificate issued by the nonexistent Snake Oil CA not only expired long ago but is issued to a bogus domain. Nevertheless, the user can choose to view the

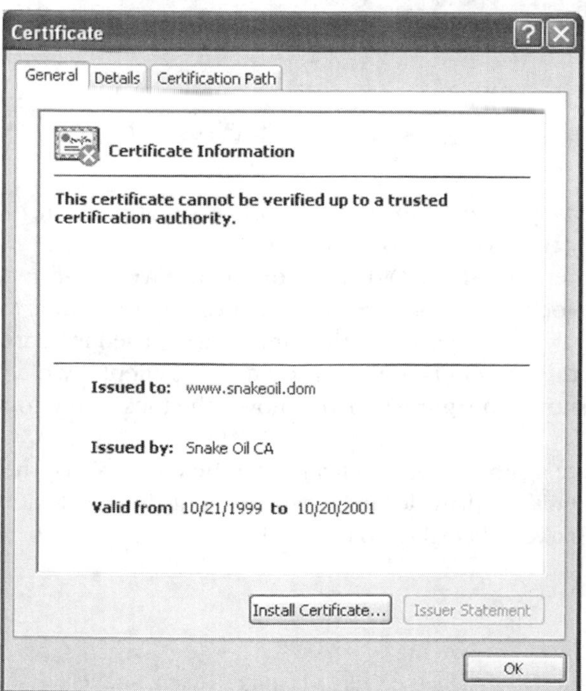

FIGURE 23.4

Apache SSL test certificate, which fails on all three counts.

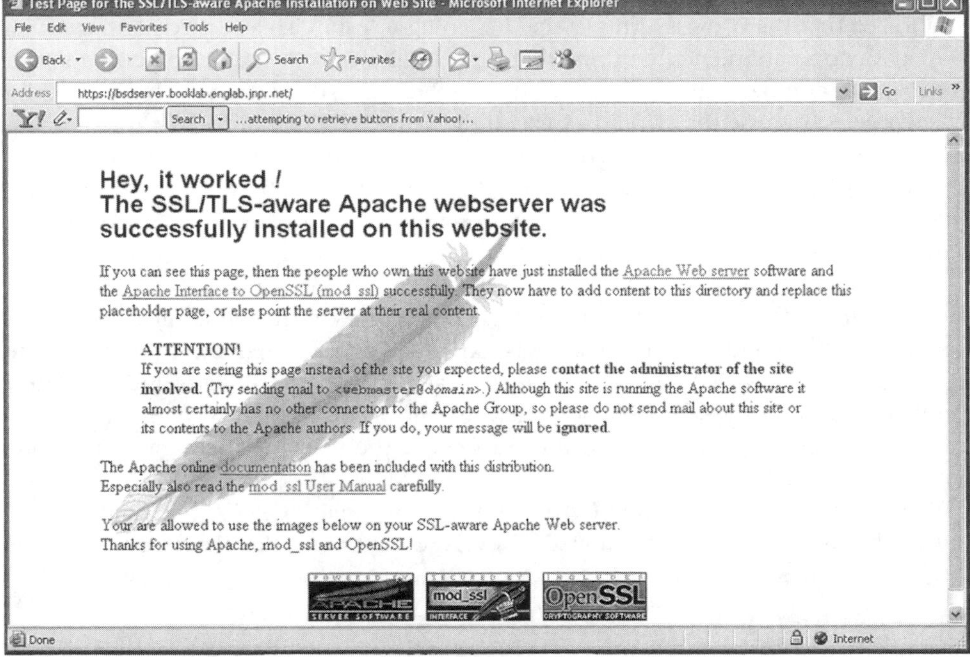

FIGURE 23.5

The secure Web page and lock (IE 7 moves it to the top of the page). Note the use of `https`.

details of the certificate fields, optionally store a copy of the certificate on the client, or choose to proceed (users cannot say they have not been warned!).

Clicking on `OK` finally (after another longish wait) delivers the secure Web page and displays the familiar browser secure lock in the lower right-hand corner of the window. We haven't actually installed any "real" secure pages, so the same page is used for content as in the last chapter. However, the content is sent encrypted to the client—which is the point. The page and lock are shown in Figure 23.5. IE7 moves the lock to the top of the page, but it's the same lock.

We can always view the certificate again by double-clicking on the lock. We see the same view as in Figure 23.4. The Details tab provides information about the certificate. The following are the fields in the Snake Oil certificate in detail.

- *Version*—V3 (SSLv3)
- *Serial Number*—01
- *Signature algorithm*—md5RSA
- *Issuer*—`ca@snakeoil.dom`, Snake Oil CA, Snake Oil, Ltd, Snake Town, Snake Desert, XY

- *Valid From*—Thursday, October 21, 1999 11:21:51 AM
- *Valid To*—Saturday, October 20, 2001 11:21:51 AM
- *Subject*—`www@snakeoil.dom`, `www.snakeoil.dom`, Webserver Team, Snake Oil, Ltd, Snake Town, Snake Desert, XY
- *Public key*—RSA (1024 bits; all 128 bytes follow)
- *Subject alternative name*—RFC822 Name=`www@snakeoil.dom`
- *Netscape comment*—mod ssl generated custom server certificate
- *Netscape Cert Type*—SSL Server Authentication (40)
- *Thumbprint algorithm*—sha1
- *Thumbprint*—20 bytes displayed

The Ethereal capture of the session shows that it takes 98 packets between client and server for an entire secure exchange. It also took almost 3 *minutes* to load the SSL page, but much of this time was "user think time" spent examining the warnings and alerts for the purposes of this book.

There is much more that could be explored in SSL, but the procedures become complex very quickly. Interested readers are referred to texts devoted to security issues. The rest of this chapter explores in more detail what we've just seen.

The Lock

The lock in the browser always gives users the strength of encryption used. Passing the mouse over the lock and pausing it will display a message box with text such as `SSL Secured (128 Bit)` in Internet Explorer (IE). This means that the keys used for encryption and decryption are 128 bits long, barely respectable today. Other browsers have other ways of revealing this information.

If you double-click on the lock, you'll be able to see the certificate information and purpose—which is usually to verify the identity of the server (remote computer). The information should also show the domain for which the certificate was issued (such as `www.example.com`), which should match the Web site. The issuer of the certificate is available, as well as the dates the certificate is valid.

Modern browsers have a built-in security feature that displays a warning message when you try to send information to a Web site that has a certificate "problem." The certificate could have expired, or the name on the certificate might not match the Web site. The user can choose to proceed, or not, or view the certificate itself.

Servers use the certificate to derive two keys, public and private. The public key is part of the digital certificate sent to the client browser. The public key is used to encrypt initial data sent to the server to set up session keys for the transaction. The reason the public key is not used throughout will be examined later in this chapter.

Some people get their own personal certificates and use them to secure a lot of what they do on the Internet, even protecting their email messages. Let's take a closer look at how SSL works as a protocol layer in TCP/IP.

Secure Socket Layer

The SSL protocol was invented as a way to secure Web sites, but the status of SSL as a protocol layer allows it to be used for any client–server transactions as long as they use TCP. SSL is the basis of a related method, Transport Layer Security (TLS), defined in RFC4346. Both form a complete socket layer sitting above TCP and UDP and add authentication (you are who you say you are), integrity (messages have not been changed between client-server pairs), and privacy (through encryption) to the Internet.

Figure 23.6 shows the relationship between SSL/TLS and the socket interface. SSL and TLS are so closely related that they both use the same well-known port. Many implementations of SSL support TLS. In fact, Ethereal often parses bits as "TLS" instead of the expected "SSL" in many places.

Typical SSL implementations on the Internet only authenticate the server. That is, SSL is used as the de facto standard way client users can be sure that when they log on to *www.mybank.com* the server is really an official entity of MyBank and not a phony Web site set up by hackers to entice users to send account, Social Security, PIN, or other information hackers always find useful. SSL used by a server is indicated by the little "lock" symbol that appears in the lower right-hand corner of most Web browsers.

TLS 1.0 can be considered an extension of SSL 3.0 to include the client side of the transaction. SSL is still used in the Netscape and Internet Explorer browsers, and in most Web server software. Not all Web pages need to be protected with SSL or TLS, and SSL can be used free for noncommercial use or licensed for commercial applications.

Why would a Web server need to authenticate and protect the client? Well, consider the liability of and bad publicity for MyBank if *www.mybank.com* accepted a request on the part of a fake client user who transferred someone's assets to an offshore account and closed the accounts? Today, many activities that could easily be done over the Internet require a phone call or fax or letter with signature (or several of these!) to protect the server from phony clients.

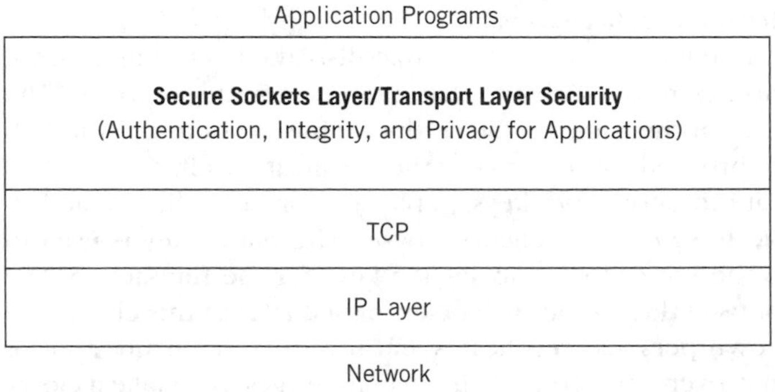

Application Programs

Secure Sockets Layer/Transport Layer Security (Authentication, Integrity, and Privacy for Applications)
TCP
IP Layer

Network

FIGURE 23.6

SSL/TLS as a "socket layer" protocol, showing how it sits on top of TCP.

PRIVACY, INTEGRITY, AND AUTHENTICATION

Before exploring SSL and TLS in more depth, an introduction to the methods they use to provide authentication, integrity, and privacy is necessary. A more complete discussion of these methods, especially certificates and public key cryptography, is presented in the chapter on IPSec.

Privacy

Privacy is the easiest for most to understand. Coded messages based on "conventional" or "traditional" secret keys have been used since ancient times, and anyone who has played with a "secret decoder ring" from a cereal box knows that the point is that only the sender and receiver know the *shared secret* key needed to code and decode the message. Most people also understand that such codes can be broken (some easily, some only with difficulty) by extensive analysis of the messages (the more text available, the better) or by simply finding out the "secret" key (the basis of many old spy movies). The key is the weakest point of the system: You can't use the code to protect the key for the same code because it is sent to other communication partners!

Today, public key (or asymmetrical) cryptography addresses the "key exchange problem" by using two keys—either one of which can be used to encrypt a message. One key remains private (i.e., known only to one party), whereas the other key is made public and available to anyone. Either key, public or private, can be used to encrypt a message—but then only the *other* key can be used to decrypt the message. (That's right, the key used for encryption can't even be used to "undo" the initial coding. Be careful when deleting the uncoded messages that the encrypted texts are based on!) A complete example of public key encryption is given later in this chapter.

Messages encrypted with the public key can only be decrypted by the private key, which means that the key exchange problem is solved. And if you give your public key to someone careless, it doesn't really matter: Anyone can learn the public key and the method is still secure as long as your private key remains private. Even better, we can now exchange old-fashioned shared secret keys this way and use them for a while (the longer a secret key is used, and the more text accumulates to analyze, the less secure the secret key). For instance, you can use your bank's public key to send transactions across the Internet and remain confident that only the bank can decrypt the message using its secret key.

Integrity

Traditional methods of making sure that the message sent is the one received left a lot to be desired. Witnessing documents with other signers, using public notaries, and other methods all had problems that could be circumvented. Traditional message integrity simply relied on the strength of the encryption method to make sure that no one "in the middle" had changed the message in transit. It is one thing to tell MyBank "transfer $10,000 to pay off my credit cards" and another to find out MyBank thought you said "transfer $10,000 to Harry Hacker."As fascinating as your broken bank correspondence might be to read, hackers usually really want to do some damage. Then, as soon as the wire transfer has cleared, Harry can close his account and move on to the next victim.

Those who have been around networks know the concept of a frame *checksum* or *one-way hash*. The checksum is a fixed number of extra bits appended to a frame (message) to verify that no bits have been altered by errors on the network while the frame is in transit. Even the checksum itself is included in the "protection." The modern equivalent of the checksum hash, extended to many more bits and applied to the message text itself (or layers of the message plus headers added), is called a *message digest*. A message digest is just a big one-way hash, which means that the original text cannot be recovered from the hash value. On the other hand, the changes made *might* just yield the same hash value as the original message. Message digests understand this and are mathematically designed to make sure the chances of this happening are very slim, on the order of one chance in a million or better.

An associated use of message digests is as a *digital signature*. After all, the message digest hash only says that the message to MyBank arrived unaltered. It doesn't guarantee that the message really came from me. Anyone in the middle knowing the message digest algorithm can simply substitute the entire message, append the proper message digest, and sent it on to the bank.

But a digital signature involves more than just a hash on the message. A digital signature is used with public key encryption to encrypt not only the text and hash value but other information (such as a sequence number) with my private key. The digital signature is appended to the encrypted message and is valid *only* for that message. The digital signature can be decrypted with my public key, which might sound like defeating the purpose—but the point is that only you can create a digital signature using the message digest, and no one can change the digest and still sign it as you have (as long as my private key remains private, of course). No one else can use this signature later, for the same reason. Digital signatures provide the receivers with *nonrepudiation*, meaning that MyBank can be sure that you sent the message and that it's really the message you sent (again, as long as you protect your private key).

Authentication

There is only one more concept that remains in understanding how SSL and TLS work. This is the idea of a certificate. Thus far, we have developed a way for an individual to send encrypted, unalterable, signed messages to MyBank at *www.mybank.com*. We do this using the bank's public key, available to anyone. (Of course, the digital signature depends on the public key—although the certificate concept applies here as well.) But how do you know that the public key provided is really the bank's key? Where does MyBank's public key come from?

It comes from a certificate, of course. The bank provides me with a certificate confirming the public key and the identity of the holder of the key. How do you know the certificate is real? After all, all forms of encryption and authentication are susceptible to the "man-in-the-middle" exploit—where someone is busily intercepting messages between client and server and substituting their own certificates (with their own keys) to both parties. One solution would be to hardcode the certificates into every browser, but this solution does not scale.

A more practical answer to the "man-in-the-middle" threat is that you know the certificate is real because you got it from a *certificate authority* (CA). The CA is a trusted third-party agency whose job it is to distribute certificates, usually on behalf of commercial enterprises that pay for their services. Certificates associate a public key with the identity of a *subject* (server or user), along with the public key. The CA issuer digital signature is included, as well as a period of validity (start and end), version and serial number of the certificate, and sometimes "extension" information.

CAs often require that certificate information be delivered in person by more than one validated representative of the company being "certified." This *root level* CA is also covered by a certificate, but one that is *self-signed*. Even on the Internet, someone has to be trusted implicitly. Other CAs can issue the certificate in a *certificate chain*. Some certification users refuse to accept a certificate if the chain is too long (the longer the chain, the greater the risk that one certificate in the chain might be bad).

Before central bank regulation became common, anyone could found a bank just by getting people to trust them with their money. Today, anyone can follow a few rules and be a CA and issue certificates—and that is especially true for private intranets in a large organization. Among the rules are procedures for validating, managing, and revoking certificates through *certificate revocation lists* (CRLs). CRLs are needed because certificates are passed around a lot and it is impossible to tell just by examination that a certificate is no longer valid because things have changed or it has been compromised or abused.

If the concepts of public key encryption, message digests, digital signatures, and certificates still seem somewhat vague and abstract, that's only to be expected. These are difficult concepts that take time to assimilate. The IPSec chapter revisits the concepts in more detail, and gives examples of how these concepts all work together.

PUBLIC KEY ENCRYPTION

Public key encryption, using a private key to recover what is encrypted with a public key, is based on complex mathematical principles. But that doesn't mean that the use of public key encryption is all that difficult to perform. After all, computers do it with ease.

Let's use something no more complex than an ordinary pocket calculator to perform this type of encryption. Along the way, several important points about public key encryption will be uncovered.

Pocket Calculator Encryption at the Client

The security that public key encryption provides is a consequence of the difficulty of factoring large numbers, not the complexity of the method. You can do PKI on any pocket calculator. The "how" is shown in the "Three Magic Numbers" sidebar and explained in material following.

Three Magic Numbers

1. Start with three magic numbers: Public "normalizer" N = 33, public encryption key E = 3, and private decryption key D = 7.
2. Encrypt plain-text letter "O" (15th letter of the alphabet) from certificate N and E values.
3. Write down "O" value E times and multiply:
   15 × 15 × 15 = 3375
4. Divide by N and compute remainder:
   3375/33 = 102.27272...
   0.27272... × 33 = 8.99976 = 9
5. Send 9, the cipher text for plain-text 15, over the network.

We have to start with three "magic" numbers, and two of them must be prime numbers. Usually, you choose two large primes first (hundreds of digits) and derive a third huge number called N (for "normalizer") through a very complex process. N is never called a key in the documentation, but N is necessary for both encrypting and decrypting. The security comes from the fact that given a large N and one of the keys, it is next to impossible to derive the second prime key number. In this example, N = 33, and the two primes are 3 and 7. There is no obvious relationship between 33 and 3 and 7, although with these small numbers, a code cracker could figure it out in a minute or two.

One of the two primes becomes the public key (it doesn't matter which), and the other becomes the private key. Never consistently assign the smaller number as the public key. This speeds up client encryption, but is a security risk if people know one factor must be larger than the other. In this example, N = 33, the public encryption key E = 3, and the private decryption key D = 7.

Example

To encrypt the plain-text letter "O," first convert it to a number. "O" is the 15th letter of the alphabet; we can use that. Of course, we have to obtain the values of the server's N and E values. We can get those from a certificate, in that the values of N and E must match up properly with the D that the receiver retains.

Now write down the "O" value E times and multiply, using any suitable calculator with at least eight (8) positions. So, 15 × 15 × 15 = 3375. This is not too large, so the encryption does not need N yet.

Divide by N and compute remainder. This is just 3375/33 = 102.27272. The fraction is there because calculators do not give remainders directly. We can get it by subtracting 102, leaving 0.27272. Then, 0.27272 × 33 = 8.99976 = 9. We have to round a little due to the limited precision of the decimal fraction. The client sends 9, which is the cipher text for the 15 ("O") plain text, over the network.

At the Server

1. Get back "O" without using E, but only N = 33 and D = 7. The receiver gets cipher-text **9** over the network.
2. Write down cipher-text value D (7) times and multiply, applying "normalizer" whenever number gets large:

   $9 \times 9 \times 9 \times 9 \times 9 \times 9 \times 9 = (531{,}441) \times 9$

   But $531{,}441/33 = 16{,}104.272$ and $0.272 \times 33 = 8.976 = 9$.

   So, $(9) \times 9 = 81$.

   Divide the final result by N and compute the remainder:

   $81/33 = 2.4545454\ldots$

   $0.4545454 \times 33 = 14.99998 = \mathbf{15}$
3. Thus, **15** plain text is the letter "O" sent securely.

Pocket Calculator Decryption at the Server

Thus far, the client has used the proper N and E from the server to encrypt "O" (15) as cipher-text 9. This is what is sent on the network. The magic of PKI is being able to get back "O" without using E, only N and D. (Because N is known to and used by both parties, it is never called a key itself.) In this example, N = 33, E = 3, and D = 7. The following is how to get back "P" using only N = 33 and D = 7 at the server end.

1. Write down the cipher-text value (9) D times and multiply. If the number gets too large for the calculator, we can apply N to get back a more useable number.

   9 3 9 3 9 3 9 3 9 3 9 3 9 5 (531,441) 3 9

   If we don't want to risk overflowing the calculator, we can apply N at any time as follows:

   $531{,}441/33 = 16{,}104.272$ (subtract 16,104) and $0.272 \times 33 = 8.976 = 9$

   (Again, rounding is needed to deal with the annoying decimal fractions that calculators insist on providing.)

   So, $(9) \times 9 = 81$. Note how the single (9) replaces 531,441. It is just a coincidence that this turned out to be 9 also.
2. Divide the final result by N and compute remainder:

   81/33 5 2.4545454, so subtract 2

   $0.4545454 \times 33 = 14.99998 = 15$

3. Thus, the plain-text 15 is the letter "O" sent securely using PKI. That's all there is to it! Of course, usually it's a number that's encrypted—but so what? Try the number 19 for yourself. You might have to "normalize" on the encryption side as well, but it still works.

The security in PKI is in the difficulty of finding D given the values of E and N. This example is mathematically trivial to hackers and crackers. But try N = 49,048,499 and E = 61. The answer is D = 2,409,781. Usually, N, E, and D are anywhere from 140 to 156 or more digits long. To deal with text messages, strings of letters can be thought of as numbers. So, "OK" becomes 1511. ASCII is typically used.

Digital signatures employ the same public keys as well. Either key, E or D, can be used to encrypt or decrypt. You just need to use the other to reverse the process (try it with "O"). So, any message *encrypted* with D can only be *decrypted* with E (my public key). So, any text that can be decrypted with E (and N) *had* to come from me as long as my private key D remains secure.

PUBLIC KEYS AND SYMMETRICAL ENCRYPTION

As has just been pointed out, public key encryption is done routinely by computers—but it's not an easy task, even for modern processors. Computers are really an engineering tool and were generally scorned by mathematicians until relatively recently. In fact, sometimes a mathematician will ask a computer scientist what value of π is used in computations. Any value that contains less than an infinite number of digits is incorrect, of course. At some point the loss of accuracy is fine for engineers, but not for "pure" mathematicians.

So, the length of the strings encrypted with public keys must be limited to what a computer can handle. We have to admit, the first time we heard about "128-bit encryption," we thought it would be interesting because no programming languages at the time supported "integers" longer than 64 bits—let alone powers involving 128-bit numbers. Normalization helps, of course, but the computational drain of public keys on general processors is substantial.

For this reason, SSL uses public key encryption as little as possible—typically only to establish symmetrical keys that can be used much more efficiently with existing algorithms and processors. Naturally, the symmetrical keys are *much* less secure than public key encryption, but they are changed more often and used for shorter periods of time.

SSL AS A PROTOCOL

SSL is a protocol layer all on its own that is placed between a connection-oriented, network layer protocol (almost always TCP) and the application layer protocol (such as HTTP) or program. Connections are useful to provide a convenient way to

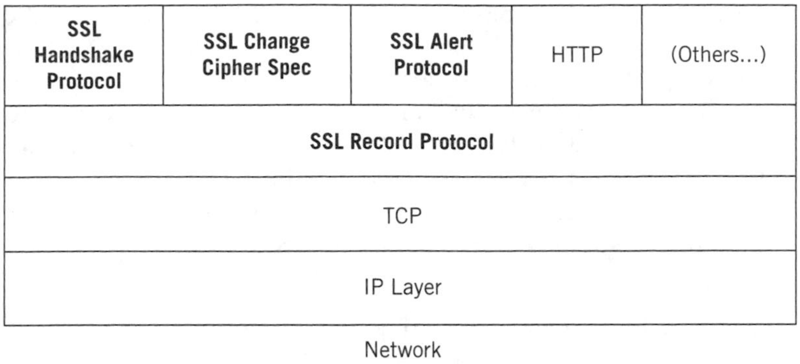

SSL Handshake Protocol	**SSL Change Cipher Spec**	**SSL Alert Protocol**	HTTP	(Others...)
SSL Record Protocol				
TCP				
IP Layer				

Network

FIGURE 23.7

The SSL protocol stack in detail showing its relationship to HTTP and other protocols.

associate security parameters with a specific flow of packets. SSL uses certificates for authentication, digital signatures and message digests for integrity, and encryption for privacy. Each of the three security areas has a range of choices allowed in order to respect local laws regarding cryptographic algorithms and new technologies to be included as developed. Specific choices in each area are negotiated when a protocol session (connection) is set up.

SSL Protocol Stack

The SSL protocol stack is shown in Figure 23.7. TLS can be regarded as an enhanced version of the SSL protocol stack, but the components are essentially the same.

SSL usually uses Diffie-Hellman (a secure key exchange method used on unsecure networks) to exchange the keys. The handshake procedure itself uses three SSL protocol processes: the *SSL Handshake Protocol* for the overall process, the *SSL Change Cipher Spec Protocol* for Cipher Suite specification and negotiation, and the *SSL Alert Protocol* for error messages.

All three of these protocols use the *SSL Record Protocol* to encapsulate their messages, as well as the application data flowing on the session once established. The nice thing about the SSL Record Protocol is that it provides a way to renegotiate active session parameters or establish a new session using a secure path. Initial session handshakes without a functioning and secure SSL Record Protocol must use a *NULL Cipher Suite* (plain text), which is of course a risk.

SSL Session Establishment

Established SSL sessions can be reused, which is good because the SSL session establishment process requires the exchange of many messages. Sessions are established after a complex handshake routine between client and server. There are many variations in the details of SSL session establishment, but Figure 23.8 shows one of the most common.

By default, SSL uses TCP port 443. Of course, a user typically just uses `http://` (or nothing at all) when accessing a Web page. Rather than making users remember to type in the port number at the end of the URL, SSL is invoked with a URL starting with `https://`. This should not be confused with Web pages distinguished by the `.shtml` ending, which means that the Server Side Includes (SSIs) are in use for that page. There are four major phases to the SSL session establishment process.

1. Initial Hello exchange
2. Optional server certificate presentation and request (authentication of server to client)
3. Presentation of client certificate if requested (authentication of client to server)
4. Finalize Cipher Suite negotiation and finish session establishment handshake

Usually, only the server presents its certificate to the client (user). Most users don't have certificates to authenticate themselves to the server, but this will change with TLS. Regarding Cipher Suite negotiation, SSL 3.0 defines 31 Cipher Suites consisting of a key exchange method, the cipher (encryption method) to use for data transfer, and the

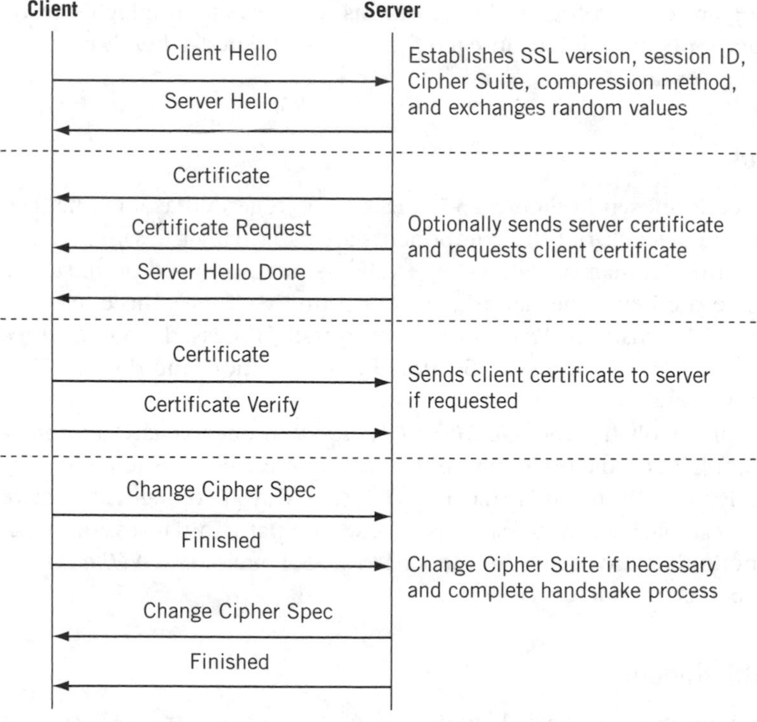

FIGURE 23.8

One form of SSL session establishment. There can be others, but this form is very common.

message digest method to use to create the SSL *Message Authentication Code* (MAC). There are nine choices for the traditional shared secret key encryption used in SSL.

- No encryption
- 40-bit key RSA Data Security, Inc. Code (RC4) stream cipher
- 128-bit key RC4 stream cipher
- 40-bit key RC2 Cipher Block Chaining (CBC)
- The venerable Data Encryption Standard (DES), DES40, and Triple DES (3DES), all with CBC
- Idea
- Fortezza

CBC uses a portion of the previously encrypted cipher text to encrypt the next block of text. There are three choices of message digest.

- No message digest
- 128-bit hash Message Digest 5 (MD5)
- 160-bit hash Secure Hash Algorithm (SHA)

SSL Data Transfer

All application data and SSL control data use the SSL Record Protocol for message transfer. Details vary, but usually the SSL Record Protocol will fragment the application data stream (perhaps a Web page) into record protocol units. Each unit is typically compressed (compression adds a layer of complexity to unauthorized decryption attempts), and the MAC is computed before the entire unit is encrypted. The end result is tucked into a TCP segment and IP packet and sent on its way. This process is illustrated in Figure 23.9.

SSL Implementation

Few programmers write an SSL implementation from scratch. SSL is usually implemented as a *toolkit library*, and patented cryptographic functions must be licensed anyway. Public key packages are patented as well, and there are export restrictions on cryptographic algorithms in the United States. All of these factors combine to discourage individuals from implementing SSL (as opposed to plain sockets) on their own.

Two public key toolkits are popular. RSARef is the RSA "reference" public key package, including RSA encryption and Diffie-Hellman key exchange. It also features unsupported, but free, source code and is to be used for noncommercial applications. BSAFE3.0 ("Be-safe," not an acronym) is the commercial version of RSARef. The public key toolkits can be combined with any SSL toolkits, including:

SSLRef—An example SSL 3.0 implementation from Netscape Communications Corp.

SSLava—An SSL 3.0 toolkit from Phaos Technology written in Java.

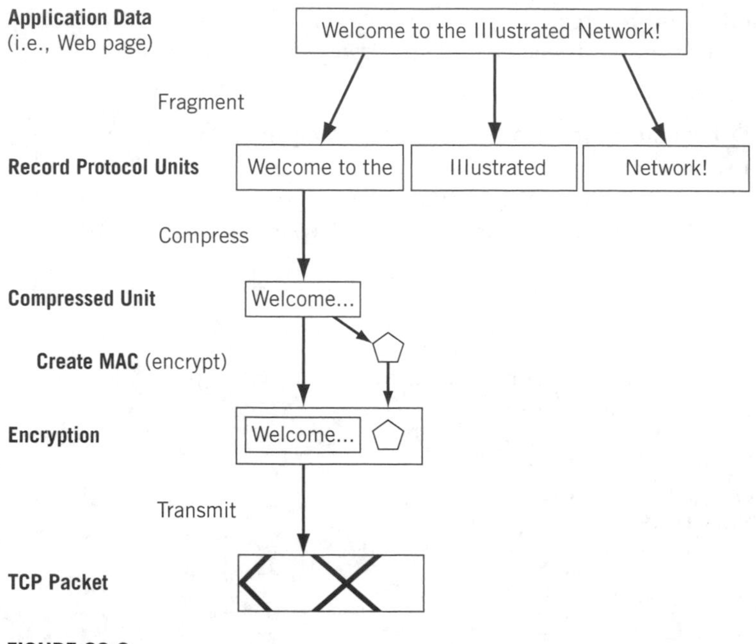

FIGURE 23.9

The SSL record protocol showing how protocol units are compressed and encrypted.

OpenSSL—A free noncommercial implementation of SSL 3.0 (and 2.0) and TLS 2.0) that can be used outside the United States. In the United States, patent restrictions require use of RSARef or BSAFE3.0.

SSL Issues and Problems

SSL is not perfect, of course. SSL suffers from a number of limitations, most of which can be overcome with careful planning and attention to detail. The sections that follow discuss a representative list of SSL issues.

Computational Complexity

As we've seen, public key encryption is so processor intensive that we avoid it whenever we can. And because the server must perform the SSL handshake for every connection, OpenSSL struggles under heavy workloads. Hardware acceleration with special cards helps, and load balancing among multiple servers all representing the same Web site helps as well.

Clear Private Keys

The server has to store the private key somewhere, and usually in clear form (otherwise, we just move the issue to the next key, or the next, and restarts become a real problem unless the actual key is somewhere on the system). The point is, of course, that data might be *transmitted* over the network in encrypted form but it is seldom *stored* on the server in an encrypted form. The physical security of the server is essential, and a technique called *perfect forward secrecy* is also helpful. We'll meet forward secrecy again in a discussion of IPSec.

Stolen Credentials

Certificate revocation lists are fine, but if a private key or certificate is stolen it can take a while for the organization to figure out that there is a bogus *www.example.com* site out there stealing people's money and identities. It's better to query the CA with a special protocol, such as the Online Certificate Status Protocol (OCSP)—defined in RFC 2560—but that's not common (and may never be). Again physical security is of paramount importance.

Pseudorandom Numbers and "Entropy"

In SSL, clients and servers both have to generate random numbers and data to use for session keys. The problem is that most computers' *pseudorandom number generators* (PRNGs) are not adequate for true security because they are predictable (one of the reasons they are *pseudo*random in the first place). The *seed* number used as input to the PRNG must itself be as random as possible, and many SSL implementations use seeds that do not have enough "entropy" (a measure of disorder or randomness). There are software-based workarounds for this.

Works Only with TCP

SSL only protects applications that use TCP. This is fine for HTTP, but more and more critical data on the Internet uses UDP and not TCP. We've already noted that multicast uses UDP, and we'll see that VoIP does as well. These data streams need protection, but SSL cannot currently provide it.

Inadequate Nonrepudiation

Suppose you purchase a product over the Internet that has a rebate. You have to send proof that you are the person that purchased the product to the rebate "fulfillment center" to receive the rebate. This is nonrepudiation in the sense that the company cannot say to the rebate center you didn't purchase the product. However, SSL cannot provide this nonrepudiation. The workaround, which involves the company *and* you having certificates, is relatively easy (but this will take a while to become the standard).

When using any security method, all of the system's "vulnerabilities" are difficult to seal. It's just difficult to detect and patch up all cracks in a complex system.

I once worked in an organization with a coworker who was famous for "playing" with the servers and their users by simply intercepting messages on the LAN. When the organization switched to encrypted communications, I tried to console him, thinking his hacking days were over. "That's all right," he told me, "I know where the backups are. Those aren't encrypted."

Where *are* those frequent backups of the Web servers' information? How secure are *they*? Security is always a never-ending battle where one side or the other seems to gain an advantage for a while, but never for long. Many of the limitations of SSL are addressed in TLS 1.1, but TLS is new and most clients are not as sophisticated as servers when it comes to security.

A Note on TLS 1.1

The biggest shortcoming of SSL is the fact that as typically implemented only the server is authenticated to the user. That is, the server certificate with the server's public key and other information is presented to the client. But clients such as Web browsers seldom have certificates to present to the server to authenticate the user. Server authentication is fine for Internet commerce (encrypted personal and credit card information is sent to the server) but not so good for on-line banking and other applications where mutual authentication is desired, if not indispensable.

Implementation of TLS 1.1 (RFC4346) allows clients (users) to use the full capabilities of the standardized PKI. This topic is explored more fully in the chapter on IPSec.

SSL and Certificates

Let's take a close look at how SSL handles certificates. Ordinarily, once SSL is installed on a server you have to generate a certificate request to one of the major CAs (such as VeriSign). There are many types of certificates available, such as personal (mainly for email), code signing (for downloaded programs), and Web site (which is what we're talking about here).

Of course, the certificate has to be distributed by a CA, which also has to be set up. In OpenSSL, most CA operations can be done at the CLI, but this method is not really suitable for a production environment.

No matter which SSL server software is used, they all tell you how to generate a certificate signing request (CSR). Once this is done, the software generates a public/private key pair. You send the public key and the CSR to the certificate-issuing authority.

If all is in order when reviewed, including related documentation, the response is emailed to the applicant and loaded into the server SSL software. You usually get three things in the response:

- The CA's certificate containing the public key
- The local certificate identifying the server
- A certificate revocation list with a list of certificates revoked by the CA

For testing purposes, it is not necessary in most cases to obtain a "real" certificate. OpenSSL, for example, includes the testing certificate from the Snake Oil CA that is functional but not intended for use (hopefully, the "snake oil" name, used for useless tonics or medications, will be a tip-off to users).

QUESTIONS FOR READERS

Figure 23.10 shows some of the concepts discussed in this chapter and can be used to answer the following questions.

```
▷ Frame 9 (132 bytes on wire, 132 bytes captured)
▷ Ethernet II, Src: 00:02:b3:27:fa:8c, Dst: 00:0e:0c:3b:87:32
▷ Internet Protocol, Src Addr: 10.10.12.222 (10.10.12.222), Dst Addr: 10.10.12.77 (10.10.12.77)
▷ Transmission Control Protocol, Src Port: 2986 (2986), Dst Port: https (443), Seq: 1, Ack: 1, Len: 78
▽ Secure Socket Layer
  ▽ SSLv2 Record Layer: Client Hello
      Length: 76
      Handshake Message Type: Client Hello (1)
      Version: TLS 1.0 (0x0301)
      Cipher Spec Length: 51
      Session ID Length: 0
      Challenge Length: 16
    ▽ Cipher Specs (17 specs)
        Cipher Spec: TLS_RSA_WITH_RC4_128_MD5 (0x000004)
        Cipher Spec: TLS_RSA_WITH_RC4_128_SHA (0x000005)
        Cipher Spec: TLS_RSA_WITH_3DES_EDE_CBC_SHA (0x00000a)
        Cipher Spec: SSL2_RC4_128_WITH_MD5 (0x010080)
        Cipher Spec: SSL2_DES_192_EDE3_CBC_WITH_MD5 (0x0700c0)
        Cipher Spec: SSL2_RC2_CBC_128_CBC_WITH_MD5 (0x030080)
        Cipher Spec: TLS_RSA_WITH_DES_CBC_SHA (0x000009)
        Cipher Spec: SSL2_DES_64_CBC_WITH_MD5 (0x060040)
        Cipher Spec: TLS_RSA_EXPORT1024_WITH_RC4_56_SHA (0x000064)
        Cipher Spec: TLS_RSA_EXPORT1024_WITH_DES_CBC_SHA (0x000062)
        Cipher Spec: TLS_RSA_EXPORT_WITH_RC4_40_MD5 (0x000003)
        Cipher Spec: TLS_RSA_EXPORT_WITH_RC2_CBC_40_MD5 (0x000006)
        Cipher Spec: SSL2_RC4_128_EXPORT40_WITH_MD5 (0x020080)
        Cipher Spec: SSL2_RC2_CBC_128_CBC_WITH_MD5 (0x040080)
        Cipher Spec: TLS_DHE_DSS_WITH_3DES_EDE_CBC_SHA (0x000013)
        Cipher Spec: TLS_DHE_DSS_WITH_DES_CBC_SHA (0x000012)
        Cipher Spec: TLS_DHE_DSS_EXPORT1024_WITH_DES_CBC_SHA (0x000063)
      Challenge
```

FIGURE 23.10

Ethereal capture of an SSL Client Hello frame. Note the list of encryption methods and details in the cipher suite.

1. Which port is used by `https`?
2. Which version of SSL is used at the record layer?
3. The capture says the "version" of SSL used is TLS 1.0. Why is that?
4. Which message should be sent in response to a Client Hello?
5. Is SSLv2 DES encryption with SHA supported by the client?

PART

V

Network Management

Network management is an important aspect of networking, and the Internet is no exception. This part of the book explores SNMP, RMON, and the MIB.

CHAPTER

Simple Network Management Protocol

24

What You Will Learn

In this chapter, you will learn how SNMP is used to manage devices on a TCP/IP network. We'll explore the SNMP model with many servers (agents) and few clients (managers).

You will learn about MIBs and the SMI tree for designating management information. We also briefly discuss RMON (remote monitor) and private management information bases (MIBs).

Network management, like network security, is often treated like an adjunct to the true task of networking, which is to relentlessly shuttle bits about (i.e., until something goes wrong). Then everyone wonders why it couldn't be easier to figure out what went haywire. Without network management facilities, the network is like driving a car without fuel-level, water-temperature, or oil-pressure gauges. When the car slowly glides to a halt, there are few clues of even where to start looking.

The Internet outgrew the humble go-have-a-look-at-it school of network management by the late 1980s, when it seemed like colleges and universities were sticking routers in every other building around the campus and then finding someone who would not object to being placed in charge of the devices. Little did they realize that they would be expected to ensure that the out-of-the-way device was functional day and night, 365 days a year. They ran their portion of the Internet on a PING and a prayer.

It's not that management of network devices was unknown at the time, or deemed unnecessary. Vendors always had some sort of management functions tucked away in their software. The problem was that each vendor's interface was different (sometimes in the same product line), the client software expensive and proprietary, and the network operations centers (NOCs) that existed tended to consist of rooms full of equipment that no one knew how to operate equally well.

But knowing that network management was essential and creating a standard for network management on the Internet were two different things. The international

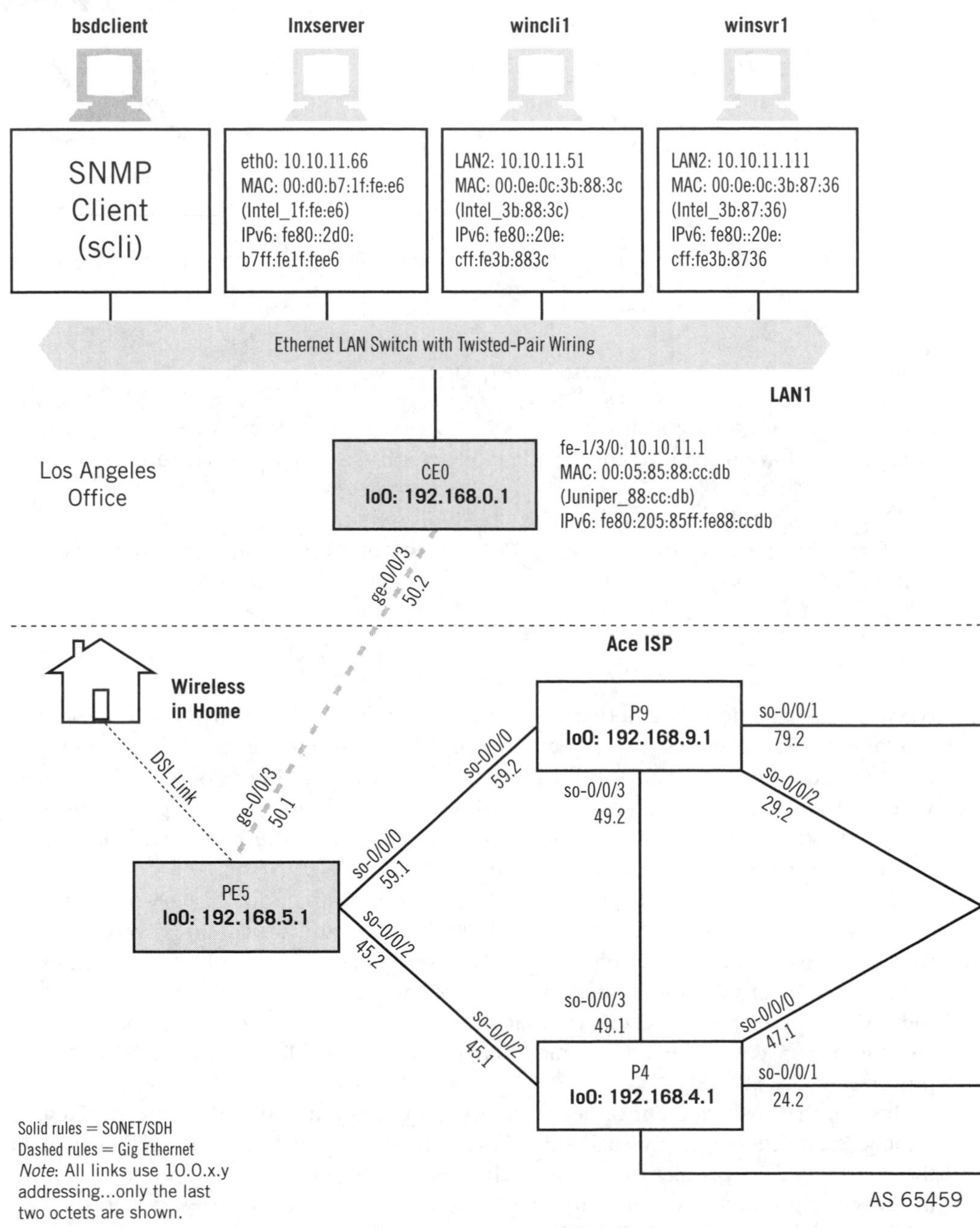

FIGURE 24.1

SNMP on the Illustrated Network, showing the hosts used as SNMP clients and the router with SNMP enabled.

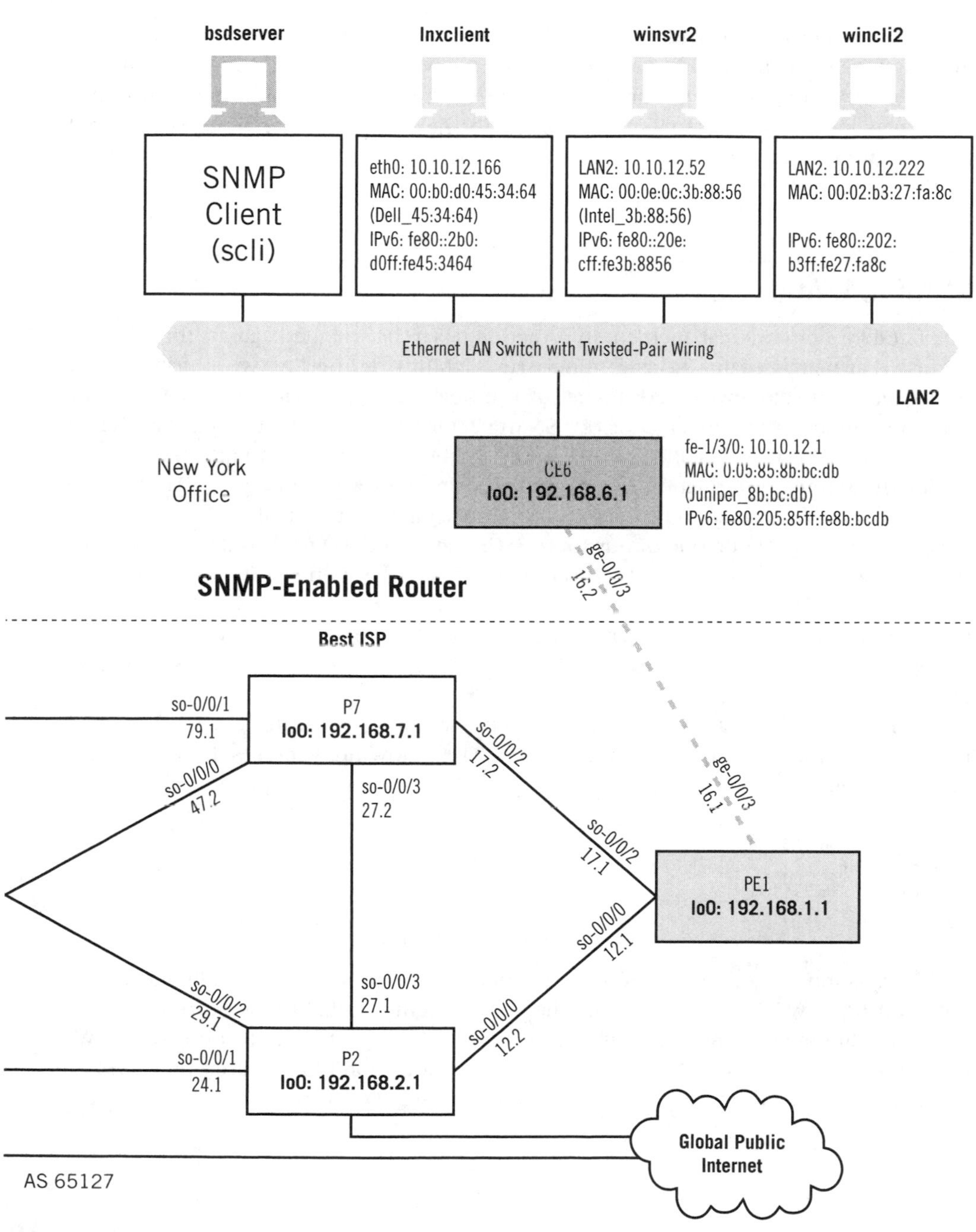
bsdserver
lnxclient
winsvr2
wincli2
SNMP Client (scli)
eth0: 10.10.12.166
MAC: 00:b0:d0:45:34:64
(Dell_45:34:64)
IPv6: fe80::2b0:
d0ff:fe45:3464
LAN2: 10.10.12.52
MAC: 00:0e:0c:3b:88:56
(Intel_3b:88:56)
IPv6: fe80::20e:
cff:fe3b:8856
LAN2: 10.10.12.222
MAC: 00:02:b3:27:fa:8c
IPv6: fe80::202:
b3ff:fe27:fa8c
Ethernet LAN Switch with Twisted-Pair Wiring
LAN2
New York Office
CE6
lo0: 192.168.6.1
fe-1/3/0: 10.10.12.1
MAC: 0:05:85:8b:bc:db
(Juniper_8b:bc:db)
IPv6: fe80:205:85ff:fe8b:bcdb
ge-0/0/3
16.2
SNMP-Enabled Router
Best ISP
so-0/0/1
79.1
P7
lo0: 192.168.7.1
so-0/0/0
47.2
so-0/0/3
27.2
so-0/0/2
17.2
ge-0/0/3
16.1
so-0/0/2
17.1
PE1
lo0: 192.168.1.1
so-0/0/0
12.1
so-0/0/2
29.1
so-0/0/3
27.1
so-0/0/0
12.2
so-0/0/1
24.1
P2
lo0: 192.168.2.1
Global Public Internet
AS 65127

standard for network management, itself a new creation at the time, was the Common Management Information Services/Common Management Information Protocol (CMIS/CMIP). However, this standard (geared to the needs of public telephony carriers) was loaded with features unnecessary to the Internet at the time. So, Internet administrators took what they could from the ISO specifications and created SNMP fairly independently.

SNMP CAPABILITIES

The need for network management information has to be weighed against the need for security. Yet many organizations routinely run SNMPv1 on their network nodes, hubs, or routers, and seldom take advantage of the heightened security available in many SNMPv1 implementations or consider SNMPv2. Organizations routinely block Telnet access to their routers, yet allow SNMP access without too much worry.

Just how much information can be gathered from a router running SNMPv1when no steps have been taken to protect information? Quite a bit, actually.

Let's enable SNMP on one of our routers, CE6, attached to LAN2, and use `bsdclient` on LAN1 and `bsdserver` on LAN2 to see what we can do with SNMP. There are many nifty GUIs available for SNMP, but we'll use FreeBSD's `scli` application to maximize information and minimize clutter on the screen. We won't be interested in traffic histograms or historical data anyway. The equipment used in this chapter is shown in Figure 24.1.

Enabling SNMP on a Juniper router is very straightforward (just setting values to the proper variables) and need not be shown. The following is the result of our initial configuration.

```
admin@CE6# show snmp
name Router_CE6;
description M71-Router;
contact WalterG;
```

There is much more we could have configured, and in fact this is really more than we need. But it will allow us to ensure that it's the right router. Now we can run a Unix command-line management application on `bsdclient` called `scli` to router CE6. (We haven't put the routers in DNS, and many organizations don't for security purposes, so we'll access the router by an interface IP address instead of by name.)

```
bsdclient# scli 10.10.12.1
100-scli version 0.2.12 (c) 2001-2002 Juergen Schoenwaelder
100-scli trying SNMPv2c ... good
(10.10.12.1) scli >
```

We are now running SNMPv2 to the router. Note that `scli` is an interactive application with its own > prompt, like `nslookup`, so we can execute all types of commands (known through `help`) at this point until an `exit` takes us out to the shell again. Let's ensure that we have the right router and examine the system information.

```
(10.10.12.1) scli > show system info
Name:               Router_CE6
Address:            10.10.12.1:161
Description:        M7i-router
Contact:             WalterG
Location:
Vendor:             unknown (enterprises.2636)
Services:           network
Current Time:       2008-02-28 20:11:36 -07:00
Agent Boot Time:    2008-02-21 20:44:12 -08:00
System Boot Time:   2008-02-21 20:43:27 -08:00
System Boot Args:   /kernel
Users:              3
Processes:          61 (532 maximum)
Memory:             256M
Interfaces:         50
Interface Swap:     2008-02-21 20:45:31 -08:00
(10.10.12.1) scli >
```

That's the router all right. Note that we get a lot more information than we entered. And some people would be very nervous about the system details that SNMP has gathered from this router. But let's look at SNMP in action first. Figure 24.2 shows the SNMP messages and details. One response is of particular interest—the one that has the information we entered on the router. Most of the information displayed at the start of the `show` command can be picked out of the lower pane in the figure.

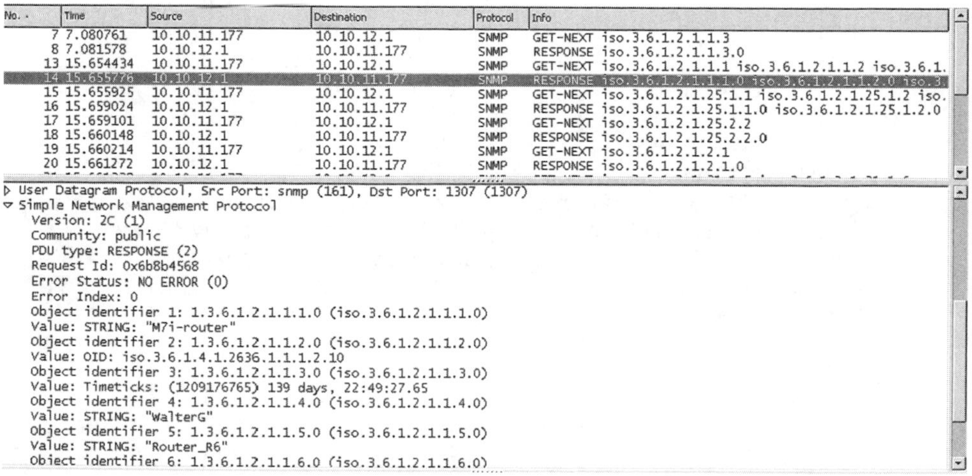

No.	Time	Source	Destination	Protocol	Info
7	7.080761	10.10.11.177	10.10.12.1	SNMP	GET-NEXT iso.3.6.1.2.1.1.3
8	7.081578	10.10.12.1	10.10.11.177	SNMP	RESPONSE iso.3.6.1.2.1.1.3.0
13	15.654434	10.10.11.177	10.10.12.1	SNMP	GET-NEXT iso.3.6.1.2.1.1.1 iso.3.6.1.2.1.1.2 iso.3.6.1.
14	15.655776	10.10.12.1	10.10.11.177	SNMP	RESPONSE iso.3.6.1.2.1.1.1.0 iso.3.6.1.2.1.1.2.0 iso.3.
15	15.655925	10.10.11.177	10.10.12.1	SNMP	GET-NEXT iso.3.6.1.2.1.25.1.1 iso.3.6.1.2.1.25.1.2 iso.
16	15.659024	10.10.12.1	10.10.11.177	SNMP	RESPONSE iso.3.6.1.2.1.25.1.1.0 iso.3.6.1.2.1.25.1.2.0
17	15.659101	10.10.11.177	10.10.12.1	SNMP	GET-NEXT iso.3.6.1.2.1.25.2.2
18	15.660148	10.10.12.1	10.10.11.177	SNMP	RESPONSE iso.3.6.1.2.1.25.2.2.0
19	15.660214	10.10.11.177	10.10.12.1	SNMP	GET-NEXT iso.3.6.1.2.1.2.1
20	15.661272	10.10.12.1	10.10.11.177	SNMP	RESPONSE iso.3.6.1.2.1.2.1.0

```
▷ User Datagram Protocol, Src Port: snmp (161), Dst Port: 1307 (1307)
▽ Simple Network Management Protocol
    Version: 2C (1)
    Community: public
    PDU type: RESPONSE (2)
    Request Id: 0x6b8b4568
    Error Status: NO ERROR (0)
    Error Index: 0
    Object identifier 1: 1.3.6.1.2.1.1.1.0 (iso.3.6.1.2.1.1.1.0)
    Value: STRING: "M7i-router"
    Object identifier 2: 1.3.6.1.2.1.1.2.0 (iso.3.6.1.2.1.1.2.0)
    Value: OID: iso.3.6.1.4.1.2636.1.1.1.2.10
    Object identifier 3: 1.3.6.1.2.1.1.3.0 (iso.3.6.1.2.1.1.3.0)
    Value: Timeticks: (1209176765) 139 days, 22:49:27.65
    Object identifier 4: 1.3.6.1.2.1.1.4.0 (iso.3.6.1.2.1.1.4.0)
    Value: STRING: "WalterG"
    Object identifier 5: 1.3.6.1.2.1.1.5.0 (iso.3.6.1.2.1.1.5.0)
    Value: STRING: "Router_R6"
    Object identifier 6: 1.3.6.1.2.1.1.6.0 (iso.3.6.1.2.1.1.6.0)
```

FIGURE 24.2

SNMP session to router CE6.

Let's see what harm we can cause with SNMP by changing something.

```
(10.10.12.1) scli > set system contact NotMe
500 noResponse 1.00 vpm
(10.10.12.1) scli >
```

The `noResponse` tells us that our request was ignored by CE6. Most devices will enable SNMP with read-only access unless told otherwise. Still, there's a lot of information available about good old router CE6, such as the following:

```
(10.10.12.1) scli > show interface
# show interface info [10.10.12.1] [2008-02-28 20:43:38 -07:00]

INTERFACE STATUS  MTU TYPE                 SPEED NAME        DESCRIPTION
        1  UUCN  1514 ethernetCsmacd        100m fxp0        fxp0
        2  UUCN  1514 ethernetCsmacd        100m fxp1        fxp1
        4  UUNN  1496 mplsTunnel               0 lsi         lsi
        5  UUNN 2147483647 other                  0 dsc         dsc
        6  UUNN 2147483647 softwareLoopback       0 lo0         lo0
        7  UUNN 2147483647 other                  0 tap         tap
        8  UUNN 2147483647 tunnel                 0 gre         gre
        9  UUNN 2147483647 tunnel                 0 ipip        ipip
       10  UUNN 2147483647 tunnel                 0 pime        pime
       11  UUNN 2147483647 tunnel                 0 pimd        pimd
       12  UUNN 2147483647 tunnel                 0 mtun        mtun
       13  UUNN  1500 propVirtual           100m fxp0.0      fxp0.0
       14  UUNN  1514 propVirtual           100m fxp1.0      fxp1.0
       16  UUNN 2147483647 softwareLoopback       0 lo0.0       lo0.0
       21  UUCN  4474 sonet                 155m so-0/0/0    so-0/0/0
       22  UUNN  4470 ppp                   155m so-0/0/0.0  so-0/0/0.0
       23  UUCN  4474 sonet                 155m so-0/0/1    so-0/0/1
       24  UUNN  4470 ppp                   155m so-0/0/1.0  so-0/0/1.0
       25  UUCN  4474 sonet                 155m so-0/0/2    so-0/0/2
       26  UUNN  4470 ppp                   155m so-0/0/2.0  so-0/0/2.0
       27  UUCN  4474 sonet                 155m so-0/0/3    so-0/0/3
       28  UUNN  4470 ppp                   155m so-0/0/3.0  so-0/0/3.0
       29  UUNN 2147483647 softwareLoopback       0 lo0.16385   lo0.16385
       30  UUNN 2147483647 tunnel           800m pd-1/2/0    pd-1/2/0
       31  UUNN 2147483647 tunnel           800m pe-1/2/0    pe-1/2/0
       32  UUNN 2147483647 tunnel           800m gr-1/2/0    gr-1/2/0
       33  UUNN 2147483647 tunnel           800m ip-1/2/0    ip-1/2/0
       34  UUNN 2147483647 tunnel           800m vt-1/2/0    vt-1/2/0
       35  UUNN 2147483647 tunnel           800m mt-1/2/0    mt-1/2/0
       36  UUNN     0 tunnel                800m lt-1/2/0    lt-1/2/0
       37  UUCN  1514 ethernetCsmacd        100m fe-1/3/0    fe-1/3/0
       38  UDCN  1514 ethernetCsmacd        100m fe-1/3/1    fe-1/3/1
       39  UUNN 2147483647 tunnel           800m pd-0/3/0    pd-0/3/0
       40  UUNN 2147483647 tunnel           800m pe-0/3/0    pe-0/3/0
       41  UUNN 2147483647 tunnel           800m gr-0/3/0    gr-0/3/0
```

```
      42  UUNN 2147483647 tunnel          800m ip-0/3/0    ip-0/3/0
      43  UUNN 2147483647 tunnel          800m vt-0/3/0    vt-0/3/0
      44  UUNN 2147483647 tunnel          800m mt-0/3/0    mt-0/3/0
      45  UUNN      0 tunnel              800m lt-0/3/0    lt-0/3/0
      46  UDCN   1504 e1                    2m e1-0/2/0    e1-0/2/0
      47  UDCN   1504 e1                    2m e1-0/2/1    e1-0/2/1
      48  UDCN   1504 e1                    2m e1-0/2/2    e1-0/2/2
Byte 2969
```

And this is only *part* of it. Just imagine if someone managed to break in and . . . but wait: All we did is use a router interface's IP address. No breaking in was needed.

What can we do to tighten things up? Let's limit SNMP access to a single interface on the router, and a single host reachable through the interface. The interface will be LAN2, on `fe-1/3/0`, not surprisingly. We'll use the LAN2 host `bsdserver` so that we can still use `scli`. We'll also let an administrator with `root` privileges on `bsdserver` make changes with the `set` request in the SNMP *community* (a sort of SNMP "password," but it's really not) called `locallan`. Almost all of this is configured on the router, not the host. The `scli` limitation to execute a remote `set` command is a function of the application. The following presents the new router configuration.

```
set snmp name Router_CE6;
set snmp description M7i router;
set snmp contact WalterG;
set snmp interface fe-1/3/0.0; # restrict SNMP to the LAN2 interface
set snmp view syscontact oid sysContact include; # let the manager change
   the sysContact
set snmp community locallan view sysContact; # establish new community
   string and add sysContact to view. . .
set snmp community locallan authorization read-write; # . . .and let it be
   read and write access. . .
set snmp community locallan clients 10.10.12.77/32; # . . .but only from
   bsdserver for the locallan community string
```

We have to explicitly add the `sysContact` object ID to a "view" for the community string `locallan` if we are going to allow the network manager on `bsdserver` to change the value of that object. Back on `bsdclient`, the effects of these changes are immediate.

```
(10.10.12.1) scli > show ip
500 noResponse
500 noResponse
500 noResponse
500 noResponse
500 noResponse
(10.10.12.1) scli >
```

But things are different once we switch to `bsdclient` (and remember to use the community string `locallan`).

```
> bsdserver# scli
100-scli version 0.2.12 (c) 2001-2002 Juergen Schoenwaelder
scli > open 10.10.12.1 locallan
100-scli trying SNMPv2c ... good
(10.10.12.1) scli > set system contact NotMe
(10.10.12.1) scli > show system
# show system info [10.10.12.1] [2008-02-28 21:02:07 -07:00]

Address:          10.10.12.1:161
Contact:          NotMe
(10.10.12.1) scli >
```

If we forget to add the object explicitly to the community on the router, `bsdserver` still has access but will not be able to write to the object.

```
(10.10.12.1) scli > set system contact NotMe
500 noAccess @ varbind 1
(10.10.12.1) scli >
```

By now it should be obvious that SNMP can be a powerful network management tool, independent of remote-access or vendor-specific management techniques. However, all of this talk about objects, community strings, SNMPv1, and v2 can be confusing. SNMP introduces a lot of terms and concepts. Let's start at the beginning and see just what SNMP can do and how it does it.

THE SNMP MODEL

This section takes a more detailed look at how SNMP, versions 1 and 2, works. This chapter identifies the shortcomings of SNMPv1 that led to the creation of SNMPv2, and then shows what SNMPv3 will add to SNMP. SNMP remains the most popular and most viable method of managing networks today, let alone the Internet.

All network management standards, not just SNMP, work by means of what is known as the *agent/manager model*. This is not really a new term or concept. The term "agent/manager model" is essentially the client/server model idea extended to network management. A manager is just a management console in the NOC running the network management software, not an actual human being. An *agent* is software that runs on all manageable devices on the network. As in the client/server model, managers "talk" and the agents "listen." So, managers are clients for network management purposes and agents are servers for network management purposes. Obviously, a major difference in the agent/manager model from traditional client/server is that in a network management situation, there are many servers (agents) and generally only a few clients (management consoles).

The manager running in the network management station (or any host setup to run it) sends commands to the agent software on the managed device using a network management protocol that both the manager and agent understand. The agent responds and then waits (or "listens") for a further command, and so on. The command may be generated by the manager software periodically, without human intervention, and the results

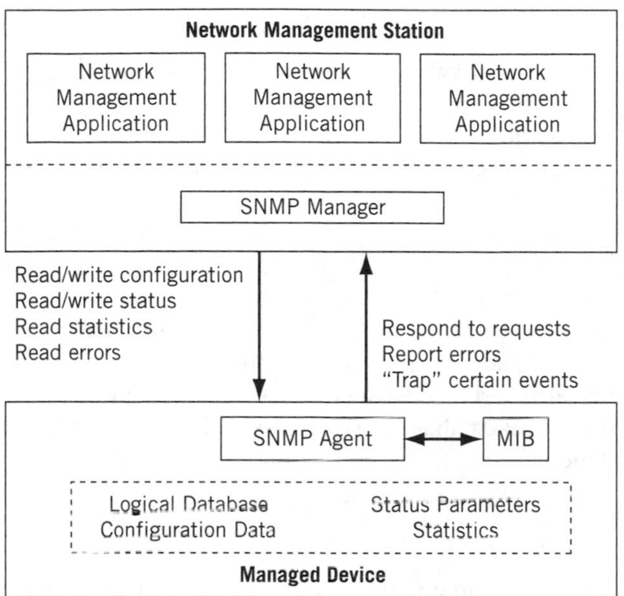

FIGURE 24.3

SNMP model, showing that an agent has access to a MIB in the managed devices.

stored in a manager console database for future reports or reference. Alternatively, the commands may be generated by NOC personnel using the manager console to solve outstanding network problems, perform routine testing, and so forth. In the case of a serious event, such as major link failure, an alarm (called a *trap* in SNMP) is generated without anyone asking. Most servers, hubs, routers, and even end-user devices sold today have built-in SNMP agent software that does not usually have to be purchased separately. The SNMP model of network management is shown in Figure 24.3.

Note that network managers can both monitor the status of the device and actually change the configuration (a dangerous capability that requires careful considerations if it is to be allowed at all). The network management station typically keeps the historical information about the network device (devices have better things to do), and has a number of applications whose main goal is to provide detailed reports about the network's performance, often in a graphical format designed for visual impact.

In addition, all network management standards provide for a special type of agent (known as the *proxy agent*) to provide the manager console with management information about network devices that do not understand the network management protocol. Of course, the network devices must understand *some* type of network management protocol or they would not be manageable at all. But the proxy agent performs a type of gateway function to translate back and forth between the network manager console protocol and the different network management protocol, often proprietary, understood by the network devices accessed by the proxy agent.

The MIB and SMI

The agent software has access to the current value of various *objects* in the managed device. The exact function and meaning of an object, and the relationship of one object to another, is described in the MIB for the managed device. The MIB is a crucial concept in all network management standards, not only in SNMP, although there are many MIBs for devices used on the Internet.

The MIB is a *database* description of all fields (objects) that make up the totality of information an agent can furnish to a manager console when requested. So, a MIB is most often just a piece of paper (RFC) that says things such as "the first field is alphanumeric, 20 characters long, and contains the name of the vendor" and "the fifth field is an integer and contains the number of bad packets received." Not that this is rendered in plain English. A special ISO "language" called ASN.1 (Abstract Syntax Notation version 1) is used to represent all fields of the MIB database in very terse and cryptic language that all MIB implementers understand.

The SMI

The problem with trying to manage all possible network device agents with a single management protocol is that there are so many different types of network devices. Some deal with packets (routers), and some with frames (bridges). Some are quite simple (hubs), and some are very complex (switches). The challenge is to find a way to sort out all of the possible MIB variables in a standard fashion so that any implementation of the network manager console protocol will be able to request the value of any particular object accessible by any agent. Fortunately, standards organizations have all agreed on and defined a standard structure for network management information.

The SNMP developers defined a Structure of Management Information (SMI) tree in RFC 1155. The same SMI is defined in ISO 10165, where it is called the Management Information Model (MIM), and in ITU-T X.720, X.721, and X.722.

MIB information is structured through the use of a *naming tree* known as the SMI conceptual tree. Figure 24.4 shows the SMI conceptual tree with the emphasis on SNMP MIB definitions.

The root of the tree is unlabeled. All branches of the tree from the root have both labels and numbers associated with them. All SNMP MIB objects are under the branch that leads from ISO (1) to Identified Organizations (3) to the Department of Defense (DoD) (6) to the Internet (1). At the lowest branches of the tree are the MIB objects themselves. These are organized into MIB-I (the original SNMP definitions) and MIB-II (extended SNMP definitions).

The system group of MIB-II is probably the most commonly used and easily understood of all MIB objects in SNMP. The System(1) group contains seven objects that provide a general description of the network device. The seven objects are:

- sysDescr(1)—A description of the network device ("router," "hub," etc.)
- sysObjectID(2)—The identifier of the device's private MIB location, if any (discussed more fully in material following)

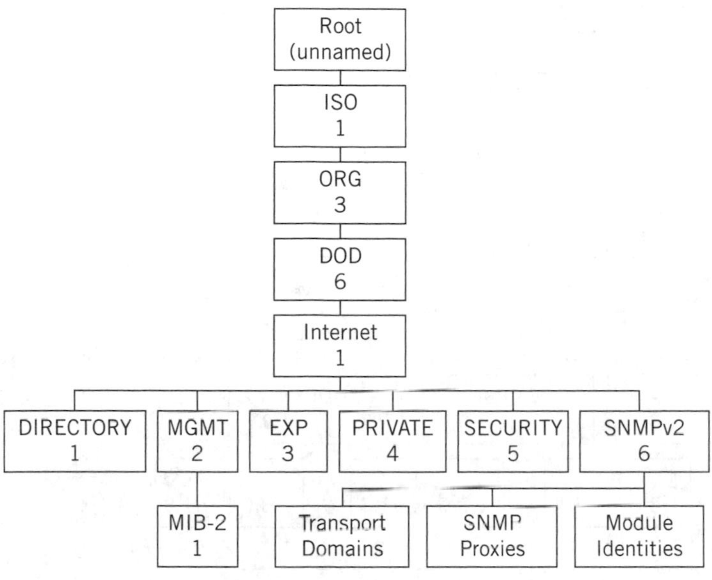

FIGURE 24.4

SMI tree, showing how the names are organized.

- sysUpTime(3)—The time, measured in 100ths of a second, since the network management software (not necessarily the device!) was reinitialized
- sysContact(4)—The name of the local contact person responsible for the network device
- sysName(5)—The name of the manufacturer of the network device
- sysLocation(6)—The physical location of the network device
- sysServices(7)—The services the network device is capable of rendering

The importance of MIBs in network management should not be overlooked. From a single console, a network manager can merely point a mouse at an icon and with a click determine that the device is a router located at 1194 North Mathilda Avenue in Sunnyvale, California; that the person responsible for the device is Walter Goralski; and so on. All of this information is provided over the network, on the fly, from the device itself (as long as it is entered and maintained on the device, of course).

The numbers and labels referred to previously are technically called object identifiers and object descriptors in SMI. The SMI tree is used by the network management protocol to designate objects in the MIB. Object identifiers are numeric, and all SNMP manageable devices commonly found on a network begin with `1.3.6.1...` (shown in Figure 24.4). Identifiers are used by the network management software. Object descriptors, on the other hand, are labels, and all SNMP manageable devices also begin with `ISO.ORG.DOD.INTERNET...`, which is the exact equivalent of the numeric string. This view of the MIB tree is shown in Figure 24.5.

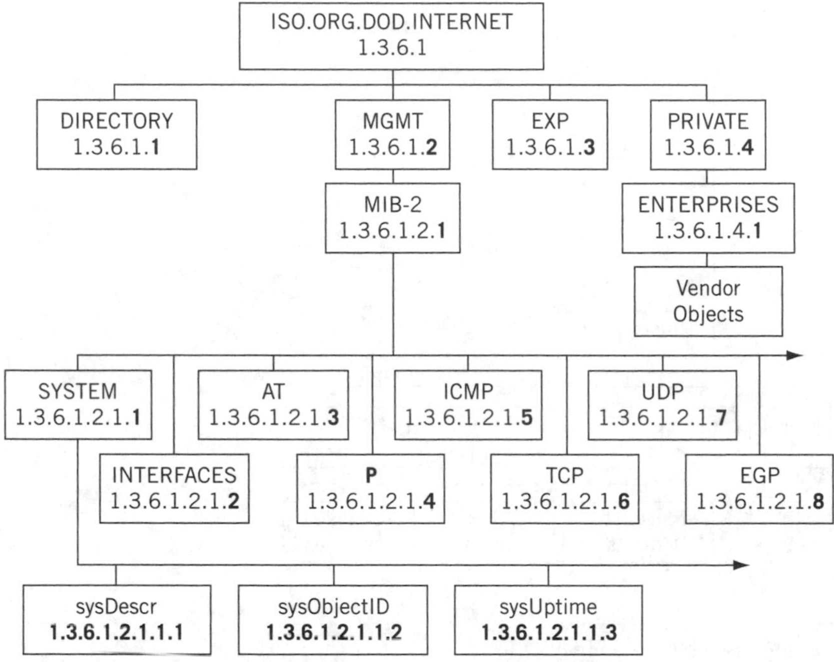

FIGURE 24.5

MIB tree by number and name. The numeric strings can quickly become very long.

As an example of the use of object identifiers, consider the case in which a network manager may need to change the system contact for a particular network device. An SNMP command, in this case a `get` request, is used to retrieve the current value of the sysDescr object. The SNMP message requests the current value of the object `1.3.6.1.2.1.1.1`, which is the object identifier equivalent of the object descriptor `iso.org.dod.internet.mgmt.mib-2.system.sysDescr`. The device knows to reply with the current value of the sysDescr object and no other. If permitted, the network manager can even use the SNMP `set` command to replace to current value of the sysDescr object with the name of the new local contact for the network device (if there is a reason to change it, perhaps to reflect an upgrade).

The MIB

All of the MIB objects in SNMP are defined in ISO ASN.1, a presentation layer (OSI-RM Layer 6) standard syntax. The definition of a managed object in a network device's agent MIB consists of the following seven fields.

- *Syntax*—An ASN.1 data type such as integer, time ticks (hundredths of a second), string, and so on.

- *Access*—If the object is read-write, read-only, not-accessible, and so on.
- *Status*—Objects may be mandatory, optional, obsolete, or deprecated (replaced by newer).
- *Description*—An optional text string describing the object type.
- *Reference*—An optional cross reference to another MIB definition (e.g., a CMIP branch).
- *Index*—If the object is a table, this defines how SNMP access a unique logical row.
- *Defval*—An optional default value assigned to the object.

In the following are two sample MIB object definitions in ASN.1, ifMTU and sysUpTime.

```
OBJECT:   ifMtu { ifEntry 4 }
Syntax:   INTEGER
Definition:  The size of the largest IP datagram that can be sent/received
   on the interface, specified in octets.
Access:   read-only.
Status:   mandatory.

OBJECT:   sysUpTime { system 3 }
Syntax:   TimeTicks
Definition:  The time (in hundredths of a second) since the network
   management portion of the system was last reinitialized.
Access:   read-only.
Status:   mandatory.
```

The ifMtu object is from the interface (ifEntry) group, and gives the maximum transmission unit size, a key TCP/IP parameter. The object is the fourth entry in the group (an integer); may only be read by the network manager software, not changed; must be in all SNMP compliant equipment that uses TCP/IP; and gives the size in bytes of the largest IP datagram that can be sent or received by this network device on this particular interface (port).

The sysUpTime object is the third in the system group, and gives the time the network management agent software has been running. The units are a special type of integer called time ticks. The object is read-only, and must be present.

MIBs are technically just pieces of paper, like a customer database data field description. MIBs must be coded and implemented in the agent software and installed in the network device before the network device can be managed by a manager console. Typically, a MIB is coded by the programmers of the network device's software in a C-language module and compiled into an object-code module with a special compiler known (not surprisingly) as a *MIB compiler*. The MIB object-code module is then linked with the SNMP protocol model to yield the entire executable module, which can be installed in the memory of the network device. All of this is usually done before the network device is sold, of course.

There are exceptions to this rule, however. MIBs exist for a variety of purposes and network types. For instance, a router may have both an Ethernet MIB and a SONET/SDH MIB if the router supports both types of network connections, and even a frame-relay

MIB on the SONET/SDH port of the router. Sometimes, though, a network device may be sold with only an Ethernet port (for example) and then upgraded to provide SONET/SDH connectivity as well, usually through the addition of a new interface card. In this case, the router may have included only the Ethernet MIB because no SONET/SDH MIB was needed. When the new SONET/SDH card is added, the SONET/SDH MIB must be added as well.

Not all modifications to network devices involve hardware. In some cases, a new MIB may have to be installed when a new software feature is activated on the network device. In many SNMP implementations, the *extensible MIB* may be activated or installed over the network without even being present at the network device site.

RMON

One additional aspect of SNMP MIBs should be discussed, in that this concept is extremely helpful in managing large networks. There is a potential problem with managing SNMP devices on a network over the network itself (security is another matter). The problem is simply this: What if the link to the network device is down? How is the status of the network device to be determined under these conditions? The answer is provided by means of a special optional MIB: the *RMON MIB*. RMON stands for "remote monitor," and this MIB provides for a dial-in port to the network device that may be used by the manager console to communicate with the network device regardless of other network link availability.

RMON may also be used with leased lines to provide another benefit for large IP networks. The larger the enterprise network, the more network devices there are that need managing. Network managers will try to monitor network device performance and workload to prevent congestion on the network. The problem is that all of these SNMP messages flowing over the network back and forth to all of the network devices can add a considerable load to a network at the worst possible time, when things are going suspiciously wrong. If RMON is configured to run on separate leased lines to critical network devices, the SNMP messages add no load at all to the enterprise network itself.

Unfortunately, not many organizations can afford the additional expense of the necessary leased lines to many of these important network devices (usually the routers). Still, RMON remains a useful option for heavily loaded or delay-sensitive IP networks.

The Private MIB

Standard MIB objects are designed for a wide variety of technologies and network devices. These MIB objects cover a large range of possibilities, but there are always situations and conditions that a network manager should be aware of that are not covered by a standard MIB object. These are usually very low-level, device-specific hardware functions, such as whether a network device's cooling fan has failed, whether the device has battery backup or a redundant power supply, or any of a number of other vendor hardware-implementation choices and options.

To cover all of these vendor-specific situations, the SMI conceptual tree includes a branch for private MIB extensions.The SMI path to the private MIB is `1.3.6.1.4.1`.This leads to the *enterprise* branch of the SMI tree, where each vendor may obtain a branch number (identifier) and label (descriptor) from the Internet Assigned Number Authority (IANA) for the vendor's private MIB. For example, all IBM private MIB objects reside at `1.3.6.1.4.1.2...` on the SMI tree because "2" is IBM's enterprise number. Cisco routers use `1.3.6.1.4.1.9...`, Hewlett-Packard has `1.3.6.1.4.1.11...`, and so forth. More than 700 enterprise code numbers have been assigned by the IANA, showing the wide availability of SNMP-compliant products.

This system of private MIBs makes sense because only the manufacturer of the network device could possibly know whether the device even has a cooling fan, battery backup, or other hardware feature. Obviously, a network manager would like to know if a device's fan has failed, especially if the device is in a closet where it may overheat and fail after a few hours.The private MIB offers a way of allowing this information to be accessed by the network manager.

SNMP manager software will generally have no concept of just where the private MIB objects are and what these objects represent. Some vendors would actually "hide" their private MIB descriptions by limiting their availability, and just what the number `2` in a private MIB field might mean (Status code? Error code? Two minutes to failure?) often remained a mystery. In most cases, this means that this vendor's network device could only be completely manageable using that vendor's network manager software, which would have a built-in description of this private MIB. Private MIBs are an effective way to "lock in" a company to using only a specific vendor's SNMP software as a network manager.

Few companies go to that extent anymore. But the problem of how any particular manager console software could know just where any vendor's private MIB is located and what the vendor's private MIB means still exists. This is where the system group `sysObjectID` object can be helpful. Accessing the object `1.3.6.1.2.1.1.2` (the second object in the system group: `sysObjectID`) from the management console will return a string such as `1.3.6.1.4.1.999.1.1...`. This is, of course, the location of the private MIB objects for the vendor of the particular device. Further requests to that SMI tree location might yield the private MIB description implemented by that vendor (`1` means fan failure, `2` means fan normal).

Manufacturers may extend private MIBs with as many objects in whatever structure they desire. Many vendors publish (on the Internet) their private MIB descriptions so that makers of SNMP management console software can easily build in private MIB support without having to follow `sysObjectID` links.

SNMP OPERATION

All of the foregoing discussion on SMI, MIBs, and private MIBs applies equally to any standard network management package that may be used on a network. Granted, there are a few differences between SNMP network management terminology and the others. Specifically, the SMI objects in network management protocols other than SNMP may not all necessarily start with `1.3.6.1...` because these are by definition TCP/IP Internet objects and the MIB in CMIP is referred to as MIM (Management Information Model). There are other minor differences as well, but the point is that all of the previous material and concepts apply to network management in general.

However, this section will deal entirely with the specifics of SNMP as the most widespread, cost-efficient, and viable network management standard for IP networks in use today. For the remainder of this section, SNMP without qualification means SNMPv1. SNMPv2 and SNMPv3 will always be qualified with the version number.

SNMP was invented to manage routers on the Internet, and early versions of SNMP had few MIB objects suitable for managing other network devices. The latest SNMP MIB definitions have been extended to include objects defined for most LAN and WAN technologies, even ATM and frame relay. SNMP was initially intended as an interim solution until ISO's CMIP network management standard was completed, at which time SNMP was supposed to merge with CMIP. But SNMP has had such success independently of CMIP that this is unlikely to happen.

SNMP is part of the TCP/IP protocol stack and is considered a standard TCP/IP application like FTP or Telnet. Of course, SNMP is a very special type of application, one that is seldom bundled with TCP/IP software as FTP and Telnet are. Due to its TCP/IP origins, the original SNMP did suffer from one annoying limitation that severely hampers the use of SNMP for managing mission-critical networks that should not fail.

The limitation is bound up with the fact that SNMP is defined as a request–response protocol, similar to DNS. Each message sent was expected to generate a reply before the next request was sent. This made perfect sense for SNMP: Why send a stream of messages to a device that has failed? And like any request–response protocol, SNMP used speedy and connectionless UDP for its messages.

But there is a price to be paid for connectionless speed. What if an SNMP message is sent and no reply received? There can be at least three causes. First, the data may have been lost by the network on the way to the destination (due to network faults or congestion). Second, the destination network device itself may be down or powered off. Third, the data may have been lost by the network on the way back from the destination (for the same reasons as the first two causes).

On the other hand, connection-oriented networks and applications that first establish a connection across the network with a remote device have a better chance of figuring out just what is wrong if a reply to a particular message is not received. If a device accepts a connection request, it means the device is turned on and ready to communicate and the network between the two devices linked by the connection is up and running. It is important to realize that this knowledge is established *even before any messages have been sent from a source to a destination*.

Obviously, toward obtaining a more robust and effective network management protocol network, managers would rather that SNMP be connection oriented, as is clear from the previous discussion. A lot could be found out just from establishing a connection between a manager console and a network device's agent. However, SNMPv1 was

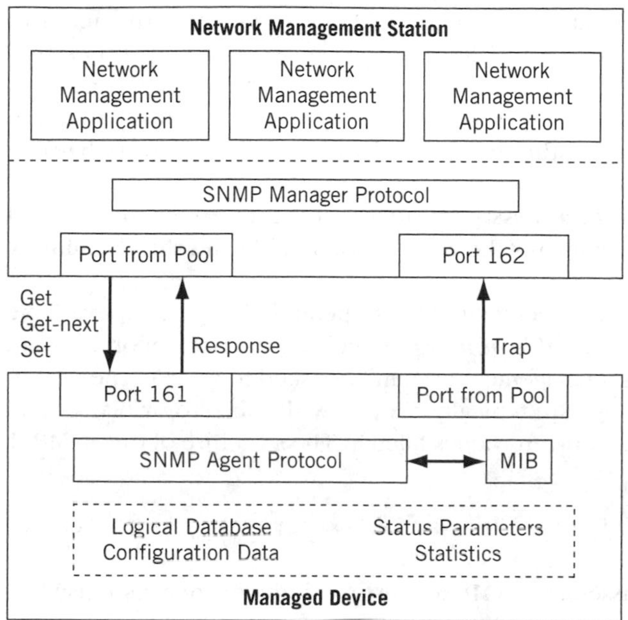

FIGURE 24.6

SNMPv1 protocol operation, showing ports for the five SNMP message types.

a connectionless TCP/IP application, which limited its effectiveness on many enterprise networks. The operation of the SNMPv1 protocol is shown in Figure 24.6.

SNMP is an extremely simple protocol. There are only five types of messages defined: `GetRequest` (or `Get`) to ask an agent to return the current value of an object (based on the SMI tree), `GetNextRequest` (or `GetNext`) to ask an agent to return the current value of the very next object, `GetResponse` (or `Response`) to return the current value of an object to the manager, `SetRequest` (or `Set`) to tell an agent to replace the current value of an object with a new value, and `Trap` to allow an agent to send a message to a manager without being asked.

The agent device accepts SNMP requests on port 161 and replies using that port. The manager chooses a source port from a pool, often restricted to SNMP only. Traps are sent via port 162 on the manager, also using a source port chosen from a pool.

Traps are used to address another quirk of SNMP. Generally, agents tell the manager console absolutely nothing without being asked. In view of this, it is normal for the SNMP manager software to periodically generate `GetRequest` messages to every manageable device's agent on the network just to ensure that everything is all right. This process is known as *SNMP polling*, and not only adds traffic to the network, but means that long periods of time may elapse between successive polls on a complex SNMP enterprise network.

Traps help to remedy this situation. These are messages sent from the agent to the manager without waiting for a poll. There are seven generic trap types that include such events as link failures and the fact that the agent network device is being reinitialized, and so on. An *enterprise-specific* trap type is included to allow vendors to extend traps to include other events (such as fan failure, battery backup activated, etc.).

All SNMPv1 messages consist of a message header and the actual SNMP protocol data unit (PDU). The header only contains the version number (1) and the community string (default is `public`).

The PDUs contain the command specifics and their operands. The fields are variable in length, and end with strings of *variable bindings,* which are the pairs of objects and their current values the network management system has asked to see. On the way to the managed device, these bindings are typically filled in with the zero or blanks, and naturally they come back with the current values filled in. The structure of the SNMPv1 PDU is shown in Figure 24.7.

- *PDU Type*—Specifies the PDU Type: `GetRequest`, `GetNextRequest`, `GetResponse`, and `Setrequest`.
- *Request ID*—A field used to associate SNMP requests with the proper response.
- *Error Status*—Only a `GetResponse` sets a numeric error code in this field. Otherwise, the field is zero.
- *Error Index*—Associates the error code with a particular object in the bindings. Only a `GetResponse` sets a numeric index in this field. Otherwise, the field is zero.
- *Variable Bindings*—The data field of the Simple Network Managment Protocol PDU. Each pair associates the object with its current value, except of course in the `GetRequest` and `GetNextRequest`.

`Traps` are not included in the figure because in SNMPv1 they have a distinctive (and annoying) structure all their own. In the previous discussion, at least two limitations of SNMPv1 have been identified. First, SNMPv1 is connectionless, which means that SNMP is much less effective than it could be. Second, SNMP must poll devices in most cases for effective network management because the traps are few and not very helpful.

There is a third aspect of SNMP that makes the protocol less effective than it could be for managing large IP networks, especially portions of the Internet. This is the fact

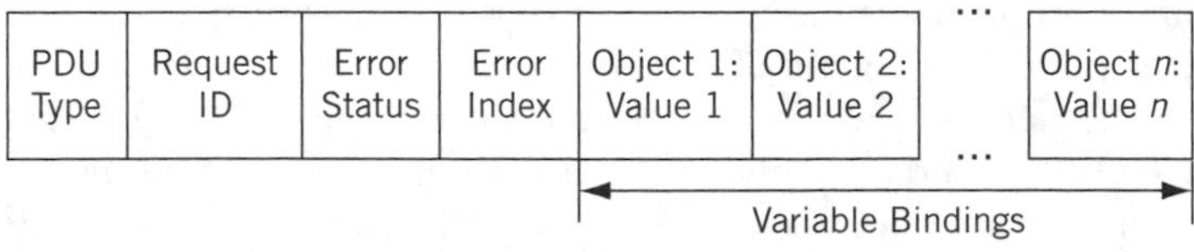

FIGURE 24.7

SNMPv1 PDU. Variable bindings allow the response to deliver a lot of information in one message.

that SNMPv1 had only rudimentary password and authentication features and even lacked a good encryption technique.

The greatest threat that network management poses to a network, ironically, comes from exploiting remote configuration capabilities, one of the most useful things in network management. Activating additional ports on hubs and routers, changing IP addresses, and modifying other operational functions over the network rather than by actually having a technician present at the network device location is a much sought-after feature of network management. But the routine practice of remote configuration is tied up with the establishment on the network of secure network management protocols to prevent hackers and other unauthorized persons from making such changes to these devices.

SNMPv1 has only rudimentary features that can be used to try to prevent this from happening. The SNMP protocol does include the use of a simple password scheme, known as the *community string*. All SNMP messages from a management console to an agent must include a community string field that is compared by the agent with the community string configured at installation in the network device. If the community strings do not match, the agent presumes that the message is not from the legitimate network management console software and discards the message.

The problem with expecting SNMP community strings to provide adequate password protection against unauthorized agent access is twofold. First, many agents are simply configured to respond to the community string `public`, which is essentially the SNMP default and might not be changed. Of course, hackers will quickly determine this fact and make immediate use of this. Second, even if the community string is altered to a more enterprise-specific string such as `Example Inc.`, the SNMP messages exchanged constantly on the enterprise network due to the SNMP polling process will make no effort to hide this fact: The community strings are not encrypted in SNMP but sent in plain text.

The problem of authentication is related to the use of passwords for network management. All SNMPv1 agents accept any SNMP messages and commands if the community string is correct. With an authentication scheme for network management, more should be needed for an agent to accept messages as proper commands sent from a valid network management console. Matching passwords is not enough: The message must come from the IP address of the network management console or consoles.

SNMPv2 Enhancements

SNMPv2 was widely anticipated in the network management community since its initial proposals. SNMPv1 also suffered from an annoying problem with the request–response system of polling. If one variable was not in the agent's database, the entire operation failed. In addition, as MIB grew and grew, SNMPv1 responses often exceeded the maximum size of a message (UDP doesn't fragment) and the operation failed.

To address these issues, SNMPv2 added a `GetBulk` message to the SNMP repertoire, which allowed the device to supply as much information as it could in response to the request. There was also a greatly expanded list of error codes used when an SNMP request failed.

`Inform` allows one network management system to trap information sent by another network management system and then get a response. In addition, the format of the `Trap` was changed to make it more like the other PDU type.

SNMPv2 can still run as a connectionless UDP application on IP networks. But implementers have the option of making SNMPv2 a connection-oriented TCP application. In addition, SNMPv2 includes very robust and standardized methods for true passwords, authentication, and encryption.

Yet the use of SNMPv1 remains common on the Internet. The problem with SNMPv2 is exactly the opposite of the simplicity of SNMPv1: SNMPv2 is very complex. This complexity translates to implementation expense, not only in the management console software but in the agent software installed by every vendor of SNMP-manageable network equipment. For very simple networks, SNMPv2 is overkill.

In addition, SNMPv2 is incompatible with SNMPv1. The message formats are different, and there are two new message types (`GetBulk` and `Inform`). RFC 1908 recommends the use of proxy agents, or simply running both when this incompatibility becomes an issue. Many Internet devices, such as routers, make use of SNMPv1 or SNMPv2 (or both) as a configuration option.

SNMPv3

A few words should be said about SNMPv3. SNMPv1 had little or no security to speak of, and SNMPv2 adds security to the basic operation of SNMP. However, SNMPv3 will essentially make network management and SNMP part of the overall *security framework* for a network. SNMP will have very strict requirements for authentication, encryption, and privacy of information. Discussions of SNMPv3 are best handled by texts devoted to the topic of security.

QUESTIONS FOR READERS

Figure 24.8 shows some of the concepts discussed in this chapter and can be used to answer the following questions.

```
▷ Frame 14 (230 bytes on wire, 230 bytes captured)
▷ Ethernet II, Src: 00:05:85:88:cc:db, Dst: 00:0e:0c:3b:8f:94
▷ Internet Protocol, Src Addr: 10.10.12.1 (10.10.12.1), Dst Addr: 10.10.11.177 (10.10.11.177)
▷ User Datagram Protocol, Src Port: snmp (161), Dst Port: 1307 (1307)
▽ Simple Network Management Protocol
    Version: 2C (1)
    Community: public
    PDU type: RESPONSE (2)
    Request Id: 0x6b8b4568
    Error Status: NO ERROR (0)
    Error Index: 0
    Object identifier 1: 1.3.6.1.2.1.1.1.0 (iso.3.6.1.2.1.1.1.0)
    Value: STRING: "M7i-router"
    Object identifier 2: 1.3.6.1.2.1.1.2.0 (iso.3.6.1.2.1.1.2.0)
    Value: OID: iso.3.6.1.4.1.2636.1.1.1.2.10
    Object identifier 3: 1.3.6.1.2.1.1.3.0 (iso.3.6.1.2.1.1.3.0)
    Value: Timeticks: (1209176765) 139 days, 22:49:27.65
    Object identifier 4: 1.3.6.1.2.1.1.4.0 (iso.3.6.1.2.1.1.4.0)
    Value: STRING: "WalterG"
    Object identifier 5: 1.3.6.1.2.1.1.5.0 (iso.3.6.1.2.1.1.5.0)
    Value: STRING: "Router_R6"
    Object identifier 6: 1.3.6.1.2.1.1.6.0 (iso.3.6.1.2.1.1.6.0)
    Value: ""
    Object identifier 7: 1.3.6.1.2.1.1.7.0 (iso.3.6.1.2.1.1.7.0)
    Value: INTEGER: 4
    Object identifier 8: 1.3.6.1.2.1.2.1.0 (iso.3.6.1.2.1.2.1.0)
    Value: INTEGER: 50
```

FIGURE 24.8

Ethereal capture of an SNMP response message. Note the object identifiers.

1. Which version of SNMP is used here?
2. Which router IP address and port are responding?
3. Express the SMI tree to the sysDescr group in English instead of numbers. It starts with "iso.org..."
4. The actual time ticks value of 1209176765 is interpreted. What does this value represent?
5. Where is the response telling the management application to go for more device-specific information?

PART

VI

Security

Security is a major concern in networking today. This part of the book continues the theme begun with SSL, and explores the basic aspects of security used on the Internet today.

- Chapter 25—Secure Shell (Remote Access)
- Chapter 26—MPLS-Based Virtual Private Networks
- Chapter 27—Network Address Translation
- Chapter 28—Firewalls
- Chapter 29—IP Security

CHAPTER

Secure Shell (Remote Access)

25

What You Will Learn

In this chapter, you will learn how the secure shell (SSH) is used as a more secure method of remote access than Telnet. We'll talk about the SSH model, features, and architectures.

You will learn how the SSH protocols operate and how keys are distributed. We'll do a simple example of Diffie-Hellman key distribution using only a pocket calculator and no advanced mathematics.

Not too long ago, most TCP/IP books would routinely cover Telnet as the Internet application for remote access. But today, with the focus on security the Telnet daemon is considered just too dangerous to leave running on hosts and routers, mainly because it is such a tempting target even when password encryption is mandated. There are ways to "enhance" Telnet with security mechanisms, much as the control connection used for FTP (which is little more than a Telnet session) has done.

This is not to say that remote access itself is not an essential Internet and TCP/IP tool. This book could not have been written without Telnet remote access. But more and more today, the preferred application for remote access is SSH.

Windows users should not let the use of the Unix term "shell" scare them. SSH is not really a Unix shell, such as the Bourne shell or other Unix interfaces. It's really a protocol that runs, like most things, over IPv4 or IPv6. Yet the use of the word "shell" in SSH is a good one because there is a lot more to SSH than just remote access. Perhaps the term "secure suite" would have been better, but SSH is what it is.

USING SSH

Most people know SSH as just another way to access the remote host of a router. For example, to access router `CE0` from host `bsdclient` and log in as `admin`, we would use the `-l` option as follows:

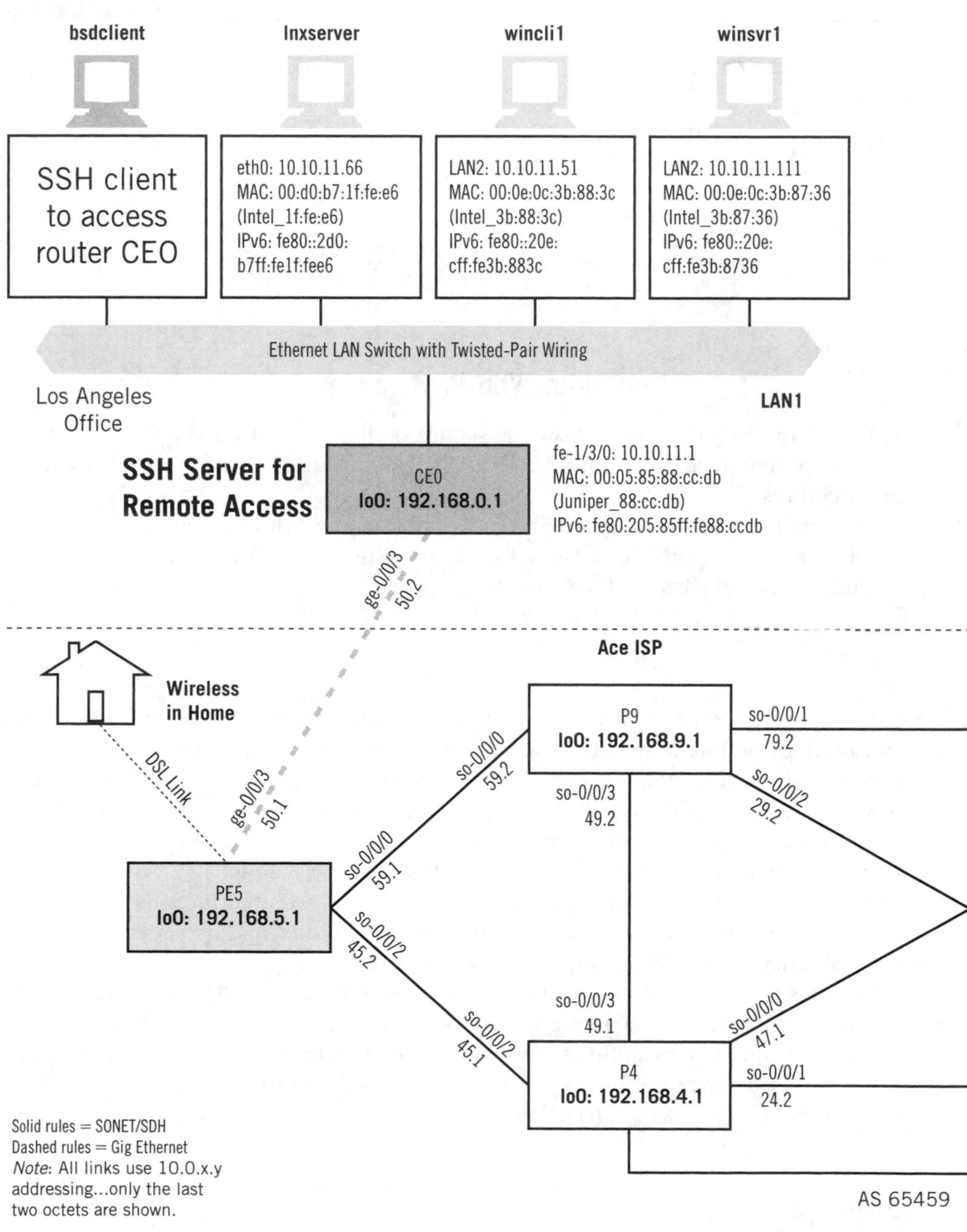

FIGURE 25.1

Using SSH on the Illustrated Network showing the host used as the SSH client and the target router used as the SSH server for remote access.

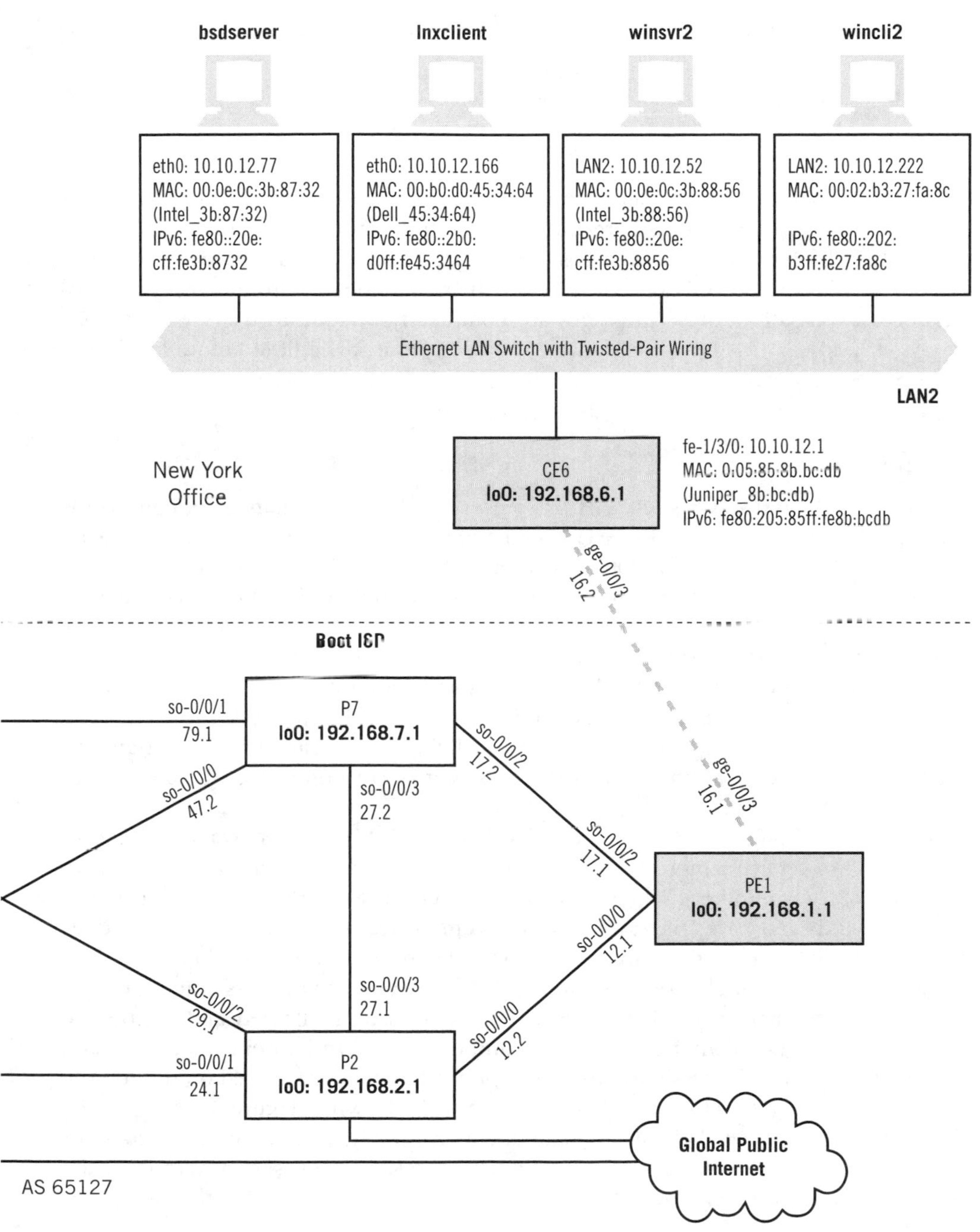
bsdserver
lnxclient
winsvr2
wincli2
eth0: 10.10.12.77
MAC: 00:0e:0c:3b:87:32
(Intel_3b:87:32)
IPv6: fe80::20e:
cff:fe3b:8732
eth0: 10.10.12.166
MAC: 00:b0:d0:45:34:64
(Dell_45:34:64)
IPv6: fe80::2b0:
d0ff:fe45:3464
LAN2: 10.10.12.52
MAC: 00:0e:0c:3b:88:56
(Intel_3b:88:56)
IPv6: fe80::20e:
cff:fe3b:8856
LAN2: 10.10.12.222
MAC: 00:02:b3:27:fa:8c
IPv6: fe80::202:
b3ff:fe27:fa8c
Ethernet LAN Switch with Twisted-Pair Wiring
LAN2
New York
Office
CE6
lo0: 192.168.6.1
fe-1/3/0: 10.10.12.1
MAC: 0:05:85:8b.bc:db
(Juniper_8b:bc:db)
IPv6: fe80:205:85ff:fe8b:bcdb
ge-0/0/3
16.2
P7
lo0: 192.168.7.1
so-0/0/1
79.1
so-0/0/0
47.2
so-0/0/3
27.2
so-0/0/2
17.2
ge-0/0/3
16.1
so-0/0/2
17.1
PE1
lo0: 192.168.1.1
so-0/0/0
12.1
so-0/0/2
29.1
so-0/0/3
27.1
so-0/0/0
12.2
P2
lo0: 192.168.2.1
so-0/0/1
24.1
Global Public
Internet
AS 65127

```
bsdclient# ssh -l admin 10.10.11.1
admin@10.10.11.1's password: (not shown)
--- JUNOS 8.4R1.3 built 2007-08-06 06:58:15 UTC
admin@CE0>
```

You might notice a longer wait after issuing the `ssh` command than other commands before being asked for the password, but if the network is fast enough this delay is marginal. In fact, a blizzard of messaging is crisscrossing the network between command and password requests, and even more before the remote device prompt appears. Without some explanation, these messages are completely opaque to users. So, let's use `bsdclient` and `CE0` (as shown in Figure 25.1) to explore SSH a little before looking at the messages in detail.

SSH Basics

Although not technically a shell, SSH lets a user do all of the things Unix commands such as `rsh`, `rlogin`, and `rcp` do. (SSH is sometimes implemented as `slogin`.) SSH is an application that allows users to log on to another host over the network, execute commands on the remote host, and move files around. But unlike the older "r commands" it is intended to replace, SSH provides secure communication over unsecure channels, strong authentication and encryption, and other security features.

The "r commands" were vulnerable to many different types of attacks. Anyone without root access to the hosts or access to the packets on the network can gain unauthorized access to the hosts in several ways. Malicious users can also log all traffic to and from the host, including other users' passwords. (In contrast, SSH *never* sends passwords in clear text.)

The popular X Windows GUI for Unix is also vulnerable in many ways. SSH allows the creation of secure remote X Windows sessions that are transparent to the user. In fact, using SSH for remote X Window clients is easier for users. Users can still use their old `rhosts` and `/etc/hosts` files for this type of remote access, and if a remote host does not support SSH there is a way for the session to fall back to *rsh*.

SSH is a traditional client/server protocol. The SSH server process waits for commands (requests) from SSH clients, executes the command if allowed, and returns the result (reply) to the client. Users are often authenticated with an encrypted key and *passphrase* instead of a password, and these public key files are placed on the remote computers users can access. The overall use of SSH is shown in Figure 25.2.

SSH consists of several client programs and a few configuration files. The programs the user runs are `ssh` or `slogin` (both essentially the same) and `scp` or `sftp` (also the same), depending on implementation. Secure shell keys are managed with `ssh-keygen`, `ssh-agent`, and `ssh-add`.

There have been two major versions of SSH. SSH1 was developed by Tatu Ylonen at the Helsinki University of Technology in Finland in 1995 after a network attack. It was released as free software and source code. It also became an Internet draft, but several

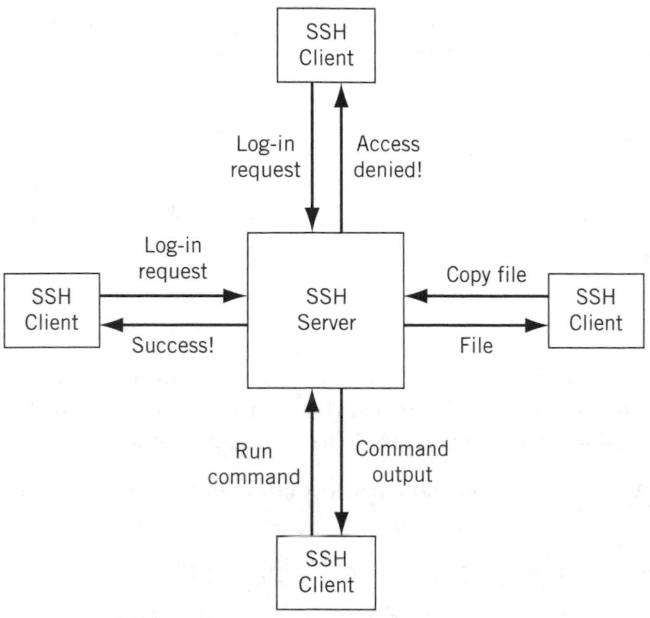

FIGURE 25.2

SSH model. Note that a way to run commands and copy files is included in the model.

issues with the original (which was not systematically developed) were addressed as SSH2 in 1996. SSH2 has new methods and is not compatible with SSH1. Unfortunately, users still liked a lot of the features of SSH1 that were lacking in SSH2, and because some security is better than none, they felt little reason to switch (licensing played a role as well).

OpenSSH is now available as a free implementation of the SSH2 protocol, and it is this version that has been ported to many operating systems. People still talk about the "Ylonen SSH," "SSH1.5," or "OpenSSH" implementations of the basic SSH protocol. SSH was an Internet draft status for a long time, and this chapter describes SSH2. SSH is now defined in a series of RFFCs from RFC 4250 through RFC 4256. This group of RFCs details various aspects of SSH operation.

SSH Features

SSH has excellent protection features. The major ones follow:

Secure client/server communication—All data are encrypted on the network.

Varied authentication—Users can be authenticated by password (encrypted), the host, or a public key.

Authentication integration—SSH can be optionally integrated (and often is) with other authentication systems such as Kerberos, PAM, PGP, and SecureID.

Security add-on—SSH can be used to add security to applications such as NNTP, Telnet, VNC, and a lot of other TCP/IP protocols and applications.

Transparency and versatility—SSH can be transparent to the user and there are implementations for almost all operating systems (including Windows with OpenSSH implementations).

SSH protects users against:

IP spoofing—A remote host can send IP packets pretending to come from somewhere else, such as a trusted host. Spoofers on LANs can even pretend to be the local routers to the outside world, which SSH protects against as well.

IP source routing—This is another way for hackers to claim that a packet came from another host.

DNS spoofing—Hackers can forge name server records supplied to a host.

Intermediate device control—This is an old favorite. A hacker can take control of a router or host between hosts and execute many types of data manipulation.

Clear text interception—Data or passwords sent in clear text are always targets for hackers.

X Windows attacks—Hackers can listen to X Windows authentication exchanges and spoof server connections.

SSH *never* trusts the network. Even if hackers took over the entire network, all that can happen is that SSH is forced to disconnect. Hackers cannot decrypt, play back, or compromise data on the connection.

This is not to say that the SSH is perfect. Like any other tool, SSH is only as good as those setting it up and using it. For example, SSH does have an option for encryption type (`none`), but this is only to be used for testing purposes. (There is no real enforcement of this, of course.) And SSH does nothing to prevent someone who had gained access to the host another way (perhaps by sitting down in front of the unprotected host itself) from doing a lot of damage with root access. In that case, SSH is often the first target of a local hacker.

In addition, a lot of organizations with their own firewall devices are nervous when users rely on SSH to connect to hosts. Remember, everything in the SSH stream is encrypted, and fairly well at that. What SSH does is offer users a direct pipeline to their internal machines right through the firewall, an invisible tunnel into the organization.

There are ways to work around this through a SSH proxy gateway, including the "mute shell" and "SSH-in-SSH" approaches. But nothing is ever perfect or 100% secure.

SSH Architecture

Many SSH components interact to allow secure client-server exchanges. These components, not all of which are distinct programs or processes, are shown in Figure 25.3.

The following is a *brief* overview of the major components of SSH.

Server—The program that authenticates and authorizes SSH connections, usually `sshd`.

Client—The program run on the client (user) device, often `ssh`, but also `scp`, `sftp`, and so on.

Session—The client/server connection, which can be interactive or batch. The session begins after successful authentication to the server and ends when the connection terminates.

Key generator—A program (usually `ssh-keygen`) that generates persistent keys. (Key types are discussed later in this chapter.)

Known hosts—A database of host keys. This is the major authentication mechanism in SSH.

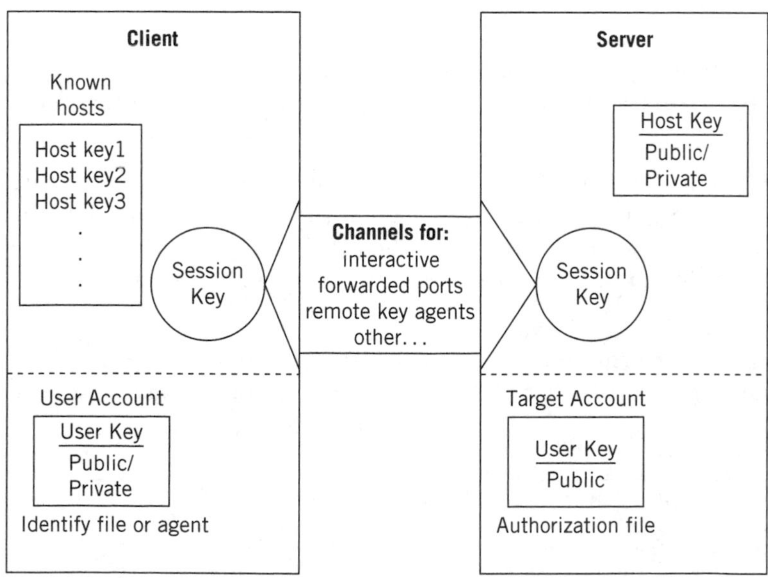

FIGURE 25.3

An overview of the SSH architecture. Note that a lot of space is devoted to the distribution and use of encryption keys.

Agent—A caching program for user keys to spare users the need to repeat passphrases. The agent is only a convenience and does not disclose the keys. The usual agent is `ssh-agent`, and `ssh-add` loads and unloads the key cache.

Signer—This program signs the host-based authentication packets used instead of password authentication.

Random seed—Random data used by SSH components to initialize the pseudorandom number generators (PRNG) used in SSH.

Configuration files—Settings to determine the behavior of SSH clients and servers.

SSH Keys

Keys are a crucial part of SSH. Almost everything that SSH does involves a key, and often more than one key. SSH keys can range from tens of bits to almost 2000. Keys are used as parameters for SSH algorithms such as encryption or authentication. SSH keys are used to bind the operation to a particular user.

There are two types of SSH keys: symmetric (shared secret keys) and asymmetric (public and private key pairs). As in all public key systems, asymmetric keys are used to establish and exchange short-duration symmetric keys. The three types of keys used in SSH are outlined in Table 25.1. As mentioned, user and host keys are typically created by the `ssh-keygen` program.

User key—This persistent asymmetric key is used by the SSH clients to validate the user's identity. A single user can have multiple keys and "identities" on a network.

Host key—This persistent asymmetric key is used by the SSH servers to validate their identity, as well as the client if host-based authentication is used. If the device runs a single SSH server process, the host key uniquely identifies the device. Devices running multiple SSH servers can share a key or use different host keys.

Session key—This transient symmetric key is generated to encrypt the data sent between client and server. It is shared during the SSH connection setup to use

Table 25.1 SSH Key Name Types and Major Characteristics

Key Name	Lifetime	Creator	Type	Purpose
User key	Persistent	User	Public	Identify user to server
Host key	Persistent	Administrator	Public	Identify a server or device
Session key	One session	Client and server	Secret	Secure communications

for encrypted data streams during the session. When the session ends, the key is destroyed. There are several session keys, actually—one in each direction and others to check integrity of communications.

SSH Protocol Operation

This section describes the operations of SSH2 and not the older, and incompatible, SSH1. There are four major pieces to SSH, and they are documented separately and theoretically have nothing whatsoever to do with one another. In practice, they all function together to provide the set of features and functions that make up SSH. Each is still an Internet draft, but these should all become RFCs some day.

There are some other documents that extend these four protocols, but these make up the heart of SSH. The major protocols follow:

- SSH Transport Layer Protocol (SSH-TRANS)
- SSH Authentication Protocol (SSH-AUTH)
- SSH Connection Protocol (SSH-CONN)
- SSH File Transfer Protocol (SSH-SFTP)

The relationships between the protocols, and their major functions, are shown in Figure 25.4.

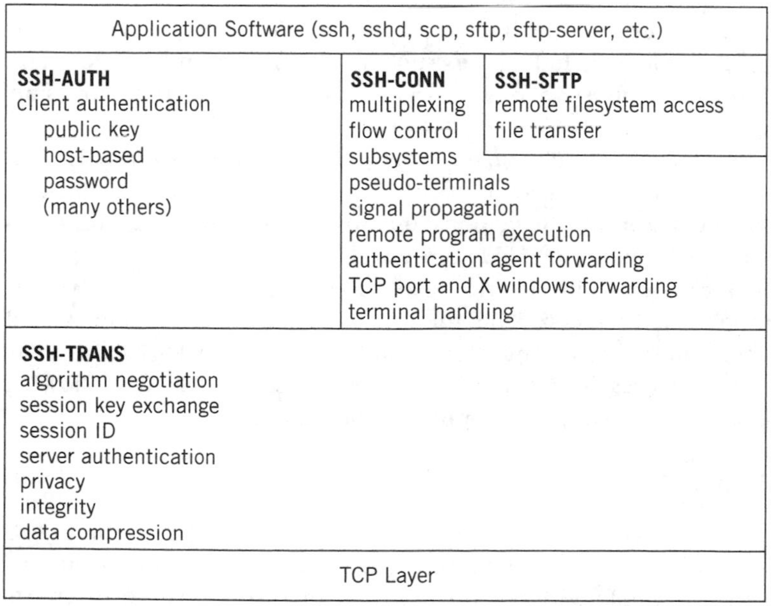

<table>
<tr><td colspan="3">Application Software (ssh, sshd, scp, sftp, sftp-server, etc.)</td></tr>
<tr><td rowspan="2">SSH-AUTH
client authentication
public key
host-based
password
(many others)</td><td>SSH-CONN
multiplexing
flow control</td><td>SSH-SFTP
remote filesystem access
file transfer</td></tr>
<tr><td colspan="2">subsystems
pseudo-terminals
signal propagation
remote program execution
authentication agent forwarding
TCP port and X windows forwarding
terminal handling</td></tr>
<tr><td colspan="3">SSH-TRANS
algorithm negotiation
session key exchange
session ID
server authentication
privacy
integrity
data compression</td></tr>
<tr><td colspan="3">TCP Layer</td></tr>
</table>

FIGURE 25.4

SSH protocols, showing how they relate to one another and the TCP transport layer.

All critical parameters used in all of the protocols are negotiated. These parameters include the ways and algorithms used for:

- User authentication
- Server authentication
- Session key exchange
- Data integrity and privacy
- Data compression

In most categories, clients and servers are required to support one or more methods, thereby promoting interoperability. Support is not the same as implementation, however, and specific clients and servers still have to find a "match" to accomplish their goals.

Initial connections (including server authentication, basic encryption, and integrity services) are established with SSH-TRANS, which is the fundamental piece of SSH. An SSH-TRANS connection provides a single and secure data stream operating full-duplex between client and server.

Once the SSH-TRANS connection is made, the client can use SSH-AUTH for authentication to the server. Multiple authentication methods can be used, and SSH-AUTH establishes things such as the format and order of requests, conditions of success or failure, and so on. Protocol extensions are defined to allow the methods to be extended in the future as other authentication methods are developed. Only one method is *required* in SSH-AUTH: public key using the digital signature standard (DSS). Two more methods are *defined*: password and host-based (but we'll concentrate on public key in this chapter).

Once authenticated, SSH clients use the SSH-CONN protocol over the "pipe" established by SSH-TRANS. There are multiple interactive or batch (noninteractive) sessions over SSH *channels*. The sessions include things such as X Windows and TCP forwarding (tunneling), control signaling (such as `^C`) over the connection, data compression, and related activities.

If file transfer or remote file manipulation is needed, this is provided by the SSH-SFTP protocol. The sequence of invoking these protocols is not rigid, and there is considerable variation in implementation, mostly in "nonstandard" or customized environments where global client access is neither needed nor desired.

Note that the SSH protocols only define what should happen on the network. Internals such as how keys are stored on the local disk, user authorization, and key forwarding (which most people think of as intimate parts of SSH), are really implementation-dependent pieces that are usually completely incompatible. The following sections describe some of the key aspects of protocol operation.

Transport Layer Protocol

Clients normally access the SSH process on the server at well-known TCP port 22. The server announces the SSH version in a text string, and there are certain conventions built into this string. For example, SSH version "1.99" means that the server supports both SSH1 and SSH2, and the client can choose to use either one from then on. Of course, if the client and server are not compatible, either can break the connection at that point.

If the connection goes forward, SSH-TRANS shifts into the *binary packet protocol*—a record-oriented non-text protocol defined for SSH-TRANS. The first activity here is *key exchange*, which precedes the negotiation of the basic security properties of the SSH session.

The key exchange often employs some form of the *Diffie-Hellman* procedure for key agreement, although there are others. Diffie-Hellman describes a way to securely exchange information (such as a shared secret key) over an unsecured network such as the Internet by using asymmetric public/private keys established beforehand. The key exchange itself should be authenticated to guard against "man-in-the-middle" attacks.

Pocket Calculator Diffie-Hellman

In the SSL chapter, we did an exercise in "pocket calculator public key encryption" to show that although the mathematical theory behind the use of asymmetric public/private key encryption was complex its use was not. We've mentioned Diffie-Hellman several times, and when first popularized in 1976 Diffie-Hellman was so revolutionary some doubted it actually worked (not mathematicians, of course!). How could secure shared secret keys possibly be sent over an unsecure network where anyone can make copies of the packets?

Let's show how Diffie-Hellman can be used to allow users to share a secret key and yet no one else knows what the key is (even the "man-in-the-middle" vulnerability does not really "crack" the key, just hijacks it). Again, we'll use small non-real-world numbers just to make the math easy enough to do on a pocket calculator. We've already shown how to raise the numbers to a power, and to compute the modular remainder from division, so that is not repeated.

Like public key encryption, Diffie-Hellman depends on properties of prime numbers. There are two important ones: the very large prime itself (P) and a related number (derived by formula) called the "primitive root of P," which is usually called Q. A large prime P will have many primitive roots, but only one is used. For this example, let's use P = 13 and Q = 11 (I didn't use a formula: There are tables on primes and primitive roots all over the Internet).

According to usual security example practice, let's call our two correspondents Alice (A) and Bob (B). A and B exchange these two numbers publicly over the network, without worrying if anyone else knows them (they have no choice, because the network is by definition unsecure anyway).

A and B each pick, independently, a random number (naturally, in reality this is done by software without users "picking" anything). Let's use A = 4 and B = 7 (they can even pick the same number by chance, of course). Now each calculates A* and B* according to the following formulas:

- A computes $A^* = Q^A \bmod (P) = 11^4 \bmod (13) = 14{,}641 \bmod 13 = 3$
- B computes $B^* = Q^B \bmod (P) = 11^7 \bmod (13) = 19{,}487{,}171 \bmod 13 = 2$

Now, all A and B have to do is exchange their A* and B* numbers over the network—not caring who sees them (which they can't help anyway). But wait, couldn't someone easily figure out the A and B values in the example? Yes, of course, with the small numbers used here. But when large enough primes and well-chosen primitive roots are selected, and A and B choose random enough numbers (one reason you don't let A and B pick their own numbers), there are many numbers that give the values 3 and 2.

Now A and B simply calculate the shared secret key to use:

- A's secret key = $(B^*)^A$ mod (P) = 2^4 mod (13) = 16 mod 13 = 3
- B's secret key = $(A^*)^B$ mod (P) = 3^7 mod (13) = 2187 mod 13 = 3

Given enough time, the shared secret key can be broken. So, the Diffie-Hellman process is repeated constantly (at fixed intervals), recomputing new keys, sometimes every few seconds. By the time the key is broken, a new one is in use.

The key exchange is usually repeated during a session because "stale" keys that are used too long might allow a malicious user to break the encryption that much faster. The more often the kcys are changed the less likely this becomes, and even if broken only that portion of the session is compromised. Usually SSH key exchanges occur every hour or after every gigabyte of data.

The use of the "null" cipher, which means no encryption at all, is a valid choice for SSH clients and servers, but this is only to be used for testing. However, many SSH administrators never disable it. A favorite OpenSSH trick is to gain root access to a host and edit the user's configuration file (`~/.ssh/config`) so that all hosts use the null cipher only. If client or server do *not* support "null," this evil trick is not possible.

Key exchange and encryption choice are followed by more security parameter choices. Methods of integrity, server authentication, and compression (a marginal feature still considered part of SSH security) are agreed on. Public key systems are popular choices, but the issue is always how to verify proper ownership of the public key, as discussed in Chapter 23, where certificates were introduced as a way to provide server authentication. At the end of the process, methods for cipher/integrity/compression are established for client-to-server and server-to-client exchanges.

Authentication Protocol

SSH-AUTH is simpler than SSH-TRANS. The authentication protocol defines a framework for these exchanges, defines a number of actual mechanisms (but only a few of them), and allows for extensions. The three defined methods are public-key, password, and host-based authentication.

The authentication process is framed by client requests and server responses. The "authentication" request actually includes elements of authorization (access rights are checked as well). A request contains:

Username, U—The claimed identity of the user. On Unix systems, this is typically the user account. However, the interpretation context is not defined by the protocol.

Server name, S—The user is requesting access to a "server," which is really the protocol to run on the SSH-TRANS connection after authentication finishes. This is usually "ssh-connection," which represents all services (remote log-in, command execution, etc.) provided by the SSH-CONN protocol.

Method name, M, and method-specific data, D—The particular authentication method used for the request and any data needed with it. For example, if the method is `password`, the data provided are the password itself.

There can be other messages exchanged, depending on the authentication request. But ultimately the server issues an authentication response. The response can be `SUCCESS` or `FAILURE`, and the success message has no other content. The failure response includes

- a list of the authentication methods that can continue the process
- a "partial success" flag

The `FAILURE` response can be misleading. If the partial success flag is not set (false), the message means that the preceding authentication method has failed for some reason (incorrect password, invalid account, and so on). However, if the partial success flag is set (true), the message means that the method has *succeeded* (odd in a failure message!), but the server requires that additional methods also succeed before access is granted. In other words, the server can require multiple successful authentication methods. OpenSSH does not support this feature.

But how does the client know which methods to start with? The client starts with a "none" authentication request, which prompts the server to reply with a list of the authentication methods the client can choose to continue the process. In other words, if the server requires any authentication at all, the "none" method fails. If not, a `SUCCESS` is immediate and a lot of time is saved.

The Connection Protocol

Clients usually request to use "ssh-connection" after a successful authentication exchange. Once the server starts the service, SSH uses the SSH-CONN protocol. This is really when SSH starts to do things.

The basic SSH-CONN service is multiplexing: the creation of dynamic logical *channels* over the SSH-TRANS connection. Channels are identified by numbers and can be created and destroyed by either side of the connection. Channels are flow controlled and have a *type*, which are also extensible. The defined channels types follow:

Session—These are for the remote execution of a program. Opening a channel does not start a program, but when started several session channels can be in operation at once.

x11—These channels are for X Windows operations.

forwarded-tcpip—These inbound channels are for forwarded TCP ports. *(Port forwarding* in SSH just means that SSH transparently encrypts and decrypts data on a TCP port.) The server opens this channel type back to the client to carry remotely forwarded TCP port data.

direct-tcpip—These outbound TCP channels are used to connect to a socket. The client simply starts listening on the port indicated.

SSH-CONN defines a set of channel or global requests in addition to traditional channel operations such as open, close, send, and so on. The global requests follow:

tcpip-forward—Used to request remote TCP port forwarding. This feature is not yet supported by Open SSH.

cancel-tcpip-forward—Used to cancel remote TCP port forwarding.

The channel requests are more elaborate and are only summarized in the following. Most refer to the remote side of the session channel.

pty-req—Requests a pseudo-terminal for the channel (usually for interactive applications). Includes window size and terminal mode information.

x11-req—Requests X Window forwarding.

Env—Sets an environmental variable. This can be risky, so it is carefully controlled.

shell, exec, subsystem—Run the default shell for the account, a program, or service. This connects the channel to the standard input and output and error streams. A "subsystem" is used, for example, with file transfers, and the subsystem name is `SFTP` in this case.

window-change—Changes the terminal window size.

xon-xoff—Uses client ^S/^Q flow control.

Signal—Sends a signal (such as the Unix *kill* command) to the remote side.

exit-status—Returns the program's exit status.

exit-signal—Returns the signal that terminated the program.

Although these channel requests can technically be sent from server to client, the use of SSH as a remote access tool means that most of these requests are issued by the client and expect the server to perform in a certain way. Clients usually ignore these requests from a server, just for security reasons.

The File Transfer Protocol

The last piece of the SSH protocol "suite" is SSH-SFTP. Oddly, SSH-SFTP does not really implement any file transfers at all because it has no file transfer capability. What the protocol does is to use SSH to start a remote file transfer agent and then work with it over the secure connection.

Initially, SSH used a secure version of the remote copy (rcp) Unix program to implement secure copy (scp). As rcp ran the remote shell (rsh), so scp ran the secure shell (SSH). But rcp was a very limited program compared to FTP. A session only transferred a group of files in one direction, and it did not allow directory listings, browsing, or any of the other features associated with FTP.

Thus, SSH2 eventually incorporated the idea of SFTP to secure the file transfer process. The SSH-SFTP protocol describes how this happens. Unfortunately, SFTP isn't just using SSH to connect to a remote FTP server. SFTP has absolutely nothing to do with the FTP protocol described in an earlier chapter of this book.

SSH and FTP are not a good match, one reason being that separate connections are used in FTP for control and data transfer. FTP itself (like Telnet) can be made more secure with SSL, but few FTP servers provide these functions. So, an FTP server can also be an SSH server (providing files in unsecure and secure manners)—and that's about a close as SSH and FTP can get.

How does SSH-SFTP work? Well, there are really two ways to transfer files over an SSH connection: with *scp* or with *sftp* (the names might be different, but it's the procedure that's important).

When a client uses *scp*, the transfer begins by running *ssh* with certain options, such as when a forwarding agent is in use. This process in turn runs another version on the remote host, which is, of course, running *sshd*. That copy of *scp* is run with its own (undocumented) options, such as "to" (-t) and "from" (-f). SSH then uses *scp*, now running on client and server, to transfer the file over the secure SSH connection.

Figure 25.5 shows how SSH uses *scp* to transfer a file called `mywebpage.html` to a server and rename it `index.html`. Naturally, the transfer is encrypted and secure.

SSH can even do a trick that FTP does not allow. SSH can be used for "third-party" transfers, a capability never implemented in FTP beyond the testing phase (for security reasons). In other words, when run locally, SSH can transfer a file between two remote hosts (as long as the authentication succeeds).

Consequently, users can perform the Web page transfer to the server even if the page is on their office desktop and they are sitting with a laptop at an airport gate waiting for a flight.

```
scp lnxclient:mywebpage.html lnxserver:index.html
```

Using *sftp* is similar, but the syntax and options for the command are different. This method starts an SSH subsystem, and that means that the SSH server must be specifically configured to run the SFTP protocol. Figure 25.6 shows how the same file

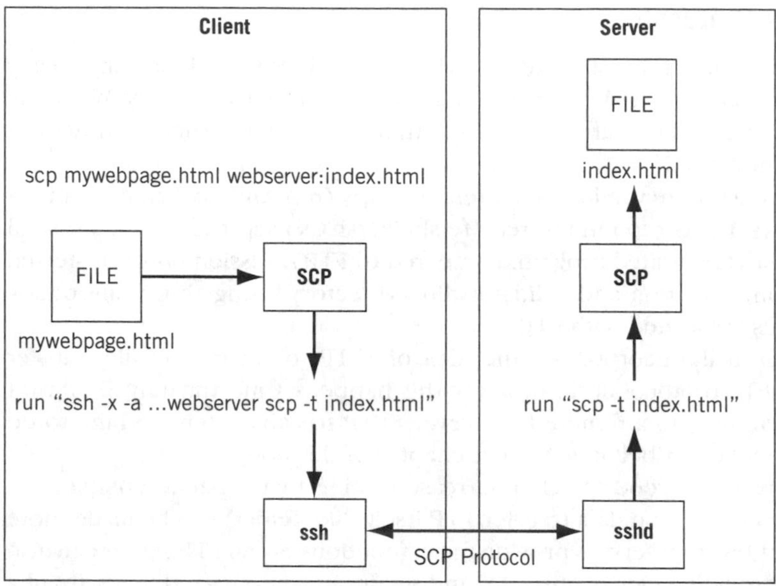

FIGURE 25.5

Transferring files with SCP, showing how SSH is used with the file copy.

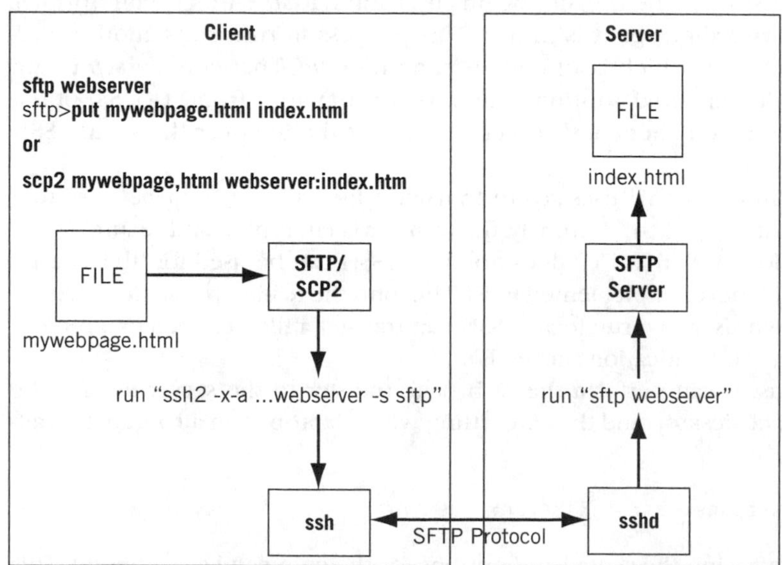

FIGURE 25.6

A file transfer with SFTP, showing the same results as when using SCP.

transfer would be done with *sftp* (in the SSH implementation known as Tectia, *sftp* is confusingly invoked with the command *scp2*).

The point here is that both methods will transfer the file as long as everything else is set up correctly. The best book on SSH—*SSH: The Secure Shell,* by Daniel J. Barrett, Richard E. Silverman, and Robert G. Byrnes (O'Reilly Media)—is about as long as this one. Interested readers are referred to this text for more detailed information on SSH.

SSH IN ACTION

If there is one thing that was used more than FTP to produce this book, it's SSH. In fact, all of the file transfers used to consolidate output for these examples could just as easily have been done with SCP or SFTP. This is especially true when routers are the remote systems: Only in special circumstances will organizations allow or use Telnet for router access.

Let's use SSH to contact the routers on the Illustrated Network. Naturally, the routers have been set up ahead of time to allow administrator access from certain hosts on LAN1 and LAN2 and are running *sshd*. But on the client side, we'll run *ssh* "out of the box" and see what happens.

Ethereal captures are not the best way to look at SSH in action. The secure and encrypted transfers make packet analysis difficult (and often impossible). Fortunately, we can use the debug feature of SSH itself to analyze the exchange in very verbose form (using the `-vv` option).

Let's see if we can catch SSH-TRANS, SSH-AUTH, and SSH-CONN in action when we access router TP2 (`10.10.11.1`) from `bsdclient`. We'll log in (the `-l` option) as `admin`.

```
bsdclient# ssh -vv -l admin 10.10.11.1
OpenSSH_3.5p1 FreeBSD-20030924, SSH protocols 1.5/2.0, OpenSSL 0x0090704f
debug1: Reading configuration data /etc/ssh/ssh_config
debug1: Rhosts Authentication disabled, originating port will not be trusted.
debug1: ssh_connect: needpriv 0
debug1: Connecting to 10.10.11.1 [10.10.11.1] port 22.
debug1: Connection established.
debug1: identity file /root/.ssh/identity type -1
debug1: identity file /root/.ssh/id_rsa type -1
debug1: identity file /root/.ssh/id_dsa type -1
debug1: Remote protocol version 1.99, remote software version OpenSSH_3.8
debug1: match: OpenSSH_3.8 pat OpenSSH*
debug1: Enabling compatibility mode for protocol 2.0
debug1: Local version string SSH-2.0-OpenSSH_3.5p1 FreeBSD-20030924
debug1: SSH2_MSG_KEXINIT sent
debug1: SSH2_MSG_KEXINIT received
debug2: kex_parse_kexinit: diffie-hellman-group-exchange-sha1,diffie-
 hellman-
 group1-sha1
debug2: kex_parse_kexinit: ssh-dss,ssh-rsa
debug2: kex_parse_kexinit: aes128-cbc,3des-cbc,blowfish-cbc,cast128-cbc,
 arcfour,aes192-cbc,aes256-cbc,rijndael-cbc@lysator.liu.se
```

```
debug2: kex_parse_kexinit: aes128-cbc,3des-cbc,blowfish-cbc,cast128-cbc,
 arcfour,aes192-cbc,aes256-cbc,rijndael-cbc@lysator.liu.se
debug2: kex_parse_kexinit: hmac-md5,hmac-sha1,hmac-ripemd160,hmac-ripemd160@
 openssh.com,hmac-sha1-96,hmac-md5-96
debug2: kex_parse_kexinit: hmac-md5,hmac-sha1,hmac-ripemd160,hmac-ripemd160@
 openssh.com,hmac-sha1-96,hmac-md5-96
debug2: kex_parse_kexinit: none,zlib
debug2: kex_parse_kexinit: none,zlib
debug2: kex_parse_kexinit:
debug2: kex_parse_kexinit:
debug2: kex_parse_kexinit: first_kex_follows 0
debug2: kex_parse_kexinit: reserved 0
debug2: kex_parse_kexinit: diffie-hellman-group-exchange-sha1,diffie-
 hellman-
 group1-sha1
debug2: kex_parse_kexinit: ssh-rsa,ssh-dss
debug2: kex_parse_kexinit: aes128-cbc,3des-cbc,blowfish-cbc,cast128-cbc,
 arcfour,aes192-cbc,aes256-cbc,rijndael-cbc@lysator.liu.se,aes128-
 ctr,aes192-ctr,aes256-ctr
debug2: kex_parse_kexinit: aes128-cbc,3des-cbc,blowfish-cbc,cast128-
 cbc,arcfour,aes192-cbc,aes256-cbc,rijndael-cbc@lysator.liu.se,aes128-
 ctr,aes192-ctr,aes256-ctr
debug2: kex_parse_kexinit: hmac-md5,hmac-sha1,hmac-ripemd160,hmac-ripemd160@
 openssh.com,hmac-sha1-96,hmac-md5-96
debug2: kex_parse_kexinit: hmac-md5,hmac-sha1,hmac-ripemd160,hmac-ripemd160@
 openssh.com,hmac-sha1-96,hmac-md5-96
debug2: kex_parse_kexinit: none,zlib
debug2: kex_parse_kexinit: none,zlib
debug2: kex_parse_kexinit:
debug2: kex_parse_kexinit:
debug2: kex_parse_kexinit: first_kex_follows 0
debug2: kex_parse_kexinit: reserved 0
debug2: mac_init: found hmac-md5
debug1: kex: server->client aes128-cbc hmac-md5 none
debug2: mac_init: found hmac-md5
debug1: kex: client->server aes128-cbc hmac-md5 none
debug1: SSH2_MSG_KEX_DH_GEX_REQUEST sent
debug1: expecting SSH2_MSG_KEX_DH_GEX_GROUP
debug1: dh_gen_key: priv key bits set: 136/256
debug1: bits set: 1042/2049
debug1: SSH2_MSG_KEX_DH_GEX_INIT sent
debug1: expecting SSH2_MSG_KEX_DH_GEX_REPLY
debug1: Host '10.10.11.1' is known and matches the DSA host key.
debug1: Found key in /root/.ssh/known_hosts:1
debug1: bits set: 1049/2049
debug1: ssh_dss_verify: signature correct
debug1: kex_derive_keys
debug1: newkeys: mode 1
debug1: SSH2_MSG_NEWKEYS sent
debug1: waiting for SSH2_MSG_NEWKEYS
debug1: newkeys: mode 0
debug1: SSH2_MSG_NEWKEYS received
```

```
debug1: done: ssh_kex2.
debug1: send SSH2_MSG_SERVICE_REQUEST
debug1: service_accept: ssh-userauth
debug1: got SSH2_MSG_SERVICE_ACCEPT
debug1: authentications that can continue: publickey,password,keyboard-
 interactive
debug1: next auth method to try is publickey
debug1: try privkey: /root/.ssh/identity
debug1: try privkey: /root/.ssh/id_rsa
debug1: try privkey: /root/.ssh/id_dsa
debug2: we did not send a packet, disable method
debug1: next auth method to try is keyboard-interactive
debug2: userauth_kbdint
debug2: we sent a keyboard-interactive packet, wait for reply
debug1: authentications that can continue: publickey,password,keyboard-
 interactive
debug2: we did not send a packet, disable method
debug1: next auth method to try is password
admin@10.10.11.1's password: (not shown)
debug2: we sent a password packet, wait for reply
debug1: ssh-userauth2 successful: method password
debug1: channel 0: new [client-session]
debug1: send channel open 0
debug1: Entering interactive session.
debug2: callback start
debug1: ssh_session2_setup: id 0
debug1: channel request 0: pty-req
debug1: channel request 0: shell
debug1: fd 3 setting TCP_NODELAY
debug2: callback done
debug1: channel 0: open confirm rwindow 0 rmax 32768
debug2: channel 0: rcvd adjust 131072
--- JUNOS 8.4R1.3 built 2007-08-06 06:58:15 UTC
admin@CEO>
```

The substantial output captures all three phases of SSH protocol operation (all but SSH-SFTP). Let's see what the major portions of this listing are saying.

Roughly speaking, the first half of the output is SSH-TRANS negotiation to establish the methods to use for key exchange, and what to use for cipher, integrity, and compression. The next quarter is used for SSH-AUTH to decide on a user authentication method to be used (its password). The last quarter, after the password is entered, is SSH-CONN (setting up SSH channel 0 from router to client).

It's not necessary to parse this line by line. Generally, the exchange starts by parsing the version string supplied by the router and starting the negotiation. The router announces support for SSH1 or SSH2 (version 1.99).

```
debug1: Remote protocol version 1.99, remote software version OpenSSH_3.8
debug1: match: OpenSSH_3.8 pat OpenSSH*
debug1: Enabling compatibility mode for protocol 2.0
```

The client announces OpenSSH support as well.

```
debug1: Local version string SSH-2.0-OpenSSH_3.5p1 FreeBSD-20030924
```

Now the process shifts to binary packet mode and begins in earnest. The next major section presents the router and client support set for key exchange, cipher, integrity, and compression.

```
debug1: SSH2_MSG_KEXINIT sent
debug1: SSH2_MSG_KEXINIT received
debug2: kex_parse_kexinit: diffie-hellman-group-exchange-sha1,diffie-
  hellman-group1-sha1
debug2: kex_parse_kexinit: ssh-dss,ssh-rsa
debug2: kex_parse_kexinit: aes128-cbc,3des-cbc,blowfish-cbc,cast128-
  cbc,arcfour,aes192-cbc,aes256-cbc,rijndael-cbc@lysator.liu.se
debug2: kex_parse_kexinit: aes128-cbc,3des-cbc,blowfish-cbc,cast128-
  cbc,arcfour,aes192-cbc,aes256-cbc,rijndael-cbc@lysator.liu.se
debug2: kex_parse_kexinit: hmac-md5,hmac-sha1,hmac-ripemd160,hmac-ripemd160@
  openssh.com,hmac-sha1-96,hmac-md5-96
debug2: kex_parse_kexinit: hmac-md5,hmac-sha1,hmac-ripemd160,hmac-ripemd160@
  openssh.com,hmac-sha1-96,hmac-md5-96
debug2: kex_parse_kexinit: none,zlib
debug2: kex_parse_kexinit: none,zlib
```

The first two lines exchange the messages, which are parsed in pairs in the following. The first pair establishes the key exchange algorithms that the client understands (`diffie-hellman-group-exchange-sha1,diffie-hellman-group1-sha1`), and the second establishes the key types (ssh-dss, ssh-rsa). The other three pairs show that the client and server both support the same methods in the other three categories. (It's not unusual for servers to support methods more than clients.) A long section of back-and-forth negotiation takes place to pare down the possibilities, and finally the client and server agree on what three methods to use for cipher, integrity, and compression.

```
debug1: kex: server->client aes128-cbc hmac-md5 none
debug1: kex: client->server aes128-cbc hmac-md5 none
```

Still, in SSH-TRANS, the actual key exchange and server authentication now begin. Fortunately, it's really the correct router.

```
debug1: SSH2_MSG_KEX_DH_GEX_REQUEST sent
debug1: expecting SSH2_MSG_KEX_DH_GEX_GROUP
debug1: dh_gen_key: priv key bits set: 136/256
debug1: bits set: 1042/2049
debug1: SSH2_MSG_KEX_DH_GEX_INIT sent
debug1: expecting SSH2_MSG_KEX_DH_GEX_REPLY
debug1: Host '10.10.11.1' is known and matches the DSA host key.
debug1: Found key in /root/.ssh/known_hosts:1
debug1: bits set: 1049/2049
debug1: ssh_dss_verify: signature correct
```

The router is known because we've accessed it before (many times, in fact). If we go somewhere we've never been before, we have the option to break off the session because the server cannot be authenticated.

```
debug1: SSH2_MSG_KEX_DH_GEX_REQUEST sent
debug1: expecting SSH2_MSG_KEX_DH_GEX_GROUP
debug1: dh_gen_key: priv key bits set: 145/256
debug1: bits set: 1006/2049
debug1: SSH2_MSG_KEX_DH_GEX_INIT sent
debug1: expecting SSH2_MSG_KEX_DH_GEX_REPLY
debug2: no key of type 0 for host 10.10.12.1
debug2: no key of type 1 for host 10.10.12.1
The authenticity of host '10.10.12.1 (10.10.12.1)' can't be established.
DSA key fingerprint is 51:5f:da:41:41:9d:b1:c0:3f:a7:d0:a8:b9:7c:99:aa.
Are you sure you want to continue connecting (yes/no)?
```

At last we're finished with SSH-TRANS. Now SSH-AUTH is used to authenticate the "user account" to the server. We derive some new keys for the process, and finally (because nothing else "works") allow the user to type in a password for the router.

```
debug1: kex_derive_keys
debug1: newkeys: mode 1
debug1: SSH2_MSG_NEWKEYS sent
debug1: waiting for SSH2_MSG_NEWKEYS
debug1: newkeys: mode 0
debug1: SSH2_MSG_NEWKEYS received
debug1: done: ssh_kex2.
debug1: send SSH2_MSG_SERVICE_REQUEST
debug1: service_accept: ssh-userauth
debug1: got SSH2_MSG_SERVICE_ACCEPT
debug1: authentications that can continue: publickey,password,keyboard-
  interactive
debug1: next auth method to try is publickey
debug1: try privkey: /root/.ssh/identity
debug1: try privkey: /root/.ssh/id_rsa
debug1: try privkey: /root/.ssh/id_dsa
debug2: we did not send a packet, disable method
debug1: next auth method to try is keyboard-interactive
debug2: userauth_kbdint
debug2: we sent a keyboard-interactive packet, wait for reply
debug1: authentications that can continue: publickey,password,keyboard-
  interactive
debug2: we did not send a packet, disable method
debug1: next auth method to try is password
admin@10.10.11.1's password:
```

Although it is difficult to tell from the debug messages, there is a significant wait after the password is typed in while SSH-CONN sets up channel 0 over the SSH-TRANS connection. But finally we're in an interactive session and all set to go.

```
debug2: we sent a password packet, wait for reply
debug1: ssh-userauth2 successful: method password
debug1: channel 0: new [client-session]
debug1: send channel open 0
debug1: Entering interactive session.
debug2: callback start
debug1: ssh_session2_setup: id 0
debug1: channel request 0: pty-req
debug1: channel request 0: shell
debug1: fd 3 setting TCP_NODELAY
debug2: callback done
debug1: channel 0: open confirm rwindow 0 rmax 32768
debug2: channel 0: rcvd adjust 131072
--- JUNOS 8.4R1.3 built 2007-08-06 06:58:15 UTC
admin@CEO>
```

Note that SSH does not bypass the router's own authentication method (log-in ID and password) in any way. But it *does* ensure that what the user types in is not sent in plain text over the network.

Let's quickly show `sftp` in action to fetch a file called `tp2` from the router. This shows obvious similarities with FTP use, but is much more secure.

```
bsdclient# sftp admin@10.10.11.1
Connecting to 10.10.11.1...
admin@10.10.11.1's password: (not shown)
sftp> ls
.
..
.ssh
CEO-base
mw-graceful-restart
richard-ASP-manual-SA
richard-base
tp2
wjg-ORA-base
wjg-bgp-try
wjg-ipv6-mcast
wjg-with-ipv6
sftp> get tp2
Fetching /var/home/remote/tp2 to tp2
sftp> quit
bsdclient#
```

The SSH debug sequence for Linux is almost identical to the one for FreeBSD, and also uses OpenSSH. Although not used here, OpenSSH for Windows XP exists and is called PuTTY.

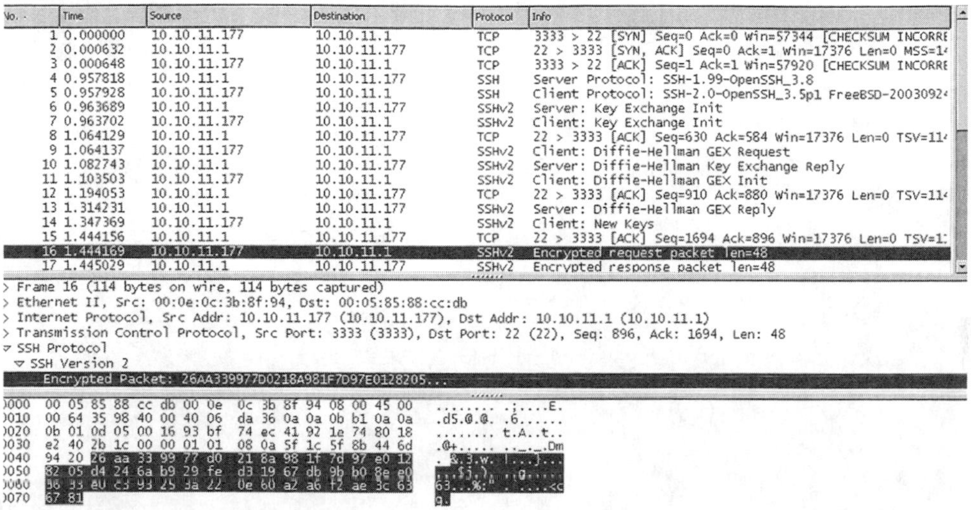

No.	Time	Source	Destination	Protocol	Info
1	0.000000	10.10.11.177	10.10.11.1	TCP	3333 > 22 [SYN] Seq=0 Ack=0 Win=57344 [CHECKSUM INCORRE
2	0.000632	10.10.11.1	10.10.11.177	TCP	22 > 3333 [SYN, ACK] Seq=0 Ack=1 Win=17376 Len=0 MSS=1
3	0.000648	10.10.11.177	10.10.11.1	TCP	3333 > 22 [ACK] Seq=1 Ack=1 Win=57920 [CHECKSUM INCORRE
4	0.957818	10.10.11.1	10.10.11.177	SSH	Server Protocol: SSH-1.99-OpenSSH_3.8
5	0.957928	10.10.11.177	10.10.11.1	SSH	Client Protocol: SSH-2.0-OpenSSH_3.5p1 FreeBSD-2003092
6	0.963689	10.10.11.1	10.10.11.177	SSHv2	Server: Key Exchange Init
7	0.963702	10.10.11.177	10.10.11.1	SSHv2	Client: Key Exchange Init
8	1.064129	10.10.11.1	10.10.11.177	TCP	22 > 3333 [ACK] Seq=630 Ack=584 Win=17376 Len=0 TSV=11
9	1.064137	10.10.11.177	10.10.11.1	SSHv2	Client: Diffie-Hellman GEX Request
10	1.082743	10.10.11.1	10.10.11.177	SSHv2	Server: Diffie-Hellman Key Exchange Reply
11	1.103503	10.10.11.177	10.10.11.1	SSHv2	Client: Diffie-Hellman GEX Init
12	1.194053	10.10.11.1	10.10.11.177	TCP	22 > 3333 [ACK] Seq=910 Ack=880 Win=17376 Len=0 TSV=11
13	1.314231	10.10.11.1	10.10.11.177	SSHv2	Server: Diffie-Hellman GEX Reply
14	1.347369	10.10.11.177	10.10.11.1	SSHv2	Client: New Keys
15	1.444156	10.10.11.1	10.10.11.177	TCP	22 > 3333 [ACK] Seq=1694 Ack=896 Win=17376 Len=0 TSV=1
16	1.444169	10.10.11.177	10.10.11.1	SSHv2	Encrypted request packet len=48
17	1.445029	10.10.11.1	10.10.11.177	SSHv2	Encrypted response packet len=48

```
> Frame 16 (114 bytes on wire, 114 bytes captured)
> Ethernet II, Src: 00:0e:0c:3b:8f:94, Dst: 00:05:85:88:cc:db
> Internet Protocol, Src Addr: 10.10.11.177 (10.10.11.177), Dst Addr: 10.10.11.1 (10.10.11.1)
> Transmission Control Protocol, Src Port: 3333 (3333), Dst Port: 22 (22), Seq: 896, Ack: 1694, Len: 48
▽ SSH Protocol
  ▽ SSH Version 2
      Encrypted Packet: 26AA339977D0218A981F7D97E0128205...

0000  00 05 85 88 cc db 00 0e  0c 3b 8f 94 08 00 45 00   ........ .;....E.
0010  00 64 35 98 40 00 40 06  da 36 0a 0a 0b b1 0a 0a   .d5.@.@. .6......
0020  0b 01 0d 05 00 16 93 bf  74 ec 41 92 1e 74 80 18   ........ t.A..t..
0030  e2 40 2b 1c 00 00 01 01  08 0a 5f 1c 5f 8b 44 6d   .@+..... .._._.Dm
0040  94 20 26 aa 33 99 77 d0  21 8a 98 1f 7d 97 e0 12   . &.3.w. !...}...
0050  82 05 d4 24 6a b9 29 fe  d3 19 67 db 9b b0 8e e0   ...$j.). ..g.....
0060  36 33 e0 c3 93 25 3a 22  0e 60 a2 a6 f2 ae 3c 63   63...%:" .`....<c
0070  67 81                                              g.
```

FIGURE 25.7

SSH capture with Ethereal, showing how the packet content is encrypted and therefore not parsed by the utility.

What does SSH look like "on the wire"? Figure 25.7 shows what Ethereal sees at the start of SSH-TRANS, including a look at an encrypted packet.

QUESTIONS FOR READERS

Figure 25.8 shows some of the concepts discussed in this chapter and can be used to answer the following questions.

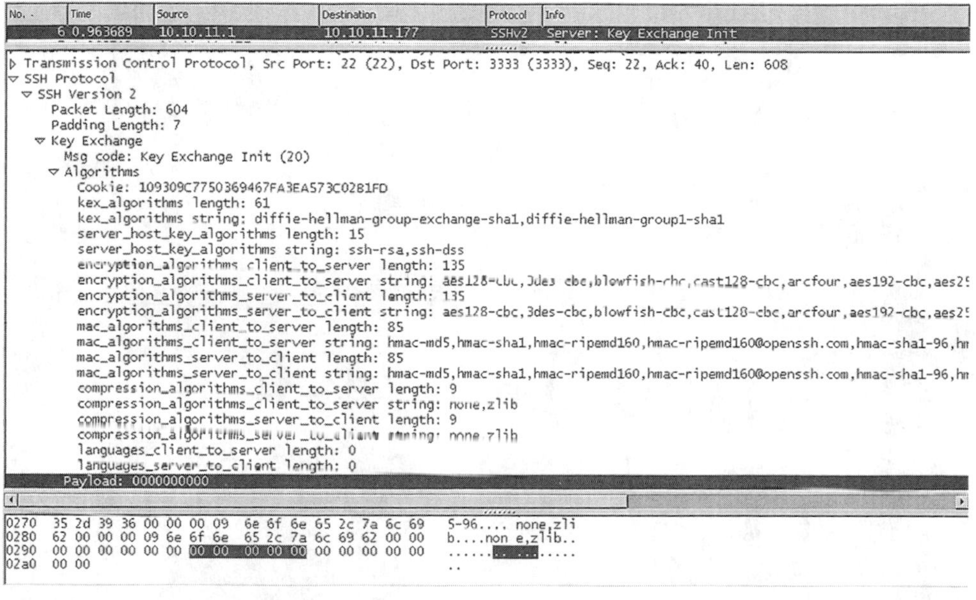

FIGURE 25.8

SSH capture with Ethereal.

1. Which devices are communicating here? Is this message from the server to the client or in the opposite direction?
2. Which ports are used on the devices? Is one the usual SSH server port?
3. Which version of SSL is used? What type of message is parsed in the figure?
4. Which two server host key algorithms are supported?
5. How many compression algorithms are supported?

CHAPTER

26

MPLS-Based Virtual Private Networks

What You Will Learn

In this chapter, you will learn one type of virtual private network architecture: the MPLS-based VPN, and in particular, a Layer 2 VPN (L2VPN). We'll also briefly look at using PPTP over DSL for remote access, another type of arrangement that is often considered a VPN.

You will learn how an L2VPN can make CE1 and CE2 appear to be connected by a single LAN, creating a virtual private LAN service (VPLS) between them. We'll also configure a complete VPLS based on L2VPNs.

In Chapter 17 on Internet Protocol (IP) switching, we introduced the idea of Multiprotocol Label Switching (MPLS) and configured a static label-switched path (LSP). That chapter showed how the LSP could be used for traffic engineering (TE) to steer transit traffic away from the least-cost hops traversed by local traffic. This chapter builds on those concepts and explores the security provided by one type of Virtual Private Network (VPN) Protocol, the Point-to-Point Tunneling Protocol (PPTP), and one type of VPN architecture, the MPLS-based VPN.

This chapter creates an L2VPN supporting VPLS. It does not create what is known as an L3VPN or BGP/MPLS IP VPN, which is actually more common. There are a few reasons we will describe an L3VPN but not configure it. Many introductions to VPNs start with L2VPNs before moving on the more complex L3VPNs. In addition, there is a much more complete book written about BGP/MPLS VPNs available: *MPLS-Enabled Applications,* 2nd edition, by Ina Minei and Julian Lucek (Wiley). We urge all interested readers to obtain this book after completing this one.

This chapter deals with more general aspects of security (and privacy) on the Internet, as companies, individuals, and government organizations blend increasingly sensitive traffic onto a single global public network. PPTP allows workers in home offices to access remote corporate resources such as servers and files over a public ISP's unsecure network. MPLS-based VPNs allow ISP to offer "private" (virtually private) networks to customers, while maintaining the global reachabilty and universal connectivity that Internet users have come to take for granted.

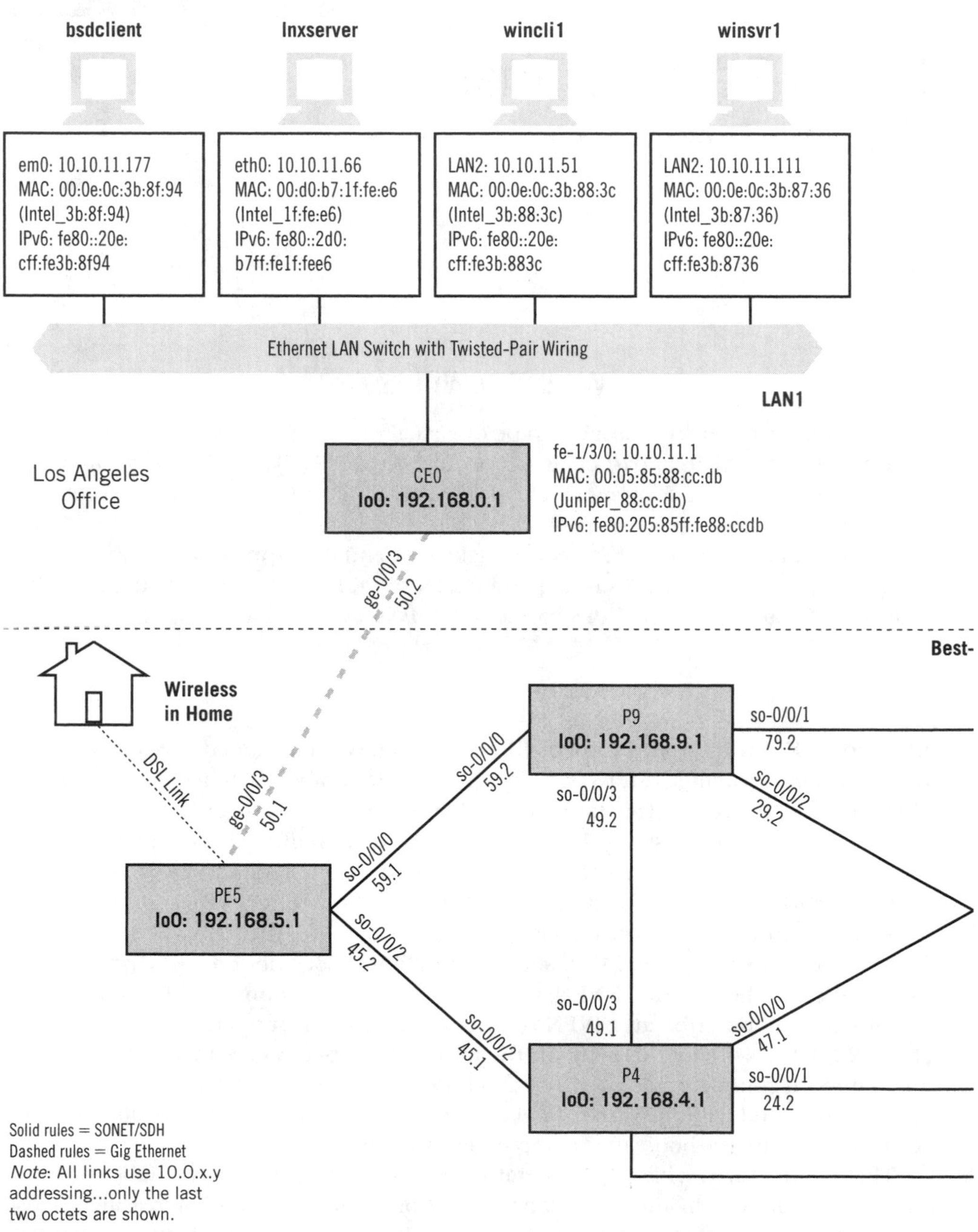

FIGURE 26.1

VPNs on the Illustrated Network. MPLS-based VPNs are based on routers (not hosts), whereas PPTP can be used with DSL.

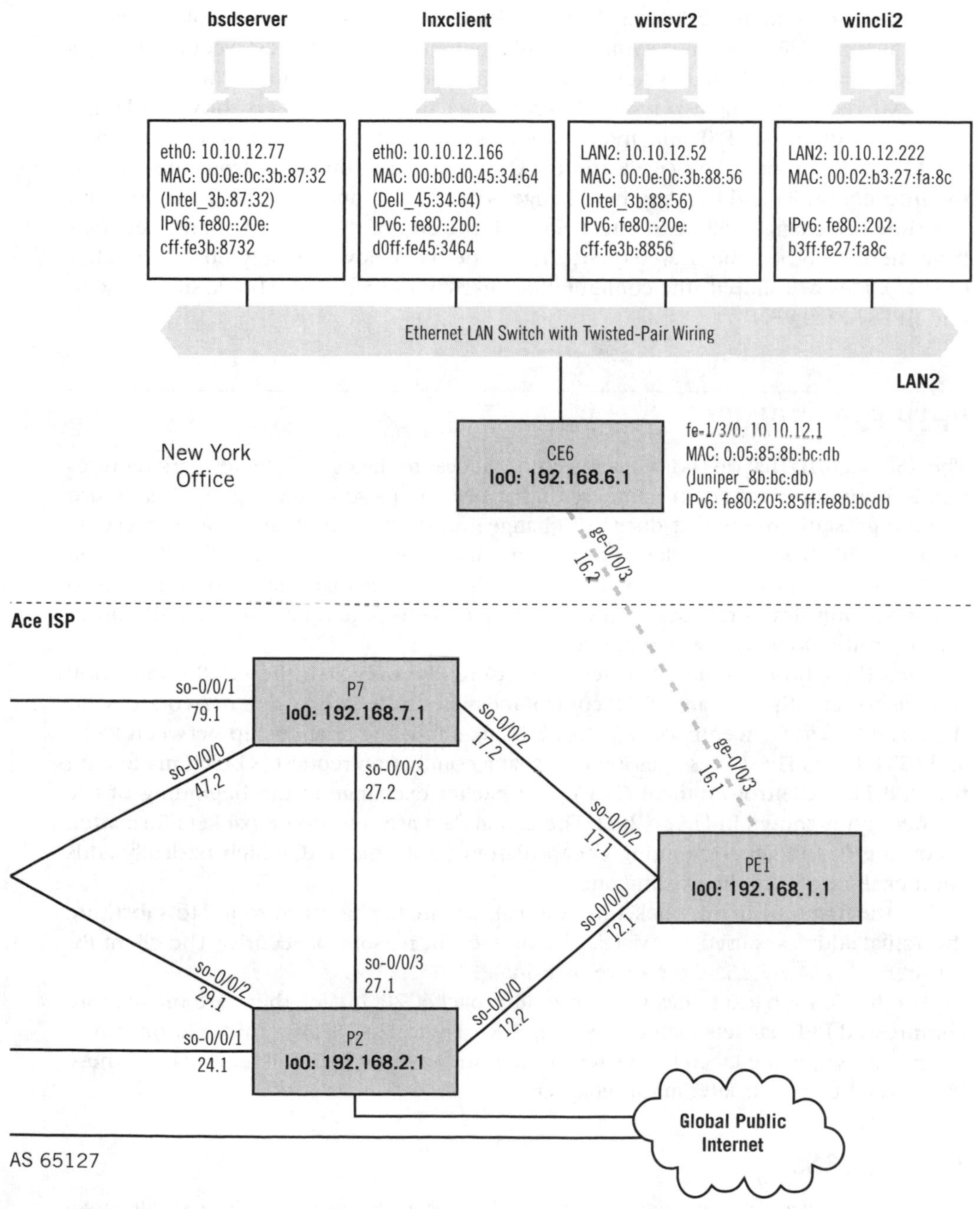
bsdserver
lnxclient
winsvr2
wincli2
eth0: 10.10.12.77
MAC: 00:0e:0c:3b:87:32
(Intel_3b:87:32)
IPv6: fe80::20e:
cff:fe3b:8732
eth0: 10.10.12.166
MAC: 00:b0:d0:45:34:64
(Dell_45:34:64)
IPv6: fe80::2b0:
d0ff:fe45:3464
LAN2: 10.10.12.52
MAC: 00:0e:0c:3b:88:56
(Intel_3b:88:56)
IPv6: fe80::20e:
cff:fe3b:8856
LAN2: 10.10.12.222
MAC: 00:02:b3:27:fa:8c
IPv6: fe80::202:
b3ff:fe27:fa8c
Ethernet LAN Switch with Twisted-Pair Wiring
LAN2
New York
Office
CE6
lo0: 192.168.6.1
fe-1/3/0: 10.10.12.1
MAC: 0:05:85:8b:bc:db
(Juniper_8b:bc:db)
IPv6: fe80:205:85ff:fe8b:bcdb
ge-0/0/3
16.2
Ace ISP
so-0/0/1
79.1
P7
lo0: 192.168.7.1
so-0/0/0
47.2
so-0/0/3
27.2
so-0/0/2
17.2
ge-0/0/3
16.1
so-0/0/2
17.1
PE1
lo0: 192.168.1.1
so-0/0/0
12.1
so-0/0/2
29.1
so-0/0/3
27.1
so-0/0/0
12.2
so-0/0/1
24.1
P2
lo0: 192.168.2.1
Global Public
Internet
AS 65127

Before we build an L2VPN for LAN1 and LAN2, let's take a quick look at remote access using PPTP while employing a popular adjunct device, the RSA SecureID. That's how we access the Illustrated Network from the comfort of our home offices.

So, we're really doing two types of VPN at once in this chapter (as shown in Figure 26.1). Both the home DSL link and the routers are highlighted, because this is where we'll be building our VPNs (we'll route LAN1 to LAN2 traffic away from the links to the Internet on P4 and P2). Another change is necessary (one we've seen before), and this time the change will be in effect through the end of the book. Ace and Best ISPs have merged to become Best-Ace ISP, and the network now has only one AS number (65127). This will simplify the configurations used in the rest of the book, starting with our MPLS-based VPN.

PPTP FOR PRIVACY

The RSA SecurID that one is issued for remote access to the corporate network requires one to copy the six random numbers that appear on its screen at log-in. There's also a four-digit static prefix that does not change, but the last six digits change every 30 seconds. This has been challenging for some users, who cannot copy the digits correctly and exceed their retry count (usually three). After that, the account is locked until an administrator releases it. Newer SecurID tokens plug right into the USB port of the computer, so no typing is required.

Even though our home office access is using PPP over DSL, the PPTP connection still has to send the PPP and PPTP control messages to the corporate network device, the L2TP Access Concentrator (LAC). (We'll talk about the relationship between PPTP and L2TP later.) These messages indicate that a connection request is being made with the PPP Link Control Protocol (LCP). The packet exchange at the beginning of the connection is shown in Figure 26.2. The actual data are sent inside packets formatted according to the generic routing encapsulation (GRE) method, which basically adds another IP header to the existing one.

For the first time in this book, this Ethereal capture file has been edited to substitute the actual addresses used for "Martian" addresses for reasons of security. The client PC is using `169.254.99.1` and the server is using `250.99.111.4`.

The first GRE packet does not come until packet 20. In fact, there are many more compressed PPP packets than those using GRE. Figure 26.3 shows this relationship in the packet sequence taken from later in the same session. We'll talk more about these PPP and GRE packets later in this chapter.

Types of VPNs

A VPN is a private communications network most often used within a single organization to communicate over a public network. VPN traffic is carried over a public network infrastructure, such as the Internet, using standard and unsecure protocols.

No.	Time	Source	Destination	Protocol	Info
1	0.000000	192.168.21.171	169.254.99.1	Messenger	NetrSendMessage request
2	7.114812	169.254.99.1	250.99.111.4	TCP	3692 > pptp [SYN] Seq=0 Ack=0 Win=64512 [CHECKSUM I!
3	7.155746	250.99.111.4	169.254.99.1	TCP	pptp > 3692 [SYN, ACK] Seq=0 Ack=1 Win=65535 [CHECK!
4	7.155824	169.254.99.1	250.99.111.4	PPTP	Start-Control-Connection-Request
5	7.199352	250.99.111.4	169.254.99.1	PPTP	Start-Control-Connection-Reply
6	7.199447	169.254.99.1	250.99.111.4	PPTP	Outgoing-Call-Request
7	7.242919	250.99.111.4	169.254.99.1	PPTP	Outgoing-Call-Reply
8	7.250723	169.254.99.1	250.99.111.4	PPTP	Set-Link-Info
9	7.254135	169.254.99.1	250.99.111.4	PPP LCP	Configuration Request
10	7.298130	250.99.111.4	169.254.99.1	PPP LCP	Configuration Request
11	7.298457	250.99.111.4	169.254.99.1	PPP LCP	Configuration Nak
12	7.303449	169.254.99.1	250.99.111.4	PPP LCP	Configuration Reject
13	7.303798	169.254.99.1	250.99.111.4	PPP LCP	Configuration Request
14	7.347835	250.99.111.4	169.254.99.1	PPP LCP	Configuration Request
15	7.348253	250.99.111.4	169.254.99.1	PPP LCP	Configuration Nak
16	7.350942	169.254.99.1	250.99.111.4	PPP LCP	Configuration Ack
17	7.351199	169.254.99.1	250.99.111.4	PPP LCP	Configuration Request
18	7.396074	250.99.111.4	169.254.99.1	PPTP	Set-Link-Info
19	7.396719	250.99.111.4	169.254.99.1	PPP LCP	Configuration Ack
20	7.397128	250.99.111.4	169.254.99.1	GRE	Encapsulated PPP
21	7.397243	169.254.99.1	250.99.111.4	PPTP	Set-Link-Info
22	7.397486	169.254.99.1	250.99.111.4	PPP LCP	Identification
23	7.397643	169.254.99.1	250.99.111.4	PPP LCP	Identification
24	7.398195	250.99.111.4	169.254.99.1	EAP	Request, Identity [RFC3748]

```
▽ Generic Routing Encapsulation (PPP)
  ▸ Flags and version: 0x2081
    Protocol Type: PPP (0x880b)
    Payload length: 0
    Call ID: 32768
    Acknowledgement number: 4
```

FIGURE 26.2

Start of a PPTP over DSL session, showing the content of the first GRE packet.

No.	Time	Source	Destination	Protocol	Info
472	43.189239	250.99.111.4	169.254.99.1	PPP Comp	Compressed data
473	43.191030	250.99.111.4	169.254.99.1	PPP Comp	Compressed data
474	43.200791	250.99.111.4	169.254.99.1	PPP Comp	Compressed data
475	43.200836	250.99.111.4	169.254.99.1	GRE	Encapsulated PPP
476	43.205455	169.254.99.1	250.99.111.4	PPP Comp	Compressed data
477	43.205488	169.254.99.1	250.99.111.4	PPP Comp	Compressed data
478	43.205500	169.254.99.1	250.99.111.4	PPP Comp	Compressed data
479	43.218382	169.254.99.1	250.99.111.4	PPP Comp	Compressed data
480	43.235842	169.254.99.1	250.99.111.4	PPP Comp	Compressed data
481	43.235878	169.254.99.1	250.99.111.4	PPP Comp	Compressed data
482	43.265467	250.99.111.4	169.254.99.1	PPP Comp	Compressed data
483	43.284070	250.99.111.4	169.254.99.1	PPP Comp	Compressed data
484	43.285119	169.254.99.1	250.99.111.4	PPP Comp	Compressed data
485	43.285148	169.254.99.1	250.99.111.4	PPP Comp	Compressed data
486	43.286619	250.99.111.4	169.254.99.1	PPP Comp	Compressed data
487	43.296830	169.254.99.1	250.99.111.4	GRE	Encapsulated PPP
488	43.296865	169.254.99.1	250.99.111.4	PPP Comp	Compressed data
489	43.338487	250.99.111.4	169.254.99.1	PPP Comp	Compressed data
490	43.349370	250.99.111.4	169.254.99.1	PPP Comp	Compressed data
491	43.461649	169.254.99.1	250.99.111.4	GRE	Encapsulated PPP
492	43.461702	169.254.99.1	250.99.111.4	PPP Comp	Compressed data
493	43.542279	169.254.99.1	250.99.111.4	PPP Comp	Compressed data
494	43.608927	250.99.111.4	169.254.99.1	GRE	Encapsulated PPP

```
▷ Internet Protocol, Src Addr: 250.99.111.4 (250.99.111.4), Dst Addr: 169.254.99.1 (169.254.99.1)
▽ Generic Routing Encapsulation (PPP)
  ▷ Flags and version: 0x2081
    Protocol Type: PPP (0x880b)
    Payload length: 0
    Call ID: 32768
    Acknowledgement number: 176
```

FIGURE 26.3

PPP and GRE packets, showing GRE encapsulation of PPP in IP.

However, the VPN mechanisms make the network look and feel like a private network composed of network nodes owned and operated by the organization and the leased lines connecting them, which carry the organization's traffic only.

In truth, the "private" network was never really as private as customers thought. Carriers did a good marketing job, but in fact every customer's bits were freely mixed on high-bit-rate backbones, although *users* could not tell whether this was the case. But when a massive microwave link was compromised in some way, hundreds or thousands of customers' data were at risk. Once the carriers all became ISPs, the marketing material for private circuits was retooled to support the use of *virtual* circuits over the public network.

Chapter 17, on frame relay and ATM networks, which also covered MPLS, mentioned the idea of a virtual circuit (or channel or connection) as something that is "not really a private circuit/channel/connection, but acts just like one," at least as far as the customer is concerned. This chapter extends that concept into the general area of VPNs.

The chapter on MPLS introduced the idea of using MPLS LSP "tunnels" as the basis for a VPN, because MPLS LSPs are pretty much invisible to IP hackers on the network. This chapter elaborates on that idea.

Are MPLS LSP Tunnels?

Sometimes MPLS LSPs are loosely called "MPLS tunnels," and most people will not object, knowing that LSPs are intended. But some object strenuously, claiming that the term *tunnel* is more properly reserved for different types of encapsulation than in MPLS—such as frame in frame, packet in packet, or some others. MPLS merely adds a small "shim header" between L3 packet and L2 frame, they claim, and therefore is not a full encapsulation (some call it "Layer 2.5").

Of course, if tunneling is defined as a "violation of the normal data-packet-frame encapsulation sequence at some endpoint devices," MPLS LSPs are certainly tunnels. Then again, VLAN tagging (the Layer 2 analog to MPLS labeling) is not called "VLAN tunneling," even though it could be.

In this chapter, we'll use the terms *MPLS LSP* and *VLAN tagging*, while avoiding the term *tunnel*.

Security and VPNs

On modern networks, a *firewall* of some type is used as a security device and sits between clients and servers. The firewall can pass authentication data to an authentication service for the local network, such as RADIUS. A trusted person with privileged access (such as root, often only using trusted devices that are physically secure) is allowed to access resources not available to general users, such as the routers and the firewall itself.

We'll talk more about firewalls in Chapter 28. For now, we'll just mention them and note that VPNs *can* use firewalls, and indeed they can be built up from firewalls but don't have to be. For many people, any type of VPN implies the purchase and use of specialized devices that form the endpoints of the VPN. To these users, the VPN is created by the customer; in brief, it is not offered as a service by the ISP. The exception, of course, is MPLS-based VPNs, which we will explore in this chapter.

VPNs do not have to be secure. An organization that uses MPLS to create the appearance of the virtual-circuit, network-like frame relay or ATM might call the result a VPN, but this is not really more secure than any other type of network. Secure VPNs use encrypted tunneling protocols to add confidentiality (a counter-sniffing notion), user and resource authentication (to prevent spoofing), and message integrity (to detect message alteration) to achieve the levels of security and privacy desired (or affordable).

It should be noted that no code is unbreakable (rumors persist to the contrary); no network is entirely protected against hackers; and some simple attacks, such as denial-of-service (DoS) attacks, are still painfully effective. What network security seeks to do is raise the *work factor* for the bad guys to the point where it takes so long to break the code that the information is useless and it's easier to attack another network whose administrators are less diligent in security areas.

If this sounds too defeatist, consider the fact that Kevin Mitnick (a hacker guru) admitted in his book, *The Art of Intrusion*, that most of his exploits relied on manipulating people ("social engineering") and not frontal attacks on equipment and software ("I'm with security. We have to change your password. What is it again?"). A lot of security dollars are spent protecting users from themselves.

VPNs and Protocols

There are several types of VPNs that can be built, and the choice of which type to use is not trivial. Many VPN schemes have a lot to do with security. But secure VPN technologies can be the basis for a *security overlay* and used to enhance security on the network.

We'll just talk generally about all types of VPNs, create an MPLS-based VPN on the Illustrated Network at the end of the chapter, and consider ways to "harden" it in the next few chapters. All VPNs are in some sense "trusted" more than simple IP router networks. Secure VPN protocols include the following:

IPSec (IP security)—IPSec has been aptly described as "a piece of IPv6 that fell into IPv4." A mandatory part of IPv6, IPSec was rushed into the IPv4 world as an advanced security measure.

SSL—SSL can be used to tunnel the entire network stack, as in the OpenVPN approach, or to create an *SSL VPN* to secure certain pieces of the network.

PPTP—A tunneling method developed by Microsoft for remote access to network resources through a special server.

L2F (Layer 2 forwarding)—Another secure remote-access method developed by Cisco.

L2TP (Layer 2 tunneling protocol)—A sort of "compromise" method that includes contributions by both Cisco and Microsoft. Today, L2TP has pretty much replaced L2F.

VPNs do not rely on one protocol or another for everything. For example, networks dominated by Windows software generally use VPNs that employ PPTP and L2TP (along with IPsec) to construct a secure VPN.

We've already talked about SSL, and IPSec is covered (and featured) in the next chapter. Let's take a look at PPTP and L2TP methods, which are for securing intermittent remote user access through dial-up links or (increasingly) from home offices over DSL.

PPTP

PPTP was developed by Microsoft as an extension to PPP and is now defined in RFC 2637. It is a Layer 2 tunneling protocol, meaning that the payload is the Layer 2 frame itself, encrypted and preceded by a small PPTP header based on extensions to the generic routing encapsulation (GRE) header described in RFC 2784. This frame, with header and trailer, is placed inside another packet and sent over the network between what PPTP calls a PPTP access concentrator (PAC) and a PPTP network server (PNS).

PPTP is a client/server protocol with the PAC as the client and the PNS as the server. Control messages are exchanged over TCP port 1723. Encryption is provided by underlying PPP mechanisms. Encryption keys are generated from the authentication process, which normally uses the Challenge Handshake Authentication Protocol (CHAP)—a three-way handshake using encrypted passwords (defined in RFC 1994).

In PPTP, PPP uses compressed data, which is not a form of encryption but does present an obstacle to unsophisticated hackers who only dabble in eavesdropping. The GRE encapsulated data are secure. PPTP is still widely used today, often in conjunction with some type of user authentication token such as an RSA SecurID numerical passcode generator. Users dial in to the PAC and log in using the passcode, which changes every 30 seconds. Dial-in connections are usually very secure because they can follow any path over the PSTN and use any PAC port available. PPTP covers communication between the PAC (which might be supporting traveling sales agents on the east coast) and the main network with the PNS (which might be on the west coast). In addition to controlling costs, PPTP used this way can use a VPN setup for that purpose.

Today, home workers with DSL often use PPTP to tunnel through the ISP's unsecure network to reach the relative security of the organization's more protective environment. Additional security is needed to reach the PAC from the user location. Between PAC and PNS, a VPN tunnel itself can be built using *double encryption*; that is, taking the PPTP data and encrypting it once again. It all depends on how paranoid the organization is (as the doomed Kurt Cobain noted, just because you're paranoid doesn't mean they're not out to get you).

L2TP

Cisco first used their L2F as an alternative to Microsoft's PPTP. But eventually both companies combined the best of both worlds to produce L2TP, a more flexible version of PPTP. L2TP is also a way to send encrypted frames between client and server over the Internet, and again the client is a remote access point and the server on a protected network. In L2TP, these are now the L2TP access concentrator (LAC) and L2TP network server (LNS).

L2TP is designed to work with more than dial-in users seeking Internet connectivity. The LAC and LNS can be linked not only over the Internet but over frame relay and ATM networks (L2TP calls them "non-IP WAN technologies"). A special L2TP device, the LAC client, can attach to the LNS directly without going through the dial-in LAC device. The overall architecture is shown in Figure 26.4.

Encryption in L2TP is provided with IPSec (why always reinvent the wheel?). There is a two-step L2TP encapsulation. An initial L2TP frame encapsulation with PPP is used to build a new IP packet using UDP port 1701 on the server side and an L2TP header. This step is followed by the IPSec encapsulation. Although it is technically allowed to send L2TP data without this step, it defeats the purpose. L2TP is defined in RFC 2661.

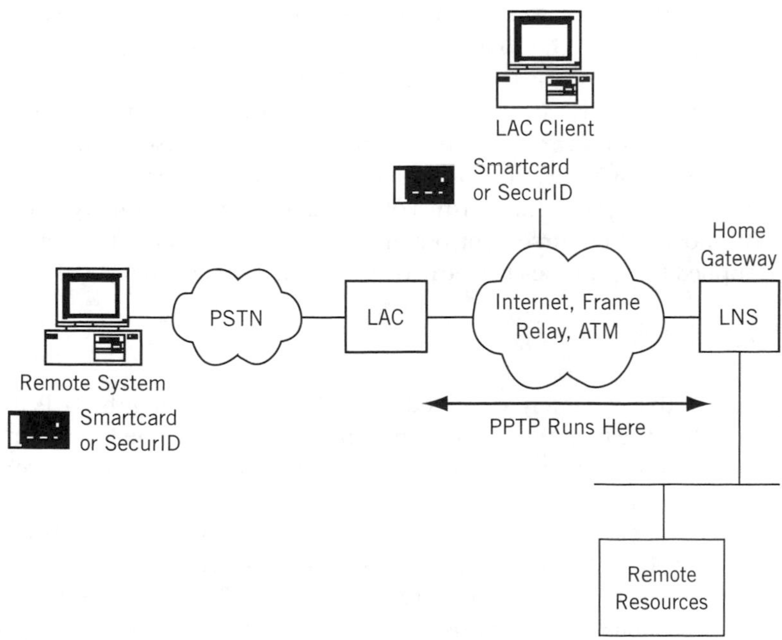

FIGURE 26.4

PPTP architecture, showing how PPTP runs between LAC and LNS.

PPTP and L2TP Compared

There are many differences between PPTP and L2TP, but the following comprise the main ones.

- PPTP cannot support a non-IP network directly, whereas L2TP works with any network that can provide point-to-point connectivity.
- PPTP supports only a single tunnel from client to server, whereas L2TP can support multiple tunnels—perhaps used as part of a multilevel security and QoS scheme.
- PPTP does not support header compression, whereas L2TP can compress its header for efficiency purposes.

Nevertheless, PPTP remains more popular than L2TP, and organizations that support many remote users (traveling or at home) with Windows-based laptops or PCs generally still use PPTP. The main alternative to PPTP and L2TP to add security to a VPN connecting an organization's sites is IPSec. IPSec is discussed in the next chapter.

TYPES OF MPLS-BASED VPNs

Now that MPLS and security protocols have been defined, let's look at the types of VPNs that can be built from these pieces. There are two major types of VPN: Those that operate at Layer 3 (the same layer as the routers that make up the network), and those that operate at Layer 2, the level of LANs linked over the VPN.

Which is "better"? There is no easy answer, and even the question should be framed more clearly in terms of what is meant by "better." Better in terms of cost, complexity (or simplicity), cryptographic sophistication, or something else altogether?

This section describes the major characteristics of each and configures one type on the Illustrated Network, not as an endorsement, but just as an example. The often bewildering terminology applied to VPN types has now been standardized in RFC 4364.

Layer 3 VPNs

Consider an organization with two widely separated sites with LANs running the TCP/IP protocol suite and using all of the techniques and applications we've described earlier in this book. What would a totally *private* IP network connecting the two sites look like? Well, the organization could contract with a carrier for a long link connecting the sites and install customer routers at each location. Security is provided by the isolated nature of the traffic on the leased private line (although that isolation is rarely absolute, as has been pointed out) and restricted access at the sites themselves. There is no Internet access, of course, unless a separate router or port is provided for this purpose.

But many carriers have evolved beyond the stage of mere "bandwidth mongers" and want to provide more sophisticated services as ISPs. Private lines are usually paid for by the mile as well as by bandwidth, and the bandwidth use for bursty IP applications is wildly erratic and thus wasted much of the time. Private networks are designed for peak loads, such as end-of-month or end-of-quarter frenzies, and sit idle most of the time. The PSTN is no exception, by the way, and is designed (in the United States) for the 5 days of maximum calling volume: Mother's Day, Christmas, New Year's Day, Thanksgiving, and Father's Day. Only unpredictable major disasters can swamp the PSTN at other times.

Adding sites can be a problem in this scenario. Organizations with many sites can always contract floor space at some central point and install their own routers and leased lines there in a hub configuration instead of a mesh to cut down on point-to-point mileage costs and the number of ports required on each router.

Of course, the isolation of the private network is always attractive to customers. But what if the ISP can promise a network that looks like the rented-floor-space router hub solution with leased private line connectivity? In other words, the ISP provides a solution that *looks like* a private router network to the customer—complete with what appear to be dedicated links and routers that contain routing information for that customer and that customer only. This is, of course, a VPN.

But what we have described is not just any type of VPN—it's a *Layer 3 VPN* (L3VPN) because the virtual nature of the network is apparent at Layer 3 (the IP layer). It's really a network of virtual routers because in reality the ISP is selling the same router resources to hundreds and even thousands of customers if the router and links are hefty enough to handle the loads. The different L3VPN customers cannot see each other at all, or even communicate unless special arrangements are made (this is sometimes called an "extranet," the closed VPN being an "intranet"). Each can only see the information in its own *virtual routing and forwarding* (VRF) tables, as if the router were divided into many tiny logical pieces.

L3VPNs are one of the most complicated entities that can be set up on a router network. They are built on MPLS LSPs, as might be expected, and carefully distribute routing information only to the VRFs that should receive it. (There is still a "master" routing table that receives *all* routing information: Someone has to *run* the L3VPN itself.)

Basic L3VPN connectivity is bad enough. It is much worse when multicast capabilities must be added to the tunnels, which are essentially point-to-point connections that do not easily replicate packets.

The RFCs and drafts for L3VPNs, which are numerous, use MPLS and BGP as the foundations for these types of VPNs—also called PPVPNs (provider-provisioned VPNs). They also introduce a distinctive architecture and terminology, as shown in Figure 26.5. The figure shows a simple two-site arrangement, but the same terms apply to more complicated configurations.

Customer Edge

Each site has a customer-edge (CE) router, designated CE1, CE2, ... CEn as needed. These routers are owned and operated by the customer and are at the "edge" of the VPN. At least one link runs to the ISP and carries customer data to and from the ISP's network. The data on the link can be in plain text (the link is generally short, point to point, and not considered a high security risk) or encrypted with IPSec, SSL, or some other VPN

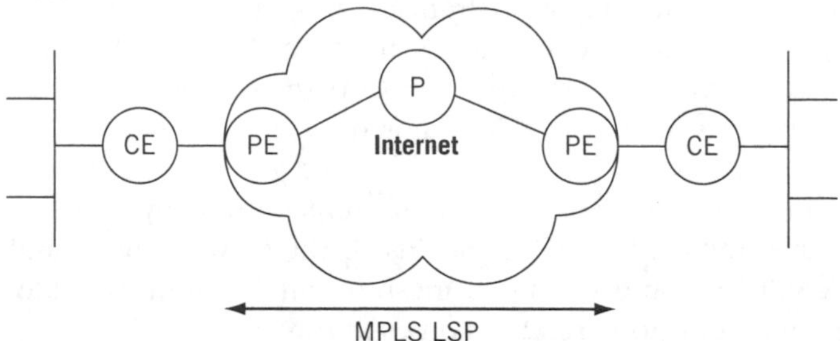

FIGURE 26.5

Basic MPLS-based VPN architecture and terminology. Note that we've been using this terminology all along.

protocol. The CEs still run a routing protocol, but only to gather information about other CE routers belonging to their own L3VPN.

Provider Edge

Each customer site connects to a provider-edge (PE) router, designated PE1, PE2, ... PEn as necessary. These are owned and operated by the ISP and are at the provider "edge" of the VPN. A PE router can carry traffic to and from many CE routers, and even carry "regular" Internet traffic for other customers. These are routers with the VRFs and run MPLS to the other PE routers and BGP to carry customer routing information. In MPLS terms, these are the ingress and egress routers, but a PE router on one VPN can be a transit (P) router on another.

Provider

The provider (P) routers are the MPLS transit routers that carry VPN traffic through the provider "core" or backbone. As in MPLS, there must be at least one P router, but there are usually quite a few, depending on the popularity of the L3VPN service. As with PE routers, the P routers can carry general ISP traffic that has nothing to do with VPNs.

The major L3VPN is RFC 4364, and Internet drafts are important for understanding how MPLS and BGP combine to make an L3VPN. MPLS LSPs connect the PE routers through the P routers, and BGP is used with *route distinguishers* to ensure that routing updates go into the proper VRFs.

The routing tables on the CE routers are generally quite simple. They contain just a few routes to the other CE router sites and a default for generic Internet access, which might be through a separate router or through the VPN itself (one tunnel leads to an Internet router "gateway"). If the Internet access (few VPNs can afford to cut themselves off from the Internet entirely) is on another router at the customer site, a *firewall* is typically used to protect this "back door" to the VPN. Firewalls are discussed in the next chapter.

Layer 2 VPNs

In an L3VPN, the two CE routers are still on two separate networks—just like LAN1 and LAN2 on the Illustrated Network. CE0 and CE6 use different IP network addresses, such as `10.0.50.2/24` and `10.0.16.2/24`, on their links to PE5 and PE1 toward the network backbone.

LANs are Layer 2 constructs at heart. Ethernet frames only care about MAC layer addresses, not IP addresses. Why not just build the VPN at Layer 2 and connect the two CE routers into one big "virtual" LAN that seems to be as private as both LANs would be separately? This is the idea behind an L2VPN.

Even though an L2VPN service is delivered over an ISP's collection of routers (just like an L3VPN), the end result is much simpler than an L3VPN. This is because there is no need to maintain separate virtual routing information for each customer. Both customer routers can use one IP address space (perhaps `10.99.99.0/24`), and do not need to run a routing protocol between the CE routers at all because they appear to be directly connected and at opposite ends of the same "link."

The L2VPN architecture still uses the CE-PE-P terminology and uses MPLS LSPs, but the basic content of the tunnels are Ethernet frames (other "emulated" LANs are sometimes supported). The backbone routers in an L2VPN are essentially transformed into LAN bridges. The VPLS tables on the PE routers are now long lists of MAC layer addresses more similar to ARP caches than to routing tables.

L2VPN service offerings have a variety of names. A popular offering from many ISPs is some form of *virtual private LAN service* (VPLS). The LANs are now *virtual* LANs (VLANs), and the Ethernet frames between CE and PE routers must employ *VLAN tagging* to allow the ISP to tell the frames apart at Layer 2. The PE routers are configured with a *VPLS virtual port* that forms the endpoint of the MPLS tunnel (LSP) that carries the frames from one LAN to the other.

There are many other variations on the basic VPN types described here. RFC 4026 lists (in addition to L3VPNs, L2VPNs, and VPLS) seven other types of VPN, mostly variations on the L2VPN theme.

- Virtual Private Wire Service (VPWS)
- IP-only LAN-like Service (IPLS)
- Pseudo Wire (PW)
- Transparent LAN Service (TLS)
- Virtual LAN (VLAN)
- Virtual Private Switched Network (VPSN)

Why all the interest in linking CE routers over Layer 2 through an ISP's router network? The trend today is to extend Ethernet's reach and speed to incredible distances (about 25 miles) and bandwidths (10 Gbps). Some see Ethernet as the ultimate "universal" network, and one without all the risks inherent in IP-based router networks. How many malicious users are busily crafting phony Ethernet frames?

Of course, malicious users followed networking from the PSTN (where they were first active in securing free long-distance service) onto the Internet, and there is no reason to think they won't follow the action anywhere else. But VPNs and virtual LANs are at least prepared to address security issues from the start.

VPLS: AN MPLS-BASED L2VPN

To make a good configuration for VPLS, we'll have to get a little creative with our network. The two routers attached to LAN1 and LAN2, customer-edge routers CE1 and CE2, will now support VLAN tagging (not difficult to do). With VPLS configured, both LANs still use addresses `10.10.11.0/24` and `10.10.12.0/24`. (In other words, we'll start the VPLS at the ISP, not at the customer routers—not all users want to renumber all of their IP devices.)

But now it will look like the CE routers are directly connected with a gigabit Ethernet LAN sharing a common IP network address. In this example, that address is `10.99.99.0/24` (which should be distinctive enough to easily pick out). So, this is where the "virtual LAN" comes in—on the link between CE1 and CE2. We've also merged Best-Ace ISP into one AS (the number is not important) so that we can use IBGP to distribute the routes and avoid more complex configurations.

The simplified Illustrated Network configuration for VPLS, along with interface designations and IP addresses, is shown in Figurc 26.6. The figure also shows an example of the VPLS table on router PE1. This table shows how the MAC addresses on the interfaces to the CE routers map to MPLS labels instead of IP addresses, as in an L3VPN.

The VPLS *virtual port* interfaces on PE1 and PE2 are designated with the `vt-` (virtual tunnel) prefix. These are not physical interfaces on the routers, of course, but logical interfaces that form the endpoints of the MPLS LSP connecting the routers over the ISP core backbone. This interface is not configured directly, but is the *result* of the VPLS configuration steps.

Router-by-Router VPLS Configuration

Let's look at each router individually and show the sections of the configuration files that directly create the VPLS service between LAN1 and LAN2. Keep in mind that there could be much more to the configuration than just these statements.

CE0 Router

All that is needed on the CE0 router is the interface to the PE router and the VLAN identifier and IP address associated with it. These values must match the configuration on router CE0. (The LAN1 interface is still `fe-1/3/0` and is still using `10.10.11.1/24`.)

```
set interfaces ge-0/0/3 vlan-tagging;
set interfaces ge-0/0/3 unit 0 vlan-id 600; # the VLAN ID must must match
    throughout the configurations
set interfaces ge-0/0/3 unit 0 family inet address 10.99.99.1/24;
    # this address space must match the CE6 link address we use
```

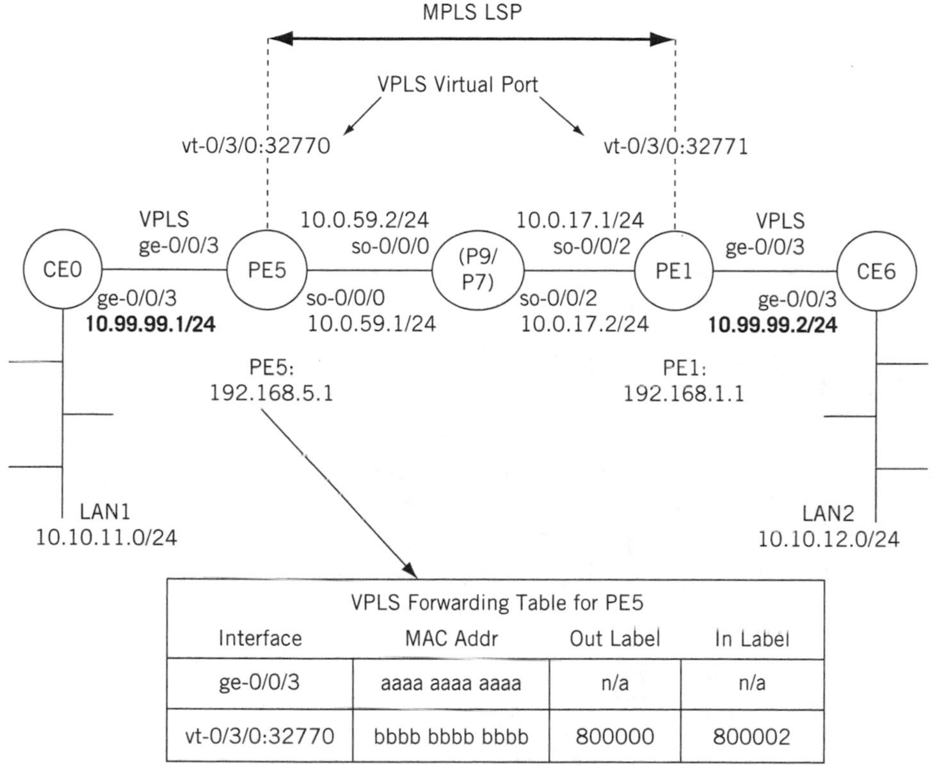

VPLS Forwarding Table for PE5			
Interface	MAC Addr	Out Label	In Label
ge-0/0/3	aaaa aaaa aaaa	n/a	n/a
vt-0/3/0:32770	bbbb bbbb bbbb	800000	800002

FIGURE 26.6

Illustrated Network topology for the VPLS configuration. Note the "new" address space.

PE5 Router

The PE router configurations are the most elaborate among the VPLS routers. These configurations are rather lengthy, so comments are used throughout. The PE routers need BGP, MPLS, OSPF, and RSVP to be configured properly for the LSP to work correctly. RSVP sets up the MPLS LSPs, OSPF handles routine routing chores, and BGP is used to carry the VPLS MAC layer information between the PE routers.

The PE routers also need to configure VLAN tagging and VPLS encapsulation on the interfaces (physical *and* logical) to the CE routers. The VLAN ID must match as well, but no IP address is needed for this "Layer 2" interface. There is a space between major sections of the configuration and liberal comments to help track what is being configured.

```
set interfaces ge-0/0/3 vlan-tagging; #interface to CE0
set interfaces ge-0/0/3 encapsulation vlan-vpls;
set interfaces ge-0/0/3 unit 0 encapsulation vlan-vpls;
set interfaces ge-0/0/3 unit 0 vlan-id 600; # must match across the network
set interfaces so-0/0/0 unit 0 family inet address 10.0.59.1; # interface to P9
set interfaces so-0/0/0 unit 0 family mpls;
```

```
set routing-options autonomous-system 65127;
set routing-options forwarding-table export exp-to-fwd;
    # used to distinguish VPLS "routes"

set protocols rsvp interface all; # turn on RSVP

set protocols mpls label-switched-path PE5-to-PE1 to 192.168.1.1;
    # The LSP to connect VPLS routers thru loopback addresses
set protocols mpls interface all;
set protocols bgp group vpls-pe type internal;
set protocols bgp group vpls-pe local-address 192.168.5.1;
set protocols bgp group vpls-pe family l2vpn unicast;
    # this VPLS is an L2VPN type and only cares about unicast traffic
set protocols bgp group vpls-pe neighbor 192.168.9.1;
    # IBGP peer router P9
set protocols bgp group vpls-pe neighbor 192.168.7.1;
    # IBGP peer router P7
set protocols bgp group vpls-pe neighbor 192.168.1.1;
    # IBGP peer router PE1

set protocols ospf traffic-engineering;
set protocols ospf area 0.0.0.0;
set protocols ospf interface all; # run OSPF to all routers

set policy-options policy-statement exp-to-fwd term A
    from community green-community;
    # policy to load forwarding table - the community must also match
set policy-options policy-statement exp-to-fwd term A
    then install-nexthop lsp PE5-to-PE1;
    # makes this LSP the next hop for the VPLS
set policy-options policy-statement exp-to-fwd term A
    then accept;
    # accepts only community = green-community

set policy-options community green-community;
    # sets the community value on BGP routes for the VPLS

set routing-instances green instance-type vpls;
    # creates a special forwarding table for VPLS traffic
set routing-instances green interface fe-0/1/0.0;
set routing-instances green route-distinguisher 10.10.10.1;
set routing-instances green vrf-target target:11111:1;
    # this value must match the community
set routing-instances green protocols vpls site-range 10;
    # this starts the main VPLS configuration
set routing-instances green protocols vpls site greenPE1 site-identifier 1;
    # after the protocols, communities, and the rest, this is simple...
```

P Router (P9)

The P routers still need the same BGP, MPLS, OSPF, and RSVP to become a transit router between PE5 and PE1. But at least no major policies need to be applied or tables created. The configuration shown, on P9, is mirrored by the one on P7 (which is not shown).

```
set interfaces so-0/0/1 unit 0 family inet address 10.0.79.2; # interface to P7
set interfaces so-0/0/1 unit 0 family mpls; #needed for the VPN
set interfaces so-0/0/2 unit 0 family inet address 10.0.59.2; # interface to PE5
set interfaces so-0/0/1 unit 0 family mpls; #needed for the VPN

set protocols rsvp interface all; # turn on RSVP for signaling
set protocols mpls interface all; # turn on MPLS for packet parsing
set protocols bgp group vpls-pe type internal; # create IBGP group for VPLS
set protocols bgp group vpls-pe local-address 192.168.9.1 # P9 router
  address
set protocols bgp group vpls-pe family l2vpn unicast # VPLS is for unicast
  traffic
set protocols bgp group vpls-pe neighbor 192.168.5.1 # IBGP peer router PE5
set protocols bgp group vpls-pe neighbor 192.168.7.1 # IBGP peer router P7
set protocols bgp group vpls-pe neighbor 192.168.1.1 # IBGP peer router PE1

set protocols ospf traffic-engineering; # needed to divert VPN packets
set protocols ospf area 0.0.0.0 interface all;  # run OSPF everywhere
```

Note that we've added the P routers to the IBGP mesh. Technically, the P routers do not need to be part of the BGP mesh for the VPN, although the P routers might need to run BGP for other purposes (which is why we are running it here). All that is needed for the VPN is a full mesh between the PE routers. This configuration does no harm on this little network, but when PEs have thousands of VPNs the signaling and information moved by BGP can create resource issues. In these cases, it is advisable to have a BGP-free core (unless, of course, BGP is needed on the P routers for other non–VPN-related purposes).

PE1 Router

The VPLS configuration on the PE1 router mirrors the configuration on the PE5 router. It is shown because of its importance in the VPLS configuration.

```
set interfaces ge-0/0/3 vlan-tagging; #interface to CE6
set interfaces ge-0/0/3 encapsulation vlan-vpls;
set interfaces ge-0/0/3 unit 0 encapsulation vlan-vpls;
set interfaces ge-0/0/3 unit 0 vlan-id 600; # must match across the network
set interfaces so-0/0/2 unit 0 family inet address 10.0.17.1; # interface to P7
set interfaces so-0/0/2 unit 0 family mpls;

set routing-options autonomous-system 65127;
set routing-options forwarding-table export exp-to-fwd;
    # used to distinguish VPLS "routes"

set protocols rsvp interface all; # turn on RSVP

set protocols mpls label-switched-path PE1-to-PE5 to 192.168.5.1;
    # The LSP to connect VPLS routers thru loopback addresses
set protocols mpls interface all;

set protocols bgp group vpls-pe type internal;
set protocols bgp group vpls-pe local-address 192.168.5.1;
```

```
set protocols bgp group vpls-pe family l2vpn unicast;
    # this VPLS is an L2VPN type and only cares about unicast traffic
set protocols bgp group vpls-pe neighbor 192.168.9.1;
    # IBGP peer router P9
set protocols bgp group vpls-pe neighbor 192.168.7.1;
    # IBGP peer router P7
set protocols bgp group vpls-pe neighbor 192.168.5.1;
    # IBGP peer router PE5

set protocols ospf traffic-engineering;
set protocols ospf area 0.0.0.0;
set protocols ospf interface all; # run OSPF to all routers

set policy-options policy-statement exp-to-fwd term A
    from community green-community;
    # policy to load forwarding table - the community must also match
set policy-options policy-statement exp-to-fwd term A
    then install-nexthop lsp PE5-to-PE1;
    # makes this LSP the next hop for the VPLS
set policy-options policy-statement exp-to-fwd term A
    then accept;
    # accepts only community = green-community

set policy-options community green-community;
    # sets the community value on BGP routes for the VPLS

set routing-instances green instance-type vpls;
    # creates a special forwarding table for VPLS traffic
set routing-instances green interface fe-0/1/0.0;
set routing-instances green route-distinguisher 10.10.10.4;
set routing-instances green vrf-target target:11111:1;
    # this value must match the community
set routing-instances green protocols vpls site-range 10;
    # this starts the main VPLS configuration
set routing-instances green protocols vpls site greenPE1 site-identifier 2;
    # after the protocols, communities, and the rest, this is simple...
```

CE6 Router

Finally, the router that connects to LAN2 mirrors the configuration of the CE0 router. (The LAN2 interface is still `fe-1/3/0` and is still using `10.10.12.1/24`.)

```
set interfaces ge-0/0/3 vlan-tagging;
set interfaces ge-0/0/3 unit 0 vlan-id 600; # the VLAN ID must must match
    throughout the configurations
set interfaces ge-0/0/3 unit 0 family inet address 10.99.99.2/24;
    # this address space must match the CE0 link address we use
```

DOES IT REALLY WORK?

Complex configurations always pose challenges for verification. How do we know this VPLS is really working? Well, one way is to see whether the PE routers are learning MAC addresses.

```
admin@PE5> show system statistics vpls | match mac
6 mac route learning requests
6 mac router learnt
0 mac routers aged
0 mac router moved
```

There are many other commands that show VPLS information. But the most important information is from the hosts on LAN1 and LAN2 themselves, which now think their site routers are connected by a single Ethernet LAN instead of six routers.

```
bsdclient# traceroute 10.10.12.77
traceroute to 10.10.12.77 (10.10.12.77), 64 hops max, 44 byte packets
 1  10.10.11.1 (10.10.11.1)  0.419 ms  0.256 ms  0.343 ms
 2  10.99.99.2 (10.99.99.2)  0.328 ms  0.294 ms  0.346 ms
 3  10.10.12.77 (10.10.12.77)  0.331 ms  0.297 ms  0.346 ms
bsdclient#
```

The bsdclient and all the other hosts on LAN1 now think that the bsdserver on LAN2 is only three hops away, although we know there are actually six routers between the source and destination! The only intermediate address that shows up is the IP address on the link address on CE6, which is where the MPLS LSP ends.

QUESTIONS FOR READERS

Figure 26.7 shows some of the concepts discussed in this chapter and can be used to answer the following questions.

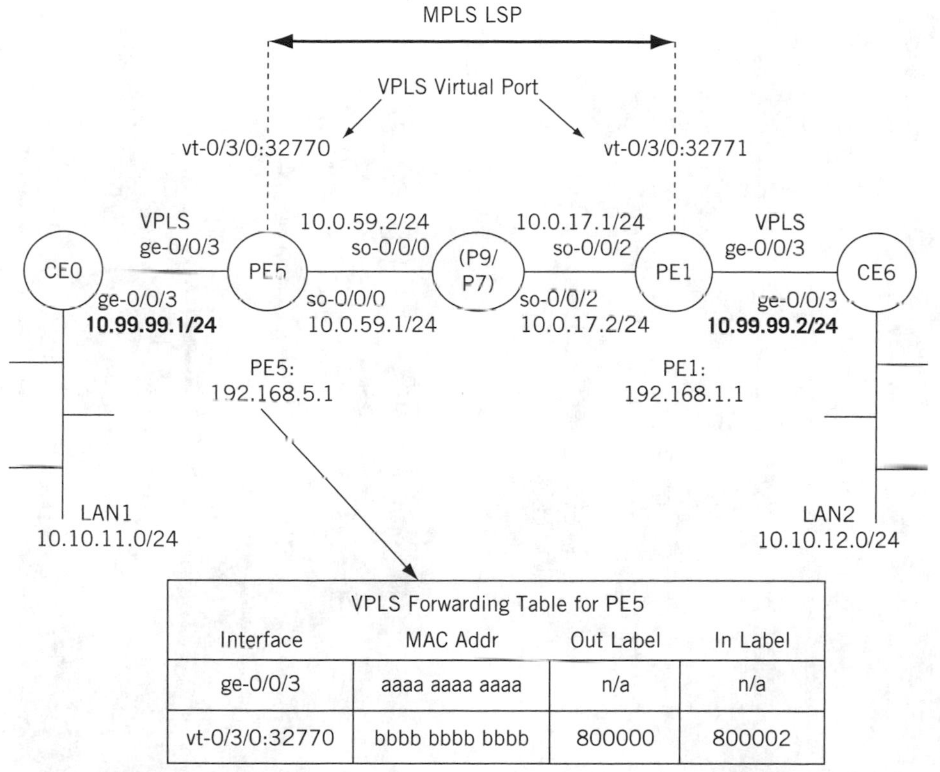

Interface	MAC Addr	Out Label	In Label
ge-0/0/3	aaaa aaaa aaaa	n/a	n/a
vt-0/3/0:32770	bbbb bbbb bbbb	800000	800002

FIGURE 26.7

Topology for the VPLS configuration.

1. How many LSPs are used to connect the two routers at the ends of the VPLS?
2. Where does the LSP connecting the site router CE0 to CE6 begin and end?
3. Why is the configuration on the PE router so complex?
4. What is the function of the VPLS virtual port?
5. What if a ***third*** site router using the `10.99.99.2/24` address space joined the network? Could the VPLS be extended to that site as well? If so, how?

CHAPTER

27 Network Address Translation

What You Will Learn

In this chapter, you will learn how NAT (originally used to address the shortage of IPv4 addresses) is now used to conceal public IPv4 addresses. We'll talk about the advantages and disadvantages of using NAT for this purpose.

You will learn that there are four types of NAT and find that using NAT for security is not the best use of NAT. We'll also configure the popular NATP and see how and where the IPv4 addresses on the Illustrated Network are translated.

This chapter deals with a common TCP/IP practice, network address translation (NAT). NAT is used to conceal the true public IPv4 addresses of a device by using substitute IPv4 addresses in packet headers. NAT is usually performed by customer-edge (site) routers or hubs, and is more sophisticated today than the older methods of simply using private RFC 1918 addresses whenever one liked.

Although often presented as a security feature, NAT (properly called "IP NAT" because there are many types of network addresses that can be translated) was invented in RFC 1631 to address the shortage of IPv4 addresses while the world waited for IPv6. NAT is still not an official Internet standard, but it is a very common practice and a feature of many routers, hubs, and remote access devices.

When NAT was introduced, it was immediately embraced to address the simple fact that IPv4 addresses were limited. Any organization that had only a Class C address (back then) would be attracted to a way to allow more than 250 or so devices to access the Internet at the same time.

In this chapter, we'll be using the equipment shown in Figure 27.1. We'll configure the CE0 at the edge of the network router to do NAT for the clients on LAN1 (`bsdclient` and `wincli1`). Before we configure NAT, we'll have to explore all of the types of NAT we could use and then configure one of these types for LAN1.

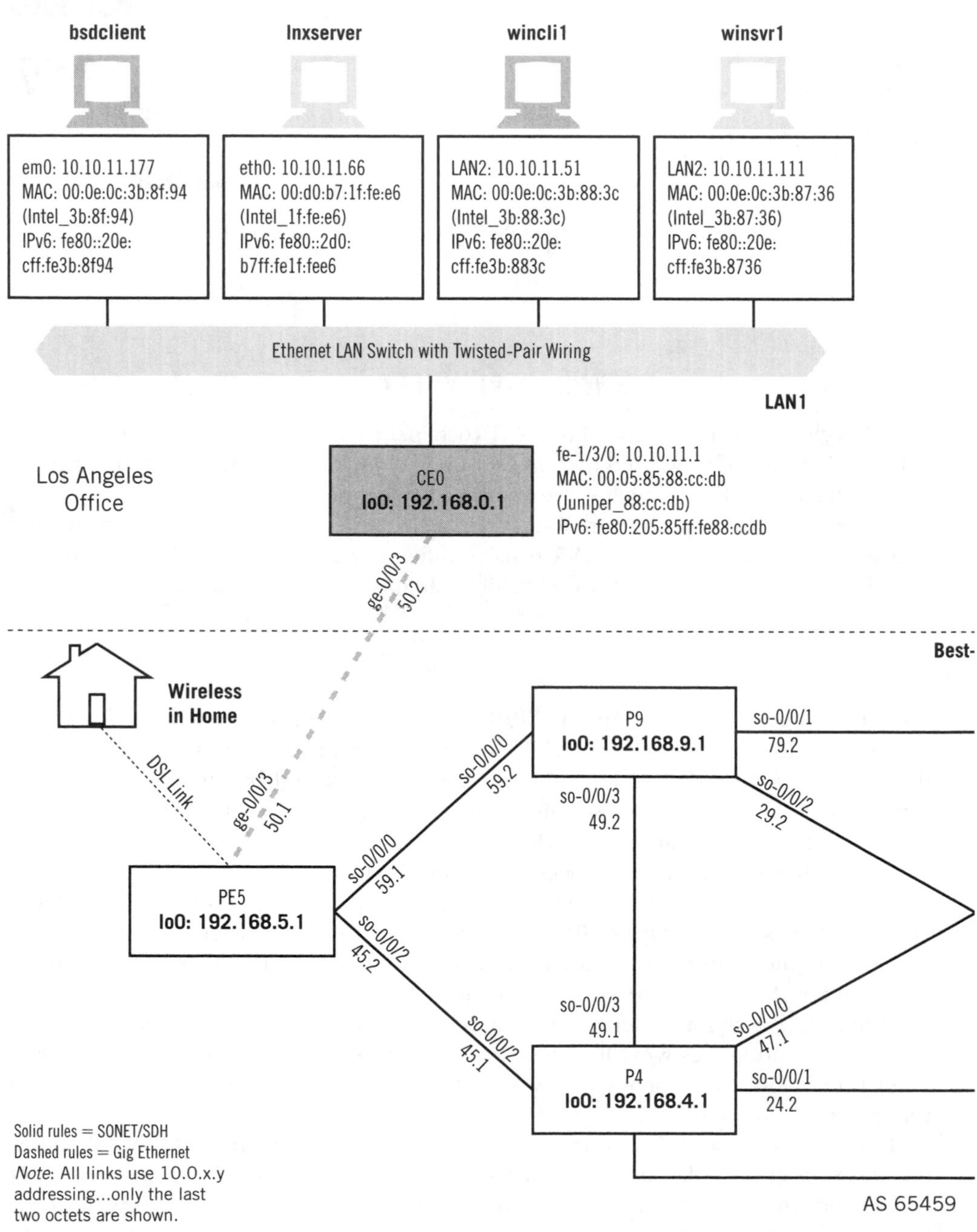

FIGURE 27.1

NAT on the Illustrated Network showing NAT configured on CE0 for the use of two hosts on LAN1.

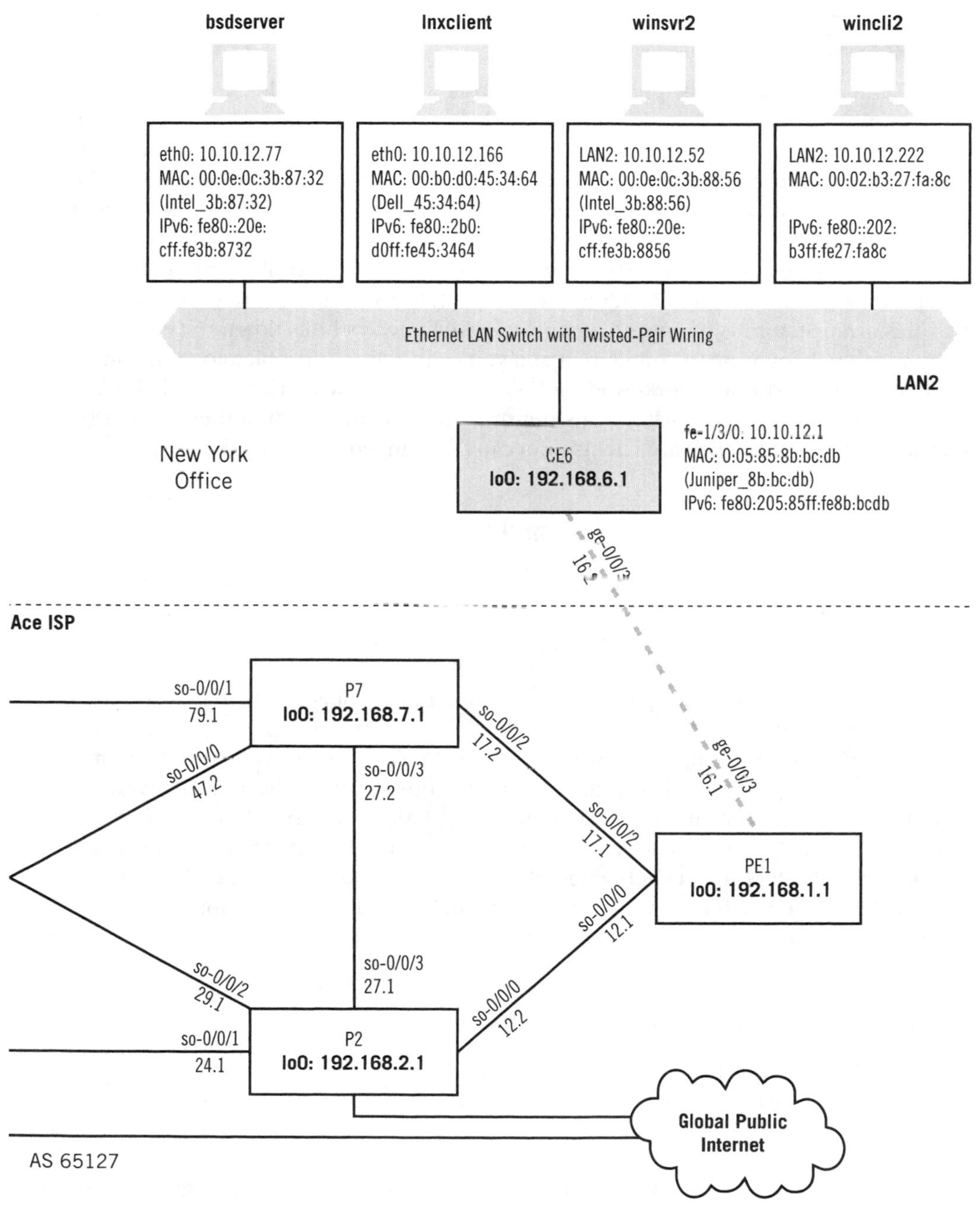
bsdserver
lnxclient
winsvr2
wincli2
eth0: 10.10.12.77
MAC: 00:0e:0c:3b:87:32
(Intel_3b:87:32)
IPv6: fe80::20e:
cff:fe3b:8732
eth0: 10.10.12.166
MAC: 00:b0:d0:45:34:64
(Dell_45:34:64)
IPv6: fe80::2b0:
d0ff:fe45:3464
LAN2: 10.10.12.52
MAC: 00:0e:0c:3b:88:56
(Intel_3b:88:56)
IPv6: fe80::20e:
cff:fe3b:8856
LAN2: 10.10.12.222
MAC: 00:02:b3:27:fa:8c
IPv6: fe80::202:
b3ff:fe27:fa8c
Ethernet LAN Switch with Twisted-Pair Wiring
LAN2
New York
Office
CE6
lo0: 192.168.6.1
fe-1/3/0: 10.10.12.1
MAC: 0:05:85:8b:bc:db
(Juniper_8b:bc:db)
IPv6: fe80:205:85ff:fe8b:bcdb
ge-0/0/3
16.2
Ace ISP
so-0/0/1
79.1
P7
lo0: 192.168.7.1
so-0/0/2
17.2
ge-0/0/3
16.1
so-0/0/0
47.2
so-0/0/3
27.2
so-0/0/2
17.1
PE1
lo0: 192.168.1.1
so-0/0/0
12.1
so-0/0/2
29.1
so-0/0/3
27.1
so-0/0/0
12.2
so-0/0/1
24.1
P2
lo0: 192.168.2.1
Global Public
Internet
AS 65127

USING NAT

With NAT, a network could support 500 or so hosts with private addresses, and the NAT router could translate these to the public IP address range when the client needed Internet access. After all, the remote server replied blindly to the source IP address, which only needed to be routable and not private. NAT devices could even allow ports to be part of the process (and know that a server's reply to `10.10.11.177:30567` is different from a reply to `10.10.11.177:31420`), even though the IP addresses were the same.

Many DSL access devices ("DSL routers") still use this "trick" to allow multiple home computers to share a single IP address from the ISP. Many ISPs are careful to point out that this arrangement is often *not supported*, which always boils down to two things: They won't tell you how to configure it and you can't report a problem on it if you do configure it and it doesn't work. Modern NAT devices know which addresses belong to servers (and should be translated consistently so that clients can find them, or not be translated at all) and which are clients (and can be changed with abandon).

NAT and IPv6

Why does this chapter only talk about NAT and IPv4? What happened to IPv6? What happened is that RFC 4864 released in May 2007 contained more than 30 pages in which it was patiently explained that NAT is *not* a security feature (as pointed out in this chapter) and should be thought of solely as a way to extend the availability of IPv4 address space. Once the huge address space in IPv6 is available, there is no need for NAT.

RFC 4864 points out that everything NAT does can be done in IPv6 without any additional protocols. These native IPv6 features include the use of privacy addresses (RFC 3041), unique local addresses (ULAs, as described in RFC 4193), the use of DHCPv6, and so on. In other words, they are things that we have already talked about which can enable internal addressing masking from the global network. For these reasons, as well as the limitations of space, we will not deal with IPv6 in this chapter.

Advantages and Disadvantages of NAT

Today, NAT still offers advantages, but these often have to be balanced against some disadvantages, especially when coupled with current security practices. The advantages to using NAT follow:

Address sharing—A small number of IP addresses can support a larger pool of devices.

Ease of expansion—If the number of hosts grows beyond the public IPv4 space assigned, it's easy to add hosts.

Local control—Administrators essentially run their own private piece of the public Internet.

Easy ISP changeover—When host addresses are private, public ISP addresses can be changed more easily.

Mainly transparent—Usually, only a handful of devices have to know the NAT rules for a site.

Security—Oversold, but still seen as an advantage. Hackers don't know the "real" client's IP address, true, but the true targets are often servers and the NAT "firewalls" themselves.

These NAT pluses have to be balanced against the current list of disadvantages.

Complexity—NAT adds management complexity and makes even routine troubleshooting more difficult.

Public address sensitivity—Private addresses are favored by hackers. Some applications and devices raise flags when presented with private addresses. (One FTP application used for this book insisted on needing to know the "real" public network IP address of the host before it would work properly!)

Application compatibility issues—NAT is not totally transparent. Applications such as FTP, which embed IP addresses and port numbers in data (such as the PASV and PORT messages), must be handled with special care by NAT routers.

Poor host accessibility—NAT makes it difficult to contact local devices from the outside world. NAT is not a good solution for Web sites, FTP servers, or even peer protocols (VoIP) running on a local LAN.

Performance concerns—The burden of hundreds of simultaneous Internet access users today often degrades NAT router performance for its main task: routing packets.

Security—Both a plus and a minus. Modern protocols such as IPSec raise alarms when packet fields are changed between end systems. You can still combine NAT and IPsec (carefully), but keeping NAT as a "security feature" in addition to IPSec can be tricky.

Four Types of NAT

NAT is still a popular thing to do on a network. There are even the following four slightly different versions of NAT that are supported in many routers, and most are known by a number of unofficial names.

- Unidirectional NAT (outbound or "traditional" NAT)
- Bidirectional NAT (inbound or "two-way" NAT)
- Port-based ("overloaded" NAT, or NAPT or PAT)
- Overlapping NAT ("twice NAT")

All of these methods are a little different, but all involve use of the same terms to describe the addresses that are translated. An address can be *inside* or *outside*, based on whether it is used on the local LAN (inside) or on the Internet (outside). Addresses can also be local or global, based on whether they are drawn from the private RFC 1918 address ranges (local) or publicly registered or obtained from an ISP (global).

NAT therefore encompasses about four address "types," which are listed in Table 27.1. In the table, the Martian address ranges `169.254.0.0/16` (used for IPv4 autoconfiguration) and `250.0.0./8` (experimental) are used as "public" addresses to preserve the Illustrated Network's policy of never using public IP addresses as examples.

In addition, the translational *mappings* that NAT performs can be static or dynamic. Static translations establish a fixed relationship between inside and outside addresses, whereas dynamic mappings allow this relationship to change between one translation and another. These can be mixed, using static mapping for servers (for example) and dynamic for clients, much like DHCP. DNS can be used for NAT purposes as well. Let's look at how each NAT variation uses these address translation terms and procedures.

Table 27.1 Address Types Used in NAT with Chapter's Example Values

Type of Address	Example	Common Use
Inside local	10.100.100.27	Client's "native" address used as source in outbound packets and destination inbound
Outside local	172.16.100.13	Destination address used by client
Inside global	169.254.99.1	Client's public address, range assigned by ISP
Outside global	250.99.111.4	Source and destination address used on Internet

Unidirectional NAT

Let's examine an example for outbound or traditional NAT that will repeat addresses from one NAT type to the other as we show how they differ. Assume that the LAN has 250 hosts that use private (inside local) addresses in the `10.100.100.0/24` range. These hosts use dynamic NAT to share a pool of 20 inside global addresses in the range `169.254.99.1` through `169.254.99.20`.

Suppose client host `10.100.100.27` accesses the Web server at public address `250.99.111.4` using unidirectional NAT. What will the router do to the packet addresses and what will the addresses look like at each step along the way—inside to NAT, NAT to outside, outside to NAT, and NAT to inside? Figure 27.2 shows the four steps.

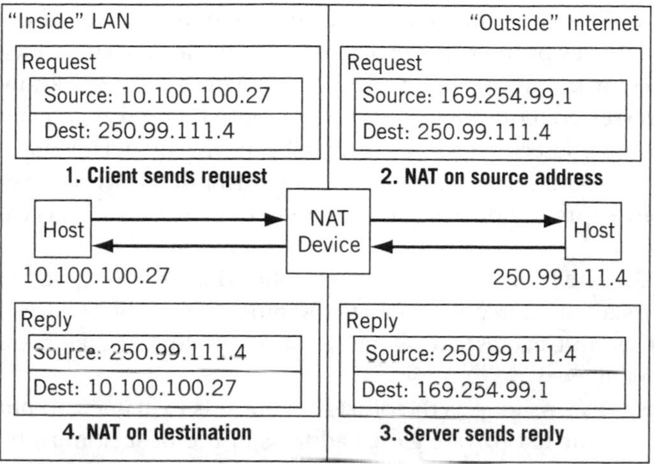

FIGURE 27.2

Unidirectional NAT. Note that only the LAN source address is translated, and in one direction.

The client's packet to the server at `250.99.111.4` has its source address changed from `10.100.100.27` (inside private) to `169.254.99.1` (outside global, which must be a routable address). The server replies by swapping source and destination address, and the reply (matching up in the NAT device to the request) is translated back to `10.100.100.27`. No one outside the organization knows which host "really" has address `10.100.100.27`, although dynamic NAT is better at this concealment than a static NAT mapping.

It might seem that dynamic mapping would always be the proper NAT choice. However, a complication arises when there are two site routers (as is often the case). If the request is sent by one NAT router and the reply received by another NAT router, the translation tables must be the same or chaos will result. Unless the routers constantly communicate NAT information (how?), this makes it difficult to use dynamic mapping.

NAT also handles adjustments other than address translation. The IP checksum must be changed, as well as UPD/TCP checksums. FTP embeds address and port information in data, and these should be changed as well. Finally, ICMP messages include initial header bytes, and even these should be changed when an ICMP message is the reply to a request.

Traditional NAT only handles this type of outbound translation. It cannot handle requests from a device on the public Internet to access a server on the private network (LAN).

Bidirectional NAT

Let's use the same basic scenario that we employed in the unidirectional NAT example, but upgrade the NAT router to use inbound or two-way NAT. The major difference is that bidirectional NAT allows requests to be initiated from the global public Internet to hosts on the private inside LAN.

This type of NAT is more difficult to implement because, whereas inside users generally know the public addresses of Internet devices, outside devices have no idea what private addresses represent the device on the LAN. And even if they *did* know them, private RFC 1918 addresses are not routable, so there would be no way to get a packet there anyway. (Home DSL routers, which normally all use NAT by default, have led to an explosion of `10.0.0.0/8` and `192.168.0.0/16` devices around the world—yet another reason ISPs refuse to support home servers unless covered by the service offering.)

Static NAT mapping, one for one from local device to public address, is one way to handle the "outside request" issue. Of course, this defeats the more-than-public-address-space support that NAT offers, and makes any security claims hollow. (Packets are blindly forwarded to the target anyway.)

The other solution is to use DNS. As long as the outside request is by name and not IP address, DNS can provide the current private global address of the host (it must be global because it must be routable). In other words, DNS and NAT can work together (as described in RFC 2694), which adds extensions for NAT to DNS. This solution uses dynamic NAT and is a four-step process. The outside client sends a request to DNS to get the IP address that goes, for instance, with `www.natusedhere.com`.

The authoritative DNS server for the `natusedhere.com` domain resolves the name into an inside local (private) address for the host, perhaps `10.100.100.27`, as before. The inside local address is now sent to the local NAT device to create a dynamic mapping between this private address and an inside global (public and routable) address. This mapping is used in the NAT translation table. For this example, we'll use `169.254.99.1`, as before.

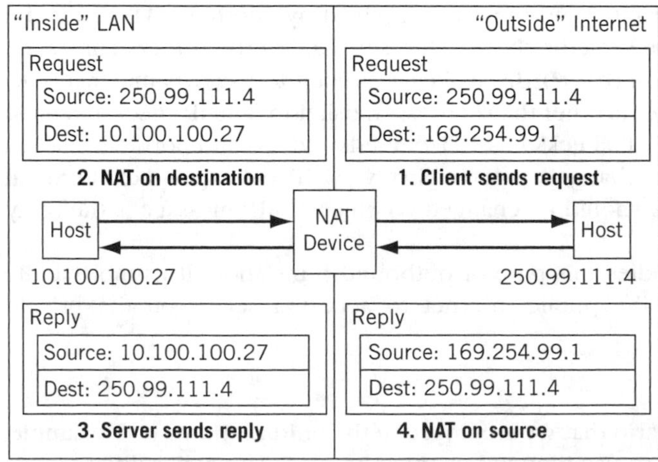

FIGURE 27.3

Bidirectional NAT, showing the direction in reverse from the previous figure. Note the reversal of number sequence and initiating client location.

The DNS server replies not with the private (nonroutable) address, but with the mapped address in the NAT reply (in this case, 169.254.99.1), as established in the previous step. Once this DNS/NAT procedure is complete, the transaction in bidirectional NAT continues (as shown in Figure 27.3).

Naturally, requests from local LAN devices are still handled as in unidirectional NAT.

Port-Based NAT

In both unidirectional and bidirectional NAT, the address translation is always one to one. Even when dynamic mapping is used, the entire inside address is always swapped out for an outside address. But we set up our examples by saying that 250 LAN hosts are going to share only 20 public IP addresses.

Unidirectional and bidirectional NAT handles 20 or fewer simultaneous Internet users on the LAN. But what happens when more than 20 hosts are trying to access the Internet all at the same time?

That's where port-based NAT, also called overloaded NAT, comes in. Some devices even advertise this as network/port address translation (NAPT) or port address translation (PAT), but we'll just call it port-based NAT.

We are now essentially translating *sockets* from inside to outside. With port-based NAT, we can easily have all 250 devices with outstanding requests on the Internet all at the same time and never come close to running out of port numbers (which run from 0 to 65,535).

Let's say that one host on the LAN is already using private address 10.100.100.27 and source port 17000 (perhaps the browser always uses that source port number) to contact a Web site. No problem. Port-based NAT just translates both IP address and port, as shown in Figure 27.4.

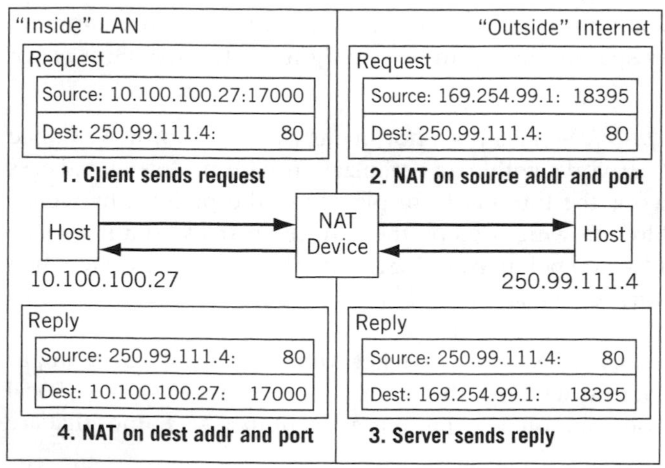

FIGURE 27.4

Port-based NAT, showing translation on both address and port.

Port-based NAT is usually how DSL routers share a single ISP address among four or more home PCs. Most NAT implementations today are capable of port-based operation. However, this does not mean it's always done when available. Not all applications or their packets use UDP or TCP ports, and port-based NAT cannot be done on these packets.

Overlapping NAT

This last type of NAT, also called "Twice NAT," is quite different from the three other types. All three previous types used private nonroutable IP addresses as a "substitute" for global routable IP addresses. NAT routers immediately assume that any packets drawn from the local LAN's private IP address space are a reference to a host within the local LAN. Anything else belongs to the outside world.

But what if the inside addresses *overlap* entirely or in part with addresses used in the outside world? In other words, what if there is another `10.100.100.0/24` address range on the "outside" that the local device using that private address space must communicate with? There are three major cases where inside addresses on a LAN might be duplicated in the outside world.

Private network to private network—NAT routers tend to use the same private address ranges, such as `10.0.0.0/8` (Cisco DSL routers and more) or `192.168.0.0/16` (Linksys products and others). So, this situation arises in DSL router configurations (such as neighbor to neighbor) all the time. And organizations often merge and find two sites now using the same private IP address ranges.

Reassigned addresses—Many customers get their IP address space from their ISP. But what if they change ISPs? The ISP is certainly free to offer that space to someone else. Instead of flash-cutting every IP address on the network, NAT can be used for the new ISP until cut-over is complete. And even if customers pay for their own address spaces, these can be reassigned if the payment is not up to date.

Private IP networks going "public"—This does not occur as often, but it was once common to have huge IP networks within an organization with no Internet access at all. (Networks are for work, the Internet is for play, or so the philosophy went.) So who cared what IP addresses were used on the private network? But if a space such as `9.0.0.0/8` is used (which belonged to IBM) something must be done when Internet connections become essential.

Thus, when a host on the local LAN sends a packet from `10.100.100.27` going to `10.100.100.10`, how does it know whether the address is truly local or not? Local frames have local MAC addresses, but "outside" packets are sent in MAC frames that are sent to the router.

Someone has to know where the other address is or there will be no solution. As before, DNS will coordinate with NAT to supply the answer. Overlapping NAT translates *both* source and destination address.

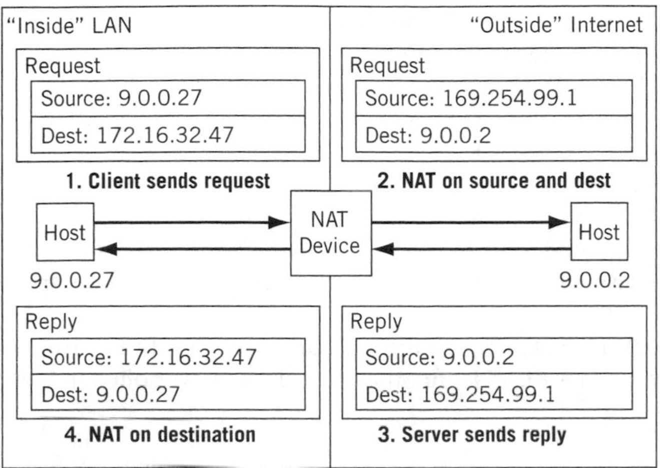

FIGURE 27.5

Overlapping NAT showing how a large corporation can use this form with public and private addresses.

Let's consider a new example. Our local host is on a LAN that uses the public IP address space `9.0.0.0/8` as a private address. Local host `9.0.0.27` needs to send to a server that turns out to be at IBM and is also `9.0.0.2`. The following is what happens.

Local client `9.0.0.27` sends a DNS request to get the address of the Web server at *www.twicenatusedhere.com*. The NAT router (which must support overlapping NAT, of course) on the local network intercepts the DNS request and uses a table to construct a special mapping for this query. Let's assume that it will translate `www.twicenatusedhere.com` into address `172.16.32.47` (another private IP address space). The NAT router knows the real public address of the IBM server, of course.

The NAT router returns this private address to the client, which uses it as the destination address. The NAT router now knows that packets sent to this IP address are for the Web server *outside* the LAN.

The NAT operation now functions as shown in Figure 27.5. Note the use of the `169.254.99.1` address, which is within the public IP address space of the local LAN.

The NAT is still useful for port-based operations where overloading makes sense (as with home LANs and DSL) and overlapping IP address spaces. However, NAT should never be used as a security method, if only because it gives a false sense of security to users and network administrators.

NAT IN ACTION

What type of NAT should we configure for the Illustrated Network? This could get tricky because we've been using private IP addresses as public addresses all along. To make it clear what we're doing, we'll limit our NAT activities to LAN1 and use part of the 172.16.0.0/16 private address space as a public address space for our NAT pool (which we've not used much so far). Because some applications are more sensitive to substituted addresses than others (such as FTP), we'll limit our NAT implementation to clients. Because the servers are affected, we'll use dynamic source NAT. Finally, we'll configure the popular port-based NAT (NATP).

First, we have to configure a pool of addresses called NATP-address-pool to use for NAT on CE0. We'll map our 10.10.11.0/24 address space to the range from 172.16.11.0 to 172.16.11.255. We'll set port selection to automatic so that we don't have to worry about the port range used. We also have to create the "rule" that subjects' packets arriving on the LAN1 interface to NAT.

The AS PIC is smart enough to match up returning traffic. (We apply the rule in both the input and output direction for LAN1.) In others words, NAT is applied in both directions for NATP.

```
set services nat pool NATP-address-pool address-range low 172.16.11.0
    high 172.16.11.255; # establish to address range to use
set services nat pool NATP-address-pool port automatic;
    # port translaton will be done automatically
set services nat rule SOURCE-NAT match-direction input-output;
    # NATP will be applied to all packets in either direction
set services nat rule SOURCE-NAT term NO-NAT-FOR-SERVERS from
    source-address 10.10.11.66; # lnxserver should not be translated
set services nat rule SOURCE-NAT term NO-NAT-FOR-SERVERS from
    source-address 10.10.11.111; # winsrvr1 should not be translated
set services nat rule SOURCE-NAT term NO-NAT-FOR-SERVERS then
    no-translation; # this is a keyword for this action
set services nat rule SOURCE-NAT term SOURCE-NAT then translated
    translation-type source dynamic; # if not a server, translate
set services nat rule SOURCE-NAT term SOURCE-NAT then translated
    source-pool NATP-address-pool; # use automatic port assignments
```

The absence of a from clause in the term SOURCE-NAT means that the then clause actions are applied to all packets that do not match the term NO-NAT-FOR-SERVERS, which is what we want to do. On the Juniper Networks router model used on our network, NAT (and several other specialized services) is performed by a special internal interface card called an Adaptive Service Physical Interface Card (AS PIC). This architecture allows the router to forward packets as fast as it can and off-loads any special packet processing to this service's interface.

Once configured, packets arriving on the LAN1 interface that are subject to NAT are not forwarded right away but sent to the AS PIC interface, which has an internal IP address. Once NAT has been performed, the packets are sent back into the main part of the router for normal table lookups and forwarding.

To get the packet to the AS PIC interface (sp-0/2/0 on CE0), we give the internal interface an IP address (just as any other interface). Then we apply the configured NAT "service set" (which we'll call SOURCE-NATP) to the LAN interface we want to apply NAT source address translation to. Another static "next-hop" routing rule gets the translated packets back to the forwarding portion of the router. (We also have to advertise a static route for the NAT address space so that the other routers know where to send packets sent back to the 172.16.11.0/24 address space, but the complete CE0 router configuration for NAT is not shown.) The interface to LAN1 and the AS PIC interface are configured as follows.

```
set interface fe-1/3/0 unit 0 family inet service input service-set
  SOURCE-NATP;
    # lconfiguration of the SOURCE-NATP service set is not shown
set interface fe-1/3/0 unit 0 family inet service output service-set
  SOURCE-NATP;
set interface fe-1/3/0 unit 0 family inet address 10.10.11.1/24;
    # this is a regular LAN1 interface address

set interface sp-0/2/0 unit 0 family inet address 172.16.1.1/24;
    # the sp- interface needs and IP address too
```

We'll say a little more about the "next-hop" configuration and service sets in Chapter 28 (on stateful firewalls). How do we know that the NAT translation is working? Let's use our little echo test program from the UDP chapter to send packets from bsdclient on LAN1 at IP address 10.10.11.177 to lnxclient on LAN2 at IP address 10.10.12.166. We'll capture the packets on lnxclient with tethereal. As expected, the source address *has* been translated to one in the 172.16.11.0/24 range.

```
[root@lnxclient admin]# /usr/sbin/tethereal -V
Capturing on eth0
Frame 1 (60 bytes on wire, 60 bytes captured)
    Arrival Time: Feb  6, 2008 11:16:03.822845000
    Time delta from previous packet: 0.000000000 seconds
    Time relative to first packet: 0.000000000 seconds
    Frame Number: 1
    Packet Length: 60 bytes
    Capture Length: 60 bytes
Ethernet II, Src: 00:0e:0c:3b:8f:94, Dst: 00:b0:d0:45:34:64
    Destination: 00:b0:d0:45:34:64 (Intel_45:34:64)
    Source: 00:0e:0c:3b:8f:94 (Intel_3b:8f:94)
    Type: IP (0x0800)
    Trailer: 000000000000000000000000000
Internet Protocol, Src Addr: 172.16.11.177 (172.16.11.177), Dst Addr:
    10.10.12.166 (10.10.12.166)
    Version: 4
    Header length: 20 bytes
...
```

However, LAN1 traffic from the servers is not translated. This time, we'll run the echo test program from lnxserver on LAN1 at IP address 10.10.11.66 to lnxclient on LAN2 at IP address 10.10.12.166. We'll capture the packets on lnxclient with tethereal. As expected, the source address has *not* been translated to one in the 172.16.11.0/24 range.

```
[root@lnxclient admin]# /usr/sbin/tethereal -V
Capturing on eth0
Frame 1 (60 bytes on wire, 60 bytes captured)
    Arrival Time: Feb  6, 2008 14:37:24.487934000
    Time delta from previous packet: 0.000000000 seconds
    Time relative to first packet: 0.000000000 seconds
    Frame Number: 1
    Packet Length: 60 bytes
    Capture Length: 60 bytes
Ethernet II, Src: 00:d0:b7:1f:fe:e6, Dst: 00:b0:d0:45:34:64
    Destination: 00:b0:d0:45:34:64 (Intel_45:34:64)
    Source: 00:05:85:88:cc:db (Intel_1f:fe:e6)
    Type: IP (0x0800)
    Trailer: 0000000000000000000000000000
Internet Protocol, Src Addr: 10.10.11.66 (10.10.11.66), Dst Addr:
    10.10.12.166 (10.10.12.166)
    Version: 4
    Header length: 20 bytes
...
```

QUESTIONS FOR READERS

The captured listing here shows some of the concepts discussed in this chapter and can be used to answer the following questions.

```
[root@lnxclient admin]# /usr/sbin/tethereal -V port 7
Capturing on eth0
Frame 1 (60 bytes on wire, 60 bytes captured)
    Arrival Time: Feb  6, 2008 16:43:22.458233000
    Time delta from previous packet: 0.000000000 seconds
    Time relative to first packet: 0.000000000 seconds
    Frame Number: 1
    Packet Length: 60 bytes
    Capture Length: 60 bytes
Ethernet II, Src: 00:d0:b7:1f:fe:e6, Dst: 00:b0:d0:45:34:64
    Destination: 00:b0:d0:45:34:64 (Intel_45:34:64)
    Source: 00:05:85:88:cc:db (Intel_1f:fe:e6)
    Type: IP (0x0800)
    Trailer: 000000000000000000000000000
Internet Protocol, Src Addr: 176.16.11.78 (176.16.11.78), Dst Addr:
    10.10.12.166 (10.10.12.166)
    Version: 4
    Header length: 20 bytes
...
```

1. Which host has this capture been run on?
2. Which host is responding to the echo?
3. What is the translated address used on the LAN1 host that responded to the echo?
4. What is the host name of the device on LAN1 that responded to the echo?
5. The port numbers are not displayed in the listing. Based on the NAT configuration on CE0, should the port number be translated as well?

CHAPTER

Firewalls

28

What You Will Learn

In this chapter, you will learn how firewalls add security to TCP/IP networks. We'll be working with both kinds of router-based firewalls: packet filters and stateful inspection.

You will learn about the types of dedicated firewalls that run on purpose-built hardware. We'll also examine firewall architectures and the use of DMZs. And because filtering works exactly the same with IPv6 as with IPv4, we will not have a special section on IPv6 firewalls.

If all data traveled the Internet encrypted inside VPNs, and all hosts only sent or received such data, the Internet would be a safer place. But the reality is messy—very messy—and denial of service attacks, hacker raids, spyware, spam, viruses, and worms make life interesting for everyone on-line.

As we write these words, teams are assembled in Las Vegas, Nevada, for the annual Defcon "contest." The name derives from Cold War "defense condition" levels and implies that hackers could have broken into military computers and started WW III, a plot device in several movies and books. Teams pay a small entry fee and compete in local and regional contests, all culminating in the finale in Las Vegas. The idea is to capture the secure "flags" or tokens on target systems set up for Defcon. All competitors' tokens are fair game, but, of course, you have to protect your own. (Taking over a competing team's network or Web server is considered a great coup.) Points are awarded for various successful exploits, and the winner is admired by all.

A certain percentage of people learning about networks and TCP/IP seem to indulge in some form of hacking at one time or another. It seems to be a rite of passage, like clubbing and drug experimentation. But most slackers eventually settle down and get real jobs, whereas a few others continue their dissolute ways. Some even make a career of their activities, as "white" or "black" hackers, and show up at places like Defcon. Hackers should never be judged solely on their appearance or demeanor, but only on their actions, which usually have consequences for everyone—intended or not.

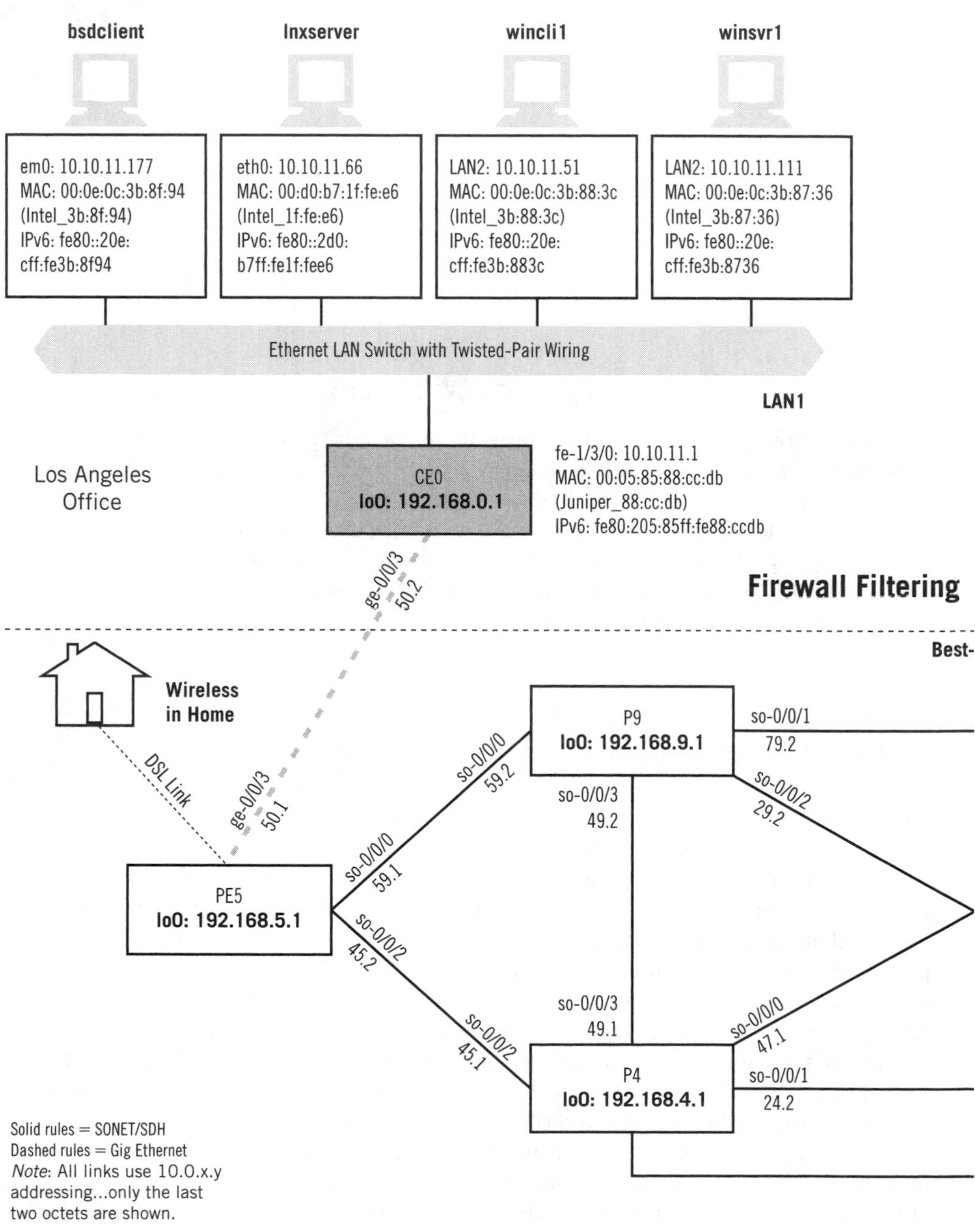

FIGURE 28.1

Firewalls on the Illustrated Network, showing how the firewall filtering is performed on the site routers.

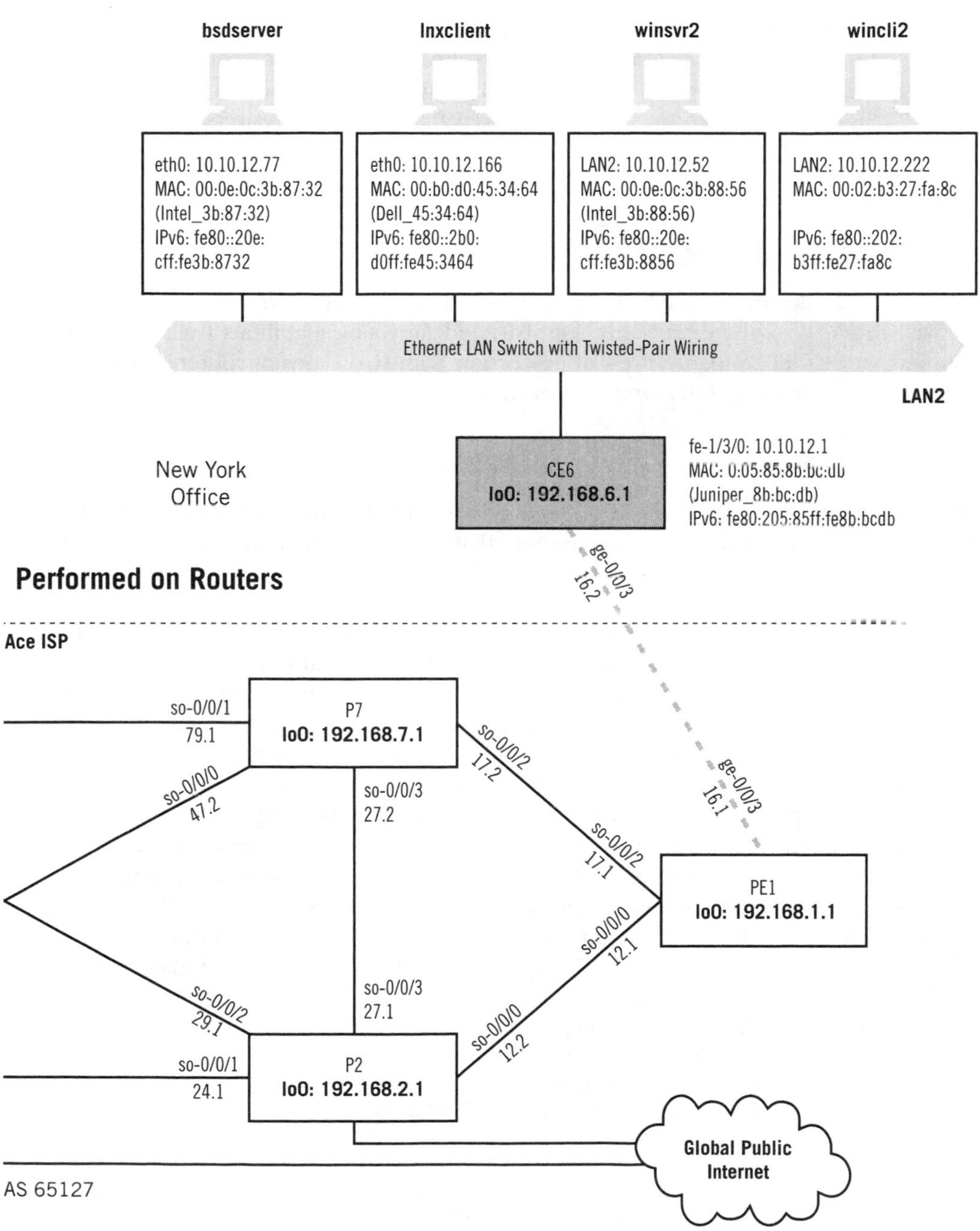

bsdserver
lnxclient
winsvr2
wincli2
eth0: 10.10.12.77
MAC: 00:0e:0c:3b:87:32
(Intel_3b:87:32)
IPv6: fe80::20e:
cff:fe3b:8732
eth0: 10.10.12.166
MAC: 00:b0:d0:45:34:64
(Dell_45:34:64)
IPv6: fe80::2b0:
d0ff:fe45:3464
LAN2: 10.10.12.52
MAC: 00:0e:0c:3b:88:56
(Intel_3b:88:56)
IPv6: fe80::20e:
cff:fe3b:8856
LAN2: 10.10.12.222
MAC: 00:02:b3:27:fa:8c
IPv6: fe80::202:
b3ff:fe27:fa8c
Ethernet LAN Switch with Twisted-Pair Wiring
LAN2
New York
Office
CE6
lo0: 192.168.6.1
fe-1/3/0: 10.10.12.1
MAC: 0:05:85:8b:bc:db
(Juniper_8b:bc:db)
IPv6: fe80:205:85ff:fe8b:bcdb
ge-0/0/3
16.2
Performed on Routers
Ace ISP
so-0/0/1
79.1
P7
lo0: 192.168.7.1
so-0/0/2
17.2
ge-0/0/3
16.1
so-0/0/0
47.2
so-0/0/3
27.2
so-0/0/2
17.1
PE1
lo0: 192.168.1.1
so-0/0/0
12.1
so-0/0/2
29.1
so-0/0/3
27.1
so-0/0/0
12.2
so-0/0/1
24.1
P2
lo0: 192.168.2.1
Global Public
Internet
AS 65127

This chapter takes a look at firewalls, one technique for adding security to TCP/IP and the Internet. Firewalls can be hardware or software designed to protect individual hosts, clients, and servers or entire LANs from the one or more of the threats previously cited. We'll implement a couple of types of firewalls on our site routers, as shown in Figure 28.1.

WHAT FIREWALLS DO

Although the Illustrated Network has no dedicated firewall device (often called a firewall *appliance*), there are fairly sophisticated firewall capabilities built into our routers. So, we will configure firewall protection with two types of router-based firewall rules: *packet filters* and *stateful inspection*.

A Router Packet Filter

Let's do something fairly simple yet effective with a firewall packet filter on the Juniper Networks router on LAN2, CE6. Assume that malicious users on LAN1 are trying to harm `bsdserver` (`10.10.12.77`) on LAN2. We'll have to "protect" it from some of the hosts on LAN1.

We'll allow remote access with Telnet (this is just an example) or SSH from the `bsdclient` (`10.10.11.177`), and allow similar access attempts from `wincli1` (`10.10.11.51`), but log them. (What do those Windows guys want on the FreeBSD server?) We'll deny and log access from `lnxserver` (`10.10.11.66`) and `winsrv1` (`10.10.11.111`) because security policy for the organization has decided that users attempting remote access from servers are not allowed to do so.

The following is the firewall filter configured on CE6 and applied to the LAN2 interface. This filters IPv4 addresses, but we could easily make another to do the same thing for these hosts' IPv6 addresses. It is a good idea to keep in mind that `from` is more in the sense of "out of all packets," especially when the filter is applied on the output side of an interface. We also have to apply the filter to the `fe-1/3/0` interface, but this configuration snippet is not shown. There is a space between the three major terms of the `remote-access-control` filter: `allow-bsdclient`, `log-wincli`, and `deny-servers`. These names are strictly up to the person configuring the firewall filter.

```
set firewall family inet filter remote-access-control term
    allow-bsdclient from address 10.10.11.177/32; # bsdclient
set firewall family inet filter remote-access-control term
    allow-bsdclient from protocol tcp; # telnet and ssh use tcp
set firewall family inet filter remote-access-control term
    allow-bsdclient from port [ ssh telnet ]; # we could use numbers too
set firewall family inet filter remote-access-control term
    allow-bsdclient then accept; # allow bsdclient access

set firewall family inet filter remote-access-control term
    log-wincli1 from address 10.10.11.51/32; # wincli1
```

```
set firewall family inet filter remote-access-control term
    log-wincli1 from protocol tcp; # telnet and ssh use tcp
set firewall family inet filter remote-access-control term
    log-wincli1 from port [ ssh telnet ]; # we could use numbers too
set firewall family inet filter remote-access-control term
    log-wincli1 then log; # log wincli1 access attempts...
set firewall family inet filter remote-access-control term
    log-wincli then accept; # ...and allow wincli1 access

set firewall family inet filter remote-access-control term
    deny-servers from address 10.10.11.66/32; # lnxserver
set firewall family inet filter remote-access-control term
    deny-servers from address 10.10.11.111/32; # winsrv1
set firewall family inet filter remote-access-control term
    deny-servers from protocol tcp; # telnet and ssh use tcp
set firewall family inet filter remote-access-control term
    deny-servers from port [ ssh telnet ]; # we could use numbers too
set firewall family inet filter remote-access-control term
    deny-servers then log; # log server access attempts...
set firewall family inet filter remote-access-control term
    deny-servers then discard; # ...and silently discard those packets
```

When we try to remotely log in from bsdclient or wincli1, we succeed (and wincli1 is logged). But when we attempt access from the servers, the following is what happens.

```
lnxserver# ssh 10.10.12.77
```

Nothing! We set the action to discard, which silently throws the packet away. A reject action at least sends an ICMP destination unreachable message back to the host. When we examine the firewall log on CE6, this is what we see. Action "A" is accept, and "D" is discard. We didn't log bsdclient, but caught the others. (The filter name is blank because not all filter names that are configured are available for the log.)

```
admin@CE6> show firewall log
Time      Filter     A Interface     Pro Source address    Destination Address
08:36:09 -           A fe-1/3/0.0    TCP 10.10.11.51       10.10.12.77
08:37:24 -           D fe-1/3/0.0    TCP 10.10.11.66       10.10.12.77
```

Stateful Inspection on a Router

Simple packet filters do not maintain a history of the streams of packets, nor do they know anything about the relationship between sequential packets. They cannot detect flows or more sophisticated attacks that rely on a sequence of packets with specific bits set. This degree of intelligence requires a different type of firewall, one that performs stateful inspection. (There are three types of firewall, as we'll see later.)

In contrast to a stateless firewall filter that inspects packets singly and in isolation, stateful filters consider state information from past communications and applications to make dynamic decisions about new communications attempts. To do this, stateful firewall filters look at *flows* or *conversations* established (normally) by five properties of TCP/IP headers: source and destination address, source and destination port, and protocol. TCP and UDP conversations consist of two flows: *initiation* and *responder*. However, some conversations (such as with FTP) might consist of two control flows and many data flows.

On a Juniper Networks router, stateful inspection is provided by a special hardware component: the Adaptive Services Physical Interface Card (AS PIC). We've already used the AS PIC to implement NAT in the previous chapter. This just adds some configuration statements to the services (such as NAT) provided by the special internal `sp-` (services PIC) interface.

Stateful firewalls do not just check a few TCP/IP header fields as packets fly by on the router. Stateful firewalls are intelligent enough that they can recognize a series of events as anomalies in five major categories.

1. IP packet anomalies
   - Incorrect IP version
   - Too-small or too-large IP header length field
   - Bad header checksum
   - Short IP total packet-length field
   - Incorrect IP options
   - Incorrect ICMP packet length
   - Zero TTL field
2. IP addressing anomalies
   - Broadcast or multicast packet source address
   - Source IP address identical to destination address (land attack)
3. IP fragmentation anomalies
   - Overlapping fragments
   - Missing fragments
   - Length errors
   - Length smaller or larger than allowed
4. TCP anomalies
   - Port 0
   - Sequence number 0 and flags field set to 0
   - Sequence number 0 with FIN/PSH/RST flags set
   - Disallowed flag combinations [FIN with RST, SYN/(URG/FIN/RST)]
   - Bad TCP checksum

5. UDP anomalies
   - Port 0
   - Bad header length
   - Bad UDP checksum

In addition, stateful firewall filters detect the following events, which are only detectable by following a flow of packets.

- SYN followed by SYN-ACK packets without an ACK from initiator
- SYN followed by RST packets
- SYN without SYN-ACK
- Non-SYN first packet in a flow
- ICMP unreachable errors for SYN packets
- ICMP unreachable errors for UDP packets

Stateful firewall filters, like other firewall filters, are also applied to an interface in the outbound or inbound direction (or both). However, the traffic on the interface must be sent to the AS PIC in order to apply the stateful firewall filter rules.

The AS PIC's `sp-` interface must be given an IP address, just as any other interface on the router. Traffic then makes its way to the AS PIC by using the AS PIC's IP address as a next hop for traffic on the interface. The next hop for traffic leaving the AS PIC (assuming the packet has not been filtered) is the "normal" routing table for transit traffic, `inet0`.

Stateful firewall filters follow the same `from` and `then` structure of other firewall filters. Keep in mind that `from` is more in the sense of "out of all packets," especially when the filter is applied on the output side of an interface. When applied to the LAN1 interface on the CE0 interface, in addition to detecting all of the anomalies previously listed, this stateful firewall filter will allow only FTP traffic onto the LAN unless it is from LAN2 and silently discards (rejects) and logs all packets that do not conform to any of these rules.

```
set stateful-firewall rule LAN1-rule match direction input-output;
set stateful-firewall rule LAN1-rule term allow-LAN2
  from address 10.10.12.0/24; # find the LAN2 IP address space
set stateful-firewall rule LAN1-rule term allow-LAN2
  then accept; # ...and allow it

set stateful-firewall rule LAN1-rule term allow-FTP-HTTP
  from application ftp; # find ftp flows
set stateful-firewall rule LAN1-rule term allow-FTP-HTTP
  then accept; #  ...and allow them

set stateful-firewall rule LAN1-rule term deny-other
  then syslog; # no 'from' matches all packets
set stateful-firewall rule LAN1-rule term deny-other
  then discard; # ...and syslogs and discards them
```

In the term deny-other, the lack of a from means that the term matches all packets that have not been accepted by previous terms. The syslog statement is the way that the stateful firewalls log events. We've also configured the interface sp-1/2/0 and applied our stateful rule as stateful-svc-set (but the details are not shown).

Now when we try to run FTP to (for example) lnxserver from bsdclient or wincli1, we succeed. But watch what happens when we attempt to run FTP from one of the routers (the routers all support both FTP client and server software).

```
admin@CE6> ftp 10.10.11.66
```

Nothing! As before, this packet is silently discarded. But the stateful firewall filter gathers statistics on much more than simply "captured" packets.

```
admin@CE0> show services stateful-firewall statistics extensive
Interface: sp-1/2/0
  Service set: stateful-svc-set
    New flows:
      Accept: 7, Discard: 1, Reject: 0
    Existing flows:
      Accept: 35, Discard: 0, Reject: 0
    Drops:
      IP option: 0, TCP SYN defense: 0
      NAT ports exhausted: 0
    Errors:
      IP: 0, TCP: 0
      UDP: 0, ICMP: 0
      Non-IP packets: 0, ALG: 0
    IP errors:
      IP packet length inconsistencies: 0
      Minimum IP header length check failures: 0
      Reassembled packet exceeds maximum IP length: 0
      Illegal source address: 0
      Illegal destination address: 0
      TTL zero errors: 0, IP protocol number 0 or 255: 0
      Land attack: 0, Smurf attack: 0
      Non IP packets: 0, IP option: 0
      Non-IPv4 packets: 0, Bad checksum: 0
      Illegal IP fragment length: 0
      IP fragment overlap: 0
      IP fragment reassembly timeout: 0
TCP errors:
      TCP header length inconsistencies: 0
      Source or destination port number is zero: 0
      Illegal sequence number, flags combination: 0
      SYN attack (multiple SYNs seen for the same flow): 0
      First packet not SYN: 0
```

```
      TCP port scan (Handshake, RST seen from server for SYN): 0
      Bad SYN cookie response: 0
    UDP errors:
      IP data length less than minimum UDP header length (8 bytes): 0
      Source or destination port is zero: 0
      UDP port scan (ICMP error seen for UDP flow): 0
    ICMP errors:
      IP data length less than minimum ICMP header length (8 bytes): 0
      ICMP error length inconsistencies: 0
      Ping duplicate sequence number: 0
      Ping mismatched sequence number: 0

ALG drops:
      BOOTP: 0, DCE-RPC: 0, DCE-RPC portmap: 0
      DNS: 0, Exec: 0, FTP: 1
      H323: 0, ICMP: 0, IIOP: 0
      Login: 0, Netbios: 0, Netshow: 0
      Realaudio: 0, RPC: 0, RPC portmap: 0
      RTSP: 0, Shell: 0
      SNMP: 0, Sqlnet: 0, TFTP: 0
      Traceroute: 0
```

In the last section, ALG drops stands for application-level gateway drops, and we find the dropped FTP flow we attempted from the CE6 router. This shows the power and scope of stateful firewall filters.

TYPES OF FIREWALLS

Whether implemented as application software or as a special combination of hardware and software, firewalls are categorized as one of three major types, all of which have variations. Software firewalls can be loaded onto each host, but this only protects the individual host. Other software-based firewalls can be loaded onto a generic platform (Windows or Unix based) and used in conjunction with routers to protect the entire site. Alternatively, routers can be configured with policies (similar to routing policies), but designed to protect the networks attached to the router.

Most effective are very sophisticated packages of specialized hardware and state-of-the-art software, such as Juniper Networks Security Products. These dedicated devices are often called *appliances*, and operate much faster and scale much better than their general-purpose relatives. Software is updated frequently, as often as every 2 weeks, to ensure that customers have the latest capabilities for the effort to secure a site.

The three major types of firewall are the packet filter, application proxy, and stateful inspection. We've seen examples of packet filters and stateful firewalls, but each type has distinctive properties that should be described in some detail.

Packet Filters

Packet filters are the oldest and most basic form of firewall. Packet filters establish site security access rules (or *policies*) that examine the TCP/IP header of each packet and decide if it should be allowed to pass through the firewall. Policies can differ for inbound and outbound packets, and usually do. Many of the fields of the IP, TCP, or UDP header can be examined, but there is no concept of a session or flow of packets in this type of firewall.

Even basic DSL routers do a good job of implementing packet filters. For home networks, this might be adequate. But packet filters do not know much about the application that the packet represents or look at the value of the TCP flags. Packet filters cannot *dynamically* create access rules that allow responses which are associated with specific requests, for example.

Application Proxy

An application proxy is one of the most secure firewall types that can be deployed. The proxy sits between the protected network and the rest of the world. Every packet sent outbound is intercepted by the proxy, which initiates its own request and processes the response. If benign, the response is relayed back to the user. Thus, clients and servers never interact directly and the entire content of the packet can be inspected byte by byte if necessary. Even tricky applications such as Java code can be checked in a *Java sandbox* to assess effects before passing the applet on to a host.

Yet many organizations do anticipate employing application proxies today, and many that once did have abandoned them. Why? Well, proxies do not scale well and must handle twice the number of connections ("inside" and "outside") as all simultaneous users on the protected network. The obvious solution to all network load-related issues—multiple proxies—do not work well because there is no way to guarantee that a response is handled by the same proxy that handled the request.

The proxy also has trouble with proprietary or customized TCP/IP applications, where threats are not obvious or even well defined. But for limited use, such as protecting a Web site, an application proxy is a very attractive solution.

Stateful Inspection

A stateful inspection firewall is the choice for network protection today. Stateful inspection is really a very sophisticated version of a packet filter. All packets can be filtered, and almost every field and flag of the header at the IP and TCP layers can be inspected in a policy.

Moreover, this form of firewall understands the concept of the *state* of the session. So, when a client accesses a Web server, the firewall recognizes the response and can associate all of the packets sent in reply. This is a *dynamic* or *reflexive* firewall operation, and all reputable firewall products use this approach.

Of course, there are TCP/IP protocols, such as UDP or ICMP (and connectionless protocols in general), that have no defined "state" associated with them. Firewall vendors are free to be creative with how they handle these protocols, but the results have been remarkably consistent.

Many stateful inspection firewalls employ a form of application proxy for certain applications. For example, if the firewall is set to do URL filtering, an application proxy function can be coupled with this. This approach is often used with email today because many attachments are malicious either by accident or on purpose. However, as with any application proxy, this solution is difficult to scale or generalize (email attachment scanning is typically done apart from the firewall).

Today, some firewalls can also perform *deep inspection* of packet flows. These rules dig deep into the content of the packet, beyond the IP and TCP/UDP headers, and perform application-level scanning. If a firewall allows access to port 80 because there is a Web server on site, hackers will quickly find out that these packets pass right through the firewall. These firewalls not only protect Web sites, but can find email worms quickly and create regular expression (regex) rules to keep them from spreading. The general architecture of a stateful inspection firewall implemented as specialized hardware and software (an appliance) is shown in Figure 28.2.

An example of this architecture is the firewall product from Juniper Networks Security Products. It had been developed from the start with performance in mind, and runs an integrated security application to provide VPN, firewall, denial-of-service countermeasures, and traffic management.

The operating system is a specialized real-time OS that can preallocate memory to speed up task execution and help maintain a given rate of service. And in contrast

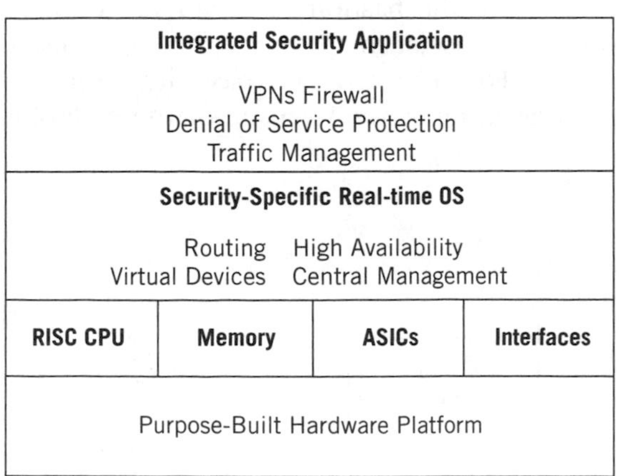

FIGURE 28.2

Firewall appliance general architecture, showing how special hardware and software is used.

to packages built on an open-source Unix-based OS no one can review the source code looking for vulnerabilities. The OS is not distributed as widely as popular proprietary packages, and can support routing and virtual device multiplication—along with central management and high availability. (Larger firewalls pretty much have to support virtual devices, so this is really making a virtue out of a necessity.) The hardware is RISC based, with very fast memory (SDRAM) and ASICs—all designed to keep up with the interfaces' traffic flows.

DMZ

The biggest question facing firewall deployment is how to place the device to best protect publicly accessible servers. Cost and number of firewalls are related to decisions made in this area.

The answer to this location question usually involves the construction of a network DMZ ("demilitarized zone," another term like many others in the security field borrowed from the military). The DMZ is most useful when site protection is not absolute—that is, when it is not possible to deny *all* probes into the site from outside on the Internet (such as when a Web server or FTP server is available for general use). Without this requirement, the position of the firewall is almost always simply behind the router (as shown in Figure 28.3).

Even without a DMZ, it is possible to protect servers that require general Internet access. However, this protection is usually placed on the server itself, which then becomes a *bastion host*, which is still an untrusted host from the viewpoint of the internal network. A bastion host and firewall are shown in Figure 28.4.

It might sound odd that the bastion host, which might be the public Web server for the organization, needs a firewall to protect the internal network from the bastion host itself. But this is absolutely essential, and the bastion host should never be considered part of the internal network. Otherwise, if this host were compromised, the entire internal network would be at risk. For this reason, the bastion host in this configuration is not a good candidate for an e-commerce Web site or the endpoint of a VPN.

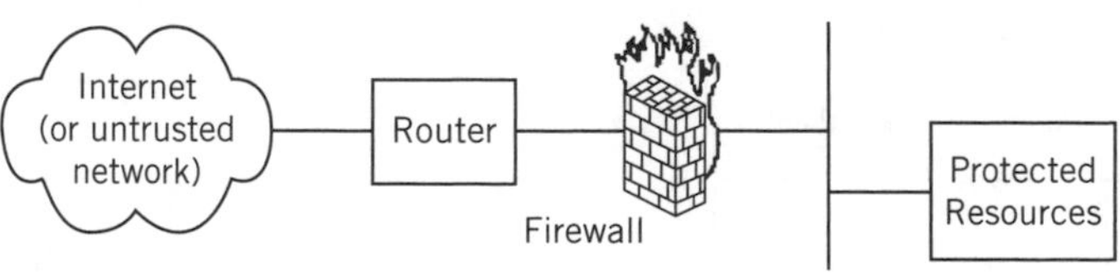

FIGURE 28.3

A single firewall positioned between router and LAN.

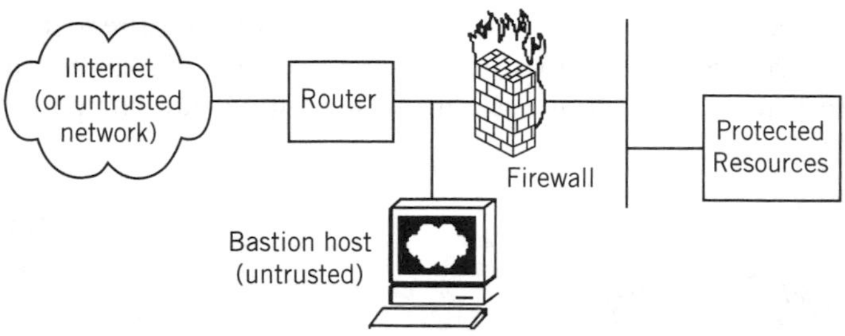

FIGURE 28.4

A firewall with bastion host between router and firewall (and therefore untrusted).

The DMZ concept has the ability to offer multiple types of protection—all in a flexible, scalable, and robust package. (DMZs can be designed with failover capabilities as well.) DMZs can be constructed with one or two firewalls, and two are better for security purposes.

With one firewall, the bastion host is reached only through the firewall itself, usually on a separate interface. The firewall can screen outside traffic (a "screened subnet"), perhaps allowing only access to port 80 for a Web server. Nothing is allowed in, of course, except in reply to an internal query (and even that is typically allowed only from specific hosts or on certain ports). This arrangement is shown in Figure 28.5.

The dual-firewall DMZ is the most sophisticated arrangement. There are both inner and outer firewalls, and the LAN between them is a true DMZ. Multiple servers, such as an anonymous FTP download server and a public Web server, can be protected in many ways. These devices can still be bastion hosts, but the protection on the DMZ servers

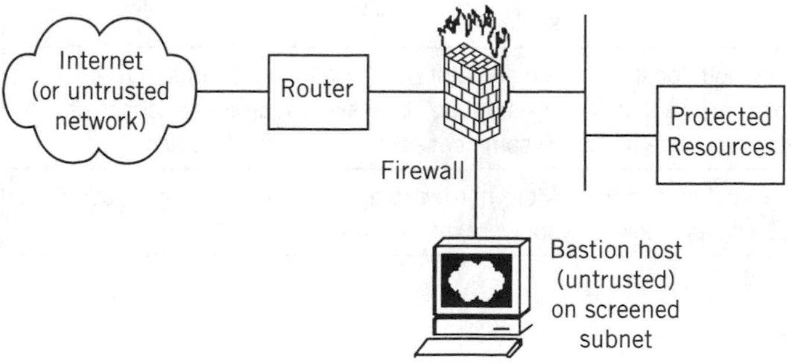

FIGURE 28.5

Firewall with bastion host and DMZ. Note the bastion host relation to the firewall.

themselves can be minimal because they all have the full protection of a firewall in whatever direction the traffic comes from or goes to. The dual-firewall DMZ is shown in Figure 28.6. The characteristics of these four basic firewall positions are compared in Table 28.1.

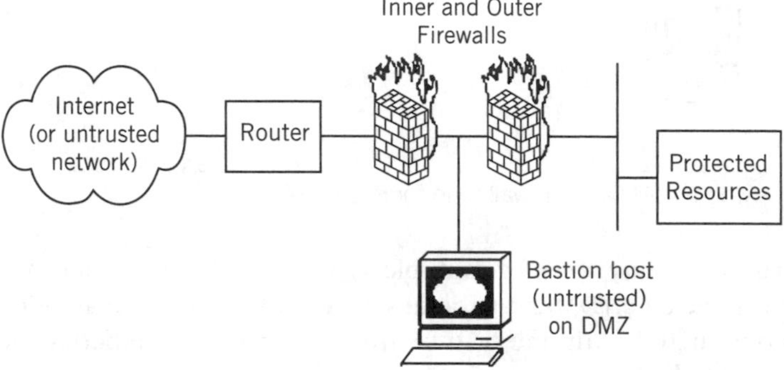

FIGURE 28.6

Dual firewalls with DMZ, showing how the bastion host is positioned on the DMZ.

Table 28.1 Advantages and Disadvantages of the Basic Firewall Designs

Type	Advantages	Disadvantages	Good for...
Single firewall	Inexpensive, easy to configure and maintain	Low security level, difficult to scale	Home or small office, no servers
Single firewall and bastion host	Lower cost than most alternatives	Bastion host vulner-able, difficult to scale	Small business with static content
Single firewall with screened subnet	Protects both local network and bastion host to some extent	Single point of failure, uses public addresses in some cases	Networks that need protected access to bastion host
Dual firewall and DMZ	Best control and very robust, scales nicely	More hardware and software, more work	Larger organizations

QUESTIONS FOR READERS

The filter listing that follows shows some of the concepts discussed in this chapter and can be used to answer the following questions.

```
set firewall family inet filter TEST term A from address 10.10.11.0/24;
set firewall family inet filter TEST term A from address 10.10.12.0/24;
set firewall family inet filter TEST term A from protocol [ udp tcp ];
set firewall family inet filter TEST term A from port [ 20 21 22 ];
set firewall family inet filter TEST term A then log;
set firewall family inet filter TEST term A then reject;
```

1. In the listing, which IP address will be selected out of all packets seen by the filter?
2. Which transport layer protocols will be selected by the filter?
3. Which applications are selected based on the port numbers given?
4. Will a log be kept of the selected packets?
5. Will the sender receive any notice that the packets have been blocked by a firewall filter?

CHAPTER

IP Security

29

What You Will Learn

In this chapter, you will learn how IPSec adds another level of security to a TCP/IP network by adding IPSec to the MPLS-based VPN that we built in Chapter 26. We'll investigate the IPSec architecture and how its features are usually implemented.

You will learn about security associations and how authentication and encapsulation work in IPSec. We'll briefly mention the Internet key exchange (IKE) as a secure way to move keys around the network.

IPSec, as has been pointed out, is really a piece of IPv6 that was pressed into service for IPv4, mostly out of desperation after businesses began to use the Internet for more than just amusement. The formats for IPv4 and IPv6 IPSec are different, given the difference in header and address formats, but they are still very similar. Optional in IPv4, support for IPSec is mandatory in IPv6. IPSec is part of a public key infrastructure (PKI) architecture based on several things that we've talked about before: public key encryption, secure key exchange for the Internet (IKE), and several related concepts and protocols.

There are several key concepts in IPSec, as with anything else in TCP/IP. We'll talk about IPSec modes first, followed by security associations (SAs) and a closely related concept, the security parameter index (SPI). Then we'll focus on the three main "protocols" that make up IPSec: the authentication header (AH), the encapsulating security payload (ESP), and the IKE.

IPSec consists of two main "core protocols"—AH and ESP—although it is often pointed out that they are not really protocols at all because they cannot function on their own. AH allows a receiver to verify that the claimed originator of the message actually did send it, and that none of the data has been altered while in transit. It also prevents captured messages from being used again in the future (e.g., when a hacker cannot *read* the password but knows that this packet will log in the user when sent). This is called a *replay* attack.

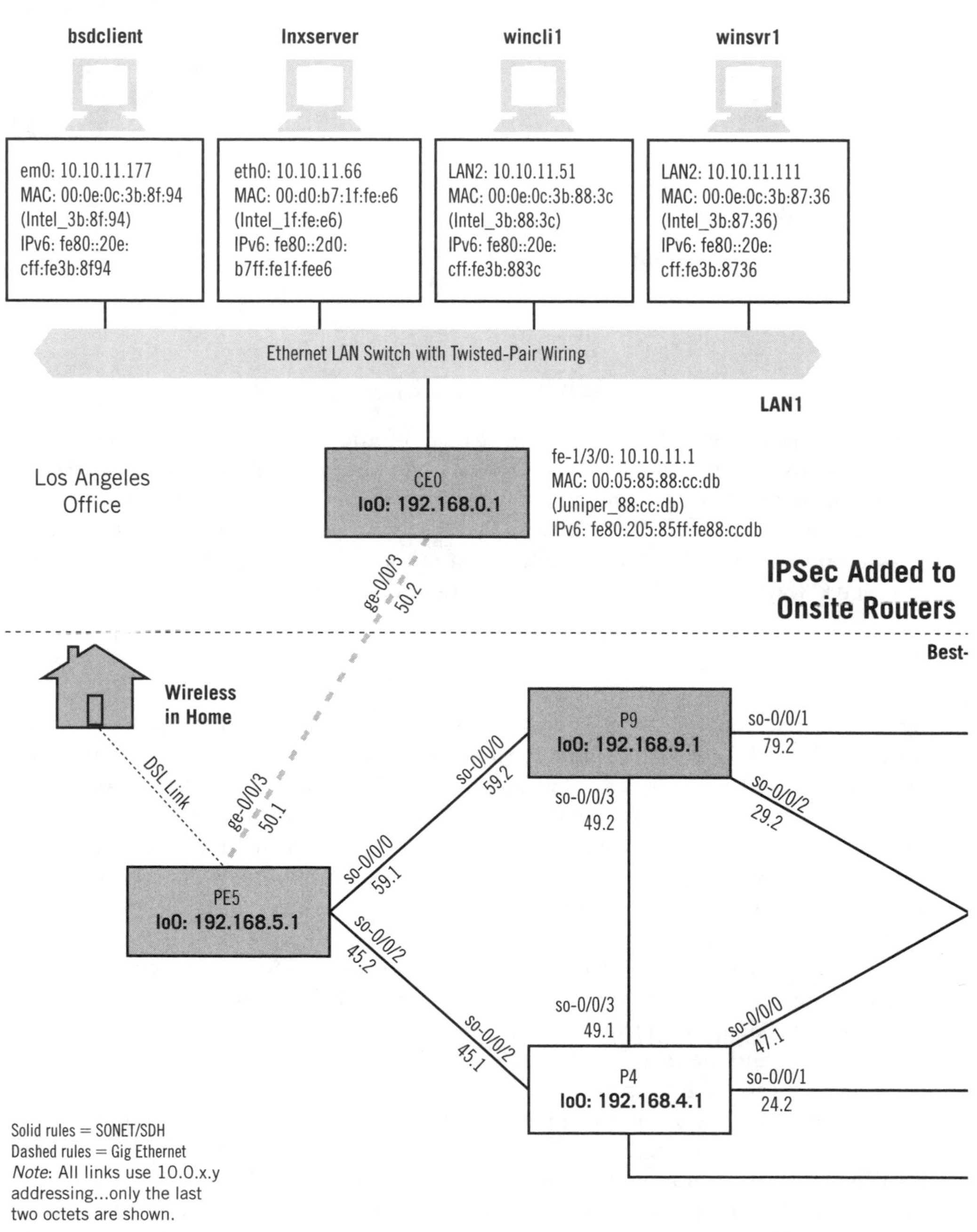

FIGURE 29.1

IPSec on the Illustrated Network, showing how IPSec adds security to the site routers connected by the MPLS-based VPN.

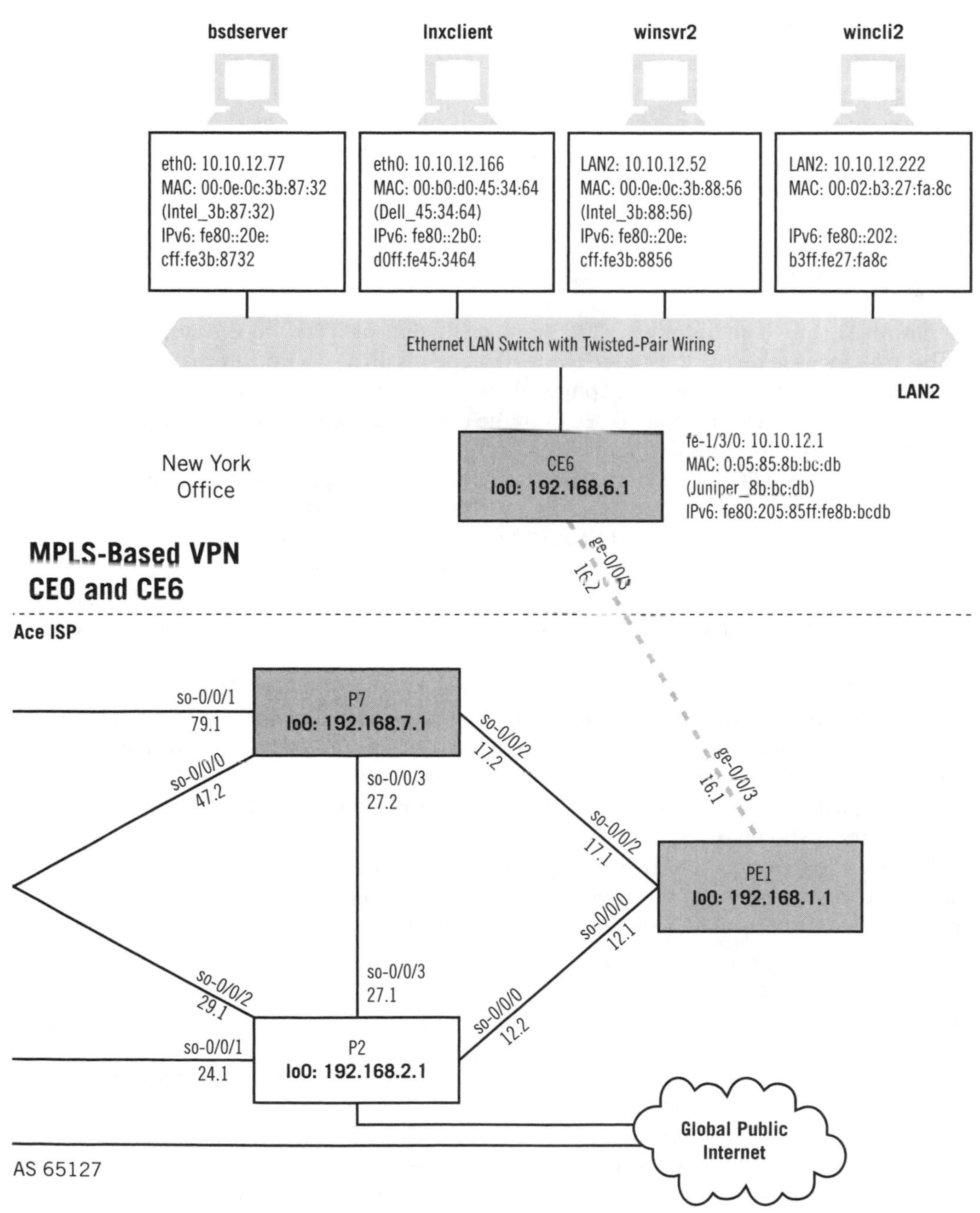

bsdserver
lnxclient
winsvr2
wincli2
eth0: 10.10.12.77
MAC: 00:0e:0c:3b:87:32
(Intel_3b:87:32)
IPv6: fe80::20e:
cff:fe3b:8732
eth0: 10.10.12.166
MAC: 00:b0:d0:45:34:64
(Dell_45:34:64)
IPv6: fe80::2b0:
d0ff:fe45:3464
LAN2: 10.10.12.52
MAC: 00:0e:0c:3b:88:56
(Intel_3b:88:56)
IPv6: fe80::20e:
cff:fe3b:8856
LAN2: 10.10.12.222
MAC: 00:02:b3:27:fa:8c
IPv6: fe80::202:
b3ff:fe27:fa8c
Ethernet LAN Switch with Twisted-Pair Wiring
LAN2
New York
Office
CE6
lo0: 192.168.6.1
fe-1/3/0: 10.10.12.1
MAC: 0:05:85:8b:bc:db
(Juniper_8b:bc:db)
IPv6: fe80:205:85ff:fe8b:bcdb
MPLS-Based VPN
CEO and CE6
ge-0/0/3
16.2
Ace ISP
so-0/0/1
79.1
P7
lo0: 192.168.7.1
so-0/0/2
17.2
so-0/0/0
47.2
so-0/0/3
27.2
ge-0/0/3
16.1
so-0/0/2
17.1
PE1
lo0: 192.168.1.1
so-0/0/0
12.1
so-0/0/2
29.1
so-0/0/3
27.1
so-0/0/0
12.2
so-0/0/1
24.1
P2
lo0: 192.168.2.1
Global Public
Internet
AS 65127

ESP encrypts the payload of the message itself. It might sound odd that authentication and encryption are separate processes in IPSec, and in practice both are normally used together. Separating the processes allows them to evolve independently, however, so advances in encryption do not require changes in authentication (and vice versa).

We'll add IPSec to the MPLS-based VPN we created in the VPN chapter, as shown in Figure 29.1. We'll still use that same configuration on the routers, but add to it.

IPSec IN ACTION

As with NAT and stateful firewalls, the implementation of IPSec on the Juniper Networks routers used on the Illustrated Network depends on a special "internal interface" supported by an adaptive services physical interface card (AS PIC). All of the routers have these PICs, so we can build IPSec onto the configuration used for the MPLS-based VPN that we built for VPLS in Chapter 26.

Our goal here will be to add an IPSec tunnel using ESP between the CE0 and CE6 routers attached to LAN1 and LAN2, and at the same time preserve the VPLS VPN between routers PE5 at LAN1 and PE1 at LAN2. The packets flowing between LAN1 and LAN2 on the links between routers PE5 and PE1 will be encapsulated and encrypted (with IPSec), and then encapsulated again (for VPLS). Is this paranoia? Perhaps. But the idea is to raise the hacker work factor on these packets high enough so that the hackers give up and move on to less protected traffic.

We could configure manual SAs on each router and configure IKE to carry this information over the network, but such a procedure is overly complex for this chapter. We have to configure the SAs anyway, so we'll just (securely) configure manual SAs on routers CE0 and CE6 to run IPSec with ESP in tunnel mode between them, thereby dispensing with IKE. The VPLS is still there, but transparent to IPSec. The network topology appears as shown in Figure 29.2.

Then we'll show that the IPSec is up and running. (We could show some garbled Ethereal captures between the routers showing that IPSec encryption is in use, but these are not very enlightening.) Again, we'll show the configuration on each router, with comments.

CE0

This router has normal interface configurations, naturally. But we'll define a bidirectional manual SA in a "rule" called `rule-manual-SA-BiESP` and reference it to a "service set" associated with the interface. We'll use ESP, and a value of 261 for the SPI. We'll talk more about security algorithms later, but we'll also use HMAC-SHA1-96 for authentication, DES-CBC for encryption, a 20-bit ASCII authentication key for SHA-1, and an 8-bit ASCII key for DES-CBC authentication.

To get traffic onto the PIC and the IPSec tunnel, we have to match the LAN traffic with our IPSec VPN selector rule. Fortunately, this rule is already referenced in the

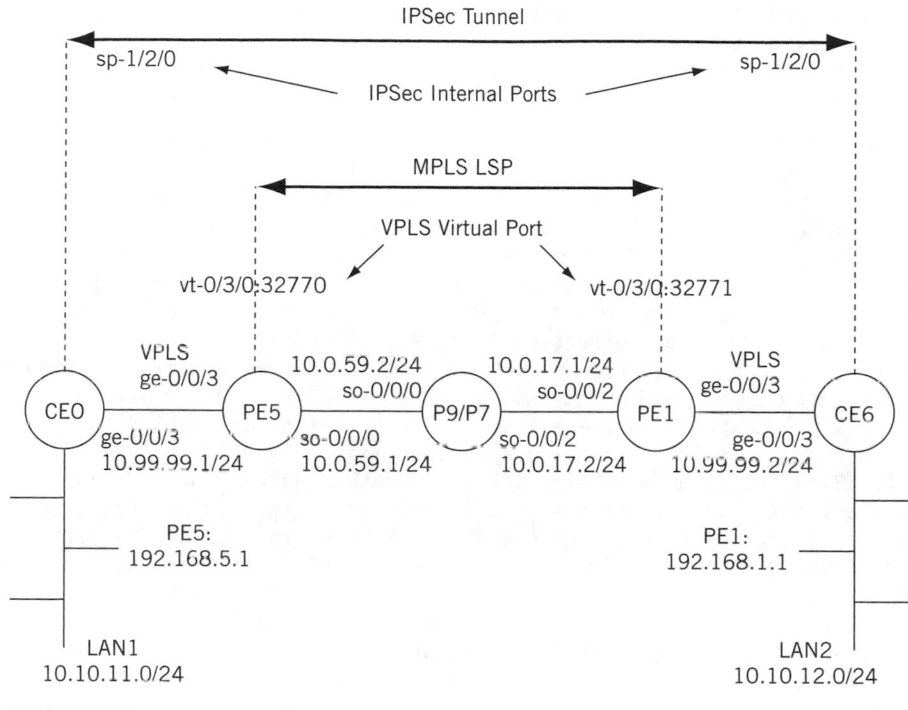

FIGURE 29.2

IPSec topology, showing how it relates to the MPLS LSP and VPLS.

service set from the VPN configuration. We'll also use a firewall filter to count the packets entering the IPSec tunnel.

```
set interfaces ge-0/0/3 vlan-tagging;
set interfaces ge-0/0/3 unit 0 vlan-id 600;
set interfaces ge-0/0/3 unit 0 family inet
    service input service-set service-set-manual-BiESP;
set interfaces ge-0/0/3 vlan-tagging unit 0 family inet
    service output service-set service-set-manual-BiESP;
    # applies the BiESP service set to input and output traffic
set interfaces ge-0/0/3 unit 0 family inet address 10.99.99.1/24;

set interface sp-1/2/0 unit 0 family inet filter input ipsec-tunnel;
    # configure the internal IPSec tunnel interface
set firewall filter ipsec-tunnel term 1 then count ipsec-tunnel;
set firewall filter ipsec-tunnel term 1 then accept;
    # configure a filter to count and process traffic

set services service-set service-set-manual-BiESP interface-service
    service-interface sp-1/2/0;
    # defines the main IPSec tunnel service set applied above
```

```
set services service-set service-set-manual-BiESP ipsec-vpn-options
    local-gateway 10.99.99.1; # the local IPSec tunnel addr
set services service-set service-set-manual-BiESP ipsec-vpn-rules
    rule-manual-SA-BiESP; # references the IPSec rule defined below

set services ipsec-vpn rule rule-manual-SA-BiESP term term-manual-SA-BiESP
    from source address 10.10.11.0/24; # find LAN1 traffic for IPSec
set services ipsec-vpn rule rule-manual-SA-BiESP term term-manual-SA-BiESP
    then remote-gateway 10.99.99.2; # far-end IPSec tunnel address
set services ipsec-vpn rule rule-manual-SA-BiESP term term-manual-SA-BiESP
    then manual direction bidirectional protocol esp; # use ESP for IPSec
set services ipsec-vpn rule rule-manual-SA-BiESP term term-manual-SA-BiESP
    then manual direction bidirectional spi 261; # the SPI is 261
set services ipsec-vpn rule rule-manual-SA-BiESP term term-manual-SA-BiESP
    then manual direction bidirectional authentication algorithm hmac-sha1-96;
set services ipsec-vpn rule rule-manual-SA-BiESP term term-manual-SA-BiESP
    then manual direction bidirectional authentication key ascii-text
    "$9$v.s8xd24Zk.5bs.5QFAtM8XNVYLGifT3goT3690BxNdw2ajHmFnCZUnCtuEh";
    # the authentication key was enters as 'juniperjuniperjunipe' (20 chars)
set services ipsec-vpn rule rule-manual-SA-BiESP term term-manual-SA-BiESP
    then manual direction bidirectional encryption algorithm des-cbc;
set services ipsec-vpn rule rule-manual-SA-BiESP term term-manual-SA-BiESP
    then manual direction bidirectional encryption key ascii-text
    "$9$3LJW/A0EclLxdBlxdbsJZn/CpOR"; # entered as juniperj (8 characters)
set services ipsec-vpn rule rule-manual-SA-BiESP match-direction output;}
```

We need a manual SA key entry because this example is not using IKE. Note that although we type the key in plain text, the result is always displayed in encrypted form.

CE6

We can use exactly the same configuration on router CE6 by just swapping the local and remote gateway addresses on the `ge-0/0/3` interface and under `ipsec-vpn-options` and `ipsec-vpn`, so that `10.99.99.1` and `10.99.99.2` are swapped, and changing the `fe-1/3/0` address to `10.10.12.1`. So, in the interest of brevity, we won't show the CE6 listing.

How do we know that the IPSec VPN tunnel is working? Everything works as before, but that proves nothing. How do we know that traffic between LAN1 and LAN2 is now encrypted? An Ethereal trace can verify that, and we can display the value of the traffic counter (as long as it is non-zero) on the firewall filter we set up on the CE routers.

```
admin@CE6> show firewall filter ipsec-tunnel
Filter: ipsec-tunnel
Counters:
Name                     Bytes          Packets
ipsec-tunnel               252                3
```

These counts reflect three pings that were sent from LAN1 to LAN2 over the IPSec tunnel. Other commands can be used to give parameters and details of the SA itself, but the latter just repeats information stored in the configuration file.

Let's see what the major portions of the configuration listing are accomplishing. To do that, we'll have to consider some concepts used in IPSec.

INTRODUCTION TO IPSec

There are three IPSec *support components* in addition to the transport services provided by AH and ESP. One of these components is a set of encryption and hashing algorithms, most of which we've met already in the SSL and SSH chapters. AH and ESP are generic and do not mandate the use of any specific mechanism. IPSec endpoints on a *secure path* negotiate the ones they will use, as does SSH. For example, two common hashing methods are Message Digest 5 (MD5) and Secure Hash Alogrithm 1 (SHA-1), and the endpoints decide which to use with IPSec.

Other important support pieces are the security policies and the SAs that embody them. The flexibility allowed in IPSec still has to be managed, and security relationships between IPSec devices are tracked by the SA and its security policy.

Finally, an IPSec key exchange framework and mechanism (IKE) is defined so that endpoints can share the keys they need to decrypt data. A way to securely send SA information is provided as well. In summary, IPSec provides the following protection services at the IP layer itself:

- Authentication of message integrity to detect changes of the content on the network
- Encryption of data for privacy
- Protection against some forms of attacks, such as replay attacks
- Negotiation of security methods and keys used between devices
- Differing security modes, called transport and tunnel, for flexibility

IPSec RFCs

When it comes to RFCs, aspects of IPSec are covered in a collection of RFCs that define the architecture, services, and protocols used in IPSec. These are listed in Table 29.1.

IPSec Implementation

Okay, IPSec is wonderful and we all should have it and use it. But how? Where? There are two places (at least) and three ways that IPSec can be implemented on a network.

First, IPSec can be implemented host to host or end to end. Every host has IPSec capabilities, and no packets enter or leave the hosts with encryption and authentication. This seems like an obvious choice; however, the fact is that there are many hosts and, as with "personal" firewalls, this can be a maintenance and management nightmare.

Table 29.1 IPSec RFCs with Title and Purpose

RFC	Name	Purpose
2401	Security Architecture for the Internet Protocol	Main document, describes architecture and how components fit together
2402	IP Authentication Header	AH "protocol" for integrity
2403	The Use of HMAC-MD5-96 within ESP and AH	Describes a popular algorithm for use in AH and ESP
2404	The Use of HMAC-SHA-1-96 within ESP and AH	Describes another popular algorithm for use in AH and ESP
2406	IP Encapsulating Security Payload	The ESP "protocol" for privacy
2408	Internet Security Association and Key Management Protocol (ISAKMP)	Defines ISAKMP methods for key exchange and negotiating SAs
2409	The Internet Key Exchange (IKE)	Describes IKE as ISAKMP method
2412	The OAKLEY Key Determination Protocol	Describes a generic protocol for key exchange, which is used in IKE

And because most data are stored on servers in "plain text" formats, all of this work is often in vain if there is a way into the server itself.

IPSec can also be implemented from router to router, and this approach makes a lot of sense. There are few routers compared to hosts, and perhaps offsite packets are the only ones that really need protection. On the local LAN, the network risks are lower (or *should* be!), and more damage is caused by users leaving themselves logged in and leaving their work locations for breaks or lunch than sniffing "on the wire." When used in combination, IPSec VPNs are a formidable barrier to attacks originating on the Internet. (This is not to say that site security can be *ignored* when IPSec and VPNs are used between routers, but it certainly can be *different*.)

Ideally, in a host or a router, IPSec would be integrated into the architecture of the device. Where IPv6 is concerned, this is exactly the case. But IPSec is still an IPv4 "add-on" and so can be implemented in hosts and routers in different ways that mainly concern where in the network the actual IPSec protection actually kicks in.

There are two common ways to look at IPSec architecture in IPv4. These are sometimes called "bump in the stack" (BITS) and "bump in the wire" (BITW).

In the BITS architecture, IPSec bits are a separate layer between the IP layer and the frames. IPSec "intercepts" the IP packets inbound and outbound and processes them. The nice thing about this approach is that it can be easily added to (and upgraded on) IPv4 hosts.

The BITW technique is common when IPSec is implemented site to site by routers, and devices located next to routers. This architecture is shown in Figure 29.3.

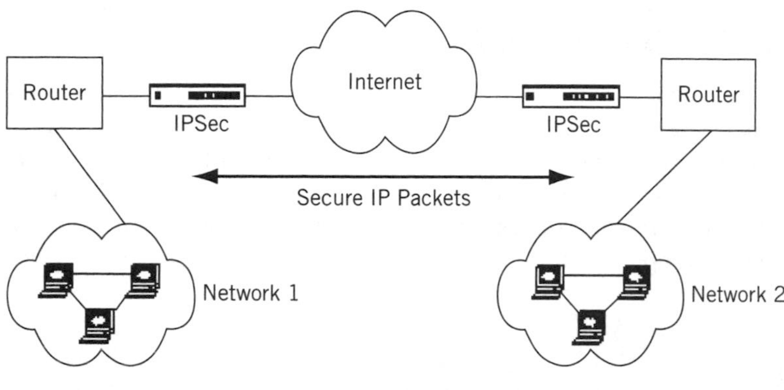

FIGURE 29.3

IPSec and routers, showing how separate devices can be used to apply IPSec to a network.

The IPSec "device" can be implemented in router software or as a separate appliance. The secure packets can be sent over a VPN or simply routed through the Internet, although a VPN adds another layer of protection to the data stream. The two approaches are similar, but have a different impact on each of the two IPSec modes.

IPSec Transport and Tunnel Mode

IPSec modes define the changes IPSec can make to a packet when it is processed for delivery. Modes in turn affect SAs, so the difference is not trivial by any means.

Transport mode—In this mode, the packet is handled as a unit from the transport layer (TCP/UDP). The segment is processed by AH/ESP and the appropriate header added along with a "normal" IP header before being passed down to the frame layer. The main point is that in transport mode, the IP header itself is *not* part of the AH/ESP process.

Tunnel mode—In this mode, IPSec performs its magic on an entire IP packet (original header included). The IPSec headers are placed in front of the encrypted IP packet and then a *new* IP header is placed in front of the entire construction. A nice feature is that the original IP address is encrypted and the new address can be seen as a form of NAT.

Transport mode is feasible only for host-to-host IPSec operation because only hosts have easy access to the transport layer segments. On the other hand, router implementations make use of tunnel mode because routers handle entire IP packets, tunnels are a familiar concept in the router world, and this form of IPSec works well with VPNs. (Some equipment vendors say that tunnel mode is "better" than transport mode, but that is really making a virtue out of necessity.)

SECURITY ASSOCIATIONS AND MORE

An IPSec device negotiates the precise methods and manages keys used for packets sent and received. Here comes a packet from somewhere else. So how will we decrypt it? What is its precise structure (mode)? The same issues come up with outbound packets. How do we know what was negotiated (or possible) for the partner at the other end of the secure path? This is turning out to be much more difficult in practice than in theory. We need help to keep it all straight. The following material describes how it's done in IPSec.

Security Policies

Security policies are general rules that tell IPSec how it can process packets. The security policy can also allow packets to pass untouched or link to places where yet more detail is provided. Security policies are stored in the device's *security policy database* (SPD).

SAs—This is a set of security information describing a particular type of secure path between one specific device and another. It is a type of "contractual agreement" that defines the security mechanisms used between the two endpoints. SAs are unidirectional, so there is one for each direction (inbound and outbound). So, there are at least *four* (and often eight!) SAs that apply to communications between a pair of devices. The SAs are kept in the device's *security association database* (SAD).

Selectors—Which packets does a given SA apply to? The rule sets are called *selectors*. A selector might be configured that applies a certain SA to a packet from a particular range of source IP addresses, or that is going to a certain destination network. SAs don't have names, however. SAs are *indexed* by number, and the number is really a representation (a "triple") of three parameters and not just the SPI.

Security parameter index—The SPI is a 32-bit number picked to uniquely identify an SA for a connected device. The SPI is placed in the AH or ESP headers and links the packet to a particular SA. Once the receiver knows some general information about the packet content, the SPI provides a clue to the rest of it.

IP destination address—The IP address of the device at the "other end" of the SA path.

Security protocol identifier—Tells whether this SA is for AH or ESP. If both are used, they need separate SAs.

The nice thing about using this combination is that any one of the parameters can change to form a "new" entity based on existing pieces. But it can still be confusing.

Authentication Header

AH authenticates by associating a header with a piece of data. The scope of the operation, and the exact placement of the header, depends on the IP version (IPv4 or IPv6) and mode (transport or tunnel). As with many other authentication schemes, AH relies on a hash operation similar in concept to the CRC used on frames. The specific hash (called an *integrity check value* [ICV]) used is stored in the SA and is known only to source and destination. The AH provides authentication, but not privacy. No direct content encryption is used in the AH operation.

AH authentication is simpler for IPv6 than for IPv4 because it was designed for IPv6. In IPv6, the AH is inserted as an extension header using the usual rules for extension header linking. The AH value of 51 is inserted into the IPv6 `Next Header` field. In transport mode, the AH is in the *main* IP header and precedes any destination options and follows an ESP header (if present). In tunnel mode, the AH is an extension header in the *new* IP packet header. These differences are shown in Figure 29.4, with routing (43) and destination option (60) headers in use with a TCP segment.

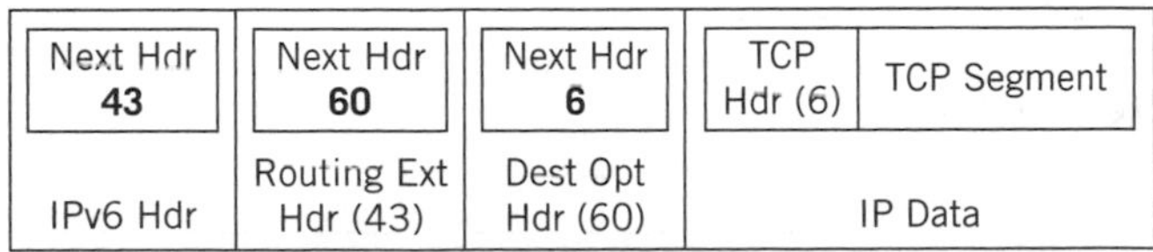

Original IPv6 Packet

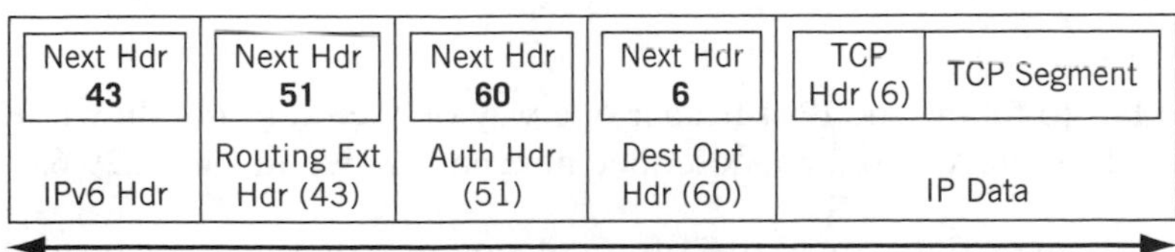

IPv6 AH Packet (transport mode)

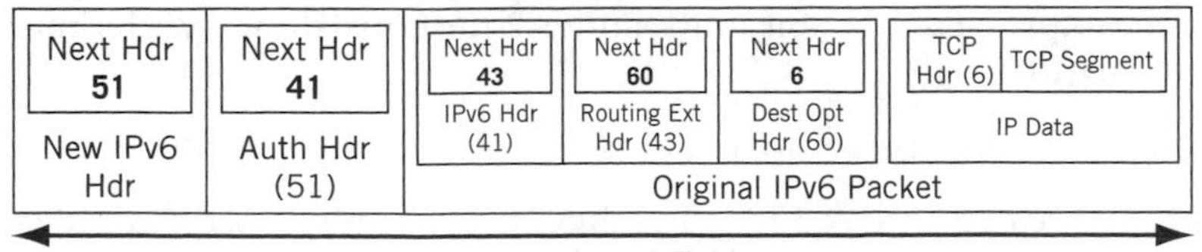

IPv6 AH Packet (tunnel mode)

FIGURE 29.4

IPv6 AH packet formats, showing how the various fields and headers relate to one another.

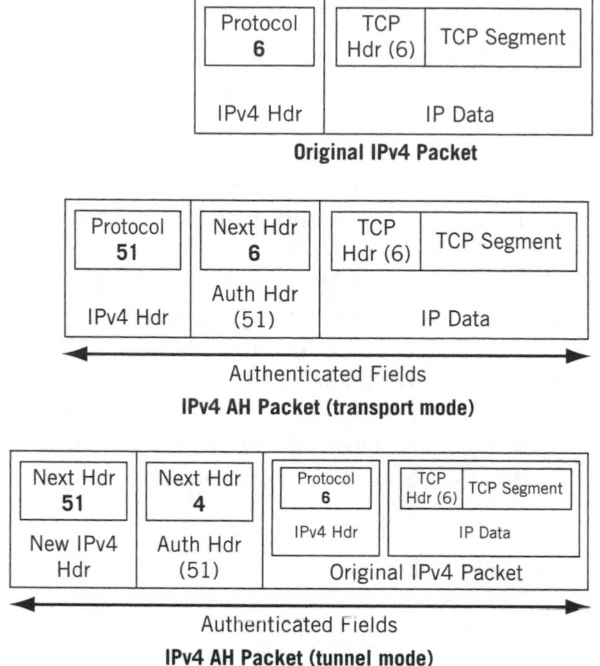

FIGURE 29.5

IPv4 AH packet formats showing how the various fields and headers relate to one another.

In IPv4, the AH has to follow the IPv4 header one way or the other (as shown in Figure 29.5). The fields of the AH itself are described next and shown in Figure 29.6.

Next Header—This 1-byte field gives the protocol number of the *next* header after the AH, *not* the protocol number of the current one.

Payload Length—This 1-byte field measures the length of the AH itself, not really the "payload." It is expressed in 32-bit units, minus 2 for consistency with other IPv6 header calculations.

Reserved—These 2 bytes must be set to all zeros.

Security Parameter Index (SPI)—A 32-bit number that combines with the destination address and type (AH in this case) to identify the SA used for this packet.

Sequence Number—A 32-bit counter that starts at zero when the SA is formed and increments with each packet sent using that SA. This prevents replay attacks with captured packets.

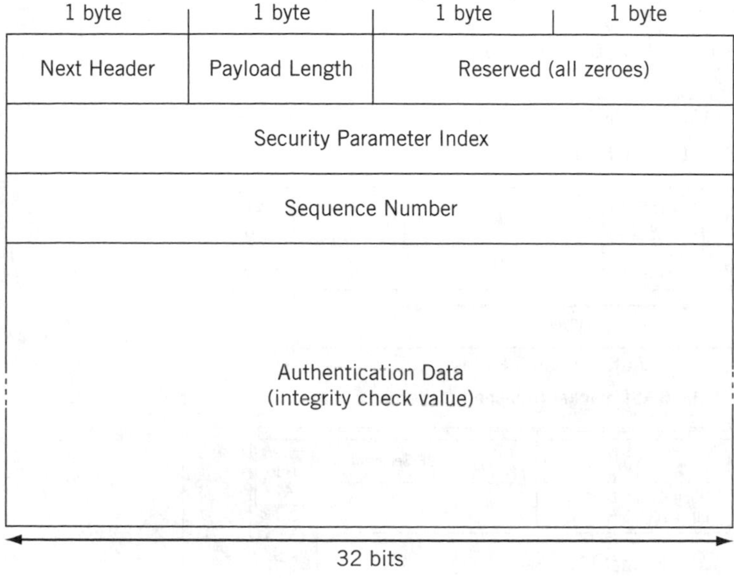

FIGURE 29.6

IPSec AH fields.

Authentication Data—This is the ICV hash and varies in size depending on hashing algorithm used. It must end on a 32-bit (IPv4) or 64-bit (IPv6) boundary, and so is padded with zeros as needed.

Encapsulating Security Payload

ESP encrypts data and adds a header and trailer to the result. ESP has its *own* optional authentication scheme, and can be used in conjunction with AH or not. Unlike the AH "unit," ESP is split up into three distinct pieces. The ESP *header* precedes the encrypted data, and its placement depends on whether IPv6 or IPv4 is used and on mode. The ESP *trailer* follows the encrypted data because some encryption algorithms require that any needed padding follow the encryption. The ESP authentication data with ICV is optional (and redundant when AH is used), so its separation makes sense. It authenticates the ESP header and trailer (and so cannot appear *in* them). This field follows *everything* else.

Placing the ESP headers is different in IPv6 and IPv4, but similar to AH. The trick is finding the ESP trailer because there is no field in the ESP header to give length to or location of the ESP trailer. If it sounds difficult to figure out where the trailer is, that's one of the points. But it can be done, given the correct SA, and the ESP trailer *does* have a next header field to "point back" to the front of the data. Figure 29.7 might make this clearer for IPv6. In transport mode, the ESP trailer value of 60 "points" (it's really in no

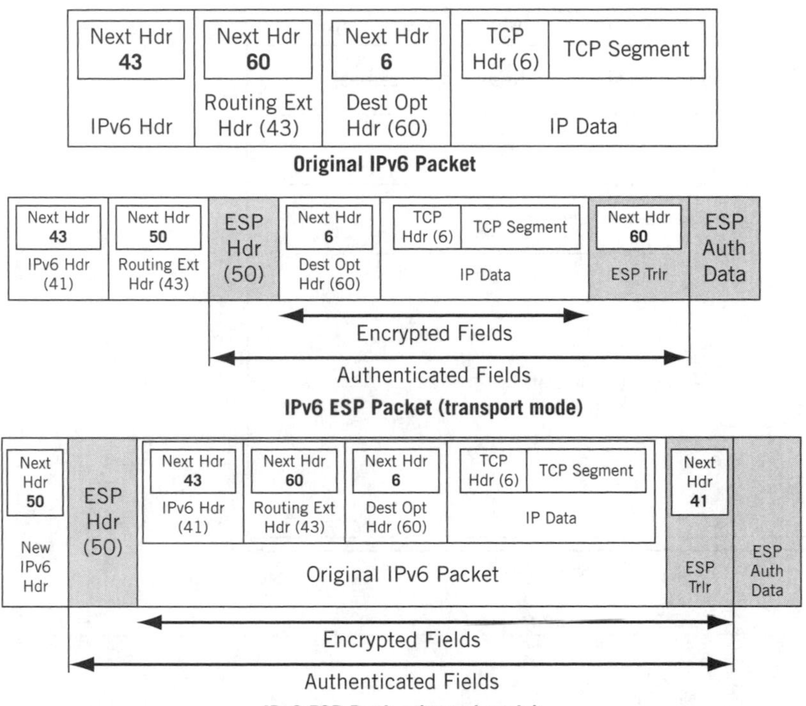

FIGURE 29.7

IPv6 ESP packet formats, showing how the various fields and headers relate to one another.

sense a pointer) to the Destination Options field (value 60) and from there to the TCP header (IP protocol value 6). In tunnel mode, the ESP trailer next header value is 41 and indicates that an IPv6 header comes next.

Figure 29.8 shows the same process for IPv4. In this case, the ESP trailer next header value is 6 for transport mode (TCP header comes next). The value is 4 in tunnel mode, to indicate that an Ipv4 packet is between the ESP header and trailer.

How it all fits together in ESP is shown in Figure 29.9. Note that several fields are only authenticated and not encrypted.

SPI—This 32-bit number is part of the ESP header and is used with destination address and type (ESP, in this case) to be used for this packet.

Sequence Number—This 32-bit number is part of the ESP header and is initialized to zero when the SA is formed and incremented to prevent replay attacks (the same is true in AH).

Payload Data—This is the encrypted data itself and varies in size. Sometimes it contains an *initialization vector*, depending on encryption method.

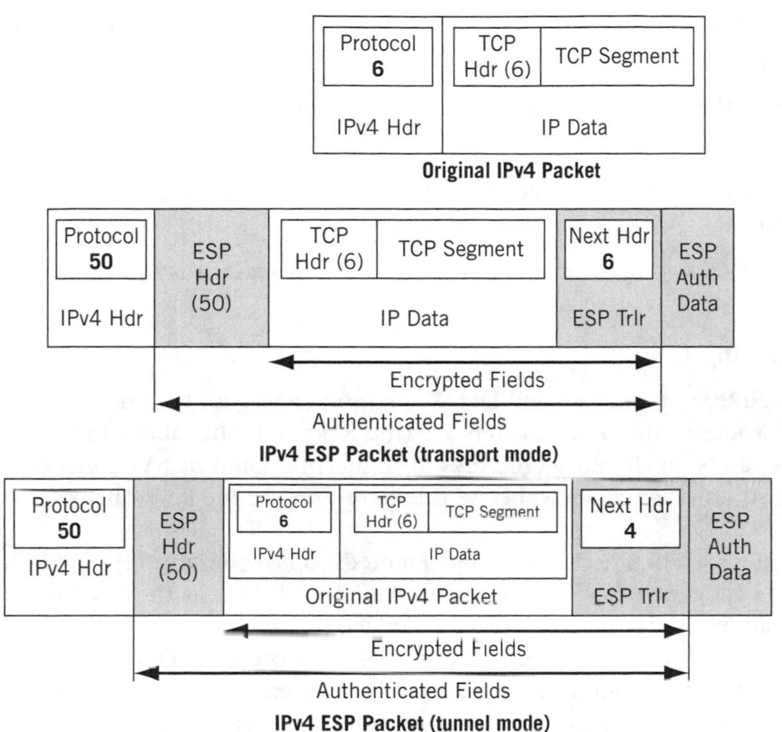

FIGURE 29.8

IPv4 ESP packet formats, showing how the various fields and headers relate to one another.

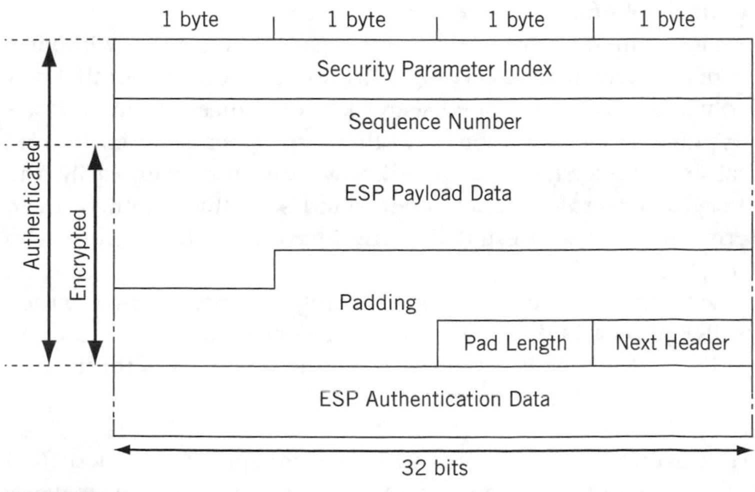

FIGURE 29.9

IPSec ESP fields, showing which fields are authenticated and encrypted.

Padding—This field, from 0 to 255 bytes long, is part of the ESP trailer and is used to align the data as needed.

Pad Length—This 1-byte field is part of the ESP trailer and gives the length of the padding.

Next Header—This 1-byte field is part of the ESP trailer and often "points" to the TCP header (6).

ESP Authentication Data—A variable-length ICV (authentication is optional).

Internet Key Exchange

Our journey through IPSec is almost complete. We've found a way for the endpoints to decide what the formats of the IPSec packets are (the SAs). But what about the keys? Like SSH, IPSec depends on shared secret keys for encryption and decryption. Obviously, the entire method is as secure as the steps taken to secure the keys. That's what IKE is for.

IPSec was actually used before IKE was implemented. So how did the keys get into the SAs and the SAs get everywhere they were needed? An "off-Net" method had to be used. Large organizations used to fly everyone who needed them to a central location and simply hand them out (in sealed envelopes, of course). Smaller organizations used FedEx or some other delivery service. Usually multiple keys, often a great many, were distributed this way, and they changed on a basis known only to those who had to change them.

This method of manual SA definition is still valid and widely used. Sometimes security personnel fly around the country configuring the SAs locally on each router. Few trust "secure" remote access methods for this sensitive task because many millions in financial resources might be at risk. For example, IPSec might have to protect corporate payroll records sent to the banks for employee direct deposit.

IKE is one of the most baffling protocols to understand and explain without a fairly deep knowledge of mathematics and cryptography. Some pieces are not that bad: Diffie-Hellman is the obvious choice for shared secret key exchange, although it says nothing about private/public key distribution. But other components are far beyond the abilities of generalists to understand, let alone know how to explain easily. And there are those who say that you don't really understand something until you can explain it in simple terms to someone else. If that is true, I have yet to find anyone who really understands IKE.

IKE allows IPSec devices to simply send their SAs securely over the Internet to each other. In other words, IKE populates the SAD so that both ends know what to do to send and receive with IPSec. IKE combines (and adds to) the functions of three other protocols.

ISAKMP—The Internet Security Association and Key Management Protocol *is a general* framework protocol for exchanging SAs and key information by negotiation and in phases. Many different methods can be used.

OAKLEY—This extends ISAKMP by describing a specific mechanism for key exchange through different defined "modes." Most of IKE's key exchange is directly based on OAKLEY.

SKEME—This defines a key exchange process different from that of OAKLEY. IKE uses some SKEME features, such as public key encryption methods and the "fast rekeying" feature.

IKE takes ISAKMP and adds the details of OAKLEY and SKEME to perform its magic. IKE has the two ISAKMP phases.

Phase 1—The first stage is a "setup" process in which two devices agree on how they will exchange further information securely. This creates an SA for IKE itself, although it's called an ISAKMP SA. This special bidirectional SA is used for Phase 2.

Phase 2—Now the ISAKMP SA is used to create the *other* SAs for the two devices. This is where the parameters such as secret keys are negotiated and shared.

Why two phases? Phase 1 typically uses public key encryption and is slow, but technically only has to be done once. Phase 2 is faster and can conjure different but very secure secret keys every hour or every 10 minutes (or more frequently for very sensitive transactions).

QUESTIONS FOR READERS

Figure 29.10 shows some of the concepts discussed in this chapter and can be used to answer the following questions.

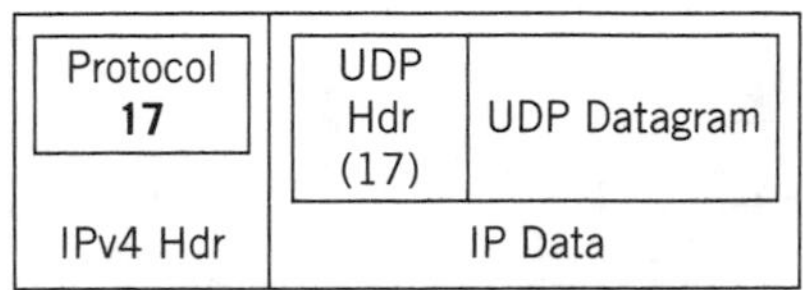

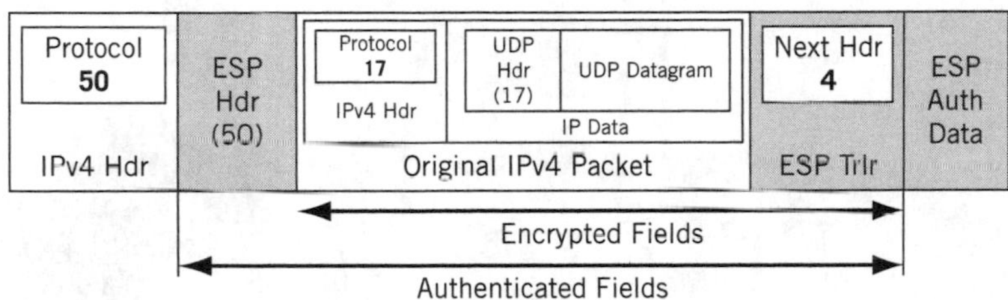

FIGURE 29.10

IPSec ESP used with an IPv4 packet.

1. Which IPSec ESP mode is used in the figure—transport or tunnel?
2. Which IP protocol is being tunneled?
3. What does the ESP trailer next header value of 4 indicate?
4. Could NAT also be used with IPSec to substitute the IPv4 addresses *and* encrypt them?
5. Is the SPI field encrypted? Is it authenticated?

PART

VII

Media

The Internet is not just for data anymore. This part of the book examines how voice communication has transitioned to the Internet.

CHAPTER

Voice over Internet Protocol

30

What You Will Learn

In this chapter, you will learn how VoIP is becoming more and more popular as an alternative to the traditional public switched telephone network (PSTN). We'll look at one form of "softphone" that lets users make "voice" calls (voice is really many things) over an Internet connection to their PC.

You will learn about the protocols used in VoIP, especially for the "data" (RTP and RTCP) and for signaling (H.323 and SIP). We'll put it all together and look at a complete architecture for carrying media other than data on the Internet.

In November 2006, when a person in Cardiff, Wales, made a local telephone call, no part of the British Telecom (BT) PSTN was involved. Only the "last mile" of the circuit was the same: No telephone central office, voice switches, or channelized trunks were used to carry the voice call. Instead, the calls were handled by multiservice access nodes (MSANs) and carried with IP protocols over the same type of network that handles BT's Internet traffic.

BT was so happy with the results that by 2011 they say their entire PSTN will be replaced with an IP network using MPLS to both secure and provide QoS for the calls. Many countries use IP voice on their backbones (such as Telecom Italia), but this is the first time a national system has decided to spend a huge amount of money (almost US$20 billion, BT says) to convert everything.

It's old news that many people, both around the world and in the United States, use the Internet to talk over the telephone. Not many of these customers know it, however, because various factors combine to make the use of voice over IP (VoIP) technology a sensitive subject. There are those who intentionally use the Internet for voice calls, and many software packages (such as those from Vonage and Avaya) are available. But not many people know that a percentage of calls (perhaps the majority) made over the PSTN are carried for part of their journey over the Internet using VoIP. The cellular telephone network is converging on IP protocols even faster than the landline network.

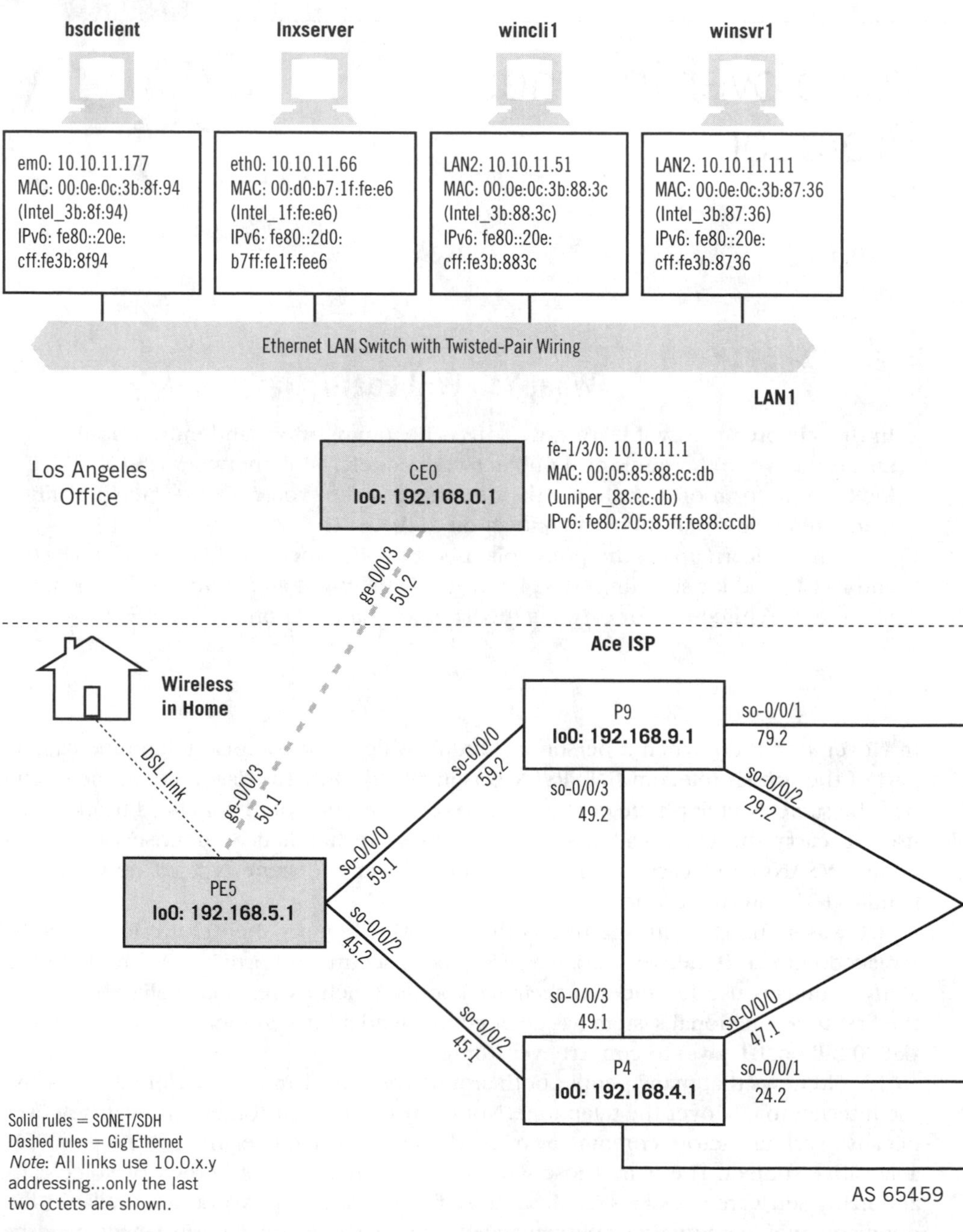

FIGURE 30.1

VoIP setup on the Illustrated Network, showing the host using an Internet telephony package.

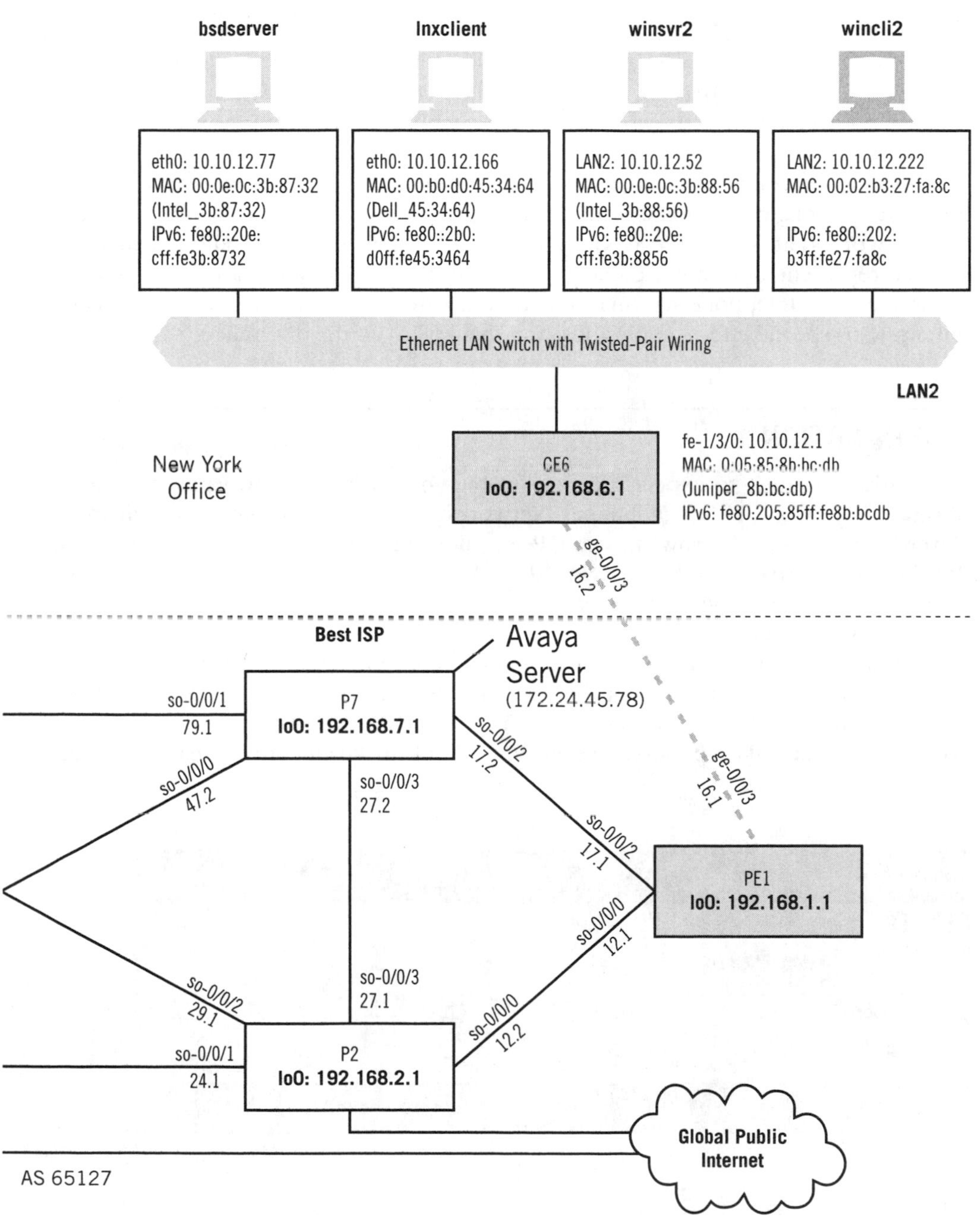

bsdserver
lnxclient
winsvr2
wincli2
eth0: 10.10.12.77
MAC: 00:0e:0c:3b:87:32
(Intel_3b:87:32)
IPv6: fe80::20e:
cff:fe3b:8732
eth0: 10.10.12.166
MAC: 00:b0:d0:45:34:64
(Dell_45:34:64)
IPv6: fe80::2b0:
d0ff:fe45:3464
LAN2: 10.10.12.52
MAC: 00:0e:0c:3b:88:56
(Intel_3b:88:56)
IPv6: fe80::20e:
cff:fe3b:8856
LAN2: 10.10.12.222
MAC: 00:02:b3:27:fa:8c
IPv6: fe80::202:
b3ff:fe27:fa8c
Ethernet LAN Switch with Twisted-Pair Wiring
LAN2
New York
Office
CE6
lo0: 192.168.6.1
fe-1/3/0: 10.10.12.1
MAC: 0:05:85:8b:bc:db
(Juniper_8b:bc:db)
IPv6: fe80:205:85ff:fe8b:bcdb
ge-0/0/3
16.2
Best ISP
Avaya
Server
(172.24.45.78)
so-0/0/1
79.1
P7
lo0: 192.168.7.1
so-0/0/2
17.2
ge-0/0/3
16.1
so-0/0/0
47.2
so-0/0/3
27.2
so-0/0/2
17.1
PE1
lo0: 192.168.1.1
so-0/0/0
12.1
so-0/0/2
29.1
so-0/0/3
27.1
so-0/0/0
12.2
so-0/0/1
24.1
P2
lo0: 192.168.2.1
Global Public
Internet
AS 65127

The exact percentage of PSTN traffic using VoIP is very difficult to pin down because some telephony carriers are relatively open about this fact and others are not, and all are as wary of their competitors as they ever were. The use of VoIP is also controversial because not too long ago the voice quality of such calls was (might as well admit it) horrible.

This chapter concerns voice, not audio, a distinction often glossed over by users but never by engineers. Voice is concerned primarily with comprehension of the spoken word, that is, of *what* is said rather than how it "sounds." Audio is generally a stereo representation of more than just speech. Think of audio as a motion picture soundtrack. The telephone system is "tuned" to the frequencies used in human speech, not music or special effects explosions. And that makes all the difference.

VoIP IN ACTION

It's a little too much to expect seeing a full-blown VoIP server and gateway on the Illustrated Network, although Juniper Networks does indeed make such software. Nevertheless, we can "borrow" an Avaya IP Softphone server for our network and install the client software on `wincli2` (`10.10.112.222`). Then we can use the VoIP software to place a call to a desk phone and capture the exchange of signaling and voice packets. This is shown in Figure 30.1.

Naturally, the server can place the call anywhere in the world, but having a conversation with a telephone in a local cubicle makes it easier to complete the call, talk, hang up, and so on. Figure 30.2 shows the main screen for the Avaya VoIP software. It doesn't look much like a phone, and some VoIP clients make an effort to make the user

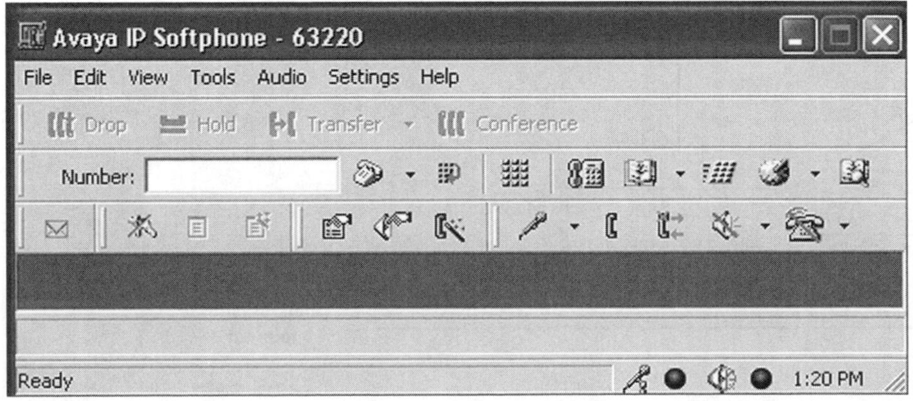

FIGURE 30.2

Avaya IP Softphone client interface. Note that this is not very "phone-like."

interface look like a "real" telephone. The best that Avaya does is place a small "keypad" on the screen so that you don't have to type the numbers in.

Before you can make a call, you have to log in to the server. A simple log-in ID and password is used, and then the screen shown in Figure 30.3 appears. It shows the extension the computer is acting as, its IP address (this capture is not from `wincli2`, so the addresses have been changed to the private range), the VoIP server's IP address, and the gateway "VoIP" address. The call status is shown also, and this screen was captured while the call was in progress.

The first thing that becomes obvious when capturing VoIP sessions is the blizzard of packets presented. The actual session, from "dialing" through conversation to "hang-up") lasted less than 30 seconds, and the log-in process, registration, and call setup took only a few seconds of that time. Yet in this 30-second window, some 756 packets passed back and forth from the VoIP client to server.

Most of them were small packets using the Real-Time Protocol (RTP), which carries 20 bytes of voice coded at 8 Kbps (the G.729 standard). A portion of the

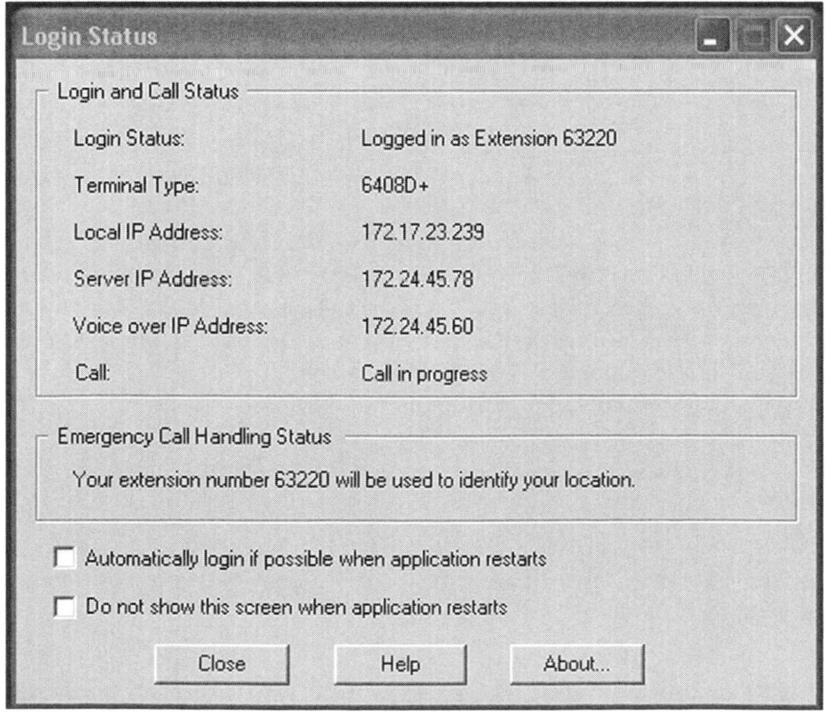

FIGURE 30.3

Avaya log-on screen with a call in progress.

```
No.   Time       Source         Destination    Protocol Info
  519 36.134534  172.24.45.65   10.10.12.222   RTP      Payload type=ITU-T G.729, SSRC=4202493579, Seq=114, Tim
  520 36.147911  10.10.12.222   172.24.45.65   RTP      Payload type=ITU-T G.729, SSRC=432397683, Seq=7268, Tim
  521 36.154530  172.24.45.65   10.10.12.222   RTP      Payload type=ITU-T G.729, SSRC=4202493579, Seq=115, Tim
  522 36.167901  10.10.12.222   172.24.45.65   RTP      Payload type=ITU-T G.729, SSRC=432397683, Seq=7269, Tim
  523 36.174524  172.24.45.65   10.10.12.222   RTP      Payload type=ITU-T G.729, SSRC=4202493579, Seq=116, Tim
  524 36.187920  10.10.12.222   172.24.45.65   RTP      Payload type=ITU-T G.729, SSRC=432397683, Seq=7270, Tim
  525 36.194570  172.24.45.65   10.10.12.222   RTP      Payload type=ITU-T G.729, SSRC=4202493579, Seq=117, Tim
  526 36.207876  10.10.12.222   172.24.45.65   RTP      Payload type=ITU-T G.729, SSRC=432397683, Seq=7271, Tim
  527 36.214566  172.24.45.65   10.10.12.222   RTP      Payload type=ITU-T G.729, SSRC=4202493579, Seq=118, Tim
  528 36.227950  10.10.12.222   172.24.45.65   RTP      Payload type=ITU-T G.729, SSRC=432397683, Seq=7272, Tim
  529 36.234505  172.24.45.65   10.10.12.222   RTP      Payload type=ITU-T G.729, SSRC=4202493579, Seq=119, Tim
  530 36.247902  10.10.12.222   172.24.45.65   RTP      Payload type=ITU-T G.729, SSRC=432397683, Seq=7273, Tim
  531 36.254515  172.24.45.65   10.10.12.222   RTP      Payload type=ITU-T G.729, SSRC=4202493579, Seq=120, Tim
  532 36.267957  10.10.12.222   172.24.45.65   RTP      Payload type=ITU-T G.729, SSRC=432397683, Seq=7274, Tim

▷ User Datagram Protocol, Src Port: 2048 (2048), Dst Port: 3376 (3376)
▿ Real-Time Transport Protocol
  ▿ [Stream setup by H245 (frame 271)]
      [Setup frame: 271]
      [Setup Method: H245]
    10.. .... = Version: RFC 1889 Version (2)
    ..0. .... = Padding: False
    ...0 .... = Extension: False
    .... 0000 = Contributing source identifiers count: 0
    0... .... = Marker: False
    .001 0010 = Payload type: ITU-T G.729 (18)
    Sequence number: 7269
    Timestamp: 18400
    Synchronization Source identifier: 432397683
    Payload: 2473FECB9C5D3E46680C7F41728458FB...

0010  00 3c 27 86 00 00 80 11  00 00 0a 0a 0c de ac 18   .<'..... ........
0020  2d 41 08 00 0d 30 00 28  6f fe 80 12 1c 65 00 00   -A...0.( o....e..
0030  47 e0 19 c5 dd 73 24 73  fe cb 9c 5d 3e 46 68 0c   G....s$s ...]>Fh.
0040  7f 41 72 84 58 fb 8e 6b  c2 68                     .Ar.X..k .h
```

FIGURE 30.4

RTP packets carrying 20 bytes of voice, shown highlighted in the bottom pane.

conversation between client and gateway is shown in Figure 30.4. (The gateway address `172.24.45.65` is now accessed from `wincli2`, and therefore different from that shown in Figure 30.3.)

In addition to the TCP packets (which are used to set up the connection to the server), and the RTP packets carrying the voice bits (and the RTCP packets with status information), there are other control packets that serve to remind us that we are not in the data world anymore. The voice world uses a unique language, and an often obscure one at that. This VoIP implementation speaks H.323, a signaling protocol family for voice. The main signaling protocols seen during the call follow.

H.225.0 RAS packets—These are the registration, admission, and status packets used to register the VoIP host on the VoIP server and allow it to use the system to make calls.

H.225.0 CS packets—The call status packets trace the progress of the call. (Is the other phone ringing? Did someone answer?)

Q.931 signaling packets—These are not strictly H.323 signaling packets. Q.931 is the "normal" signaling method with packets used on the PSTN. These are passed from the VoIP client to the server by this VoIP implementation.

Some packets of each type are shown in Figure 30.5, which only shows the expanded upper pane of a full Ethereal capture window. Signaling protocols in VoIP, as opposed to the voice "data" itself, use TCP for its sequencing and resending features.

No.	Time	Source	Destination	Protocol	Info
79	11.478372	172.24.45.78	10.10.12.222	TCP	1720 > 46182 [ACK] Seq=1 Ack=2 Win=8192 [CHECKSUM IN
82	11.950669	10.10.12.222	172.24.45.78	H.225.0	RAS: gatekeeperRequest
83	11.973718	172.24.45.78	10.10.12.222	H.225.0	RAS: gatekeeperConfirm
84	11.977533	10.10.12.222	172.24.45.78	H.225.0	RAS: registrationRequest
85	11.995277	172.24.45.78	10.10.12.222	H.225.0	RAS: registrationConfirm
86	12.024786	10.10.12.222	172.24.45.78	H.225.0	RAS: nonStandardMessage
87	12.052165	172.24.45.78	10.10.12.222	H.225.0	RAS: nonStandardMessage
88	12.052794	10.10.12.222	172.24.45.78	H.225.0	RAS: nonStandardMessage
89	12.076103	172.24.45.78	10.10.12.222	H.225.0	RAS: nonStandardMessage
90	12.091761	10.10.12.222	172.24.45.78	H.225.0	RAS: nonStandardMessage
93	12.115053	172.24.45.78	10.10.12.222	H.225.0	RAS: nonStandardMessage
94	12.124639	10.10.12.222	172.24.45.78	H.225.0	RAS: nonStandardMessage
95	12.151922	172.24.45.78	10.10.12.222	H.225.0	RAS: nonStandardMessage
96	12.161533	10.10.12.222	172.24.45.78	H.225.0	RAS: nonStandardMessage
97	12.172982	172.24.45.78	10.10.12.222	H.225.0	RAS: nonStandardMessage
98	12.187098	10.10.12.222	172.24.45.78	H.225.0	RAS: nonStandardMessage
100	12.212341	172.24.45.78	10.10.12.222	H.225.0	RAS: nonStandardMessage
101	12.215846	10.10.12.222	172.24.45.78	H.225.0	RAS: nonStandardMessage
102	12.232554	172.24.45.78	10.10.12.222	H.225.0	RAS: nonStandardMessage
103	12.261100	10.10.12.222	172.24.45.78	TCP	35654 > 1720 [SYN] Seq=0 Ack=0 Win=64512 [CHECKSUM I
104	12.262746	172.24.45.78	10.10.12.222	TCP	1720 > 35654 [SYN, ACK] Seq=0 Ack=1 Win=8192 [CHECKS
105	12.262775	10.10.12.222	172.24.45.78	TCP	35654 > 1720 [ACK] Seq=1 Ack=1 Win=64512 [CHECKSUM I
107	12.345161	10.10.12.222	172.24.45.78	Q.931	[Short Frame]
108	12.346724	172.24.45.78	10.10.12.222	TCP	1720 > 35654 [ACK] Seq=1 Ack=5 Win=8192 [CHECKSUM IN
109	12.346762	10.10.12.222	172.24.45.78	TCP	35654 > 1720 [PSH, ACK] Seq=5 Ack=1 Win=64512 [CHECK
110	12.349581	172.24.45.78	10.10.12.222	TCP	1720 > 35654 [ACK] Seq=1 Ack=322 Win=8131 [CHECKSUM
111	12.373179	172.24.45.78	10.10.12.222	H.225.0	CS: callProceeding
113	12.563662	10.10.12.222	172.24.45.78	TCP	35654 > 1720 [ACK] Seq=322 Ack=114 Win=64399 [CHECKS
114	12.565420	172.24.45.78	10.10.12.222	H.225.0	CS: connect OpenLogicalChannel CS: empty CS: empty C
116	12.764293	10.10.12.222	172.24.45.78	TCP	35654 > 1720 [ACK] Seq=322 Ack=620 Win=64512 [CHECKS
117	12.765510	172.24.45.78	10.10.12.222	H.225.0	CS: empty
118	12.964908	10.10.12.222	172.24.45.78	TCP	35654 > 1720 [ACK] Seq=322 Ack=667 Win=64465 [CHECKS
129	14.556457	10.10.12.222	172.24.45.78	Q.931	[Short Frame]
130	14.557966	172.24.45.78	10.10.12.222	TCP	1720 > 35654 [ACK] Seq=667 Ack=326 Win=8192 [CHECKSU
131	14.558005	10.10.12.222	172.24.45.78	TCP	35654 > 1720 [PSH, ACK] Seq=326 Ack=667 Win=64465 [C

FIGURE 30.5

H.225 and Q.931 signaling packets. Note the presence of TCP packets for signaling.

We've done little more than scratch the surface of VoIP, but it is enough to show that VoIP is acceptable and commercially viable today. Let's see why, and explore some of the architectures and protocols in a little more detail.

The Attraction of VoIP

In a very short period of time, we've transitioned from a world where data rode on links optimized for voice by masquerading as sound (that's what a modem is for) to a world where voice rides on links optimized for data (unchannelized) by masquerading as data packets. VoIP is a grand scheme to make this process as easy as possible.

The trick is to have the voice packets preserve the quality-of-service parameters that regulated telephone companies always have to keep an eye on (or their next request for a rate increase might be rejected, and some companies have even been forced to send customers rebates due to poor voice service). In the discussion that follows in this chapter, it will be a good thing to remember that when engineers say "voice" they really mean four things (and no, one of them is *not* audio).

What Is "Voice"?

The PSTN can carry one of four types of "voice" traffic.

1. *Two people talking*—This is what most people think of when they say "voice."
2. *Fax*—Fax machines use low-speed modems to make digital representations of images look like sound. And fax traffic is growing like never before as a result of several social factors (faxes have higher legal standing than email, for one

thing) and the fact that many languages are still not particularly email and keyboard friendly.

3. *Modem data*—Not everyone is on DSL, and a good percentage of users around the world (and, sadly, in the United States) still use analog modems to push perhaps 30 to 50 Kbps back and forth to their ISP.
4. *Touch tone*—Officially, these are the dual-tone multifrequency (DTMF) sounds you hear when you press buttons on a telephone keypad. The familiar beeps are analog (sound) representations of the numbers (digits) pressed.

There are also some economic factors pertinent to VoIP, and VoIP is one reason that premium long-distance telephone calls (which used to cost many dollars per *minute*) are seldom an issue in anyone's budget. (You used to ask before making a long-distance call from someone else's phone, and people rushed out of the shower dripping wet to take a long-distance call because the rates were higher initially.) The use of VoIP as a PSTN bypass method has become less attractive, but the goal of convergence remains strong.

VoIP is also attractive to carriers if what is often called in the United States "toll-quality voice" can be delivered at a reduced bit rate as a stream of TCP/IP packets. Bandwidth savings directly translates into network savings, which is something anyone can understand.

The Problem of Delay

Voice quality is tied to more than just bit rate. Two key parameters in assessing voice quality are *latency* (delay) and *jitter* (delay variation). Voice is much more sensitive to the values of these two network parameters, much more so than the most rigid interactive data requirements. This is because data are usually not processed until the "whole" of something has arrived, and it makes no difference if the first packets that represent a file arrive faster than the last few packets (this is the jitter). And as long as the delay remains below a certain timeout threshold the application will work fine (this is the overall delay).

Delay and latency are often used interchangeably, and they will be here. End-to-end network delays consist of two components: *serial* delay and *nodal processing* delay.

Nodal processing delay is the amount of time it takes for the bits that enter a network node (end node or intermediate node alike) to emerge. End nodes can measure this between application and link, and intermediate nodes as link-to-link delays. Today's routers operate in many cases at "line speeds," but this is a relatively recent development. Early routers operated at much too leisurely a pace to route voice packets at anywhere near the pace required for telephony services (that's what circuit-switched voice switches were for), which basically had to span the globe in about one-quarter of a second. And this had to include the serial delay.

Nodal processing delay also occurs when the analog voice is first digitized. The algorithm used to digitize voice might be complex, adding delay to the entire process. And the more bits needed to be gathered into a packet (bigger packets mean fewer packets than can get lost), the higher the nodal processing delay. This initial delay is often called the *packetization delay*, but it is just another form of nodal delay.

Serial delay is simply an acknowledgment of the fact that bits are sent on a link one by one, so it takes a certain amount of time to send a given number of bits at a given bit rate. If the serial delay is too high for a given application, there are only two ways to lower it: Put fewer bits in a packet or raise the link bit rate. Of course, you can do both. You can put fewer bits in voice packet by lowering the bit rate of the voice inside (or sending more packets—it's a tradeoff).

Jitter is the variation of the end-to-end delay across the network. As the delay varies, bits arrive either early or late at the destination. If they arrive too quickly, bits might overflow a buffer. If they arrive too late, silence results. Gaps in the conversation occur either way. And even less extreme jitter can distort the analog voice that results from the bits. To smooth out arriving voice, a "jitter buffer" is used to add the delay necessary to make the voice sound like it all arrives with the same delay.

The delay issues in VoIP are shown in Figure 30.6. Naturally, the same process works in the other direction.

Just like overall delay, and apart from jitter buffers, jitter can be handled in a couple of ways. Delay variations usually result from nodal processing load variations and buffer queue depth. In other words, when the node is busy, things slow down. This effect can be minimized by splitting off the voice for special handling, getting faster network nodes, or by increasing link bandwidth. (Note that constant appearance of "increased

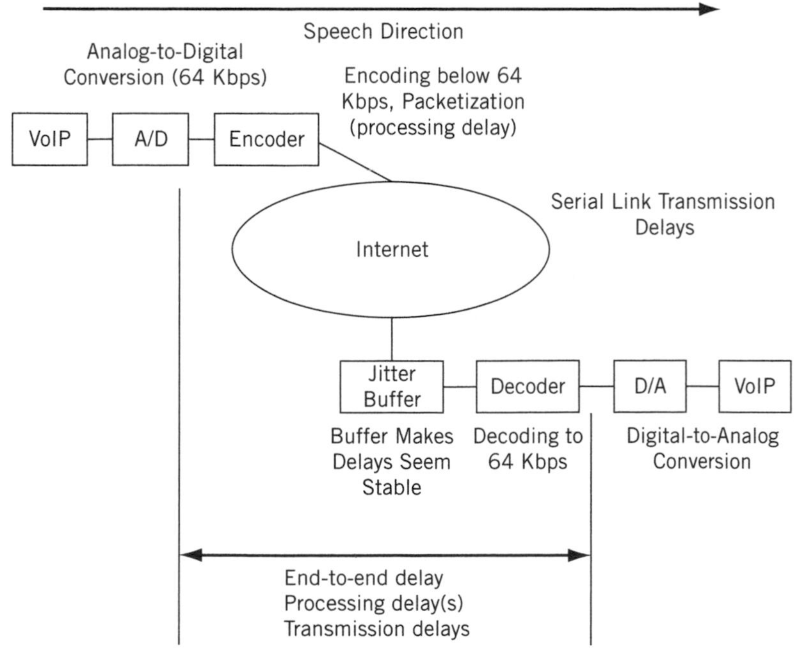

FIGURE 30.6

VoIP processing and transmission delays. Note that the jitter buffer compensates for differences in delays during different parts of the call.

link bandwidth" as a solution to networking problems, a fact that has slowed development of alternative solutions to many issues.)

The key to VoIP is not so much digitizing voice at a low bit rate, but rather TCP/IP and the Internet carrying packetized voice with acceptable latency and jitter as perceived by the humans using it. (Related issues, such as replacing silence with "comfort noise" and detecting "voice activation," are beyond the scope of this chapter.)

Packetized Voice

Voice on the PSTN is usually a streaming bidirectional connection at a fixed 64 Kbps. Once digitized, there was little incentive to play around with voice too much because any reduction in bit rate was offset by a loss in voice quality. Regulated carriers had to maintain certain voice quality levels or risk customers not having to pay for the call. However, if the "slope" of the decline of voice could be leveled so that quality at 16 Kbps or even 8 Kbps was not that much different than at 64 kbps, more calls could be carried over the same facilities. Not only that, but any bandwidth not used for carrying voice calls could be used for data (packets).

However, low-bit-rate voice with acceptable quality—something achieved with modern digital signal processing (DSP) chips—is not the same as packetized voice. Using "spare" voice bandwidth for data was the idea behind ISDN and eventually DSL. But the voice stayed on the voice channel and the data stayed on the data channel. Only by truly packetizing voice can voice and data be combined in an efficient manner.

A "voice" service really consists of two major components: content—which can take on four different meanings (as we have seen)—and signaling. This signaling is not the same as touch tones, although the intent is similar. This signaling is already packetized, and is how the number you dial and other information (such as the number you dialed from) makes its way through the voice signaling network.

This signaling network is as packetized as TCP/IP, uses special network nodes (which still route), and is known as Signaling System 7 (SS7). The real issue in VoIP is not so much how to packetize the voice content (gather bits and stick a header on them and send them out) but how the SS7 signaling packets relate to the Internet and TCP/IP.

The main stumbling block to universal VoIP service today is not so much that there are many ways to packetize voice content (there are options in many other TCP/IP protocols) but that there are many ways (and many *architectures*) to carry voice signaling information in a TCP/IP environment. These VoIP protocol controversies are important enough for a detailed look.

PROTOCOLS FOR VoIP

Voice, like audio and video, is a "real-time" application. And, as in multicast TCP is a poor choice for voice connections over the Internet. This sounds odd because voice is as connection oriented as TCP and requires handshaking overhead to complete a "call." (Humans handshake with a ring and a vocalized shared "Hello.")

The problem is not just TCP overhead, it's the fact that TCP will *always* resend missing data units. That's what it's for. However, the meaningful resending of voice bits is impossible in VoIP given the real-time nature of voice. So, UDP (which blithely accepts lost data units with a shrug) is used in VoIP—just as in multicast.

But TCP headers contain a number of fields that are very helpful for end-to-end communications, which are fields lost in UDP, such as a sequence number to detect lost voice packets. So we'll have to take what fields we need from TCP and stick them inside (after) the UDP header. This new header will have to have a name and a place in the TCP/IP protocol stack. We'll call it the Real-Time Protocol (RTP) and use it for the transport of digitized voice inside our IP packets.

Signaling, however, is another matter. We might want to keep TCP for that because resending lost signaling packets is actually a good idea (calls that are not completed do not generate revenue for metered service or friends in the user community). In addition, the delays for signaling in regulated voice services are much less stringent than the delays for voice packets, which make TCP connection overhead tolerable. So, in some cases (especially over a WAN), TCP is acceptable for voice signaling.

But what form should TCP/IP voice signaling packets take? How should voice-capable TCP/IP devices find each other by IP address? How are VoIP calls handed off to (or received from) the PSTN network with SS7? Where are the voice gateways? Who runs the gateways—the customer or the service provider? In other words, what is the overall architecture of the TCP/IP voice-signaling network?

Unfortunately, we live in a world where there are competing answers to all of these signaling questions. Let's start by looking at RTP and then examining the major differences between the various systems of VoIP signaling.

RTP for VoIP Transport

RTP grew out of efforts to improve the Streams 2 (ST2) protocol defined in RFC 1819. ST2 was known as IPv5 and is why IPv4 evolved into IPv6. RTP was defined in RFC 1889 and deliberately left open-ended to allow room for the protocol to evolve.

RTP is really a framework using *application layer framing* and was initially aimed at audio (and video) multicast sessions. However, two-way phone calls are just special cases of audio multicast, so RTP is a good fit for VoIP.

RTP can replace TCP for many applications, but in VoIP it is used with UDP. The RTP architecture also includes another protocol, the Real-Time Control Protocol (RTCP), which uses IP directly to monitor the job RTP is doing in terms of delay and voice quality.

IP port numbers 5004 and 5005 are used for RTP and RTCP, respectively, and the ports are the same on both ends of the connection. The overall RTP architecture is shown in Figure 30.7.

There are many audio and video codecs supported by RTP, but not all of them are needed for VoIP (especially video codecs, naturally). In addition, the RTP architecture establishes devices called *mixers* (to mix multiple sources for conferences) and *translators* (to compensate for low and high bit-rate links and LANs). These functions can be implemented in some type of "voice and audio server" on a LAN, but are not used in VoIP.

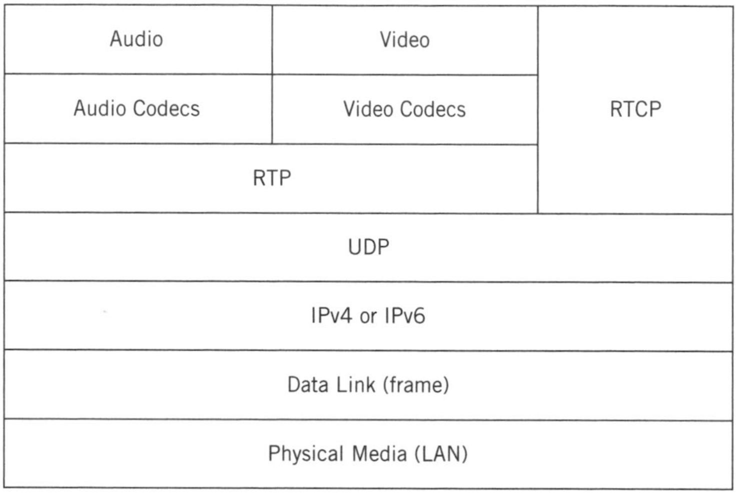

Audio
Video
Audio Codecs
Video Codecs
RTCP
RTP
UDP
IPv4 or IPv6
Data Link (frame)
Physical Media (LAN)

FIGURE 30.7

RTP and RTCP protocol stack, showing how these protocols use UDP instead of TCP.

The structure of the basic RTP header is shown in Figure 30.8. Only the fields that apply to two-party calls (point to point) are fully described.

V (version)—This 2-bit field gives the current version of RTP.

Pad (padding)—This 2-bit field aligns the packet to a specific boundary. The actual padding byte count is given in the last byte of the RTP data.

E (extension)—This 1-bit field extends the length of the RTP header, mostly for experimental purposes, and is almost always set to zero.

M (marker)—This 1-bit field is used in the first packet sent after a period of silence.

Payload type—This 7-bit field is used to define 128 types of RTP payloads. Some are static, and can only be used for the defined type, but newer ones are dynamic and are assigned by the control protocol (such as SIP).

Sequence number—This 16-bit field increases by one for each RTP packet sent. Receivers can use this field to detect missing or out-of-sequence packets.

Timestamp—This 32-bit field is most useful for video (all bits from the same frame have the same timestamp), but it is used for the voice sampling rate as well.

The count field gives the number of "contributors" to a conference. For multiparty calls, the synchronization source identifier (SSRC) and a series of contributing source identifiers (CSRC) matching the count are not used. The VoIP RTP header adds 8 bytes to the voice stream. The format of the payload in the RTP data field is determined by the values in the categories listed in Table 30.1.

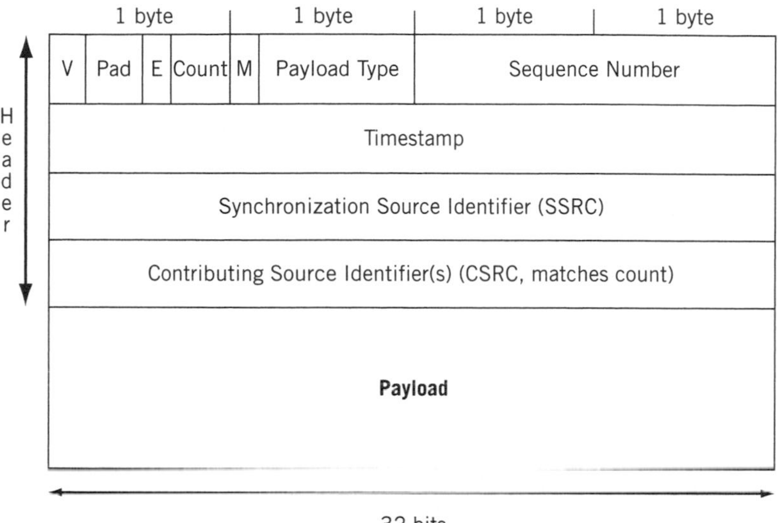

FIGURE 30.8

RTP header fields, which preserve some aspects of TCP fields.

Table 30.1 RTP Payload Formats and Their Meanings

Type	Meaning
0–34	Static assignment (most popular bit rates and formats here)
35–71	Unassigned
72–76	Reserved
77–95	Unassigned
96–127	Dynamic assignment (under the control of a call control protocol)

RTP is a pure transport mechanism. Feedback on quality and immediate network conditions is provided by the receiver to the sender with RTCP. RTCP doesn't say what senders should *do* with this information, such as the revelation that a router is becoming overloaded and dropping more packets than it is sending, but at least the ability to detect problems is there.

RTP generates periodic "reports" about the RTP session. There are five RTCP message types.

1. *Sender report*—Contains transmission and reception statistics from conference participants that are active senders.

2. *Receiver report*—Reception statistics from conference participants that are *not* active senders.
3. *Source description*—Items relating to the source, including the canonical DNS name.
4. *Bye*—Used to end a session.
5. *Application specific*—Contains any information that the applications agree to share.

The possible payload formats that can be used to carry voice bits following the RTP header are complex, seemingly fiendishly so. These are defined in RFC 2833. Fortunately, they are usually of interest only to telephony engineers.

Signaling

I first encountered voice over IP around the same time I encountered the Web, in the early 1990s. It was in a university setting, where the absolute utility and cost effectiveness of things are not as rigid as in the business world. In the fluid environment of an educational institution, many things happen because they are instructive, groundbreaking, and just, well, cool.

A graduate student of mine was in the lab one day, busily chattering into a microphone hooked up to a PC and intently listening to the garbled voice coming out of the PC's speakers. Much of the conversation consisted of "What?" and "Huh?"

When I asked, he informed me that he was talking over the Internet to an old friend in a similar lab at RPI in Troy, New York, about 150 miles north of us—and in those days usually an expensive long-distance call away (especially for graduate students). I asked him how the friend in Troy knew to be in the lab at the right time to answer his PC. "Oh," my student said, "I called his dorm room from your office and told him to go there."

Things have come a long way since the early 1990s. The trouble back then was that the world of Internet telephony was a closed world, limited to Internet-attached devices. There were no signaling gateways to translate phone numbers to IP addresses and back, and so no way to enable calls with one end on the Internet and the other end in the PSTN to complete calls.

This is not to say that there were not VoIP gateways. There were. But these used proprietary protocols for the most part, and only connected to their cousin devices from the same vendor. So, there was a need to create standard signaling protocols for VoIP.

Today, the issue seems to be *not* a lack of proposed standard protocols for VoIP but their proliferation. There are three general protocol stacks that can be used for VoIP. These are shown in Figure 30.9.

Note that the third stack combines two methods known as the Multimedia Gateway Control Protocol (MGCP) and Megaco/H.248 into a single stack. The two are similar enough to allow this.

However, things are not as bad as they might seem at first. All three of the signaling protocols could have a role in the "converged" VoIP architecture of Internet and PSTN. Before we see how this is possible, let's take a look at each of the protocols in turn.

H.225 RAS
H.225 Call Status
H.245 Control
UDP
TCP
IP
Data Link
Physical Media

H.323 Signaling Stack

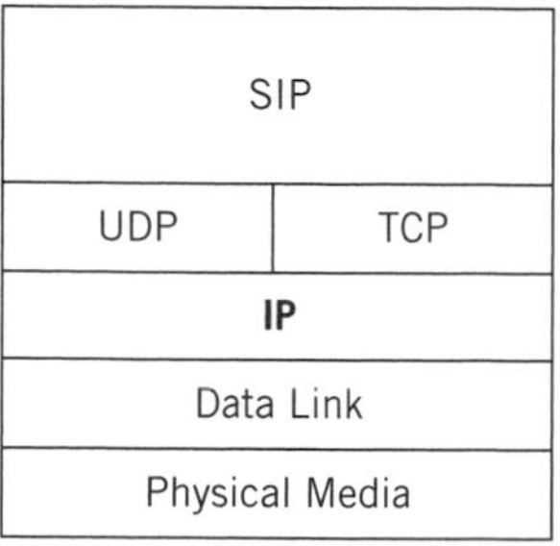

SIP Signaling Stack

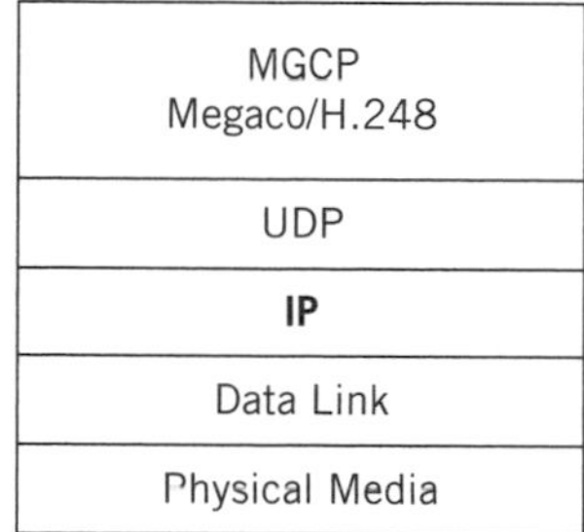

MGCP, Megaco/H.248 Signaling Stack

FIGURE 30.9

Three VoIP signaling architectures.

H.323, the International Standard

The H.323 signaling protocol framework is the international telephony standard for all telephony signaling over the packet network (not just the Internet). When work on H.323 began, the packet network most commonly mentioned for H.323 was X.25, then ATM, and not the Internet. In a sense, H.323 doesn't care—it's just an umbrella term for what needs to be done.

Like RTP, H.323 was designed for audio and video conferencing, not just point-to-point voice conversations. A LAN with devices that support H.323 capabilities (H.323 terminals, which have many different subtypes) also has an H.323 multipoint control unit (MCU) for conference coordination. The LAN includes an H.323 *gateway* to send bits to other H.323 *zones* and an H.323 *gatekeeper*. The gatekeeper is optional, and is needed only if the terminals are so underpowered they cannot generate or understand H.323 messages on their own. (Most can, although H.323 is not trivial.) The H.323 gateway is essentially a router, but with the ability to support packetized voice to PSTN connections (and the terminals are computers, of course).

The main H.323 signaling protocols used with VoIP are H.225 RAS (Registration, Admission, and Status), which is used to register the VoIP device with the gatekeeper, and H.255 CS (call status), which is used to track the progress of the call. The structure

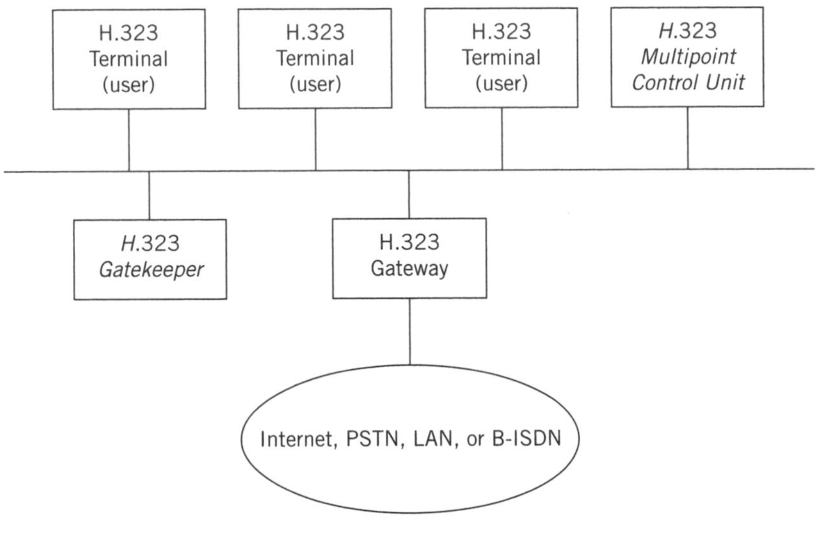

FIGURE 30.10

H.323 zone components. (Optional components are shown in italic.)

of a typical H.323 zone is shown in Figure 30.10. H.323 signaling uses both UDP and TCP when run on an IP network, and uses RTP and RTCP for transport. Components that are not strictly needed for VoIP are shown in italics.

H.323 supports not only audio and video conferencing but also *data* conferencing, where users can all see the same information on their PCs and changed data are updated across the network. Cursors are usually distinguished by distinctive colors.

The trouble with H.323 was that it is complete overkill for VoIP. Data and video support are not needed for VoIP, and some wondered why H.323 was needed in VoIP at all given its telephony roots and the hefty amount of power needed to run it. Maybe the Internet people could come up with something better.

SIP, the Internet Standard

The Session Initiation Protocol (SIP), defined in RFC 3261, is the official Internet signaling protocol for IP networks. Each session can also include audio and video conferencing, but right now SIP is mainly used for simple voice over the Internet. SIP is a text-based protocol similar to HTTP and SMTP, uses multicast Session Description Protocol (SDP) for the characteristics of the media, and is technically independent of any particular packet protocol.

Both H.323 and SIP define mechanisms for the formal processes of call signaling, call routing (the path the voice bits will follow), capabilities exchange (the bit rate that should be used), and supplementary services (such as collect calling). However, SIP attempts to perform these functions in a more streamlined fashion than H.323.

VoIP combines the worlds of the telephony carriers (H.323) and the Internet (SIP). Not surprisingly, both telephony carriers and Internet people see their way as the best way for a unified signaling protocol suitable for both environments.

The SIP architecture is client-server in nature, as expected, but with adaptation for the peer-to-peer nature of telephony. The main SIP components are the user agent (the "endpoint" device), the "intermediate servers" (which can be proxy servers or redirect servers), and the registrar.

Proxy servers forward SIP requests from the user agent to the next SIP server or user agent and retain accounting and billing information. User agents can be clients (UACs) when they send SIP requests, and servers (UASs) when they receive them. SIP redirect servers respond to client requests and tell the UACs the requested server's address.

The SIP registrar stores information about user agents, such as their location. This information is not maintained or accessed by SIP, but by a separate "location service" that is still part of the SIP framework. SIP is flexible enough to support stateless requests or to remember them, and is not tied to any one directory method to locate SIP users and components.

The general SIP architecture is shown in Figure 30.11. The only piece that is missing is the registrar, which takes the SIP register request information and uses it to update the information stored in the location server. The figure shows the sequence of SIP requests and responses to establish a session (call). The details of each step are beyond the scope of this chapter, but the point is that a lot of messages are required to complete the call. Once the called party is found and alerted in Step 8, however, the call is quickly completed from proxy to proxy and back to the calling party.

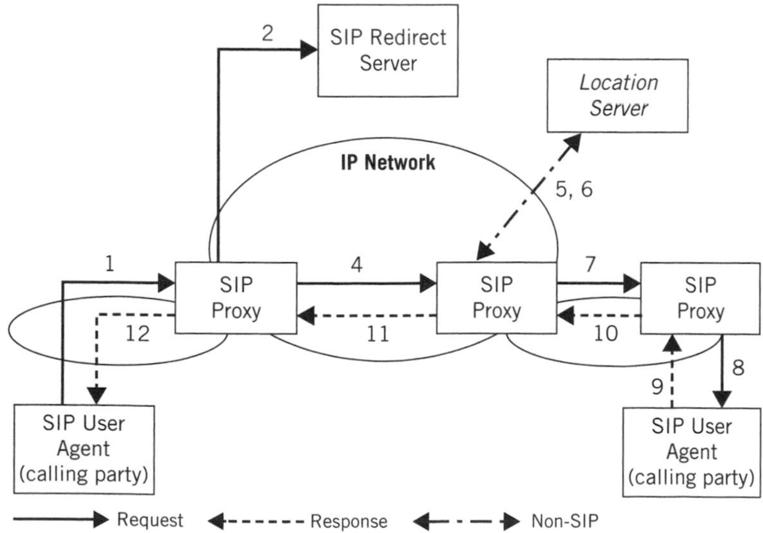

FIGURE 30.11

SIP session initiation steps.

There are six basic types of SIP requests.

1. *Invite*—Start a session.
2. *ACK*—Confirms that the client has received a final response to an invitation.
3. *Options*—Provides capabilities information, such as voice bit rates supported.
4. *BYE*—Release a call.
5. *Cancel*—Cancel a pending request.
6. *Register*—Sends information about a user's location to the SIP registrar server.

SIP responses follow the familiar three-digit codes used in many other TCP/IP protocols. The major response categories in SIP follow:

- 1xx Provisional, used for searching, ringing, queuing, and so on
- 2xx Success
- 3xx Redirection, forwarding
- 4xx Server failure
- 5xx Global failure

SIP even allows PSTN signaling messages (packets) to use the Internet to set up calls that use the PSTN on both ends, so telephony carriers can send calls directly over the Internet. This version of SIP is called SIP-T (SIP for Telephony).

MGCP and Megaco/H.248

It's one thing to describe a network of media gateways leading to the PSTN (as in H.323), or a series of servers that relay call setup packets across the Internet, as in SIP. But these elements do not function independently, despite the fact that H323 Media gateways and SIP proxy servers are on the customer premises and on LANs. If VoIP must handle the most general situations with endpoints anywhere on the Internet or PSTN, some type of overall control protocol must be developed.

That's what the Media Gateway Control Protocol (MGCP) is for. Despite the H.323 terminology, MGCP was defined in RFC 2705 as a way to control VoIP gateways from "external call control elements." In other words, MGCP allows the service providers (telephony carriers or ISPs) to control the VoIP aspects of the customer's network, whether it uses H.323 or SIP. These control points are known as call agents, and MGCP only defines how a call agent talks to the media gateway—not how the call agents talk to each other. Call agent communication uses H.323 or SIP, so this is not a limitation.

The terminology for all of these signaling protocols is starting to get confusing. Let's back up and see what we've got so far.

Media gateways—The H.323 component that handles all voice bits sent to and from the "zone" (usually a LAN).

Proxy servers—The SIP components that handle requests for SIP-capable user agents on the LAN.

Call agents—The MGCP components that control the media gateways and can do so over the Internet link itself.

But wait, didn't SIP have a media gateway? No, SIP defines a signaling framework that can tell you where the gateway *is*, but doesn't include that device in its framework. If you think about it, it all makes sense and all of the pieces are needed to make VoIP as useful as possible.

The biggest clash is between parts of H.323 and SIP. You don't need to have *both* running on the "terminals" or "user agents," no matter which terminology you use. However, many vendors are hedging their bets and supporting both H.323 and SIP right now. The funny thing is that they usually don't support MGCP.

How's that? Well, MGCP was modified into something called *Megaco* to make it more palatable to the telephone carriers. Megaco was standardized as H.248, so the result often appears as Magaco/H.248. The architecture of Megaco/H.248 is very similar to that of MGCP.

PUTTING IT ALL TOGETHER

How do H.323, SIP, and Megaco/H.248 relate to one another today? Well, they all have a place in a VoIP network that can place or take calls to and from the PSTN and handle IP transport of what appear to customers to be PSTN calls. Figure 30.12 shows the overall architecture of such a converged VoIP network.

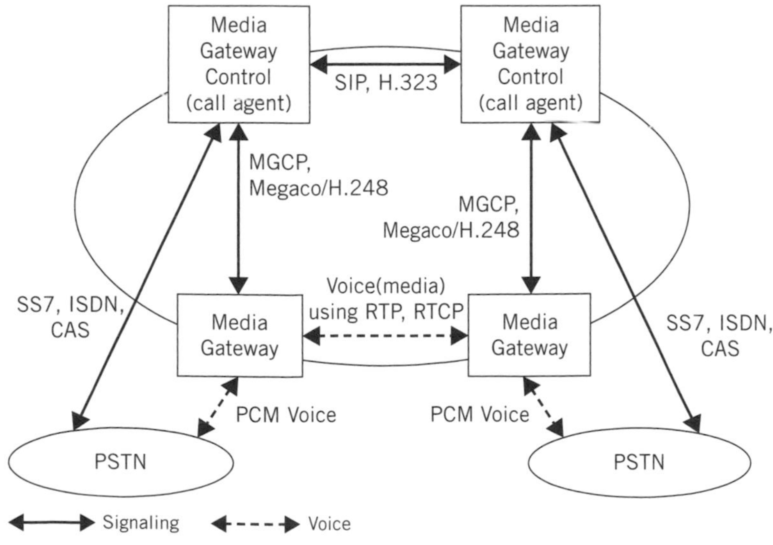

FIGURE 30.12

VoIP converged network architecture, showing how VoIP protocols can work together.

We've seen ISDN and SS7 signaling before, and channel-associated signaling (CAS) is used on aggregate circuits with many voice channels. Pulse code modulation (PCM) is a common way to carry the voice bits on the PSTN. Therefore, the "upper" path through the figure describes the signaling, and the "lower" path shows the "media" channel using RTP and RTCP over the Internet (or private IP network).

QUESTIONS FOR READERS

Figure 30.13 shows some of the concepts discussed in this chapter and can be used to answer the following questions.

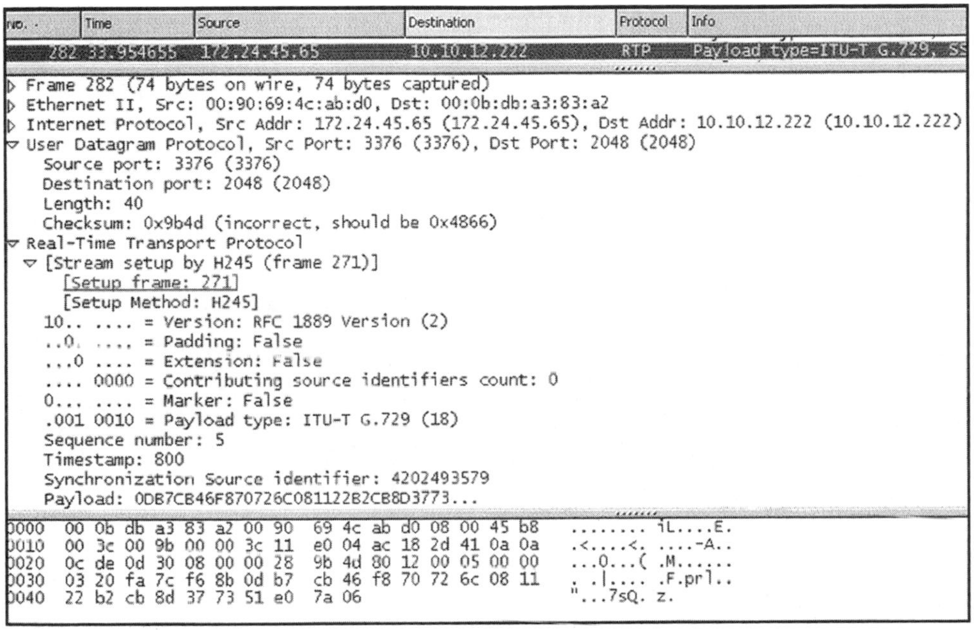

```
No. .  Time         Source          Destination      Protocol  Info
  282 33.954655    172.24.45.65    10.10.12.222     RTP       Payload type=ITU-T G.729, SS

▷ Frame 282 (74 bytes on wire, 74 bytes captured)
▷ Ethernet II, Src: 00:90:69:4c:ab:d0, Dst: 00:0b:db:a3:83:a2
▷ Internet Protocol, Src Addr: 172.24.45.65 (172.24.45.65), Dst Addr: 10.10.12.222 (10.10.12.222)
▽ User Datagram Protocol, Src Port: 3376 (3376), Dst Port: 2048 (2048)
    Source port: 3376 (3376)
    Destination port: 2048 (2048)
    Length: 40
    Checksum: 0x9b4d (incorrect, should be 0x4866)
▽ Real-Time Transport Protocol
  ▽ [Stream setup by H245 (frame 271)]
      [Setup frame: 271]
      [Setup Method: H245]
    10.. .... = Version: RFC 1889 Version (2)
    ..0. .... = Padding: False
    ...0 .... = Extension: False
    .... 0000 = Contributing source identifiers count: 0
    0... .... = Marker: False
    .001 0010 = Payload type: ITU-T G.729 (18)
    Sequence number: 5
    Timestamp: 800
    Synchronization Source identifier: 4202493579
    Payload: 0DB7CB46F870726C081122B2CB8D3773...

0000  00 0b db a3 83 a2 00 90  69 4c ab d0 08 00 45 b8   ........ iL....E.
0010  00 3c 00 9b 00 00 3c 11  e0 04 ac 18 2d 41 0a 0a   .<....<. ....-A..
0020  0c de 0d 30 08 00 00 28  9b 4d 80 12 00 05 00 00   ...0...( .M......
0030  03 20 fa 7c f6 8b 0d b7  cb 46 f8 70 72 6c 08 11   . .|.... .F.prl..
0040  22 b2 cb 8d 37 73 51 e0  7a 06                     "...7sQ. z.
```

FIGURE 30.13

Frame 282 using RTP captured from a VoIP call.

1. What are the four types of "voice" carried by VoIP?
2. In the figure, is `wincli2` sending (talking) or receiving (listening)?
3. Which UDP port is the client using for the call?
4. Which international standard protocol is used to set up the stream?
5. Which voice coding standard is used for the "data" in the voice packet?

List of Acronyms

AA	Authoritative Answer
AAAA	IPv6 DNS record
ABR	Area Border Router
ACD	Automatic Call Distribution
ACELP	Algebraic-Code-Excited Linear Prediction
ACK	Acknowledgment
AD	Active Directory
ADPCM	Adaptive Differential Pulse Code Modulation
ADSL	Asymmetric Digital Subscriber Loop
AF	Address Family
AFI	Address Family Identifier (RIP);Authority and Format Identifier (IS-IS)
AfriNIC	African Network Information Center
AH	Authentication Header
AIX	Advanced Interactive Executive (IBM's Unix)
AMI	Alternate Mark Inversion
ANS	Advanced Network Service
ANSI	American National Standards Institute
AOL	America On-Line
API	Application Program Interface
APNIC	Asian Pacific Network Information Center
APPC	Advanced Program-to-Program Communications
APPN	Advanced Peer-to-Peer Networking
ARIN	American Registry for Internet Numbers
ARP	Address Resolution Protocol
ARPA	Advanced Research Projects Agency
AS	Autonomous System
ASBR	Autonomous System Boundary Router
ASCII	American Standard Code for Information Interchange (IA-5)
ASIC	Application Specific Integrated Circuit
ASM	Any Source Multicast
ASN.1	Abstract Syntax Notation 1
ASP	Active Server Page
AT	Advanced Technology
ATM	Asynchronous Transfer Mode
ATT	Attach segment
AUI	Attachment Unit Interface
AUP	Acceptable Use Policy
AUX	Auxiliary
BBN	Bolt, Baranek, and Newman, Inc.
BBS	Bulletin Board System
BDR	Backup Designated Router
BECN	Backward Explicit Congestion Notification
BER	Bit Error Rate
BGP	Border Gateway Protocol
BIND	Berkeley Internet Name Domain
BIOS	Basic Input/Output System
B-ISDN	Broadband Integrated Services Digital Network
BITNET	Because It's Time Network

BITS	Bump in the Stack
BITW	Bump in the Wire
BOOTP	Bootstrap Protocol
BPSK	Binary Phase Shift Keying
BRI	Basic Rate Interface
BSD	Berkeley Systems (or Software) Distribution
CA	Certificate Authority
CABS	Carrier Access Billing System
CAR	Committed Access Rate
CAS	Channel Associated Signaling
CBC	Cipher Block Chaining
CBGP	Confederation Border Gateway Protocol
CBT	Core-Based Tree
CCITT	Consultative Committee on International Telegraphy and Telephony (French original)
CCS	Common Channel Signaling
CD	Call Disconnect; Collision Detection
CDMA	Code Division Multiple Access
CDR	Call Detail Record
CE	Customer Edge
CED	Called Station Identification
CELP	Code Excited Linear Prediction
CERN	European Council for Nuclear Research
CGI	Common Gateway Interface
CHAP	Challenge Handshake Authentication Protocol
CIA	Central Intelligence Agency
CIDR	Classless Interdomain Routing
CIP	Connector Interface Panel
CIR	Committed Information Rate
CIX	Commercial Internet Exchange
CLEC	Competitive Local Exchange Carrier
CLI	Command Line Interface
CLNP	Connectionless Network Protocol
CLNS	Connectionless Network Service
CLP	Cell Loss Priority
CLV	Code/Length/Value
CMIP	Common Management Information Protocol
CMIS	Common Management Information Services
CMOT	Common Management Information Services and Protocol Over TCP/IP
CNAME	Canonical Name
CNG	Calling Number
CO	Central Office
CoS	Class of Service
CPU	Central Processing Unit
CRC	Cyclical Redundancy Check
CRL	Certificate Revocation List
CRM	Customer Relationship Management
CS	Call Status
CSLIP	Compressed Serial Line Interface Protocol
CSMA	Carrier Sense Multiple Access
CSNP	Complete Sequence Number PDU
CSR	Certificate Signing Request

CSRC	Contributing Source Identifier
CSU	Channel Service Unit
CTI	Computer Telephony Integration
DAM	Diagnostic Acceptability Measure
DARPA	Defense Advanced Research Project Agency
DC	Direct Current; Demand Circuit
DCA	Defense Communication Agency
DCE	Data Circuit-terminating Equipment; Distributed Computing Environment
DD	Database Description
DDDS	Dynamic Delegation Discovery System
DDN	Defense Data Network
DE	Discard Eligible
DES	Data Encryption Standard
DF	Don't Fragment
DHAAD	Dynamic Home Agent Address Discovery
DHCP	Dynamic Host Configuration Protocol
DIS	Designated Intermediate System
DNA	Digital Network Architecture
DIX	Digital, Intel, and Xerox Ethernet
DLCI	Data Link Connection Identifier
DLL	Dynamic Link Library
DLP	Data Link Protocol
DM	Delta Modulation
DM	Dense Mode
DME	Distributed Management Environment
DMZ	Demilitarized Zone
DNS	Domain Name System
DNSSEC	Domain Name System Security
DoD	Department of Defense
DOS	Disk Operating System
DPCM	Differential Pulse Code Modulation
DR	Designated Router
DRAM	Dynamic Random Access Memory
DRT	Diagnostic Rhyme Test
DS	Digital Signal
DSAP	Destination Service Access Point
DSL	Digital Subscriber Line
DSP	Digital Signal Processor
DSU	Digital Service Unit
DTE	Data Terminal Equipment
DTMF	Dual Tone Multifrequency
DVMRP	Distance Vector Multicast Routing Protocol
DWDM	Dense Wavelength Division Multiplexing
EA	External Attributes; Extended Address
EBGP	External Border Gateway Protocol
ECC	Error Correction Code
ECM	Error Correction Mode
ECN	Explicit Congestion Notification
EGP	Exterior Gateway Protocol
EIGRP	Enhanced Interior Gateway Routing Protocol
EIR	Excess Information Rate

EoF	End of File
EoR	End of Record
ES	End System
ESMTP	Extensions to Simple Mail Transfer Protocol
ESF	Extended Superframe Format
ESP	Encapsulating Security Payload
EUI	Extended Unique Identifier
EXEC	Executive (mode)
FA	Foreign Agent
FAQ	Frequently Asked Questions
FCC	Federal Communication Commission
FCS	Frame Check Sequence
FDDI	Fiber Distributed Data Interface
FDM	Frequency Division Multiplexing
FE	Fast Ethernet
FEB	Forwarding Engine Board
FEC	Forward Error Correction, Fast EtherChannel
FECN	Forward Explicit Congestion Notification
FEIP	Fast Ethernet Interface Processor
FIN	Final segment
FIX	Federal Internet Exchange
FM	Frequency Modulation
FPC	Flexible PIC Concentrator
FQDN	Fully Qualified Domain Name
FRAD	Frame Relay Access Device
FT	Forwarding Table
FTAM	File Transfer, Access, and Management
FTP	File Transfer Protocol
GBE	Gigabit Ethernet
GE	Gigabit Ethernet
GEO	Geosynchronous Earth Orbit
GFC	Generic Flow Control
GGP	Gateway-to-Gateway Protocol
GIF	Graphics Interchange Format
GIP	Gateway Interface Protocol
GLP	Gateway Location Protocol
GPS	Global Positioning System
GRE	Generic Routing Encapsulation
GSM	Global System for Mobile
GSTN	Global Switched Telephone Network
GTLD	Generic Top Level Domain
GUI	Graphical User Interface
HA	Home Agent
HDLC	High-Level Datalink Control
HEC	Header Error Control
HF	High Frequency
HMAC	Hashed Message Authentication Check
HTML	Hypertext Markup Language
HTTP	Hypertext Transfer Protocol
IA	Implementation Agreement; International Alphabet (ASCII is IA.5); Inter-Area
IAB	Internet Activities Board; Internet Architecture Board

IANA	Internet Assigned Numbers Authority
ICANN	Internet Corporation for Assigned Names and Numbers
ICMP	Internet Control Message Protocol
ICV	Integrity Check Value
ID	Identifier
IDNS	Internationalization of the Domain Name Space
IDRP	Inter-domain Routing Protocol
IEEE	Institute of Electrical and Electronics Engineers
IEN	Internet Engineering Notes
IESG	Internet Engineering Steering Group
IETF	Internet Engineering Task Force
IGMP	Internet Group Management Protocol
IGP	Interior Gateway Protocol
IGRP	Interior Gateway Routing Protocol
IKE	Internet Key Exchange
ILEC	Incumbent Local Exchange Carrier
IMAP	Internet Mail Access Program
IMP	Interface Message Processor
IN	Intelligent Network
InARP	Inverse Address Resolution Protocol
IOS	Internetwork Operating System
IP	Internet Protocol
IPLS	IP-only LAN-like Service
IPSec	IP Security
IRC	Internet Relay Chat
IRR	Internet Routing Registry
IRTF	Internet Research Task Force
IS	Information Systems
ISAKMP	Internet Security Association and Key Management Protocol
ISATAP	Intra-site Automatic Tunnel Addressing Protocol
ISBN	International Standard Book Number
ISDN	Integrated Services Digital Network
IS–IS	Intermediate System to Intermediate System
ISN	Initial Sequence Number
ISO	International Organization for Standardization (ISO means "equal")
ISP	Internet Service Provider
IT	Information Technology
ITU	International Telecommunication Union
ITSP	Internet Telephony Service Provider
ITU	International Telecommunications Union
IVR	Interactive Voice Response
JPEG	Joint Photographic Experts' Group
KB	Kilobyte
L2F	Layer 2 Forwarding
L2TP	Layer 2 Tunneling Protocol
LAC	L2TP Access Concentrator
LAN	Local Area Network
LAPB	Link Access Procedure Balanced
LAPD	Link Access Procedure on the D-channel
LATA	Local Access and Transport Area
LCD	Liquid Crystal Diode

LCP	Link Control Protocol
LDAP	Lightweight Directory Access Protocol
LDP	Label Distribution Protocol
LEC	Local Exchange Carrier
LLC	Logical Link Control
LNS	L2TP Network Server
LOC	Location
LPC	Linear Predictive Coding
LS	Link State
LSA	Link State Advertisement
LSB	Least Significant Bit (Byte)
LSP	Label Switched Path; Link State PDU
MAC	Media Access Control
MAN	Metropolitan Area Network
MAU	Media Access Unit
MB	Megabytes
MBGP	Multiprotocol Border Gateway Protocol
MBONE	Multicast Backbone
MC	Multipoint Controller; Multicast
MCS	Miscellaneous Control System
MCU	Multipoint Control Unit
MD5	Message Digest 5
MED	Multi-Exit Discriminator
MF	More Fragments
MGCP	Multimedia Gateway Control Protocol
MIB	Management Information Base
MIME	Multipurpose Internet Mail Extensions
M-ISIS	Multicast IS–IS
MLD	Multicast Listener Discovery
MN	Mobile Node
MOSPF	Multicast OSPF
MP-BGP	Multiprotocol BGP (sometimes)
MPLS	Multiprotocol Label Switching
MSDP	Multicast Source Discovery Protocol
MSS	Maximum Segment Size
MTA	Mail Transfer Agent
MTU	Maximum Transmission Unit
MUA	Mail User Agent
MX	Mail Exchange
NAP	Network Access Point
NAPT	Network Address Port Translation
NAT	Network Address Translation
NBMA	Non-Broadcast, Multi-Access
NCP	Network Control Protocol
NCSA	National Center for Supercomputing Applications
ND	Neighbor Discovery
NDP	Neighbor Discovery Protocol
NET	Network Entity Title
NFS	Network File System
NIC	Network Interface Card/Network Information Center
NID	Network Intrusion Detection

NLA	Next Level Aggregator
NLRI	Network Layer Reachability Information
NOC	Network Operations Center
NSAP	Network Service Attachment Point
NSF	National Science Foundation
NSP	Network Service Provider
NSSA	Not-So-Stubby-Area
NVRAM	Non-Volatile Random Access Memory
NVT	Network Virtual Terminal
OACK	Option Acknowledgment
OAM&P	Operations, Administration, Maintenance & Provisioning
OC	Optical Carrier
OFDM	Orthogonal Frequency Division Multiplexing
OL	OverLoad
ONC	Open Network Computing
OSI	Open Systems Interconnection
OSI-RM	Open Systems Interconnection Reference Model
OSPF	Open Shortest Path First
OUI	Organizationally Unique Identifier
P	Provider
PAC	PPTP Access Concentrator
PARC	Palo Alto Research Center
PAT	Port Address Translation
PC	Personal Computer
PCG	PFE Clock Generator
PCI	Peripheral Component Interconnect
PCM	Pulse Code Modulation
PD	Packet Director
PDA	Personal Digital Assistant
PDU	Protocol Data Unit
PE	Provider Edge
PFE	Packet Forwarding Engine
PGM	Pretty Good Multicast
PHP	Penultimate Hop Popping
PIC	Physical Interface Card
PIM	Protocol Independent Multicast
PKI	Public Key Infrastructure
PLCP	Physical Layer Convergence Protocol
PLP	Packet Layer Protocol
PNS	PPTP Network Server
POP	Point of Presence/Post Office Protocol
POS	Packet over SONET/SDH
PPDU	Physical Protocol Data Unit
PPP	Point-to-Point Protocol
PPPoE	PPP over Ethernet
PPTP	Point-to-Point Tunneling Protocol
PSDU	Physical Layer Service Data Unit
PSH	Push
PSNP	Partial Sequence Number PDU
PSTN	Public Switched Telephone Network
PTI	Payload Type Indicator

PTR	Pointer
PW	Pseudo-Wire
QoS	Quality of Service
QR	Query Response
RA	Routing Arbiter/Recursion Available (DNS)
RADIUS	Remote Access Dial-In User Service
RAM	Random Access Memory
RARP	Reverse Address Resolution Protocol
RAS	Registration, Admission, and Status
RD	Recursion Desired
RE	Routing Engine or Regular Expression
RFC	Request for Comment
RIB	Routing Information Base
RIP	Routing Information Protocol
RIPE NCC	Reséaux IP Européens Network Coordination Center
RISC	Reduced Instruction Set Computing
ROMMON	Read-Only Memory Monitor
RMON	Remote Monitor
RP	Rendezvous Point (PIM)/Responsible Person (DNS)
RPC	Remote Procedure Call
RPF	Reverse Oath Forwarding
RPT	Rendezvous Point Tree
RQ	Request
RR	Route Reflector (BGP)/Resource Records (DNS)
RRQ	Read Request
RST	Reset
RSVP	Resource Reservation Protocol
RT	Routing Table
RTCP	Real-Time Control Protocol
RTMP	Routing Table Maintenance Protocol
RTP	Real-time Protocol or Reliable Transport Protocol (Cisco)
RTT	Round Trip Time
SA	Security Association
SAP	Service Access Point/Session Announcement Protocol
SASL	Simple Authentication and Security Layer
SCB	System Control Board (M40)
scp	secure copy
SDH	Synchronous Digital Hierarchy
SDK	Software Development Kit
SDLC	Synchronous Data Link Control
SDP	Session Description Protocol
SDU	Service Data Unit
SFM	Switching and Forwarding Module (M160)
SFTP	Secure File Transfer Protocol
SGML	Standard Generalized Markup Language
SHA	Secure Hash Algorithm
SIG	Signature
SIP	Session Initiation Protocol
SKA	Sender Keeps All
SKIP	Simple Key Management for Internet Protocols
SLIP	Serial Line Interface Protocol

SM	Sparse Mode
SMDS	Switched Multimegabit Data Services
SMI	Structure of Management Information
S/MIME	Multipurpose Internet Mail Extensions Security
SMTP	Simple Mail Transfer Protocol
SNA	Systems Network Architecture
SNAP	Sub-Network Access Protocol
SNMP	Simple Network Management Protocol
SNP	Sequence Number PDU
SNPA	Subnetwork Point of Attachment
SOHO	Small Office/Home Office
SONET	Synchronous Optical Network
SPF	Shortest Path First
SPI	Security Parameter Index
SPT	Shortest Path tree
SRV	Services
SS7	Signaling System 7
SSAP	Source Service Access Point
SSB	System Switching Board (M20)
SSH	Secure Shell
SSM	Source-Specific Multicast
SSRC	Synchronization Source Identifier
STP	Signaling Transfer Point
SYN	Synchronize
TACACS+	Terminal Access Controller Access Control Systems Plus
TC	Truncated
TCP	Transmission Control Protocol
TE	Traffic Engineering
TFTP	Trivial File Transfer Protocol
TGZ	tar and gzip
TLA	Top Level Aggregator
TLI	Transport Layer Interface
TLV	Type/Length/Value
TLS	Transparent LAN Service
ToS	Type of Service
TTL	Time To Live
TTY	Teletype
TXT	Text
UA	User Agent
UAC	User Agent Client
UAS	User Agent Server
UDP	User Datagram Protocol
UI	Unnumbered Information
UIUC	University of Illinois Urbana/Champaign
URG	Urgent
URI	Uniform Resource Identifier
URL	Universal (or Uniform) Resource Locator
URN	Uniform Resource Name
UTP	Unshielded Twisted Pair
VCI	Virtual Channel Identifier
VLAN	Virtual Local Area Network

VLSM	Variable-Length Subnet Masking
VoIP	Voice over IP
VPI	Virtual Path Identifier
VPLS	Virtual Private LAN Service
VPN	Virtual Private Network
VPSN	Virtual Private Switched Network
VPWS	Virtual Private Wire Service
VRF	Virtual Routing and Forwarding table
VTY	Virtual Teletype
WAN	Wide Area Network
WEP	Wired Equivalent Privacy
WiFi	Wireless Fiber/Wireless Fidelity
WRQ	Write Request
XDR	External Data Representation
XML	eXtensible Markup Language

Bibliography

Books

Comer, Douglas E., *The Internet Book*, 4th ed., Pearson/Prentice Hall, 2007.

Comer, Douglas E., *Internetworking with TCP/IP, Volume I: Principles, Protocols, and Architectures*, 5th ed., Prentice Hall, 2006.

Comer, Douglas E., and David L. Stevens, *Internetworking with TCP/IP, Volume II: Design, Implementation, and Internals*, Prentice Hall, 1991.

Comer, Douglas E., and David L. Stevens, *Internetworking with TCP/IP, Volume III: Client-Server Programming and Applications*, Prentice Hall, 1993.

Costales, Bryan, with Eric Allman, *sendmail*, 3rd ed., O'Reilly, 2002.

Donahoo, Michael J., and Kenneth L. Calvert, *TCP/IP Sockets in C:A Practical Guide for Programmers*, Morgan Kaufmann, 2001.

Doraswamy, Naganand, and Dan Harkins, *IPSec*, Prentice Hall PTR, 1999.

Doyle, Jeff, *OSPF and IS-IS*, Addison-Wesley, 2006.

Doyle, Jeff, *Routing TCP/IP*, Volume I, Cisco Press, Macmillan, 1998.

Doyle, Jeff, and Jennifer DeHaven Carroll, *Routing TCP/IP*, Volume II, Cisco Press, Macmillan, 2001.

Forouzan, Behrouz A., *TCP/IP Protocol Suite*, 3rd ed., McGraw-Hill, 2006.

Goralski, Walter, *Juniper and Cisco Routing*, Wiley, 2002.

Goralski, Walter, *ADSL and DSL Technologies*, 2nd ed., McGraw-Hill, 2000.

Goralski, Walter, *Introduction to ATM Networking*, McGraw-Hill, 1995.

Goralski, Walter, *SONET/SDH*, 3rd ed., McGraw-Hill/Osborne, 2002.

Gredler, Hannes, and Walter Goralski, *The Complete IS-IS Routing Protocol*, Springer, 2005.

Greene, Barry Raveendran, and Philip, Smith, *Cisco ISP Essentials*, Cisco Press, 2002.

Hall, Eric A., *Internet Core Protocols*, O'Reilly, 2000.

Huston, Geoff, *ISP Survival Guide*, Wiley, 1999.

Kozierok, Charles M., *The TCP/IP Guide*, No Starch Press, 2005.

Kumar, Vineet, and Markku Korpi, and Senthil Sengodan, *IP Telephony with H.323*, Wiley, 2001.

Kurose, James F., and Keith W. Ross, *Computer Networking: A Top-Down Approach Featuring the Internet*, 3rd ed., Pearson Addison-Wesley, 2005.

Loshin, Pete, *Big Book of Border Gateway Protocol (BGP) RFCs*, Morgan Kaufmann, 2000.

Lui, Cricket, and Paul Albitz, *DNS and BIND*, 5th ed., O'Reilly, 2006.

Naugle, Matthew, *Illustrated TCP/IP:A Graphic Guide to the Protocol Suite*, Wiley, 1999.

Nemeth, Evi, Garth Snyder, Scott Seebass, Trent R. Hein, et al., *UNIX System Administration Handbook*, Prentice Hall PTR, 2001.

Perlman, Radia, *Interconnections*, 2nd ed., Addison-Wesley, 2000.

Pullen, J. Mark, *Understanding Internet Protocols through Hands-On Programming*, Wiley, 2000.

Rhoton, John, *Programmer's Guide to Internet Mail*, Digital Press, 2000.

Ruvalcaba, Zak, *Build Your Own ASP.NET Website Using C# and VB.NET*, Sitepoint, Victoria, Australia, 2004.

Shah, Stave, and Soyinka Wale, *Linux Administration: A Beginner's Guide*, 4th ed., McGraw-Hill/Osborne, 2005.

Stallings, William, *SNMP, SNMPv2, and CMIP*, Addison-Wesley, 1993.

Stevens, W. Richard, *TCP/IP Illustrated, Volume 1: The Protocols*, Addison-Wesley, 1994.

Stevens, W. Richard, *TCP/IP Illustrated, Volume 2: The Implementation*, Addison-Wesley, 1995.

Stevens, W. Richard, *TCP/IP Illustrated, Volume 3: TCP for Transactions, HTTP, NNTP, and the UNIX Domain Protocols*, Addison-Wesley, 1996.

Stewart, John W. III, *BGP4*, Addison-Wesley1999.

Tanenbaum, Andrew S., *Computer Networks*, 4th ed., Prentice Hall PTR, 2003.

Wood, David, *Programming Internet Email*, O'Reilly, 1999.

Zeltserman, David, *A Practical Guide to SNMPv3 and Network Management*, Prentice Hall, 1999.

RFCs and Internet Drafts

All RFCs can be obtained from *www.ietf.org/rfc.html*

Internet drafts are available at *www.ietf.org/ID.html*

An interesting archive of expired drafts can be found at *www.watersprings.org/pub/id/index-all.html*

Related Standards Documents

American National Standards Institute, Inc. (ANSI): *www.ansi.org;* 11 West 42nd Street, New York, NY 10036

ITU-T (and CCITT) Recommendations

International Telecommunication Union General Secretariat, Sales Section: *www.itu.int;* Place des Nations, CH1211, Gweneva 20, Switzerland; +41 22 730 5285

ETSI, ISO, and IEEE Documents

ETSI Infocentre—Interprets ITU-T standards for application in the European telecommunications environment. The website for downloads or purchase on paper or CD-ROM: *www.etsi.org*; 06921 Sophia Antipolis, Cedex, France; +33(0)4 92 42 22

American National Standards Institute, Inc.: *www.ansi.org;* 1430 Broadway, New York, NY 10018

IEEE Standards Publications: *www.ieee.org;* (800) 678-IEEE or (908) 981-1393

Index

D

E

M

N

O

S

U

X